2022

UNDERSTANDING HEALTH INSURANCE

A GUIDE TO BILLING AND REIMBURSEMENT

MICHELLE A. GREEN

MPS, RHIA, FAHIMA, CPC

Cengage

Australia • Brazil • Canada • Mexico • Singapore • United Kingdom • United States

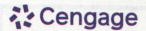

Understanding Health Insurance: A Guide to Billing and Reimbursement: 2022, **17th Edition**

Michelle A. Green

SVP, Higher Education Product Management
Erin Joyner

VP, Product Management, Learning Experiences: Thais Alencar

Product Director: Jason Fremder

Senior Product Manager: Stephen G. Smith

Product Assistant: Dallas Wilkes

Learning Designer: Kaitlin Schlicht

Senior Content Manager: Kara A. DiCaterino

Digital Delivery Quality Partner: Lisa Christopher

VP, Product Marketing: Jason Sakos

Director, Product Marketing: Neena Bali

IP Analyst: Ashley Maynard

Production Service: MPS Limited

Designer: Felicia Bennett

Cover Image Source:
VikaSuh/Shutterstock.com

Interior Image Source:
s_maria/Shutterstock.com

For product information and technology assistance, contact us at **Cengage Customer & Sales Support, 1-800-354-9706 or support.cengage.com.**

For permission to use material from this text or product, submit all requests online at **www.copyright.com.**

Library of Congress Control Number: 2021918820

ISBN: 978-0-357-62135-6

Cengage
200 Pier 4 Boulevard
Boston, MA 02210
USA

Cengage is a leading provider of customized learning solutions with employees residing in nearly 40 different countries and sales in more than 125 countries around the world. Find your local representative at: **www.cengage.com.**

To learn more about Cengage platforms and services, register or access your online learning solution, or purchase materials for your course, visit **www.cengage.com.**

Notice to the Reader

Publisher does not warrant or guarantee any of the products described herein or perform any independent analysis in connection with any of the product information contained herein. Publisher does not assume, and expressly disclaims, any obligation to obtain and include information other than that provided to it by the manufacturer. The reader is expressly warned to consider and adopt all safety precautions that might be indicated by the activities described herein and to avoid all potential hazards. By following the instructions contained herein, the reader willingly assumes all risks in connection with such instructions. The publisher makes no representations or warranties of any kind, including but not limited to, the warranties of fitness for particular purpose or merchantability, nor are any such representations implied with respect to the material set forth herein, and the publisher takes no responsibility with respect to such material. The publisher shall not be liable for any special, consequential, or exemplary damages resulting, in whole or part, from the readers' use of, or reliance upon, this material.

Printed at CLDPC, USA, 01-23

Table of Contents

Preface vii
About the Author xiv
Reviewers xv
Acknowledgments xvi
How to Use This Text xvii
SimClaim™ CMS-1500
Software User Guide xix

Chapter 1: Health Insurance Specialist Career 1

Health Insurance Overview........2
Career Opportunities 4
Education and Training..........5
    Student Internship 6
Job Responsibilities 8
    Health Insurance Specialist
    Job Description 8
Independent Contractor
and Employer Liability 9
Professionalism 11
    Attitude, Self-Esteem,
    and Etiquette 11
    Communication 12
    Conflict Management 12
    Customer Service 12
    Diversity Awareness.............12
    Leadership 12
    Managing Change 13
    Productivity 13
    Professional Ethics 13
    Team-Building 13
    Professional Appearance........14
Telephone Skills for the
Health Care Setting 15
Professional Associations
and Credentials...............18

Chapter 2: Introduction to Health Insurance and Managed Care 23

Overview of Health
Insurance and Managed Care... 25
    Health Insurance Coverage
    Statistics 28
Major Developments in
Health Insurance and
Managed Care................ 29
    The First Health Insurance
    Plans 29
    Legislation and Regulations in
    the Twenty-First Century........31
    The Affordable Care Act 32
    Health Insurance Marketplace.....32

Managed Care............... 33
    Managed Care Organizations
    and Plans.....................34
    Managed Care Models 35
    Effects of Managed Care
    on a Physician's Practice 37
Characteristics of Health
Plans and Managed Care 37
    Primary Care Provider 38
    Quality Assurance and
    Performance Measurement 38
    Utilization Management 41
    Case Management...............41
    Second Surgical Opinions.......41
    Second and Third Opinions......41
    Prescription Management 41
Consumer-Directed
Health Plans................. 43
Health Care Documentation 44
    Patient Records 44
    Problem-Oriented Record (POR)...46
Electronic Health Record
(EHR) 46
    Meaningful EHR Users...........47
    Electronic Clinical Quality
    Measures (eCQMs) 49

Chapter 3: Introduction to Revenue Management 61

Revenue Management 62
Managing Patients 65
    Managing New Patients.........65
    Managing Established
    Patients 72
Encounter Form and
Chargemaster 73
    Encounter Form 73
    Chargemaster 75
Processing an Insurance
Claim 77
    Management of Accounts
    Receivable.....................79
    Completing the CMS-1500
    Claim 81
Posting Charges to Patient
Accounts 81
Monitoring and Auditing for
Revenue Management 83
    Quarterly Provider Updates......83
    Utilization Management
    and Case Management.........84
    Revenue Monitoring............84
    Revenue Auditing..............85
    Resource Allocation
    and Data Analytics 85

Chapter 4: Revenue Management: Insurance Claims, Denied Claims and Appeals, and Credit and Collections 91

Insurance Claim Cycle 92
    Claims Submission and Electronic
    Data Interchange (EDI) 93
    Claims Processing..............98
    Claims Adjudication.............99
    Remittance Advice Reconciliation
    and Payment of Claims 102
Maintaining Insurance
Claim Files...................105
    Tracking Unpaid Claims.........106
    Storing Remittance Advice
    Documents 106
Denied Claims and the
Appeals Process 106
    Appealing Denied Claims 107
Credit and Collections 111
    Credit 111
    Collections 112
    State Insurance Regulators 115
    Improper Payments Information
    Act (IPIA) of 2002.............116

Chapter 5: Legal Aspects of Health Insurance and Reimbursement 122

Overview of Laws and
Regulations..................124
Federal Laws and Events
That Affect Health Care 128
Retention of Records 136
Health Care Audit and
Compliance Programs 136
    Compliance Programs..........137
    Medicare Integrity Program.....138
    Medicaid Integrity Program......139
    Recovery Audit Contractor
    Program.......................140
    Health Care Fraud Prevention
    and Enforcement Action Team ... 141
    Medicare Shared Savings
    Program.......................142
    Reducing Overpayments
    Program.......................143
    National Correct Coding
    Initiative 146
Health Insurance Portability
and Accountability Act
(HIPAA) 147
    HIPAA Title I—Health Care
    Access, Portability, and
    Renewability 147

HIPAA Title II—Preventing
Health Care Fraud and
Abuse.........................148
HIPAA Title II (continued)—
Administrative Simplification....150
Title II (continued)—Medical
Liability Reform..............165
Title III—Tax-Related Health
Provisions...................165
Title IV—Application and
Enforcement of Group Health
Plan Requirements...........166
Title V—Revenue Offsets
Governing Tax Deductions
for Employers...............166

**Chapter 6: ICD-10-CM
Coding   171**
**General Equivalence
Mappings....................172**
**Overview of ICD-10-CM
and ICD-10-PCS..............173**
ICD-10-PCS...................175
Coding Manuals..............176
Updating ICD-10-CM and
ICD-10-PCS.................176
Mandatory Reporting of
ICD-10-CM and ICD-10-PCS
Codes......................177
Medical Necessity...........177
**ICD-10-CM Coding
Conventions.................181**
The Alphabetic Index and
Tabular List................181
Format and Structure.........182
Use of Codes for Reporting
Purposes...................183
Placeholder Character........183
Seventh Characters..........183
Abbreviations...............183
Punctuation.................184
Other and Unspecified Codes....185
Includes Notes..............185
Inclusion Terms.............185
Excludes Notes..............186
Etiology and Manifestation
Convention.................187
And.........................187
With........................188
Cross References............189
Code Also Note..............189
Default Code................190
Code Assignment and Clinical
Criteria....................190
**ICD-10-CM Index and
Tabular List.................190**
ICD-10-CM Index to Diseases
and Injuries................190
ICD-10-CM Tabular List of
Diseases and Injuries........204
ICD-10-CM Chapter 22: Codes for
Special Purposes
(U00–U85).................208

**Official Guidelines for
Coding and Reporting........209**
ICD-10-CM Official Guidelines
for Coding and Reporting......209

Chapter 7: CPT Coding   230
Organization of CPT.........231
Relative Value Units..........233
Changes to CPT..............233
CPT Sections................233
CPT Code Number Format.....234
CPT Appendices..............234
CPT Symbols................235
CPT Sections, Subsections,
Categories, and Subcategories.238
CPT Index..................241
Main Terms..................241
Modifying Terms.............242
Code Ranges................242
Conventions.................242
Coding Procedures
and Services...............243
CPT Modifiers..............245
**Evaluation and Management
Section.....................255**
Overview of Evaluation and
Management Section.........256
Evaluation and Management
Services Guidelines..........258
Evaluation and Management
Subsections................267
Anesthesia Section..........274
Assigning Anesthesia Codes.....274
Qualifying Circumstances
for Anesthesia..............274
Anesthesia Modifiers.........275
Anesthesia Time Reporting....276
Surgery Section.............278
Surgical Package.............278
Separate Procedure..........281
Radiology Section...........282
Complete Procedure.........284
Professional versus Technical
Component.................285
**Pathology and Laboratory
Section.....................286**
Medicine Section............289
**CPT Category II and
Category III Codes...........292**
CPT Category II Codes........292
CPT Category III Codes.......293

**Chapter 8: HCPCS
Level II Coding   298**
**Purpose of HCPCS
Level II Codes...............299**
Responsibility for HCPCS
Level II Codes..............300
**Organization of HCPCS
Level II Codes...............301**
Permanent National Codes.....301

Miscellaneous Codes..........302
Temporary Codes............302
Modifiers...................303
HCPCS Level II Index and
Table of Drugs..............304
HCPCS Level II Code
Sections...................306
Basic Steps for Using
the HCPCS Level II Index
and Code Sections..........306
**Documentation and
Submission Requirements
for Reporting HCPCS
Level II Codes...............307**
Patient Record Documentation...308
DMEPOS Requirements........309
**Assigning HCPCS Level II
Codes and Modifiers.........311**

**Chapter 9: CMS
Reimbursement
Methodologies   316**
CMS Reimbursement........317
Data Analytics...............320
Case-Mix Management........321
CMS Payment Systems........322
Changes to CMS
Reimbursement Methods......323
CMS Fee Schedules.........323
Ambulance Fee Schedule......323
Clinical Laboratory
Fee Schedule...............324
Durable Medical Equipment,
Prosthetics/Orthotics,
and Supplies Fee Schedule....325
Medicare Physician
Fee Schedule...............326
CMS Payment Systems.......332
Ambulatory Surgical
Center Payment System......332
End-Stage Renal Disease
Prospective Payment
System (ESRD PPS).........334
Federally Qualified Health
Centers Prospective Payment
System (FQHC PPS).........335
Home Health Prospective
Payment System............336
Hospice Payment System......338
Hospital Inpatient Prospective
Payment System............339
Hospital Outpatient Prospective
Payment System............348
Inpatient Psychiatric
Facility Prospective
Payment System............350
Inpatient Rehabilitation
Facility Prospective
Payment System............352
Long-Term (Acute) Care
Hospital Prospective
Payment System............352
Skilled Nursing Facility
Prospective Payment System...354

Chapter 10: Coding Compliance Programs, Clinical Documentation Improvement, and Coding for Medical Necessity   361

Coding Compliance Programs . . 362

Comprehensive Error Rate Testing Program 363

Medical Review (MR) 364

National Correct Coding Initiative. 365

Recovery Audit Contractor Program 370

Clinical Documentation Improvement 370

DRG Coding Validation and Claims Denials 371

Coding for Medical Necessity. . .372

Applying Coding Guidelines 373

Coding and Billing Considerations 378

Patient Record Documentation . . .378

Advance Beneficiary Notice of Noncoverage (ABN). 378

Auditing Process 379

Medicare Coverage Database (MCD) 379

Medicare Code Editor (MCE) and Outpatient Code Editor (OCE). 380

Coding from Case Scenarios and Patient Records 381

Coding from Case Scenarios. 381

Coding from Patient Records 384

Reports. .389

Procedure for Coding Operative Reports. 389

Chapter 11: CMS-1500 and UB-04 Claims   400

General Claims Information 401

CMS-1500 and 837P 404

UB-04 (CMS-1450) and 837. 404

Claims Attachments. 407

CMS-1500 Data Entry 407

Entering Patient and Policyholder Names 409

Entering Provider Names. 409

Entering Mailing Addresses. 409

Recovery of Funds from Responsible Payers. 410

National Provider Identifier (NPI) . .410

Assignment of Benefits versus Accept Assignment. 413

Reporting Diagnoses: ICD-10-CM Codes 413

Reporting Procedures and Services: HCPCS Level II and CPT Codes. 415

CMS-1500 Block 24— Shaded Lines. 415

National Standard Employer Identifier. 419

Reporting the Billing Entity 420

Processing Secondary CMS-1500 Claims 420

Common Errors that Delay CMS-1500 Claims Processing 421

Final Steps in Processing CMS-1500 Claims 422

Maintaining CMS-1500 Insurance Claim Files for the Medical Practice. 422

Insurance File Set-Up 423

Processing Assigned Paid Claims 423

Federal Privacy Act 423

UB-04 Claim 423

UB-04 Claims and ICD-10-CM, ICD-10-PCS, CPT, and HCPCS Level II Coding. 424

UB-04 Claim Development and Implementation 425

National Uniform Billing Committee (NUBC) 425

UB-04 Claims Submission. 425

Correcting and Supplementing UB-04 Claims 436

Chapter 12: Commercial Insurance   444

Commercial Health Insurance 445

Individual Health Insurance 445

Group Health Insurance. 445

Automobile, Disability, and Liability Insurance 446

Automobile Insurance 446

Disability Insurance 446

Liability Insurance 447

Commercial Claims Instructions. 449

Commercial Secondary Coverage Claims Instructions . .457

Commercial Group Health Plan Coverage Claims Instructions. 461

Chapter 13: BlueCross BlueShield   467

BlueCross BlueShield. 468

Origin of BlueCross and BlueShield 468

BlueCross BlueShield Association 468

Business Structure. 469

Network Participation and Utilization Management 469

BlueCross BlueShield Plans 470

Traditional Fee-for-Service Plans .470

Indemnity Plans 471

Managed Care Plans 471

Federal Employee Program® 472

Medicare Supplemental Plans. . . .472

Health Care Anywhere 473

BlueCross BlueShield Billing Notes 473

Claims Processing 473

Deadline for Submitting Claims. . .473

Claim Used. 473

Inpatient and Outpatient Coverage 473

Deductible 474

Copayment/Coinsurance. 474

Allowable Fee Determination. 474

Assignment of Benefits 474

Special Handling 474

BlueCross BlueShield Claims Instructions 474

BlueCross BlueShield Secondary Coverage Claims Instructions. 482

Chapter 14: Medicare   490

Medicare Eligibility and Enrollment. 492

Medicare Eligibility. 492

Medicare Enrollment 492

Medicare Coverage. 494

Medicare Part A. 494

Medicare Part B. 497

Medicare Part C. 499

Medicare Part D. 502

Other Medicare Health Plans. 504

Employer and Union Health Plans 505

Medigap. .505

Experimental and Investigative Procedures. 506

Medicare Participating, Nonparticipating, and Opt-Out Providers 507

Participating Providers 507

Nonparticipating Providers 507

Opt-Out Providers 510

Mandatory Claims Submission . . .510

Advance Beneficiary Notice of Noncoverage 511

Medicare as Primary and Secondary Payer. 513

Medicare as Primary Payer 513

Medicare as Secondary Payer . . .515

Medicare Summary Notice 517

Medicare Billing Notes 518

Medicare Administrative Contractor (MAC) 518

Medicare Split/Shared Visit Payment Policy 519

Durable Medical Equipment Claims 519

Deadline for Submitting Claims. . .519

Claim Used. 519

Special Handling 520

Telehealth. 520

Medicare Claims Instructions. 520

Medicare and Medigap Claims Instructions. 528

Medicare-Medicaid
(Medi-Medi) Crossover
Claims Instructions. 530

Medicare as Secondary Payer
Claims Instructions. 532

Medicare Roster Billing
for Mass Vaccination
Programs Claims Instructions . . 535

   Provider Enrollment Criteria. 535
   Completing the CMS-1500
    Claim for Roster Billing
    Purposes 535

Chapter 15: Medicaid   542

Medicaid Eligibility 543
   Medically Needy Program 544
   Special Groups 544
   Children's Health Insurance
    Program. 545
   Programs of All-inclusive Care
    for the Elderly (PACE) 545
   Spousal Impoverishment
    Protection 546
   Confirming Medicaid Eligibility . . .546
Medicaid Coverage 547
   Mandatory Medicaid Benefits 547
   Optional Medicaid Benefits 548
   Preventive Health Care Services . .548
Medicaid Reimbursement. 549
   Medicare-Medicaid Relationship . .550
   Medicaid as a Secondary
    Payer 550
   Participating Providers 550
   Medicaid and Managed Care 550
   Medicaid Eligibility
    Verification System 551
   Medicaid Remittance Advice. 552
   Utilization Review. 553
   Medical Necessity 553
Medicaid Billing Notes 554
   Fiscal Agent 554
   Claim Used. 554
   Timely Claims Submission
    Deadline. 554
   Accept Assignment 554
   Deductibles 554
   Copayments. 554
   Inpatient Benefits. 554
   Major Medical/Accidental
    Injury Coverage 554
   Medicaid Eligibility. 555
   Medicaid Cards 555
   Remittance Advice. 555
Medicaid Claims
Instructions. 555

Medicaid as Secondary
Payer Claims Instructions. 562

Medicaid Parent/Newborn
Claims Instructions. 565

CHIP Claims Instructions 568

Chapter 16: TRICARE   574
TRICARE History. 575
   TRICARE 576
   Transitional Health Care Options. .577
TRICARE Administration. 578
   TRICARE Service Centers 578
   Military Treatment Facilities 579
   Case Management. 579
   Program Integrity Office 579
CHAMPVA 580
   Eligibility for CHAMPVA 580
   Veterans Choice Program 581
TRICARE Coverage 581
   TRICARE Options. 581
   TRICARE Special Programs 583
   Supplemental Health Care
    Programs. 584
TRICARE Billing Notes 584
   TRICARE Contractors 584
   Claim Used. 584
   Claims Submission Deadline 585
   Allowable Fee Determination 585
   Deductibles 585
   Confirmation of Eligibility 585
   Accepting Assignment. 585
   TRICARE Limiting Charges 587
   Special Handling 587
   Military Time. 587
TRICARE Claims
Instructions. 588

TRICARE as Secondary
Payer Claims Instructions. 596

TRICARE and Supplemental
Coverage Claims
Instructions. 599

Chapter 17: Workers'
Compensation   604

Federal and State Workers'
Compensation Programs 605
   Federal Workers'
    Compensation Programs 605
   Federal Department
    of Labor Programs 607
   Employees' Compensation
    Appeals Board. 607

   State Workers' Compensation
    Programs 608
Eligibility for Workers'
Compensation Coverage. 608
Classification and Billing
of Workers' Compensation
Cases. 609
   Classification of Workers'
    Compensation Cases 609
   Billing Workers'
    Compensation Cases 610
Workers' Compensation
and Managed Care 610
Forms and Reports 611
   First Report of Injury Form. 611
Appeals and Adjudication. 614
Fraud and Abuse. 616
Workers' Compensation
Billing Notes 616
   Eligibility .616
   Identification Card 616
   Fiscal Agent 616
   Underwriter 616
   Forms and Claim Used 617
   Claims Submission Deadline. 617
   Deductible 617
   Copayment. 617
   Premium. .617
   Approved Fee Basis. 617
   Accept Assignment 618
   Special Handling 618
   Private Payer Mistakenly Billed . . .618
Workers' Compensation
Claims Instructions. 618

Appendix I: Forms   629
CMS-1500 630
UB-04 631
Appendix II: Dental Claims
Processing   632
Dental Claims Processing. 632
Current Dental Terminology
(CDT) 632
Appendix III: Abbreviations 635
Bibliography   640
Glossary   642
Index   670

Introduction

Accurate processing of health insurance claims has become more exacting and rigorous as health insurance plan options have rapidly expanded. These changes, combined with modifications in state and federal regulations affecting the health insurance industry, are a constant challenge to health care personnel. Those responsible for processing health insurance claims require thorough instruction in all aspects of medical insurance, including plan options, payer requirements, state and federal regulations, abstracting of source documents, accurate completion of claims, and coding of diagnoses and procedures/services. *Understanding Health Insurance* provides the required information in a clear and comprehensive manner.

The text was designed and revised to support core learning objectives with chapter objectives, content, and assessments aligned to ensure students learn and practice the concepts and skills they'll need on the job. Student learning is supported through chapter outlines and measurable objectives identified at the beginning of each chapter, as well as chapter headings and assessments that clearly map to those chapter outlines and objectives.

Special attention was focused on selecting appropriate Bloom's taxonomy levels for each chapter objective along with mapping assessment items (e.g., exercises, exam questions) to each objective. In addition, the *Workbook to Accompany Understanding Health Insurance* contains assignments that map to higher Bloom's taxonomy levels to provide students with more advanced activity-based learning experiences such as completing additional claims, assigning of APCs and DRGs, and interpreting remittance advice documents.

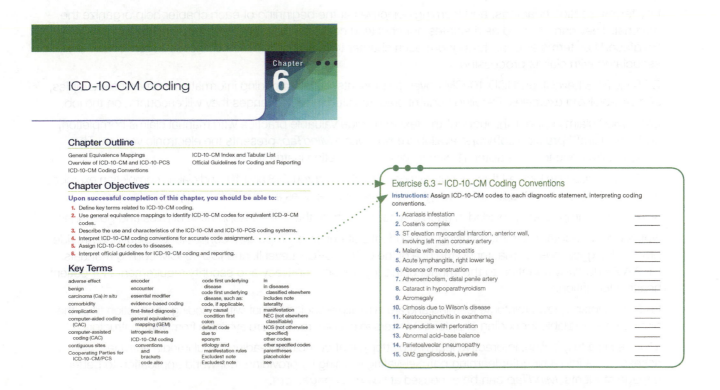

ICD-10-CM Coding

Chapter 6

Chapter Outline

General Equivalence Mappings
Overview of ICD-10-CM and ICD-10-PCS
ICD-10-CM Coding Conventions
ICD-10-CM Index and Tabular List
Official Guidelines for Coding and Reporting

Chapter Objectives

Upon successful completion of this chapter, you should be able to:

1. Define key terms related to ICD-10-CM coding.
2. Use general equivalence mappings to identify ICD-10-CM codes for equivalent ICD-9-CM codes.
3. Describe the use and characteristics of the ICD-10-CM and ICD-10-PCS coding systems.
4. Interpret ICD-10-CM coding conventions for accurate code assignment.
5. Assign ICD-10-CM codes to diseases.
6. Interpret official guidelines for ICD-10-CM coding and reporting.

Key Terms

adverse effect
benign
carcinoma (Ca) *in situ*
comorbidity
complication
computer-aided coding (CAC)
computer-assisted coding (CAC)
contiguous sites
Cooperating Parties for ICD-10-CM/PCS

encoder
encounter
essential modifier
evidence-based coding
first-listed diagnosis
general equivalence mapping (GEM)
iatrogenic illness
ICD-10-CM coding conventions and brackets
code also

code first underlying disease
code first underlying disease, such as:
code, if applicable, any causal condition first
colon
default code
due to
eponym
etiology and manifestation rules
Excludes1 note
Excludes2 note

in
in diseases classified elsewhere
includes note
laterality
manifestation
NEC (not elsewhere classifiable)
NOS (not otherwise specified)
other codes
other specified codes
parentheses
placeholder
see

Exercise 6.3 – ICD-10-CM Coding Conventions

Instructions: Assign ICD-10-CM codes to each diagnostic statement, interpreting coding conventions.

1. Acariasis infestation _____
2. Costen's complex _____
3. ST elevation myocardial infarction, anterior wall, involving left main coronary artery _____
4. Malaria with acute hepatitis _____
5. Acute lymphangitis, right lower leg _____
6. Absence of menstruation _____
7. Atheroembolism, distal penile artery _____
8. Cataract in hypoparathyroidism _____
9. Acromegaly _____
10. Cirrhosis due to Wilson's disease _____
11. Keratoconjunctivitis in exanthema _____
12. Appendicitis with perforation _____
13. Abnormal acid–base balance _____
14. Parietoalveolar pneumopathy _____
15. GM2 gangliosidosis, juvenile _____

Objectives

The objectives of this text are to:

1. Introduce information about major insurance programs and federal health care legislation.

2. Provide a basic knowledge of national diagnosis and procedure/service coding systems.

3. Explain the impact of coding compliance, clinical documentation improvement (CDI), and coding for medical necessity on health care settings.

4. Simplify the process of completing CMS-1500 and UB-04 claims.

This text is designed to be used by college and vocational school programs to train medical assistants, medical insurance specialists, coding and reimbursement specialists, and health information technicians. It can also be used as an in-service training tool for new medical office personnel and independent billing services, or individually by claims processors in the health care field who want to develop or enhance their skills.

 NOTE:

Claims completion instructions located in Chapters 11 through 17 of the textbook are based on the National Uniform Claims Committee's CMS-1500 reference instruction manual. For teaching purposes, instructions provide specific guidance for student claims completion. When employed, claims completion instructions specific to payers and government programs that reimburse your providers should be used.

Features of the Text

Major features of this text include:

- Key terms, section headings, and learning objectives at the beginning of each chapter help organize the material. They can be used as a self-test for checking comprehension and mastery of chapter content. Boldfaced key terms appear throughout each chapter to help learners master the technical vocabulary associated with claims processing.

- CPT, HCPCS Level II, and ICD-10-CM coverage presents the latest coding information, numerous examples, and skill-building exercises. Detailed content prepares students for changes they will encounter on the job.

- CMS-1500 claims appear throughout the text to provide valuable practice with manual claims completion, and SimClaim™ practice software, available online within *MindTap*, presents the electronic version. The UB-04 claim appears in Chapter 11 with its claims completion instructions.

- Coding exercises are located throughout textbook Chapters 6 through 8 and 10, and claims completion exercises are located throughout Chapters 11 through 17. Answers to exercises are available from your instructor.

- Numerous examples are provided in each chapter to illustrate the correct application of rules and guidelines.

- Notes clarify chapter content, focusing the student's attention on important concepts. Coding Tips provide practical suggestions for mastering the use of the CPT, HCPCS Level II, and ICD-10-CM coding manuals. HIPAA Alerts draw attention to the impact of this legislation on privacy and security requirements for patient health information.

- End-of-chapter reviews reinforce learning and are in multiple-choice format with a coding completion fill-in-the-blank format available for coding chapters. Answers to chapter reviews are available from your instructor.

- *MindTap* is a fully online, interactive learning platform that combines readings, multimedia activities, and assessments into a singular learning path, elevating learning by providing real-world application to better engage students. *MindTap* can be accessed at www.cengage.com.

- SimClaim™, the practice software available online within *MindTap*, contains case studies that include billing data and patient histories, and allow for data entry on CMS-1500 claims, with immediate feedback. Instructions for using SimClaim™ are located at the end of this Preface.

New to this Edition

Shorter Chapters 2 and 3 from the last edition were consolidated into Chapter 2, Introduction to Health Insurance. Lengthy Chapter 4 from the last edition was split into Chapter 3, Introduction to Revenue Management, and Chapter 4, Revenue Management: Insurance Claims, Credit, and Collections. Application-based assignments were added to the Review at the end of each chapter.

 N O T E :

Review questions were revised in accordance with added and updated content in each chapter.

- Chapter 1: Content about the American Disability Act (e.g., flexible work hours, job sharing, and telecommuting) and professional etiquette was added. The chapter Review contains two new assignments: Professionalism and Documenting Telephone Messages.

- Chapter 2: The chapter is now titled Introduction to Health Insurance and Managed Care and includes managed care content from the previous edition's Chapter 3 (Managed Care).

  o Insurance terms (schedule of benefits, covered services, carve-out plan, express contract, implied contract, premium, stop-loss insurance, guaranteed renewal [of health insurance contracts], institutional billing, and professional billing) were added.

  o Content about 21st Century Cures Act provisions of risk adjustment model reporting and prohibition of information blocking, Medicare Improvement for Patients and Providers Act (MIPPA) legislation, consumer-directed health plans, performance measurement, pharmacy management, physician referral, managed care contractual withhold arrangements, and risk pools was added.

  o Key terms Medicare, Medicaid, and CHAMPUS Reform Initiative (CRI) were relocated to Chapter 14, 15, and 16, respectively.

  o The chapter Review contains two new assignments: Introduction to Health Insurance Reimbursement, and Creating a Customized NCQA Health Plan Report Card.

- Chapter 3: The chapter is now titled Introduction to Revenue Management and includes content from the first half of the previous edition's Chapter 4 (Revenue Cycle Management). The previous edition's Chapter 3 (Managed Care) content was incorporated into Chapter 2.

  o Content about accounts payable, copayment (copay), discharged not final billed (DNFB), discharged not final coded (DNFC), facility billing, institutional billing, professional billing, and single-path coding was added.

- Chapter 4: The chapter is now titled Revenue Management: Insurance Claims, Denied Claims and Appeals, and Credit and Collections and includes content from the second half of the previous edition's Chapter 4 (Revenue Cycle Management).

  o Content about emancipated minors, suspended claim; third-party payer peer review by a medical reviewer, medical director, independent external reviewer (or Medicare qualified independent contractor), fragmentation, and skip tracing (or skip tracking) was added.

  o The chapter Review contains three new assignments: Interpreting an Explanation of Benefits, Interpreting a Remittance Advice, and Writing an Appeal Letter.

- Chapter 5: Content about MIPS was removed because it is covered in Chapter 2. Content about the Emergency Medical Treatment and Labor Act, Medicaid Fraud Control Unit (MFCU), minimum necessary standard (of the HIPAA Privacy Rule), and Notice of Privacy Practices (NPP) was added. The following content was updated: False Claim Act of 1863, Privacy Act of 1974, HIPAA Security Rule, HITECH Act, map of the Medicare fee-for-service RAC regions, HIPAA Title II (Preventing Health Care Fraud and Abuse), and designated record set. The following content was added: availability and integrity of electronic protected health information (e-PHI) (associated with the HIPAA Security Rule); Office for Civil Rights periodic audit to ensure compliance with HIPAA privacy, security, and breach notification rules; HIPAA civil and criminal penalties; Health Care Fraud and Abuse Control Program; HIPAA breach notification rule; direct and indirect treatment relationship between providers and patients; de-identification of protected health information; and treatment, payment, and health care operations (TPO). Content about the National Correct Coding Initiative (NCCI) program was expanded to provide clarification about its use. The Chapter 5 Review contains two new assignments: HIPAA Fraud and Abuse, and HIPAA Privacy and Security Rules.

- Chapter 6: ICD-10-CM guidelines and codes were updated, and applicable general coding guidelines were incorporated into outpatient coding guidelines within shaded boxes to bring attention to them. (*3-2-1 Code It!* is a comprehensive coding textbook that can be referenced for coding clarification.)

- Chapter 7: CPT coding guidelines and codes were updated. Coding step 7 (Review Appendix B in the CPT coding manual to assign appropriate modifiers) was added below the Coding Procedures and Services heading. Clarification was provided about entering CPT codes on the CMS-1500 claim based on highest to lowest reimbursement, along with content about the global period.

- Chapter 8: HCPCS Level II guidance and codes were updated.

- Chapter 9: Content about Never Events, ambulatory surgery center value-based purchasing, and value-based purchasing (VBP) was added, along with an image that summarizes VBP programs. Content about hospital value-based purchasing was clarified. The chapter Review contains three new assignments: Data Analytics for Medicare Part B Reimbursement, Interpreting Medicare Status Indicators and Procedure Discounting Data for Ambulatory Payment Classifications, and Interpreting Medicare-Severity Diagnosis-Related Groups Data.

- Chapter 10: Content about the National Correct Coding Initiative (NCCI) program was clarified. ICD-10-CM, HCPCS Level II, and CPT codes were updated.

- Chapters 11 to 17: ICD-10-CM, HCPCS Level II, and CPT codes were updated. Chapter 13 through 17 content was revised to simplify explanations, and chapter Reviews were revised accordingly. Insurance claims completion instructions and completed CMS-1500 claims were revised according to the latest industry guidelines and standards, as follows:

  o Dates are now entered as a six-character-with-spaces format (e.g., MM DD YY) *except for Blocks 3 and 11a, which require eight-digit dates for dates of birth, and Block 31 that requires no spaces, as MMDDYY.*

  o Hyphens were deleted from 9-digit ZIP codes (e.g., 123456789).

  o More than one diagnosis pointer may be entered in Block 24E *without spaces*, when applicable (e.g., ABC).

- Chapter 11: Content about the UB-04 claim was clarified to indicate that it is used to report institutional services, such as inpatient and outpatient hospital services. The diagnosis pointer letter definition was clarified to explain that it is entered in Block 24E to indicate the medical necessity of the procedure performed or service provided. Clarification about the Administrative Simplification Compliance Act (ASCA) of 2003 was added to describe the continued use of paper claims. The chapter Review contains two new assignments: Identifying CMS-1500 Claims Completion Errors, and Completing the UB-04 Claim for Hospital Outpatient Care.

- Chapter 12: Content about commercial health insurance was clarified, including the addition of new key term *private health insurance*.

- Chapter 13: Content about network participation, BCBS preferred provider networks, utilization management were added.

- Chapter 14: Medicare was changed to a key term, information about Medicare observation status was clarified, an image of the Medicare MAC A/B jurisdiction map was added, and the mandatory claim submission rule was added.

- Chapter 15: Content about applying for Medicaid coverage when relocating to a new state was added.

- Chapter 16: CHAMPUS Reform Initiative (CRI) was changed to a key term, and content about the Privacy Act of 1974 and the Computer Matching and Privacy Protection Act of 1988 was added.

- Chapter 17: Workers' compensation content was updated to reflect current practices.

Organization of This Textbook

- Chapter outlines, key terms, objectives, chapter exercises, end-of-chapter summaries, and reviews facilitate student learning.

- Chapter 1, Health Insurance Specialist Career, contains an easy-to-read table that delineates training requirements for health insurance specialists.

- Chapter 2, Introduction to Health Insurance and Managed Care, contains content about basic health insurance and managed care concepts, the history of significant health insurance legislation, managed care plans, consumer-directed health plans, and health care documentation methods. Meaningful use content remains in the chapter to serve as a background for content about the new quality payment program (e.g., Advanced APMs, eCQMs, MIPS).

- Chapter 3, Introduction to Revenue Management, provides an overview of the revenue management process, including information about patient management, using encounter forms and chargemasters, processing insurance claims from patient appointment through claims submission, and posting charges to patient accounts. An introduction to methods of monitoring and auditing for revenue management is also included.

- Chapter 4, Revenue Management: Insurance Claims, Denied Claims and Appeals, and Credit and Collections, explains the stages of the insurance claim cycle, describes how insurance claim files are maintained, outlines the appeals process for denied claims, and explains the role of credit and collections in processing claims.

- Chapter 5, Legal and Regulatory Issues, emphasizes confidentiality of patient information, retention of patient information and health insurance records, the Federal False Claims Act, the Health Insurance Portability and Accountability Act of 1996, and federal laws and events that affect health care.

- Chapter 6, ICD-10-CM Coding, contains coding conventions and coding guidelines with examples. An overview about ICD-10-PCS is also provided. The coding conventions for the ICD-10-CM Index to Disease and Injuries and ICD-10-CM Tabular List of Diseases and Injuries are clearly explained and include examples. In addition, examples of coding manual entries are included.

  The chapter review includes coding statements, which are organized according to the ICD-10-CM chapters.

 NOTE:

The ICD-10-CM chapter is sequenced before the CPT and HCPCS Level II chapters in this textbook because diagnosis codes are reported for medical necessity (to justify procedures and/or services provided).

- Chapter 7, CPT Coding, follows the organization of CPT sections. The chapter review includes coding statements organized by CPT section.

- Chapter 8, HCPCS Level II Coding, contains content about the development and use of the HCPCS Level II coding system and its modifiers. The chapter review includes coding statements organized by HCPCS Level II section.

- Chapter 9, CMS Reimbursement Methodologies, contains information about reimbursement systems implemented since 1983 (including the Medicare physician fee schedule).

- Chapter 10, Coding Compliance Programs, Clinical Documentation Improvement, and Coding for Medical Necessity, contains information about the components of an effective coding compliance plan, and content about clinical documentation improvement and coding for medical necessity. Coding exercises (e.g., case scenarios, patient reports) are also included.

- Chapter 11, CMS-1500 and UB-04 Claims, contains general instructions that are followed when entering data on the CMS-1500 claim, a discussion of common errors made on claims, guidelines for maintaining the practice's insurance claim files, and the processing of assigned claims. UB-04 claims instructions are included, along with a case study.

- Claims completion instructions in Chapters 12 through 17 are located in an easy-to-read table format, and students can follow along with completion of the John Q. Public claims in each chapter (and complete the Mary Sue Patient claims as homework) by printing the blank CMS-1500 claim (according to instructions in Appendix I) or using *MindTap*.

Resources for the Instructor

Additional instructor resources for this product are available online. Instructor assets include an Instructor's Manual, Educator's Guide, Solution and Answer Guide, PowerPoint® slides, a test bank powered by Cognero®, and a transition guide.

Sign up or sign in at www.cengage.com to search for and access this product and its online resources.

Resources for the Student

Student Workbook
(ISBN 978-0-357-62136-3)

The Workbook follows the text's chapter organization and contains application-based assignments. Each chapter assignment includes a list of objectives, an overview of content relating to the assignment, and instructions for completing the assignment. Other components may be present depending on the assignment.

Each chapter contains review questions, in multiple-choice format, to emulate credentialing exam questions. In Chapters 11 through 17, additional case studies allow more practice in completing the CMS-1500 claim.

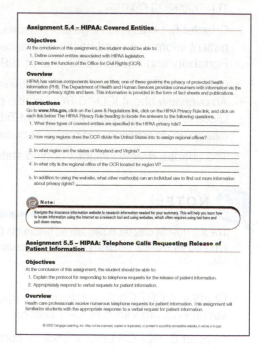

Student Resources

Additional student resources for this product are available online. Student assets include:

- CMS-1500 and UB-04 claims (blank fill-in forms), additional content related to textbook chapters, and SimClaim™ Case Studies

- CMS Evaluation and management services guidance document

- Revisions to the textbook and workbook due to coding updates

Sign up or sign in at www.cengage.com to search for and access this product and its online resources.

MindTap

MindTap is a fully online, interactive learning experience built upon authoritative Cengage content. By combining readings, multimedia activities, and assessments into a singular learning path, *MindTap* elevates learning by providing real-world application to better engage students. Instructors customize the learning path by selecting Cengage resources and adding their own content via apps that integrate into the *MindTap* framework seamlessly with many learning management systems.

The *MindTap* includes:

- Auto-graded Exercises and Chapter Review from the textbook
- Video Quizzes that walk students step-by-step through coding patient cases
- SimClaim™ activities to practice completing CMS-1500 claim forms
- Medical Office Simulation Software Training and Assessment activities to learn how to complete various billing tasks in EHR/PM software
- Learning Labs, a multimedia program designed to engage students in realistic on-the-job scenarios
- Writing Assignments to further engage students in on-the-job scenarios and encourage critical thinking
- Chapter Quizzes

To learn more, visit www.cengage.com/training/mindtap.

About the Author

Michelle A. Green, MPS, RHIA, FAHIMA, CPC, is an educational consultant for health information management academic programs, which involves mentoring program directors as they pursue CAHIIM accreditation, building new online courses (e.g., Blackboard, Moodle, TopClass), and reviewing existing online course content. She taught traditional classroom-based courses at Alfred State College from 1984 until 2000, when she transitioned all of the health information technology and coding/reimbursement specialist courses to an Internet-based format and continued teaching full-time online until 2016. Upon relocating to Syracuse, New York, she has taught for the health information technology program at Mohawk Valley Community College, Utica, New York, since 2017. Prior to 1984, she worked as a director of health information management at two acute care hospitals in the Tampa Bay, Florida, area. Both positions required her to assign codes to inpatient cases. Upon becoming employed as a college professor, she routinely spent semester breaks coding for a number of health care facilities so that she could further develop her inpatient and outpatient coding skills.

Special thanks are extended to the reviewers, digital contributors, and technical reviewers who provided recommendations and suggestions for improvement throughout the development of the text. Their experience and knowledge have been a valuable resource for the author.

Reviewers

Deborah Bigelow

MOA Instructor
Concorde Career Colleges
Jacksonville, FL

Edeedson Ciné, MBA, CMRS

Medical Office Administration/Billing/Coding
    Professor & Chair
Hunter Business School
Levittown, NY

Eva Hearn, CPC, MPH

Medical Programs Coordinator-Office Technology
    Department
Central Texas College
Killeen, TX

Kathleen Sobel

Adjunct Faculty
Purdue University Global
Mechanicsville, VA

Wanda Tenpenny, RHIA, CPC, CPMA

Curriculum Coordinator, Medical Office
    Administration
Pitt Community College
Greenville, NC

Digital Contributors

Angela R Campbell, MSHI, RHIA

AHIMA-Approved ICD-10-CM/PCS Trainer
Health Information Technology Instructor
San Juan College
Farmington, NM

Eva Davis

Instructor
Walters State Community College
Morristown, TN

Marsha Diamond, CPC, COC, CCS, CPMA, AAPC Fellow

Instructor
City College
Altamonte Springs, Florida

and
Manager
Coding/Compliance, Physician/Outpatient Services
Medical Audit Resource Services, Inc.
Orlando, Florida

Leah Grebner, PhD, RHIA, CCS, FAHIMA

Program Director, Health Information Technology
Illinois Central College
Peoria, Illinois

Molly A. Snowberger, RHIA, CPC, CCA

Outpatient Coder/Auditor
Medical Audit Resource Services, Inc.

Technical Reviewer

Yvonne McNabb, CMAA-NHA CCA - AHIMA

Allied Health Program Director
Remington College
Fort Worth, TX

Acknowledgments

In memory of my son, Eric, who always kept me "on task" by asking, "How much did you get finished in the chapter today, Mom?" Thank you for truly understanding my need to pursue my passion for teaching and writing. You always proudly introduced me as your mom, the teacher and writer. You remain forever in my heart, Eric.

A special thank you to my brother, Dave Bartholomew, for his encouragement and support. You are my rock!

To my students, located throughout the world! You always ask me the toughest questions, and you also make me want to find the answers. You are such wonderful critical thinkers!

To my technical reviewer, reviewers, and digital contributors, thank you for your incredible attention to detail and wonderful knowledge about all things coding and reimbursement!

To my learning designer, Kaitlin Schlicht, thank you for patiently walking me through crucial learning design methods!

To my senior content manager, Kara DiCaterino, I truly appreciate every single thing you do!

To my mom, Alice B. Bartholomew, for writing real-life case studies for my textbooks and helping me select a health care career. I so appreciate your guidance! I miss you.

Special appreciation is expressed to Optum Publishing Group for granting permission to reprint selected tables and pages from:

- *CPT Professional*
- *HCPCS Level II Professional*
- *ICD-10-CM Professional*
- *ICD-10-PCS Professional*

Feedback

Contact the author at michelle.ann.green@gmail.com with questions, suggestions, or comments about the text or supplements.

Objectives and Key Terms

The **Objectives** section lists the outcomes expected of the learner after a careful study of the chapter. Review the Objectives before reading the chapter content. When you complete the chapter, read the Objectives again to see if you can say for each one, "Yes, I can do that." If you cannot, go back to the appropriate content and reread it.

Key Terms represent new vocabulary in each chapter. Each term is highlighted in color in the chapter, is used in context, and is defined on first usage. A complete definition of each term appears in the Glossary at the end of the text.

Chapter Objectives

Upon successful completion of this chapter, you should be able to:

1. Define key terms related to the health insurance specialist career.
2. Briefly summarize health insurance claims processing and the parties involved.
3. Identify career opportunities available for health insurance specialists.
4. List the education and training requirements of a health insurance specialist.
5. Describe the job responsibilities of a health insurance specialist.
6. Differentiate among types of insurance purchased by contractors and employers.
7. Explain the role of workplace professionalism for a health insurance specialist.
8. Demonstrate telephone skills for the health care setting.
9. Identify coding and reimbursement professional associations and credentials offered.

Key Terms

AAPC

American Association of Medical Assistants (AAMA)

Centers for Medicare

bonding insurance

business liability insurance

embezzle

errors and omissions insurance

ethics

Healthcare Common Procedure Coding System (HCPCS)

hold harmless clause

Introduction

The career of a health insurance specialist (or reimbursement specialist) is a challenging one, with opportunities for professional advancement. Individuals who understand claims processing and billing regulations, possess accurate coding skills, have the ability to successfully appeal underpaid or denied insurance claims, and demonstrate workplace professionalism are in demand. A review of medical office personnel help-wanted advertisements indicates the need for individuals with all of these skills.

 NOTE:

Breach of patient confidentiality can result in termination of the internship, which means failing the internship course. Suspension or expulsion from your academic program are other possible consequences. Be sure to ask about your academic program's requirements regarding this issue.

During the internship, students are expected to report to work on time. Students who cannot participate in the internship on a particular day, or who arrive late, should contact their internship supervisor or program faculty, whoever is designated for that purpose. Students are also required to make up any lost time. Because the internship

 HIPAA Alert!

Traditionally, claims attachments containing medical documentation that supported procedures and services reported on claims were copied from patient records and mailed to payers. Providers now submit electronic attachments with electronic claims or send electronic attachments in response to requests for medical documentation (e.g., scanned images of paper records) to support submitted claims.

How to Avoid Resubmitting Claims

Delayed claims contain incomplete and inaccurate information and require resubmission after correction, which delays payment to the provider. Although hospitals and large group practices collect data about these problems and address them, smaller provider practices often do not have the tools to evaluate their claims submission processes. A major reason for delays in claims processing is incompleteness or inaccuracy of the information necessary to coordinate benefits among multiple payers. If the remittance advice from the primary payer is not attached to the claim submitted to the secondary payer, the result will be payment delays.

 Coding Tip

A short blank line is located after some of the codes in the encounter form (Figure 3-5) to allow entry of additional character(s) to report the specific ICD-10-CM diagnosis code. Medicare administrative contractors reject claims with missing, invalid, or incomplete diagnosis codes.

Introduction

The **Introduction** provides a brief overview of the major topics covered in the chapter.

The Introduction and the Objectives provide a framework for your study of the content.

Notes

Notes appear throughout the text and serve to bring important points to your attention. The Notes may clarify content, refer you to reference material, provide more background for selected topics, or emphasize exceptions to rules.

Icons

Icons draw attention to critical areas of content or provide experience-based recommendations. For example, the **HIPAA ALERT!** identifies issues related to the security of personal health information in the medical office.

The **Coding Tip** provides recommendations and hints for selecting codes and for the correct use of the coding manuals. Other icons include **Managed Care Alert, Hint, Remember!,** and **Caution**.

Claims Instructions

Claims Instructions simplify the process of completing the CMS-1500 for various types of payers. These instructions are provided in tables in Chapters 12 to 17. Each table consists of step-by-step instructions for completing each block of the CMS-1500 for commercial, BlueCross BlueShield, Medicare, Medicaid, TRICARE, and Workers' Compensation payers.

Block	Instructions
1	Enter an X in the *Other* box if the patient is covered by an individual or family health plan. Or, enter an X in the *Group Health Plan* box if the patient is covered by a group health plan.
	Note: The patient is covered by a group health plan if a group number is printed on the patient's insurance identification card (or a group number is included on case studies located in this textbook, workbook, and SimClaim™ software).
	Other indicates automobile, commercial, health maintenance organization (and managed care), liability, or workers' compensation insurance.
1a	Enter the health insurance identification number as it appears on the patient's insurance card (e.g., DOE, JANE, M).
2	Enter the patient's last name, first name, and middle initial (separated by commas)
3	Enter the patient's birth date as MM DD YYYY (with spaces). Enter an X in the appropriate box to indicate the patient's sex. If the patient's sex is unknown, leave blank.
4	Enter the policyholder's last name, first name, and middle initial (separated by commas) (e.g., DOE, JANE, M).
5	Enter the patient's mailing address. Enter the street address on line 1, enter the city and state on line 2, and enter the five- or nine-digit zip code on line 3. *Do not enter the hyphen or a space for a 9-digit ZIP code. Do not enter the telephone number.*
6	Enter an X in the appropriate box to indicate the patient's relationship to the policyholder. If the patient is an unmarried domestic partner, enter an X in the *Other* box.

Internet Links

AAPC: **www.aapc.com**
American Association of Medical Assistants (AAMA): **www.aama-ntl.org**
American Health Information Management Association (AHIMA): **www.ahima.org**
Ascend Learning's National Healthcareer Association (NHA): **www.nhanow.com**
Centers for Medicare and Medicaid Services (CMS): **www.cms.gov**
U.S. Department of Labor, Bureau of Labor Statistics (BLS): **www.bls.gov**

Review

1.1 – Multiple Choice

Select the most appropriate response.

1. The document submitted to the payer requesting reimbursement is called a(n)
   a. explanation of benefits.
   b. health insurance claim.
   c. remittance advice.
   d. prior approval form.

2. The Centers for Medicare and Medicaid Services (CMS) is an administrative agency within the

Exercise 6.2 – Overview of ICD-10-CM and ICD-10-PCS

Instructions: Complete each statement.

1. The *International Classification of Diseases, 10th Revision, Clinical Modification* (ICD-10-CM) codes and classifies _____ or morbidity data from inpatient and outpatient encounters.
2. The *International Classification of Diseases, 10th Revision, Procedure Classification System* (ICD-10-PCS) codes and classifies _____ data from inpatient hospital admissions only.
3. The Centers for Medicare and Medicaid Services (CMS) abbreviates ICD-10-CM and ICD-10-PCS as _____.
4. The intent of ICD-10-CM is to describe the _____ picture or findings of the patient, which means codes assigned are more precise than those needed for ICD-9-CM's statistical groupings and trend analysis.
5. ICD-10-CM codes require up to _____ characters, are entirely alphanumeric, and have unique coding conventions.
6. ICD-10-CM uses an alphabetic index to initially locate codes for conditions and a _____ list to verify codes.
7. The reporting of ICD-10-CM/PCS codes was mandated by _____ legislation.
8. Reporting ICD-10-CM codes on submitted claims ensures the medical _____ of procedures and services provided to patients during an encounter, which is defined as "the determination that a service or procedure rendered is reasonable and necessary for the

Summary

A health insurance specialist's career is challenging and requires professional training to understand claims processing and billing regulations, possess accurate coding skills, and develop the ability to successfully appeal underpaid or denied insurance claims. A health insurance claim is submitted to a third-party payer or government program to request reimbursement for health care services provided. Many health insurance plans require prior approval for treatment provided by specialists.

While the requirements of health insurance specialist programs vary, successful specialists develop skills that allow them to work independently and ethically, focus on attention to detail, and think critically. Medical practices and health care facilities employing health insurance specialists require them to perform various functions. Smaller practices and facilities require specialists to process claims for all types of payers, while larger practices and facilities expect specialists to process claims for a limited number of payers.

Internet Links

Internet Links are provided to encourage you to expand your knowledge at various state and federal government agency sites, commercial sites, and organization sites. Some exercises require you to obtain information from the Internet to complete the exercise.

Reviews and Exercises

The **Reviews** test student understanding about chapter content and critical thinking ability. Reviews in coding chapters require students to assign correct codes and modifiers using coding manuals. Answers are available from your instructor.

Exercises provide practice applying critical thinking skills. Answers to exercises are available from your instructor.

Summary

The **Summary** at the end of each chapter recaps the key points of the chapter. It also serves as a review aid when preparing for tests.

SimClaim™ CMS-1500 Software User Guide

SimClaim™ software is an online educational tool designed to familiarize you with the basics of the CMS-1500 claims completion. Because in the real-world there are many rules that can vary by payer, facility, and state, the version of *SimClaim* included in this *MindTap* maps to the specific instructions found in your *Understanding Health Insurance* textbook readings.

How to Access

Student practice software is available online through *MindTap*, accessed at www.cengage.com.

There are three types of SimClaim™ activities in this *MindTap*:

- **SimClaim™ Exercises**—Exercises are included within the chapter reading and are named "Exercise" followed by the chapter number and case number (e.g., Exercise 13.1). These exercises include the diagnosis and procedure codes that will need to be entered on the claim form.
- **SimClaim™ Cases, Set One**—Cases from Set One have a 1 at the beginning of the case study number (e.g., SimClaim™ Case **1**-1). These cases include the diagnosis and procedure codes that will need to be entered on the claim form.
- **SimClaim™ Cases, Set Two**—Cases from Set Two have a 2 at the beginning of the case study number (e.g., SimClaim™ Case **2**-1.). These cases require you to assign ICD-10-CM and CPT codes.

General Instructions

- **Blocks 3 and 11a**—Enter dates of birth as MM DD YYYY (with spaces).
- **Blocks 5, 7, 32, and 33**—Do not enter a hyphen or a space for a 9-digit ZIP code.
- **Blocks 14, 15, 16, 18, and 24A**—Enter dates as MM DD YY (with spaces).
- **Block 21**—Do *not* enter decimal points in ICD-10-CM codes.
- **Block 24D**—Enter appropriate multiple diagnosis pointer letters *without spaces*, as ABC, from Block 21. Otherwise, enter a single diagnosis pointer letter.
- **Block 27**—Enter an X in the Yes box.
- **Block 29**—If there is no amount paid indicated on the case study, *leave the field blank*.
- **Block 31**—Enter date as MMDDYY (without spaces).
- **Block 32**—Enter data as required for all Medicare claims. For all the other health insurance payers, enter data only when the facility is *other than the office setting*, as indicated on the case study.
- **Secondary insurance claims**—If a case study indicates that a patient's primary health insurance payer has paid an amount, complete a second claim for the secondary insurance payer that reflects the amount reimbursed by the primary insurance payer when indicated. The second claim is available on the Form 2 tab near the top of the CMS-1500 claim in SimClaim™.

For additional help using SimClaim™, refer to the specific health insurance payer guidelines found in your textbook.

Abbreviations

Blocks 5, 7, 32, 33, (Address Blocks) and the **Payer Address Block** contain, among other information, address information. These fields allow for the user to enter the address using full spelling and abbreviations as follows:

- "Street" allows for the following entries:
  - ○ STREET
  - ○ ST
- "Avenue" allows for the following entries:
  - ○ AVENUE
  - ○ AVE
- "Road" allows for the following entries:
  - ○ ROAD
  - ○ RD
- "Court" allows for the following entries:
  - ○ COURT
  - ○ CT
- "Highway" allows for the following entries:
  - ○ HIGHWAY
  - ○ HWY
- "Apartment" allows for the following entries:
  - ○ APARTMENT
  - ○ APT
- "Lane" allows for the following entries:
  - ○ LANE
  - ○ LN
- "Drive" allows for the following entries:
  - ○ DRIVE
  - ○ DR

Punctuation is **NEVER** allowed in address blocks.

Non-Entry Fields

Blocks 8, 24C, 24H, and 24I are non-entry fields. These blocks prohibit **ANY** input, meaning users will not even be allowed to select them.

Health Insurance Specialist Career

Chapter Outline

Health Insurance Overview

Career Opportunities

Education and Training

Job Responsibilities

Independent Contractor and Employer Liability

Professionalism

Telephone Skills for the Health Care Setting

Professional Associations and Credentials

Chapter Objectives

Upon successful completion of this chapter, you should be able to:

1. Define key terms related to the health insurance specialist career.
2. Briefly summarize health insurance claims processing and the parties involved.
3. Identify career opportunities available for health insurance specialists.
4. List the education and training requirements of a health insurance specialist.
5. Describe the job responsibilities of a health insurance specialist.
6. Differentiate among types of insurance purchased by contractors and employers.
7. Explain the role of workplace professionalism for a health insurance specialist.
8. Demonstrate telephone skills for the health care setting.
9. Identify coding and reimbursement professional associations and credentials offered.

Key Terms

AAPC

American Association
of Medical Assistants
(AAMA)

American Health
Information
Management
Association
(AHIMA)

American Medical Billing
Association (AMBA)

bonding insurance

business liability
insurance

Centers for Medicare
and Medicaid Services
(CMS)

claims examiner

coding

*Current Procedural
Terminology* (CPT)

embezzle

errors and omissions
insurance

ethics

HCPCS Level II codes

health care provider

health information
technician

health insurance claim

health insurance specialist

Healthcare Common
Procedure Coding
System (HCPCS)

hold harmless clause

independent contractor

*International Classification
of Diseases,
10th Revision,
Clinical Modification
(ICD-10-CM)*

*International
Classification of
Diseases, 10th
Revision, Procedural
Coding System
(ICD-10-PCS)*

internship

medical assistant

medical malpractice
  insurance

medical necessity

national codes

professional liability
  insurance

professionalism

property insurance

reimbursement
  specialist

respondeat superior

scope of practice

workers' compensation
  insurance

Introduction

The career of a health insurance specialist (or reimbursement specialist) is a challenging one, with opportunities for professional advancement. Individuals who understand claims processing and billing regulations, possess accurate coding skills, have the ability to successfully appeal underpaid or denied insurance claims, and demonstrate workplace professionalism are in demand. A review of medical office personnel help-wanted advertisements indicates the need for individuals with all of these skills.

Health Insurance Overview

Most health care practices in the United States accept responsibility for filing health insurance claims, and some third-party payers (e.g., BlueCross BlueShield) and government programs (e.g., Medicare) require providers to file claims. A **health insurance claim** is the documentation that is electronically or manually submitted to a third-party payer or government program requesting reimbursement for health care procedures and services provided. In the past few years, many practices have increased the number of employees assigned to some aspect of claims processing. This increase is a result of more patients having some form of health insurance, many of whom require *prior approval* for treatment by specialists and documentation of post-treatment reports. If prior approval requirements are not met, payment of the claim is denied. According to BlueCross BlueShield, if an insurance plan has a **hold harmless clause**, which means the patient is not responsible for paying what the insurance plan denies; the clause is specified in the contract, and the health care provider cannot collect those fees from the patient. It is important to realize that not all insurance policies contain *hold harmless* clauses. However, many policies contain a *no balance billing* clause that protects patients from being billed for amounts not reimbursed by payers (except for copayments, coinsurance amounts, and deductibles). (Chapter 2 contains more information about these concepts.) In addition, patients referred to nonparticipating providers (e.g., a physician who does not participate in a particular health care plan) incur significantly higher out-of-pocket costs than they may have anticipated. Competitive insurance companies are fine-tuning procedures to reduce administrative costs and overall expenditures. This cost-reduction campaign forces closer scrutiny of the entire claims process, which in turn increases the time and effort medical practices must devote to billing and filing claims according to the insurance policy filing requirements. Poor attention to claims requirements will result in lower reimbursement rates to the practices and increased expenses.

A number of health care providers sign managed care contracts as a way to combine health care delivery and financing of services to provide more affordable quality care. A **health care provider** (Figure 1-1) is a physician or other health care practitioner (e.g., nurse practitioner, physician's assistant). Each new provider-managed care contract increases the practice's patient base, the number of claims requirements and reimbursement regulations, the time the office staff must devote to fulfilling contract requirements, and the complexity of referring patients for specialty care. Each insurance plan has its own authorization requirements, billing deadlines, claims requirements, and list of participating providers or networks. If a health care provider has signed 10 participating contracts, there are 10 different sets of requirements to follow and 10 different panels of participating health care providers from which referrals can be made.

Rules associated with health insurance processing, especially government programs, change frequently; to remain up-to-date, insurance specialists should be sure they are on mailing lists to receive newsletters from third-party payers. It is also important to remain current regarding news released from the **Centers for Medicare and Medicaid Services (CMS)**, which is the administrative agency within the

FIGURE 1-1 Health care providers viewing an electronic image of a patient's chest x-ray.

federal Department of Health and Human Services (DHHS). The Secretary of the DHHS, as often reported on by the news media, announces the implementation of new regulations about government programs (e.g., Medicare, Medicaid).

The increased hiring of insurance specialists is a direct result of employers' attempts to reduce the cost of providing employee health insurance coverage. Employers renegotiate benefits with existing plans or change third-party payers altogether. The employees often receive retroactive notice of these contract changes; in some cases, they must then wait several weeks before receiving new health benefit booklets and new insurance identification cards. These changes in employer-sponsored plans have made it necessary for the health care provider's staff to check on patients' current eligibility and benefit status at each office visit.

Health insurance claims must include accurate codes. **Coding** is the process of assigning ICD-10-CM, ICD-10-PCS, CPT, and HCPCS Level II codes to diagnoses, procedures, services, and supplies. Codes contain alphanumeric and numeric characters (e.g., A01.1, 0DTJ0ZZ, 99202, K0003). Diagnoses are documented conditions or disease process (e.g., hypertension). Procedures are performed for diagnostic (e.g., lab test) and therapeutic (e.g., cholecystectomy) purposes, and services are provided to evaluate and manage patient care.

Coding systems include the following:

- *International Classification of Diseases, 10th Revision, Clinical Modification* (**ICD-10-CM**): coding system used to report diseases, injuries, and other reasons for inpatient and outpatient encounters, such as an annual physical examination performed at a physician's office

- *International Classification of Diseases, 10th Revision, Procedural Coding System* (**ICD-10-PCS**): coding system used to report procedures and services on inpatient hospital claims

- **Healthcare Common Procedure Coding System** (**HCPCS**, pronounced "hick picks"), which currently consists of two levels:

  o *Current Procedural Terminology* (**CPT**): coding system published by the American Medical Association that is used to report procedures and services performed during outpatient and physician office encounters, and professional services provided to inpatients

  o **HCPCS Level II codes** (or **national codes**): coding system published by CMS that is used to report procedures, services, and supplies not classified in CPT

(On December 31, 2003, CMS phased out the use of HCPCS Level III codes [or local codes]. However, some third-party payers continue to use the codes.)

Medical necessity involves linking every procedure or service code reported on the claim to a condition code (e.g., disease, injury, sign, symptom, other reason for encounter) that justifies the need to perform that procedure or service (Figure 1-2).

Example 1: The provider will *not* receive reimbursement when a claim is submitted with a CPT code for a right knee x-ray and an ICD-10-CM code for shoulder pain. For medical necessity purposes, the provider must document a valid reason for the knee x-ray (e.g., fracture, right patella).

PROCEDURE: Knee x-ray, right

DIAGNOSIS: Shoulder pain

Example 2: The provider will receive reimbursement when a claim is submitted with a CPT code for a chest x-ray and an ICD-10-CM code for severe shortness of breath because medical necessity has been met.

PROCEDURE: Chest x-ray

DIAGNOSIS: Severe shortness of breath

Career Opportunities

According to the *Occupational Outlook Handbook* published by the U.S. Department of Labor—Bureau of Labor Statistics, the employment growth of claims adjusters and examiners will result from more claims being submitted on behalf of a growing older adult population. Rising premiums and attempts by third-party payers to minimize costs will also result in an increased need for examiners to scrupulously review claims. Although technology reduces the amount of time it takes an adjuster to process a claim, demand for these jobs will increase anyway because many tasks cannot be easily automated (e.g., review of patient records to determine medical necessity of procedures or services rendered).

Health insurance specialists (or **reimbursement specialists**) review health-related claims to match medical necessity to procedures or services performed before payment (reimbursement) is made to the provider. A **claims examiner** employed by a third-party payer reviews health-related claims to determine whether the charges are reasonable and for medical necessity.

The claims review process requires verification of the claim for completeness and accuracy, as well as comparison with third-party payer guidelines to (1) authorize appropriate payment or (2) refer the claim to an investigator for a more thorough review.

A **medical assistant** (Figure 1-3) is employed by a provider to perform administrative and clinical tasks that keep the office or clinic running smoothly. Medical assistants who specialize in administrative aspects of

FIGURE 1-2 Health insurance specialist locating codes for entry on CMS-1500.

FIGURE 1-3 Medical assistant performing the administrative task of reviewing a record for documentation completeness.

the profession answer telephones, greet patients, update and file patient medical records, complete insurance claims, process correspondence, schedule appointments, arrange for hospital admission and laboratory services, and manage billing and bookkeeping.

Health insurance specialists and medical assistants obtain employment in clinics, health care clearinghouses (process health insurance claims), health care facility billing departments, insurance companies, and physician offices, as well as with third-party administrators (TPAs) (process health insurance claims and provide employee benefits management and other services). When employed by clearinghouses, insurance companies, and TPAs, employees often have the opportunity to work at home, where they process and verify health care claims using an Internet-based application server provider (ASP). (Information about salaries and job opportunities are located at www.bls.gov, www.aapc.com, and www.ahima.org.) Health information technicians also perform insurance specialist functions by assigning codes to diagnoses and procedures and, when employed in a provider's office, by processing claims for reimbursement. (**Health information technicians** manage patient health information and medical records, administer computer information systems, and code diagnoses and procedures for health care services provided to patients.)

In addition to an increase in insurance specialist positions available in health care practices, opportunities are also increasing in other settings. These opportunities include the following:

- Claims benefit advisors in health, malpractice, and liability insurance companies
- Coding or insurance specialists in state, local, and federal government agencies, legal offices, private insurance billing offices, and medical societies
- Medical billing and insurance verification specialists in health care organizations
- Educators in schools and companies specializing in medical office staff training
- Writers and editors of health insurance textbooks, newsletters, and other publications
- Self-employed consultants who assist medical practices with billing practices and claims appeal procedures
- Consumer claims assistance professionals who file claims and appeal low reimbursement for private individuals. In the latter case, individuals may be dissatisfied with the handling of their claims by the health care provider's insurance staff.
- Practices with poorly trained health insurance staff who are unwilling or unable to file a proper claims appeal
- Private billing practices dedicated to claims filing for patients with disabilities or who are older adults

According to the U.S. Equal Employment Opportunity Commission, the federal Americans with Disabilities Act (ADA) prohibits discrimination against individuals with disabilities, and Title I of the ADA covers employment by private employers and state/local government employers with 15 or more employees. (Section 501 of the federal Rehabilitation Act of 1973 prohibits employment discrimination against individuals with disabilities in the federal sector.) A qualified individual is protected from disparate treatment or harassment based on disability and is entitled to reasonable accommodation to perform, or apply for, a job or to enjoy the benefits and privileges of employment unless such accommodation would result in undue hardship to the employer. Some states also enact laws that prohibit employment discrimination due to disability, and they may also provide protections in addition to those enacted by the ADA.

Education and Training

Training and entry requirements vary widely for health insurance specialists, and the Bureau of Labor Statistics' *Occupational Outlook Handbook* states that opportunities will be best for those with a college degree. Academic programs should include coursework (Table 1-1) in general education (e.g., anatomy and physiology, English composition, oral communications, human relations, computer applications,

TABLE 1-1 Training requirements for health insurance specialists

Coursework	Description
Anatomy and Physiology, Medical Terminology, Pharmacology, and Pathophysiology	Knowledge of anatomic structures and physiological functioning of the body, medical terminology, and essentials of pharmacology are necessary to recognize abnormal conditions (pathophysiology). Fluency in the language of medicine and the ability to use a medical dictionary as a reference are crucial skills.
Diagnosis and Procedure/Service Coding	Understanding the rules, conventions, and applications of coding systems ensures proper selection of diagnosis and procedure/service codes, which are reported on insurance claims for reimbursement purposes.
	Example: Patient undergoes a simple suture treatment of a 3-cm facial laceration. CPT Index main term Suture does not contain a subterm for facial laceration. However, a cross reference below main term Suture directs you to main term Repair. Go to CPT Index main term Repair, subterm Skin, qualifier Wound, and qualifier Simple. Then, go to the appropriate CPT section, subsection, and category (or heading) to review listed codes and select the correct code.
Verbal and Written Communication	Health insurance specialists explain complex insurance concepts and regulations to patients and must effectively communicate with providers regarding documentation of procedures and services to reduce coding and billing errors. Written communication skills are necessary when preparing effective appeals for unpaid claims.
Critical Thinking	Differentiating among technical descriptions of similar procedures requires critical thinking skills.
	Example: Patient is diagnosed with spondy*losis*, which is defined as any condition of the spine. A code from category M47 of ICD-10-CM is assigned. If the diagnosis was mistakenly coded as spondy*lolysis*, which is a defect of the articulating portion of the vertebra, ICD-10-CM category Q76 (if congenital) or M43 (if acquired) codes would be reported in error.
Data Entry	Federal regulations require electronic submission of most government claims, which means that health insurance specialists need excellent keyboarding skills and basic finance and math skills. Because insurance information screens with different titles often contain identical information, the health insurance specialist must carefully and accurately enter data about patient care.
	Example: Primary and secondary insurance computer screens require entry of similar information. Claims are rejected by insurance companies if data are missing or erroneous.
Internet Access	Online information sources provide access to medical references, insurance company manuals, and procedure guidelines. The federal government posts changes to reimbursement methodologies and other policies on websites. Internet forums allow health insurance specialists to network with other professionals.

and so on) and health insurance specialist education (e.g., health information management, medical terminology, pharmacology, coding and reimbursement, insurance processing, and so on). The characteristics of a successful health insurance specialist include an ability to work independently, a strong sense of ethics, attention to detail, and the ability to think critically. The *American Heritage Concise Dictionary* defines **ethics** as the principles of right or good conduct, and rules that govern the conduct of members of a profession.

Student Internship

An **internship** benefits students and facilities that accept students for placement. Students receive on-the-job experience prior to graduation, and the internship assists them in obtaining permanent employment.

Facilities benefit from the opportunity to participate in and improve the formal education process. Quite often, students who complete internships obtain employment at the internship facility. The students report to the internship supervisor at the site. Students are often required to submit a professional résumé to the internship supervisor and schedule an interview prior to acceptance for placement. While this process can be intimidating, students gain experience with the interview process, which is part of obtaining permanent employment. Students should research résumé writing and utilize interview technique services available from their school's career services office. This office typically reviews résumés and provides interview tips. Some offices even videotape mock interviews for students.

The internship is on-the-job training even though it is unpaid, and students should expect to provide proof of immunizations (available from a physician) and possibly undergo a preemployment physical examination and participate in an orientation. In addition, because of the focus on privacy and security of patient information, the facility will likely require students to sign a nondisclosure agreement (to protect patient confidentiality), which is kept on file at the college and by the internship site.

 NOTE:

Breach of patient confidentiality can result in termination of the internship, which means failing the internship course. Suspension or expulsion from your academic program are other possible consequences. Be sure to ask about your academic program's requirements regarding this issue.

During the internship, students are expected to report to work on time. Students who cannot participate in the internship on a particular day, or who arrive late, should contact their internship supervisor or program faculty, whoever is designated for that purpose. Students are also required to make up any lost time. Because the internship is a simulated job experience, students are to be well groomed and should dress professionally (Figure 1-4). Students should show interest in all aspects of the experience, develop good working relationships with coworkers, and react appropriately to criticism and direction. If any concerns arise during the internship, students should discuss them with their internship supervisor or program faculty.

FIGURE 1-4 Medical assistant and internship student prepare for their next patient.

Job Responsibilities

This section provides an overview of the major responsibilities delegated to health insurance specialists. In practices where just one or two persons work with insurance billing, each individual must be capable of performing all the listed responsibilities. In multispecialty practices that employ many health insurance specialists, each usually processes claims for a limited number of insurance companies (e.g., an insurance specialist may be assigned to processing only Medicare claims). Some practices have a clear division of labor, with specific individuals accepting responsibility for only a few assigned tasks. The following job description lists typical tasks. Regardless of the employment setting, health insurance specialists are guided by a **scope of practice** that defines the profession, delineates qualifications and responsibilities, and clarifies supervision requirements (Table 1-2).

Health Insurance Specialist Job Description

1. Review patient record documentation to accurately code all diagnoses, procedures, and services using ICD-10-CM for diagnoses and CPT and HCPCS Level II for procedures and services. (ICD-10-PCS codes are reported for inpatient hospital procedures only.)

    The accurate coding of diagnoses, procedures, and services rendered to the patient allows a medical practice to

    - Communicate diagnostic and treatment data to a patient's insurance plan to assist the patient in obtaining maximum benefits.
    - Facilitate analysis of the practice's patient base to improve patient care delivery and efficiency of practice operations to contain costs.

2. Research and apply knowledge of all insurance rules and regulations for major insurance programs in the local or regional area.

3. Accurately post charges, payments, and adjustments to patient accounts and accounts receivable records.

4. Prepare or review claims generated by the practice to ensure that all required data are accurately reported and to ensure prompt reimbursement for services provided (contributing to the practice's cash flow).

TABLE 1-2 Scope of practice elements and definitions for health insurance specialists

Element	Definition
Definition of Professional	One who interacts with patients to clarify health insurance coverage and financial responsibility, completes and processes insurance claims, and appeals denied claims.
Qualifications	Graduate of health insurance specialist certificate or degree program or equivalent. One year of experience in health insurance or related field. Detailed working knowledge and demonstrated proficiency in at least one insurance company's billing and/or collection process. Excellent organizational skills. Ability to manage multiple tasks in a timely manner. Proficient use of computerized registration and billing systems and personal computers, including spreadsheet and word processing software applications. Certification through AAPC, AHIMA, AMBA, or NHA.
Responsibilities	Use medical management computer software to process health insurance claims, assign codes to diagnoses and procedures/services, and manage patient records. Communicate with patients, providers, and insurance companies about coverage and reimbursement issues. Remain up-to-date regarding changes in health care industry laws and regulations.
Supervision Requirements	Active and continuous supervision of a health insurance specialist is required. However, the physical presence of the supervisor at the time and place that responsibilities are performed is not required.

5. Review all insurance payments and remittance advice documents to ensure proper processing and payment of each claim. The patient receives an *explanation of benefits (EOB)* from the third-party payer, which is a report detailing the results of processing a claim (e.g., payer reimburses provider $80 on a submitted charge of $100). The provider receives a *remittance advice* (or *remit*), which is a notice sent by the insurance company that contains payment information about a claim.

 NOTE:

Chapter 4 contains additional information about EOBs and remits, including samples of each.

6. Correct all data errors and resubmit all unprocessed or returned claims.

7. Research and prepare appeals for all underpaid, unjustly recoded, or denied claims.

8. Rebill all claims not paid within 30 to 45 days, depending on individual practice policy and the payers' policies.

9. Inform health care providers and staff of changes in fraud and abuse laws, coding changes, documentation guidelines, and third-party payer requirements that may affect the billing and claims submission procedures.

10. Assist with timely updating of the practice's internal documents, patient registration forms, and billing forms as required by changes in coding or insurance billing requirements.

11. Maintain an internal audit system to ensure that required pretreatment authorizations are received and entered into the billing and treatment records.

12. Perform audits to compare provider documentation with assigned codes.

13. Explain insurance benefits, policy requirements, and filing rules to patients.

14. Maintain confidentiality of patient information.

Independent Contractor and Employer Liability

Health insurance specialists who are self-employed are considered independent contractors (Figure 1-5). The *'Lectric Law Library's Lexicon* defines an **independent contractor** as "a person who performs services for another under an express or implied agreement and who is not subject to the other's control, or right to control, of the manner and means of performing the services. The organization that hires an independent contractor is not liable for the acts or omissions of the independent contractor."

Independent contractors should purchase **professional liability insurance** (or **errors and omissions insurance**), which provides protection from liability as a result of errors and omissions when performing their professional services (e.g., coding audits). Professional associations often include a membership benefit that allows the purchase of liability insurance coverage at reduced rates.

Example: The American Health Information Management Association makes information about the purchase of a professional liability plan available to its membership. If a member is sued, the plan covers legal fees, court costs, court judgments, and out-of-court settlements. The available coverage varies by state.

A health care facility (or physician) that employs health insurance specialists is legally responsible for employees' actions performed within the context of their employment. This is called *respondeat superior*,

FIGURE 1-5 Self-employed health
insurance specialist.

Latin for "let the master answer," which means that the employer is liable for the actions and omissions of employees as performed and committed within the scope of their employment. Employers purchase many types of insurance to protect their business assets and property (Table 1-3).

Determining Independent Contractor Status

One way to determine independent contractor status is to apply the common law "right to control" test, which includes five factors:

- Amount of control the hiring organization exerted over the worker's activities
- Responsibility for costs of operation (e.g., equipment and supplies)
- Method and form of payment and benefits
- Length of job commitment made to the worker
- Nature of occupation and skills required

The Internal Revenue Service applies a 20-factor independent contractor test to decide whether an organization has correctly classified a worker as an independent contractor for purposes of wage withholdings. The Department of Labor uses the "economic reality" test to determine worker status for purposes of compliance with the minimum wage and overtime requirements of the Fair Labor Standards Act.

TABLE 1-3 Types of professional insurance purchased by employers

Insurance	Description
Bonding Insurance	An insurance agreement that guarantees repayment for financial losses resulting from an employee's act or failure to act. It protects the financial operations of the employer.
	Note: Physician offices should bond employees who have financial responsibilities. The National White Collar Crime Center estimates $400 billion in annual losses to all types of employers due to employees who **embezzle**, or steal, money from an employer.
Business Liability Insurance	An insurance agreement that protects business assets and covers the cost of lawsuits resulting from bodily injury (e.g., customer slips on wet floor), personal injury (e.g., slander or libel), and false advertising. **Medical malpractice insurance**, a type of professional liability insurance, covers physicians and other licensed health care professionals for liability relating to claims arising from patient treatment.
	Note: Liability insurance does not protect an employer from nonperformance of a contract, sexual harassment, race and gender discrimination lawsuits, or wrongful termination of employees.
	Note: An alternative to purchasing liability insurance from an insurance company is to *self-fund*, which involves setting aside money to pay damages or paying damages with current operating revenue should the employer ever be found liable. Another option is to join a *risk retention* or *risk purchasing group*, which provides lower-cost commercial liability insurance to its members. A third option is to obtain coverage in a *surplus lines market* that has been established to insure unique risks.
Property Insurance	An insurance agreement that protects business contents (e.g., buildings and equipment) against fire, theft, and other risks.
Workers' Compensation Insurance	Protection mandated by state law that covers employees and their dependents against injury and death occurring during the course of employment. Workers' compensation is not health insurance, and it is not intended to compensate for disabilities other than those caused by illnesses or injuries arising from employment. The purpose of workers' compensation is to provide financial and medical benefits to those with work-related illnesses or injuries, and their families, regardless of fault.

Example: Dr. Pederson's office employs Linda Starling as a health insurance specialist. As part of the job, Linda has access to confidential patient information. While processing claims, Linda notices that a friend has been a patient and later tells her spouse about the diagnosis and treatment. The friend finds out about the breach of confidentiality and contacts a lawyer. Legally, the friend can sue Dr. Pederson. Although Linda could also be named in the lawsuit, termination by her employer is more likely.

Professionalism

The *Merriam-Webster Dictionary* defines **professionalism** as the conduct, aims, or qualities that characterize a professional person. Health care facility managers establish rules of professional behavior (e.g., codes of conduct, policies, and procedures), so employees know how to behave professionally. Employees are expected to develop the following skills to demonstrate workplace professionalism, which results in personal growth and success.

Attitude, Self-Esteem, and Etiquette

"For success, attitude is equally as important as ability."   Harry F. Banks

Attitude impacts an individual's capacity to effectively perform job functions, and employers or colleagues can perceive an employee's attitude as positive, negative, or neutral. This subconscious transfer of feelings results in colleagues determining whether someone has a positive attitude about work. Self-esteem impacts attitude;

low self-esteem causes lack of confidence, and higher self-esteem leads to self-confidence, improved relationships, self-respect, and a successful career. Etiquette is the demonstration of good manners along with behavior that is considered polite among members of a profession. For example, medical assistants should refer to patients by title (e.g., Mrs. Brown) instead of their first name.

Communication

"And he goes through life, his mouth open, and his mind closed."

William Shakespeare

Successful interpersonal communication includes self-expression and active listening to develop understanding about what others are saying. To listen effectively, be sure to understand the message instead of just hearing words. This active involvement in the communication process helps avoid miscommunication.

Conflict Management

"When angry, count to ten before you speak; if very angry, a hundred."

Thomas Jefferson

Conflict occurs as a part of the decision-making process, and the way a person handles it makes it positive or negative. People often have different perspectives about the same situation, and actively listening to the other's viewpoint helps neutralize what could become negative conflict.

Customer Service

"If we don't take care of our customers, someone else will."

Unknown

Health insurance specialists serve as a direct point of contact for a provider's patients, and they are responsible for ensuring that patients receive an excellent level of service or assistance with questions and concerns. It is equally important to remember that colleagues deserve the same respect and attention as patients.

Diversity Awareness

"The real death of America will come when everyone is alike."

James T. Ellison

Diversity is defined as differences among people and includes demographics of age, education, ethnicity, gender, geographic location, income, language, marital status, occupation, parental status, physical and mental ability, race, religious beliefs, sexual orientation, and veteran status. Developing tolerance, which is the opposite of bigotry and prejudice, means dealing with personal attitudes, beliefs, and experiences. Embracing the differences that represent the demographics of our society is crucial to becoming a successful health professional.

Leadership

"The difference between a boss and a leader: a boss says, 'Go!' A leader says, 'Let's go!'"

E. M. Kelly

Leadership is the ability to motivate team members to complete a common organizational goal display. Leaders have earned the trust of their team, which is the reason the entire team is able to achieve its objective and set the standard for productivity, as well as revenue goals. Interestingly, the leader identified by the team might not be the organization's manager or supervisor. Leaders emerge from within the organization because they have demonstrated beliefs, ethics, and values with which team members identify. Managers who are not threatened by the natural emergence of leaders benefit from team harmony and increased productivity. They receive credit for excellent management skills, and they begin the process to leadership when they begin to acknowledge the work ethic of the team and its leader.

Managing Change

"If we don't change, we don't grow. If we don't grow, we aren't really living."

Gail Sheehy

Change is crucial to the survival of an organization because it is a necessary response to the implementation of new and revised federal and state programs, regulations, and so on. While the organization that does not embrace change becomes extinct, such change disrupts the organization's workflow (and productivity) and is perceived as a threat to employees. Therefore, it is the role of the organization's leadership team to provide details about the impending change, including periodic updates as work processes undergo gradual revision. Employees also need to understand what is being changed and why, and the leadership team needs to understand employees' reluctance to change.

Productivity

"Even if you are on the right track, you'll get run over if you just sit there."

Will Rogers

Health care providers expect health insurance and medical coding/billing specialists to be productive regarding completion of duties and responsibilities. Productivity can include a willingness to work flexible hours (e.g., confirming patient appointments during early evening hours) and participate in job sharing (e.g., two or more employees who work part time to accomplish tasks associated with a position). In addition, employees who have demonstrated an ability to work independently may be allowed to *telecommute* (work from home) in the areas of billing and medical coding; such employees are usually required to attend meetings and perform some tasks on site at the health care organization. Pursuing professional certification and participating in continuing education helps ensure individual compliance with the latest coding rules and other updates. Increased knowledge leads to increased productivity and performance improvement on the job.

Professional Ethics

"Always do right—this will gratify some and astonish the rest."

Mark Twain

The characteristics of a successful health insurance specialist include an ability to work independently, attention to detail, ability to think critically, and a strong sense of ethics. The *American Heritage Concise Dictionary* defines ethics as the principles of right or good conduct, and rules that govern the conduct of members of a profession.

Team-Building

"Michael, if you can't pass, you can't play."

Coach Dean Smith to Michael Jordan in his freshman year

Colleagues who share a sense of community and purpose work well together and can accomplish organizational goals more quickly and easily because they rely on one another. This means colleagues provide help to, and receive help from, other members of the team. Sharing the leadership role and working together to complete difficult tasks facilitates team-building.

Professional Appearance

Appropriate professional attire and personal presentation (Figure 1-6) provide an employee's first impression to colleagues, managers, physicians, patients or clients, and others. Well-groomed employees convey professional images about themselves and the quality of services provided by the organization. Employers establish the dress code policy, which is usually conservative and stylish but not trendy, and some require a uniform.

An employee's appearance provides that important first impression, and well-groomed professionals look self-confident, display pride in themselves, and appear capable of performing whatever duties need to be done. We have all experienced days when we did not feel good about the way we looked, which, in turn, affected our performance. To present yourself in the best possible light, be sure to adhere to the following general guidelines for a professional appearance:

- *Cleanliness* is the first essential for good grooming. Take a daily bath or shower. Use a deodorant or antiperspirant. Shampoo your hair often. Brush and floss your teeth daily.

- *Hand care* is critical. Take special care of your hands. Keep hand cream or lotion in convenient places to use after washing your hands. Because this is done frequently, hands tend to chap and crack, which can allow organisms entry into your body—a risk you cannot afford. Also, keep your fingernails manicured at a moderate length. Those who provide health care services to patients should not use false nails because bacteria and fungi can grow beneath such nails. If you work in a uniform and your organization's policy allows you to use nail polish, choose clear or light shades. Even when wearing street clothes, bright or trendy colors are not appropriate for the office.

- *Hair* must be clean and away from your face. Long hair should be worn up or at least fastened back. It is not appropriate to keep pushing your hair out of the way while working because you can add organisms to your environment and perhaps take them home with you. Patients who receive health care services from employees may also be susceptible to "receiving" something from your hair if you touch them after arranging your hair.

- *Proper attire* may vary with medical specialty. When a uniform is not required, it may be appropriate to wear a white laboratory coat over a dress shirt and slacks or a skirt. Depending on the organization

FIGURE 1-6 Present a professional appearance.

(e.g., pediatric office), it might also be acceptable for the laboratory coat to be a color other than white. For instance, many pediatric practices prefer that medical assistants wear colorful prints with patterns of cartoon characters that children will recognize to help them feel more at ease. Psychiatry and psychology medical office assistants may not be required to wear uniforms, as their clinical duties would be limited. Dressing in professional attire will not only encourage the respect of others for your profession, but will also help you feel like an integral part of the health care team. When uniforms are required, they must be clean, fit well, and be free from wrinkles. Uniform shoes should be kept clean and have clean shoestrings; hose must not have runs. Pay attention to the undergarments that you wear beneath the uniform so that they do not show through the fabric of your uniform.

- *Jewelry*, except for a watch or wedding ring, is not appropriate with a uniform. Small earrings may be worn but still may get in the way when you use the telephone. Not only does jewelry look out of place, but it is a great collector of microorganisms. Novelty piercings, such as nose rings and tongue studs, are not appropriate for professional grooming. Save the wearing of these for after work hours.

- *Fragrances*, such as perfumes, colognes, and aftershave lotions, may be offensive to some patients, especially if they are suffering from nausea. Thus, it is recommended that you not use fragrances.

- *Cosmetics*, if used, should be tasteful and skillfully applied.

- *Gum chewing* is very unprofessional. A large piece of gum interferes with speech, and cracking gum is totally unacceptable. If you feel you need gum for a breath concern, use a breath mint or mouthwash instead.

- *Posture* affects not only your appearance but also the amount of fatigue you experience. The ease at which you move around reflects your poise and confidence. To check your posture, back up to a wall, place your feet apart (straight down from your hips), and try to insert your hand through the space between your lower back and the wall. Pull your stomach in, tuck under your buttocks, and try to place your spine against the wall. Your shoulders should be relaxed with your head held erect. This will probably feel very unnatural, but practice keeping your body straight and head erect when you walk and you will see how much better you look and feel.

Remember! Maintaining personal hygiene benefits patient health and reduces risks of cross-contamination. Daily showering, clean hair, and neatly manicured nails show others that you take pride in yourself and provide a model that others can imitate. A lot of different elements compose our personal characteristics, and each has an impact about how we feel about ourselves and how others perceive us. It is important to evaluate yourself and help identify what you can do to improve your effectiveness when interacting with people. Your course instructor is an excellent resource with whom you could have a private conversation, asking whether there is anything you should be doing differently to improve your professional appearance (and communication skills). For example, during class, an instructor noticed that a student who was otherwise impeccably dressed and groomed frequently flipped long hair from one side to the other. It was recommended to the student that their hair be pulled back for interviews, internships, and employment. Prior to an on-campus interview for employment, the student stopped into the office to ask the instructor whether the hairstyle was appropriate; this was something the instructor did not ask the student to do, and it was impressive that the student incorporated constructive criticism about grooming. And, most importantly, the student got the job!

Telephone Skills for the Health Care Setting

The telephone can be an effective means of patient access to the health care system because a health care team member serves as an immediate contact for the patient. Participating in telephone skills training and following established protocols (policies) allow health care team members to respond appropriately to patients. When processes for handling all calls are developed *and* followed by health care team members, the result is greater office efficiency and less frustration for health care team members and patients. Avoid problems with telephone communication in your health care setting by implementing the following protocols:

Establish a telephone-availability policy that works for patients and office staff. Telephone calls that are unanswered, result in a busy signal, and/or force patients to be placed on hold for long periods frustrate callers (Figure 1-7). The outcome can be an administrative assistant who sounds impatient and too busy to properly resolve callers' questions and concerns. Avoid such problems by increasing telephone availability so that the calls are answered outside of the typical 9 to 5 workday (which often includes not answering the telephone during lunch). Consider having employees (who have undergone telephone skills training) answer calls on a rotating basis one hour before the office opens, during the noon hour, and one hour after the office closes. This telephone protocol will result in satisfied patients (and other callers) and office employees who do not have to return calls to individuals who otherwise leave messages on voicemail.

 NOTE:

Although an administrative assistant is the initial point of contact for the office, all health care team members must effectively handle or transfer telephone calls. This requires sensitivity to patient concerns about health care problems, and the health care professional must communicate a caring environment that leads to patient satisfaction.

Set up an appropriate number of dedicated telephone lines (e.g., appointment scheduling, insurance and billing) based on the function and size of the health care setting. Publish the telephone numbers on the office's website and in an office brochure or local telephone directory, and instruct employees to avoid using the lines when making outgoing calls. Another option is to install an interactive telephone response system that connects callers with appropriate staff (e.g., appointment scheduling, insurance and billing, and so on) based on the caller's keypad or voice responses to instructions provided.

Inform callers who ask to speak with the physician (or another health care provider) that the physician (or provider) is with a patient. Do *not* state, "The physician is busy," which implies that the physician is too busy for the patient and could offend the caller. Ask for the caller's name, telephone number, and reason for the call, and explain that the call will be returned.

Assign 15-minute time periods every 2 to 3 hours when creating the schedule, to allow time for physicians (and other health care providers) to return telephone calls. This allows the administrative assistant to tell callers an approximate time when calls will be returned (and patient records can be retrieved).

 NOTE:

Assigning the 15-minute time periods must be approved by physicians because they may prefer to return telephone calls prior to the first appointment of the day or after the last appointment of the day.

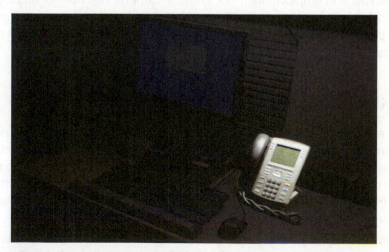

FIGURE 1-7 Unanswered telephone calls frustrate callers.

Physically separate front desk check-in/check-out and administrative assistant/patient appointment scheduling offices. It is unlikely that an employee who manages the registration of patients as they arrive at the office (and the check-out of patients at the conclusion of an appointment) has time to answer telephone calls. Office receptionists and appointment schedulers who work in private offices will comply with federal and state patient privacy laws when talking with patients. In addition, appointment scheduling, telephone management, and patient check-in (registration) and check-out procedures will be performed with greater efficiency.

Require office employees to learn professional telephone skills. Schedule professional telephone skills training as part of new employee orientation, and arrange for all employees to attend an annual workshop to improve skills. Training allows everyone to learn key aspects of successful telephone communication, which include developing an effective telephone voice that focuses on tone. During a telephone conversation, each person forms an opinion based on *how* something is said (rather than *what* is said). Therefore, speak clearly and distinctly, do not speak too fast or too slow, and vary your tone by letting your voice rise and fall naturally. The following rules apply to each telephone conversation:

- When answering the telephone, state the name of the office and your name (e.g., "Hornell Medical Center, Shelly Dunham speaking").
- Do not use slang (e.g., nope, yep, uh-huh) or health care jargon (e.g., ICU—the patient hears "eye see you").
- Use the caller's name (e.g., Betty Smith calls the office, and the administrative assistant asks, "How may I help you today, Mrs. Smith?").
- Provide clear explanations when responding to patients (e.g., "The physician will return your call between 3 and 4 PM today").
- Be pleasant, friendly, sincere, and helpful (e.g., smile as you talk with the caller and your tone will be friendly) (Figure 1-8).
- Give the caller your undivided attention to show personal interest, and do not interrupt.
- Before placing the caller on hold or transferring a call, ask for permission to do so (e.g., "May I place you on hold?," "May I transfer you to the appropriate office?").
- When the caller wants to speak with an individual who is unavailable, ask if you can take a message (e.g., "Dr. Smith is with a patient right now. May I take a message and have your call returned after 3 PM?").
- Use a preprinted message form (or commercial message pad) when taking a message (Figure 1-9). Document the following about each call, and file it in the patient's record: date of call, name of patient, name and credentials of individual talking with patient, and a brief note about the contents of the telephone conversation.

FIGURE 1-8 Smile as you talk with a caller so your tone is pleasant.

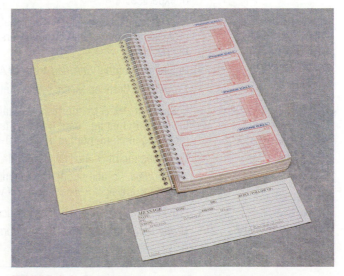

FIGURE 1-9 Message pads with carbonless copy.

Professional Associations and Credentials

The health insurance specialist who joins one or more professional associations (Table 1-4) receives useful information available in several formats, including professional journals and newsletters, access to members-only websites, notification of professional development, and so on. A key feature of membership is an awareness of the importance of professional certification. Once certified, the professional is responsible for maintaining that credential by fulfilling continuing education requirements established by the sponsoring association. Join professional associations by going to their websites to locate membership links. Membership fees (and testing fees) vary, and some associations allow students to join for a reduced fee. Professional certification examination fees also vary according to association. Once students decide where they want to seek employment (e.g., physician's office, hospital), they can research each professional association's website (located in Internet links in this chapter) to research certification examinations offered. For example, a physician's office will require different certifications as compared with hospitals. It is important for students to have an excellent understanding about the career path they want to pursue so as to obtain the appropriate certification credentials. For example, hospitals may prefer the AHIMA credentials, while physician's offices may prefer the AAPC credentials. Other organizations that offer professional certification include the American Medical Billing Association (AMBA) and Ascend Learning's National Healthcareer Association (NHA). AMBA provides industry and regulatory education and networking opportunities for members and offers the Certified Medical Reimbursement Specialist (CMRS) certification. The NHA is a national professional certification agency for health care workers and offers the Certified Billing & Coding Specialists (CBCS) certification.

TABLE 1-4 Professional associations that offer coding and reimbursement credentials

Professional Association	Description, Publications, and Credentials
AAPC	• Founded to elevate the standards of medical coding by providing certification, ongoing education, networking, and recognition for coders • Publishes the *Healthcare Business Monthly* newsmagazine and hosts continuing education • Previously known as the American Academy of Professional Coders • *Credentials:* Certified Professional Biller (CPB), Certified Professional Coder (CPC), Certified Outpatient Coder (COC), Certified Inpatient Coder (CIC), Certified Risk Adjustment Coder (CRC), Certified Professional Coder-Payer (CPC-P), and specialty credentials in many different fields of expertise
American Association of Medical Assistants (AAMA)	• Enables medical assisting professionals to enhance and demonstrate knowledge, skills, and professionalism required by employers and patients, and protects medical assistants' right to practice • Publishes monthly *Certified Medical Assistant* journal • *Credential:* Certified Medical Assistant, abbreviated as CMA (AAMA)
American Health Information Management Association (AHIMA)	• Founded in 1928 to improve the quality of medical records, and currently advances the health information management (HIM) profession toward an electronic and global environment, including implementation of ICD-10-CM and ICD-10-PCS • Publishes monthly *Journal of AHIMA* • *Credentials:* Certified Coding Assistant (CCA), Certified Coding Specialist (CCS), and Certified Coding Specialist-Physician-based (CCS-P) (Additional HIM credentials are offered by AHIMA)
American Medical Billing Association (AMBA)	• Provides industry and regulatory education and networking opportunities for members • *Credential:* Certified Medical Reimbursement Specialist (CMRS)

Summary

A health insurance specialist's career is challenging and requires professional training to understand claims processing and billing regulations, possess accurate coding skills, and develop the ability to successfully appeal underpaid or denied insurance claims. A health insurance claim is submitted to a third-party payer or government program to request reimbursement for health care services provided. Many health insurance plans require prior approval for treatment provided by specialists.

While the requirements of health insurance specialist programs vary, successful specialists develop skills that allow them to work independently and ethically, focus on attention to detail, and think critically. Medical practices and health care facilities employing health insurance specialists require them to perform various functions. Smaller practices and facilities require specialists to process claims for all types of payers, while larger practices and facilities expect specialists to process claims for a limited number of payers.

Health insurance specialists are guided by a scope of practice, which defines the profession, delineates qualifications and responsibilities, and clarifies supervision requirements. Self-employed health insurance specialists are independent contractors who should purchase professional liability insurance. Health care providers and facilities typically purchase bonding, liability, property, and workers' compensation insurance to cover their employees. Employees who demonstrate professional behavior are proud of their work, and they are recognized as having integrity and discipline. They earn the respect of their colleagues, develop a reputation for being loyal and trustworthy, and are considered team players. The AAMA, AAPC, AHIMA, AMBA, and Ascend Learning's NHA offer exams leading to professional credentials. Becoming credentialed demonstrates competence and knowledge in the field of health insurance processing as well as coding and reimbursement.

Internet Links

AAPC: *www.aapc.com*

American Association of Medical Assistants (AAMA): *www.aama-ntl.org*

American Health Information Management Association (AHIMA): *www.ahima.org*

Ascend Learning's National Healthcareer Association (NHA): *www.nhanow.com*

Centers for Medicare and Medicaid Services (CMS): *www.cms.gov*

U.S. Department of Labor, Bureau of Labor Statistics (BLS): *www.bls.gov*

Review

1.1 – Multiple Choice

Select the most appropriate response.

1. The document submitted to the payer requesting reimbursement is called a(n)
   a. explanation of benefits.
   b. health insurance claim.
   c. remittance advice.
   d. prior approval form.

2. The Centers for Medicare and Medicaid Services (CMS) is an administrative agency within the
   a. Administration for Children and Families.
   b. Department of Health and Human Services.
   c. Food and Drug Administration.
   d. Office of the Inspector General.

3. A health care practitioner is also called a health care
    a. dealer.
    b. provider.
    c. purveyor.
    d. supplier.

4. Which is the most appropriate response to a patient who calls the office and asks to speak with the physician?
    a. Politely state that the physician is busy and cannot be disturbed.
    b. Explain that the physician is unavailable, and ask if the patient would like to leave a message.
    c. Transfer the call to the exam room where the physician is located.
    d. Offer to schedule an appointment for the patient to be seen by the physician.

5. The process of assigning diagnoses, procedures, and services using numeric and alphanumeric characters is called
    a. coding.
    b. data processing.
    c. programming.
    d. reimbursement.

6. If a health insurance plan's prior approval requirements are not met by providers and the claim is submitted for reimbursement, then
    a. administrative costs are reduced.
    b. patients' coverage is cancelled.
    c. payment of the claim is denied.
    d. they pay a fine to the health plan.

7. Which coding system is used to report diagnoses and conditions on claims?
    a. CPT
    b. HCPCS Level II
    c. ICD-10-CM
    d. ICD-10-PCS

8. Which organization publishes CPT?
    a. ADA
    b. AHIMA
    c. AMA
    d. CMS

9. National codes are associated with
    a. CDT.
    b. CPT.
    c. HCPCS Level II.
    d. ICD.

10. The process of linking procedure/service and condition codes on a CMS-1500 claim justifies
    a. coding.
    b. hold harmless.
    c. medical necessity.
    d. scope of practice.

11. The medical practice that employs a health insurance specialist is legally responsible for their actions when performed within the context of their employment, which is called
    a. *per se.*
    b. *res gestae.*
    c. *respondeat superior.*
    d. subpoena *duces tecum.*

12. Which type of insurance guarantees repayment for financial losses resulting from an employee's act or failure to act?
    a. Bonding
    b. Liability
    c. Property
    d. Workers' compensation

13. Physicians and other health care professionals purchase _____ insurance to protect them from liability relating to claims arising from patient treatment.
    a. bonding
    b. medical malpractice
    c. third-party payer
    d. workers' compensation

14. Which requires health insurance specialists to differentiate among the technical descriptions of similar procedures in the CPT coding manual?
    a. Critical thinking
    b. Data entry
    c. Pathophysiology
    d. Verbal and written communication

15. The American Association of Medical Assistants offers which certification exam?
    a. CCS
    b. CMA
    c. CPC
    d. RHIT

1.2 – Professionalism

Instructions: Complete each statement by entering the appropriate professionalism skill.

1. Increased professional knowledge leads to increased _____ and performance improvement on the job.
    a. ethics
    b. leadership
    c. management
    d. productivity
    e. service

2. An employee who uses active listening to resolve issues as part of the decision-making process is demonstrating effective conflict _____ skills.
    a. ethics
    b. leadership
    c. management
    d. productivity
    e. service

3. An employee who motivates team members so that organizational goals are achieved demonstrates
    a. ethics.
    b. leadership.
    c. management.
    d. productivity.
    e. service.

4. An employee who provides excellent service when addressing questions and concerns from patients and colleagues demonstrates customer
   a. ethics.
   b. leadership.
   c. management.
   d. productivity.
   e. service.

5. Rules that govern conduct of members of a profession are called professional
   a. ethics.
   b. leadership.
   c. management.
   d. productivity.
   e. service.

1.3 – Telephone Messages

Review the voice message case scenario below, which was recorded on Dr. Sickmann's office telephone voicemail during lunch. Enter key elements on the telephone message form provided, including the (1) name of person for whom the message was left; (2) caller's name (obtain correct spelling), company or department, and return telephone number; (3) date and time of the call; (3) message for the health care team member; and (4) action to be taken (e.g., please call ..., will call back, urgent, and so on).

Case Scenario: Devon Shane, Front Office Manager, answered the phone. Tristan N. Shout, a returning patient, called at 1:00 PM on 9/20/YYYY to let the office know of a recent job change and new insurance coverage. The message was, "Tristan can now return to our office since Dr. Sickmann is a participating provider in their new insurance network. An annual exam needs to be scheduled before the year is up. Tristan would like to make an appointment for the latest time available on a Friday. Please call (123) 319-6531 as soon as we get the message."

DATE _____ TIME _____

TO _____

WHILE YOU WERE OUT

NAME _____

FROM _____

PHONE _____

TELEPHONED _____ PLEASE CALL BACK _____

CALLED TO SEE YOU _____ WILL CALL AGAIN _____

RETURNED YOUR CALL _____ URGENT _____

MESSAGE:

_____

_____

_____

TAKEN BY _____

Introduction to Health Insurance and Managed Care

Chapter Outline

Overview of Health Insurance and Managed Care

Major Developments in Health Insurance and Managed Care

Managed Care

Characteristics of Health Plans and Managed Care

Consumer-Directed Health Plans

Health Care Documentation

Electronic Health Record

Chapter Objectives

Upon successful completion of this chapter, you should be able to:

1. Define key terms related to an introduction to health insurance.

2. Summarize basic health insurance and managed care concepts.

3. Identify major developments in U.S. health insurance.

4. Describe the history, role, and effects of managed care in health care.

5. Explain the characteristics of health insurance and managed care.

6. Describe consumer-directed health plans.

7. Describe health care documentation methods.

8. Discuss the impact of the electronic health record (EHR) on health care.

Key Terms

accreditation

advanced alternative payment models (advanced APMs)

adverse selection

alternative payment models (APMs)

Amendment to the HMO Act of 1973

American Recovery and Reinvestment Act of 2009 (ARRA)

benchmarking

cafeteria plan

capitation

carve-out plan

case manager

clinical practice guidelines

closed-panel HMO

CMS-1500 claim

coinsurance

competitive medical plan (CMP)

Consolidated Omnibus Budget Reconciliation Act of 1985 (COBRA)

consumer-directed health plan (CDHP)

continuity of care

copayment (copay)

covered services

customized subcapitation plan (CSCP)

deductible

direct contract model HMO

electronic clinical quality measures (eCQMs)

electronic health record (EHR)

electronic medical record (EMR)

Employee Retirement Income Security Act of 1974 (ERISA)

enrollee

excess insurance

exclusive provider organization (EPO)

express contract

external quality review organization (EQRO)

Federal Employee Health Benefits Program (FEHBP)

Federal Employees' Compensation Act (FECA)

Federal Employers' Liability Act (FELA)

federally qualified HMO

fee schedule

fee-for-service

fee-for-service plans

flexible benefit plan

flexible spending account (FSA)

gag clause

gatekeeper

group health insurance

group model HMO

group practice without walls (GPWW)

guaranteed renewal

health care

Health Care and Education Reconciliation Act (HCERA)

health care reimbursement account (HCRA)

Health Information Technology for Economic and Clinical Health Act (HITECH Act)

health insurance

health insurance exchange

health insurance marketplace

health maintenance organization (HMO)

Health Maintenance Organization (HMO) Assistance Act of 1973

health reimbursement arrangement (HRA)

health savings account (HSA)

Healthcare Effectiveness Data and Information Set (HEDIS)

Hill-Burton Act

implied contract

indemnity plan

independent practice association (IPA) HMO

individual health insurance

individual practice association (IPA) HMO

integrated delivery system (IDS)

integrated provider organization (IPO)

legislation

lifetime maximum amount

major medical insurance

managed care

managed care organization (MCO)

managed health care

management service organization (MSO)

mandate

meaningful EHR user

meaningful use

medical care

medical foundation

medical record

Medicare contracting reform (MCR) initiative

Medicare Improvement for Patients and Providers Act (MIPPA)

Medicare Prescription Drug, Improvement, and Modernization Act (MMA)

Medicare risk programs

Merit-Based Incentive Payment System (MIPS)

National Committee for Quality Assurance (NCQA)

network model HMO

network provider

Obamacare

Office of Managed Care

Omnibus Budget Reconciliation Act of 1981 (OBRA)

open-panel HMO

Patient Protection and Affordable Care Act (PPACA)

patient record

payer mix

performance measurements

personal health record (PHR)

physician incentive plan

physician incentives

physician referral

physician-hospital organization (PHO)

point-of-service plan (POS)

policyholder

Preferred Provider Health Care Act of 1985

preferred provider organization (PPO)

premium

prepaid health plan

prescription management

preventive services

primary care provider (PCP)

problem-oriented record (POR)

Promoting Interoperability (PI) Programs

public health insurance

quality assessment and performance improvement (QAPI)

quality assurance program

quality improvement (QI)

quality improvement organization (QIO)

Quality Improvement System for Managed Care (QISMC)

quality management program

quality payment program (QPP)

record linkage

report card

rider

risk adjustment model

risk adjustment program

risk contract

risk pool

risk transfer formula

schedule of benefits

second surgical opinion (SSO)

self-insured (or self-funded) employer-sponsored group health plans

self-referral

single-payer health system

socialized medicine

staff model HMO

standards

stop-loss insurance

subscriber (enrollee)

sub-capitation payment

third-party administrators (TPAs)

third-party payer

total practice management software (TPMS)

triple option plan

universal health insurance

utilization review organization (URO)

value-based reimbursement methodology

withhold arrangement

Introduction

According to the *American Heritage Concise Dictionary*, insurance is a contract that protects the insured from loss. An insurance company guarantees payment to the insured for an unforeseen event (e.g., death, accident, and illness) in return for the payment of premiums. In addition to health insurance, types of insurance include automobile, disability, liability, malpractice, property, and life (discussed in Chapter 12 of this textbook). In the United States, insurance oversight is conducted at the state level (with insurance laws enacted by state legislators and signed by governors), and state regulators enforce the laws to ensure insurance company *solvency* (financial ability to pay submitted claims) and implement marketplace regulation (e.g., premium pricing). This chapter includes information about terms and concepts as an introduction to health insurance processing. These terms and concepts are explained in greater detail in later chapters of this text. *Managed health care (managed care)* manages health care costs, utilization, and quality by delivering health plan benefits and additional services through contracted arrangements between individuals or health care programs (e.g., Medicaid) and managed care organizations (MCOs), which accept a predetermined *per member per month* (*capitation*) payment for services. (Managing costs is also called *cost containment*.)

 NOTE:

Chapters 12 to 17 of this textbook contain content about different types of health insurance, including definitions, claims completion instructions, and sample completed CMS-1500 claims. Chapter 11 of this textbook contains content about the UB-04 claim, which contains data that is autopopulated by an electronic health record or abstracted by the health information management department, such as for inpatient hospital admissions and outpatient hospital encounters, including emergency department visits.

Overview of Health Insurance and Managed Care

To understand the meaning of the term *health insurance* as used in this text, you must differentiate between medical care and health care. **Medical care** includes the identification of diseases and the provision of care and treatment to persons who are sick, injured, or concerned about their health status. **Health care** expands the definition of medical care to include **preventive services**, which are designed to help individuals avoid health and injury problems. Preventive examinations may result in the early detection of health problems, allowing less drastic and less expensive treatment options. When a health care facility or provider registers a patient, they establish an agreement to provide treatment, resulting in an

- **express contract**, which includes provisions that are stated in the health insurance contract, such as performing an annual physical examination; and
- **implied contract**, which results from actions taken by the health care facility or provider, such as agreeing to provide treatment to a patient.

Stop-loss insurance (or **excess insurance**) provides protection against catastrophic or unpredictable losses and include

- *aggregate stop-loss plans*, which provide a maximum dollar amount eligible expenses during a contract period (e.g., numerous employees who incur inpatient hospitalization expenses during a pandemic); and
- *specific stop-loss plans*, which provide protection against a high claim on an individual (e.g., patient diagnosed with cancer that requires extensive treatment).

Health care insurance or **health insurance** is a contract between a policyholder and a third-party payer or government health program to reimburse the policyholder for all or a portion of the cost of medically necessary treatment or preventive care provided by health care professionals.

Health insurance covers groups (e.g., employer group health plans) and individuals (e.g., private health insurance), with group health insurance usually costing far less for employees because the employer incurs a larger percentage of the premium cost. The employee or individual pays a **premium**, which is the amount paid for a health insurance policy. A **schedule of benefits**, also called **covered services**, includes services covered by a health insurance plan. (*Non-covered services*, such as plastic surgery, are also described in a health insurance policy.) A **carve-out plan** is an arrangement that a health insurance company provides to offer a specific health benefit (usually at an additional cost) that is managed separately from the health insurance plan. The traditional model of health care reimbursement is called **fee-for-service**, for which providers receive payment according to a fee schedule after covered procedures and services are provided to patients. Health plans create a **fee schedule**, which is a list of predetermined payments for health care services provided to patients (e.g., fee assigned to each CPT code). An **indemnity plan** allows patients to seek health care from any provider, and the health plan reimburses the provider according to a *fee schedule; indemnity plans* are sometimes called *fee-for-service plans*.

> **Example:** Davis Vision is a health insurance company that offers vision health plans only. Delta Dental is a health insurance company that offers dental health plans only. While most insurance companies offer behavioral health (mental health) care as part of an overall plan, special support and resources are also available. Optum's UnitedHealthcare assists subscribers in finding behavioral health specialists, provides telephone support, and contracts with Beacon health options, which focuses on behavioral health care and life/work services.

 NOTE:

> Health insurance plans previously excluded coverage for *pre-existing conditions*, such as diabetes mellitus or hypertension, which are health problems diagnosed prior to the date that new health insurance coverage started. Effective January 1, 2014, health insurance companies are *not* permitted to charge more or deny coverage for pre-existing conditions, and benefits for such conditions cannot be limited. (The exception is individual health insurance policies that were purchased prior to March 2010.)

Managed health care (managed care) are *prepaid health plans* that combine health care delivery with the financing of services provided. Its intent is to manage cost and utilization by providing more affordable quality care to health care consumers and providers who agreed to certain restrictions (e.g., patients would receive care only from providers who are members of a managed care organization). A **prepaid health plan** establishes a capitation contract between a managed health care plan and network providers (e.g., facilities, physicians, and other health care practitioners within a community) who provide specified medical services for a predetermined amount paid on a monthly or yearly basis. The providers are responsible for managing all health care needs of their patient population for that capitated amount. Patients that require less care create a profit for providers, while patients who require more care can create a loss.

A **policyholder** signs a contract with a health insurance company and owns the health insurance policy. An **enrollee** or **subscriber** joins a managed care plan. (Enrollees and subscribers are also associated with traditional health insurance plans. Medicare uses beneficiaries.) The policyholder, enrollee, or subscriber is the insured, and the policy or plan might include coverage for dependents.

A **third-party payer** is a health insurance company that provides coverage, such as BlueCross BlueShield. Because both the government and the general public speak of "health insurance," this text uses that term exclusively. Health insurance is available to individuals who participate in group (e.g., employer sponsored), individual (or personal insurance), or prepaid health plans (e.g., managed care). Chapters 12 to 17 of this textbook contain content about the following types of health insurance, including definitions, claims completion instructions, sample completed CMS-1500 claims *for professional billing*, and so on. The CMS-1500 claim (2) is submitted to third-party payers for reimbursement physician office procedures and services and inpatient professional services; the electronic version of the claim is abbreviated as ANSI ASC X12N 837P.

CMS refers to the Centers for Medicare & Medicaid Services, which manage government health programs (e.g., Medicaid, Medicare). The UB-04 claim is submitted as part of *institutional billing* for inpatient and outpatient facility care, including emergency department care, and it is covered in Chapter 11 of this textbook. (UB refers to Uniform Bill, and the UB-04 is also called the CMS-1450.) The UB-04 is autopopulated with data from an electronic health record or abstracted data collected by the health information management department. (*Professional billing* and *institutional billing* are covered in Chapter 3 of this textbook.)

Different types of health insurance payments comprise the provider's **payer mix**, and it is important that providers determine the percentage of reimbursement received from each type of payer (e.g., commercial plan, government plan) as part of *revenue management*, which helps ensure the financial viability of a health care facility or medical practice.

The policyholder receives a notice from the insurance company or managed care plan that contains an insurance card and details about the health plan's coverage (often in a separate booklet written in plain language). A certificate of insurance may be provided as proof of insurance, and a summary of benefits and coverage is also included. While medical codes are reported on insurance claims for reimbursement purposes (as part of HIPAA's provision for reporting *treatment, payment, and health care operations [TPO]* on health claims), an insurance company or a managed care plan may request copies of patient records to clarify claims data, and patients are typically required to sign an *authorization to release patient information*. Some plans *may* include an *authorization for the release of patient information* clause in the original contract, which facilitates auditing (reviewing) patient records before processing a claim for reimbursement. In addition, when a health insurance contract contains a **guaranteed renewal** provision, the health insurance company must offer to renew the policy as long as premiums continue to be paid. (Except in some states, guaranteed renewal does not limit how much the individual can be charged to renew coverage.)

Employees who process patient registrations and insurance claims may be required to assist patients with information about copayments, coinsurance, and so on. For detailed information about the patient's insurance coverage, it would be appropriate to refer the patient to their health insurance representative.

A **deductible** is the amount for which the patient is financially responsible before an insurance policy provides payment. A **lifetime maximum amount** is the maximum benefits payable to a health plan participant. Insurance programs can also include **riders**, which increase, limit, delete or clarify the scope of insurance coverage, such as

- *dependent continuation*, which provides continued health insurance coverage for children who meet certain conditions, such as full-time college attendance and under age 26; and
- *special accidental injury riders*, which cover 100 percent of nonsurgical care sought and rendered within 24 to 72 hours (varies according to policy) of an accidental injury.

A **copayment (copay)** is a provision in a health or managed care plan that requires the policyholder or patient to pay a specified dollar amount to a health care provider for each encounter or medical service received. **Coinsurance** is the percentage of costs a patient shares with the health or managed care plan; for example, the plan pays 80 percent of costs, and the patient pays 20 percent. The patient pays a *copayment or coinsurance* amount for services rendered, the payer reimburses the provider according to its *fee schedule*, and the remainder is a *write-off* (or loss).

> **Example 1:** The primary care provider meets with a patient for a follow-up treatment of their recently diagnosed asthma. The physician's fee is $100. The patient pays a copayment of $20 to the provider on the day of the encounter, and per the patient's health plan owes nothing more to the provider. If the payer reimburses the provider $60 for the encounter, the provider will *write off* $20.
>
> If the patient is required to pay coinsurance (instead of a copayment), that is typically calculated as 20 percent of the reimbursement allowed by the payer. In this case, if the payer approves $80 as reimbursement for the encounter, the patient pays a coinsurance of $16 on the day of the encounter. The payer reimburses the provider $64, and the provider will *write off* $20.

Example 2: A patient receives preventive care evaluation and management services from the family practitioner. The total charges are $125, and the patient pays a $20 copayment during the office visit. The third-party payer reimburses the physician the fee schedule amount of $75. The business records the remaining $30 owed as a *write-off.*

Health Insurance Coverage Statistics

In the United States, individuals have many options for obtaining health insurance (or managed care) coverage. The most common forms of health care coverage include group health insurance, individual health insurance, public health insurance, and universal health insurance (as offered through the health insurance marketplace) (Table 2-1). The latest release of U.S. Census Bureau data is from 2020. It is estimated that 91.4 percent of people in the United States are covered by some form of health insurance, with more than 70 million Americans enrolled in some type of managed care program in response to regulatory initiatives affecting health care costs and quality, such as Medicaid managed care state contracts and Medicare Advantage (or Medicare Part C).

- 66.5 percent are covered by private health insurance.
  - 54.4 percent are covered by employment-based plans.
  - 10.5 percent are covered by direct-purchase health insurance plans, which includes marketplace coverage.
- 17.8 percent are covered by Medicaid.
- 18.4 percent are covered by Medicare.
- 3.7 percent are covered by military health care (e.g., CHAMPVA, TRICARE, VA).

The reason the insurance coverage breakdown of covered persons is greater than 100 percent is because some people are covered by more than one insurance plan (e.g., employment-based plan plus direct-purchase health insurance plan, employment-based plan plus Medicare). Thus, they are counted more than once when percentages are calculated.

TABLE 2-1 Glossary of health insurance terms

Term	Definition
Group health insurance	Private health insurance model that provides coverage, which is subsidized by employers and other organizations (e.g., labor unions, rural and consumer health cooperatives). These plans distribute the cost of health insurance among group members to lessen the cost and provide broader coverage than that offered through individual health insurance plans. The Patient Protection and Affordable Care Act (PPACA) of 2010 includes a tax credit to help small businesses and small, tax-exempt organizations afford the cost of covering their employees.
Individual health insurance	A type of private health insurance policy purchased by individuals or families who do not have access to group health insurance coverage (e.g., Aetna).
Public health insurance	Federal and state government health programs (e.g., Medicare, Medicaid, CHAMPVA, CHIP, TRICARE) available to eligible individuals.
Single-payer health system	National health service model adopted by some Western nations (e.g., Canada) and funded by taxes. The government pays for each resident's health care, which is considered a basic social service.
Socialized medicine	A type of single-payer health system in which the government owns and operates health care facilities and providers (e.g., physicians) receive salaries (e.g., Finland, Great Britain).
Universal health insurance	Social insurance model that has the goal of providing every individual with access to health coverage, regardless of the system implemented to achieve that goal, such as a combination of private and public health insurance. For example, the PPACA of 2010 extended health coverage to millions of uninsured Americans by (originally) requiring them to purchase health insurance.

Major Developments in Health Insurance and Managed Care

Since the early 1900s, when solo practices prevailed, managed care and group practices have increased in number, and health care services (like other aspects of society in this country) have undergone tremendous changes (Figure 2-1). This includes *managed care*, which was originally developed as a way to provide affordable, comprehensive, prepaid health care services. Today, many of the features associated with managed care also apply to traditional health insurance and government health plans.

The First Health Insurance Plans

The first health insurance policy was written in 1850 by the Franklin Health Assurance Company of Massachusetts, which provided private health care coverage for injuries that did not result in death. Then, federal legislation was enacted to implement additional health plans. (**Legislation** includes laws, which are rules of conduct enforced by threat of punishment if violated.)

Early in the twentieth century, the **Federal Employers' Liability Act (FELA)** was implemented to protect and compensate railroad workers who are injured on the job, and the **Federal Employees' Compensation Act (FECA)** was implemented to provide civilian employees of the federal government with medical care, survivors' benefits, and compensation for lost wages. The original *Blue Cross* and *Blue Shield* plans (now called *BlueCross BlueShield*), which originated as separate plans for institutional services and professional services, and group health insurance plans were offered for the first time.

- The Blue Shield concept grew out of lumber and mining camps in the region of the Pacific Northwest during the turn of the twentieth century.
- Group health insurance is typically offered by employers.

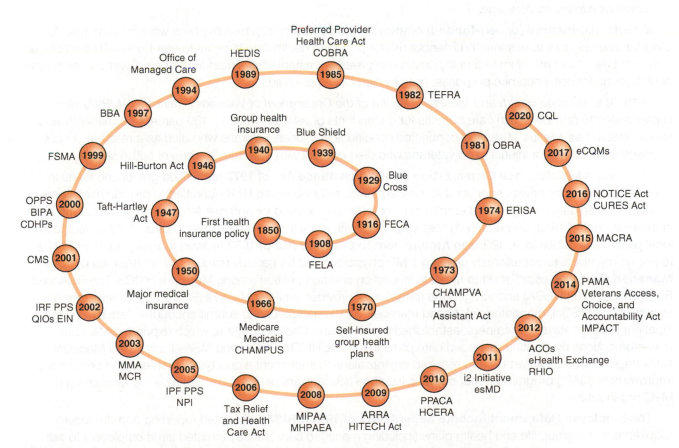

FIGURE 2-1 Timeline of dates and significant events in health care reimbursement.

During the mid-twentieth century, the **Hill-Burton Act** provided federal grants to modernize hospitals that had become obsolete due to the lack of capital investment during the Great Depression and World War II, and in return for federal funds, facilities were required to provide services for free or at reduced rates to patients unable to pay for care. In 1947, the Taft-Hartley Act balanced relationships between labor and management and indirectly resulted in the creation of **third-party administrators (TPAs)**, which administered health care plans, processed claims, and served as a system of checks and balances for labor and management. TPAs also contracted with employers to provide employee benefits management and other services. Insurance companies began offering **major medical insurance**, which provided coverage for catastrophic or prolonged illnesses and injuries. Most of these programs incorporate large deductibles and lifetime maximum amounts.

In 1959, the **Federal Employee Health Benefit Plan (FEHBP)** was enacted by Congress to allow federal employees, retirees, and their survivors to select appropriate health plans that meet their needs. Types of plans include consumer-driven and high deductible plans (that offer catastrophic risk protection with higher deductibles), health savings/reimbursable accounts with lower premiums, fee-for-service (FFS) plans and their preferred provider organizations (PPO), or health maintenance organizations (HMO), depending on where the individual lives and works (and the area serviced by plans).

The Lyndon B. Johnson administration's *War on Poverty* resulted in 1965 legislation that implemented

- *Medicare* (Title XVIII of the Social Security Amendments of 1965): Health care services to Americans over the age of 65;

- *Medicaid* (Title XIX of the Social Security Amendments of 1965): Cost-sharing program between federal and state governments to provide health care services to Americans with low incomes;

- *Civilian Health and Medical Program–Uniformed Services (CHAMPUS)*: Originally designed as a benefit for dependents of personnel serving in the armed forces, uniformed branches of the Public Health Service, and the National Oceanic and Atmospheric Administration. *This program is now known as TRICARE and contains expanded coverage.*

In 1970, **self-insured (or self-funded) employer-sponsored group health plans** were implemented to allow large employers to assume the financial risk for providing health care benefits to employees. (The employer does not pay a fixed premium to a health insurance payer, but establishes a trust fund of employer and employee contributions for self-insurance purposes, out of which claims are paid.)

In 1973, the *Civilian Health and Medical Program of the Department of Veterans Affairs (CHAMPVA)* was implemented to provide health care benefits for dependents of veterans rated as 100 percent permanently and totally disabled as a result of service-connected conditions or injuries, veterans who died as a result of service-connected conditions or injuries, and veterans who died on duty with less than 30 days of active service.

The **Health Maintenance Organization (HMO) Assistance Act of 1973** authorized grants and loans to develop HMOs under private sponsorship, defined a **federally qualified HMO** (certified to provide health care services to Medicare and Medicaid enrollees) as one that has applied for and met federal standards established in the HMO Act of 1973, and required most employers with more than 25 employees to offer HMO coverage if local plans were available. In 1985, an **Amendment to the HMO Act of 1973** allowed federally qualified HMOs to permit members to occasionally use non-HMO physicians and be partially reimbursed. In 1994, an **Office of Managed Care** was established to facilitate innovation and competition among Medicare HMOs. The Balanced Budget Act of 1997 (BBA) encouraged the formation of provider service networks (PSNs) and provider service organizations (PSOs); mandated risk-based managed care organizations to submit encounter data related to inpatient hospital stays of members; established the Medicare+Choice program, which expanded Medicare coverage options by creating managed care plans to include HMOs, PPOs, and MSAs (now called Medicare Advantage or Medicare Part C); and required organizations to implement a quality assessment and performance improvement (QAPI) program so that quality assurance activities are performed to improve the functioning of M+C organizations.

The **Employee Retirement Income Security Act of 1974 (ERISA)** mandated reporting and disclosure requirements for group life and health plans (including managed care plans), permitted large employers to self-insure employee health care benefits, and exempted large employers from taxes on health insurance premiums.

A **mandate** is an official directive, instruction, or order to take or perform a certain action; they are also authoritative commands, such as by courts, governors, and legislatures.

The **Omnibus Budget Reconciliation Act of 1981 (OBRA)** expanded the Medicare and Medicaid programs and requires providers to keep copies of government insurance claims and attachments for a period of five years. The *Tax Equity and Fiscal Responsibility Act of 1982 (TEFRA)* modified the HMO Act of 1973, creating **Medicare risk programs**, which allowed federally qualified HMOs and competitive medical plans that met specified Medicare requirements to provide Medicare-covered services under a risk contract. TEFRA defined a **risk contract** as an arrangement among providers to provide capitated (fixed, prepaid basis) health care services to Medicare beneficiaries. TEFRA defined a **competitive medical plan (CMP)** as an HMO that meets federal eligibility requirements for a Medicare risk contract but is not licensed as a federally qualified plan. Another important component of TEFRA is the implementation of *diagnosis-related groups*, which is part of the *inpatient prospective payment system* (covered in Chapter 9 of this textbook).

The **Consolidated Omnibus Budget Reconciliation Act of 1985 (COBRA)** allows employees to continue health care coverage beyond the benefit termination date by paying appropriate premiums. COBRA also established an employee's right to continue health care coverage beyond the scheduled benefit termination date (including HMO coverage).

The **Preferred Provider Health Care Act of 1985** eased restrictions on preferred provider organizations (PPOs) and allowed subscribers to seek health care from providers outside of the PPO. The *Balanced Budget Act of 1997 (BBA)* encouraged the formation of *provider service networks (PSNs)* and *provider service organizations (PSOs)* and mandated risk-based managed care organizations to submit encounter data related to inpatient hospital stays of members. The BBA also established the Medicare+Choice program (now called *Medicare Advantage* or *Medicare Part C*), which expanded Medicare coverage options by creating managed care plans to include HMOs, PPOs, and MSAs. A **quality assessment and performance improvement (QAPI) program** was implemented so that quality assurance activities are performed to improve the functioning of Medicare Advantage (or Medicare Part C) organizations.

Legislation and Regulations in the Twenty-First Century

In 2002, CMS announced that **quality improvement organizations (QIOs)** will perform utilization and quality control review of health care furnished, or to be furnished, to Medicare beneficiaries. (QIOs replaced peer review organizations or PROs, which previously performed this function.) In 2003, The **Medicare Prescription Drug, Improvement, and Modernization Act (MMA)** added new prescription drug and preventive benefits, and provided extra assistance to people earning low incomes. A **Medicare contracting reform (MCR) initiative** was also implemented to improve and modernize the Medicare fee-for-service system and to establish a contractual competitive bidding process to appoint Medicare administrative contractors (MACs). The result was an integration of the administration of Medicare Parts A and B fee-for-service benefits, replacing Medicare carriers, DMERCs, and fiscal intermediaries with Medicare Administrative Contractors (MACs). The *Recovery Audit Contractor (RAC) program* was also created to identify and recover improper Medicare payments paid to health care providers under fee-for-service Medicare plans. (RAC program details are covered in Chapter 5 of this textbook.) The *Hospital Inpatient Quality Reporting (Hospital IQR) program* authorized CMS to pay hospitals that successfully report designated quality measures based on a higher annual update to payment rates.

In 2008, the **Medicare Improvement for Patients and Providers Act (MIPPA)** helped lower costs of Medicare premiums and deductibles to benefit eligible Medicare beneficiaries, and the *Mental Health Parity and Addiction Equity Act (MHPAEA)* prevents group health plans and health insurance issuers that provide mental health or substance use disorder (MH/SUD) benefits from imposing less-favorable benefit limitations on those benefits than on medical/surgical benefits. The **American Recovery and Reinvestment Act of 2009 (ARRA)** authorized an expenditure of $1.5 billion for grants for construction, renovation, and equipment, and for the acquisition of health information technology systems. The **Health Information Technology for Economic and Clinical Health Act (HITECH Act)** (included in American Recovery and Reinvestment Act of 2009) established an Office of National Coordinator for Health Information Technology (ONC) within HHS to improve health care quality, safety, and efficiency. (In 2012, the NHIN evolved into the eHealth Exchange.)

The Affordable Care Act

In 2010, the **Patient Protection and Affordable Care Act (PPACA)** (also called the *Affordable Care Act*) focused on private health insurance reform to provide better coverage for individuals with pre-existing conditions, improve prescription drug coverage under Medicare, and extend the life of the Medicare Trust fund by at least 12 years. Its goal was to provide Americans with quality affordable health care, improve the role of public programs, improve the quality and efficiency of health care, and improve public health. Americans purchase health coverage that fits their budget and meets their needs by accessing the **health insurance marketplace** (or **health insurance exchange**) in their state. The marketplace indicates if individuals qualify for free or low-cost coverage available through Medicaid or the Children's Health Insurance Program (CHIP). (Refer to Chapter 5 for more information about risk adjustment models.) The goal is improved coverage so that consumers—whether they are healthy or sick—can select the best plan for their needs.

The **Health Care and Education Reconciliation Act (HCERA)** amended the PPACA to implement health care reform initiatives, such as increasing tax credits to buy health care insurance, eliminating special deals provided to senators, closing the Medicare "donut hole," delaying taxes on "Cadillac health care plans" until 2018, implementing revenue changes (e.g., 10 percent tax on indoor tanning services) and so on. HCERA also modified higher education assistance provisions, such as implementing student loan reform.

The PPACA implemented the **risk adjustment program** to lessen or eliminate the influence of risk selection on premiums charged by health plans and includes the following:

- **Risk adjustment model**, which provides payments to health plans that disproportionately attract higher-risk enrollees (e.g., individuals with chronic conditions). It uses an actuarial tool to predict health care costs based on the relative actuarial risk of enrollees in risk adjustment covered health plans. For example, the HHS-Hierarchical Condition Categories (HHS-HCC) risk adjustment model uses a hierarchical condition category (HCC) system to summarize diagnosis codes into levels of severity for calculating risk scores. (*Risk adjustment* is a method of adjusting capitation payments to health plans, accounting for differences in expected health costs of enrollees.)

- **Risk transfer formula**, which transfers funds from health plans with relatively lower-risk enrollees to health plans that enroll relatively higher-risk individuals, protecting such health plans against adverse selection. Enrollee risk scores are based on demographic and health status information, and it is calculated as the sum of demographic and health factors, weighted by estimated marginal contributions to total risk, and calculated relative to average expenditures. Thomson Reuters MarketScan® data is the primary source for risk adjustment model calibration, and its database includes data from all 50 states.

> **Example:** An average risk score is 1.0, and the formula for calculating the total risk score is demographic risk factor + health status risk factor. If a 57-year-old patient has a 0.5 demographic risk factor and a 0.7 health status risk factor, the total risk score is 1.2, resulting in the health plan receiving higher payments for care because the risk score is greater than the average. This provides an incentive to the health plan to enroll individuals with higher demographic and health status risk factors. To monetize this example, if the value of 1.0 is $1,000, this individual's risk score monetary average is calculated as $(0.5 \times \$1,000) + (0.7 \times \$1,000) = \$500 + \$700 = \$1,200$.

Health Insurance Marketplace

The *Patient Protection and Affordable Care Act (PPACA)* was signed into federal law on March 23, 2010, and resulted in the creation of a *Health Insurance Marketplace* (or *health insurance exchange*), abbreviated as the Marketplace, effective October 1, 2013. The PPACA is abbreviated as the *Affordable Care Act (ACA)*, and it was nicknamed **Obamacare** (because it was signed into federal law by President Obama). *The Health Insurance Marketplace does* <u>not</u> *replace other health insurance programs (e.g., individual and group commercial health insurance, Medicaid, Medicare, TRICARE).*

The Marketplace allows Americans to purchase health coverage that fits their budget and meets their needs. It is a resource where individuals, families, and small businesses can

- learn about their health coverage options;
- compare health insurance plans based on costs, benefits, and other important features;
- choose a plan;
- enroll in coverage;

The Marketplace includes information about programs to help people earning a low-to-moderate income and resources pay for health coverage. Information includes ways to save on the monthly premiums and out-of-pocket costs of coverage available through the Marketplace and information about other programs, including Medicaid and the Children's Health Insurance Program (CHIP). The Marketplace encourages competition among private health plans, and it is accessible through websites, call centers, and in-person assistance. In some states it is run by the state, and in others it is run by the federal government.

Most individuals who do not currently have health insurance through their place of work or otherwise are eligible to use the Health Insurance Marketplace (www.healthcare.gov) to compare and choose a plan. To be eligible for health coverage through the marketplace, individuals must

- be a U.S. citizen or national (or be lawfully present);
- live in the United States;
- not be incarcerated.

In 2017, the Department of Health and Human Services (DHHS) reviewed regulations and guidance related to the Affordable Care Act (ACA) and released the following changes:

- *Helping Patients Keep Their Plan*: DHHS permitted people with ACA-noncompliant plans in the individual and small group markets to renew them, and that policy was set to expire in 2017. On February 23, 2017, DHHS announced that people will be allowed to keep their pre-ACA plans if they like them.
- *More Calendar Flexibility = More Options for Patients*: In 2017, DHHS pushed back a range of deadlines for decisions to be made by insurers, allowing insurers to provide better choices to consumers. DHHS also eliminated a step in the approval process, allowing insurers to reduce regulatory costs and pass the savings on to the individual.
- *Tax Cuts and Job Acts of 2017*: The *health care mandate* was repealed, eliminating the tax penalty under the ACA for individuals who do not buy health insurance.

In 2018, DHHS issued a final rule to allow the sale and renewal of short-term, limited-duration health insurance plans that cover longer periods than the previous maximum period of less than three months. Such coverage includes an initial period of less than 12 months, with a maximum duration of no longer than 36 months in total. It can provide coverage for those transitioning among different coverage options (e.g., individual who is between jobs, student taking time off from school, middle-class families who do not have access to subsidized ACA plans). New legislation also allows states to use federal funding for subsidizing premiums for association health plans and short-term health insurance plans. Consumers can purchase ACA plans with the subsidies, and coverage for pre-existing conditions remains in place (and insurers may not charge higher premiums for individuals with pre-existing conditions).

Managed Care

Managed care (or **managed health care**) is a health care delivery system that is organized to manage cost, quality, and utilization. The delivery of services is provided through contractual arrangements established between individuals or health care programs (e.g., Medicaid) and managed care organizations (MCOs), which accept a predetermined per member per month (capitation) payment for services. In addition, *annual and lifetime* *maximum benefit amounts* may be established, which limit the total amount a managed care plan must pay for all health care services provided to a patient annually or during their lifetime.

Managed care originally focused on cost reductions by restricting health care access through utilization management and availability of limited benefits. Managed care now requires providers to assume risk because enrollees may cost more to treat than anticipated, and payers such as Medicare Advantage (Medicare Part C) transfer that risk (to providers) by using a **withhold arrangement**, which allows the payer to retain a percentage of payments *or* pre-established dollar amounts that are deducted from a provider's service/procedure fee, capitation payment, or salary payment. Those amounts may or may not be returned to the provider, depending on specific predetermined factors (e.g., contract language). Medicare Advantage plans also transfer risk to providers by using **risk pools**, which combine a group of enrollees' medical costs to calculate managed care premiums (for enrollees). The resultant risk pools allow the higher costs of less healthy patients to be offset by the relatively lower costs of healthy patients. Managed care organizations (MCOs) were created to manage benefits and to develop participating provider networks.

History of Managed Care

Managed care originated when physicians and organizations created prepaid health plans in regions of the United States during the twentieth century. The most recognizable organization is Kaiser-Permanente, based in California, which created prepaid plans for enrollees and offered what became the first health maintenance organizations (HMOs) (before HMO was even part of health care literature). The HMO Assistance Act of 1973 created the phrase *health maintenance organization*.

- Originally a *health maintenance organization (HMO)* was a combined insurance company and health care facility that entered into contracts with enrollees who received medical services from providers at that facility.

- The original HMOs arranged for enrollees to receive other services needed (e.g., emergency department, outpatient surgery, inpatient hospitalizations) from a network of providers in the community.

- HMOs later evolved into the concept of *managed care*, which is a health care delivery system organized to manage health care costs, utilization and quality.

For additional information about the history of managed care, go to ncd.gov, click on the Publications link, click on 2013 Publications link, click on the "Medicaid Managed Care for People with Disabilities" link, and click on the "Appendix B. A Brief History of Managed Care" link.

Typically, the administration of managed care includes

- managed care organizations and plans;
- managed care models;
- accreditation of managed care organizations.

Managed Care Organizations and Plans

A **managed care organization (MCO)** is responsible for the health of a group of enrollees and can be a health plan, health system, hospital, or physician group. Traditional health insurance company *fee-for-service plans*, which reimburse providers for individual health care services provided. Managed care is financed according to a prospective payment method called **capitation**, which requires providers to accept pre-established payments for providing health care services to enrollees over a period of time (usually one year or monthly). If services provided by the managed care provider cost less than the capitation amount, the provider profits. If services provided cost more than the capitation amount, the provider takes a loss.

A **customized sub-capitation plan (CSCP)** uses insurance coverage to fund health care expenses, and the individual selects one of each type of provider to create a customized network and pays the resulting customized insurance premium. Each provider is paid a fixed amount per month to provide only the care that an individual needs; specialist care is reimbursed according to a **sub-capitation payment**, which is a "carve-out" contracted amount paid to specialists from the primary care provider's capitation payment on a per member per month basis (PMPM).

Example: In June, Hillcrest Medical Group received a capitated payment of $15,000 for the 150 members (enrollees) of the ABC Managed Care Health Plan. The Group spent $12,500 of the capitated payment on preventive, chronic, and acute health care services provided to member patients. The services were provided at the Group's office and local hospital, which included inpatient, outpatient, and emergency department care. (The Group is responsible for paying the enrollees' hospital bills.) In this scenario, health care services provided to enrollees cost less than the capitated payment received. The Hillcrest Medical Group, therefore, made a profit of $2,500. If health care services had cost more than the capitated amount of $15,000, the Group would have experienced a loss.

Managed Care Models

Managed care models are categorized as follows:

- Exclusive provider organization (EPO)
- Health maintenance organization (HMO)
- Integrated delivery system (IDS)
- Point-of-service plan (POS)
- Preferred provider organization (PPO)
- Triple option plan

An **exclusive provider organization (EPO)** is a managed care plan that provides benefits to subscribers who are required to receive services from network providers. A **network provider** is a physician or health care facility under contract to the managed care plan.

A **health maintenance organization (HMO)** is an alternative to traditional group health insurance coverage and provides comprehensive health care services to voluntarily enrolled members on a prepaid basis. In contrast, traditional health insurance coverage is usually provided on a fee-for-service basis in which reimbursement increases if the health care service fees increase, if multiple units of service are provided, or if more expensive services are provided instead of less expensive ones (e.g., brand-name versus generic prescription medication). HMOs provide preventive care services to promote "wellness" or good health, thus reducing the overall cost of medical care. Annual physical examinations are encouraged for the early detection of health problems. Health risk assessment instruments (surveys) and resources are also available to subscribers.

- A **closed-panel HMO** provides health care at an HMO-owned center or satellite clinic or by physicians who belong to a specially formed medical group that serves the HMO; includes group model and staff model HMOs.
  - **Group model HMO**: Closed-panel HMO that contracts health care services for delivery to subscribers by participating physicians who are members of an independent multispecialty group practice. The HMO reimburses the physician group, which is then responsible for reimbursing physician members and contracted health care facilities (e.g., hospitals). The physician group can be owned or managed by the HMO, or it can simply contract with the HMO.
  - **Staff model HMO**: Health care services are provided to subscribers by physicians employed by the HMO. Premiums and other revenue are paid to the HMO. Usually, all ambulatory services are provided within HMO corporate buildings.
- An **open-panel HMO** provides health care by individuals who are not employees of the HMO or who do not belong to a specially formed medical group that serves the HMO; includes direct contract model HMO, individual practice association HMO, and network model HMO.

- ○ **Direct contract model HMO**: Contracted health care services are delivered to subscribers by individual physicians in the community.

- ○ **Individual practice association (IPA) HMO**: Also called **independent practice association (IPA) HMO**, contracted health services are delivered to subscribers by physicians who remain in their independent office settings. The IPA HMO is an intermediary (e.g., physician association) that negotiates the HMO contract and receives and manages the capitation payment from the HMO, so that physicians are paid on either a fee-for-service or capitation basis.

- ○ **Network model HMO**: Contracted health care services are provided to subscribers by two or more physician multispecialty group practices, and include the direct contract model, group model, individual practice association, network model, and staff model.

An **Integrated delivery system (IDS)** is an organization of affiliated providers' sites, such as hospitals, ambulatory surgical centers, or physician groups that offer joint health care services to subscribers. An integrated delivery system may also be referred to as follows: integrated service network (ISN), delivery system, vertically integrated plan (VIP), vertically integrated system, horizontally integrated system, health delivery network, or accountable health plan. Models include physician-hospital organizations, management service organizations, group practices without walls, integrated provider organizations, and medical foundations.

- • **Physician-hospital organization (PHO)**: Owned by hospital(s) and physician groups that obtain managed care plan contracts; physicians maintain their own practices and provide health care services to plan members

- • **Management service organization (MSO)**: Usually owned by physicians or a hospital that provides practice management (administrative and support) services to individual physician practices

- • **Group practices without walls (GPWW)**: Establishes a contract that allows physicians to maintain their own offices and share services (e.g., appointment scheduling, billing)

- • **Integrated provider organization (IPO)**: Manages delivery of health care services offered by hospitals, physicians (who are employees of the IPO), and other health care organizations (e.g., an ambulatory surgery clinic and a nursing facility)

- • **Medical foundation**: Nonprofit organization that contracts with and acquires clinical and business assets of physician practices; assigned a provider number and manages practice's business

A **point-of-service (POS) plan** creates flexibility for managed care plans and has been implemented by some HMOs and preferred provider organizations. Patients have freedom to use the managed care panel of providers or to self-refer to out-of-network providers. If enrollees choose to receive all medical care from the managed network of health care providers, or obtain an authorization from their POS primary care provider for specialty care with an out-of-network provider, they pay only the regular copayment or a small charge for the visit and they pay no deductible or coinsurance costs. When an enrollee seeks care from a specialist who does not participate in the managed care plan, and without a referral from the primary care physician, this is known as a **self-referral**. The enrollee will have greater out-of-pocket expenses, as both a large deductible (usually $200 to $250) and 20 to 25 percent coinsurance charges must be paid, similar to those paid by persons with fee-for-service plans.

A **preferred provider organization (PPO)** (sometimes called a *participating provider organization*) is a managed care network of physicians and hospitals that have joined together to contract with insurance companies, employers, or other organizations to provide health care to subscribers for a discounted fee. PPOs do not routinely establish contracts for laboratory or pharmacy services, but they do offer reduced-rate contracts with specific hospitals. Most PPOs are open-ended plans allowing patients to use non-PPO providers in exchange for larger out-of-pocket expenses. Premiums, deductibles, and copayments are usually higher than those paid for HMOs, but lower than those paid for regular fee-for-service plans.

A **triple option plan** is offered by a single insurance plan or as a joint venture among two or more insurance payers and provides subscribers or employees with a choice of HMO, PPO, or traditional health insurance plans. This is also called a **cafeteria plan** (or **flexible benefit plan**) because of the different benefit plans and extra coverage options provided through the insurer or third-party administrator. Triple option plans are intended to prevent the problem of covering members who are sicker than the general population (called **adverse selection**), creating a risk pool.

Effects of Managed Care on a Physician's Practice

Managed care organizations (MCOs) impact a practice's administrative procedures by requiring

- separate bookkeeping systems for each capitated plan to ensure financial viability of the contract;

- a tracking system for preauthorization of specialty care and documented requests for receipt of the specialist's treatment plan or consultation report;

- preauthorization and/or precertification for all hospitalizations and continued certification if the patient's condition requires extension of the number of authorized days;

- up-to-date lists for referrals to participating health care providers, hospitals, and diagnostic test facilities used by the practice;

- up-to-date lists of special administrative procedures required by each managed care plan contract;

- up-to-date lists of patient copayments and fees for each managed care plan contract;

- special patient interviews to ensure preauthorization and to explain out-of-network requirements if the patient is self-referring;

- additional paperwork for specialists to complete and the filing of treatment and discharge plans;

- some case managers employed by the MCO to monitor services provided to enrollees and to be notified if a patient fails to keep a preauthorized appointment;

- the attachment of preauthorization documentation to health insurance claims submitted to some MCOs.

Characteristics of Health Plans and Managed Care

Health insurance is available to individuals who participate in group plans (e.g., employer-sponsored), individual plans (or personal or private health insurance), or prepaid health plans (e.g., managed care). **Fee-for-service plans** reimburse providers according to a *fee schedule* after covered procedures and services have been provided to patients. Health plans are now implementing a **value-based reimbursement methodology**, which compensates providers for the quality of care provided to patients as measured by patient outcomes. This type of methodology requires a team-oriented approach and the coordination of patient care *across the continuum* by requiring providers to collaborate with other health care practitioners (e.g., patient-centered medical home), resulting in the best health outcome for patients.

Example: The Centers for Medicare and Medicaid Services has implemented value-based reimbursement programs, such as the *Hospital Readmission Reduction Program*, which provides incentives for hospitals to coordinate patient post-discharge care to prevent readmission. A reduction in inpatient prospective payment system (IPPS) hospital reimbursement is applied upon readmission of the patient to the hospital within a certain period of time. More information about value-based reimbursement programs is included in Chapter 9 of this textbook.

A *third-party payer* is a health insurance company that provides coverage, such as BlueCross BlueShield. Different types of health insurance payments comprise the health care provider's *payer mix*, and it is important that providers determine the percentage of reimbursement received from each type of payer as part of revenue management:

- Commercial health plans, including BlueCross BlueShield

- Government health plans (e.g., Indian Health Services, Medicaid, Medicare, TRICARE)

- Liability plans (e.g., medical coverage for an automobile accident)

- Medical disability plans (e.g., Medicare for individuals who receive Social Security disability payments)

- Workers' compensation

Many characteristics of health plans and managed care plans are similar, and they include the following areas:

- Primary care provider (gatekeeper role)
- Quality assurance and performance measurement
  - National Committee for Quality Assurance
  - Quality Improvement System for Managed Care
- Utilization management
- Case management
- Second surgical opinions
- Second and third opinions
- Prescription management

Primary Care Provider

Health insurance and managed care plan patients select a **primary care provider (PCP)** who is responsible for supervising and coordinating health care services for enrollees and arranging referrals to specialists (Figure 2-2) and inpatient hospital admissions (except in emergencies). Managed care plans and Medicare require beneficiaries to select a primary care provider, and other plans may also implement this requirement. A **physician referral** is a written order by the primary care provider that facilitates patient evaluation and treatment by a physician specialist. For managed care plans, the PCP serves as a **gatekeeper** by providing essential health care services at the lowest possible cost, avoiding nonessential care, and referring patients to specialists. (Managed care organizations typically do not provide reimbursement for specialist services without a physician referral. Other health care plans may also require physician referrals.)

 NOTE:

- Medicare and many states prohibit managed care contracts from containing **gag clauses**, which prevent providers from discussing all treatment options with patients, whether or not the plan would provide reimbursement for services. Medicare beneficiaries are entitled to advice from their physicians on medically necessary treatment options that may be appropriate for their condition or disease. Because a gag clause would have the practical effect of prohibiting a physician from giving a patient the full range of advice and counsel that is clinically appropriate, it would result in the managed care plan not providing all covered Medicare services to its enrollees, in violation of the managed care plan's responsibilities.

- **Physician incentives** include payments made directly or indirectly to health care providers to encourage them to reduce or limit services (e.g., discharge an inpatient from the hospital more quickly) so as to save money for the managed care plan. The federal **physician incentive plan** requires Medicare and Medicaid managed care plans to disclose physician incentives to CMS or state Medicaid agencies before a new or renewed contract receives final approval.

Quality Assurance and Performance Measurement

Health insurance and managed care plans participate in quality assurance and performance measurement with goals of improving patient care by measuring effectiveness of health care delivery. The Patient Protection and Affordable Care Act (PPACA) requires health insurance plans to demonstrate how health care quality is rewarded (e.g., market-based incentives for benefit design and provider reimbursement structures). Managed care plans that are "federally qualified" and those that must comply with state quality review *mandates* are required to establish quality assurance programs. (**Mandates** are authoritative commands, such as by courts, governors, and legislatures.)

A **quality assurance program** (or **quality management program**) includes activities that assess the quality of care provided in a health care setting and evaluate enrollee complaints about the quality of care received. **Performance measurements** strengthen organization accountability and support performance improvement initiatives by assessing the degree to which evidence-based treatment guidelines are followed and include an evaluation of results of care.

Guardian Managed Care Plan

101 Main St. ■ Anywhere, US 12345 ■ (101) 555-1234

PRIMARY CARE PROVIDER PREAUTHORIZATION REFERRAL FORM FOR CONSULTATION

Patient Name (Last, First, MI)	Patient Birthdate	Preauthorization Number
Member Identification Number	Member Name (Last, First, MI)	Member Birthdate
Primary Care Provider ID or NPI Number	Name of Primary Care Provider (PCP)	PCP Phone Number
Consulting Physician ID or NPI Number	Name of Consulting Physician	Consulting Physician Phone Number

This referral authorizes the services listed below. All services must be rendered by provider stated below.

Diagnosis: ICD-10-CM code(s):

Medical History:

Reason for Referral:

Consultant may provide services listed below. All authorized visits must occur within 90 days of date authorized by PCP. If surgical procedure is listed below, Consultant Treatment Plan is not required. For initial consultation, specialist must submit Consultant Treatment Report of findings and treatment recommendations.

Diagnostic tests indicated: CPT / HCPCS Level II code(s):

Procedure(s) to be performed: CPT / HCPCS Level II code(s):

Primary Care Provider Signature	Date

Consultant billing procedures for services authorized by Primary Care Physician:
1. Enter Preauthorization Number listed above in Block 23 of the CMS-1500 claim.
2. For first submission, submit CMS-1500 claim with original PCP Preauthorization Referral Form for Consultation.
3. For subsequent submissions, no attachments are required.
4. Consultant must complete Consultant Treatment Plan to obtain authorization for any surgical procedure not specified on this form.

Improperly completed forms will be returned.

Care Management Use Only
Expiration date: _____
Referral number: _____

FIGURE 2-2 Sample primary care provider preauthorization referral for consultation with a specialist.

Many states have enacted *legislation* requiring an **external quality review organization (EQRO)**, such as quality improvement organizations (QIOs), to review health care provided by managed care organizations. The types of quality reviews performed include government oversight, patient satisfaction surveys, data collected from grievance procedures, and reviews conducted by independent organizations. Independent organizations that perform reviews include accreditation agencies, such as the National Committee for Quality Assurance and the

Joint Commission. **Accreditation** is a voluntary process that a health care facility or organization undergoes to demonstrate that it has met standards beyond those required by law.

National Committee for Quality Assurance

The **National Committee for Quality Assurance (NCQA)** of Washington, DC, is a private, not-for-profit organization that assesses the quality of managed care plans in the United States and releases the data to the public for consideration when selecting a managed care plan. The NCQA developed the **Healthcare Effectiveness Data and Information Set (HEDIS)** to create standards and performance measures that assess and evaluate managed care systems in terms of membership, utilization of services, quality, access, health plan management and activities, and financial indicators. (**Standards** are requirements created by accreditation organizations.)

The NCQA reviews managed care plans and creates report cards that allow health care consumers to make informed decisions when selecting a plan. The **report card** contains data about a managed care plan's quality, utilization, customer satisfaction, administrative effectiveness, financial stability, and cost control.

Quality Improvement

Quality improvement (QI) involves continuous and systematic actions that result in measurable improvement in the provision of health care services and the health status of targeted patient groups. To implement a QI program, a health care organization needs to understand its own delivery system and key processes. Thus, QI serves to recognize that *resources* (inputs) and *activities completed* (processes) are addressed together to ensure or improve the *quality of patient care* (outputs/outcomes). The focus is on patients and meeting their needs and expectations. Services designed to meet the needs and expectations of patients and their community include systems that affect patient access (e.g., patient registration, preauthorization, precertification), evidence-based care provision, patient safety, support for patient engagement, coordination of care with other parts of the larger health care system, cultural competence (e.g., assessing patient's health literacy, use of patient-centered communication, and offering linguistically appropriate care).

> **Example:** The Original Medicare plan (Medicare Part A and Part B) provides information and resources to providers through a *coordination of care* model, which helps prevent medical errors and duplicate services. Medicare's coordinated care programs include accountable care organizations (ACOs) and an oncology care model.
>
> In an *accountable care organization (ACO)*, local health care providers and hospitals work together to communicate with each other and partner with the patient in making health care decisions. Providers share information and may use an EHR, which helps prevent repeated medical tests and may save time on paperwork.
>
> For the *oncology care model*, the Original Medicare plan works with hundreds of oncology practices that serve cancer patients to provide the patient and family with patient-focused, coordinated care, resulting in quality care being delivered to cancer patients who are receiving chemotherapy or hormonal therapy.

CMS established the **Quality Improvement System for Managed Care (QISMC)** to ensure the accountability of managed care plans in terms of objective, measurable standards (requirements). Plans are required to meet minimum performance levels and to show demonstrable and measurable improvement in specified broad clinical areas (e.g., preventive services, acute ambulatory care, chronic care, and hospital care) based on performance improvement projects that each plan identifies. Beginning in 2006, the Physician Quality Reporting System (formerly called Physician Quality Reporting Initiative or PQRI system) established a financial incentive for eligible professionals who participate in a voluntary quality reporting program.

 NOTE:

Quality improvement programs use *clinical practice guidelines* to assist providers in making decisions about the appropriate course of treatment for patient cases. **Clinical practice guidelines** define modalities for the diagnosis, management, and treatment of patients. They include recommendations based on a methodical and meticulous evaluation and synthesis of published medical literature. The guidelines are *not* protocols that must be followed but instead are to be considered.

Utilization Management

Health plans (e.g., government health programs, managed care plans, BlueCross BlueShield) use *utilization management* (or *utilization review*) as a method of controlling health care costs and quality of care. The appropriateness, efficiency, and medical necessity of health care provided to patients is reviewed on a prospective and retrospective basis. Utilization management activities include preadmission certification (PAC) or preadmission review, preauthorization (or prior approval), concurrent review, and discharge planning. (Utilization management activities are covered in Chapter 3 of this textbook.)

Some managed care plans contract out utilization management services to a **utilization review organization (URO)**, an entity that establishes a utilization management program to perform external utilization review services. Other plans contract with a *third-party administrator (TPA)*, an organization that provides health benefits claims administration and other outsourced services (e.g., employee benefits management) for self-insured companies.

 NOTE:

Health care facilities employ utilization review managers (or utilization review coordinators) to work with physicians to ensure that patients receive care appropriate to their illnesses and conditions. They review patient treatment plans and the status of preadmission certification (PAC) or preadmission review and preauthorization (or prior approval). UR coordinators also perform concurrent reviews and discharge planning functions.

Case Management

Managed care plans require the development of patient care plans to coordinate and provide for complicated cases in a cost-effective manner, which is part of *case management*. For example, instead of admitting a patient to the hospital, a managed care plan might authorize 24-hour home health care services when appropriate. The managed care plan's **case manager** (e.g., physician, physician's assistant, nurse practitioner, nurse, or social worker) submits written confirmation to the provider, authorizing treatment (Figure 2-3). (Health care organizations also employ nurses and social workers as *case managers* to help patients and families navigate complex health care and support systems. In addition, *case managers* coordinate health care services in an effort to improve patient outcomes while considering financial implications, which part of *severity of illness and intensity of services (SI/IS)* that address the balance of medical necessity, procedures/services provided, and level of care needed.)

Second Surgical Opinions

Prior to scheduling elective surgery, managed care plans often require a **second surgical opinion (SSO)**, which involves a second physician being asked to evaluate the necessity of surgery and recommend the most economical, appropriate facility in which to perform the surgery (e.g., outpatient clinic or physician's office versus inpatient hospitalization).

Second and Third Opinions

Managed care organizations (MCOs) provide the opportunity for a second opinion for certain diagnoses or treatments, especially when the patient's condition is unclear, the patient has doubts about the treatment plan for a serious health care problem, or when a treatment is not working. MCOs also provide a third opinion when the first and second opinions differ.

Prescription Management

Prescription management controls medication costs using the following strategies:

- *Pharmacy benefit managers* are prescription drug program administrators, and they are private organizations that contract with health plans to administer a health plan's prescription drug program
- *Cost sharing copayments or coinsurance* are fixed amounts or percentages of costs that a patient pays for a medication

---

Guardian Managed Care Plan

101 Main St. ■ Anywhere, US 12345 ■ (101) 555-1234

DATE: _____

RE: _____
DATE OF BIRTH: _____
IDENTIFICATION NUMBER: _____
START TREATMENT DATE: _____

NAME OF CONSULTANT: _____
MAILING ADDRESS: _____

Dear Dr. _____

_____ was referred to you by the Guardian Managed Care Plan on _____.
I am authorizing the following medically necessary treatment. This is subject to patient eligibility and contract limitations at the time treatment is performed.

Procedure	Units	From	To	Preauthorization Number
_____	_____	____	___	_____

When requesting reimbursement, please send the CMS-1500 claim to the Guardian Managed Care Plan at the above address. In order to expedite payment, please be certain to include in Block 23 the pre-authorization number indicated above.

Please note that any services provided beyond those listed in this letter require additional preauthorization. If you anticipate that the patient will require additional services, you must complete an outpatient treatment report two weeks prior to rendering any additional treatment. If the patient fails to keep appointments, please inform us by telephone. If treatment is discontinued, submit a written discharge summary within two weeks of termination.

Although eligibility and benefit information has been corroborated to the best of our ability, certification for medically necessary care does not guarantee financial reimbursement related to these matters. If you need further information, or if there are any significant changes in the patient's medical status, please contact me at the Guardian Managed Care Plan at (800) 555-1212, extension 1234.
Thank you for your cooperation.

Sincerely,

Case Manager
Original:
cc:

FIGURE 2-3 Sample case manager written confirmation order.

- *Disease management programs*: Ensures proper treatment and reduces patient risk of overdosing, underdosing, or missing medications
- *Electronic prescribing* (e-prescribing): Providers transmit prescriptions to a pharmacy electronically
- *Drug formularies*: List of brand name and generic prescription medications covered by a health plan
- *Drug utilization review*: Interprets patterns of drug use to promote patient safety
- *Generic substitution*: Different, and less expensive, formulation of the brand-name drug is substituted
- *Manufacturer drug rebates*: Participating drug manufacturers offset of prescription drug costs
- *Negotiated prices*: Drug price reduction, such as for network pharmacies
- *Prescription mail services*: Efficient distribution-oriented pharmacy that ships medications to patients

NOTE:

A *prescription drug monitoring program (PDMP)* is an electronic database that tracks controlled substance prescriptions in a state (e.g., provides health authorities with information about prescribing patterns and patient behaviors that contribute to the opioid epidemic).

Consumer-Directed Health Plans

Consumer-directed health plans (CDHPs) define employer contributions and ask employees to be more responsible for health care decisions and cost-sharing. You might think of a CDHP as a sort of "401(k) plan for health care" (recalling the shift from employer defined-benefit pension plans to employer defined-contribution 401(k) plans). Consumer-directed health plans (CDHPs) include many choices that provide individuals with an incentive to control the costs of health benefits and health care. Individuals have greater freedom in spending health care dollars, up to a designated amount, and receive full coverage for in-network preventive care. In return, individuals assume significantly higher cost-sharing expenses after the designated amount has been expended. (The catastrophic limit is usually higher than those common in other plans.) CDHPs have become a popular alternative to the increased costs of traditional health insurance premiums and the limitations associated with managed care plans. They include the following tiers:

- Tax-exempt account, which is used to pay for health care expenses and provides more flexibility than traditional managed care plans in terms of access to providers and services
- Out-of-pocket payments for health care expenses, which are made after the tax-exempt account is expended and before the deductible for high-deductible insurance has been met; this tier actually represents a gap in coverage
- High-deductible insurance policy, which reimburses allowable health care expenses after the high deductible has been paid

CDHPs usually provide Internet-based support so individuals can track health care expenses, improve their health by viewing useful information and learning about preventive services, obtain information about provider quality, and receive notification about provider group-rate pricing. Various CDHPs are available to individuals, all of which are subject to modification as legislation is passed and payers alter program requirements. Consumer-directed health plans (CDHPs) including the following types:

- **Flexible spending account (FSA)**: Tax-exempt accounts offered by employers to any number of employees, which are used to pay health care bills
  - Employees contribute funds to the FSA through a salary reduction agreement and withdraw funds to pay medical bills.
  - Funds in an FSA are exempt from both income tax and Social Security tax (employers may also contribute to FSAs).
  - Per PPACA legislation, employers can allow employees to carry over up to $550 of unspent funds remaining in the FSA at the end of the year or a have grace period of up to two and a half months (but neither is required).
- **Health care reimbursement account (HCRA)**: Tax-exempt account that is used to pay for health care expenses
  - The individual decides, in advance, how much money to deposit in the HCRA.
  - Unused funds are forfeited.
- **Health reimbursement arrangement (HRA)**: Tax-exempt accounts funded by employers, which individuals use to pay health care bills
  - The *Individual Coverage HRA (ICHRA)* was introduced in 2020, providing greater flexibility and allowing employers to reimburse employees tax-free for individual insurance and medical expenses.

   o Money must be used for qualified health care expenses and allows individuals to accumulate unspent money for future years.

   o If an employee changes jobs, the remaining HRA amount can continue to be spent down to pay for qualified health care expenses.

- **Health savings account (HSA)**: Participants enroll in a relatively inexpensive *high-deductible health plan (HDHP)*, and a tax-deductible savings account is opened to cover current and future medical expenses.

   o Money deposited (and earnings) is tax-deferred, and money withdrawn to cover qualified medical expenses is tax-free.

   o Money can be withdrawn for purposes other than health care expenses after payment of income tax plus a 20-percent penalty.

   o Unused balances "roll over" from year to year; if an employee changes jobs, the HSA can continue to be used to pay for qualified health care expenses.

Health Care Documentation

Health care providers are responsible for documenting and authenticating legible, complete, and timely patient records in accordance with acceptable standards of medical care, federal regulations (e.g., Medicare *Conditions of Participation*), and accrediting organization standards (e.g., The Joint Commission). The provider is also responsible for correcting or altering errors in patient record documentation.

 NOTE:

Clinical documentation improvement is covered in Chapter 10 of this textbook.

Patient Records

A **patient record** (or **medical record**) documents health care services provided to a patient and includes patient demographic (or identification) data, documentation to support diagnoses and justify treatment provided, and the results of treatment provided. The primary purpose of the record is to provide for **continuity of care**, which involves documenting patient care services so that others who treat the patient have a source of information to assist with additional care and treatment. The record also serves as a communication tool for physicians and other patient care professionals and assists in planning individual patient care and documenting a patient's illness and treatment.

    Secondary purposes and uses of the record do not relate directly to patient care and include

- evaluating the quality of patient care;
- providing data for use in clinical research, epidemiology studies, education, public policy making, facilities planning, and health care statistics;
- providing information to third-party payers for reimbursement;
- serving the medico-legal interests of the patient, facility, and providers of care.

    In a teaching hospital, general documentation guidelines allow both residents and teaching physicians to document physician services in the patient's medical record.

- A *teaching hospital* participates in an approved Graduate Medical Education Residency Program in medicine, osteopathy, dentistry, or podiatry.

- A *teaching physician* is a physician, other than an intern or resident, who involves residents in patient care. Generally, the teaching physician must be present during all critical or key portions of the procedure and immediately available to furnish services during the entire service (for services to be payable under the Medicare Physician Fee Schedule).

Guidelines for Teaching Physicians, Interns, and Residents

Go to www.cms.gov, and keyboard "Guidelines for Teaching Physicians" in the Search CMS box. Click Search. Click on the 2018-03 | CMS link, and then click on the *Guidelines for Teaching Physicians, Interns, and Residents (PDF)* file, which cover documentation guidelines for Medicare reimbursement.

Documentation in the patient record serves as the basis for coding. The information in the record must support codes submitted on claims for third-party payer reimbursement processing. The patient's diagnosis must also justify diagnostic and/or therapeutic procedures or services provided. This is called *medical necessity* and requires providers to document services or supplies that are

- proper and needed for the diagnosis or treatment of a medical condition;
- provided for the diagnosis, direct care, and treatment of a medical condition;
- consistent with standards of good medical practice in the local area;
- not mainly for the convenience of the physician, patient, or health care facility.

It is important to remember the familiar phrase "If it wasn't documented, it wasn't done." The patient record serves as a medico-legal document and a business record. If a provider performs a service but does not document it, the patient (or third-party payer) can refuse to pay for that service, resulting in lost revenue for the provider. In addition, because the patient record serves as an excellent defense of the quality of care administered to a patient, missing documentation can result in problems if the record has to be admitted as evidence in a court of law.

Example:

Missing Documentation: A representative from XYZ Insurance Company reviewed 100 outpatient claims submitted by the Medical Center to ensure that all services billed were documented in the patient records. Upon reconciliation of claims with patient record documentation, the representative denied payment for 13 services (totaling $14,000) because reports of the services billed were not found in the patient records. The facility must pay back the $14,000 it received from the payer as reimbursement for the claims submitted.

Lack of Medical Necessity: The patient underwent an x-ray of the right knee, and the provider documented severe right shoulder pain in the record. The coder assigned a CPT code to the right knee x-ray and an ICD-10-CM code to the right shoulder pain. In this example, the third-party payer will deny reimbursement for the submitted claim because the *reason* for the x-ray (shoulder pain) does not match the *type* of x-ray performed. For medical necessity, the provider should have documented a diagnosis such as right knee pain.

Support of Medical Necessity: The patient underwent a chest x-ray, and the provider documented severe shortness of breath in the record. The coder assigned a CPT code to chest x-ray and an ICD-10-CM code to severe shortness of breath. In this example, the third-party payer will reimburse the provider for services rendered because medical necessity for performing the procedure has been shown.

Problem-Oriented Record (POR)

The **problem-oriented record (POR)** is a systematic method of documentation that consists of four components:

- Database
- Problem list
- Initial plan
- Progress notes

The POR database contains the following information collected on each patient:

- Chief complaint
- Present conditions and diagnoses
- Social data
- Past, personal, medical, and social history
- Review of systems
- Physical examination
- Baseline laboratory data

The POR problem list serves as a table of contents for the patient record because it is filed at the beginning of the record and contains a numbered list of the patient's problems, which helps index documentation throughout the record.

The POR initial plan contains the strategy for managing patient care, as well as any actions taken to investigate the patient's condition and to treat and provide education about illnesses and injuries. The initial plan consists of three categories:

- *Diagnostic/management plans:* Plans to learn more about the patient's condition and the management of the conditions
- *Therapeutic plans:* Specific medications, goals, procedures, therapies, and treatments used to treat the patient
- *Patient education plans:* Provides education to patients about conditions for which they are being treated

The POR progress notes are documented for each problem assigned to the patient, using the SOAP format:

- *Subjective (S):* Patient's statement of signs and symptoms, including severity and duration [e.g., "I have had a very painful headache for the past three days"]
- *Objective (O):* Observations about the patient, such as physical findings, or lab or x-ray results [e.g., chest x-ray negative]
- *Assessment (A):* Judgment, opinion, or evaluation made by the health care provider [e.g., acute headache]
- *Plan (P):* Diagnostic, therapeutic, and education plans to resolve the problems [e.g., patient to take Tylenol as needed for pain]

Electronic Health Record (EHR)

Although the terms *electronic health record (EHR)* and *electronic medical record (EMR)* are often used interchangeably, the **electronic health record (EHR)** is a more global concept that includes the collection of patient information documented by a number of providers at different facilities regarding one patient. The EHR uses multidisciplinary (many specialties) and multi-enterprise (many facilities) recordkeeping approaches to facilitate **record linkage**, which allows patient information to be created at different locations according to a unique patient identifier or identification number. The electronic health record:

- provides access to complete and accurate patient health problems, status, and treatment data, and promotes coordination of patient care;

- allows access to evidence-based decision support tools (e.g., drug interaction alerts) that assist providers with decision making;

- automates and streamlines a provider's workflow, ensuring that all clinical information is communicated;

- prevents delays in health care response that result in gaps in care (e.g., automated prescription renewal notices);

- supports the collection of data for uses other than clinical care (e.g., billing, outcome reporting, public health disease surveillance/reporting, and quality management).

 NOTE:

Some disadvantages of the EHR include concerns about initial purchase costs, direct and indirect training costs, and on-going maintenance costs; issues of privacy and security expressed by patients and providers; and the possibility that evaluation and management elements not actually performed during an encounter will be automatically documented (populated) by the software.

The **electronic medical record (EMR)** has a more narrow focus because it is the patient record created for a single medical practice using a computer, keyboard, mouse, optical pen device, voice recognition system, scanner, and/or touch screen. The electronic medical record:

- includes a patient's medication lists, problem lists, clinical notes, and other documentation;

- allows providers to prescribe medications, as well as order and view results of ancillary tests (e.g., laboratory, radiology);

- alerts the provider about drug interactions, abnormal ancillary testing results, and when ancillary tests are needed.

 NOTE:

The **personal health record (PHR)** is a web-based application that allows individuals to maintain and manage their health information (and that of others for whom they are authorized, such as family members) in a private, secure, and confidential environment.

Total practice management software (TPMS) (Figure 2-4) is used to generate the EMR, automating the following medical practice functions:

- Registering patients
- Scheduling appointments
- Generating insurance claims and patient statements
- Processing payments from patient and third-party payers
- Producing administrative and clinical reports

Meaningful EHR Users

From 2011 through 2016, Medicare provided annual incentives to physicians and group practices for being a **meaningful EHR user**, defined by Medicare as

- physicians who demonstrated that *certified EHR technology* was used for the purposes of electronic prescribing, electronic exchange of health information in accordance with law and health information technology (HIT) standards, and submission of information on clinical quality measures;

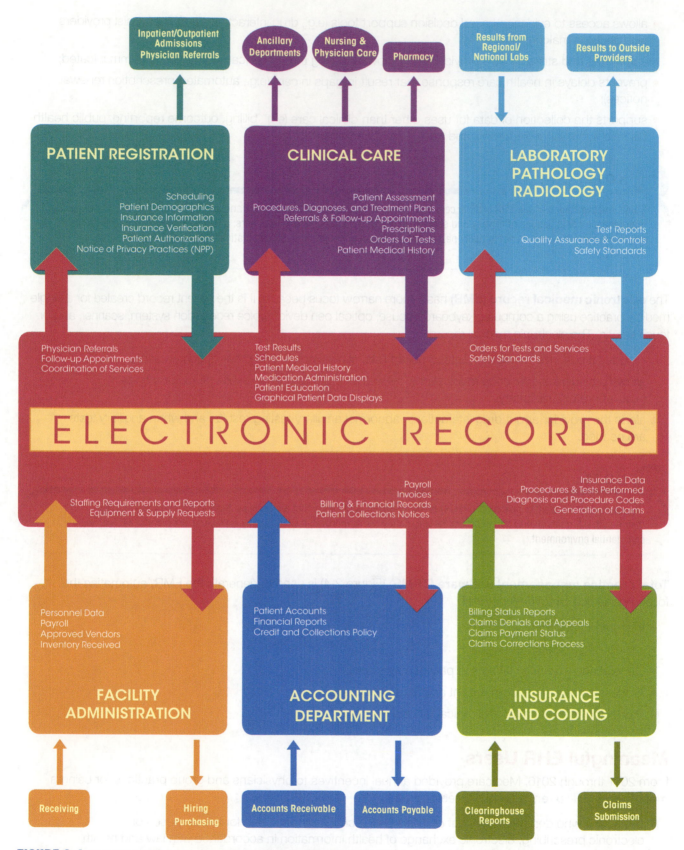

FIGURE 2-4 Total practice management software (TPMS) data flow.

- hospitals that demonstrated that *certified EHR technology* was connected in a manner that provided for the electronic exchange of health information to improve the quality of health care (e.g., promoting care coordination) and that *certified EHR technology* was used to submit information on clinical quality measures according to stages of **meaningful use** (objectives and measures that achieve goals of improved patient care outcomes and delivery through data capture and sharing, advance clinical processes, and improved patient outcomes).

The secretary of the Department of Health and Human Services determined whether physicians and hospitals had satisfactorily demonstrated "meaningful EHR use," and the secretary also selected criteria upon which clinical quality measures were based.

Meaningful Use Measures

The *American Recovery and Reinvestment Act (ARRA)*, enacted in 2009, implemented measures to modernize the nation's infrastructure, including the *Health Information Technology for Economic and Clinical Health (HITECH) Act*, which supported the concept of EHRs/meaningful use. *Meaningful use* required the use of certified EHR technology in a meaningful manner (e.g., electronic prescribing) to ensure that certified EHR technology is connected so as to provide for the electronic exchange of health information to improve the quality of care. Health care providers that use certified EHR technology submitted information about quality of care and other measures to the Secretary of Health and Human Services (HHS). The concept of meaningful use included the following health outcomes policy priorities:

- Engaging patients and families in their health
- Ensuring adequate privacy and security protection for personal health information
- Improving care coordination
- Improving population and public health
- Improving quality, safety, and efficiency and reducing health disparities

CMS implemented an incentive payment to eligible professionals (EPs) and eligible hospitals (EHs) that demonstrated they engaged in efforts to adopt, implement, or upgrade certified EHR technology. To encourage widespread EHR adoption, promote innovation, and avoid imposing excessive burden on health care providers, *meaningful use* was implemented using a phased-in approach, subdivided into three stages from 2011 and 2012 (data capture and sharing) through 2014 (advance clinical processes) and 2016 (improved outcomes).

Electronic Clinical Quality Measures (eCQMs)

CMS maintains **electronic clinical quality measures (eCQMs)**, which use data from electronic health records (EHR) and health information technology systems to measure health care quality. Measures apply to processes, observations, treatments, and outcomes, which serve to quantify the *quality of care* provided by health care systems. Measuring and reporting eCQMs data helps ensure that care is delivered safely, effectively, equitably, and timely. **Promoting Interoperability (PI) Programs** (previously called EHR incentive programs) focus on improving patient access to health information and reducing the time and cost required of providers to comply with the programs' requirements.

Quality Payment Program (QPP)

The *Medicare Access and CHIP Reauthorization Act (MACRA) of 2015* ended the *sustainable growth rate (SGR) formula* and *meaningful use payment adjustments* (and its separate quality reporting incentives). MACRA consolidated certain current law performance programs, implementing a new **quality payment program (QPP)**, which helps providers focus on the quality of patient care and making patients healthier that includes *advanced alternative payment models (Advanced APMs)* and a *merit-based incentive payment* *system (MIPS)*. (The hospital inpatient and outpatient quality reporting programs are discussed in Chapter 5 of this textbook)

 NOTE:

> The SGR law capped Medicare spending increases and included a modest allowance for inflation. As clinicians increased utilization of services, reimbursement was adjusted downward to hold costs constant, resulting in unsustainable decreases in the Medicare Physician Fee Schedule (MPFS). To avoid decreases in reimbursement, Congress was required to pass a new law every year authorizing the current fee schedule and a small increase for inflation. MACRA eliminated the SRG law and the Congressional requirement for annual MPFS legislation.

An **alternative payment model (APM)** is a payment approach that gives added incentive payments to provide high-quality and cost-efficient care; APMs can apply to a specific clinical condition, a care episode, or a population. **Advanced alternative payment models (Advanced APMs)** are a subset of APMs and include new ways for CMS to reimburse health care providers for care provided to Medicare beneficiaries. Providers who participate in an Advanced APM through Medicare Part B may earn an incentive payment for participating in the innovative payment model. Advanced APMs include

- lump-sum incentive payment (2019–2024) to some participating health care providers;
- increased transparency of physician-focused payment models;
- higher annual payments (beginning in 2026) to some participating health care providers.

Examples of APMs include accountable care organizations (ACOs), patient-centered medical homes, and bundled payment models.

> **Example:** *Comprehensive Primary Care Plus (CPC+)* is a national advanced primary care medical home innovative model, approved by CMS, which aims to strengthen primary care through regionally based multi-payer payment reform and care delivery transformation. CPC+ includes two primary care practice tracks with incrementally advanced care delivery requirements and payment options to meet the diverse needs of primary care practices in the United States (U.S.). CPC+ seeks to improve quality, access, and efficiency of primary care. Practices in both tracks will make changes in the way they deliver care, centered on key CPC+ functions: access and continuity; care management; comprehensiveness and coordination; patient and caregiver engagement; and planned care and population health. To support the delivery of comprehensive primary care, CPC+ includes three payment elements: care management fee (CMF), performance-based incentive payment, and payment under the Medicare physician fee schedule (MPFS).

The **Merit-Based Incentive Payment System (MIPS)** combines parts of the *Physician Quality Reporting System (PQRS),* the *Value Modifier (VM or Physician Value-based Payment Modifier)*, and the *Medicare Electronic Health Record (EHR)* incentive program into one single program that allows providers to earn a performance-based payment adjustment that considers

- quality;
- resource use;
- clinical practice improvement;
- meaningful use of certified EHR technology.

 NOTE:

> The EHR incentive program was renamed the *Promoting Interoperability (PI) Programs* to highlight enhanced goals of the program, better contextualize program changes, and because the incentive payments have ended for Medicare and Medicaid.

MIPS participants must decide whether to report data as an individual or with a group.

- An *individual* is defined as a single clinician, identified by a single National Provider Identifier (NPI) number tied to a single Tax Identification Number (TIN). When reporting as an individual, the payment adjustment is based on performance and data for each MIPS category.
- A *group* is defined as a single TIN with two or more eligible clinicians as identified by their NPIs (including at least one MIPS-eligible clinician) who have reassigned their Medicare billing rights to the TIN. When reporting as a group, the payment adjustment is based on the group's performance.

 NOTE:

Originally, MIPS-eligible clinicians included physicians, physician assistants, nurse practitioners, clinical nurse specialists, and certified nurse anesthetists. In 2019, the following MIPS-eligible clinicians were added: physical therapists, occupational therapists, qualified speech-language pathologists, qualified audiologists, clinical psychologists, and registered dieticians/nutrition professionals.

Data reporting for individual and group MIPS participants is conducted through a variety of methods. All MIPS participants are permitted to use the following data reporting methods:

- *Qualified registry*: CMS-approved entity that collects clinical data and submits measures and activities data for certain performance categories to CMS; in 2018, the Quality, Program Interoperability, and Improvement Activities performance categories were used to collect and report data (Program Interoperability replaced Advancing Care Information as the performance category name in 2019.)
- *Qualified clinical data registry (QCDC)*: CMS-approved entity that collects and reports clinical data for the purpose of patient and disease tracking to foster improvement in patient quality of care; data collected covers quality measures across multiple payers and is not limited to Medicare beneficiaries
- *Electronic health record (EHR) vendor*: Use of *Certified Electronic Health Record Technology (CEHRT)*, which is required for participation in the Program Interoperability performance category of MIPS
- *Attestation*: Using the https://qpp.cms.gov website to verify that measures associated with certain MIPS components, Program Interoperability, and Improvement Activities, were conducted

Individual participants are also permitted to use the following data reporting methods:

- *Routine administrative Medicare claims process*: Submission of CPT category II quality data codes and HCPCS Level II G-codes on eligible claims that demonstrate compliance with Quality performance measures; reporting such codes indicates which patients should be added to the calculation based on quality measures, such as reporting data about age-appropriate colonoscopy screenings

Group participants are also permitted to use the following data reporting methods:

- *CMS Web Interface*: Secure Internet-based data submission mechanism (portal) available only to groups with 25 or more MIPS-eligible clinicians; reporting all 15 sets of performance measures is required
- *Consumer Assessment of Healthcare Providers and Systems (CAHPS) for MIPS Survey*: Optional Quality performance measure available only to groups with 2 or more eligible clinicians; MIPS-eligible clinicians may be awarded points under the Improvement Activities performance measure category for administering the survey

The CMS comprehensive initiative entitled *Meaningful Measures* was implemented in 2017 to identify high-priority areas for quality measurement and improvement. Its purpose is to improve outcomes for patients, their families, and providers while also reducing burden on clinicians and providers. The intent is to move toward value-based payments by focusing efforts on the same quality areas and provide specificity (e.g., address high impact measure areas that safeguard public health, provide patient-centered and meaningful care to patients).

 NOTE:

Clinicians can participate in *MIPS APMs* if (1) they are participating in an Advanced APM but do not meet Medicare patient or payment count thresholds for a *qualifying Advanced APM participant (QP)* or a *partially qualifying Advanced APM participant (PQ)* or (2) if they are participating in an APM that is not considered an Advanced APM. MIPS APMs are a hybrid of MIPS and Advanced APMs, and they have different reporting requirements and scoring (as compared with MIPS or Advanced APMs).

The *merit-based incentive payment system (MIPS)* allows providers to earn a performance-based payment adjustment that considers quality, resource use, clinical practice improvement, and meaningful use of certified electronic health record technology. MIPS participants decide whether to report data as an individual (e.g., single clinician with a national provider identifier) or with a group (e.g., two or more eligible clinicians who have reassigned their Medicare billing rights to a single tax identification number). (Clinicians can also participate in *MIPS APMs*, a hybrid of MIPS and Advanced APMs, for which there are different reporting requirements and scoring.)

MIPS contains the following four performance categories, each of which is scored and weighted, with the result a MIPS final score that impacts clinician Medicare payments: quality, cost, improvement activities, and promoting interoperability (PI) (Figure 2-5). (Bonus points can also be earned.) The electronic clinical quality measures (eCQMs) reported to CMS are updated annually; the data is electronically extracted from electronic health records (EHRs) and/or health information technology systems to measure the quality of health care provided. (Some data is reported on CMS-1500 claims.) Clinicians also review benchmarked data for quality, improvement activities, and PI measures to compare their results to national and regional data. **Benchmarking** allows an entity to measure and compare its own data against that of other agencies and organizations for the purpose of continuous improvement.

- Ensure that selected *quality* measures (Table 2-2) are supported by the practice's reporting method. Clinicians must ensure that quality measures are supported by the reporting method selected (e.g., EHR allows for reporting of selected measures), adhere to documentation requirements to achieve targeted measures, and strive to meet benchmarks (comparative data) to achieve optimal results

FIGURE 2-5 MIPS performance categories.

TABLE 2-2 Sample quality measures: 50 percent of final score

Measure Name	Measure Description	Data Submission	Specialty
Age appropriate screening colonoscopy	Percentage of patients greater than 85 years of age who received a screening colonoscopy from January 1 to December 31	Registry	Gastroenterology
Biopsy follow-up	Percentage of new patients whose biopsy results have been reviewed and communicated to the primary care/referring physician and patient by the performing physician	Registry	Dermatology Obstetrics/Gynecology Otolaryngology Urology
Breast cancer screening	Percentage of women 50–74 years of age who had a mammogram to screen for breast cancer	Claims CMS Web Interface EHR Registry	Family Medicine Obstetrics/Gynecology Preventive Medicine

Courtesy of the Centers for Medicare & Medicaid Services, www.cms.gov.

- Review results of prior *cost* reports to determine whether changes can be made to improve results. There is no data submission requirement for the cost performance category.
  - Cost measures are evaluated automatically through administrative claims data.
  - CMS calculates the Medicare spending per beneficiary (MSPB) and total per capita cost (TPCC) measures (Figure 2-6).
  - MSPB and TPCC results are sent to each clinician.
  - Clinicians compare their scores with national median scores and percentile ranks, identify areas of needed improvement, and implement a cost improvement plan.
- Select *improvement activities* and implement required processes to achieve, measure, and report targeted results (Table 2-3). Clinicians must ensure that the measures are supported by the reporting method selected (e.g., EHR allows for reporting of selected measures), adhere to documentation requirements to achieve targeted measures, and strive to meet benchmarks (comparative data) to achieve optimal results.
- Select *promote interoperability (PI)* activities and review electronic health record (EHR) capabilities to achieve, measure, and report targeted results (Table 2-4). Clinicians must ensure that necessary functionality has been activated in the practice's EHR (e.g., e-prescribing, patient portal, direct messaging between patients and clinicians).

TABLE 2-3 Sample improvement activities: 15 percent of final score

Measure Name	Measure Description	Data Submission	Specialty
Age appropriate screening colonoscopy	Percentage of patients greater than 85 years of age who received a screening colonoscopy from January 1 to December 31	Registry	Gastroenterology
Biopsy follow-up	Percentage of new patients whose biopsy results have been reviewed and communicated to the primary care/referring physician and patient by the performing physician	Registry	Dermatology Obstetrics/Gynecology Otolaryngology Urology
Breast cancer screening	Percentage of women 50–74 years of age who had a mammogram to screen for breast cancer	Claims CMS Web Interface EHR Registry	Family Medicine Obstetrics/Gynecology Preventive Medicine

Courtesy of the Centers for Medicare & Medicaid Services, www.cms.gov.

Cost Measures (10% of final score)

Medicare Spending Per Beneficiary (MSPB) Clinician Measure Report

Arthur McKay, M.D., New York
National Provider Identifier (NPI): 1234567890
Last four digits of your Taxpayer Identification Number (TIN): 1234
Measurement Period: January 1, YYYY – December 31, YYYY

Your TIN's MSPB Clinician Field Test Report Measure Score:

	MSPB Clinician Measure
Your TIN's Score	$16,000
National Median	$18,696
Percentile Rank	95

The *Medicare Spending Per Beneficiary (MSPB)* measure assesses the average amount spent for Medicare services performed by providers/groups per episode of care, which is the period immediately prior to, during, and following a patient's inpatient hospital stay.

Total Per Capita Cost (TPCC) Clinician Measure Report

Arthur McKay, M.D., New York
Last four digits of your Taxpayer Identification Number (TIN): 1234
Measurement Period: October 1, YYYY – September 30, YYYY

Your TIN's MSPB Clinician Field Test Report Measure Score:

	MSPB Clinician Measure
Your TIN's Score	$891.95
National Median	$755.38
Percentile Rank	17

The *Total Per Capita Cost (TPCC)* measure is a payment-standardized, annualized, risk-adjusted, and specialty-adjusted measure that evaluates the overall efficiency of care provided to beneficiaries attributed to solo practitioners and groups, as identified by their Medicare Taxpayer Identification Number (TIN).

Courtesy of the Centers for Medicare & Medicaid Services, www.cms.gov.

FIGURE 2-6 Sample cost measures reports.

TABLE 2-4 Sample promoting interoperability (PI) activities: 25 percent of final score

Measure Name	Measure Description	Objective	Required	Performance Score
e-Prescribing	At least one permissible prescription written by the MIPS-eligible clinician is queried for a drug formulary and transmitted electronically using certified EHR technology.	Electronic Prescribing	Yes	0
Patient-generated health data	Patient-generated health data or data from a non-clinical setting is incorporated into the certified EHR technology for at least one unique patient seen by the MIPS eligible clinician during the performance period.	Coordination of Care Through Patient Engagement	No	Up to 10%

(continues)

TABLE 2-4   (continued)

Measure Name	Measure Description	Objective	Required	Performance Score
PI bonus for submission of eligible *Improvement Activities* using CEHRT	Provider attests that an eligible Improvement Activity using certified EHR technology (CEHRT) was submitted.	None	No	Up to 10%
Public health registry reporting	The MIPS eligible clinician is in active engagement with a public health agency to submit data to public health registries. To earn a 5% bonus in the promoting interoperability performance category score for submitting to one or more public health or clinical data registries, also attest to public health registry reporting for multiple registry engagement.	Public Health and Clinical Data Registry Reporting	No	Up to 10%

Summary

Health insurance is a contract between a policyholder and a third-party payer or government program for the purpose of providing reimbursement of all or a portion of medical and health care costs.

The history of health care reimbursement can be traced back to 1850 when the Franklin Health Assurance Company of Massachusetts wrote the first health insurance policy. Subsequent years, through the present, have seen significant changes and advances in health care insurance and reimbursement, from the development of the first BlueCross and BlueShield plans for separate institutional and professional services to legislation that resulted in government health care programs (e.g., to cover individuals age 65 and older), managed care, payment systems to control health care costs (e.g., diagnosis-related groups), and regulations to govern privacy, security, and electronic transaction standards for health care information. The *Patient Protection and Affordable Care Act (PPACA)* was signed into federal law by President Obama on March 23, 2010, and resulted in the creation of a health insurance marketplace (or health insurance exchange) effective October 1, 2013. The PPACA is abbreviated as the Affordable Care Act (ACA).

Health insurance is available to individuals who participate in group (e.g., employer sponsored), individual (or personal insurance), or prepaid health plans (e.g., managed care). Consumer-directed health plans (CDHPs) provide incentives for controlling health care expenses and give individuals an alternative to traditional health insurance and managed care coverage. Many characteristics of health plans and managed care plans are similar, and they include primary care provider (gatekeeper role), quality assurance and performance measurement, utilization management, case management, second surgical opinions, second and third opinions, and prescription management.

Managed care delivers health benefits and additional services through contracted arrangements between individuals or health care programs (e.g., Medicaid) and managed care organizations (MCOs), which accept a predetermined capitation (e.g., per member per month) payment for services. Managed care organizations range from structured staff model HMOs to less structured preferred provider organizations (PPOs). A managed care organization (MCO) is responsible for the health of its enrollees, which can be administered by the MCO that serves as a health plan or contracts with a hospital, physician group, or health system. Managed care enrollees are assigned to or select a primary care provider who serves as the patient's gatekeeper. Managed care is categorized according to models that include exclusive provider organizations, integrated delivery systems, health maintenance organizations, point-of-service plans, preferred provider organizations, and triple option plans. Accreditation organizations, such as the NCQA, evaluate MCOs according to preestablished standards.

A *patient record* (or *medical record*) documents health care services provided to a patient, and health care providers are responsible for documenting and authenticating legible, complete, and timely entries according to federal regulations and accreditation standards. The records include patient demographic (or identification) data, documentation to support diagnoses and justify treatment provided, and the results of treatment provided. The primary purpose of the record is to provide for continuity of care, which involves documenting patient care services so that others who treat the patient have a source of information to assist with additional care and treatment. The *problem-oriented record (POR)* is a systematic method of documentation that consists of four components: database, problem list, initial plan, and progress notes (documented using the SOAP format).

The *electronic health record (EHR)* is a global concept (as compared with the EMR) that includes the collection of patient information documented by a number of providers at different facilities regarding one patient. The EHR uses multidisciplinary (many specialties) and multi-enterprise (many facilities) recordkeeping approaches to facilitate *record linkage*, which allows patient information to be created at different locations according to a unique patient identifier or identification number. The *personal health record* (PHR) is a web-based application that allows individuals to maintain and manage their health information (and that of others for whom they are authorized, such as family members) in a private, secure, and confidential environment. The electronic medical record (EMR) has a more narrow focus (as compared with the EHR) because it is the patient record created for a single medical practice and uses total practice management software (TPMS) to generate the EMR and automate medical practice functions.

Internet Links

Beacon Health Options: *www.beaconhealthoptions.com*

Consolidated Omnibus Budget Reconciliation Act (COBRA): *www.cobrainsurance.com*

eCQI Resource Center: *ecqi.healthit.gov*

Fairview Health Services: Go to *www.healtheast.org* to view information about the Fairview Health Services health system, which is an integrated health system that provides a full spectrum of health care services.

Great Plains Regional Medical Center: Go to *www.gprmc-ok.com* and select the About link to learn more about Dr. Shadid and the history of the Great Plains Regional Medical Center, a managed care system started in 1929.

Healthcare Insurance Marketplace: *www.healthcare.gov*

Kaiser Permanente: Go to *healthy.kaiserpermanente.org* to learn about the history of the country's first HMO, Kaiser Permanente.

National Committee for Quality Assurance (NCQA): Go to *ncqa.org* to learn about the NCQA.

NCQA's Health Plan Report Card: Go to *reportcards.ncqa.org* and click the Health Plans link to use an interactive tool to create a customized report card of managed care plans.

Rochester Regional Health Information Organization (RHIO): *www.rochesterrhio.org*

The Joint Commission: *www.jointcommission.org*

The Joint Commission Quality Check: Go to *www.qualitycheck.org* and conduct a search to identify health care organizations that meet The Joint Commission's patient safety and quality standards.

UnitedHealthcare: *www.uhc.com*

Review

2.1 – Multiple Choice

Select the most appropriate response.

1. The Hill-Burton Act provided federal grants for modernizing hospitals that had become obsolete because of a lack of capital investment during the Great Depression and World War II (1929 to 1945). In return for federal funds,
    a. facilities were required to provide services free or at reduced rates to patients unable to pay for care.
    b. medical group practices were formed to allow providers to share equipment, supplies, and personnel.
    c. national coordinating agencies for physician-sponsored health insurance plans were created.
    d. universal health insurance was provided to those who could not afford private insurance.

2. Third-party administrators (TPAs) administer health care plans and process claims, serving as a
    a. clearinghouse for data submitted by government agencies.
    b. Medicare administrative contractor (MAC) for business owners.
    c. system of checks and balances for labor and management.
    d. third-party payer (insurance company) for employers.

3. Major medical insurance provides coverage for _____ illnesses and injuries, incorporating large deductibles and lifetime maximum amounts.
    a. acute care (short-term care)
    b. catastrophic or prolonged
    c. recently diagnosed
    d. work-related

4. The percentage of costs a patient shares with the health plan (e.g., plan pays 80 percent of costs and patient pays 20 percent) is called
    a. coinsurance.
    b. copayment.
    c. deductible.
    d. maximum.

5. Which allows employees to continue health care coverage beyond the benefit termination date by paying appropriate premiums and established an employee's right to continue health care coverage beyond the scheduled benefit termination date (including HMO coverage)?
    a. COBRA
    b. ERISA
    c. FSMA
    d. OBRA

6. The *Patient Protection and Affordable Care Act (PPACA)* was signed into federal law by President Obama on March 23, 2010, and resulted in creation of a(n)
    a. accountable health care organization.
    b. federal health insurance program.
    c. group health savings plan.
    d. health insurance marketplace.

7. Which is a primary purpose of the patient record?
    a. Ensure continuity of care
    b. Evaluate quality of care
    c. provide data for use in research
    d. Submit data to third-party payers

8. The problem-oriented record (POR) includes the following four components
   a. chief complaint, review of systems, physical examination, laboratory data
   b. database, problem list, initial plan, progress notes
   c. diagnostic plans, management plans, therapeutic plans, patient education plans
   d. subjective, objective, assessment, plan

9. The electronic health record (EHR) allows patient information to be created at different locations according to a unique patient identifier or identification number, which is called
   a. evidence-based decision support.
   b. health data management.
   c. record linkage.
   d. surveillance and reporting.

10. When a patient states, "I haven't been able to sleep for weeks," the provider documents that statement in the _____ portion of the SOAP note.
    a. assessment
    b. objective
    c. plan
    d. subjective

11. The provider who uses the SOAP format documents the physical examination in the _____ portion of the clinic note.
    a. assessment
    b. objective
    c. plan
    d. subjective

12. The original intent of managed health care was to
    a. dramatically improve the health care delivery system in the United States.
    b. have patients who participate in managed care take better care of themselves.
    c. replace fee-for-service plans with affordable, quality care to health care consumers.
    d. retrospectively reimburse patients for health care services provided.

13. The Patient Protection and Affordable Care Act (PPACA) risk adjustment program was implemented to lessen or eliminate the influence of risk selection on premiums charged by health plans and has a risk transfer formula, which calculates enrollee risk scores. If an average risk score is 1.0 and has a value of $1,500, and the formula for calculating the total risk score is demographic risk factor + health status risk factor, a 77-year-old patient who has a 0.7 demographic risk factor and a 0.9 health status risk factor has a risk score monetary average of
    a. $384.
    b. $2,400.
    c. $3,900.
    d. $4,800.

14. The Medical Center received a $100,000 capitation payment in January to cover the health care costs of 150 managed care enrollees. By the following January, $80,000 had been expended to cover services provided. The remaining $20,000 is
    a. distributed equally among the 150 enrollees.
    b. retained by the Medical Center as profit.
    c. returned to the managed care organization.
    d. turned over to the federal government.

15. A nonprofit organization that contracts with, and acquires the clinical and business assets of, physician practices is called a
    a. medical foundation.
    b. Medicare risk program.
    c. physician-hospital organization.
    d. triple option plan.

16. Which is responsible for supervising and coordinating health care services for health insurance and managed care enrollees?
    a. Case manager
    b. Primary care provider
    c. Third-party administrator
    d. Utilization review manager

17. The term that describes requirements created by accreditation organizations is
    a. laws.
    b. mandates.
    c. regulations.
    d. standards.

18. Which administrative procedure should a medical practice follow when it contracts with a managed care organization (MCO)?
    a. Conduct patient interviews for the managed care organization.
    b. Discontinue completing referral paperwork for specialists.
    c. Employ case managers to monitor services provided to patients.
    d. Maintain a separate bookkeeping system for each capitated plan.

19. Which is a consumer-directed health plan?
    a. Alternate payment model
    b. Capitation plan
    c. Flexible spending account
    d. Health insurance marketplace

20. In managed care, the primary care provider (PCP) typically receives a capitation payment and is responsible for managing all of an individual's health care; when the PCP arranges for the individual to receive care from a specialist), the specialist receives a(n) _____ payment on a PMPM basis to provide only the care needed by the individual.
    a. episodic
    b. flexible
    c. per encounter
    d. sub-capitation

2.2 – Managed Care Models

Instructions: Enter the managed care model for each definition.

1. A contracted network of health care providers that provide care to subscribers for a discounted fee is called a(n) _____.

2. An organization of affiliated providers' sites that offer joint health care services to subscribers is called a(n) _____.

3. The managed care model that provides benefits to subscribers who are required to receive services from network providers is called a(n) _____.

4. The managed care model that provides comprehensive health care services to voluntarily enrolled members on a prepaid basis is called a(n) _____.

5. The managed care model that allows patients to use the managed care panel of providers or self-refer to out-of-network providers is called a(n) _____.

2.3 – Introduction to Calculating Health Care Reimbursement

Instructions: Review each the case, and calculate the reimbursement amounts.

Case 1: The patient undergoes arthroscopic surgery at an ambulatory surgical center. The physician's fee is $890. The patient's coinsurance is 20 percent of the $700 fee schedule, and the patient is not required to pay any additional amount to the physician. The payer reimburses the physician 80 percent of the $700 fee schedule.

_____ **1.** Which amount is the fee schedule for the arthroscopic procedure?

_____ **2.** What percentage of the fee schedule does the patient reimburse the physician?

_____ **3.** Calculate the amount the patient pays the physician.

_____ **4.** Calculate the amount the payer reimburses the physician.

_____ **5.** Calculate the amount the physician "writes off" on this account.

Case 2: The patient was referred to an orthopedic specialist for evaluation of chronic ankle pain. The physician's fee is $150. The patient's coinsurance is 30 percent of the $100 fee schedule, and the patient is not required to pay any additional amount to the physician. The payer reimburses the physician 70 percent of the $100 fee schedule for this service.

_____ **6.** Which amount is the fee schedule?

_____ **7.** What percentage of the fee schedule does the payer reimburse the surgeon?

_____ **8.** Calculate the amount the patient pays the physician.

_____ **9.** Calculate the amount the payer reimburses the physician.

_____ **10.** Calculate the amount the physician "writes off" on this account.

2.4 – Creating a Customized NCQA Health Plan Report Card

Instructions: Create a customized report card about a health plan in your state by going to reportcards.ncqa.org, moving your mouse over the Report Cards heading, clicking on the Health Plans link, and clicking on the Health Plan Report Card link. Next, enter your state (e.g., New York) in the Search box. When a list of health plan names display, click on one of them to answer the questions below. (Be sure to scroll down the entire page of the health plan you selected to review all Report Card information about it.)

_____ **1.** Which state did you enter in the Search box?

_____ **2.** Which health plan did you click on?

_____ **3.** Was that health plan accredited?

_____ **4.** What additional information did you view about the health plan?

_____ **5.** Briefly summarize the results of each the report card generated.

Introduction to Revenue Management

Chapter Outline

Revenue Management

Managing Patients

Encounter Form and Chargemaster

Processing an Insurance Claim

Posting Charges to Patient Accounts

Monitoring and Auditing for Revenue
Management

Objectives

Upon successful completion of this chapter, you should be able to:

1. Define key terms related to revenue management.
2. Explain the revenue management process.
3. Explain how new and established patients are managed.
4. Explain the use of an encounter form and a chargemaster.
5. Describe the processing of an insurance claim from patient appointment through claims submission.
6. Explain how to post charges to patient accounts.
7. Summarize methods of monitoring and auditing for revenue management.

Key Terms

accept assignment

accounts payable

accounts receivable

accounts receivable
 management

accrual accounting

assignment of benefits

birthday rule

case management

charge description
 master (CDM)

chargemaster

chargemaster
 maintenance

chargemaster team

claims denial

claims rejection

concurrent review

data analysis

data analytics

data mining

data warehouse

day sheet

discharge planning

discharged not final
 billed (DNFB)

discharged not final
 coded (DNFC)

encounter form

facility billing

guarantor

institutional billing

integrated revenue cycle
 (IRC)

manual daily accounts
 receivable journal

metrics

nonparticipating
 provider (nonPAR)

out-of-pocket payment

participating provider (PAR)

patient account record

patient ledger

preadmission certification (PAC)

preadmission review

preauthorization

precertification

primary health insurance

prior approval

prior authorization

professional billing

prospective review

Quarterly Provider Update (QPU)

requisition form

resource allocation

resource allocation monitoring

retrospective review

revenue auditing

revenue code

revenue cycle management

revenue management

revenue monitoring

secondary health insurance

single-path coding

superbill

utilization management

utilization review

Introduction

This chapter provides an introduction to revenue management, which results in accurate, optimum, and timely reimbursement for health care services provided to patients.

Revenue Management

Revenue management is the process by which health care facilities and providers ensure their financial viability by increasing revenue, improving *cash flow* (accounts receivable and accounts payable, which involves the movement of money received and spent), and enhancing the patient's experience (including quality of patient care). The revenue management process that begins prior to inpatient hospital admission as a result of pre-admission testing and pre-admission authorization, includes the revenue cycle, and it is pursued after the posting of all collected reimbursement when post-discharge and post-care audits are performed to improve the management of revenue.

Revenue cycle management (Figure 3-1) is a revenue cycle process that typically begins upon appointment scheduling or physician order for an inpatient hospital admission, and it concludes when reimbursement obtained through collections has been posted.

In a physician practice, revenue management is also called **accounts receivable management**.

Accounts receivable involves payment owed to a business for services or goods provided. **Accounts payable** involves the amount a business owes creditors and suppliers, and health care organizations often adopt an **accrual accounting** method that focuses on anticipated revenue and associated expenses. Revenue earned and expenses billed are recorded even though third-party payer reimbursement has not been received and expenses have not been paid. (The *cash accounting* method records revenue and expenses as reimbursement is received and expenses are paid.)

Revenue cycle management includes the following features, typically in the following order:

- *Appointment scheduling* (for provider office encounters) or *physician ordering* (for inpatient admission or outpatient services as documented by the responsible physician)
- *Patient registration*
  - Appropriate consents for treatment and release of information are obtained and the patient is provided with the provider's *Notice of Privacy Practices*, which communicates how *protected health information (PHI)* may be used or shared (e.g., claims data submitted to third-party payer to obtain reimbursement for procedures and services provided).
  - Patient demographic, financial, and health care insurance information is collected, and patients receive clarification (e.g., financial counseling) about the payment of deductibles, coinsurance, and copayments.

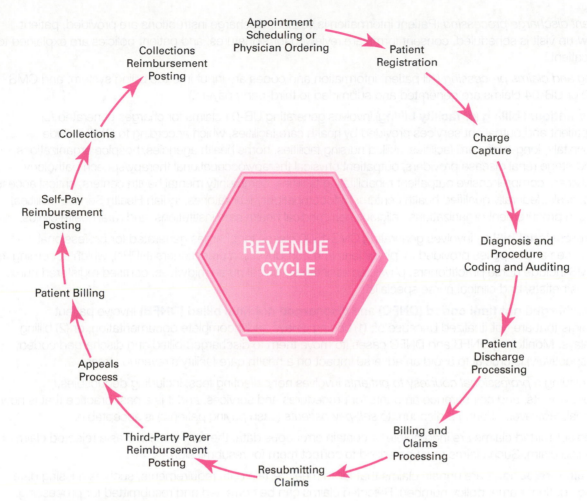

FIGURE 3-1 The revenue cycle.

o Patient's insurance coverage is validated and utilization management is performed (e.g., clinical reviews) to determine medical necessity.

o Preadmission clearance (e.g., precertification, preauthorization, screening for medical necessity) is provided.

 NOTE:

A **requisition form** is a document that is electronically or manually submitted to a health care organization, which serves as provider orders for outpatient services (e.g., laboratory test). When registering for outpatient services such as laboratory tests, patients provide the health care facility with requisition forms (e.g., physician orders) for procedures/services. Occasionally, patients forget to provide the paper-based requisition form, and providers and facilities who have implemented an electronic health record (EHR) can retrieve the electronic requisition from the EHR so that the registration process is not delayed.

● *Charge capture* (or *data capture*) (Providers use chargemasters or encounter forms to select procedures or services provided. Ancillary departments, such as the laboratory, use automated systems that link to the chargemaster.)

● *Diagnosis and procedure/service coding and auditing* (Assignment of appropriate ICD-10-CM and ICD-10-PCS or CPT/HCPCS Level II codes is performed by qualified personnel, such as medical coders, and computer-assisted coding (CAC) software-generated codes are audited for accuracy. For inpatient stays, DRGs or MS-DRGs are determined, and for outpatient encounters, APCs are determined. The assignment of DRGs, MS-DRGs, and APCs are audited to ensure accuracy, and provider documentation is reviewed to ensure accuracy of code and DRG/APC assignment. Refer to Chapter 9 of this textbook for information about DRGs, MS-DRGs, and APCs.)

- *Patient discharge processing* (Patient information is verified, discharge instructions are provided, patient follow-up visit is scheduled, consent forms are reviewed for signatures, and patient policies are explained to the patient.)

- *Billing and claims processing* (All patient information and codes are input into the billing system, and CMS-1500 or UB-04 claims are generated and submitted to third-party payers.)

  o **Institutional billing** (or **facility billing**) involves generating UB-04 claims for charges generated for inpatient and outpatient services provided by health care facilities, which according to CMS include hospitals, long-term care facilities, skilled nursing facilities, home health agencies, hospice organizations, end-stage renal disease providers, outpatient physical therapy/occupational therapy/speech pathology services, comprehensive outpatient rehabilitation facilities, community mental health centers, critical access hospitals, federally qualified health centers, histocompatibility laboratories, Indian Health Service facilities, organ procurement organizations, religious non-medical health care institutions, and rural health clinics.

  o **Professional billing** involves generating CMS-1500 claims for charges generated for professional services and supplies provided by physicians and non-physician practitioners (NPPs), which according to CMS include nurse practitioners, physician assistants, clinical nurse midwives, certified registered nurse anesthetists, and clinical nurse specialists.

  o **Discharged not final coded (DNFC)** and **discharged not final billed (DNFB)** involve patient claims that are not finalized because of: (1) coding delays and incomplete documentation, or (2) billing delays. Monitoring DNFB and DNFC cases (to move them to discharged billed and discharged coded, respectively) is crucial to avoid an adverse impact on a health care facility's revenue stream.

  o Providing a *professional courtesy to patients* involves not collecting fees, including deductibles, copayments, and coinsurance amounts for procedures and services, and it is a past practice that is now illegal. However, offering a discount to *self-pay patients* (cash paying patients) is acceptable.

- When submitted claims are incomplete or contain erroneous data, they are classified as a rejected claim or a denied claim. Such claims must be edited to correct them for resubmission.

  o **Claims rejections** are unpaid claims that fail to meet certain data requirements, such as missing data (e.g., patient name, policy number). Rejected claims can be corrected and resubmitted for processing.

  o **Claims denials** are unpaid claims that contain beneficiary identification errors (e.g., policy number does not match patient name), coding errors, diagnoses that do not support the medical necessity of procedures/services performed, duplicate claims, global days of surgery E/M coverage issues (e.g., claim for E/M service submitted when it fell within global surgery period, for which provider is not eligible for payment), national correct coding initiative (NCCI) program edits and outpatient code editor (OCE) issues (that result in denied claims), and other patient coverage issues (e.g., procedure or service required preauthorization; procedure is not included in patient's health plan contract, such as cosmetic surgery).

 NOTE:

Denied claims are reviewed, and a determination is made about whether to submit an appeal letter for reconsideration of payment. Denied claims are often categorized as technical or clinical, and that results in the need for appropriate health care facility staff involvement in the appeals process.

- *Technically denied claims* usually include errors in payer name or address or codes, and health insurance and billing staff can generate such appeals.

- *Clinically denied claims* include not meeting medical necessity for procedures/services reported, not having to obtain written preauthorization for procedures/services performed (but having obtained telephone preauthorization from the payer), and incorrect codes reported; coding and clinical staff need to be involved in generating these appeals.

- *Resubmitting claims* (Before reimbursement is received from third-party payers, late charges, lost charges, or corrections to previously processed CMS-1500 or UB-04 claims are entered, and claims are resubmitted to payers—this may result in payment delays and claims denials and rejections.)

- *Third-party payer reimbursement posting* (Payment from third-party payers is posted to appropriate accounts to reconcile charges with payments, and rejected claims are resubmitted with appropriate documentation; this process includes electronic remittance, which involves receiving reimbursement from third-party payers electronically; third-party payer contractual adjustments are made to patient accounts, such as the difference between allowed amounts and the actual charge for treatment.)

- *Appeals process* (Analysis of reimbursement received from third-party payers identifies variations in expected payments or contracted rates and may result in submission of appeal letters to payers.)

- *Patient billing* (Self-pay balances are billed to the patient; these include deductibles, copayments, and noncovered charges.)

- *Self-pay reimbursement posting* (Self-pay balances received from patients are posted to appropriate accounts.)

- *Collections* (Payments not received from patients in a timely manner result in collection letters being mailed to patients until payment is received; if payment is still not received, the account is turned over to an outside collections agency.)

- *Collections reimbursement posting* (Payments received from patients are posted to appropriate accounts.)

Integrated Revenue Management

Revenue management has traditionally been associated with just the financial management of a health care facility or a provider's medical practice. Today, an **integrated revenue cycle (IRC)** is developed by facilities and providers because clinical, coding, and information management decisions impact financial management. When case and utilization management, clinical documentation improvement, coding, and health information management are coordinated as part of the revenue management process, there is an opportunity to ensure revenue integrity and improve third-party payer reimbursement.

Example: A patient registers for an outpatient radiology procedure at her local hospital. The appropriate radiology procedure requisition from the patient's primary care provider was given to the hospital registration associate, who confirmed health plan coverage of the procedure. The patient undergoes the radiology procedure, and a review of the results leads to the hospital's radiologist performing a magnetic resonance imaging (MRI). Upon submission of the hospital claim for the radiology procedure and the MRI, the billing department receives a remittance advice that delineated payment of the radiology procedure but denial of the MRI because precertification was required. With an integrated revenue cycle, the electronic health record prompts the radiologist to obtain precertification prior to performing the MRI. This results in the patient returning to the hospital's registration office to undergo the precertification process, ensuring that the hospital is paid for the MRI.

Managing Patients

Managing New Patients

The interview and check-in procedure for a patient who is new to the provider's practice is more extensive than for a returning (or established) patient. The purpose of the new patient interview and check-in procedure is to obtain information, schedule the patient for an appointment, and generate a patient record. Basic office policies and procedures (e.g., copayments must be paid at the time of visit) should also be explained to each new patient.

(To increase office efficiency, mail new patients an information form to be completed and brought to the office 15 minutes prior to the scheduled appointment.)

Step 1   Preregister the new patient who calls to schedule an appointment. After determining that the patient has contacted the appropriate office, obtain the following information:

- Patient's name (last, first, and middle initial)
- Home address and telephone number
- Name of employer, as well as employer's address and telephone number
- Date of birth
- **Guarantor** (person responsible for paying the charges)

NOTE:

- For a minor, obtain the name, address, and signature of the parent or guardian.
- Emancipated minor laws vary by state, and they are usually married, on active duty status in the military, or living separately from their parents or legal guardians and independently managing their own financial affairs. Minors may or may not require a formal court declaration of emancipation to change their legal status, and they are legally responsible for covering the financial cost of their medical care.
- Circumstances other than emancipation status allow minors to consent to medical care without parental permission, and such exceptions to parental consent include emancipation, "mature minor" doctrine, and the provision of federally regulated public health service and state-regulated public health services.

- Social Security number
- Spouse's or partner's name, occupation, and place of employment
- Referring provider's name
- Emergency contact (e.g., relative), including address and telephone number
- Health insurance information (so the claim can be processed)
  - Name and phone number of health insurance company
  - Name of *policyholder* (which is the person in whose name the insurance policy is issued)
  - Health insurance identification number, which is sometimes the policyholder's Social Security number (SSN)
  - Health insurance group number
  - Whether health care treatment must be preauthorized

NOTE:

Instruct the patient to bring their health insurance card (Figure 3-2) to the appointment because the office will need to make a copy of its front and back. The card contains the subscriber's insurance and group number, as well as payer telephone numbers and provider network information.

Be sure to explain office policies regarding appointment cancellations, billing and collections (e.g., copayments are to be paid at the time of the office visit), and health insurance claims submission. (The patient is responsible for copayments and/or deductibles, but does not pay more than the allowed negotiated charge.) Patients may ask whether the provider participates in their health insurance plan. A **participating provider (PAR)** contracts with a health insurance plan and accepts whatever the plan pays for procedures or services performed. PARs are not allowed to bill patients for the difference between the contracted rate and their normal fee.

A **nonparticipating provider (nonPAR)** (or out-of-network provider) does not contract with the insurance plan, and patients who elect to receive care from nonPARs will incur higher out-of-pocket expenses. The patient is usually expected to pay the difference between the insurance payment and the provider's fee.

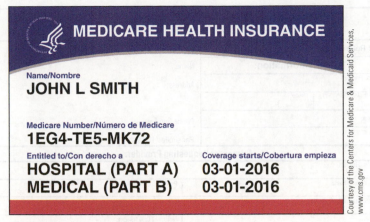

FIGURE 3-2 Sample Medicare card.

Example 1: Dr. Smith is a *participating provider (PAR)* who treats Kathe Bartron in the office. A $50 fee is charged, and $40 is the allowable charge. Dr. Smith collects an $8 copayment from the patient and is reimbursed a total of $40.

PAR provider fee	$50
PAR allowable charge	$40
Patient copayment	−$8
Insurance payment	$32
PAR provider write-off amount	$10

Example 2: Dr. Jones is a *nonparticipating provider (nonPAR)* who treats Lee Noffsker in the office and charges a $50 fee. Dr. Jones treats Lee Noffsker in the office and charges a $50 fee. Dr. Jones collects a $7.60 copayment from the patient and is reimbursed a total of $38 (because Dr. Jones does not participate in the health insurance plan and can collect the difference between Dr. Jones's fee and the patient's coinsurance plus the insurance payment).

nonPAR provider fee	$50
nonPAR allowable charge	$38
Patient copayment	−$7.60
Insurance payment	$30.40
nonPAR provider write-off amount	$12

 Managed Care Alert!

Prior to scheduling an appointment with a specialist, a managed care patient must obtain a referral from the primary care provider (Figure 3-3) or case manager (i.e., preauthorization number is required). In addition, depending on the managed care plan, certain procedures and services must be preauthorized before the patient undergoes treatment.

Step 2   Upon arrival for the office appointment, have the patient complete a patient registration form (Figure 3-4).

The patient registration form is used to create the patient's financial and medical records. Be sure to carefully review the completed form for identification, financial, health insurance, and medical history information. Sometimes patients do not know how to answer a question or they feel that the requested information does

Consultation Referral Form

Date of Referral:

Patient Information:

Name (Last, First, MI)

Date of Birth (MM/DD/YYYY)   Phone:
                              (   )

Member #:

Site #:

Payer Information:

Name:

Address:

Phone Number: (   )

Facsimile / Data #: (   )

Primary or Requesting Provider:

Name: (Last, First, MI)   Specialty:

Institution / Group Name: Provider ID or NPI #:   Provider ID or NPI #:

Address: (Street #, City, State, Zip)

Phone Number: Facsimile / Data Number:
          (   )   (   )

Consultant / Facility / Provider:

Name: (Last, First, MI)   Specialty:

Institution / Group Name: Provider ID or NPI #:   Provider ID #:

Address: (Street #, City, State, Zip)

Phone Number: Facsimile / Data Number:
          (   )   (   )

Referral Information:

Reason for Referral:

Brief History, Diagnosis and Test Results: _____

_____

Services Desired: Provide Care as indicated: **Place of Service:**

☐ Initial Consultation Only   ☐ Office
☐ Diagnostic Test: (specify) _____   ☐ Outpatient Medical/Surgical Center*
☐ Consultation with Specific Procedures: (specify) _____   ☐ Radiology   ☐ Laboratory
                                                 ☐ Inpatient Hospital*
_____   ☐ Extended Care Facility*
☐ Specific Treatment: _____   ☐ Other: (explain)
☐ Global OB Care & Delivery   *(Specific Facility Must Be Named)
☐ Other: (explain) _____

Number of visits: Authorization #: (If Required)   Referral Is Valid Until: (Date)
(If blank, 1 visit   (See Payer Instructions)
is assumed)

Signature: (Individual Completing This Form)   Authorizing Signature (If Required)

Referral certification is not a guarantee of payment. Payment of benefits is subject to a member's eligibility on the date that the service is rendered and to any other contractual provisions of the plan.

See Health Care Plan Manual For Specific Instructions.

FIGURE 3-3 Sample consultation referral form.

not apply to their situation. If information is missing, be sure to interview the patient appropriately to complete the form.

NOTE:

It is fraudulent for patients to withhold information about secondary health insurance coverage, and penalties may apply.

Step 3   Photocopy the front and back of the patient's insurance identification card(s), and file the copy in the patient's financial record.

Step 4   Confirm the patient's insurance information and eligibility status by contacting the payer via telephone, Internet, or fax. (Payer contact information can be found on the insurance card.) Collect copayment from the patient.

PHYSICIANS GROUP • MAIN STREET • ANYWHERE, NY 12345   PATIENT REGISTRATION FORM

PATIENT INFORMATION

Last Name	First Name	Middle Name
Street	City	State/Zip Code
Patient's Date of Birth	Social Security Number	Home Phone Number

Student Status ☐ Full-time ☐ Part-time	Employment Status ☐ Full-time ☐ Part-time ☐ Unemployed	Marital Status ☐ Single ☐ Married ☐ Separated ☐ Divorced ☐ Widowed
Sex ☐ Male ☐ Female	Name/Address of Employer	Occupation
Employer Phone Number	Referred by	
Emergency Contact	Address	Telephone Number

Visit is related to on-the-job injury ☐ No ☐ Yes Date: _____
Prior treatment received for injury ☐ No ☐ Yes Physician: _____ WC Number: _____

Visit is related to automobile accident ☐ No ☐ Yes Date: _____   Name & Address of Insurance Company/Policy Number

GUARANTOR'S BILLING INFORMATION

Last Name	First Name	Middle Name
Street	City	State/Zip Code
Relationship to Patient	Social Security Number	Home Phone Number
Employer	Employer Address	Employer Phone Number

INSURANCE INFORMATION

PRIMARY INSURED INFORMATION		SECONDARY INSURED INFORMATION	
Last Name	First Name/Middle Initial	Last Name	First Name/Middle Initial
Address	City/State/Zip Code	Address	City/State/Zip Code
Relationship to Insured ☐ Self ☐ Spouse ☐ Child ☐ Other		Relationship to Insured ☐ Self ☐ Spouse ☐ Child ☐ Other	
Sex ☐ Male ☐ Female		Sex ☐ Male ☐ Female	
Insured's Date of Birth	Home Phone Number	Insured's Date of Birth	Home Phone Number
Name and Address of Insurance Company		Name and Address of Insurance Company	
Insured Identification Number Group Number Effective Date		Insured Identification Number Group Number Effective Date	
Name of Employer Sponsoring Plan		Name of Employer Sponsoring Plan	

CONSENT TO PAYMENT

I have listed all health insurance plans from which I may receive benefits. I hereby authorize payment of medical benefits billed to my insurance to the Physicians Group. I hereby accept responsibility for payment for any service(s) provided to me that is not covered by my insurance. I also accept responsibility for fees that exceed the payment made by my insurance, if the Physicians Group does not participate with my insurance. I agree to pay all copayments, coinsurance, and deductibles at the time services are rendered. I, (Patient's Name), hereby authorize the Physicians Group to use and/or disclose my health information which specifically identifies me or which can reasonably be used to identify me to carry out my treatment, payment, and health care operations.

I understand that while this consent is voluntary, if I refuse to sign this consent, the Physicians Group can refuse to treat me.

I have been informed that the Physicians Group has prepared a notice ("Notice") that more fully describes the uses and disclosures that can be made of my individually identifiable health information for treatment, payment and health care operations. I understand that I have the right to review such Notice prior to signing this consent. I understand that I may revoke this consent at any time by notifying the Physicians Group, in writing, but if I revoke my consent, such revocation will not affect any actions that the Physicians Group took before receiving my revocation.

I understand that the Physicians Group has reserved the right to change privacy practices and that I can obtain such changed notice upon request. I understand that I have the right to request that the Physicians Group restrict how my individually identifiable health information is used and/or disclosed to carry out treatment, payment or health operations. I understand that the Physicians Group does not have to agree to such restrictions, but that once such restrictions are agreed to, the Physicians Group must adhere to such restrictions.

Signature of Patient or Patient's Representative _____   Date _____

Printed Name of Patient: _____   Relationship of representative to patient: _____

FIGURE 3-4 Sample patient registration form.

NOTE:

Per HIPAA privacy standards, when contacting the payer to verify insurance eligibility and benefit status, be prepared to provide the following information:

- Beneficiary's last name and first initial
- Beneficiary's date of birth
- Beneficiary's health insurance claim number (HICN)
- Beneficiary's sex

Step 5   Enter all information using computer data entry software. Verify information with the patient or subscriber, and make appropriate changes.

When the patient has more than one policy, perform a *coordination of benefits (COB)* to be sure the patient has correctly determined which policy is primary, secondary, and so on. The determination of primary or secondary status for patients with two or more commercial policies is different for adults than for children.

- *Adult patient named as policyholder:* The patient is the policyholder.
- *Adult patient named as dependent on policy:* The patient is a dependent on the insurance policy.

> **Example:** Laquisha Jones works for Anywhere College and is enrolled in the group health insurance's family plan. Laquisha is named as the primary policyholder on this plan. Laquisha's wife, Jill, is a full-time college student and is named as a dependent on Laquisha's health insurance plan. (Jill does not have other health insurance coverage.)

- *Primary versus secondary insurance:* **Primary health insurance** is the insurance plan responsible for paying health care insurance claims first. **Secondary health insurance** is the insurance plan that is billed after the primary health insurance plan has paid its contracted amount (e.g., 80 percent of billed charges) and the provider's office has received a remittance advice from the primary payer. (Depending on office policy, providers may be required to submit secondary claims to Medicare.)

 NOTE:

Certain insurance plans are always considered primary to other plans (e.g., workers' compensation insurance is primary to an employee's group health care plan if the employee is injured on the job). These situations are discussed in Chapters 12 to 17.

Determination of primary and secondary coverage for one or more government-sponsored programs is discussed in detail in the respective Medicare, Medicaid, and TRICARE chapters.

- Provider offices should share with patients their policy about submitting claims to a secondary payer, which is often courtesy service because providers are often not required to submit claims to secondary payers. Larger provider group practices might employ insurance specialists who process secondary payer claims, but smaller group practices often require patients to submit secondary claims because projected reimbursement may not justify employing dedicated staff for such processing (even though such processing results in faster reimbursement by secondary payers).

- When the patient is responsible for submitting claims to secondary payers, they are responsible for submitting an explanation of benefits (EOB) received from the primary payer. The EOB communicates to the secondary payer the reimbursement amount the provider received from the primary payer; then, the secondary payer calculates any additional reimbursement to be paid to the provider (or to the patient).

- Both primary and secondary health insurance plans provide reimbursement for qualified procedures or services only, which are those that meet medical necessity. If the patient's primary payer denies coverage due to a determination that medical necessity provisions were not met for procedures and services provided, then the secondary payer is likely to do the same. When patients are covered by group health insurance plans (e.g., employer health plans), reimbursement cannot exceed the total cost of procedures and services rendered.

Example: Cindy Thomas has two health insurance policies: a group health insurance plan through her full-time employer and another group health insurance plan through her spouse's employer. Cindy's health plan through her own employer is primary, and the health plan through her spouse's employer is secondary. When Cindy receives health care services at the physician's office, the office first submits the insurance claim to Cindy's employer's health plan; once that health plan has paid, the insurance claim can be submitted to Cindy's secondary health insurance (her spouse's group health insurance plan).

 NOTE:

Total reimbursement cannot exceed the total charges for health care services rendered by Cindy's physician.

- *Child of divorced parents:* The custodial parent's health plan is primary. If the parents are remarried, the custodial parent's health plan is primary, the custodial step-parent's plan is secondary, and the noncustodial parent's health plan is tertiary (third). An exception is made if a court order specifies that a particular parent must cover the child's medical expenses.

- *Child living with both parents:* If each parent subscribes to a different health plan, the primary and secondary policies are determined by applying the birthday rule. Physician office staff must obtain the birth date of each policyholder because the **birthday rule** states that the policyholder whose birth month and day occurs earlier in the calendar year holds the primary policy for dependent children. The year of birth is not considered when applying the birthday rule determination. If the policyholders have identical birthdays, the policy in effect the longest is considered primary.

Example 1: A child is listed as a dependent on the group policy of each parent. Which policy is primary?

Parent1—birthdate 03/06/89—works for IBM

Parent2—birthdate 03/20/87—works for General Motors

Answer: Parent1's policy is primary because Parent1's birthday is earlier in the calendar year.

Example 2: A child is listed as a dependent on Parent1's group health plan and Parent2's group health plan. Parent1 was born on 01/01/86, and Parent2 was born on 03/04/85. Which policy is considered primary?

Answer: Parent1's policy is primary because Parent1's birthday is earlier in the calendar year.

Example 3: A dependent child is covered by both parents' group policies. The parents were born on the same month, day, and year. Which policy is primary?

Parent1's policy took effect 03/06/86.

Parent2's policy took effect 09/06/92.

Answer: Parent1's policy is primary because it has been in effect six years longer.

 NOTE:

In 2021, U.S. Representative Sharice Davids, D-Kansas, introduced the Empowering Parents' Healthcare Choices Act, which is a bill that would eliminate the birthday rule and must be passed by the House and Senate before being signed by the President and implemented.

- *Gender rule:* Some self-funded health plans use the *gender rule*, which states that the father's health plan is always primary when a child is covered by both parents. This provision can cause problems if one parent's coverage uses the *birthday rule* and the other uses the *gender rule*. Be sure to contact the health plan administrators to determine which rule to follow.

Step 6   Create a new patient's medical record.

NOTE:

At this point, clinical assessment and/or treatment of the patient is performed, after which the provider documents all current and pertinent diagnoses, services rendered, and special follow-up instructions on the encounter form. The medical record and encounter form are then returned to the employee responsible for checking out patients.

Managing Established Patients

Step 1   Depending on the provider's plan of treatment, either schedule a return appointment when checking out the patient or when the patient contacts the office.

Example: The highlighted phrase in this example indicates that a follow-up visit is scheduled only if the patient contacts the office.

S: Patient describes stomach pain and vomiting.

O: Abdominal exam reveals mild tenderness. The throat is red.

A: Flu.

P: Bed rest. Return to office if symptoms worsen.

(SOAP notes are typically used in a provider's office to document patient visits. S = subjective, O = objective, A = assessment, and P = plan. SOAP notes are discussed in Chapter 10.)

Managed Care Alert!

Approximately one week prior to an appointment with a specialist for nonemergency services, the status of preauthorization for care must be verified. If the preauthorization has expired, the patient's nonemergency appointment may have to be postponed until the required treatment reports have been filed with the primary care provider or case manager and a new preauthorization for additional treatment has been obtained.

Step 2   Verify the patient's registration information when the patient registers at the front desk.

As the cost of health care increases and competition for subscribers escalates among insurers, many employers who pay a portion of health care costs for their employees purchase health insurance contracts that cover only a three- or six-month period. Therefore, it is important to ask all returning (or established) patients if there have been any changes in their name, address, phone number, employer, or health insurance plan. If the answer is yes, a new registration form should be completed and the computerized patient database should be updated.

Step 3   Collect copayment from the patient.

Step 4   Generate an encounter form for the patient's current visit.

Attach the encounter form to the front of the patient's medical record so it is available for clinical staff when the patient is escorted to the treatment area.

NOTE:

Once clinical assessment and/or treatment has been completed, the patient enters the postclinical phase of the visit. Services and diagnosis(es) are selected on the encounter form, and the patient's medical record and encounter form are given to the employee responsible for checking out patients.

Encounter Form and Chargemaster

Along with patient registration, the *encounter form* and *chargemaster* (or *charge description master*, or *CDM*) serve as the starting point for medical coding and patient billing of outpatient and physician office health care services and procedures. Each health care setting (e.g., physician office, hospital outpatient department) creates an encounter form or chargemaster unique to its organization. The ongoing maintenance of each is necessary to ensure the accurate reporting of medical codes for reimbursement purposes. Because medical codes are routinely updated, the organization's encounter form or chargemaster committee reviews them to ensure that appropriate codes are associated with services and procedures provided. This helps eliminate the possibility of reporting erroneous or outdated medical codes, reducing the incidence of claims denials.

> **Example:** The hospital's chargemaster committee contains members from information technology and all of the facility's ancillary departments (e.g., radiology, pathology, and laboratory). A patient is registered for hospital outpatient radiology treatment, and the radiologist cannot locate an appropriate CPT code (or description) for the new service on the electronic chargemaster. The radiologist contacts the chargemaster committee chairperson, who has the hospital switchboard operator announce a chargemaster stat meeting in the radiology department.
>
> Available members of the committee gather to talk with the radiologist about the new service, the medical coding representative selects an appropriate CPT code, and the electronic chargemaster is updated in real time to reflect the change. Hence, the radiologist will be able to select an appropriate code for the next patient who presents for the same new service. Although these stat meetings may appear to be inconvenient, they are necessary to the financial viability of the organization. If the radiologist had selected an unlisted CPT code (instead of the specific CPT code added by the chargemaster committee), the third-party payer would have initially denied the claim pending submission of copies of patient records for review.

 NOTE:

- *Professional coding* captures the complexity and intensity of procedures performed and services provided during an outpatient or physician office encounter. *Institutional (or facility) coding* captures the *intensity of services* used to provide patient care (e.g., intensive care unit) and *severity of illness* to classify how sick patients are (e.g., respiratory failure).
- An increase in multi-hospital systems that provide physician office services (along with traditional inpatient, outpatient, and emergency department hospital care) has resulted in the introduction of a concept called **single-path coding**, which combines professional and institutional coding to improve productivity and ensure the submission of clean claims, leading to improved reimbursement. Instead of separate professional and institutional coders (who are typically employed at different health care settings), a single-path coder will manage both professional and institutional coding for the same patient using computer-assisted coding (CAC) software and accessing all documents required for inpatient institutional (ICD-10-CM and ICD-10-PCS) and outpatient professional fee (ICD-10-CM, CPT, and HCPCS Level II) coding.
- Early in her career, as a health information manger in Florida, your author provided her hospital's medical staff with copies of discharged inpatient record face sheets that contained ICD codes. Each inpatient discharge generated a UB-04 on which ICD-10-CM diagnosis codes were reported by the hospital, and physicians who provided inpatient care generated a CMS-1500 that contained those same ICD-10-CM codes. The health information management committee approved this process that improved diagnosis coding accuracy on physicians' CMS-1500 claims, while also ensuring that the reported ICD-10-CM codes mapped to those reported on the institution's UB-04 claim.

Encounter Form

The **encounter form** (Figure 3-5) is the financial record source document used by health care providers and other personnel to record treated diagnoses and services rendered to the patient during the current encounter. In the physician's office, it is also called a **superbill**; in the hospital it is called a *chargemaster*.

The minimum information entered on an encounter form is the date of service and patient's name. The encounter form is attached to the front of the patient record so that it is available for clinical staff when the patient is escorted to the treatment area. When using medical practice management computer software to schedule patient appointments, generate encounter forms for all patients on a given day by selecting the "print encounter forms" function.

ENCOUNTER FORM

Tel: (101) 555-1111   Kim Donaldson, M.D.   EIN: 11-9876543
Fax: (101) 555-2222   INTERNAL MEDICINE   NPI: 1234567890
                             101 Main Street, Suite A
                             Alfred, NY 14802

OFFICE VISITS	NEW	EST	OFFICE PROCEDURES		INJECTIONS	
☐ Level I		99211	☐ EKG with interpretation	93000	☐ Influenza virus vaccine	
☐ Level II	99202	99212	☐ Spirometry	94010	☐ Admin of Influenza vaccine	G0008
☐ Level III	99203	99213	**LABORATORY TESTS**		☐ Pneumococcal vaccine	90732
☐ Level IV	99204	99214	☐ Blood, occult (feces)	82270	☐ Admin of pneumococcal vaccine	G0009
☐ Level V	99205	99215	☐ Skin test, Tb, intradermal (PPD)	86580	☐ Hepatitis B vaccine	90746
					☐ Admin of Hepatitis B vaccine	G0010
					☐ Tetanus and diptheria toxoids vaccine	90714
					☐ Immunization administration	90471

DIAGNOSIS

☐ Abnormal heart sounds	R00.__	☐ Chronic ischemic heart disease	I25.9	☐ Hypertension	I10
☐ Abdominal pain	R10.__	☐ Chronic obstructive lung disease	J44.9	☐ Hormone replacement	Z79.890
☐ Abnormal feces	R19.5	☐ Congestive heart failure	I50.9	☐ Hyperlipidemia	E78.5
☐ Allergic rhinitis	J30.9	☐ Cough	R05.9	☐ Hyperthyroidism	E05.9__
☐ Anemia, pernicious	D51.0	☐ Depression	F32.A	☐ Influenza	J11.1
☐ Anxiety	F41.9	☐ Diabetes mellitus, type 2	E11.____	☐ Loss of weight	R63.4
☐ Asthma	J45.909	☐ Diarrhea	R19.7	☐ Nausea	R11.0
☐ Atrophy, cerebral	G31.9	☐ Dizziness	R42	☐ Nausea with vomiting	R11.2
☐ B-12 deficiency	D51.9	☐ Emphysema	J43.__	☐ Pneumonia	J18.__
☐ Back pain	M54.9	☐ Fatigue	R53.83	☐ Sore throat	J02.9
☐ Bronchitis	J40	☐ Fever	R50.9	☐ Vaccine, hepatitis B	Z23
☐ Cardiovascular disease	I25.1__	☐ Gastritis	K29.50	☐ Vaccine, influenza	Z23
☐ Cervicalgia	M54.2	☐ Heartburn	R12	☐ Vaccine, pneumococcus	Z23
☐ Chest pain	R07.9	☐ Hematuria	R31.9	☐ Vaccine, tetanus toxoid	Z23
☐	_____	☐	_____	☐	_____

PATIENT IDENTIFICATION		FINANCIAL TRANSACTION DATA	
PATIENT NAME:		INVOICE NO.	
PATIENT NUMBER:		ACCOUNT NO.	
DATE OF BIRTH:		TOTAL FOR SERVICE:	$
ENCOUNTER DATE		AMOUNT RECEIVED:	$
DATE OF SERVICE:	/ /	PAID BY:	☐ Cash
RETURN VISIT DATE			☐ Check
			☐ Credit Card
DATE OF RETURN VISIT:	/ /	CASHIER'S INITIALS:	

FIGURE 3-5 Sample encounter form (superbill).

Coding Tip

A short blank line is located after some of the codes in the encounter form (Figure 3-5) to allow entry of additional character(s) to report the specific ICD-10-CM diagnosis code. Medicare administrative contractors reject claims with missing, invalid, or incomplete diagnosis codes.

Chargemaster

The **chargemaster** (or **charge description master [CDM]**) is a document that contains a computer-generated encounter form that includes a list of procedures, services, supplies, and revenue codes with charges for each. Chargemaster form data are entered in a health care facility's (e.g., hospital) patient accounting system, and charges are automatically posted to the patient's claim. The claim is then submitted to the payer to generate payment for inpatient, outpatient, ancillary, and other services (e.g., emergency department, laboratory, radiology, and so on).

The chargemaster allows the facility or provider to accurately and efficiently submit a claim to the payer for services rendered, and it usually contains the following:

- Department code: refers to the specific ancillary department where the service is performed
- Service code: internal identification of specific service rendered
- Service description: narrative description of the service, procedure, or supply
- Revenue code: UB-04 revenue code that is assigned to each procedure, service, or product
- CPT code: current codes that reflect procedures and services performed
- Charge amount: dollar amount facility charges for each procedure, service, or supply
- Relative value units (RVUs): numeric value assigned to a procedure; based on difficulty and time consumed

A **revenue code** is a four-digit code preprinted on a facility's chargemaster to indicate the location or type of service provided to an institutional patient. (Revenue codes are reported in form locator 42 of the UB-04 claim.)

Chargemaster					
Goodmedicine Hospital Anywhere US 12345 Department Code: 01-855 Department: Radiology					Printed on: 0415YYYY
Service Code	**Service Description**	**Revenue Code**	**CPT Code**	**Charge**	**RVU**
8550001	Chest x-ray, single view	0324	71045	74.50	0.70
8550002	Chest x-ray, two views	0324	71046	82.50	0.95
8550025	Computed tomography, lumbar spine; with contrast material	0350	72132	899.50	8.73
8550026	Computed tomography, lumbar spine; without contrast material followed by contrast material(s) and further sections	0350	72133	999.50	11.10

Chargemaster maintenance is the process of updating and revising key elements of the chargemaster (or charge description master [CDM]) to ensure accurate reimbursement. Because a chargemaster allows a health care facility to capture charges as procedures are performed and services are provided, inaccurate and outdated chargemasters can result in claims rejection, fines and penalties (for submitting false information on a claim), and overpayment or underpayment.

A **chargemaster team** jointly shares the responsibility of updating and revising the chargemaster to ensure its accuracy, and it consists of representatives of a variety of departments, such as coding compliance financial services (e.g., billing department), health information management, information services, other departments (e.g., laboratory, pharmacy, radiology, and so on), and physicians. Chargemaster maintenance requires expertise in billing regulations, clinical procedures, coding guidelines, and patient record documentation. While the entire chargemaster is reviewed periodically (e.g., annually to incorporate coding updates), the chargemaster team could be gathered any time a new procedure or service is offered by the facility so that appropriate data can be added to the chargemaster.

Revenue Code	Complete Description	Abbreviated Description
0270	Medical/surgical supplies	MED-SUR SUPPLIES
0450	Emergency department services	EMERG ROOM
0981	Emergency department physician fee	PRO FEE/ER

Personnel who render services to institutional patients (e.g., inpatient or outpatient hospital nursing, laboratory, radiology) enter data into the commercial software product. The data reside in the patient's computerized account; upon discharge from the institution, the data are verified by billing office personnel and transmitted electronically (Figure 3-6) as a UB-04 claim to a third-party payer. (The UB-04 claim is covered in Chapter 11 of this textbook.) When submitted directly to the payer, the claim is processed to authorize reimbursement to the facility.

UB-04 data elements in ASC X12N (837) format	Description of data elements
ST*837*123456~ BHT*0019*00*A98765*YYYY0504*0830~	Header
NM1*41*2*GOODMEDICINE HOSPITAL*****54*888229999~	Submitter name
NM1*40*2*CAPITAL BLUE CROSS*****54*16000~	Receiver name
HL*1**20*1~	Service provider hierarchical level for submitter
NM1*85*2*GOODMEDICINE HOSPITAL*****54*888229999~ REF*1J*898989~	Service provider name
HL*2*1*22*1~ SBR*P********BL~	Subscriber (patient) hierarchical level
NM1*IL*1*PUBLIC*JOHN*Q**MI*GRNESSC1234~ N3*1247 HILL STREET~ N4*ANYWHERE*US*12345~ DMG*D8*19820805*M**::RET:3::RET:2~ REF*SY*150259874~	Subscriber (patient) name
NM1*PR*2*CAPITAL BLUE CROSS*****PI*00303~	Payer name
CLM*ABH123456*5015***11:A:1~ DTP*096*TM*1200~ DTP*434*RD8*YYYY0504-YYYY0510~ DTP*435*DT*YYYY05101100~ CL1*2*1*01~ HI*BK:66411*BJ:66411~ HI*BF:66331:::::::Y*BF:66111:::::::N*BF:V270:::::::N~ HI*BR:7569:D8:YYYY0510~	Claim information
SE*91*123456~	Trailer

FIGURE 3-6 Portion of UB-04 data submitted in ASC X12N health care claim (837) in an electronic protocol format.

Example: During an inpatient admission, the attending physician documents an order in the patient's record for a blood glucose level to be performed by the laboratory. The patient's nurse processes the order by contacting the laboratory (e.g., telephone or computer message), which sends a technician to the patient's room to perform a *venipuncture* (blood draw, or withdrawing blood from the patient's arm using a syringe). The blood specimen is transported to the laboratory by the technician where the blood glucose test is completed. The technician enters the results into the electronic health record using a computer, and UB-04 data elements are populated from the patient's account. This data resides in the electronic health record until it is verified by the billing office (at patient discharge) and is then transmitted to a clearinghouse that processes the claim and submits it to the third-party payer. The clearinghouse also uses the network to send an acknowledgment to the institution upon receipt of the submitted claim.

Processing an Insurance Claim

The processing of an insurance claim is initiated when the patient contacts a health care provider's office and schedules an appointment. (Procedures for obtaining information on new and established patients are discussed next in this chapter.) The insurance claim used to report professional and technical services is known as the *CMS-1500 claim* (Figure 3-7). (Hospitals and other health care facilities generate the *UB-04 claim* for inpatient stays and outpatient encounters, which is covered in Chapter 11 of this textbook.) The provider's claim for payment is generated from information located on the patient's encounter form (or superbill), ledger/account record, and source document (e.g., patient record or chart). Information from these documents is transferred to the CMS-1500 claim. Such information includes patient and insurance policy identification, CPT and HCPCS Level II codes and charges for procedures and/or services, and ICD-10-CM codes for diagnoses treated and/or managed during the encounter. (The selection of CPT and HCPCS Level II codes for procedures, services, and diagnoses is discussed in later chapters.) The CMS-1500 claim requires responses to standard questions pertaining to whether the patient's condition is related to employment, an auto accident, or any other accident; additional insurance coverage; use of an outside laboratory; and whether the provider accepts assignment. To **accept assignment** means the provider agrees to accept what the insurance company allows or approves as payment in full for the claim. The patient is responsible for paying any copayment and/or coinsurance amounts.

NOTE:

To *accept assignment* is *sometimes* confused with **assignment of benefits**, which means the patient and/or insured authorizes the payer to reimburse the provider directly.

Health insurance plans may include an **out-of-pocket payment** provision, which usually has limits of $1,000 or $2,000. The physician's office manager must be familiar with the out-of-pocket payments provision of a patient's health insurance plan so that when the patient has reached the limit of an out-of-pocket payment for the year, appropriate patient reimbursement to the provider is determined. The patient may still be responsible for another out-of-pocket provision, such as 20 percent of the cost for services or procedures performed. (Not all health insurance plans include an out-of-pocket payments provision.)

Example: A patient's annual deductible has been met for their health insurance plan, but they are still required to pay a $20 copayment per encounter. Thus, the office staff no longer collects an annual deductible out-of-pocket payment from the patient; however, they do continue to collect a $20 copayment for each encounter (e.g., office visit).

NOTE:

The Affordable Care Act eliminated the *pre-existing conditions clause*, which determined patient eligibility for health plan coverage. Thus, coverage for treatment of pre-existing conditions (e.g., asthma, diabetes mellitus, hypertension) begins as of the health plan's effective date. (Prior to The Affordable Care Act, treatment of pre-existing conditions was not covered until one year after the health plan's effective date.)

HEALTH INSURANCE CLAIM FORM

APPROVED BY NATIONAL UNIFORM CLAIM COMMITTEE (NUCC) 02/12

PICA | PICA

CARRIER

1. MEDICARE (Medicare#) MEDICAID (Medicaid#) TRICARE (ID#/DoD#) CHAMPVA (Member ID#) GROUP HEALTH PLAN (ID#) FECA BLKLUNG (ID#) OTHER (ID#) | 1a. INSURED'S I.D. NUMBER (For Program in Item 1)

2. PATIENT'S NAME (Last Name, First Name, Middle Initial) | 3. PATIENT'S BIRTH DATE MM DD YY SEX M F | 4. INSURED'S NAME (Last Name, First Name, Middle Initial)

5. PATIENT'S ADDRESS (No., Street) | 6. PATIENT RELATIONSHIP TO INSURED Self Spouse Child Other | 7. INSURED'S ADDRESS (No., Street)

CITY | STATE | 8. RESERVED FOR NUCC USE | CITY | STATE

ZIP CODE | TELEPHONE (Include Area Code) ( ) | | ZIP CODE | TELEPHONE (Include Area Code) ( )

9. OTHER INSURED'S NAME (Last Name, First Name, Middle Initial) | 10. IS PATIENT'S CONDITION RELATED TO: | 11. INSURED'S POLICY GROUP OR FECA NUMBER

a. OTHER INSURED'S POLICY OR GROUP NUMBER | a. EMPLOYMENT? (Current or Previous) YES NO | a. INSURED'S DATE OF BIRTH MM DD YY SEX M F

b. RESERVED FOR NUCC USE | b. AUTO ACCIDENT? YES NO PLACE (State) | b. OTHER CLAIM ID (Designated by NUCC)

c. RESERVED FOR NUCC USE | c. OTHER ACCIDENT? YES NO | c. INSURANCE PLAN NAME OR PROGRAM NAME

d. INSURANCE PLAN NAME OR PROGRAM NAME | 10d. CLAIM CODES (Designated by NUCC) | d. IS THERE ANOTHER HEALTH BENEFIT PLAN? YES NO If yes, complete items 9, 9a and 9d.

READ BACK OF FORM BEFORE COMPLETING & SIGNING THIS FORM.

12. PATIENT'S OR AUTHORIZED PERSON'S SIGNATURE I authorize the release of any medical or other information necessary to process this claim. I also request payment of government benefits either to myself or to the party who accepts assignment below. SIGNED ___ DATE ___ | 13. INSURED'S OR AUTHORIZED PERSON'S SIGNATURE I authorize payment of medical benefits to the undersigned physician or supplier for services described below. SIGNED ___

PATIENT AND INSURED INFORMATION

14. DATE OF CURRENT ILLNESS, INJURY, or PREGNANCY (LMP) MM DD YY QUAL. | 15. OTHER DATE QUAL. MM DD YY | 16. DATES PATIENT UNABLE TO WORK IN CURRENT OCCUPATION MM DD YY MM DD YY FROM TO

17. NAME OF REFERRING PROVIDER OR OTHER SOURCE | 17a. 17b. NPI | 18. HOSPITALIZATION DATES RELATED TO CURRENT SERVICES MM DD YY MM DD YY FROM TO

19. ADDITIONAL CLAIM INFORMATION (Designated by NUCC) | 20. OUTSIDE LAB? YES NO $ CHARGES

21. DIAGNOSIS OR NATURE OF ILLNESS OR INJURY Relate A-L to service line below (24E) ICD Ind. A. B. C. D. E. F. G. H. I. J. K. L. | 22. RESUBMISSION CODE ORIGINAL REF. NO.

23. PRIOR AUTHORIZATION NUMBER

24. A. DATE(S) OF SERVICE From MM DD YY To MM DD YY | B. PLACE OF SERVICE | C. EMG | D. PROCEDURES, SERVICES, OR SUPPLIES (Explain Unusual Circumstances) CPT/HCPCS MODIFIER | E. DIAGNOSIS POINTER | F. $ CHARGES | G. DAYS OR UNITS | H. EPSDT Family Plan | I. ID. QUAL. | J. RENDERING PROVIDER ID. #

1 | | | | | | | | | NPI

2 | | | | | | | | | NPI

3 | | | | | | | | | NPI

4 | | | | | | | | | NPI

5 | | | | | | | | | NPI

6 | | | | | | | | | NPI

PHYSICIAN OR SUPPLIER INFORMATION

25. FEDERAL TAX I.D. NUMBER SSN EIN | 26. PATIENT'S ACCOUNT NO. | 27. ACCEPT ASSIGNMENT? (For govt. claims, see back) YES NO | 28. TOTAL CHARGE $ | 29. AMOUNT PAID $ | 30. Rsvd for NUCC Use

31. SIGNATURE OF PHYSICIAN OR SUPPLIER INCLUDING DEGREES OR CREDENTIALS (I certify that the statements on the reverse apply to this bill and are made a part thereof.) SIGNED ___ DATE ___ | 32. SERVICE FACILITY LOCATION INFORMATION a. NPI b. | 33. BILLING PROVIDER INFO & PH # ( ) a. NPI b.

NUCC Instruction Manual available at: www.nucc.org | **PLEASE PRINT OR TYPE**

Courtesy of the Centers for Medicare & Medicaid Services, www.cms.gov

FIGURE 3-7 Blank CMS-1500 claim (for instructional use only).

Management of Accounts Receivable

Accounts receivable management assists providers in the overall collection of appropriate reimbursement for services rendered, and includes the following functions:

- Insurance eligibility verification (confirming the patient's health insurance plan and eligibility information with the third-party payer to determine the patient's financial responsibility for services rendered)

INSURANCE ELIGIBILITY VERIFICATION FORM

Patient's Last Name, First Name, Middle Initial   Patient's DOB   Patient's Mailing Address

Insurance Specialist or Office Manager's Name   Date of Call   Physician's Name

Health Insurance Plan Name   Group No.   Health Insurance Policy Number

Health Insurance Plan Effective Date   PlanID   Health Insurance Plan Termination Date

Plan Type (circle one):   PPO   HMO   Regular   Group   MC   Capitated   WC

$ _____ $ _____ $ _____
Deductible Amount   Amount Not Satisfied   Copayment Amount

Percentage of Reimbursement: _____ %   ☐ Yes ☐ No
                                    Coinsurance   Pre-existing Clause

List plan exclusions: _____

Name of plan representative: _____

NOTE:

During the insurance verification and eligibility process, patient payments are determined. During the check-out process, all copayments, coinsurance, and deductibles are collected.

- Patient and family counseling about insurance and payment issues (assessing patient financial requirements; advising patients and families about insurance benefits, copayments, and other financial obligations; resolving patient billing questions and complaints; adjusting accounts as necessary; and establishing financial arrangements for patients as necessary)
- Patient and family assistance with obtaining community resources (assisting patients in researching financial resources, housing, transportation, and medications and pharmaceutical supplies)
- Preauthorization of services (contacting third-party payers to obtain approval before services are provided, ensuring appropriate reimbursement)
- Capturing charges and posting payments (entering charges for services and procedures in the billing system, entering adjustments to patient accounts for payments received, generating balance receipts, reconciling daily work batches, preparing an audit trail, and preparing bank deposits)
- Billing and claims submission (completing, submitting, and processing CMS-1500 claims for payment; and researching and resolving claims payment delay issues)
- Account follow-up and payment resolution (reviewing explanation of benefits and remittance advice documents, contacting payers to resolve claims denials, resubmitting CMS-1500 claims, responding to payer and patient correspondence, following up on assigned accounts, and using collection techniques to maintain current accounts, including monitoring for delinquent payments)

Example: The patient's health insurance plan has a $200 deductible, and just $100.00 has been met so far this year. The insurance specialist will inform the patient that the remaining deductible amount must be met (in addition to any copayments, coinsurance, and other out-of-pocket payments).

The patient's health insurance information is verified by the insurance specialist (or office manager) by calling the health insurance company and completing an insurance verification form.

Preauthorization

Preauthorization is a prior review of health care services (e.g., durable medical equipment, prescription drugs, surgical procedures, or treatment plans) related to an episode of care by a health plan to determine medical necessity. The health plan requires preauthorization prior to a patient receiving certain services, except in an emergency. (Preauthorization is also called precertification, prior approval, or prior authorization.) In addition, health plans may also require *referral approvals* prior to a patient receiving health care services from a specialist. The failure to obtain preauthorization or referral approval from health plans prior to providing certain services usually results in denial of payment for reported services; this means the provider will not receive reimbursement for services provided to patients.

To obtain preauthorization, the provider (or staff) contacts the patient's health plan to determine whether preauthorization for a health care service is needed. The process of obtaining preauthorization varies among health plans and typically involves the completion and faxing of the plan's preauthorization form. Some health plans (e.g., UnitedHealthcare®) have implemented an electronic preauthorization and referral process, which streamlines the process and reduces provider administrative costs. (HIPAA mandated the method for submitting health care services preauthorization review requests, and the transaction method is abbreviated as ASC X12N 278. It is part of the *electronic submission of Medical Documentation* [*esMD*] prior authorization program, which was implemented as a result of the *2011 Investing in Innovations Initiative*, discussed in Chapter 2 of this textbook.)

After review of submitted preauthorization and referral approval documentation or transactions, the health plan approves or rejects the submission. The health plan may also request additional information. When a preauthorization or referral approval request is rejected, the provider may submit an appeal.

Example 1: A health plan precertifies inpatient medical admissions and certain procedures, assists with discharge planning, and provides inpatient and outpatient medical case management. The patient is required to call the health plan prior to a scheduled (nonemergency) inpatient hospital or skilled nursing facility admission, prior to a maternity inpatient hospital admission, and within 48 hours after a hospital emergency department encounter or urgent inpatient hospital admission. If the medical services are not precertified, the patient is responsible for the entire cost of care determined not to be medically necessary. A monetary penalty is assigned if medical services are determined to be medically necessary but not precertified.

Because the health care benefits management program is included in the patient's health plan contract, it is the patient's responsibility to obtain preauthorization (precertification) of medical services. Otherwise, the responsible provider would initiate preauthorization of medical services (via fax or electronic transmission, if permitted).

Example 2: Medicare mandates physician certification of inpatient services of hospitals (other than inpatient psychiatric facilities), which requires: (1) authentication of the practitioner order (physician certifies that inpatient services were ordered in accordance with Medicare regulations, are reasonable and necessary, and are appropriately provided in accordance with the 2-midnight benchmark regulation; (2) reason for inpatient services (e.g., hospitalization for inpatient medical treatment); (3) estimated time the patient requires inpatient hospitalization; and (4) plans for posthospital care, if appropriate. Certification begins with the order for inpatient admission and must be completed, signed, dated, and documented in the patient record prior to discharge (except for outlier cases, which is discussed in Chapter 9 of this textbook).

Completing the CMS-1500 Claim

The health insurance specialist completes the claim (e.g., identify the type of insurance, patient's sex, patient's relationship to insured, provider's federal tax identification number, and so on). The CMS-1500 claim includes several areas that require the signature of the patient and the provider. When submitting claims, "SIGNATURE ON FILE" can be substituted for the patient's signature (as long as the patient's signature is actually on file in the office). The completed claim is proofread and double-checked for accuracy (e.g., verification that a signature statement is on file, and so on). Any supporting documentation that has to be attached to the claim is copied from the patient's chart (e.g., operative report) or developed (e.g., letter delineating unlisted service provided, referred to in the CPT coding manual as a "special report").

The Privacy Act of 1974 prohibits payers from notifying providers about payment or rejection information on claims for which the provider did not accept assignment. Therefore, *providers who do not accept assignment of Medicare benefits do not receive a copy of the Medicare Summary Notice (MSN) information (called a provider remittance notice, or PRN)* that is sent to the Medicare beneficiary (patient). Information released to providers is limited to whether the claim was received, processed, and approved or denied. To assist in an appeal of a denied claim, the patient must furnish the nonparticipating provider with a copy of the MSN. In addition, a letter signed by the patient must accompany the request for review. If the beneficiary writes the appeal, the provider must supply supporting documentation (e.g., copy of patient record).

Posting Charges to Patient Accounts

The following steps are the same for new and established patients:

Step 1   Assign CPT and HCPCS Level II (national) codes to procedures and services, and assign ICD-10-CM codes to diagnoses documented on the encounter form. (Coding is discussed in Chapters 6 through 8.)

Step 2   Use the completed encounter form or chargemaster to determine the charges for procedures performed and/or services provided, and total all charges.

Coding Tip

Make sure that diagnoses, procedures, and services selected on the encounter form are documented in the patient's medical record before reporting codes on the insurance claim.

Step 3   Post all charges to the patient account record (or patient ledger) and the daily accounts receivable journal, either manually (e.g., day sheet) or electronically by using practice management software (for provider office encounters). (Charges for hospital-based encounters are managed by the patient billing department.)

NOTE:

Practice management software makes use of the patient ledger and manual daily accounts receivable journal (or day sheet) obsolete. However, discussion about these items, with figures, is included to familiarize students with them in the event that they are required to use them on the job.

The **patient ledger** (Figure 3-8), known as the **patient account record** (Figure 3-9) in a computerized system, is a permanent record of all financial transactions between the patient and the practice. The charges, along with personal or third-party payments, are posted on the patient's account.

Each procedure performed must be individually described and priced on the patient's ledger/account record.

The **manual daily accounts receivable journal**, also known as the **day sheet**, is a chronologic summary used to manually track all transactions posted to individual patient ledgers/accounts on a specific day (Figure 3-10).

Medical Practice Management Software

Schedule Appointment	Patient Registration	Payer Information	Patient Ledger	Claims

Patient Name: John Q. Public

Date	Transaction	Type	CPT Code	Charges	Credits	Balance
04/05/YYYY	22042017	Invoice	99214	260.00		260.00
04/05/YYYY	22052017	Copayment	99214		20.00	240.00
05/23/YYYY	22172017	Payment	99214		240.00	0.00
06/25/YYYY	22452017	Invoice	99213	190.00		190.00
06/25/YYYY	22462017	Copayment	99213		20.00	170.00
08/01/YYYY	22672017	Payment	99213		170.00	0.00

FIGURE 3-8 Sample medical practice management software patient ledger screen.

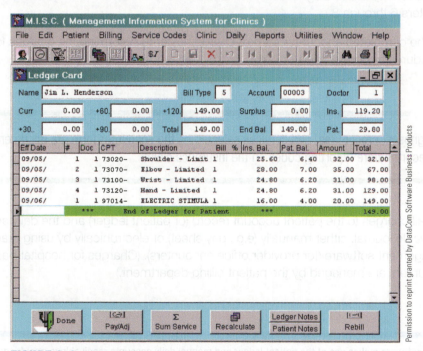

FIGURE 3-9 Sample patient account record generated from computerized practice management software.

Permission to reprint granted by DataCom Software Business Products

Medical Practice Management Software					
Day Sheet					
Date: 06/25/YYYY	**Location:** 5 Main St, Anywhere US 12345			**NPI:** 123456789A	
Account Number	**Patient Name**	**Charge**	**Adjustment**	**Credit**	**Net Change**
987654321	Patient, Ima	190.00	20.00	170.00	0.00
876543219	Public, John Q.	240.00	48.00	192.00	0.00
765432198	Smith, Mary	140.00	5.00	135.00	0.00
654321987	Taylor, Timothy	90.00	0.00	0.00	90.00
543219876	Ulrich, Stephen	360.00	72.00	148.00	140.00
	Totals:	**1,020.00**	**145.00**	**654.00**	**230.00**

FIGURE 3-10 Sample medical practice management software day sheet.

Monitoring and Auditing for Revenue Management

As part of revenue management, monitoring and auditing procedures are performed to ensure compliance with regulations and financial viability of the medical practice or health care facility. The following assist in monitoring and auditing processes:

- Quarterly provider updates (QPUs) are published to clarify CMS regulations, policies, and instructions.
- Utilization management controls health care costs and quality of care.
- Revenue monitoring ensures financial viability.
- Revenue audits identify areas of poor performance so they can be corrected.
- Data analytics are used for resource allocation monitoring and performance measurement.

Quarterly Provider Updates

CMS publishes **Quarterly Provider Updates (QPUs)** to simplify the process of understanding proposed or implemented changes to its programs (e.g., Medicare, Medicaid, CHIP). The following are published in QPUs:

- Regulations and major policies implemented or cancelled, such as revisions to the Medicare *National Coverage Determinations (NCDs)*
- New and revised manual instructions, such as revisions to the *Medicare Claims Processing Manual*
- Regulations that establish or modify the way CMS administers its programs, such as revisions to Medicare's fee-for-service payment regulations

CMS generally limits the number of days it publishes regulations and notices in the *Federal Register* to the fourth Friday of each month. This adds an element of predictability to its communications and reduces the time it takes to research changes (and implement changes in the health care setting). Because statutory requirements mandate some of CMS's regulatory work (e.g., annual revision to ICD-10-CM and ICD-10-PCS coding systems), such notices may be published in the *Federal Register* on a day other than the fourth Friday of the month. For example, the new October 1, 2015 compliance date for implementing ICD-10-CM and ICD-10-PCS was published in the Thursday, August 4, 2014, edition of the *Federal Register*, to extend the implementation date by one year.

To subscribe to receive CMS.gov updates via email, go to www.cms.gov, scroll down to the bottom right corner of the page, enter your email address in the *Receive Email Updates* box, and click *Submit*. You will be taken to a website where you can finish registering and select the types of updates you wish to receive.

Utilization Management and Case Management

Utilization management (or **utilization review**) is a method of controlling health care costs and quality of care by reviewing the appropriateness and medical necessity of care provided to patients prior to the administration of care (**prospective review**) or after care has been provided (**retrospective review**). **Case management** involves the development of patient care plans for the coordination and provision of care for complicated cases in a cost-effective manner. *Utilization managers,* who are often registered nurses and physician advisors, perform utilization management activities. These activities include the following:

- **Preadmission certification (PAC)** or **preadmission review**: a review for medical necessity of inpatient care prior to the patient's admission.

- **Preauthorization**: a review by health plans to grant prior approval for reimbursement of health care services (e.g., durable medical equipment, prescription medications, surgical procedures, treatment plans). (Preauthorization is also known as **precertification**, **prior approval**, or **prior authorization**.)

- **Concurrent review**: a continued-stay review for continued appropriateness of care and medical necessity of tests and procedures ordered during an inpatient hospitalization.

- **Discharge planning**: involves arranging appropriate health care services for the discharged patient (e.g., home health care).

Revenue Monitoring

Revenue monitoring involves assessing the revenue cycle to ensure financial viability and stability using the following **metrics**, which are standards of measurement:

- *Cash flow*: total amount of money transferred into and out of a business; measure of liquidity, which is the amount of capital available for investment and expenditures

- *Days in accounts receivable*: number of days outstanding money is owed to the organization; measure of how long it usually takes for a service/procedure to be paid by all financially responsible parties, such as third-party payers, government health programs, and patients

Example: Last year, the medical practice's gross charges for procedures/services totaled $750,000. The current accounts receivables (A/R) are $95,000, and the credit balance (from the previous year) is $9,500. The formula for calculating Days in A/R = [Receivables − (Credit Balance)] ÷ [Gross Charges ÷ 365 days]. Thus, [$95,000 − ($9,500)] ÷ [$750,000 ÷ 365] = $85,500 ÷ $2,055 = 42 days. According to national standards, A/R should average 35 days or less. Therefore, this medical practice needs to audit its revenue management processes to identify and improve areas of poor performance so that the number of days in A/R decreases.

- *Percentage of accounts receivable older than 30, 60, 90, and 120 days*: measure of the organization's ability to get procedures/services paid in a timely manner. According to national standards, A/R > 120 should be less than 12 percent. An organization's A/R > 120 that is 3.5 percent is excellent.

Report of Percentage of Accounts Receivable Older Than 30, 60, 90, and 120 Days

Days	0–30	31–60	61–90	91–120	>120	TOTAL A/R
Amounts Due	$66,500	$55,000	$9,000	$7,500	$5,000	$143,000
Percentage Due	46.5%	38.5%	6.3%	5.2%	3.5%	100%

- *Net collection rate*: percentage received of allowed reimbursement; measure of the organization's effectiveness in collecting reimbursement

> **Example:** The hospital's payments received is $945,000. Refunds paid to payers and patients (for charges not supported by documentation in the patient record) total $30,000. The total charge for inpatient and outpatient services is $1,500,000. Total write-offs are $525,000. The formula for calculating the Net Collection Rate = [(Payments − Refunds) ÷ (Charges − Write-offs)] × 100. Thus, [($945,000 − $30,000) ÷ ($1,500,000 − $525,000)] × 100 = [$915,000 ÷ $975,000] × 100 = 0.938 × 100 = 93.8 percent. The calculated net collection rate of 93.8 percent is very poor, which means the hospital needs to audit its revenue management processes to identify and correct areas of poor performance such as chargemaster accuracy, submitting claims in a timely manner, obtaining preauthorization, and so on.

- *Denial rate*: percentage of claims denied by payers; measure of the organization's effectiveness in submitting *clean claims*, which are claims paid in full upon initial submission; the formula for calculating the denial rate = [total dollar amount of denied claims ÷ total dollar amount of claims submitted] × 100; denial rates should be less than 5 percent

> **Example:** The hospital's total dollar amount of denied claims is $250,000, and the total dollar amount of claims submitted is $2,500,000. The formula for calculating the Denial Rate = [total dollar amount of denied claims ÷ total dollar amount of claims submitted] × 100. Thus, [$250,000 ÷ $2,500,000] × 100 = 10 percent. The calculated denial rate of 10 percent is unacceptable, which means the hospital needs to audit its revenue management processes to identify and correct areas related to claims submission in a timely manner, following up on rejected and unpaid claims, and so on.

Revenue Auditing

Revenue auditing is an assessment process that is conducted as a follow-up to revenue monitoring so that areas of poor performance can be identified and corrected. The auditing process includes the following elements:

- *Claims scrubbing*: using software that compares completed claims with edits to identify and correct errors prior to submission ensures accurate claims (clean claims) (e.g., demographic data, incomplete medical codes)
- *Compliance monitoring*: level of compliance with established managed care contracts is monitored; provider performance per managed care contractual requirement is monitored; compliance risk is monitored
- *Denials and rejections management*: claims denials and rejections are analyzed to prevent future denials/rejections; denied or rejected claims are resubmitted with appropriate data and/or documentation
- *Tracking resubmitted claims and appeals for denied claims*: resubmitted claims and appealed claims are tracked to ensure payment by payers
- *Posting late charges and lost charges*: performed after reimbursement for late claims is received and appeals for denied claims have been exhausted

Resource Allocation and Data Analytics

Resource allocation is the distribution of financial resources among competing groups (e.g., hospital departments, state health care organizations). **Resource allocation monitoring** uses data analytics to measure whether a health care provider or organization achieves operational goals and objectives within the confines of the distribution of financial resources, such as appropriately expending budgeted amounts as well as conserving resources and protecting assets while providing quality patient care.

Data analytics (or **data analysis**) use tools and systems to analyze, examine, and study clinical and financial data, conduct research, and evaluate the effectiveness of disease treatments:

- **Data warehouses:** databases that use *reporting interfaces* to consolidate multiple databases, allowing reports to be generated from a single request; data is accumulated from a wide range of sources within an organization and is used to guide management decisions
- **Data mining:** extracting and analyzing data to identify patterns, whether predictable or unpredictable

Example 1: The quality manager at a medical center has been charged with performing a study to determine the quality of care and costs of providing procedures and services to the practice's patient population. The manager will access and study clinical and financial data that is located in reports generated by the facility's electronic health record, and pre-established criteria will be used when conducting the study. The manager submits a report request to the information technology department, which then uses a data warehouse to generate the results. The request submitted by the manager is specific as to patient demographics, conditions, procedures and services, and so on. The manager uses the generated reports to conduct data mining, which results in the identification of quality-of-care issues associated with providing patient care as well as procedures/services that are profitable and nonprofitable. The manager then prepares a report of findings for discussion with the quality management committee (consisting of facility staff and physicians). The result is an action plan to:

- Eliminate deficiencies in quality of care to its patient population (e.g., in-service education to facility staff, purchase of technologically advanced equipment)

- Increase the number of profitable procedures/services (e.g., increase human and other resources)

- Decrease or eliminate nonprofitable procedures/services (e.g., partner with another health care organization that offers such procedures/services)

Example 2: The Department of Veterans Affairs (VA) provides health care services to almost three million veterans annually, but veterans nationwide have traditionally not had equitable access to these services. Congress enacted legislation in 1996 requiring the VA to develop a plan for equitably allocating resources to ensure that veterans who have similar economic status and eligibility priority and who are eligible for medical care have similar access to such care regardless of the region of the United States in which such veterans reside. In response, the VA implemented the *Veterans Equitable Resource Allocation (VERA)* resource allocation monitoring system to improve equity of access to veterans' health care services. VERA allocated resources to regional VA health care networks, known as *Veterans Integrated Service Networks (VISN)*, which allocate resources to their hospitals and clinics. The VA continuously assesses the effectiveness of VERA by monitoring changes in health care delivery and overseeing the network allocation process used to provide veterans with equitable access to services.

Summary

Revenue management ensures health care facility and provider financial viability by increasing revenue, improving cash flow, and enhancing the patient's experience (including quality of patient care). In a physician practice, it is also called accounts receivable management.

The insurance claim used to report professional and technical services is called the CMS-1500 claim. The processing of an insurance claim begins when the new or established patient contacts the medical practice to schedule an appointment for health care. New patients should be preregistered so that identification and health insurance information can be obtained prior to the scheduled office visit. Established patients are usually rescheduled at checkout of a current appointment.

The encounter form is the financial record source document used by health care providers and other personnel to record treated diagnoses and services rendered to the patient during the current encounter. In the physician's office, it is also called a superbill; in the hospital it is called a chargemaster. The chargemaster or charge description master (CDM) is a document that contains a computer-generated list of procedures, services, and supplies with charges for each. A revenue code is a four-digit code preprinted on a facility's chargemaster to indicate the location or type of service provided to an institutional patient.

Chargemaster maintenance is the process of updating and revising key elements of the chargemaster, and a chargemaster team jointly shares the responsibility of updating and revising the chargemaster.

Revenue management monitoring assesses the revenue cycle to ensure financial viability and stability using metrics. Revenue management auditing is conducted as follow-up to revenue cycle monitoring. Resource allocation is the distribution of financial resources among competing groups, and resource allocation monitoring uses data analytics to measure whether a health care facility or provider achieves operational goals and objectives. Data analytics are used to analyze clinical and financial data, conduct research, and evaluate the effectiveness of disease treatments. Data warehouses use reporting interfaces to consolidate multiple databases. Data mining extracts and analyzes data to identify patterns.

Internet Links

Apex EDI (health insurance clearinghouse): Go to *apexedi.com*, scroll over the Medical heading, and click on the Medical Claims link to learn how a national clearinghouse processes a medical practice's electronic insurance claims.

National Association of Insurance Commissioners: Go to *naic.org*, click on the Map link, and click on your state to explore how insurance regulators protect consumer rights and ensure the financial solvency of insurers.

National Uniform Billing Committee (NUBC): Go to *nubc.org* to learn more about the implementation of the UB-04.

National Uniform Claim Committee (NUCC): Go to *nucc.org* to learn more about the implementation of the CMS-1500.

Review

3.1 – Multiple Choice

1. Which means that the payer has been authorized to reimburse the provider directly?
    a. Accept assignment
    b. Assignment of benefits
    c. Coordination of benefits
    d. Medical necessity

2. Providers who do not accept assignment of Medicare benefits do not receive information included on the _____, which is sent to the patient.
    a. electronic flat file
    b. encounter form
    c. ledger
    d. Medicare Summary Notice

3. A patient received services on April 5, totaling $1,000. The patient paid a $90 coinsurance at the time services were rendered. (The payer required the patient to pay a 20 percent coinsurance of the reasonable charge at the time services were provided.) The physician accepted assignment, and the insurance company established the reasonable charge as $450. On July 1, the provider received $360 from the insurance company. On August 1, the patient received a check from the insurance company in the amount of $450. The overpayment was _____, and the _____ must reimburse the insurance company. (Remember! Coinsurance is the percentage of costs a patient shares with the health plan.)
    a. $450, patient
    b. $450, physician
    c. $550, patient
    d. $640, physician

4. The chargemaster is a(n)
   a. computer-generated list used by facilities, which contains procedures, services, supplies, revenue codes, and charges.
   b. data entry screen used by coders to assign diagnosis and procedure codes to generate a diagnosis-related group.
   c. document used by third-party payers and government plans to generate national provider identification numbers.
   d. encounter form used by physicians and other providers to collect data about office procedures provided to inpatients.

5. Which is a group health insurance policy provision that prevents multiple payers from reimbursing benefits covered by other policies?
   a. Accept assignment
   b. Assignment of benefits
   c. Coordination of benefits
   d. Pre-existing condition

6. Which must accept whatever a payer reimburses for procedures or services performed?
   a. Nonparticipating provider
   b. Out-of-network provider
   c. Participating provider
   d. Value-added provider

7. Which is an interpretation of the birthday rule regarding two group health insurance policies when the parents of a child covered on both policies are married to each other and live in the same household?
   a. The parent whose birth month and day occurs earlier in the calendar year is the primary policyholder.
   b. The parent who was born first is the primary policyholder.
   c. Both parents are primary policyholders.
   d. The parent whose income is higher is the primary policyholder.

8. Which is the financial record source document usually generated by a hospital?
   a. Chargemaster
   b. Day sheet
   c. Encounter
   d. Superbill

9. A 50-year-old patient reports to the hospital's registration department to begin the patient registration process. The patient tells the patient registration clerk that their physician wants them to undergo a screening mammogram. The clerk asks the patient for the requisition form (physician order for screening mammogram) and is told that the patient left it at home. The registration clerk is aware that the patient's physician office has implemented use of the electronic health record, and so the patient registration process is
   a. continued after the patient returns from having obtained a new paper-based requisition form from the physician's nearby office.
   b. continued because an electronic version of the requisition form is available from the physician office in the hospital's EHR system.
   c. halted until the radiology department approves performing the screening mammogram procedure without the requisition form.
   d. halted so the switchboard operator can page the physician to ask that a telephone order for the mammogram be called in.

10. An 18-year-old patient arrives at the hospital's registration department to begin the patient registration process for scheduled wisdom teeth extraction under anesthesia. In addition to obtaining appropriate consents for treatment and release of information along with collecting patient demographic and insurance information, the patient registration clerk
    a. authorizes preadmission clearance for the patient.
    b. conducts utilization management for medical necessity.
    c. posts charges associated with the surgical procedure.
    d. validates the patient's health insurance coverage.

11. A patient is properly registered for scheduled blood work and arrives at the hospital's laboratory department. The laboratory technician who performs venipuncture
    a. assigns diagnosis and laboratory procedure codes using ICD-10-CM and CPT/HCPCS Level II.
    b. captures charge data by using an automated system that links to the hospital's chargemaster.
    c. determines ambulatory payment classification (APC) revenue the hospital can expect to receive.
    d. forwards the record generated to the billing department so an encounter form can be completed.

12. During the patient discharge processing stage of revenue management
    a. all patient information and codes are verified and/or input into the billing system, and CMS-1500 or UB-04 claims are generated and submitted to third-party payers.
    b. late charges, lost charges, or corrections to previously processed CMS-1500 or UB-04 claims are entered, and claims are resubmitted to payers.
    c. patient information is verified, discharge instructions are provided, patient follow-up visit is scheduled, consent forms are reviewed for signatures, and patient policies are explained to the patient.
    d. reimbursement from third-party payers is posted to appropriate accounts, and rejected claims are resubmitted with appropriate documentation.

13. Charges for services, procedures, patient payments, and third-party payments are entered in the computerized
    a. chargemaster.
    b. day sheet.
    c. encounter form.
    d. patient account record.

14. Which is a manual-based chronological summary of all transactions posted to individual patient accounts on a specific day?
    a. Charge description master
    b. Daily accounts receivable journal
    c. Insurance claim
    d. Preauthorization form

15. Which process best describes the provider's financial viability, which includes methods such as increasing accounts receivable, improving cash flow, and enhancing the patient's experience?
    a. Accepting assignment
    b. Quality assurance
    c. Revenue management
    d. Utilization review

3.2 – Utilization Management and Case Management

Instructions: Complete each statement by entering the appropriate utilization management or case management concept.

1. Arranging appropriate health care services for discharged patients is called discharge _____.

2. Assessing the medical necessity of inpatient care prior to admission is called _____ review.

3. The continued-stay evaluation of the medical necessity of tests/procedures ordered during inpatient hospitalization is called _____ review.

4. The process that grants prior approval for reimbursement of a health care service is called _____.

5. Reviewing the appropriateness and necessity of care provided to patients after care has been provided is called _____ review.

Revenue Management: Insurance Claims, Denied Claims and Appeals, and Credit and Collections

Chapter Outline

Insurance Claim Cycle

Maintaining Insurance Claim Files

Denied Claims and the Appeals Process

Credit and Collections

Objectives

Upon successful completion of this chapter, you should be able to:

1. Define key terms related to revenue management: insurance claims, denied claims and appeals, and credit and collections.
2. Explain the stages of the insurance claim cycle.
3. Describe how insurance claim files are maintained.
4. Outline the appeals process for denied claims.
5. Explain the role of credit and collections in processing claims.

Key Terms

accounts receivable aging report

allowed charge

ANSI ASC X12N

appeal

bad debt

beneficiary

claims adjudication

claims adjustment reason codes (CARC)

claims attachment

claims management

claims processing

claims submission

clean claim

clearinghouse

closed claim

common data file

Consumer Credit Protection Act of 1968

coordination of benefits (COB)

covered entity

delinquent account

delinquent claim

delinquent claim cycle

denied claim

downcoding

electronic data interchange (EDI)

electronic flat file format

electronic funds transfer (EFT)

Electronic Funds Transfer Act

Electronic Healthcare Network Accreditation Commission (EHNAC)

electronic media claim

electronic remittance advice (ERA)

Equal Credit Opportunity Act

explanation of benefits (EOB)

Fair Credit and Charge Card Disclosure Act

Fair Credit Billing Act

Fair Credit Reporting Act

Fair Debt Collection Practices Act (FDCPA)

Financial Services Modernization Act (FSMA)

fragmentation

Gramm-Leach-Bliley Act

litigation

Medicare Remittance Advice

noncovered benefit

open claim

outsource

past-due account	remittance advice	source document	unassigned claim
peer review	remittance advice	suspense	unauthorized service
pre-existing condition	remark codes (RARC)	Truth in Lending Act	unbundling
remit	skip tracing	two-party check	value-added network
	skip tracking		(VAN)

Introduction

This chapter continues coverage of revenue management by describing the insurance claim cycle, which includes maintaining insurance claim files, processing claims denials by writing appeals, and processing credit and collections.

Insurance Claim Cycle

The cycle of a claim consists of four stages (Figure 4-1):

- Claims submission and electronic data interchange (EDI)
- Claims processing
- Claims adjudication
- Payment

Claims management as part of revenue management is performed to complete, submit, and follow-up on claims for procedures and services provided. Upon completion of the insurance claim, a review is performed to ensure accuracy of completed claims prior to submission.

> **Example:** Upon reviewing a recently completed claim for newborn care, Barbara noticed that the patient (policyholder) was 58 years old. Upon further review, Barbara discovered that during the pregnancy, the policyholder's 28-year-old daughter had used her mother's health insurance information. The result was the denial of all previous claims paid to the provider, and the provider was required to pay back all reimbursement paid by the payer. Although the provider was allowed to bill the patient for unpaid claims, the patient was unable to pay and the account was submitted to collections for processing.

Supporting documentation is also attached to the claim if required (e.g., special report for reported CPT unlisted code) prior to submission. For electronic claims, payers and clearinghouses provide procedures for the electronic submission of supporting documentation.

At the conclusion of the patient's encounter, the source of payment is identified along with the type of patient payment (.g., check, credit card) for coinsurance, copayments, and deductibles. When payment is not provided at the conclusion of an encounter, the patient is billed for any coinsurance, copayment, or deductible amounts due.

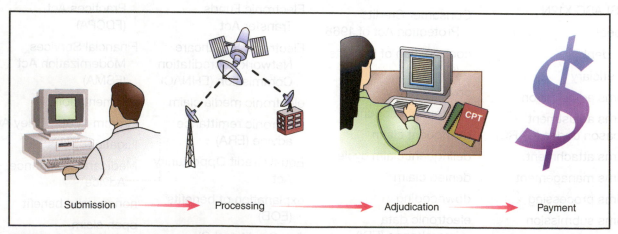

FIGURE 4-1 Cycle of an insurance claim.

Example: A patient received health care services on July 1, totaling $500. The patient's health care plan requires a 20 percent coinsurance payment directly to the provider at the time services were provided. The coinsurance amount is based on the payer's established reasonable charge of $300. So, the patient paid $60 at the time services were provided. The provider accepted assignment of the payer's established the reasonable charge of $300. On September 1, the provider received a $450 check from the payer. The overpayment was $150, which the provider must pay back to the payer.

After submitting the claim, a copy is maintained on file by the medical practice or health care facility, usually electronically, to ensure that follow-up is performed to ensure that payment was received.

Claims Submission and Electronic Data Interchange (EDI)

The cycle of an insurance claim begins in the provider's office when the health insurance specialist completes CMS-1500 claims using medical management software. **Claims submission** is the electronic or manual transmission of claims data to payers or clearinghouses for processing. Prior to submitting a claim to a clearinghouse, third-party administrator, or third-party payer, *claim scrubber software* is used to review medical claims for coding and billing accuracy before submitting it to the third-party payer. When errors are identified, the corrections are made and the claim is then ready for submission.

 NOTE:

Providers can purchase software from a vendor, contract with a billing service or clearinghouse that will provide software or programming support, or use HIPAA-compliant free billing software that is supplied by Medicare administrative contractors.

A **clearinghouse** is an agency or organization that collects, processes, and distributes claims. Claims are edited and validated to ensure that they are error-free, and are also reformatted to the specifications of the payer. A clearinghouse processes or facilitates the processing of nonstandard data elements into standard data elements (e.g., electronic claim). Claims are then submitted electronically to the appropriate payer for further processing to generate reimbursement to the provider. Clearinghouses also convert standard transactions (e.g., electronic remittance advice) received from payers to nonstandard formats (e.g., remittance advice that looks like an explanation of benefits) so providers can read them.

- An **explanation of benefits (EOB)** is sent to the *patient* by the payer and provides details about the results of claims processing, such as provider charge, payer fee scheduled, payment made by the payer, and patient financial responsibility (e.g., copayment, coinsurance). (The Medicare EOB is called a *Medicare Summary Notice* or *MSN*.)

- A **remittance advice** (also called **remit**) is an *electronic remittance advice (ERA)* or *standard paper remit (SPR)* sent to providers by third-party payers, including Medicare administrative contractors (as a **Medicare Remittance Advice**), and contains details about claims adjudication, including information about payments, deductibles and copayments, adjustments, denials, missing or incorrect data, refunds, and claims withheld due to secondary payer, third-party liability, or penalty situations.

Clearinghouses use secure networks to receive and remit electronic transactions that flow among payers, providers, and employees. A **value-added network (VAN)** is a clearinghouse that involves value-added vendors, such as banks, in the processing of claims. Using a VAN is more efficient and less expensive for providers than managing their own systems to send and receive transactions directly from numerous entities.

 NOTE:

Health care clearinghouses perform centralized claims processing for providers and health care plans. They receive claims from providers, transmit claims to payers, receive remittance advice and payment instructions from payers, and transmit that information to providers (all in a HIPAA-compliant format). A health care clearinghouse also conducts eligibility and claim status queries in the format prescribed by HIPAA.

When selecting a clearinghouse, it is important to determine which one processes a majority of claims for health plans billed by the provider. Although a provider might be able to contract with just one clearinghouse *if a health plan does not require submission of claims to a specific clearinghouse*, some plans have established their own clearinghouses, and providers must submit claims to them. Clearinghouses typically charge providers a start-up fee, a monthly flat fee, and/or a per-claim transaction fee based on volume. They also offer additional services, such as claims status tracking, insurance eligibility determination, and secondary billing services. (Providers may also want to determine whether a clearinghouse is accredited by the **Electronic Healthcare Network Accreditation Commission [EHNAC]**.)

Clearinghouses process claims in an electronic flat file format, which requires conversion of CMS-1500 claims data to a standard format. Providers can also use software to convert claims to an **electronic flat file format** (or **electronic media claim**) (Figure 4-2), which is a series of fixed-length records (e.g., 25 spaces for patient's name) submitted to payers as a bill for health care services.

> **Example:** Insurance claims processing is simplified by using a clearinghouse, which allows for direct entry of claims data online or batch uploading of claims completed using medical practice management software. (Batch uploading includes all CMS-1500 claims generated for a given period of time, such as 24 hours.) The clearinghouse generates reports to facilitate claims tracking, from submission through payment or denial (e.g., patient roster reports) to ensure claims for all patients treated on a given day were submitted.

Electronic Data Interchange (EDI)

Electronic data interchange (EDI) is the computer-to-computer transfer of data between providers and third-party payers (or providers and health care clearinghouses) in a data format agreed upon by sending and receiving parties. HIPAA's administrative simplification provisions directed the federal government to adopt national electronic standards for the automated transfer of certain health care data among health care payers (e.g., Medicare administrative contractors), payers (e.g., BCBS), and providers (e.g., hospitals, physicians). These provisions enable the entire health care industry to communicate electronic data using a single set of standards. (Electronic claims data submission has almost entirely replaced the paper-based claims processing.) Health care providers submit standard transactions for eligibility, authorization, referrals, claims, or attachments to any payer. This "simplifies" clinical, billing, and other financial applications and reduces costs. Three electronic formats are supported for health care claims transactions:

- UB-04 flat file format
- National Standard Format (NSF)
- ANSI ASC X12N 837 format (American National Standards Institute, Accredited Standards Committee, Insurance Subcommittee X12, claims validation table 837)

```
MSG_HDR|BCBS|ECM_Y06|SndApp|SndFac|RcApp|RcFac|YYYY01052369|56941
INS_CLM||||562697|YYYY0105|YYYY0110|ADLO5691|125.00
PRV_DT1|M_P|Smith|DKSL23659
PRV_DT1|M_H|Jones|DLEP65915
PAT_IDF|DCB5432|Green|19941205
CRD_STS|Y|Y|N
SRV_CMN|GM|YYYY0105|50.00
SRV_FEE|CP|45.00
SRV_FEE|CK|12.00
SRV_CMN|GM|YYYY0106|55.00
SRV_FEE|CO|10.00
SRV_FEE|RK|
```

FIGURE 4-2 Sample electronic flat file format.

NOTE:

ANSI ASC X12N is an electronic format standard that uses a variable length file format to process transactions for institutional, professional, dental, and drug claims. The ANSI organization facilitates the development of standards for health informatics and other industries (e.g., international exchange of goods and services).

The Health Insurance Portability and Accountability Act of 1996 (HIPAA) mandated national standards for the electronic exchange of administrative and financial health care transactions (e.g., CMS-1500 claim) to improve the efficiency and effectiveness of the health care system. Standards were adopted for the following transactions:

- Eligibility for a health plan
- Enrollment and disenrollment in a health plan
- First report of injury
- Health care payment and remittance advice
- Health claim status
- Health claims and equivalent encounter information
- Health claims attachments
- Health plan premium payments
- Referral certification and authorization
- Coordination of benefits (COB)

Covered entities (Figure 4-3) are required to use mandated national standards when conducting any of the defined transactions covered under HIPAA. **Covered entities** process electronic claims and include all private-sector health plans (excluding certain small self-administered health plans); managed care organizations; ERISA-covered health benefit plans (those covered by the Employee Retirement Income Security Act of 1974); government health plans (including Medicare, Medicaid, Military Health System for active duty and civilian

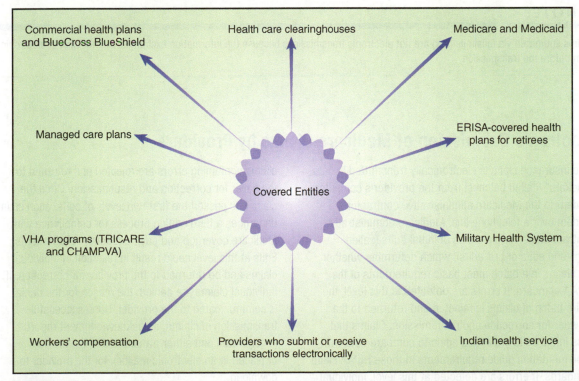

FIGURE 4-3 Covered entities.

personnel, Veterans Health Administration, and Indian Health Service programs); all health care clearinghouses; and all health care providers that choose to submit or receive these transactions electronically.

 NOTE:

HIPAA's health care transaction standards require covered entities to submit electronic transactions using the same format.

The following are advantages of electronic claims processing:

- Reduction in payment turnaround time
- Reduction in claims submission error rates

Electronic claims are submitted directly to the payer after being checked for accuracy by billing software or a health care clearinghouse, and this audit/edit process reduces the normal rejection rate to 1 to 2 percent. The audit/edit process results in a **clean claim**, which contains all required data elements needed to process and pay the claim (e.g., valid diagnosis and procedure/service codes, modifiers, and so on). In addition, if an electronic claim is rejected due to an error or omission, the provider is notified, and the claim can be edited and resubmitted for processing. As part of the *revenue integrity* process maintained by a health care organization, a *clean claim rate* is calculated to ensure compliance with needed claims edits prior to claims submission.

Electronic claims are submitted using the following transmission media:

- *Dial-up* (telephone line or digital subscriber line [DSL] is used for claims submission, and providers install software on office computers)
- *Extranet* (direct submission of claims to payers using Internet technology that emulates a system connection; provider can access information about collaborating parties only, such as payer and patient data elements)
- *Internet* (secure transmission of claims over the Internet, eliminating the need for additional software)
- *Magnetic tape, disc, or compact disc media* (physical movement of transmissions from one location to another using media)

 NOTE:

Claims submitted via facsimile (fax) are not electronic transmissions because the information exchanged did not exist in electronic form before the transmission.

Electronic Submission of Medicare Claims by Providers

The insurance claim is electronically transmitted in data "packets" (called batches) from the provider's computer modem to the Medicare administrative contractor's modem over a telephone line. Medicare administrative contractors perform a series of initial edits (called front-end edits or pre-edits), which determine whether the claims in a batch meet basic requirements of the HIPAA standard. If errors are detected at this level, the entire batch of claims is rejected and returned to the provider for correction and resubmission. Claims that pass initial edits are edited again to compare data with implementation guide requirements in those HIPAA claim standards. If errors are detected at this level, individual claims containing errors are rejected and returned to the payer for correction and resubmission. Once the claim has passed the first two levels of edits, each claim undergoes a third editing process for compliance with Medicare coverage and payment policy requirements. Edits at this level could result in rejection of individual claims and be returned to the provider for correction. If individual claims are denied, the reason for the denial is communicated to the provider. Upon successful transmission of claims, an acknowledgment report is generated and either transmitted to the provider or placed in an electronic mailbox for the provider to download.

Claims Attachments

A **claims attachment** is a set of supporting documentation or information associated with a health care claim or patient encounter. Claims attachment information can be found in the remarks or notes fields of an electronic claim. Claims attachments are used for:

- Medical evaluation for payment
- Past payment audit or review
- Quality control to ensure access to care and quality of care

 NOTE:

Claims are sometimes delayed or rejected because the payer needs to obtain a copy of patient records for review prior to making a determination. In this situation, the provider is notified of the request for information and has an opportunity to submit supporting documentation from the record to justify the medical necessity of procedures or services performed. This delay in claims processing can sometimes be avoided if the practice contacts payers to request a list of CPT and HCPCS Level II codes that require supporting documentation.

Example 1: CPT modifiers are reported on claims to provide clarification about procedures and services performed, and they are entered as two-digit numbers. Providers that submit supporting documentation when reporting the following modifiers on claims assist the payer in making payment determinations:

- -22 (Increased Procedural Services)
- -53 (Discontinued Procedure)
- -59 (Distinct Procedural Service)

Example 2: When a provider performs a procedure for which there is no CPT or HCPCS Level II code and an unlisted code is reported on the claim, supporting documentation must be submitted (e.g., copy of operative report).

 HIPAA Alert!

Traditionally, claims attachments containing medical documentation that supported procedures and services reported on claims were copied from patient records and mailed to payers. Providers now submit electronic attachments with electronic claims or send electronic attachments in response to requests for medical documentation (e.g., scanned images of paper records) to support submitted claims.

How to Avoid Resubmitting Claims

Delayed claims contain incomplete and inaccurate information and require resubmission after correction, which delays payment to the provider. Although hospitals and large group practices collect data about these problems and address them, smaller provider practices often do not have the tools to evaluate their claims submission processes. A major reason for delays in claims processing is incompleteness or inaccuracy of the information necessary to coordinate benefits among multiple payers. If the remittance advice from the primary payer is not attached to the claim submitted to the secondary payer, the result will be payment delays.

Coordination of benefits (COB) is a provision in group health insurance policies intended to keep multiple insurers from paying benefits covered by other policies; it also specifies that coverage will be provided in a specific sequence when more than one policy covers the claim. Some payers electronically transfer data to facilitate the coordination of benefits on a submitted claim. (Medicare calls this concept "crossover.") Becoming educated about how to correctly process claims for crossover patients will reduce payment delays and improve accounts receivable.

Claims Processing

Claims processing involves sorting claims upon submission to collect and verify information about the patient and provider (Figure 4-4). Clearinghouses and payers use software to automate the scanning and imaging functions associated with claims processing. Scanning technology "reads" the information reported on the claim and converts it to an image so that claims examiners can analyze, edit, and validate the data. The claims examiner views the image (or electronic data if submitted in that format) on a split computer screen (Figure 4-5) that contains the claim on the top half and information verification software on the bottom half.

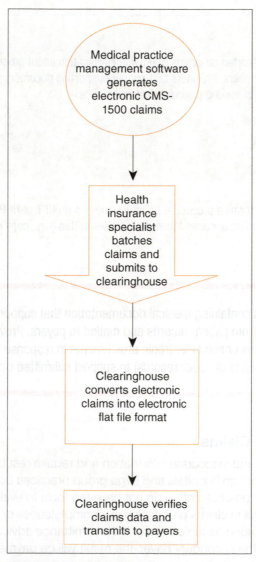

FIGURE 4-4 Claims submission and processing.

Insurance Identification Number		Payer	Payer PlanID Number
123456789		BCBS	987654321

First Name	Middle Name	Last Name	Home Phone
Maria	Antonia	Patient	(101) 111-1234

Address	City	State	ZIP Code	Work Phone
2 Tiger Street	Anywhere	NY	12345-1234	(101) 111-9876

1. MEDICARE MEDICAID TRICARE CHAMPVA GROUP HEALTH PLAN FECA BLKLUNG OTHER	1a. INSURED'S I.D. NUMBER (For Program in Item 1)
☐(Medicare#) ☐(Medicaid#) ☐(ID#DoD#) ☐(Member ID#) ☐(ID#) ☐(ID#) ☒(ID#)	123456789

2. PATIENT'S NAME (Last Name, First Name, Middle Initial)	3. PATIENT'S BIRTH DATE SEX	4. INSURED'S NAME (Last Name, First Name, Middle Initial)
PATIENT, MARIA, A	MM 10 DD 05 YY 1935 M☐ F☒	PATIENT, MARIA, A

5. PATIENT'S ADDRESS (No., Street)	6. PATIENT RELATIONSHIP TO INSURED	7. INSURED'S ADDRESS (No., Street)
2 TIGER STREET	Self ☒ Spouse☐ Child☐ Other☐	2 TIGER STREET

CITY	STATE	8. RESERVED FOR NUCC USE	CITY	STATE
ANYWHERE	NY		ANYWHERE	NY

ZIP CODE	TELEPHONE (Include Area Code)		ZIP CODE	TELEPHONE (Include Area Code)
123451234	(101) 1111234		123451234	(101) 1111234

Courtesy of the Centers for Medicare & Medicaid Services, www.cms.gov; claim data created by author.

FIGURE 4-5 Sample split screen viewed by claims examiner.

 NOTE:

Edits and validation at the claims processing stage are limited to verification of insured status, patient identification number and demographic information, provider identification number, and the like. If analysis of the claim reveals incorrect or missing information that cannot be edited by the claims examination, the claim is rejected and returned to the provider. The provider can correct the errors and omissions and resubmit the claim for processing.

Claims Adjudication

After the claim has been validated by the payer's claims examiner, it undergoes the **claims adjudication** process (Figure 4-6), in which the claim is compared to payer edits and the patient's health plan benefits to verify that the:

- Required information is available to process the claim.
- Claim is not a duplicate.
- Payer rules and procedures have been followed.
- Procedures performed and services provided are covered benefits.

The payer analyzes each claim for patient and policy identification and compares data with its computerized database. Claims are automatically rejected if the patient and subscriber names do not match exactly with names in the computerized database. Using nicknames or including typographical errors on claims will cause rejection and return, or delay in reimbursement to the provider, because the claim cannot be matched. Procedure and service codes reported on the claim are compared with the policy's master benefit list to determine if they are covered. Any procedure or service reported on the claim that is not included on the master benefit list is a **noncovered benefit** and will result in denial (rejection) of the claim. This means that the patient's insurance plan will not reimburse the provider for having performed those procedures or services. Procedures and services provided to a patient without proper preauthorization from the payer, or that were not covered by a current preauthorization, are **unauthorized services**. This means that the payer requires the provider to obtain preauthorization before performing certain procedures and services; and because it was not obtained, the claim is denied (rejected).

 NOTE:

Patients can be billed for noncovered procedures but not for unauthorized services. Providers process denials of unauthorized services as a business loss.

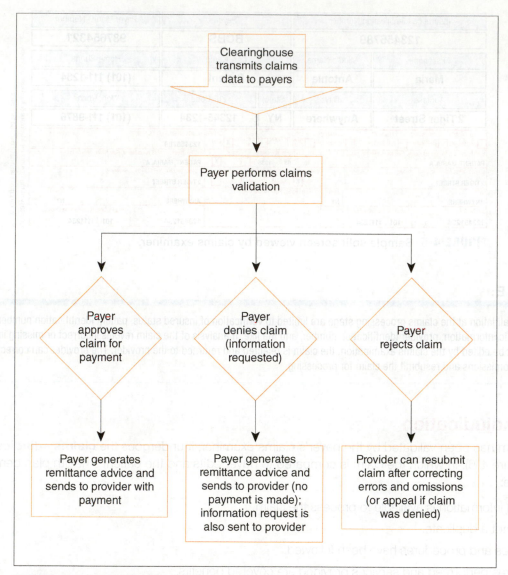

FIGURE 4-6 Claims adjudication and payment.

 Managed Care Alert! ━━━━━━━━━

For managed care claims, both procedures and dates of service are verified to ensure that the services performed were both preauthorized and performed within the preauthorized time frame.

The payer matches procedure and service codes (e.g., CPT) with diagnosis codes reported on the CMS-1500 claim to ensure the medical necessity of all procedures and services provided. Any procedure or service that is not medically necessary is denied. The claim is also checked against the **common data file**, which is a summary abstract report of all recent claims filed on each patient. This process determines whether the patient is receiving concurrent care for the same condition by more than one provider, and it identifies services that are related to recent surgeries, hospitalizations, or liability coverage.

NOTE:

Payers will identify a claim as a third-party liability responsibility based on review of codes. For example, submitting a claim on a patient who was injured in an automobile accident will trigger the payer to identify the automobile insurance as the primary payer on the claim.

A determination is made as to **allowed charges**, which is the maximum amount the payer will allow for each procedure or service, according to the patient's policy. If no irregularity or inconsistency is found on the claim, the allowed charge for each covered procedure is determined. Allowed charges vary from policy to policy, and they are less than or equal to the fee charged by the provider. This means that payment is never greater than the fee submitted by the provider. A determination of the patient's annual deductible, copayment, and/or coinsurance amounts is also made. The *deductible* is the total amount of covered medical expenses a policyholder must pay each year out-of-pocket before the insurance company is obligated to pay any benefits. A policyholder (or subscriber) is the person in whose name the insurance policy is issued; a **beneficiary** is eligible to receive health care benefits and includes the policyholder (subscriber) and eligible dependents. *Coinsurance* is the percentage the patient pays for covered services after the deductible has been met and the copayment has been paid. For example, with an 80/20 plan, the insurance company pays 80 percent and the patient pays 20 percent. A *copayment* (or *copay*) is the fixed amount the patient pays each time health care services are provided.

Example 1: The patient received preventive services for an annual physical examination on April 7. The third-party payer determines the allowed charge for preventive services to be $112, for which the payer reimburses the physician 80 percent of that amount. The patient is responsible for paying the remaining 20 percent directly to the physician. Thus, the physician will receive a check in the amount of $89.60 from the payer, and the patient will pay $22.40 to the physician.

Example 2: The patient underwent office surgery on September 8, and the third-party payer determined the allowed charge to be $680. The patient paid the 20 percent coinsurance at the time of the office surgery. The physician and patient each received a check for $544, and the patient signed the check over to the physician. The overpayment was $544, and the physician must reimburse the third-party payer.

Once the claims adjudication process has been completed, the payer generates a remittance advice that contains information about payment, denials, and pending status of claims. If a claim is denied, the provider can appeal the decision by resubmitting the claim and attaching supporting documentation. Claims that are assigned pending status contain errors and omissions, and providers can correct those problems and resubmit the claim for processing.

During the adjudication process, the status location of a claim can be monitored and providers can track claims within a health plan's internal claims processing, adjudication, and payment systems. (HIPAA standardized the status locations for all health care claims transactions.) Providers can even verify, through a batch transmission, the status of multiple claims. Providers can also verify patients' insurance coverage and eligibility for services, and they can find out when to expect reimbursement for processed claims.

NOTE:

Physician claims are adjudicated by line item (not for total charges), which means that payers bundle and edit code numbers for individual procedures and services. Because rules and procedures vary among payers, what one payer bundles, another may not. In addition, payers routinely change the rules and procedures that affect coverage policies and reimbursement to the provider. Another concern is that payers often do not apply official coding guidelines for diagnosis and procedure/service coding. Thus, CPT and HCPCS Level II codes reported on a claim are sometimes changed by the payer, affecting payment to the provider.

Example: CPT contains laboratory panel codes (e.g., electrolyte panel), which bundle several laboratory tests into one code number. Some payers prefer to receive claims that contain individual code numbers for each laboratory test performed as part of the panel (e.g., carbon dioxide, chloride, potassium, and sodium). The payer's rationale is that a provider could order a series of tests and call it a panel, which is reimbursed at a higher rate than individual tests, even if not all of the panel tests were actually performed.

Example: As part of their job as a health insurance specialist for a physician's office, the specialist queries the status of any claim that is 60 days old or older. A typical onscreen display appears as follows:

```
ABC1234 MEDICARE B ONLINE SYSTEM
SC CLAIM SUMMARY INQUIRY

HIC PROVIDER 123456 S/LOC TOB
OPERATOR ID ABCDE FROM DATE TO DATE DDE SORT
MEDICAL REVIEW SELECT

HIC PROV/MRN S/LOC TOB ADM DT FRM DT THRU DT
REC DT
SEL LAST NAME FIRST INIT TOT CHG PROV REIMB PD DT
CAN DT REAS NPC #DAYS
449999999A 179999 T B9997 131 0726YY 0726YY
SMITH M R 250.00 F1
```

The health insurance specialist verifies that this is the Medicare Part B claim status for M. R. Smith, a patient who was seen in the office on July 26, YY, for a service that was billed for $250. The specialist notes that the claim has been paid, which is the interpretation of the F1 code on the last line. Because the specialist queried the status of the claim, thinking that it was 60 days old or older, an investigation as to whether the provider actually received the payment will need to be conducted.

Remittance Advice Reconciliation and Payment of Claims

Once the adjudication process has been finalized, the claim is either denied or approved for payment. A remittance advice (RA) (Figure 4-7) is sent to the provider, and an explanation of benefits (EOB) (Figure 4-8) is mailed to the policyholder and/or patient. A remittance advice submitted by the third-party payer to the provider electronically is called an **electronic remittance advice (ERA)**. Providers use remittance advice information to process payments and adjustments to patient accounts. The remittance advice should be reviewed to make sure there are no processing errors (e.g., code changes, denial of benefits, and so on). (Patients should review EOBs to find out whether claims were paid; if denied, the patient should contact the provider's office to determine

From:	To: Sam Miskik, M.D.
Medicare Administrative Contract # 09999	Medicare Provider NPI # 1234567890
-------------------------------------	Physician's Group
EDI Exchange # 000000999	Main Street
Jun 16, YYYY @ 9:00 A.M.	Anywhere, NY 12345
Claim Number: 986532	(101) 123-1234

Adjustment applied: $0.00
Payment of $200.00 by CHECK #999999 dated Jun 16, YYYY

Patient Ref #	12345SANDERS	Internal Control #	99S7654321
Patient Name:	Jane Sanders	Paid as:	PRIMARY
Patient HICN	98765432	Claim Total:	$ 500.00
Date of Claim:	May 08, YYYY	Amount Paid:	$ 200.00

Service # 1--

Date of Service:	May 08, YYYY	Allowable:	$ 200.00
Diagnosis Code:	L70.0 (Cystic acne)	Deductible:	$ 0.00
Procedure Code:	10040 (Acne surgery)	Coinsurance:	$ 0.00
Units:	1	Copayment:	$ 0.00
Charge:	$ 400.00	Paid:	$ 200.00
Provider NPI:	1234567890	Reasons:	Amount $200 above fee schedule

Service # 2 --

Date of Service:	May 08, YYYY	Allowable:	$ 60.00
Diagnosis Code:	J45.909 (Asthma)	Deductible:	$ 0.00
Procedure Code:	99215 (Level 5 Office Visit)	Coinsurance:	$ 0.00
Units:	1	Copayment:	$ 0.00
Charge:	$ 100.00	Paid:	$ 0.00
Provider NPI:	1234567890	Reasons:	Medical necessity not met

FIGURE 4-7 Sample remittance advice for one patient (two office visits).

THE KEYSTONE PLAN

P.O. BOX 900
ALFRED, NY 14802-0900
(800) 555-9000

DATE: 04/05/YY
PATIENT ID #: BLS123456789
ENROLLEE: MORGAN PATIENT
CONTRACT: 300500
BENEFIT PLAN: STATE OF NEW YORK

MORGAN PATIENT
100 MAIN ST
ALFRED, NY 14802

EXPLANATION OF BENEFITS

SERVICE DETAIL

PATIENT/RELAT CLAIM NUMBER	PROVIDER/ SERVICE	DATE OF SERVICE	AMOUNT BILLED	AMOUNT NOT COVERED	AMOUNT ALLOWED	COPAY/ DEDUCTIBLE	%	PLAN BENEFITS	REMARK CODE
ENROLLEE 5629587	D MILLER OFFICE VISITS	04/05/YYYY	80.00	39.75	40.25	8.00	100	32.25*	D1
							PLAN PAYS	32.25	

*THIS IS A COPY OF INFORMATION SENT TO THE PROVIDER. THANK YOU FOR USING THE PARTICIPATING PROVIDER PROGRAM.

REMARK CODE(S) LISTED BELOW ARE REFERENCED IN THE *SERVICE DETAIL* SECTION UNDER THE HEADING *REMARK CODE*
(D1)   THANK YOU FOR USING A NETWORK PROVIDER. WE HAVE APPLIED THE NETWORK CONTRACTED FEE. THE MEMBER IS NOT RESPONSIBLE FOR THE DIFFERENCE BETWEEN THE AMOUNT CHARGED AND THE AMOUNT ALLOWED BY THE CONTRACT.

BENEFIT PLAN PAYMENT SUMMARY INFORMATION
D MILLER $32.25

PATIENT NAME	MEDICAL/SURGICAL DEDUCTIBLE		MEDICAL/SURGICAL OUT OF POCKET		PHYSICAL MEDICINE DEDUCTIBLE	
	ANNUAL DEDUCT	YYYY YEAR TO-DATE	ANNUAL MAXIMUM	YYYY YEAR TO-DATE	ANNUAL DEDUCT	YYYY YEAR TO-DATE
ENROLLEE	$249.00	$249.00	$1804.00	$121.64	$250.00	$0.00

THIS CLAIM WAS PROCESSED IN ACCORDANCE WITH THE TERMS OF YOUR EMPLOYEE BENEFITS PLAN. IN THE EVENT THIS CLAIM HAS BEEN DENIED, IN WHOLE OR IN PART, A REQUEST FOR REVIEW MAY BE DIRECTED TO THE KEYSTONE PLAN AT THE ALFRED ADDRESS OR PHONE NUMBER SHOWN ABOVE. THE REQUEST FOR REVIEW MUST BE SUBMITTED WITHIN 60 DAYS AFTER THE CLAIM PAYMENT DATE, OR THE DATE OF THE NOTIFICATION OF DENIAL OF BENEFITS. WHEN REQUESTING A REVIEW, PLEASE STATE WHY YOU BELIEVE THE CLAIM DETERMINATION OR PRE-CERTIFICATION IMPROPERLY REDUCED OR DENIED YOUR BENEFITS. ALSO, SUBMIT ANY DATA OR COMMENTS TO SUPPORT THE APPEAL.

THIS IS NOT A BILL.

FIGURE 4-8 Sample explanation of benefits (EOB).

whether the claim was resubmitted, requested information was sent to the payer, and so on.) After reviewing the remittance advice and posting payments and adjustments, any code changes, denials, and partial payments should be followed up on. The payer may need additional information to make a determination about a claim, and prompt compliance with such requests will expedite payment.

NOTE:

Chapter 4 of the *Workbook to Accompany Understanding Health Insurance* contains assignments to help students interpret data located on EOB and RA or ERA documents.

It is common for payers to include multiple patients on one remittance advice and to send the provider one check for multiple claims. Providers also have the option of arranging for **electronic funds transfer (EFT)**, which means that payers electronically deposit funds to the provider's bank account.

NOTE:

Medicare calls the remittance advice a *Medicare Remittance Advice* and the explanation of benefits a *Medicare Summary Notice (MSN)*. (The MSN is defined in Chapter 14, where a sample is also provided.)

State Prompt Payment Laws and Regulations

The Prompt Payment Act of 1982 requires federal agencies to pay their bills on time or risk paying penalty fees if payments are late. Many states have also enacted prompt pay laws that apply to health insurance plans, requiring them to either pay or deny claims within a specified time frame (e.g., electronic claims must typically be paid within 30 days). In addition, many states apply penalty fees for late payments.

A federal regulation requires that Medicare Advantage organizations (previously called Medicare Choice, M+C, or Medicare Part C) make prompt payments for services provided by nonparticipating providers. Such organizations must pay 95 percent of clean claims within 30 days of submission, and the organization must pay interest on clean claims not paid within 30 days. (All other claims must be paid or denied within 60 days from the date of the receipt.)

Medicare claims must also be paid promptly by Medicare administrative contractors. Clean claims must be paid or denied within 30 days from receipt, and interest must be paid on claims that are paid after 30 days. The count starts on the day after the receipt date and ends on the date payment is made.

Example: If a clean claim received October 1 of this year is paid within 30 days, then the Medicare requirement is met.

Interpreting a Remittance Advice (REMIT) and an Explanation of Benefits (EOB)

Third-party payers review submitted claims to determine whether services are covered by the patient's insurance plan (e.g., cosmetic surgery is usually not covered) and for coordination of benefits to determine which payer is responsible for reimbursement (e.g., services provided to a patient treated for a work-related injury are reimbursed by the employer's workers' compensation payer). Once a payer has completed the claims adjudication (decision-making) process, the claim is denied or approved for payment. The provider receives a remittance advice (remit), and the patient receives an explanation of benefits (EOB). (Some payers send providers an EOB instead of a remittance advice.) The remit and EOB each contains information about denied services, reimbursed services, and the patient's responsibility for payment (e.g., copayment). The remittance advice typically includes the following items:

- Third-party payer's name and contract number

- Electronic data interchange (EDI) information, including EDI exchange number, date and time remittance advice was generated, and EDI receipt identifier

- Provider's name and mailing address

- Adjustments applied to the submitted claim (e.g., reduced payment, partial payment, zero payment, and so on)

- Amount and date of payment

- Patient's reference number, name and health insurance contract number, claim date, internal control

number, paid status (e.g., primary, secondary, supplemental), claim total, and amount paid

- Date and place of service, procedure/service code, units, charge(s), provider identification number, allowable charges, deductible and coinsurance amounts, amount paid, and reasons (to explain payment amount)

The explanation of benefits typically includes the following items:

- Third-party payer's name, mailing address, and telephone number

- Date the EOB was generated, payer's identification number, contract number, and benefit plan

- Patient's name and mailing address

- Details of services reported on claim, including claim number, name of provider, date of service, amount charged, amount not covered by plan, amount allowed by plan, copayment and/or deductible amounts (that are the responsibility of the patient), amount paid under plan's benefits, and any remark codes (e.g., reason for denied claim)

- Benefit plan payment summary information, including provider's name and amount paid under plan's benefits

- Summary information about plan deductible and out-of-pocket amounts (paid by patient)

- Statement (at the bottom or top) that says THIS IS NOT A BILL

Out with the Old and In with the New

Yesterday: Traditional Claims Processing

Payers received health claim forms by mail, and they were opened, date-stamped, sorted, and grouped according to physician specialty. Data from the claim forms were keyed into a claims database, and the validity of the claim was determined. If valid, payment was mailed to the physician. If not valid, an exception report was printed, the claim was manually retrieved from the file system and faxed to a review panel of physicians. The physician may have received a request for information from the payer so that further review could occur prior to approval for payment. (The *Administrative Simplification Compliance Act [ACSA]* permits paper claims to be submitted in unusual situations, such as due to an interruption in electricity or communication service, small provider entities with fewer than 25 full-time equivalent employees, and dental claims. ACSA exceptions are detailed in Chapter 11 of this textbook.)

Today: Electronic Claims Processing

Claims are generated using medical practice management software for electronic routing and processing. Tracking of claims is automated; when a claim has to be retrieved for review, instead of searching through paper files, the image is quickly located and viewed onscreen. Medicare has enforced the mandatory submission of electronic claims, which means paper claims are denied.

Maintaining Insurance Claim Files

CMS requires providers to retain copies of any government insurance claims and copies of all attachments filed by the provider for a period of six years (unless state law stipulates a longer period). (The provider could be audited during that period.)

 NOTE:

Medicare *Conditions of Participation* require providers to maintain medical records for at least five years, and state retention laws are sometimes stricter (e.g., New York State requires medical records to be maintained for at least six years).

CMS stipulated in March 1992 that providers and billing services that submit claims electronically can comply with this federal regulation by retaining the financial **source document** (routing slip, charge slip, encounter form, or superbill) from which the insurance claim was generated. In addition, the provider should keep the emailed report of the summary of electronic claims received from the insurance company.

It is recommended that the following types of claims and files be securely stored as electronic claims files (e.g., folders created using a computer) or manual claims files (e.g., labeled folders):

1. **Open claims** are organized by month and insurance company. They have been submitted to the payer, but are not completely processed. Open claims include those that were rejected (denied) due to an error or omission and must be reprocessed.

2. **Closed claims** are filed according to year and insurance company, and include those for which all processing, including appeals, has been completed.

3. *Remittance advice documents* are organized according to date of service because payers often report the results of insurance claims processed on different patients for the same date of service and provider. This mass report is called a *batched remittance advice*.

 NOTE:

If a patient requests a copy of the remittance advice received by the provider, all patient identification except that of the requesting patient must be removed.

> **Example:** A patient contacts the office to request a copy of the transmittal notice for the last date of service. Because the information is on a batched remittance advice, the insurance specialist makes a copy of the page on which the patient's information is found. Using the copy, the insurance specialist removes information about other patients, and mails the redacted (edited) copy to the patient who requested it. The rest of the copy, which contains other patients' information, is shredded.

4. **Unassigned claims** are organized by year and are generated for providers who do not accept assignment; the file includes all unassigned claims for which the provider is not obligated to perform any follow-up work.

5. **Denied claims** are rejected by payers due to coding errors, missing information, and patient coverage issues (e.g., incorrect policy number, invalid CPT code). They are unpaid claims that have been returned to the provider by clearinghouses, third-party administrators, or third-party payers. Payers usually explain the reason a claim has been denied in the remittance advice (remit) or explanation of benefits (EOB), such as coding errors, missing information, and patient coverage issues. Denied/rejected claims are considered *open claims* until the appeal process for reconsideration of payment has been exhausted.

Tracking Unpaid Claims

The insurance specialist is responsible for tracking insurance claims submitted to third-party payers and clearinghouses, and tracking unpaid claims is especially important. To ensure that claims are processed in a timely manner (and payment is received), effective claims tracking requires the following activities:

- Maintaining an electronic copy of each submitted claim
- Logging information about claims submitted in an insurance claims registry (e.g., using medical practice management software)
- Reviewing the remittance advice (remit) to ensure that accurate reimbursement was received

The remittance advice contains reason codes for *denied claims*, which are interpreted by the insurance specialist. If the claim was denied because the service is not covered by the payer, the claim is not resubmitted. (A bill is mailed to the patient, who receives an explanation of benefits from the payer that indicates the reason for the denial.) If the claim was denied due to errors, a corrected claim is submitted to the payer. The insurance specialist should carefully review the entire claim prior to resubmission because processing of the original claim was halted by the payer (or clearinghouse) upon activation of a reason for denial. Other errors may exist in that claim, which need to be corrected prior to resubmission. The health care organization also calculates *denied claims rates* (or *denial rates*) to ensure that clean claims are submitted; this *metric* (standard of measurement) ensures accurate and timely reimbursement.

Storing Remittance Advice Documents

When the remittance advice and payment has been received, and payments have been posted to the patient accounts, be sure to post the date payment was received, amount of payment, processing date, and any applicable transmittal notice number. Claims containing no errors are moved to the *closed claims* file. Batched remittance advices are placed in the *batched remittance advice* file.

Denied Claims and the Appeals Process

Claims denials include an *administrative denial* (e.g., submitted claim contains errors, such as missing data) or a *clinical denial* (e.g., medical necessity of procedures performed or services provided is not supported).

NOTE:

Clinical and coding validation denials are associated with the inpatient prospective payment system, which uses diagnosis-related groups to determine reimbursement. *Clinical validation denials* occur when patient records are reviewed by third-party payers, such as physician reviewers, and a determination is made that there is no clinical evidence to support documented medical conditions. *Coding validation denials* occur when patient records are reviewed and the decision is that provider documentation did not support reported codes or their sequencing. The denial of payment or a reduction in payment to hospitals has resulted in the establishment of clinical and coding validation processes prior to the submission of claims, involving the health information and utilization management departments along with the facility's medical staff. (Detailed content about the inpatient prospective payment system and diagnosis-related groups is contained in Chapter 9 of this textbook.)

It is important to process claims denials as they are identified to recoup lost revenue for the provider. According to Optum's *Denial Management: Field-Tested Techniques That Get Claims Paid*, by Elizabeth W. Woodcock, MBA, FACMPE, CPC, effective claims denial management includes the following:

- *Identification*: Identify the reason for claims denials and rejections; correct the issues that resulted in denied or rejected claims; interpret **claims adjustment reason codes (CARC)** (reasons for denied or rejected claims as reported on the remittance advice or explanation of benefits) and **remittance advice remark codes (RARC)** (additional explanation of reasons for denied/rejected claims); for example, when a procedure code is inconsistent with the reported reason for the procedure (diagnosis), the claim will be denied because the diagnosis does not meet medical necessity for the procedure performed.

- *Management*: Design a work process that resolves denied or rejected claims, such as sorting by type (e.g., coding issues); forward denied claims to the appropriate staff person (e.g., coder); and implement a standard work process for processing denied or rejected claims (e.g., determining which types of denials are most common).

- *Monitoring*: Maintain a log of denied and rejected claims and the response to each, routinely review the log to follow-up on the status of corrected claims that were resubmitted and appeals of denied claims, review samples of submitted appeals to identify work processes that need revision, and proactively review claims prior to submission to ensure accuracy and to reduce claims denials and rejections by clearinghouses and third-party payers.

- *Prevention*: Involve provider staff, providers, and patients at the appropriate level of the claims process to ensure submission of accurate claims and successful appeals of denied claims; for example, if payer preauthorizations are not obtained prior to providing services, conduct in-service education to retrain staff.

An **appeal** is documented as a letter (Figure 4-9) and signed by the provider to explain why a claim should be reconsidered for payment. If appropriate, copies of medical record documentation are attached (for which the patient has signed a release-of-information authorization).

NOTE:

Medicare appeals are now called redeterminations or reconsiderations per BIPA-mandated changes.

Appealing Denied Claims

A remittance advice may indicate that payment was denied for a reason other than a processing error. The reasons for denials may include (1) procedure or service not medically necessary, (2) pre-existing condition not covered, (3) noncovered benefit, (4) termination of coverage, (5) failure to obtain preauthorization, (6) out-of-network provider used, (7) lower level of care could have been provided, (8) incorrect codes or incorrectly linked codes reported on claim, (9) bundled service or global period service is not eligible for separate payment, or (10) claim contained incomplete information or another insurance plan is primary.

NOTE:

When questioning the payer about a remittance advice that includes multiple patients, circle the pertinent patient information. Do not use a highlighter, because payer scanning equipment does not recognize highlighted information.

Redetermination 1st Level Appeal

Physician's Group
Main Street
Anywhere, US 12345
(101) 123-1234
March 15, YYYY

Medicare Part B Review Department
P.O. Box 1001
Anywhere, US 12345

NAME OF PROVIDER: _____
PROVIDER NPI NUMBER: _____
NAME OF PATIENT: _____
MEDICARE BENEFICIARY NUMBER (MBN): _____
I do not agree with the determination you made on Claim Number: _____

The reason I disagree with this determination is/are: (Check all that apply.)

❑ Service/Claim underpaid/reduced   ❑ Service(s) medically necessary   ❑ Other:

_____
_____
_____
_____

Services in question are delineated as follows:

Date(s) of Service:	Quantity Billed:	Amount Billed:	Procedure Code(s):
_____	_____	_____	_____
_____	_____	_____	_____

Attachments to consider:

❑ Medical Records   ❑ Ambulance Record   ❑ Remittance Advice   ❑ CMN*   ❑ Other:

*CMN = Certificate of Medical Necessity (for durable medical equipment)

_____   _____
Signature of Claimant or Representative   Telephone Number

FIGURE 4-9 Sample appeal letter.

The following steps should be taken to appeal each type of denial:

1. *Procedure or service not medically necessary:* The payer has determined that the procedure performed or service rendered was not medically necessary based on information submitted on the claim. To respond, first review the original source document (e.g., patient record) for the claim to determine whether significant diagnosis codes or other important information have been clearly documented or may have been overlooked. Next, write an appeal letter to the payer providing the reasons the treatment is medically necessary.

NOTE:

If the medical record does not support medical necessity, discuss the case with the office manager and provider.

2. *Pre-existing condition:* The payer has denied this claim based on the wording of the pre-existing condition clause in the patient's insurance policy. A **pre-existing condition** is any medical condition that was diagnosed and treated within a specified period of time immediately preceding the enrollee's effective date of coverage. The wording associated with these clauses varies from policy to policy (e.g., length of time pre-existing condition clause applies). It is possible for an insurance company to cancel a policy (or at least deny payment on a claim) if the patient failed to disclose pre-existing conditions. Respond to this type of denial by determining whether the condition associated with treatment for which the claim was submitted was indeed pre-existing. If it is determined that an incorrect diagnosis code was submitted on the original claim, for example, correct the claim and resubmit it for reconsideration of payment.

NOTE:

> Beginning in 2014, health insurance plans cannot refuse to cover individuals or charge more because of a pre-existing condition. An exception includes *individual* health insurance plans that individuals purchase privately (*not* through an employer).
>
> Office staff must be familiar with federal regulations regarding insurance coverage of pre-existing conditions when a patient changes jobs and/or an employer switches insurance plans.

3. *Noncovered benefit:* The claim was denied based on a list developed by the insurance company that includes a description of items covered by the policy as well as those excluded. Excluded items may include procedures such as cosmetic surgery. Respond to this type of denial by determining whether the treatment submitted on the claim for payment is indeed excluded from coverage. If it is determined, for example, that an incorrect procedure code was submitted, then correct the claim and resubmit it for reconsideration of payment along with a copy of medical record documentation to support the code change.

4. *Termination of coverage:* The payer has denied this claim because the patient is no longer covered by the insurance policy. Respond to this type of denial by contacting the patient to determine appropriate coverage, and submit the claim accordingly. For example, a patient may have changed jobs and may no longer be covered by a former employer's health insurance plan. The office needs to obtain correct insurance payer information and submit a claim accordingly. This type of denial reinforces the need to interview patients about current address, telephone number, employment, and insurance coverage each time they come to the office for treatment.

5. *Failure to obtain preauthorization:* Many health plans require patients to call a toll-free number located on the insurance card to obtain prior authorization for particular treatments. Problems can arise during an emergency situation when there is a lack of communication between provider and health plan (payer), because treatment cannot be delayed while awaiting preauthorization. Although such a claim is usually paid, payment might be less and penalties may apply because preauthorization was not obtained. If failure to obtain preauthorization was due to a medical emergency, it is possible to have penalties waived. Respond to this situation by requesting a retrospective review of a claim, and be sure to submit information explaining special circumstances that might not be evident from review of the patient's chart.

> **Example:** The patient is admitted to the labor and delivery unit for an emergency cesarean section. The patient's EOB contains a $250 penalty notice (patient's responsibility) and a reduced payment to the provider (surgeon). The remittance advice states that preauthorization for the surgical procedure (cesarean section) was not obtained. The provider appealed the claim, explaining the circumstances of the emergency surgery, and the payer waived the $250 penalty and reimbursed the provider at the regular rate.

6. *Out-of-network provider used:* The payer has denied payment because treatment was provided outside the provider network. This means that the provider is not eligible to receive payment for the services/procedures performed. Respond to this denial by writing a letter of appeal explaining why the patient sought treatment from outside the provider network (e.g., medical emergency when patient was out of town). Payment received could be reduced and penalties could also apply.

NOTE:

Failure to obtain preauthorization and *out-of-network provider used* are *not* restricted to managed care plans.

7. *Lower level of care could have been provided:* This type of denial applies when: (a) care rendered on an inpatient basis is normally provided on an outpatient basis, (b) outpatient surgery could have been performed in a provider's office, or (c) skilled nursing care could have been performed by a home health agency. Respond to this type of denial by writing a letter of appeal explaining why the higher level of care was required. Be prepared to forward copies of the patient's chart for review by the insurance payer.

8. *Incorrect codes or incorrectly linked codes reported on claim:* When the payer denies payment because an incorrect code (e.g., CPT code reported on Medicare claim instead of HCPCS Level II G code) was reported or the diagnosis and procedure/service codes are incorrectly linked on a claim, resubmit the claim with correct codes and/or correct linkage of diagnosis to procedure/service codes.

9. *Bundled service or global period service is not eligible for separate payment:* The payer will deny reimbursement when it is determined that multiple CPT or HCPCS Level II codes were reported when just one code should have been reported for a bundled service. Likewise, the payer will deny payment for claims that contain codes for services that are not eligible for separate payment because they were performed during a global period. (Bundled services and global periods are discussed further in Chapter 7 of this textbook.)

10. *Claim contained incomplete information or another insurance plan is primary:* When the payer denies payment because the claim was incomplete, resubmit the claim with complete information. When another insurance plan is primary, submit the claim to that third-party payer; when a remittance advice (RA) is received from the primary payer, submit a claim with a copy of the RA to the secondary payer.

Appeals undergo third-party payer **peer review**, which is an evaluation process performed to determine whether to reverse or uphold a claims denial. Evaluation of the appeal is performed by a medical reviewer (e.g., nurse) or a medical director (e.g., physician), and if an appeal is escalated, an independent external reviewer (e.g., physician with same specialty as provider) may assess the appeal. *Peer-to-peer review* occurs when a patient's health care provider communicates directly with a third-party payer's medical professional about reasons for which services and treatments are medically necessary. This can help prevent the need to submit an appeal letter for a denied claim.

The Medicare appeal process contains five levels. Initial appeals to Medicare administrative contractors result in a *Medicare Redetermination Notice.* Level two appeals result in a *Medicare Reconsideration Notice* for which a(n) *qualified independent contractor (QIC), qualified independent organization (QIO),* or *independent review entity (IRE)* is used as part of the appeal review process. When reconsideration decisions are not satisfactory, a hearing before an *Administrative Law Judge (ALJ)* or a review of the administrative record by an attorney *adjudicator* within the Office of Medicare Hearings and Appeals (OMHA) may be requested as a third level of appeal. If the ALJ decision is not satisfactory, or if the appeal was dismissed, review by a *Medicare Appeal Council* may be requested as a fourth level of appeal. The Medicare Appeal Council's final decision may then be appealed to federal district court as a level five appeal (if the case meets the minimum dollar amount).

Medicare's *Quality Improvement Organization (QIO) Program* is distinct from the Medicare appeals process because it is charged with inpatient quality improvement (e.g., promoting quality of care to ensure the "right care at the right time, every time") and case review (e.g., improving health and health care for Medicare beneficiaries). The QIO Program focuses on improving inpatient quality of care for people with specific health conditions and helping people who have Medicare exercise their right to high-quality inpatient health care (e.g., handling cases in which Medicare patients want to appeal a health care provider's decision to discharge them from the hospital or discontinue other types of services).

NOTE:

When a patient presents a new insurance card during a visit, edit third-party payer information in the patient's file so that claims are submitted to the appropriate payer.

Credit and Collections

Health care providers establish patient billing policies to routinely collect payments from patients that are due at the time services are delivered (e.g., copayments). Because most of a provider's fees are reimbursed by insurance plans, implementing consistent credit and collection practices is crucial to the operation of the organization.

Credit

Ideally, all payments are collected at the time the patient receives health care services. The reality is that alternate payment options are offered to patients (e.g., credit card billing, payment plans, and so on) to improve the organization's accounts receivable and reduce the need for collection practices. (*Accounts receivable* are the amounts owed to a business for services or goods provided.) If credit arrangements are available for patients, they must be consistently offered to all patients in accordance with the following federal laws:

- **Consumer Credit Protection Act of 1968** (or **Truth in Lending Act**), which requires providers to make certain written disclosures concerning all finance charges and related aspects of credit transactions (including disclosing finance charges expressed as an annual percentage rate; it required creditors to communicate the cost of borrowing money in a common language so that consumers could understand the charges, compare costs, and shop for the best credit deal).

- **Electronic Funds Transfer Act**, which establishes the rights, liabilities, and responsibilities of participants in electronic fund transfer systems. Financial institutions are required to adopt certain practices respecting such matters as transaction accounting, preauthorized transfers, and error resolution. The act also sets liability limits for losses caused by unauthorized transfers. (This law applies to financial institutions that partner with providers to process electronic funds transfers.)

- **Equal Credit Opportunity Act**, which prohibits discrimination on the basis of race, color, religion, national origin, sex, marital status, age, receipt of public assistance, or good-faith exercise of any rights under the Consumer Credit Protection Act.

- **Fair Credit and Charge Card Disclosure Act**, which amended the Truth in Lending Act and requires credit and charge card issuers to provide certain disclosures in direct mail, telephone, and other applications and solicitations for open-ended credit and charge accounts and under other circumstances (Figure 4-10). (This law applies to providers that accept credit cards.)

- **Fair Credit Billing Act**, which amended the Truth in Lending Act and requires creditors to provide prompt written acknowledgment of consumer billing complaints and investigation of billing errors.

- **Fair Credit Reporting Act**, which protects information collected by consumer reporting agencies such as credit bureaus, medical information companies, and tenant screening services. Organizations that provide information to consumer reporting agencies also have specific legal obligations, including the duty to investigate disputed information.

- **Fair Debt Collection Practices Act (FDCPA)**, which states that third-party debt collectors are prohibited from employing deceptive or abusive conduct in the collection of consumer debts incurred for personal, family, or household purposes. Such collectors may not, for example, contact debtors at odd hours, subject them to repeated telephone calls, threaten legal action that is not actually contemplated, or reveal to other persons the existence of debts.

- **Financial Services Modernization Act (FSMA)** (or **Gramm-Leach-Bliley Act**), which prohibits sharing of medical information among health insurers and other financial institutions *for use in making credit decisions*.

 NOTE:

The provider is also responsible for adhering to any state laws that affect credit and collection policies.

Forest Hills Medical Center
Forest Hills, NY 10001

TRUTH-IN-LENDING STATEMENT

Account Number _____   Date _____

Name of Patient (or Responsible Party) _____

Address _____

ANNUAL PERCENTAGE RATE (cost of your credit as a yearly rate)	FINANCE CHARGE (dollar amount credit will cost you)	AMOUNT FINANCED (amount of credit provided to you or on your behalf)	TOTAL OF PAYMENTS (amount you will have paid if you make all of the payments as scheduled)
_____ %	$ _____	$ _____	$ _____

Your payment schedule is as follows:

NUMBER OF PAYMENTS	AMOUNT OF PAYMENTS	WHEN PAYMENTS ARE DUE

Late Charge: If a payment is late, you may be charged $ _____

Repayment: If you pay off early, there will be no penalty.

Itemization of the amount financed of $ _____

$ _____ Amount given to you directly.

$ _____ Amount paid to the institution on your behalf.

I have received a copy of this statement.

_____
Signature of Patient (or Responsible Party)

FIGURE 4-10 Sample Truth-in-Lending statement.

Collections

As important as it is for a provider's employees to adhere to billing policies (e.g., verify current insurance information for each patient at the time of visit), following up on past-due accounts is crucial to the success of the business. A **past-due account** (or **delinquent account**) is one that has not been paid within a certain time frame (e.g., 120 days). Providers also track the status of **delinquent claims**, which have not been paid within a certain time frame (also about 120 days) (Table 4-1). The **delinquent claim cycle** advances through aging periods (e.g., 30 days, 60 days, 90 days, and so on), and providers typically focus internal recovery efforts on older delinquent claims (e.g., 120 days or more). As a result, many accounts in the earlier stages of the delinquency cycle are overlooked as they begin to age.

 NOTE:

Delinquent claims awaiting payer reimbursement are never outsourced. They are resolved with the payer.

The best way to deal with delinquent claims is to prevent them by:

- Verifying health plan identification cards on all patients
- Determining each patient's health care coverage (e.g., to ensure that a pre-existing condition is not submitted for reimbursement on the claim)
- Electronically submitting a *clean claim* that contains no errors
- Contacting the payer to determine that the claim was received
- Reviewing records to determine whether the claim was paid, denied, or is in **suspense** (pending) (e.g., subject to recovery of benefits paid in error on another patient's claim)
- Submitting supporting documentation requested by the payer to support the claim

TABLE 4-1 Reasons to track claims

Problem	Description
Coding errors	• **Downcoding** (assigning lower-level codes than documented in the record) • Incorrect code reported (e.g., incomplete or truncated code) • Incorrect coding system used (e.g., CPT code reported when HCPCS Level II national code should have been reported) • Medical necessity does not correspond with procedure and service codes • **Unbundling** (or **fragmentation**) (submitting multiple CPT codes when just one code should have been submitted) Note: Unbundling is associated with the National Correct Coding Initiative (NCCI) program, which is further explained in Chapter 7 of this textbook. • Unspecified diagnosis codes are reported
Delinquent payment	• Payment is overdue, based on practice policy
Denied claim	• Medical coverage cancelled • Medical coverage lapsed beyond renewal date • Medical coverage policy issues prevent payment (e.g., pre-existing condition, noncovered benefit) • No-fault, personal injury protection (PIP), automobile insurance applies • Payer determines that services were not medically necessary • Procedure performed was experimental and therefore not reimbursable • Services should have been submitted to workers' compensation payer • Services were not preauthorized, as required under the health plan • Services were provided before medical coverage was in effect
Lost claim	• Claim was not received by payer
Overpayment	• Payer may apply offsets to future provider payments to recoup funds • Payer overpays provider's fee or managed care contract rate • Provider receives payment intended for patient • Provider receives duplicate payments from multiple payers • Payment is received on a claim not submitted by the provider
Payment errors	• Patient is paid directly by the payer when the provider should have been paid • Patient cashes a **two-party check** in error (check made out to both patient and provider)
Pending claim (or suspended claim)	• Claim contains an error • Need for additional information • Review required by payer (e.g., high reimbursement, utilization management, complex procedures)
Rejected claim	• Also called *soft denials* • Claim contains a technical error (e.g., transposition of numbers; missing, incomplete, or incorrect data; duplicate charges or dates of service) • Payer instructions when submitting the claim were not followed • Resubmitted claim is returned (consider submitting a review request to payer)

 NOTE:

Payers establish time frames after which they will not process a claim, such as 180 days from the date of service. Once the claims submission date has passed, it is extremely difficult to obtain reimbursement from the payer, and *the provider is prohibited from billing the patient for payment.*

To determine whether a claim is delinquent, generate an **accounts receivable aging report** (Figure 4-11), which shows the status (by date) of outstanding claims from each payer, as well as payments due from patients. At this point, many practices **outsource** (contract out) delinquent accounts to a full-service collections agency that utilizes collection tactics, including written contacts and multiple calls from professional collectors. (Collection agencies are regulated by federal laws, such as the FDCPA, which specifies what a collection source may or may not do when pursuing payment of past-due accounts.) The collections process may involve **skip tracing** (or **skip tracking**), which is the practice of locating patients to obtain payment of a bad debt; this can involve using credit reports, databases, criminal background checks, and other methods. Agencies that collect past-due charges directly from patients can add a fee to the delinquent account balance *if the practice originally notified the patient that a fee would be added if the account was sent to an outside collection source for resolution.*

An account receivable that cannot be collected by the provider or a collection agency is called a **bad debt**, and to deduct it (write it off) the amount must have been previously included in the provider's income. Providers cannot deduct bad debts for money they expected to receive but did not (e.g., for money owed for services performed) because that amount was never included in their income.

1500 A/R Aging All

SOFTAID DEMO DATA
03/19/YYYY   16:11:34

Options
Entry Date 03/01/YYYY to 03/10/YYYY

Status Payer Code	Claim ID	Last Bill	Current	31 to 60	61 to 90	91 to 120	>120
CLAIM STATUS: PRIMARY							
AETNA OF CALIFORNIA – AETNA5						510 382-8563	
PETERS, GEORGE 58698775501	135741	03/05/YYYY	160.00	0.00	0.00	0.00	0.00
AETNA OF CALIFORNIA			160.00	0.00	0.00	0.00	0.00
HOME HEALTH AGENCY - AG						958 855-4454	
REYNOLDS, SAMUEL 56969885625	135740	03/04/YYYY	60.00	0.00	0.00	0.00	0.00
HOME HEALTH AGENCY			60.00	0.00	0.00	0.00	0.00
BLUE CROSS BLUE SHIELD OF FLOR - BCBS						305 336-3727	
LANGE, MATTHEW 12536521588	135735	03/01/YYYY	160.00	0.00	0.00	0.00	0.00
MAJORS, MARTIN 56236598541	135736	03/01/YYYY	240.00	0.00	0.00	0.00	0.00
NEVERETT, WILLIAM 56213598471	135738	03/10/YYYY	80.00	0.00	0.00	0.00	0.00
SANDERS, JOHN 56236985214	135739	03/04/YYYY	113.00	0.00	0.00	0.00	0.00
BLUE CROSS BLUE SHIELD OF FLOR			593.00	0.00	0.00	0.00	0.00
TOTAL: PRIMARY			813.00	0.00	0.00	0.00	0.00
CLAIM STATUS: SECONDARY							
MEDICAID - MCD							
TINDER, VERONICA 52623659814	135737	03/03/YYYY	1,580.00	0.00	0.00	0.00	0.00
MEDICAID			1,580.00	0.00	0.00	0.00	0.00
TOTAL: SECONDARY			1,580.00	0.00	0.00	0.00	0.00

Current	31 to 60	61 to 90	91 to 120	>120	Grand Total
2,393.000	0.00	0.00	0.00	0.00	2,393.00
100.00%	0.00%	0.00%	0.00%	0.00%	

FIGURE 4-11 Sample accounts receivable aging report.

NOTE:

Litigation (legal action) to recover a debt is usually a last resort for a medical practice. If legal action is taken, it usually occurs in small claims court where individuals can sue for money only without a lawyer. (Each state establishes limits for small claims, ranging from $2,000 to $25,000.)

Example: An insurance company mails a check in the amount of $350 to the patient because the physician who treated the patient is a nonparticipating provider (nonPAR) for that health plan. The check is reimbursement for CRNA anesthesia services provided to the patient during outpatient surgery. The patient cashes the check and spends it on a weekend vacation. When the patient receives the bill for CRNA anesthesia services, the money received from the insurance company is no longer available to pay it. That account becomes delinquent and is outsourced to a collection agency, which attempts to collect the payment. The collection agency is unable to obtain payment from the patient, and the amount is considered a bad debt for the provider's practice.

NOTE:

The *largest* past-due charges from the aging report are sent to collections first, followed by past-due charges in descending order. In Figure 4-11, the collections order would be MCD, BCBS, AG, and AETNA.

Ten Steps to an Effective Collection Process

Steps	Effective Collection Processes
Step 1	Call the patient within one week after providing services to determine patient satisfaction, and mention that an invoice for the outstanding balance is payable upon receipt.
Step 2	Mail a duplicate invoice ten days after the due date with "past due" stamped on it to alert the patient that the due date has passed.
Step 3	Mail a reminder letter with a duplicate invoice as the second overdue notice to remind the patient that the account needs attention.
Step 4	Make the first collection call, determine the reason for nonpayment, and obtain a promise to pay.
Step 5	Mail the first collection letter to the patient.
Step 6	Make the second collection call to the patient to request full payment, and obtain a promise to pay.
Step 7	Mail the second collection letter.
Step 8	Make the third collection phone call, and explain that the account will be submitted to a collection agency if payment is not made.
Step 9	Mail the final collection letter, and state that the account is being turned over to a collection agency.
Step 10	Submit the account to a collection agency.

State Insurance Regulators

Insurance is regulated by the individual states, not the federal government. State regulatory functions include registering insurance companies, overseeing compliance and penalty provisions of the state insurance code, supervising insurance company formation within the state, and monitoring the reinsurance market. State regulators ascertain that all authorized insurance companies meet and maintain financial, legal, and other requirements for doing business in the state. Regulators also license a number of insurance-related professionals, including agents, brokers, and adjusters.

If the practice has a complaint about an insurance claim, contact the state insurance regulatory agency (e.g., state insurance commission) for resolution. Although the commissioner will usually review a health care policy to determine whether the claims denial was based on legal provisions, the commissioner does not have legal authority to require a payer to reimburse a specific claim.

Example: State insurance regulators establish standards and best practices, conduct peer review, and coordinate regulatory oversight. As a result, they are monitoring the Anthem BlueCross BlueShield cyber security breach (unauthorized access to personal information) of more than 91 million policyholders, which was reported in January 2015. Data accessed illegally included consumer names, addresses, birth dates, email addresses, employment information, identification numbers, income data, birth dates, Social Security numbers, and telephone numbers.

Anthem notified the Federal Bureau of Investigation of the breach and is working with a cyber security firm to evaluate the extent of the attack. Consumers were informed about the security breaches and provided with free credit monitoring and identity theft protection services. They were told they should monitor their personal financial information, and report any fraudulent activity immediately. Consumers were also encouraged to place security freezes on their credit reports (and those of family members affected by the breaches) with the three major credit reporting agencies, Equifax, Experian, and TransUnion; this restricts access to credit reports, making it difficult for identity thieves to open new accounts in their names.

From a health insurance perspective, consumers were instructed to carefully review explanation of benefits (EOB) documents received from third-party payers and government programs. If charges for health care services not received are reported on EOB documents, consumers should contact their third-party payer or government program.

Improper Payments Information Act (IPIA) of 2002

IPIA legislated the Comprehensive Error Rate Testing (CERT) program, which was implemented in 2003 to assess and measure improper payments in the Medicare fee-for-service program. CERT produces a national *paid claims error rate*, which is used to target improvement efforts.

Summary

The cycle of a claim includes four stages: claims submission and electronic data interchange (EDI), claims processing, claims adjudication, and payment. Remittance advice reconciliation is an essential medical practice function that allows providers to determine the status of outstanding claims. Insurance claims processing problems arise as the result of a variety of issues including coding errors, delinquent claims, denied claims, lost claims, overpayment, payment errors, pending (suspense) claims, and rejected claims.

Internet Links

Cigna: Go to *cigna.com*, hover over the Health Care Providers menu item, click on Coverage and Claims, and click on the Coverage and Claims Overview link to learn more about related topics, such as prior authorizations, claims, and appeals and disputes.

EDI Basics: Go to *edibasics.com* to learn more about electronic data interchange (EDI).

Electronic Billing & EDI Transactions: Go to *cms.gov*, click on Medicare, scroll to the Billing heading, and click on the Electronic Billing & EDI Transactions link.

HIPAA-Related Code Lists: Go to *wpc-edi.com* and click on the "X12.org/Codes" link below the Code Lists section to view health care EDI code lists (e.g., claim adjustment reason codes), which contain narrative descriptions that assist in interpreting claims status data and information on a remittance advice.

Medicare Remit Easy Print (MREP) software: Go to *cms.gov*; click on the Research, Statistics, Data and Systems link; click on the Access to CMS Data & Application link; and click on the Medicare Remit Easy Print (MREP) link to learn how to download the free (to Medicare providers and suppliers) software that is used to access and print remittance advice information, including special reports.

National Association of Insurance Commissioners: Go to *www.naic.org*, click on the Map link, and click on your state to explore how insurance regulators protect consumer rights and ensure the financial solvency of insurers.

National Uniform Billing Committee (NUBC): Go to **www.nubc.org** to learn more about the implementation of the UB-04.

National Uniform Claim Committee (NUCC): Go to **www.nucc.org** to learn more about the implementation of the CMS-1500.

Review

4.1 – Multiple Choice

Select the most appropriate response.

1. The electronic or manual transmission of claims data to payers or clearinghouses is called claims
   a. adjudication.
   b. attachment.
   c. processing.
   d. submission.

2. A series of fixed-length records submitted to payers to bill for health care services is an electronic
   a. flat file format.
   b. funds transfer.
   c. remittance advice.
   d. source document.

3. Which is considered a covered entity?
   a. Organizations that accredit clearinghouses
   b. Private-sector payers that process electronic claims
   c. Providers that submit paper-based CMS-1500 claims
   d. Small self-administered health plans that processes manual claims

4. A claim that is rejected because of an error or omission is considered a(n)
   a. clean claim.
   b. closed claim.
   c. delinquent claim.
   d. open claim.

5. Which supporting documentation is associated with submission of an insurance claim?
   a. Accounts receivable aging report
   b. Claims attachment
   c. Common data file
   d. Electronic remittance advice

6. The sorting of claims upon submission to collect and verify information about the patient and provider is called claims
   a. adjudication.
   b. preauthorization.
   c. processing.
   d. submission.

7. Which of the following steps would occur first during the insurance claim cycle?
   a. The clearinghouse converts electronic claims into electronic flat file format.
   b. The clearinghouse verifies claims data and transmits to payers.
   c. The health insurance specialist batches claims and submits to clearinghouse.
   d. The medical practice management software generates electronic claims.

8. Comparing the claim to payer edits and the patient's health plan benefits is part of claims
   a. adjudication.
   b. processing.
   c. submission.
   d. transmission.

9. Which describes any procedure or service reported on a claim that is not included on the payer's master benefit list?
   a. Medically unnecessary
   b. Noncovered benefit
   c. Pre-existing condition
   d. Unauthorized service

10. Which is a summary abstract report of all recent claims filed on each patient, which is used by the payer to determine whether the patient is receiving concurrent care for the same condition by more than one provider?
   a. Common data file
   b. Encounter form
   c. Patient ledger
   d. Remittance advice

11. Which is the fixed amount patients pay each time they receive health care services?
   a. Coinsurance
   b. Copayment
   c. Deductible
   d. Insurance

12. Which of the following steps would occur first?
   a. The clearinghouse transmits claims data to payers.
   b. The payer approves claim for payment.
   c. The payer generates remittance advice.
   d. The payer performs claims validation.

13. Refer to Figure 4-11 in this chapter. Which payer's claim should be followed up first to obtain reimbursement?
   a. Aetna of California
   b. BlueCross BlueShield of Florida
   c. Home Health Agency
   d. Medicaid

14. Which requires providers to make certain written disclosures concerning all finance charges and related aspects of credit transactions?
   a. Equal Credit Opportunity Act
   b. Fair Credit Reporting Act
   c. Fair Debt Collection Practices Act
   d. Truth in Lending Act

15. Which protects information collected by consumer reporting agencies?
   a. Equal Credit Opportunity Act
   b. Fair Credit Reporting Act
   c. Fair Debt Collection Practices Act
   d. Truth in Lending Act

16. Which is the best way to prevent delinquent claims?
   a. Attach supporting medical documentation on all claims.
   b. Enter all claims data in the practice's suspense file.
   c. Submit closed claims to all third-party payers.
   d. Verify health plan identification information on all patients.

17. Which is a characteristic of delinquent commercial claims awaiting payer reimbursement?
    a. Delinquent claims are outsourced to a collection agency.
    b. The delinquent claims are resolved directly with the payer.
    c. The accounts receivable aging report was not submitted.
    d. The provided remittance advice was delayed by the payer.

18. Providers can also use software to convert claims to electronic media claims, which contain a series of _____ records submitted to payers as a bill for health care services.
    a. adaptable-length
    b. fixed-length
    c. movable-length
    d. variable-length

19. Any procedure or service that is not medically necessary is denied, and claims are also checked against the payer's abstract of all recent claims filed on each patient, which is called a(n)
    a. classification system.
    b. common data file.
    c. data abstracting system.
    d. electronic health record.

20. An electronic remittance advice (ERA) is submitted to the
    a. patient.
    b. payer.
    c. plan.
    d. provider.

4.2 – Interpreting an Explanation of Benefits

Refer to Figure 4-8 to answer each of the questions below.

_____ 1. What is the patient's identification number?

_____ 2. What is the patient's copayment amount?

_____ 3. What amount did the payer pay to the provider?

_____ 4. Is the provider a network provider?

_____ 5. What amount was billed for the patient's encounter?

4.3 – Interpreting a Remittance Advice

Review the remittance advice below, and locate payment denial reason codes for each patient along with their meanings. (Payment "Reason Code[s]" are listed for each patient, and the legend at the bottom of the remittance advice provides the meaning of each code.)

_____ 1. RHIANNON MEDINA: Could the patient be billed for the service provided as a result of the reason code listed on the remittance advice? (Yes or No)

_____ 2. CHANTEL ADDAI: Reason code 001 indicates "Patient receives discount—care received from in-network provider." Should the patient be billed the $11 adjustment amount? (Yes or No)

_____ 3. KWADZO MENSAH: Which reason code listed for this patient indicates "Denied—invalid HICN number?"

_____ 4. KWADZO MENSAH: Reason code 003 indicates "Denied—termination of coverage." What amount should the patient be billed as a result of this denied claim?

_____ 5. CHYOU WONG: What is the reason code for "Denied—service not medically necessary."

US HEALTH
100 MAIN STREET
ALFRED NY 14802

Remittance Advice

DATE: 05/25/YYYY
(800) 555-1234
FAX: (800) 555-4321

ERIN A HELPER MD
101 MEDIC DRIVE
ANYWHERE NY 12345

PAGE#: 1 OF 1

PROVIDER#: 98979697
CHECK#: 1121314

PATIENT: MEDINA, RHIANNON   **POLICY#:** DOVER123456-01
                                   HICN: 1231199091

Service Date	POS	CPT	Billed	Allowed	Copay/Coins	ASG	Paid	Adjustment	Reason Code(s)
0416YYYY	11	99212	45.00	34.00	0.00	Y	34.00	11.00	004
Totals:			45.00	34.00	0.00		34.00	11.00	NET: 34.00

PATIENT: ADDAI, CHANTEL   **POLICY#:** SHOWER778899-01
                                   HICN: 1234587702

Service Date	POS	CPT	Billed	Allowed	Copay/Coins	ASG	Paid	Adjustment	Reason Code(s)
0409YYYY	11	99211	40.00	35.00	10.00	Y	25.00	5.00	001
0409YYYY	11	81003	12.00	0.00	0.00	Y	0.00	12.00	005
Totals:			52.00	35.00	10.00		25.00	17.00	NET: 25.00

PATIENT: MENSAH, KWADZO   **POLICY#:** LOTT556633-01
                                   HICN: 5758594631

Service Date	POS	CPT	Billed	Allowed	Copay/Coins	ASG	Paid	Adjustment	Reason Code(s)
0407YYYY	11	99213	60.00	0.00	0.00	Y	0.00	0.00	002, 003
Totals:			60.00	0.00	0.00		0.00	0.00	NET: 0.00

PATIENT: WONG, CHYOU   **POLICY#:** PAYNE223344-01
                                   HICN: 4263355970

Service Date	POS	CPT	Billed	Allowed	Copay/Coins	ASG	Paid	Adjustment	Reason Code(s)
0429YYYY	11	74270	118.00	0.00	0.00	Y	0.00	0.00	005
Totals:			118.00	0.00	0.00		0.00	0.00	NET: 0.00

LEGEND

ASG   Accept assignment
                 Y = Provider accepts assignment
                 N = Provider does not accept assignment
Copay/Coins Copayment or coinsurance amount paid by patient
CPT   Current Procedural Terminology (CPT code number)
POS   Place of Service
             11 = Provider's office
Reason Codes

001 Patient receives discount—care received from in-network provider
002 Denied—invalid policy number
003 Denied—termination of coverage
004 Denied—procedure or service not covered
005 Denied—service not medically necessary
006 Covered service—no charge

4.4 – Writing an Appeal Letter

Refer to the remittance advice in Figure 4-7 and the sample appeal letter in Figure 4-9 to prepare a letter of appeal based on the case scenario.

Case Scenario: Upon review of the remittance advice in Figure 4-7, identify the reimbursement amount denied by the third-party payer and the reason for the denial. Then, using the sample appeal letter in Figure 4-9, prepare a letter of appeal requesting that the payer review the denied claims for reconsideration. Be sure to indicate in the letter of appeal exactly why the payer should reconsider the claim to provide additional reimbursement. In this case, the reason for reconsideration of the claim is that an "incorrect ICD-10-CM (J45.909) was reported for *asthma* instead of the code for *acute exacerbation of mild intermittent asthma* (J45.21); code J45.21 meets medical necessity for CPT service code 99215 (Level 5 office visit). In addition, CPT modifier -25 should have been added to CPT code 99215 to indicate the provision of an *unrelated evaluation and management service by the same physician or other qualified health care professional during a post-operative period.*"

Chapter 5

Legal Aspects of Health Insurance and Reimbursement

Chapter Outline

Overview of Laws and Regulations

Federal Laws and Events That Affect
   Health Care

Retention of Records

Health Care Audit and Compliance
   Programs

Health Insurance Portability and
   Accountability Act (HIPAA)

Chapter Objectives

Upon successful completion of this chapter, you should be able to:

1. Define key terms related to legal aspects of health insurance and reimbursement.
2. Identify sources of laws and regulations related to health care reimbursement.
3. Summarize federal legislation and regulations affecting health care.
4. Explain how record retention is determined.
5. Describe health care audit and compliance programs.
6. Explain the provisions of HIPAA legislation.

Key Terms

21st Century Cures Act

abuse

accounting of
   disclosures

ANSI ASC X12N 837

audit

authorization

black box edit

breach notification

breach of
   confidentiality

case law

civil law

Clinical Data Abstracting
   Center (CDAC)

Clinical Laboratory
   Improvement Act
   (CLIA)

CMS Internet-only
   manual (IOM)

CMS Online Manual
   System

CMS transmittal

common law

compliance program

Comprehensive Error
   Rate Testing (CERT)
   program

Conditions for Coverage
   (CfC)

Conditions of
   Participation (CoP)

confidentiality

criminal law

Cures Act

*Current Dental
   Terminology (CDT)*

decrypt

deeming

Deficit Reduction
   Act of 2005

de-identification of
   protected health
   information

deposition

designated record set

digital

eHealth Exchange

electronic Clinical
   Quality Measure
   (eCQM)

Electronic Submission of Medical Documentation System (esMD)

electronic transaction standards

encrypt

False Claims Act (FCA)

Federal Claims Collection Act (FCCA)

Federal Register

First-look Analysis for Hospital Outlier Monitoring (FATHOM)

fraud

Health Care Fraud Prevention and Enforcement Action Team (HEAT)

Health Insurance Portability and Accountability Act (HIPAA)

HIPAA Privacy Rule

HIPAA Security Rule

Hospital Inpatient Quality Reporting (Hospital IQR) program

Hospital Outpatient Quality Reporting Program (Hospital OQR)

Hospital Payment Monitoring Program (HPMP)

hospital value-based purchasing (VBP) program

Improper Payments Information Act of 2002 (IPIA)

Investing in Innovations (i2) Initiative

interrogatory

listserv

Medicaid Fraud Control Unit (MFCU)

Medicaid integrity contractor (MIC)

Medicaid Integrity Program (MIP)

medical identity theft

medical review (MR)

Medicare administrative contractor (MAC)

Medicare Drug Integrity Contractors (MEDIC) Program

Medicare Integrity Program (MIP)

Medicare Shared Savings Program

message digest

minimum necessary standard

National Drug Code (NDC)

National Individual Identifier

National Plan and Provider Enumeration System (NPPES)

National Practitioner Data Bank (NPDB)

National Provider Identifier (NPI)

National Standard Employer Identification Number (EIN)

National Standard Format (NSF)

Notice of Privacy Practices (NPP)

overpayment

Part A/B Medicare administrative contractor (A/B MAC)

Patient Safety and Quality Improvement Act

Payment Error Prevention Program (PEPP)

payment error rate

Payment Error Rate Measurement (PERM) program

physician self-referral law

Physicians at Teaching Hospitals (PATH)

precedent

privacy

Privacy Act of 1974

privileged communication

Program for Evaluating Payment Patterns Electronic Report (PEPPER)

protected health information (PHI)

qui tam

record retention

Recovery Audit Contractor (RAC) program

regulation

regulatory law

release of information (ROI)

release of information log

rural health information organization (RHIO)

security

Stark I

statutes

statutory law

subpoena

subpoena *duces tecum*

Tax Relief and Health Care Act of 2006 (TRHCA)

treatment, payment, and health care operations (TPO)

UB-04 flat file

unique bit string

United States Core Data for Interoperability (USCDI)

upcoding

whistleblower

Zone Program Integrity Contractor (ZPIC)

Introduction

The health insurance specialist must be knowledgeable about laws and regulations for maintaining patient records and processing health insurance claims. This chapter defines legal and regulatory terminology and summarizes laws and regulations that affect health insurance processing. Internet links are also included as a resource for remaining up-to-date and obtaining clarification of legal and regulatory issues.

Overview of Laws and Regulations

Federal and state **statutes** (or **statutory law**) are laws passed by legislative bodies (e.g., federal Congress and state legislatures). These laws are then implemented as **regulations** (or **regulatory law**), which are mandated guidelines written by administrative agencies (e.g., CMS). A *mandate* is an official directive, instruction, or order to take or perform a certain action, such as a federal regulation. Mandates are also authoritative commands, such as by courts, governors, and legislatures. **Case law** (or **common law**) is based on court decisions that establish a **precedent**, which is based on a court decision that is legally binding and follows the doctrine of *stare decisis* for deciding subsequent cases involving identical or similar facts. *Stare decisis* is Latin for "the thing speaks for itself," which means it requires courts to apply precedent law in the same manner to cases with the same facts. Thus, a precedent serves as "the standard" for similar cases.

> **Example:** When originally passed, New York State Public Health Law (PHL) sections 17 and 18 allowed a *reasonable charge* to be imposed for copies of patient records. Health care facilities, therefore, charged fees for locating the patient's record and making copies. These fees were later challenged in court, and reasonable charge language in the PHL was interpreted in *Hernandez v. Lutheran Medical Center* (1984), *Ventura v. Long Island Jewish Hillside Medical Center* (1985), and *Cohen v. South Nassau Communities Hospital* (1987). The original interpretation permitted charges of $1.00 to $1.50 per page, plus a search and retrieval fee of $15. However, sections 17 and 18 of the PHL were amended in 1991 when the phrase, the reasonable fee for paper copies shall not exceed seventy-five cents per page was added to the law.

Federal laws and regulations affect health care in that they govern programs such as Medicare, Medicaid, TRICARE, and the Federal Employees Health Benefit Plans (FEHBP). State laws regulate insurance companies, recordkeeping practices, and provider licensing. State insurance departments determine coverage issues for insurance policies (contracts) and state workers' compensation plans.

Civil law deals with all areas of the law that are not classified as criminal law. **Criminal law** is public law (statute or ordinance) that defines crimes and their prosecution. A **subpoena** is an order of the court that requires a witness to appear at a particular time and place to testify. A **subpoena** *duces tecum* requires documents (e.g., patient record) to be produced. A subpoena is used to obtain witness testimony at trial and at **deposition**, which is testimony under oath taken outside of court (e.g., at the provider's office). In civil cases (e.g., malpractice), the provider might be required to complete an **interrogatory**, which is a document containing a list of questions that must be answered in writing.

Qui tam is an abbreviation for the Latin phrase *qui tam pro domino rege quam pro sic ipso in hoc parte sequitur*, meaning "who as well for the king as for himself sues in this matter." It is a provision of the Federal False Claims Act, which allows a private citizen to file a lawsuit in the name of the U.S. government, charge government contractors and other entities that receive or use government funds with fraud, and share in any money recovered. Common defendants in *qui tam* actions involving Medicare/Medicaid fraud include physicians, hospitals, HMOs, and clinics.

To accurately process health insurance claims, especially for government programs like Medicare and Medicaid, you should become familiar with the *Code of Federal Regulations* (Figure 5-1). Providers and health insurance specialists can locate legal and regulatory issues found in such publications as the *Federal Register* and *Medicare Bulletin*. The **Federal Register** (Figure 5-2) is a legal newspaper published every business day by the National Archives and Records Administration (NARA). It is available in paper form, on microfiche, and online.

> **Example 1:** Federal Statute, Implemented as State Program
>
> Congress passed Title XXI of the Social Security Act as part of the Balanced Budget Act of 1997, which called for implementation of the State Children's Health Insurance Program. In response, New York implemented Child Health Plus, which expanded insurance eligibility to children under age 19 who are not eligible for Medicaid and have limited or no health insurance. Even if family income is high, children can be eligible to enroll in Child Health Plus; an insurance premium in the form of a monthly family contribution may be required (e.g., a family of two with an income ranging from $24,977 to $25,920 pays $15 per month per child).

Title 42—Public Health

CHAPTER IV—CENTERS FOR MEDICARE & MEDICAID SERVICES, DEPARTMENT OF HEALTH AND HUMAN SERVICES (Parts 400 – 498)

TOC – Table Of Contents

Subchapter A – GENERAL PROVISIONS (Parts 400 – 403)

Subchapter B – MEDICARE PROGRAM (Parts 405 – 424)

Subchapter C – MEDICAL ASSISTANCE PROGRAMS (Parts 430 – 456)

Subchapter D – STATE CHILDREN'S HEALTH INSURANCE PROGRAMS (SCHIPs) (Part 457)

Subchapter E – PROGRAMS OF ALL-INCLUSIVE CARE FOR THE ELDERLY (PACE) (Part 460)

Subchapter F – QUALITY IMPROVEMENT ORGANIZATIONS (Parts 475 – 480)

Subchapter G – STANDARDS AND CERTIFICATION (Parts 482 – 498)

FIGURE 5-1 Portion of table of contents from *Code of Federal Regulations*, Title 42, Public Health, Chapter IV, Centers for Medicare & Medicaid Services.

Example 2: Federal Statute, Implemented as a Federal Regulation, and Published in the *Federal Register*

Congress passed the Balanced Budget Refinement Act of 1999 (Public Law No. 106-113), which called for a number of revisions to Medicare, Medicaid, and the State Children's Health Insurance Program. On May 5, 2000, the Department of Health and Human Services published a proposed rule in the *Federal Register* to revise the Medicare hospital inpatient prospective payment system for operating costs. This proposed rule was titled Medicare Program; Changes to the Hospital Inpatient Prospective Payment Systems and Fiscal Year 2001 Rates; Proposed Rule. The purpose of publishing the proposed rule is to allow for comments from health care providers. Once the comment period has ended, the final rule is published in the *Federal Register*.

CMS transmittals (Figure 5-3) contain new and changed Medicare policies and procedures that are to be incorporated into a specific CMS program manual (e.g., *Medicare Claims Processing Manual*). The cover page of a transmittal summarizes new and changed material, and subsequent pages provide details. The *CMS quarterly provider update (QPU)* includes regulations and major policies that have been implemented or canceled and new/ revised Internet-only Manual (IOM) instructions. The **CMS Internet-only manual (IOM)** (or **CMS Online Manual System**) replaced paper-based manuals (except for the *Provider Reimbursement Manual* and the *State Medicaid Manual*); includes program issuances, day-to-day operating instructions, policies, and procedures that are based on statutes, regulations, guidelines, models, and directives; and is used by CMS program components, providers, contractors, Medicare Advantage organizations, and state survey agencies to administer CMS programs. The transmittals are sent to each **Medicare administrative contractor (MAC)** (or **Part A/B Medicare administrative contractor**, **[A/B MAC]**), which is an organization (e.g., insurance company) that contracts with CMS to process fee-for-service health care claims and perform program integrity tasks for both Medicare Part A and Part B. MACs also process home health and hospice claims (HHH MACs) and durable medical equipment, prosthetics, orthotics, and supplies claims (DMEPOS MACs). (DMEPOS MACs are covered in Chapter 8 of this textbook.) Each contractor makes program coverage decisions and publishes a newsletter, which is sent to providers who receive Medicare reimbursement.

20972   **Federal Register**/ Vol. 83, No. 89 / Tuesday, May 8, 2018 / Proposed Rules

DEPARTMENT OF HEALTH AND HUMAN SERVICES

Centers for Medicare & Medicaid Services

42 CFR Part 412

[CMS–1688–P]

RIN 0938–AT25

Medicare Program; Inpatient Rehabilitation Facility Prospective Payment System for Federal Fiscal Year 2019

AGENCY: Centers for Medicare & Medicaid Services (CMS), HHS.
ACTION: Proposed rule.

SUMMARY: This proposed rule would update the prospective payment rates for inpatient rehabilitation facilities (IRFs) for federal fiscal year (FY) 2019. As required by the Social Security Act (the Act), this proposed rule includes the classification and weighting factors for the IRF prospective payment system's (PPS) case-mix groups and a description of the methodologies and data used in computing the prospective payment rates for FY 2019. We are also proposing to alleviate administrative burden for IRFs by removing the Functional Independence Measure (FIM™) instrument and associated Function Modifiers from the IRF Patient Assessment Instrument (IRF–PAI) and revising certain IRF coverage requirements to reduce the amount of required paperwork in the IRF setting. In addition, we are soliciting comments on removing the face-to-face requirement for rehabilitation physician visits and expanding the use of nonphysician practitioners (that is, nurse practitioners and physician assistants) in meeting the IRF coverage requirements. For the IRF Quality Reporting Program (QRP), we are proposing to adopt a new measure removal factor, remove two measures from the IRF QRP measure set, and codify in our regulations a number of requirements.

DATES: To be assured consideration, comments must be received at one of the addresses provided below, not later than 5 p.m. on June 26, 2018.

ADDRESSES: In commenting, please refer to file code CMS–1688–P. Because of staff and resource limitations, we cannot accept comments by facsimile (FAX) transmission.
Comments, including mass comment submissions, must be submitted in one of the following three ways (please choose only one of the ways listed):

1. *Electronically.* You may submit electronic comments on this regulation to *http://www.regulations.gov.* Follow the "Submit a comment" instructions.
2. By regular mail. You may mail written comments to the following address ONLY: Centers for Medicare & Medicaid Services, Department of Health and Human Services, Attention: CMS–1688–P, P.O. Box 8016, Baltimore, MD 21244–8016.
Please allow sufficient time for mailed comments to be received before the close of the comment period.
3. *By express or overnight mail.* You may send written comments to the following address ONLY: Centers for Medicare & Medicaid Services, Department of Health and Human Services, Attention: CMS–1688–P, Mail Stop C4–26–05, 7500 Security Boulevard, Baltimore, MD 21244–1850.
For information on viewing public comments, see the beginning of the

SUPPLEMENTARY INFORMATION section.
FOR FURTHER INFORMATION CONTACT:
Gwendolyn Johnson, (410) 786–6954, for general information.
Catie Kraemer, (410) 786–0179, for information about the proposed payment policies and payment rates.
Kadie Derby, (410) 786–0468, for information about the IRF coverage policies.
Christine Grose, (410) 786–1362, for information about the quality reporting program.

SUPPLEMENTARY INFORMATION:
Inspection of Public Comments: All comments received before the close of the comment period are available for viewing by the public, including any personally identifiable or confidential business information that is included in a comment. We post all comments received before the close of the comment period as soon as possible after they have been received at *http:// www.regulations.gov.* Follow the search instructions on that website to view public comments.
The IRF PPS Addenda along with other supporting documents and tables referenced in this proposed rule are available through the internet on the CMS website at *http:// www.cms.hhs.gov/Medicare/Medicare-Fee-for-Service-Payment/Inpatient RehabFacPPS/.*
To assist readers in referencing sections contained in this document, we are providing the following Table of Contents.
Table of Contents
Executive Summary
    A. Purpose
    B. Summary of Major Provisions
    C. Summary of Impacts

    D. Improving Patient Outcomes and Reducing Burden Through Meaningful Measures
I. Background
    A. Historical Overview of the IRF PPS
    B. Provisions of the PPACA Affecting the IRF PPS in FY 2012 and Beyond
    C. Operational Overview of the Current IRF PPS
    D. Advancing Health Information Exchange
II. Summary of Provisions of the Proposed Rule
III. Proposed Update to the Case-Mix Group (CMG) Relative Weights and Average Length of Stay Values for FY 2019
IV. Facility-Level Adjustment Factors
V. Proposed FY 2019 IRF PPS Payment Update
    A. Background
    B. Proposed FY 2019 Market Basket Update and Productivity Adjustment
    C. Proposed Labor-Related Share for FY 2019
    D. Proposed Wage Adjustment for FY 2019
    E. Description of the Proposed IRF Standard Payment Conversion Factor and Payment Rates for FY 2019
    F. Example of the Methodology for Adjusting the Proposed Prospective Payment Rates
VI. Proposed Update to Payments for High-Cost Outliers Under the IRF PPS for FY 2019
    A. Proposed Update to the Outlier Threshold Amount for FY 2019
    B. Proposed Update to the IRF Cost-to-Charge Ratio Ceiling and Urban/Rural Averages for FY 2019
VII. Proposed Removal of the FIM™ Instrument and Associated Function Modifiers From the IRF–PAI Beginning With FY 2020 and Proposed Refinements to the Case-Mix Classification System Beginning With FY 2020
    A. Proposed Removal of the FIM™ Instrument and Associated Function Modifiers From the IRF–PAI Beginning With FY 2020
    B. Proposed Refinements to the Case-Mix Classification System Beginning With FY 2020
VIII. Proposed Revisions to Certain IRF Coverage Requirements Beginning With FY 2019
    A. Proposed Changes to the Physician Supervision Requirement Beginning With FY 2019
    B. Proposed Changes to the Interdisciplinary Team Meeting Requirement Beginning With FY 2019
    C. Proposed Changes to the Admission Order Documentation Requirement Beginning With FY 2019
    D. Solicitation of Comments Regarding Additional Changes to the Physician Supervision Requirement
    E. Solicitation of Comments Regarding Changes to the Use of Non-Physician Practitioners in Meeting the Requirements Under § 412.622(a)(3), (4), and (5)
IX. Proposed Revisions and Updates to the IRF Quality Reporting Program (QRP)
    A. Background
    B. General Considerations Used for Selection of Measures for the IRF QRP

FIGURE 5-2 Sample page from the *Federal Register*.

CMS Manual System

Pub. 100-08 Program Integrity Manual

Department of Health & Human Services (DHHS)
Centers for Medicare & Medicaid Services (CMS)

Transmittal 91	Date: DECEMBER 10, YYYY

CHANGE REQUEST 3560

SUBJECT: Revision of Program Integrity Manual (PIM), Section 3.11.1.4

I. SUMMARY OF CHANGES: Revising the PIM to correct inconsistencies with section 3.4.1.2.

NEW/REVISED MATERIAL – EFFECTIVE DATE*: January 1, YYYY
IMPLEMENTATION DATE: January 3, YYYY

MANUALIZATION/CLARIFICATION – EFFECTIVE/IMPLEMENTATION DATES: Not Applicable.

Disclaimer for manual changes only: The revision date and transmittal number apply to the red italicized material only. Any other material was previously published and remains unchanged. However, if this revision contains a table of contents, you will receive the new/revised information only, and not the entire table of contents.

II. CHANGES IN MANUAL INSTRUCTIONS:
(R = REVISED, N = NEW, D = DELETED)

R/N/D	CHAPTER/SECTION/SUBSECTION/TITLE
R	3/11.1.4/Requesting Additional Documentation

III. FUNDING: Medicare contractors shall implement these instructions within their current operating budgets.

IV. ATTACHMENTS:

X	Business Requirements
X	Manual Instruction
	Confidential Requirements
	One-Time Notification
	Recurring Update Notification

*Unless otherwise specified, the effective date is the date of service.

FIGURE 5-3 Sample Medicare program transmittal.

 NOTE:

In 2010, all 17 *carriers* (processed Medicare Part B claims) and all 23 *fiscal intermediaries (FI)* (processed Medicare Part A claims) were eliminated to create 16 Medicare administrative contractors (MACs). *Durable Medical Equipment Carriers (DMERCs)* that process durable medical equipment, prosthetics, orthotics, and supplies (DMEPOS) have been replaced with DME MACs. Home health and hospice claims are processed by HH&H MACs. New jurisdictions were created for administration by MACs, which consolidate the administration of Medicare Parts A and B benefits so that Medicare beneficiaries have claims processed by one contractor.

Membership in professional associations can also prove helpful in accessing up-to-date information about the health insurance industry (refer to Chapter 1 for information on joining professional associations). Newsletters and journals published by professional associations routinely include articles that clarify implementation of new legal and regulatory mandates. They also provide resources for obtaining the most up-to-date information about such issues. Another way to remain current is to subscribe to a **listserv**, a subscriber-based question-and-answer forum available through email.

The Centers for Medicare and Medicaid Services (CMS) publishes **Conditions of Participation (CoP)** and **Conditions for Coverage (CfC)**, which are requirements that health care organizations must meet in order to begin and continue participating in the Medicare and Medicaid programs. (Medicare and Medicaid participation allows health care organizations to be reimbursed for procedures and services provided to patients.) These health and safety regulations are the foundation for improving quality of patient care and protecting the health and safety of patients. CMS also ensures that accreditation organization standards (e.g., The Joint Commission) are recognized by CMS through a process called **deeming**, which requires that standards meet or exceed CoP and CfC requirements.

Conditions of Participation are met by the following:

- Clinics, rehabilitation agencies, and public health agencies as providers of outpatient physical therapy and speech-language pathology services
- Community mental health centers (CMHCs)
- Comprehensive outpatient rehabilitation facilities (CORFs)
- Critical access hospitals (CAHs)
- Home health agencies
- Hospices
- Hospital swing beds
- Hospitals
- Intermediate care facilities for individuals with intellectual disabilities (ICF/IID)
- Programs for All-inclusive Care for the Elderly organizations (PACE)
- Psychiatric hospitals
- Religious nonmedical health care institutions
- Transplant centers

Conditions for Coverage are met by the following:

- Ambulatory surgical centers (ASCs)
- End-stage renal disease facilities
- Federally qualified health centers
- Long-term care facilities
- Occupational therapists in independent practice
- Organ procurement organizations (OPOs)
- Portable x-ray suppliers
- Rural health clinics

Federal Laws and Events That Affect Health Care

The health care industry is heavily regulated by federal and state legislation (Figure 5-4). Table 5-1 summarizes major federal laws and events that affect health care. (Because state laws vary, it is recommended that they be researched individually.)

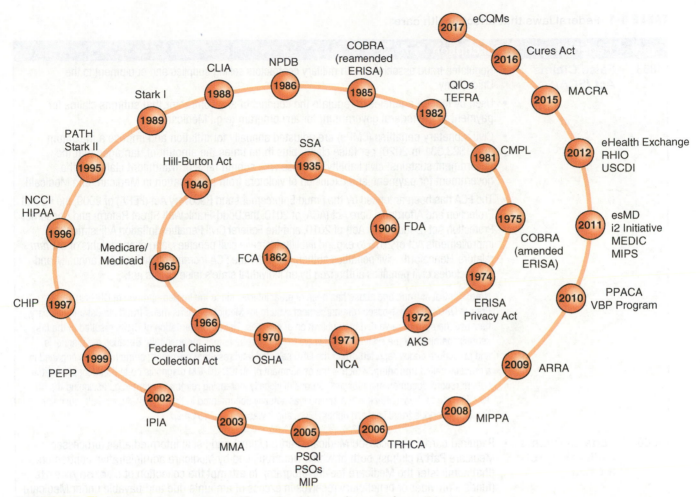

FIGURE 5-4 Timeline of dates and significant health care laws and events.

Example: When the President of the United States declares a disaster or emergency under the Stafford Act or the National Emergencies Act, and the HHS Secretary declares a public health emergency under Section 319 of the Social Security Act, the Secretary is authorized to implement waivers under section 1135 of the Social Security Act (called *1135 waivers*), such as temporarily waiving or modifying certain Medicare, Medicaid, and Children's Health Insurance Program (CHIP) requirements. The purpose is to ensure that sufficient health care items and services are available to meet the needs of individuals enrolled in Social Security Act programs in the emergency area and time periods and so that providers are reimbursed and exempted from sanctions (absent any determination of fraud or abuse) for services provided in good faith.

Examples of these *1135 waivers* or modifications include: conditions of participation or other certification requirements, program participation and similar requirements, preapproval requirements, requirements that physicians and other health care professionals be licensed in the state in which they are providing services (so long as they have equivalent licensing in another state), and so on. (The licensure waiver is for purposes of Medicare, Medicaid, and CHIP reimbursement only; state law governs whether a non-Federal provider is authorized to provide services in the state without state licensure.) The *1135 waivers* typically end upon termination of the emergency period.

During the COVID-19 pandemic, nurses and physicians traveled to other states to provide health care services in shortage areas and to relieve other nurses and physicians due to what was termed combat fatigue. The *1135 waivers* facilitated this process in Massachusetts where licensed, out-of-state medical professionals were provided with a Massachusetts license to practice within one day. In Colorado, state regulators allowed licensed medical professionals from another state to immediately begin working in their state.

TABLE 5-1 Federal laws that affect health care

Year	Federal Law	Description
1863	**False Claims Act (FCA)**	• Regulated fraud associated with military contractors selling supplies and equipment to the Union Army • Used by federal agencies to regulate the conduct of any contractor that submits claims for payment to the federal government for any program (e.g., Medicare) • Civil monetary penalties (CMPs) are adjusted annually for inflation and impose a maximum (e.g., $23,331 in 2020) per false claim, plus three times the amount of damages that the government sustains; civil liability on those who submit false or fraudulent claims to the government for payment; and exclusion of violators from participation in Medicare and Medicaid. • The FCA has been amended by the Fraud Enforcement and Recovery Act (FERA) of 2009, the Patient Protection and Affordable Care Act (ACA) of 2010, the Dodd-Frank Wall Street Reform and Consumer Protection Act (Dodd-Frank Act) of 2010, and the Federal Civil Penalties Inflation Adjustment Act Improvements Act of 2015 to expand liability, increase civil penalties, and expand rights of *qui tam* relators. Henceforth, civil penalties authorized under the FCA incrementally increase annually, and that includes civil penalties authorized by an individual state's false claims act. Note: Control of fraud and abuse has been of great interest since the implementation of DRGs in 1983. Prior to DRGs, the cost-based reimbursement system for Medicare claims made fraud almost unnecessary, because the system rewarded high utilization of services. The implementation of DRGs resulted in the first serious "gaming" of the system to find ways to maximize revenues for hospitals. Because the diagnosis and procedure codes reported affect the DRG selected (and resultant payment), some hospitals engaged in a practice called **upcoding,** which is the assignment of an ICD-10-CM diagnosis code that does not match patient record documentation for the purpose of illegally increasing reimbursement (e.g., assigning the ICD-10-CM code for heart attack when angina was actually documented in the record). As a result, upcoding became a serious fraud concern under DRGs, and it was called *DRG creep.*
1966	**Federal Claims Collection Act (FCCA)**	• Required carriers (processed Medicare Part B claims) and fiscal intermediaries (processed Medicare Part A claims), both of which were replaced by Medicare administrative contractors (that administer the Medicare fee-for-program), to attempt the collection of **overpayments** (funds a provider or beneficiary receives in excess of amounts due and payable under Medicare and Medicaid)
1970	Occupational Safety and Health Act	• Created the Occupational Safety and Health Administration (OSHA), whose mission is to ensure safe and healthful workplaces in America • Since the agency was created in 1971, workplace fatalities have been cut in half and occupational injury and illness rates have declined 40 percent; at the same time, U.S. employment has doubled from 56 million workers at 3.5 million work sites to 111 million workers at 7 million sites.
1972	Anti-Kickback Statute (AKS)	• Criminal statute that protects patients and federal health care programs from fraud and abuse by curtailing the corrupting influence of money on health care decisions • Violations of the law are punishable by up to 10 years in prison, fines and penalties that are adjusted for inflation (e.g., over $100,000), and exclusion from participation in federal health care programs. • In 1987, DHHS published regulations designating specific "safe harbors" for various payment and business practices that, while potentially prohibited by the law, would not be prosecuted (e.g., investments in group practices).
	Drug Abuse and Treatment Act	• Required that drug and alcohol abuse patient records be kept confidential and not subject to disclosure except as provided by law • Applied to federally assisted alcohol or drug abuse programs, which are those that provide diagnosis, treatment, and referral for treatment of substance and alcohol abuse Note: General medical care facilities are required to comply with this legislation only if they have an identified substance/alcohol abuse treatment unit or their personnel provide drug/alcohol diagnosis, treatment, or referral.

(continues)

TABLE 5-1 (continued)

Year	Federal Law	Description
1972 (*cont'd*)	Social Security Amendments	• Strengthened the utilization review process by creating professional standard review organizations (PSROs), which were independent peer review organizations that monitored the appropriateness, quality, and outcome of the services provided to beneficiaries of the Medicare, Medicaid, and Maternal and Child Health Programs (MCHPs) • PSROs are now called quality improvement organizations (QIOs).
1974	**Privacy Act of 1974**	• Implemented to protect the privacy of individuals identified in information systems maintained by federal government hospitals (e.g., military hospitals) and to give individuals access to records concerning themselves (e.g., review records, dispute inaccuracies in records) • Does not preempt state laws that are more restrictive **Note:** Although this law has no effect on records maintained by nonfederal hospitals, effective April 14, 2003, the Health Insurance Portability and Accountability Act of 1996 (HIPAA) requires all health plans, health care clearinghouses, and health care providers that conduct electronic financial or administrative transactions (e.g., electronic billing) to comply with national patient privacy standards, which contain safeguards to protect the security and confidentiality of patient information.
1981	Civil Monetary Penalties Law (CMPL)	• Imposes civil monetary penalties (CMPs), assessments, and program exclusions against individuals and entities that submit false, fraudulent, or otherwise improper claims for Medicare or Medicaid payment. "Improper claims" include claims submitted by an excluded individual or entity for items or services furnished during a period of program exclusion. (In 1977, the Medicare-Medicaid Anti-Fraud and Abuse Amendments, Public Law 95-142, mandated the exclusion of physicians and other practitioners convicted of program-related crimes from participation in Medicare and Medicaid.)
1982	Peer Review Improvement Act	• Replaced PSROs with peer review organizations (PROs) (now called QIOs), which were statewide utilization and quality control peer review organizations • In 1985, PROs incorporated a focused second-opinion program, which referred certain cases for diagnostic and treatment verification.
1986	Health Care Quality Improvement Act (HCQIA)	• Established the **National Practitioner Data Bank (NPDB)**, which improves the quality of health care by encouraging state licensing boards, hospitals and other health care entities, and professional societies to identify and discipline those who engage in unprofessional behavior; restricts the ability of incompetent physicians, dentists, and other health care practitioners to move from state to state without disclosure or discovery of previous medical malpractice payment and adverse action history; and impacts licensure, clinical privileges, and professional society memberships as a result of adverse actions • The *Health Integrity and Protection Data Base (HIPDB)*, established in 1996 as a result of HIPAA, was merged into the NPDB on May 6, 2013; the HIPDB combats fraud and abuse in health insurance and health care delivery by serving as a national data collection program for reporting and disclosing certain final adverse actions taken against health care practitioners, providers, and suppliers • Authorized entities use an *Integrated Querying and Reporting Service (IQRS)* to report adverse actions and submit a single query to obtain information from the NPDB (www.npdb.hrsa.gov)
	Emergency Medical Treatment and Labor Act (EMTALA)	• Ensures public access to emergency services regardless of ability to pay, specifically prohibiting *patient dumping*, which occurs when a facility that is capable of providing necessary medical care refuses care or transfers a patient to another facility because the patient is unable to pay for services. Facilities that fail to comply with EMTALA are subject to monetary penalties and exclusion from the Medicare program.
1988	**Clinical Laboratory Improvement Act (CLIA)**	• Established quality standards for all laboratory testing to ensure accuracy, reliability, and timeliness of patient test results regardless of where the test was performed.

(continues)

TABLE 5-1 (continued)

Year	Federal Law	Description
1989	Omnibus Budget Reconciliation Act (OBRA 1989)	• Enacted a **physician self-referral law** (or **Stark I**) that prohibits physicians from referring Medicare patients to *clinical laboratory services* in which the physicians or their family members had a financial ownership/investment interest and compensation arrangement • In 1994, because some providers routinely waived coinsurance and copayments, the DHHS Office of Inspector General (OIG) issued the following fraud alert: "Routine waiver of deductibles and copayments by charge-based providers, practitioners or suppliers is unlawful because it results in: (1) false claims, (2) violations of the anti-kickback statute, and (3) excessive utilization of items and services paid for by Medicare."
1995	**Physicians at Teaching Hospitals (PATH)**	• Audits implemented by DHHS that examine the billing practices of physicians at teaching hospitals • Focus was on two issues: (1) compliance with the Medicare rule affecting payment for physician services provided by residents (e.g., whether a teaching physician was present for Part B services billed to Medicare between 1990 and 1996), and (2) whether the level of the physician service was coded and billed properly
	Stark II Physician Self-Referral Law	• Stark II (physician self-referral law) expanded Stark I by including referrals of Medicare and Medicaid patients for the following designated health care services (DHCS): clinical laboratory services, durable medical equipment and supplies, home health services, inpatient and outpatient hospitalization services, occupational therapy services, outpatient prescription drugs, parenteral and enteral nutrients, equipment and supplies, physical therapy services, prosthetics, orthotics and prosthetic devices and supplies, radiation therapy services and supplies, and radiology services, including MRIs, CAT scans, and ultrasound services. • Hospitals must also comply with Stark II regulations because of relationships they establish with physicians. • In 2001, new regulations clarified what a *designated health service* was and under what circumstances physicians can have a financial relationship with an organization and still make referrals of Medicare patients for services or products provided by that organization. **Example:** Home care physicians who served as home health agency medical directors were prohibited from making in excess of $25,000/year if they wanted to make referrals to that agency. That cap was removed in the revised Stark II regulations.
1996	National Correct Coding Initiative (NCCI) program	• Developed by CMS to reduce Medicare program expenditures by detecting inappropriate codes on claims and denying payment for them
	Health Insurance Portability and Accountability Act (HIPAA)	• Mandated *administrative simplification* regulations that govern privacy, security, and electronic transaction standards for health care information • Amended ERISA and COBRA to improve portability and continuity of health insurance coverage in connection with employment; protects health insurance coverage for workers and their families when they change or lose their jobs • Created the Healthcare Integrity and Protection Data Bank (HIPDB), which was merged with the National Practitioner Data Bank (NPDB) on May 6, 2013 • Established the **Medicare Integrity Program (MIP)**, which authorizes CMS to enter into contracts with entities to perform cost report auditing, medical review, anti-fraud activities, and the Medicare Secondary Payer (MSP) program • Expanded DHHS OIG sanction authorities by extending the application and scope of current civil monetary penalty (CMP) and exclusion authorities to all Federal health care programs
1999	**Payment Error Prevention Program (PEPP)**	• Initiated by DHHS to require facilities to identify and reduce improper Medicare payments and, specifically, the Medicare **payment error rate** (number of dollars paid in error out of the total dollars paid for inpatient prospective payment system services) • Established **Clinical Data Abstracting Centers (CDACs)**, which became responsible for initially requesting and screening medical records for PEPP surveillance sampling for medical review, DRG validation, and medical necessity; medical review criteria were developed by peer review organizations (now called quality improvement organizations or QIOs)

(continues)

TABLE 5-1 (continued)

Year	Federal Law	Description
1999 (cont'd)	Program Safeguard Contractors (PSCs)	• CMS transferred responsibility for fraud and abuse detection from carriers and fiscal intermediaries (FIs) to Program Safeguard Contractors (PSCs). (PSCs were replaced by the Zone Program Integrity Contractor, or ZPIC, program in 2009.)
2002	**Improper Payments Information Act of 2002 (IPIA)**	• Established the **Payment Error Rate Measurement (PERM) program** to measure improper payments in the Medicaid program and the Children's Health Insurance Program (CHIP) • Established the **Comprehensive Error Rate Testing (CERT) program** to assess and measure improper Medicare fee-for-service payments (based on reviewing selected claims and associated medical record documentation) • Established the **Hospital Payment Monitoring Program (HPMP)** to measure, monitor, and reduce the incidence of Medicare fee-for-service payment errors for short-term, acute care, inpatient PPS hospitals, which included development of the: ◦ **First-look Analysis for Hospital Outlier Monitoring (FATHOM)** data analysis tool, which provides administrative hospital and state-specific data for specific CMS target areas ◦ **Program for Evaluating Payment Patterns Electronic Report (PEPPER)**, which contains hospital-specific administrative claims data for a number of CMS-identified problem areas (e.g., specific DRGs, types of discharges). (A hospital uses PEPPER data to compare their performance with that of other hospitals.)
2003	Medicare Prescription Drug, Improvement, and Modernization Act (MMA)	• Mandated implementation of the **Recovery Audit Contractor (RAC) program** to find and correct improper Medicare payments paid to health care providers participating in fee-for-service Medicare • CMS created the **Zone Program Integrity Contractor (ZPIC)** program to review billing trends and patterns, focusing on providers whose billings for Medicare services are higher than the majority of providers in the community. CMS programs for detecting fraud and abuse were originally assigned to carriers' fiscal intermediaries (FIs), all of which were replaced by Medicare administrative contractors (MACs) by 2009. ZPICs are assigned to the MAC jurisdictions, replacing Program Safeguard Contractors (PSCs). (RAC and ZPIC programs were implemented in 2009.) • Developed the **Hospital Inpatient Quality Reporting (Hospital IQR) program** to equip consumers with quality of care information so they can make more informed decisions about health care options. The Hospital IQR program requires hospitals to submit specific quality measures data about health conditions common among Medicare beneficiaries and that typically result in hospitalization. Eligible hospitals that do not participate in the Hospital IQR program will receive an annual market basket update with a 2.0 percentage point reduction. (The Hospital IQR program was previously called the *Reporting Hospital Quality Data for Annual Payment Update program*.)
	FACT Act	• The *Fair and Accurate Credit Transaction Act of 2003 (FACT Act)* includes the Federal Trade Commission's *Identity Theft Red Flags Rule* (or *Red Flags Rule*), which requires businesses and organizations to implement a written *Identity Theft Prevention Program* designed to detect the warning signs (or red flags) of identity theft in their day-to-day operations. Health care organizations are required to comply with the Red Flags Rule because they extend credit to patients. Their *Identity Theft Prevention Program* will help prevent **medical identity theft**, which occurs when someone uses another person's name and insurance information to obtain medical and surgical treatment, prescription drugs, and medical durable equipment; it can also occur when dishonest people who work in a medical setting use another person's information to submit false bills to health care plans. The program must include the following four criteria: (1) what patterns, practices, or specific activities the business or organization will identify as red flags indicating potential identity theft; (2) how the business or organization intends to detect the red flags it has identified; (3) how the business or organization will respond to the detection of a red flag it has identified; and (4) how the business or organization intends to evaluate the success of its program and maintain it in the future.

(continues)

TABLE 5-1 (continued)

Year	Federal Law	Description
2005	**Patient Safety and Quality Improvement Act**	• Amends Title IX of the Public Health Service Act to provide for improved patient safety by encouraging voluntary and confidential reporting of events that adversely affect patients (e.g., preventable medical errors known as *never events* or *adverse events*, which include surgery performed on the wrong site, medications administered in error, and so on) • Creates Patient Safety Organizations (PSOs) to collect, aggregate, and analyze confidential information reported by health care providers • Designates information reported to PSOs as privileged and not subject to disclosure (except when a court determines that the information contains evidence of a criminal act or each provider identified in the information authorizes disclosure)
	Deficit Reduction Act of 2005	• Created **Medicaid Integrity Program (MIP)**, which increased resources available to CMS to combat abuse, fraud, and waste in the Medicaid program. CMS contracts with **Medicaid integrity contractors (MICs)** to review provider claims, audit providers and others, identify overpayments, and educate providers, managed care entities, beneficiaries, and others with respect to payment integrity and quality of care.
2006	**Tax Relief and Health Care Act of 2006 (TRHCA)**	• Created the **Hospital Outpatient Quality Reporting Program (Hospital OQR)**, a "pay for quality data reporting program" that was implemented by CMS for outpatient hospital services; also created the *Physician Quality Reporting System*, which was replaced by Merit-based Incentive Payment System (MIPS) in 2011
2009	ARRA	• The *American Recovery and Reinvestment Act (ARRA)* protects **whistleblowers**, who are individuals that make specified disclosures relating to funds covered by the act (e.g., Medicare payments). ARRA prohibits retaliation (e.g., termination) against such employees who disclose information that they believe is: ◦ Evidence of gross mismanagement of an agency contract or grant relating to covered funds ◦ A gross waste of covered funds ◦ A substantial and specific danger to public health or safety related to the implementation or use of covered funds ◦ An abuse of authority related to the implementation or use of covered funds ◦ A violation of law, rule, or regulation related to an agency contract or grant awarded or issued relating to covered funds
	HITECH Act	• The *Health Information Technology for Economic and Clinical Health Act (HITECH Act) of 2009* published final rules in the January 2013 *Federal Register*, which impact the HIPAA privacy and security rules. (Content about specific provisions is included in the HITECH Act section of this chapter.)
2010	PPACA	• The *Patient Protection and Affordable Care Act (PPACA)* implemented the **hospital value-based purchasing (VBP) program** to promote better clinical outcomes and patient experiences of care. Value-based incentive payments are made to hospitals that meet performance standards with respect to a performance period for the fiscal year involved. Thus, reimbursement for inpatient acute care services is based on care *quality* (instead of *quantity* of services provided). The program's measures are a subset of those adopted for the *Hospital Inpatient Quality Reporting Program* (Hospital IQR program). • The *hospital reimbursement repayment program* was implemented to require CMS to reduce payments to IPPS hospitals with excess readmissions using readmission measures, such as defining a *readmission* as the admission of a patient to a *subsection (d) hospital* (general, acute care, short-term hospital) within 30 days of a previous discharge from the same or another subsection (d) hospital. • The *risk adjustment program* was implemented to lessen or eliminate the influence of risk selection on premiums charged by health plans and was discussed in Chapter 3 of this textbook.
2011	MEDIC	• The **Medicare Drug Integrity Contractors (MEDIC) program** was implemented to assist with CMS audit, oversight, anti-fraud, and anti-abuse efforts related to the Medicare Part D benefit. The goal is to identify cases of suspected fraud and abuse, investigate them thoroughly and in a timely manner, and take immediate action to ensure that the Medicare Trust Fund does not inappropriately pay claims and that inappropriate payments are recommended for recoupment.

(continues)

TABLE 5-1 (continued)

Year	Federal Law	Description
2011 (cont'd)	Medicare Access and CHIP Reauthorization Act	• Implemented the *merit-based incentive payment system (MIPS)*, which combines parts of PQRS, value-based payment modifier, and the Medicare EHR incentive program into a single program based on quality, resource use, clinical practice improvement, and meaningful use of certified EHR technology
	Investing in Innovations (i2) Initiative	• Facilitated innovations in health information technology (health IT) by promoting research and development to enhance competitiveness in the United States.
	Electronic Submission of Medical Documentation System (esMD)	• Implemented to: (1) reduce provider costs and cycle time by minimizing and eventually eliminating paper processing and mailing of medical documentation to review contractors, and to (2) reduce costs and time for review contractors
2012	**eHealth Exchange**	• Transitioned from federal *Office of the National Coordinator for Health IT* to a private sector initiative that facilitates the transformation of health care delivery in the United States through simplified, standardized electronic information and technology. The goal is to achieve improved quality of care, better health outcomes, and reduced costs by establishing a health information exchange (HIE) network to securely share clinical information over the Internet nationwide. Participants include large provider networks, hospitals, pharmacies, regional health information exchanges, and many federal agencies. A **rural health information organization (RHIO)** is a type of health information exchange network that brings together health care stakeholders within a defined geographic area and governs health information exchange among them for the purpose of improving health and care in that community.
		• eHealth Exchange has implemented the **United States Core Data for Interoperability (USCDI)**, which is the standardized set of health *data classes* and constituent data elements for nationwide, interoperable health information exchange (HIE). Data classes are the aggregation of various data elements by a common theme or use, such as patient demographics (e.g., current and previous addresses, phone number, email address), EHR entry provenance (e.g., author organization name and documentation time stamp), and substance reactions (e.g., substance/medication name, substance/medication drug class, reaction to substance/medication). *Data elements* are the most granular level at which a piece of data is represented in the USCDI for exchange, such as patient date of birth.
2016	**21st Century Cures Act (Cures Act)**	• Prohibits *information blocking* of electronic health information (EHI) by actors, which include health care providers, health information exchanges (HIE), health information networks, and health information technology (Health IT) vendors. (Also requires submission of reports about Medicare Advantage and ESRD program risk adjustment model.) *Information blocking* prevents access to and the exchange and use of electronic health information by actors (e.g, vendor). Violations of the Cures Act are subject to civil monetary penalties and DHHS disincentives.
		Example: Providers are prohibited from restricting access to or the exchange and use of electronic health information (EHI) in a patient portal. Thus, documented EHI (e.g., lab results, medication list) must be made available to patients in the portal when results are available.
		• DHHS has identified reasonable and necessary activities that do not constitute information blocking and are considered *exceptions* to information blocking prohibitions. Exceptions involve those related to: (1) not fulfilling requests to access, exchange, or use EHI to prevent harm to the patient or another person; (2) protecting privacy and security, infeasibility (e.g., public health emergency); and (3) Health IT performance exception (e.g., ransomware interferes with HIE). The Cures Act also allows exceptions that involve procedures for fulfilling requests to access, exchange, or use EHI, such as limiting content of response to a request to access, exchange, charging fees, and licensing EHI interoperability elements.
2017	Electronic Clinical Quality Measures (eCQMs)	• Integration of eCQI Resource Center and USHIK allows users to compare different versions and metadata of **electronic Clinical Quality Measures (eCQMs)**, which are processes, observations, treatments, and outcomes that quantify the quality of care provided by health care systems. Measuring such data helps ensure that care is delivered safely, effectively, equitably, and timely. eCQMs contain measures and specifications for calculating quality metrics established for federal payment reimbursements.

(continues)

TABLE 5-1 (continued)

Year	Federal Law	Description
2018	UPIC	• *Unified Program Integrity Contractors (UPICs)* were created to perform Medicare and Medicaid program integrity functions for durable equipment prosthetics, orthotics, and supplies; home health and hospice; and Medicaid and Medicare/Medicaid data matching. UPICs work under the direction of CMS's Center for Program Integrity (CPI).
	SMRC	• The *Supplemental Medical Review Contractor (SMRC)* program was created to help lower improper payment rates and increase efficiencies of Medicare and Medicaid medical review. The SMRC (e.g., Noridian Healthcare Solutions, LLC) conducts a medical review of Medicare Part A and B claims nationwide by evaluating patient records to determine whether Medicare claims were billed in compliance with Medicare's billing, coding, coverage, and payment billing practices. The focus of the medical reviews may include vulnerabilities identified by CMS internal data analysis, the Comprehensive Error Rate Testing (CERT) program, professional organizations, and Federal oversight agencies. The SMRC notifies CMS of identified improper payments and noncompliance with documentation requests, and the appropriate Medicare Administrative Contractor (MAC) initiates claims adjustments and overpayment recoupment actions through the standard overpayment recovery process.

Retention of Records

Record retention is the storage of documentation for an established period of time, usually mandated by federal or state law. (The state in which the health care provider practices determines whether federal or state law mandates the retention period.) Its purpose is to ensure records are available for use by government agencies and other third parties (e.g., insurance audit, quality of care review). It is acceptable to store medical records and insurance claims (including attachments submitted to third-party payers) in a format other than original hard copy if the storage medium (e.g., microfilm, scanned images) accurately reproduces all original documents.

- Medicare *Conditions of Participation* mandate the retention of patient records in their original or legally reproduced form (e.g., microfilm) for a period of at least five years. (Individual state laws may require retention of patient records for a longer period, such as six years in New York State.)
- The Health Insurance Portability and Accountability Act (HIPAA) mandates the retention of health insurance claims and accounting records for a minimum of six years, unless state law specifies a longer period.
- HIPAA also mandates that health insurance claims be retained for a minimum of two years after a patient's death.

Example 1: Community Hospital is located in North Carolina (NC), which mandates that hospital medical records be retained for a minimum of 11 years following the discharge of an adult, and for a minor the record must be retained until the patient's 30th birthday. Because NC law is stricter than the HIPAA mandate regarding retention of records, Community Hospital must retain adult patient records for a period of 11 years and minor patient records until the patient's 30th birthday.

Example 2: Dr. Smith practices in Alabama (AL), which mandates that medical records be retained for five years. Because the HIPAA mandate is stricter than AL state law, Dr. Smith must retain patient records for a period of six years. For any patient who has died, Dr. Smith must retain the record for a period of two years after the date of death.

Health Care Audit and Compliance Programs

Health care audit and compliance programs have been established by the Department of Health and Human Services (DHHS) to ensure the integrity of government health care programs by:

- Combating fraud, waste, and abuse, and finding and correcting improper payments (e.g., overpayments)
- Coordinating intelligence sharing among investigators, agents, prosecutors, analysts, and policymakers

- Facilitating coordination and cooperation among providers to improve quality of care and reduce unnecessary costs
- Detecting inappropriate codes submitted on claims and eliminating improper coding practices

An **audit** is an objective evaluation to determine the accuracy of submitted financial statements (e.g., CMS-1500, UB-04). Audits are conducted to assess the accuracy of submitted medical codes and procedures/services and the quality of care provided to patients. A **compliance program** contains internal policies and procedures that an organization follows to meet mandated requirements. DHHS publishes *compliance program guidance* documents on their website to assist providers in the development of internal compliance programs. (Go to https://oig.hhs.gov/compliance/compliance-guidance/index.asp to view compliance program guidance documents for all health care settings.)

Compliance Programs

The DHHS Office of Inspector General (OIG) published the final *Compliance Program Guidance for Individual and Small Group Physician Practices* in the October 5, 2000, *Federal Register.* (The *Compliance Program Guidance for Hospitals* was published in the February 23, 1998, *Federal Register.*) The intent of the guidance documents is to help physicians in individual and small group practices design voluntary compliance programs that best fit the needs of their individual practices. By law, physicians are not subject to civil, administrative, or criminal penalties for innocent errors, or even negligence. The civil False Claims Act covers only offenses that are committed with *actual knowledge* of the falsity of the claim, or *reckless disregard* or *deliberate ignorance* of the truth or falsity of a claim. (The False Claims Act does not cover mistakes, errors, or negligence.) The OIG has stated that it is mindful of the difference between innocent errors (e.g., erroneous claims) and reckless or intentional conduct (e.g., fraudulent claims).

Example: A Medicare Part C managed care plan in Florida hired a consulting company to review patients' records. The purpose was to identify additional patient diagnoses (and related ICD-10-CM codes) that would increase risk capitation payments from CMS. The consulting company identified diagnoses (and related ICD-10-CM codes) previously submitted to Medicare that were undocumented or unsupported by patient record documentation. The plan failed to inform Medicare about the undocumented or unsupported diagnosis codes to Medicare, which had inflated its risk capitation payments. As a result, the plan agreed to pay $22.6 million to settle False Claims Act allegations.

The owner-operator of a medical clinic in California used marketers to recruit individuals for medically unnecessary office visits by promising free, medically unnecessary equipment or free food. The clinic billed Medicare more than $1.7 million for the scheme, and the owner-operator was consequently sentenced to 37 months in prison.

The OIG also published a *Self-Disclosure Protocol (SDP)*, which established a process for providers to voluntarily identify, disclose, and resolve instances of potential fraud (e.g., false claims, overpayments) that involve federal health care programs (e.g., Medicare). The word "voluntarily" does *not* mean that the provider can opt out of the self-disclosure of potential fraud; the SDP must be followed if providers or their staff self-identify potential fraud. The OIG has stated that it believes the health care industry must be encouraged to conduct voluntary self-evaluations (e.g., compliance program), and submitting the SDP when appropriate is a viable opportunity for self disclosure.

A voluntary compliance program can help physicians avoid generating erroneous and fraudulent claims by ensuring that submitted claims are true and accurate, expediting and optimizing proper payment of claims, minimizing billing mistakes, and avoiding conflicts with self-referral and antikickback statutes. Unlike other guidance previously issued by the OIG (e.g., *Compliance Program Guidance for Third-Party Medical Billing Companies*), the physician compliance guidance does not require that physician practices implement all seven standard components of a full-scale compliance program. (Although the seven components provide a solid basis upon which a physician practice can create a compliance program, the OIG acknowledges that full implementation of all components may not be feasible for smaller physician practices.) Instead, the guidance emphasizes a step-by-step approach for those practices to follow in developing and implementing a voluntary compliance program.

As a first step, physician practices can begin by identifying risk areas which, based on a practice's specific history with billing problems and other compliance issues, might benefit from closer scrutiny and corrective or educational measures. The step-by-step approach is as follows:

1. Perform periodic audits to internally monitor billing practices.

2. Develop written practice standards and procedures.

3. Designate a compliance officer to monitor compliance efforts and enforce practice standards.

4. Conduct appropriate training and education about practice standards and procedures.

5. Respond appropriately to detected violations by investigating allegations and disclosing incidents to appropriate government entities.

6. Develop open lines of communication (e.g., discussions at staff meetings regarding erroneous or fraudulent conduct issues) to keep practice employees updated regarding compliance activities.

7. Enforce disciplinary standards through well-publicized guidelines.

The final guidance further identifies four specific compliance risk areas for physicians: (1) proper coding and billing; (2) ensuring that services are reasonable and necessary; (3) proper documentation; and (4) avoiding improper inducements, kickbacks, and self-referrals. These risk areas reflect areas in which the OIG has focused its investigations and audits related to physician practices. The final guidance also provides direction to larger practices in developing compliance programs by recommending that they use both the physician guidance and previously issued guidance, such as the *Third-Party Medical Billing Company Compliance Program Guidance* or the *Clinical Laboratory Compliance Program Guidance*, to create a compliance program that meets the needs of the larger practice.

Medicare Integrity Program

In 1996, HIPAA mandated the *Medicare Integrity Program (MIP)* that gives CMS-specific contracting authority to enter into contracts with entities to promote the integrity of the Medicare program, such as medical review (MR), which requires Medicare administrative contractors (MACs) to verify inappropriate billing and to develop interventions to correct the problem. CMS' Center for Program Integrity (CPI) oversees Medicare medical review contractors. CPI conducts contractor oversight activities, such as providing broad direction on medical review policy, reviewing and approving Medicare contractors' annual medical review strategies, facilitating Medicare contractors' implementation of recently enacted Medicare legislation, facilitating compliance with current regulations, ensuring Medicare contractors' performance of CMS operating instructions, conducting continuous monitoring and evaluation of Medicare Contractors' performance in accord with CMS program instructions as well as contractors' strategies and goals, and providing ongoing feedback and consultation to contractors regarding Medicare program and medical review issues.

Medical review (MR) is defined by CMS as a review of claims to determine whether services provided are medically reasonable and necessary, as well as to follow up on the effectiveness of previous corrective actions. The national objectives and goals of medical review (MR) are to:

- Increase the effectiveness of medical review payment safeguard activities.

- Exercise accurate and defensible decision making on medical review of claims.

- Place emphasis on reducing the paid claims error rate by notifying individual billing entities (e.g., providers, DME suppliers) of medical review findings and making appropriate referrals to provider outreach and education.

- Collaborate with other internal components and external entities to ensure correct claims payment and to address situations of potential fraud, waste, and abuse.

If a MAC reviews a small sample of claims and verifies that an error exists, the MAC classifies the severity of the problem as minor, moderate, or significant. Then, the MAC imposes corrective actions that are appropriate for the severity of the infraction. The following types of corrective actions can result from medical review:

- *Provider Notification/Feedback*: Problems detected at minor, moderate, or significant levels require the MAC to inform the provider of appropriate billing procedures.

- *Prepayment Review*: When medical review of a claim prior to payment results in identified problems, the provider may be placed on prepayment review, which means a percentage of claims are subjected to medical review before payment is authorized. Once providers have reestablished the practice of submitting claims correctly, they are removed from prepayment review.

- *Post-payment Review*: Medical review of claims after payment has been made is commonly performed by using statistically valid sampling, which allows underpayments or overpayments (if they exist) to be estimated without requesting the provider to submit copies of patient records for all claims submitted. This reduces the administrative burden for Medicare and costs for both Medicare and providers.

New signature guidelines for MR purposes require all health care services provided or ordered to be authenticated by the author (e.g., provider). Reviewers will disregard an entry that has a missing or illegible signature, and they will make claims review determinations based on authenticated documentation only. This means that providers can no longer use signature stamps, and their signatures must be handwritten or generated electronically, except for:

- Facsimiles of original written or electronic signatures for terminal illness for hospice care

- Clinical diagnostic test orders, which do not require a signature (but do require authenticated documentation)

- In cases where the relevant regulation, National Coverage Determination (NCD), Local Coverage Determination (LCD), and *Medicare Claims Processing Manual* have specific signature requirements, those take precedence.

Targeted Probe and Educate (TPE) Process for Medical Review

CMS's *Targeted Probe and Educate (TPE) Process for Medical Review* is designed to help providers and suppliers reduce claim denials and appeals by providing one-on-one help. The intent of the TPE process is to increase claims accuracy through MAC data analysis of specific areas, including: (1) providers and suppliers who have high claim error rates or unusual billing practices, and (2) items and services that have high national error rates and are a financial risk to Medicare. When a high rate of claims denials persists after the TPE process, providers are referred to CMS for additional action, which may include extrapolation, referral to the Zone Program Integrity Contractor (ZPIC) or Unified Program Integrity Contractor (UPIC), referral to the Recovery Auditor (RA) contractor, and so on.

Medicaid Integrity Program

The *Medicaid Integrity Program (MIP)* was mandated by the Deficit Reduction Act of 2005, which provides funds ($5 million in 2007 to $75 million by 2009 and each year thereafter) to combat fraud, waste, and abuse. Contractors will review the actions of those seeking payment from Medicaid (e.g., providers), perform audits, identify overpayments, and educate providers and others about program integrity and quality of care. Congress mandated that CMS devote at least 100 full-time staff members to the project, who will collaborate with state Medicaid officials. The MIP is based on four key principles:

- Accountability for the MIP's activities and those of its contractors and the states

- Collaboration with internal and external partners and stakeholders

- Flexibility to address the ever-changing nature of Medicaid fraud

- National leadership in Medicaid program integrity

The major strategies will include:

- Balancing the role of the MIP between providing training and technical assistance to states while conducting oversight of their activities; and between supporting criminal investigations of suspect providers while concurrently seeking administrative sanctions

- Collaborating and coordinating with internal and external partners

- Consulting with interested parties in the development of the comprehensive Medicaid integrity plan
- Developing effective return on investment strategies
- Employing lessons learned in developing guidance and directives aimed at fraud prevention
- Targeting vulnerabilities in the Medicaid program

In addition, **Medicaid Fraud Control Units (MFCUs)** investigate and prosecute Medicaid provider fraud as well as patient abuse or neglect in health care facilities and board and care facilities in all 50 States, the District of Columbia, Puerto Rico, and the U.S. Virgin Islands. MFCUs are usually part of a State Attorney General's office, which employs teams of investigators, attorneys, and auditors. MFCUs are also constituted as single, identifiable entities, and they must be separate and distinct from the state's Medicaid agency. The Office of Inspector General (OIG) provides oversight for the MFCUs by providing annual recertification, assessment of performance and compliance with federal requirements, and administration of a federal grant award to fund a portion of operational costs.

Recovery Audit Contractor Program

The *Recovery Audit Contractor (RAC) program* is mandated by the Medicare Prescription Drug, Improvement, and Modernization Act of 2003 (MMA) to find and correct improper Medicare payments paid to health care providers participating in Medicare fee-for-service (FFS), Part C, and Part D. The *Patient Protection and Affordable Care Act of 2009* requires state Medicaid programs to contract with RACs to identify and recoup overpayment and underpayment of fees to providers. The Medicaid RAC program was implemented in January 2012.

Medicare processes more than 1.2 billion Medicare claims annually, submitted by more than one million health care providers, including hospitals, skilled nursing facilities, physicians, and medical equipment suppliers. (*The federal surety bond*, a contract established between DME suppliers and Medicare, is now up to $500,000. In previous years, it was just $25,000.) Errors in claims submitted by these health care providers for services provided to Medicare beneficiaries can account for billions of dollars in improper payments each year.

The goal of the RAC program is to identify improper payments made on claims of health care services provided to Medicare beneficiaries. *Improper payments* include:

- *Overpayments* (e.g., submitted claims do not meet Medicare's National Correct Coding Initiative program or medical necessity policies, documentation in the patient record does not support codes reported on the claim, or Medicare administrative contractors reimburse providers more than once for the same patient encounter or calculate reimbursement using an incorrect fee schedule) (Table 5-2)

TABLE 5-2 Provider options for RAC program overpayment determinations

Element	Discussion Period	Rebuttal	Redetermination
Which option should I use?	The discussion period offers an opportunity for the provider to submit additional information to the RAC to indicate why recoupment should not be initiated. It also offers the opportunity for the RAC to explain the rationale for the overpayment decision. After reviewing the additional documentation submitted, the RAC could decide to reverse their decision. A letter will go to the provider detailing the outcome of the discussion period.	The rebuttal process allows the provider an opportunity to submit a statement with accompanying evidence (e.g., copies of patient records), indicating why the overpayment action will cause a financial hardship and should not occur. A rebuttal is *not* intended to review supporting medical documentation or disagreement with the overpayment decision. A rebuttal should *not* duplicate the redetermination process.	A redetermination is the first level of an appeal. The provider may request a redetermination when dissatisfied with an overpayment decision. A redetermination must be submitted within 30 days to prevent an offset on day 41.
Who do I contact?	Recovery Audit Contractor (RAC)	Claim Processing Contractor	Claim Processing Contractor

Courtesy of the Centers for Medicare & Medicaid Services, www.cms.gov.

(**continues**)

TABLE 5-2 Provider options for RAC program overpayment determinations (continued)

Element	Discussion Period	Rebuttal	Redetermination
Timeframe	Day 1–40	Day 1–15	Day 1–120 Must be submitted within 120 days of receipt of demand letter. To prevent offset on day 41, the redetermination must be filed within 30 days.
Timeframe Begins	*Automated Review:* upon receipt of demand letter *Complex Review:* upon receipt of review results letter	Date of demand letter	Upon receipt of demand letter
Timeframe Ends	Day 40 (offset begins on day 41)	Day 15	Day 120

- *Underpayments* (e.g., submitted claims report codes for simple procedures when review of the record indicates a more complicated procedure was performed)

Example: In one year, more than 600,000 claims with improper payments were collectively identified, resulting in the correction of more than $440 million in improper payments. Almost $360 million in overpayments were collected by providers, and $81 million in underpayments were repaid to providers. This represented an 83 percent decrease from RAC program corrections in the previous year, which were $2.5 billion. The RAC Program returned over $141 million to the Medicare Trust Funds, which represents a 91 percent decrease from the previous fiscal year, when the returned amount was $1.6 billion.

Health care providers subject to review include hospitals, physician practices, nursing homes, home health agencies, durable medical equipment suppliers, and any other provider or supplier that bills Medicare Parts A and B.

The national RAC program is an outgrowth of a successful demonstration program that used RACs to identify Medicare overpayments and underpayments to health care providers and suppliers in California, Florida, New York, Massachusetts, South Carolina, and Arizona. The demonstration project resulted in over $900 million in overpayments that were returned to the Medicare Trust Fund between 2005 and 2008 as well as nearly $38 million in underpayments that were returned to health care providers.

The RAC program uses *program integrity contractors (RAC auditors)* who review billing trends and patterns across Medicare programs. RAC auditors will focus on facilities and organizations (e.g., home health agency, hospitals) and individuals (e.g., providers) where billings for Medicare services are higher than the majority of providers and suppliers in the community. CMS awarded fee-for-service recovery audit program contracts (Figure 5-5) to:

- Region 1—Performant Recovery, Inc.
- Region 2—Cotiviti, LLC
- Region 3—Cotiviti, LLC
- Region 4—HMS Federal Solutions
- Region 5—Performant Recovery, Inc.

Health Care Fraud Prevention and Enforcement Action Team

In 2009, the PPACA created the **Health Care Fraud Prevention and Enforcement Action Team (HEAT)**, which is a joint effort between the DHHS and Department of Justice (DOJ) to fight health care fraud by increasing coordination, intelligence sharing, and training among investigators, agents, prosecutors, analysts, and policymakers. A key component of HEAT includes Medicare Strike Force teams, which are comprised of interagency teams of analysts, investigators, and prosecutors who can target emerging or migrating fraud

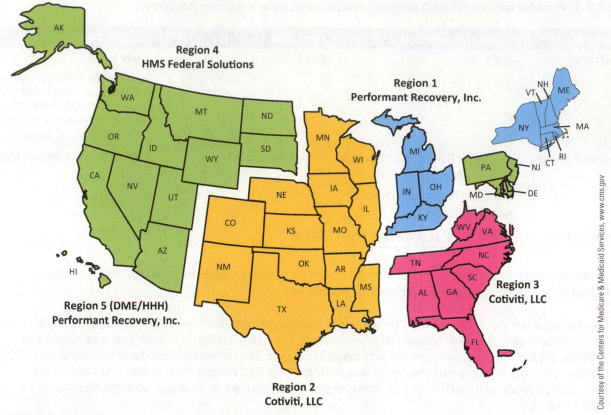

FIGURE 5-5 Medicare fee-for-service RAC regions.

Courtesy of the Centers for Medicare & Medicaid Services, www.cms.gov

schemes, including fraud by criminals masquerading as health care providers or suppliers. This effort received a boost in 2012 with the formation of a ground-breaking new Healthcare Fraud Prevention Partnership among DHHS, DOJ, and private organizations designed to find and stop scams that cut across public and private payers. This partnership facilitates industry anti-fraud efforts through shared insights among investigators, prosecutors, policymakers, and others.

Example: In September 2020, the Department of Health and Human Services' Office of Inspector General, along with state and federal law enforcement partners, participated in a health care fraud takedown of more than 345 defendants in 51 judicial districts. They were charged with participating in health care fraud schemes involving more than $4 billion in alleged losses to federal health care programs. Telemedicine executives had paid medical practitioners to write unnecessary prescriptions, either without any patient interaction or during brief telephonic conversation with patients they had never seen. Pharmacies, labs, and medical equipment companies purchased the prescriptions and sent the medications or products to patients, billing Medicare and Medicaid more than $4.5 billion. As a result, over 250 medical practitioners had their Medicare and Medicaid billing privileges revoked.

Medicare Shared Savings Program

The *Patient Protection and Affordable Care Act (PPACA)* required CMS to establish a Medicare shared savings program to facilitate coordination and cooperation among providers so as to improve the quality of care for Medicare fee-for-service beneficiaries and to reduce unnecessary costs. The Medicare shared savings program is designed to improve beneficiary outcomes and increase value of care by:

- Promoting accountability for the care of Medicare fee-for-service beneficiaries
- Requiring coordinated care for all services provided under Medicare fee-for-service
- Encouraging investment in infrastructure and redesigned care processes

Eligible providers, hospitals, and suppliers can participate in the shared savings program by creating or joining an *Accountable Care Organization (ACO)*, which is a recognized legal entity under state law that is comprised of a group of ACO participants (providers of services and suppliers). ACOs have established a mechanism for shared governance, and they work together to coordinate care for Medicare fee-for-service beneficiaries. ACOs enter into a three-year agreement with CMS, which holds them accountable for the quality, cost, and overall care of traditional fee-for-service Medicare beneficiaries who may be assigned to it. Under the **Medicare Shared Savings Program**:

- Medicare continues to pay individual providers and suppliers for specific items and services as it currently does under the fee-for-service payment systems.
- CMS develops a level of savings that must be achieved by each ACO *if the ACO is to receive shared savings*.
- CMS develops a level of losses realized by an ACO *if it is held liable for losses*.
- An ACO is accountable for meeting or exceeding quality performance standards to be eligible to receive any shared savings.

Reducing Overpayments Program

Overpayments are funds a provider or beneficiary receives in excess of amounts due and payable under Medicare and Medicaid statutes and regulations. Once a determination of overpayment has been made, the amount so determined is a debt owed to the U.S. government. The Federal Claims Collection Act of 1966 requires Medicare administrative contractors (MACs) (as agents of the federal government) to attempt the collection of overpayments. The PPACA of 2010 (Affordable Care Act) established the *60-day overpayment rule*, which requires providers to report and return overpayments within 60 days of identification or be subject to civil monetary penalties and exclusion from federal health care programs such as Medicare. (The 60-day overpayment rule is sometimes called the *voluntary disclosure rule*, but the process is not actually voluntary.) Examples of overpayments include:

- Payment based on a charge that exceeds the reasonable charge
- Duplicate processing of charges or claims
- Payment to a physician on a nonassigned claim or to a beneficiary on an assigned claim (payment made to wrong payee)
- Payment for noncovered items and services, including medically unnecessary services
- Incorrect application of the deductible or coinsurance
- Payment for items or services rendered during a period of nonentitlement
- Primary payment for items or services for which another entity is the primary payer
- Payment for items or services rendered after the beneficiary's date of death (post-payment reviews are conducted to identify and recover payments with a billed date of service that is after the beneficiary's date of death)

When a Medicare administrative contractor determines that an overpayment was made, it proceeds with recovery by issuing an overpayment demand letter (Figure 5-6) to the provider. The letter contains information about the review and statistical sampling methodology used, as well as corrective actions the provider can take. (An explanation of the sampling methodology that was followed is included.) Corrective actions include payment suspension, imposition of civil money penalties, institution of pre- or post-payment review, additional edits, and so on.

Providers and beneficiaries can receive a *waiver of overpayment recovery* if one or more of the following provisions apply:

- Overpayment was discovered subsequent to the third calendar year after the year of payment.
- If an overpaid physician is found to be without fault or is deemed without fault, overpayment shifts to the beneficiary (e.g., medically unnecessary services).
- When both provider and beneficiary are without fault with respect to an overpayment on an assigned claim for medically unnecessary services, liability is waived for the overpayment (e.g., no action is taken to recover the overpayment).

[Insert Medicare administrative contractor letterhead here]

May 15, YYYY

Seok Kim, M.D.
393 Main St
Anywhere, US 12345

RE: SSN: 123-45-6789
      PATIENT: Nathan A. Sanders
      CLAIM #:   939395SLD0005

Dear Provider:

Please be advised that an overpayment of benefits has been made for the above named patient. In order to resolve this matter we are asking you to make reimbursement. Please make your check payable to:

EMPIRE STATE HEALTH PLAN

in the amount of

$675.00

and forward it to:

EMPIRE STATE HEALTH PLAN
P.O. BOX 93902
ANYWHERE, US 12345

We are requesting this refund due to the following reason:

CLAIM WAS PROCESSED UNDER THE WRONG PATIENT FOR DATES OF SERVICE 4/15 &
4/20/YYYY.

If you have any questions, please feel free to contact us.

Sincerely,

Anya Doyle
Claims Analyst (39-392)

FIGURE 5-6 Sample overpayment recovery letter.

- If a beneficiary is liable for an incorrect payment, CMS or SSA may waive recovery if the beneficiary was without fault with respect to the overpayment and recovery would cause financial hardship or would be against equity and good conscience.

Medicare administrative contractors are prohibited from seeking overpayment recovery when the following two time limitations apply:

- Overpayment is not reopened within four years (48 months) after the date of payment, unless the case involves fraud or similar fault.
- Overpayment is discovered later than three full calendar years after the year of payment, unless there is evidence that the provider or beneficiary was at fault with respect to the overpayment.

Provider Liability for Overpayments

Providers are liable for refunding an overpayment in the following situations:

- Overpayment resulted from incorrect reasonable charge determination (because providers are responsible for knowing Medicare reasonable charges for services).

Exception: If the provider's reasonable charge screen was increased and the physician had no reason to question the amount of the increase, the physician is not liable and the case is referred to CMS for review.

- Provider received duplicate payments from the Medicare administrative contractor (because the claim was processed more than once, or the provider submitted duplicate claims).
- Provider received payment after agreeing to accept assignment (the provider agreed to accept as payment whatever the payer deemed a reasonable charge), and a beneficiary received payment on an itemized bill and submitted that payment to the provider.

> **Example:** The patient underwent office surgery on May 15, performed by the physician. Medicare determined the reasonable charge for the office surgery to be $360. In July, the physician and the patient each received a check from Medicare in the amount of $300. The patient then signed that $300 check over to the physician. Thus, the physician received a total of $600 for services provided on May 15, an overpayment of $240 (the amount received in excess of the reasonable charge). The patient is liable for the remaining $60 of the duplicate payment. (If the patient had also previously paid the physician the $60 as coinsurance, the physician would be liable for the entire $300 overpayment. Remember! *Coinsurance* is the percentage of costs a patient shares with the health plan.) The physician *is responsible for contacting the Medicare administrative contractor (MAC) to report the overpayment and make arrangements to provide a refund.*

- Provider received duplicate payments from Medicare and another payer directly or through the beneficiary, which happens to be the primary payer (e.g., automobile medical or no-fault insurer, liability insurer, or workers' compensation).
- Provider was paid but does not accept assignment.
- Provider furnished erroneous information, or provider failed to disclose facts known or that should have been known and that were material to the payment of benefits.

> **Example 1:** A beneficiary is referred to a provider by an employer for a fracture that occurred during a fall at work. The physician billed Medicare and neglected to indicate on the claim that the injury was work related (although that information had been provided by the patient). If Medicare benefits are paid to the provider for services and the injury would have been covered by workers' compensation, the provider is liable for an overpayment because of failure to disclose that the injury was work related. Thus, the provider is liable whether or not the beneficiary was also paid.

> **Example 2:** A provider submitted an assigned claim showing total charges of $1,000. The provider did not indicate on the claim that any portion of the bill had been paid by the patient. The MAC determined the reasonable charge to be $600 and paid the physician $480 (80 percent of $600) on the assumption that no other payment had been received. The MAC later learned that the beneficiary had paid the physician $200 (which included the $120 coinsurance amount) before the provider submitted the claim. Thus, the payment should have been split between provider and beneficiary, with $400 paid to the provider and an $80 overpayment refund to the beneficiary. The provider is liable for causing the $80 overpayment, as the amount received from the beneficiary was not reported on the claim. (Remember! *Coinsurance* is the percentage of costs a patient shares with the health plan.)

- Provider submitted a claim for services other than medically necessary services, but should have known they would not be covered (e.g., conversation with a relative of a beneficiary).
- Provider submitted a claim for medically unnecessary services.
- Items or services were furnished by a provider or supplier not qualified for Medicare reimbursement.

> **Example 1:** A lab test is performed by a nonqualified independent laboratory.

> **Example 2:** Services are rendered by a naturopath (practitioner who uses natural remedies instead of drugs and surgery).

- Overpayment was due to a mathematical or clerical error. (Failing to properly collect coinsurance, copayment, or deductible amounts is not a mathematical or clerical error.)
- Provider does not submit documentation to substantiate services billed, or there is a question as to whether services were actually performed (e.g., fraud is suspected).

- Overpayment was for rental of durable medical equipment, and supplier billed under the one-time authorization procedure. Suppliers of durable medical equipment that have accepted assignment can be reimbursed for rental items on the basis of a one-time authorization by the beneficiary (without the need to obtain the beneficiary's signature each month).

Absence of Provider Liability for Overpayments

A provider is liable for overpayments received unless found to be *without fault* as determined by the Medicare administrative contractor (MAC). A provider can be considered without fault if reasonable care was exercised in billing for and accepting payment, and the provider had a reasonable basis for assuming that payment was correct. In addition, if the provider had reason to question the payment and promptly brought the question to the attention of the MAC, the provider may be found without liability.

These criteria are always met in the case of overpayments due to an error with respect to the beneficiary's entitlement to Medicare benefits and the MAC's failure to properly apply the deductible. Normally, it is clear from the circumstances of the overpayment whether the provider was without fault in causing the overpayment. When this is not clear from the record, the MAC must review the issue (as long as the review occurs within three calendar years after the year in which the overpayment was made).

National Correct Coding Initiative

The Centers for Medicare and Medicaid Services (CMS) developed the *National Correct Coding Initiative (NCCI)* program in 1996 to reduce Medicare program expenditures by detecting inappropriate codes submitted on claims and denying payment for them, promote national correct coding methodologies, and eliminate improper coding practices. NCCI program guidance applies to the assignment of CPT codes for ambulatory surgery center and hospital outpatient settings. The NCCI program includes three types of edits, which can result in claims denials:

- NCCI procedure-to-procedure (PTP) edits
- Medically unlikely edits (MUEs)
- Add-on code (AOC) edits

Integrated *outpatient code editor (OCE)* software is used to process claims (after ICD-10-CM, CPT and HCPCS Level II codes are entered) for all outpatient institutional providers, whether they are subjective to the Outpatient Prospective Payment System (OPPS) or not (non-OPPS). CMS also publishes the NCCI program guidelines as documents that map to CPT and HCPCS Level II coding manual sections. (The National Correct Coding Initiative program is covered in more detail in Chapter 10 of this textbook.)

NCCI program code edits (Table 5-3) are used to process Medicare Part B claims, and NCCI program coding policies are based on the:

- Analysis of standard medical and surgical practice
- Coding conventions included in CPT
- Coding guidelines developed by national medical specialty societies (e.g., CPT advisory committee, which contains representatives of major medical societies)

TABLE 5-3 **Partial listing of National Correct Coding Initiative (NCCI) program edits in outpatient code editor (OCE) software**

NCCI /OCE Edit	Description	Disposition of Claim
1	Invalid diagnosis code	Return to provider
2	Diagnosis and age conflict	Return to provider
3	Diagnosis and sex conflict	Return to provider
4	Medicare secondary payer alert	Suspend

- Local and national coverage determinations
- Review of current coding practices

 NOTE:

Under a previous CMS contract, a private company refused to publish NCCI program code edits it developed because it considered them proprietary; these nonpublished code edits were called **black box edits**. Use of these edits was discontinued when CMS did not renew its contract with the company, and future CMS contracts do not allow for such restrictions.

Health Insurance Portability and Accountability Act (HIPAA)

In 1996, Congress passed the Health Insurance Portability and Accountability Act (HIPAA) because of concerns about fraud (e.g., coding irregularities, medical necessity issues, and waiving of copays and deductibles). While the Federal False Claims Act provides CMS with regulatory authority to enforce fraud and abuse statutes for the Medicare program, HIPAA extends that authority to all federal and state health care programs.

The Health Insurance Portability and Accountability Act of 1996 (HIPAA), Public Law No. 104-191, amended the Internal Revenue Code of 1986 to:

- Improve the portability and continuity of health insurance coverage in the group and individual markets.
- Combat waste, fraud, and abuse in health insurance and health care delivery.
- Promote the use of medical savings accounts.
- Improve access to long-term care services and coverage.
- Simplify the administration of health insurance by creating unique identifiers for providers, health plans, employers, and individuals.
- Create standards for electronic health information transactions.
- Create privacy standards for health information.

A discussion on each HIPAA component follows. Although HIPAA standards are still being finalized, health care organizations should develop and implement a response to each component.

HIPAA legislation is organized according to five titles (Figure 5-7):

- *Title I—Health Care Access, Portability, and Renewability*
- *Title II—Preventing Health Care Fraud and Abuse, Administrative Simplification, and Medical Liability Reform*
- *Title III—Tax-Related Health Provisions*
- *Title IV—Application and Enforcement of Group Health Plan Requirements*
- *Title V—Revenue Offsets*

HIPAA Title I—Health Care Access, Portability, and Renewability

HIPAA provisions were designed to improve the portability and continuity of health coverage by:

- Limiting exclusions for pre-existing medical conditions
- Providing credit for prior health coverage and a process for transmitting certificates and other information concerning prior coverage to a new group health plan or issuer
- Providing new rights that allow individuals to enroll for health coverage when they lose other health coverage, change from group to individual coverage, or gain a new dependent
- Prohibiting discrimination in enrollment and premiums against employees and their dependents based on health status

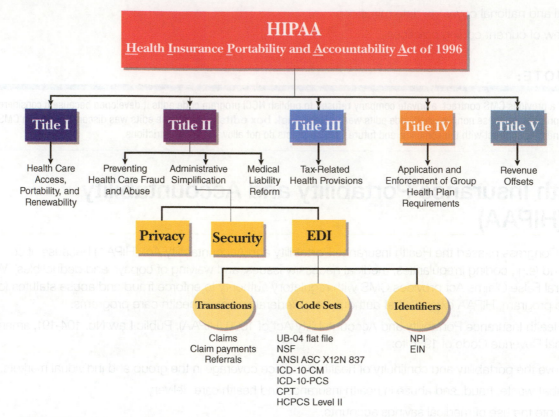

FIGURE 5-7 HIPAA provisions.

- Guaranteeing availability of health insurance coverage for small employers and renewability of health insurance coverage in both the small and large group markets
- Preserving, through narrow preemption provisions, the states' traditional role in regulating health insurance, including state flexibility to provide greater protections

HIPAA Title II—Preventing Health Care Fraud and Abuse

HIPAA defines **fraud** as "an intentional deception or misrepresentation that someone makes, knowing it is false, that could result in an unauthorized payment." The attempt itself is considered fraud, regardless of whether it is successful. **Abuse** "involves actions that are inconsistent with accepted, sound medical, business, or fiscal practices. Abuse directly or indirectly results in unnecessary costs to the program through improper payments." The difference between fraud and abuse (Table 5-4) is the individual's intent; however, both have the same impact of stealing valuable resources from the health care industry.

HIPAA consolidated and strengthened efforts to combat fraud and abuse by establishing a national *Health Care Fraud and Abuse Control Program (HCFAC)*, which coordinates federal, state, and local law enforcement activities. Billions of dollars in health care fraud judgments and settlements have been won or negotiated, and funds were returned to the federal government or to private persons, including the Medicare Trust Fund.

As part of Medicare's fraud and abuse program, the Office of Inspector General (OIG) issues *advisory opinions* to provide meaningful advice about the application of the anti-kickback statute and other OIG sanction statutes. For example, in response to a letter from a charitable pediatric clinic about their plan to waive cost-sharing amounts in certain circumstances, the OIG issued an advisory opinion that concluded, "although the arrangement could potentially generate prohibited remuneration under the anti-kickback statute if the requisite intent to induce or reward referrals of Federal health care program business were present, the OIG will not impose administrative sanctions" on the pediatric clinic (because the intent was not to induce or reward referrals of Federal health care programs such as Medicare).

TABLE 5-4 Fraud and abuse examples and possible outcomes

Examples of Fraud	Possible Outcomes of Fraud

• Accepting or soliciting bribes, kickbacks, and rebates
• Altering claims to increase reimbursement
• Billing for services or supplies not provided
• Misrepresenting codes to justify payment (e.g., upcoding)
• Entering a health insurance identification number other than the patient's to ensure reimbursement
• Falsifying certificates of medical necessity, plans of treatment, and patient records to justify payment
• Billing noncovered services as covered services
• Billing or claim processing errors
• Reporting duplicative charges on a claim
• Charging excessively for services, equipment, and supplies
• Improper billing that results in payment by a government program when another payer is responsible
• Submitting claims for services not medically necessary
• Violating participating provider agreements with third-party payers
	• Administrative sanctions
	• Civil monetary penalties
	• Exclusion from the health program (e.g., Medicare)
	• Referral to the Office of Inspector General:
	  ◦ Exclusion from Medicare program
	  ◦ Sanctions and civil monetary penalties
	  ◦ Criminal penalties (e.g., fines, incarceration, loss of license to practice, restitution, seizure of assets)
	• Education
	• Referral for Medical Review:
	  ◦ Prepayment review of submitted claims
	  ◦ Post-payment review (audit) of submitted claims
	• Recoup overpaid funds:
	  ◦ Provider refunds payer
	  ◦ Payment is withheld from future processed claims
	  ◦ Suspension of payer payments (e.g., MAC holds checks)
	• Warnings

When a Medicare provider commits fraud, an investigation is conducted by the Department of Health and Human Services (DHHS) Office of the Inspector General (OIG). The OIG Office of Investigations prepares the case for referral to the Department of Justice for criminal and civil prosecution. A person found guilty of Medicare fraud faces criminal, civil, and administrative sanction penalties, including:

- Civil monetary penalties that are adjusted for inflation and organized according to four penalty tiers and culpability levels. Penalties range from more than $100, $1,000, $10,000 and $60,000, representing the four penalty tiers, for each HIPAA violation to over $1.7 million for the maximum annual penalty (of HIPAA violations in totality). Levels of culpability include no knowledge, reasonable cause, willful neglect–corrective action taken, and willful neglect–no corrective action taken.

- Criminal penalties for HIPAA violations, which include three tiers with fines and imprisonment of up to 10 years if convicted of the crime of health care fraud as outlined in HIPAA or, for violations of the Medicare/Medicaid Anti-Kickback Statute, imprisonment of up to 10 years and a criminal penalty fine of up to $250,000 (for individuals) or $500,000 (for organizations)

In addition to these penalties, those who commit health care fraud can also be tried for mail and wire fraud.

Example 1 (Fraud): A Durable Medical Equipment (DME) business owner served almost six years in prison and paid $1.9 million in restitution after pleading guilty to conspiracy to commit health care fraud and aggravated identity theft. The DME company owner created several different companies and submitted more than 1,500 false and fraudulent claims to Medicare for unnecessary medical equipment.

Example 2 (Fraud): A court sentenced a home health agency provider/owner to 14 years in prison for submitting $45 million in false claims to Medicare. The provider submitted claims to Medicare for twice-daily injections to supposedly homebound diabetic patients. The investigation revealed most patients were not homebound or insulin-dependent diabetics.

Example 3 (Abuse): Medicare recouped $656,000 from a clinic that had submitted claims for lipid panel tests and cholesterol tests (on the same patients) when, upon review of patient records, there was no documentation of medical necessity for the cholesterol tests.

Example 4 (Abuse): A new coder mistakenly submitted inaccurate ICD-10-CM codes on several submitted claims, which was discovered upon routine audit (as part of the office's compliance program). The coder was retrained, and the claims were corrected and resubmitted to ensure accurate payment from Medicare.

 NOTE:

Operation Restore Trust was a special HHS initiative against fraud, waste, and abuse that launched in May 1995, targeting three areas of high-spending growth: durable medical equipment suppliers, home health agencies, and nursing facilities. Efforts were targeted at five states, which comprised more than one-third of all Medicare and Medicaid beneficiaries: California, Florida, Illinois, New York, and Texas. Over $24 million was paid back into the Medicare Trust Fund as a result of court-ordered criminal restitutions, fines, and recoveries. Over $14 million was paid back into the Fund as a result of civil judgments, settlements, and civil monetary penalties. Criminal convictions and civil judgments also resulted, with individuals sentenced to prison.

HIPAA Title II (continued)—Administrative Simplification

HIPAA was part of a congressional attempt at incremental health care reform, with the *administrative simplification* aspect requiring DHHS to develop standards for maintenance and transmission of health information required to identify individual patients. These standards are designed to:

- Improve efficiency and effectiveness of the health care system by standardizing the interchange of electronic data for specified administrative and financial transactions
- Protect the security and confidentiality of electronic health information

 NOTE:

California implemented a regulation that prohibits the use of Social Security numbers on health plan ID cards and health-related correspondence. In 2018, a *Medicare Beneficiary Identifier (MBI)* replaced Social Security numbers on Medicare cards.

The requirements outlined by law and the regulations implemented by DHHS require compliance by *all* health care organizations that maintain or transmit electronic health information (e.g., health plans; health care clearinghouses; and health care providers, from large integrated delivery networks to individual physician offices).

The law also establishes significant financial penalties for violations:

- Each violation: $100
- Maximum penalty for identical violations may not exceed $50,000
- Maximum penalty for identical violations during a calendar year may not exceed $1,500,000

Unique Identifiers

The administrative simplification (AS) provision of HIPAA requires establishment of standard identifiers for third-party payers (e.g., insurance companies, Medicare, and Medicaid), providers, and employers, as follows:

- *Health Plan Identifier (HPID)* (formerly called PAYERID and PlanID) is assigned to third-party payers; it was rescinded in 2019 as part of administrative simplification. The voluntary *other entity identifier (OEID)* and its implementation specifications were also rescinded.
- **National Individual Identifier** (patient identifier) has been put on hold. Several bills in Congress eliminated the requirement to establish a National Individual Identifier.
- **National Provider Identifier (NPI)** is assigned to health care providers as a unique 10-digit numeric identifier, including a check digit in the last position.
- **National Standard Employer Identification Number (EIN)** is assigned to employers who, as sponsors of health insurance for their employees, must be identified in health care transactions. It is the federal employer identification number (EIN) assigned by the Internal Revenue Service (IRS) and has nine digits with a hyphen (00-0000000). EIN assignment by the IRS began in January 1998.

The Centers for Medicare and Medicaid Services (CMS) developed the **National Plan and Provider Enumeration System (NPPES)** to assign unique identifiers to health care providers and health plans. Providers can apply for the national provider identifier (NPI) online, on paper, or through an organization (e.g., professional association). When applying for the NPI, it is important to remember that providers must:

- Apply just once because every health plan, including Medicare and Medicaid, will use the same NPI for the provider.
- Obtain an NPI even if they use a billing agency to prepare standard insurance transactions.
- Continue to participate in health plan enrollment and credentialing processes.
- Safeguard the NPI because it is a private identification number.

Electronic Health Care Transactions

HIPAA requires payers to implement **electronic transaction standards** (or transaction rules), which result in a uniform language for electronic data interchange. *Electronic data interchange (EDI)* is the process of sending data from one party to another using computer linkages. The CMS Standard EDI Enrollment Form must be completed prior to submitting electronic media claims (EMC) to Medicare. The agreement must be executed by each provider of health care services, physician, or supplier that intends to submit EMC.

> **Example:** Health care providers submit electronic claims data to payers on computer tape or disk, or by computer modem or fax. The payer receives the claim, processes the data, and sends the provider the results of processing electronic claims (an electronic remittance advice).

The proposed standard for electronic signature is **digital**, which applies a mathematical function to the electronic document, resulting in a **unique bit string** (computer code) called a **message digest** that is encrypted and appended to the electronic document. (**Encrypt** means to encode a computer file, making it safe for electronic transmission so that unauthorized parties cannot read it.) The recipient of the transmitted electronic document **decrypts** (decodes data or converts data to a language that can be read) the message digest and compares the decoded digest with the transmitted version. If they are identical, the message is unaltered and the identity of the signer is proven.

The final rule on transactions and code sets was effective October 16, 2002, for large plans and October 16, 2003, for small plans. It requires the following to be used by health plans, health care clearinghouses (which perform centralized claims processing for providers and health plans), and health care providers who participate in electronic data interchanges:

- Three electronic formats are supported for health care claim transactions: the UB-04 flat file format, the National Standard Format (NSF), and the **ANSI ASC X12N 837** (American National Standards Institute [ANSI], Accredited Standards Committee [ASC], Insurance Subcommittee [X12N], Claims validation tables [837], and further subdivided into 837I and 837P formats).
  - The **UB-04 flat file** is a series of fixed-length records that is used to bill institutional services, such as services performed in hospitals. (The UB-04 is discussed in Chapter 11 of this textbook.)
  - The **National Standard Format (NSF)** flat file format is used to bill physician and noninstitutional services, such as services reported by a general practitioner on a CMS-1500 claim.
  - The ANSI ASC X12N 837I variable-length file format is used to submit institutional claims, and the ANSI ASC X12N 837P is used to submit professional claims.
- Dental services use *Current Dental Terminology (CDT)* codes. **Current Dental Terminology (CDT)** is a medical code set maintained and copyrighted by the American Dental Association.
- Diagnoses and inpatient hospital services are reported using *ICD-10-CM*.
- Physician services are reported using *Current Procedural Terminology (CPT)* codes.
- Procedures are reported using ICD-10-PCS (hospital inpatient) and CPT and HCPCS Level II (outpatient and physician office).

- Institutional and professional pharmacy transactions are reported using *HCPCS Level II (national)* codes.
- Retail pharmacy transactions are reported using the *National Drug Code* manual. No standard code set was adopted for nonretail pharmacy drug claims.

The **National Drug Code (NDC)**, maintained by the Food and Drug Administration (FDA), identifies prescription drugs and some over-the-counter products. Each drug product is assigned a unique 11-digit, three-segment number, which identifies the vendor, product, and trade package size. The Deficit Reduction Act (DRA) of 2005 requires states to collect Medicaid rebates for physician-administered medications. Effective 2007, National Drug Codes (NDC) are reported on Medicaid CMS-1500 claims (in addition to the HCPCS Level II codes) when physicians administer medication(s) to a patient during an encounter.

> **Example:** During an office encounter, a physician administered 4 mg of Zofran intravenously (IV) to a Medicaid patient. Enter the following codes on the CMS-1500 claim:
>
> - J2405 as the HCPCS Level II code for ondansetron hydrochloride, per 1 mg, which is the generic form of Zofran. (Also enter the number 4 in the Units field of the CMS-1500 claim.)
> - 00173044202 as the National Drug Code for Zofran 2 mg/mL in solution form. (The NDC is located on the medication container.)

Privacy and Security Standards

Any information communicated by a patient to a health care provider is considered **privileged communication**, and HIPAA provisions address the privacy and security of protected health information. **Protected health information (PHI)** is information that is identifiable to an individual (individual identifiers) such as name, address, telephone numbers, date of birth, Medicaid ID number, medical record numbers, Social Security number (SSN), and name of employer. In most instances, covered entities (providers, payers, and clearinghouses) are required to obtain an individual's **authorization** prior to disclosing the individual's health information, and HIPAA has established specific requirements for an authorization form. **Privacy** is the right of individuals to keep their information from being disclosed to others.

Providers have either a *direct treatment relationship* with a patient that does not require the order of another provider (e.g., treating physician) or an *indirect treatment relationship* with a patient that does require the order of another provider (e.g., pathologist, radiologist). Interestingly, pharmacists have a direct treatment relationship with patients because, even though they fill prescriptions written by other providers, they furnish those prescriptions along with advice about them directly to the patient.

 NOTE:

> Providers should develop a policy that prohibits taking cell phone pictures of patients unless taken with the patient's own phone at the patient's request. Cell phone pictures of patients have appeared on the Internet, and employees have been terminated as a result because that is a breach of patient privacy.
>
> The increasing adoption of health information technologies (e.g., electronic health record) facilitates beneficial studies that combine large, complex data sets from multiple sources. The HIPAA Privacy Rule was designed to protect individually identifiable health information (or protected health information, PIH). The **de-identification of protected health information** is a process that removes identifiers from health information to mitigate privacy risks for individuals and thus supports the secondary use of data for comparative effectiveness studies, policy assessment, life sciences research, and other endeavors.

Once information is disclosed (e.g., for the purpose of obtaining health care), it is essential that confidentiality of the information be maintained. **Confidentiality** involves restricting patient information access to those with proper authorization and maintaining the security of patient information. **Security** involves the safekeeping of patient information by:

- Controlling access to hard copy and computerized records (e.g., implementing password protection for computer-based patient records)
- Protecting patient information from alteration, destruction, tampering, or loss (e.g., establishing office policies)

- Providing employee training in confidentiality of patient information (e.g., conducting annual in-service education programs)
- Requiring employees to sign a confidentiality statement that details the consequences of not maintaining patient confidentiality (e.g., employee termination)

Because patient information is readily available through computerized databases and other means, it is essential to take steps to maintain confidentiality. **Breach of confidentiality**, often unintentional, involves the unauthorized release of patient information to a third party, as in the following examples:

- Discussing patient information in public places (e.g., elevators)
- Leaving patient information unattended (e.g., computer screen display)
- Communicating patient information to family members without the patient's consent
- Publicly announcing patient information in a waiting room or registration area
- Accessing patient information without a job-related reason

Although HIPAA privacy regulations do not require providers to obtain patient authorization for the release of health care information to payers for processing insurance claims, many providers continue to obtain patient authorization. The best practice is to advise patients that they have the right to restrict the release of their health care information (e.g., patient writes a letter informing the provider that medical records are not to be released to insurance companies). When a patient restricts the release of health care information, the provider should obtain the patient's signature on a consent form accepting financial responsibility for the cost of treatment. An insurance company that is prohibited from reviewing patient records will probably refuse to reimburse the provider for a submitted claim. The signed consent form accepting financial responsibility allows the provider to collect payment from the patient.

 NOTE:

A dated, signed special release form is generally considered valid for one year, and the patient must sign and date the special release form each year. Undated signed forms are assumed to be valid until revoked by the patient or guardian. CMS regulations permit government programs to accept both dated and undated authorizations. Established medical practices must update patient information and obtain the necessary authorization forms. Patients who regularly seek care must sign a new authorization each year.

If patient authorization is obtained, be sure the patient has signed an "authorization for release of medical information" statement before completing the claim. The release can be obtained in one of two ways:

- Ask the patient to sign a special release form that is customized by each practice and specifically names the patient's insurance company (Figure 5-8); or
- Ask the patient to sign Block 12, "Patient's or Authorized Person's Signature," on the CMS-1500 claim (Figure 5-9).

 NOTE:

Computerized practices must obtain the patient's signature on the special release form and provide a copy to the patient's insurance company upon request. With this method, the CMS-1500 claim generated will contain "SIGNATURE ON FILE" in Block 12 (Figure 5-9).

When third parties (e.g., attorneys, family members, and others) request copies of patient information, be sure to obtain the patient's signature on an authorization to release medical information (Figure 5-10). Exceptions to the expectation of privacy include information released via subpoena *duces tecum* and according to statutory reporting requirements (e.g., communicable disease reporting).

Release of PHI for Legal Proceedings

It is usually acceptable to submit a copy of the medical record for legal proceedings. If the original record is required, obtain a receipt from the court clerk and retain a copy of the record in the storage area. Be sure to protect the original record when transporting it to court by placing it in a locked storage container.

[Insert letterhead]

Authorization for Release of Medical Information to the Payer and Assignment of Benefits to Physician

COMMERCIAL INSURANCE

I hereby authorize release of medical information necessary to file a claim with my insurance company and ASSIGN BENEFITS OTHERWISE PAYABLE TO ME TO *(fill in provider's name)*

I understand that I am financially responsible for any balance not covered by my insurance carrier. A copy of this signature is as valid as the original.

Signature of patient or guardian_______________ Date ________

MEDICARE

BENEFICIARY _______________ Medicare Number ________

I request that payment of authorized Medicare benefits be made on my behalf to *(fill in provider's name)* for any service furnished to me by that provider. I authorize any custodian of medical information about me to release to the Centers for Medicare & Medicaid Services and its agents any information needed to determine these benefits or the benefits payable for related services.

Beneficiary Signature _______________ Date ________

MEDICARE SUPPLEMENTAL INSURANCE

BENEFICIARY _______________ Medicare Number ________

Medigap ID Number ________

I hereby give *(Name of Physician or Practice)* permission to bill for Medicare Supplemental Insurance payments for my medical care.

I understand that *(Name of Medicare Supplemental Insurance Carrier)* needs information about me and my medical condition to make a decision about these payments. I give permission for that information to go to *(Name of Medicare Supplemental Insurance Company)*.

I request that payment of authorized Medicare Supplemental benefits be made either to me or on my behalf to *(Name of Physician or Practice)* for any services furnished me by that physician. I authorize any holder of medical information about me to release to *(Name of Medicare Supplemental Insurance Company)* any information required to determine and pay these benefits.

Beneficiary Signature _______________ Date ________

FIGURE 5-8 Sample authorization form for release of medical information and assignment of benefits.

READ BACK OF FORM BEFORE COMPLETING & SIGNING THIS FORM.

12. PATIENT'S OR AUTHORIZED PERSON'S SIGNATURE I authorize the release of any medical or other information necessary to process this claim. I also request payment of government benefits either to myself or to the party who accepts assignment below.

SIGNED SIGNATURE ON FILE DATE ________

Courtesy of the Centers for Medicare & Medicaid Services, www.cms.gov; claim data created by author.

FIGURE 5-9 Release of medical information (Block 12 on a CMS-1500 claim).

AUTHORIZATION FOR DISCLOSURE OF PROTECTED HEALTH INFORMATION (PHI)

(1) I hereby authorize Alfred Medical Center to disclose/obtain information from the health records of:

_____   _____   _____
Patient Name   Date of Birth   Telephone (w/ area code)
                                                               (mmddyyyy)

_____   _____   _____
Patient Address   Medical Record Number

(2) Covering the period(s) of health care:

_____   _____   _____   _____
From (mmddyyyy)   To (mmddyyyy)   From (mmddyyyy)   To (mmddyyyy)

(3) I authorize the following information to be released by (Name of Provider) (check applicable reports):

☐ Face Sheet   ☐ Physicians Orders   ☐ Scan Results   ☐ Mental Health Care   ☐ Other:

☐ Discharge Summary   ☐ Progress Notes   ☐ Operative Report   ☐ Alcohol Abuse Care   _____

☐ History & Physical Exam ☐ Lab Results   ☐ Pathology Report   ☐ Drug Abuse Care   _____

☐ Consultation   ☐ X-ray Reports   ☐ HIV Testing Results   ☐ Nurses Notes   _____

This information is to be disclosed to or obtained from:

_____   _____   _____
Name of Organization   Address of Organization   Telephone Number

for the purpose of: _____

Statement that information used or disclosed may be subject to redisclosure by the recipient and may no longer be protected by this rule. I understand that I have a right to revoke this authorization at any time. I understand that if I revoke this authorization I must do so in writing and present my written revocation to the Health Information Management Department. I understand that the revocation will not apply to information that has already been released in response to this authorization. I understand that the revocation will not apply to my insurance company when the law provides my insurer with the right to contest a claim under my policy. Unless otherwise revoked, this authorization will expire on the following date, event, or condition:

_____   _____   _____
Expiration Date   Expiration Event   Expiration Condition

If I fail to specify an expiration date, event or, condition, this authorization will expire within six (6) months.

Signature of individual and date. I understand that authorizing the disclosure of this health information is voluntary. I can refuse to sign this authorization. I need not sign this form in order to ensure treatment. I understand that I may inspect or copy the information to be used or disclosed, provided in CFR 164.534. I understand that any disclosure of information carries with it the potential for an unauthorized redisclosure and may not be protected by federal confidentiality rules. If I have questions about disclosure of my health information, I can contact the Privacy Officer at Alfred Medical Center.

Signed:

_____   _____
Signature of Patient or Legal Representative   Date

If signed by legal representative:

_____   _____
Relationship to Patient   Signature of Witness

FIGURE 5-10 Sample authorization to release medical information.

Make sure that the original record remains in the custody of the health care personnel transporting the record until the record is entered into evidence.

Release of PHI for Patients with HIV

Discussing, diagnosing, and treating HIV is a sensitive, private issue between a patient and provider. This privacy is especially important because any breach of privacy may result in stigmatization or discrimination against patients living with HIV. Patients who are concerned that their health information will not be held private or secure may be discouraged from being tested for HIV and may be dissuaded from pursuing or adhering to recommended treatment regimens.

The need for privacy and security must be carefully balanced with the appropriate sharing of patient information. Health information technology poses risks for maintaining patient privacy and security, but also offers providers and patients living with HIV potential benefits. There are instances in which providers must reveal patient information to someone other than the patient, such as reporting the names of persons who have a positive HIV test to public health authorities for infectious disease surveillance. In some states, providers are also required to report the names of partners of those who test positive for HIV.

Medical information may also need to be shared with the patient's other medical providers to coordinate care and to manage HIV as a chronic condition. Established regulations allow providers to share patient health information when necessary and appropriate, while maintaining the confidentiality, privacy, and security of this information.

Patients who undergo screening for the human immunodeficiency virus (HIV) should sign an additional authorization statement for release of information regarding their HIV status (Figure 5-11). Several states require very specific wording on this form. Be sure to determine if your state requires a special form.

[Insert letterhead]
Name and address of facility/provider obtaining release:
Name of person whose HIV-related information will be released:
Name(s) and address(es) of person(s) signing this form (if other than above):
Relationship to person whose HIV information will be released:
Name(s) and address(es) of person(s) who will be given HIV-related information:
Reason for release of HIV-related information:
Time during which release is authorized: From: To:
The Facility/Provider obtaining this release must complete the following:
Exceptions, if any, to the right to revoke consent for disclosure: (for example, cannot revoke if disclosure has already been made)
Description of the consequences, if any, of failing to consent to disclosure upon treatment, payment, enrollment, or eligibility for benefits:
(Note: Federal privacy regulations may restrict some consequences.)
My questions about this form have been answered. I know that I do not have to allow release of HIV-related information, and that I can change my mind at any time and revoke my authorization by writing the facility/provider obtaining this release.
Date   Signature

This form and any updates to it are available to the public on the New York State Department of Health Web site at www.health.state.ny.us

FIGURE 5-11 Sample authorization for release of confidential HIV-related information.

Release of PHI for Patients with Substance and Alcohol Abuse Disorders

The Drug Abuse and Treatment Act of 1972 is a federal law that requires patient records be kept confidential and not subject to disclosure except as provided by law. This law applies to federally assisted alcohol or substance abuse programs, which are those that provide diagnosis, treatment, or referral for treatment of substance or alcohol abuse. General medical care facilities are required to comply with the legislation only if they have an identified drug or alcohol abuse treatment unit or their personnel provide drug or alcohol diagnosis, treatment, or referral.

HIPAA Privacy Rule

The **HIPAA Privacy Rule** creates national standards to protect individuals' medical records and other *personal health information (PHI)*. This rule also gives patients greater access to their own medical records and more control over how their personal health information is used. The rule addresses the obligations of health care providers and health plans to protect health information, requiring physicians, hospitals, and other health care providers to obtain a patient's written consent and an authorization before using or disclosing the patient's protected health information to carry out *treatment, payment, or health care operations (TPO)*.

Treatment, payment, and health care operations (TPO) are activities defined by the HPAA Privacy Rule, including *treatment* (provision, coordination, or management of health care and related services among health care providers or by a health care provider with a third party, consultation between health care providers regarding a patient, or the referral of a patient from one health care provider to another); *payment* (various activities health care providers take to obtain payment or be reimbursed for their services and of a health plan to obtain premiums, to fulfill their coverage responsibilities and provide benefits under the plan, and to obtain or provide reimbursement for the provision of health care); and *health care operations* (certain administrative, financial, legal, and quality improvement activities necessary to run its business and to support the core functions of *treatment* and payment). Covered entities are required to provide individuals with a **Notice of Privacy Practices (NPP)**, which includes an individual's health privacy rights related to protected health information (PHI) and communicates how health information may be used and shared (e.g., claims data submitted to a third-party payer to receive reimbursement for patient services provided).

Examples of payment activities include determining eligibility or coverage under a plan and adjudicating claims; risk adjustments; billing and collection activities; reviewing health care services for medical necessity, coverage, justification of charges, and so on; utilization review activities; and disclosures to consumer reporting agencies. Examples of health care operations activities include quality assessment and improvement activities; reviewing the competence or qualifications of health care professionals; conducting or arranging for medical review, legal, and auditing services, including fraud and abuse detection and compliance programs; and business planning and development, such as conducting cost-management and planning analyses related to managing and operating the entity.

According to the Department of Health and Human Services, a key protection of the HIPAA Privacy Rule is the **minimum necessary standard**, which requires organizations to "ensure that protected health information (PHI) is not used or disclosed when it is not necessary to satisfy a particular purpose or carry out a function." Covered entities are expected to evaluate organizational practices to enhance safeguards so as to limit unnecessary or inappropriate access to and disclosure of protected health information. The minimum necessary standard does not apply to:

- Disclosures to or requests by a health care provider for treatment purposes
- Disclosures to the individual who is the subject of the information
- Uses or disclosures made pursuant to an individual's authorization
- Uses or disclosures required for compliance with the Health Insurance Portability and Accountability Act (HIPAA) Administrative Simplification Rules
- Disclosures to the Department of Health and Human Services (HHS) when disclosure of information is required under the Privacy Rule for enforcement purposes.
- Uses or disclosures that are required by other law"

Example: In any health care setting, a medical coder needs access to the entire patient record to assign accurate ICD-10-CM, CPT, and HCPCS Level II codes. Conversely, hospital patient registration employees and outpatient clinic administrative assistants need to access patient pre-registration information and patient registration data screens but not to the entire patient record; providing access to the entire patient record would be a violation of the minimum necessary standard. (The HIPAA Security Rule supports the minimum necessary standard's prohibitions against improper access to protected health information to maintain availability and integrity of electronic PHI.)

Privacy violations are subject to a penalty of no more than $100 per person per violation, not to exceed $50,000 per person per year per violation of a single standard, with a calendar year maximum of $1,500,000. More serious violations are subject to more severe penalties, including the following:

- $50,000 and up to one year in prison for persons who knowingly obtain and disclose protected health information
- $100,000 and up to five years in prison for persons who under "false pretense" obtain and disclose protected health information
- $250,000 and up to 10 years in prison for persons with intent to sell, transfer, or use PHI for malicious reasons or personal gain

Example: The DHHS Office for Civil Rights announced in 2011 that it has imposed a $4.3 million civil monetary penalty for violations of the HIPAA Privacy Rule on Cignet Health of Prince George's County, Maryland, as follows:

- $1.3 million for failing to grant 41 individuals access to their health records within 30 days
- $3 million for willful negligence when the organization failed to cooperate with the investigation

 HIPAA Alert!

Patient Access to Records. The HIPAA Privacy Rule states that "an individual has the right to inspect and obtain a copy of the individual's protected health information (PHI) in a designated record set," except for the following:

- Psychotherapy notes
- Information compiled in anticipation of use in a civil, criminal, or administration action or proceeding
- PHI subject to the Clinical Laboratory Improvements Amendments (CLIA) of 1988, which is the federal law that delineates requirements for certification of clinical laboratories
- PHI exempt from CLIA (e.g., information generated by facilities that perform forensic testing procedures)

A **designated record set** is a group of records *maintained by or for* a covered entity and includes medical and billing records about individuals maintained by or for a covered health care provider; enrollment, payment, claims adjudication, and case or medical management record systems maintained by or for a health plan; or other records that are used by or for the covered entity to make decisions about individuals.

HIPAA Security Rule

The **HIPAA Security Rule** adopts standards and safeguards to protect health information that is collected, maintained, used, or transmitted *electronically*. Covered entities affected by this rule include health plans, health care clearinghouses, and certain health care providers. The Security Rule helps maintain availability and integrity of electronic protected health information (e-PHI). Maintaining *availability* means that e-PHI is accessible and usable on demand by an authorized person. Maintaining *integrity* means that e-PHI is not altered or destroyed in an unauthorized manner.

> **Example:** A clinician is provided with an appropriate level of access by the information technology department of a health care facility for e-PHI access and documentation purposes, which ensures availability. A physician would be permitted to view the entire patient record and enter documentation while a medical technologist would be limited to viewing and entering laboratory data.
>
> When a clinician logs into the electronic health record (EHR) and documents a progress note in an inpatient hospital record, a date and time stamp along with the name of the clinician is generated for each entry to ensure integrity of e-PHI. The EHR system also requires the clinician to authenticate (electronically sign) the entry. If the clinician later attempts to edit the submitted progress note, the EHR system will require the clinician to document an amendment or addendum to the original progress note (instead of overwriting original documentation) along with a reason (e.g., lab data now available that impacts treatment plan). The original progress note can be viewed, and the amendment or addendum has a new date and time stamp generated.

Effective with implementation of the HITECH Act of 2009, health care business associates and their subcontractors must also follow the HIPAA Security Rule for electronic protected health information (PHI). Business associates are individuals or organizations that work for or with covered entities (e.g., collection agency, medical billing company) and must obtain HIPAA-compliant agreements with their subcontractors (instead of the business associate's covered entity doing so).

In general, security provisions should include the following policies and procedures:

- Define authorized users of patient information to control access.
- Implement a tracking procedure to sign out records to authorized personnel.
- Limit record storage access to authorized users.
- Lock record storage areas at all times.
- Require the original medical record to remain in the facility at all times.

 NOTE:

Individual states (e.g., New York) may have passed laws or established regulations for patient access to records; providers must follow these laws or regulations if they are stricter than HIPAA provisions.

HITECH Act

The *Health Information Technology for Economic and Clinical Health Act (HITECH Act) of 2009* published final rules in the January 2013 *Federal Register*, which impacts HIPAA as follows:

- Health care business associates and their subcontractors must comply with the HIPAA Security Rule for electronic protected health information (PHI). This means that business associates must obtain HIPAA-compliant agreements with their subcontractors (instead of the business associate's covered entity doing so).
- Patients must authorize any health marketing they receive, except for notices such as prescription refill reminders, and business associates must obtain patient authorization prior to marketing.
- The sale of PHI by a covered entity or business associate (and their subcontractors) is prohibited.
- Compound authorizations for research are permitted, with adherence to applicable rules.
- Individually identifiable health information of a person deceased for more than 50 years is no longer considered PHI under the HIPAA Privacy Rule.

- Covered entities are permitted to disclose a decedent's PHI to family members and others who were involved in the care or payment for care of a decedent prior to death, unless doing so is inconsistent with any known prior expressed preference of the individual.

- Covered entities can disclose proof of immunization to a school where state or other law requires it prior to admitting a student. Written authorization is no longer required, but an agreement must still be obtained, and it can be oral.

- Covered entities must provide recipients of fundraising communication with a clear and conspicuous opportunity to opt out of receiving further such communications.

- Patients can restrict health plan (third-party payer) access to medical records that pertain to treatment paid for by the patient out of pocket.

- Patient access to electronic PHI is required, which means covered entities must provide a copy of protected health information that is maintained electronically and located in one or more designated record sets.

  ○ Covered entities must produce a copy of the electronic record in the format requested by the patient (or authorized individual).

  ○ Fees for paper and electronic copies are defined, which means providers can charge for costs of labor and materials required to copy PHI (whether in paper or electronic form). A reasonable cost-based fee for skilled technical staff time spent creating and copying the electronic file can be included in labor costs.

  ○ A covered entity cannot withhold copies of records due to the failure to pay for services above and beyond copying costs.

  ○ Timeliness for the provision of paper and electronic records was defined.

  ○ The HIPAA **breach notification** rule requires HIPAA covered entities and their business associates to provide patient notification following a breach of unsecured protected health information. Similar breach notification provisions implemented and enforced by the Federal Trade Commission (FTC) apply to vendors of personal health records and their third party service providers, pursuant to the HITECH Act. The breach notification rule's "harm threshold" was replaced with the new "low probability standard" with respect to breach of patient information notifications. This standard, which is used to determine whether a disclosure constitutes a breach, requires covered entities and business associates (and their subcontractors) to send breach notification letters to all individuals whose information has been compromised and report the incident (including detailed, publicly reported information about the breach based on the risk assessment system) to the Office of Civil Rights (OCR). (The OCR conducts periodic audits of covered entities and business associates to ensure compliance with HIPAA privacy, security, and breach notification rules.)

  ○ DHHS adopted a new risk assessment system that must be used to assess a possible breach, and it is mandatory that the following four factors are addressed during risk assessment analysis:

    1. What are the nature and extent of the PHI involved in the breach (e.g., types of identifiers, likelihood of reidentification of PHI involved in the breach)?

    2. Who is the unauthorized person who used the PHI or to whom was the disclosure made?

    3. Was PHI actually acquired or viewed by an inappropriate recipient?

    4. To what extent has risk to the PHI been mitigated (e.g., disclosing entity received receipt of assurances from recipient that PHI was not used inappropriately)?

- Changes were made to the Genetic Information Nondiscrimination Act (GINA). Title I of GINA required a revision of the HIPAA Privacy Rule. Genetic information is defined as health information, and it may not be used or disclosed for underwriting purposes.

- Revised Notice of Privacy Practices (NPP) requirements require providers to revise the document patients read and sign before their first visit. Providers are *not* required to print and distribute a revised NPP to all individuals seeking treatment. However, providers are required to provide a copy of the NPP and obtain a good faith acknowledgement of receipt from *new patients*. The revised NPP must be posted in a clear and prominent location with copies available for individuals to easily take one. (Individuals should not have to ask the administrative assistant for a copy of the revised NPP.) The NPP contains the following new requirements:

- ○ Statement indicating that most uses and disclosures of psychotherapy notes (where appropriate) require patient (or authorized individual) authorization

- ○ Statement indicating that uses and disclosures of PHI for marketing purposes require patient (or authorized individual) authorization

- ○ Statement that disclosures constituting a sale of PHI require patient (or authorized individual) authorization

- ○ Statement that other uses and disclosures *not* described in the NPP will be made only upon authorization from the patient (or authorized individual)

- ○ Statement about fundraising communications and an individual's right to opt out

- ○ Statement informing individuals about their new right to restrict certain disclosures of PHI to a health plan if they pay for a service in full and out of pocket

- ○ Statement about an individual's right to be notified of a breach of unsecured PHI in the event the individual is affected

Protecting Patients from Identify Theft

According to the Federal Trade Commission (FTC), medical identity theft is a concern for patients, health care providers, and health care plans, and the victims of medical identity theft are typically identified when they are contacted by a debt collector about medical debt they do not owe, find erroneous listings of office visits or treatments on an explanation of benefits (EOB), have been denied insurance because their patient records document a condition they do not have, receive a bill for medical services that they did not receive, see medical collection notices on their credit report that they do not recognize, or were informed by their health care plan that they have reached their limit on benefits. Health care providers and insurers can help minimize the risk to patients who report one or more of the above occurrences by:

- *Conducting an investigation.* If patients report they were billed for services not received, review financial and medical records relating to services performed to verify identities of persons receiving services. If medical identity theft is identified, notify everyone who accessed the patient's records to let them know what information is inaccurate and ask them to correct the records.

- *Understanding provider obligations under the Fair Credit Reporting Act (FCRA).* If patients report that debts have been reported to credit reporting companies, determine how the medical identity theft affects the provider's responsibilities under FCRA. If patients provide identity theft reports detailing thefts, FCRA states that debt associated with thefts cannot be reported to credit reporting companies. An *identity theft report* is a police report that contains enough detail for credit reporting companies and businesses involved to verify that the consumer is a victim, and it also states which accounts and inaccurate information resulted from the theft.

- *Reviewing data security practices.* Even if information used to commit the fraud was not generated by the provider, it is important to periodically review data security practices and compliance with information safeguard provisions associated with HIPAA privacy and security rules.

- *Providing any necessary breach notifications.* If an investigation reveals that the provider improperly used or shared protected health information (PHI) (e.g., health information was improperly shared with an identity thief), determine whether a breach occurred under the HIPAA Breach Notification Rule (45 CFR part 164 subpart D) or any applicable state breach notification law.

Some practical tips for assisting patients with correcting medical, billing, and financial records include the following:

- *Provide patients with a copy of the provider's notice of privacy practices.* The notice should include contact information for someone who can respond to questions or concerns from patients about the privacy of their health information. Hospitals may also put the person in touch with a patient representative or ombudsman.

- *Provide patients with copies of their records in accordance with the HIPAA Privacy Rule.* Patients may ask for copies of their medical and billing records to help identify the impact of the theft and to review their records for inaccuracies before seeking additional medical care. There is no central source for medical records, so patients need to contact each provider they do business with, including physicians, clinics, hospitals, pharmacies, laboratories, and health plans. For example, if a thief obtained a prescription in your patient's name, the victim may want a copy of the record from the pharmacy that filled the prescription and the health care provider who wrote the prescription. Explain to the patient that there may be fees and mailing costs to obtain copies of medical or billing files.

- *Educate patients about their right to have their medical and billing records amended or corrected.* Encourage patients to write to their health plan or provider to dispute the inaccurate information. Tell them to include copies (because they should keep the originals) of any documents that support their position. Their letter should identify each disputed item, the reasons for disputing it, and a request that each error be corrected or deleted. Patients may want to include a copy of medical or billing records with items in question circled.

- *Send an accounting of disclosures to patients.* An **accounting of disclosures** about medical information provided to third parties (e.g., attorneys, third-party payers, and Social Security disability offices) may help indicate to patients whether there has been an inappropriate release of their medical information. HIPAA allows patients to order one free copy of the accounting from each of their providers and health plans every 12 months. The accounting includes a record of the date of the disclosure, the name of the person or entity who received the information, a brief description of the information disclosed, and a brief statement about the purpose of the disclosure or a copy of the request for disclosure.

- *Inform patients that they have the right to file a complaint if they believe their privacy rights have been violated.* For example, it would be a violation if a medical provider refused to provide someone with a copy of their own medical record. Patients can file a complaint with the U.S. Department of Health and Human Services' Office for Civil Rights (www.hhs.gov/ocr).

- *Encourage your patients to notify their health plan if they suspect medical identity theft.* Obtaining a list of benefits paid in their name can help patients determine whether there are any fraudulent charges. Patients also should carefully review EOB statements that third-party payers send after treatment is provided, and patients should verify that the claims paid match care received, ensuring that the name of the provider, dates of service, and services provided are correct. Patients should report discrepancies to their third-party payer.

- *Tell your patients to file a complaint with the FTC.* Patients can file a complaint with the FTC. They also should file a report with local police and send copies of the report to their health plan's fraud department, health care provider(s), and the three nationwide credit reporting companies.

- *Encourage patients to look for signs of other misuses of their personal information.* Someone who engages in medical identity theft also may use their victim's personal information to commit more traditional forms of identity theft, such as opening a credit card account in the victim's name. Tell patients to order copies of credit reports and to review them carefully. Once victims have their reports, they should look for inquiries from companies they did not contact, accounts they did not open, and debts that they cannot explain. They also should verify that their Social Security number, address(es), name or initials, and employers' names are listed correctly.

Release of Information

Release of information (ROI) by a covered entity (e.g., provider's office) about protected health information (PHI) requires the patient (or representative) to sign an authorization to release information, which is reviewed for authenticity (e.g., comparing the signature on the authorization form to documents signed in the patient record) and processed within a HIPAA-mandated 60-day time limit. Requests for ROI include those from patients, physicians and other health care providers, third-party payers, Social Security disability, attorneys, and so on. A **release of information log** is used to document patient information released to authorized requestors, and data are entered manually (e.g., three-ring binder) or using ROI tracking software.

The HIPAA Privacy Rule requires covered entities to track the release of protected health information (PHI) so that individuals can obtain an accounting of disclosures for the six years prior to the date of their request, retroactive to April 16, 2003. To respond to this requirement, each covered entity must establish a tracking mechanism and reporting process that includes the date of disclosure, name and address of the entity or person who received the PHI, description of the PHI disclosed, and statement of reason for disclosure (or a copy of the written request for disclosure). If an entity releases PHI to the same entity for the same reason, the first disclosure is documented along with the number of disclosures made during the accounting period and the date of the last disclosure in the accounting period. An individual has the right to receive an accounting of all PHI disclosures made by a covered entity during the six years prior to the date an accounting is requested, *except* for disclosures to:

- Carry out treatment, payment, and health care operations (TPO)
- Comply with requests that occurred prior to the compliance date for the covered entity
- Create entries in the facility's directory
- Fulfill requests from correctional institutions or law enforcement officials
- Individuals (e.g., patients), themselves
- Persons involved in the individual's care
- Send notifications to national security for intelligence purposes

Telephone Inquiries

One area of concern regarding breach of confidentiality involves the clarification of insurance data by telephone. A signed release statement from the patient may be on file, but the office has no assurance of the identity or credentials of a telephone inquirer. It is very simple for a curious individual to place a call to a physician's office and claim to be an insurance company benefits clerk. The rule to follow is, *always require written requests for patient information.* (The only circumstance that would allow the release of information over the telephone is an emergency situation that involves patient care. In this situation, be sure to authenticate the requesting party by using the "call-back method," which involves calling the facility's switchboard and asking to be connected to the requesting party.)

Facsimile Transmission

Great care must be taken to ensure that sensitive information sent by fax reaches the intended receiver and is handled properly. It is recommended that health information be faxed only when there is:

1. An urgent need for the health record and mailing the record will cause unnecessary delays in treatment, or
2. Immediate authorization for treatment required from a primary care physician or other third-party case manager.

In such cases, information transmitted should be limited only to the information required to satisfy the immediate needs of the requesting party. Each transmission of sensitive material should have a cover sheet that includes the following information:

- Name of the facility to receive the facsimile
- Name and telephone number of the person authorized to receive the transmission
- Name and telephone number of the sender
- Number of pages being transmitted
- A confidentiality notice or disclaimer (Figure 5-12)
- Instructions to authorized recipient to send verification of receipt of transmittal to the sender

The practice should keep a dated log of the transmission of all medically sensitive facsimiles and copies of all "receipt of transmittal" verifications signed and returned by the authorized recipient. Take special care to ensure that proper facsimile destination numbers are keyed into the fax machine prior to transmission.

If you have received this transmittal in error, please notify the sender immediately.

The material in this transmission contains confidential information that is legally privileged. This information is intended only for the use of the individual or entity named above.

If you are not the intended recipient, you are hereby notified that any disclosure, copying, distribution, or action taken based on the contents of this transmission is strictly prohibited.

FIGURE 5-12 Sample fax confidentiality notice.

Confidentiality and the Internet

At present, there is no guarantee of confidentiality when patient records are transmitted via the Internet. If time constraints prevent sending sensitive information through a more secure delivery system, special arrangements may be made with the requesting party to transmit the document after deleting specific patient identification information. It is best to call the party requesting the documents to arrange for an identifier code to be added to the document so that the receiving party is assured that the information received is that which was requested. This transmission should be followed by an official unedited copy of the record, sent by overnight delivery, that includes specific patient material that was deleted from the previous transmission. In 1998, the *HCFA Internet Security Policy* issued guidelines for the security and appropriate use of the Internet for accessing and transmitting sensitive information (e.g., Medicare beneficiary information). The information must be encrypted so that information is converted to a secure language format for transmission, and authentication or identification procedures must be implemented to ensure that the sender and receiver of data are known to each other and are authorized to send and receive such information.

 NOTE:

Carefully review all emails before sending to ensure receipt by intended recipients only. Sending an email to an unintended recipient can result in a breach of confidentiality (e.g., patient, facility). For example, when an investigator selected "reply all" to an email that included claims abuse information about several providers, state and CMS officials had to be notified and an investigation was conducted.

Breach of Confidentiality

Health care providers are required to notify patients when the security of their protected health information has been breached. (A breach occurs when protected health information (PHI) is acquired, accessed, used, or disclosed in a way that poses "significant risk of financial, reputational, or other harm to the individual.") The following rules apply:

- Providers must notify individuals to whom the PHI pertains within 60 days after discovery of the breach.
- Providers also have a duty to notify the media of any breach that affects more than 500 individuals residing in one state or jurisdiction.

Some situations of unauthorized disclosure, access, or use of unsecured PHI do not constitute a breach requiring notification. Examples include:

- Employees who unintentionally access PHI within the scope of their authority
- PHI that is inadvertently disclosed to an employee who normally has access to certain types of PHI
- Individuals to whom PHI was disclosed but who cannot readily retain the information

Title II (continued)—Medical Liability Reform

The threat of excessive awards in medical liability cases has increased providers' liability insurance premiums and resulted in increased health care costs. As a result, some providers stop practicing medicine in areas of the country where liability insurance costs are highest, and the direct result for individuals and communities across the country is reduced access to quality medical care. Although medical liability reform was included in HIPAA legislation, no final rule was published. Individual states, such as Ohio, have passed medical liability reform, and the U.S. Congress is also formulating separate federal medical liability reform legislation.

 NOTE:

The Patient Safety and Quality Improvement Act allows providers to report health care errors on a voluntary and confidential basis. Patient safety organizations (PSOs) analyze the problems, identify solutions, and provide feedback to avoid future errors. A database tracks national trends and recurring problems.

Title III—Tax-Related Health Provisions

HIPAA's *Title III—Tax-Related Health Provisions* provides for certain deductions for medical insurance, and makes other changes to health insurance law. The HIPAA *Title III* includes the following subtitles:

- *Subtitle A:* Medical Savings Accounts
  - *Section 302:* Medical Savings Accounts
- *Subtitle B:* Increase in Deduction for Health Insurance Costs of Self-Employed Individuals
  - *Section 311:* Increase in deduction for health insurance costs of self-employed individuals
- *Subtitle C:* Long-Term Care Services and Contracts, such as Long-Term Care Insurance
  - *Part I:* General Provisions
    - *Section 321:* Treatment of long-term care insurance
    - *Section 322:* Qualified long-term care services treated as medical care
    - *Section 323:* Reporting requirements
  - *Part II:* Consumer Protection Provisions
    - *Section 325:* Policy requirements
    - *Section 326:* Requirements for issuers of qualified long-term care insurance contracts
    - *Section 327:* Effective dates
- *Subtitle D:* Treatment of Accelerated Death Benefits
  - *Section 331:* Treatment of accelerated death benefits by recipient
  - *Section 332:* Tax treatment of companies issuing qualified accelerated death benefit riders
- *Subtitle E:* State Insurance Pools
  - *Section 341:* Exemption from income tax for state-sponsored organizations providing health coverage for high-risk individuals
  - *Section 342:* Exemption from income tax for state-sponsored worker's compensation reinsurance organizations
- *Subtitle F:* Organizations Subject to Section 833 (Section 833 of the United States Code covers treatment of BlueCross BlueShield organizations, etc.)
  - *Section 351:* Organizations subject to Section 833
- *Subtitle G:* IRA Distributions to the Unemployed
  - *Section 361:* Distributions from certain plans may be used without additional tax to pay financially devastating medical expenses

- *Subtitle H:* Organ and Tissue Donation Information Included with Income Tax Refund Payments
  - o *Section 371:* Organ and tissue donation information included with income tax refund payments

Title IV—Application and Enforcement of Group Health Plan Requirements

HIPAA's *Title IV—Application and Enforcement of Group Health Plan Requirements* specifies conditions for group health plans regarding coverage of persons with pre-existing conditions and modifies continuation of coverage requirements. The HIPAA *Title IV* includes the following subtitles and sections:

- *Subtitle A:* Application and Enforcement of Group Health Plan Requirements
  - o *Section 401:* Group health plan portability, access, and renewability requirements
  - o *Section 402:* Penalty on failure to meet certain group health plan requirements
- *Subtitle B:* Clarification of Certain Continuation Coverage Requirements
  - o *Section 421:* COBRA clarifications

Title V—Revenue Offsets Governing Tax Deductions for Employers

HIPAA's *Title V—Revenue Offsets* includes provisions related to company-owned life insurance and treatment of individuals who lose U.S. citizenship for income tax purposes. It also repeals the financial institution transition rule to interest allocation rules. For example, regulations were established regarding how employers can deduct company-owned life insurance premiums for income tax purposes. The HIPAA *Title V* includes the following subtitles and sections:

- *Subtitle A:* Company-Owned Life Insurance
  - o *Section 501:* Denial of deduction for interest on loans with respect to company-owned life insurance
- *Subtitle B:* Treatment of Individuals Who Lose U.S. Citizenship
  - o *Section 511:* Revision of income, estate, and gift taxes on individuals who lose U.S. citizenship
  - o *Section 512:* Information on individuals losing U.S. citizenship
  - o *Section 513:* Report on tax compliance by U.S. citizens and residents living abroad
- *Subtitle C:* Repeal of Financial Institution Transition Rule to Interest Allocation Rules
  - o *Section 521:* Repeal of financial institution transition rule to interest allocation rules

Summary

Federal and state statutes are laws passed by legislative bodies and implemented as regulations (guidelines written by administrative agencies). The *Federal Register* is a legal newspaper published every business day by the federal government. Medicare program transmittals are legal notices about Medicare policies and procedures, and they are incorporated into the appropriate CMS program manual (e.g., *Medicare Claims Processing Manual*). Federal and state legislation have regulated the health care industry since 1863, when the False Claims Act (FCA) was enacted.

Record retention is the storage of documentation for an established period of time, usually mandated by federal and state law. HIPAA mandates the retention of health insurance claims for a minimum of six years, unless state law specifies a longer period. Health care audit and compliance programs ensure the integrity of government health care programs by combating fraud, waste, and abuse, and finding and correcting improper payments; coordinating intelligence sharing among investigators, agents, prosecutors, analysts, and policymakers; facilitating coordination and cooperation among providers to improve quality of care and reduce unnecessary costs; and detecting inappropriate codes submitted on claims and eliminating improper coding practices. An audit is an objective evaluation to determine the accuracy of submitted financial statements, and a compliance program contains internal policies and procedures that an organization follows to meet mandated requirements.

The Health Insurance Portability and Accountability Act (HIPAA) includes the following provisions: health care access, portability, and renewability; prevention of health care fraud and abuse, administrative simplification, and medical liability reform; tax-related health provisions; application and enforcement of group health plan requirements; and revenue offsets.

HIPAA's administrative simplification regulations established the HIPAA Security and Privacy Rules. Do not confuse the purpose of each rule. The *HIPAA Security Rule* defines administrative, physical, and technical safeguards to protect the availability, confidentiality, and integrity of electronic protected health information (PHI). The *HIPAA Privacy Rule* establishes standards for how PHI should be controlled by indicating authorized uses (e.g., continuity of care) and disclosures (e.g., third-party reimbursement) and patients' rights with respect to their health information (e.g., patient access).

Internet Links

Administrative Simplification in the Health Care Industry (HIPAA): Go to *http://aspe.hhs.gov*, enter HIPAA in the Search box, click Search, and click on the Health Care Administrative Simplification link.

Comprehensive Error Rate Testing (CERT): *www.cms.gov/cert*

Federal Register: *www.federalregister.gov*

Health Care Compliance Association (HCCA): Go to *https://www.hcca-info.org*, mouse over the Publications heading, click on the Newsletters link, click on *Compliance Weekly News*, and click on the Subscribe link to subscribe for free.

Health care policy and regulatory resources, such as HIPAA: *http://healthcare.findlaw.com*

HIPAA Privacy: Go to *www.hhs.gov*, click on the A-Z Index link, and then click on the H link to learn more about HIPAA privacy and security.

Medical Identify Theft brochure: Go to *www.consumer.ftc.gov*, click on the Privacy, Identity & Online Security link, click on the Identity Theft link, and then scroll down and click on the Medical Identity Theft link.

National Plan and Provider Enumeration System (NPPES): *https://nppes.cms.hhs.gov*

Notice of Privacy Practices (NPP): Go to hhs.gov, enter "model notice of privacy practices" in the Search field, click the Search icon, click on the *Model Notices of Privacy Practices | HHS.gov* link, and click on one of the NPP Provider Files to view a sample model NPP.

Office of Inspector General, US Department of Health and Human Services: *http://oig.hhs.gov*

Payment Error Rate Measurement (PERM): *www.cms.gov/PERM*

QualityNet: Go to *www.qualitynet.org* to view the CMS-approved health care quality improvement news, resources, and data reporting tools and applications used by health care providers and others.

Sample health care forms: Go to *www.healthcare-information-guide.com*, and click on the Forms link to locate sample health care forms, including a HIPAA release form for the release of patient information.

Review

5.1 – Multiple Choice

Select the most appropriate response.

1. Record retention is the storage of documentation for an established period of time, usually mandated by federal law and
   a. internal policy.
   b. local regulations.
   c. policy and procedure.
   d. state law.

2. An attorney calls the physician's office and requests that a copy of a client's medical record be immediately faxed to the attorney's office. The insurance specialist should
   a. call the HIPAA hotline number to report a breach of confidentiality.
   b. explain to the attorney that the office does not fax or copy patient records.
   c. instruct the attorney to obtain the patient's signed authorization.
   d. retrieve the patient's medical record and fax it to the attorney.

3. An insurance company calls the office to request information about a claim. The insurance specialist confirms the patient's dates of service and the patient's negative HIV status. The insurance specialist
   a. appropriately released the dates of service, but not the negative HIV status.
   b. breached patient confidentiality by confirming the dates of service.
   c. did not breach patient confidentiality because the patient's HIV status was negative.
   d. was in compliance with HIPAA provisions concerning release of dates of service and HIV status.

4. A patient's spouse comes to the office and requests diagnostic and treatment information about the patient. The spouse is the primary policyholder on a policy for which the patient is named as a dependent. The insurance specialist should
   a. allow the patient's spouse to review the actual record in the office, but not release a copy.
   b. inform the patient's spouse that the information must be requested from the insurance company.
   c. obtain a signed patient authorization from the patient before releasing their information.
   d. release a copy of the information to the patient's spouse who is the primary policyholder.

5. Which is considered Medicare fraud?
   a. Billing for services that were not furnished and misrepresenting diagnoses to justify payment
   b. Charging excessive fees for services, equipment, or supplies provided by the physician
   c. Submitting claims for services that are not medically necessary to treat a patient's condition
   d. Violating participating provider agreements with government programs such as Medicare

6. Which is considered Medicare abuse?
   a. Falsifying certificates of medical necessity, plans of treatment, and medical records to justify payment
   b. Improper billing practices that result in Medicare payment when the claim is the legal responsibility of another third-party payer
   c. Soliciting, offering, or receiving a kickback for procedures or services provided to patients in the physician's office
   d. Unbundling codes, which is reporting multiple CPT codes on a claim to increase reimbursement from a payer

7. The 66-year-old patient was treated in the emergency department (ED) for a fractured arm. The patient said, "I was moving a file cabinet for my boss when it tipped over and fell on my arm." The facility billed Medicare and received reimbursement of $550. The facility later determined that Medicare was not the payer because this was a workers' compensation case. Therefore, the facility
   a. is guilty of both HIPAA fraud and abuse because they accepted the $550.
   b. must give the $550 check to the patient, who should contact workers' compensation.
   c. should have billed the employer's workers' compensation payer for the ED visit.
   d. was appropriately reimbursed $550 by Medicare for the emergency department visit.

8. Federal and state statutes are
   a. also known as common law.
   b. based on court decisions.
   c. guidelines written by CMS.
   d. passed by legislative bodies.

9. Which term describes guidelines written by administrative agencies (such as CMS) that are based on laws passed by legislative bodies?
   a. Interrogatories
   b. Regulations
   c. Statutes
   d. Subpoenas

10. Case law is based on court decisions that establish precedent, and is also called _____ law.
    a. common
    b. mandated
    c. regulatory
    d. statutory

11. Which term describes an individual's right to keep health care information from being disclosed to others?
    a. Confidentiality
    b. Privacy
    c. Privilege
    d. Security

12. The safekeeping of patient information by controlling access to hard-copy and computerized records is a form of
    a. administrative simplification.
    b. electronic data interchange.
    c. privacy rule standards.
    d. security rule management.

13. Information that is converted to a secure language format for electronic transmission is _____ data.
    a. decrypted
    b. electronic
    c. encrypted
    d. secure

14. Which federal legislation was enacted in 1995 to restrict the referral of patients to organizations in which providers have a financial interest?
    a. Anti-Kickback Statute
    b. Hill-Burton Act
    c. HIPAA
    d. Stark II laws

15. Testimony taken under oath outside of a courtroom environment is a(n)
    a. deposition.
    b. interrogatory.
    c. precedent.
    d. subpoena.

16. Which act of legislation requires Medicare administrative contractors to attempt the collection of overpayments made under the Medicare or Medicaid programs?
    a. False Claims Act
    b. Federal Claims Collection Act
    c. Payment Error Prevention Program
    d. Utilization Review Act

17. The recognized difference between fraud and abuse is the
    a. cost.
    b. intent.
    c. payer.
    d. timing.

18. When a Medicare provider commits fraud, which entity conducts the investigation?
    a. Centers for Medicare and Medicaid Services
    b. Medicare administrative contractor
    c. Office of the Inspector General
    d. U.S. Attorney General

19. A provider or beneficiary can receive a waiver of overpayment recovery in which situation?
    a. The beneficiary was without fault regarding overpayment, and recovery would cause financial hardship.
    b. The overpaid physician was found to be at fault, but the overpayment amount was nominal.
    c. The overpayment was discovered within the same year as the year of payment.
    d. The provider was not informed by the office manager that a demand letter had been received.

20. As part of the administrative simplification provision of HIPAA, which of the following unique identifiers is assigned to providers?
    a. National Health Plan Identifier (HPID)
    b. National Individual Identifier
    c. National Provider Identifier (NPI)
    d. National Standard Employer Identifier Number (EIN)

5.2 – HIPAA Fraud and Abuse

Instructions: Analyze each of the situations below, and enter Fraud or Abuse on the blank line to indicate which applies.

_____ 1. An insurance company breached its Medicare contract by failing to report errors identified in the quality assurance process. It concealed its true error rate by deleting claims selected for review by CMS and replacing them with claim files that would not significantly affect the error rate (and thus preserve its standing within payer performance rankings).

_____ 2. A chiropractor performed ultrasonography to follow the progress of a patient treated for back pain. Medicare denied the payment because back pain does not support medical necessity for ultrasonography.

_____ 3. An ambulance company submitted false claims for reimbursement to Medicare.

_____ 4. A consulting firm submitted false hospital cost reports, upon which reimbursement formulas are based, to the Medicare and Medicaid programs on behalf of its client hospitals. The consulting firm knowingly made claims that were false, exaggerated, or ineligible for payment, and it concealed errors from government auditors, thereby permitting the client hospitals to retain funds to which they were not entitled.

_____ 5. A spinal videofluoroscopy was performed to demonstrate the extent to which joint motion of a patient was restricted. Medicare determined that physical examination procedures (e.g., asking the patient to bend) provided enough information to guide treatment of the patient and denied reimbursement.

5.3 – HIPAA Privacy and Security

Instructions: Analyze each of the statements below, and enter Privacy or Security on the blank line to indicate which applies.

_____ 1. Creating national standards to protect individuals' patient records and other personal health information.

_____ 2. Requiring patient record storage areas to be locked at all times.

_____ 3. Requiring patients to complete and sign a release of information authorization before disclosing PHI to a third party.

_____ 4. Exempting psychotherapy notes from a patient's right to access their own records.

_____ 5. Prohibiting original patient records from leaving the facility except in accordance with court order or subpoena *duces tecum*.

ICD-10-CM Coding

Chapter Outline

General Equivalence Mappings

Overview of ICD-10-CM and ICD-10-PCS

ICD-10-CM Coding Conventions

ICD-10-CM Index and Tabular List

Official Guidelines for Coding and Reporting

Chapter Objectives

Upon successful completion of this chapter, you should be able to:

1. Define key terms related to ICD-10-CM coding.
2. Use general equivalence mappings to identify ICD-10-CM codes for equivalent ICD-9-CM codes.
3. Describe the use and characteristics of the ICD-10-CM and ICD-10-PCS coding systems.
4. Interpret ICD-10-CM coding conventions for accurate code assignment.
5. Assign ICD-10-CM codes to diseases.
6. Interpret official guidelines for ICD-10-CM coding and reporting.

Key Terms

adverse effect

benign

carcinoma (Ca) *in situ*

comorbidity

complication

computer-aided coding (CAC)

computer-assisted coding (CAC)

contiguous sites

Cooperating Parties for ICD-10-CM/PCS

encoder

encounter

essential modifier

evidence-based coding

first-listed diagnosis

general equivalence mapping (GEM)

iatrogenic illness

ICD-10-CM coding conventions and brackets code also

code first underlying disease

code first underlying disease, such as:

code, if applicable, any causal condition first

colon

default code

due to

eponym

etiology and manifestation rules

Excludes1 note

Excludes2 note

in

in diseases classified elsewhere

includes note

laterality

manifestation

NEC (not elsewhere classifiable)

NOS (not otherwise specified)

other codes

other specified codes

parentheses

placeholder

see

see also
see category
see condition
Table of Drugs and
 Chemicals
Table of Neoplasms
unspecified codes
use additional code
 with
ICD-10-CM Diagnostic
 Coding and
 Reporting Guidelines
 for Outpatient
 Services—Hospital-
 Based Outpatient
 Services and
 Provider-Based
 Office Visits
ICD-10-CM Index
 to Diseases and
 Injuries

ICD-10-CM Index of
 External Causes of
 Injury
ICD-10-CM Official
 Guidelines for Coding
 and Reporting
ICD-10-CM Tabular
 List of Diseases and
 Injuries
ICD-10-CM/PCS
 Coordination
 and Maintenance
 Committee
ICD-10-PCS Official
 Guidelines for Coding
 and Reporting
International
 Classification of
 Diseases,
 11th Revision (ICD-11)

legacy classification
 system
legacy coding system
lesion
main term
malignant
metastasis
morbidity
morphology
mortality
neoplasm
nonessential modifier
outpatient
overlapping sites
physician query process
poisoning: accidental
 (unintentional)
poisoning: assault

poisoning: intentional
 self-harm
poisoning: undetermined
preadmission testing
 (PAT)
primary malignancy
principal diagnosis
qualified diagnosis
qualifiers
re-excision
secondary diagnosis
secondary malignancy
sequela
subterm
trust the index
uncertain behavior
underdosing
unspecified nature

Introduction

ICD-10-CM codes are reported for all diagnoses regardless of health care setting. These settings include physician offices and clinics, outpatient care, stand-alone clinics, home health care, hospice, hospitals, long-term care facilities, and skilled nursing facilities.

NOTE:

ICD-10-PCS codes are reported for hospital inpatient procedures only. (CPT and HCPCS Level II codes are reported by all other health care providers, and this content is covered in Chapters 7 and 8 of this textbook.)

The health insurance specialist employed in a provider's office assigns ICD-10-CM codes to diagnoses, conditions, signs, and symptoms documented by the health care provider. Reporting ICD-10-CM codes on insurance claims results in uniform reporting of medical reasons for health care services provided. (CPT and HCPCS Level II codes are reported by the provider's office and outpatient health care settings for procedures and services; Chapters 7 and 8 of this textbook cover those coding systems.)

General Equivalence Mappings

Upon implementation of the ICD-10-CM and ICD-10-PCS coding systems, the *International Classification of Diseases, 9th Revision, Clinical Modification* (ICD-9-CM) became a **legacy coding system** (or **legacy classification system**), which means it is used to archive data but is no longer supported or updated. Because ICD-9-CM was used since 1979 in the United States to classify inpatient and outpatient/provider-based office diagnoses and inpatient procedures, *general equivalence mappings (GEMs)* were annually published through 2018 by the National Center for Health Statistics (NCHS) and Centers for Medicare and Medicaid Services (CMS).

ICD-9-CM was over 30 years old, contained outdated and obsolete terminology, used outdated codes that produced inaccurate and limited data, and was inconsistent with current medical practice. It could not accurately describe diagnoses or inpatient procedures for care delivered in the twenty-first century. (Hospitals use ICD-10-PCS to code inpatient procedures. Provider-based offices and outpatient health care settings continue to use CPT and HCPCS Level II to code procedures and services.)

The National Center for Health Statistics (NCHS) and Centers for Medicare and Medicaid Services (CMS) published **general equivalence mappings (GEMs)**, which are translation dictionaries or crosswalks of codes that can be used to roughly identify ICD-10-CM codes for their ICD-9-CM equivalent codes (and vice versa). (GEMs published by the NCHS and CMS do not contain code descriptions; however, other publishers include code descriptions to facilitate code translation.) GEMs facilitate the location of corresponding diagnosis codes between two code sets. In some areas of the classification, the correlation between codes is close; since the two code sets share the conventions of organization and formatting common to both revisions of ICD, translating between them is straightforward.

Example 1: There is straightforward correspondence between the two code sets for infectious diseases, neoplasms, eye diseases, and ear diseases.

General Equivalence Mapping

ICD-9-CM Diagnosis Code and Description	ICD-10-CM Diagnosis Code and Description
003.21 Salmonella meningitis	A02.21 Salmonella meningitis
205.01 Acute myeloid leukemia in remission	C92.01 Acute myeloblastic leukemia, in remission

Example 2: In other areas of the two code sets, such as obstetrics, entire chapters are organized according to a different axis of classification. Translating between them offers a series of possible codes that must be verified in the appropriate tabular list (ICD-9-CM or ICD-10-CM) or table of codes (ICD-10-PCS) to identify the correct code. (Consider translating the English language into Chinese or any other language, and you will see the problems inherent in such translation.)

General Equivalence Mapping

ICD-9-CM Diagnosis Code and Description	ICD-10-CM Diagnosis Code and Description
649.51 Spotting complicating pregnancy, delivered, with or without mention of antepartum condition	O26.851 Spotting complicating pregnancy, first trimester
	O26.852 Spotting complicating pregnancy, second trimester
	O26.853 Spotting complicating pregnancy, third trimester
	O26.859 Spotting complicating pregnancy, unspecified trimester

Overview of ICD-10-CM and ICD-10-PCS

The World Health Organization (WHO) publishes ICD-10, which is used to classify **mortality** (death) data from death certificates. The National Center for Health Statistics (NCHS) developed a clinical modification of ICD-10, entitled the *International Classification of Diseases, 10th Revision, Clinical Modification* (ICD-10-CM), to classify **morbidity** (disease) data from inpatient and outpatient records, including provider-based office records. The *International Classification of Diseases, 10th Revision, Procedure Classification System* (ICD-10-PCS) is used to code and classify procedure data from hospital inpatient records only. The Centers for Medicare and Medicaid Services (CMS) abbreviates ICD-10-CM and ICD-10-PCS as ICD-10-CM/PCS.

Exercise 6.1 – General Equivalence Mappings

Instructions: Use the diagnosis GEM depicted in the following table to complete each statement.

ICD-9-CM to ICD-10-CM General Equivalence Mapping

ICD-9-CM Diagnosis Code and Description	ICD-10-CM Diagnosis Code and Description
078.81 Epidemic vertigo	A88.1 Epidemic vertigo
078.82 Epidemic vomiting syndrome	R11.11 Vomiting without nausea
078.88 Other specified diseases due to *Chlamydiae*	A74.89 Other chlamydial diseases

1. ICD-10-CM code A88.1 maps to ICD-9-CM code _____.
2. ICD-9-CM code 078.81 maps to ICD-10-CM code _____.
3. ICD-9-CM code 078.88 maps to ICD-10-CM code _____.
4. ICD-10-CM code A74.89 maps to ICD-9-CM code _____.
5. ICD-10-CM code R11.11 maps to ICD-9-CM code _____.

ICD-10-CM includes many more codes and applies to more users than ICD-9-CM because it is designed to collect data on every type of health care encounter (e.g., inpatient, outpatient, hospice, home health care, and long-term care). ICD-10-CM also enhances accurate payment for services rendered and facilitates evaluation of medical processes and outcomes. The term *clinical* emphasizes the modification's intent, which is to:

- Describe the clinical picture of the patient, which means codes are more precise (when compared with classification systems designed for statistical data groupings and health care trend analysis)
- Serve as a useful tool in the area of classification of morbidity data for indexing patient records, reviewing quality of care, and compiling basic health statistics

ICD-10-CM was developed by the Centers for Disease Control and Prevention (CDC) for use in *all* U.S. health care treatment settings. ICD-10-CM codes require up to seven characters, are entirely alphanumeric, and have unique *coding conventions*, rules that apply to the assignment of codes, such as Excludes1 and Excludes2 notes.

ICD-10-CM and ICD-10-PCS (Figure 6-1) incorporate much greater specificity and clinical information, which results in:

- Decreased need to include supporting documentation with claims
- Enhanced ability to conduct public health surveillance
- Improved ability to measure health care services
- Increased sensitivity when refining grouping and reimbursement methodologies

ICD-10-CM and ICD-10-PCS also include updated medical terminology and classification of diseases, provide codes to allow for the comparison of mortality and morbidity data, and provide better data for:

- Conducting research
- Designing payment systems
- Identifying fraud and abuse
- Making clinical decisions
- Measuring care furnished to patients
- Processing claims
- Tracking public health

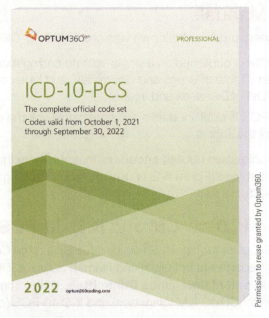

FIGURE 6-1 ICD-10-CM and ICD-10-PCS coding manuals.

To ensure accurate coding, health care professionals should assess their coding staff to determine their needs and offer appropriate education and training to:

- Apply advanced knowledge of anatomy and physiology, medical terminology, and pathophysiology.
- Effectively communicate with members of the medical staff (e.g., physician queries).
- Interpret patient record documentation (e.g., operative reports).
- Interpret and apply coding guidelines that apply to the assignment of ICD-10-CM/PCS codes.

 Coding Tip

When coders have questions about documented diagnoses or procedures/services, they should use a **physician query process** to contact the responsible physician to request clarification about documentation and the code(s) to be assigned. The process is activated when the coder notices a problem with documentation quality (e.g., an incomplete diagnostic statement when clinical documentation indicates that a more specific ICD-10-CM code should be assigned).

ICD-10-PCS

ICD-10-PCS is a procedure classification system developed by CMS for use in inpatient hospital settings *only*. ICD-10-PCS uses a *multiaxial* seven-character alphanumeric code structure (e.g., 047K04Z) that provides a unique code for all substantially different procedures. It also allows new procedures to be easily incorporated as new codes. ICD-10-PCS has more than 87,000 seven-character alphanumeric procedure codes.

 Coding Tip

In ICD-10-PCS, *multiaxial* means the codes contain independent characters, with each axis retaining its meaning across broad ranges of codes to the extent possible. (There is no decimal used in ICD-10-PCS codes.)

Coding Manuals

Many publishers produce their own versions of ICD-10-CM and ICD-10-PCS:

- ICD-10-CM is published as a single-volume coding manual with the Index to Diseases and Injuries, Neoplasm, Table of Drugs and Chemicals, and Index of External Causes of Injury located in front of the Tabular List of Diseases and Injuries.

- ICD-10-PCS is published as a separate single-volume coding manual with the Index to Procedures located in front of the Tables.

Some companies also publish **encoders** that automate the coding process. This means that computerized or web-based software (Figure 6-2) is used instead of coding manuals. (Coders use the software's Search feature to locate and verify codes.)

Updating ICD-10-CM and ICD-10-PCS

The National Center for Health Statistics (NCHS) and the Centers for Medicare and Medicaid Services (CMS) are the U.S. Department of Health and Human Services (DHHS) agencies that comprise the **ICD-10-CM/PCS Coordination and Maintenance Committee**. That committee is responsible for overseeing all changes and modifications to ICD-10-CM (diagnosis) and ICD-10-PCS (procedure) codes.

- NCHS works with the World Health Organization (WHO) to coordinate official disease classification activities for ICD-10-CM, including the use, interpretation, and periodic revision of the classification system.

- CMS is responsible for annually revising and updating the ICD-10-PCS procedure classification.

- Updates to ICD-10-CM and ICD-10-PCS are available at the official CMS (www.cms.gov) and NCHS (www.cdc.gov/nchs) websites.

- A CD-ROM version of the code sets that contain official coding guidelines is available for purchase from the U.S. Government Bookstore (bookstore.gpo.gov).

Permission to reuse granted by Optum360.

FIGURE 6-2 Encoder software.

The *Medicare Prescription Drug, Improvement, and Modernization Act (MMA)* requires all code sets (e.g., ICD-10-CM, ICD-10-PCS) to be valid at the time services are provided. This means that midyear (April 1) and end-of-year (October 1) coding updates (for new technologies) must be implemented immediately so accurate codes are reported on claims. In 2021, CMS began is considering implementation of all coding updates on April 1 and October 1 each year (instead of October 1), which means April updates would be expanded to include all possible coding revisions, not just those associated with new technologies. At the time of textbook publication, CMS had not yet made a decision.

It is crucial that updated coding manuals be purchased and/or billing systems be updated with coding changes so that billing delays (e.g., due to waiting for new coding manuals to arrive) and claims rejections are avoided. If outdated codes are submitted on claims, providers and health care facilities will incur administrative costs associated with resubmitting corrected claims and delayed reimbursement for services provided.

- Updateable coding manuals are available from publishers as a subscription service, and they are usually stored in a three-ring binder so outdated pages can be removed and new pages can be added.

- Encoder software is also available as a subscription service. Coders routinely download the most up-to-date encoder software, which contains edits for new, revised, and discontinued codes. An *encoder* automates the coding process using computerized or web-based software; instead of manually looking up conditions (or procedures) in the coding manual index, the coder uses the software's search feature to locate and verify diagnosis and procedure codes.

- Automating the medical coding process is the goal of **computer-assisted coding (CAC)** (or **computer-aided coding (CAC))** (Figure 6-3), which uses a natural language processing engine to "read" patient records and generate ICD-10-CM, ICD-10-PCS, CPT, and HCPCS Level II codes. Because of this process, coders become coding auditors responsible for ensuring the accuracy of codes reported to payers. Coding auditors performed **evidence-based coding**, which involves clicking on codes that CAC software generates to review electronic health record documentation (evidence) used to generate the code. After determining that documentation supports the CAC-generated code, the coding auditor clicks to accept the code. When documentation does not support the CAC-generated code, the coding auditor replaces it with an accurate code. For example, when the CAC-generated ICD-10-CM code does not indicate laterality or does not include a manifestation code, the coding auditor edits codes to ensure accurate reporting. (CAC can be compared to speech recognition technology that has transitioned the role of medical transcriptionists in certain fields, such as radiology, to that of medical editors.) (ICD-10-CM codes that indicate **laterality** specifically classify conditions that occur on the left, right, or bilaterally. If a bilateral ICD-10-CM code is not provided *and the condition is bilateral*, assign separate codes for both the left and right side. If the side is not identified in the patient record, assign a code for unspecified side.)

Mandatory Reporting of ICD-10-CM and ICD-10-PCS Codes

The *Medicare Catastrophic Coverage Act of 1988* mandated the reporting of ICD-9-CM diagnosis codes on Medicare claims; in subsequent years, private third-party payers adopted similar requirements for claims submission. The Administrative Simplification subtitle of the Health Insurance Portability and Accountability Act of 1996 (HIPAA) mandated the adoption of code set standards in the Transactions and Code Sets final rule published in the *Federal Register*. The final rule modifies the standard medical data code sets for coding diagnoses and inpatient hospital procedures by concurrently adopting ICD-10-CM for all diagnosis coding and ICD-10-PCS for inpatient hospital procedure coding. *Effective October 1, 2015, ICD-10-CM and ICD-10-PCS replaced ICD-9-CM.*

Medical Necessity

The concept of medical necessity determines the extent to which individuals with health conditions receive health care services. Reporting diagnosis codes (ICD-10-CM) on claims ensures the medical necessity of procedures and services (CPT and/or HCPCS Level II) provided to patients during an encounter. (ICD-10-CM diagnosis codes

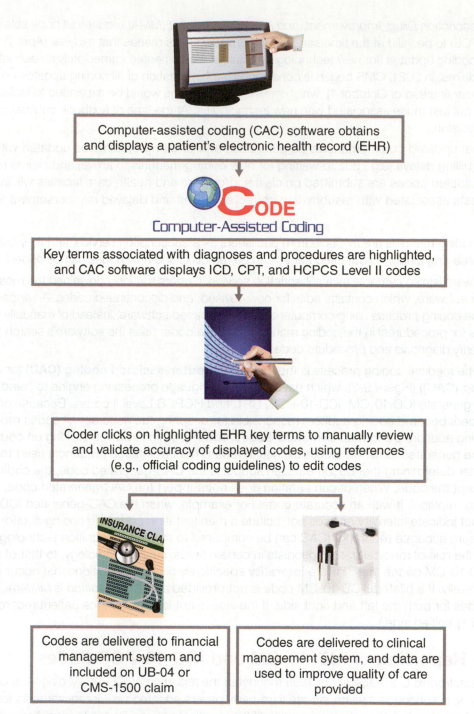

Computer-assisted coding (CAC) software obtains and displays a patient's electronic health record (EHR)

CODE
Computer-Assisted Coding

Key terms associated with diagnoses and procedures are highlighted, and CAC software displays ICD, CPT, and HCPCS Level II codes

Coder clicks on highlighted EHR key terms to manually review and validate accuracy of displayed codes, using references (e.g., official coding guidelines) to edit codes

Codes are delivered to financial management system and included on UB-04 or CMS-1500 claim

Codes are delivered to clinical management system, and data are used to improve quality of care provided

FIGURE 6-3 Computer-assisted coding (CAC).

are linked to CPT and HCPCS Level II procedure and service codes on the CMS-1500 claim.) Medicare defines *medical necessity* as "the determination that a service or procedure rendered is reasonable and necessary for the diagnosis or treatment of an illness or injury." If it is possible that scheduled tests, services, or procedures may be found "medically unnecessary" by Medicare, the patient must sign an advance beneficiary notice (ABN), which acknowledges patient responsibility for payment if Medicare denies the claim. (Chapter 14 contains a complete explanation about the ABN, including a sample form.)

An **encounter** is a face-to-face contact between a patient and a health care provider (e.g., physician, nurse practitioner) who assesses and treats the patient's condition. Thus, medical necessity is the measure of whether a health care procedure or service is appropriate for the diagnosis and/or treatment of a condition.

This decision-making process is based on the third-party payer contractual language and treating provider documentation. Generally, the following criteria are used to determine medical necessity:

- *Purpose.* The procedure or service is performed to treat a medical condition.
- *Scope.* The most appropriate level of service is provided, taking into consideration potential benefit and harm to the patient.
- *Evidence.* The treatment is known to be effective in improving health outcomes.
- *Value.* The treatment is cost-effective for this condition when compared to alternative treatments, including no treatment. (Cost-effective does not necessarily mean least expensive.)

Example: An older adult patient with type 1 diabetes mellitus is treated at the physician's office for severe wrist pain resulting from a fall. When the physician asks the patient whether they have been regularly taking their insulin and checking their blood glucose levels, the patient says that most of the time they take their insulin and sometimes they forget to check their blood glucose levels. The physician orders a blood glucose test to be done in the office, which reveals elevated blood glucose levels. The physician provides counseling and education to the patient about the importance of taking their daily insulin and checking their blood glucose levels. The physician also orders an x-ray of the wrist, which proves to be negative for a fracture. The physician provides the patient with a wrist brace and instructs the patient to follow up in the office within four weeks.

The insurance specialist reports ICD-10-CM codes for type 1 diabetes mellitus and sprained wrist along with CPT and HCPCS Level II codes for an office visit, blood glucose lab test, and the wrist brace. If the only diagnosis reported on the claim was a sprained wrist, the blood glucose lab test would be rejected for payment by the insurance company as an unnecessary medical procedure.

ICD-11 Classification System

The **International Classification of Diseases, 11th Revision (ICD-11)** was developed by the World Health Organization (WHO) and released in 2018 so that the implementation process can begin, such as translation into languages other than English. ICD-11 was revised for the purpose of recording, reporting, and analyzing health information. It contains improved usability, which means it contains more clinical detail and requires less training time. Other improvements include classification of all clinical detail, eHealth readiness for the electronic health record, linkage to other classifications and terminologies (e.g., SNOMED-CT), multilingual support, and updated scientific content.

The structure of ICD-11 is different from ICD-10, with the biggest changes focused on stem codes; extension codes; a supplementary section for the assessment of (patient) functioning; multiple parenting; and precoordination, postcoordination, and cluster coding. The number of chapters was expanded from 22 in ICD-10-CM to 26 in ICD-11, and while the ICD-11 *coding scheme* remains alphanumeric, codes range from 1A00.00 through ZZ9Z.ZZ. The second character of

ICD-11 always contains a letter to differentiate the codes from ICD-10, and the third character is always a number (referred to as a *forced number*) so that the spelling of "undesirable words" is prevented. The first character of an ICD-11 code indicates the related chapter, and letters "I" and "O" are omitted to prevent confusion with numbers "1" and "0" (just like in ICD-10-PCS).

Multiple parenting allows a condition to be correctly classified in two different places (e.g., site or etiology). For example, esophageal cancer is classified in both the neoplasm chapter and the digestive system chapter. Thus, stem code 2B70.Z (malignant neoplasms of esophagus) appears in each chapter.

Stem codes are clinical conditions described by one single category to ensure the assignment of one code per case, resulting in the (data) collection of a *meaningful minimum of information. Precoordination coding* is the assignment of stem codes, which contain all pertinent information in a pre-combined manner. For example, pneumonia due to *Mycoplasma pneumoniae* includes the disease and its histopathology in ICD-11 stem (or stand-alone) code CA40.04.

(continues)

Extension codes standardize the way additional information (e.g., anatomy, histopathology) is added to a stem code, begin with the letter "X," and can never be reported without a stem code. *Cluster coding* is used to indicate that more than one code is reported together using either a forward slash (/) or an ampersand (&) to separate multiple codes that describe a clinical case. *Postcoordination coding* is the process of combining or linking multiple (stem and extension) codes to completely describe a clinical case. For example, duodenal ulcer with acute hemorrhage is classified as stem codes DA63

(duodenal ulcer) and ME24.90 (acute gastrointestinal bleeding, NEC), and extension code XA9780 is added to indicate duodenum as the anatomic location. The codes are reported as DA63/ME24.90&XA9780.

Coding conventions such as code also, use additional code, includes, excludes, NEC, NOS, residual categories (e.g., certain, other, unspecified), and/or, due to, and with also appear in ICD-11 to provide additional information.

While ICD-11 was ready for distribution in 2018, there is no time line established for its adoption by the United States.

Exercise 6.2 – Overview of ICD-10-CM and ICD-10-PCS

Instructions: Complete each statement.

1. The *International Classification of Diseases, 10th Revision, Clinical Modification* (ICD-10-CM) codes and classifies _____ or morbidity data from inpatient and outpatient encounters.

2. The *International Classification of Diseases, 10th Revision, Procedure Classification System* (ICD-10-PCS) codes and classifies _____ data from inpatient hospital admissions only.

3. The Centers for Medicare and Medicaid Services (CMS) abbreviates ICD-10-CM and ICD-10-PCS as _____.

4. The intent of ICD-10-CM is to describe the _____ picture or findings of the patient, which means codes assigned are more precise than those needed for ICD-9-CM's statistical groupings and trend analysis.

5. ICD-10-CM codes require up to _____ characters, are entirely alphanumeric, and have unique coding conventions.

6. ICD-10-CM uses an alphabetic index to initially locate codes for conditions and a _____ list to verify codes.

7. The reporting of ICD-10-CM/PCS codes was mandated by _____ legislation.

8. Reporting ICD-10-CM codes on submitted claims ensures the medical _____ of procedures and services provided to patients during an encounter, which is defined as "the determination that a service or procedure rendered is reasonable and necessary for the diagnosis or treatment of an illness or injury."

9. The face-to-face contact between a patient and a health care provider who assesses and treats the patient's condition is called a(n) _____.

10. The criteria used to determine medical necessity include purpose, scope, evidence, and _____.

ICD-10-CM Coding Conventions

ICD-10-CM coding conventions are general rules used in the classification, and they are independent of official coding guidelines. (Refer to the ICD-10-CM *Official Guidelines for Coding and Reporting* for General Coding Guidelines and Chapter-specific Guidelines located at www.cms.gov or by accessing the online Student Resources for *Understanding Health Insurance* by signing in at www.cengage.com The Diagnostic Coding and Reporting Guidelines for Outpatient Services are located later in this textbook chapter.) The conventions are incorporated into ICD-10-CM as instructional notes, and they include the following:

- The alphabetic index and tabular list
- Format and structure
- Use of codes for reporting purposes
- Placeholder character
- Seventh characters
- Abbreviations
- Punctuation
- Other and unspecified codes
- Includes notes
- Inclusion terms
- Excludes notes
- Etiology and manifestation convention
- And
- With
- See and see also
- Code also note
- Default codes
- Code assignment and clinical criteria

The Alphabetic Index and Tabular List

ICD-10-CM includes an alphabetic index, an alphabetical list of terms and corresponding codes, and a tabular list, a structured list of codes organized into chapters based on body system or condition. The alphabetic index contains the following: Index of Diseases and Injuries, Index of External Causes of Injury, Table of Neoplasms, and Table of Drugs and Chemicals. The tabular list is called the Tabular List of Diseases and Injuries.

Eponyms

Eponyms are diseases or syndromes that are named for people. They are listed in alphabetical order as main terms in the ICD-10-CM Index to Diseases and Injuries. They are also listed as subterms below main terms *Disease and Syndrome* in the index. A description of the disease, syndrome, or procedure is usually included in parentheses following the eponym.

> **Example:** ICD-10-CM INDEX TO DISEASES AND INJURIES—EPONYM: The Index to Diseases and Injuries entry for *Christmas disease* can be located in alphabetical order. It can also be located under main term *Disease*. (Upon review of code D67 and its description in the Tabular List of Diseases and Injuries, Christmas disease is included as an synonym below the code description.)

Boxed Notes

Certain main terms in the ICD-10-CM disease index, including the Table of Neoplasms, are followed by *boxed notes* that define terms and provide coding instruction.

> **Example:** The ICD-10-CM Index to Diseases and Injuries main term Epilepsy contains a boxed note that includes terms that are to be considered equivalent to intractable, such as *pharmacoresistant*. The ICD-10-CM Table of Neoplasms contains a boxed note that clarifies how to use the columns and rows in the table.

Tables

The ICD-10-CM index includes tables which organize subterms, second qualifiers, and third qualifiers and their codes in columns and rows to make it easier to select the proper code. (Tables do not appear in the ICD-10-PCS index.) ICD-10-CM organizes the following main terms in tables, which are located at the end of the Index to Diseases and Injuries (before the Index of External Causes of Injury):

- Table of Neoplasms
- Table of Drugs and Chemicals

The **Table of Neoplasms** is an alphabetic index of anatomic sites for which there are six possible code numbers according to whether the neoplasm in question is malignant primary, malignant secondary, malignant *in situ*, benign, of uncertain behavior, or of unspecified nature. The description of the neoplasm will often indicate which of the six columns is appropriate (e.g., malignant melanoma of skin, benign fibroadenoma of breast, carcinoma *in situ* of cervix uteri).

The **Table of Drugs and Chemicals** is an alphabetic index of medicinal, chemical, and biological substances that result in poisonings and adverse effects. The first column of the table lists generic names of drugs and chemicals (although some publishers have added brand names) with six columns:

- Poisoning: Accidental (Unintentional)
- Poisoning: Intentional Self-harm
- Poisoning: Assault
- Poisoning: Undetermined
- Adverse Effect
- Underdosing

Format and Structure

The ICD-10-CM alphabetic index uses an indented format for ease in reference. Index subterms associated with an index entry's main term are indented two spaces, with second and third qualifiers associated with the main term further indented by two and four spaces, respectively. If an index entry requires more than one line, the additional text is printed on the next line and indented five spaces.

> **Example:** Locate main term Ulcer in the ICD-10-CM index, and notice that subterm aphthous (oral) (recurrent) K12.0 is indented two spaces below the U of main term Ulcer. Then, notice that second qualifier genital organ(s) is further indented two spaces.

The ICD-10-CM tabular list contains categories, subcategories, and (valid) codes. Characters for categories, subcategories, and codes consist of letters and numbers. All categories contain three characters, and a three-character category that has no further subdivision is equivalent to a (valid) code. Subcategories contain either four or five characters. Valid codes may contain three, four, five, six, or seven characters. The final level of subdivision is a (valid) code.

N O T E :

> A code that has an applicable seventh character is considered invalid without the seventh character.

In the tabular list, additional terms are indented below the term to which they are linked. If a definition or disease requires more than one line, the additional text is printed on the next line and indented five spaces.

> **Example:** Locate subcategory code P07.3 Preterm [premature] newborn [other] in the ICD-10-CM tabular list, and notice that the code and description are boldfaced and its definition and synonym (e.g., Prematurity NOS) are indented. A fifth character is required to report a valid code for subcategory P07.3, such as P07.31, Preterm newborn, gestational age 28 completed weeks.

Boldface type and a capitalized first letter is used for main term entries in the alphabetic index and all codes and descriptions of codes in the tabular list. Italicized type is used for all tabular list exclusion notes and to identify manifestation codes, which are never reported as the first-listed diagnoses.

Use of Codes for Reporting Purposes

For reporting purposes, only (valid) codes are permissible, not categories or subcategories that require additional characters. Any applicable seventh character is also required (to create a valid code).

Placeholder Character

ICD-10-CM utilizes the character X as a **placeholder** for certain codes to allow for future expansion, and it is used when a code contains fewer than six characters and a seventh character applies. For example, codes reported for poisonings, adverse effects and underdosings (categories T36–T50) often require entry of placeholder X to create a valid code.

> **Example:** Code T36.0X1A, Poisoning by penicillins, accidental (unintentional), requires the entry of X as a placeholder in the fifth-character position. Thus, reporting T36.01A (without the X placeholder in the fifth-character position) is an invalid code, which will result in a denied claim for third-party payer reimbursement.

Seventh Characters

Certain ICD-10-CM categories contain applicable seventh characters, which are required for all codes within the category, *or* as instructed by notes in the tabular list. The seventh character must always be entered in the seventh character data field, and if a code that requires a seventh character does not contain six characters, placeholder X is entered to fill in the empty character(s).

Abbreviations

The index and tabular list contains abbreviations to save space. The ICD-10-CM index and tabular list contain abbreviation **NEC (not elsewhere classifiable)**, which means "other specified" and identifies codes that are assigned when information needed to assign a more specific code cannot be located in ICD-10-CM. When a specific code is not available in the index for a condition, the coder is directed to the "other specified" code in the tabular list.

> **Example 1:** The index entry for main term Aberrant, subterm artery, and second qualifier basilar contains the NEC abbreviation in front of code Q28.1, which means a more specific code cannot be assigned. When verifying code Q28.1 in the tabular list, notice that the code description is Other malformations of precerebral vessels and that the NEC abbreviation does not appear in the code description. Code Q28.1 is assigned to the aberrant basilar artery condition because the index's NEC abbreviation provides direction to that code.

> **Example 2:** Locate code Q28.8 in the tabular list, and notice use of the NEC abbreviation next to Congenital aneurysm, specified site NEC in an inclusion term below the code description.

The ICD-10-CM index and tabular list also contain the abbreviation **NOS (not otherwise specified)**, which is the equivalent of "unspecified." It identifies codes that are to be assigned when information needed to assign a more specific code cannot be obtained from the provider. Because selecting a code from the index based on limited documentation results in the coder being directed to an "unspecified" code in the tabular list, the coder should contact the physician to request that additional documentation be provided so that a more specific diagnosis or procedure code can be assigned. A review of the patient record to assign a more specific code is also an important part of the coding process (e.g., laboratory data, radiology reports, operative report, pathology report).

> **Example 1:** The index entry for Bronchomycosis NOS B49 *[J99]* provides direction to category B49, which is an unspecified code. (Code J99 is also reported second for the condition.)

> **Example 2:** Locate code A03.9 in the tabular list, and notice that below the code description, the NOS abbreviation appears as part of inclusion term, Bacillary dysentery NOS.

Punctuation

The index includes the following punctuation:

- Colons
- Parentheses
- Brackets

A **colon** is used after an incomplete term or phrase in the index and tabular list when one or more modifiers (additional terms) is needed to assign a code.

> **Example:** Second qualifier with retinal: (located after index main term Detachment and subterm retina (without retinal break) (serous) H33.2-) requires the type of retinal detachment to be documented in the patient record so that a specific code can be selected, such as retinal break H33.00-.

Parentheses are used in the index and tabular list to enclose *nonessential modifiers*, which are supplementary words that may be present in or absent from the physician's statement of a disease or procedure without affecting the code number to which it is assigned.

> **Example 1:** The index entry Abasia (-astasia) (hysterical) F44.4 contains two nonessential modifiers in parentheses, which means that the terms may be present or absent from the provider's diagnostic statement.

> **Example 2:** In the tabular list, code I47.9 contains nonessential modifier (-Hoffman) in parentheses for inclusion term *Bouveret (-Hoffman) syndrome*, which means that the nonessential modifier may be present or absent from the provider's diagnostic statement.

Brackets are used in the index to identify manifestation codes and in the index and tabular list to enclose abbreviations, synonyms, alternative wording, or explanatory phrases. A **manifestation** is a condition that occurs as the result of another condition, and manifestation codes are always reported as secondary codes. The code and description may or may not appear in italics in the tabular list. When code descriptions are not italicized in the tabular list, make sure you sequence the codes according to the sequence in the index entry.

Example 1: The index entry for Amyloid heart (disease) E85.4 *[I43]* indicates that two codes should be reported. Because code I43 appears in slanted brackets, it is reported as a secondary code. When verifying code I43 in the tabular list, the *Code first underlying disease, such as:* instruction below the code description prompts you to report code I43 as the second code.

Example 2: The index entry for Abnormal, electrocardiogram [ECG] [EKG] R94.31 encloses abbreviations in square brackets.

Example 3: Code I45.89 in the tabular list uses square brackets to enclose the abbreviation for atrioventricular as [AV].

Other and Unspecified Codes

Other codes or **other specified codes** are assigned when patient record documentation provides detail for which a specific code does not exist in ICD-10-CM. Index entries that contain the abbreviation NEC are classified to "other" codes in the tabular list. These index entries represent specific disease entities for which no specific code exists in the tabular list, so the term is included within an "other" code.

Unspecified codes are assigned when patient record documentation is insufficient to assign a more specific code. (Before assigning an unspecified code, ask the provider to document additional information so that a more specific code can be reported.) When an ICD-10-CM tabular list category does not contain an unspecified code, the "other specified" code may represent both "other and unspecified." In ICD-10-CM, "other and unspecified" category and subcategory codes require assignment of extra character(s) to classify the condition.

When the index directs the coder to an "other, other specified, or unspecified code" in the tabular list, it is important to review the record carefully (or ask the physician for clarification of documentation) to determine if a more specific code can be assigned. This is referred to as "moving up the ladder" of codes in the tabular list.

Example 1:

- D64.89 is an *other specified* code.
- D64.9 is an *unspecified* code.
- D75 is a category of other and unspecified diseases of blood and blood-forming organs.

Example 2: For a diagnosis of polyalgia, assign code M79.89 even though the code description indicates it is an other specified code. (*Polyalgia* is an inclusion term below the code description.)

Includes Notes

An **includes note** appears in the ICD-10-CM tabular lists below certain three-character categories to further define, clarify, or provide examples of the content of a code category.

Example: The *includes note* located below category code H80 Otosclerosis in the tabular list indicates that otospongiosis is classified to that same category. This means that the provider could document otosclerosis or otospongiosis, and a code from category H80 would be assigned.

Inclusion Terms

Lists of inclusion terms are located below certain codes in the ICD-10-CM tabular list. These terms are the conditions for which that code is to be assigned. The inclusion terms may be synonyms of the code title, or, in the case of "other specified" codes, the terms are a list of various conditions assigned to that code. The list of inclusion terms in the tabular lists is not exhaustive. The ICD-10-CM index may provide additional terms also assigned to a given code.

> **Example:** The following inclusion terms are located in the ICD-10-CM Tabular List of Diseases and Injuries for diagnosis code M54.5, Low back pain:
>
> - Loin pain
> - Lumbago NOS

 NOTE:

> Inclusion terms listed below codes in the tabular list are not meant to be exhaustive, and additional terms found only in the index may also be associated with a code. This concept is called **trust the index**.
>
> > **Example:** The provider documents "infection due to fish tapeworm, larval" as the patient's diagnosis. To locate the code, go to ICD-10-CM index main term Infection, subterm fish tapeworm, and second qualifier larval B70.1. Upon verifying the code in the ICD-10-CM tabular list, notice that "infection due to fish tapeworm, larval" is not listed as an inclusion term. The coder has to *trust the index* and assign code B70.1 for the documented condition.

Excludes Notes

Two types of excludes notes are used in the tabular list, and each note has a different definition for use. However, they are similar in that they both indicate that codes excluded from each other are independent of each other. An **Excludes1 note** is a "pure" excludes. It means "not coded here" and indicates mutually exclusive codes; in other words, two conditions that cannot be reported together. However, an exception to the Excludes1.

> **Example 1:** ICD-10-CM code Q03 Congenital hydrocephalus contains an Excludes1 note for *acquired hydrocephalus (G91.-).* For hydrocephalus that develops later in life, which is an acquired form of the disease, a code from G91.- is assigned. The congenital form of the disease is *not* reported with an acquired form of the same condition. Thus, code G91.- is never reported with a code from category Q03.

> **Example 2:** ICD-10-CM code E10 Type 1 diabetes mellitus contains an Excludes1 note for *type 2 diabetes mellitus (E11.-).* Type 1 diabetes mellitus is classified to a code from category E10. Thus, a code for type 2 diabetes mellitus (category E11) is never reported with a code for type 1 diabetes mellitus.

An **Excludes2 note** means "not included here" and indicates that, although the excluded condition is not classified as part of the condition it is excluded from, a patient may be diagnosed with all conditions at the same time. Therefore, when an Excludes2 note appears under a code, it may be acceptable to assign both the code and the excluded code(s) together if supported by the medical documentation.

> **Example:** ICD-10-CM subcategory code M19.14- Post-traumatic osteoarthritis, hand contains an Excludes2 note for *post-traumatic osteoarthritis of first carpometacarpal joint (M18.2-, M18.3-).* The Excludes2 note means that because a patient can be diagnosed with both post-traumatic osteoarthritis of the hand and post-traumatic osteoarthritis of the first carpometacarpal joint, it is acceptable to assign codes to both conditions if supported by medical documentation. A sixth character is required to report a valid code from subcategory M19.14, such as M19.141 (Post-traumatic osteoarthritis, right hand).

Etiology and Manifestation Convention

Etiology and manifestation rules include the following notes in the ICD-10-CM Tabular List of Diseases and Injuries:

- Code first underlying disease
- Code first underlying disease, such as:
- Code, if applicable, any causal condition first
- Use additional code
- In diseases classified elsewhere

To classify certain conditions completely, codes must be assigned to the underlying *etiology* (cause or origin of disease) and multiple body system *manifestations* (resulting symptoms or conditions) due to the underlying etiology. For such conditions, the underlying condition is sequenced first, followed by the manifestation. Wherever an etiology and manifestation combination of codes exists, the tabular list etiology code contains a **use additional code** note and the manifestation code contains a **code first underlying disease** or **code first underlying disease, such as:** note. These instructional notes assist coders in the proper sequencing of the codes: etiology code followed by manifestation code. In most cases, the manifestation code will have in its title **in diseases classified elsewhere**, which indicates that the manifestation code is a component of the etiology/manifestation coding convention. A manifestation code that does not contain "in diseases classified elsewhere" in its title will contain a "use additional code" note. (A manifestation code is never reported as the first-listed or principal diagnosis.)

The instruction to **code, if applicable, any causal condition first** requires the causal condition to be sequenced first if present. A causal condition is a disease (e.g., diabetes mellitus) that manifests (or results in) another condition (e.g., diabetic cataracts). If no causal condition is documented, the code that contains the instruction (code, if applicable, any causal condition first) may be reported without the causal condition code. (This differs from the instruction to code first underlying condition, which does not allow for the code that contains the instruction to be reported without first sequencing the underlying condition.)

Example 1: Diagnostic statement idiopathic pulmonary hemosiderosis includes two codes in the ICD-10-CM index: E83.1- *[J84.03]*. Code J84.03 is enclosed in slanted brackets in the index, which indicates it is the manifestation code and is reported second. The ICD-10-CM tabular list entry for J84.03 contains a code first underlying disease, such as: note that prompts you to report the code second.

Example 2: The patient is diagnosed with benign hypertrophy of the prostate with urge and stress incontinence. Locate code N40.1 in the ICD-10-CM tabular list, and notice that the use additional code for . . . urinary incontinence (N39.4-) note instructs you to report an additional code. Therefore, assign codes N40.1 and N39.46 when both conditions are documented.

Next, notice that subcategory N39.4- in the tabular list includes a code also any associated overactive bladder (N32.81) note. Because the diagnostic statement (above) does not document overactive bladder, do not assign code N32.81.

Example 3: A 56-year-old male patient with an alcohol dependence (F10.20) was seen in the office, complaining of urinary incontinence. The physician determined that the condition was nonorganic in origin and most likely the result of the patient being too inebriated to realize he had urinated while unconscious. Thus, code F98.0 is assigned to urinary incontinence (or *enuresis*) that is of nonorganic origin.

And

When the word **and** appears in category titles and code descriptions in the ICD-10-CM Tabular List of Diseases and Injuries, it is interpreted as meaning and/or.

Example: Subcategory code H61.0 Chondritis and perichondritis of external ear is interpreted as Chondritis of external ear *and/or* Perichondritis of external ear. This means that code H61.0 can be assigned for both conditions or either condition, depending upon documentation.

With

When the word **with** appears in the ICD-10-CM index, it is located immediately below the main term or subterm, not in alphabetical order. To assign a code from the list of qualifiers below the word *with*, the physician must document the presence of both conditions in the patient's record.

ICD-10-CM presumes a causal relationship between the two conditions linked by the term "with" in the index or tabular list. Such conditions should be coded as related even in the absence of provider documentation explicitly linking them, *unless the documentation clearly states the conditions are unrelated*. For conditions not specifically linked by these relational terms in the classification, provider documentation must link the conditions in order to code them as related.

Example: Locate the main term measles in the index, and notice that the word *with* appears above a list of second qualifiers. To assign a code from the list, the physician must document both conditions, such as measles with keratitis (B05.81). The physician could also document:

- Measles keratitis
- Measles associated with keratitis
- Measles and keratitis
- Measles with keratoconjunctivitis

 NOTE:

The word *with* is interpreted to mean "associated with" or "due to" when it appears in a code title, the index, or an instructional note in the tabular list. When the word *with* is included in disease code descriptions in the ICD-10-CM tabular list, the physician must document both conditions for the code to be assigned.

Due to

The subterm **due to** is located in the index in alphabetical order below a main term to indicate the presence of a cause-and-effect (or causal) relationship between two conditions. When the index includes *due to* as a subterm, the code is assigned *only if* the physician documented the causal relationship between two conditions, such as meningitis due to adenovirus. It is possible that a patient could have meningitis along with an unrelated adenovirus at the same time. (The due to phrase is included in tabular list code descriptions, but it is not a coding instruction.)

ICD-10-CM occasionally presumes a causal relationship between two conditions. This means that the physician is not required to document "due to" in the diagnostic statement, such as when the patient has hypertension and chronic renal failure. This condition is coded as hypertensive chronic renal failure, which is interpreted as hypertension due to chronic renal failure.

Example: When the physician documents pneumonitis due to inhalation of regurgitated food, a causal relationship exists, and code J69.0 is assigned. (Code J69.0 also contains an instruction to code also any associated foreign body in respiratory tract, T17.-. This code is assigned only if documentation indicates retention of a foreign body.)

In

When the word **in** appears in the ICD-10-CM index, it is located in alphabetical order below the main term. To assign a code from the list of qualifiers below the word *in*, the physician must document both conditions in the patient's record. ICD-10-CM classifies certain conditions as if there were a cause-and-effect relationship present because they occur together much of the time (e.g., pneumonia in Q fever).

> **Example:** Locate the main term pneumonia in the index, and notice that the word *in (due to)* appears in alphabetical order above a list of second qualifiers. To assign a code from the list, the physician must document a relationship between both conditions, such as pneumonia in measles (or postpneumonia measles) for which combination code B05.2 is assigned. (Other conditions that occur together may require the assignment of multiple codes, one for the etiology and another for the manifestation.)

Cross References

The ICD-10-CM index includes cross-references, which instruct the coder to refer to another entry in the index (e.g., *see, see also, see* condition) or to the tabular list (e.g., *see* category) to assign the correct code.

- The **see** instruction after a main term directs the coder to refer to another term in the ICD-10-CM index to locate the code. The coder must go to the referenced main term to locate the correct code.

- The **see also** instruction is located after a main term or subterm in the ICD-10-CM index and directs the coder to another main term (or subterm) that may provide additional useful index entries. The *see also* instruction does *not* have to be followed if the original main term (or subterm) provides the correct code.

- The **see category** instruction directs the coder to the ICD-10-CM tabular list, where a code can be selected from the options provided there.

- The **see condition** instruction directs the coder to the main term for a condition, found in the ICD-10-CM disease index.

> **Example 1:** Locate category C25, Malignant neoplasm of pancreas, in the ICD-10-CM tabular list, and the Code also if applicable exocrine pancreatic insufficiency (K86.81) instruction below the description. This means that when a provider documents exocrine pancreatic insufficiency along with malignant neoplasm of head of pancreas (C25.0), two codes are reported.

> **Example 2:** Locate the main term Laceration and subterm blood vessel in the ICD-10-CM index. Notice that a cross-reference directs you to *—see* Injury, blood vessel, a different location in the index where the code can be found.

> **Example 3:** The *see also* instruction is optional if the correct code can be located below the main term (e.g., ICD-10-CM index entry Addiction*—see also* Dependence F19.20). If the correct code cannot be located, the *see also* cross-reference directs the coder to a different location in the index where the code can be found.

> **Example 4:** Locate the main term Pyelitis, subterm with, and second qualifier calculus in the ICD-10-CM index. Notice that a cross-reference directs you to *see category* N20. To assign the correct code, review category N20 in the tabular list to select the appropriate fourth digit.

> **Example 5:** Locate the main term Accidental in the ICD-10-CM index, and notice that a cross-reference directs you to*— see* condition, which means the patient record needs to be reviewed to determine the exact condition (e.g., fracture).

Code Also Note

The **code also** note in the ICD-10-CM tabular list provides instruction that two codes may be required to fully describe a condition, but the note does not provide sequencing direction. Sequencing of reported codes depends on the circumstances of the encounter as documented by the provider.

Default Code

A **default code** is listed next to a main term in the ICD-10-CM alphabetic index and represents the condition that is most commonly associated with the main term or is the unspecified code for the condition. If a condition is documented without any additional information (e.g., appendicitis), such as acute or chronic, the default code should be assigned.

Code Assignment and Clinical Criteria

The assignment of a diagnosis code is based on the provider's diagnostic statement that the condition exists. The provider's statement that the patient has a particular condition is sufficient. Code assignment is *not* based on clinical criteria used by the provider to establish the diagnosis.

Exercise 6.3 – ICD-10-CM Coding Conventions

Instructions: Assign ICD-10-CM codes to each diagnostic statement, interpreting coding conventions.

1. Acariasis infestation   _____
2. Costen's complex   _____
3. ST elevation myocardial infarction, anterior wall, involving left main coronary artery   _____
4. Malaria with acute hepatitis   _____
5. Acute lymphangitis, right lower leg   _____
6. Absence of menstruation   _____
7. Atheroembolism, distal penile artery   _____
8. Cataract in hypoparathyroidism   _____
9. Acromegaly   _____
10. Cirrhosis due to Wilson's disease   _____
11. Keratoconjunctivitis in exanthema   _____
12. Appendicitis with perforation   _____
13. Abnormal acid–base balance   _____
14. Parietoalveolar pneumopathy   _____
15. GM2 gangliosidosis, juvenile   _____

ICD-10-CM Index and Tabular List

The *International Classification of Diseases, 10th Revision, Clinical Modification* (ICD-10-CM) contains an Index of Diseases and Injuries (index) and a Tabular List of Diseases and Injuries (tabular list). The index includes an alphabetic listing of terms and codes, a table of neoplasms, table of drugs and chemicals, and an index of external causes of injury. The tabular list consists of 22 chapters, which contain categories, subcategories, and valid codes.

ICD-10-CM Index to Diseases and Injuries

The **ICD-10-CM Index to Diseases and Injuries** (Figure 6-4) is an alphabetical listing of terms and their corresponding codes, which include:

- Specific illnesses (e.g., hypertension)
- Injuries (e.g., fracture)

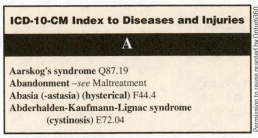

FIGURE 6-4 ICD-10-CM Index to Diseases and Injuries (partial).

- **Eponyms** (diseases and procedures named for people, such as Barlow's disease)
- Abbreviations (e.g., BMI)
- Other descriptive diagnostic terms (e.g., acute)

The index is subdivided as follows:

- Index to Diseases and Injuries
  - Table of Neoplasms
  - Table of Drugs and Chemicals
- Index of External Causes of Injury

Main Terms, Subterms, and Qualifiers

Main terms in the index are boldfaced and listed in alphabetical order, which means hyphens within main terms are ignored, but a single space within a main term is not ignored. A code listed next to a main term in the ICD-10-CM index is referred to as a *default code*. The default code represents the code for the condition most commonly associated with the main term, or it may represent an unspecified code for the condition. (The ICD-10-CM Tabular List of Diseases and Injuries must always be referenced so that the most accurate and complete code is assigned.) When a condition is documented without any additional information (e.g., appendicitis), such as acute or chronic, the *default code* is assigned (after verifying the code in the ICD-10-CM Tabular List of Diseases and Injuries).

> **Example 1:** The hyphen in Cat-scratch is ignored, resulting in sequencing that main term after Catatonic.
>
> **Catatonic**
> **Cat-scratch**

> **Example 2:** The space between bee and sting is considered, resulting in that main term being sequenced above Beer-drinkers' heart (disease)
>
> **Bee sting (with allergic or anaphylactic shock)** –*see* Toxicity, venom, arthropod, bee
>
> **Beer drinkers' heart (disease)** I42.6

Main terms may or may not be followed by a listing of parenthetical terms that serve as nonessential modifiers of the main term. **Nonessential modifiers** are supplementary words located in parentheses after a main term that do not have to be included in the diagnostic statement for the code to be assigned. **Qualifiers** are supplementary terms that further modify subterms and other qualifiers. **Subterms** (or **essential modifiers**) qualify the main term by listing alternative sites, etiology, or clinical status. A subterm is indented two spaces under the main term. Second qualifiers are indented two spaces under a subterm, and third qualifiers are indented two spaces under a second qualifier (Figure 6-5). Care must be taken when moving from the bottom of one column to the top of the next column or when turning to the next page of the index. The main term will be repeated and followed by —*continued*. When moving from one column to another, watch carefully to determine whether the subterm has changed *or* new second or third qualifiers appear.

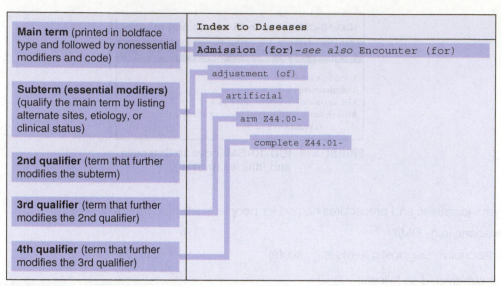

FIGURE 6-5 Display of main terms, subterms (nonessential modifiers), and qualifiers in the ICD-10-CM index.

Example: Index to Diseases and Injuries entries are organized according to main terms, subterms, second qualifiers, and third qualifiers. Refer to the index entry for stricture, aqueduct of Sylvius, with spina bifida, acquired (G91.1), and note the indented subterm and qualifiers. Notice that when the main term continues at the top of a column (or on the next page of the Index to Diseases and Injuries), the word —*continued* appears after the main term. Subterms and qualifiers are then indented below the main term.

Start of Main Term in Index to Diseases and Injuries		Continuation of Main Term (Next Column)	
Main term:	Stricture (–*see also* Stenosis)	**Main Term:**	Stricture—*continued*
Subterm:	aqueduct of Sylvius (congenital) Q03.0	**Subterm:**	bronchus J98.09
Second qualifier:	with spina bifida –*see* spina bifida,	**Second qualifier:**	congenital Q32.3
Continuation line:	by site, with hydrocephalus	**Second qualifier:**	syphilitic A52.72
Second qualifier:	acquired G91.1	**Subterm:**	cardia (stomach) K22.2

Table of Neoplasms

Neoplasms are new growths, or tumors, in which cell reproduction is out of control. For coding purposes, the provider should specify whether the tumor is *benign* (noncancerous, nonmalignant, noninvasive) or **malignant** (cancerous, invasive, capable of spreading to other parts of the body). It is highly advisable that neoplasms be coded directly from the pathology report (generated by a hospital's or stand-alone laboratory's pathology department and mailed to the provider's office); however, until the diagnostic statement specifies whether the neoplasm is benign or malignant, coders should code the patient's sign (e.g., breast lump) or report a subcategory code from the "unspecified nature" column of the documented site using the ICD-10-CM Index to Diseases Table of Neoplasms.

Another term associated with neoplasms is **lesion**, defined as any discontinuity of tissue (e.g., skin or organ) that may or may not be malignant. Disease index entries for "lesion" contain subterms according to anatomic site (e.g., organs or tissue), and that term should be referenced if the diagnostic statement does not confirm a malignancy. In addition, the following conditions are examples of benign lesions and are listed as separate Index to Diseases entries:

- Adenosis
- Cyst

- Dysplasia
- Mass (unless the word *neoplasm* is included in the diagnostic statement)
- Polyp

The *Table of Neoplasms* (Figure 6-6) is indexed by anatomic site and contains four cellular classifications: malignant, benign, uncertain behavior, and unspecified nature. The malignant classification is subdivided into three divisions: primary, secondary, and carcinoma *in situ*. The six neoplasm classifications are defined as follows:

- **Primary malignancy**—The original tumor site. All malignant tumors are considered primary unless otherwise documented as metastatic or secondary.

- **Secondary malignancy**—The tumor has metastasized (spread) to a secondary site, either adjacent to the primary site or to a remote region of the body.

- **Carcinoma (Ca)** *in situ*—A malignant tumor that is localized, circumscribed, encapsulated, and noninvasive (has not spread to deeper or adjacent tissues or organs).

- **Benign**—A noninvasive, nonspreading, nonmalignant tumor.

- **Uncertain behavior**—It is not possible to predict subsequent morphology or behavior from the submitted specimen. In order to assign a code from this column, the pathology report must specifically indicate the "uncertain behavior" of the neoplasm.

- **Unspecified nature**—A neoplasm is identified, but no further indication of the histology or nature of the tumor is reflected in the documented diagnosis. Assign a code from this column when the neoplasm was destroyed or removed and a tissue biopsy was performed and results are pending.

To go directly to the Table of Neoplasms, you must know the classification and the site of the neoplasm. Some diagnostic statements specifically document the "neoplasm" classification; others will not provide a clue. If the diagnostic statement classifies the neoplasm, the coder can refer directly to the Table of Neoplasms to assign the proper code (after verifying the code in the tabular list, of course).

	Malignant Primary	Malignant Secondary	Ca *in situ*	Benign	Uncertain Behavior	Unspecified Nature

Notes—The list below gives the code numbers for neoplasms by anatomical site. For each site there are six possible code numbers according to whether the neoplasm in question is malignant, benign, *in situ*, of uncertain behavior, or of unspecified nature. The description of the neoplasm will often indicate which of the six columns is appropriate; e.g., malignant melanoma of skin, benign fibroadenoma of breast, carcinoma *in situ* of cervix uteri.

Where such descriptors are not present, the remainder of the Index should be consulted where guidance is given to the appropriate column for each morphologic (histological) variety listed; e.g., Mesonephroma—*see* Neoplasm, malignant; Embryoma (*see also* Neoplasm, uncertain behavior, by site); Disease, Bowen's—*see* Neoplasm, skin, *in situ*. However, the guidance in the Index can be overridden if one of the descriptors mentioned above is present; e.g., malignant adenoma of colon is coded to C18.9 and not to D12.6 as the adjective "malignant" overrides the Index entry (Adenoma—*see also* Neoplasm, benign).

Codes listed with a dash - following the code have a required fifth character for laterality. The tabular must be reviewed for the complete code.

	Malignant Primary	Malignant Secondary	Ca *in situ*	Benign	Uncertain Behavior	Unspecified Nature
Neoplasm, neoplastic	C80.1	C79.9	D09.9	D36.9	D48.9	D49.9
abdomen, abdominal	C76.2	C79.8-	D09.8	D36.7	D48.7	D49.89
cavity	C76.2	C79.8-	D09.8	D36.7	D48.7	D49.89
organ	C76.2	C79.8-	D09.8	D36.7	D48.7	D49.89
viscera	C76.2	C79.8-	D09.8	D36.7	D48.7	D49.89
wall—*see also* Neoplasm, abdomen,						
wall, skin	C44.509	C79.2	D04.5	D23.5	D48.5	D49.2
connective tissue	C49.4	C79.8-	—	D21.4	D48.1	D49.2
skin	C44.509	—	—	—	—	—
basal cell carcinoma	C44.519	—	—	—	—	—
specified type NEC	C44.599	—	—	—	—	—
squamous cell carcinoma	C44.529	—	—	—	—	—

FIGURE 6-6 ICD-10-CM Table of Neoplasms (partial).

Example:

Diagnostic Statement	Table of Neoplasms Reference
Tracheal carcinoma *in situ*	trachea (cartilage) (mucosa), Malignant, Ca *in situ* (D02.1)
Cowper's gland tumor, uncertain behavior	Cowper's gland, Uncertain Behavior (D41.3)
Metastatic carcinoma	unknown site or unspecified, Malignant Secondary (C79.9)
Cancer of the breast, primary	breast, Malignant Primary (C50.9-)

If the diagnostic statement *does not* classify the neoplasm, the coder must refer to the disease index entry for the condition documented (instead of the Table of Neoplasms). That entry will either contain a code number that can be verified in the tabular list or will refer the coder to the proper Table of Neoplasms entry under which to locate the code.

Example:

Diagnostic Statement	Index to Diseases Entry
non-Hodgkin's lymphoma	**Lymphoma (of) (malignant) C85.90** non-Hodgkin (*—see also* Lymphoma, by type) C85.9- specified NEC C85.8-
Adrenal adenolymphoma	**Adenolymphoma** specified site *—see* Neoplasm, benign, by site unspecified site D11.9

 Coding Tip

1. Assigning codes from the Table of Neoplasms is a two-step process. First, classify the neoplasm by its behavior (e.g., malignant, secondary) and then by its anatomic site (e.g., acoustic nerve).

2. To classify the neoplasm's behavior, review the provider's diagnostic statement such as carcinoma of the throat, and look up "carcinoma" in the index. The entry will classify the behavior for you, directing you to the proper column in the Table of Neoplasms. (If malignant, you will still need to determine whether it is primary, secondary, or *in situ* based on documentation in the patient record.)

Primary Malignancy

A malignancy is coded as the primary site if the diagnostic statement documents:

- Metastatic *from* a site
- Spread *from* a site
- *Primary neoplasm of* a site
- A malignancy for which *no specific classification is documented*
- A *recurrent* tumor

Example: For carcinoma of cervical lymph nodes, metastatic from the left (male) breast, assign two codes:

- Primary malignancy of left breast (male) (C50.922)
- Secondary malignancy of cervical lymph nodes (C77.0)

Secondary Malignancy

Secondary malignancies are *metastatic* and indicate that a primary cancer has spread (*metastasized*) to another part of the body. Sequencing of neoplasm codes depends on whether the primary or secondary cancer is being managed or treated. To properly code secondary malignancies, consider the following: Cancer described as *metastatic* from a site is *primary* of that site. Assign one code to the primary neoplasm and a second code to the secondary neoplasm of the specified site (if the secondary site is known) or unspecified site (if the secondary site is unknown).

Example: For metastatic carcinoma from the right breast (female) to right lung, assign two codes:

- Primary malignant neoplasm of right breast (C50.911)
- Secondary malignant neoplasm of right lung (C78.01)

Cancer described as *metastatic* to a site is considered *secondary* of that site. Assign one code to the secondary site and a second code to the specified primary site (if the primary site is known) or unspecified site (if the primary site is unknown).

Example: For metastatic carcinoma from the liver to left lung, assign two codes:

- Primary malignant neoplasm of liver (C22.9)
- Secondary malignant neoplasm of left lung (C78.02)

When anatomic sites are documented as *metastatic*, assign *secondary* neoplasm code(s) to those sites, and assign an *unspecified* site code to the primary malignant neoplasm when that site is not specified.

Example: For metastatic renal cell carcinoma of the right kidney, assign two codes:

- Primary malignant neoplasm of right kidney (C64.1)
- Secondary malignant neoplasm of unspecified site (C79.9)

If the diagnostic statement does not specify whether the neoplasm site is primary or secondary, code the site as primary *unless the documented primary site is unknown*. Sometimes, when a metastatic (secondary) cancer is diagnosed, the origin of that cancer in the body cannot be found. Thus, the primary site is considered a *cancer of unknown primary (CUP)* or *occult primary tumor*. For coding purposes, the primary site is classified as unspecified (while the metastatic site is classified as secondary).

Example 1: For left lung cancer, assign one code (because *lung* does not appear in the above list of secondary sites):

- Primary malignant neoplasm of left lung (C34.92)

Example 2: For spinal cord cancer with cancer of unknown primary, assign two codes:

- Primary malignant neoplasm of unspecified site (C80.1)
- Secondary malignant neoplasm of spinal cord (C79.49)

Anatomic Site Is Not Documented

If the cancer diagnosis does not contain documentation of the anatomic site, but the term *metastatic* is documented, assign a code for *unspecified site.*

> **Example:** For metastatic chromophobe pituitary gland adenocarcinoma with unspecified secondary site, assign two codes as follows:
>
> - Primary malignant neoplasm of pituitary gland (C75.1)
> - Secondary malignant neoplasm of unspecified site (C79.9)

Primary Malignant Site Is No Longer Present

If the primary site of malignancy is no longer present, do not assign the code for "primary of unspecified site." Instead, classify the previous primary site by assigning the appropriate code from category Z85, "Personal history of malignant neoplasm."

> **Example:** For metastatic carcinoma to right lung from left breast (left radical mastectomy performed last year), assign two codes as follows:
>
> - Secondary malignant neoplasm of right lung (C78.01)
> - Personal history of malignant neoplasm of left breast (Z85.3)

Contiguous or Overlapping Sites

Contiguous sites (or **overlapping sites**) occur when the origin of the tumor (primary site) involves two adjacent sites. Neoplasms with overlapping site boundaries are classified to the fourth-digit subcategory .8, "Other."

> **Example:** For cancer of the jejunum and ileum, go to the index entry for intestine, small, overlapping lesion in the Table of Neoplasms. Locate code C17.8 in the *Malignant Primary* column, and verify the code in the tabular list.

Re-excision of Tumors

A **re-excision** of a tumor occurs when the pathology report recommends that the surgeon perform a second excision to widen the margins of the original tumor site. The re-excision is performed to ensure that all tumor cells have been removed and that a clear border (margin) of normal tissue surrounds the excised specimen. Use the diagnostic statement found in the report of the original excision to code the reason for the re-excision. The pathology report for the re-excision may not specify a malignancy at this time, but the patient is still under treatment for the original neoplasm.

 Coding Tip

1. Read all notes in the Table of Neoplasms that apply to the malignancy that you are coding.
2. Never assign a code directly from the Table of Neoplasms or Index to Diseases and Injuries.
3. Be certain you are submitting codes that represent the current status of the neoplasm.
4. Assign a code from the Table of Neoplasms if the tumor has been excised *and the patient is still undergoing radiation or chemotherapy treatment.*
5. Assign a Z code if the tumor is no longer present or if the patient is not receiving treatment, but is returning for follow-up care.
6. Classification stated on a pathology report overrides the morphology classification stated in the Index to Diseases and Injuries.
7. ICD-10-CM codes assigned to neoplasm sites are reported according to the reason for the encounter. (The designation of primary site and secondary site of neoplasm do not impact reporting order.)

Exercise 6.4 – Table of Neoplasms

Exercise 6.4A – Neoplasm Primary and Secondary Sites

Instructions: Select the most appropriate response.

1. For *oat cell carcinoma of the right lung with spread to the brain*, the secondary site is

   a. brain

   b. lung, right

   c. oat cell carcinoma

   d. unknown site or unspecified

2. For *metastatic carcinoma to right breast (female)*, the primary site is

   a. breast, right (female)

   b. carcinoma

   c. metastatic carcinoma

   d. unknown site or unspecified

3. For *metastatic carcinoma from right kidney to left femur (bone)*, the primary site is

   a. bone (left femur)

   b. kidney, right

   c. metastatic carcinoma

   d. unknown site or unspecified

4. For *metastatic malignant melanoma of left humerus (bone)*, the primary site is

   a. bone (left humerus)

   b. metastatic malignancy

   c. skin

   d. unknown site or unspecified

5. For *frontal lobe metastatic brain cancer*, the secondary site is

   a. brain

   b. frontal lobe

   c. metastatic cancer

   d. unknown site or unspecified

Exercise 6.4B – Assigning Neoplasm Codes

Instructions: Assign code(s) to each diagnostic statement, sequencing the primary site code first when two codes are required.

1. Oat cell carcinoma of the right lung with spread to the brain _____

2. Metastatic carcinoma to right breast (female) _____

3. Metastatic carcinoma from right kidney to left femur _____

4. Metastatic malignant melanoma of humerus _____

5. Brain cancer, frontal lobe _____

Table of Drugs and Chemicals

The Table of Drugs and Chemicals (Figure 6-7) is an alphabetic index of medicinal, chemical, and biological substances that result in poisonings and adverse effects. The first column of the table lists generic names of drugs and chemicals (although some publishers have added brand names) with six columns for:

- **Poisoning: Accidental (Unintentional)** (poisoning that results from an inadvertent overdose, wrong substance administered/taken, or intoxication that includes combining prescription drugs with nonprescription drugs or alcohol)

- **Poisoning: Intentional Self-harm** (poisoning that results from a deliberate overdose, such as a suicide attempt, of substance(s) administered or taken, or intoxication that includes purposely combining prescription drugs with nonprescription drugs or alcohol)

- **Poisoning: Assault** (poisoning inflicted by another person who intended to kill or injure the patient)

- **Poisoning: Undetermined** (subcategory used if the patient record does not document whether the poisoning was intentional or accidental)

- **Adverse Effect** (development of a pathologic condition that results from a drug or chemical substance that was properly administered or taken)

- **Underdosing** (taking less of a medication than is prescribed by a provider or a manufacturer's instruction)

> **Example 1:** For *hives due to penicillin taken as prescribed* (initial encounter), report codes T36.0X5A (adverse effect, penicillin, initial encounter) and L50.0 (hives).

> **Example 2:** For *coma due to overdose of barbiturates, which was the result of an attempted suicide* (initial encounter), report codes T42.3X2A (poisoning intentional self-harm, barbiturates, initial encounter) and R40.20 (coma).

 Coding Tip

The term *intoxication* indicates that either alcohol was involved (e.g., alcohol intoxication) or that an accumulation effect of a medication in the patient's bloodstream occurred (e.g., Coumadin intoxication). When *alcohol intoxication* occurs, assign an appropriate poisoning code. When an accumulation effect of a medication occurs (because the patient was taking the drug as prescribed), assign the adverse effect code (e.g., daily Coumadin use).

Substance	Poisoning, Accidental (unintentional)	Poisoning, Intentional Self-harm	Poisoning, Assault	Poisoning, Undetermined	Adverse Effect	Underdosing
14-Hydroxydihydromorphinone	T40.2X1	T40.2X2	T40.2X3	T40.2X4	T40.2X5	T40.2X6
1-Propanol	T51.3X1	T51.3X2	T51.3X3	T51.3X4	—	—
2,3,7,8-Tetrachlorodibenzo-p-dioxin	T53.7X1	T53.7X2	T53.7X3	T53.7X4	—	—
2,4-5-T (-toluene diisocyanate)	T60.1X1	T60.1X2	T60.1X3	T60.1X4	—	—
2,4,5-Trichlorophenoxyacetic acid	T60.3X1	T60.3X2	T60.3X3	T60.3X4	—	—
2,4-D (dichlorophenoxyacetic acid)	T60.3X1	T60.3X2	T60.3X3	T60.3X4	—	—
—						
ABOB	T37.5X1	T37.5X2	T37.5X3	T37.5X4	T37.5X5	T37.5X6
Abrine	T62.2X1	T62.2X2	T62.2X3	T62.2X4	—	—
Abrus (seed)	T62.2X1	T62.2X2	T62.2X3	T62.2X4	—	—
Absinthe	T51.0X1	T51.0X2	T51.0X3	T51.0X4	—	—
beverage	T51.0X1	T51.0X2	T51.0X3	T51.0X4	—	—
Acaricide	T60.8X1	T60.8X2	T60.8X3	T60.8X4	—	—
Acebutolol	T44.7X1	T44.7X2	T44.7X3	T44.7X4	T44.7X5	T44.7X6
Acecarbromal	T42.6X1	T42.6X2	T42.6X3	T42.6X4	T42.6X5	T42.6X6
Aceclidine	T44.1X1	T44.1X2	T44.1X3	T44.1X4	T44.1X5	T44.1X6
Acedapsone	T37.0X1	T37.0X2	T37.0X3	T37.0X4	T37.0X5	T37.0X6
Acefylline piperazine	T48.6X1	T48.6X2	T48.6X3	T48.6X4	T48.6X5	T48.6X6

FIGURE 6-7 ICD-10-CM Table of Drugs and Chemicals (partial).

NOTE:

An **iatrogenic illness** can result from a medical intervention, such as an adverse reaction to contrast material injected prior to a scan, and is classified within individual ICD-10-CM chapters. For example, code E71.43 (iatrogenic carnitine deficiency) is classified in ICD-10-CM Chapter 4, Endocrine, nutritional and metabolic diseases (E00–E90).

Codes in ICD-10-CM (tabular list) categories T36–T65 are combination codes that include the substances related to adverse effects, poisonings, toxic effects, and underdosing, as well as the external cause. (No additional external cause code is required for poisonings, toxic effects, adverse effects, and underdosing codes.) A code from categories T36–T65 is sequenced first, followed by the code(s) that specify the nature of the poisoning. *The exception to this rule is the sequencing of adverse effects and underdosing codes (e.g., T36.0x6-) when the condition treated is sequenced first followed by the adverse effect or underdosing code.*

 NOTE:

The Table of Drugs and Chemicals lists drugs and chemicals along with codes that identify the drug or chemical intent. *No additional external cause of injury and poisoning codes are assigned in ICD-10-CM.*

Official Guidelines for Coding and Reporting Adverse Effects, Poisoning, Underdosing, and Toxic Effects

According to official coding guidelines, the occurrence of drug toxicity is classified in ICD-10-CM as follows:

1. *Adverse Effect*
   When coding an adverse effect of a drug that has been correctly prescribed and properly administered, assign the appropriate code for the nature of the adverse effect followed by the appropriate code for the adverse effect of the drug (T36–T50). The code for the drug should have a fifth or sixth character "5" (e.g., T36.0X5-). Examples of the nature of an adverse effect are tachycardia, delirium, gastrointestinal hemorrhaging, vomiting, hypokalemia, hepatitis, renal failure, or respiratory failure.

2. *Poisoning*
   When coding a poisoning or reaction to the improper use of a medication (e.g., overdose, wrong substance given or taken in error, wrong route of administration), assign the appropriate code from categories T36–T50. The poisoning codes have an associated intent as their fifth or sixth character (accidental, intentional self-harm, assault, and undetermined). Use additional code(s) for all manifestations of poisonings. If there is also a diagnosis of abuse or dependence of the substance, the abuse or dependence is coded as an additional code. Examples of poisoning include:

   (i) *Error was made in drug prescription*
   Errors made in drug prescription or in the administration of the drug by provider, nurse, patient, or other person.

   (ii) *Overdose of a drug intentionally taken*
   If an overdose of a drug was intentionally taken or administered and resulted in drug toxicity, it would be coded as a poisoning.

   (iii) *Nonprescribed drug taken with correctly prescribed and properly administered drug*
   If a nonprescribed drug or medicinal agent was taken in combination with a correctly prescribed and properly administered drug, any drug toxicity or other reaction resulting from the interaction of the two drugs would be classified as a poisoning.

   (iv) *Interaction of drug(s) and alcohol*
   When a reaction results from the interaction of a drug(s) and alcohol, this would be classified as poisoning.

3. *Underdosing*
   Underdosing refers to taking less of a medication than is prescribed by a provider or a manufacturer's instruction. Discontinuing the use of a prescribed medication on the patient's own initiative (not directed by the patient's provider) is also classified as an underdosing. For underdosing, assign the code from categories T36–T50 (fifth or sixth character "6"). *Codes for underdosing should never be assigned as principal or first-listed codes.* If a patient has a relapse or exacerbation of the medical condition for which the drug is prescribed because of the reduction in dose, then the medical condition itself should be coded. Noncompliance (Z91.12-, Z91.13-, and Z91.14-) or complication of care (Y63.8–Y63.9) codes are to be used with an underdosing code to indicate intent, if known.

4. *Toxic Effects*
   When a harmful substance is ingested or comes in contact with a person, this is classified as a toxic effect. The toxic effect codes are in categories T51–T65. Toxic effect codes have an associated intent: accidental, intentional self-harm, assault, and undetermined.

Coding Tip

Complications due to insulin pump malfunction include:

(a) *Underdose of insulin due to insulin pump failure*

An underdose of insulin due to an insulin pump failure should be assigned to a code from subcategory T85.6-, Mechanical complication of other specified internal and external prosthetic devices, implants and grafts, that specifies the type of pump malfunction as the principal or first-listed code, followed by code T38.3X6-, Underdosing of insulin and oral hypoglycemic [antidiabetic] drugs. Additional codes for the type of diabetes mellitus and any associated complications due to the underdosing should also be assigned.

(b) *Overdose of insulin due to insulin pump failure*

The principal or first-listed code for an encounter due to an insulin pump malfunction resulting in an overdose of insulin should also be T85.6-, Mechanical complication of other specified internal and external prosthetic devices, implants and grafts, followed by code T38.3X1-, Poisoning by insulin and oral hypoglycemic [antidiabetic] drugs, accidental (unintentional).

Exercise 6.5 – Table of Drugs and Chemicals

Instructions: Assign ICD-10-CM code(s) to each diagnostic statement.

1. Myalgia of the neck as an adverse reaction to pertussis vaccine, initial encounter _____
2. Cardiac arrhythmia caused by interaction between prescribed ephedrine and wine (accident), initial encounter _____
3. Stupor, due to overdose of Nytol (suicide attempt), initial encounter _____
4. High blood pressure due to prescribed albuterol, initial encounter _____
5. Rash due to combining prescribed amoxicillin with prescribed Benadryl, initial encounter _____

Index of External Causes of Injury

The **ICD-10-CM Index of External Causes of Injury** (Figure 6-8) is arranged in alphabetical order by main term indicating the event. These codes are secondary codes for use in any health care setting. External cause codes are intended to provide data for injury research and evaluation of injury prevention strategies.

These codes are assigned to capture the following:

- *Cause of injury* ("how" the injury occurred, such as abuse, accident, assault, burn, collision, and so on)
- *Activity being performed* ("what" the patient was doing at the time of injury, such as playing a sport, gardening, sleeping, using a cell phone, and so on)
- *Place of occurrence* ("where" the patient was when the injury occurred, such as at home or work, in a post office, on a highway, and so on)
- *Patient status at the time of injury* (indicates if injury is related to leisure, military, student, volunteer, and so on, as applicable)

ICD-10-CM INDEX TO EXTERNAL CAUSE OF INJURIES

Abandonment (causing exposure to weather conditions) (with intent to injure or kill) NEC X58
Abuse (adult) (child) (mental) (physical) (sexual) X58
Accident (to) X58

    aircraft (in transit) (powered) *–see also* Accident, transport, aircraft

      due to, caused by cataclysm *–see* Forces of nature, by type

    animal-drawn vehicle *–see* Accident, transport, animal-drawn vehicle occupant

    animal-rider *–see* Accident, transport, animal-rider

    automobile *–see* Accident, transport, car occupant

    bare foot water skiier V94.4

    boat, boating *–see also* Accident, watercraft

      striking swimmer

        powered V94.11

        unpowered V94.12

ICD-10-CM TABULAR LIST OF DISEASES AND INJURIES

CHAPTER 20: External causes of morbidity (V00-Y99)

V94 Other and unspecified water transport accidents

> **EXCLUDES1:** military watercraft accidents in military or war operations (Y36, Y37)

> The appropriate 7th character is to be added to each code from category V94
> A   Initial encounter
> D   Subsequent encounter
> S   Sequela

    V94.0 **Hitting object or bottom of body of water due to fall from watercraft**

>   **EXCLUDES2:** drowning and submersion due to fall from watercraft (V92.0-)

    V94.1 **Bather struck by watercraft**
        Swimmer hit by watercraft

        V94.11 Bather struck by powered watercraft

        V94.12 Bather struck by nonpowered watercraft

FIGURE 6-8 ICD-10-CM External Causes (partial).

Coding Tip

ICD-10-CM Index of External Causes of Injury main terms to begin the process of assigning an external cause code. Common main terms include:

○ Accident

○ Injury, injured

○ Misadventure(s) to patient(s) during surgical or medical care

Before assigning an ICD-10-CM external cause code, review the notes located at the beginning of Chapter 21 in the ICD-10-CM tabular list.

Example: A 2-year-old patient fell off the toilet in the downstairs bathroom of their single-family house during an attempt to coax their cat to come down from the top of a medicine cabinet. It apparently worked because the cat jumped off the cabinet and landed on the patient. However, the patient was so surprised that they screamed and fell off the toilet onto the floor. The patient landed on their left arm due to the fall and experienced extremely sharp pain. They were evaluated in the emergency department where they were diagnosed with a *closed nondisplaced comminuted fracture of the humerus, left*. They received treatment and was discharged home to follow-up with their primary care physician in the office.

For ICD-10-CM, report the injury (fracture) (S42.355A), cause of injury (fall) (W18.11XA), place of injury (bathroom of patient's home) (Y92.012), activity (other activity involving animal care) (Y93.K9), external cause status (other external cause status) (Y99.8).

ICD-10-CM's level of specificity results in different codes for other locations in the patient's home (e.g., bathroom). For ICD-10-CM code W18.11XA (fall from toilet), the seventh character (A) indicates she received initial treatment. ICD-10-CM place of injury codes for this case indicate that the patient's health insurance policy should be billed (not a homeowner's, liability, or workers' compensation policy). If a guest of a homeowner had been injured in this manner, the homeowner's insurance would be billed. If the place of injury had been at a grocery store or another place of business, that business's liability insurance would be billed instead of the patient's health insurance.

Basic Steps for Using the Index to Diseases and Injuries

It is important to remember that you should never code directly from the Index to Diseases and Injuries. After locating a code in the index, go to that code in the Tabular List of Diseases and Injuries to find important instructions (e.g., includes notes and excludes notes) and to verify the code selected. Instructions may require the assignment of additional codes or indicate conditions that are classified elsewhere.

Step 1   Locate the main term in the Index to Diseases and Injuries.

Begin the coding process in the ICD-10-CM Index to Diseases and Injuries by locating the condition's main term and then reviewing the subterms listed below the main term to locate the proper disorder.

Example: The underlined terms in the following conditions are main terms:
Allergens <u>investigation</u>
Auditory <u>agnosia</u> secondary to organic lesion
<u>Intussusception</u>, ileocolic
<u>Status</u> (post) angioplasty

Step 2   If the instructional phrase –*see* condition is found after the main term, a descriptive term (an adjective) or the anatomic site has been mistakenly referenced instead of the disorder or the disease (the condition) documented in the diagnostic statement.

Example: The provider's diagnostic statement is *upper respiratory infection*. In the ICD-10-CM Index to Diseases and Injuries, look up the phrase *upper respiratory*. Notice that the instructional phrase –*see condition* appears next to the phrase *upper respiratory*. This instruction directs you to the condition, which is *infection*.

Step 3   When the condition in the diagnostic statement is not easily found in the index, use the main terms below to locate the code.

- Abnormal
- Anomaly
- Complication
- Delivery
- Disease
- Disorder

- Findings
- Foreign body
- Infection
- Injury
- Late effect(s)
- Lesion

- Neoplasm
- Obstruction
- Pregnancy
- Puerperal
- Syndrome
- Wound

Step 4   Sometimes terms found in the Index to Diseases and Injuries are not found in the Tabular List of Diseases and Injuries when the code number is reviewed for verification. When this occurs, the coder should *trust the index* because, to save space in the tabular list, more terms are listed in the index than in the tabular list.

> **Example:** For the condition generalized gum attrition, main term attrition, and subterm gum direct you to *see* Recession, gingival in the ICD-10-CM index (where code K06.020 for generalized gingival recession is found). When code K06.020 is verified in the tabular list, the term attrition is missing; however, code K06.020 is still the correct code. (This is an example of *trust the index*.)

 NOTE:

> To locate a code that classifies an external cause of injury, refer to the separate Index of External Causes of Injury, which is located after the Table of Drugs and Chemicals (after the Index to Diseases and Injuries).

Exercise 6.6 – ICD-10-CM Index to Diseases and Injuries

Instructions: Complete each statement.

1. The ICD-10-CM alphabetical listing of main terms or conditions printed in boldfaced type that may be expressed as nouns, adjectives, or eponyms is called the _____ to Diseases and Injuries.

2. Codes for adverse effects, poisonings, and underdosings associated with medicinal, chemical, and biological substances are initially located in the ICD-10-CM _____ of Drugs and Chemicals.

3. Main terms in the ICD-10-CM index are listed in alphabetical order, which means a single _____ between words is ignored when locating main terms in the ICD-10-CM indexes.

4. For the following list of main terms found in the ICD-10-CM Index to Diseases and Injuries, main term _____ is *not* in alphabetical order.

   a. Aerodontalgia

   b. Aeroembolism

   c. Aero-otitis media

   d. *Aerogenes capsulatus* infection

5. When numerical characters and words appear below a main term in the ICD-10-CM Index to Diseases and Injuries, they are listed in _____ order.

6. Main terms in the ICD-10-CM Index to Diseases and Injuries are printed in boldfaced type and followed by the _____ code.

7. Words contained in parentheses after a main term in the ICD-10-CM Index to Diseases and Injuries do not have to be included in the provider's diagnostic statement for the code listed after the parentheses to be assigned; such words are called _____ modifiers.

8. ICD-10-CM Index to Diseases and Injuries subterms that qualify a main term by listing alternative sites, etiology, or clinical status are called _____ modifiers.

9. When the provider documents "acute angina pectoris," the main term in the ICD-10-CM index is _____.

10. When the provider documents "past history of nutritional deficiency," the main term in the ICD-10-CM index is _____.

ICD-10-CM Tabular List of Diseases and Injuries

The **ICD-10-CM Tabular List of Diseases and Injuries** (Table 6-1) is a chronological list of codes contained within 22 chapters, which are based on body system or condition. ICD-10-CM codes are organized within:

- *Major topic headings*, also called a *code block*, are printed in bold uppercase letters and followed by groups of three-character disease categories within a chapter (e.g., Intestinal Infectious Diseases, A00–A09).

- *Categories, subcategories, and codes*, which contain a combination of letters and numbers
  - All categories contain three characters (e.g., A09).
  - A three-character category that has no further subdivision is a valid code.
  - Subcategories contain either four or five characters.
  - Codes may contain three, four, five, six, or seven characters.
    - The final level of subdivision is a code.
    - All codes in the ICD-10-CM tabular list are boldfaced.
  - Codes that have an applicable seventh character are referred to as codes (not subcategories).
  - Codes that have an applicable seventh character are considered invalid without the seventh character.

TABLE 6-1 ICD-10-CM Tabular List of Diseases and Injuries

Chapter Number	Range of Codes	Chapter Title
Chapter 1	A00–B99	Certain Infectious and Parasitic Diseases
Chapter 2	C00–D49	Neoplasms
Chapter 3	D50–D89	Diseases of the Blood and Blood-forming Organs and Certain Disorders Involving the Immune Mechanism
Chapter 4	E00–E89	Endocrine, Nutritional, and Metabolic Disorders
Chapter 5	F01–F99	Mental, Behavioral and Neurodevelopment Disorders
Chapter 6	G00–G99	Diseases of the Nervous System
Chapter 7	H00–H59	Diseases of the Eye and Adnexa
Chapter 8	H60–H95	Diseases of the Ear and Mastoid Process
Chapter 9	I00–I99	Diseases of the Circulatory System
Chapter 10	J00–J99	Diseases of the Respiratory System
Chapter 11	K00–K95	Diseases of the Digestive System
Chapter 12	L00–L99	Diseases of the Skin and Subcutaneous Tissue
Chapter 13	M00–M99	Diseases of the Musculoskeletal System and Connective Tissue
Chapter 14	N00–N99	Diseases of the Genitourinary System
Chapter 15	O00–O9A	Pregnancy, Childbirth, and the Puerperium
Chapter 16	P00–P96	Certain Conditions Originating in the Perinatal Period
Chapter 17	Q00–Q99	Congenital Malformations, Deformations, and Chromosomal Abnormalities
Chapter 18	R00–R99	Symptoms, Signs, and Abnormal Clinical and Laboratory Findings, Not Elsewhere Classified
Chapter 19	S00–T88	Injury, Poisoning, and Certain Other Consequences of External Causes
Chapter 20	V00–Y99	External Causes of Morbidity
Chapter 21	Z00–Z99	Factors Influencing Health Status and Contact with Health Services
Chapter 22	U00–U85	Codes for Special Purposes

Structure

The ICD-10-CM tabular list contains three-character categories, four-, five-, or six-character subcategories, and four-, five-, six-, or seven-character codes (Figure 6-9), which contain letters and numbers. Each level of subdivision within a category is called a subcategory, and the final level of subdivision is a code. Codes that have applicable seventh characters are referred to as codes (not subcategories or subclassifications), and a code that has an applicable seventh character is considered invalid without the seventh character.

- *Use of codes for reporting purposes.* For reporting purposes, only codes are permissible (not categories or subcategories), and any applicable seventh character is required.

- *Placeholder character.* ICD-10-CM utilizes the character "X" as a placeholder for certain codes to allow for future expansion without disturbing the code structure (e.g., H62.8X1, other disorders of right external ear in diseases classified elsewhere). When a placeholder exists, the X must be entered in order for the code to be considered a valid code.

- *Seventh characters.* Certain ICD-10-CM categories contain applicable seventh characters, which are required for all codes within the category (or as instructed by notes in the tabular list). The seventh character

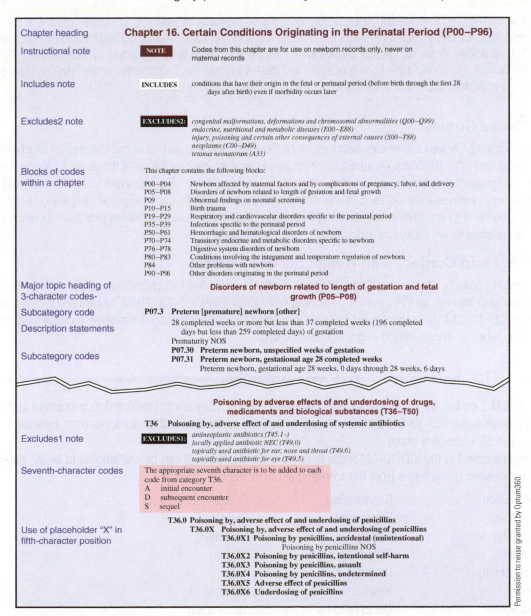

FIGURE 6-9 Sample page from ICD-10-CM Tabular List of Diseases and Injuries.

must always be located in the seventh-character data field. If a code that requires a seventh character is not six characters in length, the placeholder X is entered to fill in the empty character(s) (e.g., M48.46XS, reporting sequelae of fracture for previous fatigue fracture of lumbar vertebrae; an additional code is assigned to the sequelae, such as pain).

Example 1: ICD-10-CM CATEGORY AND SUBCATEGORY CODES: Go to Figure 6-9, refer to the Disorders of newborn related to length of gestation and fetal growth (P05–P08) section, and locate the four-character subcategory code (P07.3-) and the five-character subcategory codes (P07.30, P07.31, P07.32, and so on).

Example 2: ICD-10-CM SIX-CHARACTER AND SEVEN-CHARACTER CODES: Go to Figure 6-9, refer to the Poisoning by, adverse effects of and underdosing of drugs, medicaments and biological substances (T36–T50) section, and locate the six-character subcategory codes (T36.0X1, T36.0X2, T36.0X3, T36.0X4, T36.0X5, and T36.0X6), which also contain X as a placeholder to allow for future expansion. Then, locate the seventh characters (A, D, and S), one of which is to be added to each code from category T36 (depending on the status of encounter or whether the condition is a sequela). (**Sequela** is defined as the residual late effects of an injury or illness.)

Example 3: THE LETTER X AS A PLACEHOLDER: Go to Figure 6-9, refer to code T36.0X1A, and notice that it requires X as a placeholder in the fifth-character position. The letter A is added to code T36.0X1 to indicate an initial encounter. (Letters A, D, and S are located in the pink shaded area of Figure 6-9; one of these characters is added to code T36.0X1 to indicate the type of encounter.) If the code is reported as T36.01A (without the X placeholder in the fifth-character position), it is an invalid code that results in a denied claim for third-party payer reimbursement.

External Cause Codes

Injury, Poisoning, and Certain Other Consequences of External Causes and *External Causes of Morbidity* are incorporated into ICD-10-CM's Tabular List of Diseases and Injuries as Chapter 19 (S and T codes) and Chapter 20 (V through Y codes), respectively. External cause codes are also reported for environmental events, industrial accidents, injuries inflicted by criminal activity, and so on. While assigning the codes does not directly impact reimbursement to the provider, reporting them can expedite insurance claims processing because the circumstances related to an injury are indicated.

Health Status and Contact with Health Services Codes

Factors Influencing Health Status and Contact with Health Services are incorporated into ICD-10-CM's Tabular List of Diseases and Injuries as Chapter 21 (Z codes) (Z00-Z99) (Figure 6-10). The Z codes are located in the last chapter of the ICD-10-CM tabular list, and they are reported for patient encounters when a circumstance other than disease or injury is documented (e.g., well-child visit).

 Billing Tip

- ICD-10-CM Z codes are always reported as diagnosis codes. They are not reported as procedure codes even though some ICD-10-CM Z codes classify situations associated with procedures (e.g., canceled procedure Z53 category code).
- Although indexed in the ICD-10-CM Index to Diseases and Injuries, it can be challenging to locate main terms. Consider using terms from the following list to locate the codes:

○ Admission	○ Examination	○ Outcome of delivery
○ Aftercare	○ Exposure to	○ Problem
○ Attention to	○ Fitting	○ Screening
○ Contact	○ Follow-up	○ Status
○ Counseling	○ History	○ Test
○ Donor	○ Newborn	○ Therapy
○ Encounter	○ Observation	○ Vaccination

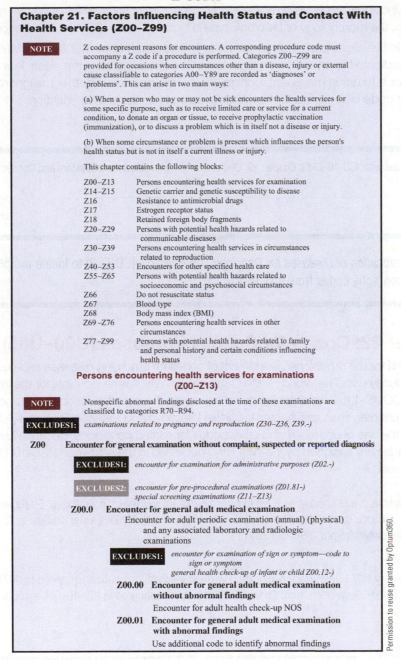

Z Codes

Chapter 21. Factors Influencing Health Status and Contact With Health Services (Z00–Z99)

NOTE Z codes represent reasons for encounters. A corresponding procedure code must accompany a Z code if a procedure is performed. Categories Z00–Z99 are provided for occasions when circumstances other than a disease, injury or external cause classifiable to categories A00–Y89 are recorded as 'diagnoses' or 'problems'. This can arise in two main ways:

(a) When a person who may or may not be sick encounters the health services for some specific purpose, such as to receive limited care or service for a current condition, to donate an organ or tissue, to receive prophylactic vaccination (immunization), or to discuss a problem which is in itself not a disease or injury.

(b) When some circumstance or problem is present which influences the person's health status but is not in itself a current illness or injury.

This chapter contains the following blocks:

Z00–Z13	Persons encountering health services for examination
Z14–Z15	Genetic carrier and genetic susceptibility to disease
Z16	Resistance to antimicrobial drugs
Z17	Estrogen receptor status
Z18	Retained foreign body fragments
Z20–Z29	Persons with potential health hazards related to communicable diseases
Z30–Z39	Persons encountering health services in circumstances related to reproduction
Z40–Z53	Encounters for other specified health care
Z55–Z65	Persons with potential health hazards related to socioeconomic and psychosocial circumstances
Z66	Do not resuscitate status
Z67	Blood type
Z68	Body mass index (BMI)
Z69–Z76	Persons encountering health services in other circumstances
Z77–Z99	Persons with potential health hazards related to family and personal history and certain conditions influencing health status

Persons encountering health services for examinations (Z00–Z13)

NOTE Nonspecific abnormal findings disclosed at the time of these examinations are classified to categories R70–R94.

EXCLUDES1: *examinations related to pregnancy and reproduction (Z30–Z36, Z39.-)*

Z00 **Encounter for general examination without complaint, suspected or reported diagnosis**

EXCLUDES1: *encounter for examination for administrative purposes (Z02.-)*

EXCLUDES2: *encounter for pre-procedural examinations (Z01.81-)*
special screening examinations (Z11–Z13)

Z00.0 **Encounter for general adult medical examination**
Encounter for adult periodic examination (annual) (physical) and any associated laboratory and radiologic examinations

EXCLUDES1: *encounter for examination of sign or symptom—code to sign or symptom*
general health check-up of infant or child Z00.12-)

Z00.00 **Encounter for general adult medical examination without abnormal findings**
Encounter for adult health check-up NOS

Z00.01 **Encounter for general adult medical examination with abnormal findings**
Use additional code to identify abnormal findings

FIGURE 6-10 Sample page of Z codes from ICD-10-CM Tabular List of Diseases and Injuries.

Morphology of Neoplasm Codes

Morphology indicates the tissue type of a neoplasm (e.g., adenocarcinoma and sarcoma); and while they are not reported on insurance claims, they are reported to state cancer registries. Neoplasms are new growths, or tumors, in which cell reproduction is out of control. A basic knowledge of morphology coding can be helpful to a coder because the name of the neoplasm documented in the patient's record does not always indicate whether the neoplasm is benign (not cancerous) or malignant (cancerous).

ICD-10-CM Chapter 2 classifies neoplasms primarily by site (topography), with broad groupings for behavior, malignant, *in situ*, benign, and so on. The ICD-10-CM Table of Neoplasms in its Index to Diseases and Injuries is used to identify the correct topography code. Morphology codes for most of ICD-10-CM's Chapter 2 (Neoplasms) codes do not include histologic type. Thus, a comprehensive separate set of morphology codes is used from the *International Classification of Diseases for Oncology, 3rd Revision* (ICD-O-3). (In a few cases, such as for malignant melanoma and certain neuroendocrine tumors, the morphology or histologic type is included in the ICD-10-CM category and code.)

Morphology codes contain five digits preceded by the letter M and range from M8000/0 to M9989/3. The first four digits (e.g., M8000) indicate the specific histologic term. The fifth digit, after the slash, is a behavior code, which indicates whether a tumor is malignant, benign, *in situ,* or uncertain whether malignant or benign. In addition, a separate one-digit code is assigned for histologic grading to indicate differentiation.

 NOTE:

Do not confuse morphology codes with ICD-10-CM's Chapter 13, Diseases of the Musculoskeletal System and Connective Tissue (M00–M99) codes.

 Coding Tip

Use the *International Classification of Diseases for Oncology, 3rd Revision* (ICD-O-3) to locate morphology codes when assigning topography codes from ICD-10-CM.

ICD-10-CM Chapter 22: Codes for Special Purposes (U00–U85)

This ICD-10-CM chapter is used for the *provisional* assignment of codes for emerging diseases and new diseases of uncertain etiology or for emergency use. The World Health Organization (WHO) is responsible for the initial assignment of the provisional codes (e.g., COVID-19). Official coding guidelines about these codes for special purposes are located in the appropriate ICD-10-CM chapter, such as Chapter 1: Certain Infectious and Parasitic Diseases (A00–B99) where guidance can be found about the use of code U07 and other codes for related conditions. Because U codes are temporary, new permanent codes are assigned by the WHO and published in the next year's ICD-10-CM (along with updated official coding guidelines).

Example 1: In 2016, code U06.9 was created by WHO to classify *Zika virus disease, unspecified.* Effective 2017, the ICD-10 Coordination and Maintenance Committee created new code A92.5 to classify Zika virus disease in Chapter 1 of ICD-10-CM. (Code U06.9 was deleted from ICD-10-CM 2021.)

Example 2: In 2020, category U07 (Emergency Use of U07) was established, and subcategory codes U07.0 (Vaping-related disorder) and U07.1 (COVID-19) were created. Codes U07.0 and U07.1 appeared in ICD-10-CM encoder software as of April 1, 2020.

Exercise 6.7 – ICD-10-CM Tabular List of Diseases and Injuries

Instructions: Complete each statement.

1. The *ICD-10-CM Tabular List of Diseases and Injuries* is a chronological list of codes contained within _____ chapters, which are based on body system or condition.

2. ICD-10-CM Chapter 22: Codes for Special Purposes (U00–U85) is used for the _____ assignment of codes for new diseases of uncertain etiology or for emergency use.

3. ICD-10-CM categories, subcategories, and codes contain a combination of _____ and numbers.

4. All of ICD-10-CM's categories contain a minimum of _____ characters.

(continues)

Exercise 6.7 – continued

5. A three-character ICD-10-CM category that has no further subdivision is a _____ code.

6. ICD-10-CM codes that contain 4 or 5 characters are considered _____ codes when additional characters are required.

7. ICD-10-CM valid _____ may contain 3, 4, 5, 6, or 7 characters.

8. Codes that have an applicable seventh character are considered _____ without the seventh character.

9. The seventh character must always be located in the seventh-character data field, and if a code that requires a seventh character is not six characters in length, placeholder letter _____ is entered to fill in the empty character(s).

10. *Factors Influencing Health Status and Contact with Health Services* are incorporated into ICD-10-CM's Tabular List of Diseases and Injuries as codes that begin with the letter _____.

Official Guidelines for Coding and Reporting

The **ICD-10-CM Official Guidelines for Coding and Reporting** and the **ICD-10-PCS Official Guidelines for Coding and Reporting** are prepared by the Centers for Medicare and Medicaid Services (CMS) and the National Center for Health Statistics (NCHS). The guidelines are approved by the **Cooperating Parties for ICD-10-CM/PCS**, which include CMS, NCHS, American Hospital Association (AHA), and American Health Information Management Association (AHIMA). The official guidelines contain rules that accompany and complement ICD-10-CM and ICD-10-PCS coding conventions and instructions. HIPAA regulations require adherence to the guidelines when assigning diagnosis and procedure codes.

- ICD-10-CM diagnosis codes were adopted under HIPAA for all health care settings.
- ICD-10-PCS procedure codes were adopted for inpatient procedures reported by hospitals.

 NOTE:

> Official coding advice (e.g., interpretation of ICD-10-CM/PCS coding principles) is published in the AHA's *Coding Clinic for ICD-10-CM and ICD-10-PCS*.

A joint effort between the health care provider and the coder is essential for complete and accurate: (1) documentation, (2) code assignment, and (3) reporting of diagnoses and procedures. The importance of consistent, complete documentation in the medical record cannot be overemphasized because without such documentation, accurate coding cannot be achieved. Review all documentation in the patient record to determine the specific reason for the encounter as well as conditions treated. Official guidelines use the following terms:

- *Encounter* to indicate all health care settings, including inpatient hospital admissions
- *Provider* to refer to physicians or any qualified health care practitioners who are legally accountable for establishing the patient's diagnosis

ICD-10-CM Official Guidelines for Coding and Reporting

ICD-10-CM official guidelines are organized in the following sections:

- Section I: Conventions, general coding guidelines, and chapter-specific guidelines
- Section II: Selection of principal diagnosis
- Section III: Reporting additional diagnoses

- Section IV: Diagnostic coding and reporting guidelines for outpatient services
- Appendix I: Present on admission reporting guidelines

 NOTE:

Content about coding conventions was included previously in this chapter.

Diagnostic Coding and Reporting Guidelines Outpatient Services—Hospital-Based Outpatient Services and Provider-Based Office Visits

The **ICD-10-CM Diagnostic Coding and Reporting Guidelines for Outpatient Services—Hospital-Based Outpatient Services and Provider-Based Office Visits** were developed by the federal government and approved for use by hospitals and providers for coding and reporting hospital-based outpatient services and provider-based office visits. Although the guidelines were originally developed for use in submitting government claims, insurance companies have also adopted them (sometimes with variation).

The terms *encounter* and *visit* are often used interchangeably when describing outpatient service contacts and, therefore, appear together in the official guidelines without distinguishing one from the other. Though the coding conventions and general coding guidelines apply to all health care settings, coding guidelines for outpatient hospital-based and provider-based office reporting of diagnoses differ from reporting of inpatient diagnoses.

- The *Uniform Hospital Discharge Data Set (UHDDS)* definition of principal diagnosis applies *only* to inpatients in acute, short-term, long-term care, and psychiatric hospitals. The inpatient **principal diagnosis** is defined as "the condition determined after study which resulted in the patient's admission to the hospital," and it is reported in Form Locator 67 of the UB-04 (CMS-1450) claim.

- Coding guidelines for inconclusive diagnoses (or qualified diagnoses) (e.g., possible, probable, suspected, rule out) were developed for inpatient reporting *only* and do not apply to outpatients.

A. Selection of First-Listed Condition

In the outpatient setting, the **first-listed diagnosis** is reported (instead of the inpatient hospital *principal diagnosis*) in Block 21 of the CMS-1500 claim; it reflects the reason for the encounter, which often is a sign or symptom. (First-listed diagnosis replaced the outdated primary diagnosis term some years ago.) Physicians do not usually have time during a single encounter to establish a definitive diagnosis. Thus, the first-listed diagnosis code indicates to third-party payers why the physician provided the services. It is determined in accordance with ICD-10-CM *coding conventions* (or rules) as well as general and disease-specific coding guidelines. Because diagnoses are often not established at the time of the patient's initial encounter or visit, two or more visits may be required before a diagnosis is confirmed. An **outpatient** is a person treated in one of four settings:

- *Ambulatory Surgery Center:* Patient is released prior to a 24-hour stay and length of stay must be 23 hours, 59 minutes, and 59 seconds or less.
- *Health Care Provider's Office* (e.g., physician)
- *Hospital Clinic, ED, Outpatient Department, Same-day Surgery Unit:* Length of stay must be 23 hours, 59 minutes, and 59 seconds or less.
- *Hospital Observation Status or Hospital Observation Unit:* Patient's length of stay is 23 hours, 59 minutes, and 59 seconds or less unless documentation for additional observation time is medically justified.

NOTE:

You may see *principal diagnosis* referred to as *first-listed diagnosis* in medical literature. Remember! An outpatient setting reports the first-listed diagnosis, *not* the principal diagnosis.

Outpatient Surgery

When a patient presents for outpatient surgery (same-day surgery), code the reason for the surgery as the first-listed diagnosis (reason for the encounter), even if the surgery is not performed due to a contraindication.

Observation Stay

When a patient is admitted for observation for a medical condition, assign a code for the medical condition as the first-listed diagnosis. When a patient presents for outpatient surgery and develops complications requiring admission to observation, code the reason for the surgery as the first-listed diagnosis (reason for the encounter), followed by codes for the complications as secondary diagnoses.

> **Example:** A patient received emergency department care for an injury to the right arm, which upon x-ray revealed a closed displaced oblique fracture of the shaft of the right humerus. The first-listed diagnosis code is S42.331A, and it justifies the medical necessity of the x-ray.

NOTE:

- *Outpatient Surgery:* When a patient presents for outpatient surgery, the first-listed diagnosis is the reason for the surgery even if the surgery is cancelled due to a contraindication (e.g., patient's blood pressure increases unexpectedly upon administration of anesthesia).
- *Observation Stay:* When a patient is admitted for observation of a medical condition, the first-listed diagnosis is the medical condition being observed.

When a patient presents for outpatient surgery and then develops complications requiring admission for observation, the first-listed diagnosis is the reason for the surgery. The secondary diagnosis is the complication(s) (e.g., respiratory distress).

B. Codes from A00–T88.9, Z00–Z99, U00–U85

The appropriate code or codes from the ICD-10-CM Tabular List of Diseases and Injuries (A00–T88, Z00–Z99) must be used to identify diagnoses, symptoms, conditions, problems, complaints, or other reason(s) for the encounter/visit. (Codes from ICD-10-CM Chapter 22, U codes, are also used to classify diagnoses.)

C. Accurate Reporting of ICD-10-CM Diagnosis Codes

For accurate reporting of ICD-10-CM diagnosis codes, the documentation should describe the patient's condition, using terminology that includes specific diagnoses as well as symptoms, problems, or reasons for the encounter. There are ICD-10-CM codes to describe all of these.

D. Codes That Describe Signs and Symptoms

Codes that describe symptoms and signs, as opposed to definitive diagnoses, are acceptable for reporting purposes when the physician has not documented an established diagnosis or confirmed diagnosis. ICD-10-CM Chapter 18 (Symptoms, Signs, and Abnormal Clinical and Laboratory Findings Not Elsewhere Classified) (R00–R99) contain many, but not all, codes for symptoms. Some symptom codes are located in other ICD-10-CM chapters, which can be found by properly using the ICD-10-CM Index to Diseases and Injuries.

General Coding Guidelines to Consider when Assigning Codes to Signs and Symptoms

The following general coding guidelines should be considered when assigning codes for signs and symptoms:

- Codes that describe symptoms and signs are reported when a related definitive diagnosis has not been established (or confirmed) by the provider.

- Signs and symptoms that are associated with a definitive disease process should *not* be assigned as additional codes unless otherwise instructed by ICD-10-CM because they are included in the disease process.

- Conditions that are not considered an integral part of a (definitive) disease process, such as additional signs and symptoms that may not be associated routinely with a disease process, should be coded when present (e.g., severe headache for which treatment or medical management is provided is coded when the patient is diagnosed with pneumonia).

- When a definitive diagnosis is *not* established during an encounter, report codes for signs and/or symptoms instead.

E. Encounters for Circumstances Other than a Disease or Injury (Z Codes)

ICD-10-CM provides codes to deal with encounters for circumstances other than a disease or an injury. In ICD-10-CM, Factors Influencing Health Status and Contact with Health Services (Z00–Z99) classifies occasions when circumstances other than a disease or injury are recorded as diagnosis or problems.

F. Level of Detail in Coding

ICD-10-CM diagnosis codes contain three, four, five, six, or seven characters.

1. *ICD-10-CM codes with three, four, five, six, or seven characters:* Disease codes with three characters are included in ICD-10-CM as the heading of a category of codes that may be further subdivided by the use of fourth, fifth, sixth, or seventh characters to provide greater specificity.

2. *Use of full number of characters required for a code:* A three-character code is to be assigned only if it cannot be further subdivided. A code is invalid if it has not been coded to the full number of characters required for that code, including the seventh-character extension, if applicable.

3. *Highest level of specificity:* Code to the highest level of specificity when supported by the medical record documentation.

G. ICD-10-CM Code for the Diagnosis, Condition, Problem, or Other Reason for Encounter/Visit

Report first the ICD-10-CM code for the diagnosis, condition, problem, or other reason for encounter/visit shown in the medical record to be chiefly responsible for the services provided. Then report additional codes that describe any coexisting conditions that were treated or medically managed or that influenced the treatment of the patient during the encounter. In some cases, the first-listed diagnosis may be a symptom when a diagnosis has not been established (confirmed) by the provider.

General Coding Guidelines to Consider When Assigning ICD-10-CM Codes

- If the same condition is described as both acute (or subacute) and chronic and separate subentries exist in the ICD-10-CM index at the same indentation level, code both *and sequence the acute (or subacute) code first*.

(continues)

General Coding Guidelines to Consider When Assigning ICD-10-CM Codes (*continued*)

- Assign combination codes when available and multiple codes as needed.
  - A *combination* code is a single code that is used to classify two diagnoses, a diagnosis with an ssociated secondary process (manifestation), or a diagnosis with an associated complication.
  - Assign two or more *multiple codes* to completely classify the elements of a complex diagnosis statement, which contain words or phrases such as *due to, incidental to, secondary to, and with*.

- A *sequela* is the *residual effect* (condition produced) after the acute phase of an illness or injury has terminated. *There is no time limit on when a sequela code can be used*.

- ICD-10-CM codes that indicate *laterality* specifically classify conditions that occur on the left, right, or bilaterally. If a bilateral ICD-10-CM code is not provided a*nd the condition is bilateral*, assign separate codes for both the left and right side. If the side is not identified in the patient record, assign a code for unspecified side.

- Code assignment is based on the documentation by patient's provider (e.g., physician or other qualified health care practitioner legally accountable for establishing the patient's diagnosis). Exceptions to to this guideline include codes for:
  - Body mass index (BMI),
  - Depth of nonpressure chronic ulcers

  - Pressure ulcer stage
  - Coma scale
  - NIH stroke scale (NIHSS)

  Such codes codes may be based on documentation from clinicians who are not the patient's provider *because such information is typically documented by other clinicians involved in the care of the patient* (e.g., dietitians document BMI, nurses document pressure ulcer stages, emergency medical technician documents coma scale).

- Follow the alphabetic index guidance when coding syndromes. In the absence of index guidance, assign codes for the documented manifestations of the syndrome. Additional codes for manifestations that are *not an integral part of the disease process* may also be assigned when the condition does not have a unique code.
  - Complications of care codes are based upon documentation of a relationship between a condition and the procedure unless otherwise instructed by ICD-10-CM. Not all conditions that occur during or following medical care or surgery are classified as complications. There must be a cause-and-effect relationship between the condition and procedure or service provided along with documentation that the condition is a complication. If a complication is not clearly documented, query the provider for clarification.

H. Uncertain Diagnoses

Do not code diagnoses documented as borderline, probable, suspected, questionable, rule out, compatible with, consistent with, or working diagnosis, or other similar terms indicating uncertainty, all of which are considered **qualified diagnoses**. Instead, code condition(s) to the highest degree of certainty for that encounter/visit, such as symptoms, signs, abnormal test results, or other reasons for the visit.

For Qualified Diagnosis	Code the Following Signs or Symptoms
Suspected pneumonia	Shortness of breath
Questionable Raynaud's	Numbness of hands
Possible wrist fracture, right	Wrist pain, right
Rule out pneumonia	Shortness of breath

NOTE:

When assigning codes to physician services provided to inpatients, adhere to the outpatient "Uncertain Diagnosis" guideline so that codes for signs and symptoms are reported instead of qualified diagnoses.

Qualified or uncertain diagnoses are a necessary part of the hospital and office chart until a specific diagnosis can be determined. Although qualified diagnoses are routinely coded for hospital inpatient admissions and reported on the UB-04 claim, CMS *specifically prohibits the reporting of qualified diagnoses on the CMS-1500 claim submitted for outpatient care*. CMS regulations permit the reporting of patients' signs and symptoms instead of the qualified diagnoses.

 NOTE:

Coding guidelines for inpatient stays allow codes for qualified diagnoses to be reported on the UB-04.

An additional incentive for not coding qualified diagnoses resulted from the Missouri case of *Stafford v. Neurological Medicine Inc., 811 F. 2d 470 (8th Cir., 1987)*. In this case, the diagnosis stated in the physician's office chart was *rule out brain tumor*. The claim submitted by the office listed the diagnosis code for *brain cancer* (instead of appropriate codes for signs and symptoms related to the qualified diagnosis, "rule out brain tumor") although test results were available that proved a brain tumor did not exist. The physician assured the patient that although they had lung cancer, there was no **metastasis** (spread of cancer from primary to secondary sites) to the brain. Sometime after the insurance company received the provider's claim, it was inadvertently sent to the patient. When the patient received the claim, they were so devastated by the diagnosis that they took their own life. The patient's spouse sued and was awarded $200,000 on the basis of *negligent paperwork* because the physician's office had reported a *qualified or uncertain diagnosis*.

I. Chronic Diseases

Chronic diseases treated on an ongoing basis may be coded and reported as many times as the patient receives treatment and care for the condition(s).

J. Code All Documented Conditions that Coexist

Code all documented conditions that coexist at the time of the encounter/visit and that require or affect patient care, treatment, or management. Do not code conditions that were previously treated and no longer exist. However, history codes (ICD-10-CM categories Z80–Z87) may be reported as secondary codes if the historical condition or family history has an impact on current care or influences treatment.

Secondary diagnoses include comorbidities and complications. A **comorbidity** is a concurrent condition that coexists with the first-listed diagnosis for outpatient care or principal diagnosis, for inpatient care, has the potential to affect treatment of the first-listed or principal diagnosis, and is an active condition for which the patient is treated and/or monitored. (Insulin-dependent diabetes mellitus is an example of a comorbidity.) A **complication** is a condition that develops after outpatient care has been provided (e.g., ruptured sutures after office surgery) or during an inpatient admission, such as development of a postoperative wound infection. Secondary diagnoses are reported in Block 21 of the CMS-1500 claim for outpatient and physician office care, and Form Locators 67A–67Q of the UB-04 for inpatient care.

Example: A patient seeks care at the health care provider's office for an injury to the right leg that, upon x-ray in the office, is diagnosed as a fractured tibia. While in the office, the physician also reviews the current status and treatment of the patient's type 2 diabetes.

- What is the first-listed diagnosis?

(continues)

- What is the secondary diagnosis?
- Which diagnosis justifies medical necessity of the right leg x-ray?
- Which diagnosis justifies medical necessity of the office visit?

Answer: The first-listed diagnosis is *fracture, shaft, right tibia,* and it justifies medical necessity for the *right leg x-ray.* The secondary diagnosis is *type 2 diabetes mellitus,* and it justifies medical necessity for the *office visit.*

NOTE:

Third-party payers review claims for *family history of codes* to determine reimbursement eligibility. Some plans reimburse for conditions that may not normally be eligible for payment when family history of a related condition is documented in the patient's record and reported on the claim.

K. Patients Receiving Diagnostic Services Only

For patients receiving diagnostic services *only* during an encounter, report first the diagnosis, condition, problem, or other reason for encounter/visit that is documented in the medical record as being chiefly responsible for the outpatient services provided during the encounter/visit. (This is the *first-listed diagnosis.*) Codes for other diagnoses (e.g., chronic conditions) may be reported as additional diagnoses.

For encounters for routine laboratory/radiology testing in the absence of any signs, symptoms, or associated diagnosis, assign Z01.89, Encounter for other specified special examinations. If routine testing is performed during the same encounter as a test to evaluate a sign, symptom, or diagnosis, it is appropriate to assign both the Z code and the code describing the reason for the nonroutine test.

For outpatient encounters for diagnostic tests that have been interpreted by a physician and for which the final report is available at the time of coding, code any confirmed or definitive diagnoses documented in the interpretation. *Do not code related signs and symptoms as additional diagnoses.*

NOTE:

Do not report codes for qualified diagnoses on outpatient cases; instead, report codes for documented signs and symptoms. This differs from coding practices in hospital inpatient settings regarding abnormal findings on test results, for which the physician may document a qualified diagnosis that is coded and reported.

L. Patients Receiving Therapeutic Services Only

For patients receiving *therapeutic services only* during an encounter/visit, sequence first the diagnosis, condition, problem, or other reason for encounter/visit shown in the medical record to be chiefly responsible for the outpatient services provided during the encounter/visit.

Assign codes to other diagnoses (e.g., chronic conditions) that are treated or medically managed or that would affect the patient's receipt of therapeutic services during this encounter/visit.

The only exception to this rule is when the reason for admission or encounter is for chemotherapy or radiation therapy. For these services, the appropriate Z code for the service is listed first and the diagnosis or problem for which the service is being performed is reported second.

M. Patients Receiving Preoperative Evaluations Only

For patients receiving *preoperative evaluations only*, assign and report first the appropriate code from ICD-10-CM subcategory Z01.81- (encounter for pre-procedural examinations) to describe the pre-op consultations.

Assign an additional code for the condition that describes the reason for the surgery. Also assign additional code(s) to any findings discovered during the preoperative evaluation.

N. Ambulatory Surgery

For *ambulatory surgery* (or *outpatient surgery*), assign a code to the diagnosis for which the surgery was performed. If the postoperative diagnosis is different from the preoperative diagnosis when the diagnosis is confirmed, assign a code to the postoperative diagnosis instead (because it is more definitive).

 NOTE:

Preadmission testing (PAT) is routinely completed prior to an inpatient admission or outpatient surgery to facilitate the patient's treatment and reduce the length of stay. As an incentive to facilities that perform PAT, some payers provide higher reimbursement for PAT, making it important to assign codes properly.

O. Routine Outpatient Prenatal Visits

For routine outpatient prenatal visits when no complications are present:

- Report a code from ICD-10-CM category Z34 (encounter for supervision of normal pregnancy) as the first-listed diagnosis.
- Do not report a code from category Z34 in combination with ICD-10-CM Chapter 15 codes.

For routine prenatal outpatient visits for patients with high-risk pregnancies, report an ICD-10-CM code from category O09 (supervision of high-risk pregnancy) as the first-listed diagnosis. A code from ICD-10-CM Chapter 15 may also be reported as a secondary diagnosis, if appropriate.

P. Encounters for General Medical Examinations with Abnormal Findings

Subcategories for *encounters for general medical examinations, Z00.0-* and *encounter for routine child health examination, Z00.12-* provide codes for *with abnormal findings* and *without abnormal findings*. When a general medical examination results in an abnormal finding, the code for *general medical examination with abnormal finding* is assigned as the first-listed diagnosis. An *examination with abnormal findings* refers to a condition or diagnosis that is newly identified or a change in the severity of a chronic condition (e.g., uncontrolled hypertension, acute exacerbation of chronic obstructive pulmonary disease) during a routine physical examination. A secondary code for the abnormal finding is also assigned.

Q. Encounters for Routine Health Screenings

ICD-10-CM Z codes are assigned for any health care setting, and they may be reported as either a first-listed or secondary code, depending on the circumstances of the encounter. (Certain Z codes may only be reported as the first-listed diagnosis.) Z codes indicate a reason for an encounter or provide additional information about a patient encounter. They are *not* procedure codes, and a corresponding procedure or service code must be reported with a Z code to describe any procedure or service provided. Categories of Z codes include:

- Contact with, and suspected exposure to, communicable diseases
- Inoculations and vaccinations
- Status (of a condition)
- History (of)
- Screening
- Observation (for a suspected condition that has been ruled out)
- Aftercare
- Follow-up
- Donor (status)
- Counseling
- Encounters for obstetrical and reproductive services

- Newborns and infants
- Routine and administrative examinations
- Miscellaneous (e.g., prophylactic organ removal)
- Nonspecific (for which assign a sign or symptom code is preferred)
- Z codes that may only be reported for principal or first-listed diagnosis
- Social determinants of health

Example 1: Personal history Z codes may be reported in conjunction with follow-up codes, and family history Z codes may be reported in conjunction with screening codes to explain the need for a test or procedure. History codes contain important information that may alter the type of treatment ordered.

Example 2: *Screening* is the testing for disease or disease precursors in seemingly well individuals so that early detection and treatment can be provided for those who test positive for the disease (e.g., screening mammogram).

A screening code may be reported as a *first-listed code* if the reason for the visit is specifically the screening exam. It may also be used as an additional code if the screening is done during an office visit for other health problems. A screening code is not necessary if the screening is inherent to a routine examination, such as a Pap smear done during a routine pelvic examination.

Should a condition be discovered during the screening, then the code for the condition may be assigned as an additional diagnosis.

 NOTE:

ICD-10-CM Z codes are *not* procedure codes and are reported on CMS-1500 and UB-04 claims to justify medical necessity of CPT and HCPCS Level II procedure and service codes.

Example: The provider admitted the patient for observation of documented COVID-19, which was ruled out. In addition to codes for the patient's signs and symptoms (e.g., fever, difficulty breathing), a code from ICD-10-CM category Z03, Encounter for medical observation for suspected diseases and conditions ruled out, is reported instead of the code for COVID-19.

Exercise 6.8 – Official Guidelines for Coding and Reporting

Exercise 6.8A – Coding Guidelines
Instructions: Complete each statement.

1. The official guidelines for coding and reporting using ICD-10-CM and ICD-10-PCS have been approved by the four organizations that comprise the _____ Parties for the ICD-10-CM/PCS.
2. The abbreviations for the four organizations that develop and approve the coding guidelines are _____, _____, _____, and _____.
3. Adherence to the official coding guidelines when assigning ICD-10-CM and ICD-10-PCS diagnosis and procedure codes is required by _____ legislation.
4. The official coding guidelines use the term _____ to indicate all health care settings, including inpatient hospital admissions.
5. The official coding guidelines refer to physicians and qualified health care practitioners who are legally accountable for establishing the patient's diagnosis as _____.

(continues)

Exercise 6.8 – continued

Exercise 6.8B – First-listed Diagnosis Selection

Instructions: Select the first-listed diagnosis for each scenario.

1. The physician treated the patient's chronic asthma during an office visit, at which time renewed prescriptions for diabetes mellitus, hypertension, and hypercholesterolemia were provided.

   a. Chronic asthma

   b. Diabetes mellitus

   c. Hypertension

   d. Hypercholesterolemia

2. The physician ordered an ultrasound to rule out cholecystitis; the patient had presented to the office with severe abdominal pain. During the encounter, the nurse performed venipuncture for an ordered blood glucose test.

   a. Abdominal pain

   b. Cholecystitis

   c. Ultrasound

   d. Venipuncture

3. The patient slipped on ice and fell while walking down the steps of the porch. The patient was treated in the emergency department for severe swelling of the left leg, and x-ray of the left leg was negative for fracture.

   a. Fall walking down steps

   b. Fracture, left leg

   c. Slip on ice

   d. Swelling, left leg

4. The patient presented to the office with a fever and was treated for nausea and vomiting. The physician diagnosed gastroenteritis.

   a. Fever

   b. Gastroenteritis

   c. Nausea

   d. Vomiting

5. The patient was treated during outpatient encounter for a sore throat, which was cultured. The physician documented possible strep throat in the record.

   a. Outpatient encounter

   b. Sore throat

   c. Strep throat

   d. Throat culture

6. The patient was treated during an outpatient encounter for both acute and chronic bronchitis, for which each was assigned an ICD-10-CM diagnosis code. Upon examination, wheezing and rales were documented.

   a. Acute bronchitis

   b. Chronic bronchitis

   c. Rales

   d. Wheezing

(continues)

Exercise 6.8 – continued

7. The patient was treated for acne in the physician's office during this encounter. The physician also documented that the patient's previously diagnosed hives had totally resolved.

    a. Acne

    b. Acne treatment

    c. Encounter

    d. Hives

8. The patient was seen for complaints of fainting, and they also said that they had previously experienced nausea and vomiting. The patient's blood was drawn and sent to the lab to have a blood glucose level performed. Lab results were normal. The patient was scheduled for outpatient testing to rule out seizure disorder.

    a. Fainting

    b. Nausea

    c. Seizure disorder

    d. Vomiting

9. The patient underwent outpatient radiation therapy for treatment of prostate cancer during today's encounter; the patient had previously complained of painful and bloody urination.

    a. Bloody urination

    b. Outpatient radiation therapy

    c. Painful urination

    d. Prostate cancer

10. The patient's preoperative diagnosis was possible appendicitis and right lower quadrant pain; laparoscopic appendectomy was performed. The postoperative diagnosis was acute appendicitis.

    a. Acute appendicitis

    b. Laparoscopic appendectomy

    c. Possible appendicitis

    d. Right lower quadrant pain

Summary

ICD-10-CM is used to classify *morbidity* (disease) data from inpatient and outpatient records, including provider-based office records. ICD-10-PCS is used to code and classify *procedures* from hospital inpatient records only. All provider offices, outpatient health care settings, and health care facilities report ICD-10-CM diagnosis codes.

Implementation of the ICD-10-CM and ICD-10-PCS coding systems resulted in ICD-9-CM becoming a *legacy coding system* (or *legacy classification system*), which means it will be used as archive data but it will no longer be supported or updated. *General equivalence mappings (GEMs)* are translation dictionaries or crosswalks of codes that can be used to roughly identify ICD-10-CM/PCS codes for their ICD-9-CM equivalent codes (and vice versa).

The ICD-10-CM Index to Diseases and Injuries is organized according to alphabetical main terms (boldfaced conditions), nonessential modifiers (in parentheses), and subterms (essential modifiers that are indented below main terms). The index also contains a Table of Neoplasms, a Table of Drugs and Chemicals, and an Index of External Causes of Injury. To properly assign an ICD-10-CM code, locate the main term in the index, apply coding conventions and official coding guidelines, and verify the code in the ICD-10-CM Tabular List of Diseases and Injuries.

The ICD-10-PCS Index is organized according to alphabetic main terms and subterms. To properly assign an ICD-10-PCS code, locate the main term in the index, apply cross-reference terms, and locate the corresponding ICD-10-PCS table. ICD-10-PCS Tables are used to construct the seven-character codes.

Medical necessity is the measure of whether a health care procedure or service is appropriate for the diagnosis and/or treatment of a condition. Third-party payers use medical necessity measurements to make a decision about whether or not to pay a claim.

Outpatient care includes any health care service provided to a patient who is not admitted to a facility. Such care may be provided in a physician's office, a stand-alone health care facility, a hospital outpatient or emergency department, or the patient's home. ICD-10-CM and ICD-10-PCS Official Guidelines for Coding and Reporting were established by CMS and NCHS, and they are used as companion documents to official versions of ICD-10-CM and ICD-10-PCS. The CMS *Diagnostic Coding and Reporting Guidelines for Outpatient Services: Hospital-Based and Provider-Based Office* are used for coding and reporting hospital-based outpatient services and provider-based office visits. The ICD-10-PCS coding guidelines are used for coding and reporting hospital inpatient procedures only.

Internet Links

CDC Topics A–Z: Go to **www.cdc.gov** and click on a letter from the A–Z Index link (e.g., letter I to locate ICD-10-CM content).

EncoderPro.com: www.encoderpro.com

HCPro: Go to **www.hcmarketplace.com** and click on the *Sign up for our FREE e-Newsletters* link. Click on the box located in front of *JustCoding News Outpatient* (along with other e-Newsletters of interest) to subscribe.

ICD-10-CM search tool: https://icd10cmtool.cdc.gov

ICD-10-CM MS-DRG Definitions (Draft) (free): Go to **www.cms.gov** click on the Medicare link, click on the ICD-10 link under Coding, click on the ICD-10 MS-DRG Conversion Project link, and click on a definitions manual link.

Web-based training courses (free): Go to **https://learner.mlnlms.com** and register to complete Web-Based Training Courses.

Review

The ICD-10-CM coding review is organized according to ICD-10-CM chapters. The ICD-10-PCS coding review is organized according to ICD-10-PCS sections.

Instructions: For 6.1–6.19, use the ICD-10-CM index and tabular list to assign codes to each condition. Apply coding conventions and guidelines to ensure proper assignment of codes, entering the first-listed diagnosis code first. Although the review is organized by chapter or section, codes from outside a particular chapter or section may be required to completely classify a case.

6.1 – Certain Infectious and Parasitic Diseases

1. Aseptic meningitis due to AIDS   _____

2. Asymptomatic HIV infection   _____

3. Septicemia due to streptococcus   _____

4. Dermatophytosis of the foot   _____

5. Measles; no complications noted   _____

6. Nodular pulmonary tuberculosis   _____

7. Acute cystitis due to *Escherichia coli (E. coli)*   _____

8. Tuberculous osteomyelitis of left lower leg   _____

9. Gas gangrene   _____

10. Rotaviral enteritis   _____

6.2 – Neoplasms

1. Primary malignant melanoma of skin of scalp   _____

2. Lipoma of face   _____

3. Glioma of the parietal lobe of the brain   _____

4. Primary adenocarcinoma of prostate   _____

5. Carcinoma *in situ* of vocal cord   _____

6. Hodgkin's granuloma of intra-abdominal lymph nodes   _____

7. Paget's disease with primary infiltrating duct carcinoma of nipple and
    areola of right breast (female)   _____

8. Secondary liver cancer   _____

9. Metastatic adenocarcinoma from breast to brain (right mastectomy performed
    five years ago; breast cancer is no longer present)   _____

10. Cancer of the pleura (primary site)   _____

6.3 – Diseases of the Blood and Blood-Forming Organs and Certain Disorders Involving the Immune Mechanism

1. Sickle cell disease with crisis   _____

2. Iron deficiency anemia secondary to chronic blood loss   _____

3. Von Willebrand disease   _____

4. Chronic congestive splenomegaly   _____

5. Congenital nonspherocytic hemolytic anemia   _____

6. Essential thrombocytopenia   _____

7. Malignant neutropenia   _____

8. Fanconi's anemia   _____

9. Microangiopathic hemolytic anemia   _____

10. Aplastic anemia secondary to antineoplastic medication (initial encounter) for
    left lower female breast cancer   _____

6.4 – Endocrine, Nutritional, and Metabolic Diseases

1. Cushing's syndrome   _____

2. Hypokalemia   _____

3. Type 2 diabetes mellitus with malnutrition   _____

4. Hypogammaglobulinemia   _____

5. Hypercholesterolemia   _____

6. Type 2 diabetes mellitus with intracapillary glomerulonephrosis   _____

7. Toxic diffuse goiter with thyrotoxic crisis   _____

8. Cystic fibrosis

9. Panhypopituitarism

10. Rickets

6.5 – Mental and Behavioral Disorders

1. Acute exacerbation of chronic undifferentiated schizophrenia

2. Reactive major depressive psychosis due to the death of a child, single episode

3. Hysterical neurosis

4. Anxiety reaction manifested by fainting

5. Alcoholic gastritis due to chronic alcoholism (episodic)

6. Juvenile delinquency; patient was caught shoplifting

7. Depression

8. Hypochondria; patient also has continuous laxative habit

9. Acute senile dementia with Alzheimer's disease

10. Epileptic psychosis with generalized grand mal epilepsy

6.6 – Diseases of the Nervous System

1. *Neisseria* meningitis

2. Intracranial abscess

3. Postvaricella encephalitis

4. Hemiplegia following cerebral infarction affecting right dominant side

5. Acute encephalitis

6. Spastic diplegic cerebral palsy

7. Tonic-clonic epilepsy

8. Bell's palsy

9. Functional quadriplegia

10. Intraspinal abscess

6.7 – Diseases of the Eye and Adnexa

1. Retinal detachment with single retinal break, right eye

2. Borderline glaucoma, right eye

3. Senile cataract, right eye

4. Blepharochalasis of right upper eyelid

5. Xanthelasma of right lower eyelid

6. Lacrimal gland dislocation, bilateral lacrimal glands

7. Stenosis of bilateral lacrimal sacs

8. Cyst of left orbit

9. Acute toxic conjunctivitis, left eye _____

10. Ocular pain, right eye _____

6.8 – Diseases of the Ear and Mastoid Process

1. Acute contact otitis externa, right ear _____

2. Chronic perichondritis, left external ear _____

3. Chronic nonsuppurative serous otitis media, bilateral _____

4. Acute eustachian salpingitis, right ear _____

5. Postauricular fistula, left ear _____

6. Attic perforation of tympanic membrane, left ear _____

7. Cochlear otosclerosis, right ear _____

8. Labyrinthitis, right ear _____

9. Tinnitus, left ear _____

10. Postprocedural stenosis of right external ear canal _____

6.9 – Diseases of the Circulatory System

1. Congestive rheumatic heart failure _____

2. Mitral valve stenosis with aortic valve disease _____

3. Acute rheumatic heart disease _____

4. Hypertensive cardiovascular disease _____

5. Hypertension _____

6. Secondary hypertension; stenosis of renal artery _____

7. Hypertensive nephropathy with chronic uremia _____

8. Hypertensive end-stage renal disease with dependence on renal dialysis _____

9. Acute STEMI myocardial infarction of inferolateral wall, initial episode of care _____

10. Arteriosclerotic heart disease (native coronary artery) with angina pectoris _____

6.10 – Diseases of the Respiratory System

1. Aspiration pneumonia due to regurgitated food _____

2. Streptococcal group B pneumonia _____

3. Respiratory failure due to myasthenia gravis _____

4. Mild intrinsic asthma with status asthmaticus _____

5. COPD with emphysema _____

6. Acute tracheitis with obstruction _____

7. Chlamydial pneumonia _____

8. Chronic tonsillitis and adenoiditis _____

9. Simple chronic bronchitis _____

10. Moderate persistent asthma with (acute) exacerbation _____

6.11 – Diseases of the Digestive System

1. Supernumerary tooth _____
2. Unilateral femoral hernia with gangrene _____
3. Cholesterolosis of gallbladder _____
4. Diarrhea _____
5. Acute perforated peptic ulcer _____
6. Acute hemorrhagic gastritis with acute blood loss anemia _____
7. Acute appendicitis with peritoneal abscess _____
8. Acute cholecystitis with cholelithiasis _____
9. Aphthous stomatitis _____
10. Diverticulosis and diverticulitis of large intestine _____

6.12 – Diseases of the Skin and Subcutaneous Tissue

1. Diaper rash _____
2. Acne vulgaris _____
3. Postinfective skin cicatrix _____
4. Cellulitis of left foot; culture reveals staphylococcus _____
5. Infected ingrowing nail, thumb, left hand _____
6. Carbuncle of face _____
7. Pemphigus foliaceous _____
8. Pressure ulcer of right elbow, stage 2 _____
9. Factitial dermatitis _____
10. Seborrhea _____

6.13 – Diseases of the Musculoskeletal System and Connective Tissue

1. Displacement of thoracic intervertebral disc _____
2. Primary localized osteoarthrosis of the left hip _____
3. Acute juvenile rheumatoid arthritis _____
4. Chondromalacia of the right patella _____
5. Pathologic fracture, cervical vertebra (initial encounter for fracture) _____
6. Staphylococcal arthritis, left knee _____
7. Postimmunization arthropathy, right ankle and foot _____
8. Idiopathic chronic gout, right shoulder _____
9. Kaschin-Beck disease, left shoulder _____
10. Fibromyalgia _____

6.14 – Diseases of the Genitourinary System

1. Vesicoureteral reflux with bilateral reflux nephropathy _____

2. Acute nephritic syndrome with C3 glomerulonephritis _____

3. Acute actinomycotic cystitis _____

4. Subserosal uterine leiomyoma, cervical polyp, and endometriosis of uterus _____

5. Mild dysplasia of the cervix _____

6. Recurrent and persistent idiopathic hematuria with glomerular
lesion and C3 glomerulopathy with dense deposit disease _____

7. Chronic obstructive pyelonephritis _____

8. Acute kidney failure with medullary necrosis _____

9. Stage 3a chronic kidney disease _____

10. Urethral stricture due to childbirth _____

6.15 – Diseases of Pregnancy, Childbirth, and the Puerperium

1. Defibrination syndrome following spontaneous abortion two weeks ago _____

2. Miscarriage at 19 weeks gestation _____

3. Incompetent cervix, second trimester _____

4. Puerperal varicose veins of legs _____

5. Spontaneous breech Cesarean delivery, single liveborn fetus _____

6. Triplet pregnancy, delivered spontaneously _____

7. Spontaneous delivery of single liveborn infant, third trimester, complicated by
placental dysfunction with retained placenta _____

8. Puerperal pyrexia of unknown origin (delivery during previous admission) _____

9. Late vomiting of pregnancy, undelivered _____

10. Severe pre-eclampsia complicating childbirth, delivered this admission _____

6.16 – Certain Conditions Originating in the Perinatal Period

1. Erythroblastosis fetalis _____

2. Hyperbilirubinemia of prematurity, prematurity (birthweight 2,000 grams) _____

3. Erb's palsy _____

4. Hypoglycemia in infant with diabetic mother _____

5. Premature baby born in hospital to cocaine-dependent mother
(birthweight 1,247 grams); neonatal withdrawal; cocaine dependence _____

6. Neonatal hematemesis _____

7. Sclerema neonatorum _____

8. Failure to thrive in newborn _____

9. Grey baby syndrome _____

10. Congenital renal failure _____

6.17 – Congenital Malformations, Deformations, and Chromosomal Abnormalities

1. Congenital diaphragmatic hernia   _____

2. Single liveborn male (born in the hospital, vaginally)
   with polydactyly of fingers   _____

3. Unilateral cleft lip and palate, incomplete   _____

4. Patent ductus arteriosus   _____

5. Congenital talipes equinovarus, right foot   _____

6. Cervical spina bifida   _____

7. Coloboma of left iris   _____

8. Tetralogy of Fallot   _____

9. Atresia of vas deferens   _____

10. Klinefelter syndrome, karyotype 47,XXY   _____

6.18 – Symptoms, Signs, and Abnormal Clinical and Laboratory Findings

1. Abnormal cervical Pap smear   _____

2. Sudden infant death syndrome   _____

3. Sleep apnea   _____

4. Fluid retention and edema   _____

5. Elevated blood pressure reading (no diagnosis of hypertension)   _____

6. Epistaxis   _____

7. Acute abdomen   _____

8. Dysphagia, pharyngeal phase   _____

9. Retrograde amnesia   _____

10. Irritable infant   _____

6.19 – Injury, Poisoning, and Certain Other Consequences of External Causes

1. Open frontal fracture with traumatic subarachnoid hemorrhage and no loss
   of consciousness (initial encounter)   _____

2. Traumatic anterior dislocation, left elbow (initial encounter)   _____

3. Sprain of lateral collateral ligament, right knee (subsequent encounter)   _____

4. Chronic headaches due to old traumatic avulsion, left eye   _____

5. Traumatic amputation, between right knee and ankle (initial encounter)   _____

6.20 – Burns

Note: Burns usually require two codes:

- One code for *each* site and highest degree (which means more than one code can be assigned)
- One code for the percentage of body surface (not body part) affected

Body Surface	Percentage
Head and neck	9%
Back (trunk)	18%
Chest (trunk)	18%
Leg (each)	18%
	18%
Arm (each)	9%
	9%
Genitalia	1%
TOTAL BODY SURFACE	100%

Refer to the following chart to calculate the percentage of burns for an extent of body surface. The percentage of total body area or surface affected follows the "rule of nines," as depicted in the following chart:

1. Third-degree burn of left lower leg (calf) and second-degree burn of left thigh (initial encounter)   _____

2. Third-degree burn of right forearm (initial encounter)   _____

3. Third-degree burn of upper back (subsequent encounter)   _____

4. Thirty percent body burns with 10 percent third-degree burns (initial encounter)   _____

5. Painful scarring due to old first- and second-degree burns of right palm   _____

6.21 – Foreign Bodies

Note: Refer to the main term "Foreign body" in the ICD-10-CM Index to Diseases and Injuries to begin the process of locating each code. Then, validate each assigned code in the ICD-10-CM Tabular List of Diseases and Injuries.

1. Coin in the bronchus causing asphyxiation (initial encounter)   _____

2. Foreign body in right eye (initial encounter)   _____

3. Marble in colon (initial encounter)   _____

4. Bean in nose (initial encounter)   _____

5. Q-tip stuck in left ear (initial encounter)   _____

6.22 – Complications

Note: Refer to the main term "Complication" in the ICD-10-CM Index to Diseases and Injuries to begin the process of locating each code. Then, validate each assigned code in the ICD-10-CM Tabular List of Diseases and Injuries.

1. Infected ventriculoperitoneal shunt (initial encounter)   _____

2. Displaced left breast prosthesis (initial encounter)   _____

3. Leakage of mitral valve prosthesis (initial encounter)   _____

4. Postoperative superficial thrombophlebitis of right leg (initial encounter)
(following surgical procedure on saphenous vein)   _____

5. Dislocated left hip internal prosthesis (initial encounter)   _____

6.23 – Poisonings, Adverse Effects, and Underdosing

Note: Use the ICD-10-CM Table of Drugs and Chemicals to begin the process of locating each code. Then, validate each assigned code in the ICD-10-CM Tabular List of Diseases and Injuries.

1. Accidental lead poisoning (child discovered eating paint chips) (initial encounter)   _____

2. Anaphylactic shock due to allergic reaction to penicillin (initial encounter)   _____

3. Theophylline toxicity (initial encounter)   _____

4. Carbon monoxide poisoning from nonmoving car exhaust (suicide attempt)
(initial encounter)   _____

5. Hypertension due to underdosing of Aldomet (initial encounter)   _____

6.24 – External Causes of Morbidity

Note: Use the ICD-10-CM Index of External Causes of Injury to begin the process of locating each code. Then, validate each assigned code in the ICD-10-CM Tabular List of Diseases and Injuries. Multiple codes are assigned to report the injury (e.g., laceration) as the first-listed or principal diagnosis code and then to report secondary external causes of morbidity codes for the cause (e.g., fall), intent, if known, (e.g., accidental, intentional), place of occurrence, if known (e.g., parking lot), activity (e.g., bicycling), and patient's status, if known (civilian, military).

1. Bicyclist fell off bicycle in parking lot (as paid messenger), lacerating chin (initial encounter) _____

2. Boy wearing heelies-type sneakers used the wheels (in the sneaker's heels) to glide and collided with tree in yard of single-family home; the boy started crying excessively (initial encounter)   _____

3. Pedestrian was walking through deep snow at local college and fell down steps, spraining right wrist (initial encounter)   _____

4. Patient walked into lamppost while walking on sidewalk, striking the head causing dizziness (initial encounter)   _____

5. Patient lacerated right hand while slicing tomatoes with a kitchen knife in the college dormitory kitchen (initial encounter)   _____

6.25 – Factors Influencing Health Status and Contact with Health Services

1. Exposure to tuberculosis   _____

2. Family history of colon carcinoma   _____

3. Postoperative follow-up examination, human kidney donor   _____

4. Encounter for removal of cast from healed pathologic fracture of right ankle   _____

5. Admitted as bone marrow donor   _____

6. Encounter for chemotherapy for patient with Hodgkin lymphoma   _____

7. Encounter for reprogramming (adjustment) of cardiac pacemaker   _____

8. Encounter for replacement of tracheostomy tube   _____

9. Encounter for renal dialysis in patient with end-stage renal failure   _____

10. Encounter for speech therapy for patient with dysphasia secondary
    to an old CVA   _____

6.26 – Codes for Special Purposes

1. Patient tested positive for COVID-19   _____

2. Vaping lung damage   _____

3. Post COVID-19 condition   _____

Chapter 7

CPT Coding

Chapter Outline

Organization of CPT

CPT Index

CPT Modifiers

Evaluation and Management Section

Anesthesia Section

Surgery Section

Radiology Section

Pathology and Laboratory Section

Medicine Section

CPT Category II and Category III Codes

Chapter Objectives

Upon successful completion of this chapter, you should be able to:

1. Define key terms related to CPT coding.
2. Describe the organization of CPT.
3. Locate main terms, subterms, and cross-references in the CPT index.
4. Select appropriate modifiers to add to CPT codes.
5. Assign CPT codes from the evaluation and management section.
6. Assign CPT codes from the anesthesia section.
7. Assign CPT codes from the surgery section.
8. Assign CPT codes from the radiology section.
9. Assign CPT codes from the pathology and laboratory section.
10. Assign CPT codes from the medicine section.
11. Assign CPT codes from Category II and Category III.

Key Terms

care plan oversight services

case management services

Category I codes

Category II codes

Category III codes

comprehensive assessment

concurrent care

consultation

contributory components

coordination of care

counseling

coding conventions (CPT)

  boldface type

  cross-reference terms

    See

    See also

descriptive qualifier

guidelines

inferred words

instructional notes

italicized type

CPT Symbols

●
▲
►◄
;
+
⊘
✎

↰
↰
↰
★
✳
↑↓

critical care services

direct patient contact

emergency department services

established patient

Evaluation and Management Documentation Guidelines

Evaluation and Management (E/M) section

extent of examination (CPT)

comprehensive examination

detailed examination

expanded problem focused examination

problem focused examination

extent of history (CPT)

comprehensive history

detailed history

expanded problem focused history

problem focused history

face-to-face time

global period

global surgery

history

home services

hospital discharge services

indented code

initial hospital care

key components

level of E/M service

medical decision making

moderate (conscious) sedation

modifier

monitored anesthesia care (MAC)

multiple surgical procedures

nature of the presenting problem

new patient

newborn care

nursing facility services

observation or inpatient care services

observation services

organ- or disease-oriented panel

partial hospitalization

physical examination

physical status modifier

place of service (POS)

preoperative clearance

preventive medicine services

professional component

prolonged services

qualifying circumstances

radiologic views

referral

resequenced code

separate procedure

special report

stand-alone code

standby services

subsequent hospital care

surgical package

technical component

telemedicine

transfer of care

type of service (TOS)

unit/floor time

unlisted procedure

unlisted service

without direct patient contact

Introduction

This chapter introduces the assignment of *Current Procedural Terminology* (CPT) service and procedure codes reported on insurance claims. CPT is published by the American Medical Association and includes codes for procedures performed and services provided to patients. It is level I of the Healthcare Common Procedure Coding System (HCPCS), which also contains level II (national) codes that are covered in Chapter 8 of this textbook.

Organization of CPT

Current Procedural Terminology (CPT) is a listing of descriptive terms and identifying codes for reporting medical services and procedures provided in an outpatient setting. For *professional billing*, CPT codes are assigned to inpatient hospital services and procedures provided by physicians and other qualified health care professionals. For *institutional billing*, ICD-10-PCS codes are assigned to inpatient hospital services and procedures provided by the hospital. (ICD-10-CM codes are assigned to all diagnoses and conditions in all health care settings.)

Example: A physician provides initial and subsequent hospital inpatient evaluation and management services to a patient admitted as a hospital inpatient. The physician's practice reports ICD-10-CM and CPT codes on the CMS-1500 claim to obtain reimbursement for professional services provided and procedures performed. The hospital where the patient was an inpatient reports ICD-10-CM and ICD-10-PCS codes on the UB-04 claim to obtain reimbursement for institutional services provided and procedures performed. (When the physician's practice is owned by the hospital, a hospital-based coder may assign all of the codes for professional and institutional billing. Codes are reported on appropriate claims for reimbursement.)

CPT provides a uniform language that describes medical, surgical, and diagnostic services to facilitate communication among providers, patients, and insurers. The American Medical Association (AMA) first published CPT in 1966, and subsequent editions expanded its descriptive terms and codes for diagnostic and therapeutic procedures. Five-digit codes were introduced in 1970, replacing the four-digit classification. In 1983, CPT was adopted as part of the Healthcare Common Procedure Coding System (HCPCS), and its use was mandated for reporting Medicare Part B services. In 1986, HCPCS was required for reporting to Medicaid agencies, and in July 1987, as part of the Omnibus Budget Reconciliation Act (OBRA), CMS mandated that CPT codes be reported for outpatient hospital surgical procedures.

 HIPAA Alert!

HIPAA named CPT and HCPCS Level II as the procedure code set for physician or other qualified health care professional services, physical and occupational therapy services, radiological procedures, clinical laboratory tests, other medical diagnostic procedures, hearing and vision services, and transportation services, including ambulance. HIPAA was modified in 2009 to name ICD-10-CM as the code set for diagnosis codes and ICD-10-PCS inpatient hospital procedures and services, CDT for dental services, and NDC for drugs. It eliminated the use of HCPCS Level III local codes effective December 2003. (Some private health insurance companies continue to use HCPCS Level III codes.)

CMS enforced regulations resulting from the Medicare Prescription Drug, Improvement, and Modernization Act (MMA) on October 1, 2004, which required that new, revised, and deleted CPT codes be implemented each January 1 and April 1 (with CPT vaccine codes also released on July 1). (Molecular Pathology Tier 2 Administrative MAAA and PLA codes are released quarterly at the AMA CPT public website.) Be sure to purchase updated coding manuals to avoid billing delays and claims rejections. If outdated codes are submitted on claims, providers and health care facilities will incur administrative costs associated with resubmitting corrected claims and delayed reimbursement for services provided.

CPT codes are used to report services and procedures performed on patients by:

- Providers in offices, clinics, and private homes
- Providers who care for patients in hospitals, nursing facilities, and hospices
- Providers employed by health care facilities
- Hospital outpatient departments

Procedures and services submitted on a claim must be linked to the ICD-10-CM code that justifies the need for the service or procedure. That ICD-10-CM code must demonstrate medical necessity for the service or procedure to receive reimbursement consideration by insurance payers.

The assignment of CPT codes simplifies reporting and assists in the accurate identification of procedures and services for third-party payer consideration. CPT codes and descriptions are based on consistency with contemporary medical practice as performed by clinical providers throughout the country. CPT codes are five characters in length, and code descriptions reflect health care services and procedures performed in modern medical practice. In addition, the AMA reviews and updates CPT codes and descriptions on an annual basis.

Relative Value Units

Relative value units (RVUs) are assigned by the Centers for Medicare and Medicaid Services (CMS) to each CPT and HCPCS Level II code. RVUs represent the cost of providing a service, and include the following payment components: physician work (physician's time and intensity in providing the service), practice expense (overhead costs involved in providing a service), and malpractice expense (malpractice expenses). Medicare physician fee schedule payments are based on payment components multiplied by conversion factors and geographical adjustments.

Changes to CPT

CPT supports electronic data interchange (EDI), the electronic health record (EHR) or electronic medical record (EMR), and reference/research databases. CPT can also be used to track new technology and performance measures. Improvements to CPT address the needs of hospitals, managed care organizations, and long-term care facilities. There are three categories of CPT codes:

- **Category I codes**: five-character CPT codes and procedure/service descriptor nomenclature; these are codes traditionally associated with CPT and organized within six sections; each section contains subsections and anatomic, procedural, condition, or descriptor subheadings; and codes are presented in numerical order except for the Evaluation and Management section, which appears as the first section

- **Category II codes**: "evidence-based performance measurements" tracking codes that are assigned an alphanumeric identifier with a letter in the last field (e.g., 0012F); these codes will be located after the Medicine section, and *their use is optional*

- **Category III codes**: "emerging technology" temporary codes assigned for data collection purposes that are assigned an alphanumeric identifier with a letter in the last field (e.g., 0075T); these codes are located after the Medicine section, and they will be archived after five years unless accepted for placement within Category I sections of CPT

New *proprietary laboratory analyses (PLA)* codes are available to any clinical laboratory or manufacturer that wants to specifically identify their commercially available tests that are used on human specimens. PLA test codes are published quarterly at the www.ama-assn.org website. You can locate these by entering "CPT PLA codes" in the Search box. New codes are effective in the quarter following their publication.

CPT Sections

CPT organizes Category I procedures and services within six sections:

- Evaluation and Management (E/M) (99202–99499)
- Anesthesia (00100–01999, 99100–99140)
- Surgery (10004–69990)
- Radiology (70010–79999)
- Pathology and Laboratory (80047–89398, 0001U–0254U)
- Medicine (90281–99199, 99500–99607, 0001A–0042A)

 NOTE:

- The E/M section is located at the beginning of CPT because these codes are reported by all specialties.
- Medicine section codes (99100–99140) that classify *Qualifying Circumstances for Anesthesia Services* are explained in the Anesthesia section guidelines; they are to be reported with Anesthesia section codes.

CPT Code Number Format

A five-character code number and a narrative description identify each procedure and service listed in CPT. Most procedures and services are classified as **stand-alone codes**, which include a complete description of the procedure or service. To save space, some descriptions are not printed in their entirety next to a code number. Instead, an **indented code** appears below a stand-alone code, requiring the coder to refer back to the common portion of the code description that is located before the semicolon.

Example 1: Stand-alone code description

27870   Arthrodesis, ankle, open

Example 2: Indented code description

27780   Closed treatment of proximal fibula or shaft fracture; without manipulation
27781   with manipulation

The code description for 27781 is *closed treatment of proximal fibula or shaft fracture with manipulation.*

CPT Appendices

CPT contains appendices that are located between the Medicine section and the Index. Insurance specialists should carefully review these appendices to become familiar with coding changes that affect the practice annually (Table 7-1).

TABLE 7-1 CPT Appendices

CPT Appendix	Description
Appendix A	Detailed descriptions of each CPT modifier.
	Coding Tip: Place a marker at the beginning of Appendix A because you will refer to this appendix often.
Appendix B	Annual CPT coding changes (added, deleted, and revised CPT codes).
	Coding Tip: Carefully review Appendix B because it will serve as the basis for updating encounter forms and chargemasters.
Appendix C	Clinical examples for Evaluation and Management (E/M) section codes.
	Note: The AMA halted the project to revise E/M code descriptions using clinical examples (or vignettes) in 2004. However, previously developed clinical examples are still included in Appendix C.
Appendix D	Summary list of CPT add-on codes.
	Coding Tip: Add-on codes are identified in CPT with the + symbol.
Appendix E	Summary list of CPT codes exempt from modifier -51 reporting rules.
	Coding Tip: Exempt codes are identified in CPT with the ⊘ symbol.
Appendix F	Summary list of CPT codes exempt from modifier -63 reporting rules.
	Coding Tip: Codes that are exempt from modifier -63 is the parenthetical instruction "(Do not report modifier -63 in conjunction with . . . .)"
Appendix G	Summary list of CPT codes that include moderate (conscious) sedation was removed from CPT. The related bull's-eye symbol was also removed from the codes, and codes 99151-99157 are used for moderate (conscious) sedation reporting purposes.
Appendix H	Alphabetic clinical topics listing was removed from CPT and can be located at www.ama-assn.org by entering *CPT Category II Codes Alphabetical Clinical Topics Listing* in the Search box to view a document that includes performance measures.
Appendix I	Genetic testing code modifiers have been removed from CPT.
Appendix J	Summary electrodiagnostic medicine listing of sensory, motor, and mixed nerves (reported for motor and nerve studies codes).

(continues)

TABLE 7-1 CPT Appendices (continued)

Appendix K	Products pending Food and Drug Administration (FDA) approval but that have been assigned a CPT code. In the CPT manual, these codes are preceded by the flash symbol (✔).
Appendix L	List of vascular families to assist in selecting first-, second-, third-, and beyond third-order branch arteries.
Appendix M	Crosswalk of deleted and renumbered CPT codes and citations from 2007 to 2009. (The AMA discontinued the practice of deleting and renumbering codes in 2010.)
Appendix N	Summary list of resequenced CPT codes.
Appendix O	List of administrative codes for multianalyte assays with algorithmic analyses (MAAA) procedures, which are procedures that use multiple results generated from assays of various types, including molecular pathology assays, and so on.
Appendix P	Codes that may be used to report synchronous telemedicine services when appended with modifier -95. Such services require the use of electronic communication that facilitates interactive telecommunications via audio and video. The codes are preceded by the star (★) symbol.
Appendix Q	Table of severe acute respiratory syndrome coronavirus 2 (SARS-CoV-2) (coronavirus disease [COVID-19]) vaccines and associated vaccine product codes and immunization administration codes.
Appendix R	Table of Digital medicine—services taxonomy services for clinician-to-patient services and clinician-to-clinician services.

Telemedicine

Telemedicine is the provision of remote medical care using an interactive audio and video telecommunications system that permits real-time communication between the provider, located at the distant site (e.g., physician's office), and the patient, located at the originating site (e.g., patient's home several hours driving distance away from the provider). It is an alternative to in-person face-to-face encounters, which allows patients to receive health care services for minor medical conditions (instead of going to an emergency room), for chronic conditions that are well managed, from specialists located in other areas of the country, or when patients cannot leave work to see their provider.

The availability of *telemedicine* is the result of advancements in clinical decision making and user friendly technology. It is also seen as an affordable option for patients who have high-deductible health insurance plans.

Example: New York State Department of Health (www.health.ny.gov) data about *potentially preventable emergency department encounters* identifies common conditions (e.g., ear and sinus infections, sore throats) that represent millions of annual visits to hospital emergency departments. Such encounters could have been avoided or treated elsewhere if patients had been able to schedule an appointment with their primary care providers. Face-to-face encounters with a physician remains the ideal method for having minor conditions addressed; however, if the patient is unable to obtain an appointment for an immediate office visit, the patient can ask whether the issue could be addressed using telemedicine. This results in: (1) cost savings due to avoiding a potentially preventable emergency department encounter, and (2) treatment by the patient's primary care provider. (The patient would schedule an appointment with the provider for follow-up of the condition treated using telemedicine.)

CPT Symbols

Symbols located throughout the CPT coding book include the following (examples are included for illustrative purposes only and may not match the current CPT manual):

- ● A bullet located to the left of a code number identifies new codes for procedures and services added to CPT.

Example: CPT code 33897 was added to a new edition of the coding manual.

- ● 33897   Percutaneous transluminal angioplasty of native or recurrent coarctation of the aorta

▲ A triangle located to the left of a code identifies a code description that has been revised.

Example: CPT code 11981 was revised in a new edition of the coding manual to replace non-biodegradable in the code description and add it in parentheses.

   ▲ 11981   Insertion, drug-delivery implant (ie, bioresorbable, biodegradable, non-biodegradable)

►◄ Horizontal triangles surround revised guidelines and notes. *This symbol is not used for revised code descriptions*.

Example: The parenthetical instruction above code 80503 indicates that CPT codes 80500 and 80502 were deleted in a new edition of the coding manual.

   ► (80500, 80502 have been deleted. To report a clinical pathology consultation, limited or comprehensive, see 80503, 80504, 80505, 80506) ◄

Coding Tip

A complete list of code additions, deletions, and revisions is found in Appendix B of CPT. Revisions marked with horizontal triangles (►◄) are *not* included in Appendix B, and requires review all CPT guidelines and notes.

; A semicolon is used to save space in CPT, and some code descriptions are not printed in their entirety next to a code number. Instead, the entry is indented and the coder must refer back to the common portion of the code description that is located before the semicolon. The common portion begins with a capital letter, and the abbreviated (or subordinate) descriptions are indented and begin with lowercase letters.

Example: The code description for 67255 is *scleral reinforcement with graft*.

   67250   Scleral reinforcement (separate procedure); without graft
   67255   with graft

Coding Tip

CPT uses proportional spacing, and careful review of code descriptions to locate the semicolon is necessary.

+ The plus symbol located to the left of a code identifies add-on codes (listed in Appendix D of CPT) for procedures that are commonly, but not always, performed at the same time and by the same surgeon as the primary procedure. An add-on code is reported with its primary procedure code and cannot be reported alone. Parenthetical notes, located below add-on codes, often identify the primary procedure to which add-on codes apply. (Add-on codes are exempt from modifier -51. A complete list of codes that are exempt from modifier -51 is found in Appendix E of the CPT manual.)

Example:

   22210   Osteotomy of spine, posterior or posterolateral approach, 1 vertebral segment; cervical
  + 22216   each additional vertebral segment (List separately in addition to primary procedure)

Coding Tip

Codes identified with + are *never* reported as stand-alone codes; they are reported with primary procedure codes. Also, *do not* append add-on codes with modifier −51.

⊘   The forbidden symbol identifies codes that are *not* to be used with modifier -51. These codes are reported in addition to other codes, but they are *not* classified as add-on codes.

> **Example:**
>
> ⊘ **20974**   Electrical stimulation to aid bone healing; noninvasive (nonoperative)

↗   The flash symbol indicates codes that classify products that are pending FDA approval but have been assigned a CPT code.

> **Example:**
>
> ↗ **90671**   Pneumococcal conjugate vaccine, 15 valent (PCV15), for intramuscular use

\#   The number symbol precedes CPT **resequenced codes**, which appear out of numerical order (e.g., code 99224).

> **Example:**
>
> \# **33227**   Removal of permanent pacemaker pulse generator with replacement of pacemaker pulse generator; single lead system

⊃   The blue reference symbol located before a code description in some CPT coding manuals indicates that the coder should refer to the *CPT Changes: An Insider's View* annual publication that contains all coding changes for the current year.

⊃   The green reference symbol located below a code description in some CPT coding manuals indicates that the coder should refer to the *CPT Assistant* monthly newsletter.

⊃   The red reference symbol located below a code description in some CPT coding manuals indicates that the coder should refer to the *Clinical Examples in Radiology* quarterly newsletter.

> **Example:**
>
> **73551**   Radiologic examination, hip, unilateral, with pelvis when performed; 1 view
> > ⊃ *CPT Changes: An Insider's View* 2016
> > ⊃ *CPT Assistant* Aug 16:7, Nov 16:10
> > ⊃ *Clinical Examples in Radiology* Fall 15:9, Summer 16:8

★   The star symbol is used to identify codes that may be used to report telemedicine services when appended with modifier -95 (e.g., 90791-95).

> **Example:**
>
> ★ **90845**   Psychoanalysis

⟩(The parens symbol identifies duplicate proprietary laboratory analyses (PLA) tests. Descriptor language of some PLA codes are identical, and codes are differentiated only by reviewing proprietary names listed in Appendix O of the CPT manual.

↑↓   The double arrow symbol identifies CPT Category I PLA codes.

 NOTE:

> Although PLA codes are included in the Pathology and Laboratory section of CPT, they do not fulfill Category I criteria unless the arrow symbol precedes the code.

CPT Sections, Subsections, Categories, and Subcategories

CPT Category I codes are organized according to six sections that are subdivided into subsections, categories, and subcategories (Figure 7-1).

Guidelines

Guidelines are located at the beginning of each CPT section, and *should be carefully reviewed before attempting to code*. **Guidelines** define terms and explain the assignment of codes for procedures and services located in a particular section (Figure 7-2). This means that guidelines in one section do not apply to another section in CPT.

Unlisted Procedures/Services

An **unlisted procedure** or **unlisted service** code is assigned when the provider performs a procedure or service for which there is no CPT code. When an unlisted procedure or service code is reported, a **special report** (e.g., copy of procedure report) must accompany the claim to describe the nature, extent, and need for the procedure or service along with the time, effort, and equipment necessary to provide the service.

NOTE:

- Do not add a modifier to CPT unlisted procedure/service codes because they do not include specific descriptions that would justify modifying their meaning.
- Medicare and other third-party payers often require providers to report HCPCS Level II (national) codes instead of unlisted procedure or service CPT codes.

SYMBOL / CONVENTION	CPT ENTRY:	
Section	**Surgery**	
Subsection	**Integumentary System**	
Category / Heading	**Skin, Subcutaneous and Accessory Structures**	
Subcategory / Subheading	**Incision and Drainage**	
Note	(For excision, see 11400, et seq)	
Code number / Description	**10040**	Acne surgery (eg, marsupialization, opening or removal of multiple milia, comedones, cysts, pustules)
Use of semicolon	**11000**	Debridement of extensive eczematous or infected skin; up to 10% of body surface
Use of plus symbol	**+11001**	each additional 10% of the body surface, or part thereof (List separately in addition to code for primary procedure)
Use of -51 modifier exemption symbol	⊘ **20974**	Electrical stimulation to aid bone healing; noninvasive (nonoperative)

Current Procedural Terminology published by the American Medical Association.

FIGURE 7-1 Selection from CPT that illustrates symbols and conventions.

Surgery Guidelines

Guidelines to direct general reporting of services are presented in the **Introduction**. Some of the commonalities are repeated here for the convenience of those referring to this section on **Surgery**. Other definitions and items unique to Surgery are also listed.

Services

Services rendered in the office, home, or hospital, consultations, and other medical services are listed in **Evaluation and Management Services** section (99202-99499) beginning on page 9. "Special Services, Procedures and Reports" (99000-99082) are listed in the **Medicine** section.

Supplied Materials

Supplies and materials (eg, sterile trays/drugs) over and above those usually included with the procedure(s) rendered are reported separately. List drugs, trays, supplies, and materials provided. Identify as 99070 or specific supply code.

Reporting More Than One Procedure/Service

When more than one procedure/service is performed on the same date, same session or during a post-operative period (subject to the "surgical package" concept), several CPT modifiers may apply (see Appendix A for definition).

Current Procedural Terminology published by the American Medical Association.

FIGURE 7-2 Portion of CPT surgery guidelines.

Notes

Instructional notes appear throughout CPT sections to clarify the assignment of codes. They are typeset in two patterns (Figure 7-3):

1. A *blocked unindented note* is located below a subsection title and contains instructions that apply to all codes in the subsection.
2. An *indented parenthetical note* is located below a subsection title, code description, or code description that contains an example.

Parenthetical notes that contain the abbreviation "eg" are examples.

 N O T E :

> Parenthetical notes within a code series provide information about deleted codes. Such content does not have to be included in provider documentation.

Descriptive Qualifiers

Descriptive qualifiers are terms that clarify the assignment of a CPT code. They can occur in the middle of a main clause or after the semicolon and may or may not be enclosed in parentheses. Be sure to read all code descriptions very carefully to properly assign CPT codes that require descriptive qualifiers.

Example:

17000	Destruction (eg, laser surgery, electrosurgery, cryosurgery, chemosurgery, surgical curettement), premalignant lesions (eg, actinic keratoses); first lesion
+ 17003	<u>second through 14 lesions, each</u> (List separately in addition to code for first lesion)

The underlining identifies descriptive qualifiers in the code description for 17003.

Cardiovascular System

Blocked unindented note

Selective vascular catheterizations should be coded to include introduction and all lesser order selective catheterizations used in the approach (eg, the description for a selective right middle cerebral artery catheterization includes the introduction and placement catheterization of the right common and internal carotid arteries).

Additional second and/or third order arterial catheterizations within the same family of arteries supplied by a single first order artery should be expressed by 36218 or 36248. Additional first order or higher catheterizations in vascular families supplied by a first order vessel different from a previously selected and coded family should be separately coded using the conventions described above.

Indented parenthetical note located below subsection title

(For monitoring, operation of pump, and other nonsurgical services, see 99190-99192, 99291, 99292, 99354-99360)

(For other medical or laboratory related services, see appropriate section)

(For radiological supervision and interpretation, see 75600-75970)

(For anatomic guidance of arterial and venous anatomy, see Appendix L)

Heart and Pericardium

Pericardium

33020   Pericardiotomy for removal of clot or foreign body (primary procedure)

Parenthetical note located below code description

Current Procedural Terminology published by the American Medical Association.

FIGURE 7-3 Selection from CPT that illustrates types of instructional notes.

Coding Tip

Coders working in a provider's office should highlight descriptive qualifiers in CPT that pertain to the office's specialty. This will help ensure that qualifiers are not overlooked when assigning codes.

Foreign Body/Implant Definition

The Foreign Body/Implant Definition guideline applies to the Surgery, Radiology, and Medicine sections to clarify that (1) an object intentionally placed into the patient is considered an implant, and (2) an object unintentionally placed (due to ingestion or trauma) is considered a foreign body. However, when an implant shifts from its original position or becomes broken, it is considered a foreign body for coding purposes (especially when it becomes a hazard to a patient). The exception is when CPT coding instructions provide guidance to specific codes that describes the removal of a shifted or broken implant.

Exercise 7.1 – Organization of CPT

Instructions: Complete each statement.

1. *Current Procedural Terminology* (CPT) is a listing of descriptive terms and identifying codes for reporting medical services and _____.

(continues)

Exercise 7.1 – continued

2. CPT codes are assigned to inpatient hospital services and procedures provided by physicians and other qualified health care professionals for _____ billing.

3. Procedures and services submitted on a claim must be linked to the ICD-10-CM code that justifies the need for the service or procedure, which demonstrates the _____ necessity for the service or procedure to receive reimbursement consideration by insurance payers.

4. CPT Category I codes contain five characters and descriptor nomenclature, and they are organized into _____ sections.

5. CPT Category II codes contain five characters, are used as evidence-based performance measurements tracking codes, and are located after the _____ section in the CPT coding manual.

6. CPT Category III codes contain five characters for emerging technology, are assigned for data collection purposes, and will be _____ after five years unless accepted for placement within a CPT Category I section.

7. Most CPT procedures and services are classified as _____ codes, which include a complete description of the procedure or service.

8. Some CPT procedures and services contain a semicolon to save space, and the coder must refer back to the _____ portion of the code description (that is located before the semicolon).

9. CPT contains appendices located between the Medicine section and the Index, and coders review Appendix _____ to locate annual CPT coding changes of added, deleted, and revised CPT codes.

10. Symbols located throughout the CPT coding book, and a bullet symbol located to the left of a code number identifies new codes for procedures and services that have been _____ to CPT.

11. The triangle symbol located to the left of a code identifies a code description that has been _____ in CPT.

12. The plus symbol located to the left of a CPT code identifies add-on codes for procedures, and an add-on code must be reported with its _____ procedure code.

13. Guidelines are located at the beginning of each CPT section, and they define terms and explain the assignment of codes for procedures and services located in that particular _____.

14. When the provider performs a procedure or service for which there is no CPT code, a(n) _____ procedure or service code is assigned and a special report is attached to the claim.

15. Blocked unindented notes (below a subsection title) and indented parenthetical notes (below codes and descriptions) clarify the assignment of codes, and they are referred to as _____ notes.

CPT Index

The CPT index (Figure 7-4) is organized by alphabetical main terms printed in boldface.

Main Terms

The CPT index is organized according to main terms, which can stand alone or be followed by modifying terms. Main terms can represent:

- Procedure or service (e.g., endoscopy)
- Organ or anatomic site (e.g., colon)
- Condition (e.g., abscess)
- Synonyms, eponyms, and abbreviations (e.g., Bricker Operation, Fibrinase, EEG)

N

Cross-referenced term	**Nasal Polyp** *See* Nose, Polyp
Main term (boldface type) **Subterm (not indented)**	**Nails** Avulsion..................................11730–11732
Range of codes to investigate	Biopsy....................................11755 Debridement........................11720, 11721 Drainage...............................10060, 10061
Subterm (indented)	Evacuation Hematoma, Subungual............11740

Current Procedural Terminology published by the American Medical Association.

FIGURE 7-4 Selection from the CPT index.

Modifying Terms

A main term may be followed by subterms that modify the main term and/or terms they follow. The subterms may also be followed by additional subterms that are indented.

Code Ranges

Index code numbers for specific procedures may be represented as a single code number, a range of codes separated by a dash, a series of codes separated by commas, or a combination of single codes and ranges of codes. All listed numbers should be investigated before assigning a code for the procedure or service.

Conventions

Main terms in the CPT index are printed in **boldface type**, along with CPT categories, subcategories, headings, and code numbers. **See** and *See also* are **cross-reference terms** that directs coders to an index entry under which codes are listed. No codes are listed under the original entry. **Italicized type** is used for the cross-reference term, *See*, in the CPT index.

Example: AV Shunt
> *See* Arteriovenous Shunt

In this example, you are directed to the index entry for Arteriovenous Shunt because no codes are listed for AV Shunt.

To save space in the CPT index when referencing subterms, **inferred words** are used.

Example: Abdomen
> Exploration (of) 49000, 49010

In this example, the word (of) is inferred and does not actually appear in the CPT index.

 Coding Tip

The descriptions of *all* codes listed for a specific procedure must be carefully investigated before selecting a final code. As with ICD-10-CM (and ICD-10-PCS), CPT coding must *never* be performed solely from its index.

Exercise 7.2 – CPT Index

Instructions: Answer each item below.

1. Main terms in the CPT index can represent procedures or services, organs or anatomic sites, conditions, or synonyms, eponyms, and _____.

2. A main term may be followed by a _____, which modifies the main term.

3. CPT index codes for procedures and services may be represented as a single code number, a _____ of codes separated by a dash, a series of codes separated by commas, or a combination of single codes and ranges of codes.

4. Main terms in the CPT index are printed in _____ type, along with CPT categories, subcategories, headings, and codes.

5. The cross-reference term in italicized type, which directs coders to an index entry under which codes are listed, is called _____.

Coding Procedures and Services

Step 1   Read the introduction in the CPT coding manual.

Step 2   Review guidelines at the beginning of each section.

Step 3   Review the procedure or service listed in the source document (e.g., encounter form, progress note, operative report, laboratory report, pathology report). Code only what is documented in the source document; do not make assumptions about conditions, procedures, or services not stated. If necessary, obtain clarification from the provider.

Step 4   Refer to the CPT index, and locate the main term for the procedure or service documented. Main terms can be located by referring to the:

a. *Procedure or service* documented.

Example: Arthroscopy

b. *Organ or anatomic site.*

Example: Arm

c. *Condition documented in the record.*

Example: Hernia Repair

d. *Substance being tested.*

Example: Blood

e. *Synonym* (terms with similar meanings).

Example: Pyothorax

f. *Eponym* (procedures and diagnoses named for an individual).

Example: Collis Procedure

g. *Abbreviation.*

Example: CBC

Step 5   Locate subterms and follow cross-references.

Example: The patient underwent an Abbe-Estlander procedure that required full-thickness excision of lip with reconstruction and cross lip flap. In the CPT index, go to main term Abbe-Estlander Procedure and subterm Lip Reconstruction to look up codes 40527, 40761.

Step 6   Review descriptions of service/procedure codes, and compare all qualifiers to descriptive statements.

Example: The operative report documents an Abbe-Estlander procedure requiring full-thickness excision of lip with reconstruction and cross lip flap. Review of CPT index entries 40527, 40761 (for main term Abbe-Estlander Procedure, and subterm Lip Reconstruction) results in the assignment of code 40527 for Excision of lip; full thickness, reconstruction with cross lip flap (Abbe-Estlander). (Code 40761 is reported for a full-thickness lip repair and Abbe-Estlander procedure that is performed during the same operative episode.)

 Hint

If the main term is located at the bottom of a CPT index page, turn the page and check to see if the main term and subterm(s) continue.

Step 7   Assign the applicable code number and any add-on (+) or additional codes needed to accurately classify the statement being coded.

Step 8   Review Appendix B in the CPT coding manual to assign appropriate modifiers. (Table 7-2 provides clarification about the assignment of modifiers.)

 NOTE:

When entering CPT codes on the CMS-1500 claim, enter codes based on highest to lowest reimbursement (e.g., provider-based charge). Third-party payers will determine reimbursement based on the patient's health plan contract, and the assignment of multiple procedure/service modifiers results in discounted reimbursement.

 Coding Tip

You may have to refer to synonyms, translate medical terms to ordinary English, or substitute medical words for English terms documented in the provider's statement to find the main term in the index. Some examples are:

Procedure Statement	Word Substitution
Placement of a shunt	Insertion of shunt
Pacemaker implantation	Pacemaker insertion
Resection of tumor	Excision or removal of tumor
Radiograph of the chest	X ray of chest
Suture laceration	Repair open wound
Placement of nerve block	Injection of nerve anesthesia

Exercise 7.3 – Finding Procedures in the Index

Instructions: Using only the CPT index, enter the code or range of codes to be investigated. For example, when locating Acromioplasty in the CPT index, 23415–23420 is the answer entered.

1. Closed treatment of wrist dislocation   _____
2. Dilation of vagina   _____
3. Placement of nasogastric tube   _____
4. Radiological exam of the pharynx including fluoroscopy   _____
5. Magnetic resonance imaging (MRI), wrist   _____
6. Arthrodesis of tibiofibular joint   _____
7. Automated CBC   _____
8. Electrosurgical removal, skin tags   _____
9. Molar pregnancy excision   _____
10. Denervation, femoral hip joint   _____

CPT Modifiers

CPT **modifiers** (Table 7-2) clarify services and procedures performed by providers. Although the CPT code and description remain unchanged, modifiers indicate that the description of the service or procedure performed has been altered. CPT modifiers are reported in Block 24E of the CMS-1500 claim.

Example: A patient has a history of gallbladder disease. After several hours of acute pain, they were referred to Dr. S for an evaluation of their condition. Dr. S performed a complete history and physical examination and decided to admit the patient to the hospital for an immediate work-up for cholecystitis. After receiving the results of the laboratory tests and sonogram, the patient was scheduled for an emergency laparoscopic cholecystectomy. The surgeon was Dr. S and the assistant surgeon was Dr. A. The surgery was successful, and the patient was discharged the next day and told to return to the office in seven days. Four days later, the patient returns to Dr. S's office complaining of chest pains. Dr. S performs another examination and orders the necessary tests. After reviewing the test results and confirming with the patient's primary care physician, it is determined that the patient was suffering from mild angina.

Dr. S submits a claim (Figure 7-5) for the following services (1) Initial hospital visit, comprehensive, with medical decision making of high complexity (99223-57) (Modifier -57 indicates decision for surgery); and (2) laparoscopic cholecystectomy (47562). Dr. A submits a claim (Figure 7-6) for the laparoscopic cholecystectomy 47562-80 (Modifier 80 indicates assistant surgeon).

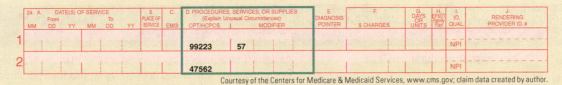

Courtesy of the Centers for Medicare & Medicaid Services, www.cms.gov; claim data created by author.

FIGURE 7-5 Completed Block 24D on CMS-1500 claim.

Courtesy of the Centers for Medicare & Medicaid Services, www.cms.gov; claim data created by author.

FIGURE 7-6 Completed Block 24D on CMS-1500 claim.

NOTE:

In an attempt to simplify the explanation of modifiers, the wording in this textbook does not correspond word-for-word with descriptions found in CPT.

TABLE 7-2 Organization of CPT modifiers according to reporting similarity

Special Evaluation and Management (E/M) Services		
Modifier	Description	Interpretation
-24	Unrelated Evaluation and Management Service by the Same Physician or Other Qualified Health Care Professional During a Postoperative Period	Assign to indicate that an E/M service was performed during the standard postoperative period for a condition unrelated to the surgery. The procedure to which the modifier is attached *must be* linked to a diagnosis that is *unrelated* to the surgical diagnosis previously submitted. Be sure to submit a copy of documentation with the claim to explain the circumstances.
	Example: One week after surgical release of a frozen shoulder, an established patient received level 3 evaluation and management services for treatment of the flu. Report code 99213-24.	
-25	Significant, Separately Identifiable Evaluation and Management Service by the Same Physician or Other Qualified Health Care Professional on the Same Day of the Procedure or Other Services	Assign when a documented E/M service was performed on the same day as another procedure because the patient's condition required the assignment of significant, separately identifiable, additional E/M services that are normally not a part of the other procedure.
		Note: The documented history, examination, and medical decision making must "stand on its own" to justify reporting modifier -25 with the E/M code. The E/M service provided must be "above and beyond" what is normally performed during a procedure.
		Many payers restrict the reporting of modifier -25. Be sure to obtain payer reporting guidelines.
	Example: During routine preventive annual examination, it was discovered that a 65-year-old established patient had an enlarged liver, necessitating expansion of the scope of level 4 E/M services. Report 99397 and 99214-25. (Be sure to submit supporting documentation to the payer.)	
-57	Decision for Surgery	Assign when the reported E/M service resulted in the *initial* decision to perform surgery on the day before *or* the day of surgery, to exempt it from the global surgery package.
	Example: The patient received level 4 E/M services for chest pain in the emergency department, and a decision was made to insert a coronary arterial stent. Report 99284-57.	
Greater, Reduced, or Discontinued Procedures or Services		
Modifier	Description	Interpretation
-22	Increased Procedural Services	Assign when a procedure *requires greater than usual service(s).* Documentation that would support using this modifier includes difficult, complicated, extensive, unusual, or rare procedure(s).
		Note: This modifier has been overused. Be sure special circumstances are documented, and send a copy of documentation with the claim.
	Example: Procedure report documents blood loss of 600 mL or greater. Operative report documents prolonged operative time, which required intraoperative transfusions. Report the CPT surgery code with modifier -22.	

(continues)

TABLE 7-2   (continued)

Greater, Reduced, or Discontinued Procedures or Services (continued)		
Modifier	Description	Interpretation
-52	Reduced Services	Report when a service has been partially reduced at the physician's discretion and does not completely match the CPT code description.
		Note: Attach a copy of documentation to the claim.
		Example: A surgeon removed a coccygeal pressure ulcer and performed a coccygectomy. However, the surgeon did not use a primary suture or perform a skin flap closure because the wound had to be cleansed for a continued period of time postoperatively. Report code 15920-52. (When the surgeon eventually performs the wound closure procedure, an appropriate code would be reported.)
-53	Discontinued Procedure	Report when a provider elects to terminate a procedure because of extenuating circumstances that threaten the well-being of the patient.
		Note: Do *not* report for procedures electively canceled prior to induction of anesthesia and/or surgical prep.
		Example: The surgeon inserted the colonoscope and removed it right away because the patient had not been properly prepared for the procedure. Report code 45378-53. (The patient received instruction about properly preparing for the colonoscopy procedure, and the procedure was rescheduled.)
-73	Discontinued Outpatient Hospital/ Ambulatory Surgery Center (ASC) Procedure Prior to Anesthesia Administration	Report to describe outpatient facility and ASC procedures discontinued *prior to the administration of any anesthesia* because of extenuating circumstances threatening the well-being of the patient. Do not report for elective cancellations.
		Note: Report a code from ICD-10-CM category Z53 to document the reason the procedure was halted.
		Example: Hospital outpatient facility patient developed heart arrhythmia prior to anesthesia administration for left breast simple complete mastectomy, and surgery was halted. Report 19303-73-LT.
-74	Discontinued Outpatient Hospital/ Ambulatory Surgery Center (ASC) Procedure After Anesthesia Administration	Report to describe outpatient hospital or ASC procedures discontinued *after the administration of anesthesia* due to extenuating circumstances.
		Note: Report a code from ICD-10-CM category Z53 to document the reason the procedure was halted.
		Example: ASU patient was prepped and draped, and general anesthesia administered prior to performance of a laparoscopic cholecystectomy. Anesthesiologist noted a sudden increase in blood pressure, and the procedure was terminated. Report 47562-74.
Global Surgery		
Modifier	Description	Interpretation

Global Surgery modifiers:

- Apply to the four areas related to the CPT surgical package (Figure 7-7), which includes the procedure; local infiltration, metacarpal/digital block or topical anesthesia when used; and normal, uncomplicated follow-up care.
- Do not apply to obstetric coding where the CPT description of specific codes clearly describes separate antepartum, postpartum, and delivery services for both vaginal and cesarean deliveries.

(continues)

TABLE 7-2 (continued)

Global Surgery (continued)		
Modifier	**Description**	**Interpretation**

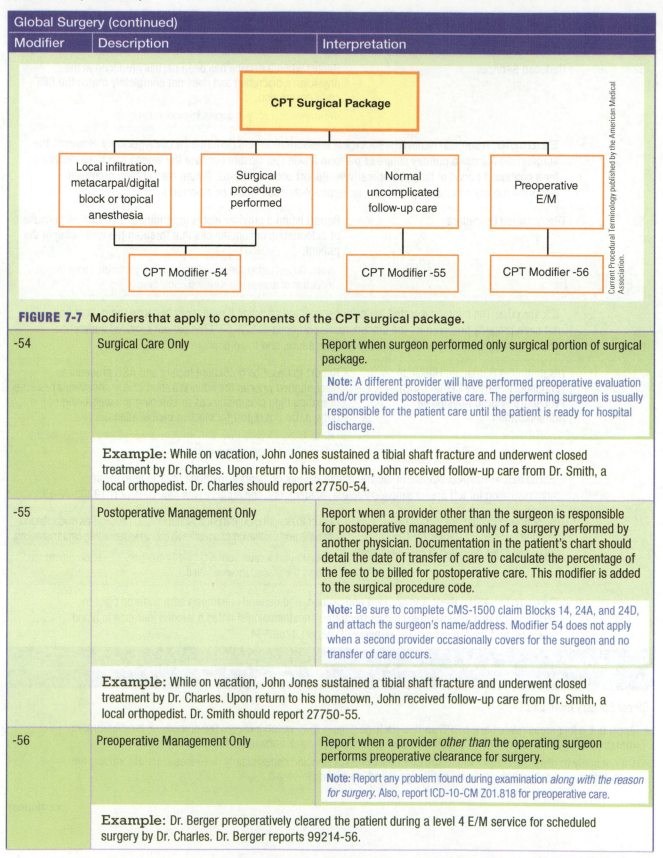

FIGURE 7-7 Modifiers that apply to components of the CPT surgical package.

-54	Surgical Care Only	Report when surgeon performed only surgical portion of surgical package. **Note:** A different provider will have performed preoperative evaluation and/or provided postoperative care. The performing surgeon is usually responsible for the patient care until the patient is ready for hospital discharge. **Example:** While on vacation, John Jones sustained a tibial shaft fracture and underwent closed treatment by Dr. Charles. Upon return to his hometown, John received follow-up care from Dr. Smith, a local orthopedist. Dr. Charles should report 27750-54.
-55	Postoperative Management Only	Report when a provider other than the surgeon is responsible for postoperative management only of a surgery performed by another physician. Documentation in the patient's chart should detail the date of transfer of care to calculate the percentage of the fee to be billed for postoperative care. This modifier is added to the surgical procedure code. **Note:** Be sure to complete CMS-1500 claim Blocks 14, 24A, and 24D, and attach the surgeon's name/address. Modifier 54 does not apply when a second provider occasionally covers for the surgeon and no transfer of care occurs. **Example:** While on vacation, John Jones sustained a tibial shaft fracture and underwent closed treatment by Dr. Charles. Upon return to his hometown, John received follow-up care from Dr. Smith, a local orthopedist. Dr. Smith should report 27750-55.
-56	Preoperative Management Only	Report when a provider *other than* the operating surgeon performs preoperative clearance for surgery. **Note:** Report any problem found during examination *along with the reason for surgery*. Also, report ICD-10-CM Z01.818 for preoperative care. **Example:** Dr. Berger preoperatively cleared the patient during a level 4 E/M service for scheduled surgery by Dr. Charles. Dr. Berger reports 99214-56.

(continues)

TABLE 7-2 (continued)

Special Surgical and Procedural Services

Modifier	Description	Interpretation
-58	Staged or Related Procedure or Service by the Same Physician or Other Qualified Health Care Professional During the Postoperative Period	Report to indicate that additional related surgery was required during the postoperative period of a previously completed surgery and was performed by the same physician. Documentation should include one of the following: • Original plan for surgery included additional stages to be performed within the postoperative period of the first stage of the procedure. • Underlying disease required performance of a second related, but unplanned, procedure. • Additional related therapy is required after the performance of a diagnostic surgical procedure. **Note:** Do *not* report modifier -58 if the CPT code description describes multiple sessions of an event.

Example: A surgical wound is not healing properly because of the patient's underlying diabetes. Patient was told prior to the original surgery that if this happened, additional surgery would be required for subcutaneous tissue debridement of the wound. Report code 11042-58 for debridement surgery.

Modifier	Description	Interpretation
-59	Distinct Procedural Service	Report when the same physician performs one or more *distinctly independent procedures* on the same day as other procedures or services, according to the following criteria: • Procedures are performed at different sessions or during different patient encounters. • Procedures are performed on different sites or organs and require a different surgical prep. • Procedures are performed for multiple or extensive injuries, using separate incisions/excisions; for separate lesions; or for procedures not ordinarily encountered/performed on the same day. However, when another modifier is appropriate, it should be reported instead of modifier -59. Modifier -59 is never added to E/M codes. **Note:** Modifier -51, multiple procedures, may also be added to reported secondary procedures codes.

Example: Patient has two basal cell carcinomas removed, one from the forehead with a simple closure (11640) and the other from the nose requiring adjacent tissue transfer (14060). Report as 14060, 11640-51 (forehead), 11640-59-51 (nose).

Note: CMS has defined HCPCS Level II modifiers to selectively identify subsets of modifier -59 (Distinct Procedural Services) for Medicare claims:

• -XE Separate Encounter, a Service that is Distinct Because it Occurred During a Separate Encounter

• -XS Separate Structure, a Service that is Distinct Because it was Performed on a Separate Organ/Structure

• -XP Separate Practitioner, a Service that is Distinct Because it was Performed by a Different Practitioner

• -XU Unusual Non-Overlapping Service, the Use of a Service that is Distinct Because it Does Not Overlap Usual Components of the Main Service

Example: A patient receives an antibiotic infusion as an outpatient and is discharged. Patient returns later that same day and receives another separate antibiotic infusion. Modifier -XE is reported with each CPT medication administration (infusion) code and each HCPCS Level II drug (e.g., clindamycin).

(continues)

TABLE 7-2 (continued)

Special Surgical and Procedural Services (continued)

Modifier	Description	Interpretation
-63	Procedure Performed on Infants Less Than 4 kg (Refer to CPT Appendix A for the list of codes to which modifier -63 applies.)	Report when infant weighs less than 4 kilograms (kg) because procedures performed may require increased complexity and provider work.
	Example: An infant's weight was 3.5 kg at the time she underwent diagnostic thoracoscopy was performed. Report 32601-63.	
-78	Unplanned Return to the Operating/Procedure Room by the Same Physician or Other Qualified Health Care Professional Following Initial Procedure for a Related Procedure During the Postoperative Period	Report for unplanned circumstances that require a return to the operating room for complications of the initial operation. **Note:** To ensure payment, an ICD-10-CM surgical complication code is also reported to justify medical necessity for the return to the operating room.
	Example: Surgical sutures of the axilla did not hold, and a 12 cm layer closure of the axillary wound was performed. Report 12034-78.	
-79	Unrelated Procedure or Service by the Same Physician or Other Qualified Health Care Professional During the Postoperative Period	Report when a new procedure or service is performed by a surgeon during the normal postoperative period of a previously performed but unrelated surgery.
	Example: Six weeks following cataract surgery performed on the left eye, the patient undergoes diathermic repair of retinal detachment, right eye. Report 67101-79.	

Bilateral and Multiple Procedures or Encounters

Modifier	Description	Interpretation
-27	Multiple Outpatient Hospital E/M Encounters on the Same Date	Report for hospital outpatients who receive multiple E/M services performed by *different providers* on the same day. **Note:** Do *not* report for multiple E/M services performed by the same provider on the same day.
	Example: A patient is treated in the hospital's emergency department and receives level 4 evaluation and management services due to a fractured ankle. The patient is treated later the same day in the urgent care center and receives level 3 evaluation and management services due to a migraine that did not respond to prescribed medication taken at home. Report codes 99284-27 and 99213-27.	
-50	Bilateral Procedure	Report this directional modifier when a procedure was performed bilaterally *during the same session and when the code description does not specify that the procedure is bilateral*. Modifier -50 is *not* reported with add-on codes, designed with a plus symbol in CPT. For bilateral procedures, report the add-on code twice.
	Example: Patient undergoes bilateral arthrodesis, knees. Report 27580-50 (or report HCPCS Level II national modifiers as codes 27580-LT and 27580-RT).	
	Coding Tip: Directional modifiers (e.g., 50, LT, RT) are reported with CPT and HCPCS Level II codes when the code description includes anatomic structures that are found bilaterally (e.g., kidneys). When code descriptions include anatomic structures that are found bilaterally along with those *not* found bilaterally (e.g., code 11300, shaving of lesion, trunk, arms or legs), do not report directional modifiers with the CPT or HCPCS Level II code.	
	Example: Laparoscopic retroperitoneal lymph node biopsy. Report code 38570. Retroperitoneal lymph nodes are located in the abdomen, which is not a paired anatomic structure; thus a directional modifier is *not* reported.	

(continues)

TABLE 7-2 (continued)

Bilateral and Multiple Procedures or Encounters (continued)

Modifier	Description	Interpretation
-51	Multiple Procedures	Report when multiple procedures *other than E/M services* are performed at the same session by the same provider. The procedures performed are characterized as: • Multiple, related surgical procedures performed at the same session • Surgical procedures performed in combination, whether through the same or another incision, or involving the same or different anatomy • Combination medical and surgical procedures performed at the same session **Note:** This modifier is reported with the secondary or lesser procedure(s).

Example: Patient underwent right tibial shaft fracture repair and arthrodesis of left knee. Report codes 27750-RT and 27580-51-LT.

Coding Tip: Do not report modifier -51 if:
• Notes at the beginning of a category instruct the coder to *report in addition to . . .* (see note before code 22310).
• The code description states *List separately in addition to the code for primary procedure* (see code 22116).
• The code description includes the words *each* or *each additional* (e.g., code 22103).
• The symbol **+** precedes a code; this designates an add-on code.

Repeat Procedures

Modifier	Description	Interpretation
-76	Repeat Procedure or Service by Same Physician or Other Qualified Health Care Professional	Report when a procedure was repeated because of special circumstances involving the original service, and the same physician performed the repeat procedure.

Example: A repeat Rhythm EKG is performed because of changes in the patient's condition or the need to assess the effect of therapeutic procedures. Report 93041-76.

Modifier	Description	Interpretation
-77	Repeat Procedure or Service by Another Physician or Other Qualified Health Care Professional	Report when a physician *other than the original physician* performs a repeat procedure because of special circumstances involving the original study or procedure.

Example: Patient underwent sterilization procedure (e.g., tubal ligation), but became pregnant. After C-section delivery, patient underwent a second sterilization procedure. Report 58611-77 (in addition to the C-section procedure code).

Multiple Surgeons

Modifier	Description	Interpretation
-62	Two Surgeons	Report when two primary surgeons are required during an operative session, each performing distinct parts of a reportable procedure. Ideally, the surgeons represent different specialties.

Example: A spinal surgeon and a general surgeon work together as primary surgeons to perform an anterior spinal fusion of L5–S1; the spinal surgeon also inserts an intervertebral synthetic cage and performs iliac bone grafting. Each surgeon reports code 22558-62. The spinal surgeon also reports codes 22853 and 20937.

Note: Surgeons should document the procedure(s) they performed in individual operative reports.

(continues)

TABLE 7-2 (continued)

Multiple Surgeons (continued)		
Modifier	Description	Interpretation
	Coding Tip: Report modifiers 62 and 50 (bilateral procedure) when co-surgery is done by surgeons of the same specialty (e.g., bilateral knee replacement that required two surgeons to operate on both knees at the same time due to the patient's condition or risk).	
	Coding Tip: If either surgeon acts as the assistant surgeon for additional unrelated procedure(s) performed during the same operative session, report modifier 80 or 81 with the additional procedures code(s).	
-66	Surgical Team	Report when surgery performed is highly complex and requires the services of a skilled team of three or more physicians or other qualified health professionals. The procedure reported on the claim for each participating physician must include this modifier. The operative reports must document the complexity of the surgery and refer to the actions of each team member.
	Example: A surgical team of three physicians performs the reattachment of a severed arm. Each surgeon reports 20805-66.	
-80	Assistant Surgeon	Report when one physician assists another during an operative session. The assistant surgeon reports the same CPT code as the operating physician.
	Example: Dr. Landry assists Dr. Bartron during single CABG surgery. Dr. Landry reports code 33510-80.	
-81	Minimum Assistant Surgeon	Report when primary operating physician planned to perform a surgical procedure alone, but circumstances arise that require the services of an assistant surgeon for a short time. The second surgeon reports the same CPT code as the operating physician.
	Example: Dr. Kelly begins an invasive cholecystectomy procedure on a patient and discovers that the gallbladder is the size of a hot dog bun, which necessitates calling Dr. Pietro to assist for a short time. Dr. Pietro reports 47600-81. (A gallbladder is supposed to be the size of your little finger.)	
-82	Assistant Surgeon (when qualified resident surgeon not available)	Report when a qualified resident surgeon is unavailable to assist with a procedure. In teaching hospitals, the physician acting as the assistant surgeon is usually a qualified resident surgeon. If circumstances arise (e.g., rotational changes) and a qualified resident surgeon is not available, another surgeon may assist with a procedure. The nonresident-assistant surgeon reports the same CPT code as the operating physician.
	Example: Resident surgeon Dr. Smith was to assist surgeon Dr. Manlin with a routine laparoscopic appendectomy. Dr. Smith was temporarily reassigned to the emergency department due to a staffing problem. Therefore, Dr. Manlin's partner, Dr. Lando, assisted with the procedure. Dr. Lando reports 44970-82.	
	Coding Tip: Do not report modifiers 80, 81, and 82 for nonphysician surgical assistant services (e.g., physician assistant, nurse practitioner) unless the payer authorizes this reporting.	

(continues)

TABLE 7-2 (continued)

Preventive Services

Modifier	Description	Interpretation
-33	Preventive Service	Alerts third-party payers that the procedure or service was preventive under applicable laws and that patient cost sharing (e.g., coinsurance, copayment, deductible) does not apply when furnished by in-network providers.

Example: The patient's primary care provider provided 20 minutes of smoking and tobacco use cessation counseling. Report code 99407-33.

Coding Tip:
- When multiple preventive procedures or services are provided on the same day, add modifier -33 to each code.
- When procedure or service code descriptions contain the word screening (e.g., screening mammography), do not add modifier -33 to the code.

Professional Components

Modifier	Description	Interpretation
-26	Professional Component	Report when the physician either interprets test results or operates equipment for a procedure. *Do not report this modifier when a specific separately identifiable code describes the professional component of a procedure (e.g., 93010).*

Example: Independent radiologist Dr. Minion interprets a three-view chest x-ray that was performed on a patient by another provider. Dr. Minion reports code 71047-26.

Mandated Services

Modifier	Description	Interpretation
-32	Mandated Services	Report when services (e.g., second or third opinion for a surgical procedure) provided were mandated by a third party (e.g., attorney, payer).

Example: A patient is seen by the primary care provider who recommends respiratory therapy. Before the payer will approve reimbursement for respiratory therapy, the patient receives a level 3 E/M service by respiratory specialist Dr. Powell. Dr. Powell reports code 99213-32.

Unusual Anesthesia or Anesthesia by Surgeon

Modifier	Description	Interpretation
-23	Unusual Anesthesia	Report when circumstances (e.g., extent of service, patient's physical condition) require anesthesia for procedures that usually require either no anesthesia or local anesthesia.

Example: The 30-year-old patient, who has an intellectual disability and is extremely apprehensive, requires general anesthesia for sliding hernia repair. Report 00832-23.

Modifier	Description	Interpretation
-47	Anesthesia by Surgeon	Report when the surgeon provides regional or general anesthesia in addition to performing the surgical procedure.

NOTE: Modifier -47 is added to the CPT surgery code. It is not reported with Anesthesia section codes 00100–01999.

Example: Instead of calling in an anesthesiologist to assist with a surgical case, Dr. Borja administers regional anesthesia and performs the spigelian hernia repair. Dr. Borja reports code 49590-47.

(continues)

TABLE 7-2 (continued)

Laboratory Services

Modifier	Description	Interpretation
-90	Reference (Outside) Laboratory	Report when a laboratory test is performed by an outside or reference laboratory.
	Example: The provider orders a complete blood count (CBC). Because the office does not perform lab testing, arrangements are made with an outside laboratory to perform the CBC and bill the physician. The physician reports the CBC as code 85025-90. Code 36415 is also reported for routine venipuncture.	
-91	Repeat Clinical Diagnostic Laboratory Test	Report when a clinical diagnostic laboratory test is repeated on the same day to obtain subsequent (multiple) test results. *This modifier is not reported when lab tests are repeated to confirm initial results* (e.g., due to equipment problems).
	Example: The patient was in the emergency department for 18 hours for observation of chest pain. Patient underwent serial (repeated) lab tests for cardiac enzyme testing every six hours. Report codes 82657, 82657-91, and 82657-91.	
-92	Alternative Laboratory Platform Testing	When a single-use disposable kit or transportable instrument is used to perform HIV laboratory testing (CPT codes 86701-86703), add modifier -92 to the reported code.
	Example: The hospital laboratory technician brought all of the HIV-1 testing materials to emergency department examination room #1 and performed an HIV-1 test on a patient Report code 86701-92.	

Telemedicine Services

Modifier	Description	Interpretation
-95	Synchronous Telemedicine Services Rendered Via a Real-Time Interactive Audio and Video Telecommunication System	Report to alert payer that synchronous telemedicine service, which is defined as a real-time interaction between provider and patient (who is located at a distant site from provider). (CPT Appendix P includes a comprehensive list of codes to which modifier -95 can be added.)
	Example: Patient underwent psychiatric diagnostic evaluation via synchronous telemedicine services. Report code 90791-95.	

Multiple Modifiers

Modifier	Description	Interpretation
-99	Multiple Modifiers	Report to alert third-party payers that more than two modifiers are being added to a procedure/service code.

Note: The CMS-1500 claim allows up to four modifiers to be listed after a CPT or HCPCS Level II code, on line 1 enter modifier 99. Then, enter the multiple modifiers assigned to the code in Block 19 (Additional Claim Information) or in the the equivalent electronic data field.

19. ADDITIONAL CLAIM INFORMATION (Designated by NUCC)							
22 47 50 80							

21. DIAGNOSIS OR NATURE OF ILLNESS OR INJURY Relate A-L to service line below (24E)   ICD Ind.

A. _____   B. _____   C. _____   D. _____
E. _____   F. _____   G. _____   H. _____
I. _____   J. _____   K. _____   L. _____

24. A. DATE(S) OF SERVICE						B. PLACE OF SERVICE	C. EMG	D. PROCEDURES, SERVICES, OR SUPPLIES (Explain Unusual Circumstances)		E. DIAGNOSIS POINTER
From MM	DD	YY	To MM	DD	YY			CPT/HCPCS	MODIFIER	
1								49540	99	

Courtesy of the Centers for Medicare & Medicaid Services, www.cms.gov; claim data created by author.

(continues)

TABLE 7-2 (continued)

Habilitative and Rehabilitative Services		
Modifier	Description	Interpretation
-96	Habilitative Services	Report for *habilitative services*, which (1) help patients learn skills and functioning for daily living that they have not yet developed, and (2) help patients keep, learn, or improve skills and functioning for daily living.
	Example: Thirty-month-old child receives speech therapy due to a limited expressive vocabulary (speech delay). Report code 92507-96.	
-97	Rehabilitative Services	Report for *rehabilitative services*, which help patients keep, relearn, or improve skills and functioning for daily living that have been lost or impaired because of illness, injury, or disability.
	Example: Patient receives 15 minutes of direct one-on-one patient contact for therapeutic activities to improve functional performance as the result of a stroke. Report code 97530-97.	

Exercise 7.4 – CPT Modifiers

Instructions: Assign just the appropriate modifier(s) to each statement below. (Do not assign the CPT code.)

_____ 1. Assistant surgeon reported patient's cesarean section, delivery only.

_____ 2. Cholecystectomy reported during postoperative period for treatment of leg fracture.

_____ 3. Treatment for chronic conditions at same time preventive medicine is provided.

_____ 4. Inpatient encounter provided by surgeon, with decision to perform surgery tomorrow.

_____ 5. Preoperative clearance for surgery by primary care provider.

_____ 6. Postoperative management of vaginal hysterectomy.

_____ 7. Repeat gallbladder x-ray series, same physician.

_____ 8. Arthroscopy of right elbow and closed fracture reduction of left wrist.

_____ 9. Needle core biopsy of right and left breast.

_____ 10. Evaluation and management service required by payer.

Evaluation and Management Section

The **Evaluation and Management (E/M) section** (codes 99202–99499) is located at the beginning of CPT because these codes describe services (e.g., office encounters) most frequently provided by physicians. Accurate assignment of *E/M codes* is essential to the success of a physician's practice because most of the revenue generated by the office is based on provision of these services. Before assigning E/M codes, make sure you review the guidelines (located at the beginning of the E/M section) and apply any notes (located below the category and subcategory titles).

Most E/M services are cognitive services—this means that the provider must acquire information from the patient, use reasoning skills to process the information, interact with the patient to provide feedback, and respond by creating an appropriate plan of care. E/M services do not include significant procedural services (e.g., diagnostic tests or surgical procedures), which are coded separately. However, some services that arise directly from the E/M service provided are included (e.g., cleansing traumatic lesions, closing lacerations with adhesive strips, applying dressings, and providing counseling and educational services).

NOTE:

The CPT star (★) symbol in front of CPT codes in the office or other outpatient services category codes may be reported for telemedicine services by adding modifier -95.

Overview of Evaluation and Management Section

The E/M section is organized according to place of service (POS) (e.g., office, hospital, home, type of service (TOS) (e.g., new or initial encounter, follow-up or subsequent encounter), and miscellaneous services (e.g., prolonged services or care plan oversight). The E/M level of service reflects the amount of work involved in providing health care to a patient, and correct coding requires determining the extent of history and examination performed as well as the complexity of medical decision making (except for Office or Other Outpatient Services where level of medical decision making *or* total time spent on the day of encounter determines code assignment.)

Between three and five levels of service are included in E/M categories, and documentation in the patient's chart must support the level of service reported. CMS often refers to E/M codes by level numbers, and the level corresponds to the last digit of the CPT code (e.g., 99205 is a level 5 E/M service).

NOTE:

Beginning with CPT 2021, for office or other outpatient services, documentation of a medically appropriate history and examination is required and E/M code selection will focus on documentation of level of medical decision making *or* total time spent on the date of encounter.

Example: Refer to the Office or Other Outpatient Services category in the E/M section, and notice that it contains two subcategories:

- New patient (contains four codes)
- Established patient (contains five codes)

Each code represents a level of E/M service, ranked from lowest to highest level. CMS would consider E/M code 99203 a level 3 code.

Accurate assignment of E/M codes depends on: (1) identifying the place of service (POS) and/or type of service (TOS) provided to the patient, (2) determining whether the patient is new or established, (3) reviewing the patient's record for documentation of level of service components, (4) applying CMS's *Documentation Guidelines for Evaluation and Management Services*, and (5) determining whether E/M guidelines (e.g., unlisted service) apply.

NOTE:

CMS developed **Evaluation and Management Documentation Guidelines**, which is a points-based system for determining history, examination, and medical decision making. E/M codes were assigned according to elements associated with comprehensive multisystem (1995) and single system specialty examinations (1997), and providers used whichever set of guidelines is most advantageous to their practice reimbursement.

Effective January 2021, CMS moved to a medical necessity-based system, eliminating the need to use either set of guidelines. (Medical necessity is the provision of health care procedures, services, and supplies required to diagnose or treat a condition, disease, illness, injury, or symptoms *and that meet accepted standards of medicine*.)

Place of Service (POS)

Place of service (POS) refers to the physical location where health care is provided to patients (e.g., office or other outpatient settings, hospitals, nursing facilities, home health care, or emergency departments).

Example 1: The provider treats the patient in the office.

Place of Service: Office

E/M Category: Office or Other Outpatient Services

Example 2: The patient receives care in the hospital's ED.

Place of Service: Hospital ED

E/M Category: Emergency Department Services

Type of Service (TOS)

Type of service (TOS) refers to the kind of health care services provided to patients. It includes critical care, consultation, initial hospital care, subsequent hospital care, and confirmatory consultation.

Example 1: The patient undergoes an annual physical examination in the provider's office.

Type of Service: Preventive care

E/M Category: Preventive Medicine Services

Example 2: The hospital inpatient is transferred to the regular medical-surgical unit for recovery from surgery. The patient suddenly stops breathing and requires respirator management by the physician.

Type of Service: Critical care

E/M Category: Critical Care Services

Sometimes *both the TOS and POS* must be identified before the proper code can be assigned.

Example 1: Dr. Smith completes Josie Black's history and physical examination on the first day of the inpatient admission.

Place of Service: Hospital

Type of Service: Initial inpatient care

E/M Category: Hospital Inpatient Services

E/M Subcategory: Initial Hospital Care

Example 2: Dr. Charles meets with Josie Black in the office to render a second opinion.

Place of Service: Office

Type of Service: Consultation

E/M Category: Consultations

E/M Subcategory: Office or Other Outpatient Consultations

 Coding Tip

Refer to the CPT Medicine section for codes that describe specialty services (e.g., ophthalmologic services, psychiatric services) that require evaluation and management. When codes for specialty services are reported from the Medicine section, a code from the CPT E/M section is not reported on the same date *unless a significant, separately identifiable E/M service was provided (and modifier -25 is attached).*

Evaluation and Management Services Guidelines

Evaluation and management (E/M) services guidelines are general instructions about the assignment of E/M section codes. Throughout the E/M section, *notes* provide specific instructions that apply to categories (or subsections) and subcategories. Reviewing E/M guidelines and notes prior to the assignment is necessary to the appropriate assignment of E/M codes. Currently, two sets of E/M section guidelines serve as the basis for selecting an appropriate code:

1. Office or other outpatient services guidelines, which use documentation of medical decision making *or* time; and
2. Remaining E/M services guidelines (e.g., Inpatient Hospital Care category), which use documentation of the history, physical examination, *and* medical decision making.

 NOTE:

The *Evaluation and Management Services Guidelines* in the CPT coding manual contains a table entitled *Summary of Guideline Differences*, which distinguishes between components for the purpose of code selection.

Classification of Evaluation and Management Services

The evaluation and management (E/M) section contains categories, many of which contain subcategories. For example, New Patient is a subcategory below the Office or Other Outpatient Services category.

Definitions of Commonly Used Terms

The E/M section contains phrases and definitions for the purpose of selecting an appropriate code. Some definitions apply to all E/M subsections, while others apply to just one or more subsections. The following phrases and definitions apply to *all* E/M subsections:

- Level of E/M service
- New patient and established patient
- Time

Level of E/M Service. Evaluation and management codes use the last number of each CPT code to represent the **level of E/M service**. Levels within categories and subcategories are not interchangeable, and each of *level of E/M service* may be reported by physicians or other qualified health care professionals.

> **Example:** CPT code 99202 classifies a level 2 office or other outpatient E/M service reported for new patients, and it requires a medically appropriate history and/or examination, straightforward medical decision making, and usually requires 15–29 minutes of physician or other qualified health care professional total time spent on the date of the encounter. CPT code 99211 classifies a level 1 office or other outpatient E/M service reported for established patients, and it is reported when the presence of the physician or other qualified health care professional may not be required (e.g., office nurse takes patient's blood pressure and documents it in the record).

New Patient and Established Patient. A **new patient** is one who has *not* received any professional services from the physician, or from another physician of the same specialty who belongs to the same group practice, within the past three years. An **established patient** is one who *has* received professional services from the physician, or from another physician of the same specialty who belongs to the same group practice, within the past three years.

 NOTE:

> The *Evaluation and Management Services Guidelines* in the CPT coding manual contains a *Decision Tree for New vs Established Patients*, which provides assistance for reporting new or established patient encounter codes.

> **Example 1:** Patient had a prescription renewed by Dr. Smith on January 1, 2020, and patient has seen another physician of the same specialty in the paractice. Patient has been Dr. Smith's patient since the initial office visit on March 15, 2017. On December 1, 2020, Dr. Smith treated the patient during an office encounter.
>
> *New Patient:* March 15, 2017.
>
> *Established Patient:* January 1, 2020, and December 1, 2020.
>
> Patient is considered a new patient on March 15, 2017, because that is the date the patient was initially seen by Dr. Smith. Then, because the patient received professional services from another physician of the same specialty in the practice (the prescription renewal) on January 1, 2020, the patient is also considered an established patient for the December 1, 2020, encounter.

Example 2: Dr. Charles and Dr. Black share a general practice. Dr. Charles treated the patient in the office on July 1, 2021. The patient was first seen by the practice on February 15, 2017, when Dr. Black provided preventive care services to them. The patient returned to the practice on November 1, 2021, for an annual physical examination conducted by Dr. Black.

New Patient: February 15, 2015, and July 1, 2021.

Established Patient: November 1, 2021.

Example 3: Dr. Corey left Alfred Medical Group to join Buffalo Physician Group as a family practitioner. At Buffalo Physician Group, when Dr. Corey provides professional services to patients, are those patients considered new or established?

Answer: Patients who have not received professional services from Dr. Corey or another physician of the same specialty at Buffalo Physician Group are considered new. Patients who have been treated by another family practitioner at Buffalo Physician Group within the past three years are considered established. If any of Dr. Corey's patients from the Alfred Medical Group choose to seek care from Dr. Corey or another physician of the same specialty at the Buffalo Physician Group, they will be considered established patients.

Time. The amount of time a physician or other qualified health care professional spends providing patient care may be used to select an appropriate level of E/M service code. Beginning with CPT 2021, except for code 99211, time alone may be used to select an appropriate level of Office or Other Outpatient Services code. **Face-to-face time** is the amount of time the office or outpatient care provider spends with the patient and/or family. When using *time* to determine the level of Office or Other Outpatient Service code, refer to descriptions of CPT codes 99202–99205 and 99212–99215 for guidance. *Remember! Face-to-face time* between the physician or other qualified health care professional and the patient is required to determine the amount of time for an Office or Other Outpatient Services encounter.

Remaining E/M categories (e.g., Hospital Inpatient Services) allow the use of time to select an appropriate level of E/M service code *only when counseling and/or coordination of care dominates the E/M service.* In addition to the length of time spent counseling the patient and coordinating care, documentation must include issues discussed and a relevant history, examination, and medical decision making (if performed). Because time is used differently in categories *other than the office or other outpatient E/M service category*, the category instructions must be reviewed to apply the use of time when selecting a code. For example, **unit/floor time** is the amount of time the provider spends at the patient's bedside and managing the patient's care on the unit or floor (e.g., documenting orders for diagnostic tests or reviewing test results). Unit/floor time applies to inpatient hospital care, hospital observation care, initial and follow-up inpatient hospital consultations, and nursing facility services.

In addition to meeting with the patient face to face, the following activities count toward total time when provided by the physician or other qualified health care professional:

- Care coordination (when not separately reported with another E/M code)
- Communicating results of ancillary tests to the patient, family, or caregiver
- Counseling and educating the patient, family, or caregiver
- Documenting clinical information in the patient record
- Obtaining and/or reviewing a separately obtained history
- Ordering medications, tests, and procedures
- Performing a medically appropriate examination or evaluation
- Preparing to see the patient (e.g., reviewing results of ancillary tests)
- Referring the patient to and communicating with other health care professionals (when not separately reported with another E/M code)

Do *not* count time spent on the following the performance of other services that are reported separately, travel, or teaching that is general and not limited to discussion required for the management of a specific patient.

NOTE:

When using *time* to determine the level of office or other outpatient service code, refer to descriptions of CPT codes 99202–99205 and 99212–99215 for guidance. *Remember! Face-to-face time* between the physician or other qualified health care professional and the patient is required to determine the amount of time for an Office or Other Outpatient Services encounter.

Concurrent Care and Transfer of Care. **Concurrent care** is the provision of similar services, such as hospital inpatient visits, to the same patient by more than one physician or other qualified health care professional on the same day. CMS permits concurrent care by two or more providers on the same day even if the providers are of the same specialty. To avoid reimbursement denials by third-party payers and Medicare administrative contracts, the attending physician is to add modifier -AI (Principal Physician of Record) to the E/M code reported. When possible, each provider should report different ICD-10-CM diagnosis codes from those reported by other providers who see the patient on the same day. **Transfer of care** occurs when a physician who is managing some or all of a patient's problems releases the patient to the care of another physician or other qualified health care professional who is providing patient care management and who is *not* providing consultative services.

Example: A patient was admitted to the hospital on October 5 for an acute myocardial infarction. On October 7, the attending physician (a cardiologist) wrote a physician's order requesting a psychiatrist to consult with the patient regarding anxiety and depression. The cardiologist's insurance specialist should report the ICD code for acute myocardial infarction to justify inpatient E/M services provided to the patient. The psychiatrist's insurance specialist should report the ICD codes for anxiety and depression to justify inpatient consultation E/M services provided to the patient. If each provider reported the ICD code for acute myocardial infarction, the provider who submitted the claim first would be reimbursed (and the other provider's claim would be denied).

Counseling. CPT defines **counseling** as a "discussion with a patient and/or family concerning one or more of the following areas: diagnostic results, impressions, and/or recommended diagnostic studies; prognosis; risks and benefits of management (treatment) options; instructions for management (treatment) and/or follow-up; importance of compliance with chosen management (treatment) options; risk factor reduction; and patient and family education."

Example: Weight management counseling services provided to a patient during an E/M encounter visit must be properly documented, along with other required elements, so that the appropriate level of E/M code can be selected.

Services Reported Separately. When procedures or services are provided on the same date as the provision of E/M services, separate CPT codes may be reported.

Example: A COVID-19 laboratory test is performed during an E/M encounter for a patient who complains of difficulty breathing and a fever. In addition to the appropriate code for the office or other outpatient E/M services encounter, a code for the COVID-19 laboratory test is reported.

Instructions for Selecting a Level of Office or Other Outpatient Service

Selecting an appropriate level of Office or Other Outpatient Service has been simplified in CPT 2021 and requires determining *either* the level of medical decision making defined for each service provided or the total time for E/M services provided on the date of encounter (*except for* CPT code 99211). A medical appropriate history and examination must also be documented, but they do not directly impact selection of an office or other outpatient service code.

Medical decision making involves establishing diagnoses, assessing the status of a patient's condition, and selecting a management option. For office or other outpatient services, three elements are used to determine level of medical decision making:

- Number and complexity of problems addressed during and encounter
- Amount and complexity of data to be reviewed and analyzed; data includes patient records, test results, and other information
- Risk of complications, morbidity, and mortality associated with patient management decisions made during the encounter

The four levels of medical decision making include: straightforward, low, moderate, and high. (Medical decision making for *other than* Office or Other Outpatient Services is also discussed later in this chapter.)

NOTE:

The Evaluation and Management Guidelines in the CPT coding manual contains an extensive table that assists in selection of *Levels of Medical Decision Making*.

Guidelines for Hospital Observation, Hospital Inpatient, Consultations, Emergency Department, Nursing Facility, Domiciliary, Rest Home, or Custodial Care, and Home Services

The following guidelines apply to the following E/M categories: Hospital Observation, Hospital Inpatient, Consultations, Emergency Department, Nursing Facility, Domiciliary, Rest Home, or Custodial Care, and Home Services.

Levels of Evaluation and Management Services

The levels of E/M services code descriptions for the Hospital Observation, Hospital Inpatient, Consultations, Emergency Department, Nursing Facility, Domiciliary, Rest Home, or Custodial Care, and Home Services categories include seven components, six of which determine the level of E/M service code to be assigned:

- History
- Examination
- Medical decision making
- Counseling
- Coordination of care
- Nature of presenting problem
- Time

   The **key components** of history, examination, and medical decision making are required when selecting an E/M level of service code. **Contributory components** include counseling, coordination of care, nature of presenting problem, and time; and they are used to select the appropriate E/M service code when patient record documentation indicates that they were the focus of the visit.

NOTE:

Medical decision making and time *only* apply to the selection of a level of Office or Other Outpatient Services.

Key Components

E/M code selection (*except for* Office or Other Outpatient Services) is based on three key components:

- Extent of history
- Extent of examination
- Complexity of medical decision making

All three key components must be considered when assigning codes for new patients. For established patients, two of the three key components must be considered. This means that documentation in the patient's chart must support the key components used to determine the E/M code selected.

NOTE:

The concept of key components does *not* apply to the selection of Office or Other Outpatient Services codes; instead, an appropriate medical history and examination is documented, and code selection is based on level of medical decision making *or* time.

Extent of History

A **history** is an interview of the patient that includes the following elements: chief complaint (patient's description of signs/symptoms, conditions/diseases/problems, or other factors) history of present illness (description of present illness from first sign/symptom to present, including location, quality, severity, timing, context, modifying factors, and associated signs/symptoms significantly related to presenting problems), a review of systems (inventory of body systems), and a past/family/social history. The **extent of history (CPT)** is categorized according to four levels:

- **Problem focused history**: chief complaint, brief history of present illness or problem

- **Expanded problem focused history**: chief complaint, brief history of present illness, problem pertinent system review

- **Detailed history**: chief complaint, extended history of present illness, problem pertinent system review extended to include a limited number of additional systems, pertinent past/family/social history directly related to patient's problem

- **Comprehensive history**: chief complaint, extended history of present illness, review of systems directly related to the problem(s) identified in the history of the present illness in addition to a review of all additional body systems, complete past/family/social history

Extent of Examination

A **physical examination** is an objective assessment of the patient's body areas (e.g., extremities) and organ systems (e.g., cardiovascular). The **extent of examination (CPT)** is categorized according to four levels:

- **Problem focused examination**: limited examination of the affected body area or organ system

- **Expanded problem focused examination**: limited examination of the affected body area or organ system and other symptomatic or related organ system(s)

- **Detailed examination**: extended examination of the affected body area(s) and other symptomatic or related organ system(s)

- **Comprehensive examination**: general multisystem examination or a complete examination of a single organ system. CPT recognizes the following body areas: head (including face), neck, chest (including breasts and axilla), abdomen, genitalia/groin/buttocks, back, each extremity. CPT also recognizes the following organ systems: eyes/ears/nose/mouth/throat, cardiovascular, respiratory, gastrointestinal, genitourinary, musculoskeletal, skin, neurologic, psychiatric, and hematologic/lymphatic/immunological.

Complexity of Medical Decision Making

Medical decision making (Figure 7-8) refers to the complexity of establishing a diagnosis, assessing the status of a patient's condition, and/or selecting a management option as measured by the:

- Number of possible diagnoses or management options to be considered

- Amount and/or complexity of data (e.g., patient records, diagnostic test results) to be obtained, reviewed, and analyzed

- Risk of significant complications, morbidity, and mortality, along with comorbidities associated with patient's presenting problems, diagnostic procedures, and possible management options

Number of Diagnoses or Management Options	Amount/Complexity of Data to Be Reviewed	Risk of Complications and/or Morbidity/Mortality	Type of Medical Decision Making
Minimal	Minimal or none	Minimal	Straightforward
Limited	Limited	Low	Low complexity
Multiple	Moderate	Moderate	Moderate complexity
Extensive	Extensive	High	High complexity

Current Procedural Terminology published by the American Medical Association.

FIGURE 7-8 Criteria to determine complexity of medical decision making.

Complexity of medical decision-making criteria reflects the provider's level of uncertainty, volume of data to review, and risk to the patient. The patient's record includes the following documentation:

- Laboratory, imaging, and other test results that are significant to the management of the patient's care
- List of known diagnoses as well as those that are suspected
- Opinions of other physicians who have been consulted
- Planned course of action for the patient's treatment (plan of treatment)
- Review of patient records obtained from other facilities

The physician is responsible for determining the complexity of medical decision making, and that decision must be supported by documentation in the patient's chart. CPT includes a table in the E/M guidelines that can assist in determining the complexity of medical decision making. Once the key components for extent of history and examination are determined, the type of medical decision making can be selected as follows:

- Straightforward
- Low complexity
- Moderate complexity
- High complexity

Selecting the Appropriate Level of Evaluation and Management Service

Once the extent of history, extent of examination, and complexity of medical decision making are determined, select the appropriate E/M code. *Remember!* This code selection process applies *only* to codes selected from the Hospital Observation, Hospital Inpatient, Consultations, Emergency Department, Nursing Facility, Domiciliary, Rest Home, or Custodial Care, and Home Services categories. Codes selected from the Office or Other Oupatient Services category require documentation of a medically appropriate history and examination, and the level of service is based on medical decision making *or* time.

Example: Follow the steps for selecting a level of E/M service, and review the progress note below (documented using the SOAP format) to determine the extent of history and examination and complexity of medical decision making for a patient who is seen by a specialist during an office consultation encounter.

Subjective: The 35-year-old patient is seen today with a chief complaint of severe snoring. This has gone on for years and finally something needs to be done about it because the patient awakens frequently during the night. Patient says upon waking in the morning, they feel exhausted and become very tired during the day. Review of systems reveals allergies. Patient denies smoking or alcohol use. Patient is on no medications.

Objective: Blood pressure is 126/86. Pulse is 82. Weight is 185. EYES: Pupils equal, round, and reactive to light and accommodation; extraocular muscles intact. EARS & NOSE: Tympanic membranes normal; oropharynx benign. NECK: Supple without jugular venous distention, bruits, or thyromegaly. RESPIRATORY: Breath sounds are clear to percussion and auscultation. EXTREMITIES: Without edema; pulses intact.

(continues)

(continued)

Assessment: Possible sleep apnea. Snoring.

Plan: Patient to undergo sleep study in two weeks. Results to be evaluated to determine whether patient is candidate for laser-assisted uvuloplasty (LAUP) surgery.

To assign the E/M code, the following is determined:

New or Established Patient: The descriptions for all consultation codes include *new or established patients*.

Extent of History: HPI elements include quality, severity, timing, and context; in the above case, an extended HPI (four elements) is documented. ROS elements *include allergic;* in the above case, a problem pertinent ROS (one body system) is documented. PFSH elements include documentation of social history; in the above case, a pertinent PFSH (one history area) is documented *for a score of* 1. Because three out of three HPI/ROS/PFHS types must be selected to determine the higher-level extent of history, an expanded problem focused history is documented.

Extent of Examination: Exam elements include Constitutional, Eyes, ENT, Neck, Respiratory, Cardiovascular; thus, an expanded problem focused examination is documented.

Complexity of Medical Decision Making: Undiagnosed new problem with uncertain prognosis is documented (possible sleep apnea). Although physiologic test not under stress (sleep study) is documented as being ordered, results are not reviewed by this provider during this encounter. Therefore, complexity of medical decision making is straightforward.

E/M Code Assigned: 99242 (Three of three key components are required.)

Contributory Components

The contributory components of counseling, coordination of care, nature of presenting illness, and time play an important role in selecting the E/M code (for E/M categories *except* Office or Other Outpatient Services) when documentation in the patient record indicates that they were the focus of the encounter for Hospital Observation, Hospital Inpatient, Consultations, Emergency Department, Nursing Facility, Domiciliary, Rest Home, or Custodial Care, and Home Services. Counseling and/or coordination of care components drive CPT code selection only when they dominate the encounter (e.g., nursing facility encounter), requiring that more than 50 percent of the provider's time be spent on such components. In such circumstances, the provider must be sure to carefully document these elements so as to support the higher-level code selected. (Some E/M code descriptions include notes about time and nature of the presenting problem to assist in determining the appropriate code number to report.)

Counseling is a discussion with a patient and/or family concerning one or more of the following areas: diagnostic results, impressions, and/or recommended diagnostic studies; prognosis; risks and benefits of management (treatment) options; instructions for management (treatment) and/or follow-up; importance of compliance with chosen management (treatment) options; risk factor reduction; patient and family education.

Coordination of care is provided when the physician or other qualified health care professional makes arrangements with other providers or agencies for services to be provided to a patient.

Nature of the Presenting Problem

CPT defines **nature of the presenting problem** as "a disease, condition, illness, injury, symptom, sign, finding, complaint, or other reason for the encounter, with or without a diagnosis being established at the time of the encounter." The *nature of the presenting problem* is considered when determining the number of diagnoses or management options for medical decision-making complexity.

Five types of presenting problems are recognized:

- Minimal (problem may not require the presence of the physician, but service is provided under the physician's supervision, such as a patient who comes to the office once a week to have blood pressure taken and recorded)

- Self-limited or minor (problem that runs a definite and prescribed course, is transient in nature, and is not likely to permanently alter health status)

- Low severity (problem where the risk of morbidity without treatment is low; there is little to no risk of mortality without treatment; full recovery without functional impairment is expected, such as a patient who is diagnosed with eczema and who does not respond to over-the-counter medications)

- Moderate severity (problem where the risk of morbidity without treatment is moderate; there is moderate risk of mortality without treatment; uncertain prognosis; increased probability of prolonged functional impairment, such as a 35-year-old patient diagnosed with chest pain on exertion)

- High severity (problem where the risk of morbidity without treatment is high to extreme; there is a moderate to high risk of mortality without treatment; high probability of severe, prolonged functional impairment, such as an infant hospitalized with a diagnosis of respiratory syncytial virus)

Instructions for Selecting a Level of E/M Service for Hospital Observation, Hospital Inpatient, Consultations, Emergency Department, Nursing Facility, Domiciliary, Rest Home, or Custodial Care, and Home Services

When selecting an E/M level of service code for the following categories, refer to Evaluation and Management Services Guidelines found in the CPT coding manual: Hospital Observation, Hospital Inpatient, Consultations, Emergency Department, Nursing Facility, Domiciliary, Rest Home, or Custodial Care, and Home Services.

Step 1. Review the level of E/M service descriptors in the selected category or subcategory. Refer to clinical examples in Appendix C of the CPT coding manual.

Step 2. Determine the extent of history obtained and examination performed.

Step 3. Determine the complexity of medical decision making.

Step 4. Select the appropriate level of E/M service based on key components and contributory components.

Unlisted Service and Special Report

Evaluation and management guidelines clarify that an *unlisted service* code is assigned when the provider furnishes an E/M service for which there is no CPT code. When an unlisted procedure or service code is reported, a special report (e.g., copy of documented encounter note record) must accompany the claim to describe the nature of, extent of, and need for the procedure or service.

 Coding Tip

Medicare and third-party payers often require providers to report HCPCS Level II national codes instead of unlisted procedure or service CPT codes. (HCPCS Level II national codes are discussed in Chapter 8 of this textbook.)

When an unlisted service code is reported, a *special report* must be submitted with the insurance claim to demonstrate medical appropriateness. The provider should document the following elements in the special report:

- Complexity of patient's symptoms
- Final diagnosis
- Pertinent physical findings

- Diagnostic and therapeutic procedures
- Concurrent problems
- Follow-up care

Clinical Examples

Appendix C of the CPT coding manual contains clinical examples of E/M service codes. Along with a careful review of the E/M code descriptions, they assist providers in selecting the appropriate code for documented E/M services. The AMA cautions providers that the clinical examples "do not encompass the entire scope of medical practice." They can be used in addition to document key components (history, examination, and/or medical decision making) that are required to determine a particular level of service.

Evaluation and Management Subsections

The E/M section (99202–99499) contains notes unique to each category and subcategory (Table 7-3). *Remember to review notes before assigning an E/M code*. (For a complete list of categories and subcategories, refer to Table 1, Categories and Subcategories of Service, in the E/M Services Guidelines of your CPT coding manual.) (CPT refers to E/M subsections and categories as categories and subcategories, respectively.)

> **Example:** Lucy Moreno is a 45-year-old established female patient who was seen in the office on April 22 for a medical history and examination as follow-up for her diagnosis of lower back pain. Patient states that she is having great difficulty managing her pain and she says that she realizes part of the problem is that she needs to lose 50 pounds. A variety of weight-loss management options were discussed with the patient, including an appropriate exercise program; and she is scheduled to return in one month for recheck. Today's visit was 30 minutes in length, more than half of which was spent discussing weight-loss management. Report code 99214.

TABLE 7-3 Evaluation and Management subsections

Subsection (Category)	Description
Office or Other Outpatient Services	E/M services provided in a physician's office, a hospital outpatient department, or another ambulatory care facility (e.g., stand-alone ambulatory care center). A medically appropriate history and examination must be documented, and the level of medical decision making as defined for each service *or* total time spent face-to-face with the patient on the date of encounter is used to select an appropriate Office or Other Outpatient Services code. (E/M subsections *other than* Office or Other Outpatient Services require documentation of level of history, examination, and medical decision making; if time is used to determine E/M code selection for such services, contributing components must be documented.) Before assigning an E/M level of service code from this category, make sure you apply the definition of *new* and *established* patient. Subcategories include: • New patient • Established patient **Note:** Code 99211 is commonly thought of as a "nurse visit" because it is typically reported when ancillary personnel provide E/M services. However, the code can be reported when the E/M service is rendered by any other provider (e.g., nurse practitioner, physician assistant, or physician). • CMS "incident to" guidelines apply when the 99211 level of service is provided by ancillary personnel (e.g., nurse). Guidelines state that the physician must be physically present in the office suite when the service is provided. • Documentation of a 99211 level of service includes a chief complaint and a description of the service provided. Because the presenting problem is of minimal severity, documentation of a history and examination is not required. When prescription drug management services are provided (with documentation of E/M key components) during an office visit, report a minimum level 3 E/M code. Reporting a level 1 or 2 E/M code is considered undercoding.

(continues)

TABLE 7-3 (continued)

Subsection (Category)	Description
Hospital Observation Services	**Observation services** are furnished in a hospital outpatient setting, and the patient is considered an outpatient. Services include use of a bed and at least periodic monitoring by a hospital's nursing or other staff that is reasonable and necessary to evaluate an outpatient's condition or determine the need for possible admission to the hospital as an inpatient. Observation services are reimbursed only when ordered by a physician (or another individual authorized by state licensure law and hospital staff bylaws to admit patients to the hospital or to order outpatient tests). Medicare requires the physician to order an inpatient admission if the duration of observation care is expected to be 48 hours or more. (Other payers require an inpatient admission order if the duration of observation care is expected to be 24 hours or more.) Subcategories include: • Observation care discharge services • Initial observation care • Subsequent observation care Note: The 2016, *Notice of Observation Treatment and Implication for Care Eligibility (NOTICE) Act* requires hospitals to provide Medicare beneficiaries who receive observation services as outpatients for more than 24 hours with a *Medicare Outpatient Observation Notice (MOON)*, which is signed by the beneficiary. The purpose of the MOON is to inform beneficiaries that their hospital stay is outpatient, not inpatient, and has resultant implications such as higher cost sharing (e.g., coinsurance payments) and post-hospitalization ineligibility for Medicare coverage of skilled nursing facility (SNF) services. (A sample MOON form is available at www.cms.gov. Click on the Medicare link, click on the Beneficiary Notices Initiatives [BNI] link, and scroll down and click on the MOON, Form CMS-10611 [ZIP] link [located at the bottom right].)
Hospital Inpatient Services	E/M services provided to hospital inpatients, including partial hospitalization services; they are indicated when the patient's condition requires services and/or procedures that cannot be performed in any other POS without putting the patient at risk. Subcategories include: • **Initial hospital care** (covers first inpatient encounter) • **Subsequent hospital care** (includes review of chart for changes in patient's condition, results of diagnostic studies, and/or reassessment of patient's condition since performance of last assessment) • **Observation or inpatient care services** (assigned only if the patient is admitted to and discharged from observation/inpatient status on the same day) • **Hospital discharge services** (include final examination of the patient, discussion of hospital stay with patient/caregiver, instructions for continued care, and preparation of discharge records, prescriptions, and referral forms) Note: A *hospital inpatient* is someone who is admitted and discharged and has a length of stay (LOS) of one or more days. **Partial hospitalization** is a short-term, intensive treatment program where individuals who are experiencing an acute episode of an illness (e.g., geriatric, psychiatric, or rehabilitative) can receive medically supervised treatment during a significant number of daytime or nighttime hours. This type of program is an alternative to 24-hour inpatient hospitalization and allows the patients to maintain their everyday life without the disruption associated with an inpatient hospital stay.
Consultations	A **consultation** is an examination of a patient by a health care provider, usually a specialist, for the purpose of advising the referring or attending physician in the evaluation and/or management of a specific problem with a known diagnosis. Consultants may initiate diagnostic and/or therapeutic services as necessary during the consultation. Subcategories include: • Office or other outpatient consultations • Inpatient consultations Coding Tip: Do not confuse a *consultation* with a **referral**, which occurs when a patient reports that another provider "referred" the patient to the provider. Because the referring provider did not schedule the appointment or document a request for the referral, the referral is *not* a consultation. **Preoperative clearance** occurs when a surgeon requests a specialist or other physician (e.g., general practitioner) to examine a patient and provide an opinion about whether the patient can withstand the expected risks of a specific surgery. If the referring surgeon documents a written request for preoperative clearance, this service is considered a consultation, even when provided by the patient's primary care physician.

(continues)

TABLE 7-3 (continued)

Subsection (Category)	Description
Consultations (*cont'd*)	**Note:** In 2010, CMS (Medicare) and the federal Office of Workers' Compensation Board eliminated reporting of CPT consultation codes. Providers are required to report codes from the "Office or Other Outpatient Services" or "Inpatient Hospital Services" subsections of CPT. For the hospital inpatient setting, the admitting or attending physician will attach modifier A1 (Principal Physician of Record) to the initial visit code. This will distinguish the admitting or attending physician's service from those who provide consultation services.

The OIG reported that most consultation services reported to Medicare in 2001 were inappropriate, and subsequent education efforts to improve reporting failed to produce desired results. Other third-party payers will likely adopt the elimination of CPT's consultation codes. It is unknown whether the AMA will eliminate the "Consultations" subsection from a future revision of CPT. |
| | **Example:** On May 1, a patient is seen in the hospital's emergency department (ED) and receives level 4 E/M services from Dr. Axel (ED physician) for complaints of severe shortness of breath, chest pain radiating down the left arm, back pain, and extreme anxiety. The patient is admitted to the hospital, and Dr. Rodney (attending physician) provides level 3 initial hospital care. Dr. Axel reports code 99284, and Dr. Rodney reports code 99222 A1. |
| Emergency Department Services | **Emergency department services** are provided in a hospital, which is open 24 hours for the purpose of providing unscheduled episodic services to patients who require immediate medical attention. Subcategories include:

- New or established patient
- Other emergency services

While ED physicians employed by the facility usually provide ED services, any physician who provides services to a patient registered in the ED may report the ED services codes. The physician does not have to be assigned to the hospital's ED.

When services provided in the ED are determined not to be an actual emergency, ED services codes (99281-99288) are still reportable if ED services were provided. Typically, the hospital reports a lower-level ED services code for nonemergency conditions.

If a physician provides emergency services to a patient in the office, it is not appropriate to assign codes from the Emergency Department Services category of E/M. If the patient is asked to meet the primary care provider in the hospital's ED as an alternative to the physician's office and the patient is not registered as a patient in the ED, the physician should report a code from the Office or Other Outpatient Services category of E/M. ED services codes are reported only if the patient receives services in the hospital's ED.

Note: Instead of developing national emergency department coding guidelines, CMS instructed hospitals to develop internal guidelines for reporting emergency department E/M visits. The guidelines must reflect hospital resources (not physician resources) used in providing the service. CMS reviews hospital claims to evaluate patterns associated with reporting different levels of emergency department E/M codes to:

- Verify appropriate billing of Medicare services
- Ensure that hospitals follow their own internally developed guidelines

A medical emergency is the sudden and unexpected onset of a medical condition, or the acute exacerbation of a chronic condition that is threatening to life, limb, or sight. It requires immediate medical treatment or manifests painful symptomatology requiring immediate palliative effort to relieve suffering.

A maternity emergency is a sudden unexpected medical complication that puts the mother or fetus at risk.

A psychiatric inpatient admission is an emergency situation in which, based on a psychiatric evaluation performed by a physician (or another qualified mental health care professional with hospital admission authority), the patient is at immediate risk of serious harm to self or others as a result of a mental disorder, and requires immediate continuous skilled observation at the acute level of care.

Coding Tip: Code 99288 (Other Emergency Services) is reported when the physician is in two-way communication contact with ambulance or rescue crew personnel located outside the hospital. |

(continues)

TABLE 7-3 (continued)

Subsection (Category)	Description
Critical Care Services	*Critical* care is the direct delivery of medical care by a physician to a patient who is critically ill or injured. **Critical care services** are reported when a physician directly delivers medical care for a critically ill or critically injured patient. Critical care services can be provided on multiple days even if no changes are made to the treatment rendered to the patient, as long as the patient's condition requires the direct delivery of critical care services by the provider. *The provider should document the total time spent delivering critical care services.* Note: It is not necessary for a patient to be admitted to a critical care unit or an intensive care unit to receive critical care services. Patients can receive critical care services in the hospital emergency department, medical/surgical unit, and so on. **Example:** Dr. Smith delivers critical care services to his patient on June 15th from 8:00 to 9:00 A.M., 10:30 to 10:45 A.M., and 3:00 to 3:45 P.M. To assign codes to this case, total the minutes of critical care services directly delivered by the provider. (Refer to the table located in the CPT coding manual's Critical Care Services category to select the codes.) Report codes 99291 and 99292 × 2. Coding Tip: When critical care service codes are reported in addition to another E/M service code (e.g., ED care and initial hospital care), add modifier -25 to the E/M service code to report it as a separately identified service provided to the patient. Remember! Critical care services are reported based on the total time the physician spends in constant attendance, and the time need not be continuous.
Nursing Facility Services	**Nursing facility services** are provided at a nursing facility (NF), skilled nursing facility (SNF), intermediate care facility (ICF), long-term care facility (LTCF), or psychiatric residential treatment facility. NFs provide convalescent, rehabilitative, or long-term care for patients. A comprehensive assessment must be completed on each patient upon admission, and then annually (unless the patient's condition requires more frequent assessments). Subcategories include: • Initial nursing facility care • Subsequent nursing facility care • Nursing facility discharge services • Other nursing facility services Note: The **comprehensive assessment** documents the patient's functional capacity, identification of potential problems, and nursing plan to enhance (or at least maintain) the patient's physical and psychosocial functions. The assessments are written when the patient is admitted or readmitted to the facility or when a reassessment is necessary because of a substantial change in the patient's status. The nursing facility assessment code (99318) is reported when the nursing facility patient's attending physician conducts an annual assessment.
Domiciliary, Rest Home (e.g., Boarding Home), or Custodial Care Services	These services are provided to residents of a facility that offers room, board, and other personal assistance services, usually on a long-term basis. These codes include E/M services provided to residents of an assisted living facility, group home, or custodial care and intermediate care facilities. Subcategories include: • New patient • Established patient
Domiciliary, Rest Home (e.g., Assisted Living Facility), or Home Care Plan Oversight Services	**Care plan oversight services** cover the time supervising a complex and multidisciplinary care treatment program for a specific patient who is under the care of a domiciliary or rest home, or who resides at home.
Home Services	**Home services** are provided to individuals in their place of residence to promote, maintain, or restore health and/or to minimize the effects of disability and illness, including terminal illness. Subcategories include: • New patient • Established patient

(continues)

TABLE 7-3 (continued)

Subsection (Category)	Description
Prolonged Services	Services involving patient contact that are considered beyond the usual service in either an inpatient or outpatient setting may be reported as **prolonged services**. Subcategories include: • Prolonged service with direct patient contact (*except with Office or Other Outpatient Services*, which means CPT codes 99354-99357 are not reported with codes 99202-99205 or 99212-99215. (**Direct patient contact** refers to face-to-face patient contact on an inpatient, observation, or outpatient (e.g., emergency department) basis, and these codes are reported in addition to other E/M services provided.) • Prolonged service without direct patient contact *except with Office or Other Outpatient Services*, which means CPT codes 99354–99357 are *not* reported with codes 99202–99205 or 99212–99215. (**Without direct patient contact** refers to nonface-to-face time spent by the provider on an inpatient, observation, or outpatient (e.g., emergency department) basis *and occurring before and/or after direct patient care*.) These codes are *not* reported with Office or Other Outpatient Services codes. • Prolonged clinical staff (e.g., registered nurse, dietitian) services with physician or other qualified health care professional supervision are reported when a prolonged E/M service is provided in the Office or Other Outpatient Setting that involves prolonged clinical staff face-to-face time. • Prolonged service with or without direct patient contact on the date of office or other outpatient service is reported by physicians or other qualified health care professionals for face-to-face or non-face-to-face patient care. The code is reported only when the code selected for Office or Other Outpatient Services was based on time alone and when the minimum time required for the highest level of service (e.g., 99205 or 99215) has been exceeded by at least 15 minutes. Note: CPT contains a Comparison of Prolonged Service Codes table, which provides direction about reporting prolonged service codes with other E/M category codes. • **Standby services** cover providers who spend prolonged periods of time without direct patient contact (Standby services code is *not* reported when the result is a procedure performed by the individual who was on standby and when that procedure is subject the surgical package.)
Case Management Services	**Case management services** include "processes in which a physician or another qualified health care professional is responsible for direct care of a patient, and for coordinating and controlling access to or initiating and/or supervising other health care services needed by the patient." Medical team conferences are included as case management services.
Care Plan Oversight Services	*Care plan oversight services* codes are reported by one individual who supervises the home health, hospice, or nursing facility care plan of a patient or resident during a given period of time (e.g., 30 days). One individual may report care plan oversight services for a given period of time, which reflects the sole or predominant supervisory role with a particular patient or resident. Codes are not reported for the supervision of residents in nursing facilities or patients receiving home health care *unless recurrent supervision of therapy is required*.

Preventive Medicine Services	**Preventive medicine services** include routine examinations or risk management counseling for children and adults who exhibit no overt signs or symptoms of a disorder while presenting to the medical office for a preventive medical physical. Such services are also called *wellness visits*. Discussion of risk factors such as diet and exercise counseling, family problems, substance abuse counseling, and injury prevention are an integral part of preventive medicine.
	
	Care must be taken to select the proper code according to the age of the patient and the patient's status (new or established). Subcategories, headings, and subheadings include:
	
	• New patient
	• Established patient
	• Counseling risk factor reduction and behavior change intervention
	  ◦ New or established patient
	    ▪ Preventive medicine, individual counseling
	    ▪ Behavior change interventions, individual
	    ▪ Preventive medicine, group counseling
	• Other preventive medicine services

(continues)

TABLE 7-3 (continued)

Subsection (Category)	Description
Non-Face-to-Face Services	Non-face-to-face services include the following subcategories: • Telephone services • Online digital evaluation and management services • Interprofessional telephone/Internet/electronic health record consultations • Digitally stored data services/remote physiologic monitoring • Remote physiologic monitoring treatment management services An *online electronic medical evaluation* is a non-face-to-face E/M service provided by a physician to a patient using Internet resources in response to a patient's online inquiry. An *interprofessional telephone/Internet consultation* is an assessment and management service that is provided when a patient's treating physician or other qualified health care professional requests the opinion and/or treatment advice of a physician with specific specialty expertise to assist in the diagnosis and/or management of the patient's problem without the need for the patient's face-to-face contact with the consultant.
Special Evaluation and Management Services	Provided for establishment of baseline information prior to basic life or disability insurance certificates being issued and for examination of a patient with a work-related or medical disability problem. During special evaluation and management services, the examining provider does *not* assume active management of the patient's health problems. Subcategories include: • Basic life and/or disability evaluation services • Work-related or medical disability evaluation services
Newborn Care Services	**Newborn care** includes services provided to newborns in a variety of health care settings (e.g., hospital, birthing center, and home birth). Also included is delivery/birthing room attendance and resuscitation services.
Delivery/Birthing Room Attendance and Resuscitation Services	These services are provided for attendance at delivery, initial stabilization of a newborn, delivery/ birthing room resuscitation, and provision of positive pressure ventilation and/or chest compression.
Inpatient Neonatal Intensive Care Services and Pediatric and Neonatal Critical Care Services	These services are provided to critically ill neonates and infants by a physician. A neonate is a newborn, up to 28 days old. An infant is a very young child, up to one year old. (The same definitions for critical care services codes apply to adult, child, and neonate.) Subcategories include: • Pediatric critical care patient transport • Inpatient neonatal and pediatric critical care • Initial and continuing intensive care services Pediatric patient transport includes the physical attendance and direct face-to-face care provided by a physician during the interfacility transport of a critically ill or critically injured patient, aged 24 months or less.
Cognitive Assessment and Care Plan Services	These services are provided when the comprehensive evaluation of a patient, who exhibits signs and symptoms of cognitive impairment, is required to confirm or establish a diagnosis, including etiology and severity of the condition.
Care Management Services	These are management and support services provided by clinical staff, under the direction of a physician or other qualified health care professional, to patients who reside at home or in a domiciliary, rest home, or assisted living facility (e.g., coordinating patient care with a home health agency). Subcategories include: • Care planning • Chronic care management services • Complex chronic care management services • Principal care management services

(continues)

TABLE 7-3 (continued)

Subsection (Category)	Description
Psychiatric Collaborative Care Management Services	These services are provided when a patient has a diagnosed psychiatric disorder that requires behavioral health care assessment; establishment, implementation, revision, and monitoring of a care plan; and provision of brief interventions.
Transitional Care Management Services	Services provided to established patients whose medical and/or psychosocial problems require moderate or high level of medical decision making during transitions in care from one setting (e.g., acute care hospital) to the patient's community setting (e.g., home).
Advance Care Planning	These are face-to-face services provided by a physician or other qualified health care professional to a patient, family member, or surrogate and include counseling and discussion of advance directives, with or without completion of r elevant legal forms. An advance directive (e.g., durable medical power of attorney, health care proxy, living will, medical orders for life-sustaining treatment) appoints an agent and documents the wishes of a patient regarding future medical treatment should the patient lack decisional capacity at that time.
General Behavioral Health Integration Care Management	These services are provided by clinical staff for patients with behavioral health and substance abuse conditions, and codes are reported by the supervising physician or other qualified health care professional. Services provided require care management services (face-to-face or non-face-to-face) of 20 or more minutes in a calendar month, a treatment plan, and specified elements of the CPT code description.
Other Evaluation and Management Services	Code 99499 is assigned when the E/M service provided is not described in any other listed E/M codes. The use of modifiers with this code is not appropriate. In addition, a special report must be submitted with the CMS-1500 claim.

Exercise 7.5 – Evaluation and Management Section

Instructions: Review each statement, and use your CPT coding manual to assign the appropriate Evaluation and Management section code(s).

1. New patient, routine preventive medicine, age 11. Risk factor discussion, 20 minutes. _____

2. Critical care, 1.5 hours _____

3. Subsequent nursing facility care encounter, expanded problem focused history and examination _____

4. Medical team conference, 50 minutes, nurse practitioner and discharge planner _____

5. Follow-up encounter, ICU patient, stable, expanded problem focused history and examination _____

6. Resuscitation of newborn in delivery room, including positive pressure ventilation and chest compressions _____

7. Telephone E/M service by established patient to physician, 10 minutes; patient's last appointment was two weeks ago _____

8. Custodial care encounter in a boarding home, established patient, detailed history and examination, high level of MDM _____

9. Pediatrician on standby, high-risk birth, 65 minutes _____

10. Heart risk factor education, group counseling, asymptomatic attendees, 65 minutes _____

Anesthesia Section

Anesthesia services are associated with the administration of analgesia and/or anesthesia as provided by an anesthesiologist (physician) or certified registered nurse anesthetist (CRNA). Services include the administration of local, regional, epidural, general anesthesia, monitored anesthesia care (MAC), and/or the administration of anxiolytics (drug that relieves anxiety) or amnesia-inducing medications. The patient's physiological parameters are also monitored during the administration of local or peripheral block anesthesia with sedation (when medically necessary), and other supportive services are provided when the anesthesiologist deems them necessary during any procedure.

Anesthesia care requires the preoperative evaluation of a patient, which includes documenting the history and physical examination to minimize the risk of adverse reactions, planning alternative approaches to administering anesthesia, and answering all questions asked by the patient about the anesthesia procedure. The anesthesiologist or CRNA is responsible for the patient's post-anesthesia recovery period until patient care is assumed by the surgeon or another physician; this occurs when the patient is discharged from the post-anesthesia recovery area.

 NOTE:

Monitored anesthesia care (MAC) is the provision of local or regional anesthetic services with certain conscious-altering drugs when provided by a physician, anesthesiologist, or medically directed CRNA. MAC requires sufficiently monitoring the patient to anticipate the potential need for administration of general anesthesia, and it requires continuous evaluation of vital physiologic functions as well as recognition and treatment of adverse changes.

Assigning Anesthesia Codes

Anesthesia codes describe a general anatomic area or service that is associated with a number of surgical procedures, often from multiple CPT sections.

- CPT codes 00100–01860 are reported for anesthesia services during surgical procedures.
- CPT codes 01916–01942 are reported for anesthesia services during radiology procedures.
- CPT codes 01951–01953 are reported for anesthesia services during burn excisions or debridement.
- CPT codes 01958–01969 are reported for anethesia services during obstetric procedures.
- CPT codes 01990–01999 are reported for anesthesia services during other procedures.

A one-to-one correspondence for Anesthesia to Surgery section codes does not exist, and one Anesthesia section code is often reported for many different surgical procedures that share similar anesthesia requirements. Anesthesia section guidelines also include four codes (99100–99140) that are located in the Medicine section, which are used to report qualifying circumstances for anesthesia.

Separate or Multiple Procedures

When multiple surgical procedures are performed during the single administration of anesthesia, report the anesthesia code that represents the most complex procedure performed. The time reported is the combined total for all procedures performed. (Content about anesthesia time reporting can be found later in this chapter.)

Qualifying Circumstances for Anesthesia

When anesthesia services are provided during situations or circumstances that make anesthesia administration more difficult, report a **qualifying circumstances** code from the CPT Medicine section (in addition to the Anesthesia section code). Difficult circumstances depend on factors such as extraordinary condition of patient, notable operative conditions, or unusual risk factors. These code(s) are reported in addition to the Anesthesia section code(s). Qualifying circumstances codes include:

- 99100 (Anesthesia for patient of extreme age, younger than one year and older than 70)
- 99116 (Anesthesia complicated by utilization of total body hypothermia)

- 99135 (Anesthesia complicated by utilization of controlled hypotension)
- 99140 (Anesthesia complicated by emergency conditions [specify]) (An *emergency condition* results when a delay in treatment of the patient would lead to a significant increase in threat to life or body part.)

> **Example:** A 92-year-old patient with hypertension received general anesthesia services from a CRNA, who was monitored by an anesthesiologist, during total left hip arthroplasty. Report codes 01214 P2 QY and 99100.

Anesthesia Modifiers

All anesthesia services require the following types of modifiers to be reviewed for assignment with reported Anesthesia section codes. HCPCS Level II provider-type modifiers are reported first, followed by physical status modifiers and CPT modifiers.

- HCPCS Level II provider-type modifiers
- Physical status modifiers
- CPT modifiers

HCPCS Level II Anesthesia Modifiers

When applicable, the following HCPCS Level II provider-type modifiers are added first to reported Anesthesia section codes:

- -AA (anesthesia services performed personally by anesthesiologist)
- -AD (medically supervised by a physician for more than four concurrent procedures)
- -G8 (monitored anesthesia care [MAC] for deep complex, complicated, or markedly invasive surgical procedure) (Report modifier -G8 with CPT codes 00100, 00400, 00160, 00300, 00532, 00920 only. Do not report modifier -G8 with modifier -QS.)
- -G9 (monitored anesthesia care [MAC] for patient who has a history of severe cardiopulmonary condition)
- -QK (medical direction of two, three, or four concurrent anesthetic procedures involving qualified individuals)
- -QS (monitored anesthesia care service) (Do not report modifier -G8 with modifier -QS.)
- -QX (CRNA service, with medical direction by physician)
- -QY (medical direction of one Certified Registered Nurse Anesthetist [CRNA] by an anesthesiologist)

> **Example:** A CRNA provided general anesthesia services to an otherwise healthy patient who underwent a vaginal hysterectomy due to uterine fibroids. The CRNA received medical direction from an anesthesiologist. Report code 00944-QY-P1.

Physical Status Modifiers

A **physical status modifier** is added to each reported Anesthesia section code to indicate the patient's condition at the time anesthesia was administered. The modifier also serves to identify the complexity of services provided. (The physical status modifier is determined by the anesthesiologist or CRNA and is documented as such in the patient record.) Physical status modifiers are represented by the letter "P" followed by a single digit, from 1 to 6, as indicated below:

- -P1 (normal healthy patient; e.g., no biochemical, organic, physiologic, psychiatric disturbance)
- -P2 (patient with mild systemic disease; e.g., anemia, chronic asthma, chronic bronchitis, diabetes mellitus, essential hypertension, heart disease that only slightly limits physical activity, obesity)
- -P3 (patient with moderate systemic disease; e.g., angina pectoris, chronic pulmonary disease that limits activity, history of prior myocardial infarction, heart disease that limits activity, poorly controlled essential hypertension, morbid obesity, diabetes mellitus, type I and/or with vascular complications)

- -P4 (patient with severe systemic disease that is a constant threat to life; e.g., advanced pulmonary/renal/hepatic dysfunction, congestive heart failure, persistent angina pectoris, unstable/rest angina)
- -P5 (moribund patient who is not expected to survive without the operation; e.g., abdominal aortic aneurysm)
- -P6 (declared brain-dead patient whose organs are being removed for donor purposes)

Example: An anesthesiologist provided general anesthesia services to a 65-year-old patient with mild systemic disease who underwent total knee replacement. Report code 01402-AA-P2.

CPT Modifiers

The following CPT modifiers should be reviewed to determine whether they should be added to the reported Anesthesia section codes:

- -23 (unusual anesthesia) (When a patient's circumstances warrant the administration of general or regional anesthesia instead of the usual local anesthesia, add modifier -23 to the Anesthesia section code [e.g., extremely apprehensive patients, individuals with intellectual disabilities, patients who have a physical condition, such as spasticity or tremors].)
- -53 (discontinued procedure)
- -59 (distinct procedural service)
- -74 (discontinued outpatient hospital/ambulatory surgery center procedure after anesthesia administration)
- -99 (multiple modifiers)

Example: An anesthesiologist provided general anesthesia services to a 49-year-old patient with chronic obstructive pulmonary disease who underwent extracorporeal shock wave lithotripsy, with water bath. The patient was extremely anxious about the procedure, which normally does not require general anesthesia. Report code 00872-AA-P2-23.

Anesthesia Time Reporting

When reporting Anesthesia section codes, be sure to report the time units in Block 24G of the CMS-1500. (*Anesthesia time units* are based on the total anesthesia time, and they are reported as one unit for each 15 minutes [or fraction thereof] of anesthesia time. For example, 45 minutes of anesthesia time equals three anesthesia time units. The number 3 is entered in Block 24G of the CMS-1500 claim.) Reimbursement for anesthesia services is based on the reported time units, which represents the continuous actual presence of the anesthesiologist or CRNA during the administration of anesthesia. Anesthesia time starts when the anesthesiologist or CRNA begins to prepare the patient for anesthesia care in the operating room or equivalent area (e.g., patient's room) and ends when the anesthesiologist or CRNA is no longer in personal attendance (e.g., patient is released for postoperative supervision by the surgeon).

 NOTE:

Anesthesia time is calculated as the continuous actual presence of the anesthesiologist or CRNA during the administration of anesthesia. Anesthesia time begins when the anesthesiologist or CRNA begins to prepare the patient for anesthesia care in the operating room or equivalent area and ends when the anesthesiologist or CRNA is no longer in personal attendance.

When calculating anesthesia time units, do *not* include:

- Examination and evaluation of the patient by the anesthesiologist or CRNA prior to administration of anesthesia (e.g., reviewing patient records prior to the administration of anesthesia). (If surgery is canceled, report an appropriate code from the CPT E/M section. Usually, a consultation code is reported.)
- Nonmonitored interval time (e.g., period of time when patient does not require monitored anesthesia care, period of time during which anesthesiologist or CRNA leaves operating room to assist with another procedure).

- Recovery room time. (The anesthesiologist or CRNA is responsible for monitoring the patient in the recovery room as part of the anesthesia service provided.)

- Routine postoperative evaluation by the anesthesiologist or CRNA. (When postoperative evaluation and management services are significant, separately identifiable services, such as postoperative pain management services or extensive unrelated ventilator management, report an appropriate code from the CPT E/M section. In addition, the management of epidural or subarachnoid medication administration is reported with CPT code 01996 because it is separately payable on dates of service subsequent to surgery *but not on the date of surgery.*)

Example: A patient undergoes cataract extraction surgery, which requires monitored anesthesia care by the CRNA. At 9:45 A.M., the CRNA administeres a sedative and then performs a retrobulbar injection to administer regional block anesthesia. From 10:00 A.M. until 10:30 A.M., the patient does not require monitored anesthesia care. The CRNA begins monitored anesthesia care again at 10:30 A.M. during the cataract extraction procedure, and monitored anesthesia care ends at 10:45 A.M. The patient is admitted to the recovery room at 10:45 A.M. for monitoring by the recovery room nurse; the patient is released from the recovery room to the surgeon for postoperative care at 11:30 A.M.

Carefully read the procedure outlined in the operative report. Sometimes the discriminating factor between one code and another will be the surgical approach or type of procedure documented.

The total time calculated for monitored anesthesia care is 30 minutes, or 2 time units. (Total time calculated does not include the 30 minutes of nonmonitored interval time [9:00–9:30 a.m.] or the 45 minutes of recovery room time [10:45–11:30 a.m.].)

Exercise 7.6 – Anesthesia Section

Instructions: Review each statement, and use your CPT coding manual to assign the appropriate Anesthesia section code, including CPT and HCPCS Level II modifiers.

1. Anesthesiologist provided anesthesia services to a 77-year-old patient with hypertension who received a corneal transplant. The patient has a history of prior stroke.

   _____

2. Anesthesiologist provided anesthesia services to a 50-year-old patient with diabetes with coronary arteriosclerosis who underwent direct coronary artery bypass grafting.

   _____

3. Anesthesiologist provided anesthesia services for hernia repair in the lower abdomen of an otherwise healthy 9-month-old infant.

   _____

4. CRNA provided anesthesia services under physician direction during an extensive procedure on the cervical spine of an otherwise healthy patient.

   _____

5. CRNA provided anesthesia services to a morbidly obese patient who underwent repair of malunion, humerus.

   _____

Surgery Section

The Surgery section contains subsections that are organized by body system. Each subsection is subdivided into categories by specific organ or anatomic site. Some categories are further subdivided by procedure subcategories in the following order:

- Incision
- Excision
- Introduction or Removal
- Repair, Endoscopy
- Revision or Reconstruction
- Destruction
- Grafts
- Suture
- Other Procedures

To code surgeries properly, three questions must be asked:

1. What body system was involved?

2. What anatomic site was involved?

3. What type of procedure was performed?

Carefully read the procedure outlined in the operative report. Sometimes the discriminating factor between one code and another will be the surgical approach or type of procedure documented.

Example 1: Surgical approach

57540	Excision of cervical stump, abdominal approach;
57545	with pelvic floor repair
57550	Excision of cervical stump, vaginal approach;
57556	with repair of enterocele

When reporting the code number for the excision of cervical stump, code 57540 would be reported for an abdominal approach, and code 57550 would be reported for a vaginal approach.

Example 2: Type of procedure

11600	Excision, malignant lesion including margins, trunk, arms, or legs; excised diameter 0.5 cm or less
17260	Destruction, malignant lesion (e.g., laser surgery, electrosurgery, cryosurgery, chemosurgery, surgical curettement), trunk, arms, or legs; lesion diameter 0.5 cm or less

When reporting the code for removal of a 0.5 cm malignant lesion of the arm, code 11600 would be reported for a surgical excision, and code 17260 would be reported for a destruction procedure (e.g., laser ablation).

Surgical Package

The **surgical package** (or **global surgery**) includes a variety of services provided by a surgeon (Figure 7-9):

- Surgical procedure performed
- Local infiltration, metacarpal, metatarsal, or digital block anesthesia, or topical anesthesia
- One related Evaluation and Management (E/M) encounter on the date immediately prior to or on the date of the procedure (including history and physical)
- Immediate postoperative care, including dictating operative notes, talking with family and other physicians, documenting postoperative orders, and evaluating the patient in the postanesthesia recovery area
- Typical postoperative follow-up care, including pain management, suture removal, dressing changes, local incisional care, removal of operative packs, cutaneous sutures, staples, lines, wires, tubes, drains, casts, or splints (However, casting supplies can usually be billed separately).

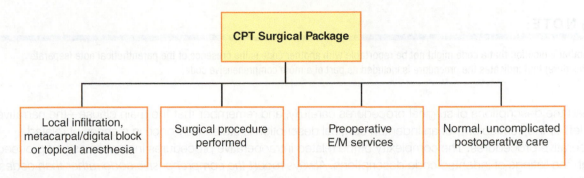

FIGURE 7-9 Components of the surgical package.

 NOTE:

The surgical package does *not* apply to treatment of patients for surgical complications. Procedures and/or services provided to treat complications are reported in addition to the surgical package CPT code.

The **global period** is the number of days associated with the surgical package (or global surgery) and is designated by the payer as 0, 10, or 90 days or as a three-character code. During the global period, all postoperative services are included in the procedure code; postoperative services (except services provided to treat complications) cannot be separately reported and billed. (Obtain global period information from each payer.) The following designations are also associated with the surgical package:

- 000 (endoscopies or some minor surgical procedures that have a zero-day post-operative period)
- 010 (minor procedures with a 10-day post-operative period)
- 090 (major surgeries with a 90-day post-operative period)
- MMM (global period policy does not apply)
- XXX (global period policy does not apply)
- YYY (payer-determined global period, specified as 0, 10, or 90 days [or 000, 010, or 090 days])
- ZZZ (add-on procedure/service is related to a primary procedure/service, falls within the global period of another procedure/service; modifier -26 may be applicable to the reported CPT code)

When different physicians in a same-specialty group practice participate in the pre- and postoperative care of a patient, the physician who performs the surgery reports the CPT code, patient care is shared by the physicians, and reimbursement is distributed within the group. Do *not* bill separately for services included in the global package, even though a different physician in a same-specialty group practice provides the service.

Coders must be aware that *unbundling* is not allowed; unbundling means assigning multiple codes to procedures/services when just one comprehensive code *should be* reported. Examples of procedures that are bundled (included) with the surgical package code include:

- Local infiltration of medication
- Closure of surgically created wounds
- Minor debridement
- Exploration of operative area
- Fulguration of bleeding points
- Application of dressings
- Application of splints with musculoskeletal procedures

NOTE:

Another indication that a code might not be reportable with another code is the presence of the parenthetical note (separate procedure) that indicates the procedure is included as part of a more comprehensive code.

Read the descriptions of surgical procedures carefully, and remember that the main clause—the narrative to the left of the semicolon—of an indented surgical description is stated only once in a series of related intraoperative procedures. The complexity of the related intraoperative procedures increases as you proceed through the listings of indented code descriptions. *Always report the comprehensive code rather than codes for individual components of a surgery.*

Example:

35001	Direct repair of aneurysm, pseudoaneurysm, or excision (partial or total) and graft insertion, with or without patch graft; for aneurysm and associated occlusive disease, carotid, subclavian artery, by neck incision
35002	for ruptured aneurysm, carotid, subclavian artery, by neck incision
35005	for aneurysm, pseudoaneurysm, and associated occlusive disease, vertebral artery
35011	for aneurysm and associated occlusive disease, axillarybrachial artery, by arm incision
35013	for ruptured aneurysm, axillary-brachial artery, by arm incision

Only one code from this series of five codes is assigned *if the procedures performed and reported were rendered during the same operative session.* Note the increasing complexity of procedures as code numbers increase within a series.

Exceptions to reporting one combination code occur either when the code number is marked by a **+** symbol (add-on code) or when a parenthetical note indicates that a code should be reported in addition to the primary code. The following statements appear in CPT code descriptions or as parenthetical notes when it is appropriate to report additional codes:

- List separately in addition to code for primary procedure.
- Use . . . in conjunction with . . .
- Each additional . . .
- Each separate/additional . . .

Exercise 7.7 – Working with the Surgical Package

Instructions: Review each statement, and use your CPT coding manual to assign the appropriate Surgery section code.

1. Incision and drainage (I&D), finger abscess   _____

2. Percutaneous image-guided drainage by catheter, abscess, appendix   _____

3. Therapeutic agent injection, L-5 paravertebral nerve, with image guidance   _____

4. Laparoscopic cholecystectomy with cholangiography   _____

5. Flexible esophagoscopy with removal of foreign body using balloon catheter and radiologic supervision and interpretation (S&I)   _____

Separate Procedure

The parenthetical note, **separate procedure**, follows a code description identifying procedures that are an integral part of another procedure or service. In addition, a *separate procedure* code is reported if the procedure or service is performed independently of the comprehensive procedure or service or is unrelated to or distinct from another procedure or service performed at the same time. The *separate procedure* code is *not* reported if the procedure or service performed is included in the description of another reported code.

Example: The patient undergoes only a cystourethroscopy (passage of an endoscope through the urethra to visualize the urinary bladder). CPT codes for cystourethroscopy include the following:

52000	Cystourethroscopy (separate procedure)
52001	Cystourethroscopy, with irrigation and evacuation of multiple obstructing clots
52005	Cystourethroscopy, with ureteral catheterization, with or without irrigation, instillation, or ureteropyelography, exclusive of radiologic service;
52007	with brush biopsy of ureter and/or renal pelvis
52010	Cystourethroscopy, with ejaculatory duct catheterization, with or without irrigation, instillation, or duct radiography, exclusive of radiologic service

Report code 52000, because only the cystourethroscopy was performed. A code from 52001–52010 would be reported *only* if the operative report documented additional procedures that were included in the code description.

The placement of the phrase "separate procedure" is critical to correct coding. When it appears after the semicolon, it applies to that specific code.

Example:

38100	Splenectomy; total (separate procedure)

The phrase that appears to the left of the semicolon applies to all indented code descriptions.

Example:

10080	Incision and drainage of pilonidal cyst; simple
10081	complicated

Multiple Surgical Procedures

Great care must be taken when billing **multiple surgical procedures** (two or more surgeries performed during the same operative session). The major surgical procedure (the procedure reimbursed at the highest level) should be reported first on the claim, and the lesser surgeries listed on the claim in descending order of expense. Modifier -51 is added to the CPT number for each lesser surgical procedure that does not have the symbol ⊘ or + in front of the code. (Appendix E in the CPT coding manual provides a complete list of modifier -51 exemptions.)

The ranking into major and minor procedures is done to accommodate the fact that most insurance companies will reduce the fee for the second surgery by 50 percent of the regular fee and for the third, fourth, and so on, by 50 to 75 percent. If a lesser procedure is listed first, it may be paid at 100 percent and the major or most expensive surgery reduced by 50 to 75 percent, resulting in a lower payment for the combined surgeries. Insurance companies reason that when multiple surgical procedures are performed during the same operative session, they share the same pre- and postoperative session; therefore, the fee is reduced because the pre- and postoperative portions are covered in the full payment for the major procedure.

 Billing Tip

Computerized practices must be sure that *multiple surgeries performed during the same operative session are entered into the computer in the proper order* to ensure that they are reported correctly on the claim.

Exercise 7.8 – Coding Separate and Multiple Procedures

Instructions: Review each statement, and use your CPT coding manual to assign the appropriate Surgery section code(s).

1. Diagnostic arthroscopy, right wrist, with synovial biopsy   _____
2. Simple vaginal mucosal biopsy   _____
3. Diagnostic nasal endoscopy, bilateral, and facial chemical peel   _____
4. Diagnostic thoracoscopy, lungs and pleural space   _____
5. Needle biopsy of testis   _____
6. Total abdominal hysterectomy with removal of ovaries and anterior colporrhaphy   _____
7. Laparoscopic appendectomy and lumbar hernia repair   _____
8. Biopsy of larynx (indirect) via laryngoscopy   _____
9. Puncture aspiration of two breast cysts, left   _____
10. Debridement of extensive eczematous skin involving 5 percent of body surface   _____

Radiology Section

The Radiology section includes subsections (Table 7-4) for diagnostic radiology (imaging), diagnostic ultrasound, radiation oncology, and nuclear medicine. These subsections are further subdivided into anatomic categories.

The number of **radiologic views** (studies taken from different angles) described in the report or on the encounter form determines the code selection for many diagnostic radiologic procedures. The term *complete* in the discussion of views is a reference to the number of views required for a full study of a designated body part. Carefully review code descriptions to understand how many views constitute a "complete study" for a specific type of radiologic procedure.

Example:

70120	Radiologic examination, mastoids; less than three views per side
70130	complete, minimum of three views per side

TABLE 7-4 Radiology subsections

Subsection (Category)	Description
Diagnostic Radiology (Diagnostic Imaging)	Codes for noninvasive (noninterventional) and invasive (interventional) diagnostic and therapeutic procedures, in addition to CT, MRI, and magnetic resonance angiography (MRA). (Interventional radiology uses image guidance to perform minimally invasive procedures, such as an angiography.) These diagnostic procedures can be as simple as a routine chest x-ray or as complex as a carotid angiography, which requires selective vascular catheterization. To code diagnostic radiology procedures accurately, identify the following: • Anatomic site • Type of procedure • Number of views • Laterality of the procedure (e.g., unilateral or bilateral) • Use of contrast media
	Example 1: Patient undergoes complete x-ray of facial bones. Report code 70150.
	Example 2: Patient undergoes CT of the cervical spine. Report code 72125. (There is no mention of contrast material in this example.)
Diagnostic Ultrasound	Use of high-frequency sound waves (e.g., mechanical oscillations) to produce an image. Codes are organized according to anatomic site; procedures are often performed as follow-up studies for inconclusive diagnostic radiology procedures, intraoperatively (e.g., during endoscopic procedures), and as guidance for biopsies, cyst localization, invasive procedures, paracentesis, pericardiocentesis, placement of radiation therapy fields, and thoracentesis.
	Example: Patient undergoes ultrasound of the spinal canal and contents. Report code 76800.
Radiologic Guidance	Performed during a procedure to visualize access to an anatomic site; contains three headings: fluoroscopic guidance, computed tomography guidance, and magnetic resonance imaging guidance.
	Example: Patient undergoes fluoroscopic guidance for needle placement prior to biopsy procedure. Report code 77002.
Breast, Mammography	Radiological examination of the soft tissue and internal structures of the breast. Screening mammography is performed when a patient presents *without* signs and symptoms of breast disease (e.g., routine annual screening for early detection of unsuspected breast cancer). Diagnostic mammography includes an assessment of suspected disease (e.g., suspicious mass is palpated on physical examination) and is reported when an abnormality is found or suspected.
	Example: Patient undergoes bilateral screening mammography, which is reviewed and interpreted by the radiologist. Report code 77067.
Bone/Joint Studies	CPT codes 77071–77086 classify bone and joint studies.
	Example: Patient, age 51, undergoes complete osseous survey. Report code 77075.
Radiation Oncology	Uses high-energy ionizing radiation to treat malignant neoplasms and certain nonmalignant conditions. Therapeutic modalities (methods) directed at malignant and benign lesions include brachytherapy, hyperthermia, stereotactic radiation, and teletherapy.
	Example: Radiation oncologist provides intermediate therapeutic radiology treatment planning services to a 49-year-old patient. Report code 77262.

(continues)

TABLE 7-4 (continued)

Subsection (Category)	Description
Nuclear Medicine	Use of radioactive elements (e.g., radionuclides and radioisotopes) for diagnostic imaging (e.g., scan) and radiopharmaceutical therapy (destroys diseased tissue, such as a malignant neoplasm). The isotope emits gamma rays as it deteriorates, which enables the radiologist to visualize internal abnormalities (e.g., tumors). The images created by the contrast media (radioactive element) are detected by a gamma camera. Nuclear medicine codes do not include the provision of radium, which means that the nuclear medicine report must be reviewed to identify the diagnostic or therapeutic radiopharmaceutical provided. Then an appropriate HCPCS Level II code is reported for the radiopharmaceutical administered. (The injection of the radionuclide is included as part of the procedure, and a separate injection code is not reported.) Common diagnostic nuclear medicine procedures include bone scans, cardiac scans (e.g., thallium scan and MUGA), renal scans, thyroid scans, and hepatobiliary scans (e.g., HIDA scans). Therapeutic nuclear medicine procedures are used to treat diseases such as chronic leukemia, hyperthyroidism, and thyroid cancer.
	Example: Patient undergoes particulate pulmonary perfusion imaging, which requires venous injection of 10 mc of radioactive Technetium Tc-99m macroaggregated albumin. Report codes 78580, 36000, and A9540.

Complete Procedure

Do not confuse use of the term *complete* in the code description with its use in a parenthetical note. When the word *complete* is found in the code description, one code is reported to "completely" describe the procedure performed.

Example: For a clavicle x-ray, one code is reported (by the radiologist).

    73000   Radiologic examination; clavicle, complete

When the word *complete* is found in a parenthetical note below a code, it may be necessary to report more than one code to "completely" describe the procedure performed. In this case, when each component is performed by the same physician (e.g., radiologist), that physician reports all codes. However, when multiple physicians (e.g., radiologist and surgeon or other physician) perform each component of the procedure, each physician reports an appropriate code.

Example: For a cervical/thoracic myelography via cervical contrast injection procedure, two codes are reported to completely describe the procedure performed.

- Code 72270 is reported for the myelography procedure with radiological supervision and interpretation.
- Review the parenthetical note located below code 72270 to determine whether additional code(s) need to be reported. Report code 61055 for the cervical contrast injection procedure.

    72270   Myelography, two or more regions (e.g., lumbar/thoracic, cervical/thoracic, lumbar/cervical, lumbar/thoracic/cervical), radiological supervision and interpretation

            (Do not report 72270 in conjunction with 62284, 62302, 62303, 62304, 62305.) (When both 62284 and 72270 are performed by the same physician or other qualified health care professional for myelography of 2 or more regions, use 62305.) (For complete myelography of 2 or more regions via injection procedure at C1-C2, see 61055, 72270.)

(continues)

(continued)

61055	Cisternal or lateral cervical (C1-C2) puncture; with injection of medication or other substance for diagnosis or treatment (Do not report 61055 in conjunction with 62302, 62303, 62304, 62305.)
	(For radiological supervision and interpretation by a different physician or qualified health care professional, see Radiology.)
62284	Injection procedure for myelography and/or computed tomography, lumbar
	(Do not report 62284 in conjunction with 62302, 62303, 62304, 62305, 72240, 72255, 72265, 72270.) (When both 62284 and 72240, 72255, 72265, 72270 are performed by the same physician or other qualified health care professional for myelography, see 62302, 62303, 62304, 62305.) (For injection procedure at C1-C2, see 61055.)
	(For radiological supervision and interpretation, see Radiology.)

Professional versus Technical Component

Another consideration in Radiology section coding involves determining which provider is responsible for the professional and technical components of an examination.

- The **professional component** of a radiologic examination covers the supervision of the procedure and the interpretation and documentation of a report describing the examination and its findings.

- The **technical component** of an examination covers the use of the equipment, supplies provided, and employment of the radiologic technicians.

When the examination takes place in a clinic or private office that owns the equipment, and professional services are performed by a physician employed by the clinic or private office, both professional and technical components are billed on the same claim. If, however, the equipment and supplies are owned by a hospital or other corporation and the radiologist performs only the professional component of the examination, two separate billings are generated: one by the physician for the professional component and one by the hospital for the technical component.

When two separate billings are required, the professional component is billed by adding the modifier 26 to the CPT code number. (HCPCS Level II modifier -TC, Technical Component, is added to the Radiology section code reported by the provider who performs the radiologic procedure.)

An exception to this rule is when the code description restricts the use of the code to "supervision and interpretation."

Coding Tip

Report code 76140 when physician consultation is requested to review x-rays produced in another facility and the consultant generates a written report.

Special care must be taken when coding interventional diagnostic procedures that involve injection of contrast media, local anesthesia, or needle localization of a mass. CPT assigns two separate codes to these interventional procedures: a 70000 series Supervision and Interpretation section code, and a Surgery section code. This is done because these procedures may be performed by two physicians, each billing separately. If only one physician is involved, the claim should still include both codes.

Example:
75710   Angiography, extremity, unilateral, radiologic supervision and interpretation

Exercise 7.9 – Radiology Coding

Instructions: Review each statement, and use your CPT coding manual to assign the appropriate Radiology section code.

1. Upper GI series, single-contrast (x-ray)   _____
2. Chest x-ray, frontal and left lateral   _____
3. Cervical spine x-ray, 6 views, with flexion and extension (spine)   _____
4. X-ray pelvis, AP   _____
5. Abdomen, flat plate, AP (x-ray)   _____
6. Colon x-ray, double-contrast with high density barium and air   _____
7. Intraoperative radiologic supervision and interpretation of cholangiography by radiologist   _____
8. Bilateral screening mammography   _____
9. Retrograde pyelography with KUB (Urography) via cystourethroscopy   _____
10. SPECT nuclear medicine liver imaging, with vascular flow imaging   _____

Pathology and Laboratory Section

This section is organized according to the type of pathology or laboratory procedure performed (Table 7-5). Within each subsection, procedures are listed alphabetically.

 NOTE:

The Clinical Laboratory Improvement Act (CLIA) established quality standards for all laboratory testing to ensure the accuracy, reliability, and timeliness of patient test results regardless of where the test was performed.

TABLE 7-5 Pathology and Laboratory subsections

Subsection(s)	Description
Organ or Disease-Oriented Panels	Single code numbers are assigned to **organ- or disease-oriented panels**, which consist of a series of blood chemistry studies routinely ordered by providers at the same time for the purpose of investigating a specific organ or disorder. The composition of the panel is very specific, and no substitutions are allowed.
	Example: Report code 80061 when the physician orders a lipid panel. The following tests are performed on the blood sample: cholesterol, serum, total (82465); lipoprotein, direct measurement, high-density cholesterol (HDL cholesterol) (83718); and triglycerides (84478).
	Note: Refer to "Blood Tests, Panels" in the CPT index to locate organ- or disease-oriented panel codes.
Drug Assay	Codes for laboratory tests that determine whether a drug or a specific classification of drugs is present in blood or urine.
	Example: Report code 80305 for a drug screen, Drug Class List A (e.g., cocaine) that is read by direct optical observation (e.g., urine dipsticks), per date of service.

(continues)

TABLE 7-5 (continued)

Subsection(s)	Description
Therapeutic Drug Assays	Codes for laboratory tests performed to monitor levels of known, prescribed, or over-the-counter medications.
	Example: Report code 80162 when the physician orders a therapeutic drug assay to determine the patient's total digoxin level. (Patient digoxin levels are routinely monitored for therapeutic purposes.)
Evocative/Suppression Testing	Codes for laboratory tests when substances are injected for the purpose of confirming or ruling out specific disorders.
	Example: Report 80400 when the physician orders an adrenocorticotropic hormone (ACTH) stimulation panel to determine whether the patient has adrenal insufficiency.
Pathology Clinical Consultations	Codes reported by pathologists who perform clinical pathology consultations requested by attending physicians when a pathology or laboratory result requires additional medical interpretive judgment. Pathology clinical consultation codes are based on medical decision making or time, and instructions for selecting a level of service are included as a table. Other pathology consultative codes are assigned for: • Face-to-face patient contact, assign an appropriate E/M code. • Consultative review of tissue specimen slides, report codes 88321–88325. • Pathologic consultation during surgery, report codes 88329–88334.
	Example: Report code 80503 when a pathologist provides a pathology clinical consultation with a limited review of the patient's history and medical record and straightforward medical decision making.
• Urinalysis • Molecular Pathology • Genomic Sequencing Procedures and Other Molecular Multianalyte Assays • Multianalyte Assays with Algorithmic Analyses • Chemistry • Hematology and Coagulation • Immunology	Codes for laboratory tests performed on body fluids (e.g., urine, blood). Tests are ordered by physicians and performed by technologists under the supervision of a physician (usually a pathologist).
	Example: Report code 81025 for a urine pregnancy test.
Transfusion Medicine	Codes reported for procedures and products (e.g., fresh frozen plasma) associated with blood transfusions.
	Example: Report code 86900 for ABO blood typing. (ABO refers to the four blood groups: A, B, AB, and O.)
	Note: Codes for transfusion of blood and blood components (e.g., packed cells) are located in the CPT Surgery section (36430–36460, except for "leukocyte transfusion," which is assigned code 86950).
Microbiology	Codes reported for bacteriology, mycology, parasitology, and virology procedures.
	Example: Report code 87086 for a urine culture that tests for bacteria.
Anatomic Pathology	Codes reported for postmortem examination (also called *autopsy* or *necropsy*).
	Example: Report code 88027 for a gross and microscopic autopsy performed on an adult, which includes the central nervous system (CNS, brain, and spinal cord).

(continues)

TABLE 7-5 (continued)

Subsection(s)	Description
• Cytopathology • Cytogenetic Studies	Codes reported for pathology screening tests (cytopathology) and for tissue cultures and chromosome analysis studies (cytogenetic studies).
	Example: Report code 88125 for forensic cytopathology of a sperm specimen.
Surgical Pathology	Codes reported when specimen(s) removed during surgery require pathologic diagnosis. Codes are organized according to level. (Refer to codes 88300–88309 for descriptions of levels and associated procedures.)
	Example 1: Report code 88304 for a gallbladder specimen removed during cholecystectomy. This subsection also includes additional codes reported for histochemistry, consultation and report on referred material, and so on.
	Example 2: Report code 88321 when a pathologist reviews tissue slides prepared elsewhere to render a second opinion regarding pathologic diagnosis.
In Vivo (e.g., Transcutaneous) Laboratory Procedures	Reported for *noninvasive* laboratory procedures that are performed transcutaneously, which means the measurement is obtained by pressing a laboratory instrument against the patient's skin or using visible and near-infrared optical bands to obtain a laboratory value.
	Example: Report code 88720 for transcutaneous total bilirubin testing.
Other Procedures	Codes reported for miscellaneous laboratory procedures, not elsewhere classified in the CPT Pathology and Laboratory section.
	Example: Report code 89230 for sweat collection by iontophoresis.
Reproductive Medicine Procedures	Codes reported for oocyte or embryo procedures are coded for the female partner, and codes involving sperm alone are coded for the male partner. They address the coding needs in the evolving reproductive medicine area. (The AMA states that, alternatively, *all* "reproductive medicine procedures" codes may also be applied to the female.)
	Example: Report code 89259 for cryopreservation of sperm. (Patient can be male or female because a male could have donated the sperm for purchase by a female who will arrange to have it stored.)
Proprietary Laboratory Analysis	Codes reported for proprietary (e.g., registered, trademarked) clinical laboratory analyses.
	Example: Report code 0009U for the proprietary laboratory analysis conducted to detect HER2 status.

Exercise 7.10 – Pathology and Laboratory Coding

Instructions: Review each statement, and use your CPT coding manual to assign the appropriate Pathology and Laboratory section code.

1. Hepatic function panel _____
2. Acute hepatitis panel _____
3. Tuberculosis skin test _____
4. Urinalysis by dip stick with microscopy, automated _____
5. WBC count with differential, automated _____
6. Stool for occult blood by peroxidase activity _____
7. Wet mount, vaginal smear _____

(continues)

Exercise 7.10 – continued

8. Glucose blood test, quantitative _____

9. Sedimentation rate, erythrocytes, automated _____

10. Aerobic blood culture, bacterial, with isolation and presumptive identification of isolate _____

11. Antibiotic sensitivity study using urine, disk method _____

12. Microhematocrit blood count, spun _____

13. Monospot test _____

14. Strep test, group A, rapid _____

15. One-year storage of sperm _____

Medicine Section

The CPT Medicine section classifies *noninvasive* or *minimally invasive* diagnostic and therapeutic procedures and services.

- Noninvasive procedures require no surgical incision or excision, and they are not open procedures.
- Minimally invasive procedures include percutaneous access.

Medicine is the last section of CPT, and its codes are reported with those from all other sections. The Medicine section includes subsections (Table 7-6) that:

- Classify procedures and procedure-oriented services (e.g., immunizations)
- Apply to various medical specialties (e.g., gastroenterology, ophthalmology, otorhinolaryngology, and psychiatry)
- Apply to different types of health care providers (e.g., physical therapists and occupational therapists)

TABLE 7-6 Medicine subsections

Medicine Subsection	Description
Immune Globulins, Serum or Recombinant Products	Reported for the *supply of the immune globulin product,* including broad-spectrum and anti-infective immune globulins, antitoxins, and other isoantibodies. (The *administration* of an immune globulin is reported separately with a code from the Therapeutic, Prophylactic, and Diagnostic Injections and Infusions subsection.)
Immunization Administration for Vaccines/Toxoids	Reported for intradermal, intramuscular, percutaneous, and subcutaneous injections and intranasal/oral administration.
Vaccines, Toxoids	Reported to identify the vaccine/toxoid product only, in addition to immunization administration for vaccines/toxoids codes.
Psychiatry	Reported by psychiatrists, psychologists, and licensed clinical social workers for provision of psychiatric diagnostic services, psychotherapy, and other services to an individual, family, or group.
Biofeedback	Reported for biofeedback services, including review of the patient's history; preparation of biofeedback equipment; placement of electrodes on patient; reading and interpreting responses; monitoring the patient; and control of muscle responses. (*Biofeedback* is a technique that trains the patient to gain some control over autonomic body functions.)
Dialysis	Reported for hemodialysis, miscellaneous dialysis procedures, end-stage renal disease services, and other dialysis procedures.
Gastroenterology	Reported for gastric physiology services and other procedures.
Ophthalmology	Reported for general ophthalmological services, special ophthalmological services, contact lens services, and spectacle services (including prosthesis for aphakia).

(continues)

TABLE 7-6 (continued)

Medicine Subsection	Description
Special Otorhinolaryngologic Services	Reported for vestibular function tests without electrical recording, vestibular function tests with recording (e.g., ENG, PENG), audiologic function tests, evaluative and therapeutic services, special diagnostic procedures, and other procedures. When otorhinolaryngologic services are performed during provision of an Evaluation and Management (E/M) service, do *not* code and report the component procedures separately (e.g., otoscopy, tuning fork test, whispered voice test). However, any special otorhinolaryngologic services located in the CPT Medicine section that are *not* typically included in a comprehensive otorhinolaryngologic evaluation *are* reported separately.
Cardiovascular	Reported for therapeutic services and procedures; cardiography; cardiovascular monitoring services; implantable, insertable, and wearable cardiac device evaluations; echocardiography; cardiac catheterization; intracardiac electrophysiological procedures/studies; peripheral arterial disease rehabilitation; noninvasive physiologic studies and procedures; and other vascular studies.
Noninvasive Vascular Diagnostic Studies	Reported for cerebrovascular arterial studies, extremity arterial and venous studies, visceral and penile vascular studies, extremity arterial-venous studies, and other noninvasive vascular diagnostic studies (e.g., a duplex scan). (A *duplex scan* is a noninvasive test that is performed to evaluate a vessel's blood flow.)
Pulmonary	Reported for ventilator management and pulmonary diagnostic testing, rehabilitation, and therapies.
Allergy and Clinical Immunology	Reported for allergy testing, ingestion challenge testing, and allergen immunotherapy.
Endocrinology	Reported for subcutaneous placement of a sensor for continual glucose (blood sugar) monitoring (up to 72 hours) and physician interpretation/report of results of monitoring.
Neurology and Neuromuscular Procedures	Reported for neurology and neuromuscular diagnostic and therapeutic services that do *not* require surgical procedures (e.g., sleep testing, EEG, EMG, motion analysis).
Medical Genetics and Genetic Counseling Services	Reported for counseling of an individual, couple, or family to investigate family genetic history and assess risks associated with genetic defects in offspring.
Adaptive Behavior Services	Reported for adaptive behavior assessments and treatment.
Central Nervous System Assessments/Tests	Reported for tests performed to measure neuro-cognitive function, mental status, and speech testing.
Health and Behavior Assessment and Intervention	Reported for tests that identify the psychological, behavioral, emotional, cognitive, and social elements involved in the prevention, treatment, or management of physical health problems.
Hydration, Therapeutic, Prophylactic, Diagnostic Injections and Infusions, and Chemotherapy and Other Highly Complex Drug or Highly Complex Biologic Agent Administration	Reported for hydration IV infusion that consists of prepackaged fluid and electrolytes (but no drugs or other substances). Codes include the administration of local anesthesia; intravenous (IV) insertion; access to catheter, IV, or port; routine syringe, tubing, and other supplies; and flushing performed upon completion of infusion. Reported for the administration of chemotherapeutic agents by multiple routes (e.g., intravenously). These codes can be separately billed when an E/M service is rendered on the same day as the chemotherapy administration. *Chemotherapy* is the treatment of cancer with drugs that serve to destroy cancer cells or slow the growth of cancer cells, keep cancer from spreading to other parts of the body, and prevent recurrence of the cancer. Chemotherapy administered in addition to other cancer treatments, such as surgery and/or radiation therapy, is called *adjuvant chemotherapy.*
Photodynamic Therapy	Reported for the administration of light therapy to destroy premalignant/malignant lesions or ablate abnormal tissue using photosensitive drugs.
Special Dermatological Procedures	Reported for dermatology procedures that are typically performed in addition to an appropriate E/M service code.
Physical Medicine and Rehabilitation	Reported for services that focus on the prevention, diagnosis, and treatment of disorders of the musculoskeletal, cardiovascular, and pulmonary systems that may produce temporary or permanent impairment.
Medical Nutrition Therapy	Reported for medical nutrition therapy, which is classified according to type of assessment, individual or group therapy, and length of time.

(continues)

TABLE 7-6 (continued)

Medicine Subsection	Description
Acupuncture	Reported for acupuncture treatment, which is classified as face-to-face patient contact in specified increments of time and according to whether electrical stimulation was provided.
Osteopathic Manipulative Treatment	Reported for manual treatment applied by a physician to eliminate or alleviate somatic dysfunction and related disorders.
Chiropractic Manipulative Treatment	Reported for manual treatments that influence joint and neurophysiological function.
Education and Training for Patient Self-Management	Reported for education and training services provided for patient self-management by a qualified, nonphysician health care professional using a standard curriculum. The codes are classified according to the length of time spent face-to-face with one or more patients.
Non-Face-to-Face Nonphysician Services	Reported for telephone services provided to an established patient, parent, or guardian; qualified nonphysician health care professional online digital assessment and management services; remote therapeutic monitoring services; and remote therapeutic monitoring treatment management services.
Special Services, Procedures, and Reports	Reported for special services, procedures, and reports (e.g., handling/conveyance of specimen for transfer from physician's office to laboratory).
Qualifying Circumstances for Anesthesia	Reported for situations that complicate the administration of anesthesia services (e.g., emergencies, extreme age, hypotension, and hypothermia). These add-on codes are reported in addition to a code from the Anesthesia section.
Moderate (Conscious) Sedation	Reported for a drug-induced depression of consciousness that requires no interventions to maintain airway patency or ventilation. • CPT specifies that moderate (conscious) sedation does not include minimal sedation (e.g., anxiolysis), deep sedation, or monitored anesthesia care (MAC). • Subsection notes specify services that are included in moderate (conscious) sedation codes (e.g., IV access, administration of agent, and monitoring oxygen saturation). • The surgeon who performs a surgical procedure usually provides moderate (conscious) sedation services. When another physician (e.g., an anesthesiologist) provides general anesthesia, regional anesthesia, or monitored anesthesia care, that other physician reports an appropriate Anesthesia section code and its modifiers. • **Moderate (conscious) sedation** is the administration of moderate sedation or analgesia, which results in a drug-induced depression of consciousness.
Other Services and Procedures	Reported for services and procedures that cannot be classified in another subsection of the Medicine section (e.g., anogenital examination, vision screening by nonoptical professionals, hypothermia treatment).
Home Health Procedures/ Services	Reported by nonphysician health care professionals who perform procedures and provide services to the patient in the patient's residence (the patient's home, assisted living facility, or group home).
Medication Therapy Management Services	Reported when a pharmacist provides individual management of medication therapy with assessment and intervention.

Exercise 7.11 – Medicine Section

Instructions: Review each statement, and use your CPT coding manual to assign the appropriate Medicine section code, including modifiers.

1. Right heart (cardiac) catheterization performed on 72-year-old patient; 15 minutes of moderate (conscious) sedation provided by physician performing procedure; and, requirement that independent trained observer assist in monitoring patient's level of consciousness and physiological status _____

2. Routine Electrocardiogram, tracing only _____

3. Spirometry _____

(continues)

Exercise 7.11 – continued

4. Cardiopulmonary resuscitation, in office   _____

5. Diagnostic psychiatric evaluation   _____

6. Influenza vaccine, trivalent 0.25 mg IM, age 18 months   _____

7. Whirlpool and paraffin bath therapy   _____

8. Brief emotional/behavioral assessment with scoring and documentation, one standardized instrument   _____

9. Office services on emergency basis   _____

10. Physical therapy evaluation, low complexity   _____

CPT Category II and Category III Codes

Category II codes were added to CPT to track "evidence-based performance measurements," and their use is optional. Category III codes were added to track "emergency technology," and they are temporary codes reported for data collection purposes.

CPT Category II Codes

CPT Category II codes are supplemental tracking codes used for performance measurement. They (as well as certain HCPCS Level II G codes defined by CMS) are assigned for certain services or test results, which support nationally established performance measures that have proven to contribute to quality patient care. CPT Category II codes are alphanumeric and consist of four digits followed by the alpha character F. (HCPCS Level II G codes are alphanumeric and consist of the alpha character G followed by four digits.) The reporting of Category II codes (and CMS-defined HCPCS Level II G codes) is optional and is *not* a substitute for the assignment of CPT Category I codes. When reported on the CMS-1500 claim, the submitted charge is zero ($0.00). CPT Category II codes are arranged according to the following categories:

- Modifiers (1P–8P), reported with CPT Category II codes only
- Composite Measures
- Patient Management
- Patient History
- Physical Examination
- Diagnostic/Screening Processes or Results
- Therapeutic, Preventive or Other Interventions
- Follow-up or Other Outcomes
- Patient Safety
- Structural Measures
- Nonmeasure Code List

The purpose of reporting Category II codes is to facilitate the collection of information about the quality of services provided to patients. The use of Category II is expected to decrease the time required for patient record abstracting and review, thus minimizing the administrative burden on health care providers (e.g., physicians, hospitals).

Example: Dr. Ryan is a dermatologist who is participating in a nationwide quality management study about malignant melanoma. CPT Category II code 0015F is reported for each patient who receives melanoma follow-up services, which include obtaining a history about new or changing moles (code 1050F), performing a complete physical skin examination (code 2029F), and providing patient counseling to perform a monthly skin self-examination (code 5005F). Thus, codes 0015F, 1050F, 2029F, and 5005F are reported on the CMS-1500 claim, and the charge for each is zero ($0.00). In addition, ICD-10-CM reason for encounter code(s) and CPT Category I service/procedure code(s) are reported on the same CMS-1500 claim with appropriate charges entered for each CPT Category I code.

CPT Category III Codes

CPT Category III codes are temporary codes that allow for utilization tracking of emerging technology, procedures, and services. (They may or may not eventually be assigned a CPT Category I code and description; in general, Category III codes are archived five years from the date of initial publication unless a modification to the date is made.) They facilitate data collection on and assessment of new services and procedures during the Food and Drug Administration (FDA) approval process or to confirm that a procedure/service is generally provided. According to the CPT coding manual, "the inclusion of a service or procedure in this section neither implies nor endorses clinical efficacy, safety, or the applicability to clinical practice." CPT Category III codes are alphanumeric and consist of four digits followed by the alpha character T. CMS designates certain CPT Category III codes as covered by Medicare, which means charges are entered when reporting the codes on a CMS-1500 claim.

In the past, researchers were hindered by the length and requirements of the CPT approval process. Thus, CPT Category III (temporary) codes facilitate the reporting of emerging technology, procedures, and services. They are generally retired if the emerging technology, procedure, or service is not assigned a CPT Category I code within five years. When a Category III code is available, it must be reported instead of an unlisted CPT Category I code (because reporting an unlisted code does not offer the opportunity for collection of specific data).

> **Example:** Cryopreservation of ovarian reproductive tissue is reported with Category III code 0058T.

Summary

CPT codes are reported for services and procedures provided by home health care and hospice agencies, outpatient hospital departments, physicians who are employees of a health care facility, and physicians who see patients in their offices or clinics and in patients' homes. CPT organizes Category I procedures and services into six sections:

- Evaluation and Management (E/M) (99202–99499)
- Anesthesia (00100–01999, 99100–99140)
- Surgery (10021–69990)
- Radiology (70010–79999)
- Pathology and Laboratory (80047–89398, 0001U–0222U)
- Medicine (90281–99199, 99500–99607)

CPT also contains Category II codes (supplemental tracking codes used for performance measurement in compliance with the Merit-based Incentive Payment System [MIPS] under the Quality Payment Program) and Category III codes (temporary codes that allow for utilization tracking of emerging technology, procedures, and services).

The CPT index is organized by alphabetical main terms printed in boldface; appendices are located between the Medicine section and the Index. CPT Category I codes are organized according to six sections that are subdivided into subsections, categories, and subcategories. Guidelines, notes, and descriptive qualifiers are also organized according to sections, subsections, categories, and subcategories. Two-character CPT and HCPCS Level II modifiers are added to five-character CPT (and HCPCS Level II) codes to clarify services and procedures performed by providers.

Internet Links

American Medical Association: *www.ama-assn.org*

E/M Documentation Guidelines: Go to *www.cms.gov*, click on the Outreach & Education link, click on Get Training, click on Medical Learning Network®(MLN), click on Publications, enter Evaluation in the Filter On: box, and click on the dated guide.

Family Practice Management: Go to *www.aafp.org*, and click on the FPM Journal link to view past and current issues in this helpful journal.

Novitas Solutions: *www.novitas-solutions.com*

Review

7.1 – Evaluation and Management Section

Instructions: Use your CPT coding manual to assign code(s) to each item.

1. Home services encounter, established patient straightforward medical decision making and problem focused interval history and examination   _____

2. Emergency department service, low complexity medical decision making and expanded problem focused history and examination   _____

3. Initial hospital care, high complexity medical decision making and comprehensive history and examination   _____

4. Subsequent hospital care, high complexity medical decision making and detailed interval history and examination   _____

5. Emergency department service, straightforward medical decision making and problem focused history and examination   _____

6. Physician-referred consultation, moderate complexity medical decision making and comprehensive history and examination   _____

7. Office consultation, high level of medical decision making and comprehensive history and examination   _____

8. Follow-up office consultation, 30 minutes   _____

9. Follow-up inpatient consultation, high complexity medical decision making and detailed interval history and examination   _____

10. Office blood pressure check by nurse for established patient   _____

11. Critical care   _____

12. Home services provided established patient who resides in a private residence by physician with moderate complexity medical decision making and detailed interval history and examination   _____

13. Patient calls physician about recent lab test results, 7 minutes   _____

14. Precollege physical examination for 18-year-old new patient   _____

15. Well-child care of 5-year-old established patient   _____

16. Preventive medicine service for 56-year-old established patient   _____

17. Inpatient hospital observation and discharge services, low complexity medical decision making and detailed history and examination   _____

18. Critical care services by attending physician, 134
    minutes on July 15   _____

19. Medical disability examination by treating physician   _____

20. Advance care planning, including explanation and discussion about advance
    directives by physician, 30 minutes, face-to-face with patient   _____

7.2 – Anesthesia Section

Instructions: Use your CPT manual to assign anesthesia codes, adding appropriate modifier(s). (Enter the provider-type modifier first, such as 00000-AA-P1.)

1. A 22-year-old patient with controlled hypertension underwent planned vaginal
   delivery for which neuraxial labor anesthesia was administered by an anesthesiologist.   _____

2. A 54-year-old otherwise healthy patient sustained multiple trauma in
   an automobile accident and was administered general anesthesia by an
   anesthesiologist for emergency cranial surgery.   _____

3. A 72-year-old with controlled diabetes mellitus received general anesthesia
   for biopsy of parotid salivary gland malignancy, lateral lobe, from a CRNA who received
   medical direction from an anesthesiologist (who was not in the same operating room
   but provided direction from an adjacent operating room).   _____

4. A 64-year-old with a long history of cirrhosis underwent liver transplant surgery
   under general anesthesia, which was administered by the anesthesiologist.   _____

5. A 34-year-old with high cholesterol developed a right upper arm lump.
   Bone cyst of the right humerus was diagnosed, and the patient underwent excision
   of the cyst for which regional anesthesia was administered by the anesthesiologist.   _____

7.3 – Surgery Section

Instructions: Use your CPT manual to assign procedure codes, adding appropriate modifier(s).

1. Percutaneous core needle biopsy, mediastinum; assistant surgeon reporting   _____

2. Electrodesiccation, basal cell carcinoma (1 cm), face   _____

3. Complicated bilateral repair of recurrent inguinal hernia   _____

4. Biopsy of anorectal wall via proctosigmoidoscopy   _____

5. Mastectomy for gynecomastia, bilateral   _____

6. Open reduction, right tibia/fibula shaft fracture, with insertion of screws   _____

7. Excision, condylomata, penis   _____

8. Replacement of breast tissue expander with breast prosthesis (permanent)   _____

9. Closed reduction of closed fracture, right clavicle   _____

10. Incision and drainage of infected bursa, right wrist   _____

11. Cystourethroscopy with brush biopsy of urinary bladder   _____

12. Endoscopic right maxillary sinusotomy with partial polypectomy   _____

13. Insertion of nontunneled Hickman central venous catheter (short-term) (age 70) _____

14. Avulsion of four nail plates, left foot, nails 2-5 _____

15. Adjacent tissue transfer, trunk, defect 20.0 sq cm in size _____

7.4 – Radiology Section

Instructions: Use your CPT manual to assign procedure and service codes, adding appropriate modifier(s).

1. Arthrography of the right shoulder, supervision and interpretation _____

2. Chest x-ray, frontal, single view (professional component only) _____

3. Transabdominal ultrasound of pregnant uterus, first pregnancy (real time with image documentation), fetal and maternal evaluation, second trimester _____

4. Application of radioactive needles (radioelement), intracavitary of uterus, intermediate _____

5. Positron emission tomography (PET) imaging, whole body _____

7.5 – Pathology and Laboratory Section

Instructions: Use your CPT manual to assign procedure and service codes, adding appropriate modifier(s).

1. Lipid panel blood test _____

2. Drug screen for opiates, dipstick (outside laboratory performed drug screen) _____

3. Blood count (manual), erythrocytes _____

4. Cervical cytopathology slides, manual screening under physician supervision _____

5. Gross and microscopic examination of gallbladder _____

7.6 – Medicine Section

Instructions: Use your CPT manual to assign procedure and service codes, adding appropriate modifier(s).

1. Complete echocardiography, transthoracic (real-time with image documentation [2D] with M-mode recording) _____

2. MMR vaccine immunization _____

3. Intermittent positive pressure breathing of a newborn _____

4. Gait training, first 30 minutes _____

5. Medical psychoanalysis _____

6. Ultraviolet light is used to treat a skin disorder _____

7. Chemotherapy, IV infusion technique, 10 hours, requiring use of portable pump _____

8. Combined right cardiac catheterization and retrograde left heart catheterization for congenital cardiac anomalies _____

9. Home (services) visit for newborn care and assessment _____

10. Therapeutic phlebotomy _____

7.7 – Category II Codes

Instructions: Use your CPT manual to assign procedure and service codes.

1. Initial prenatal care visit _____

2. Assessment of tobacco use _____

3. Recording of vital signs during emergency medicine treatment _____

4. Documentation and review of spirometry results for COPD patient _____

5. Inhaled bronchodilator prescribed for COPD patient _____

7.8 – Category III Codes

Instructions: Use your CPT manual to assign procedure and service codes, adding appropriate modifier(s).

1. Insertion of ocular telescope prosthesis including removal of crystalline lens or intraocular lens prosthesis _____

2. Extracorporeal shock wave involving musculoskeletal system, high energy _____

3. Transcervical uterine fibroid(s) ablation with ultrasound guidance, radiofrequency _____

4. Speech audiometry threshold, automated _____

5. High dose rate electronic brachytherapy, two fractions, skin surface application _____

HCPCS Level II Coding

Chapter Outline

Purpose of HCPCS Level II Codes

Organization of HCPCS Level II
Codes

Documentation and Submission Requirements
for Reporting HCPCS Level II Codes

Assigning HCPCS Level II Codes and Modifiers

Chapter Objectives

Upon successful completion of this chapter, you should be able to:

1. Define key terms related to HCPCS Level II coding.
2. Describe the purpose of HCPCS Level II codes.
3. Explain the organization of HCPCS Level II codes.
4. Identify documentation and submission requirements for reporting HCPCS Level II codes.
5. Assign HCPCS Level II codes, modifiers, and quantities.

Key Terms

certificate of medical necessity
(CMN)

CMS HCPCS Workgroup

DME MAC

durable medical equipment (DME)

durable medical equipment,
prosthetics, orthotics, and
supplies (DMEPOS)

durable medical equipment,
prosthetics, orthotics, and
supplies (DMEPOS) dealers

HCPCS Level II code types:
miscellaneous codes
modifiers
permanent national codes
temporary codes

Medicare Pricing, Data Analysis
and Coding (PDAC) contractor

orthotics

prosthetics

transitional pass-through
payments

Introduction

This chapter presents the procedure/service coding reference developed by CMS, the *Healthcare Common Procedure Coding System* (HCPCS, pronounced "hick-picks"). Two levels of codes are associated with HCPCS, commonly referred to as HCPCS Level I and II codes:

- HCPCS Level I: *Current Procedural Terminology (CPT)*
- HCPCS Level II: national codes

The majority of procedures and services are reported using CPT (HCPCS Level I) codes. However, CPT does not describe durable medical equipment, prosthetics, orthotics, and supplies (DMEPOS), nor certain other services reported on claims submitted for Medicare and some Medicaid patients. Therefore, CMS developed HCPCS Level II codes to report DMEPOS and other services. Most state Medicaid programs and many commercial payers also use the HCPCS coding system.

 NOTE:

Effective December 31, 2003, Medicare no longer required use of HCPCS Level III codes, which had the same structure as Level II codes and began with the letters W, X, Y, or Z. However, some third-party payers continue to use HCPCS Level III codes.

Purpose of HCPCS Level II Codes

HCPCS Level II (or HCPCS national codes) was created in 1983 after Medicare found that its payers used more than 100 different coding systems, making it difficult to analyze claims data. HCPCS Level II furnishes health care providers and suppliers with a standardized language for reporting professional services, procedures, supplies, and equipment. It is used to describe common medical services and supplies not classified in CPT. HCPCS Level II codes are five characters in length, and they begin with letters A–V, followed by four numbers. HCPCS Level II codes identify services performed by physician and nonphysician providers (e.g., nurse practitioners and speech therapists); ambulance companies; and durable medical equipment (DME) companies, which are called durable medical equipment, prosthetics, orthotics, and supplies (DMEPOS) dealers. When claims are to be submitted to one of the four regional MACs, DMEPOS dealers that have coding questions should check with the **Medicare Pricing, Data Analysis and Coding (PDAC) Contractor**, which is responsible for providing suppliers and manufacturers with assistance in determining HCPCS codes to be used. (PDACs were previously called *statistical analysis durable medical equipment regional carriers* or *SADMERCs*.)

- **Durable medical equipment (DME)** is defined by Medicare as equipment that can withstand repeated use, is primarily used to serve a medical purpose, is used in the patient's home, and would not be used in the absence of illness or injury.
- **Durable medical equipment, prosthetics, orthotics, and supplies (DMEPOS)** include artificial limbs, braces, medications, surgical dressings, and wheelchairs.
- **Durable medical equipment, prosthetics, orthotics, and supplies (DMEPOS) dealers** supply patients with DME (e.g., canes, crutches, walkers, commode chairs, and blood-glucose monitors). DMEPOS claims are submitted to DME Medicare administrative contractors (DME MACs) that replaced durable medical equipment regional carriers (DMERCs) that were awarded contracts by CMS. Each DME MAC covers a specific geographic region of the country and is responsible for processing DMEPOS claims for its specific region.
- **Orthotics** is a branch of medicine that deals with the design and fitting of orthopedic devices.
- **Prosthetics** is a branch of medicine that deals with the design, production, and use of artificial body parts.

When an appropriate HCPCS Level II code exists, it is often assigned instead of a CPT code (with the same or similar code description) for Medicare accounts and for some state Medicaid systems. (Other payers may not require the reporting of HCPCS Level II codes instead of CPT codes, so coders should check with individual payers to determine their policies.) CMS creates HCPCS Level II codes:

- For services and procedures that will probably never be assigned a CPT code (e.g., medications, equipment, supplies)
- To determine the volumes and costs of newly implemented technologies

New HCPCS Level II codes are reported for several years until CMS initiates a process to create corresponding CPT codes. When the CPT codes are published, they are reported instead of the original HCPCS Level II codes. (HCPCS Level II codes that are replaced by CPT codes are often deleted. If not deleted, they are probably continuing to be reported by another payer or government demonstration program.)

Example: Report HCPCS Level II device code C1725 for the surgical supply of a catheter, transluminal angioplasty, nonlaser method (may include guidance, infusion/perfusion capability) during vascular surgery. Thus, when reporting a CPT code for a transluminal balloon angioplasty procedure, also report HCPCS Level II device code C1725 for the surgical supply of the catheter.

 NOTE:

When people refer to HCPCS codes, they are most likely referring to HCPCS Level II codes. CMS is responsible for the annual updates to HCPCS Level II codes and two-character alphanumeric modifiers.

The HCPCS Level II coding system classifies similar medical products and services for the purpose of efficient claims processing. Each HCPCS Level II code contains a description, and the codes are used primarily for billing purposes.

Example: DMEPOS dealers report HCPCS Level II codes on claims to identify durable medical equipment, prosthetics, orthotics, and supplies.

HCPCS is *not* a reimbursement methodology or system, and it is important to understand that just because codes exist for certain products or services, coverage (e.g., payment) is not guaranteed. The HCPCS Level II coding system has the following characteristics:

- It ensures uniform reporting of medical products or services on claims.
- Code descriptors identify similar products or services (rather than specific products or brand/trade names).
- HCPCS is not a reimbursement methodology for making coverage or payment determinations. (Each payer makes determinations on coverage and payment outside this coding process.)

Responsibility for HCPCS Level II Codes

HCPCS Level II codes are developed and maintained by the **CMS HCPCS Workgroup**, which is composed of representatives of the major components of CMS, Medicaid State agencies, the Veterans Administration, and the Medicare Pricing, Data Analysis and Coding (PDAC) contractors. HCPCS Level II codes do not carry the copyright of a private organization. They are in the public domain, and many publishers print annual coding manuals.

Some HCPCS Level II references contain general instructions or guidelines for each section; an Appendix summarizing additions, deletions, and terminology revisions for codes (similar to Appendix B in CPT); or separate tables of drugs or deleted codes. Others use symbols to identify codes excluded from Medicare coverage, codes where payment is left to the discretion of the payer, or codes with special coverage instructions. In addition, most references provide a complete Appendix of current HCPCS Level II national modifiers. CMS has stated that it is not responsible for any errors that might occur in or from the use of these private printings of HCPCS Level II codes.

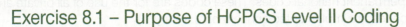

Exercise 8.1 – Purpose of HCPCS Level II Coding

Instructions: Select the most appropriate response.

1. Which of the following key terms is defined as including artificial limbs, braces, medications, surgical dressings, and wheelchairs?

   a. CMS HCPCS workgroup
   b. DME
   c. DMEPOS
   d. DMEPOS dealer
   e. HCPCS Level II

2. Which of the following key terms is defined as including codes that ensure uniform reporting of medical products or services on claims?

   a. CMS HCPCS workgroup
   b. DME
   c. DMEPOS
   d. DMEPOS dealer
   e. HCPCS Level II

3. Which of the following key terms is defined by Medicare as equipment that can withstand repeated use?

   a. CMS HCPCS workgroup
   b. DME
   c. DMEPOS
   d. DMEPOS dealer
   e. HCPCS Level II

4. Which of the following key terms is defined as developing and maintaining HCPCS Level II codes?

   a. CMS HCPCS workgroup
   b. DME
   c. DMEPOS
   d. DMEPOS dealer
   e. HCPCS Level II

5. Which of the following key terms is defined as supplying patients with DME (e.g., canes, crutches, walkers, commode chairs)?

   a. CMS HCPCS workgroup
   b. DME
   c. DMEPOS
   d. DMEPOS dealer
   e. HCPCS Level II

Organization of HCPCS Level II Codes

HCPCS Level II codes are organized by type, depending on the purpose of the codes and the entity responsible for establishing and maintaining them. The four types are:

- Permanent national codes
- Miscellaneous codes
- Temporary codes
- Modifiers

HCPCS Level II also includes an index, table of drugs, and code sections.

Permanent National Codes

HCPCS Level II **permanent national codes** are maintained by the CMS HCPCS Workgroup, which is also responsible for making decisions about additions, revisions, and deletions to the permanent national alphanumeric codes. Decisions regarding changes to the permanent national codes are made only by unanimous consent of all three parties. As HCPCS Level II is a national coding system, none of the parties, including CMS, can make unilateral decisions regarding permanent national codes. These codes are for the use of all private and public health insurers. (New permanent codes are implemented annually on January 1.)

Miscellaneous Codes

HCPCS Level II **miscellaneous codes** include *miscellaneous/not otherwise classified* codes that are reported when a DMEPOS dealer submits a claim for a product or service for which there is no existing HCPCS Level II code. Miscellaneous codes allow DMEPOS dealers to submit a claim for a product or service as soon as it is approved by the Food and Drug Administration (FDA), even though there is no code that describes the product or service. The use of miscellaneous codes also helps avoid the inefficiency of assigning codes for items or services that are rarely furnished or for which payers expect to receive few claims.

Claims that contain miscellaneous codes are manually reviewed by the payer, and the following must be provided for use in the review process:

- Complete description of product or service
- Pricing information for product or service
- Documentation to explain why the item or service is needed by the beneficiary

Before reporting a miscellaneous code on a claim, a DMEPOS dealer should check with the payer to determine if a specific code has been identified for use (instead of a miscellaneous code).

Temporary Codes

HCPCS Level II **temporary codes** are maintained by the CMS and other members of the HCPCS National Panel, independent of permanent national codes. While new permanent codes are implemented once a year on January 1, temporary codes allow payers the flexibility to establish codes that are needed before implementation of the next January 1 annual update. Approximately 35 percent of the HCPCS Level II codes are temporary codes. Certain sections of the HCPCS Level II codes were set aside to allow HCPCS National Panel members to develop temporary codes, and decisions regarding the number and type of temporary codes and how they are used are made independently by each HCPCS National Panel member. Temporary codes serve the purpose of meeting the short-time-frame operational needs of a particular payer.

 NOTE:

Decisions regarding MAC temporary codes are made by an internal CMS HCPCS workgroup, and other payers may also use these codes.

Although the HCPCS National Panel may decide to replace temporary codes with permanent codes, if permanent codes are not established, the temporary codes remain "temporary" indefinitely.

 NOTE:

Whenever a permanent code is established by the HCPCS National Panel to replace a temporary code, the temporary code is deleted and cross-referenced to the new permanent code.

Categories of Temporary Codes

C codes permit implementation of section 201 of the Balanced Budget Refinement Act of 1999, and they identify items that may qualify for **transitional pass-through payments** under the hospital outpatient prospective payment system (OPPS). These are temporary additional payments (over and above the OPPS payment) made for certain innovative medical devices, drugs, and biologicals provided to Medicare beneficiaries. These codes are used exclusively for OPPS purposes and are only valid for Medicare claims submitted by hospital outpatient departments.

G codes identify professional health care procedures and services that do not have codes identified in CPT. G codes are reported to all payers.

H codes are reported to state Medicaid agencies that are mandated by state law to establish separate codes for identifying mental health services (e.g., alcohol and drug treatment services).

K codes are reported to MACs when existing permanent codes do not include codes needed to implement a MAC medical review coverage policy.

Q codes identify services that would not ordinarily be assigned a CPT code (e.g., drugs, biologicals, and other types of medical equipment or services).

S codes are used by the BCBSA and the HIAA when no HCPCS Level II codes exist to report drugs, services, and supplies, but codes are needed to implement private payer policies and programs for claims processing.

T codes are reported to state Medicaid agencies when no permanent national codes exist, but codes are needed to administer the Medicaid program. (T codes are not reported to Medicare, but can be reported to private payers.)

Modifiers

HCPCS Level II **modifiers** are attached to any HCPCS Level I (CPT) or II (national) code to clarify services and procedures performed by providers. Although the HCPCS Level II code and description remain unchanged, modifiers indicate that the description of the service or procedure performed has been altered. HCPCS two-character alphabetic or alphanumeric modifiers are added to five-character CPT or HCPCS Level II codes.

> **Example:** Modifier UE indicates the product is used equipment.
>
> Modifier NU indicates the product is new equipment.

Coding Tip

Depending on the publisher, the HCPCS Level II coding manual includes a list of modifiers inside the front and back covers *or* as a separate appendix. (Figure 8-1 contains a brief sample listing of HCPCS Level II modifiers, regardless of location in the coding manual.)

The CPT coding manual includes an abbreviated list of all CPT modifiers inside the front cover; also included are some HCPCS Level II modifiers. Appendix A of the CPT coding manual includes a detailed list of all CPT modifiers.

Coders assign CPT and HCPCS Level II modifiers to CPT and HCPCS Level II codes. Thus, familiarity with all modifiers is crucial to reporting accurate CPT and HCPCS Level II codes for reimbursement purposes. A careful review of the patient record will help determine which modifier(s), if any, should be added to CPT and HCPCS Level II codes.

HCPCS Level II modifiers are either alphabetic (two letters) or alphanumeric (one letter followed by one number) (Figure 8-1).

> **Example 1:** A patient sees a clinical psychologist for 30 minutes of individual psychotherapy (CPT code 90832). Report:
>
> 90832 AH

24. A.	DATE(S) OF SERVICE					B.	C.	D. PROCEDURES, SERVICES, OR SUPPLIES		E.	F.	G.	H.	I.	J.
	From			To		PLACE OF		(Explain Unusual Circumstances)		DIAGNOSIS		DAYS OR	EPSDT Family	ID.	RENDERING
	MM	DD	YY	MM	DD	YY	SERVICE	EMG	CPT/HCPCS	MODIFIER	POINTER	$ CHARGES	UNITS	Plan	QUAL	PROVIDER ID. #
1									90832	AH					NPI	

Courtesy of the Centers for Medicare & Medicaid Services, www.cms.gov; claim data created by author.

HCPCS Level II Modifiers

NOTE: When CPT modifier 50 is reported, do *not* report modifiers RT and LT.

AA	Anesthesia services performed personally by anesthesiologist
AD	Medical supervision by a physician: more than four concurrent anesthesia procedures
AH	Clinical psychologist
AM	Physician, team member service
AP	Ophthalmological examination
AS	Physician assistant, nurse practitioner, or clinical nurse specialist services for assistant at surgery
AT	Acute treatment (this modifier should be used when reporting service 98940, 98941, 98942)
E1	Upper left, eyelid
E2	Lower left, eyelid
E3	Upper right, eyelid
E4	Lower right, eyelid
LT	Left side (used to identify procedures performed on the left side of the body)
RT	Right side (used to identify procedures performed on the right side of the body)

Courtesy of the Centers for Medicare & Medicaid Services, www.cms.gov.

FIGURE 8-1 Sample HCPCS Level II modifiers.

Example 2: A Medicare patient undergoes tendon excision, right palm (CPT code 26170) and left middle finger (CPT code 26180). Report:

26170 RT

26180 59 F2

24. A.	DATE(S) OF SERVICE					B.	C.	D. PROCEDURES, SERVICES, OR SUPPLIES (Explain Unusual Circumstances)		E.	F.	G.	H.	I.	J.	
	From			To		PLACE OF SERVICE	EMG	CPT/HCPCS	MODIFIER	DIAGNOSIS POINTER	$ CHARGES	DAYS OR UNITS	EPSDT Family Plan	ID. QUAL.	RENDERING PROVIDER ID #	
	MM	DD	YY	MM	DD	YY										
1									26170	RT					NPI	
2									26180	59 F2					NPI	

Courtesy of the Centers for Medicare & Medicaid Services, www.cms.gov; claim data created by author.

NOTE:

- C codes are reported for new drugs, biologicals, and devices that are eligible for transitional pass-through payments under the ambulatory payment classifications (APCs) under the outpatient prospective payment system.
- D codes are copyrighted by the American Dental Association, and the codes are included in the *HCPCS Level II Professional* publication.

HCPCS Level II Index and Table of Drugs

Because of the wide variety of services and procedures described in HCPCS Level II, the alphabetical index (Figure 8-2) is very helpful in finding the correct code. The various publishers of the reference may include an expanded index that lists additional terms, making the search for codes easier and faster. The Table of Drugs (Figure 8-3) lists codes assigned to medications, which include codes that begin with letters A, C, J, Q, and S. The table of drugs also includes medication unit amounts (e.g., 10 mg) and route of administration (e.g., IM). Some publishers print brand names beneath the generic description, and others provide a special expanded index of the drug codes. It is important never to code directly from the index and always to verify the code in the tabular section of the coding manual. You may wish to review the HCPCS Level II references from several publishers and select the one that best meets your needs and is the easiest for you to use.

Index

A

Abdomen
dressing holder/binder, A4461, A4463
pad, low profile, L1270

Abduction
control, each, L2624
pillow, E1399
rotation bar, foot, L3140–L3170

Ablation
robotic, waterjet, C2596
transbronchial, C9751
ultrasound, C9734

Abortion, S0199, S2260–S2267

AbobotulinumtoxintypeA, J0586

Absorption dressing, A6251–A6256

Permission to reuse granted by Optum360.

FIGURE 8-2 HCPCS Level II index entries (sample).

Drug Name	Unit Per	Route	Code
ABATACEPT	10 mg	IV	**J0129**
ABCIXIMAB	10 mg	IV	**J0130**
ABELCET	10 mg	IV	**J0287**
ABILIFY	0.25 mg	IM	**J0400**
ABILIFY MAINTENA® KIT	1 mg	IM	**J0401**
ABLAVAR	1 mL	IV	**A9583**
ABOBOTULINUMTOXINA	5 units	IM	**J0586**
ABRAXANE	1 mg	IV	**J9264**

Permission to reuse granted by Optum360.

FIGURE 8-3 HCPCS Level II table of drugs (sample).

NOTE:

The Food and Drug Administration (FDA) publishes the *National Drug Code (NDC) directory*, which includes drug products that are identified and reported using a unique, three-segment number. Go to www.fda.gov, click on For Health Professionals, and scroll down and click on Drugs@FDA to locate information about FDA approved drug products.

If you have difficulty locating the service or procedure in the HCPCS Level II index, review the list of codes and descriptions in the appropriate section of the tabular list of codes to locate the code. Read the code descriptions very carefully. You may need to ask the provider to help select the correct code.

HCPCS Level II Code Sections

The alphabetic first character identifies the code sections of HCPCS Level II. Some are logical, such as R for radiology, whereas others, such as J for drugs, appear to be arbitrarily assigned. The HCPCS Level II code ranges are as follows:

A0000–A0999	Transportation Services Including Ambulance
A4000–A9999	Medical and Surgical Supplies
B4000–B9999	Enteral and Parenteral Therapy
C1000–C9999	Outpatient PPS
D0000–D9999	Dental Procedures (copyrighted by the American Dental Association)
E0100–E9999	Durable Medical Equipment
G0008–G9999	Procedures/Professional Services (Temporary)
H0001–H9999	Alcohol and Drug Abuse Treatment Services
J0100–J8499	J Codes Drugs
J8501–J9999	J Codes Chemotherapy Drugs
K0000–K9999	Temporary Codes (Assigned to DME MACs)
L0100–L4999	Orthotics
L5000–L9999	Prosthetics
M0000–M0301	Other Medical Services
M1003–M1149	Quality Measures
P0000–P9999	Laboratory Services
Q0000–Q9999	Q Codes (Temporary)
R0000–R9999	Diagnostic Radiology Services
S0000–S9999	Temporary National Codes (Non-Medicare)
T1000–T9999	National T Codes Established for State Medicaid Agencies
U0001–U0005	Coronavirus (COVID-19) Laboratory Tests
V0000–V2999	Vision Services
V5000–V5999	Hearing Services

Basic Steps for Using the HCPCS Level II Index and Code Sections

1. Review the patient record to determine the procedures performed or services provided.

2. Locate the main term in the HCPCS Level II index.

3. Identify the code next to the main term in the HCPCS Level II index. There may be one code or a range of codes listed.

4. Go to the appropriate HCPCS Level II code section to locate the code(s), comparing code description to with documented procedures and services.

5. Review the list of modifiers to identify any that should be added to the code.

6. Assign the code (and any appropriate modifiers).

 NOTE:

When the main term for a procedure or service cannot be found in the index, go to the HCPCS Level II code sections to review code descriptions. Compare multiple code descriptions with documentation of procedures performed and services provided to select the proper code.

Exercise 8.2 – Organization of HCPCS Level II Codes

Instructions: Select the most appropriate response.

1. Which of the following key terms is defined as being used by all private and public health insurers?

   a. Miscellaneous codes

   b. Modifiers

   c. Permanent codes

   d. Temporary codes

   e. Transitional pass-through payments

2. Which of the following key terms is defined as being reported when there is no existing HCPCS Level II code?

   a. Miscellaneous codes

   b. Modifiers

   c. Permanent codes

   d. Temporary codes

   e. Transitional pass-through payments

3. Which of the following key terms is defined as temporary additional payments (over and above the OPPS payment)?

   a. Miscellaneous codes

   b. Modifiers

   c. Permanent codes

   d. Temporary codes

   e. Transitional pass-through payments

4. Which of the following key terms is defined as being attached to any code to clarify services and procedures performed by providers?

   a. Miscellaneous codes

   b. Modifiers

   c. Permanent codes

   d. Temporary codes

   e. Transitional pass-through payments

5. Which of the following key terms is defined as allowing payers the flexibility to establish these codes as needed before the next January 1 annual update?

   a. Miscellaneous codes

   b. Modifiers

   c. Permanent codes

   d. Temporary codes

   e. Transitional pass-through payments

Documentation and Submission Requirements for Reporting HCPCS Level II Codes

The specific HCPCS Level II code determines whether the claim is sent to the:

- MAC that processes Medicare Part A and B claims
- DME MAC that processes DMEPOS dealer claims

A *Medicare administrative contractor (MAC)* is an organization (e.g., third-party payer) that contracts with CMS to process claims and perform program integrity tasks for Medicare Part A and Medicare Part B, home health care and hospice, and DMEPOS. Each MAC uses a variety of media (e.g., website, newsletters, meetings) to inform providers about Medicare program decisions, which are based on Medicare's program transmittals and quarterly provides updates that communicate new and revised policies or procedures that are to be incorporated into CMS Internet-Only Manuals (IOMs).

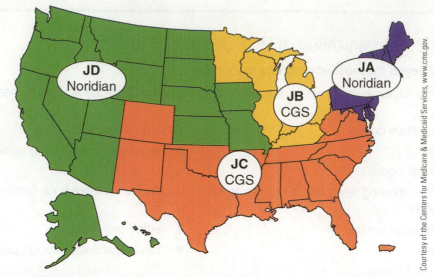

FIGURE 8-4 Map of defined geographic areas for DME claims.

All Medicare DME claims are processed by just four regional **DME MACs**, which are designated as jurisdictions A, B, C, and D and process DME claims for defined geographic areas (Figure 8-4). When CMS investigated and pursued past fraudulent DME claims, it became apparent that DME billings were out of control. Thus, reducing the number of DME MACs to four jurisdictions allowed primary MACs to focus on familiar, traditional claims submitted by providers who are billing for services, not equipment.

When the physician treats a Medicare patient for a broken ankle and supplies the patient with crutches, two claims are generated. The one for the fracture care, or professional service, is sent to the primary Medicare administrative contractor (MAC); the claim for the crutches is sent to the DME MAC. The physician must register with both, review billing rules, comply with claims instructions, and forward claims correctly to secure payment for both services. If the physician is not registered with the DME MAC to provide medical equipment and supplies, the patient is given a prescription for crutches to take to a local DMEPOS dealer.

Some services, such as most cosmetic procedures, are excluded as Medicare benefits by law and will not be covered by either MAC. Splints and casts for traumatic injuries have CPT numbers that would be used to report these supplies or services to the local MAC. Because the review procedure for adding new codes to Level II is a much shorter process, new medical and surgical services may first be assigned a Level II code and then incorporated into CPT at a later date.

Patient Record Documentation

The patient record includes documentation that justifies the medical necessity of procedures, services, and supplies coded and reported on an insurance claim. This means that the diagnoses reported on the claim must justify diagnostic and/or therapeutic procedures or services provided. The patient's record should include the following documentation:

- Patient history, including review of systems
- Physical examination, including impression
- Diagnostic test results, including analysis of findings
- Diagnoses, including duration (e.g., acute or chronic) and comorbidities that impact care
- Patient's prognosis, including potential for rehabilitation

When DMEPOS items are reported on a claim, the DMEPOS dealer must keep the following documents on file:

- Provider order for DMEPOS item, signed and dated
- Signed advance beneficiary notice (ABN) if medical necessity for an item cannot be established

An *advance beneficiary notice (ABN)* (discussed further in Chapter 14 of this textbook) is a waiver signed by the patient acknowledging that because medical necessity for a procedure, service, or supply cannot be established (e.g., due to the nature of the patient's condition, injury, or illness), the patient accepts responsibility for reimbursing the provider or DMEPOS dealer for costs associated with the procedure, service, or supply. When the provider reports DMEPOS items on a claim, the provider must keep the following documents on file:

- Diagnosis establishing medical necessity for the item
- Clinical notes that justify the DMEPOS item ordered
- Provider order for DMEPOS item, signed and dated
- Signed advance beneficiary notice if medical necessity for an item cannot be established

DMEPOS Requirements

For certain items or services reported on a claim submitted to the DME MAC, the DMEPOS dealer must receive a signed **certificate of medical necessity (CMN)** (Figure 8-5) from the treating physician before submitting a claim to Medicare. A copied, electronic, faxed, or original CMN must be maintained by the DMEPOS dealer and must be available to the DME MAC on request. The CMN is a prescription for DME, services, and supplies. DME MAC medical review policies include local coverage determinations (LCDs) and national coverage determinations (NCDs), both of which define coverage criteria, payment rules, and documentation required as applied to DMEPOS claims processed by DME MACs for frequently ordered DMEPOS equipment, services, and supplies. (National policies are included in the *Medicare Benefit Policy Manual, Medicare Program Integrity Manual,* and *Medicare National Coverage Determinations Manual.*) If DMEPOS equipment, services, or supplies do not have medical review policies established for coverage, the general coverage criteria applies. The DMEPOS equipment, services, or supplies must:

- Fall within a benefit category
- Not be excluded by statute or by national CMS policy
- Be reasonable and necessary to diagnose and/or treat an illness or injury or to improve the functioning of a malformed body

DME MACs are required to follow national policy when it exists; when there is no national policy on a subject, DME MACs have the authority and responsibility to establish local policies. Because many DMEPOS dealers operate nationally, the CMS requires that the medical review policies published by the DME MACs be identical in all four regions.

Exercise 8.3 – Documentation and Submission Requirements for Reporting HCPCS Level II Codes

Instructions: Complete each statement below.

1. The specific HCPCS Level II code determines whether the claim is sent to the MAC that processes provider claims or the _____ MAC that processes DMEPOS dealer claims.

2. Providers and DMEPOS dealers obtain annual lists of valid HCPCS Level II codes, which include _____ instructions for services.

3. CMS decided to have all DME claims processed by only four DME MACs to reduce _____ claims.

4. When a physician treats a Medicare patient for a fractured femur and supplies the patient with crutches, two claims are generated. The physician's claim for the fracture care is sent to the MAC, and the claim for the crutches is sent to the _____ MAC.

5. For certain items or services reported on a claim submitted to the DME MAC, the DMEPOS dealer must receive a signed certificate of medical _____.

DEPARTMENT OF HEALTH AND HUMAN SERVICES
CENTERS FOR MEDICARE & MEDICAID SERVICES

Form Approved OMB
No. 0938-0679
Expires 02/2024

CERTIFICATE OF MEDICAL NECESSITY
CMS-484—OXYGEN

DME 484.3

SECTION A: Certification Type/Date: INITIAL ___/___/___   REVISED ___/___/___   RECERTIFICATION___/___/___

PATIENT NAME, ADDRESS, TELEPHONE and MEDICARE ID	SUPPLIER NAME, ADDRESS, TELEPHONE and NSC or NPI #
(___)____-____ Medicare ID _____	(___)____-____ NSC or NPI #_____

PLACE OF SERVICE _____	Supply Item/Service Procedure Code(s):	PT DOB ___/___/___ Sex ____ (M/F) Ht. ____(in) Wt _____

NAME and ADDRESS of FACILITY if applicable (see reverse)	PHYSICIAN NAME, ADDRESS, TELEPHONE and UPIN or NIP #
	(___)____-____ UPIN or NPI #_____

SECTION B: Information in this Section May Not Be Completed by the Supplier of the Item Supplies.

EST. LENGTH OF NEED (# OF MONTHS): _____ 1–99 (99=LIFETIME)	DIAGNOSIS CODES: _____

ANSWERS	ANSWER QUESTIONS 1–9. (Check Y for Yes, N for No, or D for Does Not Apply, unless otherwise noted.)
a)_____mm Hg b)_____% c)____/____/____	1. Enter the result of recent test taken on or before the certification date listed in Section A. Enter (a) arterial blood gas PO2 and/or (b) oxygen saturation test; (c) date of test.
☐1 ☐2 ☐3	2. Was the test in Question 1 performed (1) with the patient in a chronic stable state as an outpatient, (2) within two days prior to discharge from an inpatient facility to home, or (3) under other circumstances?
☐1 ☐2 ☐3	3. Check the one number for the condition of the test in Question 1: (1) At Rest; (2) During Exercise; (3) During Sleep
☐Y ☐N ☐D	4. If you are ordering portable oxygen, is the patient mobile within the home? If you are not ordering portable oxygen, check D.
_____LPM	5. Enter the highest oxygen flow rate ordered for this patient in liters per minute. If less than 1 LPM, enter an "X".
a)_____mm Hg b)_____% c)____/____/____	6. If greater than 4 LPM is prescribed, enter results of recent test taken on 4 LPM. This may be an: (a) arterial blood gas PO2 and/or (b) oxygen saturation test with patient in a chronic stable state. Enter date of test (c).

ANSWER QUESTIONS 7-9 ONLY IF PO2 = 56–59 OR OXYGEN SATURATION = 89 IN QUESTION 1

☐Y ☐N	7. Does the patient have dependent edema due to congestive heart failure?
☐Y ☐N	8. Does the patient have cor pulmonale or pulmonary hypertension documented by P pulmonale on an EKG or by an echocardiogram, gated blood pool scan or direct pulmonary artery pressure measurement.
☐Y ☐N	9. Does the patient have a hematocrit greater than 56%?

NAME OF PERSON ANSWERING SECTION B QUESTIONS, IF OTHER THAN PHYSICIAN (Please Print):
NAME_____ TITLE_____ EMPLOYER_____

SECTION C: Narrative Description of Equipment and Cost

(1) Narrative description of all items, accessories and option ordered; (2) Suppliers charge; and (3) Medicare Fee Schedule Allowance for each item, accessory, and option (see instructions on back)

SECTION D: PHYSICIAN Attestation and Signature/Date

I certify that I am the treating physician identified in Section A of this form. I have received Sections A, B and C of the Certificate of Medical Necessity (including charges for items ordered). Any statement on my letterhead attached hereto, has been reviewed and signed by me. I certify that the medical necessity information in Section B is true, accurate and complete, to the best of my knowledge, and I understand that any falsification, omission, or concealment of material fact in that section may subject me to civil or criminal liability.

PHYSICIAN'S SIGNATURE_____ DATE ____/____/____

Signature and Date Stamps Are Not Acceptable.

Form CMS–484 (12/18)

Courtesy of the Centers for Medicare & Medicaid Services, www.cms.gov.

FIGURE 8-5 Sample certificate of medical necessity required of DMEPOS dealer.

Assigning HCPCS Level II Codes and Modifiers

Some services must be reported by assigning both a CPT and a HCPCS Level II code. In addition, modifiers are attached to codes to provide additional information regarding the product or service reported. Modifiers supplement the information provided by a HCPCS Level II code description to identify specific circumstances that may apply to an item or a service. (A comprehensive list of modifiers and descriptions are located in the HCPCS Level II coding manual.)

> **Example:** A clinical psychologist provides 45 minutes of interactive group psychotherapy in a partial hospitalization setting. Report HCPCS Level II code and modifier, G0411-AH.

The most common scenario uses the CPT code for administration of an injection and the HCPCS Level II code to identify the medication administered. Most drugs have qualifying terms such as dosage limits that could alter the quantity reported (see Figure 8-3). If a drug stating "per 50 mg" is administered in a 70-mg dose, the quantity billed would be "2." If you administered only 15 mg of a drug stating "up to 20 mg," the quantity is "1." Imagine how much money providers lose by reporting only the CPT code for injections. Unless the payer or insurance plan advises the provider that it does not pay separately for the medication injected, always report this combination of codes.

> **Example:** Intramuscular methylprednisolone, 40 mg, was injected into the region of the left scapula to release a trigger point of spasming, contracted, hard muscle. The physician explained that the patient's third-party payer would likely reject the submitted claim as not medically necessary, and modifier -GA (Item or service expected to be denied as not reasonable and necessary) would be attached to each submitted code. The patient agreed to be responsible for payment of treatment and signed the advance beneficiary notice. Report CPT code 96372-GA and HCPCS Level II code J1020-GA.

It is possible that a particular service would be assigned a CPT code and a HCPCS Level II code. Which one should you report? The answer is found in the instructions from the payer. Most commercial payers require the CPT code. Medicare gives HCPCS Level II codes the highest priority if the CPT code is general and the HCPCS Level II code is more specific.

> **Example:** A 45-year-old female patient received annual preventative evaluation and management services from the primary care provider, and the resident that the provider was supervising performed a pelvic and clinical breast examination. Report CPT code 99386 (Preventative evaluation and management service, 40-64 years) and HCPCS Level II code G0101-GC (Cervical or vaginal cancer screening; pelvic and clinical breast examination). The description for modifier -GC is This service has been performed in part by a resident under the direction of a teaching physician.

Most supplies are included in the charge for the office visit or the procedure. CPT provides code 99070 for all supplies and materials exceeding those usually included in the primary service or procedure performed. However, this CPT code may be too general to ensure correct payment. If the office provides additional supplies when performing a service, the HCPCS Level II codes may identify the supplies in sufficient detail to secure proper reimbursement.

Although CMS developed this system, some HCPCS Levels I and II services are not payable by Medicare. Medicare may also place qualifications or conditions on payment for some services. As an example, an ECG is a covered service for a cardiac problem but is not covered when performed as part of a routine examination. Also, the payment for some services may be left to the payer's discretion. Two CMS publications assist payers in correctly processing claims. The *Medicare National Coverage Determinations Manual* advises the MAC whether a service is covered or excluded under Medicare regulations. The *Medicare Benefit Policy Manual* directs the MAC to pay a service or reject it using a specific "remark" or explanation code.

There are more than 4,000 HCPCS Level II codes, but you may find that no code exists for the procedure or service you need to report. Unlike CPT, HCPCS Level II does not have a consistent method of establishing codes for reporting "unlisted procedure" services. If the MAC does not provide special instructions for reporting these services in HCPCS, report them with the proper "unlisted procedure" code from CPT. Remember to submit documentation explaining the procedure or service when using the "unlisted procedure" codes.

NOTE:

CMS developed the HCPCS Level II codes for Medicare, but commercial payers also adopt them.

Exercise 8.4 – Assigning HCPCS Level II Codes

Instructions: Use the sample index entries located in Figures 8-2 and 8-3 of this chapter to identify the HCPCS Level II code for each item, and then verify the code in your HCPCS Level II coding manual.

_____ 1. Abdominal pad (low profile) (as an addition to thoracic-lumbar-sacral orthotic)

_____ 2. Abduction control, left lower extremity

_____ 3. Implantable access catheter, external access

_____ 4. Abelcet, 10 milligrams intravenously

_____ 5. Paclitaxel protein-bound particles, 1 milligram intravenously

Summary

Two levels of codes are associated with HCPCS, commonly referred to as HCPCS Level I and II codes. (HCPCS Level III codes were discontinued effective December 31, 2003; however, some third-party payers continue to use them.) HCPCS Level I includes the five-digit *Current Procedural Terminology* (CPT) codes developed and published by the American Medical Association (AMA). HCPCS Level II (or HCPCS national codes) was created in the 1980s to describe common medical services and supplies not classified in CPT.

The HCPCS Level II national coding system classifies similar medical products and services for the purpose of efficient claims processing. Each code contains a description, and the codes are used primarily for billing purposes. The codes describe DME devices, accessories, supplies, and repairs; prosthetics; medical and surgical supplies; medications; provider services; temporary Medicare codes (e.g., Q codes); and other items and services (e.g., ambulance services). Some services must be reported by assigning both a CPT and a HCPCS Level II national code. The most common scenario uses the CPT code for the administration of an injection and the HCPCS code to identify the medication.

The specific HCPCS Level II code determines whether the claim is sent to the primary Medicare administrative contractor (MAC) that processes provider claims or the DME MAC that processes DMEPOS dealer claims. Providers and DMEPOS dealers obtain annual lists of valid HCPCS Level II codes, which include billing instructions for services.

Internet Links

HCPCS Level II coding files: Go to *www.cms.gov*, click on the Medicare link, scroll down to the Coding heading, and click on the HCPCS Release & Code Sets link.

Medicare Durable Medical Equipment (DME) Center: Go to *www.cms.gov*, click on the Medicare link, scroll to Provider Type, and click on Durable Medical Equipment (DME) link.

Review

8.1 – Multiple Choice

Instructions: Select the most appropriate response.

1. HCPCS Level II was introduced in 1983 after Medicare found that its payers used more than 100 different coding systems, making it
   a. difficult to analyze claims data.
   b. expensive to reimburse services.
   c. proficient to assign codes.
   d. unmanageable to publish manuals.

2. HCPCS Level II furnishes health care providers and suppliers with a _____ language for reporting professional services, procedures, supplies, and equipment.
   a. medical
   b. proficient
   c. standardized
   d. therapeutic

3. Although the majority of procedures and services are reported using CPT (HCPCS Level I), that coding system does not describe _____ reported on claims submitted for Medicare and some Medicaid patients.
   a. DMEPOS
   b. LCD/NCD
   c. PDAC
   d. SADMERC

4. HCPCS Level II codes are five characters in length, and they begin with letters _____, followed by four numbers.
   a. A–B, E–V
   b. A–V
   c. A–Z
   d. W–Z

5. Because HCPCS Level II is not a reimbursement methodology or system, its procedure, product, and service codes _____ coverage (e.g., payment).
   a. are assured
   b. bear out
   c. correspond with
   d. do not guarantee

6. HCPCS Level II codes are developed and maintained by _____ and do not carry the copyright of a private organization, which means they are in the public domain and many publishers print annual coding manuals.
   a. BCBS
   b. CMS
   c. NCCI
   d. OIG

7. The four types of HCPCS Level II codes are
   a. miscellaneous, modifier, permanent, and temporary codes.
   b. miscellaneous, investigational, permanent, and temporary codes.
   c. miscellaneous, investigational, medical/surgical supply, and transportation service codes.
   d. orthotic, prosthetic, radiology, and temporary codes.

8. A patient with diabetes received a J-cell alkaline replacement battery for a home blood glucose monitor. Assign the HCPCS Level II code.
   a. A4233
   b. A4234
   c. A4235
   d. A4236

9. Halo procedure, cervical halo incorporated into Milwaukee-type orthosis. Assign the HCPCS Level II code.
   a. L0120
   b. L0810
   c. L0820
   d. L0830

10. Assistive listening telecommunication device for the deaf (TDD). Assign the HCPCS Level II code.
    a. V5267
    b. V5269
    c. V5272
    d. V5273

8.2 – Assigning HCPCS Level II Codes

Instructions: Use your HCPCS Level II manual to assign procedure, service, or supply code(s), adding applicable modifier(s).

1. Patient received ALS 1 emergency transport ambulance service from home to hospital emergency department _____

2. Patient received supplies for self-administered injections _____

3. Patient was administered artificial saliva, 60 milliliters, orally _____

4. Stroke patient was administered four ounces of food thickener, orally _____

5. Patient underwent insertion of catheter for intravascular ultrasound (prior to scheduled ultrasound procedure) _____

6. Patient purchased a used heavy-duty wheeled walker (after being informed about purchase and rental options) _____

7. Powered bone marrow biopsy needle was used (during bone marrow procedure) _____

8. Patient underwent 60 minutes of behavioral health counseling and therapy _____

9. Patient received injection of tetracycline, 250 mg _____

10. Patient supplied with lightweight wheelchair _____

11. Patient supplied with brand new protective body sock for use under a new cervical-thoracic-lumbar-sacral-orthotic (CTLSO) (Milwaukee) spinal orthotic _____

12. Patient underwent cellular therapy _____

13. Patient underwent office screening Pap smear, cervix, which was interpreted by pathologis _____

14. Medicare patient underwent the Fern test _____

15. Provider transported portable EKG equipment to a nursing facility for the purpose of testing five patient _____

16. Patient received 10 milligrams of IV Zidovudine _____

17. Medicaid telehealth transmission _____

18. CDC 2019 Novel Coronavirus (2019-nCoV) Real-Time RT-PCR Diagnostic Panel _____

19. Aniseikonic lens, single vision _____

20. Single lens spectacle mounted low vision aid _____

8.3 – HCPCS Level II Coding and Modifiers and Units of Service Quantity

Instructions: Using the current edition of the HCPCS Level II coding manual, assign procedure, service, or supply codes, applicable HCPCS Level II modifier(s), and quantity (of units of service) to each of the following services.

1. B-12 injection not covered by Medicare, but patient agrees to pay. Patient signed "waiver of liability statement issued as required by payer policy, individual case."

   Code _____ Modifier(s) _____ Quantity _____

2. Purchase of new rolling chair with six-inch wheels. Rental declined.

   Code _____ Modifier(s) _____ Quantity _____

3. 100 reagent strips for home glucose monitor. Patient is not on insulin.

   Code _____ Modifier(s) _____ Quantity _____

4. Cervical cancer screening, including pelvic and clinical breast exam, with physician services provided in a physician-scarcity area.

   Code _____ Modifier(s) _____ Quantity _____

5. Rental of immersion external heater for nebulizer.

   Code _____ Modifier(s) _____ Quantity _____

8.4 – CPT Coding, HCPCS Level II Modifiers, and Units of Service Quantity

Instructions: Using the current editions of the CPT and HCPCS Level II coding manuals, assign procedure and service codes, applicable HCPCS Level II modifier(s), and quantity (of units of service) to each of the following scenarios.

1. Metatarsophalangeal synovectomy, third digit, left foot.

   Code _____ Modifier(s) _____ Quantity _____

2. Glucose tolerance test, three specimens (includes glucose), performed at a CLIA-waived site.

   Code _____ Modifier(s) _____ Quantity _____

3. Closed manipulation, left bimalleolar fracture, performed by physician who has opted out of Medicare.

   Code _____ Modifier(s) _____ Quantity _____

4. Anesthesiologist provides medical direction of one CRNA during radical nasal surgery.

   Code _____ Modifier(s) _____ Quantity _____

5. Clinical psychologist administered a single automated psychological test using standardized instrument and electronic platform with automated results.

   Code _____ Modifier(s) _____ Quantity _____

CMS Reimbursement Methodologies

Chapter Outline

CMS Reimbursement

CMS Fee Schedules

CMS Payment Systems

Chapter Objectives

Upon successful completion of this chapter, you should be able to:

1. Define key terms related to CMS reimbursement methodologies.
2. Compare cost-based and price-based prospective payment systems to retrospective reasonable cost systems.
3. Explain the components, rules, and differences among CMS fee schedules.
4. Summarize processes and regulations established for CMS payment systems.

Key Terms

All-Patient diagnosis-related group (AP-DRG)

All-Patient Refined diagnosis-related group (APR-DRG)

ambulance fee schedule

ambulatory payment classifications (APCs)

ambulatory surgical center (ASC)

ambulatory surgical center payment system

Ambulatory Surgical Center Quality Reporting (ASCQR) Program

balance billing

bundled payment

case mix

case-mix index

case-mix management

case rate

clinical laboratory fee schedule

CMS Quarterly Provider Update (QPU)

conversion factor

diagnosis-related groups (DRGs)

Diagnostic and Statistical Manual (DSM)

disproportionate share hospital (DSH) adjustment

durable medical equipment, prosthetics/orthotics, and supplies (DMEPOS) fee schedule

End-Stage Renal Disease prospective payment system (ESRD PPS)

episode of care (home health)

Federally Qualified Health Center (FQHC)

Federally Qualified Health Centers Prospective Payment System (FQHC PPS)

global payment

grouper software

health insurance prospective payment system (HIPPS) code set

Home Assessment Validation and Entry (HAVEN)

home health patient-driven groupings model (PDGM)

Home Health Prospective Payment System (HH PPS)

Home Health Value-Based Purchasing (HHVBP) Model

hospital-acquired condition (HAC)

Hospital-Acquired Condition (HAC) Reduction Program

hospital readmissions reduction program (HRRP)

incident to

indirect medical education (IME) adjustment

inpatient prospective payment system (IPPS)

Inpatient Psychiatric Facility Prospective Payment System (IPF PPS)

Inpatient Psychiatric Facility Quality Reporting (IPFQR) Program

Inpatient Rehabilitation Facility Prospective Payment System (IRF PPS)

Inpatient Rehabilitation Validation and Entry (IRVEN)

intensity of resources

intensity of services (IS)

IPPS 3-day payment window

IPPS 72-hour rule

IPPS transfer rule

limiting charge

long-term (acute) care hospital prospective payment system (LTCH PPS)

major diagnostic category (MDC)

Medicare physician fee schedule (MPFS)

Medicare severity diagnosis-related groups (MS-DRGs)

Medicare Summary Notice (MSN)

minimum data set (MDS)

Never Events

Outcomes and Assessment Information Set (OASIS)

outlier

outpatient encounter

Outpatient Prospective Payment System (OPPS)

outpatient visit

patient assessment instrument (PAI)

patient-driven payment model (PDPM)

pay-for-performance (P4P)

payment system

per diem

present on admission (POA)

prospective cost-based rates

prospective payment system (PPS)

prospective price-based rates

relative value units (RVUs)

Resident Assessment Validation and Entry (jRAVEN)

retrospective reasonable cost system

retrospective reimbursement methodology

risk of mortality (ROM)

severity of illness (SOI)

site of service differential

Skilled Nursing Facility Prospective Payment System (SNF PPS)

Skilled Nursing Facility Value-Based Purchasing (SNF VBP) Program

value-based purchasing (VBP)

wage index

Introduction

Since the Medicare program was implemented in 1966, expenditures have increased at an unanticipated rate, and the news media frequently report that the program will be bankrupt in a few years. In 1983, the Health Care Financing Administration (HCFA, now called CMS) implemented the first prospective payment system (PPS) to control the cost of hospital inpatient care.

In subsequent years, similar reimbursement systems were implemented for alternate care (e.g., physician office, long-term care). This chapter details CMS's reimbursement methodologies and related issues, including the data analytics and related quality reporting programs, case-mix management, CMS Fee Schedules, and CMS Payment Systems.

CMS Reimbursement

In 1964, the Johnson administration avoided opposition from hospitals for passage of the Medicare and Medicaid programs by adopting retrospective reasonable cost-basis payment arrangements originally established by BlueCross. Reimbursement according to a **retrospective reasonable cost system** or **retrospective reimbursement methodology** meant that providers reported actual charges for care after each encounter. Payers then reimbursed providers according to a fee schedule or a percentage of billed charges, or on a

TABLE 9-1 CMS reimbursement methods, year implemented, and type

Payment System	Year	Type
Ambulance Fee Schedule	2002	Cost-based
Ambulatory Surgical Center (ASC) Payment System	1994	Price-based
Clinical Laboratory Fee Schedule	1985	Cost-based
Durable Medical Equipment, Prosthetics/Orthotics, and Supplies (DMEPOS) Fee Schedule	1989	Cost-based
End-Stage Renal Disease Prospective Payment System (ESRD PPS)	2011	Price-based
Federally Qualified Health Center Prospective Payment System (FQHC PPS)	2014	Price-based
Home Health Prospective Payment System (HH PPS)	2000	Price-based
Hospice Payment Rate	1983	Cost-based
Hospital Inpatient Prospective Patient System (IPPS)	1983	Price-based
Hospital Outpatient Prospective Payment System (HOPPS)	2000	Price-based
Inpatient Psychiatric Facility Prospective Payment System (IPF PPS)	2004	Cost-based
Inpatient Rehabilitation Facility Prospective Payment System (IRF PPS)	2002	Price-based
Long-Term (Acute) Care Hospital Prospective Payment System (LTCH PPS)	2001	Price-based
Medicare Physician Fee Schedule (MPFS)[1]	1992	Cost-based
Skilled Nursing Facility Prospective Payment System (SNF PPS)	1998	Price-based

[1] MPFS was originally implemented as the Resource-Based Relative Value Scale (RBRVS) system.

per diem basis. For example, hospitals were often reimbursed 80 percent of allowed charges. Although this policy helped secure passage of Medicare and Medicaid (by enticing hospital participation), subsequent spiraling reimbursement costs ensued.

Shortly after the passage of Medicare and Medicaid, Congress began investigating a **prospective payment system (PPS)** (or *prospective reimbursement methodology*), which includes bundled payments, capitation, case rates, and global payments. A **bundled payment** is a predetermined payment amount for all services provided during an episode-of-care (e.g., inpatient hospital admission). *Capitation* is a single payment to a provider that covers for the provision of patient health care services during a specified period of time (e.g., annually, monthly), and it is typically associated with managed care. A **case rate** is a predetermined payment for an encounter, regardless of the number of services provided or length of encounter. A **global payment** is one payment that covers all services rendered by multiple providers during an episode of care.

CMS created payment systems (Table 9-1), which established predetermined rates based on patient category or the type of facility (with annual increases based on an inflation index and a geographic wage index):

- **Prospective cost-based rates** are established in advance, but they are based on reported health care costs (charges) from which a predetermined *per diem* (Latin meaning "for each day") rate is determined (e.g., ambulance fee schedule). Annual rates are usually adjusted using actual costs from the prior year.

- **Prospective price-based rates** are associated with a particular category of patient (e.g., inpatients), and rates are established prior to the provision of health care procedures and services (e.g., diagnosis-related groups [DRGs] for inpatient care).

📝 **NOTE:**

According to the American Enterprise Institute for Public Policy Research, in 1966, Medicare cost $3 billion. At that time, Congress's House Ways and Means Committee estimated that by 1990 Medicare would cost $12 billion (adjusting for inflation). However, in 1990, Medicare actually cost $107 billion.

> **Example:** Prior to 1983, acute care hospitals generated invoices based on total charges for an inpatient stay. In 1982, an eight-day inpatient hospitalization at $225 per day (including ancillary service charges) would be billed $1,800. This *per diem* reimbursement rate actually discouraged hospitals from limiting inpatient lengths of stay. In 1983, the hospital would have been reimbursed a PPS rate of $950 for the same inpatient hospitalization, regardless of length of stay. The PPS rate encourages hospitals to limit inpatient lengths of stay because any reimbursement received in excess of the actual cost of providing care is retained by the facility. (In this example, if the $950 PPS rate had been paid in 1980, the hospital would have absorbed the $850 loss.)

Effective October 2007, CMS no longer provides reimbursement for additional costs associated with the treatment of preventable errors, including those considered **Never Events**, which are medical errors that should never occur (e.g., wrong site surgery) and adverse events that are unambiguous (clearly identifiable and measurable), serious (resulting in death or significant disability), and usually preventable. *Never Events* consist of serious reportable events that are grouped into categories:

- Care management events
- Criminal events
- Environmental events
- Patient protection events
- Product or device events
- Radiologic events
- Surgical or procedural events

Never Events are also publicly reported, with goals of improving qualify of care and increasing provider accountability, and many states have also mandated their reporting. Health care facilities are accountable for correcting systematic problems that contributed to the event, with some states (e.g., Minnesota) mandating performance of a root cause analysis and reporting its results. (*Root cause analysis [RCA]* is is a structured method used to analyze serious adverse events, with the goal of identifying what happened, why it happened, and how to prevent it from happening again. It is conducted as part of a facility's quality assurance and performance improvement [QAPI] program.)

Effective October 2008, CMS implemented legislation and a number of **value-based purchasing (VBP)** programs in an effort to link Medicare payments a value-based system for the purpose of promoting better clinical outcomes for patients by improving health care quality. (Content about the VBP associated with each payment system is located in this chapter.)

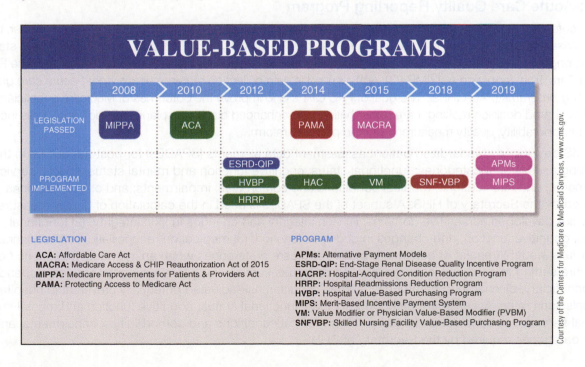

Data Analytics

Data analytics for revenue management uses information collected about claims and actual costs of health care provided, patient clinical data, patient satisfaction surveys, and research studies to assist health care facilities and providers make decisions about facility size, types of health care services offered, staffing needs, and more. The Centers for Medicare and Medicaid Services (CMS) website (www.cms.gov) contains many resources, such as Medicare Utilization for both Part A and Part B services. Data are often presented in table format, and they are ranked in order from the highest to the lowest allowed charge and allowed services. Types of data available include HCPCS codes according to specialty and type of service codes.

Example: A health information management (HIM) professional is tasked with: (1) collecting data about revenue generated from paid claims for the month of January and actual costs incurred by the facility in providing health care services to that patient population, and (2) conducting data analytics of the generated report. Facility leadership had identified a higher than previously calculated case-mix index, which means patient severity of illness and intensity of services has increased. They are interested in determining the root cause by applying data analytics.

The HIM professional worked with the information technology (IT) department to generate a report that contains needed data, which includes number of patients treated, cost of providing treatment, reimbursement received from third-party payers,and types of patient services provided. The initial data report included totals for each data element, and the HIM professional continued to work with the IT department to generate a more detailed report that contained itemized data about costs, reimbursement received, and patient services; in addition, totals for each grouping of patient services was generated.

The final data report was comprehensive, and the HIM professional then conducted data analysis, which required review and interpretation of data in the report to identify patterns and possible trends. Upon completion, the HIM professional submitted a data analytics report to facility leadership, which was tasked with examining the patterns and possible trends to determine how clinical care could be improved while limiting excessive costs.

Because the goal is to provide quality patient care at affordable costs, facility leadership also received a clinical data report generated from the electronic health record system and a patient satisfaction survey report so that these results (e.g., incidence of nosocomial infections, patient preferences) could be included in the examination process. Leadership examination results in an evaluative process, which greatly assists in the decision-making process about services to add or discontinue, staffing needs for services provided, and so on.

Post-Acute Care Quality Reporting Program

Post-acute care (PAC) includes rehabilitation or palliative services that Medicare beneficiaries receive after, or in some cases instead of, a stay in an acute care hospital. The intensity of patient care indicates whether a stay in a facility, ongoing outpatient therapy, or care provided at home is required. In 2014, the Improving Medicare Post-Acute Care Transformation Act (IMPACT Act) resulted in data collection requirements for *post-acute care quality reporting programs* (PAC QRPs). The goal of PAC QRPs is to improve the outcomes of Medicare beneficiaries through shared decision making, care coordination, and enhanced discharge planning. Additional goals include data interoperability, quality measurement, and payment reform.

CMS developed standardized patient assessment data elements (SPADEs) for post-acute care in the following assessment categories: functional status; cognitive function and mental status; special services, treatments, and interventions; medical conditions and comorbities; impairments; and other categories required by the Secretary of HHS. A subset of the SPADEs is used in the calculation of quality measures that were developed across five domains: (1) skin integrity and changes in skin integrity; (2) functional status, cognitive function, and changes in cognitive function; (3) medication reconciliation; (4) incidence of major falls; and (5) transfer of health information and care preferences when an individual transitions from one care setting to another. Resource use and other measures include total estimated Medicare spending per beneficiary, discharge to community, and all-condition risk-adjusted potentially preventable hospital readmissions rates. Assessment categories include: functional status; cognitive function and mental status; special services, treatments, and interventions; medical conditions and comorbidities; impairments; and other categories required by the Secretary of DHHS.

Assessment instruments for each type of PAC setting include the following:

- Home health agency (HHA): Outcome and Assessment Information Set (OASIS)

- Hospice: Item set (HIS)

- Inpatient rehabilitation facility (IRF): IRF patient care assessment instrument (IRF-PAI)

- Long-term care hospital (LTCH): LTCH Continuity Assessment Record and Evaluation Data Set (LTCH CARE Data Set or LCDS)

- Skilled nursing facility (SNF): Resident Assessment Intrument (RAI) and Minimum Data Set (MDS)

Content about reimbursement methodologies and the collection of SPADE for quality measures for each type of PAC setting is included later in this chapter.

Example: A Medicare patient is transferred from an acute inpatient hospital setting to a home health agency (HHA), and discharge planning requires that a list of the patient's medications be provided to the patient, family, or caregiver. The OASIS patient assessment instrument for home health agency care includes SPADE quality measures for *Provision of Current Reconciled Medication List to Patient at Discharge and Route of Current Reconciled Medication List Transmission to Patient.*

The patient is interviewed by the HHA and asked whether a current reconciled medication list was provided to the patient, family, or caregiver, and the response is indicated as Yes or No on the OASIS patient assessment instrument. The transmission method of the medication list is also determined, such as EHR, health information exchange organization, verbal (e.g., in-person, telephone, video conference), paper-based (e.g., copy, fax, printout), or some other method (e.g., compact disk or thumb drive, email, text).

OASIS data about the provision of patient medication lists generates statistical data about this SPADE quality measure, and it is used to determine with the discharge planning requirement. Statistical results may reveal that all patients are provided with a medication list upon discharge from an acute inpatient hospital setting to HHA care, but the method of transmission may be problematic. Or, statistical results may reveal noncompliance, and HHA professionals would then determine reasons for noncompliance and work with the acute inpatient hospital setting to ensure future compliance with the discharge planning requirement of providing a patient's medication list.

Case-Mix Management

With implementation of prospective payment systems, **case-mix management** has become an important function of revenue management because it allows health care facilities and providers to determine anticipated health care needs by reviewing data analytics about types and/or categories of patients treated.

The term **case mix** describes a health care organization's patient population and is based on a number of characteristics, such as age, diagnosis, gender, resources consumed, risk factors, treatments received, and type of health insurance. A facility's case mix reflects the diversity, clinical complexity, and resource needs of the patient population.

A **case-mix index** is the relative weight assigned for a facility's patient population, and it is used in a formula to calculate health care reimbursement. If 1.000 represents an average relative weight, a weight lower than 1.000 (such as 0.9271) indicates that the resource needs of a hospital's patient population are less complex. A facility's case-mix index is calculated by totaling all relative weights for a period of time and dividing by the total number of patients treated during that period of time. (The facility's case-mix index is not used in the calculation of payments because it is determined after reimbursement has been received.) Thus, a facility assigned a lower case-mix index will receive less reimbursement for services provided. Conversely, a facility assigned a higher case-mix index will receive higher reimbursement for services provided. For example, a hospital's case-mix index is calculated by totaling all DRG relative weights for a period of time and dividing by the total number of patients treated during that period of time. (A list of DRG relative weights can be found at www.cms.gov.)

Facilities typically calculate statistics for case-mix management purposes as:

- Total relative weight (relative weight × total number of cases)

- Total payment (reimbursement amount per case × total number of cases)

Example: Hospital inpatients are classified according to Medicare-severity diagnosis-related groups (MS-DRGs) based on principal and secondary diagnosis, surgical procedures performed, age, discharge status, medical complexity (e.g., existence of comorbidities and/or complications), and resource needs. Each MS-DRG has a relative weight associated with it, and that weight is related to the complexity of patient resource needs. Anywhere Medical Center's overall case-mix index (relative weight) is 1.110. In January, MS-DRG 436 had 54 cases with a reimbursement amount of $3,100 each and a relative weight of 1.135.

- Total relative weight for MS-DRG 123 is 61.29 (1.135 × 54)
- Total payment for MS-DRG 123 is $167,400 (54 × $3,100)

CMS Primary Care Initiative: Primary Care First and Direct Contracting

In 2019, CMS implemented the *CMS Primary Care Initiative*, which provides primary care practices and other providers with *primary care first (PCF)* and *direct contracting (DC)* payment model options. Both models incentivize providers to reduce hospital utilization and total cost of care by potentially significantly rewarding them through performance-based payment adjustments. The models seek to improve quality of care, specifically patients' experiences of care and key outcome-based clinical quality measures, which may include controlling high blood pressure, managing diabetes mellitus, and screening for colorectal cancer.

The primary care first (PCF) payment models test whether financial risk and performance based payments that reward primary care practitioners and other clinicians for easily understood, actionable outcomes will reduce total Medicare expenditures, preserve or enhance quality of care, and improve patient health outcomes. PCF will provide payment to practices through a simplified total monthly payment that allows clinicians to focus on caring for patients rather than their revenue cycle. PCF also includes a payment model option that provides higher payments to practices that specialize in care for high need patients, including those with complex, chronic needs and seriously ill populations (SIP).

While PCF models are focused on individual primary care practice sites, the direct contracting (DC) payment models aim to engage a wider variety of organizations that have experience taking on financial risk and serving larger patient populations (e.g., Accountable Care Organizations, Medicare Advantage plans, Medicaid managed care organizations). Depending on the DC contracting payment model, the model participant will receive a fixed monthly payment that can range from a portion of anticipated primary care costs to the total cost of care.

All five payment model options focus on supporting care for patients who have chronic conditions and serious illnesses. Through the primary care first payment model, high need patients with serious illnesses who do not have a primary care practitioner or care coordination and indicate an interest in receiving care from a practice participating in the model will be assigned to a model participant. Participating practices that choose to care for seriously ill populations (SIP) of patients will be required to provide care to clinically stabilize the patient. All payment model options include enhancements to encourage participation of providers who are focused on care for these populations.

CMS Payment Systems

The federal government administers several health care programs, some of which require services to be reimbursed according to a predetermined reimbursement methodology (**payment system**). Federal health care programs (an overview of each is located in Chapter 2) include the following:

- CHAMPVA
- Indian Health Service (IHS)
- Medicaid (including the State Children's Health Insurance Program, or SCHIP)

- Medicare
- TRICARE (formerly CHAMPUS)
- Workers' Compensation (also a state health care program)

Depending on the type of health care services provided to beneficiaries, the federal government requires that one of the payment systems listed in Table 9-1 be used for the CHAMPVA, Medicaid, Medicare, and TRICARE programs.

Changes to CMS Reimbursement Methods

Ongoing development and evaluation of CMS reimbursement methods result in changes made to them on at least an annual basis. Such changes impact each payment system by implementing new regulations.

> **Example 1:** The implementation of Medicare Severity DRGs (MS-DRGs) in fiscal year 2008 replaced traditional CMS DRGs because of the need for a payment system that focused on more than just inpatient resource intensity. (DRGs and MS-DRGs are covered later in this chapter.)

> **Example 2:** The *three-day payment window* statutory provision in fiscal year 2011 covers the three days prior to or after an inpatient admission for which an IPPS payment is generated. The provision requires a hospital (or entities wholly owned or operated by the hospital) to include the following on an inpatient beneficiary's claim: diagnoses, procedures, and charges for all outpatient diagnostic services and admission-related outpatient nondiagnostic services furnished to the beneficiary during the three-day payment window. This resulted in policies pertaining to admission-related outpatient nondiagnostic services more consistent with common hospital billing practices and made no changes to the existing policy regarding billing of outpatient diagnostic services.
>
> A similar *one-day payment window* statutory provision applies to a hospital *not paid under the IPPS,* such as psychiatric hospitals and units, inpatient rehabilitation hospitals and units, long-term care hospitals, children's hospitals, and cancer hospitals; thus, the statutory payment window for such hospitals is one day *preceding* the date of the patient's admission.

> **Example 3:** A new Federally Qualified Health Center Prospective Payment System (FQHC PPS) was implemented in 2010. (FQHC PPS is covered later in this chapter.)

 NOTE:

MS-DRGs and the three-day payment window are explained in greater detail later in this chapter.

CMS Fee Schedules

A *fee schedule* is a comprehensive listing of fee maximums used to reimburse providers and suppliers on a fee-for-service basis. CMS develops fee schedules for ambulance services; clinical laboratory services; durable medical equipment, prosthetics, orthotics and supplies; and physicians.

Ambulance Fee Schedule

The Balanced Budget Act of 1997 required establishment of an **ambulance fee schedule** payment system for ambulance services provided to Medicare beneficiaries. Starting in April 2002, the ambulance fee schedule was phased in over a five-year period replacing a retrospective reasonable cost payment system for providers and suppliers of ambulance services (because such a wide variation of payment rates resulted for the same service). This schedule requires:

- Ambulance suppliers to accept Medicare assignment
- Reporting of HCPCS codes on claims for ambulance services
- Establishment of increased payment under the fee schedule for ambulance services furnished in rural areas based on the location of the beneficiary at the time the beneficiary is placed onboard the ambulance
- Revision of the certification requirements for coverage of nonemergency ambulance services
- Medicare to pay for beneficiary transportation services when other means of transportation are contraindicated. Ambulance services are divided into different levels of ground (land and water transportation) and air ambulance services based on the medically necessary treatment provided during transport

Example: A patient is transported by ambulance from home to the local hospital for care. Under the retrospective reasonable cost payment system, the ambulance company charges $600, and Medicare pays 80 percent of that amount, or $480. The ambulance fee schedule requires Medicare to reimburse the ambulance company $425, which is an amount equal to the predetermined rate or *fee schedule*.

Clinical Laboratory Fee Schedule

The Deficit Reduction Act of 1984 established the Medicare **clinical laboratory fee schedule** (Figure 9-1), which is a data set based on local fee schedules (for outpatient clinical diagnostic laboratory services). Medicare reimburses laboratory services according to the (1) submitted charge, (2) national limitation amount, or (3) local fee schedule amount, whichever is lowest. The local fee schedules are developed by Medicare administrative contractors who are:

- Local contractors that process Medicare Part B claims, including claims submitted by independent laboratories and physician office laboratories
- Local contractors that process Medicare Part A claims, including outpatient laboratory tests performed by hospitals, nursing homes, and end-stage renal disease centers

Clinical Diagnostic Laboratory Fee Schedule
12/10/YYYY

CPT Code	Modifier	National Limit	Mid Point	N.Y.S. Rate	Short Description of HCPCS Code
78267		$10.98	$14.84	$10.98	Breath test attain/anal c-14
78268		$94.11	$127.18	$94.11	Breath test analysis, c-14
80048		$11.83	$15.98	$11.83	Basic metabolic panel
80051		$9.80	$13.24	$8.93	Electrolyte panel
80053		$14.77	$19.96	$14.77	Comprehensive metabolic panel
80061		$0.00	$0.00	$15.88	Lipid panel
80061	-QW	$0.00	$0.00	$15.88	Lipid panel
80069		$12.13	$16.39	$12.13	Renal function panel
80074		$0.00	$0.00	$64.46	Acute hepatitis panel
80076		$11.42	$15.43	$11.42	Hepatic function panel

Current Procedural Terminology published by the American Medical Association.

FIGURE 9-1 Sample clinical lab fee schedule data (modifier -QW is reported for a CLIA-waived laboratory test).

Durable Medical Equipment, Prosthetics/Orthotics, and Supplies Fee Schedule

The Deficit Reduction Act of 1984 also established the Medicare **durable medical equipment, prosthetics/orthotics, and supplies (DMEPOS) fee schedule** (Figure 9-2). Medicare reimburses DMEPOS either 80 percent of the actual charge for the item *or* the fee schedule amount, whichever is lower. (Fee schedule amounts are annually updated and legislated by Congress.)

The *Medicare Prescription Drug, Improvement, and Modernization Act of 2003 (MMA)* authorized Medicare to replace the current durable medical equipment (DME) payment methodology for *certain items* with a competitive acquisition process to improve the effectiveness of its methodology for establishing DME payment amounts. The new bidding process established payment amounts for certain durable medical equipment, enteral nutrition, and off-the-shelf orthotics. Competitive bidding provides a way to create incentives for suppliers to provide quality items and services in an efficient manner and at reasonable cost.

Durable Medical Equipment, Prosthetics, Orthotics, and Supplies (DMEPOS)
8/16/YYYY

HCPCS Code	Modifier	Jurisdiction[1]	Category[2]	Ceiling[3]	Floor[4]	N.Y.S. Rate	Short Description of HCPCS Code
A4217		D	SU	$3.13	$2.66	$2.66	Sterile water/saline, 500 mL
A4217	-AU	D	OS	$3.13	$2.66	$2.66	Sterile water/saline, 500 mL
A4221		D	SU	$22.64	$19.24	$22.64	Supplies for maint drug infus cath, per wk.
A4222		D	SU	$46.73	$39.72	$46.73	External drug infusion pump supplies, per cassette or bag
A4253		D	IN	$38.52	$32.74	$38.52	Blood glucose/reagent strips, per 50
A4255		D	SU	$4.11	$3.49	$4.11	Glucose monitor platforms, 50 per box

[1]**Jursidiction**
D (Regional DME MAC jurisdiction)
L (Local Part B administrative contractor jurisdiction)
J (Joint regional DME MAC/local MAC jurisdiction)

[2]**Category**
IN (inexpensive and other routinely purchased items)
FS (frequently serviced items)
CR (capped rental items)
OX (oxygen and oxygen equipment)
OS (ostomy, tracheostomy, & urological items)
SD (surgical dressings)
PO (prosthetics & orthotics)
SU (supplies)
TE (transcutaneous electrical nerve stimulators)

[3]**Ceiling** (maximum fee schedule amount)

[4]**Floor** (minimum fee schedule amount)

FIGURE 9-2 Sample DMEPOS fee schedule data.

NOTE:

A valid ICD-10-CM diagnosis code must be reported for each line item on electronically submitted claims. If an electronic claim that is submitted to a regional DME MAC does not contain a valid ICD-10-CM diagnosis code, it will be rejected.

Medicare Physician Fee Schedule

As of 1992, physician services and procedures are reimbursed according to a payment system originally known as the *Resource-Based Relative Value Scale (RBRVS)* system. The RBRVS system replaced the Medicare physician payment system of "customary, prevailing, and reasonable" (CPR) charges under which physicians were reimbursed according to the historical record of the charge for the provision of each service. This system, now called the **Medicare physician fee schedule (MPFS)**, reimburses providers an allowed amount according to predetermined rates assigned to services and is revised by CMS each year. All services are standardized to measure the value of a service as compared with other services provided. These standards, called **relative value units (RVUs)**, use the following components that determine MPFS pricing amounts that are adjusted to reflect the variation of practice costs from area to area.

- *Physician work*, which reflects the physician's time and intensity in providing the service (e.g., judgment, technical skill, and physical effort)
- *Practice expense*, which reflects overhead costs involved in providing a service (e.g., rent, utilities, equipment, and staff salaries)
- *Malpractice expense*, which reflects malpractice expenses (e.g., costs of liability insurance)

 NOTE:

Most third-party payers, including state Medicaid programs, have adopted aspects of the MPFS.

Payment limits were also established by adjusting the RVUs for each locality by geographic adjustment factors (GAF), called *geographic cost practice indices (GCPIs)*, so that Medicare providers are paid differently in each state and also within each state (e.g., New York state has five separate payment localities). An annual **conversion factor** (dollar multiplier) converts RVUs into payments using a formula (Figure 9-3).

Although the Medicare physician fee schedule is used to determine payment for Medicare Part B (physician) services, other services, such as anesthesia, pathology/laboratory, and radiology, require special consideration.

- Anesthesia services payments are based on the actual time an anesthesiologist spends with a patient and the American Society of Anesthesiologists' relative value system.
- Radiology services payments vary according to place of service (e.g., hospital radiology department vs. freestanding radiology center).
- Pathology services payments vary according to the number of patients served:
  - Pathology services that include clinical laboratory management and supervision of technologists are covered and paid as hospital services.
  - Pathology services that are directed to an individual patient in a hospital setting (e.g., pathology consultation) are paid under the physician fee schedule.

The *Medicare Access and CHIP Reauthorization Act of 2015 (MACRA)* repealed the long-standing sustainable growth rate (SGR) methodology for updating the Medicare physician fee schedule (MPFS) by establishing the *Quality Payment Program*, which include MIPS and APMs. All MPFS updates will be based on either the Merit-based Incentive Payment System (MIPS) or provider participation in qualified Alternative Payment Models (APMs). MIPS combines parts of the *Physician Quality Reporting System (PQRS)*, the *Value Modifier (VM)* or *Physician*

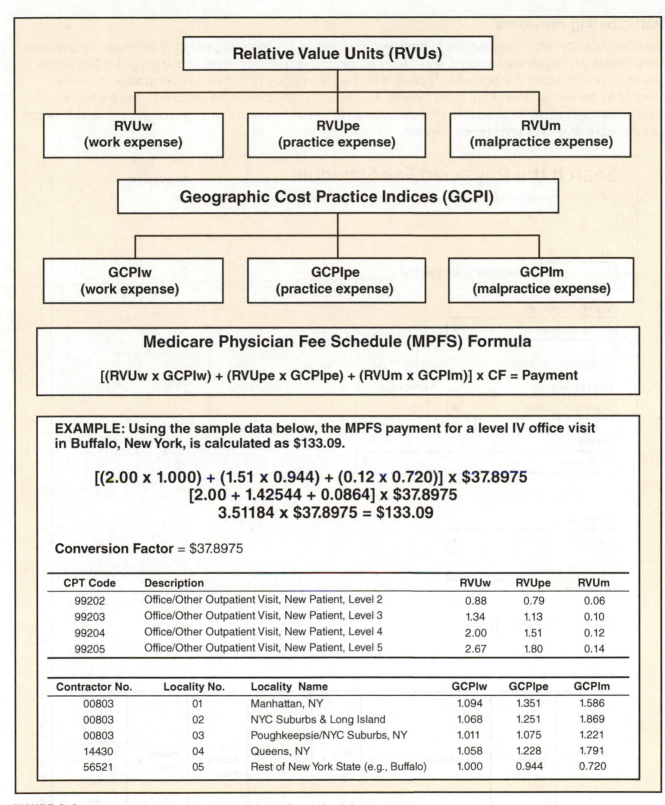

Relative Value Units (RVUs)

| RVUw (work expense) | RVUpe (practice expense) | RVUm (malpractice expense) |

Geographic Cost Practice Indices (GCPI)

| GCPIw (work expense) | GCPIpe (practice expense) | GCPIm (malpractice expense) |

Medicare Physician Fee Schedule (MPFS) Formula

[(RVUw x GCPIw) + (RVUpe x GCPIpe) + (RVUm x GCPIm)] x CF = Payment

EXAMPLE: Using the sample data below, the MPFS payment for a level IV office visit in Buffalo, New York, is calculated as $133.09.

$$[(2.00 \times 1.000) + (1.51 \times 0.944) + (0.12 \times 0.720)] \times \$37.8975$$
$$[2.00 + 1.42544 + 0.0864] \times \$37.8975$$
$$3.51184 \times \$37.8975 = \$133.09$$

Conversion Factor = $37.8975

CPT Code	Description	RVUw	RVUpe	RVUm
99202	Office/Other Outpatient Visit, New Patient, Level 2	0.88	0.79	0.06
99203	Office/Other Outpatient Visit, New Patient, Level 3	1.34	1.13	0.10
99204	Office/Other Outpatient Visit, New Patient, Level 4	2.00	1.51	0.12
99205	Office/Other Outpatient Visit, New Patient, Level 5	2.67	1.80	0.14

Contractor No.	Locality No.	Locality Name	GCPIw	GCPIpe	GCPIm
00803	01	Manhattan, NY	1.094	1.351	1.586
00803	02	NYC Suburbs & Long Island	1.068	1.251	1.869
00803	03	Poughkeepsie/NYC Suburbs, NY	1.011	1.075	1.221
14430	04	Queens, NY	1.058	1.228	1.791
56521	05	Rest of New York State (e.g., Buffalo)	1.000	0.944	0.720

FIGURE 9-3 Formula for determining physician fee schedule payments.

Value-based Modifier (PVBM) programs, and the *Medicare Electronic Health Record (EHR)* incentive program into one single program. This allows providers to earn a performance-based payment adjustment that considers quality, resource use, clinical practice improvement, and meaningful use of certified EHR technology.

Participating Providers

Medicare typically calculates payment to *participating providers (PARs)* as 80 percent of the Medicare physician fee schedule (MPFS) allowed amount, and the beneficiary (patient) is responsible for the remaining 20 percent. The *Medicare Physician Fee Schedule Look-up* tool at www.cms.gov provides information about services covered by the MPFS. Data about more than 10,000 physician services can be searched using the tool to display results (Figure 9-4). Search results are reviewed to determine pricing, limiting charges, conversion factors, associated relative value units (when relevant).

Search the Physician Fee Schedule

Data Updated: 01/20/2021

Use this search to view adjusted pricing amounts that reflect variations in pricing costs from area to area.

Select search parameters.

Year

2021

See notes for selected year

Type of Information

Pricing Information

Select Healthcare Common Procedural Coding System (HCPCS) criteria.

HCPCS Criteria	**HCPCS Code**
Single HCPCS Code	99213

Modifier

All Modifiers

Select Medicare Administrative Contractor (MAC) option.

MAC Option

National Payment Amount

Search fees   Reset search inputs

Search Results

● Show default columns   ○ Show all columns

Showing 1 - 1 of 1

HCPCS Code ▲	Modifier ▲	Short Description ⇕	Proc Stat ▲	Mac Locality ▲	Non-Facility Price ⇕	Facility Price ⇕	Non-Facility Limiting Charge ◀
99213		Office o/p est low 20-29 min	A	0000000	$92.47	$68.04	$101.02

FIGURE 9-4 Medicare physician fee schedule search (containing sample data).

Nonparticipating Providers

The nonparticipating provider (nonPAR) allowed amount is calculated as a 5 percent reduction of the Medicare physician fee schedule (MPFS) amount. In addition, when the nonPAR does not *accept assignment* Medicare requires the nonPAR to bill the patient no more than the difference between what Medicare reimburses and the **limiting charge**, which is calculated by multiplying the *reduced* MPFS by 115 percent.

 NOTE:

Quality payment program (QPP) about APMs, MIPS, QRS, and VM (or VBPM) content is located in Chapter 2.

Use the following formula to calculate the limiting charge and the amount the patient owes for a nonPAR who does not accept assignment:

[MPFS – (MPFS × 5 percent)] × 115 percent = limiting charge

For example, [$80 – ($80 × 5 percent)] × 115 percent = $76 × 115 percent = $87.40 (limiting charge).

(Medicare reimburses the nonPAR based on the $76 reduced MPFS amount, which is 80 percent of the reduced MPFS, or $60.80 [$76 × 0.80]. The patient is responsible for reimbursing the nonPAR for the difference between what Medicare reimburses the nonPAR and the limiting charge, or $26.60, which includes any copayment [$87.40 – $60.80].)

The **Medicare Summary Notice (MSN)** (Figure 9-5) notifies Medicare beneficiaries of actions taken on claims. Limiting charge information appears on the MSN, and the Medicare policy is intended to reduce the amount patients enrolled in Medicare are expected to pay when they receive health care services. If a participating (PAR) and a nonparticipating (nonPAR) physician charge the same fee for an office visit, amounts billed and reimbursement received are different for each physician.

Example: A PAR and nonPAR physician each charge $50 for an office visit (CPT code 99213). The Medicare physician fee schedule for CPT code 99213 is $40. The nonPAR 5 percent reduction of the MPFS rate is $38, and the limiting charge is $43.70 ($38 × 115 percent).

The PAR physician is reimbursed:

Medicare payment (80 percent of $40)	$32.00
Beneficiary coinsurance (20 percent of $40)	+ $8.00
TOTAL REIMBURSEMENT TO PAR $40.00	

The nonPAR physician is reimbursed:

Medicare payment (80 percent of $38)	$30.40
Beneficiary is billed the balance of the $43.70 limiting charge	+ $13.30
TOTAL REIMBURSEMENT TO NONPAR	$43.70

Generally, participating physicians report their actual fees to Medicare but adjust, or write off, the uncollectible portion of the charge when they receive payment. NonPAR physicians usually report only the *limiting charge* as their fee. Billing write-off or adjustment amounts to beneficiaries is called **balance billing** and is prohibited by Medicare regulations. In the preceding example, using CPT code 99213, the write-off amounts are:

Participating physician	$10.00 (because $50 – $40 = $10)
NonPAR physician	$6.30 (because $50 – $43.70 = $6.30)

The patient pays $5.30 more ($13.30 – $8 = $5.30) to the nonPAR, which can be significant for people living on a fixed income. Beneficiaries frequently ask, "Does the physician participate in Medicare?" when calling for an appointment. With very few exceptions, people who qualify for Medicare are not allowed to purchase other primary health insurance. CMS must be certain that Medicare beneficiaries are not required to pay excessive out-of-pocket amounts for health care services. To protect Medicare enrollees financially, providers must comply with extensive rules and regulations.

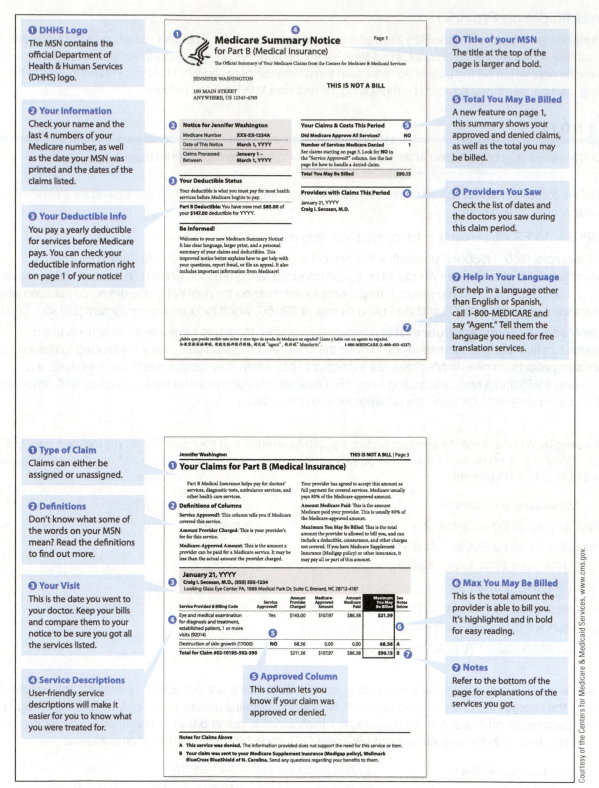

FIGURE 9-5 Sample Pages from Medicare Summary Notice (MSN) for Medicare Part B.

Nonphysician Practitioners

Medicare reimburses professional services provided by nonphysician practitioners, including nurse practitioners, clinical nurse specialists, and physician assistants.

Nonphysician practitioner reimbursement rules include the following:

- Reimbursement for services provided by nonphysician practitioners is allowed *only* if no facility or other provider is paid in connection with such services.

- Payment is based on 80 percent of the actual charge or 85 percent of the Medicare physician fee schedule, whichever is less. Medicare reimburses 80 percent of the resultant payment, and the patient pays 20 percent.

- Direct payment can be made to the nonphysician practitioner, the employer, or the contractor (except for services provided by PAs, for which payment *must* be made to the employer).

- If nonphysician practitioners provide services outside of the office setting, they must obtain their own Medicare provider numbers.

- Services provided by nonphysician practitioners may also be reported to Medicare as **incident to** the supervising physician's service. (Nonphysician practitioners *do not* have to have their own Medicare provider numbers when billing incident-to services.) *Incident-to* services are reimbursed at 100 percent of the Medicare physician fee schedule, and Medicare pays 80 percent of that amount directly to the physician.

- Reimbursement is available for services provided by nonphysician practitioners who work *in collaboration with* a physician (e.g., DO or MD), which means that a written agreement is in place specifying the services to be provided by the nonphysician practitioner, who must work with one or more physicians to deliver health care services. These providers receive medical direction and appropriate supervision as required by state law.

 NOTE:

Nonphysician practitioners that bill Medicare under an incident-to provision report the physician's provider number on the CMS-1500 claim (instead of their own provider number). This provision is based on the Medicare regulation that permits billing of ancillary personnel services under the physician's provider number (e.g., office EKG performed by a medical assistant).

The types of services nonphysician practitioners provide include those traditionally reserved to physicians, such as physical examination, minor surgery, setting casts for simple fractures, interpreting x-rays, and other activities that involve independent evaluation or treatment of the patient's condition. Also, if authorized under the scope of their state licenses, nonphysician practitioners may furnish services billed under all levels of evaluation and management codes and diagnostic tests *if furnished in collaboration with a physician*.

 NOTE:

The collaborating physician need not be present when the nonphysician practitioner provides services to patients, and the physician does not have to independently evaluate each patient seen by the nonphysician practitioner. The written agreement must be made available to Medicare upon request, and any services provided by the nonphysician practitioner that are not included in the agreement cannot be billed to Medicare.

Location of Service Adjustment

Physicians are usually reimbursed on a fee-for-service basis with payments established by the Medicare physician fee schedule (MPFS) based on the RBRVS system. When physician or other qualified health care professional office-based services are performed in a facility, such as a hospital or outpatient setting, MPFS payments are reduced because the physician or other qualified health care professional did not provide supplies, utilities, or the costs of running the facility. This is known as the **site of service differential**. Other rules govern the services performed by hospital-based providers and teaching physicians. This chapter discusses rules that affect private practice physicians and other qualified health care professionals billing under the MPFS.

CMS Manual System

The Centers for Medicare and Medicaid Services (CMS) publish Internet-only manuals (IOMs) (e.g., Medicare Claims Processing Manual) on their website. The manuals include CMS program issuances (e.g., transmittals, national coverage determinations, and so on), day-to-day operating instructions, policies, and procedures that are based on statutes, regulations, guidelines, models, and directives. The CMS program components, providers, contractors, Medicare Advantage organizations, and state survey agencies use the IOMs to administer CMS programs. They are also a good source of Medicare and Medicaid information for the general public.

CMS transmittals communicate new or changed policies and/or procedures that are being incorporated into a specific CMS Internet-only program manual. The **CMS Quarterly Provider Update (QPU)** is an online CMS publication that contains information about regulations and major policies currently under development, regulations and major policies completed or canceled, and new or revised manual instructions.

CMS Payment Systems

CMS payment systems include the composite rate payment system and prospective payment systems, as follows:

- Ambulatory surgical center payment rates
- End-stage renal disease composite rate payment system
- Federally qualified health centers prospective payment system
- Home health prospective payment system
- Hospital inpatient prospective payment system
- Hospice payment system
- Hospital outpatient prospective payment system
- Inpatient psychiatric facility prospective payment system
- Inpatient rehabilitation facility prospective payment system
- Long-term (acute) care hospital prospective payment system
- Skilled nursing facility prospective payment system

Ambulatory Surgical Center Payment System

An **ambulatory surgical center (ASC)** is a state-licensed, Medicare-certified supplier (not provider) of surgical health care services that must *accept assignment* on Medicare claims. An ASC must be a separate entity distinguishable from any other entity or facility, and it must have its own employer identifier number (EIN) as well as processes for:

- Accreditation
- Administrative functions
- Clinical services
- Financial and accounting systems
- Governance (of medical staff)
- Professional supervision
- Recordkeeping
- State licensure

An ASC can be physically located within a health care organization and still be considered separate for Medicare reimbursement purposes if all the preceding criteria are met. Hospital-based ASCs submit the UB-04 claim, while freestanding ASCs usually submit the CMS-1500 claim.

In 1980, Medicare authorized implementation of *ambulatory surgical center payment rates* as a fee paid to ambulatory surgery centers (ASCs) for facility services furnished in connection with performing certain surgical procedures. (Physician's professional services are separately reimbursed by the Medicare physician fee schedule.)

Effective January 1, 2008, the MMA of 2003 mandated implementation of a revised **ambulatory surgical center payment system** that uses the outpatient prospective payment system (OPPS) relative payment weights as a guide for ASC reimbursement. Medicare allows payment of an ASC facility fee for any surgical procedure performed at an ASC, *except those surgical procedures that Medicare has determined are not eligible for the ASC facility fee*. This means that instead of maintaining and updating an "inclusive list of procedures," Medicare maintains and updates an "exclusionary list of procedures" for which an ASC facility fee would *not* be paid (e.g., any procedure included on the OPPS inpatient list).

Under the payment system (Table 9-2), Medicare uses the ambulatory payment classification (APC) groups and relative payment weights for surgical procedures established under the OPPS as the basis of the payment groups and the relative payment weights for surgical procedures performed at ASCs. Relative payment weights are based on the average resources used to treat patients in a particular APC, with a weight of 1.000 being the average; when a relative payment weight is higher than 1.000, such as 1.435, that means more resources are required to treat the patient and, thus, the payment is correspondingly higher. These payment weights would be multiplied by an ASC conversion factor to calculate the ASC payment rates.

The ASC relative payment weights are updated each year using the national OPPS relative payment weights for that calendar year and, for office-based procedures, the practice expense payments under the physician fee schedule for that calendar year. Medicare makes the relative payment weights budget neutral to ensure that changes in the relative payment weights from year to year do not cause the estimated amount of expenditures to ASCs to increase or decrease as a function of those changes.

TABLE 9-2 Sample list of Medicare-approved ASC procedures under ASC payment system

HCPCS CODE	HCPCS Code Description	ASC Relative Payment Weight	ASC Facility Fee Payment	Patient Copayment
G0104	Colorectal cancer screening; flexible sigmoidoscopy	1.7292	$68.63	$13.73
G0105	Colorectal cancer screening; colonoscopy on individual at high risk	7.8134	$310.10	$62.02
G0121	Colorectal cancer screening; colonoscopy on individual not meeting criteria for high risk	7.8134	$310.10	$62.02
G0127	Trimming of dystrophic nails, any number	0.2665	$10.58	$2.12
G0186	Destruction of localized lesion of choroid (for example, choroidal neovascularization); photocoagulation, feeder vessel technique (one or more sessions)	4.0750	$161.73	$32.35
G0260	Injection procedure for sacroiliac joint; provision of anesthetic, steroid, and/or other therapeutic agent, with or without arthrography	5.5439	$220.03	$44.01
G0268	Removal of impacted cerumen (one or both ears) by physician on same date of service as audiologic function testing	0.5409	$21.47	$4.29

Ambulatory Surgical Center Quality Reporting (ASCQR) Program

The **Ambulatory Surgical Center Quality Reporting (ASCQR) Program** is a pay-for-reporting program that requires ambulatory surgical centers (ASCs) to meet administrative, data collection, reporting, and other program requirements, or receive a reduction of 2.0 percentage points in their annual payment update for failure to meet these program requirements. The (ASCQR) Program promotes higher quality, more efficient health care that it is linked to quality of care measurements. ASCQR Program requirements must be met by ASCs to be eligible for payment updates, and this process includes certain data collection and data submission requirements. ASCs that do not meet reporting requirements, including data that is publicly available, may incur a 2.0 percentage point reduction to any payment update provided under the revised ASC payment system for that year. In addition, a *value-based purchasing (VBP) program* for payments under the Medicare program for ambulatory surgical centers (ASCs) includes efforts to improve quality and payment efficiency in ASCs. The VBP program revises how Medicare pays for health care services, moving the program towards rewarding better value, outcomes, and innovations, instead of merely volume (of health care procedures and services provided).

Example: Two measures of hospital events following specified surgical procedures for the *ASCQR Program* measure set include data collected via administrative claims. (For the purposes of this measure, *hospital visits* include emergency department visits, observation stays, and unplanned inpatient admissions.) The purpose of data collection is to ultimately ensure that such events do not occur, and the requirement to submit such data assists ASC facilities in the implementation of protocols to prevent such events.

(1) *ASC-17: Hospital Visits after Orthopedic Ambulatory Surgical Center Procedures*, which assesses all-cause, unplanned hospital visits within seven days of an orthopedic procedure performed at an ASC (beginning with the 2022 payment determination).

(2) *ASC-18: Hospital Visits after Urology Ambulatory Surgical Center Procedures*, which assesses all-cause, unplanned hospital visits occurring within seven days of the urology procedure performed at an ASC (beginning with the 2022 payment determination).

Three measures were removed from the ASCQR Program because data submission indicated compliance with such quality measures:

(1) *ASC-5: Prophylactic Intravenous (IV) Antibiotic Timing*, which assessed whether intravenous antibiotics given for prevention of surgical site infection were administered on time.

(2) *ASC-6: Safe Surgery Checklist Use*, which was a structural measure of facility process that assesses whether an ASC employed a safe surgery checklist that covered each of the three critical perioperative periods (prior to administering anesthesia, prior to skin incision, and prior to patient leaving the operating room) for the entire data collection period.

(3) *ASC-7: ASC Facility Volume Data on Selected Procedures*, which was a structural measure of facility capacity that collects surgical procedure volume data on six categories of procedures frequently performed in the ASC setting.

The online data submission tool, *QualityNet*, allows for batch submission of *ASCQR Program* measure data and makes corresponding regulatory updates. *Batch submission* is submission of data for multiple facilities simultaneously using a single, electronic file containing data from multiple facilities submitted via one agent *QualityNet* account.

End-Stage Renal Disease Prospective Payment System (ESRD PPS)

Medicare's ESRD benefit allows patients to receive dialysis treatments, which remove excess fluids and toxins from the bloodstream. Patients also receive items and services related to their dialysis treatments, including drugs to treat conditions resulting from the loss of kidney function, such as anemia and low blood calcium. CMS traditionally divided ESRD items and services into two groups for payment purposes:

- Dialysis and associated routine services (e.g., nursing, supplies, equipment, certain drugs, and certain laboratory tests) are reimbursed according to a composite rate (one rate for a defined set of services). Paying according to a composite rate (or fixed) is a common form of Medicare payment, also known as *bundling*.

- **End-Stage Renal Disease prospective payment system (ESRD PPS)** that provides a single, per-treatment payment to ESRD facilities, covering all resources used when providing an outpatient dialysis treatment. CMS adjusts the ESRD PPS base rate to reflect patient and facility characteristics that contribute to higher per-treatment costs.

  ○ The rate is case-mix adjusted to provide a mechanism to account for differences in patients' utilization of health care resources (e.g., patient's age, documentation, and reporting of comorbidities) (Table 9-3).

TABLE 9-3 Case-mix adjustments to composite rates based on patient age

Age Range	Case-Mix Index Multiplier
18–44	1.023
45–59	1.055
60–69	1.000
70–79	1.094
80+	1.174

o The ESRD PPS includes *Consolidated Billing (CB)* requirements for limited Medicare Part B services as part of the ESRD facility's bundled payment. (The CB payment rate system bundles ESRD drugs and related laboratory tests with composite rate payments, and one reimbursement amount is paid for ESRD services provided to patients. Lists of items and services subject to CB requirements are periodically updated, at which time they are no longer separately payable.)

 NOTE:

A facility's *case mix* is a measure of the types of patients treated, and it reflects patient utilization of varying levels of health care resources. Patients are classified according to age, gender, health status, and so on.

For example, elderly patients usually require more complex care than teenage patients, which means a greater amount of money is spent on patient care provided to the elderly.

End-Stage Renal Disease Quality Improvement Program

The end-stage renal disease quality improvement program (ESRD QIP) promotes high-quality care delivered by outpatient dialysis facilities. As the first federal Value Based Purchasing (VBP) program, ESRD QIP changed the way CMS pays for treatment of ESRD patients by linking a portion of payment directly to facilities' performance on quality care measures. The ESRD QIP reduces payments to ESRD facilities that do not meet or exceed certain performance standards.

The ESRD QIP scores facility performance on a variety of clinical measures (e.g., clinical care) and reporting measures (e.g., anemia management), which are based on reimbursement claims, CROWNWeb data (ESRD national patient registry and quality measure reporting system), and data from the Center for Disease Control and Prevention's (CDC) National Healthcare Safety Network (NHSN). ESRD facilities have an opportunity to review scores and to submit a request for clarifying information and/or a formal inquiry prior to CMS finalizing the scores and applying any resultant payment reductions.

Federally Qualified Health Centers Prospective Payment System (FQHC PPS)

Federally Qualified Health Centers (FQHCs) are safety net providers that primarily provide services typically furnished in an outpatient clinic. FQHCs include community health centers, migrant health centers, health care for the homeless health centers, public housing primary care centers, and health center program "lookalikes." They also include outpatient health programs or facilities operated by a tribe or tribal organization or by an urban Indian organization. FQHCs are paid based on the FQHC PPS for medically necessary primary health services and qualified preventive health services furnished by an FQHC practitioner.

The Affordable Care Act (ACA) (also called Obamacare) established the **Federally Qualified Health Centers Prospective Payment System (FQHC PPS)** and was implemented in 2014. FQHCs include an FQHC payment code on claims submitted for payment, and they are paid 80 percent of the lesser of charges based on FQHC payment codes or the FQHC PPS rate (a national encounter-based rate with geographic and other adjustments).

Beginning in 2017, the FQHC PPS base payment rate has been updated annually using the FQHC *market basket, which replaced the Medicare Economic Index as the index for establishing Medicare values for reimbursement.* For example, in calendar year 2017, the market basket update under the FQHC PPS was 1.8 percent. In addition, the following adjustments apply to the FQHC PPS payment rate:

- FQHC Geographic Adjustment Factor
- New patient adjustment
- Initial Preventive Physical Examination (IPPE) or Annual Wellness Visit (AWV) adjustment

Exceptions to the FQHC PPS payment rate include encounters with more than one FQHC practitioner on the same day, regardless of the length or complexity of the visit. Multiple encounters with the same FQHC practitioner on the same day, constitute a single visit, except when the patient has an illness or injury requiring additional diagnosis or treatment subsequent to the first encounter *or* a qualified medical visit and a qualified mental health visit on the same day.

> **Example:** The FQHC PPS payment rate does not apply to charges incurred for encounters on the same day when a patient is treated by a practitioner during the morning (e.g., diabetes mellitus) and returns later in the day for a second encounter (e.g., trauma due to a fall).

Home Health Prospective Payment System

Home health is a covered service under the Part A Medicare benefit. It consists of part-time, medically necessary, skilled care (e.g., nursing, physical therapy, occupational therapy, and speech-language therapy) that is ordered by a physician. Home health care is reimbursed according to a Medicare **home health prospective payment system (HH PPS)**, which uses the home health patient-driven groupings model (PDGM) to establish prospective reimbursement rates for each 60-day **episode of care (home health)**, which is the period of time (two months) during which care is provided for a particular condition. If a patient is eligible for care after the end of the first episode, a second episode can begin, and there are no limits to the number of episodes of care a patient who remains eligible for the home health benefit can receive.

> **Example:** A patient is discharged from the hospital after knee replacement surgery and begins a 60-day episode of care (home health) that includes physical therapy on July 5. Home health care concludes on September 2, and the patient is mobile. A second 60-day episode of care (home health) is not needed.

The **home health patient-driven groupings model (PDGM)** was implemented in 2020, replacing the *home health resource groups (HHRGs).* The PDGM relies more heavily on clinical characteristics and other patient information to place home health periods of care into meaningful payment categories, and it also eliminated the use of therapy service thresholds. As a result of implementation of the PDGM, the unit of home health payment was reduced from a 60-day episode to a 30-day period. PDGM data is reported to Medicare on HH PPS claims using the **health insurance prospective payment system (HIPPS) code set**. Codes in this set are five-character alphanumeric codes that represent case-mix groups about which payment determinations are made for the HH PPS. The HPGM includes five main case-mix variables, including admission source, timing, clinical grouping, functional impairment level, and comorbidity adjustment. CMS originally created the HIPPS code set for the skilled nursing facility prospective payment system (SNF PPS) in 1998, and reporting requirements for the HH PPS (and inpatient rehabilitation facility PPS) were added later. HIPPS codes are determined after patient assessments using the **Outcomes and Assessment Information Set (OASIS)** are completed.

Grouper software is used to determine the appropriate HIPPS code and case mix weight after Outcomes and Assessment Information Set (OASIS) data such as diagnoses and ICD-10-CM codes (Figure 9-6), which are input for each patient. A Java-based **Home Assessment Validation and Entry (HAVEN)** (also abbreviated as jHAVEN) data entry software is then used to collect OASIS assessment data for transmission to state databases.

(M1021) Primary Diagnosis & (M1023) Other Diagnoses	
Column 1	**Column 2**
Diagnoses (Sequencing of diagnoses should reflect the seriousness of each condition and support the disciplines and services provided)	ICD-10-CM and symptom control rating for each condition. Note that the sequencing of these ratings may not match the sequencing of the diagnoses.
Description	ICD-10-CM / Symptom Control Rating
(M1021) Primary Diagnosis a. _____	**V, W, X, Y codes NOT allowed** a. ☐☐☐ ☐☐☐ ☐0 ☐1 ☐2 ☐3 ☐4
(M1023) Other Diagnoses b. _____	**All ICD-10–CM codes allowed** b. ☐☐☐ ☐☐☐ ☐0 ☐1 ☐2 ☐3 ☐4
c. _____	c. ☐☐☐ ☐☐☐ ☐0 ☐1 ☐2 ☐3 ☐4
d. _____	d. ☐☐☐ ☐☐☐ ☐0 ☐1 ☐2 ☐3 ☐4
e. _____	e. ☐☐☐ ☐☐☐ ☐0 ☐1 ☐2 ☐3 ☐4
f. _____	f. ☐☐☐ ☐☐☐ ☐0 ☐1 ☐2 ☐3 ☐4

FIGURE 9-6 Sample of OASIS items to be completed as part of recertification (follow-up) assessment or other follow-up assessment.

Example: A patient who resides in the Los Angeles-Long Beach-Glendale area was newly diagnosed by his primary care provider with diabetes mellitus, type 2, with hyperglycemia (E11.65) and received home health care for diabetic management teaching, medication review and evaluation of compliance, and response to new medications. The patient also has documented diagnoses of chronic systolic (congestive) heart failure (I50.22), cerebral atherosclerosis (I67.2), and benign prostatic hypertrophy (N40.0).

Upon completion of an initial OASIS assessment, results included:

- Risk of hospitalization (OASIS field M1033) due to two or more emergency department visits in six months
- Decline in mental, emotional, or behavioral status in the past three months
- Reported or observed history of difficulty complying with any medical instructions (e.g., medications, diet, exercise) during the past three months
- Currently taking five or more medications

The initial OASIS assessment included the following OASIS fields and functional items for this patient: M1800 Grooming, M1810 Upper body dressing, M1820 Lower body dressing, M1830 Bathing, M1840 Toilet transferring, M1850 Transferring, and M1860 Ambulation/locomotion. Entry of the patient's diagnoses and OASIS assessment into grouper software results in HIPPS code 1IA31 (Early-Community-Medication Management, Teaching and Assessment, Endocrine-Low Functional Impairment-High Comorbidity) and case-mix weight of 1.2759. Next, the grouper software calculates the total reimbursement by applying a *national, standardized 30-day period payment rate* such as $1,753.68. The initial reimbursement amount is $2,237.52 ($1,753.68 x 1.2759). However, the total reimbursement amount is calculated as a

(continues)

(continued)

result of applying the *wage-adjusted labor portion of case-mix* using pre-determined case-mix data: 0.239 (non-labor case mix index) and 1.3055 (wage case-mix index for Los Angeles-Long Beach-Glendale, CA).

- Non-labor portion of case-mix adjusted period payment amount: $2,237.52 x 0.239 = $534.77
- Wage-adjusted labor portion of case-mix adjusted period payment amount: $1,702.75 x 1.3055 = $2,222.94
- Non-labor portion of case-mix and wage-adjusted labor portion amount: $534.77 + $2,222.94 = $2,757.71
- Total reimbursement: $2,757.71

 NOTE:

ICD-10-CM codes are used to determine the appropriate HH PPS payment level.

Home Health Value-Based Purchasing Model

The **Home Health Value-Based Purchasing (HHVBP) Model** is designed to provide Medicare-certified HHAs with incentives to provide higher quality and more efficient care. CMS will adjust HHA payments for services based on quality of care, not just quantity of services provided during a given performance period. The model will test whether larger incentives for providing better quality care can result in better outcomes from home health services.

Hospice Payment System

Hospice is a comprehensive, holistic program of care and support for terminally ill patients and their families. Hospice care changes the focus to *palliative care* (comfort care) for pain relief and symptom management instead of treatment to cure the patient's illness. Medicare's hospice program was established by the *Tax Equity and Fiscal Responsibility Act (TEFRA) of 1982*, which expanded the scope of Medicare benefits by authorizing coverage for hospice care for terminally ill beneficiaries and established a fee-for-service payment rate system. The *Patient Protection and Affordable Care Act of 2010* reformed the hospice payment rate system (Table 9-4) to implement aggregate expenditures to control Medicare hospice costs.

Medicare pays a daily rate for each day a patient is enrolled in the hospice benefit, regardless of the number of services provided on a given day. Hospice payments are made based on the *level of care* required to meet the patient's and family's needs, including:

- Routine home care
- Continuous home care
- Inpatient respite care
- General inpatient care

TABLE 9-4 Sample hospice payment system rates

Level of Hospice Care	Hospice Payment Rate
Routine home care (Days 1–60)	$191 per day
Routine home care (Days 61+)	$150 per day
Continuous home care	$965 per day or $40 per hour
Inpatient respite care	$171 per day
General inpatient care	$734 per day
Aggregate reimbursement cap per beneficiary served	$28,500
Inpatient days cap	20% of total days of hospice service

NOTE:

Routine home care payments are made at a higher payment rate for the first 60 days of hospice care, and a reduced payment rate for hospice care for 61 days and over.

A service intensity add-on (SIA) payment in addition to the *per diem* RHC rate is made for services furnished during the last seven days of a patient's life. SIA eligibility criteria include the following:

- The day is a routine home care level of care day.
- The day occurs during the last seven days of the patient's life, and the patient is discharged expired.
- Direct patient care is furnished by a registered nurse (RN) or social worker, respectively, that day.

The SIA payment is equal to the continuous home care hourly payment rate multiplied by the amount of direct patient care furnished by an RN or social worker during the seven-day period for a minimum of 15 minutes and up to four hours total per day.

Daily hospice payment rates are adjusted for differences in wage rates among markets. Each level of hospice care's base rate has a labor share (adjusted by the hospice wage index) and a nonlabor share. Base rates are updated annually, based on the hospital market basket update.

Two caps affect Medicare payments under the hospice benefit:

- *Inpatient cap* (number of days of inpatient care furnished is limited to not more than 20 percent of total patient care days)
- *Aggregate* cap (limits the amount of Medicare payments a provider may receive in an accounting year, and is calculated by multiplying the number of hospice beneficiaries during the accounting year by a per-beneficiary *cap amount*)

There are two methods for counting beneficiaries:

- *Patient-by-patient proportional method* (counts only that fraction that represents the portion of a patient's total days of care in all hospices and all years that was spent in that hospice in that cap year)
- *Streamlined method* (counts those beneficiaries who received care from a single hospice in the initial year of election only)

When a beneficiary receives care from more than one hospice, the patient-by-patient proportional method is used. The aggregate payment cap is then compared with actual aggregate payments made to the hospice during the cap year; any payments in excess of the cap are considered overpayments and must be refunded to Medicare by the hospice.

Hospice Quality Reporting Program

The *Hospice Quality Reporting Program (HQRP)* was established to report quality measures that relate to care provided by hospice programs across the USA. The HQRP contains data reported using the Hospice Item Set (HIS) data collection tool, data from Medicare hospice claims, and an *experience of care survey* submitted through the *Hospice Consumer Assessment of Healthcare Providers and Systems (CAHPS®) Hospice Survey* system. All Medicare-certified hospice providers are required to comply with reporting requirements, and the HQRP has implemented a *pay-for-reporting* method, which means that timely submission and acceptance of complete data determines compliance with the HQRP. The *Hospice Abstraction Reporting Tool (HART)*, available from CMS, is free software that allows Hospice facilities to collect and maintain facility, HIS, and patient information for submission to a national data repository.

Hospital Inpatient Prospective Payment System

Before 1983, Medicare payments for hospital inpatient care were based on a *retrospective reasonable cost system*, which meant hospitals often received 80 percent of reasonable charges. Since 1983, when the **inpatient prospective payment system (IPPS)** was implemented, Medicare has reimbursed hospitals for inpatient hospital services according to a predetermined rate upon patient discharge. Each discharge was categorized into a **diagnosis-related group (DRG)**, which reimburses hospitals for inpatient stays and is based on the patient's principal and secondary diagnoses (including comorbidities and complications) as well as surgical and other procedures (if performed). Decision trees served as the basis for development of DRG grouper software, which is used to enter patient data (e.g., ICD-10-CM and ICD-10-PCS codes) to determine DRG assignment and reimbursement (Figure 9-7). (Medicare later implemented *Medicare severity diagnosis-related groups* [*MS-DRGs*] in 2008 to determine how much payment the hospital receives. MS-DRGs are discussed in detail later in this chapter.) Diagnosis-related groups are organized into mutually exclusive categories called **major diagnostic categories (MDCs)**, which are loosely based on body systems (e.g., nervous system). *Medicare code editor (MCE)* software is used to detect and report errors in ICD-10-CM/PCS coded data when inpatient hospital Medicare claims are processed.

 NOTE:

Cancer hospitals are excluded from the IPPS and continue to be paid on a reasonable cost basis subject to per-discharge limits.

Because the IPPS payment is based on an adjusted average payment rate, some cases receive Medicare reimbursement in excess of costs (rather than billed charges), whereas other cases receive payment that is less than costs incurred. The system is designed to provide hospitals with an incentive to manage their operations more efficiently by finding areas in which increased efficiencies can be instituted without affecting the quality of care and by treating a mix of patients to balance cost and payments. Note that a hospital's payment is not affected by the length of stay prior to discharge (unless the patient is transferred). It is expected that some patients will stay longer than others and that hospitals will offset the higher costs of a longer stay with the lower costs of a reduced stay.

Each DRG has a payment weight assigned to it, based on the average resources used to treat Medicare patients in that DRG. *Payment weights* are based on the average resources used to treat patients in a particular DRG, with a weight of 1.000 being the average; when a relative payment weight is higher than 1.000, such as 1.435, that means more resources are required to treat the patient and, thus, the payment is correspondingly higher. The reimbursement rate can be adjusted according to the following guidelines:

- **Disproportionate share hospital (DSH) adjustment**. Hospitals that treat a high percentage of low-income patients receive increased Medicare payments.
- **Indirect medical education (IME) adjustment**. Approved teaching hospitals receive increased Medicare payments. The adjustment varies depending on the ratio of residents-to-beds (to calculate operating costs) and residents-to-average-daily-census (to calculate capital costs).
- **Outlier**. Hospitals that treat unusually costly cases receive increased medical payments. The additional payment is designed to protect hospitals from large financial losses due to unusually expensive cases. Outlier payments are added to DSH or IME adjustments, when applicable.

Several DRG systems were developed for use in the United States, including:

- *Diagnosis-related groups (DRGs)*
  - ○ Original system used by CMS to reimburse hospitals for inpatient care provided to Medicare beneficiaries
  - ○ Based on **intensity of resources**, which is the relative volume and types of diagnostic, therapeutic, and inpatient bed services used to manage an inpatient disease
  - ○ Replaced in 2008 by Medicare severity DRGs (MS-DRGs) (discussed below)
- **All-Patient diagnosis-related groups (AP-DRGs)**
  - ○ Original DRG system adapted for use by third-party payers to reimburse hospitals for inpatient care provided to *non*-Medicare beneficiaries (e.g., BlueCross BlueShield, commercial health plans, TRICARE)
  - ○ Based on intensity of resources

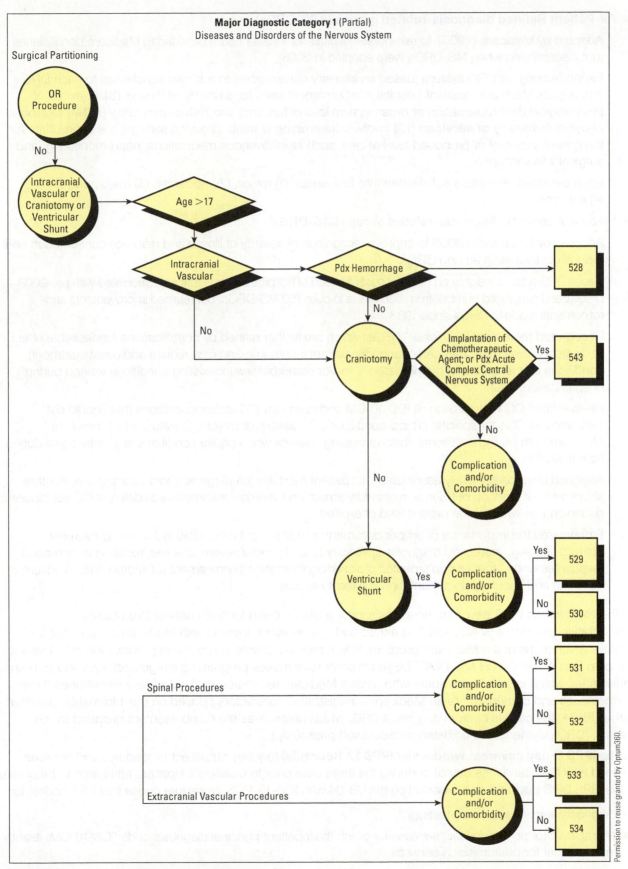

FIGURE 9-7 Sample original DRG decision tree.

- **All-Patient Refined diagnosis-related groups (APR-DRGs)**
  - Adopted by Medicare in 2007 to reimburse hospitals for inpatient care provided to Medicare beneficiaries (but discontinued when MS-DRGs were adopted in 2008)
  - Expanded original DRG system (based on intensity of resources) to add two subclasses to each DRG that adjusts Medicare inpatient hospital reimbursement rates for **severity of illness (SOI)** (extent of physiological decompensation or organ system loss of function) and **risk of mortality (ROM)** (likelihood of dying) (**Intensity of services [IS]** involves determining whether provided services are appropriate for the patient's current or proposed level of care, such as intravenous medications, heart monitoring, and surgical interventions.)
  - Each subclass, in turn, is subdivided into four areas: (1) minor, (2) moderate, (3) major, and (4) extreme

- **Medicare severity diagnosis-related groups (MS-DRGs)**
  - Adopted by Medicare in 2008 to improve recognition of severity of illness and resource consumption and reduce cost variation among DRGs
  - Bases DRG relative weights on hospital *costs* (instead of hospital charges that are associated with pre-2008 DRGs), and expanded number from 538 DRGs to over 750 MS-DRGs, but retained improvements and refinements made to DRGs since 1983
  - Recognized more than 335 "base" DRGs, which are further refined by *complications* (undesirable effect of disease or treatment that can change the patient's outcome and may require additional treatment), conditions that arise during hospitalization, and/or *comorbidities* (coexisting conditions treated during hospitalization) (CC)
  - Re-evaluated CC list to assign *all* ICD-10-CM codes as non-CC status (conditions that should not be treated as CCs for specific clinical conditions), CC status, *or* major CC status, which prevents Medicare from paying additional costs of treating patients who acquire conditions (e.g., infections) during hospitalization
  - Assigned diagnoses closely associated with patient mortality (cardiogenic shock, cardiac arrest, other shock without mention of trauma, respiratory arrest, and ventricular fibrillation) to different CC subclasses, depending on whether the patient lived or expired
  - Emphasized the importance of proper documentation of patient care, relating it to reimbursement optimization (e.g., increased diagnosis specificity to justify more severe illnesses, resulting in increased reimbursement)—facilities implemented clinical documentation improvement (CDI) programs to ensure thorough and accurate documentation in patient records

To determine an IPPS payment, hospitals submit a UB-04 claim for each patient to a Medicare administrative contractor (MAC), which is a third-party payer that contracts with Medicare to carry out the operational functions of the Medicare program. MACs process claims and perform program integrity tasks for Medicare Part A and Part B and DMEPOS; each contractor makes program coverage decisions and publishes a newsletter, which is sent to providers who receive Medicare reimbursement. (Medicare transitioned fiscal intermediaries and carriers to create Medicare administrative contractors.) Based on the information provided on the UB-04, the case is categorized into a DRG, which determines the reimbursement provided to the hospital. (DRG payments are adjusted as discussed previously.)

The **IPPS 3-day payment window** (or **IPPS 72-hour rule**) requires outpatient procedures and services provided by a hospital on the day of or during the three days prior to a patient's inpatient admission to be covered by the IPPS DRG payment and reported on the UB-04 with ICD-10-PCS procedure codes (*not* CPT codes) for:

- Diagnostic services (e.g., lab testing)
- Therapeutic (or nondiagnostic) services for which the inpatient principal diagnosis code (ICD-10-CM) exactly matches that for preadmission services

Coding for Diagnosis-Related Groups (DRGs)

Diagnoses and procedures are assigned ICD-10-CM and ICD-10-PCS codes, and they are sequenced according to CMS official coding guidelines and the Uniform Hospital Discharge Data Set (UHDDS). This means that hospitals are not required to assign codes to every diagnosis and procedure documented in the patient record. However, hospitals must evaluate their institutional data needs to develop coding policies, which will determine the assignment of ICD-10-CM and ICD-10-PCS codes to diagnoses and procedures.

When assigning codes to comorbidities (coexisting conditions) and complications (conditions that develop during inpatient admission), be sure to carefully review patient record documentation to assign the most specific code possible. Revisions to the MS-DRGs comorbidities and complications (CC) list eliminated many diagnoses that were considered CCs in the past. As a result, physicians must be educated about the importance of proper documentation practices.

EXAMPLE: Under MS-DRGs, the following apply:

- Chronic obstructive pulmonary disease (COPD) (J44.9) is not a CC. However, acute exacerbation of COPD (J44.1) is a CC.

- Congestive heart failure (CHF) (I50.9) is not a CC. However, chronic systolic heart failure (I50.22) is a CC and acute systolic heart failure (I50.21) is a major CC (MCC).

ICD-10-PCS codes are assigned for documented OR (operating room) and non-OR procedures. (Non-OR procedures are performed in the patient's room, emergency department, radiology department, and so on.) Whether ICD-10-PCS codes are assigned to other procedures, such as ancillary tests (e.g., EKG, laboratory tests, and so on), is dependent on the hospital's coding policy.

The *present on admission (POA) indicator* differentiates between patient conditions present upon inpatient admission and those that develop during the inpatient admission. Claims that do not report the POA indicator are returned to the facility for correction. Hospital-acquired conditions that are reported as not present at the time of admission are not considered when calculating the MS-DRG payment. This means that such conditions, even if included on the CC and MCC lists, are not considered a CC or MCC if diagnosed during the inpatient stay and the facility will not receive additional payment for such conditions.

Diagnostic services include examinations and procedures or hospital outpatient procedures or services that aided in the assessment of a medical condition or identified a disease. Examples include diagnostic laboratory services, such as hematology and chemistry, diagnostic x-rays, isotope studies, electrocardiograms, pulmonary function studies, thyroid function tests, psychological tests, and other tests provided to determine the nature and severity of an ailment or injury.

 NOTE:

- Services that are distinct from and unrelated to the inpatient admission are separately billed by the hospital *if documentation supports that the service is unrelated to the inpatient admission.*

- However, hospitals *must* bundle technical components of all outpatient diagnostic services and related non-diagnostic services (e.g., therapeutic services) with the claim for an inpatient stay when services are furnished to a Medicare beneficiary during the three days preceding an inpatient admission.

- The following hospital and hospital units are subject to a *1-day payment window* (instead of the 3-day payment window): cancer hospitals, children's hospitals, inpatient rehabilitation hospitals and units, long-term care hospitals, and psychiatric hospitals and units.

Medicare also requires that physician services clinically related to an inpatient admission and provided within 72 hours of the admission be paid at the lower facility rate (instead of the greater office or nonfacility rate). CMS requires that HCPCS Level II modifier -PD (diagnostic or related nondiagnostic item or service provided in a wholly owned or wholly operated entity to a patient who is admitted as an inpatient within three days) be added to CPT codes to identify claims for related services provided within 72 hours of an inpatient admission. As a result of this new requirement:

- Physician office claims must be held for at least three days prior to submission, and CMS requires hospitals to notify physician offices about related inpatient admissions.
- Modifier -PD must be added to CPT and HCPCS Level II codes that are reported on CMS-1500 claims for any inpatients who received physician office services within 72 hours prior to admission.

In practice, physician offices need to implement a process to ensure that claims submission is delayed by three days. Also, an office staff member needs to review daily list(s) of inpatient admissions received from local hospital(s) to identify patients whose claims need to be modified by adding -PD to CPT codes.

According to CMS, all *nondiagnostic* services (other than ambulance and maintenance renal dialysis services) furnished by a hospital on the date of admission or during the three-day payment window are deemed to be related to the admission and *must be bundled with the inpatient stay if the services were provided on the day of or during the three days prior to a patient's inpatient admission.* The *exception to the rule* is when a hospital determines, attests, and documents that the service furnished during the three-day payment window is clinically distinct or independent from the reason for the patient's inpatient hospital admission. Hospitals are required to report condition code 51 with the nondiagnostic service CPT or HCPCS Level II code on the submitted outpatient hospital UB-04 claim.

In addition, an **IPPS transfer rule** states that certain patients discharged to a postacute provider are treated as transfer cases, which means hospitals are paid a graduated *per diem* rate for each day of the patient's stay, not to exceed the prospective payment DRG rate. (Outliers are also recognized for extraordinarily high-cost cases.)

Hospital-Acquired Conditions and Present on Admission Indicator Reporting

Payment under the Medicare program for inpatient hospital services is generally based on the *inpatient prospective payment system* (IPPS), and hospitals receive reimbursement for each inpatient discharge based in part on diagnosis codes that identify a *Medicare severity diagnosis-related group (MS-DRG).* Assignment of an MS-DRG can take into account the presence of secondary diagnoses, and payment levels are adjusted to account for a number of hospital-specific factors. The Deficit Reduction Act of 2005 (DRA) expanded hospital quality measures collected by Medicare and allowed for the adjustment of payments to hospitals for certain preventable **hospital-acquired conditions (HACs),** which are medical conditions or complications that patients develop during inpatient hospital stays and that were not present at admission (e.g., pressure ulcers, hospital-acquired infections, pulmonary emboli). HACs are categorized as those that (1) are high cost, high volume, or both; (2) result in the assignment of a case to a MS-DRG that has a higher payment when present as a secondary diagnosis; and (3) could reasonably have been prevented through the application of evidence-based guidelines.

In 2002, the National Quality Forum (NQF) published *Serious Reportable Events in Healthcare: A Consensus Report,* which listed the previously noted adverse events, which were *serious, largely preventable, and of concern to both the public and health care providers.* These events were originally known as *never events* (now called *adverse events*). The Medicare program addressed certain *adverse events* through national coverage determinations (NCDs). Similar to any other patient population, Medicare (and Medicaid) beneficiaries may experience serious injury or death if they undergo erroneous surgical or other invasive procedures and may require additional health care to correct adverse outcomes that may result from such errors. To address and reduce the occurrence of these surgeries, CMS issued three national coverage determinations (NCDs). Under these NCDs, CMS does not cover a particular surgical or other invasive procedure performed to treat a particular medical condition when the practitioner erroneously performs (1) a different procedure altogether; (2) the correct procedure but on the wrong body part; or (3) the correct procedure but on the wrong patient. Medicare and Medicaid also do not cover hospitalizations and other services related to these noncovered procedures.

NOTE:

The never event or adverse event list contains *serious reportable events* that are grouped into seven categories: surgical or procedural events; product or device events; patient protection events; care management events; environmental events; radiological events; and criminal events.

Since October 1, 2007, hospitals subject to the IPPS have been required to submit information on Medicare claims specifying whether diagnoses were **present on admission (POA)**, which is a condition that exists at the time an order for inpatient hospital admission occurs.

All claims submitted for inpatient admissions to general acute care hospitals or other health care facilities are required to report the present on admission (POA) indicator, which is assigned by the coder to the principal and secondary diagnoses and external cause of injury code reported on the UB-04 or 837 Institutional (837I) electronic claim.

The coder reviews the patient record to determine whether a condition was present on admission or not. Any issues related to inconsistent, missing, conflicting, or unclear documentation are resolved by the provider as a result of the physical query process when coders contact responsible physicians to request clarification about documentation (so that specific codes can be assigned).

In this context, present on admission is defined as present at the time the order for inpatient admission occurs. Thus, conditions that develop during an outpatient encounter, including emergency department, observation, or outpatient surgery, are considered as present on admission upon admission of the patient as a hospital inpatient. CMS reporting options and definitions include the following, and payment is made for "Y" and "W" indicators:

- Y = Yes (diagnosis was present at the time of inpatient admission)
- N = No (diagnosis was not present at the time of inpatient admission)
- U = Unknown (documentation is insufficient to determine if the condition was present at the time of inpatient admission)
- W = Clinically undetermined (provider is unable to clinically determine whether the condition was present at the time of inpatient admission)
- Blank = Unreported/not used (exempt from POA reporting; the field is blank for factors that do not represent a current disease or for a condition that is always present on admission)

The HAC-POA indicator payment provision applies to IPPS hospitals only, and the following is a list of the Medicare HACs for which CMS does not reimburse hospitals. The Patient Protection and Affordable Care Act (PPACA) of 2010 also authorized CMS to make payment adjustments to applicable hospitals based on risk-adjustment quality measures. (Effective July 2012, Medicaid also does not reimburse hospitals for these HACs.)

- Foreign object retained after surgery
- Air embolism
- Blood incompatibility
- Stage III and IV pressure ulcers
- Falls and trauma
  - Fractures
  - Dislocations
  - Intracranial injuries
  - Crushing injuries
  - Burns
  - Other injuries

- Manifestations of poor glycemic control
  - Diabetic ketoacidosis
  - Nonketotic hyperosmolar coma
  - Hypoglycemic coma
  - Secondary diabetes with ketoacidosis
  - Secondary diabetes with hyperosmolarity
- Catheter-associated urinary tract infection (UTI)
- Vascular catheter-associated infection
- Surgical site infection, mediastinitis, following coronary artery bypass graft (CABG)
- Surgical site infection following bariatric surgery for obesity
  - Laparoscopic gastric bypass
  - Gastroenterostomy
  - Laparoscopic gastric restrictive surgery
- Surgical site infection following certain orthopedic procedures
  - Spine
  - Neck
  - Shoulder
  - Elbow
- Surgical site infection following cardiac implantable electronic device (CIED)
- Deep vein thrombosis (DVT)/pulmonary embolism (PE) following certain orthopedic procedures:
  - Total knee replacement
  - Hip replacement
- Iatrogenic pneumothorax with venous catheterization

Hospital Quality Improvement Program

The acute care hospital quality improvement program (QIP) provides a comparison of measures for five Centers for Medicare & Medicaid Services (CMS) acute care hospital quality improvement programs, including the:

- Hospital Inpatient Quality Reporting (IQR) Program (Refer to Chapter 5.)
- Hospital Value-Based Purchasing (VBP) Program
- Promoting Interoperability Program (PI Program) (Refer to Chapter 2.)
- Hospital Readmissions Reduction Program (HRRP)
- Hospital-Acquired Condition Reduction Program (HACRP)

Hospital Value-Based Purchasing Program

The hospital **value-based purchasing (VBP)** program is part of a long-standing CMS effort to link Medicare's inpatient prospective payment system (IPPS) to a value-based system for the purpose of promoting better clinical outcomes for hospital inpatients by improving health care quality, which affects payment for inpatient stays to over 3,500 hospitals. Medicare beneficiaries and all patients receive during acute-care inpatient stays by:

- Eliminating or reducing the occurrence of adverse events (health care errors resulting in patient harm).
- Adopting evidence-based care standards and protocols, which result in the best outcomes for the most patients.
- Re-engineering hospital processes that improve patients' experience of care.
- Increasing the transparency of care for consumers.
- Recognizing hospitals that are involved in the provision of high-quality care at a lower cost to Medicare.

A hospital's VPB performance in is based on measures for each fiscal year (FY), with hospital's total performance score (TPS) comprised of the following domains:

- Clinical case/clinical outcomes
- Person and community engagement
- Safety
- Efficiency and cost reduction

Participating hospitals are paid for inpatient acute care services based on quality of care, not just quantity of services provided. The inpatient hospital VBP was authorized by the Patient Protection and Affordable Care Act (PPACA).

Pay-for-Performance (P4P)

Pay-for-performance (P4P) initiatives link reimbursement to performance criteria. Traditionally, Medicare and other health plans based payment on the *process* of care. P4P strategies promote the *right* care for every patient every time and defines the *right care* as being effective, efficient, equitable, patient centered, safe, and timely. This means that despite the patient's ethnicity, gender, geographic location, and socioeconomic status, patients receive "right care." Examples of P4P initiatives include the hospital value-based purchasing program, hospital outpatient quality reporting program, and so on.

Hospital Readmissions Reduction Program

The **hospital readmissions reduction program (HRRP)** requires CMS to reduce payments to IPPS hospitals with excess readmissions. Readmission measures established by CMS:

- Define *readmission* as an inpatient admission to a subsection (d) hospital (general, acute care, short-term hospital) within 30 days of discharge from the same or another subsection (d) hospital.

- Adopt specific readmission measures for the applicable conditions and procedures of acute myocardial infarction (AMI), aspiration pneumonia, chronic obstructive pulmonary disease (COPD), coronary artery bypass graft (CABG) surgery, elective total hip arthroplasty (THA) surgery, heart failure (HF), pneumonia (PN), sepsis patients coded with pneumonia present on admission, and total knee arthroplasty (TKA) surgery.

- Establish a methodology to calculate the excess readmission ratio for each applicable condition, which results in calculation of the readmission payment adjustment. (A hospital's excess readmission ratio is a measure of a hospital's readmission performance compared to the national average for the hospital's set of patients with that applicable condition.)

- Establish a policy of using the risk adjustment methodology endorsed by the National Quality Forum (NQF) to calculate excess readmission ratios, which includes adjustments for factors that are clinically relevant, such as certain patient demographic characteristics, comorbidities, and patient frailty.

- Establish an applicable period of three years of discharge data and the use of a minimum of 25 cases to calculate a hospital's excess readmission ratio for each applicable condition.

- Included the application of an algorithm for planned readmissions in order to adjust readmissions measures.

CMS also established payment adjustment policies to determine which hospitals are subject to the HRRP, the methodology to calculate the hospital readmission payment adjustment factor, the portion of the IPPS payment used to calculate readmission payment adjustment amounts, and a process for hospitals to review readmission information and submit corrections before readmission rates are publicized.

Hospital-Acquired Condition Reduction Program (HACRP)

Effective October 1, 2015, the **Hospital-Acquired Condition (HAC) Reduction Program** encourages hospitals to reduce HACs by adjusting payments to hospitals that rank in the worst-performing 25 percent with respect to HAC quality measures. CMS is permitted may reduce these hospitals' payments by one percent and uses the

Total HAC Score to determine the worst-performing quartile of all hospitals. The score is based on data for six quality measures in two domains:

- Domain 1: CMS Recalibrated Patient Safety Indicator (PSI) 90 (CMS PSI 90)
- Domain 2: Centers for Disease Control and Prevention (CDC) National Healthcare Safety Network (NHSN) health care-associated infection (HAI) measures, which include Central Line-Associated Bloodstream Infection (CLABSI), Catheter-Associated Urinary Tract Infection (CAUTI), Surgical Site Infection (SSI) (colon and hysterectomy), Methicillin-resistant *Staphylococcus aureus* (MRSA) bacteremia, and *Clostridium difficile* Infection (CDI).

The Patient Protection and Affordable Care Act requires CMS to publicly report hospitals' performance information. Prior to publication CMS sends confidential Hospital-Specific Reports (HSRs) to hospitals, and gives them 30 days to review their HAC Reduction Program data, submit questions about the calculation of their results, and request corrections. After the Scoring Calculations Review and Corrections period, CMS publicly reports hospitals' measure scores, domain scores, and HAC Reduction Program data on the Hospital Compare website at www.Medicare.gov.

NOTE:

The *HAC Reduction Program* is distinct from the *Deficit Reduction Act: Hospital-Acquired Conditions (Present on Admission Indicator) program* (covered previously in this chapter).

Hospital Outpatient Prospective Payment System

The BBA of 1997 authorized CMS to implement an **outpatient prospective payment system (OPPS)** for hospital outpatient services provided to Medicare patients. (The OPPS was implemented in 2000.) Also reimbursed under the OPPS are certain Medicare Part B services furnished to hospital inpatients who have no Part A coverage, as well as partial hospitalization services furnished by community mental health centers. All services are paid according to **ambulatory payment classifications (APCs)**, which group services according to similar clinical characteristics and in terms of resources required. A payment rate is established for each APC and, depending on services provided, hospitals may be paid for more than one APC for a patient encounter (Figure 9-8). The Medicare beneficiary coinsurance was also recalculated under the OPPS and was based on 20 percent of the national median charge for services in the APC. (Both the total APC payment and the portion paid as coinsurance amounts are adjusted to reflect geographic wage variations.)

NOTE:

The OPPS does not cover payments for professional services, which are reported on the CMS-1500 claim and reimbursed according to a fee schedule, such as the Medicare physician fee schedule (MPFS) discussed later in this chapter. Hospitals report outpatient encounters on the UB-04 (or CMS-1450) claim using ICD-10-CM for diagnoses and HCPCS/CPT for procedures and services.

Each CPT and HCPCS Level II code is assigned a *status indicator (SI)* as a payment indicator to identify how each code is paid (or not paid) under the OPPS. For example, status indicator "S" refers to "significant procedures for which the multiple procedure reduction does not apply." This means that the CPT and/or HCPCS Level II code is paid the full APC reimbursement rate. OPPS status indicator "T" refers to "services to which the multiple procedure payment reduction applies." (CPT modifier, -51 is not added to codes reported for OPPS payment consideration.) This means that the reported CPT and/or HCPCS Level II code will be paid a discounted APC reimbursement rate when reported with other procedures on the same claim.

APC grouper software is used to assign an APC to each CPT and/or HCPCS Level II code reported on an outpatient claim, as well as to appropriate ICD-10-CM diagnosis codes. Outpatient code editor (OCE) software is used in conjunction with the APC grouper to identify Medicare claims edits and assign APC groups to reported codes.

Outpatient Prospective Payment System (OPPS) Formula

(APC Weight x Conversion Factor x Wage Index) + Add-On Payments = Payment

NOTE: When a patient undergoes multiple procedures and services on the same day, multiple APCs are generated and payments are added together. APC software automatically discounts multiple APC payments when appropriate (e.g., bilateral procedure).

EXAMPLE: Using the sample data below, the OPPS payment for a patient who underwent a cataract procedure with intraocular lens implant, chest X-ray, and ureteral reflux study in Buffalo, New York, is calculated as $1,253.73. (NOTE: Add-on payments do not apply to this example and APC payments were not discounted.)

(22.98 x $54.561 x 0.8192) + (0.78 x $54.561 x 0.8192) + (4.29 x $54.561 x 0.8192)

$1,027.12 + $34.86 + $191.75 = $1,253.73

Conversion Factor = $54.561
Wage Index = 0.8192

HCPCS Code	Description	APC	APC Weight
66984	Cataract procedure with intraocular lens implant	246	22.98
71046	Chest x-ray, 2 views	260	0.78
78740	Ureteral reflux study	292	4.29

Current Procedural Terminology published by the American Medical Association.

FIGURE 9-8 Formula for determining OPPS payments.

Example: OCE software reviews to/from dates of service to identify and reject claims that are submitted for reimbursement as hospital-based outpatient care when, in fact, the claim should be processed as inpatient care.

 NOTE:

A Medicare patient's coinsurance amount is initially calculated for each APC based on 20 percent of the national median charge for services in the APC. The coinsurance amount for an APC does not change until the amount becomes 20 percent of the total APC payment, and no coinsurance amount can be greater than the hospital in-patient deductible in a given year.

The unit of payment for the OPPS is an outpatient visit or encounter. (The unit of payment for the IPPS discussed earlier is an inpatient hospital admission.) An **outpatient encounter** (or **outpatient visit**) includes all outpatient procedures and services (e.g., same-day surgery, x-rays, laboratory tests, and so on) provided during one day to the same patient. Thus, a patient who undergoes multiple outpatient procedures and receives multiple services on the same day will be assigned to one or more outpatient groups (called *APCs*). Each APC is weighted and has a prospective payment amount associated with it; if a patient is assigned multiple APCs, the payments are totaled to provide reimbursement to the hospital for the encounter. *Weights* are based on the average resources used to treat patients in a particular APC, with a weight of 1.000 being the average; when a relative payment weight is higher than 1.000, such as 1.435, that means more resources are required to treat the patient and, thus, the payment is correspondingly higher. (APC payments may be discounted when certain procedures or services are provided, such as bilateral procedures.) A **wage index** adjusts payments to account for geographic variations in hospitals' labor costs. In addition, *add-ons* such as *pass-through payments* provide additional reimbursement to hospitals that use innovative (new and improved) biologicals, drugs, and technical devices.

Outlier payments for high-cost services, *hold harmless payments* for certain hospitals, and *transitional payments* to limit losses under the OPPS can also increase payments. (The hospital profits if the payment rate is higher than the cost of care provided; the hospital loses money if the payment rate is lower than the cost of care provided.)

NOTE:

Health care personnel routinely discuss "pass-through payments" due to new technology, such as innovative medical devices (e.g., using surgical glue instead of stitches) and new drugs and vaccines (e.g., human papillomavirus [HPV] vaccine).

NOTE:

New York State will phase in ambulatory patient groups (APGs) as a new payment methodology for most Medicaid outpatient services (e.g., outpatient clinic, ambulatory surgery, and emergency department services). Implementation of APGs will result in:

- Higher payments for higher intensity services and lower payments for lower intensity services
- The transition of funds from inpatient to outpatient services to support quality outpatient care and to address the problem of avoidable hospitalizations

Hospital Outpatient Quality Reporting Program

The *Hospital Outpatient Quality Reporting (OQR) Program* requires hospitals to report data using standardized measures of care to receive the full update to their OPPS payment rate. CMS focuses on reporting measure data that have high impact and support national priorities for improved quality and efficiency of care for Medicare beneficiaries.

The current measure set for the Hospital OQR Program includes assessment of processes of care, imaging efficiency patterns, care transitions, emergency department through-put efficiency, use of health information technology, care coordination, patient safety, and volume. Participating hospitals agree that they will allow CMS to publicly report data for the quality measures, hospitals that meet data reporting requirements receive their full OPPS payment update; hospitals that do not participate or fail to meet requirements may receive a 2 percent reduction of their payment update.

Inpatient Psychiatric Facility Prospective Payment System

The **Inpatient Psychiatric Facility Prospective Payment System (IPF PPS)** was implemented as a result of Medicare, Medicaid, and SCHIP Balanced Budget Refinement Act of 1999 (BBRA) provisions that required implementation of a *per diem* patient classification system that reflects differences in patient resource use and costs. About 1,800 inpatient psychiatric facilities, including freestanding psychiatric hospitals and certified psychiatric units in general acute care hospitals, were impacted. The IPF PPS replaced a reasonable cost-based payment system, affecting approximately 2,000 facilities, to promote long-term cost control and utilization management. Licensed psychiatric facilities and hospital-based psychiatric units were reimbursed according to the new PPS, which was phased in over a three-year period beginning in 2004. (General health care facilities that are not licensed for specialty care but that occasionally treat patients with behavioral health or chemical dependency diagnoses are exempt from the IPF PPS.)

Health information department coders will use ICD-10-CM and ICD-10-PCS to assign codes to inpatient behavioral health diagnoses and procedures and will enter data into DRG software to calculate the IPF PPS rates. Inpatient psychiatric facilities are reimbursed according to a *per diem* payment that is calculated using DRG data, wage-adjusted rates, and facility-level adjusters (Figure 9-9). (IPPS MS-DRGs reimburse acute care hospitals a flat payment based on ICD-10-CM and ICD-10-PCS codes and other data.) Providers will use the **Diagnostic and Statistical Manual (DSM)** published by the American Psychiatric Association. Although DSM codes do not affect IPF PPS rates, the manual contains diagnostic assessment criteria that are used as tools to identify psychiatric disorders. The DSM includes psychiatric disorders and codes, provides a mechanism for communicating and recording diagnostic information, and is used in the areas of research and statistics.

Inpatient Psychiatric Hospital PPS Calculator

		Adjustment Factors
Patient Age	Patient is under age 65	1
Principal Diagnosis	DRG 12: Degenerative Nervous System Disorders (select as many comorbidities that apply below)	1.07
Comorbidity	Renal Failure, Chronic	1.14
Comorbidity	Arteriosclerosis of the Extremity with Gangrene	1.17
Comorbidity	Infectious Diseases	1.08
LOS (Days)	18	
Geographic Location	Rural	1.16
Teaching Adj.	0.6	1.28
Wage Area	Utah	0.9312

After making selections (above), scroll down for payment calculation information.

Budget Neutral Base Rate	$530

Calculate Wage Adjusted Rate	
The labor portion of the base rate	$386
Apply wage index factor of 0.9312 to the labor portion of $386	$359
The non-labor portion of the Federal base rate	$144
The total wage-adjusted rate	$503

Apply Facility Level Adjusters	
Teaching Adjustment	1.28
Rural Adjustment (if applicable)	1.16

Apply Patient Level Adjusters	
DRG 12: Degenerative Nervous System Disorders	1.07
Apply age adjustment	1
Apply comorbidity adjusters:	
Renal Failure, Chronic	1.14
Arteriosclerosis of the Extremity with Gangrene	1.17
Infectious Diseases	1.08

Total PPS Adjustment Factor	2.2846

The wage-adjusted and PPS-adjusted per diem amount is $1,150 (2.2846 * $503)

Apply variable per diem adjustment for 18 days:	Per Diem Amount	Unit	Extended
Day 1 (adjustment factor=1.26):	$1,150 * 1.26 = $1,449	1	$1,449
Days 2–4 (adjustment factor=1.12):	$1,150 * 1.12 = $1,288	3	$3,865
Days 5–8 (adjustment factor=1.05):	$1,150 * 1.05 = $1,208	4	$4,831
Days over 8 (adjustment factor=1.00):	$1,150 * 1.00 = $1,150	10	$11,502

Total Inpatient Psychiatric Hospital PPS Payment:	$21,646

FIGURE 9-9 Psychiatric hospital IPF PPS calculator worksheet.

Inpatient Psychiatric Facility Quality Reporting (IPFQR) Program Overview

The **Inpatient Psychiatric Facility Quality Reporting (IPFQR) Program** is a pay-for-reporting program intended to equip consumers with quality of care information to make more informed decisions about health care options. It is also intended to encourage hospitals and clinicians to improve the quality of inpatient care provided to beneficiaries by, first, ensuring that providers are aware of and reporting on best practices for their respective facilities and type of care.

To meet IPFQR program requirements, IPFs are required to submit all quality measures to CMS, and because this is a pay-for-reporting program, eligible facilities are subject to payment reduction for non-participation (e.g., 2.0 percentage point reduction of annual update to standard federal rate).

Inpatient Rehabilitation Facility Prospective Payment System

The BBA of 1997 authorized the implementation of a per-discharge prospective payment system (PPS) for inpatient rehabilitation hospitals and rehabilitation units, also called inpatient rehabilitation facilities (IRFs). Implemented in 2002, the **Inpatient Rehabilitation Facility Prospective Payment system (IRF PPS)** utilizes information from a patient assessment instrument. Effective October 1, 2018 a **patient-driven payment model (PDPM)** was implemented as a new case-mix reimbursement system that connects payment to patients' conditions and care needs instead of the volume of services provided. (In addition to IRFs, the PDPM applies to long term acute care facility and skilled nursing facility payments.)

A **patient assessment instrument** classifies patients into IRF PPS groups based on clinical characteristics and expected resource needs. Separate IRF PPS payments are calculated for each group and include case- and facility-level adjustments. Elements of the IRF PPS include:

- *Minimum Data Set for Post Acute Care (MDS-PAC)* (patient-centered assessment instrument completed by each Medicare patient that emphasizes the patient's care needs instead of the provider's characteristics; it classifies patients for Medicare payment and contains an appropriate quality-of-care monitoring system, including the use of quality indicators)

- *Case-mix groups (CMGs)* (classification of patients into function-related groups, which predict resources needed to furnish patient care to different types of patients; data elements from the MDS-PAC are used to classify a patient into a CMG)

- *CMG relative weights* (weights that account for the variance in cost per discharge and resource utilization among CMGs; reimbursement is based on a national formula that adjusts for case mix; *weights* are based on the average resources used to treat patients in a particular CMG, with a weight of 1.000 being the average; when a relative payment weight is higher than 1.000, such as 1.435, that means more resources are required to treat the patient and, thus, the payment is correspondingly higher)

- *CMG payment rates* (predetermined, per-discharge reimbursement amount that includes all operating and capital costs associated with providing covered inpatient rehabilitation services)

Inpatient Rehabilitation Validation and Entry (IRVEN) software (Figure 9-10) is the computerized data entry system used by inpatient rehabilitation facilities to create a file in a standard format that can be electronically transmitted to a national database. The data collected are used to assess the clinical characteristics of patients in rehabilitation hospitals and rehabilitation units in acute care hospitals. It provides agencies and facilities with a means to objectively measure and compare facility performance and quality. It will also provide researchers with information to support the development of improved standards.

Long-Term (Acute) Care Hospital Prospective Payment System

The BBRA of 1999 authorized the implementation of a per-discharge DRG **long-term (acute) care hospital prospective payment system (LTCH PPS)** for cost reporting periods beginning on or after October 1, 2002 to classify patients according to long-term (acute) care DRGs, which are based on patients' clinical characteristics and expected resource needs. This new prospective payment system replaced the reasonable cost-based payment system under which long-term (acute) care hospitals (LTCHs) were previously paid. (In 2008, Medicare severity long-term care diagnosis-related groups [MS-LTC-DRGs] were adopted for the LTCH PPS.) Effective October 1, 2018, a *patient-driven payment model (PDPM)* was implemented as a new case-mix reimbursement system that connects payment to patients' conditions and care needs instead of the volume of services provided. (In addition to LTCHs, the PDPM applies to intermediate rehabilitation facility and skilled nursing facility payments.) Long-term (acute) care hospitals are defined by Medicare as having an average inpatient length of stay of greater than 25 days. The *long-term care hospital quality reporting program (LTCH QRP)* was mandated by of the Patient Protection and Affordable

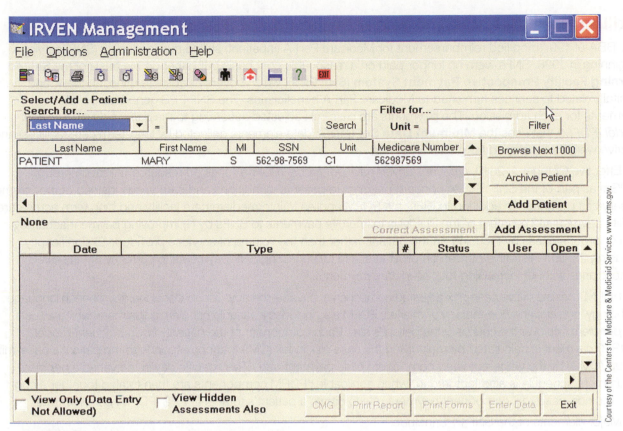

FIGURE 9-10 Opening screen from IRVEN software.

Care Act of 2010, creating LTCH quality reporting requirements. Every year, CMS publishes the quality measures that LTCHs must report. The Improving Medicare Post-Acute Care Transformation Act of 2014 (IMPACT Act) requires LTCHs to submit standardized patient assessment data for quality measures, resource use, and other measures. It specifies that data elements be standardized and interoperable to allow for the exchange of data among post-acute care providers and other providers (e.g., provide access to longitudinal information for providers to facilitate coordinated care).

Major elements of the LTCH PPS include:

- *Patient classification system* (Patients are classified according to long-term [acute] care diagnosis-related groups [LTC DRGs] based on clinical characteristics and average resource needs. The LTC DRGs are based on existing IPPS DRGs, which have been weighted to reflect the resources required to treat medically complex patients in long-term care hospitals. *Weights* are based on the average resources used to treat patients in a particular LTC DRG, with a weight of 1.000 being the average. When a relative payment weight is higher than 1.000, such as 1.435, that means more resources are required to treat the patient and, thus, the payment is correspondingly higher.)

- *Relative weights* (The MS-LTC-DRGs primary element that accounts for variations in cost per discharge, because the weights reflect severity of illness and resource consumption for each diagnosis)

- *Payment rate* (LTCH PPS payments for Medicare patients will be predetermined, per-discharge amounts for each MS-LTC-DRG.)

- *Adjustments* (LTCH PPS payments are adjusted for short stay cases, interrupted stay cases, cases discharged and readmitted to colocation providers, and high-cost outlier cases. In addition, adjustments are made for differences in area wages and a cost-of-living adjustment [COLA] for LTCHs in Alaska and Hawaii.)

Skilled Nursing Facility Prospective Payment System

The BBA of 1997 modified reimbursement for Medicare Part A (inpatient) skilled nursing facility (SNF) services. Beginning in 1998, SNFs were no longer paid on a reasonable cost basis but rather on the basis of the **Skilled Nursing Facility Prospective Payment System (SNF PPS)**, which covers all costs (routine, ancillary, and capital) related to services furnished to Medicare Part A beneficiaries. The SNF PPS generates *per diem* payments for each admission. The payments are case-mix adjusted according to the *patient-driven payment model (PDPM)* that uses the **Minimum Data Set (MDS)** (data elements collected by long-term care facilities) and relative weights developed from staff time data.

Effective October 1, 2019, a *patient-driven payment model (PDPM)* replaced resource-utilization groups (RUGs) as part of the SNF PPS to connect payment to patients' conditions and care needs instead of the volume of services provided. (In addition to IRFs, the PDPM applies to intermediate care facility and long term acute care facility payments.) The intent of the PDPM is to improve payments to SNFs by (1) improving payment accuracy and appropriateness by focusing on the patient, rather than the volume of services provided; (2) significantly reducing the administrative burden on providers; and (3) improving SNF payments to currently underserved beneficiaries without increasing total Medicare payments.

PDPM consists of five case-mix adjusted components: physical therapy, occupational therapy, speech language pathology, nursing, and non-therapy ancillaries. PDPM also includes a variable *per diem* adjustment, which adjusts the *per diem* rate over the course of the patient's stay. Each component of the *patient-driven payment model (PDPM) payment* is calculated by multiplying the case-mix index (CMI) that corresponds to the patient's case-mix group (CMG) by the wage-adjusted component base payment rate. (The specific day in the variable *per diem* adjustment schedule is also factored in, when applicable.) PDPM components are then totaled together along with the non-case-mix component payment rate to create a patient's total SNF PPS (PDPM) *per diem* rate.

Major elements of the SNF PPS include:

- *Payment rate* (Federal rates are determined using allowable costs from facility cost reports, and data are aggregated nationally by urban and rural area to determine standardized federal *Per diem* rates to which case-mix and wage adjustments apply.)

- *Case-mix adjustment* (*Per diem* payments for each admission are case-mix adjusted using the patient-driven payment model, based on data from resident assessments and relative weights developed from staff time data.)

- *Geographic adjustment* (Labor portions of federal rates are adjusted for geographic variation in wages using the hospital wage index.)

Computerized java-based data entry software entitled **Resident Assessment Validation and Entry (jRAVEN)** is used to enter MDS data about SNF patients and transmit those assessments in CMS-standard format to individual state or national databases. jRAVEN also allows facilities to generate system reports (Figure 9-11).

Skilled Nursing Facility Value-Based Purchasing Program

The **Skilled Nursing Facility Value-Based Purchasing (SNF VBP) Program** was implemented with the intent of rewarding quality and improving health care. As a result, SNFs have an opportunity to receive incentive payments based on performance. Under the SNF VBP program, SNFs will receive:

- hospital readmissions measure information (after a patient is discharged and has a hospital admission within 30 days).

- performance scores based on individual performance and in comparison to other SNFs.

- confidential quarterly and annual reports about their performance.

- payment incentives based on their performance.

The *Skilled Nursing Facility 30-Day All-Cause Readmission Measure (SNFRM)* is used in the SNF VBP program to estimate the risk-standardized rate of unplanned readmissions within 30 days for people with fee-for-service Medicare (who were inpatients at PPS, critical access, or psychiatric hospitals) and for any cause

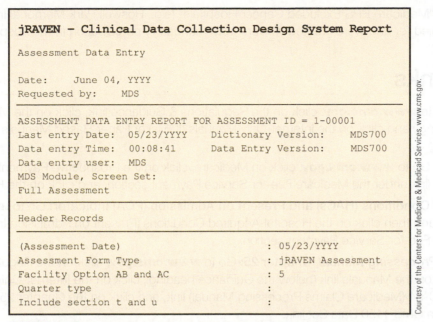

FIGURE 9-11 Sample report generated from jRAVEN software.

or condition. In particular, the SNF VBP program awards incentive payments based on performance regarding readmission measures. Those incentive payments are included on Medicare Part A claims paid according to the SNF PPS as a single line item on each claim (and no separate payments are made). Incentive payments do not apply to any other type of claim (e.g., Medicaid, Medicaid managed care, Medicare Advantage).

Summary

Health care costs increased dramatically with the implementation of government-sponsored health programs in 1965. This led to the creation and implementation of prospective payment systems and fee schedules for government health programs as a way to control costs by reimbursing facilities according to predetermined rates based on patient category or type of facility (with annual increases based on an inflation index and a geographic wage index). The Centers for Medicare and Medicaid Services (CMS) manage implementation of Medicare PPS, fee schedules, and exclusions according to prospective cost-based rates and prospective price-based rates.

Prospective cost-based rates are based on reported health care costs (e.g., charges) from which a prospective *per diem* rate is determined. Annual rates are usually adjusted using actual costs from the prior year. This method may be based on the facility's *case mix* (types and categories of patients that reflect the need for different levels of service based on acuity). Prospective payment systems based on this reimbursement methodology include the patient-driven payment model (PDPM) for inpatient rehabilitation facilities, long-term (acute) care facilities, and skilled nursing facilities.

Prospective price-based rates are associated with a particular category of patient (e.g., inpatients), and rates are established by the payer (e.g., Medicare) prior to the provision of health care services. Prospective payment systems based on this reimbursement methodology include Medicare severity diagnosis-related groups (MS-DRGs) for inpatient care.

Typically, third-party payers adopt prospective payment systems, fee schedules, and exclusions after Medicare has implemented them; payers modify them to suit their needs.

A fee schedule is cost-based, fee-for-service reimbursement methodology that includes a list of maximum fees and corresponding procedures/services, which payers use to compensate providers for health care services delivered to patients.

Exclusions are "Medicare PPS Excluded Cancer Hospitals" (e.g., Roswell Park Memorial Institute in Buffalo, New York) that applied for and were granted waivers from mandatory participation in the hospital inpatient PPS.

Internet Links

CMS manuals: Go to **www.cms.gov**, click on the Regulations & Guidance link, click on the Manuals link (below the Guidance heading), and click on the Internet-Only Manuals (IOMs) or Paper-Based Manuals link to access CMS manuals.

HIPPS rate codes: Go to **www.cms.gov**, click on Medicare, click on the Prospective Payment Systems - General Information link under the Medicare Fee-for-Service Payment section, and click on the HIPPS Codes link.

Hospital-Acquired Conditions (HACs) and Present on Admission (POA) Indicator: Go to **www.cms.gov**. Click on Medicare, and then click on the Hospital-Acquired Conditions (Present on Admission Indicator) link under the Medicare Fee-for-Service Payment section.

***Medicare Claims Processing Manual,* Chapter 25:** Go to **www.cms.gov**, click on the Regulations & Guidance link, click on the Manuals link (below the Guidance heading), click on the Internet-Only Manuals (IOMs) link, click on the 100-04 (Medicare Claims Processing Manual) link, and click on the Chapter 25 - Completing and Processing the Form CMS-1450 Data Set link.

Medicare Payment Advisory Commission: Go to **www.medpac.gov**.

Medicare payment systems: Go to **www.cms.gov**, click on the Medicare link, scroll to the Medicare Fee-for-Service Payment heading, and click on any payment system link.

Quality Payment Program: Go to **https://qpp.cms.gov** to learn more about the Quality Payment Program, which includes MIPS and APMs.

Review

9.1 – Calculating Medicare Payments, Write-Offs, Limiting Charges, and Allowed Amounts

Instructions: Complete the following.

1. Calculate the following amounts for a participating provider who bills Medicare:

Submitted charge (based on provider's regular fee for office visit)	$ 75
Medicare physician fee schedule (MPFS) allowed amount	$ 60
Coinsurance amount (paid by patient or supplemental insurance)	$ 12
a. Medicare payment (80 percent of the MPFS allowed amount)	_____
b. Medicare write-off (not to be paid by Medicare or the beneficiary)	_____

2. Calculate the following amounts for a nonPAR who bills Medicare and does not accept assignment:

Submitted charge (based on provider's regular fee)	$ 600
Medicare physician fee schedule (MPFS) allowed amount	$ 400
NonPAR MPFS reduced amount (MPFS allowed amount is reduced by 5 percent)	$ 380
($400 − ($400 × 5 percent) = $450 − $20 = $380)	
NonPAR limiting charge amount (MPFS allowed amount × 115 percent)	$ 460
($400 × 1.15 = $460)	
Medicare payment (80 percent of MPFS reduced amount)	_____
Balance of MPFS limiting charge amount (Billed to beneficiary)	$ 156
($460 − 304 = $156)	
Write-off amount (not to be paid by Medicare or the beneficiary)	_____

3. **Calculate the following amounts for a nonphysician practitioner who bills Medicare:**

Submitted charge (based on provider's regular fee for office encounter) $ 75
MPFS allowed amount $ 60

a. Nonphysician practitioner allowed amount (100 percent of MPFS allowed amount) _____

b. Medicare payment (80 percent of the MPFS allowed amount) _____

9.2 – Multiple Choice

Instructions: Select the most appropriate response.

1. Which prospective payment system (PPS) determines a preestablished payment that depends on the patient's principal diagnosis, comorbidities, complications, and principal and secondary procedures?
   a. OPPS
   b. IPPS
   c. MPFS
   d. SNF PPS

2. The skilled nursing facility prospective payment system (SNF PPS) uses a _____ model.
   a. fee-for-service-based
   b. cost-based
   c. managed care
   d. patient-driven payment

3. Which replaced the reasonable cost-based payment system to now classify patients according to long-term (acute) care DRGs based on patients' clinical characteristics and expected resource needs?
   a. IPPS
   b. LTCH PPS
   c. SNF PPS
   d. OPPS

4. The Resource-Based Relative Value Scale (RBRVS) system, originally implemented in 1992, is now referred to as the
   a. clinical laboratory fee schedule.
   b. long-term (acute) care hospital prospective payment system.
   c. Medicare physician fee schedule.
   d. outpatient prospective payment system.

5. Reviewing types and/or categories of patients treated by a facility is part of _____ management.
   a. capitation
   b. case-mix
   c. chargemaster
   d. claims

6. Diagnosis-related groups are organized into mutually exclusive categories called _____, which are loosely based on body systems.
   a. ambulatory payment classifications
   b. major diagnostic categories
   c. outcomes and assessment information sets
   d. resource utilization groups

7. Physician work, practice expense, and malpractice expense are components of
   a. conversion factors.
   b. limiting charges.
   c. relative-value units.
   d. site of service differentials.

8. Which are medical conditions or complications that patients develop during inpatient hospital stays and that were not present on admission?
   a. Case-mix index relative weights
   b. Hospital-acquired conditions
   c. Medical diagnostic categories
   d. Resource utilization groups

9. A condition that exists at the time an order for inpatient hospital admission occurs is categorized as
   a. case management.
   b. data analysis.
   c. present on admission.
   d. revenue cycle auditing.

10. A patient is admitted as a hospital inpatient with a diagnosis of possible myocardial infarction. During admission, the physician documented that the patient fell while walking to the bathroom and fractured the left hip. Which present on admission (POA) indicator applies to the left hip fracture diagnosis?
    a. Y (present at the time of inpatient admission)
    b. N (not present at the time of inpatient admission)
    c. U (documentation is insufficient to determine if condition is present on admission)
    d. W (provider is unable to clinically determine whether condition was present on admission or not)

11. A patient is admitted as a hospital inpatient with a diagnosis of pneumococcal pneumonia. The physician documented in the history and physical examination that the patient also has chronic asthma and diabetes mellitus, both of which were medically managed during the inpatient admission. Which present on admission (POA) indicator applies to the pneumococcal pneumonia?
    a. Y (present at the time of inpatient admission)
    b. N (not present at the time of inpatient admission)
    c. U (documentation is insufficient to determine if condition is present on admission)
    d. W (provider is unable to clinically determine whether condition was present on admission or not)

12. A patient is admitted as a hospital inpatient and undergoes bilateral knee replacement surgery. The responsible physician documents severe arthritis, bilateral knees. Upon discharge, the patient is provided with instructions for follow-up and care postoperatively as well as for a diagnosis of hypothyroidism. Which present on admission (POA) indicator applies to the hypothyroidism?
    a. Y (present at the time of inpatient admission)
    b. N (not present at the time of inpatient admission)
    c. U (documentation is insufficient to determine if condition is present on admission)
    d. W (provider is unable to clinically determine whether condition was present on admission or not)

13. A hospital has 290 inpatient cases that are assigned to DRG 169, which has a relative weight of 1.106. What is the total relative weight for the cases?
    a. 262.21
    b. 320.74
    c. 49,010.00
    d. 54,205.06

14. A nursing facility has 12 Medicare cases that are reimbursed at $9,995 per case. What is the total Medicare reimbursement for all of the cases?
    a. $832.92
    b. $11,054.47
    c. $119,940.00
    d. $132,653.64

15. The inpatient prospective payment system (IPPS) is a reimbursement method that is a _____ rate.
    a. capitation
    b. cost-based
    c. price-based
    d. retrospective

9.3 – Data Analytics for Medicare Part B Reimbursement

Instructions: Refer to the *Top 10 Current Procedural Terminology (CPT) Codes* table, and analyze its data by answering the following questions about the *Medicare Part B Physician and Supplier National Data*.

Rank by Charges	CPT Code	Allowed Charges	Number of Services
1	99214	$ 8,174,871,557	81,303,417
2	99213	$ 6,789,770,914	100,262,062
3	99232	$ 3,572,583,474	50,943,179
4	99223	$ 2,309,147,150	11,770,703
5	66984	$ 2,254,500,991	3,103,372
6	99233	$ 2,253,815,789	22,283,347
7	99285	$ 1,674,265,887	9,879,083
8	88305	$ 1,377,477,046	19,853,914
9	99204	$ 1,339,445,004	8,569,205
10	99215	$ 1,316,510,822	9,691,728
	TOTALS	$ 31,062,388,634	317,660,010

Top 10 Current Procedural Terminology (CPT) Codes (Medicare Part B Physician and Supplier National Data)

_____ **1.** Which CPT code is ranked last according to number of services?

_____ **2.** What was the total allowed charges for CPT code 99233?

_____ **3.** Calculate the percentage of E/M codes in the top 10 ranking.

_____ **4.** List the lowest ranking CPT Surgery code according to allowed charges.

_____ **5.** Calculate the average per service allowed charge for CPT code 99213.

9.4 – Interpreting Medicare Status Indicators and Procedure Discounting Data for Ambulatory Payment Classifications

Instructions: Refer to the *Medicare Status Indicators and Procedure Discounting Data for Ambulatory Payment Classifications* table, and analyze its data by answering the following questions about ambulatory payment classifications data.

Status Indicator	Description
T	Significant procedure, multiple procedure reduction applies
S	Significant procedure, and is not discounted when you report multiple CPT codes that group to APCs with multiple "S" status indicators
Small Intestine Endoscopy	
Codes in Range:	44360
	44361
	44363
	44364
	44365

Medicare Status Indicators and Procedure Discounting Data for Ambulatory Payment Classifications

(continues)

(continued)

Medicare Status Indicators and Procedure Discounting Data for Ambulatory Payment Classifications	
Small Intestine Endoscopy	**Description**
Status Indicator:	T
Relative Weight:	10.1857
Payment Rate:	$701.55
National Adjusted Coinsurance:	$152.78
Minimum Unadjusted Coinsurance:	$140.31

_____ 1. How many codes are contained in the range for small intestine endoscopy?

_____ 2. What is the relative weight for small intestine endoscopy?

_____ 3. What is the national adjusted coinsurance for small intestine endoscopy?

_____ 4. What is the payment rate for small intestine endoscopy?

_____ 5. What is the minimum unadjusted coinsurance for small intestine endoscopy?

9.5 – Interpreting Medicare-Severity Diagnosis-Related Groups Data

Instructions: Review the *Medicare-Severity Diagnosis-Related Groups 414–416 Data* table to answer questions about MS-DRGs 414–416.

Medicare-Severity Diagnosis-Related Groups 414–416 Data						
MS-DRG	**MDC**	**Type**	**MS-DRG Title**	**Weight**	**LOS**	**RATE**
414	07	Surg	Cholecystectomy Except by Laparoscope w/o CDE w MCC	3.6208	8.8	$5,431.20
415	07	Surg	Cholecystectomy Except by Laparoscope w/o CDE w CC	2.0173	5.8	$3,025.95
416	07	Surg	Cholecystectomy Except by Laparoscope w/o CDE w/o CDE w/o CC/MCC	1.3268	3.5	$1,990.20

_____ 1. What is the weight associated with MS-DRG 415?

_____ 2. What is the payment rate associated with MS-DRG 414?

_____ 3. What is the length of stay (LOS) for MS-DRG 416?

_____ 4. Which MS-DRG has the lowest reimbursement rate?

_____ 5. Which MS-DRG has the highest reimbursement rate?

Coding Compliance Programs, Clinical Documentation Improvement, and Coding for Medical Necessity

Chapter Outline

Coding Compliance Programs

Clinical Documentation Improvement

Coding for Medical Necessity

Coding from Case Scenarios and Patient Records

Chapter Objectives

Upon successful completion of this chapter, you should be able to:

1. Define key terms related to related to coding compliance programs, clinical documentation improvement, and coding for medical necessity.
2. Describe the components of a coding compliance program.
3. Apply clinical documentation improvement to ensure coding accuracy.
4. Apply coding for medical necessity guidance when reporting ICD-10-CM, CPT, and HCPCS Level II codes on claims.
5. Review case scenarios and patient records to determine the appropriate assignment of codes to diagnoses, procedures, and services.

Key Terms

auditing process

clinical documentation improvement (CDI)

clinical documentation integrity (CDI)

coding compliance

coding compliance program

coding for medical necessity

compliance program guidance

local coverage determination (LCD)

medically managed

medically unlikely edit (MUE)

Medicare code editor (MCE)

Medicare coverage database (MCD)

narrative clinic note

National Correct Coding Initiative (NCCI) program

national coverage determination (NCD)

operative report

outpatient code editor (OCE)

procedure-to-procedure (PTP) code pair edits

SOAP note
assessment
objective
plan
subjective

Introduction

In Chapters 7 through 9, coding practice exercises consisted of statements for which diagnosis or procedure/service codes were assigned. The next step in learning to code properly is to determine that coding compliance is met, apply clinical documentation improvement (CDI) processes, and select diagnoses and procedures/services from case studies and patient reports and link each procedure/service with the diagnosis code that justifies the medical necessity for performing it. (Coding compliance, clinical documentation improvement, and coding for medical necessity are required by payers for reimbursement consideration.)

Coding compliance, clinical documentation improvement, and coding for medical necessity require a background in patient record documentation practices and the ability to interpret provider documentation.

Coding Compliance Programs

Coding compliance is the conformity to established coding guidelines and regulations. Health information management departments (and similar areas, such as the coding and billing section of a physician's practice) develop coding compliance programs to ensure coding accuracy and conformance with guidelines and regulations. **Coding compliance programs** include:

- *Written policies and procedures,* which are updated at least annually, and address clinical documentation improvement, downcoding/unbundling/upcoding, ethical coding, physician queries, using code editing software, and so on.

- *Routine coding audits and monitoring*, both internal (performed by coding manager) and external (conducted by outside consulting agency), identify coding errors and at-risk coding practices. when performing audits, *benchmarking* is a helpful practice that allows the coding manager to establish criteria (e.g., coding error rates, coding productivity rates), which are used during coding assessment.

- *Compliance-based education and training,* which results from routine coding audits and monitoring. Education and training programs are developed to assist coders improve accuracy (e.g., decrease coding error rates) and the proper use of software (e.g., outpatient code editor).

An effective coding compliance program requires adherence to the following government programs:

- Comprehensive error rate testing (CERT) program
- Medical review (MR)
- National correct coding initiative (NCCI) program
- Recovery audit contractor (RAC) program

(Chapter 4 of this textbook also covers the CERT, MR, and RAC programs.)

The Department of Health and Human Services' Office of the Inspector General (OIG) developed voluntary **compliance program guidance** documents for the following segments of the health care industry to encourage the development and use of internal controls to monitor adherence to applicable regulations, statutes, and program requirements. Health care organizations implemented compliance programs under the management of a designated *compliance officer.*

- Hospitals (1998 and 2005)
- Home health agencies (1998)
- Clinical laboratories (1998)
- Third-party medical billing companies (1998)
- Durable medical equipment, prosthetic, orthotic, and supply industry (1999)
- Hospices (1999)
- Medicare+Choice organizations (1999)

- Nursing facilities (2000 and 2008)
- Individual and small group physician practices (2000)
- Ambulance suppliers (2003)
- Pharmaceutical manufacturers (2003)
- Recipients of Public Health Service biomedical and behavioral research awards (2005)

Voluntary compliance efforts foster an environment that promotes detection, prevention, and resolution of conduct that does not conform to facility or provider ethical business policies, federal and state laws (statutes) and regulations, and government and private third-party payer health care program requirements. A successful compliance program reduces fraud and abuse, enhances provider operations, improves quality of patient care, and reduces overall costs of providing health care services. Health care facilities establish *benchmarks* (e.g., points of reference) to demonstrate implementation of a compliance program and document achievements and action plans to address deficiencies.

Example: Hospitals review and edit the *charge description master* (CDM) (or *chargemaster*) to ensure that updated CPT codes and other data are included for ancillary services (e.g., laboratory, radiology). This internal control mechanism impacts reimbursement by eliminating erroneous claims and resultant third-party payer denials (for submission of outdated codes on claims).

 NOTE:

The Indian Health Service (IHS) website contains a sample coding compliance plan. Go to www.ihs.gov, enter Coding Resources in the Search box, click Search, click on the Coding Resources | Health Information Management (HIM) link, and click on the Coding Compliance Plan link.

Comprehensive Error Rate Testing Program

The *comprehensive error rate testing (CERT) program* was implemented as a result of the Improper Payments Elimination and Recovery Improvement Act (IPERIA) of 2012, and its purpose is to annually review programs to improve efforts to reduce and recover improper payments. *Improper payments* are those that should not have been made or included an incorrect amount. They are both overpayments and underpayments, and include:

- Duplicate payments
- Payments for an incorrect amount
- Payments for an ineligible service
- Payments for services not received
- Payments to an ineligible recipient

The objective of the CERT program is to estimate the accuracy of the Medicare fee-for-service (FFS) by calculating improper payment rate through evaluation of a statistically valid random sample of claims (e.g., 50,000 claims each year). The evaluation determines whether they were properly paid under Medicare billing, coding, and coverage rules. The CERT program process includes the following steps:

1. Claim selection from Medicare Part A, Part B, and DMEPOS
2. Medical record requests from providers and suppliers that submitted the selected claims
3. Review of claims by medical review professionals (coders, nurses, physicians) and submitted documentation (medical records) to determine whether claim was paid properly
4. Assignment of improper payment categories
   a. No documentation (e.g., provider or supplier fails to respond to request for medical records)
   b. Insufficient documentation (e.g., medical records do not support payment for services billed)

   c. Medical necessity (e.g., submitted medical records either support or do not support services billed)

   d. Incorrect coding (e.g., erroneous codes, unbundled codes)

   e. Other (e.g., duplicate payment error, noncovered or unallowable service)

5. Calculation of improper payment rate by statistical contractor

6. Centers for Medicare and Medicaid Services (CMS) and Medicare administrative contractors (MACs) analyze improper payment rate data and MACs develop *Improper Payment Reduction Strategies;* corrective actions to reduce improper payments include:

   a. Comparative Billing Reports (CBRs) (for specific providers)

   b. Provider education

   c. Improving system edits

   d. Prior authorization projects

   e. Program for Evaluating Payment Patterns Electronic Report (PEPPERs) (inpatient hospitals)

   f. Refining improper payment rate measurement processes

   g. Risk-based provider screening

   h. Updating coverage policies and manuals

> **Example:** For fiscal year (FY) 2016, the Medicare FFS program improper payment rate was 11 percent, representing over $41 billion in improper payments (compared to 12 percent for FY 2015 and over $43 billion in improper payments).

Medical Review (MR)

The goal of the Medicare *medical review (MR)* program is to reduce payment errors by identifying and addressing provider billing errors that involve coverage and coding issues. To achieve the goal, Medicare administrative contractors:

- Proactively identify patterns of potential billing errors concerning Medicare coverage and coding made by providers through data analysis and evaluation of other information (e.g., submission of complaints).
- Review CERT program data, RAC program vulnerabilities, and Office of Inspector General (OIG) and Government Accountability Office (GAO) reports.
- Take action to prevent and address identified errors.
- Publish local coverage determination (LCDs) to provide guidance about items and services that will be eligible for Medicare payment.
- Publish Medicare Learning Network (MLN) educational articles related to the MR process.

All medical review activities are based on the operational principle of *progressive correct action (PCA)*, which involves data analysis, error detection, validation of errors, provider education, determination of review type, sampling claims, and payment recovery. PCA serves as an approach to performing medical review, and it assists Medicare administrative contractors in deciding how to deploy medical review resources and tools appropriately. The Medicare administrative contractor may use any relevant information deemed necessary to generate a prepayment or postpayment claim review determination. A process called *additional documentation request (ADR)* is initiated when the Medicare administrative contractor has reviewed documentation submitted with a claim and then requests additional documentation from the provider when deemed necessary and in accordance with Medicare program manuals.

CMS medical review personnel provide MAC oversight by interpreting medical review policy. Such direction includes:

- Reviewing and approving MAC annual medical review strategies
- Facilitating MAC implementation of recently enacted Medicare legislation
- Facilitating compliance with current regulations

- Ensuring MAC performance of CMS operating instructions
- Conducting continuous monitoring and evaluation of MAC performance in accord with CMS program instructions and MAC strategies and goals
- Providing ongoing feedback and consultation to MACs regarding Medicare program and medical review issues

MACs are required to adhere to CMS policy instructions, including those found in Medicare manuals and the following:

- **National coverage determinations (NCDs)**, which are developed by CMS to describe circumstances for which Medicare will cover specific procedures, services, or technologies on a national basis. Medicare coverage is limited to items and services that are reasonable and necessary for the diagnosis or treatment of an illness or injury (and within the scope of a Medicare benefit category). If an NCD does not specifically exclude or limit an indication or circumstance, or if the item or service is not mentioned at all in an NCD or in a Medicare manual, it is up to the MAC to make the coverage decision.
- **Local coverage determinations (LCDs)**, which are determinations made by MACs to cover items and services that are not developed as an NCD, and they are based on whether the service or item is reasonable and necessary.

Example: The medical review of high utilization DMEPOS claims was conducted in 2007 because $219 million Medicare Part B claims were paid for test strips and lancets. Information submitted by DME suppliers on claims was analyzed, and it was determined that $76 million paid claims could be identified as high utilization claims. Of 100 sampled claims for test strips and lancets, 29 claims were submitted in accordance with Medicare documentation requirements. The remaining 71 claims contained one or more deficiencies, such as missing or incomplete physician orders, insufficient documentation about refill requirements, missing proof-of-delivery records, and the quantity of supplies that exceeded utilization guidelines was not supported (by documentation indicating the specific reason for additional supplies, actual frequency of testing, or treating physician's evaluation of the patient's diabetic control within six months before ordering the supplies). Based on the sample results, it was estimated that the DMEPOS MAC inappropriately allowed for payment of over $40 million in claims for test strips and lancets. Of this amount, it was estimated that the DMEPOS MAC inappropriately paid over $30 million to DME suppliers.

National Correct Coding Initiative

The Centers for Medicare and Medicaid Services (CMS) implemented the **National Correct Coding Initiative (NCCI) program** to promote national correct coding methodologies and to control the improper assignment of codes that result in inappropriate reimbursement of Medicare Part B claims. Effective October 2010, the NCCI program was implemented for state Medicaid programs. Separate edit files and manuals are published for the CMS state Medicaid NCCI program methodology. The CMS Medicare and Medicaid NCCI programs both use the term *procedure to procedure (PTP)* to identify NCCI program column one/column two edits. (Table 10-1 contains a list of NCCI program terms, definitions, and examples.) There are more than 140,000 NCCI program code pairs (or NCCI program edit pairs) that cannot be reported on the same claim for the same date of service, and providers use *outpatient code editor (OCE)* software to detect inappropriate codes and more.

- NCCI program **procedure-to-procedure (PTP) code pair edits** are automated prepayment edits that prevent improper payment when certain codes are submitted together for Part B-covered services. If a provider reports both codes associated with an edit pair for the same beneficiary on the same date of service, the Column One code is eligible for payment but the Column Two code is denied *unless a clinically appropriate CPT or HCPCS Level II modifier is also reported*.
- NCCI program **medically unlikely edits (MUEs)** are used to compare *units of service (UOS)* with CPT and HCPCS Level II codes reported on claims and indicate the maximum number of UOS allowable by the same provider for the same beneficiary on the same date of service under most circumstances.
- NCCI program *add-on code (AOC) edits* contain a list of CPT and HCPCS Level II add-on codes with their respective primary codes; a reported add-on code is eligible for payment only when its CPT primary code is also eligible for reimbursement.

TABLE 10-1 NCCI program terms and definitions

NCCI Terms	Definitions
Add-on code	CPT code preceded by a plus (+) symbol to indicate that the code is reported *only when the CPT primary code is reported as the first- listed procedure.*
NCCI program edits	Pairs of CPT and/or HCPCS Level II codes that are not separately payable except under certain circumstances (e.g., reporting an appropriate modifier). CCI edits apply to services billed by the same provider for the same beneficiary on the same date of service.
	Example: The surgeon intends to perform a laparoscopic cholecystectomy, but upon visualization of an inflamed and huge gallbladder, the procedure is changed to an open cholecystectomy. If CPT codes for open cholecystectomy and laparoscopic cholecystectomy are reported, NCCI program edits result in a claims denial. (When a laparoscopic procedure becomes an open procedure, report only the open procedure code.)
Column 1 code	The major procedure or service when reported with another code. The *column 1 code* represents greater work, effort, and time than the other code reported. Thus, higher payments are associated with column 1 codes (previously called *comprehensive codes*).
	Example: The patient undergoes a superficial biopsy and a deep biopsy of the same site (during the same operative episode). If CPT codes for both deep and superficial biopsies are reported, NCCI program edits result in claims denial. (When both deep and superficial biopsies are performed on the same site, report only the deep biopsy code.)
Column 2 code	The lesser procedure or service when reported with another code. The *column 2 code* is part of another major procedure or service, and it is often represented by a lower work relative value unit (RVU) under the Medicare Physician Fee Schedule. Thus, lower payments are associated with column 2 codes (previously called *component codes*).
	Example: The patient undergoes a superficial biopsy and a deep superficial biopsy of the same site (during the same operative episode). Documentation supports the significant work, effort, and time associated with each biopsy, which means codes for both the superficial biopsy and deep biopsy are reported. A modifier (e.g., -59, Distinct Procedural Service) is added to the superficial biopsy code so that NCCI program edits do not result in claims denial. (Reduced payment for the superficial biopsy might be processed by the payer after review of documentation.)
Column 1/ column 2 edits	Now referred to as *procedure-to-procedure code edits,* these are code pairs (or edit pairs), where one code is a component (column 1) of the more comprehensive code (column 2), and only the comprehensive code is paid. (When clinical circumstances justify reporting both codes, add an NCCI modifier to either code of the code pair so that payment of both codes might be allowed.) (*See also* NCCI procedure-to-procedure [PTP] code pair edits in this table.)
Mutually exclusive codes (Figure 10-1)	Code pairs (or edit pairs), where one of the procedures/services could not reasonably be performed with the other. (When clinical circumstances justify reporting both codes, add a modifier to either code of the code pair so that payment of both codes might be allowed.)
	Example: A claim contains CPT codes for initial inpatient E/M services and critical care E/M services (with modifier -59) for the same date of service. Documentation supports initial inpatient E/M services provided at 3 A.M. on the day of admission (when the patient did not require critical care) and critical care services later that same day (when the patient did require critical care).
Procedure-to-procedure (PTP) code pair edits (Figure 10-2)	Used by Medicare administrative contractors to adjudicate provider claims for physician services, outpatient hospital services, and outpatient therapy services; they are *not* applied to facility claims for inpatient services. (*See also* NCCI program column 1/column 2 edits in this table.)
	Example: Refer to Figure 10-1, which contains a sample listing of the NCCI PTP code pair edits. Column 1 code 10021 is reported on the CMS-1500 claim, and none of the codes from column 2 are reported on the same claim (unless an appropriate modifier is attached to one of the codes and supporting documentation justifies reporting multiple codes).

National Correct Coding Initiative Program Procedure-to-Procedure Code Pair Edits					
Column 1	Column 2	* = In	Effective	Deletion	Modifier 0 = not allowed
10021	J2001		20040701	*	1
10021	19303		20020101	*	1
10021	36000		20021001	*	1
10021	36410		20021001	*	1
10021	64415		20021001	*	1
10021	64416		20030101	*	1
10021	64417		20021001	*	1

Courtesy of the Centers for Medicare & Medicaid Services, www.cms.gov.

FIGURE 10-1 Sample NCCI program column 1/column 2 code pair edits.

National Correct Coding Initiative Program Mutually Exclusive Edits					
Column 1	Column 2	* = In existence prior to 1996	Effective Date	Deletion Date * = no data	Modifier 0 = not allowed 1 = allowed 9 = not applicable
10060	11401		19960101	*	1
10060	11402		19960101	*	1
10060	11403		19960101	*	1
10060	11404		19960101	*	1
10060	11406		19960101	*	1

Courtesy of the Centers for Medicare & Medicaid Services, www.cms.gov.

FIGURE 10-2 Sample NCCI program mutually exclusive edits.

> **Example:** A patient undergoes a cataract extraction in the left eye. The claim submitted by the provider contains a 3 in the units column of Block 24, which means the patient underwent cataract extraction surgery on three left eyes. The *medically unlikely edit* process rejects the claim (because the patient has just one left eye). If 1 had been entered in the units column of Block 24, the claim would have passed the *medically unlikely edit* and payment would have been processed.

NCCI program PTP code edit pairs (Table 10-2) are used to process Medicare Part B claims, and NCCI program coding policies are based on the:

- Analysis of standard medical and surgical practice
- Coding conventions included in CPT
- Coding guidelines developed by national medical specialty societies (e.g., CPT Advisory Committee, which contains representatives of major medical societies)
- Local and national coverage determinations
- Review of current coding practices

The NCCI program was initially developed for use by MACs that process Medicare Part B claims for physician office services. NCCI program edits were added to the outpatient code editor (OCE) in August 2000, and they are used by MACs to process Medicare Part B claims for outpatient hospital services and by contractors that process state Medicaid claims. (Some OCE edits that apply to outpatient hospital services claims differ from comparable edits in the NCCI program used to process physician office services claims.)

Carefully review parenthetical notes below CPT code descriptions to locate procedures that are separately reported (in addition to the major procedure performed). When reporting codes for outpatient hospital services and physician office services, be sure to use outpatient code editor (OCE) software or NCCI program software, respectively, to identify bundled codes for procedures and services considered necessary to accomplish the major procedure.

TABLE 10-2 Partial listing of National Correct Coding Initiative (NCCI) program edits in outpatient code editor (OCE) software

NCCI Edit	Description	Disposition of Claim
1	Invalid diagnosis code	Return to Provider
2	Diagnosis and age conflict	Return to Provider
3	Diagnosis and sex conflict	Return to Provider
4	Medicare secondary payer alert	Suspend
19	Mutually exclusive procedure that is not allowed by NCCI program even if appropriate modifier is present	Line Item Rejection
20	Component of a comprehensive procedure that is not allowed by NCCI program even if appropriate modifier is present	Line Item Rejection
39	Mutually exclusive procedure that would be allowed by NCCI program if appropriate modifier were present	Line Item Rejection
40	Component of a comprehensive procedure that would be allowed by NCCI program if appropriate modifier were present	Line Item Rejection

Courtesy of the Centers for Medicare & Medicaid Services, www.cms.gov.

NOTE:

Go to medicare.fcso.com, and enter "NCCI" in the Search box, and click on the Search icon to locate *NCCI (National Correct Coding Initiative)*, which provides access to an *NCCI Procedure-to-Procedure code pair lookup tutorial*. When entering a CPT code and the date of service, PTP search results display column 1/column 2 code edits.

Bundled procedure codes are *not* separately coded or reported with the major procedure code. Reporting bundled procedure codes in addition to the major procedure code is characterized as unbundling (fraud). The OCE edits are packaged with commercial software, such as Optum360's *EncoderPro.com Expert*. The NCCI program edits are available at www.cms.gov. (The OCE and NCCI program edits are available for purchase from the National Technical Information Service at www.ntis.gov.)

Example: Code 67911 describes the Correction of lid retraction. A parenthetical note below the code description advises that, if autogenous graft materials are used during the same operative session, tissue graft codes 15769, or 20920, 20922 are reported in addition to code 67911. According to the Medicare Code Editor (MCE), *other procedures necessary to accomplish* the correction of lid retraction are included in code 67911, such as full-thickness graft placement (15260). Other such procedures are not separately coded and reported when performed during the same operative session as the correction of lid retraction.

CMS Posts Correct Coding Initiative (CCI) Edits on Internet

Courtesy of the Centers for Medicare & Medicaid Services, www.cms.gov.

The Centers for Medicare & Medicaid Services (CMS) today make it easier for physicians and other providers to bill properly and be paid promptly for their services to people with Medicare coverage. CMS has posted on its website (www.cms.gov) the automated edits used to identify questionable claims and adjust payments to reflect what would have been paid if the claim had been filed correctly. The edits, known as the National Correct

Coding Initiative (NCCI) program procedure-to-procedure code pair edits, identify pairs of services that normally should not be billed by the same physician for the same patient on the same day. The NCCI program also promotes uniformity among the contractors that process Medicare claims in interpreting Medicare payment policies.

The posting of NCCI program edits is the most recent in a series of steps CMS has taken to use the

(continues)

CMS Posts Correct Coding Initiative (CCI) Edits on Internet (*continued*)

Internet creatively to reduce the regulatory burden on physicians and make it easier for them to work with Medicare to improve services to beneficiaries. CMS has also added a feature to its website that makes it possible for physicians to determine in advance what they will be paid for a particular service or range of services. The Medicare Physician Fee Schedule look-up provides both the unadjusted payment rates, as well as the payment rates by geographic location. While the NCCI program is a cornerstone of efforts to ensure that Medicare and beneficiaries do not pay twice for the same service or for duplicative services, CMS believes physicians should have easy access to the edits used to identify incorrect claims. The NCCI program includes two types of PTP code pair edits:

- Comprehensive/component edits (code pairs that should not be billed together because one service inherently includes the other)

- Mutually exclusive edits (code pairs that, for clinical reasons, are unlikely to be performed on the same patient on the same day; for example, two different types of testing that yield equivalent results)

CPT codes representing services denied based on NCCI program edits may not be billed to Medicare beneficiaries. Since these denials are based on incorrect coding rather than medical necessity, the provider cannot submit an Advance Beneficiary Notice (ABN) to seek payment from a Medicare beneficiary. An Advance Beneficiary Notice (ABN) is a form completed and signed by a Medicare beneficiary each time a provider believes a normally covered service will not be covered and the provider wants to bill the beneficiary directly for the service. In addition, because the denials are based on incorrect coding (rather than a legislated Medicare benefit exclusion) the provider cannot seek payment from the beneficiary even if a Notice of Exclusions from Medicare Benefits (NEMB) was obtained.

A *Notice of Exclusions from Medicare Benefits (NEMB)* is a form completed and signed by a Medicare beneficiary before items, procedures, and services excluded from Medicare benefits are provided; alerts Medicare beneficiaries in advance that Medicare does not cover certain items and services because they do not meet the definition of a Medicare benefit or because they are specifically excluded by law; NEMB is completed when an ABN is not appropriate.

The NCCI program edits, which are updated quarterly, were previously available to physicians and other providers on a paid subscription basis, but they are now available to anyone with a personal computer. The NCCI program edits are posted as a spreadsheet that will allow users to sort by procedural code and effective date. A "find" feature will allow users to look for a specific code. The NCCI program edit files are also indexed by procedural code ranges for easy navigation.

The new web page also includes links to documents that explain the edits, including the:

- Medicare Claims Processing Manual

- NCCI Edits Program Transmittals

- NCCI FAQs (frequently asked questions)

- NCCI Policy Manual for Part B MACs

Unbundling CPT Codes

Providers are responsible for reporting the CPT (and HCPCS Level II) code that most comprehensively describes the services provided. NCCI program edits determine the appropriateness of CPT code combinations for claims submitted to Medicare administrative contractors. NCCI program edits are designed to detect unbundling, which involves reporting multiple codes for a service when a single comprehensive code should be assigned. The practice of unbundling occurs because:

- Provider's coding staff unintentionally reports multiple codes based on misinterpreted coding guidelines.
- Reporting multiple codes is intentional and is done to maximize reimbursement.

Unbundling occurs when one service is divided into its component parts, and a code for each component part is reported as if they were performed as separate services.

Example: A 64-year-old female patient undergoes total abdominal hysterectomy with bilateral salpingectomy and oophorectomy. Review CPT Surgery section code descriptions for 58150, 58700, and 58720. Reporting codes 58700 and 58720 in addition to 58150 is considered unbundling. If all three codes are submitted on a claim, reimbursement for codes 58700 and 58720 would be disallowed (and the provider might be subject to allegations of fraud and abuse).

Unbundling occurs when a code for the separate surgical approach (e.g., laparotomy) is reported in addition to a code for the surgical procedure. Procedures performed to gain access to an area or organ system are not separately reported.

Example: A 54-year-old female patient undergoes excision of ileoanal reservoir with ileostomy, which requires lysis of adhesions to gain access to the site of surgery. Review CPT Surgery section code descriptions for 45136 and 44005. Report CPT code 45136 only because code 44005 is considered a component part of the total procedure (45136). Reporting both codes would be considered unbundling.

Recovery Audit Contractor Program

The Tax Relief and Health Care Act of 2006 implemented the *recovery audit contractor (RAC) program* (in 2010), which was created by CMS as part of the agency's comprehensive efforts to identify improper Medicare overpayments and underpayments and to fight Medicare fraud, waste, and abuse. Contracts were awarded to recovery audit contractors (RACs) designed to guard the Medicare Trust Fund. The RAC program is the result of a successful demonstration program that used RACs to identify Medicare overpayments and underpayments to health care providers and suppliers in California, Florida, New York, Massachusetts, South Carolina, and Arizona. The demonstration resulted in the return of over $900 million in overpayments to the Medicare Trust Fund between 2005 and 2008 and nearly $38 million in underpayments returned to health care providers.

Overpayments occur when health care providers submit claims that do not meet Medicare's coding or medical necessity policies. Underpayments occur when health care providers submit claims for a simple procedure but the medical record reveals that a more complicated procedure was actually performed. Health care providers that are subject to RAC program review include home durable medical equipment suppliers, health agencies, hospitals, nursing facilities, physician practices, and any other provider or supplier that submits claims to Medicare Parts A and B.

Example: In 2015, RACs identified and corrected over $440 million in improper payments. Over $359 million were collected in overpayments, and over $80 million were identified as underpayments (and paid back to providers). (Although RACs did not perform *any patient status reviews* on inpatient hospital claims with dates of admission in 2015, more than $278 million of overpayments collected continued to be generated by inpatient hospital claims. These resulted from coding validation and other types of inpatient hospital reviews.) As a result, a net of over $141 million was returned to the Medicare Trust Fund and takes into consideration RAC program costs, which include administrative costs, contingency fees, and amounts overturned upon appeal.

Clinical Documentation Improvement

Clinical documentation improvement (or **clinical documentation integrity**) **(CDI)** helps ensure accurate and thorough patient record documentation and identifies discrepancies between provider documentation and codes to be assigned. Coders that have questions about documented diagnoses or procedures/services use a *physician query process* to request clarification about documentation, which impacts appropriate code assignment. This results in resolution of documentation and coding discrepancies. Coders also review patient record documentation and use coding guidelines and other guidance (e.g., NCCI program) to assign the most specific codes possible.

Generating Physician Queries

A *physician query* is generated when there is an issue with the quality of documentation in the patient record, such as incomplete or inconsistent provider documentation. For example, if the provider documents an unspecified diagnostic statement, generate a query to the physician asking that additional documentation related to the diagnosis be provided (e.g., acute nature of the condition). Such documentation could result in a more specific ICD-10-CM code assignment. *CMS's rules about physician queries state that they cannot be leading or introduce new information that has not already been documented in the patient record.* Coders generate physician queries when:

- A higher degree of specificity associated with a condition needs to be documented by the physician.

- Assigning a *present on admission (POA)* indicator (for hospital inpatient cases) is difficult because of unclear documentation.

- Clinical evidence of a diagnosis is documented, but the provider did not document the diagnosis.

- Documentation in the patient record is contradictory, unclear or vague, unreadable, or unspecified.

 NOTE:

> The *ICD-10-CM Official Guidelines for Coding and Reporting* presume a causal relationship in ICD-10-CM when two conditions are linked by the terms "with," "associated with," or "due to" (index, tabular list code title, or tabular list instructional note). Even when provider documentation does not specifically link two conditions, they are coded as related unless the provider states that the conditions are not related. (Providers must continue to document a causal relationship for conditions that are not specifically linked by the relational terms in ICD-10-CM.)
>
> In addition, the guideline about "code assignment and clinical criteria" allows for the assignment of a diagnosis code based on provider documentation that the condition exists. *The provider's statement that the patient has a particular condition is sufficient.* Coders are *not* required to locate clinical criteria in the patient record to assign a code to such conditions.

Example: Hospitals created CDI programs in response to implementation of *Medicare severity diagnosis-related groups (MS-DRGs)*. Because MS-DRGs assign payment weights to hospital inpatient cases, based on average resources used to treat patient categorized to a particular MS-DRG, it is important to assign accurate and complete codes to the hospital inpatient admission diagnosis, principal diagnosis, comorbidities (coexisting conditions), complications (conditions that develop during inpatient admission), and procedures. Clinical document specialists are often hired by hospitals to manage the CDI process, and qualifications include excellent coding, reimbursement, and verbal and written communication skills.

DRG Coding Validation and Claims Denials

Revenue cycle management includes *diagnosis-related group (DRG) coding validation and claims denial* procedures, which are vital to recovering otherwise lost revenue to the facility (or reimbursing overpayments received by the hospital to third-party payers). Inpatient DRG coding validation is performed by payers to confirm the accuracy of hospital coding and reimbursement. Payers conduct:

- *Coding audits* identify incorrect code and DRG assignment that results in overpayments to hospitals

- *Level of care audits* review of short inpatient lengths of stay to determine whether the level of care was appropriate (e.g., perhaps the level of care should have been on an outpatient basis)

- *Readmission audits* review of inpatient hospital claims for patient readmissions within a specified number of days, such as five days, to determine whether the previous hospital discharge and level of care provided was appropriate

- *Transfer audits* review of inpatient hospital claims to determine whether transfer or discharge was appropriate (e.g., perhaps a patient discharged home should have been transferred to home health care)

The hospital health information management department completes the following steps as a result of the third-party payer DRG coding validation and claims denial process.

1. *Identify the reason for the claims denial.* Third-party payers submit a letter or other document of claims denial (e.g., remittance advice) to the health care facility or provider, which includes the reason for denying payment of a claim. For example, ASC X12 claims adjustment reason code N208 is for missing, incomplete, or invalid DRG code.

2. *Develop effective claims denial management policies.* For example, claims denial documents are forwarded to an employee in the health information management department who retrieves the original submitted claim, DRG, or other payment information, and the patient record so that an appeal can be prepared.

3. *Review facility documents to determine whether the claims denial is justified.* For example, a commercial third-party payer's claims denial correspondence indicates that the DRG originally assigned by the health care facility is incorrect, and the payer has modified the DRG assignment by adding, deleting, or editing ICD-10-CM or ICD-10-PCS codes. In this case, the health care facility employee who reviews documentation related to the claims denial must determine the accuracy of original codes submitted and the DRG assigned.

4. *Prepare a letter of appeal to obtain appropriate reimbursement.* For example, if the employee determines that code and DRG assignment is accurate, a letter of appeal must contain language from source documents (e.g., patient record, official coding guidelines). However, if facility-assigned code and DRG assignment is determined to be inaccurate, the letter of appeal should include corrected code and DRG assignment. Copies of pertinent reports from the patient record are attached to both types of appeal letters to support the code and DRG assignment.

5. *Follow up to ensure appropriate reimbursement.* For example, the employee prepares a spreadsheet document to track the dates of claims denials, appeals submitted, follow-up correspondence from third-party payers (and replies to such correspondence), and reimbursement received by the facility. This type of document ensures appropriate follow-up from a claims management perspective.

Computer-Assisted Coding

Computer-assisted coding (CAC) (Figure 10-3) has become a tool for accurate coding because it is software that uses natural-language processing to locate and analyze diagnoses and procedures in the patient record and assign ICD-10-CM, ICD-10-PCS, CPT, and HCPCS Level II codes to them. Traditionally, medical coding has been performed by qualified individuals who use paper-based coding manuals and encoders. Many health care facilities and providers continue to perform coding in this manner; however, as technology-driven health care continues to be implemented, electronic health record and CAC software is used to perform medical coding of routine encounters. Coders audit and validate CAC-assigned codes and assign codes to complex encounters (e.g., trauma-based inpatient admissions).

Coding for Medical Necessity

Medical necessity involves linking each procedure or service code reported on a claim to a condition code (e.g., disease, injury, sign, symptom, other reason for encounter) that justifies the need to perform or provide that procedure or service. **Coding for medical necessity** involves assigning ICD-10-CM codes to diagnoses and CPT/HCPCS Level II codes to procedures/services, and then matching an appropriate ICD-10-CM code with each CPT or HCPCS Level II code when reporting codes on CMS-1500 claims. It requires the review of patient record documentation to identify diagnoses, procedures, and services.

Example 1: Procedure: Urinalysis

Diagnosis: Stomach pain

In this example, the provider is not reimbursed because the reason for the urinalysis (stomach pain) does not match the type of procedure performed (urinalysis). To code for medical necessity, the provider would need to document a diagnosis such as urinary frequency to justify reimbursement for the urinalysis procedure.

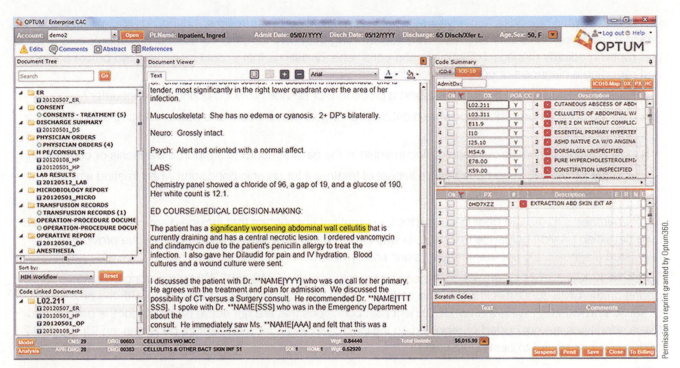

FIGURE 10-3 Sample screen from Optum Enterprise computer-assisted coding (CAC) software.

> **Example 2:** Procedure: X-ray of left humerus
>
> Diagnosis: Upper arm pain, left
>
> In this example, the provider is reimbursed because medical necessity (upper arm pain, left) for performing the procedure (x-ray of left humerus) is demonstrated.

Third-party payers do not consider all diagnoses for all procedures and services medically necessary. CMS and other payers establish health care coverage policies (e.g., national coverage determinations, covered later in this chapter), which specify diagnosis codes that support medical necessity for certain procedures and services. If a submitted claim is denied due to medical necessity, it is fraudulent to resubmit the claim with a different diagnosis code that was not documented in the patient record (but would result in reimbursement to the provider). Fraudulent practices result in criminal prosecution, fines, and penalties.

Applying Coding Guidelines

In Chapters 6 through 8, diagnosis and procedure statements were coded according to ICD-10-CM, CPT, or HCPCS Level II. In preparation for entering codes in the diagnosis blocks on the CMS-1500 claim, it is necessary to apply the *Official Coding Guidelines for Physician and Outpatient Hospital Services* and to understand the limitations of the CMS-1500 claim when billing payers. Assigning ICD-10-CM and ICD-10-PCS codes for hospital inpatient cases also requires application of the *ICD-10-CM Official Guidelines for Coding and Reporting* and the *ICD-10-PCS Official Guidelines for Coding and Reporting.* (The UB-04 claim is populated with ICD-10-CM and ICD-10-PCS codes and other data by the hospital's information technology system, except for paper claims that may be submitted by certain qualified institutions such as organizations with less than 25 full-time equivalent employees.) All of the coding guidelines are provided by the Centers for Medicare and Medicaid Services (CMS) and the National Center for Health Statistics (NCHS).

Coding may not be a problem when reviewing short, one-line diagnosis or procedure/service statements such as those that appeared in most of the earlier exercises. When working with case scenarios, sample reports, or patient records, however, you must select the diagnosis and procedure/service to code based on provider documentation.

Be sure to code and report only those diagnoses, conditions, procedures, and/or services that are documented in the patient record as having been *treated* or *medically managed.* **Medically managed** means that even though a diagnosis (e.g., hypertension) may not receive direct treatment during an encounter, the provider has to consider that diagnosis when determining treatment for other conditions. It is appropriate to code and report medically managed diagnoses and conditions. Questions that should be considered before coding and reporting a diagnosis or condition include:

1. Does the diagnosis or condition support a procedure or service provided during this encounter?

2. Did the provider prescribe a new medication or change a prescription for a new or existing diagnosis or condition?

3. Are positive diagnostic test results documented in the patient record to support a diagnosis or condition?

4. Did the provider have to consider the impact of treatment for chronic conditions when treating a newly diagnosed condition?

Remember! ICD-10-CM coding guidelines for outpatient encounters that include diagnostic tests interpreted by a physician provide guidance to assign a code to the definitive diagnosis established by the provider as the first-listed diagnosis. Do *not* code related signs and symptoms as additional diagnoses.

Up to 12 ICD-10-CM diagnosis codes can be reported on one CMS-1500. When reporting procedure/service codes on the CMS-1500, it is important to carefully match the appropriate diagnosis code with the procedure or service provided. Providers often document past conditions that are not active problems for the patient, and these conditions are not coded or reported on the claim. (However, for data capture purposes, an ICD-10-CM Z code can be assigned to past conditions.)

 NOTE:

> A diagnosis or condition code is linked with each procedure or service code reported on the CMS-1500 claim. Up to 12 ICD-10-CM codes are entered next to letters A–L in Block 21 of the CMS-1500 claim. The appropriate diagnosis pointers (letters) located next to the entered ICD-10-CM codes from Block 21 is reported in Block 24E to justify medical necessity of the procedure or service code reported in Block 24D.

Report ICD-10-CM codes on the claim, beginning with the *first-listed diagnosis* and followed by any secondary diagnoses (e.g., coexisting conditions) that were treated or medically managed. Then, link the code for each procedure or service provided with the diagnosis or condition that proves the *medical necessity* for performing the procedure or service.

Example: Tim Johnson's primary care provider performed a level 3 E/M service (99213) in the office on June 1 to evaluate Tim's symptoms of upset stomach (K30) and vomiting without nausea (R11.11). Tim's type 2 diabetes mellitus (E11.9) was medically managed during the encounter when venipuncture (36415) and a blood glucose test (82947) were performed; test results were within normal limits. Table 10-3 demonstrates how diagnoses and conditions are linked with procedures or services performed during the encounter. Figure 10-4 illustrates completion of Blocks 21 and 24A–E on the CMS-1500 claim. Note that Block 24E, line 1, contains three diagnosis code indicators from Block 21 whereas Block 24E, lines 2 and 3, each contain just one diagnosis code indicator from Block 21. If a payer allows multiple diagnosis codes to be linked to procedures/services in Block 24, enter ABC in Block 24E, line 1.

TABLE 10-3 Linking diagnosis and procedure/service codes from Block 21 with Block 24E of the CMS-1500 claim

Diagnosis	ICD-10-CM Code (Block 21 of CMS-1500)	Procedure or Service	CPT Code (Block 24D of CMS-1500)	Diagnosis Pointer (Block 24E of CMS-1500)
Upset stomach	K30	Office visit	99213	A
Vomiting	R11.11	Office visit	99213	B
Diabetes mellitus	E11.9	Office visit	99213	C
		Venipuncture	36415	C
		Blood-sugar test	82947	C

(continues)

21. DIAGNOSIS OR NATURE OF ILLNESS OR INJURY Relate A-L to service line below (24E)			ICD Ind. **0**	22. RESUBMISSION CODE		ORIGINAL REF. NO.
A. **K30**	B. **R1111**	C. **E119**	D.			
E.	F.	G.	H.	23. PRIOR AUTHORIZATION NUMBER		
I.	J.	K.	L.			

24. A. DATE(S) OF SERVICE						B. PLACE OF SERVICE	C. EMG	D. PROCEDURES, SERVICES, OR SUPPLIES (Explain Unusual Circumstances) CPT/HCPCS MODIFIER		E. DIAGNOSIS POINTER	F. $ CHARGES	G. DAYS OR UNITS	H. EPSDT Family Plan	I. ID. QUAL.	J. RENDERING PROVIDER ID. #
From MM	DD	YY	To MM	DD	YY										
1 06	01	YY				11		99213		ABC	75 00	1		NPI	
2 06	01	YY				11		36415		C	15 00	1		NPI	
3 06	01	YY				11		82947		C	35 00	1		NPI	

FIGURE 10-4 Completed Blocks 21 and 24 of the CMS-1500 claim.

Exercise 10.1 – Choosing the First-Listed Diagnosis

Select the definitive diagnosis as the first-listed diagnosis for each case scenario.

1. The patient was seen by the provider during an office encounter for sore throat. Patient has past history of urinary frequent, but is symptom free today. Rapid strep test and urinalysis tests were negative during this encounter. Diagnosis is acute pharyngitis. Select the first-listed diagnosis.

    a. Occasional bouts of urinary frequency, but symptom-free today

    b. Sore throat with swollen glands and enlarged tonsils

    c. Acute pharyngitis (with negative rapid strep test)

    d. Urinalysis test negative

2. The patient received care for a musculoligamentous sprain, left ankle during this office encounter. Patient complained of edema, left lateral malleolus and limited range of motion due to pain. X-ray was negative for fracture. Select the first-listed diagnosis.

    a. Edema, left lateral malleolus

    b. Limited range of motion due to pain

    c. Musculoligamentous sprain, left ankle

    d. X-ray, negative for fracture

3. The patient presented to the office with distended urinary bladder, enlarged prostate, and urinary retention. Prostate-specific antigen (PSA) blood test established a diagnosis of benign prostatic hypertrophy. Select the first-listed diagnosis.

    a. Benign prostatic hypertrophy (BPH)

    b. Distended urinary bladder

    c. Enlarged prostate

    d. Urinary retention

4. The patient presented as pale, diaphoretic, and in acute distress. Examination revealed pulse 112 and regular, respirations 22 with some shortness of breath, limited chest expansion, and scattered bilateral wheezes. Blood culture test established a diagnosis of bacterial endocarditis. Select the first-listed diagnosis.

    a. Bacterial endocarditis

    b. Limited chest expansion, scattered bilateral wheezes

    c. Pale, diaphoretic, and in acute distress

    d. Pulse 112 and regular, respirations 22 with some shortness of breath

5. The patient was seen in the office for right leg pain and weak right leg. Patient also complains of tightness in the lower back from difficulty walking. CT scan was negative, and after extensive examination the provider documented partial drop foot gait, right, as the diagnosis. Select the first-listed diagnosis.

    a. Pain, right leg

    b. Partial drop foot gait, right

    c. Right leg still weak

    d. Tightness in lower back

Exercise 10.2 – Linking Diagnoses with Procedures/Services to Justify Medical Necessity

Link the diagnosis/es with the procedure/service to justify medical necessity by entering letter(s) in the Diagnosis Pointer(s) column of the table provided for each case.

Example: The patient was treated by the physician in the office for a fractured thumb, and x-rays were taken. The following diagnoses and procedures were documented in the patient's chart as medically managed. Enter diagnosis pointer letter(s) to justify medical necessity of each procedure/service provided.

A. Diabetes mellitus, non-insulin-dependent, controlled

B. Benign essential hypertension

C. Simple fracture, right thumb

Diagnosis Pointer	Procedure/Service
ABC	Office encounter
C	X-ray, right thumb

Analysis: Based on the procedure performed and service delivered, the patient was seen for the thumb fracture. The diabetes and hypertension are chronic conditions that were medically managed during this encounter. Therefore, all conditions are linked to the office encounter service and just the thumb fracture is linked to the x-ray, right thumb, procedure.

1. Case: The patient was treated in the office for abdominal cramping and bloody stools. A hemoccult test was positive for blood in the stool. The patient was scheduled for proctoscopy with biopsy two days later, and Duke C carcinoma of the colon was diagnosed. The patient was scheduled for proctectomy to be performed in seven days. The following diagnoses were documented in the patient's chart. Enter diagnosis pointer letter(s) to justify medical necessity of each procedure/service provided.

A. Abdominal cramping

B. Blood in the stool

C. Duke C carcinoma, colon

Diagnosis Pointer	Procedure/Service
	Hemoccult lab test
	Proctoscopy with biopsy
	Proctectomy

2. Case: The patient was treated in the office for urinary frequency with dysuria, sore throat with cough, and headaches. The urinalysis was negative, and the strep test was positive for streptococcus infection. The patient was placed on antibiotics and was scheduled to be seen in 10 days. The following diagnoses were documented in the patient's chart. Enter diagnosis pointer letter(s) to justify medical necessity of each procedure/service provided.

A. Urinary frequency with dysuria

B. Sore throat with cough

C. Headaches

D. Strep throat

(continues)

Exercise 10.2 – continued

Diagnosis Pointer	Procedure/Service
	Office encounter
	Urinalysis
	Strep test

3. Case: The patient was treated in the office to rule out pneumonia. The patient had been experiencing wheezing and congestion, and respirations were labored. The chest x-ray done in the office was positive for pneumonia. The following diagnoses were documented in the patient's chart. Enter diagnosis pointer letter(s) to justify medical necessity of each procedure/service provided.

A. Pneumonia

B. Wheezing

C. Congestion

D. Labored respirations

Diagnosis Pointer	Procedure/Service
	Office encounter
	Chest x-ray

4. Case: The physician treated the patient in the nursing facility for the second time since admission. The patient complained of malaise. It was noted that the patient had a cough as well as a fever of 103°F and that the pharynx was erythematous (abnormally red in appearance, which is a sign of infection). The following diagnoses were documented in the patient's chart. Enter diagnosis pointer letter(s) to justify medical necessity of each procedure/service provided.

A. Malaise

B. Cough

C. Fever of 103°F

D. Erythematous pharynx

E. Acute pharyngitis

Diagnosis Pointer	Procedure/Service
	Nursing facility encounter

5. Case: The patient was treated in the emergency department for chills and fever. The physician noted left lower abdominal quadrant pain and tenderness. The physician diagnosed *acute diverticulitis*. The following diagnoses were documented in the patient's chart. Enter diagnosis pointer letter(s) to justify medical necessity of each procedure/service provided.

A. Chills

B. Fever

C. Acute diverticulitis

Diagnosis Pointer	Procedure/Service
	Emergency department encounter

Coding and Billing Considerations

In addition to applying coding guidelines and rules to accurately assign and report codes on insurance claims, you should also incorporate the following as part of practice management:

- Completion of an advance beneficiary notice of noncoverage (ABN) when appropriate
- Implementation of an auditing process
- Review of local coverage determinations (LCDs) and national coverage determinations (NCDs)
- Complete and timely patient record documentation
- Use of outpatient code editor (OCE) software (for outpatient hospital claims)

Patient Record Documentation

Patient record documentation must justify and support the medical necessity of procedures and services reported to payers. The following characteristics are associated with patient record documentation in all health care settings:

- Documentation should be generated at the time of service or shortly thereafter.
- Delayed entries within a reasonable time frame (24 to 48 hours) are acceptable for purposes of clarification, correction of errors, addition of information not initially available, and when certain unusual circumstances prevent documentation at the time of service. Delayed entries cannot be used to authenticate services or substantiate medical necessity for the purpose of reimbursement.
- The patient record cannot be altered. Doing so is considered tampering with documentation. This means that errors must be legibly corrected so that a reviewer can determine the origin of the corrections, and the use of correction fluid (e.g., Wite-Out™) is prohibited.
- Corrections or additions to the patient record must be dated, timed, and legibly signed or initialed.
- Patient record entries must be legible.
- Entries should be dated, timed, and authenticated by the author.

 NOTE:

It is recommended that an *authentication* legend be generated that contains the word-processed provider's name and, next to it, the provider's signature.

Advance Beneficiary Notice of Noncoverage (ABN)

An *advance beneficiary notice of noncoverage (ABN)* (see Chapter 14 of this textbook, Figure 14-3) is a waiver required by Medicare for all outpatient and physician office procedures/services that are not covered by the Medicare program. Before providing a procedure or service that is not medically necessary and/or that Medicare will not cover, the patient must be informed and required to sign the waiver. (Even though a provider considers a procedure or service medically necessary, Medicare may not cover that procedure or service.) Patients sign the waiver to indicate that they understand the procedure or service is not covered by Medicare and that they will be financially responsible for reimbursing the provider for the procedure or service performed. If the waiver is not signed before the procedure/service is provided *and* Medicare denies coverage, the perception is that the provider is providing free services to Medicare patients—this is considered *fraud* by the Office of the Inspector General for CMS!

Example: A Medicare patient is seen by the health care provider for severe left shoulder pain. There is no history of trauma, and in the office the patient has full range of motion with moderate pain. The patient insists that the shoulder be scanned to make sure there is no cancer. The physician explains that Medicare will reimburse for a scanning procedure *only if medically necessary* and that the patient's symptoms and past history do not justify ordering the scan. The patient insists on the scan even if Medicare will not pay. The physician explains that this is an option and that the patient can sign the facility's ABN so that if Medicare denies the claim, the facility can bill the patient for the scan. The patient signs the ABN, which the physician keeps on file in the office, and the scan is ordered. The claim is submitted to Medicare, but it is denied due to lack of medical necessity to justify the scan. The patient is billed for the scan and is responsible for paying the provider.

Auditing Process

Medical practices and health care facilities should routinely participate in an **auditing process**, which involves reviewing patient records and CMS-1500 or UB-04 claims to assess coding accuracy and completeness of documentation. Medical practices should also review encounter forms to ensure the accuracy of ICD-10-CM, CPT, and HCPCS Level II codes. In addition, health care facilities should audit chargemasters to ensure the accuracy of HCPCS Level II/CPT and UB-04 revenue codes. Physicians use an *encounter form* (or *superbill*) to select diagnoses treated or medically managed and procedures, services, and supplies provided to patients during an office visit. Physicians and other personnel use *chargemasters* to select procedures, services, and supplies provided to hospital emergency department patients and outpatients. (No diagnosis codes are included on chargemasters because diagnoses are documented in the patient record, coded by health information personnel, entered using an automated abstracting system, and reported on the UB-04 by billing office personnel. Nursing and other personnel typically use automated order-entry software to capture procedures, services, and supplies provided to health care facility inpatients.)

Example: Upon routine audit of outpatient records and UB-04 claims submitted to payers, a claim for $4,890 submitted to a commercial payer was paid based on 80 percent of total billed charges, or $3,912. Review of the patient record revealed that the patient was actually treated in the hospital for 36 hours—this case should have been billed as an inpatient at a DRG rate of $1,500 (based on the patient's diagnosis). The result of the audit was an overpayment of $2,412, which the facility has an obligation to refund to the payer.

Medicare Coverage Database (MCD)

The **Medicare coverage database (MCD)** is used by Medicare administrative contractors, providers, and other health care industry professionals to determine whether a procedure or service is reasonable and necessary for the diagnosis or treatment of an illness or injury. The MCD contains:

- National coverage determinations (NCDs), including draft policies and proposed decisions
- Local coverage determinations (LCDs), including policy articles

The MCD also includes other types of national coverage analyses (NCAs), coding analyses for labs (CALs), Medicare Evidence Development & Coverage Advisory Committee (MedCAC) proceedings, and Medicare coverage guidance documents.

CMS develops *national coverage determinations (NCDs)* on an ongoing basis, and Medicare administrative contractors create edits for NCD rules, called local coverage determinations (LCDs) (discussed below). NCDs (and LCDs) link ICD-10-CM diagnosis codes with procedures or services that are considered reasonable and necessary for the diagnosis or treatment of an illness or injury. When review of NCDs (or LCDs) indicates that a procedure or service is not medically necessary, the provider is permitted to bill the patient only if an advance beneficiary notice of noncoverage (ABN) is signed by the patient prior to providing the procedure or service.

- Claims submitted with diagnosis and procedure/service codes that fail NCD or LCD edits may be denied.
- When an LCD and an NCD exist for the same procedure or service, the NCD takes precedence.

Example: The Centers for Medicare and Medicaid Services (CMS) published national coverage determinations (NCDs) that will prevent Medicare from paying for the following surgical errors:

- Wrong surgical or other invasive procedures performed on a patient
- Surgical or other invasive procedures performed on the wrong body part
- Surgical or other invasive procedures performed on the wrong patient

Local coverage determinations (LCDs) (formerly called *local medical review policies*, LMRPs) specify under what clinical circumstances a service is covered (including under what clinical circumstances it is considered to be reasonable and necessary) and coded correctly. They list covered and noncovered codes, but they do not include coding guidelines. LCDs assist MACs and providers (e.g., hospitals, physicians, and suppliers) by outlining how contractors will review claims to ensure that they meet Medicare coverage requirements. MACs publish LCDs to provide guidance to the public and medical community within a specified geographic area. CMS requires that LCDs be consistent with national guidance (although they can be more detailed or specific), developed with scientific evidence and clinical practice, and created using specified federal guidelines. If a MAC develops an LCD, it applies only within the area serviced by that contractor. Although another MAC may come to a similar decision, CMS does not require it to do so.

Example: A Medicare administrative contractor (MAC) established an LCD for *MRI and CT Scans of Thorax and Chest* (LCD ID # L26732), which defines indications and limitations of coverage and/or medical necessity, reasons for denials, documentation requirements, and a list of ICD-10-CM codes that support medical necessity. Before submitting a claim for payment of an MRI or CT scan of thorax and chest to the MAC, the insurance specialist should review this LCD to make sure the procedure is covered, that the ICD-10-CM codes reported are accurate, and that the patient record documentation supports medical necessity of the procedure.

Medicare Code Editor (MCE) and Outpatient Code Editor (OCE)

The **Medicare code editor (MCE)** is software that detects and reports errors in ICD-10-CM/PCS coded data during the processing of inpatient hospital Medicare claims. The **outpatient code editor (OCE)** is software that edits outpatient claims submitted by hospitals, community mental health centers, comprehensive out-patient rehabilitation facilities, and home health agencies. The software is used during the assignment of ambulatory payment classifications (APCs) and to review submissions for coding validity (e.g., missing characters from codes) and coverage (e.g., medical necessity). OCE edits result in one of the following dispositions: rejection, denial, return to provider (RTP), or suspension.

Example: The OCE reviews data elements submitted on the UB-04 claim such as from/through dates, ICD-10-CM diagnosis codes, type of bill, age, gender, HCPCS/CPT codes, revenue codes, service units, and so on.

Exercise 10.3 – National Coverage Determinations

Go to www.cms.gov, scroll to the Top 5 Resources, click on the **Medicare coverage database** link, enter the procedure or service to locate its national coverage determination and carefully review its contents to determine whether Medicare covers that procedure/service. (The NCD procedure or service title is underlined in each paragraph.) Then, indicate whether procedure in each item is *covered or not covered*, and summarize the NCD language associated with the procedure or service.

Example: A 67-year-old female, status post menopause, undergoes a <u>bone (mineral) density study</u> for osteoporosis screening.

Answer: Covered. Upon review of the NCD entitled *Bone (Mineral) Density Studies*, it is noted that conditions for coverage of bone mass measurements are located in the *Medicare Benefit Policy Manual*, which indicates that bone mass measurement (BMM) is covered under certain conditions (e.g., BMM is ordered by the treating physician, is reasonable and necessary for treating the patient's condition, and so on).

(continues)

Exercise 10.3 – continued

1. A 72-year-old male undergoes left heart <u>cardiac catheterization</u> by cutdown for coronary artery disease and angina pectoris, which was performed in an ambulatory surgery center. The patient is "status post myocardial infarction" four weeks ago.

2. A 66-year-old female participates in <u>cardiac rehabilitation programs</u> with continuous ECG monitoring for status post coronary angioplasty, status post coronary bypass, and unstable angina.

3. An 81-year-old female undergoes diagnostic colonoscopy (<u>endoscopy</u>) through a stoma for history of colon cancer (treatment complete), Crohn's disease, blood in stool, and abdominal pain.

4. A 94-year-old male undergoes an FDA-approved CT (<u>computed tomography</u>) scan, on FDA-approved equipment, of the head for a laceration of the scalp, closed head trauma, contusion of the scalp, suspected brain lesion, and suspected brain metastasis.

Coding from Case Scenarios and Patient Records

Careful review of patient record documentation results in the identification of diagnoses, procedures, and services that are assigned ICD-10-CM, CPT, and HCPCS Level II codes and modifiers. (ICD-10-PCS codes are assigned to hospital inpatient cases only.) The steps to identifying diagnoses, procedures, and services from case scenarios and patient records are explained in this section.

Coding from Case Scenarios

Case scenarios summarize medical data from patient records; in this text, they introduce the student to the process of selecting (or abstracting) diagnoses and procedures. Once this technique is learned, it will be easier to move on to selecting diagnoses and procedures from patient records.

Step 1	Read the entire case scenario to obtain an overview of the problems presented and procedures/services performed. Research any word or abbreviation not understood.
Step 2	Reread the problem and highlight the diagnoses, symptoms, or health status that supports, justifies, and/or proves the medical necessity of any procedure or service performed.
Step 3	Assign codes to documented diagnoses, symptoms, procedure(s), signs, health status, and/or service(s).
Step 4	Assign modifiers to CPT and HCPCS Level II codes, if applicable.
Step 5	Identify the first-listed condition.
Step 6	Link each procedure or service to a diagnosis, symptom, or health status for medical necessity.

Case 1

The patient returned to the surgeon's office <u>during</u> the (open cholecystectomy) postoperative period because of symptoms of <u>shortness of breath, dizzy spells, and pain in the left arm</u>. A level 4 reexamination (detailed history and examination was documented) of the patient was performed. The wound is healing nicely. There is no abnormal redness or abnormal pain from the incision. A 3-lead ECG rhythm strip was performed, which revealed an <u>inversion of the T wave</u>. The abnormal ECG was discussed with the patient who agreed to an immediate referral to Dr. Cardiac for a cardiac work-up.

Answer

Procedure	CPT Code	Diagnosis (ICD-10-CM Code)
1. Office visit, established patient, level 3	99214-24	A. Postoperative status (Z98.890)
2. 3-lead ECG rhythm strip	93040	B. Shortness of breath (R06.02) and dizziness (R42)
		C. Pain, left arm (M79.602)
		D. Abnormal ECG-inverted T wave (R94.31)

Rationale

- The service provided is a level 3 office visit, established patient.
- The words "reexamination" and "during postoperative period, by same surgeon" justify the use of the -24 modifier because this examination was conducted during the postoperative period.
- Abnormal ECG illustrates an inversion of the T wave, the documented problem.
- "Shortness of breath, dizzy spells, and pain in the left arm" are symptoms of a possible cardiac condition that is causing the abnormal ECG.

Case 2

An older adult with multiple chronic conditions registered for hospital outpatient surgery and was scheduled for repair of an initial, uncomplicated left inguinal hernia. The patient was cleared for surgery by their primary care physician. General anesthesia was administered by the anesthesiologist, after which the incision was made. At this point, the patient went into shock, the surgery was halted, and the wound was closed. The patient was sent to Recovery.

Answer

Procedure	CPT Code	Diagnosis (ICD-10-CM Code)
1. Hernia repair, initial	49505-74	A. Inguinal hernia (K40.90)
		B. Shock due to surgery (T81.11XA)
		C. Surgery cancelled (Z53.09)

Rationale

- Procedure was initiated for the repair of an uncomplicated, inguinal hernia.
- Modifier -74 indicates surgery was stopped after anesthesia had been administered because of the threat to the patient's well-being from the shock.
- The first-listed diagnosis is inguinal hernia, which is the reason the patient sought health care.
- Secondary diagnoses include shock resulting from surgery (explains the discontinuation of the surgery) and cancelled surgery.

Exercise 10.4 – Coding Case Scenarios

Instructions: List and code the procedures, services, and diagnosis(es) for each of the following case scenarios. Be sure to include all necessary CPT and/or HCPCS modifiers.

1. A 66-year-old established Medicare patient came to the office for an annual physical. Patient has a past history of hypertension, controlled by medication, and new complaints of dizziness and tiredness (which the physician determined was related to today's increased blood pressure). During the course of the examination, the physician found blood pressure of 160/130. Because this was the third encounter with an elevated blood pressure, a diagnosis of hypertension was

(continues)

Exercise 10.4 – continued

established and the patient placed on prescription medication. A level 4 E/M service was provided for this established patient in addition to the preventive medicine encounter.

Procedures/Services	CPT Codes	Diagnoses	ICD-10-CM Codes

2. A 67-year-old established female patient was admitted to the outpatient hospital surgery center for a scheduled diagnostic arthroscopy of her right shoulder because of constant pain on rotation of the shoulder. Prior to entering the operating room she told the nurse, "I have been feeling weak and tired ever since my last visit." The surgeon performs a level 4 re-examination prior to the surgery. The findings were negative and the diagnostic arthroscopy, right shoulder, was performed uneventfully.

Procedures/Services	CPT Codes	Diagnoses	ICD-10-CM Codes

3. The patient was seen in the emergency department (ED) at 10:00 A.M. for right lower quadrant pain; the ED physician provided a level 3 E/M service. Ultrasound revealed an inflamed appendix. A surgeon was called in, who evaluated the patient (conducting a level 3 new patient E/M outpatient service) and performed an outpatient laparoscopic appendectomy at 1:00 P.M. for the ruptured appendix with abscess. The patient was discharged at 9:00 A.M. the next morning.

Procedures/Services	CPT Codes	Diagnoses	ICD-10-CM Codes

4. An emergency department (ED) physician performed a level 3 evaluation and management service on a patient who was seen for complaints of severe abdominal pain, nausea, and vomiting. An abdominal ultrasound revealed an enlarged gallbladder. A surgeon was called in, evaluated the patient (conducting a level 3 new patient E/M outpatient service), and performed a laparoscopic cholecystectomy, which revealed acute cholecystitis. The patient's stay was less than 24 hours.

Procedures/Services	CPT Codes	Diagnoses	ICD-10-CM Codes

5. Dr. B performed a postoperative examination on an established patient and also removed the sutures from an open appendectomy that the patient underwent while on vacation in another part of the country.

Procedures/Services	CPT Codes	Diagnoses	ICD-10-CM Codes

NOTE:

Additional coding case scenarios are found at the end of this chapter and in the Workbook that accompanies this text.

Coding from Patient Records

A patient record serves as the business record for a patient encounter, and is maintained in a manual record or automated format (e.g., electronic medical record, electronic health record). The patient record contains documentation of all health care services provided to a patient to support diagnoses, justify treatment, and record treatment results. The primary purpose of the patient record is to provide *continuity of care* (documentation of patient care services so that others who treat the patient have a source of information from which to base additional care and treatment). Secondary purposes of the patient record do not relate directly to patient care, and they include:

- Evaluating the quality of patient care
- Providing information to third-party payers for reimbursement
- Serving the medico-legal interests of the patient, facility, and providers of care
- Providing data for use in clinical research, epidemiology studies, education, public policy making, facilities planning, and health care statistics

Example 1: Information about patient medications is available in the EHR so that health care providers do not prescribe another medicine that might be harmful.

Example 2: EHR systems are backed up like most computer systems, so patients who reside in an area affected by a disaster (e.g., hurricane) can have their health information retrieved from another location.

Example 3: EHRs are available in an emergency. If a patient is in an accident and is unable to explain their health history, a hospital that has an EHR may be able to talk to the patient's physician's EHR (or EMR) system. Thus, the hospital will obtain information about patient medications, health issues, and tests, so that faster and more informed decisions about emergency care can be made.

NOTE:

Health insurance specialists review the patient record when assigning codes to diagnoses, procedures, and services. In addition, copies of reports from the patient record may be requested from third-party payers to process insurance claims.

Patient Record Documentation in the Electronic Health Record (EHR)

Electronic health records (EHRs) are electronic versions of patient records maintained in a health care setting. An EHR includes information about the patient's medical history, progress notes (e.g., SOAP notes), information about the patient's health including symptoms, diagnoses, medications, lab results, vital signs, immunizations, and reports from diagnostic tests and procedures. Providers work with other physicians, hospitals, and third-party payers to legally share that information, which enhances continuity of patient care. Patients have privacy rights whether information is stored as a paper-based record or in an EHR, and the same federal laws protect health information in both formats.

EHRs contain the ability to exchange health information electronically with providers, which can help improve health care quality and safety for patients by:

- Providing accurate, up-to-date, and complete information about patients at the point of care
- Enabling quick access to patient records for more coordinated, efficient care

(continues)

Patient Record Documentation in the Electronic Health Record (EHR) (*continued*)

- Securely sharing electronic information with patients and other clinicians

- Helping providers more effectively diagnose patients, reduce medical errors, and provide safer care

- Improving patient and provider interaction and communication, as well as health care convenience

- Enabling safer, more reliable prescribing

- Helping promote legible, complete documentation and accurate, streamlined coding and billing

- Enhancing privacy and security of patient data

- Helping providers improve productivity and work-life balance

- Enabling providers to improve efficiency and meet their business goals

- Reducing costs through decreased paperwork, improved safety, reduced duplication of testing, and improved health

Diagnoses, procedures, and services are selected and coded from clinic notes, consultation reports, and diagnostic reports. This process is the same as that used for case scenarios. The major difference is that clinic notes, consultations, and diagnostic reports contain more detail.

Clinic Notes

Health care providers use two major formats for documenting clinic notes:

- Narrative clinic notes
- SOAP notes

Diagnoses, procedures, and services can be selected and coded from either format. Both require documentation to support the level of Evaluation and Management (E/M) service coded and reported on the CMS-1500 claim, even if the provider selects the E/M code from a preprinted encounter form (e.g., superbill).

Example: Portion of an encounter form containing E/M service, date, code, and charge

| New Patient E/M Service | 01-01-YYYY | ☑99203 | $70.00 |

Narrative Clinic Note

A **narrative clinic note** is written in paragraph format.

Example: Narrative clinic note

A 21-year-old female patient comes to the office today, having been referred by Dr. Bandaid for pain in the RLQ of the abdomen, 2 days' duration. Temp: 102°F. Detailed history and physical examination revealed rebound tenderness over McBurney's point with radiation to the RUQ and RLQ. The remainder of the physical examination is normal. For additional information, see the complete history and physical in this chart. Laboratory data ordered by Dr. Bandaid (oral report given by Goodtechnique Lab) is as follows: WBC 19.1; RBC 4.61; platelets 234,000; hematocrit 42; hemoglobin 13.5; bands 15 percent, and PMNs 88 percent. UA and all other blood work were within normal limits. Patient is to be admitted to Goodmedicine Hospital for further work-up and possible appendectomy.

T.J. Stitcher, M.D.

SOAP Notes

A **SOAP note** is written in outline format ("SOAP" is an acronym derived from the first letter of the topic headings used in the note: Subjective, Objective, Assessment, and Plan).

The **subjective** part of the note contains the chief complaint and the patient's description of the presenting problem. It can also include the response to treatment prescribed earlier, past history, review of symptoms, and relevant family and social history. The documentation may appear in quotes because it represents the patient's statement verbatim.

The **objective** part of the note contains documentation of measurable or objective observations made during physical examination and diagnostic testing. Some health care providers may also include historical information obtained from previous encounters in this section.

The **assessment** contains the diagnostic statement and may include the physician's rationale for the diagnosis. If this section is missing from the report, look for positive diagnostic test results documented in the objective data or code the symptoms presented in either the subjective or objective data.

The **plan** is the statement of the physician's future plans for the work-up and medical management of the case. This includes plans for medications, diet, and therapy; future diagnostic tests to be performed; suggested lifestyle changes; items covered in the informed consent discussions; items covered in patient education sessions; and suggested follow-up care.

Example: SOAP note

3/29/YYYY

S: Pt states no complaints, no new symptoms since last visit, which was seven days ago.

O: Patient seen today, on 10th day postop. T 98.6°F; P 80; R 20; BP 120/86, right arm, sitting, WT 120 lb.

   Incision, inner aspect of left breast, healing well. No sign of inflammation or infection.

A: Papilloma with fibrocystic changes, no malignancy.

   Size 3.0 × 1.5 × 0.2 cm.

P: 1. Suture removal today.

   2. Return visit, 3 months for follow-up.

Janet B. Surgeon, M.D.

In this example, the chief complaint (S:) and the vital signs (O:) were documented by the medical assistant (or nurse). The provider then performed an examination (O:), documented the findings (A:), and established a plan for the patient (P:). Because this note documents a postoperative follow-up office visit within the global period, no diagnoses or procedures/services are selected or coded. Neither the third-party payer nor the patient is billed for this postoperative visit. However, when the patient returns in three months for follow-up, that visit is billed to the payer (because it is not within the postoperative global period).

Diagnostic Test Results

Diagnostic test results are documented in two locations:

- Clinic notes
- Laboratory reports

Laboratory reports quantify data, and diagnostic implications are summarized in *clinic notes* documented by the provider. Other diagnostic tests (e.g., x-ray and pathology reports) include an interpretation by the responsible physician (e.g., radiologist or pathologist).

MILLION, IMA	Patient No. 12345	PROVIDER: Erin Helper, M.D.

Specimen: Blood (collected 03/03/YYYY).	Test completed: 03/03/YYYY at 04:50 P.M.	Technician: 099

Test	Result		Normal Values
Sodium	142 mEq/L		(135–148)
Potassium	4.4 mEq/L		(3.5–5.1)
Chloride	105 mEq/L		(97–107)
Glucose	176 mg/dL	**H**	(70–110)
BUN	14 mg/dL		(5–20)
Creatinine	1.0 mg/dL		(0.8–1.5)

FIGURE 10-5 Sample laboratory report with abnormal glucose level.

MILLION, IMA	Patient No. 12345	PROVIDER: Erin Helper, M.D.

Baseline Mammogram

There are mild fibrocystic changes in both breasts but without evidence of a dominant mass, grouped microcalcifications, or retractions. Density on the left side is slightly greater and thought to be simply asymmetric breast tissue. There are some small axillary nodes bilaterally.

IMPRESSION: Class 1 (normal or clinically insignificant findings).

Follow-up in 1 year is suggested to assess stability in view of the fibrocystic asymmetric findings. Thereafter, biannual follow-up if stable. No dominant mass is present particularly in the upper inner quadrant of the left breast.

Maryanne Iona, M.D.

FIGURE 10-6 Sample radiology report.

The laboratory report in Figure 10-5 documents a high glucose level (denoted by the **H** on the report). Upon review of the clinic note, if the insurance specialist finds documentation of signs and symptoms like a high glucose level, the provider should be asked whether a definitive diagnosis is to be coded instead.

The x-ray in Figure 10-6 was justified by the diagnosis of mild fibrocystic changes of the breast. (If the diagnosis is not documented in the patient's record, be sure to check with the provider before coding this as the diagnosis.)

Exercise 10.5 – Coding SOAP Notes

Review the following SOAP notes, then list and assign code(s) to the diagnoses.

1. S: Patient complains of stomach pain, 3 days' duration. Patient also stated that both legs still get painful from the knees down.

O: Ht 5'6"; Wt 164 lb; BP 122/86; pulse 92 and regular; temp 97.0°F, oral; chest normal; heart normal. The Doppler arteriogram of lower extremities taken last week at the hospital is reported as within normal limits bilaterally.

A: Another episode of chronic atrophic gastritis. Leg pain, left.

P: Carafate 1 g. Take 1 tablet qid before meals and at bedtime, #120 tabs.

(continues)

Exercise 10.5 – continued

Diagnoses	ICD-10-CM Codes

2. S: Patient seems to be doing quite well, postop cholecystectomy; however, the pain experienced prior to surgery is not gone.

O: Incision is well healed. Abdomen is soft and nontender.

A: Surgical aftercare. Pathology report revealed chronic cholecystitis and cholelithiasis.

P: 1. Lengthy discussion with patient and spouse about treatment in the future. Asked that they call any time they have questions.

   2. Return visit here on a prn basis.

Diagnoses	ICD-10-CM Codes

3. S: Patient complains of generalized stiffness and being tired. Patient also notes that the left knee was swollen and felt hot to the touch last week. Patient was last seen 18 months ago on Penicillamine and 2 mg prednisone bid. Patient's other medications are loperamide for loose stool and Tagamet 300 mg bid.

O: Examination reveals some swelling of the left knee with active synovitis of the left knee and minimal fluid. Patient's present weight is 134 lb, BP 116/72. The hematocrit performed today is 37.5 and sed rate is 65.

A: This patient has active rheumatoid arthritis, left knee.

P: 1. Increase prednisone to 5 mg bid, and Penicillamine to 500 mg bid.

   2. X-ray of left knee tomorrow.

   3. Recheck CBC, sed rate, and urinalysis in 4 weeks.

   4. Discussed with patient the possibility of injecting steroids into the left knee if no improvement is shown.

Diagnoses	ICD-10-CM Codes

4. S: Patient returns today for follow-up of chronic angina and dyspnea. Patient says the angina still appears mainly when resting, and particularly upon awakening in the morning. This is accompanied by some dyspnea and pain occasionally radiating into the left jaw, but no palpitations. The angina is relieved by nitroglycerin. The patient continues to take Inderal 40 mg qid.

O: BP, left arm, sitting, 128/72; weight is 150 lb. Chest is clear. No wheezing or rales.

A: Unstable angina. Patient again refused to consider a heart catheterization.

P: New RX: Isordil Tembids 40 mg.
   Refill nitroglycerin.

Diagnoses	ICD-10-CM Codes

(continues)

Exercise 10.5 – continued

5. S: This 17-year-old patient presents to the office with a sore throat, fever, and swollen glands, 2 days' duration.

O: Oral temp 102.4°F; pulse 84; respirations 18; BP 118/78; wt 138 lb. The throat is markedly erythematous with evidence of exudative tonsillitis. Ears show normal TMs bilaterally. Few tender, submandibular nodes, bilaterally.

A: Acute tonsillitis.

P: 1. Obtained throat culture that was sent to the lab. Waiting for results.

2. Patient started on an empiric course of Pen Vee K 250 mg #40 to be taken qid × 10 days.

3. Encouraged patient to increase oral fluid intake.

4. Patient to call office in 48 hours to obtain culture results and report patient's progress.

Diagnoses	ICD-10-CM Codes

Reports

Operative reports will vary from a short narrative description of a minor procedure that is performed in the physician's office (Figure 10-7) to more formal reports dictated by the surgeon in a format required by hospitals and ambulatory surgical centers (ASCs) (Figure 10-8).

Hospital and ASC formats may vary slightly, but all contain the following information in outline form:

- Date of the surgery
- Patient identification
- Pre- and postoperative diagnosis(es)
- List of the procedure(s) performed
- Name(s) of primary and secondary surgeons who performed surgery

The body of the report contains a detailed narrative of:

- Positioning and draping of the patient for surgery
- Achievement of anesthesia
- Detailed description of how the procedure(s) was performed; identification of the incision made; and instruments, drains, dressings, special packs, and so on, used during surgery
- Identification of abnormalities found during the surgery
- Description of how hemostasis was obtained and the closure of the surgical site(s)
- Condition of the patient upon leaving the operating room
- Signature of surgeon

Procedure for Coding Operative Reports

Step 1 Make a copy of the operative report.

This will allow you to freely make notations in the margin and highlight special details without marking up the original (which must remain in the patient's record).

MILLION, IMA   **Patient No.** 12345   **PROVIDER:** Erin Helper, M.D.

12/5/YYYY

Reason for Visit: Postpartum exam and colposcopy.

Vital Signs: Temperature 97.2F. Blood pressure 88/52. Weight 107.

Labs: Glucose negative; Albumin, trace.

Patient seems to be doing fine, thinks the bleeding has just about stopped at this point. The patient's daughter is apparently also doing fine; patient is to get back chromosomal analysis in a couple of days. No other system defects have been found yet.

Examination: *Breasts:* Negative bilaterally. Patient is breastfeeding. *Abdomen:* Soft, flat, no masses, nontender. *Pelvic:* Cervix appeared clear, no bleeding noted. Uterus anteverted, small, nontender. Adnexa negative. Vagina appeared atrophic. Episiotomy healing well.

Procedure: Colposcopy of cervix performed with staining of acetic acid. Entire squamocolumnar junction could not be visualized even with aid of endocervical speculum. Exam was made more difficult because of very thick cervical mucus, which could not be completely removed, and because the vagina and cervix were somewhat atrophic appearing. Whitening of epithelium around entire circumference of cervix noted, but no abnormal vasculature noted. Numerous biopsies were taken from posterior and anterior lip of cervix. Endocervical curettage done. Repeat Pap smear of cervix also done.

Plan: Patient to call at the end of this week for biopsy results. Patient told intercourse is permitted after five days, to use condoms, or to come back to office first to have size of diaphragm checked.

Erin Helper, M.D.

FIGURE 10-7 Sample physician's office operative report.

MILLION, IMA   **Patient No.** 12345   **PROVIDER:** Gail R. Bones, M.D.
Room #: 101B   **DATE OF SURGERY:** 01/01/YYYY

Preoperative Diagnosis:	Displaced supracondylar fracture, left humerus
Postoperative Diagnosis:	Same
Procedure:	Closed reduction and casting, left humeral fracture
Surgeon:	Gail R. Bones, M.D.
Assistant Surgeon:	T.J. Stitcher, M.D.

Findings and Procedure:

After adequate general anesthesia, the patient's left elbow was gently manipulated and held at 110 degrees of flexion, at which point the patient continued to maintain a good radial pulse. X-rays revealed a good reduction; therefore, a plaster splint was applied, care being taken not to put any constriction in the antecubital fossa. X-rays were taken again, and showed excellent reduction has been maintained. Patient maintained good radial pulse, was awake, and was taken to Recovery in good condition.

Gail R. Bones, M.D.

FIGURE 10-8 Sample hospital outpatient surgery or ambulatory surgery center operative report.

Step 2   Carefully review the list of procedures performed.

Step 3   Read the narrative of the report and make a note of procedures to be coded.

Key words to look for include:

> Simple versus complicated
>
> Partial, complete, total, or incomplete
>
> Unilateral versus bilateral
>
> Initial versus subsequent
>
> Incision versus excision
>
> Open versus closed treatment, surgery, or fracture
>
> Reconstructive surgery
>
> Repair
>
> Endoscopy
>
> Biopsy
>
> Ligation
>
> Debridement
>
> Complex, simple, intermediate, repair
>
> Micronerve repair
>
> Reconstruction
>
> Graft (bone, nerve, or tendon requires additional code)
>
> Diagnostic versus surgical procedure

Be alert to the following:

1. Additional procedures documented in the narrative of the report that are not listed in the heading of the report (e.g., Procedures Performed) should be coded.

> **Example:**
>
> **Postoperative Diagnosis:** Chronic cholecystitis and cholelithiasis without obstruction
>
> **Procedures Performed:** Laparoscopic cholecystectomy with cholangiography
>
> In the body of the operative report, the surgeon describes the laparoscopic cholecystectomy and a cholangiogram. The surgeon also documents the operative findings and a biopsy of a suspicious liver nodule. The insurance specialist should contact the surgeon so that the liver biopsy is added to the *Procedures Performed* statement and then assign a CPT code to it (in addition to the laparoscopic cholecystectomy and cholangiogram).

2. When the *Procedures Performed* heading lists procedures performed that are not described in the body of the operative report, the surgeon will have to add a written addendum to the operative report documenting the performance of any listed procedure that should be coded.

> **Example:**
>
> **Procedures Performed:** Arthroscopy, right knee. Open repair, right knee, collateral and cruciate ligaments
>
> Upon review of the body of the report, the insurance specialist notes that the surgeon did not document removal of the scope. Even though the removal of a scope is not coded, the insurance specialist should instruct the surgeon to document this as an addendum to the operative report.

Step 4   Identify main term(s) and subterms for the procedure(s) to be coded.

Step 5   Underline and research any terms in the report that you cannot define.

Many coding errors are made when the coder does not understand critical medical terms in the report.

Step 6   Locate the main term(s) in the CPT index.

Check for the proper anatomic site or organ.

Step 7   Research all suggested codes.

Read all notes and guidelines pertaining to the codes you are investigating. Watch for add-on procedures described in any notes/guidelines.

Step 8   Return to the CPT index and research additional codes if you cannot find a particular code(s) that matches the description of the procedure(s) performed in the operative report.

Because a monetary value is associated with each CPT code, and to avoid bundling, never assign multiple, separate codes to describe a procedure if CPT has a single code that classifies all the individual components of the procedure described by the physician.

 Remember!

Global surgery includes the preoperative assessment (e.g., H&PE); the procedure; local infiltration, metacarpal/digital block or topical anesthesia when used; and normal, uncomplicated follow-up care.

Never assign a code number described in CPT as a "separate procedure" when it is performed within the same incision as the primary procedure and is an integral part of a larger procedure.

Step 9   Investigate the possibility of adding modifiers to a specific code description to fully explain the procedure(s) performed.

Example: Key word indicators for use of modifier -22

Extensive debridement/lysis or adhesions

Excessive bleeding (>500 mL)

Friable tissue

Prolonged procedure due to _____

Unusual anatomy, findings, or circumstances

Very difficult

Step 10   Code the postoperative diagnosis. This should explain the medical necessity for performing the procedure(s). If the postoperative diagnosis does not support the procedure performed, be sure the patient's chart contains documentation to justify the procedure.

Example: The patient is seen in the emergency department (ED) with right lower quadrant pain, and evaluation reveals elevated temperature and increased white blood count. Preoperative diagnosis is *appendicitis*, and the patient undergoes *appendectomy*; however, the postoperative diagnosis is *normal appendix*. In this situation, the documentation of the patient's signs and symptoms in the ED chart justifies the surgery performed even though the postoperative diagnosis does not support the surgery performed.

Look for additional findings in the body of the report if the postoperative diagnosis listed on the operative report does not completely justify the medical necessity for the procedure.

Compare the postoperative diagnosis with the biopsy report on all excised neoplasms to determine whether the tissue is benign or malignant.

When doing the exercises in this text and the Workbook, use any stated pathology report to determine whether excised tissue is benign or malignant if it is not covered in the postoperative diagnosis(es).

When working in a medical practice, do not code an excision until the pathology report is received.

Step 11   Review code options with the physician who performed the procedure if the case is unusual.

Before assigning an "unlisted CPT procedure" code, review HCPCS Level II codes. Remember that a description of the procedure performed must accompany the claim if an unlisted CPT code is reported.

Step 12   Assign final code numbers for procedures verified in Steps 3 and 4 and any addendum the physician added to the original report.

Step 13   Properly sequence the codes, listing first the most significant procedure performed during the episode.

Step 14   Be sure to destroy the copy of the operative report (e.g., shred it) after the abstracting and coding process is completed.

Exercise 10.6 – Coding Operative Reports

Identify diagnoses and procedures to be reported for each case, and assign ICD-10-CM and CPT codes to each. When working with the case studies in this text, code procedures as listed in the case. (When working in a medical practice, refer to the Medicare physician fee schedule or the payer's fee schedule to determine which surgical procedure receives the highest reimbursement.)

1. Case

Preoperative Diagnosis:	Questionable recurrent basal cell carcinoma, frontal scalp
Postoperative Diagnosis:	Benign lesion, frontal scalp, 0.3 cm in diameter
Operation:	Excision of possible recurrent basal cell carcinoma of frontal scalp

History: About one year ago, the patient had an excision and grafting of a very extensive basal cell carcinoma of the forehead at the edge of the scalp. The patient now has a large granular area at 12 o'clock on the grafted area. This may be a recurrence of the basal cell carcinoma.

Procedure: The patient was placed in the dorsal recumbent position and draped in the usual fashion. The skin and subcutaneous tissues at the junction of the skin grafts of the previous excision and the normal scalp were infiltrated with 1/2 percent xylocaine containing epinephrine. An elliptical excision of the normal skin and the granulating area was made.

Pathology Report: The entire specimen measures 0.7 × 0.4 × 0.3 cm depth. Part of the specimen is a slightly nodular hemorrhagic lesion measuring 0.3 cm in diameter. Resected piece of skin shows partial loss of epithelium accompanied by acute and chronic inflammation of granulation tissue from a previous excision of basal cell carcinoma. *Diagnosis:* This specimen is benign; there is no evidence of tumor.

Diagnoses/Procedures	ICD-10-CM/CPT Codes

(continues)

Exercise 10.6 – continued

2. Case

Preoperative Diagnosis:	Tumor of the skin of the back with evolving melanocyte cells
Postoperative Diagnosis:	Benign lesion, skin of the back
Operation Performed:	Wide excision
Anesthesia:	General

Indications: The 45-year-old patient had a previous biopsy of a nevus located on the back. The pathology report indicated evolving melanocyte cells in the area close to the margin of the excision. The pathologist recommended that a wide re-excision be performed. The patient was informed of the situation during an office visit last week, and the patient agreed to be readmitted for a wider excision of the tumor area.

Procedure: The patient was placed on their left side, and general anesthesia was administered. The skin was prepped and draped in a usual fashion. A wide excision, 5.0 cm in length and 4.0 cm wide, was made. The pathologist was alerted, and the specimen was sent to the lab. The frozen section was reported as negative for melanocytes on the excisional margin at this time. After the report was received, the wound was closed in layers and a dressing was applied. The patient tolerated the procedure well and was sent to Recovery in good condition.

Diagnoses/Procedures	ICD-10-CM/CPT Codes

3. Case

Preoperative Diagnosis:	Serous otitis media, bilateral
Postoperative Diagnosis:	Same
Operation Performed:	Bilateral tympanostomy with insertion of ventilating tubes
Anesthesia:	General

Procedure: The patient was placed in a supine position and induction of general anesthesia was achieved by face mask. The ears were examined bilaterally using an operating microscope. An incision was made in the anteroinferior quadrants. A large amount of thick fluid was aspirated from both ears, more so from the left side. Ventilating tubes were introduced with no difficulties. Patient tolerated the procedure well and was sent to Recovery in satisfactory condition.

Diagnoses/Procedures	ICD-10-CM/CPT Codes

4. Case

Preoperative Diagnosis:	Pilonidal cyst
Postoperative Diagnosis:	Same
Operation Performed:	Pilonidal cystectomy

(continues)

Exercise 10.6 – continued

Anesthesia:	Local with 4 mL of 1/2 percent xylocaine
Estimated Blood Loss:	Minimal
Fluids:	550 mL intraoperatively

Procedure: The patient was brought to the operating room and placed in a jackknife position. After sterile prepping and draping, 40 mL of 1/2 percent xylocaine was infiltrated into the surrounding tissue of the pilonidal cyst that had a surface opening on the median raphe over the sacrum. After adequate anesthesia was obtained and 1 gram of IV Ancef administered intraoperatively, the surface opening was probed. There were no apparent tracks demonstrated upon probing. Next, a scalpel was used to make an approximately 8 × 8 cm elliptical incision around the pilonidal cyst. The incision was carried down through subcutaneous tissue to the fascia and the tissue was then excised. Attention was turned to achieving hemostasis with Bovie electrocautery. The pilonidal cyst was then opened and found to contain fibrous tissue. The wound was closed with 0 Prolene interrupted vertical mattress. Estimated blood loss was minimal, and the patient received 550 mL of crystalloid intraoperatively. The patient tolerated the procedure well and was sent to Recovery in stable condition.

Diagnoses/Procedures	ICD-10-CM/CPT Codes

5. Case

Preoperative Diagnosis:	Incarcerated right femoral hernia
Postoperative Diagnosis:	Same
Operation Performed:	Right femoral herniorrhaphy
Anesthesia:	General

Procedure: Patient is a 37-year-old male. Initially, the patient was placed in the supine position, and the abdomen was prepped and draped with Betadine in the appropriate manner. Xylocaine (1 percent) was infiltrated into the skin and subcutaneous tissue. Because of the patient's reaction to pain, general anesthesia was also administered. An oblique skin incision was performed from the anterior superior iliac spine to the pubic tubercle. The skin and subcutaneous tissues were sharply incised. Dissection was carried down until the external oblique was divided in the line of its fibers with care taken to identify the ilioinguinal nerve to avoid injury. Sharp and blunt dissection were used to free the inguinal cord. The cremasteric muscle was transected. Attempts at reduction of the incarcerated femoral hernia from below were unsuccessful.

The femoral canal was opened in an inferior to superior manner, and finally this large incarcerated hernia was reduced. The conjoint tendon was then sutured to Cooper's ligament with 0 Prolene interrupted suture. The conjoint tendon was somewhat attenuated and of poor quality. A transition suture was placed from the conjoint tendon to Cooper's ligament and then to the inguinal ligament with care taken to obliterate the femoral space without stenosis of the femoral vein. The conjoint tendon was then sutured laterally to the shelving border or Poupart's ligament. The external oblique was closed over the cord with 0 chromic running suture. 3-0 plain was placed in the subcutaneous tissue and the skin was closed with staples. Sterile dressings were applied. The patient tolerated the operative procedure well and was gently taken to Recovery in satisfactory condition.

Diagnoses/Procedures	ICD-10-CM/CPT Codes

Summary

The Office of the Inspector General (OIG) developed voluntary *compliance program guidance* documents for segments of the health care industry to encourage the development and use of internal controls to monitor adherence to applicable regulations, statutes, and program requirements. *Coding compliance* is the conformity to established coding guidelines and regulations. Health information management departments (and similar areas, such as the coding and billing section of a physician's practice) develop coding compliance programs to ensure coding accuracy and conformance with guidelines and regulations. Coding compliance programs include written policies and procedures, routine coding audits and monitoring, compliance-based education and training.

The Centers for Medicare and Medicaid Services (CMS) implemented the *National Correct Coding Initiative (NCCI)* program to promote national correct coding methodologies and to control the improper assignment of codes that result in inappropriate reimbursement of Medicare Part B claims. CMS has posted on its website the automated edits used to identify questionable claims and adjust payments to reflect what would have been paid if the claim had been filed correctly.

Clinical documentation improvement (CDI) helps ensure accurate and thorough patient record documentation when coders identify discrepancies between provider documentation and codes to be assigned. Coders that have questions about documented diagnoses or procedures/services use a *physician query process* to request clarification about documentation and codes to be assigned. This results in resolution of documentation and coding discrepancies. Coders also review patient record documentation and use coding guidelines and other guidance to assign the most specific codes possible.

Medically managed means that even though a diagnosis may not receive direct treatment during an encounter, the provider has to consider that diagnosis when determining treatment for other conditions. Up to 12 diagnosis codes can be reported on one CMS-1500, and the appropriate diagnosis code must be linked to the procedure or service provided. Patient record documentation must justify and support the medical necessity of procedures and services reported to payers for reimbursement. Medical practices and health care facilities should routinely participate in an auditing process, which involves reviewing patient records and CMS-1500 or UB-04 claims to assess coding accuracy and completeness of documentation. Medical practices should also review encounter forms to ensure the accuracy of ICD-10-CM and HCPCS/CPT codes. In addition, health care facilities should audit chargemasters to ensure the accuracy of HCPCS/CPT and UB-04 revenue codes.

National coverage determinations (NCDs) and local coverage determinations (LCDs) specify under what clinical circumstances a service is covered, and they list covered and noncovered codes (but they do not include coding guidelines). The outpatient code editor (OCE) is software that edits outpatient claims, assigns ambulatory payment classifications (APCs), and reviews submissions for coding validity and coverage. NCDs and LCDs comprise the Medicare coverage database (MCD).

Health care providers document narrative clinic notes and SOAP notes, and diagnostic test results are documented in clinic notes and laboratory reports. Operative reports can include a short narrative description of a minor procedure or dictated reports as typically required by hospitals and ambulatory surgical centers (ASCs).

Internet Links

Compliance Program Guidance: To locate compliance program guidance documents, go to *www.oig.hhs .gov*, click on the Compliance menu item, and click on Compliance Guidance. The website also contains a Compliance 101 and Provider Education link.

Comprehensive Error Rate Testing (CERT) Program: Go to *certprovider.admedcorp.com* to locate provider documentation information, such as sample (medical record) request letters and more.

Medicare Coverage Database (MCD): Go to *www.cms.gov*, click on the Regulations & Guidance link, click on the Medicare Coverage Center link under the Special Topics heading and click on the Medicare Coverage Database link.

National Correct Coding Initiative (NCCI) Program: Go to *www.cms.gov*, click on Medicare, scroll to the Coding heading, and click on the National Correct Coding Initiative Edits link.

Payment Accuracy: Go to **www.paymentaccuracy.gov** to view the current payment accuracy rate and improper payment data that is displayed in chart format.

The FPM Toolbox: Go to **www.aafp.org**, click on the FPM Journal link, scroll down and click on the Toolbox link, and then click on any of the category links to locate checklists, decision trees, forms, and so on.

WorldVistA electronic health record (EHR) (open source software): Go to **worldvista.org** and click on the About VistA and About WorldVistA links.

Review

10.1 – Coding Compliance: Ensuring Coding Accuracy

Instructions: Review each case scenario to identify the coding error, and select the corresponding letter to describe the error.

Example: A patient is treated for excision of a 1-cm skin lesion on the right arm. The pathology diagnosis is benign nevus. The physician documents benign nevus as the final diagnosis.

Procedure Code	Diagnosis Code
11401	D22.6

Identify the coding error:

a. Code is inappropriate for patient's age

b. Code is incomplete

c. Medical necessity was not met

d. Procedure codes are unbundled

Select b because the coder referred to Nevus, Skin, Arm D22.6- in the ICD-10-CM Index to Diseases and Injuries. That code requires assignment of fifth-character 1 to report D22.61 as the correct code.

---

1. The physician performed an automated urinalysis without microscopy in the office on a patient who complained of dysuria. The urinalysis revealed more than 100,000 white cells and was positive for bacteria.

Procedure Code	Diagnosis Code
81003	B96.20

Identify the coding error.
   a.   Code is inappropriate for patient's age
   b.   Code is incomplete
   c.   Code reported is incorrect
   d.   Procedure codes are unbundled

2. An office single-view frontal chest x-ray was performed on a patient referred for shortness of breath. The radiologist reported no acute findings, but an incidental note was made of a small diaphragmatic hiatal hernia.

Procedure Code	Diagnosis Code
71045	K44.9

Identify the coding error.
   a.   Code is inappropriate for patient's age
   b.   Code is incomplete
   c.   Code reported is incorrect
   d.   Procedure codes are unbundled

3. A healthy 20-year-old male underwent a physical examination performed by his family physician, prior to starting soccer training.

Procedure Code	Diagnosis Code
99394	Z02.5

Identify the coding error.
- a. Code is inappropriate for patient's age
- b. Code is incomplete
- c. Medical necessity was met
- d. Procedure codes are unbundled

4. The patient was diagnosed with incipient cataract, and on March 5 underwent extracapsular cataract removal that required phacoemulsification, with insertion of intraocular lens prosthesis.

Procedure Code	Diagnosis Code
66984	H26.9
66985-51	H26.9

Identify the coding error.
- a. Code is inappropriate for patient's age
- b. Code is incomplete
- c. Medical necessity not met
- d. Procedure codes are unbundled

5. Patient underwent physical therapy high complexity evaluation for right dominant side hemiplegia due to CVA (stroke).

Procedure Code	Diagnosis Code
97163	I69.35

Identify the coding error.
- a. Code inappropriate for patient's age
- b. Code is incomplete
- c. Medical necessity not met
- d. Procedure codes are unbundled

10.2 – Multiple Choice

1. The National Correct Coding Initiative program has resulted in numerous code pairs that cannot be reported on the same claim for the same
- a. date of service.
- b. health care facility.
- c. national provider identifier.
- d. third-party payer.

2. The Department of HHS's Office of the Inspector General developed voluntary _____ program guidance documents for the health care industry to encourage the development and use of internal controls to monitor adherence to applicable regulations, statutes, and program requirements.
- a. accreditation
- b. compliance
- c. regulatory
- d. statutory

3. *Benchmarking* allows coding managers to establish criteria for coding _____ purposes.
   a. assessment
   b. education
   c. reimbursement
   d. validation

4. *Clinical documentation improvement* is part of an effective coding compliance program because it helps ensure accurate and thorough
   a. accounts receivables.
   b. benchmarking.
   c. medical coder credentials.
   d. patient record documentation.

5. The *comprehensive error rate testing (CERT)* program conducts annual reviews to
   a. ensure that ICD-10-CM and HCPCS codes are accurate.
   b. facilitate timely reimbursement to health care providers.
   c. improve efforts to reduce and recover improper payments.
   d. limit the number of claims submitted to third-party payers.

Chapter 11

CMS-1500 and UB-04 Claims

Chapter Outline

General Claims Information

CMS-1500 Data Entry

Processing Secondary CMS-1500 Claims

Common Errors that Delay CMS-1500 Claims
  Processing

Final Steps in Processing CMS-1500 Claims

Maintaining CMS-1500 Insurance Claim Files
  for the Medical Practice

UB-04 Claim for Inpatient and Outpatient Care

Chapter Objectives

Upon successful completion of this chapter, you should be able to:

1. Define key terms related to CMS-1500 and UB-04 claims.
2. Explain general purposes and completion processes for CMS-1500 (837P) and UB-04 (CMS-1450) (837) claims.
3. Describe data entry requirements for the CMS-1500 claim.
4. Explain how CMS-1500 secondary claims are processed.
5. Describe common errors that delay CMS-1500 claims processing.
6. State the final steps in CMS-1500 claims processing.
7. Explain how CMS-1500 claims are maintained for a medical practice.
8. Complete a UB-04 claim for inpatient and outpatient care.

Key Terms

Administrative Simplification
  Compliance Act (ASCA)

ANSI ASC X12N 837I (837I)

ANSI ASC X12N 837P (837P)

billing entity

data packet

diagnosis pointer letter

Federal Privacy Act

hospitalist

Medicare supplemental plan

National Council for Prescription
  Drug Programs (NCPCP)
  Telecommunication Standard

supervising physician

UB-04

Introduction

This chapter covers general completion and submission requirements of CMS-1500 and UB-04 (CMS-1450) claims, including their electronic versions (837P and 837I, respectively).

General Claims Information

CMS-1500 claims for professional services and UB-04 claims for inpatient and outpatient institutional health care services are submitted for reimbursement according to the payment system established for each type of provider (e.g., physician fee-for-service payment, inpatient prospective payment system). The reverse of the CMS-1500 claim contains special instructions for government programs (Figure 11-1).

Paper CMS-1500 Claims

The **Administrative Simplification Compliance Act (ASCA)** was implemented in October 2003 to prohibit payment of initial health care CMS-1500 claims that were not sent electronically, except in the following situations:

- *Dental Claims.* Dentists are permitted to submit paper dental claims as an exception to HIPAA's electronic claim requirement because (1) they are required to submit electronic transactions to other payers using a format that differs from that generally used by Medicare, and (2) because Medicare does not generally cover dental services, the allowance for submission of paper claims minimizes the burden on dentists who may, at times, need to bill Medicare.

- *Disruption in Electricity or Communication.* Paper claims are permitted when an interruption in electrical or communication service occurs, but only for the period of the interruption.

- *Medicare Beneficiaries.* Paper claims may be submitted by Medicare beneficiaries.

- *Medicare Demonstration Projects.* Paper claims are permitted for Medicare demonstration projects, which often allow for unusual situations that are not normally handled by HIPAA's transactions standards.

- *Medicare Secondary Payer.* For claims where more than one health plan is responsible for payment *before* Medicare, paper claims continue to be permitted.

- *Roster Billing.* To promote an increase in vaccinations for Medicare beneficiaries, Medicare allows mass immunizers to submit a single claim with an attached list of beneficiaries to whom a vaccine was administered. Many mass immunizers bill electronically in a non-standard format, and roster billing simplifies provider billing that is not otherwise available in an electronic form.

- *Small Provider Claims.* Paper claims may be submitted by a (1) provider with fewer than 25 full-time equivalent (FTE) employees that submits claims to a Medicare administrative contract (MAC); or (2) facility, physician, practitioner, or supplier with fewer than 10 FTE employees who submit claims to a MAC or a Durable Medical Equipment Regional Carrier (DMERC).

- *Unusual Cases.* The requirement to submit electronic claims may be waived when the provider (1) submits, on average, less than 10 claims per month; or (2) furnishes services or supplies outside of the U.S. territory and is a non-U.S. provider.

Providers are responsible for determining whether they meet one or more of these situations, and a waiver request does not need to be submitted. Some of these situations are temporary or apply only to certain claims, and when the temporary situation expires or when billing other types of claims, providers must submit claims electronically and in accordance wwith the HIPAA transaction standard.

BECAUSE THIS FORM IS USED BY VARIOUS GOVERNMENT AND PRIVATE HEALTH PROGRAMS, SEE SEPARATE INSTRUCTIONS ISSUED BY APPLICABLE PROGRAMS.

NOTICE: Any person who knowingly files a statement of claim containing any misrepresentation or any false, incomplete or misleading information may be guilty of a criminal act punishable under law and may be subject to civil penalties.

MEDICARE AND TRICARE PAYMENTS

A patient's signature requests that payment be made and authorizes release of any information necessary to process the claim and certifies that the information provided in Blocks 1 through 12 is true, accurate and complete. In the case of a Medicare claim, the patient's signature authorizes any entity to release to Medicare medical and nonmedical information and whether the person has employer group health insurance, liability, no-fault, worker's compensation or other insurance which is responsible to pay for the services for which the Medicare claim is made. See 42 CFR 411.24(a). If item 9 is completed, the patient's signature authorizes release of the information to the health plan or agency shown. In Medicare assigned or TRICARE participation cases, the physician agrees to accept the charge determination of the Medicare carrier or TRICARE fiscal intermediary as the full charge and the patient is responsible only for the deductible, coinsurance and non-covered services. Coinsurance and the deductible are based upon the charge determination of the Medicare carrier or TRICARE fiscal intermediary if this is less than the charge submitted. TRICARE is not a health insurance program but makes payment for health benefits provided through certain affiliations with the Uniformed Services. Information on the patient's sponsor should be provided in those items captioned in "Insured"; i.e., items 1a, 4, 6, 7, 9, and 11.

BLACK LUNG AND FECA CLAIMS

The provider agrees to accept the amount paid by the Government as payment in full. See Black Lung and FECA instructions regarding required procedure and diagnosis coding systems.

SIGNATURE OF PHYSICIAN OR SUPPLIER (MEDICARE, TRICARE, FECA AND BLACK LUNG)

In submitting this claim for payment from federal funds, I certify that: 1) the information on this form is true, accurate and complete; 2) I have familiarized myself with all applicable laws, regulations, and program instructions, which are available from the Medicare contractor; 3) I have provided or will provide sufficient information required to allow the government to make an informed eligibility and payment decision; 4) this claim, whether submitted by me or on my behalf by my designated billing company, complies with all applicable Medicare and/or Medicaid laws, regulations, and program instructions for payment including but not limited to the Federal anti-kickback statute and Physician Self-Referral law (commonly known as Stark law); 5) the services on this form were medically necessary and personally furnished by me or were furnished incident to my professional service by my employee under my direct supervision, except as otherwise expressly permitted by Medicare or TRICARE; 6) for each service rendered incident to my professional service, the identity (legal name and NPI, license #, or SSN) of the primary individual rendering each service is reported in the designated section.

For services to be considered "incident to" a physician's professional services, 1) they must be rendered under the physician's direct supervision by his/her employee, 2) they must be an integral, although incidental part of a covered physician service, 3) they must be of kinds commonly furnished in physician's offices, and 4) the services of non-physicians must be included on the physician's bills.

For TRICARE claims, I further certify that I (or any employee) who rendered services am not an active duty member of the Uniformed Services or a civilian employee of the United States Government or a contract employee of the United States Government, either civilian or military (refer to 5 USC 5536).

For Black-Lung claims, I further certify that the services performed were for a Black Lung-related disorder.

No Part B Medicare benefits may be paid unless this form is received as required by existing law and regulations (42 CFR 424.32).

NOTICE: Anyone who misrepresents or falsifies essential information to receive payment from Federal funds requested by this form may upon conviction be subject to fine and imprisonment under applicable Federal laws.

NOTICE TO PATIENT ABOUT THE COLLECTION AND USE OF MEDICARE, TRICARE, FECA, AND BLACK LUNG INFORMATION
(PRIVACY ACT STATEMENT)

We are authorized by CMS, TRICARE and OWCP to ask you for information needed in the administration of the Medicare, TRICARE, FECA, and Black Lung programs. Authority to collect information is in section 205(a), 1862, 1872 and 1874 of the Social Security Act as amended, 42 CFR 411.24(a) and 424.5(a) (6), and 44 USC 3101;41 CFR 101 et seq and 10 USC 1079 and 1086; 5 USC 8101 et seq; and 30 USC 901 et seq; 38 USC 613; E.O. 9397.

The information we obtain to complete claims under these programs is used to identify you and to determine your eligibility. It is also used to decide if the services and supplies you received are covered by these programs and to insure that proper payment is made.

The information may also be given to other providers of services, carriers, intermediaries, medical review boards, health plans, and other organizations or Federal agencies, for the effective administration of Federal provisions that require other third parties payers to pay primary to Federal program, and as otherwise necessary to administer these programs. For example, it may be necessary to disclose information about the benefits you have used to a hospital or doctor. Additional disclosures are made through routine uses for information contained in systems of records.

FOR MEDICARE CLAIMS: See the notice modifying system No. 09-70-0501, titled, 'Carrier Medicare Claims Record,' published in the Federal Register, Vol. 55 No. 177, page 37549, Wed. Sept. 12, 1990, or as updated and republished.

FOR OWCP CLAIMS: Department of Labor, Privacy Act of 1974, "Republication of Notice of Systems of Records," Federal Register Vol. 55 No. 40, Wed Feb. 28, 1990, See ESA-5, ESA-6, ESA-12, ESA-13, ESA-30, or as updated and republished.

FOR TRICARE CLAIMS: PRINCIPLE PURPOSE(S): To evaluate eligibility for medical care provided by civilian sources and to issue payment upon establishment of eligibility and determination that the services/supplies received are authorized by law.

ROUTINE USE(S): Information from claims and related documents may be given to the Dept. of Veterans Affairs, the Dept. of Health and Human Services and/or the Dept. of Transportation consistent with their statutory administrative responsibilities under TRICARE/CHAMPVA; to the Dept. of Justice for representation of the Secretary of Defense in civil actions; to the Internal Revenue Service, private collection agencies, and consumer reporting agencies in connection with recoupment claims; and to Congressional Offices in response to inquiries made at the request of the person to whom a record pertains. Appropriate disclosures may be made to other federal, state, local, foreign government agencies, private business entities, and individual providers of care, on matters relating to entitlement, claims adjudication, fraud, program abuse, utilization review, quality assurance, peer review, program integrity, third-party liability, coordination of benefits, and civil and criminal litigation related to the operation of TRICARE.

DISCLOSURES: Voluntary; however, failure to provide information will result in delay in payment or may result in denial of claim. With the one exception discussed below, there are no penalties under these programs for refusing to supply information. However, failure to furnish information regarding the medical services rendered or the amount charged would prevent payment of claims under these programs. Failure to furnish any other information, such as name or claim number, would delay payment of the claim. Failure to provide medical information under FECA could be deemed an obstruction.

It is mandatory that you tell us if you know that another party is responsible for paying for your treatment. Section 1128B of the Social Security Act and 31 USC 3801-3812 provide penalties for withholding this information.

You should be aware that P.L. 100-503, the "Computer Matching and Privacy Protection Act of 1988", permits the government to verify information by way of computer matches.

MEDICAID PAYMENTS (PROVIDER CERTIFICATION)

I hereby agree to keep such records as are necessary to disclose fully the extent of services provided to individuals under the State's Title XIX plan and to furnish information regarding any payments claimed for providing such services as the State Agency or Dept. of Health and Human Services may request.

I further agree to accept, as payment in full, the amount paid by the Medicaid program for those claims submitted for payment under that program, with the exception of authorized deductible, coinsurance, co-payment or similar cost-sharing charge.

SIGNATURE OF PHYSICIAN (OR SUPPLIER): I certify that the services listed above were medically indicated and necessary to the health of this patient and were personally furnished by me or my employee under my personal direction.

NOTICE: This is to certify that the foregoing information is true, accurate and complete. I understand that payment and satisfaction of this claim will be from Federal and State funds, and that any false claims, statements, or documents, or concealment of a material fact, may be prosecuted under applicable Federal or State laws.

According to the Paperwork Reduction Act of 1995, no persons are required to respond to a collection of information unless it displays a valid OMB control number. The valid OMB control number for this information collection is 0938-XXXX. The time required to complete this information collection is estimated to average 10 minutes per response, including the time to review instructions, search existing data resources, gather the data needed, and complete and review the information collection. If you have any comments concerning the accuracy of the time estimate(s) or suggestions for improving this form, please write to: CMS, 7500 Security Boulevard, Attn: PRA Reports Clearance Officer, Baltimore, Maryland 21244-1850. This address is for comments and/or suggestions only. DO NOT MAIL COMPLETED CLAIM FORMS TO THIS ADDRESS.

FIGURE 11-1 Reverse of CMS-1500, which contains special instructions for government programs.

Claims are submitted electronically to a third-party clearinghouse or payer using a computer with software that meets electronic submission requirements as established by the Health Insurance Portability and Accountability Act (HIPAA) claim standard. The claim is electronically transmitted as **data packets** (unit of data routed between provider and billing company, clearinghouse, or payer using the Internet or other packet-exchange network).

Health care settings are responsible for submitting UB-04 and CMS-1500 claims, and some settings submit both types of claims depending on services provided (Table 11-1).

Example: Anywhere Medical Center provides acute hospital inpatient, outpatient, and emergency department (ED) services. When a patient is admitted as a hospital inpatient, the UB-04 claim is submitted by the medical center for inpatient services upon discharge of the patient from the facility.

- If the medical center contracts with or employs a *hospitalist* (physician who contracts with or is employed by a hospital to provide inpatient professional services), a CMS-1500 claim is submitted by either the contracted agency or the medical center depending on the legal arrangement.

- If the patient's independent primary care physician provided inpatient professional services, a CMS-1500 claims is submitted by the physician office staff.

- If that patient primary care physician's medical practice is owned by the medical center, a CMS-1500 claims is submitted by the medical center (instead of the physician office staff), which is an example of *single-path coding and billing* (facility coder assigns ICD-10-CM, ICD-10-PCS, CPT, and HCPCS Level II codes, depending on facility and professional services, and the facility submits both the UB-04 and CMS-1500 claims for reimbursement).

TABLE 11-1 Submission of UB-04 and CMS-1500 claims by health care setting

Health Care Setting	UB-04 Claim Submission	CMS-1500 Claim Submission
Ambulatory surgical center (ASC)	ASC facility services	Responsible physician professional services (e.g., surgeon)
Durable medical equipment (DME) supplier	—	Durable medical equipment
Home health agency	Home health services	Responsible physician professional services
Hospice agency	Hospice services	Responsible physician professional services
Hospital emergency department (ED)	Hospital ED facility services	ED physician professional services
Hospital outpatient department	Hospital outpatient facility services	Responsible physician professional services (e.g., outpatient surgeon, pathology, radiologist)
Hospital[1] inpatient	Hospital inpatient facility services	Responsible physician professional services (e.g., hospitalist, attending physician)
Nursing facility[2]	Nursing facility services	Responsible physician professional services (e.g., attending physician)
Physician office[3]	—	Responsible physician (e.g., primary care provider, specialist)
Stand-alone outpatient centers[4]	—	Responsible physician(e.g., primary care provider, specialist)

[1]Hospital settings include acute care, critical access, short-term care, long-term care, psychiatric, and rehabilitation hospitals

[2]Nursing facility settings include intermediate care facilities, skilled nursing facilities.

[3]Physician office settings include solo and group medical practices, employed physician practices (e.g., hospitals that purchase and management existing solo and group practices); providers include physicians of medicine and osteopathy, dentists, physicians of podiatric medicine, optometrists, chiropractors (spinal manipulation), as well as nurse practitioners and physician assistants.

[4]Stand-alone outpatient centers include community outpatient mental health centers; comprehensive outpatient rehabilitation facilities and outpatient rehabilitation facilities; independent (outpatient) rural health clinics and freestanding federally qualified (outpatient) health centers; neighborhood outpatient health centers; stand-alone laboratory, physical therapy, radiology, renal dialysis, speech pathology; urgent care centers; and walk-in clinics. (To submit CMS-1500 claims, all of these facilities must *not* be located within hospital settings.)

Upon receipt of data packets, a series of edits is conducted to determine whether claims meet basic requirements of the HIPAA administrative simplification standard. Any errors detected at this level result in rejection of the entire data packet. Claims in a data packet that pass initial edits are next edited against HIPAA claim standards implementation guide requirements. After the data packet passes the first two levels of edits, each claim is reviewed for compliance with coverage and payment policy requirements. Rejected data packets and individual claims are returned to the submitter (e.g., provider, billing company, clearinghouse) for correction and resubmission. Rejected or denied claims that are not compliant with coverage and payment policy requirements include errors that need to be corrected or reasons for denials. (Denied claims may initiate the appeals process, discussed in Chapter 4.) Upon successful transmission, an acknowledgement report is generated and transmitted to the submitter of each claim.

Electronic claims must meet requirements adopted as the national standard under HIPAA, which include the following. (Requirements are mandated for government claims, and many third-party payers have also adopted them.)

- **ANSI ASC X12N 837P (837P)** is the standard format used for submission of electronic claims for *professional* health care services. Professional providers include physicians and suppliers. A *supplier* is a physician or other health care practitioner *or* an entity other than a provider that furnishes health care services. For example, physicians submit Medicare claims to Medicare administrative contractors (MACs) (sometimes called *carriers*), and durable medical equipment (DME) suppliers submit Medicare claims to a DMEMAC.

- **ANSI ASC X12N 837I (837I)** is the standard format for submission of electronic claims for *institutional* health care services. Institutional providers include hospitals, skilled nursing facilities, end-stage renal disease providers, home health agencies, hospices, outpatient rehabilitation clinics, comprehensive outpatient rehabilitation facilities, community mental health centers, critical access hospitals, federally qualified health centers, histocompatibility laboratories, Indian Health Service facilities, organ procurement organizations, religious non-medical health care institutions, and rural health clinics. For example, hospitals submit Medicare claims for inpatient admissions to Medicare administrative contractors (MACs) (previously called fiscal intermediaries [FIs]).

- **National Council for Prescription Drug Programs (NCPCP) Telecommunication Standard** is the standard format for retail pharmacy. (The 837P is used for retail pharmacy services, such as a pharmacist billing a payer for administration of a flu vaccination at a retail pharmacy store.) For example, a retail pharmacy submits Medicare claims to the patient's *Medicare Part D sponsor*, which is an organization that has one or more contract(s) with the Centers for Medicare and Medicaid Services to provide Part D (prescription drug) benefits to Medicare beneficiaries.

CMS-1500 and 837P

The CMS-1500 claim for professional services is submitted electronically after being generated by medical practice management software, and the 837P is the standard format used to electronically transmit health care claims. Because the CMS-1500 and 837P data elements for uniform electronic billing specifications are consistent, one processing system can handle both types of claims. Patient data from a physician's office practice management software is used to populate the CMS-1500 claim (Figure 11-2), and the claim is electronically transmitted from the computer to the third-party clearinghouse or the payer.

UB-04 (CMS-1450) and 837

The **UB-04** claim (Figure 11-3), designated as the CMS-1450 by CMS, uses 837I as its standard format to electronically transmit health care claims for inpatient and outpatient institutional services. Data elements in the UB-04 for uniform electronic billing specifications are consistent with the hard copy data set.

Patient data from an institution's electronic health record populates the UB-04 claim, which is electronically transmitted to the payer or a clearinghouse for processing. An exception allows certain institutions to submit paper UB-04 claims, such as health care facilities with less than 25 full-time equivalent (FTE) employees.

HEALTH INSURANCE CLAIM FORM

APPROVED BY NATIONAL UNIFORM CLAIM COMMITTEE (NUCC) 02/12

PICA — PICA

CARRIER

1. MEDICARE (Medicare#) MEDICAID (Medicaid#) TRICARE (ID#/DoD#) CHAMPVA (Member ID#) GROUP HEALTH PLAN (ID#) FECA BLKLUNG (ID#) OTHER (ID#)

1a. INSURED'S I.D. NUMBER (For Program in Item 1)

2. PATIENT'S NAME (Last Name, First Name, Middle Initial)

3. PATIENT'S BIRTH DATE MM DD YY SEX M F

4. INSURED'S NAME (Last Name, First Name, Middle Initial)

5. PATIENT'S ADDRESS (No., Street)

6. PATIENT RELATIONSHIP TO INSURED Self Spouse Child Other

7. INSURED'S ADDRESS (No., Street)

CITY STATE

8. RESERVED FOR NUCC USE

CITY STATE

ZIP CODE TELEPHONE (Include Area Code) ( )

ZIP CODE TELEPHONE (Include Area Code) ( )

9. OTHER INSURED'S NAME (Last Name, First Name, Middle Initial)

10. IS PATIENT'S CONDITION RELATED TO:

11. INSURED'S POLICY GROUP OR FECA NUMBER

a. OTHER INSURED'S POLICY OR GROUP NUMBER

a. EMPLOYMENT? (Current or Previous) YES NO

a. INSURED'S DATE OF BIRTH MM DD YY SEX M F

b. RESERVED FOR NUCC USE

b. AUTO ACCIDENT? PLACE (State) YES NO

b. OTHER CLAIM ID (Designated by NUCC)

c. RESERVED FOR NUCC USE

c. OTHER ACCIDENT? YES NO

c. INSURANCE PLAN NAME OR PROGRAM NAME

d. INSURANCE PLAN NAME OR PROGRAM NAME

10d. CLAIM CODES (Designated by NUCC)

d. IS THERE ANOTHER HEALTH BENEFIT PLAN? YES NO *If yes,* complete items 9, 9a, and 9d.

READ BACK OF FORM BEFORE COMPLETING & SIGNING THIS FORM.

12. PATIENT'S OR AUTHORIZED PERSON'S SIGNATURE I authorize the release of any medical or other information necessary to process this claim. I also request payment of government benefits either to myself or to the party who accepts assignment below.

SIGNED DATE

13. INSURED'S OR AUTHORIZED PERSON'S SIGNATURE I authorize payment of medical benefits to the undersigned physician or supplier for services described below.

SIGNED

PATIENT AND INSURED INFORMATION

14. DATE OF CURRENT ILLNESS, INJURY, or PREGNANCY (LMP) MM DD YY QUAL.

15. OTHER DATE QUAL. MM DD YY

16. DATES PATIENT UNABLE TO WORK IN CURRENT OCCUPATION FROM MM DD YY TO MM DD YY

17. NAME OF REFERRING PROVIDER OR OTHER SOURCE

17a. 17b. NPI

18. HOSPITALIZATION DATES RELATED TO CURRENT SERVICES FROM MM DD YY TO MM DD YY

19. ADDITIONAL CLAIM INFORMATION (Designated by NUCC)

20. OUTSIDE LAB? YES NO $ CHARGES

21. DIAGNOSIS OR NATURE OF ILLNESS OR INJURY Relate A-L to service line below (24E) ICD Ind.

A. B. C. D.
E. F. G. H.
I. J. K. L.

22. RESUBMISSION CODE ORIGINAL REF. NO.

23. PRIOR AUTHORIZATION NUMBER

24. A. DATE(S) OF SERVICE From MM DD YY To MM DD YY	B. PLACE OF SERVICE	C. EMG	D. PROCEDURES, SERVICES, OR SUPPLIES (Explain Unusual Circumstances) CPT/HCPCS MODIFIER	E. DIAGNOSIS POINTER	F. $ CHARGES	G. DAYS OR UNITS	H. EPSDT Family Plan	I. ID. QUAL.	J. RENDERING PROVIDER ID. #
1								NPI	
2								NPI	
3								NPI	
4								NPI	
5								NPI	
6								NPI	

25. FEDERAL TAX I.D. NUMBER SSN EIN

26. PATIENT'S ACCOUNT NO.

27. ACCEPT ASSIGNMENT? (For govt. claims, see back) YES NO

28. TOTAL CHARGE $

29. AMOUNT PAID $

30. Rsvd for NUCC Use

31. SIGNATURE OF PHYSICIAN OR SUPPLIER INCLUDING DEGREES OR CREDENTIALS (I certify that the statements on the reverse apply to this bill and are made a part thereof.)

SIGNED DATE

32. SERVICE FACILITY LOCATION INFORMATION

a. NPI b.

33. BILLING PROVIDER INFO & PH # ( )

a. NPI b.

PHYSICIAN OR SUPPLIER INFORMATION

NUCC Instruction Manual available at: www.nucc.org

PLEASE PRINT OR TYPE

FIGURE 11-2 CMS-1500 claim.

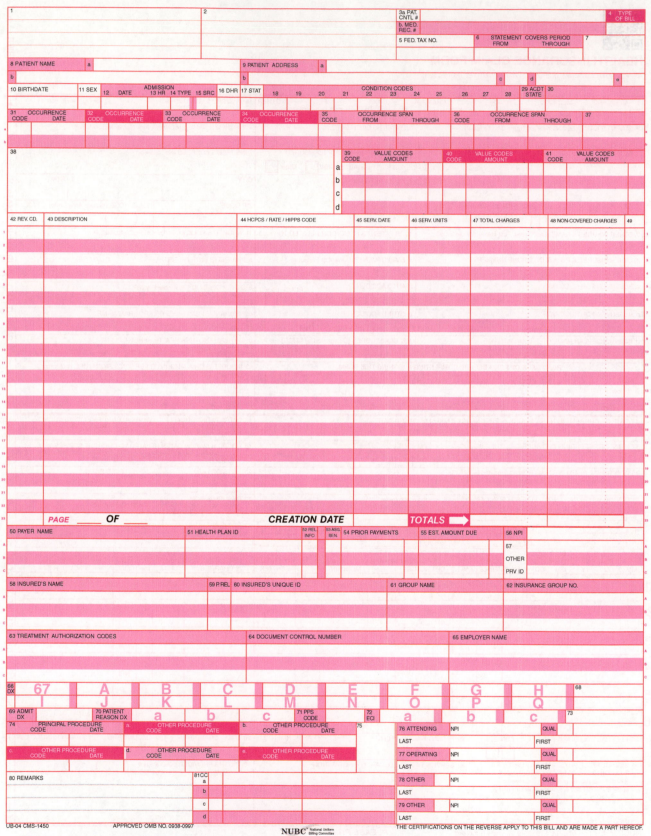

FIGURE 11-3 Blank UB-04 claim.

Claims Attachments

Some claims require attachments, such as operative reports, discharge summaries, clinic notes, or letters, to aid in determination of the reimbursement to be paid by the third-party payer. Attachments are also required when CPT unlisted codes are reported. HIPAA administrative simplification regulations require all payers to accept claim attachments. Each claims attachment (medical report substantiating the medical condition) should include patient and policy identification information. Instructions for submitting *electronic media claims (EMC)* are discussed in Chapter 4.

Any *letter* written by the provider should contain clear and simple English rather than "medicalese." The letter can describe an unusual procedure, special operation, or a patient's medical condition that warranted performing surgery in a setting different from the CMS-stipulated site for that surgery.

CMS-1500 Data Entry

Data entry for CMS-1500 claims includes requirements about the following for optical character recognition of scanned claims by computer software.

- Entering patient and policyholder names, provider names, and mailing addreses and telephone numbers
- Recovery of funds from responsible payers
- National provider identifier (NPI) and National standard employer identifier (EIN)
- Assignment of benefits versus accept assignment
- Reporting ICD-10-CM diagnosis codes and HCPCS Level II and CPT codes
- Reporting the billing entity

All data entered on the claim must fit within the borders of the data field (Figure 11-4).

- Enter all alpha characters in uppercase (capital letters).
- Do not enter the alpha character "O" for a zero (0).
- Enter a space between the CPT or HCPCS code and its modifier (instead of a hyphen). If multiple modifiers are reported enter one space between each modifier.
- Do *not* enter hyphens or spaces in the 9-digit ZIP code, social security number, employer identification number (EIN), or national provider identifier (NPI).
- Enter commas between the patient or policyholder's last name, first name, and middle initial.
- *Do not* use punctuation in a patient's or policyholder's name, except for a hyphen in a compound name.

Example: GARDNER-BEY

- *Do not* enter a person's title or other designations, such as Sr., Jr., II, or III, unless printed on the patient's insurance ID card.

Example: The name on the ID card states:

Wm F. Goodpatient, IV

Name on claim is entered as:

GOODPATIENT IV, WILLIAM, F

Courtesy of the Centers for Medicare & Medicaid Services, www.cms.gov; claim data created by author.

FIGURE 11-4 Example of correct placement of the X within a box on the CMS-1500 claim.

- For CMS-1500 claims, enter two zeroes in the cents column when a fee or a monetary total is expressed in whole dollars. *Do not* enter any leading zeroes in front of the dollar amount.

Example: Six dollars is entered as 6 00

F.
$ CHARGES
6   00

Courtesy of the Centers for Medicare & Medicaid Services, www.cms.gov; claim data created by author.

- For *all* CMS-1500 claims, birth dates are entered as eight digits with spaces between the digits representing the month, day, and the *four-digit year (MM DD YYYY)* in Blocks 3 (Figure 11-5A) and 11a. For *all* UB-04 claims, birth dates are entered as eight digits *without* spaces (e.g., MMDDYYYY) (Figure 11-5B).

3. PATIENT'S BIRTH DATE		SEX	
MM	DD	YY	
03	**08**	**YYYY**	M ☐ F ☒

Courtesy of the Centers for Medicare & Medicaid Services, www.cms.gov; claim data created by author.

FIGURE 11-5A Proper entry for CMS-1500 claim birth date and sex.

10 BIRTHDATE	11 SEX	ADMISSION 12 DATE	13 HR	14 TYPE	15 SRC
08051970	**M**	**0505YYYY**			

Courtesy of the Centers for Medicare & Medicaid Services, www.cms.gov; claim data created by author.

FIGURE 11-5B Proper entry for UB-04 claim birth date, sex, and admission date.

- All other CMS-1500 blocks that require date(s) are entered as six digits with spaces between the digits representing the month, day, and two-digit year (e.g., MM DD YY) *except for Block 31 where no spaces are entered between the digits* (e.g., MMDDYY).

 NOTE:

Medicare Claims Processing Manual Chapter 26: Completing and Processing Form CMS-1500 Data Set allows for entry of six- or eight-digit dates in all CMS-1500 blocks *except for birth dates in Blocks 3 and 11a, which require eight-digit dates*. However, consistency when entering six- or eight-digit dates throughout the claim is required. For example, do not enter a six-digit date in CMS-1500 Block 14 (date of current illness) but eight-digit dates in Blocks 12, 13, 15, 16, 18, 24A, and 31. National Uniform Claims Committee (NUCC) claims completion instructions state that dates entered in Block 24A must be six digits (MM DD YY) only, which differs from Medicare claims completion instructions. (For *Understanding Health Insurance* claims completion, six-digit dates are entered *except for birth dates in Blocks 3 and 11a, which require eight-digit dates*.)

- Two-digit code numbers for the months are:

Jan—01	Apr—04	July—07	Oct—10
Feb—02	May—05	Aug—08	Nov—11
Mar—03	June—06	Sept—09	Dec—12

- For CMS-1500 claims, Block 3 requires entry of an X in the appropriate box, M (male) or F (female) (Figure 11-5A) to designate the patient's sex. For UB-04 claims, the patient's sex requires entry of the letter M (male) or F (female) in Form Locator 11 (Figure 11-5B); some third-party payers also allow the letter U (unknown) to be entered. (Medicare Code Editor software contains listings of male- and female-related diagnosis and procedure codes and corresponding text descriptions, and inconsistencies between a patient's sex and a diagnosis or procedure reported on the UB-04 result in claims denials. For example, a claim submitted for a male patient with cervical cancer as a diagnosis or hysterectomy as a procedure will be denied.)

- For CMS-1500 claims, the third-party payer block is located from the upper center to the right margin of the form. Do not use punctuation or other symbols in the address. When entering a nine-digit zip code, do *not* include the hyphen or a space (e.g., 123456789). For the UB-04 claim, Form Locator 80 populates third-party payer information.

  Line 1–Name of third-party payer

  Line 2–First line of address

  Line 3–Second line of address, if necessary; otherwise, leave blank

  Line 4–City, state (2 characters), and nine-digit zip code that does *not* include the hyphen or a space (123451234)

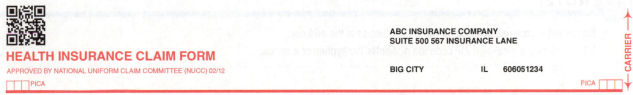

HEALTH INSURANCE CLAIM FORM
APPROVED BY NATIONAL UNIFORM CLAIM COMMITTEE (NUCC) 02/12
PICA

ABC INSURANCE COMPANY
SUITE 500 567 INSURANCE LANE

BIG CITY   IL   606051234
PICA
CARRIER →

Courtesy of the Centers for Medicare & Medicaid Services, www.cms.gov; claim data created by author.

- For the CMS-1500 claim, list only one procedure per line, starting with line one of Block 24. (To report more than six procedures or services for the same date of service, generate a new CMS-1500 claim.) The UB-04 claim allows 22 procedures or services to be entered for the same date(s) of service in Form Locator 42.

Entering Patient and Policyholder Names

For the CMS-1500 claim, when entering the patient's name in Block 2 and the policyholder's name in Block 4, separate the last name, first name, and middle initial with commas (e.g., DOE, JOHN, S). For UB-04 claims, when entering the patient's name in Form Locator 8 and the policyholder's name in Form Locator 58, separate the last name, first name, and middle initial with a space (e.g., DOE JOHN S). When the patient is the policyholder, enter name in Blocks 2 and 4 (CMS-1500) and Form Locators 8 and 58 (UB-04).

In Block 12 of the CMS-1500 claim, SIGNATURE ON FILE or SOF is entered to authorization the release of medical information to the third-party payer for the electronic transmission claims (instead of having the patient sign the claim) because a certification letter is filed with the payer; the date is not entered in Block 12.

Entering Provider Names

For the CMS-1500 claim, when entering the name of a provider, enter the first name, middle initial (if known), last name, and credentials (e.g., MARY SMITH MD). *Do not enter any punctuation.*

For the UB-04 claim, the provider's name is populated in Form Locator 70 (with the NPI).

Entering Mailing Addresses

For the CMS-1500 claim, when entering a patient's and/or policyholder's (Blocks 5 and 7) mailing address, enter the street address on line 1. Enter the city and state on line 2. Enter the five- or nine-digit zip code on line 3 (because the patient's four-digit extender for the zip code might be unknown). For the UB-04 claim, the patient's address is populated in Form Locators 9a through 9e (with 9e populated with the four-digit zip code extension, if available). When the address in Blocks 5 and 7 of the CMS-1500 are identical, leave Block 7 blank.

The patient's address refers to the patient's permanent residence. Do not enter a temporary address or a school address. (If the patient has a foreign address, contact the payer for specific reporting instructions.)

NOTE:

The National Uniform Claims Committee (NUCC) recommends that the patient's and insured's telephone number *not* be reported. That data is not captured for electronic claims purposes, which refers to the ANSI ASC X12N 837P professional health care claim transaction, v5010A1. (Phone extensions are also not supported.) *Therefore, do not enter telephone numbers in CMS-1500 Block 5 (patient) and Block 7 (insured) in this textbook, workbook, or SimClaim.*

For the CMS-1500 claim, when entering a provider's name, mailing address, and telephone number (Block 33), enter the provider's name on line 1, enter the provider's billing address on line 2, and enter the provider's city, state, and nine-digit zip code without the hyphen or a space on line 3. Enter the telephone number in the area next to the Block title. For the UB-04 claim, the institution's name, address, and telephone number are populated in Form Locators 1 and 2.

NOTE:

- Do not enter commas, periods, or other punctuation in the address.
- When entering a nine-digit ZIP code, do *not* enter the hyphen or a space.

Recovery of Funds from Responsible Payers

For CMS-1500 claims, payers flag claims for investigation when an X is entered in one or more of the YES boxes in Block 10 of the CMS-1500 claim. For CMS-1500 and UB-04 claims, when an ICD-10-CM code begins with the letter V, W, X, or Y is reported in Block 21, payers also flag claims for review. Such an entry indicates that payment might be the responsibility of a workers' compensation payer; automobile insurance company; or homeowners, business, or other liability policy insurance company. Some payers reimburse the claim and outsource (to a vendor that specializes in "backend recovery") the pursuit of funds from the appropriate payer. Other payers deny payment until the provider submits documentation to support reimbursement processing by the payer (e.g., remittance advice from workers' compensation or other liability payer denying the claim).

For the CMS-1500 claim, entering an X in any of the YES boxes in Block 10 of the CMS-1500 alerts the commercial payer that another insurance company might be liable for payment. The commercial payer will not consider the claim unless the provider submits a remittance advice from the liable party (e.g., automobile policy) indicating that the claim was denied. For employment-related conditions, another option is to attach a letter from the workers' compensation payer that documents rejection of payment for an on-the-job injury. Block 10d, Claim Codes (Designated by NUCC), are entered when required by health insurance plans and government programs. For example, COVID-19 claims contained code DR in Block 10d to indicate procedures and services provided were "disaster related."

NOTE:

In ICD-10-CM, the majority of codes assigned to external causes of morbidity are located in Chapter 20. Other conditions stated as due to external causes are also classified elsewhere in ICD-10-CM's Chapters 1–22. For these other conditions, ICD-10-CM codes from Chapter 20 are also reported to provide additional information regarding external causes of the condition (e.g., place of occurrence).

National Provider Identifier (NPI)

The *national provider identifier* (NPI) is a unique 10-digit number issued to individual providers (e.g., physicians, dentists, pharmacists) and health care organizations (e.g., group physician practices, hospitals, nursing facilities).

Even if an individual provider moves, changes specialty, or changes practices, the provider will keep the same NPI (but must notify CMS to supply the new information).

The NPI issued to a health care organization is also permanent *except in rare situations when a health care provider does not wish to continue an association with a previously used NPI.*

 NOTE:

If an NPI is used fraudulently by another, a new NPI will be issued to the individual provider or health care organization affected.

HIPAA mandated the adoption of standard unique identifiers to improve the efficiency and effectiveness of the electronic transmission of health information for:

- Employers—national standard employer identifier number (EIN)

- Health care providers—national provider identifier (NPI)

- Individuals—national individual identifier (has been placed on hold)

HIPAA *covered entities* include health plans, health care clearinghouses, and health care providers that conduct electronic transactions. HIPAA mandated use of the NPI to identify health care providers in standard transactions, which include claims processing, patient eligibility inquiries and responses, claims status inquiries and responses, patient referrals, and generation of remittance advices. Health care providers (and organizations) that transmit health information electronically to submit claims data are required by HIPAA to obtain an NPI even if the provider (or organization) uses business associates (e.g., billing agencies) to prepare the transactions.

NPI Application Process

The *National Plan and Provider Enumeration System (NPPES)* was developed by CMS to assign the unique health care provider and health plan identifiers and to serve as a database from which to extract data (e.g., health plan verification of provider NPI). Each health plan has a process by which NPI data will be accessed to verify the identity of providers who submit HIPAA transactions.

 NOTE:

Search for NPI numbers at *https://npiregistry.cms.hhs.gov.*

Providers apply for an NPI by submitting the following:

- Web-based application

- Paper-based application

- Electronic file (e.g., hospital submits an electronic file that contains information about all physician employees, such as emergency department physicians, pathologists, and radiologists)

Practices that Bill "Incident To"

For CMS-1500 claims, when a nonphysician practitioner (NPP) (e.g., nurse practitioner, physician assistant) in a group practice bills incident-to a physician, but that physician is out of the office on the day the NPP provides services to the patient, another physician in the same group can provide direct supervision to meet the incident-to requirements. A **supervising physician** is a licensed physician in good standing who, according to state regulations, engages in the direct supervision of nonphysician practitioners whose duties are encompassed by the supervising physician's scope of practice. A supervising physician is not required to be physically present in the patient's treatment room when services are provided; however, the supervising physician must be present in the office suite or facility to render assistance, if necessary.

NOTE:

A *rendering physician* provides (or renders) care to patients. A supervising physician engages in the direct supervision of nonphysician practitioners who provide care to patients. In an institutional setting, a hospitalist is a rendering physician. A **hospitalist** is a dedicated inpatient physician who works exclusively in a hospital.

For the CMS-1500 claim, when incident-to services are reported, the following entries are made:

- Enter the ordering physician's name in Block 17 (*not* the supervising physician's name). (An *ordering provider* is a physician or nonphysician practitioner who orders services [e.g., clinical laboratory tests] for the patient.)
- Enter the applicable qualifier (in the space preceding the name) to identify which provider is being reported.
  - DN (referring provider)
  - DK (ordering provider)
  - DQ (supervising provider)
- Enter the ordering physician's NPI in Block 17b.

- For Block 17a, enter the applicable qualifier (in the space preceding the name) for the ordering, referring, or supervising provider, if applicable. The following qualifiers are permitted:

  - 0B (state license number)
  - 1G (provider UPIN number)
  - G2 (provider commercial number)
  - LU (location number for supervising provider *only*)

| 17. NAME OF REFERRING PHYSICIAN OR OTHER SOURCE | 17a. | 0B | 921435 |
| DN ¦ MATEO SANTIAGO | 17b. | NPI | 9873216540 |

Courtesy of the Centers for Medicare & Medicaid Services, www.cms.gov.

- In Block 19 (Additional Claim Information, Designated by NUCC), refer to instructions from payers and government programs. If completion is required, enter the appropriate qualifier before the information being entered. (Do not enter spaces, hyphens, or other separators between the qualifier and the information entered.) For example, *NTEADDSurgery was lengthier than planned due to congenital anomaly*, with NTE entered as the beginning qualifier, ADD entered as the additional information qualifier, and the entered statement as information that clarifies reporting an "increased procedural services" CPT modifier -22 on the claim.

| 19. ADDITIONAL CLAIM INFORMATION (Designated by NUCC) |
| **NTEADD Surgery was lengthier than planned due to congenital anomaly** |

- In Block 22 (Resubmission), enter the appropriate resubmission code and original reference number, which was assigned by the payer to a previously submitted claim. For replacement of prior claim enter code 7 in the left-hand side of the block, and for void/cancel of prior claim enter 8.

| 22. RESUBMISSION CODE | ORIGINAL REF. NO. |
| 7 | 8521236547 |

- Enter the supervising physician's NPI in Block 24J.

Courtesy of the Centers for Medicare &
Medicaid Services, www.cms.gov.

- Enter the supervising physician's name (or signature) in Block 31.

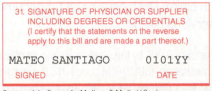

Courtesy of the Centers for Medicare & Medicaid Services, www.cms.gov.

Assignment of Benefits versus Accept Assignment

For the CMS-1500 claim, an area of confusion for health insurance specialists is differentiating between *assignment of benefits* and *accept assignment*. Patients sign Block 13 of the CMS-1500 claim to instruct the payer to directly reimburse the provider. This is called *assignment of benefits*. If the patient does not sign Block 13, the payer sends reimbursement to the patient. The patient is then responsible for reimbursing the provider. SIGNATURE ON FILE or SOF can also be entered in Block 13 for electronic claims processing. (However, when the patient's signature is *not* on file, leave Block 13 blank.)

When the YES box in Block 27 contains an X, the provider agrees to accept as payment in full whatever the payer reimburses. This is called *accept assignment*. The provider can still collect deductible, copayment, and coinsurance amounts from the patient. If the NO box in Block 27 contains an X, the provider does not accept assignment. The provider can bill the patient for the amount not paid by the payer.

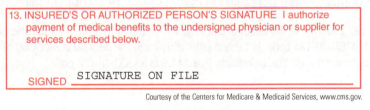

Courtesy of the Centers for Medicare & Medicaid Services, www.cms.gov.

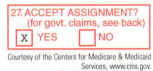

Courtesy of the Centers for Medicare & Medicaid
Services, www.cms.gov.

Reporting Diagnoses: ICD-10-CM Codes

Block 21

For CMS-1500 claims, diagnosis codes (without decimal points) are entered in Block 21 of the claim. A maximum of *12* ICD-10-CM codes may be entered on a single claim, next to letters A through L in Block 21. In the ICD Ind (ICD indicator) box, enter 0 for ICD-10-CM. Then, the appropriate **diagnosis pointer letters** from Block 21 (A through L) is entered in Block 24E of the CMS-1500 to justify medical necessity of the procedure performed or service provided. More than one diagnosis pointer letter can be entered in Block 24E, if permitted by the payer, which are entered without spaces (e.g., ABCD). (In this textbook, multiple diagnosis pointer letters are permitted.)

NOTE:

- When entering ICD-10-CM codes in Block 21 of the CMS-1500 claim, do *not* enter the decimal.
- When entering ICD-10-CM codes in Form Locator 66 of the UB-04 claim, do *not* enter the decimal.
- When a payer allows more than one *diagnosis pointer letter* to be entered from Block 21 in Block 24E of the CMS-1500 claim, do not enter a space or a comma between each letter (e.g., ABCD). The diagnosis pointer letter entered in Block 24E indicates the medical necessity of the procedure performed or service provided.

If more than 12 diagnoses are required to justify the procedures and/or services on a claim, generate additional claims. In such cases, be sure that the diagnoses justify the medical necessity for performing the procedures/services reported on each claim. Diagnoses must be documented in the patient's record to validate medical necessity of procedures or services billed.

Example: The patient was seen on January 9, YY, by the provider during an office encounter (place of service 11) due to bronchopneumonia and frequency of micturition. ICD-10-CM codes J18.0 (bronchopneumonia) and R35.0 (frequency of micturition) are reported in CMS-1500 Block 21 (without decimals). Because both conditions justify the medical necessity of the level 3 established patient evaluation and management service provided, letters A and B from Block 21 are entered in Block 24E.

CMS-1500 claim entry

Courtesy of the Centers for Medicare & Medicaid Services, www.cms.gov; claim data created by author.

For the UB-04, ICD-10-CM diagnosis codes are populated without the decimal in Form Locators 66, 69, 70, 71, and 72. (ICD-10-PCS codes that are populated in Form Locator 74 do not contain decimals.)

Example: A patient was admitted to the hospital and received inpatient treatment for chronic obstructive pulmonary disease, which is assigned ICD-10-CM code J44.9 and entered *without the decimal* in Block 66 of the UB-04 claim. (The number 0 is entered below the DX title to indicate that J44.9 is an ICD-10-CM code.)

UB-04 claim entry

 NOTE:

Coders should be aware that some chronic conditions always affect patient care because they require medical management and should, therefore, be coded and reported on the CMS-1500 claim. Examples include diabetes mellitus and hypertension.

Sequencing Multiple Diagnoses

For CMS-1500 claims, the first-listed code reported is the major reason the patient was treated by the health care provider. For the UB-04 claim, the principal diagnosis code is that condition, established after study, which was chiefly responsible for occasioning the patient's inpatient admission to the hospital. *Secondary diagnoses codes are also entered and should be included on the claim only if they are necessary to justify procedures/services reported.* Do not enter any diagnoses stated in the patient record that were not treated or medically managed (e.g., existing diagnosis that impacts treatment of a new diagnosis) during the encounter.

Be sure code numbers are placed within the designated field on the claim.

Accurate Coding

For physician office and outpatient claims processing, *never* report a code for uncertain diagnoses, which include such terms as "rule out," "suspicious for," "probable," "ruled out," "possible," or "questionable." Instead, enter ICD-10-CM codes for the patient's signs or symptoms. *For inpatient hospitalizations, it is acceptable to report codes for uncertain diagnoses when a definitive diagnosis has not been established.*

Be sure all diagnosis codes are reported to the highest degree of specificity known at the time of the treatment.

If the computerized billing system displays a default diagnosis code (e.g., condition last treated) when entering a patient's claim information, determine if the code validates the current procedure/service reported. It may frequently be necessary to edit this code because, although the diagnosis may still be present, it may not have been treated or medically managed during the current encounter.

Reporting Procedures and Services: HCPCS Level II and CPT Codes

Instructions in this section are for those CMS-1500 claim blocks that are universally required. All other blocks are discussed individually in Chapters 12 through 17.

CMS-1500 Block 24—Shaded Lines

Shaded rows were added to Block 24 because input from the health insurance industry indicated a need to report supplemental information about services reported, specifically in shaded Blocks 24A-24G. Supplemental information is entered on the shaded row above its corresponding service line. (Shaded rows are not intended to allow billing of 12 lines of service.)

The six service lines in Block 24 were also divided horizontally to accommodate entry of the NPI and another (e.g., proprietary) identifier. If another identifier is entered in shaded Block 24J, a corresponding identifying qualifier (e.g., G2 for commercial payer-assigned identifying number) is entered in Block 24I. The NPI is entered in unshaded Block 24J, and the other identifier (e.g., provider number assigned by commercial payer) is entered in shaded Block 24J.

Example: The CMS-1500 claim was submitted for dental care provided on October 15, YY. The shaded line above that date of service contains identifying qualifier ZZ, which indicates provider name, followed by the name of the provider (Margaret Miller DDS). Then ID qualifier G2, which indicates commercial payer assigned identifier, is followed by identifier number 987654321. Such information is useful to the provider for internal data capture (as well as to payers that request such information).

24. A. DATE(S) OF SERVICE From MM DD YY To MM DD YY	B. PLACE OF SERVICE	C. EMG	D. PROCEDURES, SERVICES, OR SUPPLIES (Explain Unusual Circumstances) CPT/HCPCS MODIFIER	E. DIAGNOSIS POINTER	F. $ CHARGES	G. DAYS OR UNITS	H. EPSDT Family Plan	I. ID. QUAL.	J. RENDERING PROVIDER ID. #
ZZ Margaret Miller DDS								G2	987654321
1 10 15 YY	11		E1399	AB	450 00	1		NPI	1234567890

Courtesy of the Centers for Medicare & Medicaid Services, www.cms.gov; claim data created by author.

CMS-1500 Block 24A—Dates of Service

Per the CMS-1500 claims instructions from CMS, enter date(s) of service with spaces between the month, day, and four-digit year (MM DD YY).

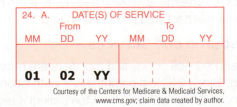

24. A. DATE(S) OF SERVICE From MM DD YY	To MM DD YY
01 02 YY	

Courtesy of the Centers for Medicare & Medicaid Services,
www.cms.gov; claim data created by author.

Example 1: Patient is admitted to the hospital on June 1. The physician reports detailed subsequent hospital visits on June 2, 3, and 4. Date of service 06 01 YY (no spaces) is entered on a separate line in Block 24 because the CPT code assigned for initial inpatient care (on the day of admission) is different from subsequent hospital visits (reported for June 2, 3, and 4 as 06 02 YY through 06 04 YY). If identical consecutive procedures fall within a two-month span, use two lines, one for the first month and one for the second.

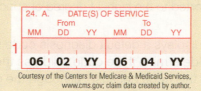

Courtesy of the Centers for Medicare & Medicaid Services, www.cms.gov; claim data created by author.

Example 2: Patient is admitted to the hospital on May 29. The physician reports an initial E/M service on May 29 and subsequent E/M services on May 30, May 31, June 1, June 2, and June 3. When reporting consecutive days on one line, the first date is reported in 24A in the *From* column and the last day in the *To* column. The *DAYS OR UNITS* column (24G) should reflect the number of days reported in 24A.

Courtesy of the Centers for Medicare & Medicaid Services, www.cms.gov; claim data created by author.

CMS-1500 Block 24B—Place of Service

All payers require entry of a place of service (POS) code on the CMS-1500 claim. The POS code reported must be consistent with the CPT procedure/service code description, and it will be one or two digits, depending on the payer.

When third-party payers and government programs (e.g., Medicaid) audit submitted claims, they require evidence of documentation in the patient's record about encounters and inpatient hospital visits. It is recommended that when a provider submits a claim for inpatient visits, a copy of hospital documentation (e.g., progress notes) supporting the visits be filed in the office patient record. Without such documentation, payers and government programs deny reimbursement for the visits.

Blueshield POS Codes	Medicare POS Codes	Description
1	21	Inpatient Hospital
2	22	Outpatient Hospital
3	11	Office
4	12	Home

CMS-1500 Block 24C—EMG

Check with the payer for their definition of emergency (EMG) treatment. If the payer requires completion of CMS-1500 claim Block 24C, and EMG treatment was provided, enter a Y (for YES). Otherwise, leave blank.

CMS-1500 Block 24D—Procedures and Services

CPT and HCPCS Level II procedure and service codes and modifiers are reported in CMS-1500 Claim Block 24D. Below the heading in claim Block 24D is a parenthetical instruction that says *(Explain Unusual Circumstances)*, which allows for entry of documentation from the patient's record.

NOTE:

Do not report procedure and/or service codes if no fee was charged.

When reporting more than one CPT Surgery code on a CMS-1500 claim, enter the code with the highest fee in line 1 of Block 24, and then enter additional codes (and modifiers) in descending order of charges. Be sure to completely enter data on each horizontal line before beginning to enter data on another line.

Identical procedures or services can be reported on the same line *if* the following circumstances apply:

- Procedures were performed on consecutive days in the same month.
- The same code is assigned to the procedures/services reported.
- Identical charges apply to the assigned code.
- Block 24G (Days or Units) is completed.

CMS-1500 Block—24H (ESPDT/Family Plan)

Early & periodic screening, diagnosis, and treatment (EPSDT) and family planning services are reported in Block 24H for Medicaid procedures and services. For EPSDT, use the following codes to identify the status of a referral:

- AV (ESPEDT available–not used; patient refused referral)
- S2 (Patient currently under treatment for referred diagnostic or corrective health problem)
- ST (New service requested) (Patient referral to another provider for diagnostic or corrective treatment)
- NU (Not Used) (Used when no EPSDT patient referral was given.)

When there is a requirement to report family planning services, enter Y for Yes in Block 24H. When there is no requirement to Family planning services, leave the block blank.

CMS-1500 Modifiers

To accurately report a procedure or service, up to four CPT/HCPCS modifiers can be entered to the right of the solid vertical line in CMS-1500 Block 24D on the claim. The first modifier is entered between the solid vertical line and the dotted line.

If additional modifier(s) are added, enter one blank space between modifiers. *Do not* enter a hyphen in front of the modifier(s).

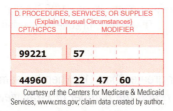

Courtesy of the Centers for Medicare & Medicaid Services, www.cms.gov; claim data created by author.

Days or Units

CMS-1500 Block 24F contains charges for services or procedures, and Block 24G requires reporting of the number of encounters, units of service or supplies, amount of drug injected, and so on, for the procedure reported on the same line in Block 24D. Block 24G has room for only three digits. (If reporting a fraction of a unit, enter the number with a decimal point, such as 1.5 in Block 24G.) When entering charges in Block 24F, when 2 or greater is entered in Block 24G (as days or units), add together the charges for all units on that line. For example, if a service is $45 and Block 24G contains 2 units, enter $45 in Block 24F and 2 in Block 24G. Then, the total charge ($90) entered in Block 28 is calculated by adding together charges on each line of Block 24F.

F. $ CHARGES	G. DAYS OR UNITS
45 : 00	2

UB-04 claim Form Locator 46 requires reporting the number of service units. The most common number entered is "1" to represent the delivery of a single procedure/service.

The entry of a number greater than "1" is required if identical procedures are reported on the same line. Do not confuse the number of units assigned on one line with the number of days the patient is in the hospital.

> **Example:** The patient is in the hospital for three days following an open cholecystectomy. The number of units assigned to the line reporting the surgery code is 1 (only one cholecystectomy was performed).

 Remember!

When a procedure is performed more than once a day, enter the appropriate modifier(s) and consider submitting supporting documentation with the claim. Rules to follow when reporting multiple days/units include:

- *Anesthesia time:* Report elapsed time as one unit for each 15 minutes (or fraction thereof) of anesthesia time. Convert hours to minutes, first.

  > **Example:** Elapsed time 3 hours and 15 minutes, reported as 13 units (195 minutes divided by 15 minutes equals 13).

- *Multiple procedures:* Enter the procedure code that will be reimbursed highest first, and then enter secondary procedure codes in descending order of charges. Enter a "1" in the units column for each procedure entered. Then enter any required modifiers to the secondary procedures (e.g., modifier 51 for multiple procedures).

- *Inclusive dates of similar services:* Report the number of days indicated in the *From* and *To* blocks (CMS-1500 claim Block 24A); the number of days is reported in CMS-1500 claim Block 24G.

  > **Example:** The physician treated Mr. Greenstalk on 01/02 through 01/04 and performed a detailed inpatient subsequent exam each day. The same E/M code is reported on one line in Block 24 and a 3 is entered as the units in Block 24G.

- *Radiology services:* Enter a number greater than "1" when the same radiology study is performed more than once on the same day. *Do not report the number of x-ray views taken for a specific study*.

  > **Example:** 71048 Chest, four views
  >
  > Enter 1 in Block 24G of the CMS-1500 claim.
  >
  > The 1 is populated in Form Locator 46 of the UB-04 claim.

Medically Unlikely Edits (MUE) Project

CMS implemented the *medically unlikely edits (MUE) project* as part of the NCCI program to improve the accuracy of Medicare payments by detecting and denying unlikely Medicare claims on a prepayment basis. The project is CMS's response to the May 2006 Office of Inspector General (OIG) report, entitled *Excessive Payments for Outpatient Services Processed by Mutual of Omaha*, which reported errors due to inappropriate units of service, accounting for $2.8 million in outpatient service overpayments from one third-party payer. The OIG determined that the payer made these overpayments because sufficient edits were not in place to detect billing errors related to units of service.

The following examples illustrate ways providers overstated the units of service on individual claims:

- A provider billed 10,001 units of service for 1 CT scan as the result of a typing error. The payer was overpaid approximately $958,000.

- A provider billed 141 units of service (the number of minutes in the operating room) for 1 shoulder arthroscopy procedure. The payer was overpaid approximately $97,000.

- A provider billed 8 units of service (the number of 15-minute time increments in the operating room) for 1 cochlear implant procedure. The payer was overpaid approximately $67,000.

MUEs are used to compare units of service with code numbers as reported on submitted claims:

- CMS-1500: Block 24G (units of service) is compared with Block 24D (code number) on the same line.

- UB-04: Form Locator 46 (service units) is compared with Form Locator 44 (HCPCS/RATE/HIPPS CODE).

National Standard Employer Identifier

CMS-1500 claim Block 25 requires entry of either the provider's Social Security number (SSN) or the employer tax identification number (EIN). If completing claims for a group practice, enter the practice's EIN in this block. Do not enter the hyphen (e.g., 111234567). The SSN is also entered without hyphens or spaces.

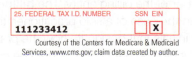

25. FEDERAL TAX I.D. NUMBER	SSN EIN
111233412	☐ ☒

Courtesy of the Centers for Medicare & Medicaid Services, www.cms.gov; claim data created by author.

NOTE:

If the EIN is unavailable, enter the provider's SSN. Reporting correct EIN and/or SSN information is crucial because payers report reimbursement to the Internal Revenue Service (IRS) according to EIN or SSN.

Exercise 11.1 – Entering Procedures in Block 24

Review the following unrelated scenarios and enter the data into columns A, D, F, and G of Block 24. If more than one service is provided on the same date, enter them on one line of Block 24.

1. 10/10/YY   Level 4 E/M office encounter   99214 $65.00
2. 10/10/YY   Level 2 E/M subsequent hospital encounter   99232 $45.00

Note: The patient had two subsequent hospital encounters on 10/10.

(continues)

Exercise 11.1 – continued

3.	10/12/YY	Level 1 E/M subsequent hospital encounter	99231	$35.00
4.	10/15/YY	X-ray, pelvis, 4 views	72190	$150.00
5.	11/09/YY	Cholecystectomy, open	47600	$900.00
6.	11/09/YY	Diagnostic arthroscopy, knee	29870-51	$500.00

24. A. DATE(S) OF SERVICE						B. PLACE OF SERVICE	C. EMG	D. PROCEDURES, SERVICES, OR SUPPLIES (Explain Unusual Circumstances) CPT/HCPCS MODIFIER		E. DIAGNOSIS POINTER	F. $ CHARGES	G. DAYS OR UNITS	H. EPSDT Family Plan	I. ID. QUAL.	J. RENDERING PROVIDER ID. #
MM	From DD	YY	MM	To DD	YY										
1														NPI	
2														NPI	
3														NPI	
4														NPI	
5														NPI	
6														NPI	

Courtesy of the Centers for Medicare & Medicaid Services, www.cms.gov.

Reporting the Billing Entity

CMS-1500 claim Block 32 contains the name, address, city, state, and ZIP code of the location where health care services were provided. This occurs when a physician or other qualified health care professional has their own NPI, and services were provided at a health care facility (that has a different NPI).

Medicare requires Block 32 to be populated along with Block 33. Block 32a contains the NPI of the service facility location, and for Medicare the physician or other qualified health care professional even when the NPI is the same for Blocks 32a and 32b.

CMS-1500 claim Block 33 requires entry of the name, address (including nine-digit ZIP code without the hyphen or a space), and telephone number of the billing entity. The **billing entity** is the legal business name of the practice (e.g., Goodmedicine Clinic). In the case of a solo practitioner, the name of the practice may be entered as the name of the physician followed by initials that designate how the practice is incorporated (e.g., Irvin M. Gooddoc, M.D., PA). The phone number, including area code, should be entered on the same line as the printed words "& PH #." Below this line is a blank space for a three-line billing entity mailing address.

The last line of CMS-1500 claim Block 33 is for entering the provider and/or group practice national provider number (NPI).

Courtesy of the Centers for Medicare & Medicaid Services, www.cms.gov.

Processing Secondary CMS-1500 Claims

The CMS-1500 claim contains blocks for entering primary and secondary payer information.

For the CMS-1500 claim, when primary and secondary information is entered on the same CMS-1500 claim, primary insurance policy information is entered in Block 11 through 11c, and an X is entered in the YES box in

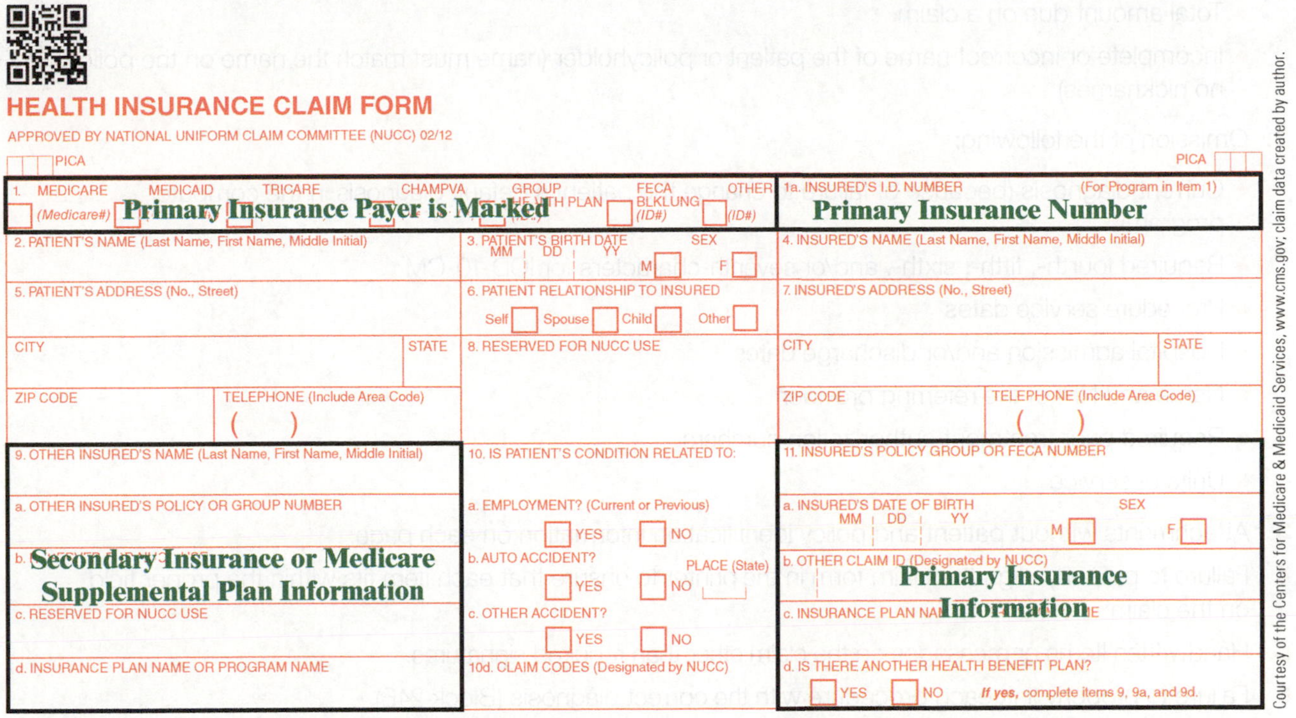

FIGURE 11-6 Entry of secondary policy information in Block 9 of primary CMS-1500 claim (primary policy information is entered in Blocks 1, 1a, and 11).

Block 11d. The secondary insurance policy information is entered in Blocks 9–9d of the same claim (Figure 11-6). **Medicare supplemental plans** usually cover deductible, copayment, and coinsurance amounts that patients pay to receive health care through Medicare, and they are known as *Medigap* plans.

When generating CMS-1500 claims from this text and the Workbook, a single CMS-1500 claim is generated when the patient's primary and secondary insurance policies are with the same payer (e.g., BlueCross BlueShield). Multiple claims are generated when the patient is covered by multiple insurance policies with different companies (e.g., Aetna and United Healthcare). For example, if the patient has both primary and secondary insurance with different payers, two claims are generated. The primary claim is completed according to step-by-step instructions, and the secondary claim is completed by following special instructions included in each chapter.

Common Errors that Delay CMS-1500 Claims Processing

After the CMS-1500 claim has been completed, check for these common errors:

1. Keyboarding errors or incorrectly entered information, as follows:

   - Procedure code number
   - Diagnosis code number
   - Policy identification numbers
   - Dates of service
   - Federal employer tax ID number (EIN)

- Total amount due on a claim
- Incomplete or incorrect name of the patient or policyholder (name must match the name on the policy; no nicknames)

2. Omission of the following:

   - Current diagnosis (because of failure to change the patient's default diagnosis in the computer program)
   - Required fourth-, fifth-, sixth-, and/or seventh-characters for ICD-10-CM
   - Procedure service dates
   - Hospital admission and/or discharge dates
   - Name and NPI of the referring provider
   - Required prior treatment authorization numbers
   - Units of service

3. Attachments without patient and policy identification information on each page.

4. Failure to properly align the claim form in the printer to ensure that each item fits within the proper field on the claim.

5. Handwritten items or messages on the claim other than required signatures.

6. Failure to properly link each procedure with the correct diagnosis (Block 24E).

 NOTE:

Because the first character of each ICD-10-CM code is alphabetic *and the letters I and O are used*, carefully enter ICD-10-CM I and O codes (so that the numbers 1 and 0 are not mistakenly entered as the first characters).

Final Steps in Processing CMS-1500 Claims

Step 1   Double-check each claim for errors and omissions.

Step 2   Add any necessary attachments.

Step 3   Post submission of the claim to the patient's account.

Step 4   Save the claim in the practice management software.

Step 5   Submit the claim to the payer or clearinghouse.

Maintaining CMS-1500 Insurance Claim Files for the Medical Practice

Medicare *Conditions of Participation (CoP)* require providers to keep copies of any government insurance claims and copies of all attachments filed by the provider for a period of five years, unless state law specifies a longer period. "Providers and billing services filing claims electronically can comply with the federal regulation by retaining the source documents (routing slip, charge slip, encounter form, superbill) from which they generated the claim and the daily summary of claims transmitted and received for" these years.

Although there are no specific laws covering retention of commercial or BlueCross BlueShield claims, health care provider contracts with specific insurance carriers may stipulate a specific time frame for all participating providers. It is good business practice to keep these claims until you are sure all transactions have been completed.

Insurance File Set-Up

Files should be organized in the following manner:

1. File *open assigned cases* by month and payer. (These claims have been sent to the payer, but processing is not complete.)
2. File *closed assigned cases* by year and payer.
3. File *batched remittance advice notices*.
4. File *unassigned or nonparticipating claims* by year and payer.

Processing Assigned Paid Claims

When the remittance advice arrives from the payer, pull the claim(s) and review the payment(s). Make a notation of the amount of payment, remittance advice notice processing date, and applicable batch number on the claim. Claims with no processing errors and payment in full are marked "closed." They are moved to the closed assigned claims file. Single-payment remittance advice notices may be attached to the claim before storing them in the closed assigned claims file. Batched remittance advice notices are refiled and if, after comparing the remittance advice notices and the claim, an error in processing is found, the following steps should be taken:

Step 1	Write an immediate appeal for reconsideration of the payment.
Step 2	Make a copy of the original claim, the remittance advice notices, and the written appeal.
Step 3	Generate a new CMS-1500 claim, and attach it to the remittance advice notices and the appeal. Make sure the date in Block 31 matches the date on the original claim.
Step 4	Mail the appeal and claim to the payer.
Step 5	Make a notation of the payment (including the check number) on the office copy of the claim.
Step 6	Refile the claim and attachments in the assigned open claims file.

Federal Privacy Act

The **Federal Privacy Act** of 1974 prohibits a payer from notifying the provider about payment or rejection of unassigned claims or payments sent directly to the patient or policyholder. If the provider is to assist the patient with the appeal of a claim, the patient must provide a copy of the explanation of benefits (EOB) received from the payer and a letter that explains the error. The letter is to be signed by the patient and policyholder, to give the payer permission to allow the provider to appeal the unassigned claim. The EOB and letter must accompany the provider's request for reconsideration of the claim. If the policyholder writes the appeal, the provider must supply the policyholder with the supporting documentation required to have the claim reconsidered.

UB-04 Claim

The **UB-04** claim (Figure 11-3) is an insurance claim or flat file used to bill institutional services, such as inpatient and outpatient services provided by hospitals. It contains data entry blocks called form locators (FLs) (and was previously called the UB-92). These are similar to the CMS-1500 claim blocks used to input information about procedures or services provided to a patient in a physician's office. UB-04 claims data for Medicare Part A reimbursement is submitted to Medicare administrative contractors (MACs, replacing carriers, DMERCs, and fiscal intermediaries) and other third-party payers. Payments are processed for hospitals, skilled nursing facilities, home health and hospice agencies, dialysis facilities, rehabilitation facilities, and rural health clinics.

UB-04 Claims and ICD-10-CM, ICD-10-PCS, CPT, and HCPCS Level II Coding

UB-04 claims are usually automatically generated when chargemaster (or encounter form) and other data is transmitted from the electronic health record to the facility's billing department. (The CMS-1500 claim continues to be completed as data entry in many physician practices.) (While the majority of UB-04 claims are autopopulated by EHR data, some institutions continue to complete the UB-04 claim by using data entry for submission to third-party payers for reimbursement [Figure 11-7].)

- For outpatient claims, physicians and other health care providers circle procedure/service CPT and HCPCS Level codes that are pre-printed on a paper-based chargemaster (after which keyboarding specialists enter the codes into the facility's computer). Or, they select codes using a tablet computer or a computer terminal (and click to transmit the codes).

Medical coders assign ICD-10-CM codes for outpatient diagnoses and enter them in the facility's EHR abstracting software. Then, the EHR data is transmitted to the UB-04 claim, populating it without the need for data entry. (UB-04 form locators 67, 69, 70, and 72 are populated with ICD-10-CM codes, and form locator 44 is populated with CPT and HCPCS Level II codes.)

- For inpatient UB-04 claims, medical coders assign ICD-10-CM for diagnoses and ICD-10-PCS codes for procedures, and they enter the codes in EHR abstracting software. EHR data is also transmitted to the UB-04 claim, populating it without the need for data entry. (UB-04 form locators 67, 69, 70, and 72 are populated with ICD-10-CM codes, and form locator 74 is populated with ICD-10-PCS codes.)

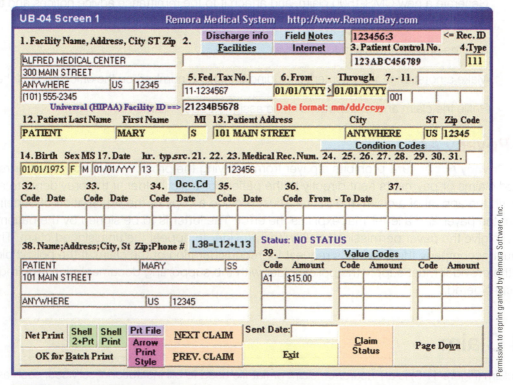

FIGURE 11-7 Sample data entry screen using UB-04 electronic data interchange software.

NOTE:

- Chapters 6, 7, and 8 of this textbook contains content about ICD-10-CM, CPT, and HCPCS Level II coding.

UB-04 Claim Development and Implementation

Institutional and other selected providers submit UB-04 (CMS-1450) claim data to payers for reimbursement of patient services. The National Uniform Billing Committee (NUBC) is responsible for developing data elements reported on the UB-04 in cooperation with State Uniform Billing Committees (SUBCs).

National Uniform Billing Committee (NUBC)

Like the role of the National Uniform Claims Committee (NUCC) in the development of the CMS-1500 claim, the National Uniform Billing Committee (NUBC) is responsible for identifying and revising data elements (information entered into UB-04 form locators or submitted by institutions using electronic data interchange). (The claim was originally designed as the first uniform bill and called the UB-82 because of its 1982 implementation date. Then, the UB-92 was implemented in 1992.) The current claim is called the UB-04 because it was developed in 2004 (although it was implemented in 2007). UB-04 revisions emphasized clarification of definitions for data elements and codes to eliminate ambiguity and to create consistency. The UB-04 also addressed emergency department (ED) coding and data collection issues to respond to concerns of state public health reporting systems. The NUBC continues to emphasize the need for data sources to continue to support public health data reporting needs.

Data Specifications for the UB-04

When reviewing data specifications for the UB-04, the NUBC balanced the payers' need to collect information against the burden of providers to report that information. In addition, the administrative simplification provisions of HIPAA are applied when developing data elements. Each data element required for reporting purposes is assigned to a unique UB-04 form locator (FL), which is the designated space on the claim identified by a unique number and title, such as the patient name in FL8.

UB-04 Claims Submission

Whether completed manually or using onscreen software, the UB-04 claim contains 81 form locators for which required, not used, and situational instructions are provided (Table 11-2). (Instructions located in Table 11-2 are based on the *Medicare Claims Processing Manual*, Chapter 3, Inpatient Hospital Billing, located at www.cms.gov.) The data is entered according to third-party payer guidelines that contain instructions for completing the UB-04. Providers that submit the UB-04 claim (or UB-04 data elements in EDI format) include the following:

- Ambulance companies
- Ambulatory surgery centers
- Home health care agencies
- Hospice organizations
- Hospitals (emergency department, inpatient, and outpatient services)
- Psychiatric drug/alcohol treatment facilities (inpatient and outpatient services)
- Skilled nursing facilities
- Subacute facilities
- Stand-alone clinical/laboratory facilities
- Walk-in clinics

TABLE 11-2 UB-04 (CMS-1450) Form Locator (FL) descriptions and Medicare claims completion instructions

FL	Description	Instructions
		Note: Form locator (FL) descriptions indicate whether data entry for Medicare claims is required (mandatory), not required (optional), not used (leave FL blank), or situational (dependent on circumstances clarified in the FL instructions). Payer-specific instructions can be located by conducting Internet searches.
1	Billing provider name, address, and telephone number (REQUIRED)	• Enter the provider name, city, state, zip code, telephone number, fax number, and country code. • Either the provider's post office box number or street name and number may be included. The state can be abbreviated using standard post office abbreviations, and five- or nine-digit zip codes are acceptable. **Note:** Payer compares FL1 information to data on file for provider number reported in FL51 (to verify provider identity).
2	Billing provider's pay-to address (SITUATIONAL)	Enter provider name, address, city, state, zip code, and identification number *if the pay-to name and address information is different from the billing provider information in FL1.* Otherwise, leave blank.
3a	Patient control number (unique claim number) (REQUIRED)	Enter the alphanumeric control number *if assigned by the provider and needed to facilitate retrieval of patient financial records and for posting payments.*
3b	Medical/health record number (SITUATIONAL)	Enter the medical record number *if assigned by the provider and needed to facilitate retrieval of patient records.* Otherwise, leave blank.
4	Type of bill (TOB) (REQUIRED)	**Note:** The four-digit alphanumeric TOB code provides three specific pieces of information after a leading zero. Digit 1 (the leading 0) is ignored by CMS. Digit 2 identifies the type of facility. Digit 3 classifies the type of care provided. Digit 4 indicates the sequence of this bill for this particular episode of care, and it is called a *frequency code.* Enter a valid four-digit TOB classification number. • Digit 1: Leading Zero • Digit 2: Type of Facility 1 Hospital 2 Skilled nursing 3 Home health (includes HH PPS claims, for which CMS determines whether services are paid from the Medicare Part A or Part B) 4 Religious nonmedical (hospital) 5 Reserved for national assignment (discontinued 10/1/05) 6 Intermediate care 7 Clinic or hospital-based renal dialysis facility (requires assignment of special information as Digit 3 below) 8 Special facility or hospital ASC surgery (requires assignment of special information as Digit 3 below) 9 Reserved for national assignment • Digit 3: Bill Classification, Except Clinics and Special Facilities 1 Inpatient (Medicare Part A) 2 Inpatient (Medicare Part B) 3 Outpatient 4 Other (Medicare Part B) 5 Intermediate Care—Level I 6 Intermediate Care—Level II 7 Reserved for national assignment (discontinued 10/1/05) 8 Swing bed 9 Reserved for national assignment

(continues)

TABLE 11-2 (continued)

FL	Description	Instructions
4	Type of bill (TOB) (REQUIRED) (cont'd)	• Digit 3 (Clinics Only)

• Digit 3 (Clinics Only)

1	Rural health clinic (RHC)
2	Hospital-based or independent renal dialysis facility
3	Freestanding provider-based federally qualified health center (FQHC)
4	Other rehabilitation facility (ORF)
5	Comprehensive outpatient rehabilitation facility (CORF)
6	Community mental health center (CMHC)
7–8	Reserved for national assignment
9	Other

• Digit 3 (Special Facilities Only)

1	Hospice (non-hospital-based)
2	Hospice (hospital-based)
3	Ambulatory surgical center services to hospital outpatients
4	Freestanding birthing center
5	Critical access hospital
6–8	Reserved for national assignment
9	Other

• Digit 4 (Frequency—Definition)

A	Admission/election notice (hospice or religious nonmedical health care institution)
B	Termination/revocation notice (hospice/Medicare coordinated care demonstration or religious nonmedical health care institution)
C	Change of provider notice (hospice)
D	Health care institution void/cancel notice (hospice)
E	Change of ownership (hospice)
F	Beneficiary initiated adjustment claim
G	Common working file (CWF) initiated adjustment claim
H	CMS initiated adjustment claim
I	Internal adjustment claim (other than QIO or provider)
J	Initiated adjustment claim (other entities)
K	OIG initiated adjustment claim
M	Medicare as secondary payer (MSP) initiated adjustment claim
P	Quality improvement organization (QIO) adjustment claim
Q	Claim submitted for reconsideration/reopening outside of timely filing
0	Nonpayment/zero claims provider
1	Admit through discharge claim
2	Interim—first claim
3	Interim—continuing claim(s)
4	Interim—last claim
5	Late charge only
(There is no code 6)	
7	Replacement of prior claim
8	Void/cancel of a prior claim
9	Final claim for HH PPS episode

(continues)

TABLE 11-2 (continued)

FL	Description	Instructions
4	Type of bill (TOB) (REQUIRED) (cont'd)	• Sample Bill Type Codes 011X Hospital inpatient (Medicare Part A) 012X Hospital inpatient (Medicare Part B) 013X Hospital outpatient 014X Hospital other (Medicare Part B) 018X Hospital swing bed 021X SNF inpatient 022X SNF inpatient (Medicare Part B) 023X SNF outpatient 028X SNF swing bed 032X Home health 033X Home health 034X Home health (Medicare Part B only) 041X Religious nonmedical health care institutions 071X Clinical rural health 072X Clinic ESRD 073X Federally qualified health centers 074X Clinic outpatient physical therapy (OPT) 075X Clinic CORF 076X Community mental health centers 081X Non-hospital-based hospice 082X Hospital-based hospice 083X Hospital outpatient (ASC) 085X Critical access hospital
5	Federal tax number (REQUIRED)	Enter the facility's federal tax identification number in 00-0000000 format.
6	Statement covers period (from-through) (REQUIRED)	Enter beginning and ending dates of the period included on this bill as MMDDYY.
7	Unlabeled (NOT USED)	Leave blank.
8a	Patient identifier (SITUATIONAL)	Enter the patient's payer identification (ID) number, *which is the subscriber/insured ID number entered in FL60.*
8b	Patient name (REQUIRED)	Enter patient's last name, first name, and middle initial (if any). Use a comma to separate the last name, first name, and middle initial. Note: When the patient's last name contains a prefix, do not enter a space after the prefix (e.g., VonSchmidt). When the patient's name contains a suffix, enter as LastName Suffix, FirstName (e.g., Smith III, James).
9a–e	Patient address (REQUIRED)	• Enter the patient's street address in 9a. • Enter the patient's city in 9b. • Enter the patient's state in 9c. • Enter the patient's five- or nine-digit zip code in 9d. • Enter the patient's country code *if the patient resides outside of the United States* in 9e.

(continues)

TABLE 11-2 (continued)

FL	Description	Instructions
10	Patient birth date (REQUIRED)	Enter the patient's date of birth as MMDDCCYY. **Note:** If birth date is unknown, enter zeros for all eight digits.
11	Patient sex (REQUIRED)	Enter the patient's sex as a one-character letter: M Male F Female U Unknown
12	Admission start of care date (REQUIRED for inpatient and home health)	Enter the inpatient date of admission (or home health start-of-care date) as MMDDYY.
13	Admission hour (SITUATIONAL)	Enter the admission hour using military time (e.g., 03 for admission hour of 3:00 through 3:59 A.M.), *if required by the payer.*
14	Type of admission/ visit (REQUIRED FOR INPATIENT CLAIMS)	Enter one-digit type of admission/visit code: 1 Emergency 2 Urgent 3 Elective 4 Newborn 5 Trauma center 6–8 Reserved for national assignment 9 Information not available
15	Point of origin for admission or visit (REQUIRED)	Enter one-digit source of admission or visit code: 1 Physician referral 2 Clinic referral 3 Managed care plan referral 4 Transfer from a hospital 5 Transfer from a skilled nursing facility 6 Transfer from another health care facility 7 Emergency room 8 Court/law enforcement 9 Information not available A Transfer from a critical access hospital B Transfer from another home health agency C Readmission to same home health agency D Transfer from hospital inpatient in the same facility resulting in a separate claim to the payer E–Z Reserved for national assignment
16	Discharge hour (SITUATIONAL)	Enter the discharge hour using military time (e.g., 03 for admission hour of 3:00 through 3:59 A.M.), *if required by the payer.*
17	Patient discharge status (REQUIRED)	Enter two-digit patient discharge status code: 01 Discharged to home or self-care (routine discharge) 02 Discharged/transferred to a short-term general hospital for inpatient care 03 Discharged/transferred to SNF with Medicare certification in anticipation of covered skilled care (effective 2/23/05) 04 Discharged/transferred to an intermediate care facility (ICF)

(continues)

TABLE 11-2 (continued)

FL	Description	Instructions
17	Patient discharge status (REQUIRED) (cont'd)	05 Discharged/transferred to another type of institution not defined elsewhere in this code list (effective 2/23/05) (e.g., cancer hospitals excluded from Medicare PPS and children's hospitals) 06 Discharged/transferred to home under care of organized home health service organization in anticipation of covered skills care (effective 2/23/05) 07 Left against medical advice or discontinued care 08 Reserved for national assignment 09 Admitted as an inpatient to this hospital **Note:** For patient status code 09, in situations where a patient is admitted before midnight of the third day following the day of an outpatient diagnostic service or a service related to the reason for the admission, the outpatient services are considered inpatient. Therefore, code 09 would apply only to services that began longer than three days earlier or were unrelated to the reason for admission, such as observation following outpatient surgery, which results in admission. 10–19 Reserved for national assignment 21 Expired (or did not recover—religious nonmedical health care patient) Discharged/transferred to court/law enforcement 22–29 Reserved for national assignment 30 Still patient or expected to return for outpatient services 31–39 Reserved for national assignment 40 Expired at home (Hospice claims only) 41 Expired in a medical facility (e.g., hospital, SNF, ICF, or freestanding hospice) (Hospice claims only) 42 Expired—place unknown (Hospice claims only) 43 Discharged/transferred to a federal health care facility (effective 10/1/03) (e.g., Department of Defense hospital, Veteran's Administration hospital) 44–49 Reserved for national assignment 50 Discharged/transferred to hospice (home) 51 Discharged/transferred to hospice (medical facility) 52–60 Reserved for national assignment 61 Discharged/transferred within this institution to a hospital-based Medicare-approved swing bed 62 Discharged/transferred to an inpatient rehabilitation facility including distinct parts/units of a hospital 63 Discharged/transferred to long-term care hospital 64 Discharged/transferred to a nursing facility certified under Medicaid *but not certified under Medicare* 65 Discharged/transferred to a psychiatric hospital or psychiatric distinct part/unit of a hospital 66 Discharged/transferred to a critical access hospital (effective 1/1/06) 67–99 Reserved for national assignment
18–28	Condition codes (SITUATIONAL, including submission of adjusted and reopened claims)	Enter the two-digit code (in numerical order) that describes any of the following conditions or events that apply to this billing period, *if required by the payer.* Otherwise, leave blank. (*Sample of condition codes listed below.*) 02 Condition is employment-related 03 Patient covered by insurance not reflected here 04 Information only bill 05 Lien has been filed **Note:** For a comprehensive list of condition codes, refer to Chapter 25 of the *Medicare Claims Processing Manual* (**www.cms.gov**).
29	Accident State (SITUATIONAL)	Enter the state (e.g., NY) in which an accident occurred, *if required by the payer.*
30	Unlabeled (NOT USED)	Leave blank.

(continues)

TABLE 11-2 (continued)

FL	Description	Instructions
31–34	Occurrence code(s) and date(s) (SITUATIONAL)	Enter occurrence code(s) and associated date(s) (MMDDYY) to report specific event(s) related to this billing period *if condition code(s) were entered in FL18–28*. Otherwise, leave blank. (*Sample of occurrence codes listed below.*) 01 = Accident/medical coverage 02 = No Fault Insurance Involved 03 = Accident/Tort Liability 04 = Accident Employment Related 05 = Accident No Medical/Liability Coverage 06 = Crime Victim **Note:** For a comprehensive list of occurrence codes, refer to Chapter 25 of the *Medicare Claims Processing Manual* (**www.cms.gov**).
35–36	Occurrence span code and dates (SITUATIONAL FOR INPATIENT CLAIMS)	Enter occurrence span code(s) and beginning/ending dates defining a specific event relating to this billing period as MMDDYY *for inpatient claims*. (*Sample of occurrence span codes listed below.*) 70 Qualifying stay dates (Medicare Part A SNF level of care only) or non-utilization dates (for payer use on hospital bills only) 71 Hospital prior stay dates 72 First/last visit (occurring in this billing period where these dates are different from those in FL6) 74 Noncovered level of care 75 SNF level of care **Note:** For a comprehensive list of occurrence span codes, refer to Chapter 25 of the *Medicare Claims Processing Manual* (**www.cms.gov**).
37	Untitled (NOT USED)	Leave blank.
38	Responsible party name and address (SITUATIONAL)	• Enter the responsible party name and address, *if required by the payer*. • Enter the responsible party last name, first name, and middle initial (if any). Use a comma to separate the last name, first name, and middle initial. • Enter responsible party street address, city, state, and zip code.
39–41	Value codes and amounts (REQUIRED)	• Enter two-character value code(s) and dollar/unit amount(s). • Codes and related dollar or unit amounts identify data of a monetary nature necessary for processing the claim. Negative amounts are not allowed, except in FL41. If more than one value code is entered for the same billing period, enter in ascending numeric sequence. Lines "a" through "d" allow for entry of up to four lines of data. Enter data in FL39a through 41a before FL39b through 41b, and so on. Codes used for Medicare claims are available from Medicare contractors. (*Sample of value codes listed below.*) 01 = Most Common Semi-Private Rooms 02 = Provider Has No Semi-Private Rooms 08 = Lifetime Reserve Amount in the First Calendar Year 45 = Accident Hour 50 = Physical Therapy Visit A1 = Inpatient Deductible Part A A2 = Inpatient Coinsurance Part A A3 = Estimated Responsibility Part A B1 = Outpatient Deductible B2 = Outpatient Coinsurance

(continues)

TABLE 11-2 (continued)

FL	Description	Instructions
39–41	Value codes and amounts (REQUIRED) (cont'd)	Note: When submitting claims for denied charges and days, enter value code *80* (number of days covered by primary payer as qualified by payer), the number of covered days in the amount field for form locators 39, 40, and 41 (e.g., entry 80 12.00 indicates that the amount of 12 days were covered). Then, enter value code *81* (days of care not covered by primary payer) and the number of days that were not covered (e.g., entry 81 1.00 indicates that the amount of one days was not covered). Do not count the day of discharge for covered days. (An inpatient length of stay counts the day of admission, but not the day of discharge.) The sum of covered days and noncovered days must equal the number of days in "From-Through" of Form Locator 6.
42	Revenue code(s) (REQUIRED)	Enter four-character revenue code(s) to identify accommodation and/or ancillary charges.
		Note: When completing UB-04 claims in this chapter, revenue codes are provided in case studies.
		Revenue codes entered in FL42 explain charges entered in FL47. They are entered in ascending numeric sequence, and do not repeat on the same bill. (*Sample revenue codes listed below.*)
		010X All-inclusive rate (e.g., 0100, 0101)
		0 All-inclusive room and board plus ancillary
		1 All-inclusive room and board
		Note: For a comprehensive list of revenue codes, refer to Chapter 25 of the *Medicare Claims Processing Manual* (**www.cms.gov**).
43	Revenue description (NOT REQUIRED)	Enter the narrative description (or standard abbreviation) for each revenue code, reported in FL42, on the adjacent line in FL43. (This information assists clerical bill review by the facility/provider and payer.)
44	HCPCS/Rates/HIPPS Rate Codes (REQUIRED if applicable)	• *For outpatient claims*, enter the HCPCS (CPT and/or HCPCS Level II) code that describes outpatient services or procedures. Modifiers are separated by spaces after the HCPCS code. • *For inpatient claims*, enter the accommodation rate. • *For SNF claims*, enter the Health Insurance Prospective Payment System (HIPPS) rate code and the two-character assessment indicator (AI) to specify the type of assessment.
45	Service date (REQUIRED FOR OUTPATIENT CLAIMS)	Enter line item dates of service, including claims where "from" and "through" dates are the same for outpatient claims.
46	Service units (SITUATIONAL)	Enter the number of units that quantify services reported as revenue codes (FL42) (e.g., number of days for type of accommodation, number of pints of blood), *if required by the payer*. When HCPCS codes are reported for procedures/services, units equal the number of times the procedure/service reported was performed.
47	Total charges (REQUIRED)	• Enter charges for procedures/services reported as revenue codes (FL42) *on each line*. Be sure to consider the units of service (FL46) in your calculations. • Enter the sum of all charges reported on the last line (same line as revenue code 0001).
		Note: When submitting claims for denied charges and days, enter the total covered charges in form locator 47 (TOTAL CHARGES) for each revenue code (e.g., 1095 00 because the room fee is a covered charge). Then, enter the total noncovered charges in form locator 48 (NONCOVERED CHARGES) for each revenue code (e.g., 25 00 because cable television is a noncovered charge). (Payers do not always require form locator 48 to be completed.)

(continues)

TABLE 11-2 (continued)

FL	Description	Instructions
48	Noncovered charges (SITUATIONAL)	Enter noncovered charge(s) (e.g., copayment, day after active care ended) *if related revenue codes were entered in FL42.* (Do not enter negative charges.)
49	Untitled (NOT USED)	Leave blank.
50A–C	Payer name (REQUIRED)	Enter the name of the health insurance payer as follows: • Line A (Primary Payer) • Line B (Secondary Payer) • Line C (Tertiary Payer)
51A–C	Payer/health plan ID (REQUIRED)	Report the payer's 10-character national health plan identifier (health plan ID).
52A–C	Release of information certification indicator (REQUIRED)	Enter the appropriate identifier for release of information certification for each payer, which is needed to permit the release of data to other organizations to adjudicate (process) the claim. I Informed consent to release medical information for conditions or diagnoses regulated by federal statutes Y Provider has on file a signed statement permitting the release of medical/billing date related to a claim
53A–C	Assignment of benefits certification indicator (SITUATIONAL)	Enter the assignment of benefits certification indicator, *if required by the payer.*
54A–C	Prior payment(s)— payer (SITUATIONAL)	Enter the sum of payments collected from the patient toward payer deductibles/coinsurance or blood deductibles, *if required by the payer.* **Example:** The first three pints of blood are treated as noncovered by Medicare. If total inpatient hospital charges were $350, including $50 for a deductible pint of blood, the hospital would enter $300 (toward the Part A deductible) and $50 (toward the blood deductible) in 54A and 54B, respectively.
55A–C	Estimated amount due—payer (SITUATIONAL)	Enter the estimated amount due from the patient, *if required by the payer.*
56	National provider identifier (NPI) (REQUIRED)	Enter the billing provider's NPI.
57A–C	Other provider ID (SITUATIONAL)	Enter other billing provider identification number(s), *if required by the payer.*
58A–C	Insured's name (REQUIRED)	Enter the insured's name (last, first, middle initial), as verified on the patient's health insurance card, *on the same lettered line (A, B, or C) that corresponds to the line on which payer information was entered in FL50A–C.*
59A–C	Patient's relationship to insured (REQUIRED)	Enter the "patient's relationship to subscriber/insured" code to indicate the relationship of the patient to the insured. 01 Spouse 18 Self 19 Child 20 Employee 21 Unknown 39 Organ Donor 40 Cadaver Donor 53 Life Partner G8 Other Relationship

(continues)

TABLE 11-2 (continued)

FL	Description	Instructions
60A–C	Insured's unique identifier (REQUIRED)	Enter the patient's health insurance identification number *on the same lettered line (A, B, or C) that corresponds to the line on which payer information was entered in FL50A–C.*
61A–C	Insured's group name (SITUATIONAL)	Enter the name of the health insurance group *on the same lettered line (A, B, or C) if workers' compensation or an employer group health plan (EGHP) was entered in FL50A–C.*
62A–C	Insured's group number (SITUATIONAL)	Enter the group number (or other identification number) of the health insurance group *on the same lettered line (A, B, or C) if workers' compensation or an employer group health plan (EGHP) was entered in FL50A–C.*
63A–C	Authorization code or referral number (SITUATIONAL)	Enter the treatment authorization code or referral number assigned by the payer *if procedures/services reported on this claim were preauthorized or a referral was required.* Note: When quality improvement organization (QIO) review is performed for Medicare outpatient preadmission, preprocedure, or home IV therapy services, enter the treatment authorization number for all approved admissions or services.
64A–C	Document control number (DCN) (SITUATIONAL)	Enter the control number assigned to the original bill by the health plan or the health plan's fiscal agent as part of their internal control *if this is not the original UB-04 submitted for procedures/services provided* (e.g., this UB-04 is a corrected claim).
65A–C	Employer name (SITUATIONAL)	Enter the name of the employer that provides health care coverage for the insured (identified on the same line in FL58) *if workers' compensation or an employer group health plan (EGHP) was entered in FL50A–C.*
66	ICD revision indicator (REQUIRED)	Enter the indicator to designate which version of ICD was used to report diagnosis codes. 0 Tenth revision (ICD-10-CM)
67	Principal diagnosis code and present on admission (POA) indicator (REQUIRED)	Enter the ICD code for the principal diagnosis (hospital inpatient) and the present on admission (POA) indicator *or* the first-listed diagnosis (hospital outpatient). Note: • Do not enter the decimal in the reported ICD-10-CM code because it is implied (e.g., E119 instead of E11.9). • Do not report ICD-10-CM diagnosis codes on *nonpatient claims for laboratory services*, where the hospital functions as an independent laboratory.
67A–Q	Other diagnosis code(s) and present on admission (POA) indicator(s) (SITUATIONAL)	Enter ICD-10-CM codes for up to eight additional diagnoses *if they coexisted (in addition to the principal diagnosis) at the time of admission or developed subsequently, and which had an effect upon the treatment or the length of stay* (hospital inpatient) or *if they coexisted in addition to the first-listed diagnosis* (hospital outpatient). Note: • Do *not* enter the decimal in the reported ICD-10-CM code because it is implied (e.g., E119 instead of E11.9). • Do *not* report ICD-10-CM diagnosis codes on *nonpatient claims for laboratory services* when the hospital functions as an independent laboratory. • Effective January 1, 2011, CMS expanded the number of other (secondary) significant diagnosis codes reported from 8 to 24. CMS is conducting an analysis of the entire claims processing system to determine the changes needed to process the additional ICD codes (e.g., increasing the number of procedure code fields required for electronic submission of UB-04 data). It is unknown whether the UB-04 claim will be similarly revised to expand the number of procedure code (and date) fields.
68	Untitled (NOT USED)	Leave blank.

(continues)

TABLE 11-2 (continued)

FL	Description	Instructions
69	Admitting diagnosis code (REQUIRED FOR HOSPITAL INPATIENT CLAIMS)	Enter the ICD-10-CM code for the admitting diagnosis, which is the condition identified by the physician at the time of the patient's admission to the hospital, *if completing an inpatient claim.*
70a–c	Patient's reason for visit (SITUATIONAL)	Enter the ICD-10-CM code for the patient's reason for visit (e.g., sign, symptom, diagnosis) *if the patient received care for an unscheduled outpatient visit* (e.g., emergency department).
71	Prospective payment system (PPS) code (SITUATIONAL)	Enter the PPS code, *if required by the payer.*
72a–c	ECI (external cause of injury) and POA indicator (SITUATIONAL)	Enter ICD-10-CM external cause of injury code(s) and POA indicator(s), *if required by the payer.* Note: Check to determine if your state (e.g., New York) requires entry of E-codes for data capture purposes (e.g., statistical analysis).
73	Untitled (NOT USED)	Leave blank.
74	Principal procedure code and date (SITUATIONAL FOR INPATIENT CLAIMS)	Enter the ICD-10-PCS code for the principal procedure *if an inpatient procedure was performed.* Enter the date as MMDDYY. (Leave blank for outpatient claims.) Note: Do *not* enter the decimal in the reported ICD code because it is implied (e.g., 1471 instead of 14.71).
74a–e	Other procedure code(s) and date(s) (SITUATIONAL)	Enter the ICD-10-PCS code *if additional inpatient procedure(s) were performed.* Enter the date as MMDDYY. (Leave blank for outpatient claims.) Note: Effective January 1, 2011, CMS expanded the number of other (secondary) significant procedure codes reported from 5 to 24. CMS is conducting an analysis of the entire claims processing system to determine the changes needed to process the additional ICD-10-PCS codes (e.g., increasing the number of procedure code fields required for electronic submission of UB-04 data). It is unknown whether the UB-04 claim will be similarly revised to expand the number of procedure code (and date) fields.
75	Untitled (NOT USED)	Leave blank.
76	Attending provider name and identifiers (SITUATIONAL)	• Enter the name and NPI of the attending provider for all claims *except those submitted for nonscheduled transportation services.* • Leave the QUAL field blank. Note: The *attending* provider is the individual who has overall responsibility for the patient's medical care and treatment reported on this claim.
77	Operating physician name and identifiers (SITUATIONAL)	Enter the name and NPI of the operating physician *if a surgical procedure ICD-10-PCS code is reported on this claim.* (Leave the QUAL field blank.)
78–79	Other provider name and identifiers (SITUATIONAL)	Enter the name and NPI number of the provider *that corresponds to the following qualifier codes*: DN Referring Provider (The provider who sends the patient to another provider for services. Required on outpatient claims when the referring provider is different from the attending provider.) ZZ Other Operating Physician (The individual who performs a secondary surgical procedure or assists the operating physician. Required when another operating physician is involved.) 82 Rendering Provider (The health care professional who delivers or completes a particular medical service or nonsurgical procedure. Required when state or federal regulations call for a combined claim, such as a claim that includes both facility and professional fee components.)

(continues)

TABLE 11-2 (continued)

FL	Description	Instructions
80	Remarks (SITUATIONAL)	Enter remarks *for the following situations*: • DME billings (provider enters rental rate, cost, and anticipated months of usage so that payer may determine whether to approve the rental or purchase of the equipment) • Medicare is not primary payer (because workers' compensation, EGHP, automobile medical, no-fault, or liability insurer is primary) • Renal dialysis facilities (provider enters first month of the 30-month period during which Medicare benefits are secondary to benefits payable under an EGHP) • Other information not entered elsewhere on the UB-04, which is necessary for proper payment
81a–d	Code-Code (SITUATIONAL)	Enter the code qualifier (from the list below) and additional codes (e.g., occurrence codes) as related to a form locator or to report from the external code list approved by the NUBC for inclusion in the institutional data set, *if required by the payer*. 01-A0 Reserved for national assignment A1 National Uniform Billing Committee condition codes—not used for Medicare A2 National Uniform Billing Committee occurrence codes—not used for Medicare A3 National Uniform Billing Committee occurrence span codes—not used for Medicare A4 National Uniform Billing Committee value codes—not used for Medicare A5-B0 Reserved for national assignment B3 Health care provider taxonomy code B4-ZZ Reserved for national assignment CODE SOURCE: ASC X12N External Code Source 682 (National Uniform Claim Committee)

The UB-04 (CMS-1450) and its data elements serve the needs of many third-party payers. Although some payers do not collect certain data elements, it is important to capture all NUBC-approved data elements for audit trail purposes. In addition, NUBC-approved data elements are reported by facilities that have established coordination of benefits agreements with the payers. An outpatient case (Figure 11-8) and completed UB-04 claim (Figure 11-9) are provided to illustrate claims completion.

Correcting and Supplementing UB-04 Claims

Two processes are used to correct and supplement a UB-04 claim. An *adjustment claim* is subject to normal claims processing timely submission requirements, such as submission within one year of the date of service. Form locators 4 (type of bill) and 18–28 (condition codes) are completed. A *reopened claim* is generated when the need for correction or supplementation is discovered *after the claims processing timely submission limit.* Claims determinations may be reopened within one year of the date of receipt of the initial determination for any reason. However, when reopened within one to four years of the date of receipt of the initial determination, good cause must be demonstrated. A reopened claim is also a separate and distinct process from the appeals process, and a reopening will not be granted if an appeal decision is pending or in process. Form locators 4 (type of bill) and 18–28 (condition codes) are completed.

 NOTE:

Many form locators will remain blank on the completed UB-04 claim.

Alfred Medical Center • 548 N Main St • Alfred, NY 14802

(607) 555-1234   **EIN:** 87-1349061   **NPI:** 9876543211   **TOB:** 0131

OUTPATIENT CASE

PATIENT NAME	DATE & START/END TIME OF VISIT		SOURCE OF ADMISSION
John Q Public	0505YY 0900	1300	Physician referral

PATIENT ADDRESS	PATIENT TELEPHONE NUMBER	BIRTH DATE	SEX
15 Hill St Alfred NY 14802	(607)555-1234	08-05-40	M (Male)

MARITAL STATUS	MEDICAL RECORD #	PATIENT CONTROL #	PATIENT DISCHARGE STATUS
Widowed	987654	859ABC451562	01 (Discharged home)

PAYER	HEALTH INSURANCE ID NUMBER (HICN)
Medicare	0DF3-SD4-LJ61

PRIMARY PAYER MAILING ADDRESS	Health Plan ID
Medicare, P.O. Box 650, Canandaigua, Ny 14424	3429872450

PATIENT RELATIONSHIP TO INSURED	EMPLOYMENT STATUS	NAME OF EMPLOYER
18 (Self)	Retired	

RESPONSIBLE PHYSICIAN	RESPONSIBLE PHYSICIAN N.P.I.	TYPE OF ADMISSION
John Smith, M.D.	1265891895	Elective

RELEASE OF INFORMATION FORM	ASSIGNMENTS OF BENEFITS FORM
Signed by patient	Signed by patient

CASE SUMMARY	DIAGNOSES	ICD CODES
Patient was registered in the outpatient clinic and underwent single view chest x-ray for chronic obstructive pulmonary disease (COPD). Patient discharged home, to be followed by primary care physician.	COPD	J44.9

CHARGE DESCRIPTION MASTER (PARTIAL)

ALFRED MEDICALCENTER
548 N MAIN ST
ALFRED, NY 14802

Printed on 05/05/YY

DEPARTMENT CODE: 01.855   DEPARTMENT: Radiology

	SERVICE CODE	SERVICE DESCRIPTION	REVENUE CODE	CPT CODE	CHARGE	RVU
X	8550001	Chest x-ray, single view	0324	71045	74.50	0.70
	8550002	Chest x-ray, two views	0324	71046	82.50	0.95

FIGURE 11-8 Outpatient case.

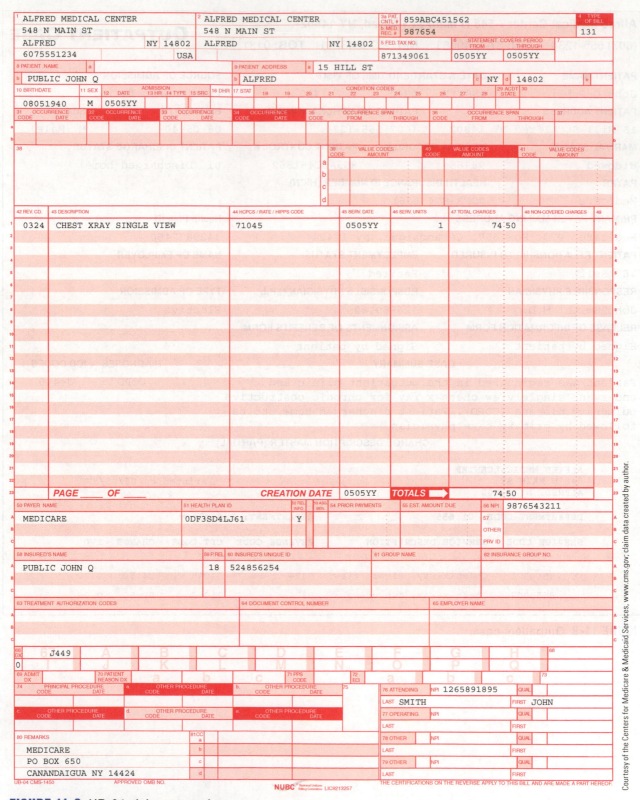

FIGURE 11-9 UB-04 claim answer key.

Summary

The CMS-1500 claim is generated by using medical practice management software. Entering data into the software using this technology greatly increases productivity associated with claims processing because the need to manually enter data from the claim into a computer is eliminated. The 10-digit *national provider identifier (NPI)* is issued to individual providers and health care organizations and replaces health care provider identifiers (e.g., PIN, UPIN) previously generated by health plans and government programs.

The *UB-04 claim* contains data entry blocks called form locators (FLs) (similar to CMS-1500 claim blocks), which are used to input information about procedures or services provided to a patient. *Revenue codes* are four-digit codes preprinted on a facility's chargemaster (or encounter form) to indicate the location or type of service provided to an institutional patient, and they are reported on the UB-04 claim.

Internet Links

National Uniform Billing Committee: *www.nubc.org*

National Uniform Claim Committee: *www.nucc.org*

Review

11.1 – Multiple Choice

Instructions: Select the most appropriate response.

1. Office and other outpatient providers submit _____ procedure and service codes to payers.
   a. CPT/HCPCS Level II
   b. DSM-5
   c. ICD-10-CM
   d. ICD-10-PCS

2. The reverse side of the CMS-1500 claim contains special instructions for the submission of _____ claims.
   a. BlueCross BlueShield
   b. commercial insurance
   c. government program
   d. state workers' compensation

3. Electronic claims must meet requirements adopted as national standards under
   a. ARRA.
   b. CLIA.
   c. HIPAA.
   d. MMA.

4. Claims are electronically transmitted as _____ packets between provider and billing company, clearinghouse, or payer using the Internet or other packet-exchange network.
   a. abstract
   b. code set
   c. data
   d. revenue

5. When entering a CPT code in Block 24, identical procedures performed can be reported on the same line if which of the following circumstances apply?
   a. Block 24G (Days or Units) contains an entry.
   b. Different charges apply to the assigned code.
   c. Procedures were performed in varying months.
   d. Unlisted codes are assigned to the procedure.

6. The CMS-1500 claim is transmitted using the 837P standard format to
   a. clearinghouses.
   b. facilities.
   c. government agencies.
   d. providers.

7. Patient and insured telephone numbers are no longer reported on the CMS-1500 claim because the
   a. data is not collected for electronic claims purposes.
   b. federal privacy and security laws require nondisclosure.
   c. National Uniform Billing Committee (NUBC) mandated it.
   d. extensions for telephone numbers are not supported.

8. Which statement is an accurate interpretation of the phrase "assignment of benefits"? If signed by the patient on the CMS-1500 claim the
   a. payer is instructed to reimburse the provider directly.
   b. payer sends reimbursement for services to the patient.
   c. provider accepts as payment what the payer reimburses.
   d. provider cannot collect copayments from the patient.

9. When an X is entered in one or more of the YES boxes of Block 10 on the CMS-1500 claim, payment might be the responsibility of a _____ insurance company.
   a. disability
   b. homeowner's
   c. life
   d. managed care

10. When a physician or other qualified health care professional has their own NPI, and procedures or services were provided at a health care facility that has a different NPI, CMS-1500 claim Block 32 contains data about the
    a. electronic claims submission data packet address.
    b. location where health care services were provided.
    c. preauthorization or utilization management company.
    d. third-party payer or government health care program.

11. A chargemaster includes services provided to a hospital outpatient as four-character _____ codes, which are populated on the UB-04 claim.
    a. disease and procedure
    b. place-of-service
    c. revenue
    d. type-of-service

12. The type of bill (TOB) four-digit code, populated in Form Locator 4 of the UB-04 claim, contains indicators for a leading 0, _____, bill classification, and frequency definition.
    a. assignment of benefits
    b. discharge status
    c. mode of charges
    d. type of facility

13. Which is responsible for developing data elements reported on the UB-04?
    a. AHA
    b. CMS
    c. NUBC
    d. NUCC

14. Which is the appropriate format for entering an ICD-10-CM code in Block 21 of the CMS-1500 claim?
    a. A01 01
    b. A0101
    c. A01.01
    d. A01-01

15. Which is the correct format for entering a CPT code and its modifier in Block 24 of the CMS-1500 claim?
    a. 99212 25
    b. 99212.25
    c. 99212-25
    d. 99212x25

16. Medicare supplemental plans usually cover deductible, copayment, and coinsurance amounts, and they are known as _____ plans.
    a. MEDIC
    b. Medicaid
    c. Medigap
    d. MIP

17. Which is a common error that can delay CMS-1500 claims processing?
    a. Attaching claims that contain proper patient and provider identification
    b. Failing to properly link each procedure with the correct diagnosis
    c. Including ICD-10-CM codes for the most current diagnoses
    d. Keyboarding entered information accurately and completely

18. Which is considered a final step for processing CMS-1500 claims?
    a. Documenting the patient encounter in the electronic medical record
    b. Entering patient registration information in medical office software
    c. Posting the patient's copayment to the office's revenue management software
    d. Submitting the completed CMS-1500 claim to the payer or clearinghouse

19. Which is maintained for claims that have been submitted to the payer, but for which processing is still incomplete?
    a. Batched remittance advice notices
    b. Closed assigned cases
    c. Open assigned cases
    d. Unassigned or nonparticipating claims

20. While it is acceptable to report codes for uncertain diagnoses when a definitive diagnosis has not been established for inpatient hospitalizations, it is never appropriate to report uncertain diagnosis codes for physician office and outpatient claims. Which is an example of an uncertain diagnosis?
    a. Acute asthma, ruled in
    b. Acute and chronic bronchitis
    c. Resolving myocardial infarction
    d. Suspicious for urinary tract infection

11.2 – Identifying CMS-1500 Claims Completion Errors

Instructions: Review the completed CMS-1500 claim to identify and circle each error.

HEALTH INSURANCE CLAIM FORM

APPROVED BY NATIONAL UNIFORM CLAIM COMMITTEE (NUCC) 02/12

PICA								PICA

1. MEDICARE (Medicare#)	MEDICAID (Medicaid#)	TRICARE (ID#/DoD#)	CHAMPVA (Member ID#)	GROUP HEALTH PLAN [X] (ID#)	FECA BLKLUNG (ID#)	OTHER (ID#)	1a. INSURED'S I.D. NUMBER (For Program in Item 1) **321987456**

2. PATIENT'S NAME (Last Name, First Name, Middle Initial)
DUNNETT, ANTHONY. L

3. PATIENT'S BIRTH DATE MM 7 DD 30 YY 1990   SEX M [X] F

4. INSURED'S NAME (Last Name, First Name, Middle Initial)
DUNNETT, ANTHONY, L

5. PATIENT'S ADDRESS (No., Street)
555 MILKY WAY

6. PATIENT RELATIONSHIP TO INSURED
Self [X] Spouse Child Other

7. INSURED'S ADDRESS (No., Street)

CITY **ANYWHERE**   STATE **NY**

8. RESERVED FOR NUCC USE

CITY   STATE

ZIP CODE **12345**   TELEPHONE (Include Area Code) ( )

ZIP CODE   TELEPHONE (Include Area Code) ( )

9. OTHER INSURED'S NAME (Last Name, First Name, Middle Initial)

10. IS PATIENT'S CONDITION RELATED TO:

11. INSURED'S POLICY GROUP OR FECA NUMBER
411

a. OTHER INSURED'S POLICY OR GROUP NUMBER

a. EMPLOYMENT? (Current or Previous) YES [X] NO

a. INSURED'S DATE OF BIRTH MM 07 DD 30 YY 1990   SEX M [X] F

b. RESERVED FOR NUCC USE

b. AUTO ACCIDENT? YES [X] NO   PLACE (State)

b. OTHER CLAIM ID (Designated by NUCC)

c. RESERVED FOR NUCC USE

c. OTHER ACCIDENT? YES [X] NO

c. INSURANCE PLAN NAME OR PROGRAM NAME
METROPLITAN

d. INSURANCE PLAN NAME OR PROGRAM NAME

10d. CLAIM CODES (Designated by NUCC)

d. IS THERE ANOTHER HEALTH BENEFIT PLAN? YES [X] NO   If yes, complete items 9, 9a and 9d.

READ BACK OF FORM BEFORE COMPLETING & SIGNING THIS FORM.

12. PATIENT'S OR AUTHORIZED PERSON'S SIGNATURE I authorize the release of any medical or other information necessary to process this claim. I also request payment of government benefits either to myself or to the party who accepts assignment below.

SIGNED **SIGNATURE ON FILE**   DATE

13. INSURED'S OR AUTHORIZED PERSON'S SIGNATURE I authorize payment of medical benefits to the undersigned physician or supplier for services described below.

SIGNED **SIGNATURE**

14. DATE OF CURRENT ILLNESS, INJURY, or PREGNANCY (LMP) MM 04 DD 01 YY YY   QUAL. 431

15. OTHER DATE QUAL.   MM DD YY

16. DATES PATIENT UNABLE TO WORK IN CURRENT OCCUPATION FROM MM DD YY TO MM DD YY

17. NAME OF REFERRING PROVIDER OR OTHER SOURCE   17a.   17b. NPI

18. HOSPITALIZATION DATES RELATED TO CURRENT SERVICES FROM MM DD YY TO MM DD YY

19. ADDITIONAL CLAIM INFORMATION (Designated by NUCC)

20. OUTSIDE LAB? YES [X] NO $ CHARGES

21. DIAGNOSIS OR NATURE OF ILLNESS OR INJURY Relate A-L to service line below (24E)   ICD Ind.

A. R350   B.   C.   D.
E.   F.   G.   H.
I.   J.   K.   L.

22. RESUBMISSION CODE   ORIGINAL REF. NO.

23. PRIOR AUTHORIZATION NUMBER

24. A. DATE(S) OF SERVICE From MM DD YY To MM DD YY	B. PLACE OF SERVICE	C. EMG	D. PROCEDURES, SERVICES, OR SUPPLIES (Explain Unusual Circumstances) CPT/HCPCS	MODIFIER	E. DIAGNOSIS POINTER	F. $ CHARGES	G. DAYS OR UNITS	H. EPSDT Family Plan	I. ID. QUAL.	J. RENDERING PROVIDER ID. #
1 04 01 YY	11		99214		A	350 00	1		NPI	
2									NPI	
3									NPI	
4									NPI	
5									NPI	
6									NPI	

25. FEDERAL TAX I.D. NUMBER 111234524   SSN [ ] EIN [X]

26. PATIENT'S ACCOUNT NO. 123456

27. ACCEPT ASSIGNMENT? (For govt. claims, see back) [X] YES NO

28. TOTAL CHARGE $ 350 00

29. AMOUNT PAID $

30. Rsvd for NUCC Use

31. SIGNATURE OF PHYSICIAN OR SUPPLIER INCLUDING DEGREES OR CREDENTIALS (I certify that the statements on the reverse apply to this bill and are made a part thereof.)

SIGNED **ERIN A HELPER MD**   DATE **MMDDYY**

32. SERVICE FACILITY LOCATION INFORMATION

a.   b.

33. BILLING PROVIDER INFO & PH # (101) 1111234
ERIN A HELPER MD
101 MEDIC STREEET
ANYWHERE NY 12345-9874

a.   b.

NUCC Instruction Manual available at: www.nucc.org   **PLEASE PRINT OR TYPE**

11.3 – Completing the UB-04 Claim for Outpatient Hospital Case Study

Instructions: Complete a UB-04 claim for the outpatient hospital case study. Use the blank UB-04 claim in Appendix I of this textbook, or print the UB-04 claim from the online Student Resources for this product. Refer to Table 11-2 UB-04 claims instructions and the sample completed UB-04 claim (Figure 11-9) for assistance completing a claim for this case study.

Alfred Medical Center ● 548 N Main St ● Alfred NY 14802   **Outpatient Case**
(607) 555-1234   EIN: 871349061   **TOB:** 131   **NPI:** 9876543211

PATIENT NAME	PATIENT CONTROL NO.	DATE/TIME OF OUTPATIENT VISIT		SOURCE OF ADMISSION
Candy Santos	215478965230	05-01-YYYY	0230	Physician referral

PATIENT ADDRESS	TELEPHONE NO.	BIRTH DATE	SEX
3902 Hatzel St, Anywhere NY 12345	(101) 111-5128	06-16-1950	Female (F)

MARITAL STATUS	MEDICAL RECORD NUMBER	PRIMARY PAYER	DISCHARGE HOUR	PATIENT STATUS
Single (S)	356478	Medicare	0500	Discharged Home

RESPONSIBLE PARTY	RESPONSIBLE PARTY ADDRESS	HEALTH INSURANCE ID NUMBER (HICN)
Candy Santos	3902 Hatzel Street, Anywhere NY 12345	241793

PATIENT RELATIONSHIP TO INSURED	EMPLOYMENT STATUS	NAME OF EMPLOYER
Self (18)	Retired	

GROUP NAME	GROUP NO.	PRIMARY PAYER MAILING ADDRESS	HEALTH PLAN ID
		Medicare, PO Box 9800, New York NY 12300	2FH5-UF6-NL83

RESPONSIBLE PHYSICIAN	RESPONSIBLE PHYSICIAN NPI	TYPE OF ADMISSION
Bill Waters, M.D.	1149678520	Elective (3)

CASE SUMMARY	DIAGNOSES	ICD CODE
Patient was registered in the outpatient clinic and underwent excision of mass of right breast. Patient discharged home, to be followed by primary care physician.	Benign neoplasm, right breast	D24.1

CHARGE DESCRIPTION MASTER

ALFRED MEDICAL CENTER
548 N MAIN ST
ALFRED NY 14802

Printed on 05/01/YYYY

DEPARTMENT CODE: 01.957   **DEPARTMENT:** Surgery

SERVICE CODE	SERVICE DESCRIPTION	REVENUE CODE	CPT CODE	CHARGE	RVU
8650101	Excision of mass, right breast	0314	19120-RT	950.00	1.05

Commercial Insurance

Chapter Outline

Commercial Health Insurance

Automobile, Disability, and Liability Insurance

Commercial Claims Instructions

Commercial Secondary Coverage Claims Instructions

Commercial Group Health Plan Coverage Claims Instructions

Chapter Objectives

Upon successful completion of this chapter, you should be able to:

1. Define key terms related to commercial, automobile, disability, and liability insurance.
2. Explain the characteristics of commercial insurance plans.
3. Differentiate among automobile, disability, and liability insurance.
4. Complete commercial insurance primary coverage claims.
5. Complete commercial insurance secondary coverage claims.
6. Complete commercial group health plan coverage claims.

Key Terms

automobile insurance policy

base period

commercial health insurance

disability income insurance

disability insurance

indemnity insurance

liability insurance

lien

private health insurance

subrogation

supplemental health plan

Introduction

This chapter contains instructions for completing fee-for-service claims that are generally accepted nationwide by most commercial health insurance companies (or private health insurance companies), including Aetna, United Healthcare, Prudential, Cigna, and others. (Instructions for submitting BlueCross BlueShield, Medicare, Medicaid, TRICARE, CHAMPVA, and workers' compensation claims are found in later chapters.)

These instructions apply to *all primary commercial and HMO fee-for-service (noncapitated) claims.* Separate instructions are provided when the patient has secondary and/or supplemental health insurance coverage.

To assist you in learning how to process commercial claims, this chapter includes:

- Separate instructions for primary, secondary, and supplemental commercial insurance plans
- Instructions in a table format for completing claims
- A case study and completed claim to illustrate the instructions
- A case-study exercise, a blank claim, and the completed claim that allows the student to practice completing a claim. The completed claim allows the student to receive immediate feedback.

 NOTE:

CMS-1500 claims completion instructions are included in this chapter. (UB-04 claims are autopopulated by data abstracted and coded from patient records *or* from an electronic health record (EHR) in hospital, skilled nursing facility, inpatient hospice, and home health care organizations. *Chapter 11 of this textbook contains general UB-04 claims completion instructions*, along with examples and a review assignment.)

Commercial Health Insurance

Commercial health insurance (or **private health insurance**) are for-profit companies, although some operate as nonprofit organizations, to which policyholders pay monthly premiums for coverage of medical expenses. Individuals (e.g., private health insurance) and groups (e.g., employer group health insurance) are covered, depending on the negotiated contract. Premiums and benefits vary according to the type of plan offered, but group health insurance usually costs less than individual private health insurance.

Individual Health Insurance

Individual health insurance policies are regulated by individual states and include the following:

- *Fee-for-service* (or *indemnity*) *insurance* is traditional health insurance that covers a portion of services, such as inpatient hospitalizations or physician office visits, with the patient paying the remaining costs.
- *High-risk pools* is "last resort" health insurance for individuals who cannot obtain coverage due to a serious medical condition; certain eligibility requirements apply, such as refusal by at least one or two insurance companies.
- *Managed care* (e.g., health maintenance organization, preferred provider organization) (Review Chapter 3 of this textbook for comprehensive information about managed care.)
- *Association health insurance* is offered to members of a professional association and marketed to small business owners as a way to provide coverage to employees. However, these plans are not subject to the same regulations as group health insurance plans and, therefore, are more risky.

Group Health Insurance

Group health insurance is available through employers and other organizations (e.g., labor unions, rural and consumer health cooperatives), and all or part of the premium costs are paid by employers. Employer-based group health insurance:

- Covers all employees, regardless of health status, and cannot be cancelled if an employee becomes ill
- Offers COBRA continuation coverage, which means when an employee resigns (or has another qualifying event) the employee must be offered COBRA continuation coverage that lasts for 18 to 36 months, depending on the employee's situation
- Has employer-limited plan options (e.g., prescription drug plan that covers a certain list of medications, called a *formulary*)

Automobile, Disability, and Liability Insurance

Automobile, disability, and liability insurance plans are included in this chapter for informational purposes. (They are not commercial health insurance plans.) It is recommended that financial records for such plans be maintained separately.

Automobile Insurance

Indemnity insurance compensates policyholders for actual economic losses, up to limiting amounts on the insurance policy, and it usually requires the insured to prove losses before payment is made. Automobile insurance is an example of indemnity insurance. An **automobile insurance policy** is a contract between an individual and an insurance company whereby the individual pays a premium and, in exchange, the insurance company agrees to pay for specific car-related financial losses during the term of the policy. Available coverage typically includes the following:

- *Collision* pays for damage to a covered vehicle caused by collision with another object or by an automobile accident; a deductible is required.

- *Comprehensive* pays for loss of or damage to a covered vehicle, such as that caused by fire, flood, hail, impact with an animal, theft, vandalism, or wind; a deductible may apply.

- *Emergency road service* pays expenses incurred for having an automobile towed as a result of a breakdown.

- *Liability* pays for accidental bodily injury and property damage to others, including medical expenses, pain and suffering, lost wages, and other special damages; property damage includes damaged property and may include loss of use.

- *Medical payments* reimburses medical and funeral expenses for covered individuals, regardless of fault, when those expenses are related to an automobile accident.

- *Personal injury protection (PIP)* reimburses medical expenses for covered individuals, regardless of fault, for treatment due to an automobile accident; also pays for funeral expenses, lost earnings, rehabilitation, and replacement of services such as child care if a parent has disabilities. Not all states require PIP insurance, and reimbursement from the PIP payer is based on individual state laws.

- *Rental reimbursement* pays expenses incurred for renting a car when an automobile is disabled because of an automobile accident.

- *Underinsured motorist* pays damages when a covered individual is injured in an automobile accident caused by another driver who has insufficient liability insurance—not available in every state.

Medical payments and PIP coverage usually reimburse, up to certain limits, the medical expenses of an injured driver and any passengers in a vehicle that was involved in an automobile accident. (Coverage might also be available for pedestrians injured by a vehicle.) The automobile insurance company's *medical adjuster* reviews health care bills submitted to the insurance company for treatment of injuries sustained as the result of a motor vehicle accident to determine coverage. Medical expenses that may be reimbursed include ambulance services; emergency department care; laboratory services; medical supplies (e.g., crutches); physical therapy; prescription drugs; services provided by chiropractors, dentists, physicians, and specialists; x-rays; and so on. (In addition, nonautomobile health insurance policies may include coverage that pays medical bills regardless of who was at fault during an automobile accident.)

Disability Insurance

Disability insurance (or **disability income insurance**) is defined as reimbursement for income lost as a result of a temporary or permanent illness or injury. (Disability insurance generally does not pay for health care services but provides financial assistance to individuals with disabilities. The person with disabilities uses private insurance, Medicare, Medicaid, and other other health care insurance plans for the payment of health care services.) When patients are treated for diagnoses related to disabilities and other medical problems, separate patient records must be maintained. Offices that generate one patient record for the treatment of diagnoses associated with disabilities as well as other medical problems often confuse the submission of diagnostic and procedural data for insurance processing. This can result in payment delays and claims denials. For example, under certain circumstances, other insurance coverage (e.g., workers' compensation) is primary to basic medical coverage.

Disability benefits are usually paid if an individual:

- Has been unable to do regular or customary work for a certain number of days (number of days depends on the policy)
- Was employed when a diagnosis associated with disabilities was established
- Has disability insurance coverage
- Was under the care and treatment of a licensed provider during initial disability; to continue receiving benefits, the individual must remain under care and treatment
- Processes a claim within a certain number of days after the date the individual with disabilities was diagnosed (number of days depends on the policy)
- Has the licensed provider complete the disability medical certification document(s)

Individuals may be found ineligible for disability benefits if they:

- Are claiming or receiving unemployment insurance benefits
- Were diagnosed with disabilities while committing a crime that resulted in a felony conviction
- Are receiving workers' compensation benefits at a weekly rate equal to or greater than the disability rate
- Are in jail, prison, or a recovery home (e.g., halfway house) because of being convicted of a crime
- Fail to have an independent medical examination when requested to do so

A disability claim begins on the date of disability, and the disability payer calculates an individual's weekly benefit amount using a base period. The **base period** usually covers 12 months and is divided into four consecutive quarters. It includes taxed wages paid approximately 6 to 18 months before the disability claim begins. The base period does not include wages being paid at the time the disability began.

A final payment notice is sent when records show that an individual has been paid through the physician's estimated date of recovery. If the individual still has disabilities, the physician must submit appropriate documentation so that the case can be reviewed. When an individual has recovered or returned to work and is diagnosed with disabilities again, a new claim should be submitted along with a report of the dates worked.

 NOTE:

The federal Social Security Disability Insurance (SSDI) and Supplemental Security Income (SSI) disability programs provide assistance to people with disabilities. Both programs are administered by the federal Social Security Administration, and only individuals with disabilities and who meet medical criteria qualify for benefits under either program. Social Security Disability Insurance pays benefits to you and certain members of your family if you are "insured," meaning that you worked long enough and paid Social Security taxes. Supplemental Security Income pays benefits based on financial need.

Liability Insurance

Although processing liability insurance claims is not covered in this text, it is important to understand how it influences the processing of health insurance claims. **Liability insurance** is a policy that covers losses to a third party caused by the insured, by an object owned by the insured, or on premises owned by the insured. Liability insurance claims are made to cover the cost of medical care for traumatic injuries and lost wages and, in many cases, remuneration (compensation) for the injured party's "pain and suffering."

Most health insurance contracts state that health insurance benefits are secondary to liability insurance. In this situation, the patient is *not* the insured. This means that the insured (e.g., employer) is responsible for payment, and the patient's health insurance plan is billed as secondary (and reimburses only the remaining costs of health care *not* covered by the insured).

When negligence by another party is suspected in an injury claim, the health insurance company will not reimburse the patient for medical treatment of the injury until one of two factors is established: (1) it is determined that there was no third-party negligence; or (2) in cases in which third-party negligence did occur, the liability payer determines that the incident is not covered by the negligent party's liability contract.

> **Example:** Dr. Small treats Jim Keene in the office for scalp lacerations (cuts) from a work-related injury. Mr. Keene is covered by an employer-sponsored group health plan called HealthCareUSA, and his employer provides workers' compensation insurance coverage for on-the-job injuries.
>
> The insurance claim for treatment of Mr. Keene's lacerations should be submitted to the employer's workers' compensation insurance payer.
>
> If the claim were submitted to HealthCareUSA, it would be subject to review because the diagnosis code submitted would indicate trauma (injury), which activates the review of patient records by an insurance company. Upon reviewing requested copies of patient records, HealthCareUSA would determine that another insurance plan should have been billed for this treatment. HealthCareUSA would deny payment of the claim, and Dr. Small's office would then submit the claim to the workers' compensation carrier payer. In this scenario, a delay in payment for treatment results.

To file a claim with a liability payer, a regular patient billing statement is often used rather than an insurance claim. Be sure to include the name of the policyholder and the liability policy identification numbers. If the liability payer denies payment, a claim is then filed with the patient's health insurance plan. *A photocopy of the written denial of responsibility from the liability payer must accompany the health insurance claim.*

> **Example:** California's Medical Care Services operates Medi-Cal, which is California's Medicaid program. Its Third Party Liability Branch is responsible for ensuring that Medi-Cal complies with state and federal laws relating to the legal liability of third parties to reimburse health care services to beneficiaries. The Branch ensures that all reasonable measures are taken to ensure that the Medi-Cal program is the *payer of last resort*. As a result, within one year, the Branch recovered more than $202 million, which was recycled back into the Medi-Cal program.

Pursuing Reimbursement from Liability Payers

Third-party payers implement a "pay and chase" method to aggressively pursue the recovery and coordination of payment for health care expenses from liability payers (e.g., malpractice cases, public property injuries, and automobile accidents). Third-party payers review diagnosis codes reported on claims (e.g., trauma) to determine whether a liability payer should be considered primary. Once this initial determination has been made, third-party payers often outsource the recovery and coordination of payment for health care expenses from liability payers to subrogation vendors, which further screen data to identify potential liability claims and recover reimbursement paid on claims by third-party payers.

Subrogation refers to the contractual right of a third-party payer to recover health care expenses from a liable party. (For example, if a patient is injured on the job, the workers' compensation payer is responsible for reimbursing the patient's health care expenses.) Third-party recovery standards for investigation of liability coverage and the process for filing a lien (securing a debtor's property as a guarantee of payment for a debt) in a potential liability case vary on federal and state bases.

Commercial Claims Instructions

The commercial claims completion instructions in this chapter are generally recognized nationwide. Some payers may require variations in a few of the CMS-1500 blocks, and their requirements should be followed accordingly. Throughout the year, commercial payers implement changes to claims completion requirements that are discovered by providers when claims are denied—commercial payers do not typically make available their billing manual or updates unless requested or the medical practice subscribes to updates.

Primary claims submission is covered in this chapter's claims completion instructions (Table 12-1), as determined by *one* of the following criteria:

- The patient is covered by just one commercial health plan.
- The patient is covered by a large employer group health plan (EGHP), *and* the patient is also a Medicare beneficiary. (EGHP is primary.)
- The patient is covered by a small *or* large employer group health plan on which the patient is designated as policyholder (or insured), *and* the patient is also listed as a dependent on another EGHP.
- The patient is a child covered by two or more plans. The primary policyholder is the parent whose birthday occurs first in the year. (*Remember!* The *birthday rule* for a child covered by two or more plans states that the policyholder whose birth month and day occur earlier in the calendar year holds the primary policy when each parent subscribes to a different health insurance plan.)

 NOTE:

- Refer to Chapter 11 for clarification of claims data entry, and enter CMS-1500 claims data using upper case.
- As you review the CMS-1500 claims instructions in Table 12-1, refer to the John Q. Public case study (Figure 12-1) and completed CMS-1500 claim (Figure 12-2). The completed claim will also assist you when you begin work on Exercise 12.1.
- Use these instructions when completing any claims associated with *Understanding Health Insurance*.

TABLE 12-1 CMS-1500 claims completion instructions for commercial payers

Block	Instructions
1	Enter an X in the *Other* box if the patient is covered by an individual or family health plan. Or, enter an X in the *Group Health Plan* box if the patient is covered by a group health plan.
	Note: The patient is covered by a group health plan if a group number is printed on the patient's insurance identification card (or a group number is included on case studies located in this textbook, workbook, and SimClaim™ software). *Other* indicates automobile, commercial, health maintenance organization (and managed care), liability, or workers' compensation insurance.
1a	Enter the health insurance identification number as it appears on the patient's insurance card. *Do not enter hyphens or spaces in the number.*
2	Enter the patient's last name, first name, and middle initial (separated by commas) (e.g., DOE, JANE, M).
3	Enter the patient's birth date as MM DD YYYY (with spaces). Enter an X in the appropriate box to indicate the patient's sex. If the patient's sex is unknown, leave blank.
4	Enter the policyholder's last name, first name, and middle initial (separated by commas) (e.g., DOE, JANE, M).
5	Enter the patient's mailing address. Enter the street address on line 1, enter the city and state on line 2, and enter the five- or nine-digit zip code on line 3. *Do not enter the hyphen or a space for a 9-digit ZIP code. Do not enter the telephone number.*
6	Enter an X in the appropriate box to indicate the patient's relationship to the policyholder. If the patient is an unmarried domestic partner, enter an X in the *Other* box.
7	If the patient's address is the same as the policyholder's address, leave blank. Otherwise, enter the policyholder's mailing address. Enter the street address on line 1, enter the city and state on line 2, and enter the five- or nine-digit zip code on line 3. *Do not enter the telephone number.*
8	Leave blank.

TABLE 12-1 (continued)

Block	Instructions
9, 9a, 9d	Leave blank. *Blocks 9, 9a, and 9d are completed if the patient has secondary insurance coverage (discussed later in this chapter).* Note: When the patient is covered by a primary commercial health insurance plan and another health insurance plan (e.g., another commercial health insurance plan, Medicaid, Medicare, and so on), complete Blocks 9, 9a, and 9d.
9b–9c	Leave blank.
10a–c	Enter an X in the appropriate boxes to indicate whether the patient's condition is related to employment, an automobile accident, and/or another type of accident. If an X is entered in the YES box for auto accident, enter the two-character state abbreviation of the patient's residence.
10d	Leave blank.
11	Enter the policyholder's commercial group number if the patient is covered by a group health plan. *Do not enter hyphens or spaces in the group number.* Otherwise, leave blank. Note: The policyholder's group number refers to the alphanumeric or numeric identifier for group health plan coverage. (The FECA number is the nine-digit alphanumeric identifier assigned to a patient claiming work-related condition(s) under the Federal Employees Compensation Act. The FECA number is discussed in Chapter 17 of this textbook.) (Entering the group number is discussed later in this chapter.)
11a	Enter the policyholder's birth date as MM DD YYYY (with spaces). Enter an X in the appropriate box to indicate the policyholder's sex. If the policyholder's sex is unknown, leave blank.
11b	Leave blank. This is reserved for property and casualty or worker's compensation claims when qualifier Y4 is entered to the left of the vertical, dotted line (with the agency claim identification number entered to the right).
11c	Enter the name of the policyholder's commercial health insurance plan.
11d	Enter an X in the NO box if the patient does not have secondary insurance coverage. Note: When the patient is covered by a primary commercial health insurance plan and another health insurance plan (e.g., another commercial health insurance plan, Medicaid, Medicare, and so on), enter an X in the YES box (discussed later in this chapter).
12	Enter SIGNATURE ON FILE. Leave the date field blank. (The abbreviation SOF is also acceptable.) Note: Entering SIGNATURE ON FILE means that the patient has previously signed an authorization to release medical information to the payer, and it is maintained "on file" by the provider. If the patient has not signed an authorization, leave blank or enter NO SIGNATURE ON FILE in the block.
13	Enter SIGNATURE ON FILE to authorize direct payment to the provider for benefits due the patient, which is called *assignment of benefits.* (The abbreviation SOF is also acceptable.)
14	Enter the date as MM DD YY (with spaces) to indicate when the patient first experienced signs *or* symptoms of the present illness, actual date of injury, *or* the date of the last menstrual period (LMP) for obstetric visits. *If the date is not documented in the patient's record, but the history indicates an appropriate date (e.g., three weeks ago), simply count back to the approximate date and enter it on the claim.* Enter the applicable qualifier to identify which date is being reported: 431 (onset of current symptoms/illness or injury) *or* 484 (last menstrual period). **Example:** For encounter date 06/08/YY, when the record documents that the patient was injured three months ago, enter 03 08 YY and 431 in Block 14.
15	Enter the date as MM DD YY (with spaces) to indicate that a prior episode of the same or similar illness began, *if documented in the patient's record. Previous pregnancies are not a similar illness.* If a date is entered in Block 15, also enter the applicable qualifier to identify which date is being reported (e.g., 454 for initial treatment). Otherwise, leave blank.
16	Enter dates as MM DD YY (with spaces) to indicate the period of time the patient was unable to work in his current occupation, *if documented in the patient's record. An entry in this block might indicate employment-related insurance coverage.* Otherwise, leave blank.

(continues)

TABLE 12-1 (continued)

Block	Instructions
17	If applicable, enter the first name, middle initial (if known), last name, and credentials of the professional who referred, ordered, or supervised health care service(s) or supplies reported on the claim. *Do not enter any punctuation.* In front of the name, enter the applicable qualifier to identify which provider is being reported, as follows: DN (referring provider), DK (ordering provider), or DQ (supervising provider). Otherwise, leave blank.
17a	Leave blank.
17b	Enter the 10-digit national provider identifier (NPI) of the provider entered in Block 17. Otherwise, leave blank.
18	Enter the admission date and discharge date as MM DD YY (with spaces) if the patient received inpatient services (e.g., hospital, skilled nursing facility). Otherwise, leave blank. *If the patient has not been discharged at the time the claim is completed, leave the discharge date blank.*
19	Leave blank. Note: Refer to third-party payer instructions regarding use of this block because some require certain identifiers and appropriate qualifiers that describe the identifier, such as photographs available upon request of the provider (e.g., XP AA).
20	Enter an X in the NO box if all laboratory procedures reported on the claim were performed in the provider's office. Enter an X in the YES box if laboratory procedures reported on the claim were performed by an outside laboratory and billed to the provider. Enter the total amount charged by the outside laboratory in $ CHARGES, and enter the outside laboratory's name, mailing address, and NPI in Block 32. (Charges are entered *without* punctuation. For example, $1,100.00 is entered as 1100 00 below $ CHARGES.)
21	Enter the ICD-10-CM code for up to 12 diagnoses or conditions treated or medically managed during the encounter. Lines A through L in Block 21 will relate to CPT/HCPCS service/procedure codes reported in Block 24E. In the *ICD Ind* (ICD indicator) box, enter 0 for ICD-10-CM.
22	Leave blank. This is reserved for resubmitted claims.
23	Enter prior authorization number, referral number, mammography precertification number, or Clinical Laboratory Improvement Amendments (CLIA) number, as assigned by the payer for the current service. *Do not enter hyphens or spaces in the number.* Otherwise, leave blank.
24A	Enter the date the procedure or service was performed in the FROM column as MM DD YY (with spaces). Enter a date in the TO column *if the procedure or service was performed on consecutive days during a range of dates. Then, enter the number of consecutive days in Block 24G.* Note: The shaded area in each line is used to enter supplemental information to support reported services *if instructed by the payer to enter such information.* Data entry in Block 24 is limited to reporting six services. *Do not use the shaded lines to report additional services.* If additional services were provided, generate new CMS-1500 claim(s) to report the additional services.
24B	Enter the appropriate two-digit place-of-service (POS) code to identify the location where the reported procedure or service was performed.
24C	Leave blank.
24D	Enter the CPT or HCPCS Level II code and applicable required modifier(s) for procedures or services performed. *Separate the CPT/HCPCS code and first modifier with one space. Separate additional modifiers with one space each. Up to four modifiers can be entered.*
24E	Enter the diagnosis pointer letter(s) from Block 21 that relate to the procedure or service performed on the date of service to *justify medical necessity* of procedures and services reported on the claim.
24F	Enter the fee charged for each reported procedure or service (e.g., 55 00). *Do not enter commas, periods, or dollar signs. Do not enter negative amounts. Enter 00 in the cents area if the amount is a whole number.*
24G	Enter the number of days or units for procedures or services reported in Block 24D. *If just one procedure or service was reported in Block 24D, enter a 1 in Block 24G.*

(continues)

TABLE 12-1 (continued)

Block	Instructions
24H	Leave blank. This is reserved for Medicaid claims.
24I	Leave blank. (The NPI abbreviation is preprinted on the CMS-1500 claim.)
24J	Enter the 10-digit NPI for the: • Provider who performed the service *if the provider is a member of a group practice.* (Leave blank if the provider is a solo practitioner.) • Supervising provider *if the service was provided incident-to the service of a physician or nonphysician practitioner* **and** *the physician or practitioner who ordered the service did not supervise the provider.* (Leave blank if the incident-to service was performed under the supervision of the physician or nonphysician practitioner.) • DMEPOS supplier or outside laboratory *if the physician submits the claim for services provided by the DMEPOS supplier or outside laboratory.* (Leave blank if the DMEPOS supplier or outside laboratory submits the claim.) Otherwise, leave blank. **Example:** Dr. Sanderlee evaluates the patient during a three-month recheck of chronic anemia. Dr. Sanderlee performs venipuncture and sends the patient's blood sample to an outside laboratory where a complete blood count test will be performed. Dr. Sanderlee's insurance specialist enters the outside laboratory's NPI in Block 24J because the complete blood count test is reported in Block 24D on that line.
25	Enter the provider's Social Security number (SSN) or employer identification number (EIN). *Do not enter hyphens or spaces in the number.* Enter an X in the appropriate box to indicate which number is reported. **Example:** • Dr. Brilliant is a solo practitioner. Enter Dr. Brilliant's EIN in Block 25. • Dr. Healer practices at the Goodmedicine Clinic. Enter Dr. Healer's EIN in Block 25.
26	Enter the patient's account number as assigned by the provider.
27	Enter an X in the YES box to indicate that the provider agrees to accept assignment. Otherwise, enter an X in the NO box.
28	Enter the total charges for services and/or procedures reported in Block 24. Note: If multiple claims are submitted for one patient because more than six procedures or services were reported, be sure the total charge reported on each claim accurately represents the total of the items on each submitted claim.
29	Enter the total amount the patient (or another payer) paid *toward covered services only.* If no payment was made, leave blank.
30	Leave blank.
31	Enter the provider's name and credential (e.g., MARY SMITH MD) and the date the claim was completed as MMDDYY (without spaces). *Do not enter any punctuation.*
32	Enter the name and address where procedures or services were provided *if at a location other than the provider's office or the patient's home, such as a hospital, outside laboratory facility, skilled nursing facility, or DMEPOS supplier.* Otherwise, leave blank. Enter the name on line 1, the address on line 2, and the city, state, and nine-digit zip code on line 3. *Do not enter the hyphen or a space for a 9-digit ZIP code.* Note: If Block 18 contains dates of service for inpatient care and/or Block 20 contains an X in the YES box, enter the name and address of the facility that provided services.
32a	Enter the 10-digit NPI of the facility or supplier entered in Block 32.
32b	Leave blank.

(continues)

TABLE 12-1 (continued)

Block	Instructions
33	Enter the provider's *billing* name, address, and telephone number. Enter the phone number in the area next to the block title. *Do not enter parentheses for the area code.* Enter the name on line 1, enter the address on line 2, and enter the city, state, and nine-digit zip code on line 3. *Do not enter the hyphen or a space for a 9-digit ZIP code.*
	Example:
	• Dr. Brilliant is a solo practitioner. Enter Dr. Brilliant's name, credential, and address in Block 33.
	• Dr. Healer practices at the Goodmedicine Clinic. Enter Goodmedicine Clinic as the billing provider along with its address and telephone number in Block 33.
33a	Enter the 10-digit NPI of the *billing* provider (e.g., solo practitioner) or group practice (e.g., clinic).
	Example: Dr. Healer (NPI: 6789012345) practices at Goodmedicine Clinic (NPI: 3345678901). Enter 3345678901 in Block 33a.
33b	Leave blank.

Courtesy of the Centers for Medicare & Medicaid Services, www.cms.gov.

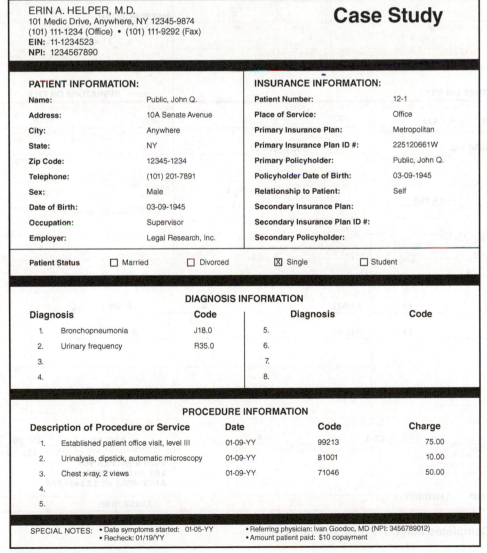

FIGURE 12-1 John Q. Public case study.

HEALTH INSURANCE CLAIM FORM

APPROVED BY NATIONAL UNIFORM CLAIM COMMITTEE (NUCC) 02/12

[ ] [ ] PICA

PICA [ ] [ ]

1. MEDICARE [ ] (Medicare#) MEDICAID [ ] (Medicaid#) TRICARE [ ] (ID#/DoD#) CHAMPVA [ ] (Member ID#) GROUP HEALTH PLAN [ ] (ID#) FECA BLKLUNG [ ] (ID#) OTHER [X] (ID#)

1a. INSURED'S I.D. NUMBER   (For Program in Item 1)
225120661W

2. PATIENT'S NAME (Last Name, First Name, Middle Initial)
PUBLIC, JOHN, Q

3. PATIENT'S BIRTH DATE MM 03 DD 09 YY 1945   SEX M [X] F [ ]

4. INSURED'S NAME (Last Name, First Name, Middle Initial)
PUBLIC, JOHN, Q

5. PATIENT'S ADDRESS (No., Street)
10A SENATE AVENUE

6. PATIENT RELATIONSHIP TO INSURED
Self [X] Spouse [ ] Child [ ] Other [ ]

7. INSURED'S ADDRESS (No., Street)

CITY
ANYWHERE

STATE
NY

8. RESERVED FOR NUCC USE

CITY

STATE

ZIP CODE
123451234

TELEPHONE (Include Area Code)
( )

ZIP CODE

TELEPHONE (Include Area Code)
( )

9. OTHER INSURED'S NAME (Last Name, First Name, Middle Initial)

10. IS PATIENT'S CONDITION RELATED TO:

11. INSURED'S POLICY GROUP OR FECA NUMBER

a. OTHER INSURED'S POLICY OR GROUP NUMBER

a. EMPLOYMENT? (Current or Previous)
YES [ ] NO [X]

a. INSURED'S DATE OF BIRTH MM 03 DD 09 YY 1945   SEX M [X] F [ ]

b. RESERVED FOR NUCC USE

b. AUTO ACCIDENT?
YES [ ] NO [X]   PLACE (State)

b. OTHER CLAIM ID (Designated by NUCC)

c. RESERVED FOR NUCC USE

c. OTHER ACCIDENT?
YES [ ] NO [X]

c. INSURANCE PLAN NAME OR PROGRAM NAME
METROPOLITAN

d. INSURANCE PLAN NAME OR PROGRAM NAME

10d. CLAIM CODES (Designated by NUCC)

d. IS THERE ANOTHER HEALTH BENEFIT PLAN?
YES [ ] NO [X] If yes, complete items 9, 9a, and 9d.

READ BACK OF FORM BEFORE COMPLETING & SIGNING THIS FORM.

12. PATIENT'S OR AUTHORIZED PERSON'S SIGNATURE I authorize the release of any medical or other information necessary to process this claim. I also request payment of government benefits either to myself or to the party who accepts assignment below.

SIGNED **SIGNATURE ON FILE**   DATE

13. INSURED'S OR AUTHORIZED PERSON'S SIGNATURE I authorize payment of medical benefits to the undersigned physician or supplier for services described below.

SIGNED **SIGNATURE ON FILE**

14. DATE OF CURRENT ILLNESS, INJURY, or PREGNANCY (LMP) MM 01 DD 05 YY QUAL. 431

15. OTHER DATE QUAL. MM DD YY

16. DATES PATIENT UNABLE TO WORK IN CURRENT OCCUPATION FROM MM DD YY TO MM DD YY

17. NAME OF REFERRING PROVIDER OR OTHER SOURCE
DN IVAN GOODOC MD

17a.
17b. NPI **3456789012**

18. HOSPITALIZATION DATES RELATED TO CURRENT SERVICES FROM MM DD YY TO MM DD YY

19. ADDITIONAL CLAIM INFORMATION (Designated by NUCC)

20. OUTSIDE LAB? YES [ ] NO [X] $ CHARGES

21. DIAGNOSIS OR NATURE OF ILLNESS OR INJURY Relate A-L to service line below (24E)   ICD Ind. **0**

A. **J180**   B. **R350**   C. _____   D. _____
E. _____   F. _____   G. _____   H. _____
I. _____   J. _____   K. _____   L. _____

22. RESUBMISSION CODE   ORIGINAL REF. NO.

23. PRIOR AUTHORIZATION NUMBER

24. A. DATE(S) OF SERVICE From MM DD YY	To MM DD YY	B. PLACE OF SERVICE	C. EMG	D. PROCEDURES, SERVICES, OR SUPPLIES (Explain Unusual Circumstances) CPT/HCPCS	MODIFIER	E. DIAGNOSIS POINTER	F. $ CHARGES	G. DAYS OR UNITS	H. EPSDT Family Plan	I. ID. QUAL.	J. RENDERING PROVIDER ID. #
1 01 09 YY		11		99213 .		AB	75 00	1		NPI	
2 01 09 YY		11		81001		B	10 00	1		NPI	
3 01 09 YY		11		71046		A	50 00	1		NPI	
4										NPI	
5										NPI	
6										NPI	

25. FEDERAL TAX I.D. NUMBER   SSN EIN [X]
111234523

26. PATIENT'S ACCOUNT NO.
12-1

27. ACCEPT ASSIGNMENT? (For govt. claims, see back) YES [X] NO [ ]

28. TOTAL CHARGE $ **135 00**

29. AMOUNT PAID $ **10 00**

30. Rsvd for NUCC Use

31. SIGNATURE OF PHYSICIAN OR SUPPLIER INCLUDING DEGREES OR CREDENTIALS (I certify that the statements on the reverse apply to this bill and are made a part thereof.)

ERIN A HELPER MD   MMDDYY
SIGNED   DATE

32. SERVICE FACILITY LOCATION INFORMATION

a. NPI   b.

33. BILLING PROVIDER INFO & PH # (101) 1111234
ERIN A HELPER MD
101 MEDIC DRIVE
ANYWHERE NY 123459874

a. **1234567890**   b.

NUCC Instruction Manual available at: www.nucc.org

PLEASE PRINT OR TYPE

FIGURE 12-2 Completed John Q. Public primary claim.

Exercise 12.1 – Completing a Commercial as Primary CMS-1500 Claim

1. Obtain a blank claim by making a copy of the CMS-1500 claim form in Appendix I.
2. Review the Mary S. Patient case study (Figure 12-3).
3. Select the information needed for Blocks 1 through 33, and enter the required information on the blank CMS-1500 claim.
4. Review the completed claim to be sure that all required blocks are completed accurately.
5. Compare your claim with the completed Mary S. Patient claim (Figure 12-4).

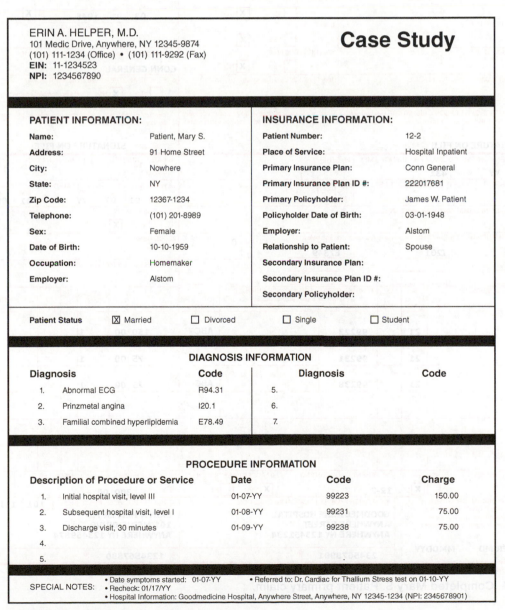

FIGURE 12-3 Mary S. Patient case study.

HEALTH INSURANCE CLAIM FORM

APPROVED BY NATIONAL UNIFORM CLAIM COMMITTEE (NUCC) 02/12

| | PICA | | | | | | | | PICA | |

1. MEDICARE ☐ (Medicare#)   MEDICAID ☐ (Medicaid#)   TRICARE ☐ (ID#/DoD#)   CHAMPVA ☐ (Member ID#)   GROUP HEALTH PLAN ☐ (ID#)   FECA BLKLUNG ☐ (ID#)   OTHER ☒ (ID#)

1a. INSURED'S I.D. NUMBER (For Program in Item 1)
222017681

2. PATIENT'S NAME (Last Name, First Name, Middle Initial)
PATIENT, MARY, S

3. PATIENT'S BIRTH DATE MM 10 DD 10 YY 1959   **SEX** M ☐ F ☒

4. INSURED'S NAME (Last Name, First Name, Middle Initial)
PATIENT, JAMES, W

5. PATIENT'S ADDRESS (No., Street)
91 HOME STREET

6. PATIENT RELATIONSHIP TO INSURED
Self ☐ Spouse ☒ Child ☐ Other ☐

7. INSURED'S ADDRESS (No., Street)

CITY NOWHERE   **STATE** NY

8. RESERVED FOR NUCC USE

CITY   **STATE**

ZIP CODE 123671234   **TELEPHONE (Include Area Code)** ( )

ZIP CODE   **TELEPHONE (Include Area Code)** ( )

9. OTHER INSURED'S NAME (Last Name, First Name, Middle Initial)

10. IS PATIENT'S CONDITION RELATED TO:

11. INSURED'S POLICY GROUP OR FECA NUMBER

a. OTHER INSURED'S POLICY OR GROUP NUMBER

a. EMPLOYMENT? (Current or Previous) YES ☐ NO ☒

a. INSURED'S DATE OF BIRTH MM 03 DD 01 YY 1948   **SEX** M ☒ F ☐

b. RESERVED FOR NUCC USE

b. AUTO ACCIDENT? YES ☐ NO ☒ PLACE (State)

b. OTHER CLAIM ID (Designated by NUCC)

c. RESERVED FOR NUCC USE

c. OTHER ACCIDENT? YES ☐ NO ☒

c. INSURANCE PLAN NAME OR PROGRAM NAME
CONN GENERAL

d. INSURANCE PLAN NAME OR PROGRAM NAME

10d. CLAIM CODES (Designated by NUCC)

d. IS THERE ANOTHER HEALTH BENEFIT PLAN? YES ☐ NO ☒ If yes, complete items 9, 9a, and 9d.

READ BACK OF FORM BEFORE COMPLETING & SIGNING THIS FORM.

12. PATIENT'S OR AUTHORIZED PERSON'S SIGNATURE I authorize the release of any medical or other information necessary to process this claim. I also request payment of government benefits either to myself or to the party who accepts assignment below.

SIGNED **SIGNATURE ON FILE**   DATE

13. INSURED'S OR AUTHORIZED PERSON'S SIGNATURE I authorize payment of medical benefits to the undersigned physician or supplier for services described below.

SIGNED **SIGNATURE ON FILE**

14. DATE OF CURRENT ILLNESS, INJURY, or PREGNANCY (LMP) MM 01 DD 07 YY   QUAL. 431

15. OTHER DATE QUAL.   MM DD YY

16. DATES PATIENT UNABLE TO WORK IN CURRENT OCCUPATION FROM MM DD YY TO MM DD YY

17. NAME OF REFERRING PROVIDER OR OTHER SOURCE

17a.   17b. NPI

18. HOSPITALIZATION DATES RELATED TO CURRENT SERVICES FROM MM 01 DD 07 YY TO MM 01 DD 09 YY

19. ADDITIONAL CLAIM INFORMATION (Designated by NUCC)

20. OUTSIDE LAB? YES ☐ NO ☒ $ CHARGES

21. DIAGNOSIS OR NATURE OF ILLNESS OR INJURY Relate A-L to service line below (24E)   ICD Ind. 0

A. R9431   B. I201   C. E7849   D.
E.   F.   G.   H.
I.   J.   K.   L.

22. RESUBMISSION CODE   ORIGINAL REF. NO.

23. PRIOR AUTHORIZATION NUMBER

24. A. DATE(S) OF SERVICE						B. PLACE OF SERVICE	C. EMG	D. PROCEDURES, SERVICES, OR SUPPLIES (Explain Unusual Circumstances) CPT/HCPCS	MODIFIER	E. DIAGNOSIS POINTER	F. $ CHARGES	G. DAYS OR UNITS	H. EPSDT Family Plan	I. ID. QUAL.	J. RENDERING PROVIDER ID. #
	From MM	DD	YY	To MM	DD	YY										
1	01	07	YY				21		99223		ABC	150 00	1		NPI	
2	01	08	YY				21		99231		ABC	75 00	1		NPI	
3	01	09	YY				21		99238		ABC	75 00	1		NPI	
4															NPI	
5															NPI	
6															NPI	

25. FEDERAL TAX I.D. NUMBER 111234523   SSN ☐ EIN ☒

26. PATIENT'S ACCOUNT NO. 12-2

27. ACCEPT ASSIGNMENT? (For govt. claims, see back) YES ☒ NO ☐

28. TOTAL CHARGE $ 300 00

29. AMOUNT PAID $

30. Rsvd for NUCC Use

31. SIGNATURE OF PHYSICIAN OR SUPPLIER INCLUDING DEGREES OR CREDENTIALS (I certify that the statements on the reverse apply to this bill and are made a part thereof.)

ERIN A HELPER MD   MMDDYY
SIGNED   DATE

32. SERVICE FACILITY LOCATION INFORMATION
GOODMEDICINE HOSPITAL
ANYWHERE STREET
ANYWHERE NY 123451234
a. 2345678901   b.

33. BILLING PROVIDER INFO & PH # (101) 1111234
ERIN A HELPER MD
101 MEDIC DRIVE
ANYWHERE NY 123459874
a. 1234567890   b.

NUCC Instruction Manual available at: www.nucc.org   **PLEASE PRINT OR TYPE**

CARRIER

PATIENT AND INSURED INFORMATION

PHYSICIAN OR SUPPLIER INFORMATION

FIGURE 12-4 Completed Mary S. Patient primary claim.

Commercial Secondary Coverage Claims Instructions

Modifications are made to the primary CMS-1500 claim instructions when patients are covered by primary and secondary or supplemental health insurance plans. *Secondary health insurance* plans provide coverage similar to that of primary plans; **supplemental health plans** usually cover only deductible, copayment, and coinsurance expenses.

When the same payer issues the primary and secondary or supplemental policies (Table 12-2), submit just one CMS-1500 claim (Figure 12-5). If the payers for the primary and secondary or supplemental policies are different (Table 12-3), submit a CMS-1500 claim to the primary payer. When the primary payer has processed the claim (e.g., provider is reimbursed), generate a second CMS-1500 claim (Figure 12-6) to send to the secondary payer, and include a copy of the primary payer's remittance advice.

 NOTE:

Use these instructions when completing any claims associated with *Understanding Health Insurance*.

TABLE 12-2 Modifications to commercial primary CMS-1500 claims completion instructions when the same commercial health insurance company provides a secondary or supplemental policy (Refer to Table 12-1 for primary CMS-1500 claims completion instructions.)

Block	Instructions
9	Enter the secondary or supplemental policyholder's last name, first name, and middle initial (if known) (separated by commas).
9a	Enter the secondary or supplemental policyholder's policy or group number.
9d	Enter the name of the secondary or supplemental policyholder's commercial health insurance plan.
11d	Enter an X in the YES box.

Courtesy of the Centers for Medicare & Medicaid Services, www.cms.gov.

TABLE 12-3 Modifications to commercial primary CMS-1500 claims completion instructions when a different commercial health insurance company provides a secondary or supplemental policy

Block	Instructions
	Note: If the primary and secondary/supplemental payers are the same, do not generate a second CMS-1500 claim. Instead, modify the primary CMS-1500 claim using the instructions in Table 12-2.
1a	Enter the secondary or supplemental policyholder's health insurance identification number (HICN) as it appears on the insurance card. *Do not enter hyphens or spaces in the number.*
4	Enter the secondary or supplemental policyholder's last name, first name, and middle initial (separated by commas).
7	If the patient's address is the same as the secondary policyholder's address, leave blank. Otherwise, enter the secondary or supplemental policyholder's mailing address. *Do not enter the hyphen or a space for a 9-digit ZIP code. Do not enter the telephone number.*
9	Enter the primary policyholder's last name, first name, and middle initial (if known) (separated by commas).
9a	Enter the primary policyholder's policy or group number.
9d	Enter the name of the primary policyholder's commercial health insurance plan.
11	Enter the secondary or supplemental policyholder's policy or group number. *Do not enter hyphens or spaces in the policy or group number.*
11a	Enter the secondary or supplemental policyholder's birth date as MM DD YYYY (with spaces). Enter an X in the appropriate box to indicate the policyholder's sex. If the policyholder's sex is unknown, leave blank.
11c	Enter the name of the secondary or supplemental policyholder's commercial health insurance plan.
11d	Enter an X in the YES box.
26	Add an S to the patient's account number to indicate the secondary policy.

Courtesy of the Centers for Medicare & Medicaid Services, www.cms.gov.

Exercise 12.2 – Completing a Commercial Secondary CMS-1500 Claim When the Same Commercial Payer Provides Primary and Secondary Coverage

1. Obtain a blank claim by making a copy of the CMS-1500 claim form in Appendix I.

2. Underline Blocks 9, 9a, 9d, and 11d on the claim.

3. Refer to the Mary S. Patient case study (Figure 12-3). Enter the following additional information in the appropriate blocks for the secondary policy (Table 12-2):

   Conn General ID # 22335544

   Policyholder: James W. Patient

   Birth date: 03/01/48

   Relationship: Spouse

4. Review the completed claim to be sure all required blocks are properly completed.

5. Compare your claim with the completed Mary S. Patient claim in Figure 12-5.

 NOTE:

Use these instructions when completing any claims associated with *Understanding Health Insurance.*

Exercise 12.3 – Completing a Commercial Secondary CMS-1500 Claim When Different Commercial Payers Provide Primary and Secondary Coverage

1. Obtain a blank claim by making a copy of the CMS-1500 claim form in Appendix I.

2. Underline Blocks 1a, 4, 7, 9, 9a, 9d, 11, 11a, 11c, 11d, and 26 on the claim.

3. Refer to the Mary S. Patient case study (Figure 12-3). Enter the following information in the appropriate blocks for the secondary policy:

   Aetna ID # 987654321

   Policyholder: James W. Patient

   Birth date: 03/01/48

   Relationship: Spouse

   Add an "S" to the patient's account number in Block 26 (e.g., 12-2S)

4. Review the completed claim to be sure all required blocks are properly completed.

5. Compare your claim with the completed Mary S. Patient claim in Figure 12-6.

HEALTH INSURANCE CLAIM FORM

APPROVED BY NATIONAL UNIFORM CLAIM COMMITTEE (NUCC) 02/12

CARRIER

| | PICA | | | | | | PICA | |

1. MEDICARE [ ] (Medicare#) MEDICAID [ ] (Medicaid#) TRICARE [ ] (ID#/DoD#) CHAMPVA [ ] (Member ID#) GROUP HEALTH PLAN [ ] (ID#) FECA BLKLUNG [ ] (ID#) OTHER [X] (ID#)

1a. INSURED'S I.D. NUMBER (For Program in Item 1)
222017681

2. PATIENT'S NAME (Last Name, First Name, Middle Initial)
PATIENT, MARY, S

3. PATIENT'S BIRTH DATE MM **10** DD **10** YY **1959** SEX M [ ] F [X]

4. INSURED'S NAME (Last Name, First Name, Middle Initial)
PATIENT, JAMES, W

5. PATIENT'S ADDRESS (No., Street)
91 HOME STREET

6. PATIENT RELATIONSHIP TO INSURED
Self [ ] Spouse [X] Child [ ] Other [ ]

7. INSURED'S ADDRESS (No., Street)

CITY **NOWHERE**   STATE **NY**

8. RESERVED FOR NUCC USE

CITY   STATE

ZIP CODE **123671234**   TELEPHONE (Include Area Code) ( )

ZIP CODE   TELEPHONE (Include Area Code) ( )

9. OTHER INSURED'S NAME (Last Name, First Name, Middle Initial)
PATIENT, JAMES, W

10. IS PATIENT'S CONDITION RELATED TO:

11. INSURED'S POLICY GROUP OR FECA NUMBER

a. OTHER INSURED'S POLICY OR GROUP NUMBER
22335544

a. EMPLOYMENT? (Current or Previous) YES [ ] NO [X]

a. INSURED'S DATE OF BIRTH MM **03** DD **01** YY **1948** SEX M [X] F [ ]

b. RESERVED FOR NUCC USE

b. AUTO ACCIDENT? YES [ ] NO [X] PLACE (State)

b. OTHER CLAIM ID (Designated by NUCC)

c. RESERVED FOR NUCC USE

c. OTHER ACCIDENT? YES [ ] NO [X]

c. INSURANCE PLAN NAME OR PROGRAM NAME
CONN GENERAL

d. INSURANCE PLAN NAME OR PROGRAM NAME
CONN GENERAL

10d. CLAIM CODES (Designated by NUCC)

d. IS THERE ANOTHER HEALTH BENEFIT PLAN? [X] YES [ ] NO If yes, complete items 9, 9a, and 9d.

READ BACK OF FORM BEFORE COMPLETING & SIGNING THIS FORM.

12. PATIENT'S OR AUTHORIZED PERSON'S SIGNATURE I authorize the release of any medical or other information necessary to process this claim. I also request payment of government benefits either to myself or to the party who accepts assignment below.

SIGNED **SIGNATURE ON FILE**   DATE

13. INSURED'S OR AUTHORIZED PERSON'S SIGNATURE I authorize payment of medical benefits to the undersigned physician or supplier for services described below.

SIGNED **SIGNATURE ON FILE**

14. DATE OF CURRENT ILLNESS, INJURY, or PREGNANCY (LMP) MM **01** DD **07** YY **YY** QUAL. **431**

15. OTHER DATE QUAL. MM DD YY

16. DATES PATIENT UNABLE TO WORK IN CURRENT OCCUPATION FROM MM DD YY TO MM DD YY

17. NAME OF REFERRING PROVIDER OR OTHER SOURCE
17a.
17b. NPI

18. HOSPITALIZATION DATES RELATED TO CURRENT SERVICES FROM MM **01** DD **07** YY **YY** TO MM **01** DD **09** YY **YY**

19. ADDITIONAL CLAIM INFORMATION (Designated by NUCC)

20. OUTSIDE LAB? YES [ ] NO [X] $ CHARGES

21. DIAGNOSIS OR NATURE OF ILLNESS OR INJURY Relate A-L to service line below (24E) ICD Ind. **0**

A. **R9431** B. **I201** C. **E7849** D.
E. F. G. H.
I. J. K. L.

22. RESUBMISSION CODE   ORIGINAL REF. NO.

23. PRIOR AUTHORIZATION NUMBER

24. A. DATE(S) OF SERVICE From MM DD YY / To MM DD YY	B. PLACE OF SERVICE	C. EMG	D. PROCEDURES, SERVICES, OR SUPPLIES CPT/HCPCS	MODIFIER	E. DIAGNOSIS POINTER	F. $ CHARGES	G. DAYS OR UNITS	H. EPSDT	I. ID. QUAL.	J. RENDERING PROVIDER ID. #
1 01 07 YY	21		99223		ABC	150 00	1		NPI	
2 01 08 YY	21		99231		ABC	75 00	1		NPI	
3 01 09 YY	21		99238		ABC	75 00	1		NPI	
4									NPI	
5									NPI	
6									NPI	

25. FEDERAL TAX I.D. NUMBER **111234523** SSN [ ] EIN [X]

26. PATIENT'S ACCOUNT NO. **12-2**

27. ACCEPT ASSIGNMENT? [X] YES [ ] NO

28. TOTAL CHARGE $ **300 00**

29. AMOUNT PAID $

30. Rsvd for NUCC Use

31. SIGNATURE OF PHYSICIAN OR SUPPLIER INCLUDING DEGREES OR CREDENTIALS (I certify that the statements on the reverse apply to this bill and are made a part thereof.)
ERIN A HELPER MD   **MMDDYY**
SIGNED   DATE

32. SERVICE FACILITY LOCATION INFORMATION
GOODMEDICINE HOSPITAL
ANYWHERE STREET
ANYWHERE NY 123451234
a. **2345678901** b.

33. BILLING PROVIDER INFO & PH # (**101**) **1111234**
ERIN A HELPER MD
101 MEDIC DRIVE
ANYWHERE NY 123459874
a. **1234567890** b.

NUCC Instruction Manual available at: www.nucc.org   PLEASE PRINT OR TYPE

FIGURE 12-5 Completed Mary S. Patient claim when primary and secondary payers are the same.

FIGURE 12-6 Completed Mary S. Patient claim when primary and secondary payers are different.

Commercial Group Health Plan Coverage Claims Instructions

Employers include group health plan coverage (Table 12-4) in fringe benefit programs to retain high-quality employees and ensure productivity by providing preventive medical care to create a healthy workforce. There are many group health plan options available to employers, including various payment options from paying 100 percent of annual premium costs for each employee to sharing a percentage (e.g., 80 percent) of the annual insurance costs with employees.

> **Example:** Linda Ryan is employed by a public school that provides individual and family group health plan coverage. Linda's employer pays 80 percent of the annual premium. The total annual premium of the family group health plan is $12,000. Linda selects family coverage for the group health plan, which means Linda's employer pays $9,600 per year ($12,000 × 0.80). Linda is responsible for 20 percent of the annual premium (or $2,400, calculated as $12,000 × 0.20), which means $92.31 is deducted from each of Linda's 26 biweekly paychecks ($2,400/26). (Copayments and deductibles also apply to Linda's group health plan, such as a $20 copayment for office visits, a $50 copayment for hospital emergency department visits, and a $35 copayment for hospital outpatient ancillary tests.)

NOTE:

Individual and family health plans cover individuals and their families, and each person covered must qualify individually. Group health plans are required to accept employees and their family members, and may be less expensive than individual or family health plans.

NOTE:

Use these instructions when completing any claims associated with *Understanding Health Insurance*.

TABLE 12-4 Modifications to commercial primary CMS-1500 claims completion instructions when the policy is a group health plan (Refer to Table 12-1 for primary CMS-1500 claims completion instructions.)

Block	Instructions
1	Enter an X in the Group Health Plans box.
11	Enter the policyholder's group number.

Note: Locate the group number on the policyholder's insurance identification card (or in case studies located in this textbook, workbook, and SimClaim™ software).

Courtesy of the Centers for Medicare & Medicaid Services, www.cms.gov.

Exercise 12.4 – Completing a Commercial Group Health Plan CMS-1500 Claim

1. Obtain a blank claim by making a copy of the CMS-1500 claim form in Appendix I.
2. Underline Blocks 1 and 11 on the claim.
3. Refer to the Mary S. Patient case study (see Figure 12-3), and complete the group health plan claim. Enter the following information in the appropriate blocks for the group health plan policy:

   Group number: 123A
4. Review the completed claim to be sure all required blocks are properly completed.
5. Compare your claim with the completed Mary S. Patient claim in Figure 12-7.

HEALTH INSURANCE CLAIM FORM

APPROVED BY NATIONAL UNIFORM CLAIM COMMITTEE (NUCC) 02/12

☐☐☐ PICA | PICA ☐☐☐

1. MEDICARE (Medicare#) ☐ MEDICAID (Medicaid#) ☐ TRICARE (ID#/DoD#) ☐ CHAMPVA (Member ID#) ☐ GROUP HEALTH PLAN (ID#) [X] FECA BLKLUNG (ID#) ☐ OTHER (ID#) ☐

1a. INSURED'S I.D. NUMBER (For Program in Item 1)
222017681

2. PATIENT'S NAME (Last Name, First Name, Middle Initial)
PATIENT, MARY, S

3. PATIENT'S BIRTH DATE MM 10 DD 10 YY 1959 SEX M ☐ F [X]

4. INSURED'S NAME (Last Name, First Name, Middle Initial)
PATIENT, JAMES, W

5. PATIENT'S ADDRESS (No., Street)
91 HOME STREET

6. PATIENT RELATIONSHIP TO INSURED
Self ☐ Spouse [X] Child ☐ Other ☐

7. INSURED'S ADDRESS (No., Street)

CITY NOWHERE STATE NY

8. RESERVED FOR NUCC USE

CITY STATE

ZIP CODE 123671234 TELEPHONE (Include Area Code) ( )

ZIP CODE TELEPHONE (Include Area Code) ( )

9. OTHER INSURED'S NAME (Last Name, First Name, Middle Initial)
PATIENT, JAMES, W

10. IS PATIENT'S CONDITION RELATED TO:

11. INSURED'S POLICY GROUP OR FECA NUMBER
123A

a. OTHER INSURED'S POLICY OR GROUP NUMBER

a. EMPLOYMENT? (Current or Previous) YES ☐ NO [X]

a. INSURED'S DATE OF BIRTH MM 03 DD 01 YY 1948 SEX M [X] F ☐

b. RESERVED FOR NUCC USE

b. AUTO ACCIDENT? YES ☐ NO [X] PLACE (State)

b. OTHER CLAIM ID (Designated by NUCC)

c. RESERVED FOR NUCC USE

c. OTHER ACCIDENT? YES ☐ NO [X]

c. INSURANCE PLAN NAME OR PROGRAM NAME
CONN GENERAL

d. INSURANCE PLAN NAME OR PROGRAM NAME

10d. CLAIM CODES (Designated by NUCC)

d. IS THERE ANOTHER HEALTH BENEFIT PLAN?
[X] YES ☐ NO If yes, complete items 9, 9a, and 9d.

READ BACK OF FORM BEFORE COMPLETING & SIGNING THIS FORM.

12. PATIENT'S OR AUTHORIZED PERSON'S SIGNATURE I authorize the release of any medical or other information necessary to process this claim. I also request payment of government benefits either to myself or to the party who accepts assignment below.

SIGNED **SIGNATURE ON FILE** DATE ____

13. INSURED'S OR AUTHORIZED PERSON'S SIGNATURE I authorize payment of medical benefits to the undersigned physician or supplier for services described below.

SIGNED **SIGNATURE ON FILE**

14. DATE OF CURRENT ILLNESS, INJURY, or PREGNANCY (LMP) MM 01 DD 07 YY YY QUAL. 431

15. OTHER DATE QUAL. MM DD YY

16. DATES PATIENT UNABLE TO WORK IN CURRENT OCCUPATION FROM MM DD YY TO MM DD YY

17. NAME OF REFERRING PROVIDER OR OTHER SOURCE
17a.
17b. NPI

18. HOSPITALIZATION DATES RELATED TO CURRENT SERVICES FROM MM 01 DD 07 YY YY TO MM 01 DD 09 YY YY

19. ADDITIONAL CLAIM INFORMATION (Designated by NUCC)

20. OUTSIDE LAB? YES ☐ NO [X] $ CHARGES

21. DIAGNOSIS OR NATURE OF ILLNESS OR INJURY Relate A-L to service line below (24E) ICD Ind. 0
A. R9431 B. I201 C. E7849 D.
E. F. G. H.
I. J. K. L.

22. RESUBMISSION CODE ORIGINAL REF. NO.

23. PRIOR AUTHORIZATION NUMBER

24. A. DATE(S) OF SERVICE From MM DD YY	To MM DD YY	B. PLACE OF SERVICE	C. EMG	D. PROCEDURES, SERVICES, OR SUPPLIES (Explain Unusual Circumstances) CPT/HCPCS MODIFIER	E. DIAGNOSIS POINTER	F. $ CHARGES	G. DAYS OR UNITS	H. EPSDT Family Plan	I. ID. QUAL.	J. RENDERING PROVIDER ID. #
1	01 07 YY		21		99223	ABC	150 00	1		NPI	
2	01 08 YY		21		99231	ABC	75 00	1		NPI	
3	01 09 YY		21		99238	ABC	75 00	1		NPI	
4										NPI	
5										NPI	
6										NPI	

25. FEDERAL TAX I.D. NUMBER 111234523 SSN ☐ EIN [X]

26. PATIENT'S ACCOUNT NO. 12-2

27. ACCEPT ASSIGNMENT? (For govt. claims, see back) [X] YES ☐ NO

28. TOTAL CHARGE $ 300 00

29. AMOUNT PAID $

30. Rsvd for NUCC Use

31. SIGNATURE OF PHYSICIAN OR SUPPLIER INCLUDING DEGREES OR CREDENTIALS (I certify that the statements on the reverse apply to this bill and are made a part thereof.)
ERIN A HELPER MD MMDDYY
SIGNED DATE

32. SERVICE FACILITY LOCATION INFORMATION
GOODMEDICINE HOSPITAL
ANYWHERE STREET
ANYWHERE NY 123451234
a. 2345678901 b.

33. BILLING PROVIDER INFO & PH # (101) 1111234
ERIN A HELPER MD
101 MEDIC DRIVE
ANYWHERE NY 123459874
a. 1234567890 b.

NUCC Instruction Manual available at: www.nucc.org **PLEASE PRINT OR TYPE**

CARRIER

PATIENT AND INSURED INFORMATION

PHYSICIAN OR SUPPLIER INFORMATION

FIGURE 12-7 Completed Mary S. Patient claim for commercial payer group health plan.

Summary

Automobile insurance coverage includes medical payments and PIP; disability insurance provides an individual with reimbursement for lost wages; liability insurance covers losses to a third party caused by the insured or on premises owned by the insured.

Although commercial claims completion instructions are generally recognized nationwide, it is important to check with each payer to determine if they require alternate information to be entered on the claim. Commercial payers also implement changes to claims completion requirements throughout the year, and most providers discover these changes when claims are denied. Commercial payers do not typically make available their billing manuals or updates, which is another reason it is important to routinely contact payers to request their specific CMS-1500 claims completion instructions.

When patients are covered by primary *and* secondary/supplemental health insurance plans, modifications are made to the CMS-1500 claim instructions:

- If the same payer provides both primary and secondary/supplemental coverage, just one claim is submitted, and information is entered in Blocks 9, 9a, 9d, 11, 11a, 11c, and 11d.
- If the secondary/supplemental payer is different from the primary payer, a primary claim is submitted to the primary payer, and a new claim is generated and submitted to the secondary payer, with information entered in Blocks 1a, 4, 7 (if applicable), 9, 9a, 9d, 11, 11a, 11c, and 11d. A copy of the primary payer's remittance advice is attached to the secondary claim.

When completing commercial CMS-1500 claims for exercises in the textbook, assignments in the workbook, and case studies in SimClaim™, the following special instructions apply:

- Block 12—Enter SIGNATURE ON FILE.
- Block 13—Enter SIGNATURE ON FILE.
- Block 20—Enter an X in the NO box.
- Block 26—Enter the case study number (e.g., 12-2). If the patient has both primary and secondary coverage, enter a P (for primary) (e.g., 12-2P) next to the number (on the primary claim) and an S (for secondary) (e.g., 12-2S) next to the number (on the secondary claim).
- Block 27—Enter an X in the YES box.
- Block 31—Enter the provider's complete name with credentials and the date as MMDDYY.

Internet Links

Aetna: **www.aetna.com**

eHealth: **www.ehealthinsurance.com**

Insurance Information Institute: **www.iii.org**

Washington State Office of the Insurance Commissioner: **www.insurance.wa.gov**

Wisconsin Office of the Commissioner of Insurance: **www.oci.wi.gov**

Review

Multiple Choice

Instructions: Select the most appropriate response.

1. When a patient is covered by a large employer group health plan (EGHP) and Medicare, which is primary?
   - **a.** EGHP
   - **b.** Medicare
   - **c.** No distinction is made between the plans.
   - **d.** The plan that has been in place longest.

2. When a child who is covered by two or more plans lives with his married parents, the primary policyholder is the parent
   a. who is older.
   b. who is younger.
   c. whose birthday occurs first in the year.
   d. whose birthday occurs later in the year.

3. When the provider's Social Security number is entered in Block 25 of the CMS-1500 claim, the number
   a. contains the hyphens associated with Social Security numbers.
   b. contains the identification number without hyphens or spaces.
   c. is left blank, because Social Security numbers are private.
   d. can contain spaces or hyphens when the number is entered.

4. When the CMS-1500 claim requires spaces for data entry of a date, the data is entered as which of the following?
   a. MM DD YYYY or MM DD YY
   b. MM-DD-YYYY or MM-DD-YY
   c. MM/DD/YYYY or MM/DD/YY
   d. MMDDYYYY or MMDDYY

5. Entering an X in the Other box on the CMS-1500 claim indicates that the patient is covered by an individual or family health plan, and can also indicate that the claim should be processed by a(n) _____ payer.
   a. automobile or liability
   b. FECA worker's compensation
   c. Medicaid or Medicare
   d. TRICARE

6. When the CMS-1500 claim requires a response to YES or NO entries, enter
   a. a checkmark.
   b. an X.
   c. either an X or a checkmark.
   d. nothing.

7. When SIGNATURE ON FILE is the appropriate entry for a CMS-1500 claim block, which is also acceptable as an entry?
   a. FILED   b. S/F   c. SIGNED   d. SOF

8. Block 14 of the CMS-1500 claim requires entry of the date the patient first experienced signs or symptoms of an illness or injury (or the date of last menstrual period for obstetric visits). Upon completion of Jean Mandel's claim, you notice that there is no documentation in the record of the date that the patient first experienced the symptom of pain. The provider does document that the pain began five days ago. Today is May 10, YY. What do you enter in Block 14?
   a. 05 05 YY
   b. 05 10 YY
   c. the word NONE
   d. nothing (leave blank)

9. Blocks 24A–24J of the CMS-1500 claim contain shaded rows, which can contain
   a. additional dates of service and codes.
   b. attachments to the CMS-1500 claim.
   c. modifiers that didn't fit in the unshaded block.
   d. supplemental information, per payer instructions.

10. If a physician is reporting level 3 subsequent hospital services provided to a hospital inpatient on 05/10/YY and 05/11/YY, which is entered in Block 24A of the CMS-1500 claim?
    a. 05 10 YY   **b.** 05 10 YY 05 11 YY   **c.** 05 11 YY   **d.** 05 11 YY 05 11 YY

11. What is entered in Block 24J of the CMS-1500 claim if the provider is a member of a group practice?
    a. Employer identification number (EIN)
    b. National Provider Identifier (NPI)
    c. Prior preauthorization number
    d. Social Security number (SSN)

12. When Block 25 of the CMS-1500 contains the provider's EIN, enter _____ after the first two digits of the EIN.
    a. a hyphen
    b. a space
    c. no punctuation or space
    d. the provider's SSN

13. When a patient is covered by the same primary and secondary commercial health insurance plan,
    a. complete and submit two different CMS-1500 claims.
    b. mail the remittance advice with the claim to the plan.
    c. send the secondary CMS-1500, but not the primary claim.
    d. submit just one completed CMS-1500 to the same plan.

14. When entering the patient's name in Block 2 of the CMS-1500 claim, separate the last name, first name, and middle initial (if known) with
    a. commas.
    b. hyphens.
    c. parentheses.
    d. slashes.

15. Block 33a of the CMS-1500 claim contains the provider's
    a. EIN.   **b.** NPI.   **c.** PIN.   **d.** SSN.

16. Which typically covers the medical expenses of individuals and groups, and is either purchased by individuals or provided by employers?
    a. Automobile insurance
    b. Commercial insurance
    c. Disability insurance
    d. Liability insurance

17. Which specifically compensates policyholders for actual economic losses, up to limiting amounts on the insurance policy, and usually requires the insured to prove losses before payment is made?
    a. Commercial insurance
    b. Disability insurance
    c. Indemnity insurance
    d. Liability insurance

18. Which is a contract between an individual and an insurance company whereby the individual pays a premium and, in exchange, the insurance company agrees to pay for specific car-related financial losses during the term of the policy?
    a. Automobile insurance
    b. Commercial insurance
    c. Disability insurance
    d. Liability insurance

19. Which covers income lost as a result of a temporary or permanent illness or injury?
    a. Automobile insurance
    b. Commercial insurance
    c. Disability insurance
    d. Liability insurance

20. Which is a policy that covers losses to a third party caused by the insured, such as by an object owned by the insured, or on premises owned by the insured?
    a. Automobile insurance
    b. Commercial insurance
    c. Disability insurance
    d. Liability insurance

21. Which specifically refers to the contractual right of a third-party payer to recover health care expenses from a liable party?
    a. Reimbursement
    b. Revenue
    c. Subrogation
    d. Substitution

22. When a patient is injured on the job, which type of insurance is responsible for reimbursing the patient's health care expenses?
    a. Commercial
    b. Disability
    c. Liability
    d. Workers' compensation

23. Third-party recovery standards for the investigation of liability coverage and the process for filing a lien in a potential liability case vary on federal and state bases. Which is an example of a lien?
    a. Arranging for an investigator to verify the existence of liability coverage
    b. Obtaining confirmation that the liable party has an appropriate income
    c. Pledging or securing a debtor's property as a guarantee of payment for a debt
    d. Securing a debtor's property as security or payment for a debt

24. Secondary health insurance plans provide coverage similar to that of _____ plans.
    a. disability
    b. liability
    c. primary
    d. supplemental

25. Which benefit program is most likely to be implemented by employers to retain high-quality employees and ensure productivity?
    a. 100 percent of annual premium costs for each employee
    b. A cost-share that totals 80 percent of annual insurance
    c. On-site health care services for employee convenience
    d. Preventive medical care to create a healthy workforce

BlueCross BlueShield

Chapter Outline

BlueCross BlueShield

BlueCross BlueShield Plans

BlueCross BlueShield Billing Notes

BlueCross BlueShield Claims Instructions

BlueCross BlueShield Secondary Coverage

Claims Instructions

Chapter Objectives

Upon successful completion of this chapter, you should be able to:

1. Define key terms related to BlueCross BlueShield.
2. Explain the purpose, origin, and features of BlueCross BlueShield.
3. Differentiate among BlueCross BlueShield plans.
4. Describe BlueCross BlueShield billing notes when completing CMS-1500 claims.
5. Complete BlueCross BlueShield primary coverage claims.
6. Complete BlueCross BlueShield secondary coverage claims.

Key Terms

BCBS preferred provider network

BlueCard©

BlueCross BlueShield (BCBS)

BlueCross BlueShield Association (BCBSA)

BlueCross BlueShield Global®

coordinated home health care

Federal Employee Program® (FEP)

for-profit corporation

GeoBlue®

Government-Wide Service Benefit Plan

health care anywhere

member

member hospital

nonprofit corporation

outpatient pretreatment authorization program (OPAP)

service location

usual, customary, and reasonable (UCR)

Introduction

BlueCross BlueShield health plans are perhaps the best known medical insurance programs in the United States. They began as two separate *prepaid health plans* selling contracts to individuals or groups for coverage of specified medical expenses as long as the premiums were paid. BlueCross plans originally covered only hospital bills, and BlueShield plans covered fees for physician services. Over the years, the programs merged and increased coverage to include almost all health care services.

 NOTE:

> CMS-1500 claims completion instructions are included in this chapter. (UB-04 claims are autopopulated by data abstracted and coded from patient records *or* from an electronic health record (EHR) in hospital, skilled nursing facility, inpatient hospice, and home health care organizations. *Chapter 11 of this textbook contains general UB-04 claims completion instructions*, along with examples and a review assignment.)

BlueCross BlueShield

BlueCross plans originally covered only hospital bills, and BlueShield plans covered fees for physician services. Today, **BlueCross BlueShield (BCBS)** has community-based, independent, and locally operated companies that provide health plan coverage to Americans in all 50 states, the Washington D.C., and Puerto Rico. Coverage is also provided to those who live, travel, and work internationally.

Origin of BlueCross and BlueShield

The forerunner of what is known today of the original *BlueCross* health plan began in 1929 when Baylor University Hospital in Dallas, Texas, approached teachers in the Dallas school district with a plan that would guarantee up to 21 days of hospitalization per year for members and each of their dependents, in exchange for a $6 annual premium. This original prepaid health plan was accepted by the teachers and worked so well that the concept soon spread across the country, and early plans specified which hospital the members and their dependents could use for care. By 1932, some plans modified this concept and organized community-wide programs that allowed the member to be hospitalized in one of several **member hospitals**, which had signed contracts to provide services for special rates. The blue cross symbol was first used in 1933 by the St. Paul, Minnesota plan, and was adopted in 1939 by the *American Hospital Association (AHA)* when it became the approving agency for accreditation of new prepaid hospitalization plans. In 1973, the AHA deeded the right to both the name and the use of the blue cross symbol to the Blue Cross Association. At that time the symbol was updated to the trademark in use today.

The original *BlueShield* health plan began as a resolution passed by the House of Delegates at an American Medical Association meeting in 1938 to support the concept of voluntary health insurance that would encourage physicians to cooperate with prepaid health care plans. In 1939, the first known plan was formed in Palo Alto, California, and it was called the California Physicians' Service. This plan stipulated that physicians' fees for covered medical services would be paid in full by the plan if the member earned less than $3,000 a year. When the member earned more than $3,000 a year, a small percentage of the physician's fee would be paid by the patient. This patient responsibility for a small percentage of the health care fee is the forerunner of today's industry-wide required patient coinsurance and copayment requirements. The blue shield design was first used as a trademark by the Buffalo New York plan in 1939. The name and symbol were formally adopted by the Associated Medical Care Plans, formed in 1948, as the approving agency for accreditation of new BlueShield plans adopting programs created in the spirit of the California Physicians' Service program.

BlueCross BlueShield Association

In 1977, the membership of the separate BlueCross and BlueShield national associations voted to combine personnel under the leadership of a single president, responsible to both boards of directors.

Further consolidation occurred in 1986 when the boards of directors of the separate national BlueCross and BlueShield associations merged into a single corporation named the BlueCross BlueShield Association (BCBSA).

The **BlueCross BlueShield Association (BCBSA)** consists of independent, community-based, and locally operated BlueCross BlueShield companies that collectively provide health care coverage to more than 100 million Americans. The BCBSA maintains offices in Chicago, Illinois, and Washington, D.C. and performs the following functions:

- Owns and manages the BlueCross and BlueShield trademarks and names
- Grants licenses to BCBS companies to use trademarks and names
- Represents BlueCross and BlueShield in national forums

Business Structure

Strong competition among all health insurance companies in the United States emerged during the 1990s and resulted in the following:

- Mergers occurred among BCBS regional corporations (within a state or with neighboring states) and names no longer had regional designations.

> **Example:** CareFirst BCBS is the name of the corporation that resulted from a merger between BCBS of Maryland and Washington, D.C., BCBS.

- The BlueCross BlueShield Association no longer required plans to be nonprofit (as of 1994).

Nonprofit and For-Profit Corporations

Regional corporations that needed additional capital to compete with commercial for-profit health insurance plans petitioned their respective state legislatures to allow conversion from their nonprofit status to for-profit corporations. **Nonprofit corporations** are charitable, educational, civic, or humanitarian organizations whose profits are returned to the corporation rather than distributed to shareholders and officers of the corporation. Because no profits of the organization are distributed to shareholders, the government does not tax the organization's income. **For-profit corporations** pay taxes on profits generated by the corporation's enterprises and pay dividends to shareholders on after-tax profits.

For BCBS plans that converted to for-profit companies, state regulators and courts scrutinized these transactions, some on a retroactive basis, to ensure that charitable assets are preserved. For example, Blue Cross of California created The California Endowment in 1996, which awards grants to community-based organizations. The California Health Care Foundation was also created to improve health care delivery systems, including the support of health equity.

 NOTE:

> For-profit commercial plans have the right to cancel a policy at renewal time if the patient moves into a region of the country in which the company is not licensed to sell insurance or if the person is a high user of benefits and has purchased a plan that does not include a noncancellation clause.

Network Participation and Utilization Management

BCBS companies contract with health care facilities, physicians, and other health care professionals to form **BCBS preferred provider networks**, which ensure that members receive accessible, appropriate, cost-effective, and quality health care services. (Members who receive care from non-network providers can expect to pay higher costs.) A *utilization management* (or *utilization review*) program evaluates accessibility, appropriateness, cost-effectiveness, medical necessity, and quality of health care services provided to patients, as well as treatment plans created for patients. Components of a utilization management program include:

- *Admission review*: A review of documentation to determine that the type of admission, emergency or urgent, is at the appropriate level of care for the patient's diagnosis
- *Case management*: Coordination of health care delivery for members between nurse case managers and physicians and other health care team members, and the provision of assistance to members in navigating the health care system
- *Concurrent review*: Inpatient hospital patient review process to assess continued appropriateness of care and medical necessity, and to initiate the discharge planning process for post-discharge patient care; this review process is in accordance with severity of illness and intensity of services (ISSI) concepts
- *Discharge planning*: Identifying, evaluating, and assisting patients with post-discharge health care requirements, such as home health care
- *Drug utilization review*: Evaluation of medications to determine whether they are being used appropriately and safely, and to determine their effectiveness
- *Preadmission review*: Evaluating medical necessity and required level of care for procedures, services, and elective admissions prior to inpatient hospital admission
- *Precertification*: Review process to grant prior approval for reimbursement of health care procedures and services
- *Prospective review*: Review of health care procedures and services *before delivery* for prior authorization purposes
- *Retrospective review* (or *claims review*): Reviewing medical necessity and appropriateness of medical procedures and services provided as part of claims processing (after provision of care) by compiling and analyzing data to determine consumer and provider patterns of care

BlueCross BlueShield Plans

BlueCross BlueShield offer the following types of health insurance plans to its **members**, which are BCBS enrollees or subscribers.

- Traditional fee-for-service plans
- Indemnity plans
- Managed care plans
  - Coordinated home health care
  - Exclusive provider organization (EPO)
  - Health maintenance organization (HMO)
  - Outpatient pretreatment authorization plan (OPAP)
  - Point-of-service (POS) plan
  - Preferred provider organization (PPO)
  - Second surgical opinion (SSO)
- Federal Employee Program® (FEP)
- Medicare supplemental plans
- Health care anywhere

Traditional Fee-for-Service Plans

Traditional *fee-for-service* plans provide reimbursement to providers according to a *fee schedule* after procedures have been performed or services are provided to BCBS members. These plans usually include basic coverage and major medical benefits.

- *BCBS basic coverage* includes minimum health procedures and services, such as physician office encounters, inpatient and outpatient hospital services, prescription drug coverage, pregnancy and childbirth services, and mental health care.
- *BCBS major medical* includes extended coverage of hospital, medical, and surgical benefits to *supplement* basic coverage benefits, such as extending hospital days and other benefits, such as dental, hearing, vision, and weight management services.

Indemnity Plans

Indemnity plans are similar to traditional fee-for-service health plans, but they provide members with the option to receive care from any provider. Indemnity plans may cost more than other health plans, including fee-for-service and managed care plans.

Managed Care Plans

Managed care is a health care delivery system that provides health care and controls costs through a network of physicians, hospitals, and other health care providers. Providers receive capitated payments from the health plan on a monthly or yearly basis, and they are responsible for providing health care services to members. BCBS managed care plans include the coordinated home health care program, exclusive provider organizations, health maintenance organizations, outpatient pretreatment authorization plans, point-of-service plans, preferred provider organizations, and second surgical opinions.

A **coordinated home health care** program is usually coordinated between an inpatient facility (e.g., hospital) and a home health agency to facilitate the patient's discharge home. The patient is provided with home health agency care by a participating provider, and the patient must require skilled nursing services (e.g., physical therapy, medical supplies) on an intermittent basis under the direction of the primary care provider.

An *exclusive provider organization (EPO)* provides health care services through a network of physicians, hospitals, and other health care providers. However, they must obtain services from EPO providers only or the patient is responsible for the charges.

BCBS *health maintenance organization (HMO)* plans share financial and health care delivery risks with providers to offer comprehensive medical services to members in return for a fixed, prepaid fee. For example, *Empire BlueCross HMO* is the trade name of *Empire HealthChoice HMO, Inc.* Because familiar BCBS names are not always used in the plan name, some HMOs may not be easily recognized as BCBS plans. The BCBS trademarks, however, usually appear on the plan's ID cards and advertisements.

The **outpatient pretreatment authorization program (OPAP)** requires preauthorization of outpatient physical, occupational, and speech therapy services; acupuncture; spinal manipulation/chiropractic; and habilitative services. (CPT modifiers -96 and -97 are reported for habilitative and rehabilitative services, respectively.) In addition, OPAP requires periodic treatment/progress plans to be filed. OPAP is a requirement for the delivery of certain health care services and is issued prior to the provision of services.

A *point-of-service (POS) plan* allows members to choose, at the time medical services are needed, whether they will go to a provider within the plan's network or outside the network. When members go outside the network to seek care, out-of-pocket expenses and copayments generally increase. POS plans provide a full range of inpatient and outpatient services, and members choose a primary care provider (PCP) from the payer's PCP list. The PCP assumes responsibility for coordinating member and dependent medical care, and the PCP is often referred to as the *gatekeeper* of the patient's medical care. The name and telephone number of the PCP appear on POS plan ID cards, and written referral notices issued by the PCP are usually mailed to the appropriate local processing address following the transmission of an electronic claim. Because the PCP is responsible for authorizing all inpatient hospitalizations, a specialist's office should contact the PCP when hospitalization is necessary and follow up that call with one to the utilization management office at the local BCBS plan.

A *preferred provider organization (PPO)* offers discounted health care services to members who use a designated network of health care providers (who contract with the PPO) but also provides coverage for services rendered by health care providers who are not part of the PPO network. *BlueCard®* provides members who live or travel outside of their BCBS plan area to use preferred provider organization (PPO) benefits when receiving health care services from a PPO provider (e.g., hospital, physician). The plan also links PPO providers with independent BCBS companies by using a single electronic network to process claims and generate provider reimbursement. In this type of plan, the member is responsible for remaining within the network of PPO providers and must request referrals to PPO specialists whenever possible. The member must also adhere to the managed care requirements of the PPO plan, such as preadmission review. Failure to adhere to these requirements will result in denial of the claim or reduced payment to the provider. In such cases, the patient is responsible for the difference or balance between the reduced payment and the normal PPO allowed rate.

The mandatory *second surgical opinion (SSO)* requirement is necessary when a patient is considering elective, nonemergency surgical care. The initial surgical recommendation must be made by a physician qualified to perform the anticipated surgery. If a second surgical opinion is not obtained prior to surgery, the patient's out-of-pocket expenses may be greatly increased. The patient or surgeon should contact the member's BCBS plan for instructions. In some cases, the second opinion must be obtained from a member of a select surgical panel. In other cases, the concurrence of the need for surgery from the patient's PCP may suffice.

Federal Employee Program®

The BlueCross BlueShield **Federal Employee Program® (FEP)** (Figure 13-1) began covering federal employees on July 1, 1960 as part of the *Federal Employee Health Benefits Program (FEHBP)*, and continues to provide benefits to millions of federal members, retirees, and their survivors. FEP is underwritten and administered by BlueCross BlueShield companies, and claims are submitted to local plans that serve the location where the patient was seen (called a **service location**), regardless of the member's FEP plan affiliation. FEP cards contain the phrase **Government-Wide Service Benefit Plan** under the insurance company's trademark, the letter "R" is located in front of the member number, and the FEP logo.

 NOTE:

> The federal government's Office of Personnel Management (OPM) oversees administration of the FEHBP, and BCBS is just one of several payers who reimburse health care services. Others include the American Postal Workers Union (APWU) Health Plan, Government Employee Hospital Association (GEHA), Mail Handlers Benefit Plan (MHBP), and National Association of Letter Carriers (NALC).

Medicare Supplemental Plans

BCBS corporations offer several federally designed and regulated *Medicare supplemental plans* (described in Chapter 14), which augment the Medicare program by paying for Medicare deductible, copayment, and coinsurance amounts. Other services that can be covered by a Medicare supplemental plan include custodial care, extended long-term care, hearing aids, routine dental care, and routine vision care. These plans are better known throughout the industry as *Medigap* plans and are usually identified by the word *Medigap* on the patient's plan ID card.

FIGURE 13-1 Mock-up of an insurance FEP PPO plan identification card.

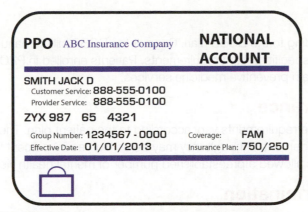

FIGURE 13-2 Mock-up of an insurance card with suitcase logo.

Health Care Anywhere

Health care anywhere is a concept that allows members of BCBS plans to access health care benefits throughout the United States and around the world, depending on their home plan benefits. A blank suitcase symbol on the member's identification card indicates out-of-area coverage, and covered procedures and services are reimbursed according to the member's benefit plan (Figure 13-2). Generally, the **BlueCard**® program enables members to obtain health care services while traveling or living in another BCBS plan's service area (within the United States or in another country) and to receive the benefits of their home plan contract and to access local provider networks. **GeoBlue**® is international health care coverage for employers, including non-profit organizations, individuals, and U.S. and non-U.S. academic institution faculty, students, or staff and who are short-term travelers and long-term expatriates. **BlueCross BlueShield Global**® includes health care plans for employers, individuals, and students who live, work, and travel internationally; it represents a collaboration with *Bupa Global* (an insurance company based in Europe) to offer international health insurance plans to individuals at home or who live, study, travel or work abroad, including expatriates.

BlueCross BlueShield Billing Notes

A summary follows of nationwide billing issues for traditional BCBS fee-for-service claims. Participating providers are required to submit claims for members.

Claims Processing

Claims for BCBS patients are submitted to the local BCBS company for processing (and not to the patient's "home" BCBS plan).

> **Example:** August Rodriguez's home health insurance coverage is an employer group health plan (EGHP) through Western New York (WNY) BCBS, which is located in Buffalo, New York. August receives health care services from a local physician in Syracuse, New York, because that is the city in which August works and resides. The physician's office submits claims to Central BCBS in Syracuse, which contacts WNY BCBS to determine contractual coverage and reimbursement rates for treatment provided to August.

Deadline for Submitting Claims

The general deadline is customarily one year from the date of service, unless otherwise specified in the member's or provider's contracts.

Claim Used

BCBS payers accept the CMS-1500 claim for professional services (and the UB-04 claim for institutional services).

Inpatient and Outpatient Coverage

Inpatient and outpatient coverage may vary according to the plan. Many plans require second surgical opinions and prior authorization for elective hospitalizations. Information on the individual program requirements can be obtained from each BCBS payer.

Deductible

The deductible will vary according to the BCBS plan. Consult the BCBS billing manual or eligibility status computerized phone bank for specific patient requirements. Patients enrolled in PPO plans may have no applicable deductibles for certain preventive medicine services.

Copayment/Coinsurance

Patient copayment/coinsurance requirements vary according to the patient plan. The most common coinsurance amounts are 20 percent or 25 percent, although they may be as high as 50 percent for mental health services on some policies. (The member is allowed a preestablished number of mental health visits.)

Allowable Fee Determination

The allowable fee varies according to the plan. Many corporations use the physician fee schedule to determine the allowed fees for each procedure. Other plans use a **usual, customary, and reasonable (UCR)** basis, which is the amount commonly charged for a particular medical service by providers within a particular geographic region for establishing their allowable rates. UCR charges that are submitted by providers contribute to national pricing databases that identify provider charges according to specialty and services in the same geographic locations. Participating providers must accept the allowable rate on all covered services and write off or adjust the difference or balance between the plan-determined allowed amount and the amount billed. Patients are responsible for any deductible and copay/coinsurance described in the policy, as well as full charges for uncovered services.

The remittance advice sent to participating provider (PAR) and preferred provider network (PPN) providers clearly states the patient's total deductible and copayment/coinsurance responsibility for each claim submission.

Nonparticipating providers (NonPARs) may collect the full fee from the patient. BCBS payments are then sent directly to the patient.

Assignment of Benefits

All claims filed by participating providers qualify for an *assignment of benefits* to the provider. This means that payment is made directly to the provider by BCBS.

Special Handling

The following special handling guidelines should be followed:

1. Make it a habit and priority to retain a current photocopy of the front and back of all patient insurance plan ID cards in the patient's file.
2. Resubmit claims not paid within 30 days.
3. Some mental health claims are forwarded to a *third-party administrator (TPA)* that provides administrative services for health care plans and specializes in mental health case management. Check the back of the ID card and billing manual for special instructions.

BlueCross BlueShield Claims Instructions

The claims instructions (Table 13-1) in this section are used for completing primary BCBS claims. (At the end of the chapter, you will find instructions for completing secondary and supplemental claims.)

BCBS has primary claim status when the patient is:

- Covered by only one BCBS plan
- Covered by a BCBS employer-group health plan (EGHP) and a government plan (e.g., Medicaid)
- Covered by a BCBS EGHP and an individual commercial plan
- Designated as the policyholder of a BCBS EGHP and is also listed as a dependent on another EGHP (that may or may not be a BCBS plan)

Your instructor may substitute local requirements for specific CMS-1500 blocks. *Enter these local instructions in the margins of this text for quick reference when working with case study assignments that are to be graded by the instructor.*

 NOTE:

As you review the CMS-1500 claims instructions in Table 13-1, refer to the John Q. Public case study (Figure 13-3) and completed CMS-1500 claim (Figure 13-4). The completed claim will also assist you when you begin work on Exercise 13.1.

Insurance companies frequently change billing rules and instructions. Obtain updates from a variety of sources (e.g., professional publications, Internet-based listservs, and payer websites).

- Refer to Chapter 11 for clarification of claims completion (e.g., entering names, mailing addresses, ICD-10-CM codes, diagnosis pointer letters, NPI, and so on).

TABLE 13-1 CMS-1500 claims completion instructions for BCBS fee-for-service plans

Block	Instructions
1	Enter an X in the *Other* box if the patient is covered by an individual or family health plan. Or, enter an X in the *Group Health Plan* box if the patient is covered by a group health plan. **Note:** The patient is covered by a group health plan if a group number is printed on the patient's insurance identification card (or a group number is included on case studies located in this textbook, workbook, and SimClaim™ software). *Other* indicates automobile, commercial, health maintenance organization (and managed care), liability, or workers' compensation insurance.
1a	Enter the BCBS plan identification number as it appears on the patient's insurance card. *Do not enter hyphens or spaces in the number.*
2	Enter the patient's last name, first name, and middle initial (separated by commas) (e.g., DOE, JANE, M).
3	Enter the patient's birth date as MM DD YYYY (with spaces). Enter an X in the appropriate box to indicate the patient's sex. If the patient's sex is unknown, leave blank.
4	Enter the policyholder's last name, first name, and middle initial (separated by commas).
5	Enter the patient's mailing address. Enter the street address on line 1, enter the city and state on line 2, and enter the five- or nine-digit zip code on line 3. *Do not enter the hyphen or a space for a 9-digit ZIP code. Do not enter the telephone number.*
6	Enter an X in the appropriate box to indicate the patient's relationship to the policyholder. If the patient is an unmarried domestic partner, enter an X in the *Other* box.
7	If the patient's address is the same as the policyholder's address, leave blank. Otherwise, enter the policyholder's mailing address. Enter the street address on line 1, enter the city and state on line 2, and enter the five- or nine-digit zip code on line 3. *Do not enter the hyphen or a space for a 9-digit ZIP code. Do not enter the telephone number.*
8	Leave blank.
9, 9a, 9d	Leave blank. *Blocks 9, 9a, and 9d are completed if the patient has secondary insurance coverage (discussed later in this chapter).*
9b–9c	Leave blank.
10a–c	Enter an X in the appropriate boxes to indicate whether the patient's condition is related to employment, an automobile accident, and/or another accident. If an X is entered in the YES box for auto accident, enter the two-character state abbreviation of the patient's residence.
10d	Leave blank.
11	Enter the policyholder's BCBS group number if the patient is covered by a group health plan. *Do not enter hyphens or spaces in the policy or group number.* Otherwise, leave blank.
11a	Enter the policyholder's birth date as MM DD YYYY (with spaces). Enter an X in the appropriate box to indicate the policyholder's sex. If the policyholder's sex is unknown, leave blank.
11b	Leave blank. This is reserved for property and casualty or worker's compensation claims.

(continues)

TABLE 13-1 (continued)

Block	Instructions
11c	Enter the name of the policyholder's BCBS health insurance plan.
11d	Enter an X in the NO box. *Block 11d is completed by entering an X in the YES box if the patient has secondary insurance coverage (discussed later in this chapter).*
12	Enter SIGNATURE ON FILE. Leave the date field blank. (The abbreviation SOF is also acceptable.)
13	Leave blank. *Assignment of benefits is a provision of BCBS contracts signed by policyholders, which authorizes BCBS to reimburse providers directly for plan benefits.*
14	Enter the date as MM DD YY (with spaces) to indicate when the patient first experienced signs or symptoms of the present illness, actual date of injury, *or* the date of the last menstrual period (LMP) for obstetric visits. Enter the applicable qualifier to identify which date is being reported: 431 (onset of current symptoms/illness or injury) or 484 (last menstrual period). *If the date is not documented in the patient's record, but the history indicates an appropriate date (e.g., three weeks ago), simply count back to the approximate date and enter it on the claim.*
15–16	Leave blank.
17	If applicable, enter the first name, middle initial (if known), last name, and credentials of the professional who referred, ordered, or supervised health care service(s) or supply(ies) reported on the claim. *Do not enter any punctuation.* In front of the name, enter the applicable qualifier to identify which provider is being reported, as follows: DN (referring provider), DK (ordering provider), or DQ (supervising provider). Otherwise, leave blank.
17a	Leave blank.
17b	Enter the 10-digit national provider identifier (NPI) of the provider entered in Block 17. Otherwise, leave blank.
18	Enter the admission date and discharge date as MM DD YY (with spaces) if the patient received inpatient services (e.g., hospital, skilled nursing facility). Otherwise, leave blank. *If the patient has not been discharged at the time the claim is completed, leave the discharge date blank.*
19	Leave blank.
20	Enter an X in the NO box if all laboratory procedures reported on the claim were performed in the provider's office. Otherwise, enter an X in the YES box and enter the total amount charged by the outside laboratory in $ CHARGES. Also enter the outside laboratory's name, mailing address, and NPI in Block 32. (Charges are entered *without* punctuation. For example, $1,100.00 is entered as 110000 below $ CHARGES.)
21	Enter the ICD-10-CM code for up to 12 diagnoses or conditions treated or medically managed during the encounter. Lines A through L in Block 21 will relate to CPT or HCPCS Level II service or procedure codes reported in Block 24E. In the *ICD Ind* (ICD indicator) box, enter 0 for ICD-10-CM.
22	Leave blank. Reserved for resubmitted claims.
23	Enter prior authorization number, referral number, mammography precertification number, or Clinical Laboratory Improvement Amendments (CLIA) number, as assigned by the payer for the current service. *Do not enter hyphens or spaces in the number.* Otherwise, leave blank.
24A	Enter the date the procedure or service was performed in the FROM column as MM DD YY (with spaces). Enter a date in the TO column *if the procedure or service was performed on consecutive days during a range of dates. Then, enter the number of consecutive days in Block 24G.* Note: The shaded area in each line is used to enter supplemental information to support reported services *if instructed by the payer to enter such information.* Data entry in Block 24 is limited to reporting six services. *Do not use the shaded lines to report additional services.* If additional services were provided, generate new CMS-1500 claim(s) to report the additional services.
24B	Enter the appropriate two-digit place-of-service (POS) code to identify the location where the reported procedure or service was performed.
24C	Leave blank.
24D	Enter the CPT or HCPCS Level II code and applicable required modifier(s) for procedures or services performed. *Separate the CPT/HCPCS code and first modifier with one space. Separate additional modifiers with one space each. Up to four modifiers can be entered.*

(continues)

TABLE 13-1 (continued)

Block	Instructions
24E	Enter the diagnosis pointer letter(s) from Block 21 that relate to the procedure or service performed on the date of service to justify medical necessity of procedures and services reported on the claim.
24F	Enter the fee charged for each reported procedure or service. *Do not enter commas, periods, or dollar signs. Do not enter negative amounts. Enter 00 in the cents area if the amount is a whole number.*
24G	Enter the number of days or units for procedures or services reported in Block 24D. *If just one procedure or service was reported in Block 24D, enter a 1 in Block 24G.*
24H	Leave blank. This is reserved for Medicaid claims.
24I	Leave blank. The NPI abbreviation is preprinted on the CMS-1500 claim.
24J	Enter the 10-digit NPI for the: • Provider who performed the service *if the provider is a member of a group practice.* (Leave blank if the provider is a solo practitioner.) • Supervising provider *if the service was provided incident-to the service of a physician or nonphysician practitioner* **and** *the physician or practitioner who ordered the service did not supervise the provider.* (Leave blank if the incident-to service was performed under the supervision of the physician or nonphysician practitioner.) • DMEPOS supplier or outside laboratory *if the physician submits the claim for services provided by the DMEPOS supplier or outside laboratory.* (Leave blank if the DMEPOS supplier or outside laboratory submits the claim.) Otherwise, leave blank.
25	Enter the provider's Social Security number (SSN) or employer identification number (EIN). *Do not enter hyphens or spaces in the number.* Enter an X in the appropriate box to indicate which number is reported.
26	Enter the patient's account number as assigned by the provider.
27	Enter an X in the YES box to indicate that the provider agrees to accept assignment. Otherwise, enter an X in the NO box.
28	Enter the total charges for services and/or procedures reported in Block 24. **Note:** If multiple claims are submitted for one patient because more than six procedures or services were reported, be sure the total charge reported on each claim accurately represents the total of the items on each submitted claim.
29–30	Leave blank.
31	Enter the provider's name and credential (e.g., MARY SMITH MD) and the date the claim was completed as MMDDYY (without spaces). *Do not enter any punctuation.*
32	Enter the name and address where procedures or services were provided *if at a location other than the provider's office or the patient's home, such as a hospital, outside laboratory facility, skilled nursing facility, or DMEPOS supplier.* Otherwise, leave blank. Enter the name on line 1, the address on line 2, and the city, state, and five- or nine-digit zip code on line 3. *Do not enter the hyphen or a space for a 9-digit ZIP code.* **Note:** If Block 18 contains dates of service for inpatient care and/or Block 20 contains an X in the YES box, enter the name and address of the facility that provided services.
32a	Enter the 10-digit NPI of the facility entered in Block 32.
32b	Leave blank.
33	Enter the provider's *billing* name, address, and telephone number. Enter the phone number in the area next to the block title. *Do not enter parentheses for the area code.* Enter the provider's name on line 1, enter the address on line 2, and enter the city, state, and nine-digit zip code on line 3. *Do not enter the hyphen or a space for a 9-digit ZIP code.*
33a	Enter the 10-digit NPI of the *billing* provider (e.g., solo practitioner) or group practice (e.g., clinic).
33b	Leave blank.

Courtesy of the Centers for Medicare & Medicaid Services, www.cms.gov.

ERIN A. HELPER, M.D.
101 Medic Drive, Anywhere, NY 12345-9874
(101) 111-1234 (Office) • (101) 111-9292 (Fax)
EIN: 11-1234523
NPI: 1234567890

Case Study

PATIENT INFORMATION:

Name:	Public, John Q.
Address:	10A Senate Avenue
City:	Anywhere
State:	NY
Zip Code:	12345-1234
Telephone:	(101) 201-7891
Sex:	Male
Date of Birth:	03-09-1945
Occupation:	Supervisor
Employer:	Legal Research Inc

INSURANCE INFORMATION:

Patient Number:	13-1
Place of Service:	Office
Primary Insurance Plan:	BlueCross BlueShield
Primary Insurance Plan ID #:	WW123456
Group #:	50698
Primary Policyholder:	Public, John Q.
Policyholder Date of Birth:	03-09-1945
Relationship to Patient:	Self
Secondary Insurance Plan:	
Secondary Insurance Plan ID #:	
Secondary Policyholder:	

Patient Status   ☒ Married   ☐ Divorced   ☐ Single   ☐ Student

DIAGNOSIS INFORMATION

Diagnosis	Code	Diagnosis	Code
1. Bronchopneumonia	J18.0	5.	
2. Urinary frequency	R35.0	6.	
3.		7.	
4.		8.	

PROCEDURE INFORMATION

Description of Procedure or Service	Date	Code	Charge
1. Established patient office visit, level III	01-12-YY	99213	75.00
2. Urinalysis, dipstick, automatic microscopy	01-12-YY	81001	10.00
3. Chest x-ray, 2 views	01-12-YY	71046	50.00
4.			
5.			

SPECIAL NOTES: Recheck 01-19-YY. Referring Physician: Ivan Gooddoc, M.D. (NPI 3456789012).

FIGURE 13-3 John Q. Public case study.

HEALTH INSURANCE CLAIM FORM

APPROVED BY NATIONAL UNIFORM CLAIM COMMITTEE (NUCC) 02/12

| | | | | PICA | | | | | | PICA | |

1. MEDICARE (Medicare#)	MEDICAID (Medicaid#)	TRICARE (ID#/DoD#)	CHAMPVA (Member ID#)	GROUP HEALTH PLAN (ID#) [X]	FECA BLKLUNG (ID#)	OTHER (ID#)	1a. INSURED'S I.D. NUMBER (For Program in Item 1)

1a. INSURED'S I.D. NUMBER: WW123456

2. PATIENT'S NAME (Last Name, First Name, Middle Initial)
PUBLIC, JOHN, Q

3. PATIENT'S BIRTH DATE MM 03 DD 09 YY 1945 SEX M [X] F

4. INSURED'S NAME (Last Name, First Name, Middle Initial)
PUBLIC, JOHN, Q

5. PATIENT'S ADDRESS (No., Street)
10A SENATE AVENUE

6. PATIENT RELATIONSHIP TO INSURED
Self [X] Spouse Child Other

7. INSURED'S ADDRESS (No., Street)

CITY ANYWHERE **STATE** NY

8. RESERVED FOR NUCC USE

CITY **STATE**

ZIP CODE 123451234 **TELEPHONE (Include Area Code)** ( )

ZIP CODE **TELEPHONE (Include Area Code)** ( )

9. OTHER INSURED'S NAME (Last Name, First Name, Middle Initial)

10. IS PATIENT'S CONDITION RELATED TO:

11. INSURED'S POLICY GROUP OR FECA NUMBER
50698

a. OTHER INSURED'S POLICY OR GROUP NUMBER

a. EMPLOYMENT? (Current or Previous) YES NO [X]

a. INSURED'S DATE OF BIRTH MM 03 DD 09 YY 1945 SEX M [X] F

b. RESERVED FOR NUCC USE

b. AUTO ACCIDENT? YES NO [X] PLACE (State)

b. OTHER CLAIM ID (Designated by NUCC)

c. RESERVED FOR NUCC USE

c. OTHER ACCIDENT? YES NO [X]

c. INSURANCE PLAN NAME OR PROGRAM NAME
BLUECROSS BLUESHIELD

d. INSURANCE PLAN NAME OR PROGRAM NAME

10d. CLAIM CODES (Designated by NUCC)

d. IS THERE ANOTHER HEALTH BENEFIT PLAN? YES NO [X] If yes, complete items 9, 9a. and 9d.

READ BACK OF FORM BEFORE COMPLETING & SIGNING THIS FORM.
12. PATIENT'S OR AUTHORIZED PERSON'S SIGNATURE I authorize the release of any medical or other information necessary to process this claim. I also request payment of government benefits either to myself or to the party who accepts assignment below.

SIGNED **SIGNATURE ON FILE** DATE

13. INSURED'S OR AUTHORIZED PERSON'S SIGNATURE I authorize payment of medical benefits to the undersigned physician or supplier for services described below.

SIGNED

14. DATE OF CURRENT ILLNESS, INJURY, or PREGNANCY (LMP) MM 01 DD 12 YY QUAL. 431

15. OTHER DATE QUAL. MM DD YY

16. DATES PATIENT UNABLE TO WORK IN CURRENT OCCUPATION FROM MM DD YY TO MM DD YY

17. NAME OF REFERRING PROVIDER OR OTHER SOURCE DN IVAN GOODOC MD
17a.
17b. NPI 3456789012

18. HOSPITALIZATION DATES RELATED TO CURRENT SERVICES FROM MM DD YY TO MM DD YY

19. ADDITIONAL CLAIM INFORMATION (Designated by NUCC)

20. OUTSIDE LAB? YES NO [X] $ CHARGES

21. DIAGNOSIS OR NATURE OF ILLNESS OR INJURY Relate A-L to service line below (24E) ICD Ind. 0

A. J180 B. R350 C. D.
E. F. G. H.
I. J. K. L.

22. RESUBMISSION CODE ORIGINAL REF. NO.

23. PRIOR AUTHORIZATION NUMBER

24. A. DATE(S) OF SERVICE From MM DD YY	To MM DD YY	B. PLACE OF SERVICE	C. EMG	D. PROCEDURES, SERVICES, OR SUPPLIES (Explain Unusual Circumstances) CPT/HCPCS | MODIFIER	E. DIAGNOSIS POINTER	F. $ CHARGES	G. DAYS OR UNITS	H. EPSDT Family Plan	I. ID. QUAL.	J. RENDERING PROVIDER ID. #
1	01 12 YY		11		99213	AB	75 00	1		NPI	
2	01 12 YY		11		81001	B	10 00	1		NPI	
3	01 12 YY		11		71020	A	50 00	1		NPI	
4										NPI	
5										NPI	
6										NPI	

25. FEDERAL TAX I.D. NUMBER 111234523 SSN EIN [X]

26. PATIENT'S ACCOUNT NO. 13-1

27. ACCEPT ASSIGNMENT? YES [X] NO

28. TOTAL CHARGE $ 135 00

29. AMOUNT PAID $

30. Rsvd for NUCC Use

31. SIGNATURE OF PHYSICIAN OR SUPPLIER INCLUDING DEGREES OR CREDENTIALS (I certify that the statements on the reverse apply to this bill and are made a part thereof.)
ERIN A HELPER MD MMDDYY
SIGNED DATE

32. SERVICE FACILITY LOCATION INFORMATION
a. NPI b.

33. BILLING PROVIDER INFO & PH # (101) 1111234
ERIN A HELPER MD
101 MEDIC DRIVE
ANYWHERE NY 123459874
a. 1234567890 b.

NUCC Instruction Manual available at: www.nucc.org **PLEASE PRINT OR TYPE**

FIGURE 13-4 Completed John Q. Public claim.

Exercise 13.1 – Completing a BCBS as Primary CMS-1500 Claim

1. Obtain a blank claim by making a copy of the CMS-1500 claim form in Appendix I.
2. Review the Mary S. Patient case study (Figure 13-5).
3. Select the information needed from the case study, and enter the required information on the claim.
4. Review the completed claim to be sure all required blocks are completed accurately.
5. Compare your claim with the completed Mary S. Patient claim (Figure 13-6).

ERIN A. HELPER, M.D.
101 Medic Drive, Anywhere, NY 12345-9874
(101) 111-1234 (Office) • (101) 111-9292 (Fax)
EIN: 11-1234523
NPI: 1234567890

Case Study

PATIENT INFORMATION:

Name:	Patient, Mary S.
Address:	91 Home Street
City:	Nowhere
State:	NY
Zip Code:	12367-1234
Telephone:	(101) 201-8989
Sex:	Female
Date of Birth:	10-10-1959
Occupation:	Manager
Employer:	Happy Farm Day Care

INSURANCE INFORMATION:

Patient Number:	13-2
Place of Service:	Office
Primary Insurance Plan:	BlueCross BlueShield
Primary Insurance Plan ID #:	WWW1023456
Primary Policyholder:	Mary S. Patient
Policyholder Date of Birth:	10-10-1959
Relationship to Patient:	Self
Secondary Insurance Plan:	
Secondary Insurance Plan ID #:	
Secondary Policyholder:	

Patient Status   ☒ Married   ☐ Divorced   ☐ Single   ☐ Student

DIAGNOSIS INFORMATION

Diagnosis		Code	Diagnosis		Code
1.	Strep throat	J02.0	5.		
2.	Type 1 diabetes mellitus	E10.9	6.		
3.			7.		
4.			8.		

PROCEDURE INFORMATION

	Description of Procedure or Service	Date	Code	Charge
1.	Office visit, level II	01-12-YY	99212	65.00
2.	Strep test	01-12-YY	87880	12.00
3.				
4.				
5.				

SPECIAL NOTES:

FIGURE 13-5 Mary S. Patient case study.

HEALTH INSURANCE CLAIM FORM

APPROVED BY NATIONAL UNIFORM CLAIM COMMITTEE (NUCC) 02/12

Courtesy of the Centers for Medicare & Medicaid Services, www.cms.gov; claim data created by author.

| | PICA | | | | | | | PICA | |

1. MEDICARE ☐ (Medicare#) MEDICAID ☐ (Medicaid#) TRICARE ☐ (ID#/DoD#) CHAMPVA ☐ (Member ID#) GROUP HEALTH PLAN ☐ (ID#) FECA BLKLUNG ☐ (ID#) OTHER ☒ (ID#)

1a. INSURED'S I.D. NUMBER (For Program in Item 1)
WWW1023456

2. PATIENT'S NAME (Last Name, First Name, Middle Initial)
PATIENT, MARY, S

3. PATIENT'S BIRTH DATE MM 10 DD 10 YY 1959 SEX M ☐ F ☒

4. INSURED'S NAME (Last Name, First Name, Middle Initial)
PATIENT, MARY, S

5. PATIENT'S ADDRESS (No., Street)
91 HOME STREET
CITY NOWHERE STATE NY
ZIP CODE 123671234 TELEPHONE (Include Area Code) ( )

6. PATIENT RELATIONSHIP TO INSURED
Self ☒ Spouse ☐ Child ☐ Other ☐

7. INSURED'S ADDRESS (No., Street)
CITY STATE
ZIP CODE TELEPHONE (Include Area Code) ( )

8. RESERVED FOR NUCC USE

9. OTHER INSURED'S NAME (Last Name, First Name, Middle Initial)

a. OTHER INSURED'S POLICY OR GROUP NUMBER

b. RESERVED FOR NUCC USE

c. RESERVED FOR NUCC USE

d. INSURANCE PLAN NAME OR PROGRAM NAME

10. IS PATIENT'S CONDITION RELATED TO:
a. EMPLOYMENT? (Current or Previous) YES ☐ NO ☒
b. AUTO ACCIDENT? YES ☐ NO ☒ PLACE (State)
c. OTHER ACCIDENT? YES ☐ NO ☒
10d. CLAIM CODES (Designated by NUCC)

11. INSURED'S POLICY GROUP OR FECA NUMBER

a. INSURED'S DATE OF BIRTH MM 10 DD 10 YY 1959 SEX M ☐ F ☒

b. OTHER CLAIM ID (Designated by NUCC)

c. INSURANCE PLAN NAME OR PROGRAM NAME
BLUECROSS BLUESHIELD

d. IS THERE ANOTHER HEALTH BENEFIT PLAN? YES ☐ NO ☒ If yes, complete items 9, 9a, and 9d.

READ BACK OF FORM BEFORE COMPLETING & SIGNING THIS FORM.
12. PATIENT'S OR AUTHORIZED PERSON'S SIGNATURE I authorize the release of any medical or other information necessary to process this claim. I also request payment of government benefits either to myself or to the party who accepts assignment below.
SIGNED **SIGNATURE ON FILE** DATE

13. INSURED'S OR AUTHORIZED PERSON'S SIGNATURE I authorize payment of medical benefits to the undersigned physician or supplier for services described below.
SIGNED

14. DATE OF CURRENT ILLNESS, INJURY, or PREGNANCY (LMP) MM 01 DD 12 YY YY QUAL. 431

15. OTHER DATE QUAL. MM DD YY

16. DATES PATIENT UNABLE TO WORK IN CURRENT OCCUPATION FROM MM DD YY TO MM DD YY

17. NAME OF REFERRING PROVIDER OR OTHER SOURCE
17a.
17b. NPI

18. HOSPITALIZATION DATES RELATED TO CURRENT SERVICES FROM MM DD YY TO MM DD YY

19. ADDITIONAL CLAIM INFORMATION (Designated by NUCC)

20. OUTSIDE LAB? YES ☐ NO ☒ $ CHARGES

21. DIAGNOSIS OR NATURE OF ILLNESS OR INJURY Relate A-L to service line below (24E) ICD Ind. 0
A. J020 B. E109 C. D.
E. F. G. H.
I. J. K. L.

22. RESUBMISSION CODE ORIGINAL REF. NO.

23. PRIOR AUTHORIZATION NUMBER

24. A. DATE(S) OF SERVICE From MM DD YY	To MM DD YY	B. PLACE OF SERVICE	C. EMG	D. PROCEDURES, SERVICES, OR SUPPLIES (Explain Unusual Circumstances) CPT/HCPCS	MODIFIER	E. DIAGNOSIS POINTER	F. $ CHARGES	G. DAYS OR UNITS	H. EPSDT Family Plan	I. ID. QUAL.	J. RENDERING PROVIDER ID. #
1	01 12 YY		11		99212		AB	65 00	1		NPI	
2	01 12 YY		11		87880		A	12 00	1		NPI	
3											NPI	
4											NPI	
5											NPI	
6											NPI	

25. FEDERAL TAX I.D. NUMBER SSN ☐ EIN ☒
111234523

26. PATIENT'S ACCOUNT NO.
13-2

27. ACCEPT ASSIGNMENT? (For govt. claims, see back) ☒ YES ☐ NO

28. TOTAL CHARGE $ 77 00

29. AMOUNT PAID $

30. Rsvd for NUCC Use

31. SIGNATURE OF PHYSICIAN OR SUPPLIER INCLUDING DEGREES OR CREDENTIALS (I certify that the statements on the reverse apply to this bill and are made a part thereof.)
ERIN A HELPER MD MMDDYY
SIGNED DATE

32. SERVICE FACILITY LOCATION INFORMATION
a. NPI b.

33. BILLING PROVIDER INFO & PH # (101) 1111234
ERIN A HELPER MD
101 MEDIC DRIVE
ANYWHERE NY 123459874
a. 1234567890 b.

NUCC Instruction Manual available at: www.nucc.org **PLEASE PRINT OR TYPE**

FIGURE 13-6 Completed Mary S. Patient claim.

BlueCross BlueShield Secondary Coverage Claims Instructions

Modifications are made to the CMS-1500 claim when patients are covered by primary and secondary or supplemental health insurance plans. Secondary health insurance plans provide coverage similar to that of primary health plans, whereas supplemental health plans usually cover only deductible, copayment, and coinsurance expenses.

When the same BCBS payer issues the primary and secondary or supplemental policies (Table 13-2), submit only one CMS-1500 claim (Figure 13-7). If BCBS payers for the primary and secondary or supplemental policies are different (Table 13-3), submit a CMS-1500 claim to the primary payer. After the primary payer processes the claim, generate a second CMS-1500 claim (Figure 13-9) to send to the secondary or supplemental payer and include a copy of the primary payer's remittance advice.

> **NOTE:**
>
> Use these instructions when completing any claims associated with *Understanding Health Insurance.*

TABLE 13-2 Modifications to BCBS primary CMS-1500 claims completion instructions when patient is covered by same BCBS payer for primary and secondary or supplemental plans (Refer to Table 13-1 for primary CMS-1500 claims completion instructions.)

Block	Instructions
9	Enter the secondary or supplemental policyholder's last name, first name, and middle initial (if known) (separated by commas).
9a	Enter the secondary or supplemental policyholder's policy or group number.
9d	Enter the name of the secondary or supplemental policyholder's commercial health insurance plan.
11d	Enter an X in the YES box.

Exercise 13.2 – Completing a BCBS CMS-1500 Claim When a Patient Is Covered by the Same BCBS Payer for Primary and Secondary Policies

1. Obtain a blank claim by making a copy of the CMS-1500 claim form in Appendix I.

2. Underline Blocks 9, 9a, 9d, 11d, and 26 on the claim.

3. Refer to the case study for Mary S. Patient (Figure 13-5). Enter the following information in the appropriate blocks for the secondary policy (Table 13-2):

    BlueCross BlueShield POLICY NO. R152748

    Policyholder: James W. Patient

    Birth date: 03/01/48

    Relationship: Spouse

    Employer: NAVAL STATION

    Add BB to the patient account number in Block 26, entering 13-2BB (to indicate two BCBS policies).

4. Complete the secondary claim on Mary S. Patient using the data from the case study (Figure 13-5), entering claims information in the blocks indicated in step 2.

5. Review the completed claim to be sure all required blocks are properly completed. Compare your claim with Figure 13-7.

HEALTH INSURANCE CLAIM FORM

APPROVED BY NATIONAL UNIFORM CLAIM COMMITTEE (NUCC) 02/12

☐☐☐ PICA | PICA ☐☐☐

| 1. MEDICARE ☐ (Medicare#) | MEDICAID ☐ (Medicaid#) | TRICARE ☐ (ID#/DoD#) | CHAMPVA ☐ (Member ID#) | GROUP HEALTH PLAN ☐ (ID#) | FECA BLKLUNG ☐ (ID#) | OTHER ☒ (ID#) | 1a. INSURED'S I.D. NUMBER (For Program in Item 1) **WWW1023456** |

| 2. PATIENT'S NAME (Last Name, First Name, Middle Initial) **PATIENT, MARY, S** | 3. PATIENT'S BIRTH DATE MM 10 DD 10 YY 1959 SEX M☐ F☒ | 4. INSURED'S NAME (Last Name, First Name, Middle Initial) **PATIENT, MARY, S** |

| 5. PATIENT'S ADDRESS (No., Street) **91 HOME STREET** | 6. PATIENT RELATIONSHIP TO INSURED Self ☒ Spouse ☐ Child ☐ Other ☐ | 7. INSURED'S ADDRESS (No., Street) |

| CITY **NOWHERE** | STATE **NY** | 8. RESERVED FOR NUCC USE | CITY | STATE |

| ZIP CODE **123671234** | TELEPHONE (Include Area Code) ( ) | | ZIP CODE | TELEPHONE (Include Area Code) ( ) |

| 9. OTHER INSURED'S NAME (Last Name, First Name, Middle Initial) **PATIENT, JAMES, W** | 10. IS PATIENT'S CONDITION RELATED TO: | 11. INSURED'S POLICY GROUP OR FECA NUMBER |

| a. OTHER INSURED'S POLICY OR GROUP NUMBER **R152748** | a. EMPLOYMENT? (Current or Previous) YES ☐ NO ☒ | a. INSURED'S DATE OF BIRTH MM 10 DD 10 YY 1959 SEX M☐ F☒ |

| b. RESERVED FOR NUCC USE | b. AUTO ACCIDENT? YES ☐ NO ☒ PLACE (State) | b. OTHER CLAIM ID (Designated by NUCC) |

| c. RESERVED FOR NUCC USE | c. OTHER ACCIDENT? YES ☐ NO ☒ | c. INSURANCE PLAN NAME OR PROGRAM NAME **BLUECROSS BLUESHIELD** |

| d. INSURANCE PLAN NAME OR PROGRAM NAME **BLUECROSS BLUESHIELD** | 10d. CLAIM CODES (Designated by NUCC) | d. IS THERE ANOTHER HEALTH BENEFIT PLAN? YES ☒ NO ☐ *If yes*, complete items 9, 9a, and 9d. |

READ BACK OF FORM BEFORE COMPLETING & SIGNING THIS FORM.

| 12. PATIENT'S OR AUTHORIZED PERSON'S SIGNATURE I authorize the release of any medical or other information necessary to process this claim. I also request payment of government benefits either to myself or to the party who accepts assignment below. SIGNED **SIGNATURE ON FILE** DATE | 13. INSURED'S OR AUTHORIZED PERSON'S SIGNATURE I authorize payment of medical benefits to the undersigned physician or supplier for services described below. SIGNED |

| 14. DATE OF CURRENT ILLNESS, INJURY, or PREGNANCY (LMP) MM 01 DD 12 YY QUAL. 431 | 15. OTHER DATE QUAL. MM DD YY | 16. DATES PATIENT UNABLE TO WORK IN CURRENT OCCUPATION FROM MM DD YY TO MM DD YY |

| 17. NAME OF REFERRING PROVIDER OR OTHER SOURCE | 17a. 17b. NPI | 18. HOSPITALIZATION DATES RELATED TO CURRENT SERVICES FROM MM DD YY TO MM DD YY |

| 19. ADDITIONAL CLAIM INFORMATION (Designated by NUCC) | 20. OUTSIDE LAB? YES ☐ NO ☒ $ CHARGES |

| 21. DIAGNOSIS OR NATURE OF ILLNESS OR INJURY Relate A-L to service line below (24E) ICD Ind. 0 A. **J020** B. **E109** C. D. E. F. G. H. I. J. K. L. | 22. RESUBMISSION CODE ORIGINAL REF. NO. |
| | 23. PRIOR AUTHORIZATION NUMBER |

24. A. DATE(S) OF SERVICE From MM DD YY To MM DD YY	B. PLACE OF SERVICE	C. EMG	D. PROCEDURES, SERVICES, OR SUPPLIES (Explain Unusual Circumstances) CPT/HCPCS MODIFIER	E. DIAGNOSIS POINTER	F. $ CHARGES	G. DAYS OR UNITS	H. EPSDT Family Plan	I. ID. QUAL.	J. RENDERING PROVIDER ID. #
1	01 12 YY	11		99212	AB	65 00	1		NPI	
2	01 12 YY	11		87880	A	12 00	1		NPI	
3									NPI	
4									NPI	
5									NPI	
6									NPI	

| 25. FEDERAL TAX I.D. NUMBER **111234523** SSN☐ EIN☒ | 26. PATIENT'S ACCOUNT NO. **13-2BB** | 27. ACCEPT ASSIGNMENT? (For govt. claims, see back) YES ☒ NO ☐ | 28. TOTAL CHARGE $ **77 00** | 29. AMOUNT PAID $ | 30. Rsvd for NUCC Use |

| 31. SIGNATURE OF PHYSICIAN OR SUPPLIER INCLUDING DEGREES OR CREDENTIALS (I certify that the statements on the reverse apply to this bill and are made a part thereof.) SIGNED **ERIN A HELPER MD** DATE **MMDDYY** | 32. SERVICE FACILITY LOCATION INFORMATION a. NPI b. | 33. BILLING PROVIDER INFO & PH # (**101**) **1111234** **ERIN A HELPER MD** **101 MEDIC DRIVE** **ANYWHERE NY 123459874** a. **1234567890** b. |

NUCC Instruction Manual available at: www.nucc.org

PLEASE PRINT OR TYPE

FIGURE 13-7 Completed Mary S. Patient claim (same BCBS payer for primary and secondary coverage).

TABLE 13-3 Modifications to BCBS secondary CMS-1500 claims completion instructions when patient is covered by BCBS secondary or supplemental plan (and primary payer is *not* BCBS)

Block	Instructions
	Note: If the primary and secondary/supplemental payers are the same, do not generate a second CMS-1500 claim. Refer to Table 13-2 instructions.
1a	Enter the secondary or supplemental policyholder's BCBS identification number as it appears on the insurance card. *Do not enter hyphens or spaces in the number.*
4	Enter the secondary or supplemental policyholder's last name, first name, and middle initial (if known) (separated by commas).
7	If the patient's address is the same as the secondary or supplemental policyholder's address, leave blank. Otherwise, enter the secondary or supplemental policyholder's mailing address. Enter the street address on line 1, enter the city and state on line 2, and enter the five- or nine-digit zip code on line 3. *Do not enter the hyphen or a space in a 9-digit ZIP code. Do not enter the telephone number.*
9	Enter the primary policyholder's last name, first name, and middle initial (if known) (separated by commas).
9a	Enter the primary policyholder's policy or group number. *Do not enter hyphens or spaces in the number.*
9d	Enter the name of the primary policyholder's health insurance plan (e.g., commercial health insurance plan name or government program).
11	Enter the secondary or supplemental policyholder's policy or group number. *Do not enter hyphens or spaces in the policy or group number.*
11a	Enter the secondary or supplemental policyholder's birth date as MM DD YYYY (with spaces). Enter an X in the appropriate box to indicate the policyholder's sex. If the policyholder's sex is unknown, leave blank.
11c	Enter the name of the secondary or supplemental policyholder's BCBS health insurance plan.
11d	Enter an X in the YES box.
29	Enter the reimbursement amount received from the primary payer.

Courtesy of the Centers for Medicare & Medicaid Services, www.cms.gov.

Exercise 13.3 – Completing a BCBS Secondary Claim for BCBS Secondary or Supplemental Plan, When Primary Payer Is *Not* BCBS

1. Obtain a blank claim by making a copy of the CMS-1500 claim form in Appendix I.
2. Underline Blocks 1a, 4, 7, 9, 9d, 11, 11a, 11c, 11d, and 29, and note the entries discussed in Table 13-3. Add an "S" to the patient's account number in Block 26 (e.g., 13-3S).
3. Review Figure 13-8. Complete the BCBS secondary claim for this case using data from the case study.
4. Review the completed claim to be sure all required blocks are properly completed.
5. Compare your claim with Figure 13-9.

ERIN A. HELPER, M.D.
101 Medic Drive, Anywhere, NY 12345-9874
(101) 111-1234 (Office) • (101) 111-9292 (Fax)
EIN: 11-1234523
NPI: 1234567890

Case Study

PATIENT INFORMATION:

Name:	Cross, Janet B.
Address:	1901 Beach Head Drive
City:	Anywhere
State:	NY
Zip Code:	12345-1234
Telephone:	(101) 201-1991
Sex:	Female
Date of Birth:	11-01-1934
Occupation:	Retired
Employer:	

INSURANCE INFORMATION:

Patient Number:	13-3
Place of Service:	Hospital Inpatient
Primary Insurance Plan:	Medicare
Primary Insurance Plan ID #:	1912AA66844
Primary Policyholder:	Cross, Janet B.
Policyholder Date of Birth:	11-01-1934
Relationship to Patient:	Self
Secondary Insurance Plan:	BlueCross BlueShield
Secondary Insurance Plan ID #:	WWW191266844
Secondary Policyholder:	Cross, Janet B.
Relationship to Patient:	Self

Patient Status   ☒ Married   ☐ Divorced   ☐ Single   ☐ Student

DIAGNOSIS INFORMATION

	Diagnosis	Code		Diagnosis	Code
1.	Intracranial hemorrhage	I62.9	5.		
2.	Dysphasia	R47.02	6.		
3.			7.		
4.			8.		

PROCEDURE INFORMATION

	Description of Procedure or Service	Date	Code	Charge
1.	Initial hospital visit, level III	01-13-YY	99223	150.00
2.	Discharge management, 60 minutes	01-14-YY	99239	100.00
3.				
4.				
5.				

SPECIAL NOTES: Patient transferred to University Medical Center via ambulance. Place of service: Goodmedicine Hospital, Anywhere Street, Anywhere, NY 12345 (NPI: 2345678901) Remittance advice received from Medicare indicated payment of $75.00.

FIGURE 13-8 Janet B. Cross case study.

HEALTH INSURANCE CLAIM FORM

APPROVED BY NATIONAL UNIFORM CLAIM COMMITTEE (NUCC) 02/12

□ □ PICA	PICA □ □

1. MEDICARE □ (Medicare#) MEDICAID □ (Medicaid#) TRICARE □ (ID#/DoD#) CHAMPVA □ (Member ID#) GROUP HEALTH PLAN □ (ID#) FECA BLKLUNG □ (ID#) OTHER [X] (ID#)

1a. INSURED'S I.D. NUMBER (For Program in Item 1)
WWW191266844

2. PATIENT'S NAME (Last Name, First Name, Middle Initial)
CROSS, JANET, B

3. PATIENT'S BIRTH DATE MM **11** DD **01** YY **1934** SEX M □ F [X]

4. INSURED'S NAME (Last Name, First Name, Middle Initial)
CROSS, JANET, B

5. PATIENT'S ADDRESS (No., Street)
1901 BEACH HEAD DRIVE

6. PATIENT RELATIONSHIP TO INSURED
Self [X] Spouse □ Child □ Other □

7. INSURED'S ADDRESS (No., Street)

CITY **ANYWHERE** STATE **NY**

8. RESERVED FOR NUCC USE

CITY STATE

ZIP CODE **123451234** TELEPHONE (Include Area Code) ( )

ZIP CODE TELEPHONE (Include Area Code) ( )

9. OTHER INSURED'S NAME (Last Name, First Name, Middle Initial)
CROSS, JANET, B

10. IS PATIENT'S CONDITION RELATED TO:

11. INSURED'S POLICY GROUP OR FECA NUMBER

a. OTHER INSURED'S POLICY OR GROUP NUMBER
1912AA66844

a. EMPLOYMENT? (Current or Previous) YES □ NO [X]

a. INSURED'S DATE OF BIRTH MM **11** DD **01** YY **1934** SEX M □ F [X]

b. RESERVED FOR NUCC USE

b. AUTO ACCIDENT? YES □ NO [X] PLACE (State)

b. OTHER CLAIM ID (Designated by NUCC)

c. RESERVED FOR NUCC USE

c. OTHER ACCIDENT? YES □ NO [X]

c. INSURANCE PLAN NAME OR PROGRAM NAME
BLUECROSS BLUESHIELD

d. INSURANCE PLAN NAME OR PROGRAM NAME
MEDICARE

10d. CLAIM CODES (Designated by NUCC)

d. IS THERE ANOTHER HEALTH BENEFIT PLAN?
[X] YES □ NO **If yes,** complete items 9, 9a, and 9d.

READ BACK OF FORM BEFORE COMPLETING & SIGNING THIS FORM.

12. PATIENT'S OR AUTHORIZED PERSON'S SIGNATURE I authorize the release of any medical or other information necessary to process this claim. I also request payment of government benefits either to myself or to the party who accepts assignment below.

SIGNED **SIGNATURE ON FILE** DATE

13. INSURED'S OR AUTHORIZED PERSON'S SIGNATURE I authorize payment of medical benefits to the undersigned physician or supplier for services described below.

SIGNED

14. DATE OF CURRENT ILLNESS, INJURY, or PREGNANCY (LMP) MM **01** DD **13** YY **YY** QUAL. **431**

15. OTHER DATE QUAL. MM DD YY

16. DATES PATIENT UNABLE TO WORK IN CURRENT OCCUPATION FROM MM DD YY TO MM DD YY

17. NAME OF REFERRING PROVIDER OR OTHER SOURCE

17a.
17b. NPI

18. HOSPITALIZATION DATES RELATED TO CURRENT SERVICES FROM MM **01** DD **13** YY **YY** TO MM **01** DD **14** YY **YY**

19. ADDITIONAL CLAIM INFORMATION (Designated by NUCC)

20. OUTSIDE LAB? YES □ NO [X] $ CHARGES

21. DIAGNOSIS OR NATURE OF ILLNESS OR INJURY Relate A-L to service line below (24E) ICD Ind. **0**

A. **I629** B. **R4702** C. D.
E. F. G. H.
I. J. K. L.

22. RESUBMISSION CODE ORIGINAL REF. NO.

23. PRIOR AUTHORIZATION NUMBER

24. A. DATE(S) OF SERVICE From / To						B. PLACE OF SERVICE	C. EMG	D. PROCEDURES, SERVICES, OR SUPPLIES (Explain Unusual Circumstances) CPT/HCPCS / MODIFIER	E. DIAGNOSIS POINTER	F. $ CHARGES	G. DAYS OR UNITS	H. EPSDT Family Plan	I. ID. QUAL.	J. RENDERING PROVIDER ID. #
MM	DD	YY	MM	DD	YY									
01	13	YY				21		99223	AB	150 00	1		NPI	
01	14	YY				21		99239	AB	100 00	1		NPI	
													NPI	
													NPI	
													NPI	
													NPI	

25. FEDERAL TAX I.D. NUMBER SSN □ EIN [X]
111234523

26. PATIENT'S ACCOUNT NO.
13-3S

27. ACCEPT ASSIGNMENT? (For govt. claims, see back) YES [X] NO □

28. TOTAL CHARGE $ **250 00**

29. AMOUNT PAID $ **75 00**

30. Rsvd for NUCC Use

31. SIGNATURE OF PHYSICIAN OR SUPPLIER INCLUDING DEGREES OR CREDENTIALS (I certify that the statements on the reverse apply to this bill and are made a part thereof.)
ERIN A HELPER MD **MMDDYY**
SIGNED DATE

32. SERVICE FACILITY LOCATION INFORMATION
GOODMEDICINE HOSPITAL
ANYWHERE STREET
ANYWHERE NY 12345
a. **2345678901** b.

33. BILLING PROVIDER INFO & PH # (**101**) **1111234**
ERIN A HELPER MD
101 MEDIC DRIVE
ANYWHERE NY 123459874
a. **1234567890** b.

PLEASE PRINT OR TYPE

CARRIER PATIENT AND INSURED INFORMATION PHYSICIAN OR SUPPLIER INFORMATION

FIGURE 13-9 Completed Janet B. Cross BCBS secondary payer claim (when BCBS is not the primary payer).

Summary

BlueCross plans were initiated in 1929 and originally provided coverage for hospital bills, whereas BlueShield was created in 1938 and originally covered fees for physician services. BlueCross and BlueShield (BCBS) plans entered into joint ventures that increased coverage of almost all health care services, and the BlueCross BlueShield Association (BCBSA) was created in 1986 when the separate BlueCross association merged with the BlueShield association. The BCBS plans were pioneers in nonprofit, prepaid health care; and competition among all health insurance payers in the United States resulted in further mergers. BCBS negotiates contracts with network providers who are designated *participating providers (PARs)*. PARs are eligible to contract with preferred provider networks and qualify for assignment of benefits. BCBS plans include fee-for-service, indemnity, managed care, Federal Employee Program®, Medicare supplemental, and BCBS Global® plans.

When completing BCBS CMS-1500 claims for exercises in the textbook, assignments in the workbook, and case studies in SimClaim™, the following special instructions apply:

- Block 12—Enter SIGNATURE ON FILE, and leave date blank.
- Block 20—Enter an X in the *NO* box.
- Block 23—Leave blank.
- Block 24E—Enter diagnosis pointer(s) on each line.
- Block 26—Enter the case study number (e.g., 13-4). If the patient has both primary and secondary coverage, enter a P (for primary) next to the case study number (on the primary claim) and an S (for secondary) next to the number (on the secondary claim); if the same BCBS plan provides both primary and secondary coverage, enter a BB next to the case study number.
- Block 27—Enter an X in the *YES* box.
- When completing secondary claims, enter REMITTANCE ADVICE ATTACHED in the top margin of the CMS-1500 claim (to simulate the attachment of a primary payer's remittance advice with a claim submitted to a secondary payer).

Internet Links

- **BCBS Federal Employee Program®: *fepblue.org***
- **BlueCross BlueShield: *bcbs.com***
- **BlueCross BlueShield Global®: *bcbsglobal.com***
- **Bupa Global: *bupaglobal.com***
- **GeoBlue®: *about.geo-blue.com***

Review

Multiple Choice

Instructions: Select the most appropriate response.

1. BCBS preferred provider networks are responsible for
   a. assessing continued appropriateness of care and medical necessity, and beginning discharge planning.
   b. ensuring that members receive accessible, appropriate, cost-effective, and quality health care services.
   c. evaluating accessibility, appropriateness, cost-effectiveness, medical necessity, and quality of health care.
   d. reviewing health care procedures and services before health care delivery for prior authorization purposes.

2. Patients who receive coordinated home health care program services must require
   a. custodial care, extended long-term care, hearing aids, routine dental care, or vision care.
   b. extended hospital coverage, such as transfer to a rehabilitation center or a nursing home.
   c. preauthorization of outpatient physical, occupational, and speech therapy services.
   d. skilled nursing services on an intermittent basis under the primary care provider's direction.

3. Patients who receive care from _____ providers can expect to pay higher costs.
   a. fee-for-service
   b. non-network
   c. participating
   d. prepaid

4. Which service is provided as part of BCBS basic coverage?
   a. Dental
   b. Hearing aids
   c. Prescription drugs
   d. Weight management

5. Which service is provided as part of BCBS major medical coverage *only*?
   a. Inpatient hospital
   b. Mental health
   c. Pregnancy and childbirth
   d. Vision

6. Traditional fee-for-service plans provide reimbursement to providers
   a. according to a fee schedule after procedures have been performed or services provided to members.
   b. on a discounted basis because they provide services to BCBS members who are not part of a PPO network.
   c. that are considered the patient's primary care provider, which is often referred to as the gatekeeper.
   d. who receive capitated payments and are responsible for providing health care services to members.

7. BCBS indemnity provide members with the option to receive care from any provider, and they may cost _____ than other health plans, such as fee-for-service and managed care plans.
   a. less
   b. more

8. The preauthorization of physical, occupational, and speech therapy services is a requirement for BCBS managed care plans as part of its _____ program.
   a. coordinated home health care
   b. fee-for-service
   c. outpatient pretreatment authorization
   d. second surgical opinion

9. Which phrase is located on a Federal Employee Program® insurance identification card?
   a. Access to Broad Provider Network
   b. Federal Employees Health Benefits (FEHB) Program
   c. Government-Wide Service Benefit Plan
   d. Standard and Basic Option

10. Which symbol is included on a BCBS identification card to indicate that members selected plans that allow them to access health care benefits throughout the United States and around the world?
    a. Blue shield
    b. Caduceus
    c. R$_x$
    d. Suitcase

11. BlueCross BlueShield claims filed by participating providers qualify for *assignment of benefits*, which means payment is made directly to the
    a. guarantor.
    b. patient.
    c. payer.
    d. provider.

12. When entering the provider's Social Security number (SSN) or employer identification number (EIN) in Block 25 of the CMS-1500 claim, a
    a. hyphen is entered.
    b. hyphen is not entered.
    c. space is entered instead of a hyphen.
    d. space or hyphen is entered.

13. When the same BCBS payer issues the primary and secondary or supplemental policies, submit _____ CMS-1500 claim(s).
    a. one combined
    b. two separate

14. When a patient receives professional services from a provider in the office setting and BCBS payers for the member's primary and secondary policies are different companies, submit
    a. both CMS-1500 claims to the primary and secondary payers at the same time, entering data in Blocks 11 through 11d on the first claim and 9, 9a, and 9d on the second claim.
    b. one single CMS-1500 claim to both the primary payer and the secondary payers, and be sure to enter data in Blocks 9, 9a, 9d, and 11, 11a, 11b, 11c, and 11d on the claim.
    c. the CMS-1500 claim to the primary payer, and then after payment, submit a second claim to the secondary payer with a copy of the primary payer's remittance advice.
    d. UB-04 (CMS-1450) claims because when a patient receives professional services from a provider in an office setting, BCBS require services to be classified as institutional services.

15. BCBS is considered secondary when the patient is covered by a
    a. BCBS EGHP plan and an individual commercial plan.
    b. Medicaid plan and a BCBS employer-group health plan.
    c. Medicare plan and a BCBS supplemental Medigap plan.
    d. single BCBS plan that the patient purchased privately.

Chapter

14

Medicare

Chapter Outline

Medicare Eligibility and Enrollment

Medicare Coverage

Medicare Participating, Nonparticipating, and
   Opt-Out Providers

Advance Beneficiary Notice of Noncoverage

Medicare as Primary and Secondary Payer

Medicare Summary Notice

Medicare Billing Notes

Medicare Claims Instructions

Medicare and Medigap Claims Instructions

Medicare-Medicaid (Medi-Medi) Crossover
   Claims Instructions

Medicare as Secondary Payer Claims
   Instructions

Medicare Roster Billing for Mass Vaccination
   Programs Claims Instructions

Chapter Objectives

Upon successful completion of this chapter, you should be able to:

1. Define key terms related to Medicare.

2. Explain Medicare eligibility and enrollment guidelines.

3. Explain the characteristics of different types of Medicare coverage, including calculation of coinsurance/copayments for hospital outpatient services.

4. Differentiate among participating, nonparticipating, and opt-out providers.

5. Recognize when a Medicare advance beneficiary notice of noncoverage is required.

6. Distinguish between Medicare as primary payer and Medicare as secondary payer.

7. Describe the purpose of a Medicare Summary Notice.

8. Describe Medicare billing notes when completing CMS-1500 claims.

9. Complete Medicare primary claims.

10. Complete Medicare and Medigap claims.

11. Complete Medicare-Medicaid (Medi-Medi) crossover claims.

12. Complete Medicare as secondary claims.

13. Complete Medicare roster billing claims.

Key Terms

accountable care organization (ACO)

advance beneficiary notice of noncoverage (ABN)

benefit period

conditional primary payer status

demonstration/pilot program

diagnostic cost group hierarchical condition category (DCG/HCC) risk adjustment model

drug formulary

employer-sponsored group health plan (EGHP)

end-stage renal disease (ESRD)

general enrollment period (GEP)

hospice

initial enrollment period (IEP)

lifetime reserve days

mass immunizer

medical necessity denial

Medicare

Medicare Advantage

Medicare-approved amount

Medicare beneficiary identifier (MBI)

Medicare Cost Plan

Medicare Hospital Insurance

Medicare-Medicaid (Medi-Medi) crossover

Medicare Medical Insurance

Medicare medical savings account (MSA)

Medicare Outpatient Observation Notice (MOON)

Medicare Part A

Medicare Part B

Medicare Part C

Medicare Part D

Medicare Part D coverage gap

Medicare Part D "donut hole"

Medicare Part D sponsor

Medicare Prescription Drug Coverage

Medicare private contract

Medicare Savings Program (MSP)

Medicare Secondary Payer (MSP)

Medicare SELECT

Medicare Shared Savings Program (MSSP)

Medicare special needs plans (SNP)

Medicare Supplementary Insurance (MSI)

Medication Therapy Management Programs

Medigap

opt-out provider

Original Medicare

palliative care

private fee-for-service (PFFS)

Programs of All-inclusive Care for the Elderly (PACE)

qualified disabled working individual (QDWI)

qualified Medicare beneficiary program (QMBP)

qualifying individual (QI)

respite care

risk adjustment

risk adjustment data validation (RADV)

roster billing

special enrollment period (SEP)

specified low-income Medicare beneficiary (SLMB)

spell of illness

Introduction

Medicare, the largest single health care program in the United States, is a federal health program authorized by Congress and administered by the Centers for Medicare and Medicaid Services for people who are 65 or older, certain younger people with disabilities, and people with **end-stage renal disease (ESRD)** (permanent kidney failure requiring dialysis or a transplant). CMS is responsible for the operation of the Medicare program and for selecting Medicare administrative contractors (MACs) to process Medicare Part A, Part B, and durable medicine equipment (DME) claims. (**Original Medicare** includes Medicare Part A and Part B.)

CMS establishes contracts with *Medicare Part C (Medicare Advantage)* plan sponsors, such as private insurance companies, and pays them a set monthly managed care capitation rate; thus, claims are not submitted by providers. CMS also establishes contracts with *Medicare Part D (Prescription Drug Coverage)* plan sponsors, such as private insurance companies and other private companies, and claims are submitted by pharmacies to plan sponsors for processing. The Medicare Prescription Drug, Improvement, and Modernization Act of 2003 (MMA) created *Medicare administrative contractors (MACs)*, which replaced carriers and fiscal intermediaries and process both Medicare Part A and Part B claims. Medicare includes:

- **Medicare Part A** (**Medicare Hospital Insurance**) helps cover inpatient hospital care, skilled nursing facility care, hospice care, and home health care. The UB-04 (CMS-1450) claim is submitted.

- **Medicare Part B** (**Medicare Medical Insurance**) helps cover physician and other qualified health care practitioner services, outpatient care, durable medical equipment, and preventive services. The CMS-1500 claim is submitted.

- **Medicare Part C** (**Medicare Advantage**), formerly called Medicare+Choice, is an alternative to the Original Medicare Plan that bundles Medicare Part A, Part B, and Part D coverage, and may offer extra benefits (e.g., dental, hearing, vision). (Claims are not submitted because contracted sponsors are paid a monthly capitation rate to provide all health care procedures and services to enrolled patients. However, reports are submitted to Medicare, and patients may pay premiums, deductibles, coinsurance, and copayments.)

- **Medicare Part D** (**Medicare Prescription Drug Coverage**) helps cover the cost of prescription brand-name and generic drugs according to a **drug formulary** (list of brand name and generic prescription drugs covered by a health plan).

Medicare beneficiaries can also obtain supplemental insurance, called *Medigap*, which helps cover costs not reimbursed by the Original Medicare Plan. Depending on the region of the country, more than one Medicare health plan may be available to enrollees. Supplemental coverage also includes coverage from a former employer or union, or Medicaid.

 NOTE:

CMS-1500 claims completion instructions are included in this chapter. (UB-04 claims are autopopulated by data abstracted and coded from patient records *or* from an electronic health record [EHR] in hospital, skilled nursing facility, inpatient hospice, and home health care organizations. *Chapter 11 of this textbook contains general UB-04 claims completion instructions*, along with examples and a review assignment.)

Medicare Eligibility and Enrollment

Medicare is the federal health insurance program for people who are 65 or older, certain younger people with disabilities, and people with *End-Stage Renal Disease (ESRD)*. The Centers for Medicare & Medicaid Services (CMS) work with the Social Security Administration to enroll people in Medicare. Medicare enrollment results from eligibility, and people are either automatically enrolled or apply for coverage.

Medicare Eligibility

General Medicare eligibility requires:

1. Individuals or their spouses to have worked at least 10 years during which time they paid the Medicare (payroll) tax
2. Individuals to be the minimum of 65 years old
3. Individuals to be citizens or permanent residents of the United States

Individuals can also qualify for coverage if they are younger than 65 *and* have a disability or end-stage renal disease. The *Social Security Administration (SSA)* (an agency of the federal government) bases its definition of *disability* on the inability of an individual to engage in any substantial gainful activity by reason of any medically determinable physical or mental impairment(s), which can be expected to result in death or which has lasted or can be expected to last for a continuous period of not less than 12 months.

Medicare Enrollment

Medicare enrollment is handled in two ways: either individuals are enrolled automatically, or they apply for coverage.

Automatic Enrollment

Individuals not yet age 65 who already receive Social Security, Railroad Retirement Board, disability benefits, or who have *amyotrophic lateral sclerosis (ALS)*, also called Lou Gehrig's disease, are automatically enrolled in

FIGURE 14-1 Sample Medicare card.

Part A and Part B effective the month of their 65th birthday. About three months before the 65th birthday or 24th month of disability, individuals are sent a Medicare card (Figure 14-1). In 2015, the *Medicare Access and CHIP Reauthorization Act (MACRA)* required CMS to remove Social Security numbers (SSNs) from all Medicare cards by April 2019. A new randomly generated **Medicare beneficiary identifier (MBI)** replaced the SSN-based health insurance claim number on new Medicare cards.

If the individual wants both Medicare Part A (hospital insurance) and Part B (supplemental medical insurance), the individual just signs the Medicare card and keeps it in a safe place. Medicare Part B premiums are deducted from Social Security check or prior to automatic bank deposit. Individuals who do *not* want Part B coverage (because there is a monthly premium associated with it) must follow the instructions that accompany the Medicare card; these instructions direct the individual to mark an "X" in the refusal box on the back of the Medicare card form, sign the form, and return it *with* the Medicare card to the address indicated. The individual is then sent a new Medicare card showing coverage for Part A only.

Applying for Medicare

Individuals who are close to age 65 and who do *not* receive Social Security, Railroad Retirement Board, or disability benefits, or who do not have ALS must apply for Medicare Part A and Part B by contacting the Social Security Administration (or, if they worked for a railroad, contact the Railroad Retirement Board) approximately three months before the month in which they turn 65 or the 24th month of disability. A seven-month **initial enrollment period (IEP)** for applying provides an opportunity for the individual to enroll in Medicare Part A and Part B. Those who wait until they actually turn 65 to apply for Medicare will cause a delay in the start of Part B coverage because they will have to wait until the next **general enrollment period (GEP)** (annual January 1 through March 31 enrollment period for Medicare Part A and Part B), and coverage starts on July 1 of that year.

Once the initial enrollment period ends, individuals may have an opportunity to enroll in Medicare Part A and Part B during a **special enrollment period (SEP)**, which is available due to special circumstances.

- Individuals covered by a group health plan *based on current employment* can enroll in Medicare Part A and Part B anytime as long as the

  - Individual or spouse (or family member if the individual has a disability) is working.

  - Individual is covered by a group health plan through the employer or union *based on that work*.

- Individuals covered by a group health plan *based on current employment* and who have one of the following occur (whichever happens first) can enroll in Medicare Part A and Part B the month after

  - Employment ends.

  - Group health plan insurance *based on current employment* ends.

- Individuals who serve as international volunteers for at least 12 months and who volunteer for a tax-exempt nonprofit organization and have health insurance during that time can enroll in Medicare Part A and Part B when one of the following occur (whichever happens first).

o Volunteer work stops.

o Health insurance outside of the United States ends.

Usually there is no *late enrollment penalty* if individuals enroll during a special enrollment period.

Medicare Coverage

Medicare coverage includes the following programs: Medicare Part A (Hospital Insurance), Medicare Part B (Medical Insurance), Medicare Part C (Medicare Advantage), Medicare Part D (Prescription Drug Coverage). Other Medicare health plans include Medicare Cost Plans, demonstration/pilot programs, Programs of All-inclusive Care for the Elderly (PACE), medication therapy management programs, and Medicare Savings Programs. Medicare coverage is impacted by employer and union health plans, and Medigap provides supplemental coverage.

Medicare Part A

Medicare Part A (Hospital Insurance) helps cover home health care, hospice care, and inpatient care in a hospital, religious nonmedical health care institution, and skilled nursing facility. Medicare Part A beneficiaries are responsible for paying copayments, coinsurance, and deductibles for procedures and services provided, as applicable.

Blood

When a health care facility obtains blood from a blood bank at no charge, Medicare beneficiaries are not required to pay for it or replace it. If the facility is required to purchase blood, the beneficiary must either reimburse facility costs for the first three units of blood in a calendar year *or* have someone else donate blood to replace it.

Hospitalizations

Medicare pays only a portion of a patient's inpatient hospitalization expenses, and the patient's out-of-pocket expenses are calculated on a benefit-period basis. This includes inpatient care received in acute care hospitals, critical access hospitals, (inpatient) rehabilitation facilities, and long-term care hospitals; psychiatric care in inpatient psychiatric facilities; and inpatient care for a qualifying clinical research study. A **benefit period** begins the day a Medicare patient is admitted as an inpatient, and it ends when the patient has not received any inpatient care for 60 days in a row. There is no limit to the number of benefit periods a patient may incur during a calendar year. (Some Medicare literature uses the term **spell of illness** instead of *benefit period*.) After 90 continuous days of hospitalization, the patient may elect to use some or all of the allotted lifetime reserve days, or pay the full daily charges for hospitalization. **Lifetime reserve days** (60 days) may be used only once during a patient's lifetime and are usually reserved for use during the patient's final, terminal hospital stay. (Inpatient psychiatric hospital care includes 190 days in a lifetime.)

 NOTE:

> Medicare Part B covers professional services provided to hospital inpatients. For example, an initial inpatient encounter with the patient's physician (in the patient's room) is a professional service that is reported on the CMS-1500 claim. (The hospital generates a UB-04 claim for inpatient care, which includes room and board, dining services, nursing care, social services, procedures, and more.)

Medicare beneficiaries pay:

- Deductible and no coinsurance for days 1–60 of each benefit period.
- Coinsurance per day for days 61–90 of each benefit period.
- Coinsurance per "lifetime reserve day" after day 90 of each benefit period (up to 60 days during Medicare beneficiary's lifetime).
- All costs for each day after all lifetime reserve days have been used.

A person who has been out of the hospital for a period of 60 consecutive days will enter a new benefit period if rehospitalized, and the person is responsible for paying the deductible again.

Hospital (Outpatient) Observation Services

Whether the Medicare beneficiary is an inpatient or an outpatient affects how much they pay for hospital services and if transferred to a skilled nursing facility (SNF), whether they qualify for Medicare Part A SNF coverage. A Medicare beneficiary is a(n):

- Inpatient *when formally admitted to the hospital with a physician's order.*
- Outpatient when receiving emergency or observation services, laboratory or radiology tests, *without a physician's order for formal inpatient admission* (even if the Medicare beneficiary spent the night in the hospital).

Each day in the hospital, the Medicare beneficiary (or their caregiver, such as a spouse) should always ask whether they are an inpatient or an outpatient. They can ask the hospital, physician, social worker, or patient advocate, each of whom can determine inpatient or outpatient status.

Sometimes physicians keep the Medicare beneficiary as an outpatient for observation services while deciding whether to admit them as an inpatient or discharge them. Medicare beneficiaries Patients kept under observation for more than 24 hours must receive a **Medicare Outpatient Observation Notice (MOON)**, which indicates why they are a hospital outpatient receiving observation services and how that affects patient financial responsibilities to the hospital after discharge.

NOTE:

Effective 2016, The *Notice of Observation Treatment and Implication for Care Eligibility Act (NOTICE Act)* requires hospitals to provide the *Medicare Outpatient Observation Notice (MOON)* to Medicare patients who receive observation services as outpatients for more than 24 hours to inform them that they are an outpatient receiving observation services and are not an inpatient of a hospital or a critical access hospital (CAH).

Religious Nonmedical Health Care Institution

For Medicare beneficiaries who qualify for inpatient hospital or skilled nursing facility care in religious nonmedical health care institutions, Medicare will cover services such as room and board, and items or services that do *not* require a physician's order or prescription (e.g., unmedicated wound dressings, use of a simple walker). Medicare does *not* cover the religious portion of care.

Skilled Nursing Facility Stays

Medicare covers semi-private rooms, meals, skilled nursing, therapy, and other medically necessary services and supplies in a skilled nursing facility (SNF) *only after a three-day minimum inpatient hospital stay that was medically necessary for a related illness or injury.* The Medicare beneficiary pays nothing for the first 20 days of each benefit period, a coinsurance per day for days 21–100 of each benefit period, and all costs for each day after day 100 in a benefit period.

NOTE:

Medicare Part B helps cover medically necessary physician services and other outpatient care for Medicare beneficiaries who are residents of SNFs. For example, a SNF resident who develops severe left shin pain is seen by their physician (at the facility), who orders a left lower leg x-ray. The SNF patient undergoes outpatient x-ray, left lower leg, at the facility. Medicare Part B helps cover the costs of the physician's professional service (SNF inpatient visit) and the x-ray, left lower leg (outpatient service).

> **Example:** An 85-year old Medicare beneficiary undergoes four-day inpatient hospitalization for acute gastroenteritis and persistent bacterial urinary tract infection (UTI). The patient is also diagnosed with late-stage Alzheimer's disease, and pelvic ultrasound reveals left ovary mass. Upon resolution of gastroenteritis and UTI after a four-day inpatient stay, the patient is transferred to a skilled nursing facility for a planned 10-day stay to receive medically necessary inpatient physical and occupational therapy. The inpatient hospitalization will be paid according to MS-DRGs, and Medicare will cover the 10-day SNF stay. The patient pays nothing for this 10-day SNF stay. (If medical necessity does not justify the entire 10-day SNF stay, Medicare will pay for the number of medically necessary days supported by documentation.)

Home Health Services

Medicare Part A (and Part B) covers medically necessary home health services, which include part-time or intermittant skilled nursing care (e.g., intravenous medication administration), physical and occupational therapy, speech-language pathology, continued occupational therapy, medical social, and part-time or intermittent home health aide services, durable medical medical equipment (DME), and medical supplies. Patients must be "homebound," which means they have trouble leaving home without help due to illness or injury or because leaving home is not recommended due to illness or injury, or they are normally unable to leave home because it is a major effort. The patient pays nothing for covered home health services, but is responsible for paying a 20 percent deductible for Medicare-approved DME.

Hospice Care

To qualify for hospice care, a hospice physician and the primary care physician must certify that the patient is terminally ill, which means the patient as a life expectancy of six months or less. **Hospice** is an autonomous, centrally administered program of coordinated inpatient and outpatient palliative (relief of symptoms) services for terminally ill patients and their families. This program provided in the home or another facility (e.g., nursing home) to patients for whom the provider can do nothing further to stop the progression of disease, and the patient receives **palliative care** (comfort care, such as pain management and symptom relief, instead of treatment to cure an illness). In addition to comfort care, a physician-directed interdisciplinary team provides medical, nursing, and social services, DME for pain and symptom management, aide and homemaker services, and other covered services (e.g., grief and spiritual counseling) are also provided. Beneficiary financial obligations are:

- $0 for hospice care, and there is no deductible
- Copayment of up to $5 per prescription for prescription drugs for pain and symptom management
- 5 percent of the *Medicare-approved amount* for inpatient **respite care** (short-term care provided by another caregiver, so the primary caregiver can rest)

The **Medicare-approved amount** for Original Medicare is the reimbursement a physician or supplier receives when they *accept assignment*. That amount may be less than the actual amount charged by the physician or supplier. Medicare pays part of the Medicare-approved amount, and the beneficiary pays the remainder.

Respite care can also include the temporary hospitalization of a terminally ill, dependent hospice patient for the purpose of providing relief for the nonpaid person who has the major day-to-day responsibility for care of that patient.

When a patient's health improves or an illness goes into remission, the patient no longer needs hospice care. Also, the patient always has the right to stop hospice care at any time for any reason. If the patient stops hospice care, the type of Medicare coverage in place prior to choosing a hospice program (e.g., treatment to cure a terminal illness) is resumed. If eligible, the patient can return to hospice care at any time.

> **Example:** A patient has terminal cancer and receives hospice care. The patient's cancer goes into remission, and it is decided that, due to remission, hospice care can be discontinued. The physician explains that if the patient becomes eligible for hospice services in the future, recertification for the return to hospice care can be provided.

Medicare Part B

Medicare Part B (Medical Insurance) helps cover medically necessary physician and other qualified health care practitioner services, outpatient care, home health services, durable medical equipment (DME), mental health services, and other medical services. Part B also covers many preventive services (e.g., vaccinations).

 NOTE:

Medicare beneficiaries pay nothing for most Medicare-covered *preventive services* if services are received from a provider who accepts assignment. However, for some preventive services, beneficiaries may be required to pay a deductible, coinsurance, or both. Such costs may also apply if the beneficiary receives a preventive service during the same encounter as a non-preventive service.

Medicare Part B covers two types of services:

- *Medically necessary services,* which are services or supplies needed to diagnose or treat medical conditions and that meet accepted standards of medical practice.

- *Preventive services,* which include health care to prevent illness (e.g., flu) or detect illness at an early stage when treatment is most likely to work best.

Example: Medicare Part B covers clinical research, ambulance services, durable medical equipment (DME), mental health (inpatient and outpatient), partial hospitalization, second surgical opinion, and limited outpatient prescription drugs.

 NOTE:

For an extensive list of Medicare Part B covered services, go to www.medicare.gov, click on the Basics link, click on the "Medicare & You" handbook link, and click on the Download "Medicare & You" link to download a PDF, eBook, audio, or Braille file. Or, call 1-800-MEDICARE to request that a paper "Medicare & You" handbook be mailed to you.

Medicare beneficiary payment requirements depends on service(s) provided. Physicians, other qualified health care practitioners, and suppliers who *accept assignment* are called *participating (PAR) providers*, and that reduces out-of-pocket costs for patients because they are required by law to charge for Medicare deductible and coinsurance amounts *only*. They usually wait for Medicare to pay its share before asking patients to pay their deductibles and copayments. Also, providers who accept assignment must submit CMS-1500 claims directly to Medicare and cannot charges patients for submitting the claim.

Nonparticipating (NonPAR) providers have *not* agreed to accept assignment, and they are *not* required by law to accept as payment in full the *Medicare-approved amount* for Medicare-covered services. NonPAR providers can can choose to accept assignment for individual services.) Medicare patients may be required to pay more for services provided, and they might also be required to to pay the entire charge at the time of service. The provider or supplier is supposed to submit a CMS-1500 claim to Medicare for any Medicare-covered services they provide, and if they do not submit the Medicare claim when asked, patients can 1-800-MEDICARE for assistance. NonPAR providers can also charge more than the *Medicare-approved amount*, but only up to the "limiting charge."

Under Medicare Part B, the beneficiary is responsible for paying an annual deductible, and they must pay all costs for services (up to the Medicare-approved amount) until the annual deductible is met. After having met the deductible, Medicare reimburses providers and suppliers the *Medicare-approved amount*, and patients typically pay 20% of that amount for the service provided (if the provider *accepts assignment*). There's no annual limit on what Medicare beneficiaries pay out-of-pocket; however, there may be limits on supplemental coverage, such as Medicaid, Medigap, or employer or union coverage.

Medicare Part B coverage is based on:

- Federal and state laws
- National coverage decisions (NCDs) made by Medicare about whether something is covered
- Local coverage decisions (LCDs) made by Medicare administrative contractors (MACs) that process claims for Medicare; MACs determine medically necessity and coverage for their region.

Providers who do not routinely collect the patient's deductible and coinsurance are in violation of Medicare regulations and are subject to large fines and exclusion from the Medicare program.

Calculating Hospital Outpatient Coinsurance and Copayment Amounts

In hospital outpatient settings, the coinsurance amount is based on a national median amount per ambulatory payment classification (APC), which could be higher than 20 percent. Hospitals have the option of charging patients either the 20 percent or the higher national median coinsurance amount. Regardless, Medicare will reimburse hospitals the difference between the Medicare-approved amount and the national coinsurance of 20 percent. However, if the hospital collects the higher median coinsurance amount from the patient, Medicare will reduce its reimbursement accordingly. Also, under the outpatient prospective payment system (OPPS), Medicare allows patients to pay either a coinsurance amount (20 percent of the charge for procedures and services) or a fixed copayment amount, *whichever is less,* when seeking care from hospital outpatient departments that are participating providers.

> **Example 1:** A patient undergoes outpatient surgery to have basal cell carcinoma removed from their forehead. The charge is $265. The fixed copayment amount for this type of procedure, adjusted for wages in the geographic area, is $25. The coinsurance amount is $53 ($265 × 0.20), and the copayment amount is $25. Thus, the patient pays the $25 copayment amount because it is less than the calculated coinsurance amount.

> **Example 2:** A patient undergoes outpatient laboratory procedures to test their blood glucose and A1C blood levels. The cost is $175. The fixed copayment for these ancillary laboratory procedures, adjusted for wages in the geographic area, is $25. The coinsurance amount is $35 ($175 × 0.20), and the copayment is $45. Thus, the patient pays the $35 calculated coinsurance amount because it is less than the copayment amount.

Physician Fee Schedule

Since 1992, Medicare has reimbursed provider services according to a *physician fee schedule* (previously called the *Resource-Based Relative Value Scale, RBRVS*), which also limits the amounts nonparticipating providers (nonPARs) can charge beneficiaries. Reimbursement under the fee schedule is based on relative value units (RVUs) that consider resources used in providing a service (physician work, practice expense, and malpractice expense). The schedule is revised annually and is organized in a table format that includes CPT/HCPCS Level II codes and the Medicare-allowed fee for each. Medicare bases payment on whichever is less, the participating physician's actual charges *or* the physician fee schedule amount. For most codes, Medicare pays 80 percent of the amount listed, and the beneficiary is responsible for 20 percent. A nonparticipating physician (nonPAR) is subject to a 5 percent reduction in the MPFS for each CPT or HCPCS Level II code. (This means that the nonPAR fee schedule is equal to 95 percent of the MPFS.) When a nonPAR does not *accept assignment* for a submitted claim, they are subject to a limiting charge, which allows them to collect a maximum of 115 percent of the nonparticipating reduced Medicare physician fee schedule amount; this is the maximum a nonPAR may charge a Medicare beneficiary on an unassigned claim.

> **Example:** A sample of CPT E/M codes are listed in the Medicare physician fee schedule (MPFS) below. Because a participating provider (PAR) is paid 80 percent of the MPFS amount, for code 99202, the PAR is paid $51.58 ($64.48 × 0.80), and the patient pays $12.90 ($64.48 × 0.20).
>
> A nonparticipating provider (nonPAR) is paid 80% of the limiting charge MPFS, which is reduced by 5 percent. For code 99202, the nonPAR is paid $49.01 ($64.48 − [0.05 × $64.48] = $64.48 − $3.22 = $61.26; $61.26 × 0.80 = $49.01).

The patient is responsible for $12.25 ($61.26 × 0.20) if the nonPAR accepts assignment. However, if the nonPAR does *not* accept assignment, the patient is responsible for $14.83 ($64.48 × 1.15 = $74.15; $74.15 × 0.20 = $14.83)

99202	$ 64.48	99212	$ 38.02
99203	$ 96.32	99213	$ 52.76
99204	$136.57	99214	$ 82.57
99205	$173.30	99215	$120.93

Medicare Part C

Medicare Part C (Medicare Advantage) coverage of hospital and medical services is provided by CMS-approved private companies that follow Medicare rules. (Most Medicare Advantage plans include prescription drug coverage, which is Medicare Part D. And, with a Medicare Advantage plan, beneficiaries are still covered by Medicare, just not Original Medicare.) To join a Medicare Advantage plan, the beneficiary must enroll in both Part A and Part B and live in the plan's service area (Figure 14-2). Beneficiaries can can join a Medicare Advantage Plan even if you have a pre-existing condition, and each year they can choose to leave the plan or make changes to services covered and what is paid (e.g., premium). (If a plan stops participating in Medicare, beneficiaries must join another Medicare Advantage plan or return to Original Medicare. And, patients with End-Stage Renal Disease (ESRD) can enrolled in a Medicare Advantage plan during the annual Medicare *open enrollment* period.)

Medicare beneficiaries need to seek care from providers who participate in the Medicare Advantage plan's network and service area. These plans establish a limit on what out-of-pocket annual costs covered services, which helps protect beneficiaries from unexpected costs. (Some Medicare Advantage plans allow out-of-network coverage, but at a higher cost to the beneficiary.) Plans also provide beneficiaries with a Medicare card, which must be presented to receive Medicare-covered services (and used to switch to Original Medicare, if the beneficiary decides to make a change).

Medicare Advantage plans cover almost all Medicare Part A and Part B benefits. In addition, the plans *must* cover all emergency and urgent care and almost all medically necessary services that Original Medicare covers. However, for a Medicare Advantage Plan, if hospice care services are required Original Medicare will cover those costs along with some new Medicare benefits and costs for clinical research studies.

Most Medicare Advantage plans coverage extra benefits (for services Original Medicare does not cover), such as dental, fitness, hearing, and vision programs. Plans can even choose to provide more benefits, such as transportation services to physician visits, over-the-counter drugs, and other services that promote health and wellness. Plans can also tailor benefit packages to certain chronically-ill enrollees, which benefits customized to treat specific conditions.

Medicare payment to Medicare Advantage plans is capitated. (*Capitation* is the payment of pre-established payments to providers for the provision of health care services to beneficiaries during a specified period of time, such as monthly or annually.) The plans must follow Medicare rules, but they can charge different out-of-pocket costs and may have different requirements for obtaining services (e.g., referrals required for care from specialists, receiving care from the plan's network of providers and suppliers). The requirements can change annually, the the plan must notify beneficiaries about any changes prior to the start of the next enrollment year. Medicare Advantage plans include:

- Health maintenance organization (HMO)
- HMO point-of-service (HMO POS)
- Medical savings account (MSA)
- Preferred provider organization (PPO)
- Private fee-for-service (PFFS)
- Special needs plan (SNP)

Comparing Original Medicare and Medicare Advantage

Step 1

Patient decides to enroll in Original Medicare or a Medicare Advantage Plan

Original Medicare includes Part A (Hospital Insurance) and/or Part B (Medical Insurance)

- Medicare provides this coverage directly.
- Patient has choice of doctors, hospitals, and other providers that accept Medicare.
- Patient or supplemental coverage pay *deductibles* and *coinsurance*.
- Patient pays a monthly premium for Part B.

Step 2

Patient decides whether to enroll in prescription drug coverage (Part D)

- To receive drug coverage, *patient must join a Medicare Prescription Drug Plan* and usually pays a monthly premium.
- These plans are run by private companies approved by Medicare.

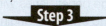
Step 3

Patient decides whether to enroll in supplemental coverage

- Patient may purchase coverage that "fills gaps" in Original Medicare coverage. Patient can choose to buy a Medicare Supplement Insurance (Medigap) policy from a private company.
- Costs vary by policy and company.
- Employers and unions may offer similar coverage.

Medicare Advantage (Part C)

Part C includes Part A (Hospital Insurance) and Part B (Medical Insurance)

- Private insurance companies approved by Medicare provide this coverage.
- In most plans, patient must use plan doctors, hospitals, and other providers; otherwise, patient pays more or all of the costs.
- Patient may pay a monthly premium (in addition to Part B premium) and a copayment or coinsurance for covered services.
- Costs, extra coverage, and rules vary by plan.

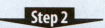
Step 2

Patient decides whether to enroll in prescription drug coverage (Part D)

- Drug coverage offered by the Medicare Advantage Plan, *in most cases must be obtained through that plan.*
- In some types of Medicare Advantage Plans that don't offer drug coverage, patient can join a Medicare Prescription Drug Plan.

Note: Patients who enroll in a Medicare Advantage Plan *cannot* use Medicare Supplement Insurance (Medigap) to pay for out-of-pocket costs required of the Medicare Advantage Plan. Patients who have a Medicare Advantage Plan cannot be sold a Medigap policy. Patients can purchase a Medigap policy only if they disenroll from their Medicare Advantage Plan and enroll in Original Medicare.

FIGURE 14-2 Determining Medicare coverage choices.

 NOTE:

Refer to Chapter 2 of this textbook for content about managed care.

A **Medicare medical savings account (MSA)** is used by an enrollee to pay health care bills, and Medicare pays the cost of a special health care policy that has a high deductible. Medicare also annually deposits into an account the difference between policy costs and what Medicare pays for an average enrollee in the patient's region. The money deposited annually by Medicare is managed by a Medicare-approved insurance company or other qualified company. It is not taxed if the enrollee uses it to pay qualified health care expenses. It may earn interest or dividends, and any funds left in the account at the end of a calendar year are carried over to the next year. The enrollee pays health care expenses using money from the Medicare MSA account until the high deductible has been met. (If the Medicare MSA is exhausted before the high deductible has been met, the enrollee pays out of pocket until the deductible has been met.) Once the deductible has been met, the insurance policy pays health care expenses.

> **Example:** Jill selects the Medicare MSA plan option, establishes an account, and selects a Medicare MSA insurance policy with a $5,000 deductible. Medicare deposits $1,200 into Jill's Medicare MSA account on January 1. During the first year of the Medicare MSA plan, Jill receives health care services for which she pays $300, leaving $900 remaining in her Medicare MSA account. On January 1, Medicare deposits another $1,200 into her account; Jill now has $2,100 that she can use for health care expenses. During that next year, Jill undergoes surgery that costs $8,000. She uses the $2,100 in her account plus $2,900 of her own money to meet the policy's high deductible of $5,000; the remaining $3,000 is reimbursed by the Medicare MSA insurance policy.

 NOTE:

Medicare MSA enrollees are required to pay the monthly Medicare Part B premium.

Private fee-for-service (PFFS) plans are offered by private insurance companies and are available in some regions of the country. Medicare pays a pre-established amount of money each month to the insurance company, which decides how much it will pay for services. Such plans reimburse providers on a fee-for-service basis and are authorized to charge enrollees up to 115 percent of the plan's payment schedule.

Medicare special needs plans (SNP) cover all Medicare Part A and Part B health care services for individuals who can benefit the most from special care for chronic illnesses, care management of multiple diseases, and focused care management. Such plans may limit membership to individuals who:

- Are eligible for both Medicare and Medicaid (Medi-Medi coverage)
- Have certain chronic or disabling conditions
- Reside in certain institutions (e.g., nursing facility)

Costs of Medicare Part C (Medicare Advantage)

When selecting a Medicare Advantage plan, beneficiaries should determine whether the plan charges a monthly premium, annual deductible, additional deductibles for certain services, copayments, or coinsurance. (Many Medicare Advantage plans have a $0 premium.) *When enrolling in a plan that charges a premium, that is paid in addition to the Medicare Part B premium. Some Medicare Advantage plans help pay all or part of Medicare Part B premiums, which is called a "Medicare Part B premium reduction."*

Medicare beneficiaries should also consider

- Type of health care services needed
- How often services are required (e.g., treatment of chronic conditions, such as renal dialysis)
- Availability of services from a network provider (because cost of services from non-network providers might be higher)
- Whether providers accept assignment
- Provision for extra benefits, such as dental, fitness, hearing, and vision (in addition to Original Medicare benefits) *and if you need to pay more to get them*
- Eligibility for Medicaid (and the available of state help through a *Medicare Savings Program*)

Medicare Advantage Plans cannot charge more than Original Medicare for certain services, such as chemotherapy, dialysis, and skilled nursing facility care. Once the plan's annual limit on out-of-pocket costs for all Medicare Part A and Part B services is reached, beneficiaries pay nothing for Medicare Part A and Part B covered services.

Risk Adjustment of Medicare Capitation Payments Using the CMS Diagnostic Cost Group Hierarchical Condition Category (DCG/HCC) Risk Adjustment Model

Historically, capitation payments to Medicare managed care plans were linked to fee-for-service expenditures by geographic area, with payments set at 95 percent of an enrollee's county's adjusted average per capita cost. In an effort to control rising health care costs to the Medicare Advantage program, the *principal inpatient diagnostic cost group (PIP-DCG) payment program* was implemented as a transition model, resulting in a feasible way to implement a *risk-adjustment model* that was based on readily available, already audited inpatient diagnostic data.

According to the American Health Information Management Association, "*risk adjustment* is a statistical process that considers the underlying health status and health spending of patients when examining their healthcare outcomes or healthcare costs." Assigning ICD-10-CM codes to diagnoses is used as part of the risk adjustment process to help predict health care costs based on patient demographics and diagnoses.

Effective 2016, the *21st Century Cures Act (Cures Act)* requires submission of reports about Medicare Advantage program and ESRD risk adjustment models every three years. **Risk adjustment** is a method of adjusting capitation payments to health plans, accounting for differences in expected health costs of enrollees. (Commercial insurers determine revenue needs based on trends in medical expenditures, benefits offered, and anticipated enrollment, and then determine how to set premiums, deductibles, and copayment and coinsurance amounts.) Medicare Advantage risk adjustment models are more comprehensive in that diagnoses and demographic information are used to adjust each enrollee's monthly capitation rate to account for expected costs associated with age, sex, and conditions. At the individual (beneficiary) level, predicted medical costs can be lower or higher than actual medical costs. At the group (of beneficiaries) level, below-average predicted costs balance above-average predicted costs. Thus, risk adjustment accuracy is intended at the group level.

Risk adjustment models applied to health care data include the CMS value-based purchasing (VBP), prescription drug hierarchical condition category (RxHCC), Medicare Advantage diagnostic cost group hierarchical condition category (DCG/HCC), and HHS hierarchical condition category (HHS-HCC) models, and the 3M all-patient refined diagnosis-related groups (APR DRGs). (The HHS-HCC model is used by CMS to determine payments made to health insurers for caring for sicker patients in the Affordable Care Act marketplace.)

CMS then evaluated risk-adjustment models that use both ambulatory and inpatient diagnoses, and selected the **diagnostic cost group hierarchical condition category (DCG/HCC) risk adjustment model** for Medicare risk-adjustment. The DCG/HCC model results in more accurate predictions of medical costs for Medicare Advantage enrollees than previously, and its use is intended to redirect money away from managed care organizations (MCOs) that select the healthy, while providing MCOs that care for the sickest patients with the resources to do so. The ultimate purpose of the DCG/HCC risk adjustment payment model is to promote fair payments to MCOs that reward efficiency and encourage excellent care for the chronically ill.

To receive fair payments under the DCG/HCC risk adjustment model, health care providers report ICD-10-CM codes for acute and chronic conditions (comorbidities) that are medically managed or impact treatment of other conditions. Providers also report ICD-10-CM codes for manifestations of conditions (e.g., ophthalmic manifestations of diabetes mellitus) and complications of treatment (e.g, postoperative wound infection). Providers do *not* report ICD-10-CM codes for patient conditions that no longer exist.

Medicare Part D

Medicare Part D (Medicare Prescription Drug Plans) offer prescription drug coverage to all Medicare beneficiaries that may help lower prescription drug costs and help protect against higher costs in the future. Medicare Part D is optional, and individuals who join a Medicare drug plan pay a monthly premium, which varies by plan. Deductible, coinsurance, and copayment amounts also vary by plan. The **Medicare Part D sponsor** is an organization (e.g., health insurance company) that has one or more contract(s) with CMS to provide Part D benefits to Medicare beneficiaries.

TABLE 14-1 Example of Medicare Part D coverage gap (for patient who pays a monthly premium throughout the year)

Costs	Patient Responsibility
Annual deductible	Patient pays first $480 of drug costs before Medicare Part D plan begins to pay its share.
Copayment or coinsurance (amount patient pays at the pharmacy)	Patient pays *copayment* and Medicare Part D plan pays its share for each covered drug until combined amount (plus *deductible*) reaches $4,430.

Coverage gap	Once a patient and the Medicare Part D plan have spent $4,430 for covered drugs, the patient is in the *coverage gap* (or "donut hole").
	  Then, the patient pays 25% of Medicare Part D plan's cost for covered brand-name prescription drugs and 44% of Medicare Part D plan's cost for covered generic prescription drugs.
	  The amount the patient pays (and the discount paid by the drug company) counts as *out-of-pocket spending*, and this helps patient get out of the coverage gap.

Catastrophic coverage	Once the patient has spent $7,050 *out-of-pocket* for the year, patient's *coverage gap* ends. Then, patient pays a small coinsurance or copayment for each covered drug until the end of the year.

(Individuals who decide not to enroll in a Medicare Prescription Drug Plan when first eligible may be required to pay a penalty if they choose to join later.)

Medicare prescription drug plans are administered by insurance companies approved by Medicare. There are two ways to obtain Medicare prescription drug coverage:

1. Join a Medicare Prescription Drug Plan that adds coverage to the Original Medicare Plan, some Medicare private fee-for-service plans, some Medicare cost plans, and Medicare medical savings account plans. This plan requires subscribers to pay a monthly premium and an annual deductible.

2. Join a Medicare Advantage plan (e.g., HMO) that includes prescription drug coverage as part of the plan. Monthly premiums and annual deductibles will vary, depending on the plan. In addition, all Medicare health care (including prescription drug coverage) is provided by such plans.

The **Medicare Part D coverage gap** (or **Medicare Part D "donut hole"**) (Table 14-1) is the difference between the initial coverage limit and the catastrophic coverage threshold for the Medicare Part D prescription drug program. Medicare beneficiaries who surpass the prescription drug-coverage limit are financially responsible for the entire cost of prescription drugs until expenses reach the catastrophic coverage threshold. Starting in 2011, the PPACA (abbreviated as the Affordable Care Act) provided for a 50 percent discount on *brand-name drugs* when Medicare beneficiaries reach the prescription drug "donut hole." Closure of the coverage gap (donut hole) does *not* mean that patients receive free medications; instead, patients pay a coinsurance amount while in the coverage gap (donut hole) that is reduced to 25 percent.

Payment Validation for Medicare Part C and Part D Programs

Payment validation ensures the accuracy of Medicare Part C and Part D program payments, and it protects the Medicare Trust Fund. The *Improper Payments Elimination and Recovery Act of 2010* requires government agencies to identify, report, and reduce erroneous payments in government programs and activities. CMS has reported a Part C *composite payment error estimate* since 2008 and conducts Medicare Advantage risk adjustment data validation activities to ensure the accuracy and integrity of risk adjustment data and Medicare Advantage risk-adjusted payments. **Risk adjustment data validation (RADV)** is the process of verifying that diagnosis codes submitted for payment by a Medicare Advantage organization are supported by patient record documentation for an enrollee. CMS has also prepared and implemented a systematic plan for identifying, measuring, and reporting erroneous payments for the Medicare Part D program.

Other Medicare Health Plans

Other Medicare health programs generally provide all of an individual's Medicare-covered health care, and some cover prescription drugs. They include:

- Medicare Cost Plans
- Demonstration/pilot program
- Programs of All-inclusive Care for the Elderly (PACE)
- Medication Therapy Management Programs

 NOTE:

The Medicare Prescription Drug, Improvement, and Modernization Act of 2003 (MMA) required implementation of *Medicare Prescription Drug Plans (Medicare Part D)* in 2006 to assist Medicare beneficiaries with outpatient prescription drug costs. The MMA also requires coordination of Medicare Part D with state pharmaceutical assistance programs (SPAP), Medicaid plans, group health plans, Federal Employee Health Benefit plans (FEHBP), and military plans such as TRICARE. Enrollment in Medicare Part D is voluntary, and beneficiaries must apply for the benefit.

A **Medicare Cost Plan** is a type of Medicare health plan available in certain areas of the country, which works in much the same way and has some of the same rules as a Medicare Advantage plan. In a Medicare Cost Plan, if the beneficiary receives health care services from a non-network provider, Original Medicare provides coverage. The beneficiary pays Medicare Part A and Part B coinsurance and deductibles.

A **demonstration/pilot program** is a special project that tests improvements in Medicare coverage, payment, and quality of care. Demonstrations usually apply to a specific group of people and/or are offered only in specific areas. They also include pilot programs for individuals with multiple chronic illnesses that are designed to reduce health risks, improve quality of life, and provide health care savings.

Programs of All-inclusive Care for the Elderly (PACE) Medicare and Medicaid program offered in many states that allows people who otherwise need a nursing home-level of care to remain in the community. To be eligible, an individual must be:

- 55 years old or older
- A resident in the service area of the PACE organization
- Able to live safely in the community with the help of PACE services
- State-certified as eligible for nursing home-level of care, which means the beneficiary is similar to an average nursing home resident (but can remain at home with PACE care)

Example: Cheyanne Blackhorse is a 78-year-old woman with insulin-dependent diabetes mellitus, hypertension, chronic asthma, all of which are controlled by prescription medications. The patient is also blind in one eye and has mild dementia, and the family supports Cheyanne's desire to remain in her home. They are able to frequently call and visit in person.

Cheyanne also has limitations in activities of daily living (ADLs) and needs help showering and with meals. PACE provides assistance with twice-weekly showering, arranges daily *Meals on Wheels*, and monitors prescription medications to ensure that they are properly taken. PACE also arranges transportation for Cheyanne to the primary care provider every three months (and as needed when additional care is required, such as treatment for influenza). While Cheyanne is provided with a high level of care by PACE at home, the patient remains a part of the community and does not need to reside in nursing home at this time.

Medication Therapy Management Programs are available to Medicare beneficiaries who participate in a drug plan so they can learn how to manage medications through a free Medication Therapy Management (MTM) program. The MTM provides a list of a beneficiary's medications, reasons why beneficiaries take them, an action plan to help beneficiaries make the best use of medications, and a summary of medication review with the beneficiary's physician or pharmacist.

Medicare Savings Programs

The **Medicare Savings Program (MSP)** was implemented as part of the Medicare Catastrophic Coverage Act of 1988 and later expanded by other legislation to provide relief for individuals who have limited income and resources. Federal, state, and county governments help pay for Medicare costs when certain income and resource limit conditions are met. Recipients of the Medicare Savings Programs must apply for Medicaid in their state, and state Medicaid offices administer all of the programs. (An additional benefit of enrollment in a Medicare Savings Program is automatic enrollment in the Medicare Part D *Extra Help* program.)

State and federal governments jointly fund the Medicare Savings Programs, with administrative costs split among federal (50 percent), state (25 percent), and county (25 percent) governments. (The costs of benefits for QMB, SLMB, and QDWI programs are split the same way. However, QI benefits are fully federally funded.)

- **Qualified Medicare beneficiary program (QMBP)** pays Medicare Part A and B or Medicare Part C premiums, deductibles, coinsurance, and copayments.
- **Specified low-income Medicare beneficiary (SLMB)** helps pay Medicare Part B premiums for people who have Part A.
- **Qualifying individual (QI)** helps pay Medicare Part B premiums for people who have Part A.
- **Qualified disabled working individual (QDWI)** pays Medicare Part A premiums only.

Medicare Shared Savings Program

In 2012, **accountable care organizations (ACOs)** were created to help physicians, hospitals, and other health care providers work together to improve care for people with the Original Medicare plan (Medicare Part A and Part B). Under the **Medicare Shared Savings Program (MSSP)**, ACOs enter into agreements with CMS to take responsibility for the quality of care furnished to Medicare beneficiaries in return for the opportunity to share in savings realized through improved care. CMS then implemented *Pathways to Success*, which redesigned participation options so that ACOs were encouraged to transition to *performance-based risk models* more quickly (and increase savings for the Medicare Trust Fund).

Employer and Union Health Plans

Some employer and union health insurance policies provide coverage for individuals who reach age 65 and who retire. Medicare has special rules that apply to beneficiaries who have group health plan coverage through their own or their spouse's current employment. Group health plans of employers with 20 or more employees must offer the same health insurance benefits under the same conditions that younger workers and spouses receive. When the individual or the individual's spouse stops working and the individual is already enrolled in Part B, individuals are responsible for:

- Notifying Medicare that their or their spouse's employment situation has changed
- Providing Medicare with the name and address of the employer plan, policy number of the plan, date the coverage stopped, and reason coverage stopped
- Telling their provider that Medicare is their primary payer and should be billed first (The individual should also provide the date their group health coverage stopped.)

Medigap

Medigap (or **Medicare Supplementary Insurance [MSI]**), sold by private (insurance) companies, is designed to supplement Medicare benefits by paying for services that Medicare does not cover (e.g., copayments, coinsurance, and deductibles). Although Medicare covers many health care costs, enrollees must still pay Medicare's deductibles and coinsurance amounts. In addition, there are many health care services that Medicare does not cover. A Medigap policy provides reimbursement for out-of-pocket costs not covered by Medicare, in addition to those that are the beneficiary's share of health care costs. Medigap policies (Table 14-2), offer a different combination of benefits, and premium amounts are determined by the private (insurance) companies.

TABLE 14-2 Example of Medigap plans (Medicare supplemental insurance)

Benefits	A	B	C	D	F*	G*	K**	L	M	N***
Medicare Part A coinsurance and hospital costs (up to an additional 365 days after Medicare benefits are used)	100%	100%	100%	100%	100%	100%	100%	100%	100%	100%
Medicare Part B coinsurance or copayment	100%	100%	100%	100%	100%	100%	50%	75%	100%	100% ***
Blood (first 3 pints)	100%	100%	100%	100%	100%	100%	50%	75%	100%	100%
Part A hospice care coinsurance or copayment	100%	100%	100%	100%	100%	100%	50%	75%	100%	100%
Skilled nursing facility care coinsurance			100%	100%	100%	100%	50%	75%	100%	100%
Medicare Part A deductible		100%	100%	100%	100%	100%	50%	75%	50%	100%
Medicare Part B deductible			100%		100%					
Medicare Part B excess charges					100%	100%				
Foreign travel emergency (up to plan limits)			80%	80%	80%	80%			80%	80%
Out-of-pocket limit							$6,620	$3,310		

*Plans F and G also offer a high-deductible plan in some states. Patients who choose this option must pay for Medicare-covered costs up to the deductible amount before their Medigap policy pays anything.

**For Plans K and L, after the patient's out-of-pocket yearly limit and yearly Part B deductible have been met, Medigap pays 100% of covered services for the rest of the calendar year.

***Plan N pays 100% of the Part B coinsurance, except for a copayment of up to $20 for some office visits and up to a $50 copayment for emergency room visits that do not result in an inpatient admission.

Courtesy of the Centers for Medicare & Medicaid Services, www.cms.gov.

Medicare SELECT is a type of Medigap insurance that requires enrollees to use a network of providers (doctors and hospitals) in order to receive full benefits. Because of this requirement, Medicare SELECT policies may have lower premiums. However, if an out-of-network provider is used, Medicare SELECT generally will not pay benefits for nonemergency services. Medicare, however, will still pay its share of approved charges. Currently, Medicare SELECT is available only in limited geographic areas of the country.

Effective 2020, Medigap plans sold to new Medicare enrollees are *not* be allowed to cover the Medicare Part B deductible. Consequently, Medigap Plans C and F are no longer available to new Medicare enrollees. However, if a Medicare enrollee purchased a Medigap Plan C or F (or the high deductible version of Plan F) prior to January 1, 2020, they will be allowed to keep their plan. Also, individuals who were eligible for Medicare prior to January 1, 2020, but had not yet enrolled may be able to purchase Medigap Plan C or F.

Experimental and Investigative Procedures

Medicare law allows payment only for services or supplies that are considered reasonable and necessary for the stated diagnosis. Medicare will not cover procedures deemed to be experimental in nature. There are cases in which the provider determines that treatments or services are fully justified and such treatment options are then explained to the patient, who must pay the full cost of the noncovered procedure. Medicare regulations specify that the provider must refund any payment received from a patient for a service denied by Medicare as investigational, unnecessary, unproved, or experimental, unless the patient agreed in writing prior to receiving the services to personally pay for such services. An appeal of the denial of payment must be made in writing, and if the appeal is not granted, a refund must be paid to the patient within 30 days. A refund is not required if the provider "could not have known a specific treatment would be ruled unnecessary."

Medicare Participating, Nonparticipating, and Opt-Out Providers

For Medicare purposes, Part B reimbursement is based on the relationship a provider has with Medicare, which is referred to as a provider type. The provider's type determines how much Medicare patients pay for Part B services. There are three provider types:

- Participating provider (PAR)
- Nonparticipating provider (nonPAR)
- Opt-out provider

The *Medicare Access and CHIP Reauthorization Act (MACRA)* of 2015 made three important changes to how Medicare pays those who provide care to Medicare beneficiaries:

- Ends Sustainable Growth Rate (SGR) formula for determining Medicare payments for health care provider services.
- Creates new framework for rewarding providers for delivering better care, not just more care.
- Combines existing quality reporting programs into one new system, the quality payment program (QPP) that includes alternate payment systems (APMs), merit-based incentive payments (MIPS), and MIPS-APMs.

Participating Providers

Medicare has established a *participating provider (PAR)*, an agreement in which the provider contracts to *accept assignment* on all claims submitted to Medicare. By 2000, more than 85 percent of all physicians, practitioners, and suppliers in the United States were PARs. Congress mandated special incentives to increase the number of health care providers signing PAR agreements with Medicare, including:

- Direct payment of all claims
- Bonuses provided to Medicare administrative contractors (MACs) for recruitment and enrollment of PARs
- Publication of an annual, regional PAR directory (MedPARD) made available to all Medicare patients
- A special message printed on all unassigned Medicare Summary Notice (MSN) forms mailed to patients, reminding them of the reduction in out-of-pocket expenses if they use PARs and stating how much they would save with PARs
- Hospital referrals for outpatient care that provide the patient with the name and full address of at least one PAR provider each time the hospital provides a referral for care
- Faster processing of assigned claims

Regardless of the type of Medicare Part B services billed, PARs have "one-stop" billing for beneficiaries who have Medigap coverage and who assign both Medicare and Medigap payments to PARs. After Medicare has made payment, the claim will automatically be sent to the Medigap insurer for payment of all coinsurance and deductible amounts due under the Medigap policy. The Medigap insurer must pay the PAR directly.

Nonparticipating Providers

Medicare *nonparticipating providers (nonPARs)* may elect to accept assignment on a claim-by-claim basis, but several restrictions must be adhered to:

- NonPARs must file all Medicare claims.
- Fees are restricted to not more than the "limiting charge" on nonassigned claims.
- Balance billing of the patient by a nonPAR is forbidden.
- Collections are restricted to only the deductible and coinsurance due at the time of service on an assigned claim.

- Patients must sign an advance beneficiary notice of noncoverage for all nonassigned surgical fees over $500.
- NonPARs must accept assignment on clinical laboratory charges.

Limiting Charge

Nonparticipating (nonPAR) providers who do not accept assignment on Medicare claims are subject to a limit regarding what can be charged to beneficiaries for covered services. The Medicare-allowed fee for nonPARs is 5 percent below the PAR Medicare fee schedule, but the nonPAR physician who does not accept assignment may charge a maximum of 15 percent above the nonPAR approved rate (or 10 percent above the PAR Medicare fee schedule). The 15 percent allowance is based on the 95 percent reduced Medicare fee schedule, which means nonPAR providers receive somewhat less than 110 percent of the allowed PAR amount. Eighty percent of the *limiting charge* is the maximum Medicare will reimburse a nonPAR for a covered service. It applies regardless of who is responsible for payment and whether Medicare is primary or secondary.

Example: Compare the PAR and nonPAR Medicare reimbursement rates for providers who accept assignment.

Participating (PAR) Provider Medicare Reimbursement		Nonparticipating (nonPAR) Provider Medicare Reimbursement	
PAR usual charge for office visit	$110	nonPAR charge for office visit	$110
PAR MPFS	$100	nonPAR MPFS limiting charge[1]	$109.25
Medicare pays 80% of MPFS	$80	Medicare pays 80% of limiting charge	$87.40
PAR writes off amount[2]	$10	nonPAR bills patient[3]	$21.85
Patient coinsurance[4]	$20	Patient coinsurance[4]	$20
Total payment to PAR	$100	Total payment to nonPAR	$109.25

[1]The nonPAR MPFS limiting charge is 5% below the PAR MPFS. (In the nonPAR example above, the $120.18 nonPAR MPFS limiting charge is calculated as: (1) $100 × 5% = $5, (2) $100 − $5 = $95, and (3) $95 x 115% = $109.25.)

[2]PAR writes off the difference between the usual charge and the MPFS amount.

[3]nonPAR can bill the patient for the difference between the limiting charge and the MPFS amount because it is less than 115 percent of the MPFS amount.

[4]This is 20% of the PAR MPFS.

Although it appears that the nonPAR is paid more than the PAR ($109.25 versus $100), the nonPAR has to collect $21.85 from the patient, whereas the PAR has to collect just $20 from the patient. (It is also more cost-effective for patients to seek treatment from PARs.)

 HIPAA Alert!

With the passage of the Health Insurance Portability and Accountability Act (HIPAA) of 1996, Congress increased the potential fine if a nonPAR does not heed Medicare administrative contractor (MAC) warnings to desist from flagrant abuse of the limiting charge rules.

Accepting Assignment on a Claim

A nonparticipating provider who agrees to accept assignment on a claim will be reimbursed the Medicare-allowed fee. The nonPAR may also collect any previously unpaid deductible and the 20 percent coinsurance determined from the Medicare Physician Fee Schedule (MPFS). If the nonPAR collects the entire charge at the time of the patient's encounter, the assigned status of the claim is voided and the nonPAR limiting charge is then in effect. The nonPAR may also be subject to a fine or may be in violation of MPFS requirements.

The nonPAR cannot revoke the agreement for an assigned claim *unless* it is by mutual written consent of the provider and the beneficiary. Even then, such an agreement must be communicated to the MAC *before* the MAC has determined the allowed amount. Providers who repeatedly violate the assignment agreement could be charged and found guilty of a misdemeanor, which is punishable by a fine, imprisonment, or both. In addition, a criminal violation may result in suspension from Medicare participation.

The following practitioners who submit claims for services must accept assignment:

- Anesthesiologist assistants
- Certified nurse midwives
- Certified registered nurse anesthetists
- Clinical nurse specialists
- Clinical psychologists
- Clinical social workers
- Mass immunization roster billers
- Nurse practitioners
- Physician assistants
- Registered dietitians

Providers who submit claims for the following services must accept assignment:

- Ambulance services
- Ambulatory surgical center services
- Clinical diagnostic laboratory services
- Home dialysis supplies and equipment
- Medications
- Physician lab services
- Physician services to Medicare-Medicaid (Medi-Medi) crossover patients

Example: A patient undergoes laboratory procedures and sees the nonPAR physician during an office visit (E/M service). If the nonPAR accepts assignment for just the laboratory procedures, two claims must be submitted: one for the laboratory services and another for the office visit.

Waiver of Medicare Billing Contracts

Medicare law specifically states that nonPARs are subject to sanctions, including fines and exclusions from the Medicare program, if they (1) require patients to sign agreements stating that the patient waives the right to have the nonPAR provider file the patient's Medicare claims, or (2) require that the patient agrees to pay charges for services that are in excess of the nonPAR charge limits.

Privacy Act of 1974

In addition to the other restrictions, the *Privacy Act of 1974* forbids the Medicare administrative contractor (MAC) from disclosing the status of any unassigned claim to the nonPAR beyond the following:

- Date the claim was received by the MAC
- Date the claim was paid, denied, or suspended
- General reason the claim was suspended

The nonPAR provider will *not* be told payment amounts or approved charge information.

Opt-Out Providers

An **opt-out provider** (e.g., psychiatrist) does not accept Medicare and has signed an agreement to be excluded from the Medicare program. Such providers are permitted to charge whatever they want for services; however, they must adhere to certain rules to do so. Medicare will not pay for care received from an opt-out provider *except for emergencies*. The patient is responsible for all costs of care received from an opt-out provider.

Patients must be provided with a copy of the private contract that describes charges. Patients sign the private contract to confirm that they understand they are responsible for all costs of health care services provided and that Medicare will not reimburse the patient. Opt-out providers do *not* submit CMS-1500 claims to Medicare for services patients receive.

Private Contract

Under the Balanced Budget Act of 1997, physicians were provided the option of withdrawing from Medicare and entering into private contracts with their Medicare patients. This **Medicare private contract** is an agreement between the Medicare beneficiary and a physician or other practitioner who has "opted out" of Medicare for two years for *all* covered items and services furnished to Medicare beneficiaries. This means that the physician or other health care practitioner will not bill for any service or supplies provided to any Medicare beneficiary for at least two years.

Under a private contract:

- No Medicare payment will be made for services or procedures provided to a patient.
- The patient is required to pay whatever the physician/practitioner charges.
- There is no limit on what the physician/practitioner can charge for Medicare-approved services (and the limiting charge does not apply).
- Medicare managed care plans will not pay for services rendered under a private contract.
- No claim is to be submitted to Medicare, and Medicare will not pay if a claim is submitted.
- Supplemental insurance (Medigap) will not pay for services or procedures provided.
- Other insurance plans may not pay for services or procedures rendered.

The private contract applies only to services and procedures rendered by the provider with whom the patient signed an agreement. Patients cannot be asked to sign a private contract when facing an emergency or urgent health situation. If patients want to pay for services that the Original Medicare Plan does not cover, the physician does not have to leave Medicare or ask the patient to sign a private contract. The patient is welcome to obtain noncovered services and to pay for those services.

A physician who enters into a Medicare private contract with one patient will be unable to bill Medicare for any patient for a period of two years with the exception of emergency or urgent care provided to a patient who has not signed an agreement with the provider to forego Medicare benefits. In emergency or urgent care cases, any claim submitted for urgent or emergency care must be accompanied by an attachment explaining the following: (1) the nature of the emergency or urgent problem, and (2) a statement affirming that this patient has not signed an agreement with the provider to forego Medicare. If a provider submits a nonemergency or urgent care claim for any patient before the opt-out agreement becomes effective, the provider must submit claims for all Medicare patients thereafter and abide by the limiting charge rules. However, if the patient files the claim, the provider will not be penalized.

Mandatory Claims Submission

Federal law requires that all providers and suppliers submit claims to Medicare if they provide a Medicare-covered service to a patient enrolled in Medicare Part B. This regulation does not apply if the:

- Patient is not enrolled in Part B.
- Patient disenrolled before the service was furnished.

- Patient or the patient's legal representative refuses to sign an authorization for release of medical information.
- Provider opts out of the Medicare program, and those patients enter into private contracts with the provider (see section on Private Contracting).

An exception may occur if a patient refuses to sign an authorization for the release of medical information to Medicare. However, if the patient later opts to sign a Medicare authorization and requests that claims for all prior services be filed with Medicare, the request must be honored.

Advance Beneficiary Notice of Noncoverage

An **advance beneficiary notice of noncoverage (ABN)** is a written document provided to a Medicare beneficiary by a supplier, physician, or provider prior to service being rendered (Figure 14-3) to inform beneficiaries in the traditional fee-for-service Medicare program about possible noncovered charges when *limitation of liability (LOL)* applies. The ABN indicates that the service is unlikely to be reimbursed by Medicare, specifies why Medicare denial is anticipated, and requests the beneficiary to sign an agreement that guarantees personal payment for services. A beneficiary who signs an ABN agreement will be held responsible for payment of the bill if Medicare denies payment. ABNs should be generated whenever the supplier or provider believes that a claim for the services is likely to receive a Medicare **medical necessity denial** (a denial of otherwise covered services that were found to be not "reasonable and necessary") or when the service would be considered custodial care. The provider is held liable for the service and cannot bill the Medicare administrative contractor (MAC) or the Medicare beneficiary *unless the beneficiary signs an ABN*, which makes the beneficiary liable for payment if they opt to receive the service after notice was provided. Providers must also have patients sign an ABN prior to providing preventative services that are usually covered by Medicare but will not be covered because the frequency of providing such services has been exceeded.

Caution

Do not obtain ABNs on every procedure or service to be rendered to a patient "just in case" Medicare denies the claim. To do so is considered fraudulent.

Billing Tip

The purpose of obtaining the ABN is to ensure payment for a procedure or service that might not be reimbursed under Medicare.

Cost estimates are unnecessary when an ABN is generated, because the purpose of the ABN is to document that the beneficiary has received notice that a service is unlikely to be reimbursed by Medicare. Hospital ABNs are called Hospital-Issued Notices of Noncoverage (HINN) or Notices of Noncoverage (NONC).

Do not have a patient sign an ABN when a service is *never* covered by Medicare. Instead, have those patients sign a different form, called the Notice of Exclusion of Medicare Benefits (NEMB). The ABN is used when the service is sometimes covered by Medicare, but the provider does not think it will be covered for that patient. It communicates that the patient will be responsible for provider charges if Medicare denies the service. The NEMB clearly states that the service is never covered by Medicare, and that the patient is responsible for paying provider charges. Unlike the ABN, providers are not required to have patients sign an NEMB for a never-covered Medicare service in order to bill the patient; however, use of the form makes it clear to the patient *before* a service is provided that the patient will have to pay for it.

A. Notifier:

B. Patient Name: **C. Identification Number:**

ADVANCE BENEFICIARY NOTICE OF NONCOVERAGE (ABN)

NOTE: If Medicare doesn't pay for **D.** _____ below, you may have to pay.

Medicare does not pay for everything, even some care that you or your health care provider have good reason to think you need. We expect Medicare may not pay for the **D.** _____ below.

D.	**E. Reason Medicare May Not Pay:**	**F. Estimated Cost:**

WHAT YOU NEED TO DO NOW:

- Read this notice, so you can make an informed decision about your care.
- Ask us any questions that you may have after you finish reading.
- Choose an option below about whether to receive the **D.** _____ listed above.
  Note: If you choose Option 1 or 2, we may help you to use any other insurance that you might have, but Medicare cannot require us to do this.

G. OPTIONS: Check only one box. We cannot choose a box for you.

☐ **OPTION 1.** I want the **D.** _____ listed above. You may ask to be paid now, but I also want Medicare billed for an official decision on payment, which is sent to me on a Medicare Summary Notice (MSN). I understand that if Medicare doesn't pay, I am responsible for payment, but I can appeal to Medicare by following the directions on the MSN. If Medicare does pay, you will refund any payments I made to you, less copays or deductibles.

☐ **OPTION 2.** I want the **D.** _____ listed above, but do not bill Medicare. You may ask to be paid now as I am responsible for payment. I cannot appeal if Medicare is not billed.

☐ **OPTION 3.** I don't want the **D.** _____ listed above. I understand with this choice I am **not** responsible for payment, and I cannot appeal to see if Medicare would pay.

H. Additional Information:

This notice gives our opinion, not an official Medicare decision. If you have other questions on this notice or Medicare billing, call **1-800-MEDICARE** (1-800-633-4227/**TTY**: 1-877-486-2048).

Signing below means that you have received and understand this notice. You also receive a copy.

I. Signature:	**J. Date:**

Form CMS-R-131 (Exp. 06/30/2023)   Form Approved OMB No. 0938-0566

Courtesy of the Centers for Medicare & Medicaid Services, www.cms.gov.

FIGURE 14-3 Advance beneficiary notice of noncoverage form approved for use by CMS.

NOTE:

Electronic ABNs allow beneficiaries to view the notice on a computer screen prior to signing, and the beneficiary is provided with a printout of the signed document.

- Providers must retain copies of ABNs for five years from the date of service, and electronic retention of the signed paper document is acceptable (e.g., scanned ABN).
- An ABN is in effect for one year from date of signature unless there are changes to what is described on the form.

There are four modifiers that can be added to codes assigned to procedures and services that may be denied. Depending on the procedure performed or the service provided and specific circumstances, the modifier may be required by Medicare or voluntarily added to the code. The following modifiers are added to codes when Medicare is expected to deny the service or item as not reasonable and necessary.

- -GA: Waiver of liability statement (ABN) issued as required by payer policy, individual case, which is used to report that a required ABN was issued for a service and is on file. Medicare will automatically deny these services and assign liability to the beneficiary. Because the provider obtained an ABN, the patient can be billed for this service.

- -GZ: Item or service expected to be denied as not reasonable and necessary, which indicates an ABN was not issued for this service. Medicare will automatically deny these services and indicate the beneficiary is not responsible for payment. Because the provider did not obtain an ABN prior to performing the service, the patient cannot be billed.

The following modifiers are added to codes when procedures and services do not meet medical necessity as determined by a Medicare Local Coverage Determination (LCD) or National Coverage Determination (NCD). These modifiers may also be added to codes for procedures and services that are statutorily (by law) excluded from the Medicare program. The use of an ABN is optional for such situations, but it is proof that the beneficiary accepts liability for payment of these services.

- -GX: Notice of liability issued, voluntary under payer policy, which is used to report that a voluntary ABN was issued for a procedure or service that is statutorily excluded from Medicare reimbursement. Medicare will reject noncovered procedures and services appended with -GX and assign liability to the beneficiary.

- -GY: Item or service statutorily excluded or does not meet the definition of any Medicare benefit, which is used when a procedure or service is excluded by Medicare and an ABN was not issued to the beneficiary. Medicare will deny these claims, and the beneficiary will be liable.

Modifiers -GX and -GY are informational only, and when used, they allow the provider to bill the beneficiary.

> **Example:** Mary Jones is a 70-year-old female Medicare beneficiary who is evaluated for possible facial cosmetic surgery. Because cosmetic surgery is excluded from the Medicare program, the provider's office has the patient sign an *advance beneficiary notice of noncoverage (ABN)* so that the Medicare beneficiary (Mary Jones) can be billed for all procedures performed and services provided. Modifier -GY is added to codes submitted for all procedures and services.

Medicare as Primary and Secondary Payer

Medicare as primary payer processes submitted claims first and reimburses providers up to the limits of coverage, while *Medicare as secondary payer (MSP)* processes submitted claims after the primary payer (e.g., employer group health plan) has reimbursed providers up to the limits of such primary coverage (Table 14-3). When an MSP claim is submitted, the primary payer's remittance advice is attached to the claim.

Medicare as Primary Payer

Medicare is considered the primary payer under the following circumstances:

- The employee is eligible for a group health plan but has declined to enroll, or has recently dropped coverage.
- The individual is currently employed, but is not yet eligible for group plan coverage or has exhausted benefits under the plan.
- The health insurance plan is only for self-employed individuals.
- The health insurance plan was purchased as an individual plan and not obtained through a group.
- The patient is also covered by TRICARE, which provides health benefits to retired members of the uniformed services and spouses/children of active duty, retired, and deceased service members.

TABLE 14-3 Determining how Medicare works with other insurance

Scenario	Medicare payment
If patient has *retiree* group health plan coverage (including from a spouse's former employment)...	Medicare pays first.
If patient is 65 or older, has group health plan coverage based on a spouse's *current* employment, and the employer has *20 or more employees*...	Group health plan pays first. Medicare pays second.
If patient is 65 or older, has group health plan coverage based on a spouse's *current* employment, and the employer has *less than 20 employees*...	Medicare pays first.
If patient is under 65 and has disabilities, has group health plan coverage based on a family member's *current* employment, and the employer has *100 or more employees*...	Group health plan pays first. Medicare pays second.
If patient is under 65 and has disabilities, has group health plan coverage based on a family member's *current* employment, and the employer has *less than 100 employees*...	Medicare pays first.
If patient has Medicare because of *end-stage renal disease (ESRD)*...	Group health plan pays first for the first 30 months after patient becomes eligible to enroll in Medicare. Then, Medicare pays first *after* this 30-month period.

- The patient is under age 65, has Medicare because of a disability or ESRD, and is not covered by an employer-sponsored plan.
- The patient is under age 65, has ESRD, and has an employer-sponsored plan but has been eligible for Medicare for more than 30 months.
- The patient has left a company and has elected to continue coverage in the group health plan under federal COBRA rules.
- The patient has both Medicare and Medicaid (Medi-Medi crossover patient).

The Consolidated Omnibus Budget Reconciliation Act of 1985 (COBRA) requires employers with 20 or more employees to allow employees and their dependents to keep their employer-sponsored group health insurance coverage for up to 18 months for any of the following occurrences:

- Death of the employed spouse
- Loss of employment or reduction in work hours
- Divorce

The employee or dependents may have to pay their share as well as the employer's share of the premium.

Medicare Conditional Primary Payer Status

Medicare will award an assigned claim **conditional primary payer status** and process the claim under the following circumstances:

- A plan that is normally considered primary to Medicare issues a denial of payment that is under appeal.
- A patient with a physical or intellectual disability fails to file a claim with the primary payer.
- A workers' compensation claim has been denied, and the case is slowly moving through the appeal process.
- There is no response from a liability payer within 120 days of submitting the claim.

Medicare is to be reimbursed immediately if payment is received from the primary payer at a later date.

Medicare as Secondary Payer

The **Medicare Secondary Payer (MSP)** rules state that Medicare is secondary when the patient is eligible for Medicare and is also covered by one or more of the following plans:

- An **employer-sponsored group health plan (EGHP)** that has more than 20 covered employees and provides coverage to employees and dependents without regard to enrollee's employment status (e.g., full-time, part-time, retired)
- Disability coverage through an employer-sponsored group health plan that has more than 100 covered employees
- An end-stage renal disease case covered by an employer-sponsored group plan of any size during the first 18 months of the patient's eligibility for Medicare
- A third-party liability policy, if the Medicare-eligible person is seeking treatment for an injury covered by such a policy (this category includes automobile insurance, no-fault insurance, and self-insured liability plans)
- A workers' compensation program; if the claim is contested, the provider should file a Medicare primary claim and include a copy of the workers' compensation notice declaring that the case is "pending a Compensation Board decision"
- Veterans Administration (VA) preauthorized services for a beneficiary who is eligible for both VA benefits and Medicare
- Federal Black Lung Program that covers currently or formerly employed coal miners

All primary plans, which are collectively described in the Medicare literature as *MSP plans*, must be billed first. Medicare is billed only after the remittance advice from the primary plan or plans has been received. (The remittance advice must be attached to the Medicare claim when the claim is submitted.)

> **Example:** An individual receives treatment from a physician who charges $250. The individual's Medicare Part B deductible has previously been met. As primary payer, the employer group health plan's (EGHP) allowed charge is $200, and the EGHP pays 80 percent of this amount (or $160). The Medicare physician fee schedule amount is $150. The Medicare secondary payment is calculated as follows:
>
> - Physician charge minus EGHP payment ($250 − $160 = $90)
> - Medicare payment (determined in usual manner) (80 percent of $150 = $120)
> - EGHP allowable charge minus EGHP payment ($200 − $160 = $40)
> - Medicare pays $40 (lowest of amounts in steps 1, 2, or 3)

 NOTE:

> Providers are required to determine whether Medicare is a primary or secondary payer for each inpatient admission of a Medicare beneficiary and each outpatient encounter with a Medicare beneficiary prior to submitting a bill to Medicare. It must accomplish this by asking the beneficiary about other insurance coverage.
>
> Be sure to submit a claim to Medicare for services paid by a primary payer, even if the primary payer reimbursed the entire amount charged. Failure to submit claims to Medicare could result in patients being denied credit toward their Medicare deductible.

Independent and hospital labs are to enter NONE in Block 11 of the CMS-1500 claim when they bill Medicare for reference lab services when there is no face-to-face encounter with a Medicare patient. CMS does not require labs to collect Medicare secondary payer information to bill Medicare if they have had no face-to-face encounter with the patient. Entering NONE in Block 11 will prevent claims from being denied as unprocessable. When independent or hospital labs have face-to-face encounters with Medicare patients, they must collect MSP information.

Federal law requires that Medicare recover any money spent for care as a secondary payer before a settlement is dispersed, and standardized options for beneficiaries to manage any settlements relating to auto, liability, and workers' compensation insurance include the following:

- The individual or beneficiary pays for all related future medical care until the settlement is exhausted and documents it accordingly.
- Medicare would not pursue future medical recoveries if the individual or beneficiary's case fits a number of conditions in the proposal.
- The individual or beneficiary acquires and provides an attestation regarding the date of care completion from the treating physician.
- The individual or beneficiary submits proposed Medicare Set-Aside Arrangement (MSA) amounts for CMS review and obtains approval.
- The beneficiary participates in one of Medicare's recovery options.
- The beneficiary makes an up-front payment.
- The beneficiary obtains a compromise or waiver of recovery.

To avoid fines and penalties for routinely billing Medicare as primary when it is the secondary payer, a more detailed Medicare secondary payer questionnaire (Figure 14-4) should be provided to all Medicare patients when they register/reregister (update demographic and/or insurance information) with the practice. This form is used to clarify primary and secondary insurance payers.

Exercise 14.1 – Medicare as Secondary Payer

Review the following cases and determine the primary payer for each.

Example: The 68-year-old patient is retired and covered by Medicare, an employer-sponsored retirement plan, and his 55-year-old spouse's employer-sponsored large group plan.

Primary payer: Employer-sponsored large group plan.

1. The 72-year-old patient is the policyholder in an employer-sponsored large group plan and has Medicare and Medigap policy. The provider is a participating provider.

   Primary payer: _____

2. The 75-year-old patient has Medicare and an employer-sponsored retirement plan. The claim is for an injury received in a car accident, for which the patient has automobile liability insurance. The provider is a participating provider.

   Primary payer: _____

3. The 70-year-old patient has an employer-sponsored retirement plan as a supplemental policy through a former employer. The patient also has Medicare. The patient is diagnosed with cancer. The spouse is deceased. The provider is a participating provider.

   Primary payer: _____

4. The patient is 67, working full-time, and covered by Medicare, an employer-sponsored large group plan, and a Medigap plan. The spouse is retired, 62, and covered by an employer-sponsored plan for 18 employees. The provider is a participating provider.

   Primary payer: _____

5. The patient is 50 and a person with a disability. The patient collects Social Security (due to the disability) and has Medicare (due to the disability) and disability coverage through an employer-sponsored group health plan that covers 50 employees.

   Primary payer: _____

Goodmedicine Clinic ■ 1 Provider St ■ Anywhere, US 12345 ■ (101) 111-2222

To: All Medicare Patients

In order for us to comply with the Medicare as Secondary Payer laws, you must complete this form before we can properly process your insurance claim.

Please complete this questionnaire and return it to the front desk. We will also need to make photocopies of all your insurance identification cards. Do not hesitate to ask for clarification of any item on this form.

CHECK ALL ITEMS THAT DESCRIBE YOUR HEALTH INSURANCE COVERAGE

1. I am working full time _____ part time _____ . I retired on ___/___/___.

2. _____ I am enrolled in a Medicare HMO plan.
   _____ I am entitled to Black Lung Benefits.
   _____ I had a job-related injury on ___/___/___.
   _____ I have a fee service card from the VA.
   _____ I had an organ transplant on ___/___/___.
   _____ I have been on kidney dialysis since ___/___/___.
   _____ I am being treated for an injury received in a car accident _____.
   _____ Other vehicle (please identify)
   _____ Other type of accident (please identify) _____

   _____.

3. _____ I am employed/My spouse is employed and I am covered by an employer-sponsored health care program covering more than 20 employees. Name of policy:

   _____

4. _____ I/My spouse has purchased a private insurance policy to supplement Medicare. Name of policy:

   _____

5. _____ I have health insurance through my/my spouse's previous employer or union. Name of previous employer or union:

   _____

6. _____ I am covered by Medicaid and my ID number is: _____

7. _____ I am retired and covered by an employer-sponsored retiree health care plan. Name of plan:

   _____

8. _____ I am retired, but have been called back temporarily and have employee health benefits while I am working. Name of plan:

   _____

Patient Signature _____   Date _____/_____/_____

FIGURE 14-4 Sample Medicare secondary payer questionnaire.

Medicare Summary Notice

The *Medicare Summary Notice* (MSN) (Figure 14-5) is an easy-to-read statement sent to Medicare patients every three months, which clearly lists Medicare claims information. It replaced the Explanation of Medicare Benefits (EOMB), the Medicare Benefits Notice (Part A), and benefit denial letters.

Medicare Summary Notice
for Part B (Medical Insurance)

Page 1 of 4

The Official Summary of Your Medicare Claims from the Centers for Medicare & Medicaid Services

THIS IS NOT A BILL

Patient Name here
Street Address
City, State 12345-6789

Notice for Your Name

Medicare Number	9999AA99999
Date of This Notice	September 16, YYYY
Claims Processed Between	June 15 – September 15, YYYY

Your Deductible Status

Your deductible is what you must pay for most health services before Medicare begins to pay.

Part B Deductible: You have now met $85 of your $XXX.XX deductible for YYYY

Be Informed!

Welcome to your new Medicare Summary Notice! It has clear language, larger print, and a personal summary of your claims and deductibles. This improved notice better explains how to get help with your questions, report fraud, or file an appeal. It also includes important information from Medicare!

Your Claims & Costs This Period

Did Medicare Approve All Services?	NO
Number of Services Medicare Denied	1

See claims starting on page 3. Look for **NO** in the "Service Approved?" column. See the last page for how to handle a denied claim.

Total You May Be Billed	$90.15

Providers with Claims This Period

June 18, YYYY
Jane Doe, M.D.

¿Sabía que puede recibir este aviso y otro tipo de ayuda de Medicare en español? Llame y hable con un agente en española.
如果需要国语帮助，请致电联邦医疗保险，请先说 "agent"，然后说" Mandarin".   **1-800-MEDICARE (1-800-633-4227)**

FIGURE 14-5 Sample Medicare Summary Notice (Page 1 of 4).

Medicare Billing Notes

Medicare Administrative Contractor (MAC)

The regional MAC for traditional Medicare claims is selected by CMS through a competitive bidding process, and jurisdictions are determined. Obtain the name and mailing address of the MAC for your region.

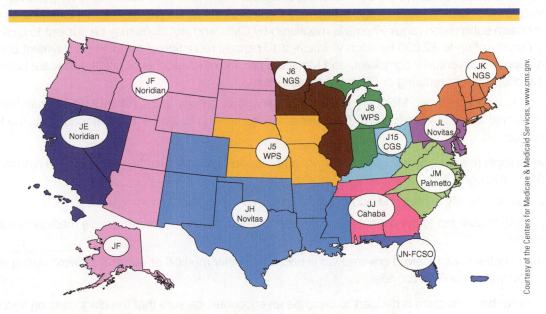

Medicare Administrative Contractor
A/B Jurisdiction Map
as of December 2015

Courtesy of the Centers for Medicare & Medicaid Services, www.cms.gov.

Medicare Split/Shared Visit Payment Policy

The *Medicare split/shared visit payment policy* applies when the physician and a qualified nonphysician provider (NPP) (e.g., nurse practitioner, physician assistant) each personally perform a substantive portion of a medically necessary evaluation and management (E/M) service for the same patient on the same date of service. A *substantive portion of an E/M visit* involves performing all or some portion of the history, examination, or medical decision making (the key components of an E/M service). The physician and qualified NPP must be in the same group practice or be employed by the same employer.

Durable Medical Equipment Claims

Durable medical equipment (DME) claims must be sent to one of four regional Medicare administrative contractors in the country. Check the Medicare manual for the one responsible for processing DME claims for your region.

Deadline for Submitting Claims

The claim submission deadline for Medicare claims is 12 months (or one calendar year) after the date of service. (The Affordable Care Act amended the time period for submitting Medicare fee-for-service [FFS] claims to one calendar year after the date of service.) Any claims received after that date will be denied due to being past the timely filing statute.

Example 1: A claim for services performed on January 28 this year must be received by the Medicare administrative contractor (MAC) by January 28 of next year.

Example 2: A claim for services performed on November 5 this year must be received by the MAC by November 5 of next year.

Claim Used

Medicare administrative contracts accept the CMS-1500 claim for professional services (and the UB-04 claim for institutional services).

Special Handling

According to the Social Security Act, a providers are required to file Medicare claims for their patients. Noncompliance with MSP rules and regulations may result in a substantial penalty or fine. Compliance with mandatory claim submission requirements is monitored by CMS, and violations may be subject to a civil monetary penalty of up to $2,000 for each violation, a 10 percent reduction of a provider's payment once the physician/supplier is eventually compliant, and Medicare program exclusion. In addition, Medicare beneficiaries may not be charged for preparing or filing a Medicare claim.

For each submission, when Medicare is the secondary payer, a copy of the primary payer's remittance advice must be attached to the Medicare claim. Two claims may be needed to describe one encounter in the following circumstances:

- When multiple referring, ordering, or supervising names and provider identifier numbers are required in Blocks 17 through 17a
- When multiple facility names and addresses are required in Block 32
- When DME is charged to the patient at the same time the patient had a reimbursable medical or surgical encounter
- When the patient has received covered lab services and other medical or surgical services during an encounter with a nonPAR provider

When more than one claim is needed to describe an encounter, be sure that the diagnoses on each claim prove the medical necessity for performing the service, and that the proper names and numbers required in Blocks 17, 17a, and 32 appear on the correct claims.

Telehealth

For claims submitted for *telehealth* (*telemedicine*) services, report CPT and HCPCS Level II codes with telehealth HCPCS Level II modifier -GT (via interactive audio and video telecommunications systems) (e.g., 99202-GT), which certifies that the beneficiary (patient) was present at an eligible originating site when the telehealth service was provided. Claims are submitted to the Medicare Administrative Contractor (MAC) for covered telehealth services, and Medicare reimburses the provider the appropriate amount under the Medicare Physician Fee Schedule (PFS) for telehealth services.

Originating sites for telehealth services are paid an *originating site facility fee* for telehealth services as described by HCPCS Level II code Q3014 (telehealth originating site facility fee). Claims are submitted to the MAC for the originating site facility fee, which is a separately billable Medicare Part B payment. (When a Community Mental Health Center [CMHC] serves as an originating site, the originating site facility fee *does not count toward the number of services used to determine payment for partial hospitalization services*.)

For providers located in a critical access hospital (CAH) who reassign billing rights to a CAH that elected the Optional Payment Method, the CAH submits claims to the MAC for telehealth services, and the payment amount is 80 percent of the Medicare PFS for telehealth services.

Federal telemedicine demonstration programs in Alaska or Hawaii allow claims submission of CPT or HCPCS Level II codes for professional services with telehealth modifier -GQ (via an asynchronous telecommunications system) (e.g., 99202-GQ), which certifies that the asynchronous medical file was collected and transmitted to the provider at a site distant from a federal telemedicine demonstration project conducted in Alaska or Hawaii.

Medicare Claims Instructions

The law requires that all Medicare claims be filed using optical character recognition, which means when scanned the data entered can be recognized by computer software. Practices must make certain that claims generated by computer software follow Medicare claims processing guidelines. Extraneous data on the claims or data appearing in blocks not consistent with Medicare guidelines will cause the claim to be rejected.

Review Chapter 11, "CMS-1500 and UB-04 Claims" before working with Medicare claims instructions.

NOTE:

Medicare Claims Processing Manual Chapter 26: Completing and Processing Form CMS-1500 Data Set allows for entry of 6- or 8-digit dates in all CMS-1500 blocks *except for birth dates in Blocks 3 and 11a, which require 8-digit dates.* However, consistency when entering 6- or 8-digit dates throughout the claim is required. For example, do not enter a 6-digit date in CMS-1500 Block 14 (date of current illness) but 8-digit dates in Blocks 12, 13, 15, 16, 18, 24A, and 31. National Uniform Claims Committee (NUCC) CMS-1500 claims completion instructions state that dates entered in Block 24A must be six digits (MM DD YY) only, which differs from Medicare claims completion instructions. (For *Understanding Health Insurance* claims completion, 6-digit dates are entered *except for birth dates in Blocks 3 and 11a, which require 8-digit dates.*)

Read the following instructions carefully. Medicare requires many details that are not required for other payers discussed in this text.

These instructions (Table 14-4) are for submitting primary Original Medicare Plan claims when the patient is not covered by additional insurance. (Instructions for submitting Medicare-HMO fee-for-service claims are found in Chapter 12.)

During review of the instructions, refer to the John Q. Public case study in Figure 14-6 and the completed CMS-1500 claim (Figure 14-7).

NOTE:

- Refer to Chapter 11 of this textbook for clarification of claims completion (e.g., entering names, mailing addresses, ICD-10-CM codes, diagnosis pointer letters, NPI, and so on).
- Use these instructions when completing any claims associated with *Understanding Health Insurance.*

TABLE 14-4 CMS-1500 claims completion instructions for Medicare primary claims

Block	Instructions
1	Enter an X in the Medicare box.
1a	Enter the Medicare beneficiary identifier (MBI) as it appears on the patient's insurance card. *Do not enter hyphens or spaces in the number.*
2	Enter the patient's last name, first name, and middle initial (separated by commas) (e.g., DOE, JOHN, J).
3	Enter the patient's birth date as MM DD YYYY (with spaces). Enter an X in the appropriate box to indicate the patient's sex. If the patient's sex is unknown, leave blank.
4	Leave blank. *Block 4 is completed if the patient has other insurance primary to Medicare (e.g., employer group health plan) (discussed later in this chapter).*
5	Enter the patient's mailing address. Enter the street address on line 1, enter the city and state on line 2, and enter the five- or nine-digit zip code on line 3. *Do not enter the hyphen or a space for a 9-digit ZIP code. Do not enter the telephone number.*
6	Leave blank.
7	Leave blank. *Block 7 is completed if the patient has other insurance primary to Medicare (e.g., employer group health plan) (discussed later in this chapter).*
8	Leave blank.
9, 9a, 9d	Leave blank. *Blocks 9, 9a, and 9d are completed if the patient has secondary insurance coverage, such as Medigap (discussed later in this chapter).*
9b–9c	Leave blank.
10a–c	Enter an X in the NO boxes. (If an X is entered in the YES box for auto accident, enter the two-character state abbreviation of the patient's residence.)
10d	Leave blank.
11	Enter NONE, which indicates the provider has made a good-faith effort to determine whether Medicare is the primary or secondary payer.
11a	Leave blank.
11b	Leave blank. This is reserved for property and casualty or workers' compensation claims.

(continues)

TABLE 14-4 (continued)

Block	Instructions
11c–d	Leave blank.
12	Enter SIGNATURE ON FILE. Leave the date field blank. (The abbreviation SOF is also acceptable.)
13	Leave blank. *Block 13 is completed if the patient has Medigap coverage.*
14	Enter the date as MM DD YY (with spaces) to indicate when the patient first experienced signs or symptoms of the present illness, actual date of injury, *or* the date of the last menstrual period (LMP) for obstetric visits. Enter the applicable qualifier to identify which date is being reported: 431 (onset of current symptoms/illness or injury) *or* 484 (last menstrual period). *If the date is not documented in the patient's record, but the history indicates an appropriate date (e.g., three weeks ago), simply count back to the approximate date and enter it on the claim.*
15	Leave blank.
16	Enter dates as MM DD YY (with spaces) to indicate the period of time the patient was unable to work in his current occupation, *if documented in the patient's record. An entry in this block might indicate employment-related insurance coverage.* Otherwise, leave blank.
17	If applicable, enter the first name, middle initial (if known), last name, and credentials of the professional who referred, ordered, or supervised health care service(s) or supply(ies) reported on the claim. *Do not enter any punctuation.* In front of the name, enter the applicable qualifier to identify which provider is being reported, as follows: DN (referring provider), DK (ordering provider), or DQ (supervising provider). Otherwise, leave blank.
17a	Leave blank.
17b	Enter the 10-digit national provider identifier (NPI) of the professional in Block 17. Otherwise, leave blank.
18	Enter the admission date and discharge date as MM DD YY (with spaces) if the patient received inpatient services (e.g., hospital, skilled nursing facility). Otherwise, leave blank. *If the patient has not been discharged at the time the claim is completed, leave the discharge date blank.*
19	Leave blank.
20	Enter an X in the NO box if all laboratory procedures reported on the claim were performed in the provider's office. Otherwise, enter an X in the YES box, enter the total amount charged by the outside laboratory in $ CHARGES, and enter the outside laboratory's name, mailing address, and NPI in Block 32. (Charges are entered *without* punctuation. For example, $1,100.00 is entered as 110000 below $ CHARGES.)
21	Enter the ICD-10-CM code for up to 12 diagnoses or conditions treated or medically managed during the encounter. Lines A through L in Block 21 will relate to CPT or HCPCS Level II service or procedure codes reported in Block 24E. In the *ICD Ind* (ICD indicator) box, enter 0 for ICD-10-CM.
22	Leave blank. This is reserved for resubmitted claims.
23	Enter the applicable quality improvement organization (QIO) prior authorization number, investigational device exemption (IDE) number, NPI for a physician performing care plan oversight services of a home health agency or hospice, referral number, mammography precertification number, 10-digit Clinical Laboratory Improvement Amendments (CLIA) certification number, or skilled nursing facility NPI. *Do not enter hyphens or spaces in the number.* Otherwise, leave blank.
24A	Enter the date the procedure or service was performed in the FROM column as MM DD YY (with spaces). Enter a date in the TO column *if the procedure or service was performed on consecutive days during a range of dates. Then, enter the number of consecutive days in Block 24G.* Note: The shaded area in each line is used to enter supplemental information to support reported services *if instructed by the payer to enter such information.* Data entry in Block 24 is limited to reporting six services. *Do not use the shaded lines to report additional services.* If additional services were provided, generate new CMS-1500 claim(s) to report the additional services.
24B	Enter the appropriate two-digit place-of-service (POS) code to identify the location where the reported procedure or service was performed.
24C	Leave blank.
24D	Enter the CPT or HCPCS Level II code and applicable required modifier(s) for procedures or services performed. *Separate the CPT/HCPCS code and first modifier with one space. Separate additional modifiers with one space each. Up to four modifiers can be entered.*

(continues)

TABLE 14-4 (continued)

Block	Instructions
24E	Enter the diagnosis pointer letter(s) from Block 21 that relate to the procedure or service performed on the date of service to justify medical necessity of procedures and services reported on the claim.
24F	Enter the fee charged for each reported procedure or service. *Do not enter commas, periods, or dollar signs. Do not enter negative amounts. Enter 00 in the cents area if the amount is a whole number.*
24G	Enter the number of days or units for procedures or services reported in Block 24D. *If just one procedure or service was reported in Block 24D, enter a 1 in Block 24G.*
24H	Leave blank. Reserved for Medicaid claims.
24I	Leave blank. The NPI abbreviation is preprinted on the CMS-1500 claim.
24J	Enter the 10-digit NPI for the: • Provider who performed the service *if the provider is a member of a group practice* (Leave blank if the provider is a solo practitioner.) • Supervising provider *if the service was provided incident-to the service of a physician or nonphysician practitioner* **and** *the physician or practitioner who ordered the service did not supervise the provider* (Leave blank if the incident-to service was performed under the supervision of the physician or nonphysician practitioner.) • DMEPOS supplier or outside laboratory *if the physician submits the claim for services provided by the DMEPOS supplier or outside laboratory* (Leave blank if the DMEPOS supplier or outside laboratory submits the claim.) Otherwise, leave blank.
25	Enter the provider's Social Security number (SSN) or employer identification number (EIN*). Do not enter hyphens or spaces in the number.* Enter an X in the appropriate box to indicate which number is reported.
26	Enter the patient's account number as assigned by the provider.
27	Enter an X in the YES box to indicate that the provider agrees to accept assignment. Otherwise, enter an X in the NO box.
28	Enter the total charges for services and/or procedures reported in Block 24. Note: If multiple claims are submitted for one patient because more than six procedures or services were reported, be sure the total charge reported on each claim accurately represents the total of the items on each submitted claim.
29	Enter the total amount the patient (or another payer) paid *toward covered services only.* If no payment was made, leave blank.
30	Leave blank.
31	Enter the provider's name and credential (e.g., MARY SMITH MD) and the date the claim was completed as MMDDYY (without spaces). *Do not enter any punctuation.*
32	Enter the name and address where procedures or services were provided, such as *a hospital, an outside laboratory facility, a physician's office, a skilled nursing facility, or a DMEPOS supplier.* Enter the name on line 1, the address on line 2, and the city, state, and nine-digit zip code on line 3. *Do not enter the hyphen or a space for a 9-digit ZIP code. If procedures or services were provided in the patient's home, leave blank.* **Example:** Dr. Brilliant is a solo practitioner. Enter Dr. Brilliant's name, credential, and address in Block 32. Dr. Healer practices at the Goodmedicine Clinic. Enter Goodmedicine Clinic and its address in Block 32. Note: If Block 18 contains dates of service for inpatient care and/or Block 20 contains an X in the YES box, enter the name and address of the facility that provided services.
32a	Enter the 10-digit NPI of the provider entered in Block 32.
32b	Leave blank.
33	Enter the provider's *billing* name, address, and telephone number. Enter the phone number in the area next to the block title. *Do not enter parentheses for the area code.* Enter the name on line 1, enter the address on line 2, and enter the city, state, and nine-digit zip code on line 3. *Do not enter the hyphen or a space for a 9-digit ZIP code.*
33a	Enter the 10-digit NPI of the *billing* provider (e.g., solo practitioner) or group practice (e.g., clinic).
33b	Leave blank.

ERIN A. HELPER, M.D.
101 Medic Drive, Anywhere, NY 12345-9874
(101) 111-1234 (Office) • (101) 111-9292 (Fax)
EIN: 11-1234523
NPI: 1234567890

Case Study

PATIENT INFORMATION:

Name:	Public, John Q.
Address:	10A Senate Avenue
City:	Anywhere
State:	NY
Zip Code:	12345-1234
Telephone:	(101) 201-7891
Sex:	Male
Date of Birth:	09-25-1930
Occupation:	
Employer:	
Spouse's Employer:	

INSURANCE INFORMATION:

Patient Number:	14-1
Place of Service:	Office
Primary Insurance Plan:	Medicare
Primary Insurance Plan ID #:	1111AA11111
Policy #:	
Primary Policyholder:	Public, John Q.
Policyholder Date of Birth:	09-25-1930
Relationship to Patient:	Self
Secondary Insurance Plan:	
Secondary Insurance Plan ID #:	
Secondary Policyholder:	

Patient Status   ☐ Married   ☐ Divorced   ☒ Single   ☐ Student

DIAGNOSIS INFORMATION

Diagnosis	Code	Diagnosis	Code
1. Abdominal pain	R10.9	5.	
2.		6.	
3.		7.	
4.		8.	

PROCEDURE INFORMATION

Description of Procedure or Service	Date	Code	Charge
1. New patient office visit, level III	01-20-YY	99203	75.00
2.			
3.			
4.			
5.			

SPECIAL NOTES: Referring physician: Ivan Gooddoc, M.D. (NPI 3456789012).

FIGURE 14-6 John Q. Public case study.

HEALTH INSURANCE CLAIM FORM

APPROVED BY NATIONAL UNIFORM CLAIM COMMITTEE (NUCC) 02/12

☐☐☐ PICA   PICA ☐☐☐

1. MEDICARE	MEDICAID	TRICARE	CHAMPVA	GROUP HEALTH PLAN	FECA BLKLUNG	OTHER	1a. INSURED'S I.D. NUMBER	(For Program in Item 1)
☒ (Medicare#)	☐ (Medicaid#)	☐ (ID#/DoD#)	☐ (Member ID#)	☐ (ID#)	☐ (ID#)	☐ (ID#)	1111AA11111	

2. PATIENT'S NAME (Last Name, First Name, Middle Initial)
PUBLIC, JOHN, Q

3. PATIENT'S BIRTH DATE MM **09** DD **25** YY **1930**   SEX M ☒ F ☐

4. INSURED'S NAME (Last Name, First Name, Middle Initial)

5. PATIENT'S ADDRESS (No., Street)
10A SENATE AVENUE

6. PATIENT RELATIONSHIP TO INSURED Self ☐ Spouse ☐ Child ☐ Other ☐

7. INSURED'S ADDRESS (No., Street)

CITY **ANYWHERE**   STATE **NY**

8. RESERVED FOR NUCC USE

CITY   STATE

ZIP CODE **123451234**   TELEPHONE (Include Area Code) ( )

9. OTHER INSURED'S NAME (Last Name, First Name, Middle Initial)

10. IS PATIENT'S CONDITION RELATED TO:

11. INSURED'S POLICY GROUP OR FECA NUMBER
NONE

ZIP CODE   TELEPHONE (Include Area Code) ( )

a. OTHER INSURED'S POLICY OR GROUP NUMBER

a. EMPLOYMENT? (Current or Previous) ☐ YES ☒ NO

a. INSURED'S DATE OF BIRTH MM DD YY   SEX M ☐ F ☐

b. RESERVED FOR NUCC USE

b. AUTO ACCIDENT? ☐ YES ☒ NO   PLACE (State)

b. OTHER CLAIM ID (Designated by NUCC)

c. RESERVED FOR NUCC USE

c. OTHER ACCIDENT? ☐ YES ☒ NO

c. INSURANCE PLAN NAME OR PROGRAM NAME

d. INSURANCE PLAN NAME OR PROGRAM NAME

10d. CLAIM CODES (Designated by NUCC)

d. IS THERE ANOTHER HEALTH BENEFIT PLAN? ☐ YES ☐ NO **If yes,** complete items 9, 9a, and 9d.

READ BACK OF FORM BEFORE COMPLETING & SIGNING THIS FORM.

12. PATIENT'S OR AUTHORIZED PERSON'S SIGNATURE I authorize the release of any medical or other information necessary to process this claim. I also request payment of government benefits either to myself or to the party who accepts assignment below.

SIGNED **SIGNATURE ON FILE**   DATE

13. INSURED'S OR AUTHORIZED PERSON'S SIGNATURE I authorize payment of medical benefits to the undersigned physician or supplier for services described below.

SIGNED

14. DATE OF CURRENT ILLNESS, INJURY, or PREGNANCY (LMP) MM **01** DD **20** YY **YY** QUAL. **431**

15. OTHER DATE QUAL. MM DD YY

16. DATES PATIENT UNABLE TO WORK IN CURRENT OCCUPATION FROM MM DD YY TO MM DD YY

17. NAME OF REFERRING PROVIDER OR OTHER SOURCE **DN   IVAN GOODOC MD**

17a.
17b. NPI **3456789012**

18. HOSPITALIZATION DATES RELATED TO CURRENT SERVICES FROM MM DD YY TO MM DD YY

19. ADDITIONAL CLAIM INFORMATION (Designated by NUCC)

20. OUTSIDE LAB? ☐ YES ☒ NO $ CHARGES

21. DIAGNOSIS OR NATURE OF ILLNESS OR INJURY Relate A-L to service line below (24E)   ICD Ind. **0**

A. **R109**   B.   C.   D.
E.   F.   G.   H.
I.   J.   K.   L.

22. RESUBMISSION CODE   ORIGINAL REF. NO.

23. PRIOR AUTHORIZATION NUMBER

24. A. DATE(S) OF SERVICE From MM DD YY / To MM DD YY	B. PLACE OF SERVICE	C. EMG	D. PROCEDURES, SERVICES, OR SUPPLIES (Explain Unusual Circumstances) CPT/HCPCS / MODIFIER	E. DIAGNOSIS POINTER	F. $ CHARGES	G. DAYS OR UNITS	H. EPSDT Family Plan	I. ID. QUAL.	J. RENDERING PROVIDER ID. #
1 01 20 YY	11		99203	A	75 00	1		NPI	
2								NPI	
3								NPI	
4								NPI	
5								NPI	
6								NPI	

25. FEDERAL TAX I.D. NUMBER **111234523** SSN ☐ EIN ☒

26. PATIENT'S ACCOUNT NO. **14-1**

27. ACCEPT ASSIGNMENT? (For govt. claims, see back) ☒ YES ☐ NO

28. TOTAL CHARGE $ **75 00**

29. AMOUNT PAID $

30. Rsvd for NUCC Use

31. SIGNATURE OF PHYSICIAN OR SUPPLIER INCLUDING DEGREES OR CREDENTIALS (I certify that the statements on the reverse apply to this bill and are made a part thereof.)

ERIN A HELPER MD   **MMDDYY**
SIGNED   DATE

32. SERVICE FACILITY LOCATION INFORMATION
ERIN A HELPER MD
101 MEDIC DRIVE
ANYWHERE NY 123459874
a. **1234567890**   b.

33. BILLING PROVIDER INFO & PH # (**101**) **1111234**
ERIN A HELPER MD
101 MEDIC DRIVE
ANYWHERE NY 123459874
a. **1234567890**   b.

NUCC Instruction Manual available at: www.nucc.org   **PLEASE PRINT OR TYPE**

FIGURE 14-7 Completed CMS-1500 claim for John Q. Public case study.

Exercise 14.2 – Completing a Medicare as Primary CMS-1500 Claim

1. Obtain a blank claim by making a copy of the CMS-1500 claim form in Appendix I.
2. Refer to the claims completion instructions in Table 14-4.
3. Review the Mary S. Patient case study (Figure 14-8).
4. Select the information needed from the case study, and enter the required information on the claim.
5. Review the claim to be sure all required blocks are properly completed.
6. Compare your claim with the completed Mary S. Patient claim in Figure 14-9.

ERIN A. HELPER, M.D.
101 Medic Drive, Anywhere, NY 12345-9874
(101) 111-1234 (Office) • (101) 111-9292 (Fax)
EIN: 11-1234523
NPI: 1234567890

Case Study

PATIENT INFORMATION:

Name:	Patient, Mary S.
Address:	91 Home Street
City:	Nowhere
State:	NY
Zip Code:	12367-1234
Telephone:	(101) 201-8989
Sex:	Female
Date of Birth:	03-08-1933
Occupation:	
Employer:	

INSURANCE INFORMATION:

Patient Number:	14-2
Place of Service:	Office
Primary Insurance Plan:	Medicare
Primary Insurance Plan ID #:	2222BB22222
Policy #:	
Primary Policyholder:	Mary S. Patient
Policyholder Date of Birth:	03-08-1933
Relationship to Patient:	Self
Secondary Insurance Plan:	
Secondary Insurance Plan ID #:	
Secondary Policyholder:	

Patient Status ☐ Married   ☐ Divorced   ☒ Single   ☐ Student

DIAGNOSIS INFORMATION

Diagnosis	Code	Diagnosis	Code
1. Pleurisy	R09.1	5.	
2. Atrial tachycardia	I47.1	6.	
3. History of pulmonary embolism	Z86.711	7.	
4.		8.	

PROCEDURE INFORMATION

Description of Procedure or Service	Date	Code	Charge
1. Office consultation, Level III, new patient	01-30-YY	99203	150.00
2. Chest x-ray, two views (frontal and lateral)	01-30-YY	71046	50.00
3. 12-lead ECG with interpretation and report	01-30-YY	93000	50.00
4.			
5.			

SPECIAL NOTES: Date of onset 01-28-YY. Referred by Ivan M. Gooddoc M.D. (NPI 3456789012). CPT office or other outpatient E/M code 99203 is reported (instead of CPT consultation E/M code 99243) because effective January 1, 2010, Medicare no longer recognizes CPT consultation codes for Medicare Part B payment.

FIGURE 14-8 Mary S. Patient case study.

HEALTH INSURANCE CLAIM FORM

APPROVED BY NATIONAL UNIFORM CLAIM COMMITTEE (NUCC) 02/12

PICA						PICA

1. MEDICARE [X] (Medicare#) MEDICAID [ ] (Medicaid#) TRICARE [ ] (ID#/DoD#) CHAMPVA [ ] (Member ID#) GROUP HEALTH PLAN [ ] (ID#) FECA BLKLUNG [ ] (ID#) OTHER [ ] (ID#)

1a. INSURED'S I.D. NUMBER (For Program in Item 1)
2222BB22222

2. PATIENT'S NAME (Last Name, First Name, Middle Initial)
PATIENT, MARY, S

3. PATIENT'S BIRTH DATE MM 03 DD 08 YY 1933 SEX M [ ] F [X]

4. INSURED'S NAME (Last Name, First Name, Middle Initial)

5. PATIENT'S ADDRESS (No., Street)
91 HOME STREET

6. PATIENT RELATIONSHIP TO INSURED
Self [ ] Spouse [ ] Child [ ] Other [ ]

7. INSURED'S ADDRESS (No., Street)

CITY **NOWHERE**   STATE **NY**

8. RESERVED FOR NUCC USE

CITY   STATE

ZIP CODE **123671234**   TELEPHONE (Include Area Code) ( )

ZIP CODE   TELEPHONE (Include Area Code) ( )

9. OTHER INSURED'S NAME (Last Name, First Name, Middle Initial)

10. IS PATIENT'S CONDITION RELATED TO:

11. INSURED'S POLICY GROUP OR FECA NUMBER
NONE

a. OTHER INSURED'S POLICY OR GROUP NUMBER

a. EMPLOYMENT? (Current or Previous) YES [ ] NO [X]

a. INSURED'S DATE OF BIRTH MM DD YY   SEX M [ ] F [ ]

b. RESERVED FOR NUCC USE

b. AUTO ACCIDENT? YES [ ] NO [X]   PLACE (State)

b. OTHER CLAIM ID (Designated by NUCC)

c. RESERVED FOR NUCC USE

c. OTHER ACCIDENT? YES [ ] NO [X]

c. INSURANCE PLAN NAME OR PROGRAM NAME

d. INSURANCE PLAN NAME OR PROGRAM NAME

10d. CLAIM CODES (Designated by NUCC)

d. IS THERE ANOTHER HEALTH BENEFIT PLAN? YES [ ] NO [ ] If yes, complete items 9, 9a, and 9d.

READ BACK OF FORM BEFORE COMPLETING & SIGNING THIS FORM.
12. PATIENT'S OR AUTHORIZED PERSON'S SIGNATURE I authorize the release of any medical or other information necessary to process this claim. I also request payment of government benefits either to myself or to the party who accepts assignment below.

SIGNED **SIGNATURE ON FILE**   DATE

13. INSURED'S OR AUTHORIZED PERSON'S SIGNATURE I authorize payment of medical benefits to the undersigned physician or supplier for services described below.

SIGNED

14. DATE OF CURRENT ILLNESS, INJURY, or PREGNANCY (LMP) MM 01 DD 28 YY YY QUAL. **431**

15. OTHER DATE QUAL. MM DD YY

16. DATES PATIENT UNABLE TO WORK IN CURRENT OCCUPATION FROM MM DD YY TO MM DD YY

17. NAME OF REFERRING PROVIDER OR OTHER SOURCE
DN **IVAN M GOODDOC MD**

17a.
17b. NPI **3456789012**

18. HOSPITALIZATION DATES RELATED TO CURRENT SERVICES FROM MM DD YY TO MM DD YY

19. ADDITIONAL CLAIM INFORMATION (Designated by NUCC)

20. OUTSIDE LAB? YES [ ] NO [X] $ CHARGES

21. DIAGNOSIS OR NATURE OF ILLNESS OR INJURY Relate A-L to service line below (24E)   ICD Ind. **0**

A. **R091**   B. **I471**   C. **Z86711**   D.
E.   F.   G.   H.
I.   J.   K.   L.

22. RESUBMISSION CODE   ORIGINAL REF. NO.

23. PRIOR AUTHORIZATION NUMBER

24. A. DATE(S) OF SERVICE / **B. PLACE OF SERVICE** / **C. EMG** / **D. PROCEDURES, SERVICES, OR SUPPLIES** (Explain Unusual Circumstances) CPT/HCPCS MODIFIER / **E. DIAGNOSIS POINTER** / **F. $ CHARGES** / **G. DAYS OR UNITS** / **H. EPSDT Family Plan** / **I. ID QUAL.** / **J. RENDERING PROVIDER ID. #**

#	From MM	DD	YY	To MM	DD	YY	B. PLACE OF SERVICE	C. EMG	CPT/HCPCS	MODIFIER	E. POINTER	$ CHARGES	DAYS/UNITS	EPSDT	ID QUAL.	RENDERING PROVIDER ID. #
1	01	30	YY				11		99203		ABC	150 00	1		NPI	
2	01	30	YY				11		71046		A	50 00	1		NPI	
3	01	30	YY				11		93000		B	50 00	1		NPI	
4															NPI	
5															NPI	
6															NPI	

25. FEDERAL TAX I.D. NUMBER SSN [ ] EIN [X]
111234523

26. PATIENT'S ACCOUNT NO.
14-2

27. ACCEPT ASSIGNMENT? (For govt. claims, see back) YES [X] NO [ ]

28. TOTAL CHARGE $ **250 00**

29. AMOUNT PAID $

30. Rsvd for NUCC Use

31. SIGNATURE OF PHYSICIAN OR SUPPLIER INCLUDING DEGREES OR CREDENTIALS (I certify that the statements on the reverse apply to this bill and are made a part thereof.)

SIGNED **ERIN A HELPER MD**   DATE **MMDDYY**

32. SERVICE FACILITY LOCATION INFORMATION
ERIN A HELPER MD
101 MEDIC DRIVE
ANYWHERE NY 123459874
a. **1234567890**   b.

33. BILLING PROVIDER INFO & PH # (**101**) **1111234**
ERIN A HELPER MD
101 MEDIC DRIVE
ANYWHERE NY 123459874
a. **1234567890**   b.

NUCC Instruction Manual available at: www.nucc.org   **PLEASE PRINT OR TYPE**

FIGURE 14-9 Completed Medicare primary CMS-1500 claim for Mary S. Patient case study.

Medicare and Medigap Claims Instructions

Modifications must be made to the Medicare primary claim (Table 14-5 and Figure 14-10) when the health care provider is a Medicare PAR, the patient has a Medigap policy in addition to Medicare, and the patient has signed an Authorization for Release of Medigap Benefits. If a separate Medigap release is on file, the words SIGNATURE ON FILE must appear in Block 13. No benefits will be paid to the PAR if Block 27, Accept Assignment, contains an X in the NO box.

 NOTE:

Use these instructions when completing any claims associated with *Understanding Health Insurance*.

TABLE 14-5 CMS-1500 claims completion instructions for Medicare and Medigap claims

Block	Instructions
1	Enter an X in the *Medicare* and the *Other* boxes.
9	Enter SAME if the patient is the Medigap policyholder.
	If the patient is *not* the Medigap policyholder, enter the policyholder's last name, first name, and middle initial (if known) (separated by commas).
9a	Enter MEDIGAP followed by the policy number and group number, separated by spaces (e.g., MEDIGAP 123456789 123). (The abbreviations MG or MGAP are also acceptable.)
9d	Enter the Medigap Plan ID number.
13	Enter SIGNATURE ON FILE. (The abbreviation SOF is also acceptable.) Leave the date field blank.

Courtesy of the Centers for Medicare & Medicaid Services, www.cms.gov.

Exercise 14.3 – Completing a Medicare and Medigap CMS-1500 Claim

Additional information needed for this case:

Dr. Helper is a Medicare PAR. The billing entity is Erin Helper, M.D.

1. Obtain a blank claim by making a copy of the CMS-1500 claim form in Appendix I.

2. Underline the block identifiers on the new claim for the blocks listed in the Medicare and Medigap claim form instructions (Table 14-5).

3. Refer to the case study for John Q. Public (see Figure 14-6). Enter the following information in the blocks for the secondary policy:

   - Aetna Medigap ID # 22233544
   - Plan ID: 11543299
   - Policyholder: John Q. Public
   - Employer: Retired

4. Complete the Medicare-Medigap claim using the data from the case study.

5. Compare the completed claim to the claim in Figure 14-10 to be sure all required blocks are properly completed.

HEALTH INSURANCE CLAIM FORM

APPROVED BY NATIONAL UNIFORM CLAIM COMMITTEE (NUCC) 02/12

▢ PICA

1. MEDICARE	MEDICAID	TRICARE	CHAMPVA	GROUP HEALTH PLAN	FECA BLKLUNG	OTHER	1a. INSURED'S I.D. NUMBER (For Program in Item 1)
[X] (Medicare#)	▢ (Medicaid#)	▢ (ID#/DoD#)	▢ (Member ID#)	▢ (ID#)	▢ (ID#)	[X] (ID#)	1111AA11111

2. PATIENT'S NAME (Last Name, First Name, Middle Initial)
PUBLIC, JOHN, Q

3. PATIENT'S BIRTH DATE MM 09 DD 25 YY 1930   SEX M [X] F ▢

4. INSURED'S NAME (Last Name, First Name, Middle Initial)

5. PATIENT'S ADDRESS (No., Street)
10A SENATE AVENUE

6. PATIENT RELATIONSHIP TO INSURED Self ▢ Spouse ▢ Child ▢ Other ▢

7. INSURED'S ADDRESS (No., Street)

CITY **ANYWHERE** STATE **NY**

8. RESERVED FOR NUCC USE

CITY STATE

ZIP CODE **123451234** TELEPHONE (Include Area Code) ( )

ZIP CODE TELEPHONE (Include Area Code) ( )

9. OTHER INSURED'S NAME (Last Name, First Name, Middle Initial)
SAME

10. IS PATIENT'S CONDITION RELATED TO:

11. INSURED'S POLICY GROUP OR FECA NUMBER
NONE

a. OTHER INSURED'S POLICY OR GROUP NUMBER
MEDIGAP 22233544

a. EMPLOYMENT? (Current or Previous) YES ▢ NO [X]

a. INSURED'S DATE OF BIRTH MM DD YY   SEX M ▢ F ▢

b. RESERVED FOR NUCC USE

b. AUTO ACCIDENT? YES ▢ NO [X] PLACE (State)

b. OTHER CLAIM ID (Designated by NUCC)

c. RESERVED FOR NUCC USE

c. OTHER ACCIDENT? YES ▢ NO [X]

c. INSURANCE PLAN NAME OR PROGRAM NAME

d. INSURANCE PLAN NAME OR PROGRAM NAME
11543299

10d. CLAIM CODES (Designated by NUCC)

d. IS THERE ANOTHER HEALTH BENEFIT PLAN? YES ▢ NO ▢ *If yes,* complete items 9, 9a, and 9d.

READ BACK OF FORM BEFORE COMPLETING & SIGNING THIS FORM.

12. PATIENT'S OR AUTHORIZED PERSON'S SIGNATURE I authorize the release of any medical or other information necessary to process this claim. I also request payment of government benefits either to myself or to the party who accepts assignment below.

SIGNED **SIGNATURE ON FILE** DATE

13. INSURED'S OR AUTHORIZED PERSON'S SIGNATURE I authorize payment of medical benefits to the undersigned physician or supplier for services described below.

SIGNED **SIGNATURE ON FILE**

14. DATE OF CURRENT ILLNESS, INJURY, or PREGNANCY (LMP) MM 01 DD 09 YY YY QUAL. **431**

15. OTHER DATE QUAL. MM DD YY

16. DATES PATIENT UNABLE TO WORK IN CURRENT OCCUPATION FROM MM DD YY TO MM DD YY

17. NAME OF REFERRING PROVIDER OR OTHER SOURCE **DN IVAN GOODDOC MD**

17a.
17b. NPI **3456789012**

18. HOSPITALIZATION DATES RELATED TO CURRENT SERVICES FROM MM DD YY TO MM DD YY

19. ADDITIONAL CLAIM INFORMATION (Designated by NUCC)

20. OUTSIDE LAB? YES ▢ NO [X] $ CHARGES

21. DIAGNOSIS OR NATURE OF ILLNESS OR INJURY Relate A-L to service line below (24E) ICD Ind. **0**

A. **R109** B. _____ C. _____ D. _____
E. _____ F. _____ G. _____ H. _____
I. _____ J. _____ K. _____ L. _____

22. RESUBMISSION CODE ORIGINAL REF. NO.

23. PRIOR AUTHORIZATION NUMBER

24. A. DATE(S) OF SERVICE From MM DD YY To MM DD YY	B. PLACE OF SERVICE	C. EMG	D. PROCEDURES, SERVICES, OR SUPPLIES (Explain Unusual Circumstances) CPT/HCPCS	MODIFIER	E. DIAGNOSIS POINTER	F. $ CHARGES	G. DAYS OR UNITS	H. EPSDT Family Plan	I. ID. QUAL.	J. RENDERING PROVIDER ID. #
1	01 20 YY	11		99203		A	75 00	1		NPI
2										NPI
3										NPI
4										NPI
5										NPI
6										NPI

25. FEDERAL TAX I.D. NUMBER **111234523** SSN ▢ EIN [X]

26. PATIENT'S ACCOUNT NO. **14-1**

27. ACCEPT ASSIGNMENT? (For govt. claims, see back) YES [X] NO ▢

28. TOTAL CHARGE $ **75 00**

29. AMOUNT PAID $

30. Rsvd for NUCC Use

31. SIGNATURE OF PHYSICIAN OR SUPPLIER INCLUDING DEGREES OR CREDENTIALS (I certify that the statements on the reverse apply to this bill and are made a part thereof.)

ERIN A HELPER MD SIGNED **MMDDYY** DATE

32. SERVICE FACILITY LOCATION INFORMATION
ERIN A HELPER MD
101 MEDIC DRIVE
ANYWHERE NY 123459874
a. **1234567890** b.

33. BILLING PROVIDER INFO & PH # (**101**) **1111234**
ERIN A HELPER MD
101 MEDIC DRIVE
ANYWHERE NY 123459874
a. **1234567890** b.

NUCC Instruction Manual available at: www.nucc.org   *PLEASE PRINT OR TYPE*

Courtesy of the Centers for Medicare & Medicaid Services, www.cms.gov; claim data created by author.

FIGURE 14-10 Completed Medicare-Medigap CMS-1500 claim for John Q. Public case study.

Medicare-Medicaid (Medi-Medi) Crossover Claims Instructions

A **Medicare-Medicaid (Medi-Medi) crossover** plan provides both Medicare and Medicaid coverage to certain eligible beneficiaries (Medicare beneficiaries with low incomes).

The following modifications are usually made to the Medicare primary claim when the patient is covered by Medicare and also has Medicaid coverage for services rendered on a fee-for-service basis (Table 14-6 and Figure 14-11). (Each state has its own Medicaid plan, so it's important to locate your state's specific claims instructions.)

 NOTE:

Use these instructions when completing any claims associated with *Understanding Health Insurance*.

TABLE 14-6 CMS-1500 claims completion instructions for Medicare-Medicaid (Medi-Medi) crossover claims

Block	Instructions
1	Enter an X in both the Medicare *and* Medicaid boxes.
	Note: According to NUCC claims instructions, an X is to be entered in just one box in Block 1. However, at the time this textbook was printed, Medicare-Medicaid crossover claims instructions require an X to be entered in both the Medicare and Medicaid boxes.
10d	Enter the abbreviation MCD followed by the patient's Medicaid ID number.
27	Enter an X in the YES box. (NonPAR providers must accept assignment on Medicare-Medicaid crossover claims.)

Courtesy of the Centers for Medicare & Medicaid Services, www.cms.gov.

Exercise 14.4 – Completing a Medicare-Medicaid Crossover CMS-1500 Claim

Additional information needed for this case:

Dr. Helper is a Medicare PAR. The billing entity is Erin Helper, M.D.

1. Obtain a blank claim by making a copy of the CMS-1500 claim form in Appendix I.
2. Underline the blocks discussed in the Medicare-Medicaid crossover claims instructions (Table 14-6).
3. Refer to the Mary S. Patient case study in Figure 14-8, and enter additional Medicaid information in the secondary policy blocks:
   - Insurance policy: Medicaid
   - ID #: 101234591XT
   - Relationship: Self
4. Complete the Medicare-Medicaid (Medi-Medi) claim.
5. Compare the completed claim with the claim in Figure 14-11.

HEALTH INSURANCE CLAIM FORM

APPROVED BY NATIONAL UNIFORM CLAIM COMMITTEE (NUCC) 02/12

☐ PICA		☐ PICA

CARRIER

1. MEDICARE MEDICAID TRICARE CHAMPVA GROUP HEALTH PLAN FECA BLKLUNG OTHER	1a. INSURED'S I.D. NUMBER (For Program in Item 1)
☒ (Medicare#) ☒ (Medicaid#) ☐ (ID#/DoD#) ☐ (Member ID#) ☐ (ID#) ☐ (ID#) ☐ (ID#)	**2222BB22222**

2. PATIENT'S NAME (Last Name, First Name, Middle Initial)	3. PATIENT'S BIRTH DATE MM DD YY SEX	4. INSURED'S NAME (Last Name, First Name, Middle Initial)
PATIENT, MARY, S	03 08 1933 M☐ F☒	

5. PATIENT'S ADDRESS (No., Street)	6. PATIENT RELATIONSHIP TO INSURED	7. INSURED'S ADDRESS (No., Street)
91 HOME STREET	Self ☐ Spouse ☐ Child ☐ Other ☐	

CITY	STATE	8. RESERVED FOR NUCC USE	CITY	STATE
NOWHERE	**NY**			

ZIP CODE	TELEPHONE (Include Area Code)		ZIP CODE	TELEPHONE (Include Area Code)
123671234	( )			( )

9. OTHER INSURED'S NAME (Last Name, First Name, Middle Initial)	10. IS PATIENT'S CONDITION RELATED TO:	11. INSURED'S POLICY GROUP OR FECA NUMBER
		NONE

a. OTHER INSURED'S POLICY OR GROUP NUMBER	a. EMPLOYMENT? (Current or Previous) ☐ YES ☒ NO	a. INSURED'S DATE OF BIRTH MM DD YY SEX M☐ F☐

b. RESERVED FOR NUCC USE	b. AUTO ACCIDENT? PLACE (State) ☐ YES ☒ NO	b. OTHER CLAIM ID (Designated by NUCC)

c. RESERVED FOR NUCC USE	c. OTHER ACCIDENT? ☐ YES ☒ NO	c. INSURANCE PLAN NAME OR PROGRAM NAME

d. INSURANCE PLAN NAME OR PROGRAM NAME	10d. CLAIM CODES (Designated by NUCC) **MCD 101234591XT**	d. IS THERE ANOTHER HEALTH BENEFIT PLAN? ☐ YES ☐ NO **If yes,** complete items 9, 9a, and 9d.

READ BACK OF FORM BEFORE COMPLETING & SIGNING THIS FORM.

12. PATIENT'S OR AUTHORIZED PERSON'S SIGNATURE I authorize the release of any medical or other information necessary to process this claim. I also request payment of government benefits either to myself or to the party who accepts assignment below.

SIGNED **SIGNATURE ON FILE** DATE

13. INSURED'S OR AUTHORIZED PERSON'S SIGNATURE I authorize payment of medical benefits to the undersigned physician or supplier for services described below.

SIGNED

PATIENT AND INSURED INFORMATION

14. DATE OF CURRENT ILLNESS, INJURY, or PREGNANCY (LMP) MM DD YY **01 28 YY** QUAL. **431**	15. OTHER DATE QUAL. MM DD YY	16. DATES PATIENT UNABLE TO WORK IN CURRENT OCCUPATION FROM MM DD YY TO MM DD YY

17. NAME OF REFERRING PROVIDER OR OTHER SOURCE **DN IVAN M GOODDOC MD**	17a. 17b. NPI **3456789012**	18. HOSPITALIZATION DATES RELATED TO CURRENT SERVICES FROM MM DD YY TO MM DD YY

19. ADDITIONAL CLAIM INFORMATION (Designated by NUCC)		20. OUTSIDE LAB? ☐ YES ☒ NO $ CHARGES

21. DIAGNOSIS OR NATURE OF ILLNESS OR INJURY Relate A-L to service line below (24E) ICD Ind. **0**		22. RESUBMISSION CODE ORIGINAL REF. NO.
A. **R091** B. **I471** C. **Z86711** D.		
E. F. G. H.		23. PRIOR AUTHORIZATION NUMBER
I. J. K. L.		

24. A. DATE(S) OF SERVICE From MM DD YY To MM DD YY	B. PLACE OF SERVICE	C. EMG	D. PROCEDURES, SERVICES, OR SUPPLIES (Explain Unusual Circumstances) CPT/HCPCS MODIFIER	E. DIAGNOSIS POINTER	F. $ CHARGES	G. DAYS OR UNITS	H. EPSDT Family Plan	I. ID. QUAL.	J. RENDERING PROVIDER ID. #
1	01 30 YY	11		99203	ABC	150 00	1		NPI	
2	01 30 YY	11		71046	A	50 00	1		NPI	
3	01 30 YY	11		93000	B	50 00	1		NPI	
4									NPI	
5									NPI	
6									NPI	

25. FEDERAL TAX I.D. NUMBER SSN EIN **111234523** ☒	26. PATIENT'S ACCOUNT NO. **14-2**	27. ACCEPT ASSIGNMENT? (For govt. claims, see back) ☒ YES ☐ NO	28. TOTAL CHARGE $ **250 00**	29. AMOUNT PAID $	30. Rsvd for NUCC Use

31. SIGNATURE OF PHYSICIAN OR SUPPLIER INCLUDING DEGREES OR CREDENTIALS (I certify that the statements on the reverse apply to this bill and are made a part thereof.) **ERIN A HELPER MD** SIGNED **MMDDYY** DATE	32. SERVICE FACILITY LOCATION INFORMATION **ERIN A HELPER MD** **101 MEDIC DRIVE** **ANYWHERE NY 123459874** a. **1234567890** b.	33. BILLING PROVIDER INFO & PH # (**101**) **1111234** **ERIN A HELPER MD** **101 MEDIC DRIVE** **ANYWHERE NY 123459874** a. **1234567890** b.

PHYSICIAN OR SUPPLIER INFORMATION

NUCC Instruction Manual available at: www.nucc.org **PLEASE PRINT OR TYPE**

FIGURE 14-11 Completed Medicare-Medicaid (Medi-Medi) CMS-1500 claim for Mary S. Patient case study.

Medicare as Secondary Payer Claims Instructions

CMS-1500 claims instructions are modified when Medicare is secondary to another insurance plan (Table 14-7). The Medicare Secondary Payer (MSP) program coordinates benefits between Medicare and other payers to determine if another insurance plan is primary. CMS awards a coordination-of-benefits (COB) contract to consolidate activities that support the collection, management, and reporting of other insurance coverage primary to Medicare. The COB contractor uses the following to identify insurance primary to Medicare:

- *Initial Enrollment Questionnaire (IEQ)*—Medicare beneficiaries complete a questionnaire about other insurance coverage about three months before they are entitled to Medicare
- *IRS/SSA/CMS Data Match*—Employers complete a questionnaire that provides group health plan (GHP) information about identified workers who are either entitled to Medicare or married to a Medicare beneficiary
- *MSP Claims Investigation*—Collects data about other health insurance that may be primary to Medicare; is based on information submitted on a CMS-1500 claim or from other sources
- *Voluntary MSP Data Match Agreements*—Voluntary agreements between CMS and employers and payers that allow the electronic data exchange of group health plan eligibility and Medicare information

 NOTE:

Use these instructions when completing any claims associated with *Understanding Health Insurance*.

TABLE 14-7 CMS-1500 claims completion instructions for Medicare as secondary payer claims

Block	Instructions
1	Enter an X in the *Medicare* and *Other* boxes. Note: According to NUCC claims instructions, an X is to be entered in just one box in Block 1. However, at the time this textbook was printed, Medicare as secondary payer claims instructions require an X to be entered in both the Medicare and Other boxes.
4	If the policyholder is the patient, enter SAME. If the patient is not the policyholder, enter the primary insurance policyholder's name.
6	Enter an X in the appropriate box to indicate the patient's relationship to the primary insurance policyholder.
7	If the address of the policyholder is the same as the patient, enter SAME.
10a–10c	Enter an X in the appropriate boxes to indicate whether the patient's condition is related to employment or an auto or other accident. Note: Entering an X in any of the YES boxes alerts the Medicare administrative contractor that another insurance plan might be liable for payment. Medicare will not process the claim until the provider submits a remittance advice from the liable party (e.g., auto insurance, workers' compensation).
11	Enter the primary policyholder's group number if the patient is covered by a group health plan. *Do not enter hyphens or spaces in the policy or group number.* Otherwise, leave blank.
11a	Enter the primary insurance policyholder's date of birth as MM DD YYYY (with spaces). Enter an X in the appropriate box to indicate the policyholder's sex.
11c	Enter the name of the primary policyholder's insurance plan. Note: Be sure to attach a copy of the remittance advice to the claim, which must contain the payer's name and address.
11d	Enter an X in the NO box. Note: Medicare is secondary, which is indicated by entering an X in the Medicare box in Block 1. However, an X is entered in the YES box if the patient is covered by a secondary or supplemental health plan (e.g., commercial health plan) in addition to a primary health plan (e.g., employer-based group health plan) and Medicare as secondary coverage.
16	If the patient is employed full time, enter the dates the patient is or was unable to work (if applicable).

Exercise 14.5 – Completing a Medicare as Secondary Payer CMS-1500 Claim

Additional information needed for this case:

Dr. Helper is a Medicare PAR. The billing entity is Erin Helper, M.D. The ambulatory surgical center NPI is 5678901234.

1. Obtain a blank claim by making a copy of the CMS-1500 claim form in Appendix I.

2. Underline the blocks discussed in the Medicare Secondary Payer claims instructions in Table 14-7. Add an "S" to the patient's account number in Block 26 (e.g., 14-3S).

3. Refer to the Jack L. Neely case study (Figure 14-12) and complete the Medicare Secondary Payer claim for this case.

4. Review the completed claim to be sure all required blocks are filled in.

5. Compare your claim with Figure 14-13.

ERIN A. HELPER, M.D.
101 Medic Drive, Anywhere, NY 12345-9874
(101) 111-1234 (Office) • (101) 111-9292 (Fax)
EIN: 11-1234523
NPI: 1234567890

Case Study

PATIENT INFORMATION:

Name:	Jack L. Neely
Address:	329 Water Street
City:	Nowhere
State:	NY
Zip Code:	12367-1234
Telephone:	(101) 201-1278
Sex:	Male
Date of Birth:	09-09-1929
Occupation:	Retired
Spouse's Employer:	Federal Investigative Service

INSURANCE INFORMATION:

Patient Number:	14-3
Place of Service:	Anywhere Surgical Center
Primary Insurance Plan:	BlueCross BlueShield
Primary Insurance Plan ID #:	R1234567
Primary Group #:	103
Primary Policyholder:	Mary Neely
Primary Policyholder Birth Date:	03-19-1935
Relationship to Patient:	Spouse
Secondary Policy:	Medicare
Secondary Insurance Plan ID #:	3333CC33333
Secondary Policyholder:	Jack L. Neely

Patient Status   ☒ Married   ☐ Divorced   ☐ Single   ☐ Student

---

DIAGNOSIS INFORMATION

Diagnosis	Code	Diagnosis	Code
1. Rectal bleeding (3 days)	K62.5	5.	
2. History of polyps, ascending colon	Z86.010	6.	
3.		7.	
4.		8.	

PROCEDURE INFORMATION

Description of Procedure or Service	Date	Code	Charge
1. Colonoscopy, flexible to ileum (cecum)	01-08-YY	45378	700.00
2.			
3.			
4.			
5.			

SPECIAL NOTES: Referring physician: Arnold Younglove M.D. (NPI 4567890123)
Anywhere Surgical Center, 101 Park St, Anywhere, NY 12345 (NPI 5678901234)

FIGURE 14-12 Jack L. Neely case study.

REMITTANCE ADVICE ATTACHED

HEALTH INSURANCE CLAIM FORM

APPROVED BY NATIONAL UNIFORM CLAIM COMMITTEE (NUCC) 02/12

CARRIER

| | | PICA | | | | | | | | | | PICA | |

1. MEDICARE [X] (Medicare#) MEDICAID [ ] (Medicaid#) TRICARE [ ] (ID#/DoD#) CHAMPVA [ ] (Member ID#) GROUP HEALTH PLAN [ ] (ID#) FECA BLKLUNG [ ] (ID#) OTHER [X] (ID#)

1a. INSURED'S I.D. NUMBER (For Program in Item 1)
3333CC33333

2. PATIENT'S NAME (Last Name, First Name, Middle Initial)
NEELY, JACK, L

3. PATIENT'S BIRTH DATE MM 09 DD 09 YY 1929   SEX M [X] F [ ]

4. INSURED'S NAME (Last Name, First Name, Middle Initial)
NEELY, MARY

5. PATIENT'S ADDRESS (No., Street)
329 WATER STREET

6. PATIENT RELATIONSHIP TO INSURED
Self [ ] Spouse [X] Child [ ] Other [ ]

7. INSURED'S ADDRESS (No., Street)
SAME

CITY NOWHERE   STATE NY

8. RESERVED FOR NUCC USE

CITY   STATE

ZIP CODE 123671234   TELEPHONE (Include Area Code) ( )

ZIP CODE   TELEPHONE (Include Area Code) ( )

9. OTHER INSURED'S NAME (Last Name, First Name, Middle Initial)

10. IS PATIENT'S CONDITION RELATED TO:

11. INSURED'S POLICY GROUP OR FECA NUMBER
103

a. OTHER INSURED'S POLICY OR GROUP NUMBER

a. EMPLOYMENT? (Current or Previous) YES [ ] NO [X]

a. INSURED'S DATE OF BIRTH MM 03 DD 19 YY 1935   SEX M [ ] F [X]

b. RESERVED FOR NUCC USE

b. AUTO ACCIDENT? YES [ ] NO [X]   PLACE (State)

b. OTHER CLAIM ID (Designated by NUCC)

c. RESERVED FOR NUCC USE

c. OTHER ACCIDENT? YES [ ] NO [X]

c. INSURANCE PLAN NAME OR PROGRAM NAME
BLUECROSS BLUESHIELD

d. INSURANCE PLAN NAME OR PROGRAM NAME

10d. CLAIM CODES (Designated by NUCC)

d. IS THERE ANOTHER HEALTH BENEFIT PLAN? YES [ ] NO [X] If yes, complete items 9, 9a, and 9d.

READ BACK OF FORM BEFORE COMPLETING & SIGNING THIS FORM.
12. PATIENT'S OR AUTHORIZED PERSON'S SIGNATURE I authorize the release of any medical or other information necessary to process this claim. I also request payment of government benefits either to myself or to the party who accepts assignment below.

SIGNED **SIGNATURE ON FILE**   DATE

13. INSURED'S OR AUTHORIZED PERSON'S SIGNATURE I authorize payment of medical benefits to the undersigned physician or supplier for services described below.

SIGNED

PATIENT AND INSURED INFORMATION

14. DATE OF CURRENT ILLNESS, INJURY, or PREGNANCY (LMP) MM 01 DD 08 YY   QUAL. 431

15. OTHER DATE QUAL. MM DD YY

16. DATES PATIENT UNABLE TO WORK IN CURRENT OCCUPATION FROM MM DD YY TO MM DD YY

17. NAME OF REFERRING PROVIDER OR OTHER SOURCE
DN ARNOLD YOUNGLOVE MD

17a.
17b. NPI 4567890123

18. HOSPITALIZATION DATES RELATED TO CURRENT SERVICES FROM MM DD YY TO MM DD YY

19. ADDITIONAL CLAIM INFORMATION (Designated by NUCC)

20. OUTSIDE LAB? YES [ ] NO [X] $ CHARGES

21. DIAGNOSIS OR NATURE OF ILLNESS OR INJURY Relate A-L to service line below (24E)   ICD Ind. 0

A. K625   B. Z86010   C.   D.
E.   F.   G.   H.
I.   J.   K.   L.

22. RESUBMISSION CODE   ORIGINAL REF. NO.

23. PRIOR AUTHORIZATION NUMBER

| 24. A. DATE(S) OF SERVICE | | | | | | B. PLACE OF SERVICE | C. EMG | D. PROCEDURES, SERVICES, OR SUPPLIES (Explain Unusual Circumstances) | | E. DIAGNOSIS POINTER | F. $ CHARGES | | G. DAYS OR UNITS | H. EPSDT Family Plan | I. ID. QUAL. | J. RENDERING PROVIDER ID. # |
From MM	DD	YY	To MM	DD	YY			CPT/HCPCS	MODIFIER							
01	08	YY				24		45378		AB	700	00	1		NPI	
															NPI	
															NPI	
															NPI	
															NPI	
															NPI	

25. FEDERAL TAX I.D. NUMBER SSN [ ] EIN [X]
111234523

26. PATIENT'S ACCOUNT NO.
14-3S

27. ACCEPT ASSIGNMENT? (For govt. claims, see back) YES [X] NO [ ]

28. TOTAL CHARGE $ 700 00

29. AMOUNT PAID $

30. Rsvd for NUCC Use

31. SIGNATURE OF PHYSICIAN OR SUPPLIER INCLUDING DEGREES OR CREDENTIALS (I certify that the statements on the reverse apply to this bill and are made a part thereof.)

ERIN A HELPER MD   MMDDYY
SIGNED   DATE

32. SERVICE FACILITY LOCATION INFORMATION
ANYWHERE SURGICAL CENTER
101 PARK ST
ANYWHERE NY 123459874

a. 5678901234 b.

33. BILLING PROVIDER INFO & PH # (101) 1111234
ERIN A HELPER MD
101 MEDIC DRIVE
ANYWHERE NY 123459874

a. 1234567890 b.

PHYSICIAN OR SUPPLIER INFORMATION

NUCC Instruction Manual available at: www.nucc.org   **PLEASE PRINT OR TYPE**

FIGURE 14-13 Completed Medicare as Secondary Payer CMS-1500 claim for Jack L. Neely case study.

Medicare Roster Billing for Mass Vaccination Programs Claims Instructions

The simplified **roster billing** process streamlines the process for submitting health care claims for a large group of beneficiaries for influenza virus or pneumococcal vaccinations. It was developed to enable Medicare beneficiaries to participate in mass pneumococcal polysaccharide vaccine (PPV) and influenza virus vaccination programs offered by public health clinics (PHCs) and other entities that bill Medicare payers. (Medicare has not yet developed roster billing for hepatitis B vaccinations.) Properly licensed individuals and entities conducting mass immunization programs may submit claims using a simplified claims submission procedure to bill for the PPV and influenza virus vaccine benefit for multiple beneficiaries if they agree to accept assignment for these claims. A **mass immunizer** as a traditional Medicare-enrolled provider/supplier or a nontraditional provider (e.g., public health clinic, supermarket) that offers influenza virus and/or pneumococcal vaccinations to a large number of individuals (e.g., general public, members of a retirement community). Entities that submit claims on roster bills (and therefore must accept assignment) may not collect any donations or other cost-sharing of any kind from Medicare beneficiaries for PPV or influenza vaccinations. However, the entity may bill Medicare for the amount not subsidized from its own budget.

 NOTE:

UB-04 institutional claims must include at least five beneficiaries immunized on the same date to submit a roster bill. Medicare Part B does not require immunization of the minimum five beneficiaries.

Example: A public health clinic (PHC) sponsors an influenza virus vaccination clinic for Medicare beneficiaries. The cost is $12.50 per vaccination, and the PHC pays $2.50 of the cost from its budget.

The PHC is therefore eligible to roster-bill Medicare the $10 cost difference for each beneficiary. The PHC submits both the roster billing form (Figure 14-14) and CMS-1500 claim (Figure 14-15).

Provider Enrollment Criteria

All individuals and entities that submit PPV and influenza virus vaccination benefit claims to Medicare on roster bills must complete Form CMS-855, the Provider/Supplier Enrollment Application. Specialized instructions must be followed to simplify the enrollment process, and providers may not bill Medicare for any services other than PPV and influenza virus vaccinations.

Completing the CMS-1500 Claim for Roster Billing Purposes

Providers that qualify for roster billing may use a preprinted CMS-1500 claim that contains standardized information about the entity and the benefit (Table 14-8). Providers that submit roster bills to carriers must complete certain blocks on a single modified CMS-1500 claim, which serves as the cover sheet for the roster bill.

NOTE:

- Roster billing is *not* used to submit single patient immunization bills.
- Providers should establish a computer edit to identify individuals and entities that plan to participate in the Medicare program only for the purpose of mass immunizing beneficiaries.
- If the provider is not charging for the vaccine or its administration, enter 0 00 or NC (for "no charge") on the appropriate line for that item. This information is required for both paper claims and electronic submissions.
- During a mass immunization clinic, beneficiaries receive either the PPV or the influenza virus vaccination, not both. (This note applies to CMS-1500 Blocks 21 and 24D.)

 NOTE:

Use these instructions when completing any claims associated with *Understanding Health Insurance*.

TABLE 14-8 CMS-1500 claims completion instructions for Medicare roster billing

Block	Instructions
1	Enter an X in the Medicare box.
2	Enter SEE ATTACHED ROSTER.
11	Enter NONE.
20	Enter an X in the NO box.
21	On line 1, enter Z23.
24A	Enter the date the service was performed in the FROM column as MM DD YY (with spaces).
24B	Enter 60 (place of service, POS, code for "mass immunization center").
24D	On line 1, enter the appropriate influenza flu vaccine or pneumococcal vaccine CPT code. On line 2, enter G0008 (administration of influenza flu vaccine) *or* G0009 (administration of pneumococcal vaccine).
24E	On lines 1 and 2, enter the diagnosis pointer letter(s) A from Block 21.
24F	On lines 1 and 2, enter the charge for each service, *not* the total charge for all patients. (The roster of patients that is attached to the CMS-1500 is used to calculate the total charge for all patients.)
27	Enter an X in the YES box.
29	Enter 0 00.
31	Have the entity's representative sign and date the claim. Enter the date as MMDDYY (without spaces).
32	Enter the name and address of the service location.
32a	Enter the NPI of the service facility.
33	Enter the name, address, and telephone number of the service provider.
33a	Enter the NPI of the billing provider or group.

Exercise 14.6 – Completing a Medicare Roster Billing for Mass Vaccination Programs Claim

1. Obtain a blank claim by making a copy of the CMS-1500 claim form in Appendix I.
2. Underline the blocks discussed in the CMS-1500 claims completion instructions for Medicare roster billing in Table 14-8.
3. Refer to the sample roster billing form (Figure 14-14) and complete the Medicare Roster Billing for Mass Vaccination Programs claim.
4. Review the completed claim to be sure all required blocks are filled in.
5. Compare your claim with Figure 14-15.

Provider	Anywhere Health Clinic
	100 Main St, Anywhere, NY 12345-1234
	(101) 555-1111
EIN	98-7654321
NPI	1123456789
Date of Service	November 15, YY
MAC Control Number	456987123
Diagnosis	Encounter for immunization (ICD-10-CM code Z23)
Type of Service	Influenza vaccine (CPT code 90686) (HCPCS Level II code G0008-33)
Cost	$10 (vaccine) and $10.00 (Administration of vaccine) ($60.00 to be billed to Medicare for each patient) (G0008-33)

Patient Information

MBI	Name	DOB	Sex	Address	Signature
1234AA12345	Doe, John A	02/05/34	M	1 Hill, Anywhere, NY 12345	*John A. Doe*
2345BB23456	Doe, Jane M	12/24/30	F	5 Main, Anywhere, NY 12345	*Jane M. Doe*
2222BB22222	Smith, May J	02/18/32	F	8 Roe, Anywhere, NY 12345	*May J Smith*
3456DD34567	Brown, Lou	05/15/20	F	2 Sims, Anywhere, NY 12345	*Lou Brown*
4567EE45678	Green, Julie	09/30/25	F	6 Pine, Anywhere, NY 12345	*Julie Green*

FIGURE 14-14 Sample roster billing form (attach to CMS-1500 claim).

HEALTH INSURANCE CLAIM FORM

APPROVED BY NATIONAL UNIFORM CLAIM COMMITTEE (NUCC) 02/12

PICA   PICA

1. MEDICARE [X] (Medicare#)   MEDICAID [ ] (Medicaid#)   TRICARE [ ] (ID#/DoD#)   CHAMPVA [ ] (Member ID#)   GROUP HEALTH PLAN [ ] (ID#)   FECA BLKLUNG [ ] (ID#)   OTHER [ ] (ID#)   1a. INSURED'S I.D. NUMBER (For Program in Item 1)

2. PATIENT'S NAME (Last Name, First Name, Middle Initial)
SEE ATTACHED ROSTER

3. PATIENT'S BIRTH DATE MM DD YY   SEX M [ ] F [ ]

4. INSURED'S NAME (Last Name, First Name, Middle Initial)

5. PATIENT'S ADDRESS (No., Street)

6. PATIENT RELATIONSHIP TO INSURED   Self [ ] Spouse [ ] Child [ ] Other [ ]

7. INSURED'S ADDRESS (No., Street)

CITY   STATE

8. RESERVED FOR NUCC USE

CITY   STATE

ZIP CODE   TELEPHONE (Include Area Code) ( )

ZIP CODE   TELEPHONE (Include Area Code) ( )

9. OTHER INSURED'S NAME (Last Name, First Name, Middle Initial)

10. IS PATIENT'S CONDITION RELATED TO:

11. INSURED'S POLICY GROUP OR FECA NUMBER
NONE

a. OTHER INSURED'S POLICY OR GROUP NUMBER

a. EMPLOYMENT? (Current or Previous) YES [ ] NO [ ]

a. INSURED'S DATE OF BIRTH MM DD YY   SEX M [ ] F [ ]

b. RESERVED FOR NUCC USE

b. AUTO ACCIDENT? YES [ ] NO [ ]   PLACE (State)

b. OTHER CLAIM ID (Designated by NUCC)

c. RESERVED FOR NUCC USE

c. OTHER ACCIDENT? YES [ ] NO [ ]

c. INSURANCE PLAN NAME OR PROGRAM NAME

d. INSURANCE PLAN NAME OR PROGRAM NAME

10d. CLAIM CODES (Designated by NUCC)

d. IS THERE ANOTHER HEALTH BENEFIT PLAN? YES [ ] NO [ ]   If yes, complete items 9, 9a, and 9d.

READ BACK OF FORM BEFORE COMPLETING & SIGNING THIS FORM.
12. PATIENT'S OR AUTHORIZED PERSON'S SIGNATURE I authorize the release of any medical or other information necessary to process this claim. I also request payment of government benefits either to myself or to the party who accepts assignment below.
SIGNED_____ DATE_____

13. INSURED'S OR AUTHORIZED PERSON'S SIGNATURE I authorize payment of medical benefits to the undersigned physician or supplier for services described below.
SIGNED_____

14. DATE OF CURRENT ILLNESS, INJURY, or PREGNANCY (LMP) MM DD YY   QUAL.

15. OTHER DATE QUAL. MM DD YY

16. DATES PATIENT UNABLE TO WORK IN CURRENT OCCUPATION FROM MM DD YY TO MM DD YY

17. NAME OF REFERRING PROVIDER OR OTHER SOURCE   17a.   17b. NPI

18. HOSPITALIZATION DATES RELATED TO CURRENT SERVICES FROM MM DD YY TO MM DD YY

19. ADDITIONAL CLAIM INFORMATION (Designated by NUCC)

20. OUTSIDE LAB? YES [ ] NO [X] $ CHARGES

21. DIAGNOSIS OR NATURE OF ILLNESS OR INJURY Relate A-L to service line below (24E)   ICD Ind. 0
A. **Z23**   B.   C.   D.
E.   F.   G.   H.
I.   J.   K.   L.

22. RESUBMISSION CODE   ORIGINAL REF. NO.

23. PRIOR AUTHORIZATION NUMBER

24. A. DATE(S) OF SERVICE From MM DD YY	To MM DD YY	B. PLACE OF SERVICE	C. EMG	D. PROCEDURES, SERVICES, OR SUPPLIES CPT/HCPCS	MODIFIER	E. DIAGNOSIS POINTER	F. $ CHARGES	G. DAYS OR UNITS	H. EPSDT Family Plan	I. ID. QUAL.	J. RENDERING PROVIDER ID. #
1 11 15 YY		60		90686		A	10 00	1		NPI	
2 11 15 YY		60		G0008	33	A	10 00	1		NPI	
3										NPI	
4										NPI	
5										NPI	
6										NPI	

25. FEDERAL TAX I.D. NUMBER   SSN [ ] EIN [ ]

26. PATIENT'S ACCOUNT NO.

27. ACCEPT ASSIGNMENT? (For govt. claims, see back) YES [X] NO [ ]

28. TOTAL CHARGE $

29. AMOUNT PAID $ 0 00

30. Rsvd for NUCC Use

31. SIGNATURE OF PHYSICIAN OR SUPPLIER INCLUDING DEGREES OR CREDENTIALS (I certify that the statements on the reverse apply to this bill and are made a part thereof.)
SIGNATURE   SIGNED   **MMDDYY**   DATE

32. SERVICE FACILITY LOCATION INFORMATION
ANYWHERE HEALTH CLINIC
100 MAIN ST
ANYWHERE NY 123451234
a. 1123456789   b.

33. BILLING PROVIDER INFO & PH # (101) 5551111
ANYWHERE HEALTH CLINIC
100 MAIN ST
ANYWHERE NY 123451234
a. 1123456789   b.

NUCC Instruction Manual available at: www.nucc.org   **PLEASE PRINT OR TYPE**

CARRIER — PATIENT AND INSURED INFORMATION — PHYSICIAN OR SUPPLIER INFORMATION

Courtesy of the Centers for Medicare & Medicaid Services, www.cms.gov; claim data created by author.

FIGURE 14-15 Completed CMS-1500 claim as cover sheet for Medicare roster billing form.

Summary

Medicare Part A reimburses institutional providers for inpatient hospital and skilled nursing facility stays; home health and hospice services; ESRD and kidney donor coverage; and heart/heart-lung, liver, and bone marrow transplants. Medicare Part B reimburses noninstitutional health care providers for all outpatient services, including physician services, diagnostic testing, ambulance services, DME, supplies used in the home and certified by a physician, and so on.

Medicare Advantage plans (Medicare Part C) include managed care plans and private fee-for-service plans that provide care under contract to Medicare and may include such benefits as coordination of care, reductions in out-of-pocket expenses, and prescription drugs. The Medicare prescription drug program consists of private prescription drug plans (PDPs) and Medicare Advantage prescription drug plans (MA–PDs), collectively referred to as Medicare Part D.

Participating providers (PARs) agree to accept assignment on all Medicare claims submitted, and PARs receive special incentives as part of the agreement. Nonparticipating providers (nonPARs) may elect to accept assignment on a claim-by-claim basis, and restrictions apply (e.g., limiting charge).

When completing Medicare CMS-1500 claims for exercises in the textbook, assignments in the workbook, and case studies in SimClaim™, the following special instructions apply:

- Block 9a—Enter MEDIGAP followed by the policy and/or group number (this instruction applies to Medigap claims only); otherwise, leave blank.
- Block 12—Enter SIGNATURE ON FILE (patients have signed a customized authorization that is filed in the patient's record), and leave date blank.
- Block 20—Enter an X in the NO box.
- Block 23—Leave blank.
- Block 26—Enter the case study number (e.g., 14-7). If the patient has both primary and secondary coverage, enter a P (for primary) next to the case study number (on the primary claim) and an S (for secondary) next to the number (on the secondary claim); if the patient is eligible for the Medicare-Medicaid crossover plan, enter MM next to the case study number.
- Block 27—Enter an X in the YES box.
- When completing secondary claims, enter REMITTANCE ADVICE ATTACHED in the top left margin of the CMS-1500 claim (to simulate the attachment of a primary payer's remittance advice with a claim submitted to a secondary payer).

Internet Links

Medicare Contractor Beneficiary and Provider Communications Manual: Go to *www.cms.gov*, scroll down to the Top 5 Resources heading, click on the Manuals link, click on the Internet-Only Manuals (IOMs) link, click on the Publication 100-09 *(Medicare Contractor Beneficiary and Provider Communications Manual)* link, and click on the Chapter 6-Medicare Administrative Contractor (MAC) Beneficiary and Provider Communications Manual (PDF) link.

Medicare coverage information: Go to *www.cms.gov*, click on the Medicare link, scroll down to the Coverage heading, and click on the Medicare Coverage - General Information link.

Medicare HCC Risk Score Calculator: Go to *www.medicareinformatics.com*, scroll down to the *HCC Risk Adjustment* heading, click on the *HCC Risk Score Calculator*, and enter ICD-10-CM codes to determine hierarchical condition categories and scores.

Medicare Learning Network® (MLN): Go to *go.cms.gov/MLNProducts* to browse available MLN products and multimedia.

Medicare physician fee schedules: Go to **www.cms.gov**, click on the Medicare link, scroll down to the Medicare Fee-for-Service Payment heading, and click on the Fee Schedules - General Information link.

Medicare program manuals: Go to **www.cms.gov**, scroll down to the Top 5 Resources heading, click on the Manuals link, click on the Internet-Only Manuals (IOMs) link, and click on Publications 100-04 (*Medicare Claims Processing Manual*) and 100-05 (*Medicare Secondary Payer Manual*) links.

Medicare Summary Notice (MSN): Go to **www.medicare.gov**, scroll over the Forms, Help, & Resources link, click on the "Free Medicare publications" link, and click on the Download Handbook link. The *Medicare & You* publication contains information about the MSN.

QualityNet health care quality data exchange: www.qualitynet.org

RBRVS EZ-Fees™ software tour: www.rbrvs.net

U.S. government site for people with Medicare: www.medicare.gov

Review

14.1 – Multiple Choice

Instructions: Select the most appropriate response.

1. When a patient has Medicare and retiree group health plan coverage, Medicare pays
   a. first.
   b. second.

2. What is the name of the statement that Medicare patients receive every three months?
   a. Medicare summary notice
   b. Remittance advice

3. Which is a characteristic of Medicare enrollment?
   a. Eligible individuals are automatically enrolled, or they apply for coverage.
   b. Individuals who qualify for SSA benefits must "buy in" to Medicare Part A.
   c. The general enrollment period is between January 1 and December 31.
   d. Those that enroll in Medicare Part A must also enroll in Medicare Part B.

4. Which processes Original Medicare claims?
   a. Carrier
   b. Centers for Medicare and Medicaid Services
   c. Fiscal intermediary
   d. Medicare administrative contractor

5. A skilled nursing facility (SNF) patient is admitted, having met medical necessity requirements after a three-day-minimum acute hospital stay. Which criterion applies to the current SNF admission?
   a. If the patient remains in the SNF for more than 24 hours, the facility must provide a Medicare Outpatient Observation Notice (MOON) to guarantee payment by Medicare.
   b. Medicare will cover services such as room and board and items/services that do not require a physician's order (e.g., unmedicated wound dressings, use of a simple walker).
   c. The Medicare beneficiary pays nothing for the first 20 days of each benefit period, a coinsurance per day for days 21–100 of each benefit period, and all costs for each day after day 100 in a benefit period.
   d. To qualify for SNF care, a SNF physician and the primary care physician must certify that the patient is terminally ill, which means the patient as a life expectancy of six months or less.

6. Which is the total number of Medicare lifetime reserve days (defined as the number of days that can be used just once during a patient's lifetime)?
    a. 20
    b. 60
    c. 100
    d. 180

7. The Original Medicare plan includes Medicare
    a. Part A only.
    b. Part A and Part B.
    c. Part C.
    d. Part D.

8. Medigap coverage is offered to Medicare beneficiaries by
    a. commercial payers.
    b. Medicaid.
    c. employers.
    d. federal health plans.

9. A Medicare nonparticipating provider is *not* allowed to
    a. apply the assignment of benefits.
    b. implement balance billing.
    c. mandate limiting charges.
    d. participate in private contracting.

10. Which is provided to a Medicare beneficiary by a physician before providing a service that is unlikely to be reimbursed by Medicare?
    a. Advance beneficiary notice of noncoverage
    b. Medical necessity denial
    c. MSP questionnaire
    d. Waiver of Medicare billing contract

14.2 – Medicare Coinsurance and Copayment Amounts for Hospital Outpatient Services

Instructions: Medicare allows patients to pay either a coinsurance amount (20 percent of the charge for procedures and services) or a fixed copayment amount, whichever is less, for hospital outpatient services (when the hospital is a participating [PAR] provider). For each of the following, calculate the amount the patient is required to pay to the PAR hospital for the outpatient service provided. (The patient has already met the annual deductible required by the payer.)

_____ 1. Sally Jones underwent outpatient surgery to have one mole removed from the upper back. The charge was $65. The fixed copayment amount for this type of procedure, adjusted for wages in the geographic area, is $15.

_____ 2. Cherie Brown underwent an outpatient chest x-ray that cost $75. The fixed copayment for this type of procedure, adjusted for wages in the geographic area, is $25.

_____ 3. James Hill underwent an outpatient oral glucose tolerance test. The charge for this procedure was $122. The fixed copayment for this type of procedure, adjusted for wages in the geographic area, is $20.

_____ 4. Scott Wills underwent toenail removal as an outpatient. The charge was $81. The fixed copayment for this type of procedure, adjusted for wages in the geographic area, is $25.

_____ 5. George Harris had a suspicious lesion removed from his left temple as an outpatient. The charge was $78. The fixed copayment amount for this type of procedure, adjusted for wages in the geographic area, is $15.

Chapter

15

Medicaid

Chapter Outline

Medicaid Eligibility

Medicaid Coverage

Medicaid Reimbursement

Medicaid Billing Notes

Medicaid Claims Instructions

Medicaid as Secondary Payer Claims
    Instructions

Medicaid Parent/Newborn Claims Instructions

CHIP Claims Instructions

Chapter Objectives

Upon successful completion of this chapter, you should be able to:

1. Define key terms related to Medicaid.
2. Explain Medicaid eligibility guidelines.
3. Describe mandatory services included with Medicaid coverage.
4. Describe Medicaid reimbursement policies.
5. Apply Medicaid billing notes when completing CMS-1500 claims.
6. Complete Medicaid primary claims.
7. Complete Medicaid secondary claims.
8. Complete Medicaid parent/newborn claims.
9. Complete CHIP claims.

Key Terms

adjusted claim

Basic Health Program (BHP)

Children's Health Insurance
    Program (CHIP)

dual eligibles

Early and Periodic Screening,
    Diagnostic, and Treatment
    (EPSDT) services

Federal Medical Assistance
    Percentage (FMAP)

federal poverty level (FPL)

Medicaid

Medicaid eligibility verification
    system (MEVS)

Medicaid remittance advice

medical assistance program

parent/newborn claim

recipient eligibility verification
    system (REVS)

surveillance and utilization review
    subsystem (SURS)

voided claim

Introduction

Medicaid provides medical and health-related services to certain individuals and families with low incomes and limited resources. It is jointly funded by the federal and state governments to assist states in providing adequate medical care to qualified individuals. Federal policy guidance specifies the Centers for Medicare & Medicaid Services (CMS) as responsible for implementing laws passed by Congress related to Medicaid, the Children's Health Insurance Program (CHIP), and the Basic Health Program. To implement these programs, CMS issues regulations that explain how laws will be implemented and what states and others need to do to comply. In addition to regulations, CMS issues sub-regulatory guidance to address policy issues as well as operational updates and technical clarifications about existing regulations and guidance.

The following **medical assistance programs** provide health care coverage to individuals with low incomes:

- **Medicaid** is a cost-sharing medical assistance program between the federal and state governments that provides health care services to eligible adults, children, pregnant people, older adults, and people with disabilities who have low incomes.

- The **Children's Health Insurance Program (CHIP)** is jointly funded by federal and state governments to provide health coverage to eligible children. States may choose between a Medicaid expansion program, a separate CHIP, or a combination of both types of programs.

- The **Basic Health Program (BPH)** is a health benefits coverage program for residents with low incomes who would otherwise be eligible to purchase coverage through the Health Insurance Marketplace. Implemented by the Affordable Care Act, BPH gives states the ability to provide more affordable coverage to residents with low incomes and improve continuity of care for people whose income fluctuates above and below Medicaid and CHIP income eligibility levels. States contract with one or more private insurance companies to provide coverage to eligible residents at affordable premiums.

Medicaid varies considerably from state to state (including the assignment of state names, such as Medi-Cal or MassHealth), and each state has modified its program over time. (Go to www.medicaid.gov, click on the Menu, click on the State Overviews link, and choose a state from the State Medicaid & CHIP Profiles drop-down menu to research the vast differences among individual state Medicaid programs.)

 NOTE:

> CMS-1500 claims completion instructions are included in this chapter. (UB-04 claims are autopopulated by data abstracted and coded from patient records or from an electronic health record (EHR) in hospitals, skilled nursing facilities, inpatient hospices, and home health care organizations. *Chapter 11 of this textbook contains general UB-04 claims completion instructions*, along with examples and a review assignment.)

Medicaid Eligibility

Medicaid policies for eligibility are complex and vary considerably, even among states of similar size and geographic proximity. Thus, a person who is eligible for Medicaid in one state may not be eligible in another state; and the services provided by one state may differ considerably in amount, duration, or scope as compared with services provided in a similar or neighboring state. In addition, state legislatures may change Medicaid eligibility requirements during the year.

Medicaid does not provide medical assistance for all persons with low incomes, and it is important to realize that low income is only one test for Medicaid eligibility. Non-financial eligibility criteria include U.S. citizenship (or certain qualified non-citizens, such as lawful permanent residents), residence of the state in which Medicaid is received, and for some eligibility groups there are limits according to age, pregnancy, or parenting status. In addition to their Medicaid programs, most states implement "state-only" programs to provide medical assistance for specified individuals with low incomes who do not qualify for Medicaid. (Federal funds are *not* provided for state-only programs.) The federal government provides matching funds to state Medicaid programs when certain health care services are provided to eligible individuals (e.g., children, individuals with disabilities, and persons 65 years or older). Each state administers its own Medicaid program. Centers for Medicare and Medicaid Services (CMS) monitors the programs and establishes requirements for the delivery, funding, and quality of services as well as eligibility criteria.

The *Modified Adjusted Gross Income (MAGI)* is the basis for determining Medicaid income eligibility for most children, pregnant people, parents, and adults. The MAGI-based methodology considers taxable income and tax filing relationships to determine financial eligibility for Medicaid. (MAGI replaced the former process for calculating Medicaid eligibility, which was based on the Aid to Families with Dependent Children program and the Temporary Assistance for Needy Families.) The MAGI-based methodology does not allow for income disregards that vary by state or by eligibility group, and it does not allow for an asset or resource test.

Medicaid eligibility includes the following eligibility groups:

- Medically needy
- Special groups

Programs that impact Medicaid include:

- Children's Health Insurance Program (CHIP)
- Programs of All-inclusive Care for the Elderly (PACE)

Medicaid eligibility is impacted by:

- Spousal Impoverishment Protection
- Confirming Medicaid Eligibility

Once an individual is eligible for Medicaid, coverage is effective either on the date of application or the first day of the month of application. Benefits may also be covered retroactively for up to three months prior to the month of application *if the individual would have been eligible during that period had they applied*. Coverage generally stops at the end of the month in which a person no longer meets requirements for eligibility.

Medically Needy Program

States that establish a *medically needy Medicaid program* expand eligibility to additional qualified persons who may have too much income to qualify under another program. (Federal matching funds are available.) This option allows currently ineligible individuals to become eligible by "spending down" the amount of income that is above a state's income eligibility standard. For example, when individuals pay the medical expenses for care not covered by health insurance, that "spend down amount" can make them eligible for Medicaid.

States must provide individuals with the opportunity to request a fair hearing to appeal a *medically needy program* eligibility denial when the individual believes an error was made or the state did not act with reasonable promptness regarding eligibility. (States must also allow a "spend down" of income to eligibility levels for groups based on blindness, disability, or age [65 and older].)

Special Groups

States are required to assist the following special groups:

- *Qualified Medicare beneficiaries (QMB)* states pay Medicare premiums, deductibles, coinsurance amounts, and copayments for individuals with low incomes.
- *Qualified working disabled individuals (QWDI)* states pay Medicare Part A premiums for certain individuals with disabilities who lose Medicare coverage because of work.

- *Qualifying individual (QI)* states pay Medicare Part B premiums for individuals with low incomes.
- *Specified low-income Medicare beneficiary (SLMB)* states pay Medicare Part B premiums for individuals with low incomes.

States may also improve access to employment, training, and placement of people with disabilities who want to work by providing expanded Medicaid eligibility to:

- Individuals who are disabled and employed between ages 16 and 65 who have income and resources greater than that allowed under the SSI program
- Individuals who are employed and who become ineligible for the group described above because their medical conditions improve (States may require these individuals to share in the cost of their medical care.)

Two additional eligibility groups are related to specific medical conditions, and states may provide coverage under their Medicaid plans:

- Time-limited eligibility for individuals who have breast or cervical cancer
- Individuals diagnosed with tuberculosis (TB) who are uninsured

Individuals with breast or cervical cancer receive all Medicaid plan services. TB patients receive only services related to the treatment of TB.

Children's Health Insurance Program

The *Children's Health Insurance Program (CHIP)* allows states to create or expand existing Medicaid programs, providing more federal funds to states for the purpose of expanding Medicaid eligibility to include a greater number of currently uninsured children. With certain exceptions, these include children in households with low incomes who would not otherwise qualify for Medicaid. CHIP may also be used to provide medical assistance to children during a presumptive eligibility period for Medicaid.

The *Affordable Care Act* strengthened the Children's Health Insurance Program (CHIP) by implementing consistent standards and systems to seamlessly and efficiently meet consumers' health care needs, improve quality, and lower costs.

> **Example:** An uninsured 45-year-old (with no children) who is employed as a restaurant host, where health insurance is not offered, could qualify for Medicaid if they earn less than $12,000 in a year.

Programs of All-inclusive Care for the Elderly (PACE)

The *Programs of All-Inclusive Care for the Elderly (PACE)* provides comprehensive medical and social services to certain community-dwelling individuals who are older adults, most of whom are dually eligible for Medicare and Medicaid benefits. An interdisciplinary team of health professionals provides PACE participants with coordinated care. PACE allows individuals to remain in the community rather than receive care in a nursing facility.

Financing for the program is capitated, which allows providers to deliver all services needed by participants (rather than only those reimbursable under Medicare and Medicaid fee-for-service plans). PACE is a Medicare program that states can elect to implement for Medicaid beneficiaries as an optional benefit.

When implemented, the PACE program is the sole source of Medicaid and Medicare benefits for participants, and the PACE model of care is established as a provider in the Medicare program.

 NOTE:

When a PACE participant needs to use a noncontract provider, physician, or other entity, there is a limit on the amount that these noncontract entities can charge the PACE program.

Spousal Impoverishment Protection

The expense of nursing facility care—which can be as much as $15,000 per month or more—can rapidly deplete the lifetime savings of older adult couples. Congress enacted provisions to prevent "spousal impoverishment," which leaves the spouse who is still living at home in the community with little or no income or resources. These provisions alleviate this situation so that community spouses are able to live out their lives with independence and dignity.

Under the Medicaid spousal impoverishment provisions, a certain amount of the couple's combined resources is protected for the spouse living in the community. Depending on how much income the community spouse has, a certain amount of income belonging to the spouse in the nursing facility can be "set aside" for the community spouse's use. Following is the minimum and maximum amount of resources and income that can be protected for a spouse in the community in 2021:

- Spousal share, up to a maximum of $130,380 in 2021
- State spousal resource standard, which a state could set at any amount between $26,075 and $130,380 in 2021
- Amount transferred to the community spouse for support as directed by court order
- Amount designated by a state officer to raise the community spouse's protected resources up to the minimum monthly maintenance needs standard

 NOTE:

The couple's home, household goods, automobile, and burial funds are *not* included in the couple's combined countable resources.

The community spouse's income is *not* available to the spouse who resides in the facility, and the two individuals are not considered a couple for income eligibility purposes. The state uses the income eligibility standard for one person rather than two, and the standard income eligibility process for Medicaid is used.

Example: John Q. Public is required to reside in a nursing facility. His wife, Nancy Public, resides in the family home. At the time of Mr. Public's Medicaid application, they have $160,000 in resources (not including the family home, which is not included in resources as long as the spouse is in residence). John Q. Public's monthly Social Security income (SSI) is $1,000, and Nancy Public's monthly SSI is $600, totaling $1,600.

- Under the *income-first approach*, the state attributes one-half of the resources (or $80,000) to Mrs. Public as her community spouse resource allowance (CSRA). This allows Mr. Public to retain $80,000, which must be reduced to $1,500 before becoming eligible for Medicaid. This means the Public family is expected to convert $80,000 in resources (e.g., stocks, bonds, summer home) to cash and spend it on nursing facility care for Mr. Public. Because the state's minimum monthly maintenance needs allowance (MMMNA) is $2,177.50 (in 2021), Mrs. Public keeps all her monthly SSI, in addition to all $1,000 of her husband's monthly SSI. None of the monthly income is expended on nursing facility care for Mr. Public.

- Under the *resources-first approach*, Mr. Public is expected to expend the $1,000 monthly SSI on nursing facility care. This means that Mrs. Public has a monthly income of only $600, and because the state's MMMNA is $2,177.50, Mr. Public can transfer $80,000 in resources to Mrs. Public. This increases the CSRA to an amount that generates an additional $1,000 per month. As a result, Mr. Public becomes immediately eligible for Medicaid, and Mrs. Public is allowed to retain all $160,000 in resources.

Confirming Medicaid Eligibility

Any time patients state that they receive Medicaid, they must present a valid Medicaid identification card.

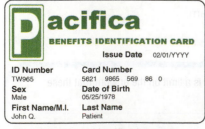

Sample Medicaid identification card

Eligibility, in many cases, will depend on the patient's monthly income. As eligibility may fluctuate from one month to the next, most states have a dedicated telephone line for verification of eligibility. Confirmation of eligibility should be obtained for each visit; failure to do so may result in a denial of payment. If residing in one of these states, be sure to access the Medicaid verification line. Some states have a point-of-service device similar to those used by credit card companies. Beneficiaries carry plastic cards containing encoded data strips. When the card is swiped, the printout indicates eligibility or ineligibility data.

Retroactive eligibility is sometimes granted to patients whose income has fallen below the state-set eligibility level and who had high medical expenses prior to applying for Medicaid. When patients notify the practice that they have become retroactively eligible for Medicaid benefits, confirm this information before proceeding. A refund of any payments made by the patient during the retroactive period must be made and Medicaid is billed for these services.

Medicaid Coverage

Because states establish and administer their own Medicaid programs, they determine the type, amount, duration, and scope of services within broad federal guidelines. Federal law requires states to provide certain mandatory benefits and allows states the choice of covering other optional benefits.

Mandatory Medicaid Benefits

Mandatory benefits include the following:

- Inpatient hospital services
- Outpatient hospital services
- Early and Periodic Screening, Diagnostic, and Treatment (EPSDT) services
- Nursing facility services
- Home health services
- Physician services
- Rural health clinic services
- Federally qualified health center services
- Laboratory and x-ray services
- Family planning services
- Nurse midwife services
- Certified pediatric and family nurse practitioner services
- Freestanding birth center services (when licensed or otherwise recognized by the state)
- Transportation to medical care
- Tobacco cessation counseling for pregnant people

 NOTE:

Early and Periodic Screening, Diagnostic, and Treatment (EPSDT) services consist of routine pediatric checkups provided to all children enrolled in Medicaid to detect potential problems, provide treatment, and conduct other measures to correct or ameliorate defects and physical and mental illnesses and conditions discovered by the screening services, whether or not such services are covered by the state Medicaid plan.

- Early: Assessing and identifying problems early
- Periodic: Checking children's health at periodic, age-appropriate intervals
- Screening: Providing physical, mental, developmental, dental, hearing, vision, and other screening tests to detect potential problems
- Diagnostic: Performing diagnostic tests to follow up when a risk is identified
- Treatment: Controlling, correcting, or reducing health problems found

Optional Medicaid Benefits

Optional Medicaid benefits that states can implement include the following:

- Prescription drugs
- Clinic services
- Physical therapy
- Occupational therapy
- Speech, hearing and language disorder services
- Respiratory care services
- Other diagnostic, screening, preventive and rehabilitative services
- Podiatry services
- Optometry services
- Dental Services
- Dentures
- Prosthetics
- Eyeglasses
- Chiropractic services
- Other practitioner services
- Private duty nursing services
- Personal care
- Hospice
- Case management
- Services for individuals age 65 or older in an institution for mental disease (IMD)
- Services in an intermediate care facility for individuals with intellectual disability (ICF/IID)
- State plan home- and community-based services
- Self-directed personal assistance services—1915(j)
- Community First Choice option—1915(k)
- Tuberculosis-related services
- Inpatient psychiatric services for individuals under age 21
- Other services approved by the Secretary of DHHS
- Health homes for enrollees with chronic conditions

Preventive Health Care Services

Preventive health care services include immunizations, screenings for common chronic and infectious diseases and cancers, clinical and behavioral interventions to manage chronic disease and reduce associated risks, and counseling to support healthy living and self-management of chronic disease. CMS assists states expand access to preventive health care by providing technical assistance and facilitating the exchange of information about practices of high quality, high impact, and effective preventive care delivery.

Medicaid's prevention initiatives include the following:

- Medicaid prevention learning network (for state-to-state learning and enhanced technical assistance to improve delivery of preventive health care)
- School-based health (SBH)
- Antipsychotic drug use in children (ADC)

- Diabetes prevention and management
- HIV health improvement
- Tobacco cessation
- Developmental and behavioral screening of young children (to identify possible delays in growth and development)
- Early and Periodic Screening, Diagnostic and Treatment (EPSDT) (e.g., vision services, dental services, hearing services)
- Immunizations
- Obesity (screenings and interventions to reduce obesity and promote healthy eating and physical activity)
- Oral health (for prevention and early treatment of dental conditions)

Medicaid Reimbursement

The Medicaid program is jointly funded by the federal government and states, and the federal government pays states for a specified percentage of program expenditures, called the **Federal Medical Assistance Percentage (FMAP)**. The FMAP is determined annually for each state using a formula that compares the state's average per capita income level with the national average. States must ensure that they can fund their share of Medicaid expenditures for care and services available under their state plan. States can also establish their own Medicaid provider payment rates within federal requirements, and they generally pay for services through fee-for-service or managed care arrangements.

States are permitted to require copayments, coinsurance, deductibles, and other similar charges for most Medicaid-covered benefits, both inpatient and outpatient services, and amounts charged can vary with income. Such out-of-pocket costs cannot be imposed for emergency services, family planning services, pregnancy-related services, or preventive services for children. In addition, children, terminally ill individuals, and individuals residing in an institution are exempt from paying out-of-pocket costs. Federal guidance about cost-sharing limits them to nominal or minimal amounts, such as a $4 managed care copayment.

 NOTE:

Federal law requires that state Medicaid programs make *Disproportionate Share Hospital (DSH)* payments to qualifying hospitals that serve a large number of Medicaid and uninsured individuals. The federal DSH allotment is established annually for each state and limits *Federal Financial Participation (FFP)* for total statewide DSH payments made to hospitals. To receive FFP for DSH payments, federal law requires states to submit an independent certified audit and an annual report to the Secretary describing DSH payments made to each DSH hospital. The report must identify each disproportionate share hospital that got a DSH payment adjustment, and it must provide any other information the DHHS Secretary needs to ensure the appropriateness of the payment amount. The annual certified independent audit includes specific verifications to make sure all DSH payments are appropriate.

Federal law also limits FFP for DSH payments through a hospital-specific DSH limit. Under that hospital-specific DSH limit, FFP is not available for state DSH payments that are more than the hospital's eligible uncompensated care cost. That is calculated as the cost of providing inpatient hospital and outpatient hospital services to Medicaid patients and the uninsured, minus payments received by the hospital on behalf of those patients.

According to Medicaid.com, "the *Indian Health Care Improvement Act (IHCIA) of 1976* amended the *Social Security Act* to permit reimbursement by Medicare and Medicaid for services provided to Indigenous Americans and Alaska Natives in Indian Health Service (IHS) and tribal health care facilities. In doing so, Congress recognized that many Indigenous Americans, especially those residing in very remote and rural locations, were eligible for but could not access Medicaid and Medicare services without traveling sometimes hundreds of miles to Medicaid and Medicare providers located off reservation."

States are provided with with a 100 percent *Federal Medical Assistance Percentage (FMAP)* for Medicaid services provided through an IHS or tribal health care facility. (The Affordable Care Act eliminated the 2000 expiration date of the IHCIA, making the Act permanent and authorizing appropriations to fund reimbursement for health care services provided to American Indians and Alaska Natives in Indian Health Service [IHS] and tribal health care facilities.) According to Medicaid.gov, "certain protections for [Indigenous Americans] that preclude states from imposing Medicaid premiums or any other Medicaid cost sharing on [Indigenous American] enrollees who have used the Indian health system. Section 5006 also emphasizes the state-tribal relationship by formally requiring that states consult with the tribal community on Medicaid and CHIP policy matters. Specifically, states must seek advice from designees of Indigenous Americans Indian health programs and urban Indian organizations in the state when Medicaid and CHIP matters have a direct effect on [Indigenous Americans], Indian health programs, or urban Indian programs."

Medicare-Medicaid Relationship

Medicare beneficiaries with low incomes and limited resources may also receive help from the Medicaid program. For those eligible for *full* Medicaid coverage, Medicare coverage is supplemented by services available under a state's Medicaid program. These additional services may include, for example, nursing facility care beyond the 100-day limit covered by Medicare, prescription drugs, eyeglasses, and hearing aids.

Dual Eligibles

Medicare beneficiaries with low incomes and limited resources may receive help with out-of-pocket medical expenses from state Medicaid programs. Various benefits are available to **dual eligibles**, which are based on the **federal poverty level (FPL)** (income guidelines established annually by the federal government). The program for individuals entitled to Medicare *and* eligible for some type of Medicaid benefit is abbreviated as Medi-Medi. Individuals eligible for full Medicaid coverage receive program supplements to their Medicare coverage via services and supplies available from the state's Medicaid program. Services covered by both programs are paid first by Medicare and the difference by Medicaid, up to the state's payment limit. Medicaid also allows coverage of the following additional services:

- Nursing facility care beyond the 100-day limit covered by Medicare
- Prescription drugs
- Eyeglasses
- Hearing aids

 NOTE:

When an individual has both Medicare and Medicaid coverage, covered services are paid by Medicare first before any payments are made by the Medicaid program. The reason for this is because Medicaid is always the *payer of last resort*.

Medicaid as a Secondary Payer

Medicaid is always the *payer of last resort*. If the patient is covered by another medical or liability policy, including Medicare, TRICARE (formerly CHAMPUS), CHAMPVA, or Indian Health Services (IHS), this coverage must be billed first. Medicaid is billed only if the other coverage denies responsibility for payment, pays less than the Medicaid fee schedule, or if Medicaid covers procedures not covered by the other policy.

Participating Providers

Any provider who accepts a Medicaid patient must accept the Medicaid-determined payment as payment in full. Providers are forbidden by law to bill *(balance billing)* patients for Medicaid-covered benefits. A patient may be billed for any service that is not a covered benefit; however, some states have historically required providers to sign formal participating Medicaid contracts. Other states do not require contracts.

Medicaid and Managed Care

Managed care is a health care delivery system that manages cost, utilization, and quality. Medicaid managed care provides for delivery of Medicaid health benefits and additional services through contracted arrangements between state Medicaid agencies and managed care organizations (MCOs) that accept a monthly *capitation payment* (pre-determined monetary amount) for these services.

The goal is for states to reduce Medicaid program costs and manage the utilization of health care services. Key objectives include an improvement in health plan performance, health care quality, and patient outcomes. Some states implement a range of initiatives to coordinate and integrate care beyond traditional managed care. Such initiatives focus on improving care for patients with chronic and complex conditions, aligning payment incentives with performance goals, and establishing accountability for high-quality care.

 NOTE:

States with *managed long term services and supports (MLTSS)* require delivery of long term services and supports capitated Medicaid managed care programs. The intent is to expand home- and community-based services, promoting community inclusion, ensuring quality, and increasing efficiency. The PACE program and Health Homes are examples of such services, which coordinate care for Medicaid beneficiaries who have chronic conditions and adopts a "whole-person" philosophy. Health Homes providers coordinate and integrate primary, acute, behavioral health, and long-term care services and support to treat the whole person.

Federal managed care regulations recognize four types of managed care entities:

- *Managed Care Organizations (MCOs)* provide a comprehensive benefit package with payment that is risk-based/capitation.

- *Primary Care Case Management (PCCM)* provide primary care case managers who contract with states to furnish case management services that are based on location, coordination, and monitoring, and they are generally paid based on fee-for-service for medical services rendered plus a monthly case management fee.

- *Prepaid Inpatient Health Plan (PIHP)* is a limited benefit package that includes inpatient hospital or institutional services, such as mental health care, with payment either risk-based/capitation or non-risk fees.

- *Prepaid Ambulatory Health Plan (PAHP)* is a limited benefit package that does not include inpatient hospital or other institutional services, such as dental or transportation, with payment either risk-based/capitation or non-risk fees.

Example: State contracts with limited-benefit plans for providing behavioral health or oral health services may include requirements regarding network development, assistance to enrollees seeking services, and development of member materials.

Medicaid Eligibility Verification System

Medicaid and CHIP agencies rely primarily on data sources to verify eligibility for Medicaid and CHIP, such as the Social Security Administration, Department of Homeland Security, and Department of Labor. The Affordable Care Act and accompanying federal regulations established a data-driven approach to the verification of financial and non-financial information needed to determine Medicaid and CHIP eligibility. The **Medicaid eligibility verification system (MEVS)**, sometimes called **recipient eligibility verification system (REVS)**, allows providers to electronically access the state's eligibility file using the following methods. Then, a "receipt ticket" (Figure 15-1) is generated upon eligibility verification by MEVS.

- *Point-of-service device* is used with the patient's medical identification card, which contains a magnetic strip; when the provider "swipes" the card through the device's reader, accurate eligibility information is displayed. (The provider purchases the point-of-service device, which includes magnetic card reader equipment.)

- *Computer software* allows the provider to enter a Medicaid recipient's identification number so that accurate eligibility information is displayed.

- *Automated voice response system* allows providers to call the state's Medicaid office to receive eligibility verification information.

 NOTE:

Go to eMedNY.org to view a web-based electronic Medicaid system.

```
                    US MEDICAID
          Eligibility
          10/19/YYYY 09:52:15
                  PAYER INFORMATION
          Payer: UNITED STATES MEDICAL SERVICES
          Payer ID: US59MCD
                 PROVIDER INFORMATION
          Provider: ANYWHERE HOSP
          Service Provider# 1111111
                SUBSCRIBER INFORMATION
          Current Trace Number: YYYY5621590000000
          Assigning Entity: 5111111111
          Insured or subscriber: Patient, John Q.
          Member ID: 555555555
          Address: Senior Assisted Living
          5400 MAIN ST
          ANYWHERE, US 12345-9999
          Date of Birth: 08/22/YYYY
          Sex: Male
         ELIGIBILITY AND BENEFIT INFORMATION
           HEALTH BENEFIT PLAN COVERAGE
          ACTIVE COVERAGE
          Insurance Type: Medicaid
          Eligibility Begin Date: 11/20/YYYY
          ACTIVE COVERAGE
          Insurance Type: Medicare Primary
          Eligibility Date Range: 11/20/YYYY – 11/20/YYYY

             HEALTH BENEFIT PLAN COVERAGE
               OTHER OR ADDITIONAL PAYER
          Insurance Type: Other
          Benefit Coord. Date Range: 11/20/YYYY – 11/20/YYYY
          Payer: BLUECROSS BLUESHIELD
          Address: 2300 MAIN ST
          PO BOX 6052
          ANYWHERE, US 12345-9999
          Information Contact:
          Telephone: (800) 123-4567
          TRANS REF #: 111111111
```

FIGURE 15-1 Sample Medicaid eligibility verification system (MEVS) receipt ticket.

Medicaid Remittance Advice

Providers receive reimbursement from Medicaid on a lump-sum basis, which means they will receive payment for several claims at once. A **Medicaid remittance advice** (Figure 15-2) is sent to the provider and contains the current status of all claims (including adjusted and voided claims). The provider should compare content on the remittance advice to claims submitted to determine whether proper payment was received. If improper payment was issued, the provider has the option to appeal the claim. An **adjusted claim** has a payment correction, resulting in additional payment(s) to the provider. A **voided claim** is one that Medicaid should not have originally paid and results in a deduction from the lump-sum payment made to the provider. If a year-to-date negative balance appears on the Medicaid remittance advice as a result of voided claims, the provider receives no payment until the amount of paid claims exceeds the negative balance amount.

```
                          State of New York Medicaid
    Provider Number: 999   Remittance Advice as of 01-06-YY              RA#: 256295987

    RECIPIENT    MEDICAID   INTERNAL     SERVICE DATES  POS    CPT    QUANTITY  BILLED   ALLOWED   CUT/    PAYMENT   ADJUSTMENT
      NAME         ID      CONTROL NO.   FROM    TO            CODE              AMOUNT   AMOUNT    BACK    AMOUNT    REASON CODE

    DOE, JOHN    123654   4400367890   0105YY  0105YY   11   99213      1        45.00    24.00    21.00    24.00      A2
    REMARK CODES: N59                  *** CLAIMS TOTALS ***             1                 24.00    21.00    24.00

    JONES, MARY  569562   5626594589   0106YY  0106YY   11   99213      1        54.00    24.00    30.00    24.00      A2
                                       0106YY  0106YY   11   82948      1        18.00     1.00    17.00     1.00      A2
    REMARK CODES: N59   MA66           0106YY  0106YY   11   36415      1         4.00     0.00     4.00     0.00      125
                                       *** CLAIMS TOTALS ***             3                 25.00    51.00    25.00

    *** CATEGORY TOTALS:               NUMBER OF CLAIMS:      2    4     121.00    49.00    72.00    49.00

                          RA# 256295987  CHECK AMOUNT: $ 49.00

    ******************************************************************************************************
    *** EARNINGS DATA ***              NO. OF CLAIMS PROCESSED YEAR TO DATE:     75
                                       DOLLAR AMOUNT PROCESSED YEAR TO DATE:     $1459.82
                                       CHECK AMOUNT YEAR TO DATE:                $1459.82

    *** CODE LEGEND ***        11 = Office
                               125 = Submission/billing error(s)
                               A2 = Contractual adjustment
                               N59 = Refer to provider manual for program/provider information
```

FIGURE 15-2 Sample Medicaid remittance advice (RA).

NOTE:

- The provider should compare content on the remittance advice to claims submitted to determine whether proper payment was received. If improper payment was issued, the provider has the option to appeal the claim.
- Remittance advice documents should be maintained according to the statute of limitations of the state in which the provider practices.

Utilization Review

The federal government requires states to verify the receipt of Medicaid services. Thus, a sample of Medicaid recipients is sent a monthly survey letter requesting verification of services paid the previous month on their behalf. (Such services are identified in nontechnical terms, and confidential services are omitted.) Federal regulations also require Medicaid to establish and maintain a **surveillance and utilization review subsystem (SURS)**, which safeguards against unnecessary or inappropriate use of Medicaid services or excess payments and assesses the quality of those services. A postpayment review process monitors both the use of health services by recipients and the delivery of health services by providers. Regardless of whether the provider or the Medicaid program caused a payment error, overpayments to providers may be recovered by the SURS unit.

The SURS unit is also responsible for identifying possible fraud or abuse, and most states organize the unit under the state's Office of Attorney General, which is certified by the federal government to detect, investigate, and prosecute fraudulent practices or abuse against the Medicaid program.

Medical Necessity

Medicaid-covered services are payable only when the service is determined by the provider to be medically necessary. Covered services must be:

- Consistent with the patient's symptoms, diagnosis, condition, or injury
- Recognized as the prevailing standard and consistent with generally accepted professional medical standards of the provider's peer group
- Provided in response to a life-threatening condition; to treat pain, injury, illness, or infection; to treat a condition that could result in physical or mental disability; or to achieve a level of physical or mental function consistent with prevailing community standards for diagnosis or condition

In addition, medically necessary services are:

- Not furnished primarily for the convenience of the recipient or the provider
- Furnished when there is no other equally effective course of treatment available or suitable for the recipient requesting the service that is more conservative or substantially less costly

Medicaid Billing Notes

Following is information on nationwide fee-for-service billing. Consult your state's Medicaid managed care organization's (MCO) billing manual to bill for noncapitated MCO services.

Fiscal Agent

The name of the state's Medicaid fiscal agent will vary from state to state. Contact the local county government for information about the Medicaid program in your area. (In some states, third-party payers contract with Medicaid to process claims.)

Claim Used

Medicaid accepts the CMS-1500 claim for professional services (and the UB-04 claim for institutional services).

Timely Claims Submission Deadline

Deadlines vary from state to state. Check with your state's Medicaid office. It is important to file a Medicaid fee-for-service claim as soon as possible. The only time a claim should be delayed is when the patient does not identify Medicaid eligibility or if the patient has applied for retroactive Medicaid coverage.

Medicare-Medicaid crossover claims follow the Medicare, not Medicaid, deadlines for claims.

Accept Assignment

Accept assignment must be selected on the CMS-1500 claim, or reimbursement (depending on state policy) may be denied. (Entering an X in Block 27 of the CMS-1500 claim also expedites Medicare reimbursement to the provider.) It is illegal to attempt collection of the difference between the Medicaid payment and the fee the provider charged, even if the patient did not reveal the Medicaid status at the time services were rendered.

 NOTE:

Medicaid patients must assign benefits to providers.

Deductibles

A deductible may be required. In such cases, eligibility cards usually are not issued until after the stated deductible has been met.

Copayments

Copayments are required for some Medicaid recipients.

Inpatient Benefits

All non-emergency hospitalizations must be preauthorized. If the patient's condition warrants an extension of the authorized inpatient days, the hospital must seek an authorization for additional inpatient days.

Major Medical/Accidental Injury Coverage

There is no special treatment for major medical or accidental injury categories. Medicaid will conditionally subrogate claims when there is liability insurance to cover a person's injuries. *Subrogation* is the assumption of an obligation for which another party is primarily liable.

Medicaid Eligibility

Because Medicaid eligibility is determined by income, patients can be eligible for one encounter and not the next. Check eligibility status on each visit. New work requirements may change this, as beneficiaries may continue coverage for a specific time even if their income exceeds the state eligibility levels. Prior authorization is required for many procedures and most non-emergency hospitalizations. Consult the current Medicaid handbook for a listing of the procedures that must have prior authorization. When in doubt, contact the state agency for clarification.

 NOTE:

> Medicaid coverage cannot transfer from state to state, and a person is not permitted to have coverage in two or more different states at the same time. This means that individuals who relocate must apply for Medicaid in the new state. Thus, after relocating, Medicaid coverage must be terminated in the first state before applying for coverage in the new state. States may offer retroactive Medicaid coverage, which allows for eligibility to about three months prior to the date of an application's approval. However, health care services may need to be paid *out of pocket* until retroactive coverage provides reimbursement.

Medicaid Cards

Cards may be issued for the "Unborn child of . . ." (the name of the pregnant individual is inserted in the blank space). These cards are good only for services that promote the life and good health of the unborn child.

Remittance Advice

Because other health and liability programs are primary to Medicaid, the remittance advice from the primary coverage must be attached to the Medicaid claim.

A combined Medicare-Medicaid (Medi-Medi) claim should be filed by the Medicare deadline on the CMS-1500 claim.

Medicaid Claims Instructions

The instructions in Table 15-1 are for submitting primary Medicaid fee-for-service claims when the patient is not covered by additional insurance. If the patient is covered by Medicare and Medicaid, follow the instructions for Medicare-Medicaid (Medi-Medi) crossover claims in Chapter 14.

Refer to the John Q. Public case study in Figure 15-3 and the completed claim in Figure 15-4 as you study Table 15-1.

 NOTE:

> - Refer to Chapter 11 for clarification of claims completion (e.g., entering names, mailing addresses, ICD-10-CM codes, diagnosis pointer letters, NPI, and so on).
> - Use these instructions when completing any claims associated with *Understanding Health Insurance.*

TABLE 15-1 CMS-1500 claims completion instructions for Medicaid primary claims

Block	Instructions
1	Enter an X in the *Medicaid* box.
1a	Enter the Medicaid identification number as it appears on the patient's Medicaid card. *Do not enter hyphens or spaces in the number.*
2	Enter the patient's last name, first name, and middle initial (separated by commas) (DOE, JANE, M).
3	Enter the patient's birth date as MM DD YYYY (with spaces). Enter an X in the appropriate box to indicate the patient's sex. If the patient's sex is unknown, leave blank.

(continues)

TABLE 15-1 (continued)

Block	Instructions
4	Leave blank.
5	Enter the patient's mailing address. Enter the street address on line 1, enter the city and state on line 2, and enter the five- or nine-digit zip code on line 3. *Do not enter the hyphen or a space for a 9-digit ZIP code. Do not enter the telephone number.*
6–8	Leave blank.
9, 9a, 9d	Leave blank. *Blocks 9, 9a, and 9d are completed if the patient has additional insurance coverage, such as commercial insurance.*
9b–9c	Leave blank.
10a–c	Enter an X in the NO boxes. (If an X is entered in the YES box for auto accident, enter the two-character state abbreviation of the patient's residence.)
10d	Leave blank. For Medicaid managed care programs, enter an E for emergency care or U for urgency care (if instructed to do so by the administrative contractor).
11–16	Leave blank.
17	If applicable, enter the first name, middle initial (if known), last name, and credentials of the professional who referred, ordered, or supervised health care service(s) or supply(ies) reported on the claim. *Do not enter any punctuation.* In front of the name, enter the applicable qualifier to identify which provider is being reported, as follows: DN (referring provider), DK (ordering provider), or DQ (supervising provider). Otherwise, leave blank.
17a	Leave blank.
17b	Enter the 10-digit national provider identifier (NPI) of the professional in Block 17. Otherwise, leave blank.
18	Enter the admission date and discharge date as MM DD YY (with spaces) if the patient received inpatient services (e.g., hospital, skilled nursing facility). Otherwise, leave blank. *If the patient has not been discharged at the time the claim is completed, leave the discharge date blank.*
19	Leave blank.
20	Enter an X in the NO box if all laboratory procedures reported on the claim were performed in the provider's office. Otherwise, enter an X in the YES box, enter the total amount charged by the outside laboratory in $ CHARGES, and enter the outside laboratory's name, mailing address, and NPI in Block 32. (Charges are entered *without* punctuation. For example, $1,100.00 is entered as 110000 below $ CHARGES.)
21	Enter the ICD-10-CM code for up to 12 diagnoses or conditions treated or medically managed during the encounter. Lines A through L in Block 21 will relate to CPT or HCPCS Level II service or procedure codes reported in Block 24E. In the *ICD Ind* (ICD indicator) box, enter 0 for ICD-10-CM.
22	Leave blank. This is reserved for submitted claims.
23	Enter the Medicaid preauthorization number, which was assigned by the payer, if applicable. If written preauthorization was obtained, attach a copy to the claim. Otherwise, leave blank.
24A	Enter the date the procedure or service was performed in the FROM column as MM DD YY (with spaces). Enter a date in the TO column *if the procedure or service was performed on consecutive days during a range of dates. Then, enter the number of consecutive days in Block 24G.* **Note:** The shaded area in each line is used to enter supplemental information to support reported services *if instructed by the payer to enter such information.* Data entry in Block 24 is limited to reporting six services. *Do not use the shaded lines to report additional services.* If additional services were provided, generate new CMS-1500 claim(s) to report the additional services.
24B	Enter the appropriate two-digit place-of-service (POS) code to identify the location where the reported procedure or service was performed.
24C	Enter an E *if the service was provided for a medical emergency,* regardless of where it was provided. Otherwise, leave blank.
24D	Enter the CPT or HCPCS Level II code and applicable required modifier(s) for procedures or services performed. *Separate the CPT/HCPCS code and first modifier with one space. Separate additional modifiers with one space each. Up to four modifiers can be entered.*

(continues)

TABLE 15-1 (continued)

Block	Instructions
24E	Enter the diagnosis pointer letter(s) from Block 21 that relate to the procedure or service performed on the date of service to justify medical necessity of procedures and services reported on the claim.
24F	Enter the fee charged for each reported procedure or service. *Do not enter commas, periods, or dollar signs. Do not enter negative amounts. Enter 00 in the cents area if the amount is a whole number.*
24G	Enter the number of days or units for procedures or services reported in Block 24D. *If just one procedure or service was reported in Block 24D, enter a 1 in Block 24G.*
24H	Enter an E if the service was provided under the EPSDT program, or enter an F if the service was provided for family planning. Enter a B if the service can be categorized as both EPSDT and family planning. Otherwise, leave blank.
24I	Leave blank. The NPI abbreviation is preprinted on the CMS-1500 claim.
24J	Enter the 10-digit NPI for the: • Provider who performed the service *if the provider is a member of a group practice* (Leave blank if the provider is a solo practitioner.) • Supervising provider *if the service was provided incident-to the service of a physician or nonphysician practitioner and the physician or practitioner who ordered the service did not supervise the provider* (Leave blank if the incident-to service was performed under the supervision of the physician or nonphysician practitioner.) • DMEPOS supplier or outside laboratory *if the physician submits the claim for services provided by the DMEPOS supplier or outside laboratory* (Leave blank if the DMEPOS supplier or outside laboratory submits the claim.) Otherwise, leave blank.
25	Enter the provider's Social Security number (SSN) or employer identification number (EIN). *Do not enter hyphens or spaces in the number.* Enter an X in the appropriate box to indicate which number is reported.
26	Enter the patient's account number as assigned by the provider.
27	Enter an X in the YES box to indicate that the provider agrees to accept assignment. Otherwise, enter an X in the NO box.
28	Enter the total charges for services and/or procedures reported in Block 24. **Note:** If multiple claims are submitted for one patient because more than six procedures or services were reported, be sure the total charge reported on each claim accurately represents the total of the items on each submitted claim.
29–30	Leave blank.
31	Enter the provider's name and credential (e.g., MARY SMITH MD) and the date the claim was completed as MMDDYY (without spaces). *Do not enter any punctuation.*
32	Enter the name and address where procedures or services were provided *if at a location other than the patient's home, such as a hospital, outside laboratory facility, skilled nursing facility, or DMEPOS supplier.* Otherwise, leave blank. Enter the name on line 1, the address on line 2, and the city, state, and nine-digit zip code on line 3. *Do not enter the hyphen or a space for a 9-digit ZIP code.* **Note:** If Block 18 contains dates of service for inpatient care and/or Block 20 contains an X in the YES box, enter the name and address of the facility that provided services.
32a	Enter the 10-digit NPI of the provider entered in Block 32.
32b	Leave blank.
33	Enter the provider's *billing* name, address, and telephone number. Enter the phone number in the area next to the Block title. *Do not enter parentheses for the area code.* Enter the name on line 1, enter the address on line 2, and enter the city, state, and nine-digit zip code on line 3. *Do not enter the hyphen or a space for a 9-digit ZIP code.*
33a	Enter the 10-digit NPI of the *billing* provider (e.g., solo practitioner) or group practice (e.g., clinic).
33b	Leave blank.

Courtesy of the Centers for Medicare & Medicaid Services, www.cms.gov.

ERIN A. HELPER, M.D.
101 Medic Drive, Anywhere, NY 12345-9874
(101) 111-1234 (Office) • (101) 111-9292 (Fax)
EIN: 11-1234523
NPI: 1234567890

Case Study

PATIENT INFORMATION:

Name:	Public, John Q.
Address:	10A Senate Avenue
City:	Anywhere
State:	NY
Zip Code:	12345-1234
Telephone:	(101) 201-7891
Sex:	Male
Date of Birth:	10-10-1959
Occupation:	
Employer:	

INSURANCE INFORMATION:

Patient Number:	15-1
Place of Service:	Office
Primary Insurance Plan:	Medicaid
Primary Insurance Plan ID #:	99811948
Policy #:	
Primary Policyholder:	Public, John Q.
Policyholder Date of Birth:	10-10-1959
Relationship to Patient:	Self
Secondary Insurance Plan:	
Secondary Insurance Plan ID #:	
Secondary Policyholder:	

Patient Status   ☒ Married   ☐ Divorced   ☐ Single   ☐ Student

DIAGNOSIS INFORMATION

	Diagnosis	Code		Diagnosis	Code
1.	Benign sebaceous cyst	L72.3	5.		
2.	Malignant lesion, skin of trunk	C44.509	6.		
3.			7.		
4.			8.		

PROCEDURE INFORMATION

	Description of Procedure or Service	Date	Code	Charge
1.	Excision, 1.4 cm malignant lesion, skin of trunk, with intermediate repair	01-21-YY	11602	75.00
			12031-51	75.00
2.	Excision, 2.1 cm benign cyst, skin of back	01-21-YY	11403-51	50.00
3.				
4.				
5.				

SPECIAL NOTES: Medicaid Preauthorization No. YY8301

FIGURE 15-3 John Q. Public case study.

HEALTH INSURANCE CLAIM FORM

APPROVED BY NATIONAL UNIFORM CLAIM COMMITTEE (NUCC) 02/12

[ ] [ ] PICA

CARRIER

1. MEDICARE (Medicare#)	MEDICAID [X] (Medicaid#)	TRICARE (ID#/DoD#)	CHAMPVA (Member ID#)	GROUP HEALTH PLAN (ID#)	FECA BLKLUNG (ID#)	OTHER (ID#)	1a. INSURED'S I.D. NUMBER (For Program in Item 1) **99811948**

2. PATIENT'S NAME (Last Name, First Name, Middle Initial)
PUBLIC, JOHN, Q

3. PATIENT'S BIRTH DATE   MM 10 DD 10 YY 1959   SEX M [X] F [ ]

4. INSURED'S NAME (Last Name, First Name, Middle Initial)

5. PATIENT'S ADDRESS (No., Street)
10A SENATE AVENUE

6. PATIENT RELATIONSHIP TO INSURED Self [ ] Spouse [ ] Child [ ] Other [ ]

7. INSURED'S ADDRESS (No., Street)

CITY **ANYWHERE**   STATE **NY**

8. RESERVED FOR NUCC USE

CITY   STATE

ZIP CODE **123451234**   TELEPHONE (Include Area Code) ( )

ZIP CODE   TELEPHONE (Include Area Code) ( )

PATIENT AND INSURED INFORMATION

9. OTHER INSURED'S NAME (Last Name, First Name, Middle Initial)

10. IS PATIENT'S CONDITION RELATED TO:

11. INSURED'S POLICY GROUP OR FECA NUMBER

a. OTHER INSURED'S POLICY OR GROUP NUMBER

a. EMPLOYMENT? (Current or Previous) YES [ ] NO [X]

a. INSURED'S DATE OF BIRTH MM DD YY   SEX M [ ] F [ ]

b. RESERVED FOR NUCC USE

b. AUTO ACCIDENT? YES [ ] NO [X] PLACE (State)

b. OTHER CLAIM ID (Designated by NUCC)

c. RESERVED FOR NUCC USE

c. OTHER ACCIDENT? YES [ ] NO [X]

c. INSURANCE PLAN NAME OR PROGRAM NAME

d. INSURANCE PLAN NAME OR PROGRAM NAME

10d. CLAIM CODES (Designated by NUCC)

d. IS THERE ANOTHER HEALTH BENEFIT PLAN? YES [ ] NO [ ] If yes, complete items 9, 9a, and 9d.

READ BACK OF FORM BEFORE COMPLETING & SIGNING THIS FORM.

12. PATIENT'S OR AUTHORIZED PERSON'S SIGNATURE I authorize the release of any medical or other information necessary to process this claim. I also request payment of government benefits either to myself or to the party who accepts assignment below.

SIGNED _____ DATE _____

13. INSURED'S OR AUTHORIZED PERSON'S SIGNATURE I authorize payment of medical benefits to the undersigned physician or supplier for services described below.

SIGNED _____

14. DATE OF CURRENT ILLNESS, INJURY, or PREGNANCY (LMP) MM DD YY QUAL.

15. OTHER DATE QUAL. MM DD YY

16. DATES PATIENT UNABLE TO WORK IN CURRENT OCCUPATION FROM MM DD YY TO MM DD YY

17. NAME OF REFERRING PROVIDER OR OTHER SOURCE   17a.   17b. NPI

18. HOSPITALIZATION DATES RELATED TO CURRENT SERVICES FROM MM DD YY TO MM DD YY

19. ADDITIONAL CLAIM INFORMATION (Designated by NUCC)

20. OUTSIDE LAB? YES [ ] NO [X] $ CHARGES

21. DIAGNOSIS OR NATURE OF ILLNESS OR INJURY Relate A-L to service line below (24E)   ICD Ind. **0**

A. **L723** B. **C44509** C. _____ D. _____
E. _____ F. _____ G. _____ H. _____
I. _____ J. _____ K. _____ L. _____

22. RESUBMISSION CODE _____ ORIGINAL REF. NO. _____

23. PRIOR AUTHORIZATION NUMBER **YY8301**

24. A. DATE(S) OF SERVICE From MM DD YY	To MM DD YY	B. PLACE OF SERVICE	C. EMG	D. PROCEDURES, SERVICES, OR SUPPLIES (Explain Unusual Circumstances) CPT/HCPCS	MODIFIER	E. DIAGNOSIS POINTER	F. $ CHARGES	G. DAYS OR UNITS	H. EPSDT Family Plan	I. ID. QUAL.	J. RENDERING PROVIDER ID. #
1	01 21 YY		11		11602		B	75 00	1		NPI	
2	01 21 YY		11		12031	51	B	75 00	1		NPI	
3	01 21 YY		11		11403	51	A	50 00	1		NPI	
4											NPI	
5											NPI	
6											NPI	

25. FEDERAL TAX I.D. NUMBER **111234523** SSN [ ] EIN [X]

26. PATIENT'S ACCOUNT NO. **15-1**

27. ACCEPT ASSIGNMENT? (For govt. claims, see back) [X] YES [ ] NO

28. TOTAL CHARGE $ **200 00**

29. AMOUNT PAID $

30. Rsvd for NUCC Use

31. SIGNATURE OF PHYSICIAN OR SUPPLIER INCLUDING DEGREES OR CREDENTIALS (I certify that the statements on the reverse apply to this bill and are made a part thereof.)

ERIN A HELPER MD   **MMDDYY**
SIGNED   DATE

32. SERVICE FACILITY LOCATION INFORMATION

a. NPI   b.

33. BILLING PROVIDER INFO & PH # (**101**) **1111234**
ERIN A HELPER MD
101 MEDIC DRIVE
ANYWHERE NY 123459874

a. **1234567890**   b.

PHYSICIAN OR SUPPLIER INFORMATION

NUCC Instruction Manual available at: www.nucc.org

PLEASE PRINT OR TYPE

PICA [ ] [ ]

FIGURE 15-4 Completed primary Medicaid CMS-1500 claim for John Q. Public case study.

Exercise 15.1 – Completing a Medicaid as Primary CMS-1500 Claim

1. Obtain a blank claim by making a copy of the CMS-1500 claim form in Appendix I.
2. Review the claims instructions in Table 15-1.
3. Review Figure 15-5, Mary S. Patient case study.
4. Select the information needed from the case study, and enter the required information on the claim.
5. Review the claim to be sure all required blocks are properly completed.
6. Compare your claim with the completed claim in Figure 15-6.

ERIN A. HELPER, M.D.
101 Medic Drive, Anywhere, NY 12345-9874
(101) 111-1234 (Office) • (101) 111-9292 (Fax)
EIN: 11-1234523
NPI: 1234567890

Case Study

PATIENT INFORMATION:

Name:	Patient, Mary S.
Address:	91 Home Street
City:	Nowhere
State:	NY
Zip Code:	12367-1234
Telephone:	(101) 201-8989
Sex:	Female
Date of Birth:	03-08-1980
Occupation:	
Employer:	

INSURANCE INFORMATION:

Patient Number:	15-2
Place of Service:	Office
Primary Insurance Plan:	Medicaid
Primary Insurance Plan ID #:	99811765
Policy #:	
Primary Policyholder:	Patient, Mary S.
Policyholder Date of Birth:	03-08-1980
Relationship to Patient:	Self
Secondary Insurance Plan:	
Secondary Insurance Plan ID #:	
Secondary Policyholder:	

Patient Status   ☒ Married   ☐ Divorced   ☐ Single   ☐ Student

DIAGNOSIS INFORMATION

Diagnosis	Code	Diagnosis	Code
1. Annual physical exam	Z00.00	5.	
2. Hypertension	I10	6.	
3.		7.	
4.		8.	

PROCEDURE INFORMATION

Description of Procedure or Service	Date	Code	Charge
1. Preventive Medicine Office Visit	01-05-YY	99386	150.00
2. Established Patient Office Visit, Level III	01-05-YY	99213-25	75.00
3.			
4.			
5.			

SPECIAL NOTES: Patient scheduled for outpatient chest x-ray and mammogram at RadioDiagnostics.

FIGURE 15-5 Mary S. Patient case study.

HEALTH INSURANCE CLAIM FORM

APPROVED BY NATIONAL UNIFORM CLAIM COMMITTEE (NUCC) 02/12

CARRIER

| | PICA | | | | | | | PICA | |

1. MEDICARE	MEDICAID	TRICARE	CHAMPVA	GROUP HEALTH PLAN	FECA BLKLUNG	OTHER	1a. INSURED'S I.D. NUMBER (For Program in Item 1)
☐ (Medicare#)	☒ (Medicaid#)	☐ (ID#/DoD#)	☐ (Member ID#)	☐ (ID#)	☐ (ID#)	☐ (ID#)	99811765

2. PATIENT'S NAME (Last Name, First Name, Middle Initial)
PATIENT, MARY, S

3. PATIENT'S BIRTH DATE MM 03 DD 08 YY 1980 SEX M ☐ F ☒

4. INSURED'S NAME (Last Name, First Name, Middle Initial)

5. PATIENT'S ADDRESS (No., Street)
91 HOME STREET

6. PATIENT RELATIONSHIP TO INSURED
Self ☐ Spouse ☐ Child ☐ Other ☐

7. INSURED'S ADDRESS (No., Street)

CITY NOWHERE   **STATE** NY

8. RESERVED FOR NUCC USE

CITY   **STATE**

ZIP CODE 123671234   **TELEPHONE (Include Area Code)** ( )

ZIP CODE   **TELEPHONE (Include Area Code)** ( )

9. OTHER INSURED'S NAME (Last Name, First Name, Middle Initial)

10. IS PATIENT'S CONDITION RELATED TO:

11. INSURED'S POLICY GROUP OR FECA NUMBER

a. OTHER INSURED'S POLICY OR GROUP NUMBER

a. EMPLOYMENT? (Current or Previous)
☐ YES ☒ NO

a. INSURED'S DATE OF BIRTH MM DD YY SEX M ☐ F ☐

b. RESERVED FOR NUCC USE

b. AUTO ACCIDENT? PLACE (State)
☐ YES ☒ NO

b. OTHER CLAIM ID (Designated by NUCC)

c. RESERVED FOR NUCC USE

c. OTHER ACCIDENT?
☐ YES ☒ NO

c. INSURANCE PLAN NAME OR PROGRAM NAME

d. INSURANCE PLAN NAME OR PROGRAM NAME

10d. CLAIM CODES (Designated by NUCC)

d. IS THERE ANOTHER HEALTH BENEFIT PLAN?
☐ YES ☐ NO *If yes,* complete items 9, 9a, and 9d.

READ BACK OF FORM BEFORE COMPLETING & SIGNING THIS FORM.

12. PATIENT'S OR AUTHORIZED PERSON'S SIGNATURE I authorize the release of any medical or other information necessary to process this claim. I also request payment of government benefits either to myself or to the party who accepts assignment below.

SIGNED _____   DATE _____

13. INSURED'S OR AUTHORIZED PERSON'S SIGNATURE I authorize payment of medical benefits to the undersigned physician or supplier for services described below.

SIGNED _____

14. DATE OF CURRENT ILLNESS, INJURY, or PREGNANCY (LMP) MM DD YY QUAL.

15. OTHER DATE QUAL. MM DD YY

16. DATES PATIENT UNABLE TO WORK IN CURRENT OCCUPATION FROM MM DD YY TO MM DD YY

17. NAME OF REFERRING PROVIDER OR OTHER SOURCE
17a.
17b. NPI

18. HOSPITALIZATION DATES RELATED TO CURRENT SERVICES FROM MM DD YY TO MM DD YY

19. ADDITIONAL CLAIM INFORMATION (Designated by NUCC)

20. OUTSIDE LAB? ☐ YES ☒ NO $ CHARGES

21. DIAGNOSIS OR NATURE OF ILLNESS OR INJURY Relate A-L to service line below (24E) ICD Ind. 0

A. Z0000   B. I10   C. _____   D. _____
E. _____   F. _____   G. _____   H. _____
I. _____   J. _____   K. _____   L. _____

22. RESUBMISSION CODE   ORIGINAL REF. NO.

23. PRIOR AUTHORIZATION NUMBER

24. A. DATE(S) OF SERVICE From MM DD YY To MM DD YY	B. PLACE OF SERVICE	C. EMG	D. PROCEDURES, SERVICES, OR SUPPLIES (Explain Unusual Circumstances) CPT/HCPCS MODIFIER	E. DIAGNOSIS POINTER	F. $ CHARGES	G. DAYS OR UNITS	H. EPSDT Family Plan	I. ID. QUAL.	J. RENDERING PROVIDER ID. #
1	01 05 YY	11		99386	A	150 00	1		NPI	
2	01 05 YY	11		99213 25	B	75 00	1		NPI	
3									NPI	
4									NPI	
5									NPI	
6									NPI	

25. FEDERAL TAX I.D. NUMBER SSN ☐ EIN ☒
111234523

26. PATIENT'S ACCOUNT NO.
15-2

27. ACCEPT ASSIGNMENT? (For govt. claims, see back)
☒ YES ☐ NO

28. TOTAL CHARGE $ 225 00

29. AMOUNT PAID $

30. Rsvd for NUCC Use

31. SIGNATURE OF PHYSICIAN OR SUPPLIER INCLUDING DEGREES OR CREDENTIALS (I certify that the statements on the reverse apply to this bill and are made a part thereof.)

ERIN A HELPER MD   MMDDYY
SIGNED   DATE

32. SERVICE FACILITY LOCATION INFORMATION

a. NPI   b.

33. BILLING PROVIDER INFO & PH # (101) 1111234
ERIN A HELPER MD
101 MEDIC DRIVE
ANYWHERE NY 123459874

a. 1234567890   b.

NUCC Instruction Manual available at: www.nucc.org

PLEASE PRINT OR TYPE

FIGURE 15-6 Completed primary Medicaid CMS-1500 claim for Mary S. Patient case study.

Medicaid as Secondary Payer Claims Instructions

Modifications are made to the CMS-1500 claim when patients are covered by Medicaid and a secondary or supplemental health insurance plan (Table 15-2), which means just one CMS-1500 claim is submitted.

 NOTE:

- These claims instructions *do not* apply to Medicare-Medicaid (Medi-Medi) crossover cases, which are discussed in Chapter 14.
- Use these instructions when completing any claims associated with *Understanding Health Insurance.*

TABLE 15-2 CMS-1500 claims completion instructions for Medicaid as secondary payer
(Refer to Table 15-1 for primary CMS-1500 claims completion instructions.)

Block	Instructions
4	Enter the primary policyholder's last name, first name, and middle initial (separated by commas).
6	Enter an X in the appropriate box to indicate the patient's relationship to the primary policyholder. If the patient is an unmarried domestic partner, enter an X in the *Other* box.
7	If the address of the patient is the same as the primary policyholder, leave blank. Otherwise, enter the primary policyholder's mailing address. Enter the street address on line 1, enter the city and state on line 2, and enter the five- or nine-digit zip code on line 3. *Do not enter the hyphen or a space for a 9-digit ZIP code. Do not enter the telephone number.*
9	Enter the primary policyholder's last name, first name, and middle initial (if known) (separated by commas). If the primary policyholder is the patient, enter SAME.
9a	Enter the primary policyholder's policy or group number. *Do not enter hyphens or spaces in the number.*
9d	Enter the name of the primary policyholder's health insurance plan (e.g., commercial health insurance plan name or government program).
10a–c	Enter an X in the appropriate box.
10d	Leave blank.
11	Enter the rejection code provided by the payer *if the patient has other third-party payer coverage and the submitted claim was rejected by that payer.* Otherwise, leave blank. Sample rejection codes and reasons are as follows: K Services Not Covered L Coverage Lapsed M Coverage Not in Effect on Service Date N Individual Not Covered Q Claim Not Filed Timely (requires documentation, such as copy of rejection from third-party payer) R No Response from Carrier Within 120 Days of Claim Submission (requires documentation, such as a statement indicating a claim submission but no response) S Other Rejection Reason Not Defined Above (requires documentation, such as a statement on the claim indicating that payment was applied to the deductible) Note: When a third-party payer has rejected the submitted claim, and a CMS-1500 claim is sent to Medicaid, enter the code that describes the reason for rejection by the payer (e.g., service not covered). The rejection code reported in Block 11 alerts Medicaid that another payer is not responsible for reimbursement of procedures/services provided. (The other payer's remittance advice or explanation of benefits may need to be submitted to Medicaid as proof.)
11d	Enter an X in the YES box.
28	Enter the total charges for services and/or procedures reported in Block 24.
29	Enter the amount paid by the primary payer. If the other payer denied the claim, enter 0 00.

Exercise 15.2 – Completing a Medicaid as Secondary Payer CMS-1500 Claim

1. Obtain a blank claim by making a copy of the CMS-1500 claim form in Appendix I.
2. Review the claims instructions in Table 15-2.
3. Review Figure 15-7, Jennifer Connelly case study.
4. Select the information needed from the case study, and enter the required information on the claim.
5. Review the claim to be sure all required blocks are properly completed.
6. Compare your claim with the completed claim in Figure 15-8.

ERIN A. HELPER, M.D.
101 Medic Drive, Anywhere, NY 12345-9874
(101) 111-1234 (Office) • (101) 111-9292 (Fax)
EIN: 11-1234523
NPI: 1234567890

Case Study

PATIENT INFORMATION:

Name:	Connelly, Jennifer
Address:	45 Main Street
City:	Nowhere
State:	NY
Zip Code:	12367-1234
Telephone:	(101) 555-5624
Sex:	Female
Date of Birth:	05-05-1955
Occupation:	
Employer:	

INSURANCE INFORMATION:

Patient Number:	15-3
Place of Service:	Office
Primary Insurance Plan:	Aetna
Primary Insurance Plan ID #:	56265897
Policy #:	
Primary Policyholder:	Thomas Connelly
Policyholder Date of Birth:	05-25-1956
Employer:	Turbodyne
Relationship to Patient:	Spouse
Secondary Insurance Plan:	Medicaid
Secondary Insurance Plan ID #:	56215689
Secondary Policyholder:	Jennifer Connelly

Patient Status ☒ Married   ☐ Divorced   ☐ Single   ☐ Student

DIAGNOSIS INFORMATION

Diagnosis	Code	Diagnosis	Code
1. Hypertension	I10	5.	
2.		6.	
3.		7.	
4.		8.	

PROCEDURE INFORMATION

Description of Procedure or Service	Date	Code	Charge
1. New patient, office visit, level III	01-07-YY	99203	150.00
2.			
3.			
4.			
5.			

SPECIAL NOTES: Aetna paid $105.00 as primary payer.

FIGURE 15-7 Jennifer Connelly case study.

REMITTANCE ADVICE ATTACHED

HEALTH INSURANCE CLAIM FORM

APPROVED BY NATIONAL UNIFORM CLAIM COMMITTEE (NUCC) 02/12

☐☐ PICA | PICA ☐☐

1. MEDICARE MEDICAID TRICARE CHAMPVA GROUP HEALTH PLAN FECA BLKLUNG OTHER	1a. INSURED'S I.D. NUMBER (For Program in Item 1)
☐ (Medicare#) ☒ (Medicaid#) ☐ (ID#/DoD#) ☐ (Member ID#) ☐ (ID#) ☐ (ID#) ☐ (ID#)	56215689

2. PATIENT'S NAME (Last Name, First Name, Middle Initial)	3. PATIENT'S BIRTH DATE / SEX	4. INSURED'S NAME (Last Name, First Name, Middle Initial)
CONNELLY, JENNIFER	MM 05 DD 05 YY 1955 M☐ F☒	CONNELLY, THOMAS

5. PATIENT'S ADDRESS (No., Street)	6. PATIENT RELATIONSHIP TO INSURED	7. INSURED'S ADDRESS (No., Street)
45 MAIN STREET	Self☐ Spouse☒ Child☐ Other☐	

CITY	STATE	8. RESERVED FOR NUCC USE	CITY	STATE
NOWHERE	NY			

ZIP CODE	TELEPHONE (Include Area Code)	ZIP CODE	TELEPHONE (Include Area Code)
123671234	( )		( )

9. OTHER INSURED'S NAME (Last Name, First Name, Middle Initial)	10. IS PATIENT'S CONDITION RELATED TO:	11. INSURED'S POLICY GROUP OR FECA NUMBER
CONNELLY, THOMAS		

a. OTHER INSURED'S POLICY OR GROUP NUMBER	a. EMPLOYMENT? (Current or Previous)	a. INSURED'S DATE OF BIRTH / SEX
56265897	☐ YES ☒ NO	MM DD YY M☐ F☐

b. RESERVED FOR NUCC USE	b. AUTO ACCIDENT? PLACE (State)	b. OTHER CLAIM ID (Designated by NUCC)
	☐ YES ☒ NO	

c. RESERVED FOR NUCC USE	c. OTHER ACCIDENT?	c. INSURANCE PLAN NAME OR PROGRAM NAME
	☐ YES ☒ NO	

d. INSURANCE PLAN NAME OR PROGRAM NAME	10d. CLAIM CODES (Designated by NUCC)	d. IS THERE ANOTHER HEALTH BENEFIT PLAN?
AETNA		☒ YES ☐ NO If yes, complete items 9, 9a, and 9d.

READ BACK OF FORM BEFORE COMPLETING & SIGNING THIS FORM.

12. PATIENT'S OR AUTHORIZED PERSON'S SIGNATURE I authorize the release of any medical or other information necessary to process this claim. I also request payment of government benefits either to myself or to the party who accepts assignment below.

SIGNED _____ DATE _____

13. INSURED'S OR AUTHORIZED PERSON'S SIGNATURE I authorize payment of medical benefits to the undersigned physician or supplier for services described below.

SIGNED _____

14. DATE OF CURRENT ILLNESS, INJURY, or PREGNANCY (LMP) QUAL.	15. OTHER DATE QUAL. MM DD YY	16. DATES PATIENT UNABLE TO WORK IN CURRENT OCCUPATION FROM MM DD YY TO MM DD YY

17. NAME OF REFERRING PROVIDER OR OTHER SOURCE	17a. / 17b. NPI	18. HOSPITALIZATION DATES RELATED TO CURRENT SERVICES FROM MM DD YY TO MM DD YY

19. ADDITIONAL CLAIM INFORMATION (Designated by NUCC)	20. OUTSIDE LAB? ☐ YES ☒ NO $ CHARGES

21. DIAGNOSIS OR NATURE OF ILLNESS OR INJURY Relate A-L to service line below (24E) ICD Ind. 0	22. RESUBMISSION CODE ORIGINAL REF. NO.
A. I10 B. C. D.	
E. F. G. H.	23. PRIOR AUTHORIZATION NUMBER
I. J. K. L.	

24. A. DATE(S) OF SERVICE From To	B. PLACE OF SERVICE	C. EMG	D. PROCEDURES, SERVICES, OR SUPPLIES (Explain Unusual Circumstances) CPT/HCPCS MODIFIER	E. DIAGNOSIS POINTER	F. $ CHARGES	G. DAYS OR UNITS	H. EPSDT Family Plan	I. ID. QUAL.	J. RENDERING PROVIDER ID. #
1	01 07 YY	11		99203	A	150 00	1		NPI
2									NPI
3									NPI
4									NPI
5									NPI
6									NPI

25. FEDERAL TAX I.D. NUMBER SSN EIN	26. PATIENT'S ACCOUNT NO.	27. ACCEPT ASSIGNMENT? (For govt. claims, see back)	28. TOTAL CHARGE	29. AMOUNT PAID	30. Rsvd for NUCC Use
111234523 ☐SSN ☒EIN	15-3S	☒ YES ☐ NO	$ 150 00	$ 105 00	

31. SIGNATURE OF PHYSICIAN OR SUPPLIER INCLUDING DEGREES OR CREDENTIALS (I certify that the statements on the reverse apply to this bill and are made a part thereof.)	32. SERVICE FACILITY LOCATION INFORMATION	33. BILLING PROVIDER INFO & PH # (101) 1111234
		ERIN A HELPER MD 101 MEDIC DRIVE ANYWHERE NY 123459874
ERIN A HELPER MD MMDDYY SIGNED DATE	a. NPI b.	a. 1234567890 b.

NUCC Instruction Manual available at: www.nucc.org   **PLEASE PRINT OR TYPE**

(right margin, vertical) CARRIER | PATIENT AND INSURED INFORMATION | PHYSICIAN OR SUPPLIER INFORMATION

(right margin, vertical) Courtesy of the Centers for Medicare & Medicaid Services, www.cms.gov; claim data created by author.

FIGURE 15-8 Completed Medicaid secondary payer CMS-1500 claim for Jennifer Connelly case study.

Medicaid Parent/Newborn Claims Instructions

The instructions in Table 15-3 are for parent/newborn claims. They modify the primary Medicaid instructions.

The infant of a Medicaid recipient is automatically eligible for Medicaid for the entire first year of life. Individual state Medicaid programs determine reimbursement procedures for services provided to newborns. When claims are submitted under the parent's *Medicaid identification number*, coverage is usually limited to the newborn's first 10 days of life (during which time an application is made so the newborn is assigned its own identification number). Medicaid usually covers newborns through the end of the month of their first birthday (e.g., newborn delivered on January 5 this year is covered until January 31 next year). The newborn must continuously live with its parent to be eligible for the full year, and the newborn remains eligible for Medicaid even if changes in family size or income occur and the parent is no longer eligible for Medicaid.

 NOTE:

> Medicaid *Baby Your Baby* programs cover the parent's prenatal care only.

A **parent/newborn claim** is submitted for services provided to a newborn under the parent's Medicaid identification number. (The parent's services are *not* reimbursed on the parent/newborn claim; they are submitted on a separate CMS-1500 claim according to the instructions in Table 15-1.)

 NOTE:

> Use these instructions when completing any claims associated with *Understanding Health Insurance*.

TABLE 15-3 CMS-1500 claims completion instructions for Medicaid parent/newborn claims

Block	Instructions
1a	Enter the parent's Medicaid ID number as it appears on the patient's Medicaid card. *Do not enter hyphens or spaces in the number.*
2	Enter the parent's last name followed by the word NEWBORN (separated by a comma).
	Example: VANDERMARK, NEWBORN
	Note: A Medicaid payer may require BABYBOY or BABYGIRL to be entered instead of NEWBORN (e.g., VANDERMARK, BABYGIRL).
3	Enter the infant's birth date as MM DD YYYY (with spaces). Enter an X to indicate the infant's sex.
4	Enter the parent's name (separated by a comma), followed by (MOM), as the responsible party.
	Example: VANDERMARK, JOYCE (MOM)
	Note: A Medicaid payer may require just the parent's last name and first name, separated by a comma (e.g., VANDERMARK, JOYCE).
21	Enter ICD-10-CM secondary diagnosis codes in fields B through L, if applicable.

Courtesy of the Centers for Medicare & Medicaid Services, www.cms.gov.

Exercise 15.3 – Completing a Medicaid Parent/Newborn CMS-1500 Claim

1. Obtain a blank claim by making a copy of the CMS-1500 claim form in Appendix I.
2. Review the claims instructions in Table 15-3.
3. Review Figure 15-9, Newborn Muracek case study.
4. Select the information needed from the case study, and enter the required information on the claim.
5. Review the claim to be sure all required blocks are properly completed.
6. Compare your claim with the completed claim in Figure 15-10.

KIM A. CARRINGTON, M.D.
900 Medic Drive, Anywhere, NY 12345-9872
(101) 111-2365 (Office) • (101) 111-5625 (Fax)
EIN: 11-5623567
NPI: 7890123456

Case Study

PATIENT INFORMATION:

Name:	Muracek, Newborn
Address:	515 Hill Street
City:	Anywhere
State:	NY
Zip Code:	12367-1234
Telephone:	(101) 555-5598
Sex:	Female
Date of Birth:	01-10-YYYY
Occupation:	
Employer:	

INSURANCE INFORMATION:

Patient Number:	15-4
Place of Service:	Inpatient Hospital
Primary Insurance Plan:	Medicaid
Primary Insurance Plan ID #:	56265987
Policy #:	
Primary Policyholder:	Yvonne Muracek
Policyholder Date of Birth:	12-24-1980
Employer:	
Relationship to Patient:	Parent
Secondary Insurance Plan:	
Secondary Insurance Plan ID #:	
Secondary Policyholder:	

Patient Status   ☐ Married   ☐ Divorced   ☒ Single   ☐ Student

---

DIAGNOSIS INFORMATION

	Diagnosis	Code		Diagnosis	Code
1.	Healthy single liveborn infant, delivered vaginally	Z38.00	5.		
2.			6.		
3.			7.		
4.			8.		

PROCEDURE INFORMATION

	Description of Procedure or Service	Date	Code	Charge
1.	History and examination of normal newborn	01-10-YY	99460	150.00
2.	Attendance at delivery	01-10-YY	99464	400.00
3.	Subsequent care for normal newborn	01-11-YY	99462	100.00
4.				
5.				

SPECIAL NOTES: Inpatient care provided at Goodmedicine Hospital, Anywhere St, Anywhere, NY 12345-1234. (NPI: 2345678901) Application for infant's Medicaid ID number has been submitted.

FIGURE 15-9 Newborn Muracek case study.

HEALTH INSURANCE CLAIM FORM

APPROVED BY NATIONAL UNIFORM CLAIM COMMITTEE (NUCC) 02/12

☐☐☐ PICA   PICA ☐☐☐

1. MEDICARE ☐(Medicare#) MEDICAID ☒(Medicaid#) TRICARE ☐(ID#/DoD#) CHAMPVA ☐(Member ID#) GROUP HEALTH PLAN ☐(ID#) FECA BLKLUNG ☐(ID#) OTHER ☐(ID#)	1a. INSURED'S I.D. NUMBER (For Program in Item 1) 56265987

2. PATIENT'S NAME (Last Name, First Name, Middle Initial) — **MURACEK, NEWBORN**

3. PATIENT'S BIRTH DATE MM **01** DD **10** YY **YYYY** SEX M☐ F☒

4. INSURED'S NAME (Last Name, First Name, Middle Initial) — **MURACEK, YVONNE (MOM)**

5. PATIENT'S ADDRESS (No., Street) — **515 HILL STREET**

6. PATIENT RELATIONSHIP TO INSURED — Self☐ Spouse☐ Child☒ Other☐

7. INSURED'S ADDRESS (No., Street)

CITY **ANYWHERE** STATE **NY**

8. RESERVED FOR NUCC USE

CITY   STATE

ZIP CODE **123671234** TELEPHONE ( )

9. OTHER INSURED'S NAME

10. IS PATIENT'S CONDITION RELATED TO:

11. INSURED'S POLICY GROUP OR FECA NUMBER

a. OTHER INSURED'S POLICY OR GROUP NUMBER

a. EMPLOYMENT? YES☐ NO☒

a. INSURED'S DATE OF BIRTH   SEX M☐ F☐

b. RESERVED FOR NUCC USE

b. AUTO ACCIDENT? YES☐ NO☒ PLACE (State)

b. OTHER CLAIM ID (Designated by NUCC)

c. RESERVED FOR NUCC USE

c. OTHER ACCIDENT? YES☐ NO☒

c. INSURANCE PLAN NAME OR PROGRAM NAME

d. INSURANCE PLAN NAME OR PROGRAM NAME

10d. CLAIM CODES

d. IS THERE ANOTHER HEALTH BENEFIT PLAN? YES☐ NO☐

12. PATIENT'S OR AUTHORIZED PERSON'S SIGNATURE SIGNED   DATE

13. INSURED'S OR AUTHORIZED PERSON'S SIGNATURE SIGNED

14. DATE OF CURRENT ILLNESS, INJURY, or PREGNANCY (LMP) QUAL.

15. OTHER DATE QUAL. MM DD YY

16. DATES PATIENT UNABLE TO WORK FROM   TO

17. NAME OF REFERRING PROVIDER OR OTHER SOURCE 17a. 17b. NPI

18. HOSPITALIZATION DATES RELATED TO CURRENT SERVICES FROM **01 10 YY** TO **01 11 YY**

19. ADDITIONAL CLAIM INFORMATION

20. OUTSIDE LAB? YES☐ NO☒ $ CHARGES

21. DIAGNOSIS OR NATURE OF ILLNESS OR INJURY ICD Ind. **0**
A. **Z3800** B. C. D.
E. F. G. H.
I. J. K. L.

22. RESUBMISSION CODE   ORIGINAL REF. NO.

23. PRIOR AUTHORIZATION NUMBER

24. A. DATE(S) OF SERVICE From MM DD YY To MM DD YY	B. PLACE OF SERVICE	C. EMG	D. PROCEDURES CPT/HCPCS MODIFIER	E. DIAGNOSIS POINTER	F. $ CHARGES	G. DAYS OR UNITS	H. EPSDT	I. ID QUAL	J. RENDERING PROVIDER ID. #
1 01 10 YY	21		99460	A	150 00	1		NPI	
2 01 10 YY	21		99464	A	400 00	1		NPI	
3 01 10 YY	21		99462	A	100 00	1		NPI	
4								NPI	
5								NPI	
6								NPI	

25. FEDERAL TAX I.D. NUMBER **115623567** SSN☐ EIN☒

26. PATIENT'S ACCOUNT NO. **15-4**

27. ACCEPT ASSIGNMENT? ☒YES ☐NO

28. TOTAL CHARGE $ **650 00**

29. AMOUNT PAID $

30. Rsvd for NUCC Use

31. SIGNATURE OF PHYSICIAN OR SUPPLIER **KIM A CARRINGTON MD MMDDYY** SIGNED DATE

32. SERVICE FACILITY LOCATION INFORMATION
GOODMEDICINE HOSPITAL
ANYWHERE ST
ANYWHERE NY 123451234
a. 2345678901 b.

33. BILLING PROVIDER INFO & PH # (**101**) **1112365**
KIM A CARRINGTON MD
900 MEDIC DRIVE
ANYWHERE NY 123459872
a. 7890123456 b.

NUCC Instruction Manual available at: www.nucc.org   PLEASE PRINT OR TYPE

FIGURE 15-10 Completed Medicaid parent/newborn CMS-1500 claim for Newborn Muracek case study.

CHIP Claims Instructions

Each state selects a payer that administers its Children's Health Insurance Program (CHIP), and the payer develops its own CMS-1500 claims instructions. General instructions included in Table 15-4 are used to complete CHIP CMS-1500 claims for case studies in this textbook and its Workbook. It is important to obtain official CMS-1500 claims completion instructions from the CHIP payer in your state.

> **Example 1:** California's Healthy Kids program is administered by the Partnership HealthPlan of California (www.PartnershipHP.org), which requires entry of an X in the *Group Health Plan* box.

> **Example 2:** New York State's Child Health Plus program is administered by Excellus BlueCross BlueShield (www.ExcellusBCBS.com), which requires entry of an X in the *Other* box.

 NOTE:

Use these instructions when completing any claims associated with *Understanding Health Insurance*.

TABLE 15-4 CMS-1500 claims completion instructions for CHIP claims

Block	Instructions
1	Enter an X in the *Other* box.
	Note: Some CHIP payers, such as California's Healthy Kids program (administered by the Partnership HealthPlan of California), require an X to be entered in the *Group Health Plan box*.
1a	Enter the CHIP identification number (assigned by the Health Plan) of the subscriber (person who holds the policy).
29	Enter the total amount the patient (or another payer) paid toward covered services only. If no payment was made, leave blank.

Courtesy of the Centers for Medicare & Medicaid Services, www.cms.gov.

Exercise 15.4 – Completing a CHIP CMS-1500 Claim

1. Obtain a blank claim by making a copy of the CMS-1500 claim form in Appendix I.
2. Review the claims instructions in Table 15-4.
3. Review Figure 15-11, Edgar Vasquez case study.
4. Select the information needed from the case study, and enter the required information on the claim.
5. Review the claim to be sure all required blocks are properly completed.
6. Compare your claim with the completed claim in Figure 15-12.

ANGELA DILALIO, M.D.
99 Provider Street • Injury, NY 12347-9875 • (101) 201-4321
EIN: 11-1982342
NPI: 4567890123

Case Study

PATIENT INFORMATION:

Name:	Edgar Vasquez
Address:	1018 Bonita Ave
City:	Anywhere
State:	US
Zipcode:	12345
Telephone:	(101) 690-5244
Sex:	Male
Date of Birth:	10-18-2018
Occupation:	
Employer:	
Spouse's Employer	

INSURANCE INFORMATION:

Patient Number:	15-5
Place of Service:	Office
Primary Insurance Plan:	CHIP
Primary Insurance Plan ID#:	CAM101919690
Group #:	987654Y
Primary Policyholder:	Edgar Vasquez
Policyholder Date of Birth:	10-18-2008
Relationship to Patient:	Self
Secondary Insurance Plan:	
Secondary Insurance Plan ID #:	
Secondary Policyholder:	

Patient status: ☐ Married   ☐ Divorced   ☒ Single   ☐ Employed   ☐ Student   ☐ Other

DIAGNOSIS INFORMATION

	Diagnosis	Code		Diagnosis	Code
1.	Asthma	J45.909	5.		
2.			6.		
3.			7.		
4.			8.		

PROCEDURE INFORMATION

	Description of Procedure or Service	Date	Code	Charge
1.	Office visit, established visit, level II	12-18-YY	99212	$40.00
2.				
3.				
4.				
5.				

SPECIAL NOTES:

FIGURE 15-11 Edgar Vasquez case study.

HEALTH INSURANCE CLAIM FORM

APPROVED BY NATIONAL UNIFORM CLAIM COMMITTEE (NUCC) 02/12

▢▢▢ PICA   PICA ▢▢▢

| 1. MEDICARE ▢ (Medicare#) MEDICAID ▢ (Medicaid#) TRICARE ▢ (ID#/DoD#) CHAMPVA ▢ (Member ID#) GROUP HEALTH PLAN ▢ (ID#) FECA BLKLUNG ▢ (ID#) OTHER ☒ (ID#) | 1a. INSURED'S I.D. NUMBER (For Program in Item 1) CAM101919690 |

| 2. PATIENT'S NAME (Last Name, First Name, Middle Initial) **VASQUEZ, EDGAR** | 3. PATIENT'S BIRTH DATE MM 10 DD 18 YY 2018 SEX M ☒ F ▢ | 4. INSURED'S NAME (Last Name, First Name, Middle Initial) |

| 5. PATIENT'S ADDRESS (No., Street) **1018 BONITA AVE** | 6. PATIENT RELATIONSHIP TO INSURED Self ▢ Spouse ▢ Child ▢ Other ▢ | 7. INSURED'S ADDRESS (No., Street) |

| CITY **ANYWHERE** | STATE **US** | 8. RESERVED FOR NUCC USE | CITY | STATE |

| ZIP CODE **12345** | TELEPHONE (Include Area Code) ( ) | | ZIP CODE | TELEPHONE (Include Area Code) ( ) |

| 9. OTHER INSURED'S NAME (Last Name, First Name, Middle Initial) | 10. IS PATIENT'S CONDITION RELATED TO: | 11. INSURED'S POLICY GROUP OR FECA NUMBER |

| a. OTHER INSURED'S POLICY OR GROUP NUMBER | a. EMPLOYMENT? (Current or Previous) YES ▢ NO ☒ | a. INSURED'S DATE OF BIRTH MM DD YY SEX M ▢ F ▢ |

| b. RESERVED FOR NUCC USE | b. AUTO ACCIDENT? YES ▢ NO ☒ PLACE (State) | b. OTHER CLAIM ID (Designated by NUCC) |

| c. RESERVED FOR NUCC USE | c. OTHER ACCIDENT? YES ▢ NO ☒ | c. INSURANCE PLAN NAME OR PROGRAM NAME |

| d. INSURANCE PLAN NAME OR PROGRAM NAME | 10d. CLAIM CODES (Designated by NUCC) | d. IS THERE ANOTHER HEALTH BENEFIT PLAN? YES ▢ NO ▢ If yes, complete items 9, 9a, and 9d. |

READ BACK OF FORM BEFORE COMPLETING & SIGNING THIS FORM.

12. PATIENT'S OR AUTHORIZED PERSON'S SIGNATURE I authorize the release of any medical or other information necessary to process this claim. I also request payment of government benefits either to myself or to the party who accepts assignment below.

SIGNED _____   DATE _____

13. INSURED'S OR AUTHORIZED PERSON'S SIGNATURE I authorize payment of medical benefits to the undersigned physician or supplier for services described below.

SIGNED _____

| 14. DATE OF CURRENT ILLNESS, INJURY, or PREGNANCY (LMP) MM DD YY QUAL. | 15. OTHER DATE QUAL. MM DD YY | 16. DATES PATIENT UNABLE TO WORK IN CURRENT OCCUPATION FROM MM DD YY TO MM DD YY |

| 17. NAME OF REFERRING PROVIDER OR OTHER SOURCE 17a. 17b. NPI | 18. HOSPITALIZATION DATES RELATED TO CURRENT SERVICES FROM MM DD YY TO MM DD YY |

| 19. ADDITIONAL CLAIM INFORMATION (Designated by NUCC) | 20. OUTSIDE LAB? YES ▢ NO ☒ $ CHARGES |

21. DIAGNOSIS OR NATURE OF ILLNESS OR INJURY Relate A-L to service line below (24E)   ICD Ind. **0**

A. **J45909**   B. _____   C. _____   D. _____
E. _____   F. _____   G. _____   H. _____
I. _____   J. _____   K. _____   L. _____

22. RESUBMISSION CODE _____ ORIGINAL REF. NO. _____

23. PRIOR AUTHORIZATION NUMBER

24. A. DATE(S) OF SERVICE From MM DD YY To MM DD YY	B. PLACE OF SERVICE	C. EMG	D. PROCEDURES, SERVICES, OR SUPPLIES (Explain Unusual Circumstances) CPT/HCPCS MODIFIER	E. DIAGNOSIS POINTER	F. $ CHARGES	G. DAYS OR UNITS	H. EPSDT Family Plan	I. ID. QUAL.	J. RENDERING PROVIDER ID. #
1	12 18 YY	11		99212	A	40 00	1		NPI	
2									NPI	
3									NPI	
4									NPI	
5									NPI	
6									NPI	

| 25. FEDERAL TAX I.D. NUMBER **111982342** SSN ▢ EIN ☒ | 26. PATIENT'S ACCOUNT NO. **15-5** | 27. ACCEPT ASSIGNMENT? (For govt. claims, see back) YES ☒ NO ▢ | 28. TOTAL CHARGE $ **40 00** | 29. AMOUNT PAID $ | 30. Rsvd for NUCC Use |

| 31. SIGNATURE OF PHYSICIAN OR SUPPLIER INCLUDING DEGREES OR CREDENTIALS (I certify that the statements on the reverse apply to this bill and are made a part thereof.) **ANGELA DILALIO MD   MMDDYY** SIGNED   DATE | 32. SERVICE FACILITY LOCATION INFORMATION a. NPI   b. | 33. BILLING PROVIDER INFO & PH # (**101**) **2014321** **ANGELA DILALIO** **99 PROVIDER STREET** **INJURY NY 123479875** a. **4567890123**   b. |

NUCC Instruction Manual available at: www.nucc.org   **PLEASE PRINT OR TYPE**

CARRIER

PATIENT AND INSURED INFORMATION

PHYSICIAN OR SUPPLIER INFORMATION

Courtesy of the Centers for Medicare & Medicaid Services, www.cms.gov; claim data created by author.

FIGURE 15-12 Completed CHIP CMS-1500 claim for Edgar Vasquez case study.

Summary

Title 19 of the SSA created Medicaid, a medical assistance program for individuals with low incomes. The federal government establishes Medicaid eligibility requirements, and individual states have discretion in determining coverage policies as well as establishing financial criteria for eligibility.

A *dual eligible* is an individual who is covered by both Medicare and Medicaid—Medicare is billed as the primary payer. Medicaid is always the *payer of last resort* when a recipient is covered by other insurance (e.g., Medicare, TRICARE, IHS, or commercial health insurance). Participating providers accept Medicaid payments as payment in full, and balance billing is illegal.

Data sources, such as MEVS (or REVS), allow providers to electronically verify a recipient's eligibility for Medicaid coverage via a point-of-service device, computer software, or an automated voice response system. The Medicaid remittance advice sent to providers contains the status of claims submitted, including paid, adjusted, and voided claims. Medicaid's surveillance utilization review system assesses unnecessary or inappropriate use of Medicaid services or excess payments, as well as the quality of services rendered.

When completing Medicaid CMS-1500 claims for exercises in the textbook, assignments in the workbook, and case studies in SimClaim™, the following special instructions apply:

- Block 20—Enter an X in the NO box.
- Block 24C—Leave blank.
- Block 24H—Leave blank.
- Block 26—Enter the case study number (e.g., 15-5). If the patient has Medicaid as secondary coverage, enter an S (for secondary) next to the number (on the secondary claim).
- Block 27—Enter an X in the YES box.
- Block 32—If Block 18 contains dates and/or Block 20 contains an X in the YES box, enter the name, address, and Medicaid NPI of the responsible provider (e.g., hospital, outside laboratory).
- When completing secondary claims, enter REMITTANCE ADVICE ATTACHED in the top margin of the CMS-1500 claim (to indicate that a primary payer's remittance advice would be attached to the claim submitted to the secondary payer).

Internet Links

BenefitsCheckUp®: Go to *www.benefitscheckup.org* to locate information useful to older adults with limited income and resources.

Children's Health Insurance Program (CHIP): Go to *www.medicaid.gov*, and click on the CHIP link.

Medicaid: Go to *www.medicaid.gov*.

Medi-Cal: Go to *www.medi-cal.ca.gov*.

Programs of All-inclusive Care for the Elderly (PACE): Go to *www.medicaid.gov*, hover over Medicaid, scroll down and click on Long Term Services & Supports, and click on PACE.

Ticket to Work and Work Incentives Improvement Act (TWWIA): Go to *www.medicaid.gov*, hover over Medicaid, click on Long Term Services & Supports, click on the Employment Initiatives link, and click on the Ticket to Work link.

Review

Multiple Choice

Instructions: Select the most appropriate response.

1. Medicaid is jointly funded by federal and state governments, and each state
   a. administers its own Medicaid program.
   b. adopts the federal scope of services.
   c. establishes uniform eligibility standards.
   d. implements managed care for payment.

2. State legislatures may change Medicaid eligibility requirements
   a. as directed by the federal government.
   b. during the year, sometimes more than once.
   c. no more than once during each year.
   d. to clarify services and payments only.

3. Which program is the basis for determining Medicaid income eligibility for most children, pregnant people, parents, and adults?
   a. Aid to Families with Dependent Children
   b. Modified Adjusted Gross Income
   c. Supplemental Security Income
   d. Temporary Assistance for Needy Families

4. States that opt to include a medically needy eligibility group in their Medicaid program allow currently ineligible individuals to become eligible by
   a. enrolling in Medicaid and agreeing to pay health plan monthly premiums to the state.
   b. paying Medicare premiums, deductibles, copayments, and coinsurance amounts.
   c. spending down the amount of income that is above a state's income eligibility standard.
   d. training for a new job, during which they will become eligible for the Medicaid program.

5. How often should providers verify a patient's Medicaid eligibility?
   a. Annually
   b. At each encounter
   c. Monthly
   d. Semi-annually

6. Which is a mandatory Medicaid benefit, which states must offer to comply with federal law?
   a. Dental services
   b. Home health services
   c. Hospice care services
   d. Prescription drugs

7. Individuals who are eligible for both Medicare and Medicaid coverage are called
   a. dual eligibles.
   b. Medicaid allowables.
   c. PACE participants.
   d. participating providers.

8. When a patient has Medicaid coverage in addition to other, third-party payer coverage, Medicaid is always considered the
   a. adjusted claim.
   b. medically necessary service.
   c. payer of last resort.
   d. remittance advice.

9. A voided claim
   a. has a negative balance and the provider receives no payment until amounts exceed the negative balance.
   b. includes a payment correction, which results in additional reimbursement being made to the provider.
   c. should not have been paid and results in a deduction from the lump-sum payment made to the provider.
   d. underwent review to safeguard against unnecessary use of Medicaid services or excess payments.

10. Medicaid-covered services are paid only when the service is determined by the provider to be medically necessary, which means the services are
    a. consistent with the patient's symptoms, diagnosis, condition, or injury.
    b. performed primarily for the convenience of the patient or the provider.
    c. provided when other equally effective treatments are available or suitable.
    d. recognized as being inconsistent with generally accepted standards.

Chapter Outline

TRICARE History

TRICARE Administration

CHAMPVA

TRICARE Coverage

TRICARE Billing Notes

TRICARE Claims Instructions

TRICARE as Secondary Payer Claims
Instructions

TRICARE and Supplemental Coverage Claims
Instructions

Chapter Objectives

Upon successful completion of this chapter, you should be able to:

1. Define key terms related to TRICARE.
2. Summarize major developments in the history of TRICARE.
3. Summarize the parties and processes involved in the administration of TRICARE.
4. Define CHAMPVA.
5. Explain the TRICARE coverage options, special programs, and supplemental plans.
6. Apply TRICARE billing notes when completing CMS-1500 claims.
7. Complete TRICARE primary claims.
8. Complete TRICARE as secondary payer claims.
9. Complete TRICARE and supplemental coverage claims.

Key Terms

beneficiary counseling
and assistance
coordinator
(BCAC)

catastrophic cap
benefit

catchment area

CHAMPUS Reform
Initiative (CRI)

Civilian Health and
Medical Program
of the Department
of Veterans Affairs
(CHAMPVA)

Civilian Health and
Medical Program–
Uniformed Services
(CHAMPUS)

clinical trial

common access card
(CAC)

Computer Matching and
Privacy Protection Act
of 1988

Continued Health Care
Benefit Program
(CHCBP)

critical pathway

customer service
representative (CSR)

debt collection
assistance officer
(DCAO)

Defense Enrollment
Eligibility Reporting
System (DEERS)

Defense Health Agency
(DHA)

demonstration project or pilot

fiscal year

health care finder (HCF)

lead agent (LA)

Military Health System (MHS)

Military Health System (MHS) Nurse Advice Line

military treatment facility (MTF)

practice guidelines

primary care manager (PCM)

Program Integrity (PI) Office

Supplemental Health Care Program (SHCP)

Transitional Assistance Management Program (TAMP)

TRICARE

TRICARE beneficiary

TRICARE Prime

TRICARE Select

TRICARE Service Centers (TSCs)

TRICARE sponsors

uniformed services

Introduction

TRICARE is a health care program for uniformed service members and their families, National Guard/Reserve members and their families, survivors, former spouses, Medal of Honor recipients and their families, and others registered in the Defense Enrollment Eligibility Reporting System (DEERS). TRICARE was created to expand health care access, ensure quality of care, control health care costs, and improve medical readiness.

 NOTE:

CMS-1500 claims completion instructions are included in this chapter. (UB-04 claims are autopopulated by data abstracted and coded from patient records *or* from an electronic health record (EHR) in hospitals, skilled nursing facilities, inpatient hospices, and home health care organizations. *Chapter 11 of this textbook contains general UB-04 claims completion instructions*, along with examples and a review assignment.)

TRICARE History

The **Civilian Health and Medical Program–Uniformed Services (CHAMPUS)** (now called TRICARE) was implemented in 1967 as the result of an initiative to provide military medical care for families of active duty members. It was designed as a benefit for dependents of personnel serving in the **uniformed services**, which includes the U.S. military branches (Army, Navy, Air Force, Marines, and Coast Guard), Public Health Service Commissioned Corps, and the National Oceanic and Atmospheric Administration (NOAA) Commissioned Corps. (TRICARE also coordinates dental, medical, and pharmacy options among military hospitals and clinics and a network of civilian providers.) The original budget was $106 million; the current budget is more than $50 billion and includes funding for the entire Military Health System (MHS) with almost 10 million beneficiaries (www.tricare.mil). The *Defense Health Program (DHP)* is the responsibility of the Office of the Assistant Secretary of Defense for Health Affairs, which appropriates funding from Congress for Military Health System (MHS) functions. These functions include health care delivery at military treatment facilities (MTFs), TRICARE, certain medical readiness activities, certain expeditionary medical capabilities, education and training programs, medical research, management and headquarters activities, facilities sustainment, procurement, and civilian personnel. The **Military Health System (MHS)**, managed by the Defense Health Agency (DHA), is the entire health care system of the U.S. uniformed services and includes MTFs as well as various programs in the civilian health care market, such as TRICARE. In the 1980s the Department of Defense (DoD) began researching ways to improve access to quality care while controlling costs and authorizing demonstration projects. A demonstration project, the **CHAMPUS Reform Initiative (CRI)** was carried out in California and Hawaii and offered military families a choice of how their health care benefits could be used. The DoD noted the successful operation and high levels of patient satisfaction associated with the CRI and determined that its concepts should be expanded to a nationwide uniform program.

The *Privacy Act of 1974* established a code of fair information practices to governs the collection, dissemination, maintenance, and use of information about individuals, which is maintained in systems of records by *federal* agencies. While the Privacy Act prohibits disclosure of an individual's record without consent from that individual (except when pursuant to statutory exception), it provides individuals with a means by which to seek access to and amendment of their records and establishes agency record-keeping requirements. The **Computer Matching and Privacy Protection Act of 1988** amended the Privacy Act of 1974 to regulate the use of computer-matching agreements by *federal* agencies when records contained within a system of records are matched with other federal, state, or local government records.

TRICARE

TRICARE is the health care program for uniformed service members, retirees, and their families around the world. TRICARE provides comprehensive coverage to all beneficiaries, and it includes health plans, special programs, prescriptions, and dental plans. TRICARE coordinates dental, medical, and pharmacy options among military hospitals and clinics and a network of civilian providers.

TRICARE partners with civilian regional contractors to administer benefits, and the regional contractor is the resource for information and assistance. There are three TRICARE regions: two in the United States and TRICARE overseas (Figure 16-1). Each is managed by a lead agent staff that is responsible for the military health system in that region. Commanders of selected military treatment facilities (MTFs) are selected as **lead agents (LA)** for the TRICARE regions. The lead agent staff serves as a federal health care team created to work with regional military treatment facility commanders, uniformed service headquarters' staff, and the Defense Health Agency (DHA) to support the mission of the Military Health System (MHS).

TRICARE Eligibility, Beneficiaries, Sponsors, Family Members, and Dependents

The following are eligible for the TRICARE health program:

- Uniformed Service members and their families
- National Guard/Reserve members and their families
- Survivors
- Former spouses
- Medal of Honor recipients and their families
- Others registered in the Defense Enrollment Eligibility Reporting System (DEERS)

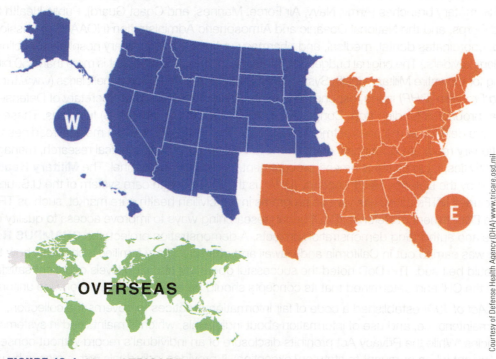

Courtesy of Defense Health Agency (DHA) www.tricare.osd.mil

FIGURE 16-1 Map of TRICARE regions.

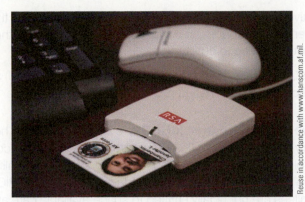

Reuse in accordance with www.hanscom.af.mil.

FIGURE 16-2 Sample uniformed services common access card (CAC) inserted into point-of-service (POS) device.

(National Guard/Reserve includes member of the Army National Guard, Army Reserve, Navy Reserve, Marine Corps Reserve, Air National Guard, Air Force Reserve, and U.S. Coast Guard Reserve.)

TRICARE beneficiaries include

- Sponsors
- Family members

TRICARE sponsors are uniformed service personnel who are active duty, deceased, retired, or members of the National Guard/Reserve. *Family members* are spouses and children who are registered in DEERS, and they include dependents of deceased sponsors. Sponsor information can be verified in the **Defense Enrollment Eligibility Reporting System (DEERS)**, a computer system that contains up-to-date Defense Department workforce personnel information. For example, sponsor information includes last name, date of birth, and *Department of Defense (DoD) Benefit Number* (11-digit number located on the reverse of the uniformed service ID card that is used to verify eligibility and file claims). When receiving care, beneficiaries present their **common access card (CAC)**, which is a "smart" scannable uniformed services identification card issued by the Department of Defense (Figure 16-2) *or* their *DoD uniformed services identification (USID) card*, which uses plastic cardstock and contains security features to deter counterfeiting and fraud. An eligibility authorization letter can also be presented when seeking health care care. (Sponsors or retirees *and* family members age 10 and older are provided with either the CAC or USID card. Children under age 10 use a parent's CAC or USID card.)

Transitional Health Care Options

The **Transitional Assistance Management Program (TAMP)** provides 180 days of premium-free transitional health care benefits after regular TRICARE benefits end. (TAMP continues to provide the minimum essential coverage that is required under the Affordable Care Act, but it is temporary, similar to COBRA benefits when an employee resigns from a non-military job.) Sponsors and eligible family members may be covered by TAMP if the sponsor is:

- Involuntarily separating from active duty under honorable conditions
- A National Guard or Reserve member separating from a period of more than 30 consecutive days of active duty served in support of a contingency operation
- Separating from active duty following involuntary retention (stop-loss) in support of a contingency operation
- Separating from active duty following a voluntary agreement to stay on active duty for less than one year in support of a contingency operation
- Receiving a sole survivorship discharge

- Separating from regular active duty service and agree to become a member of the Selected Reserve of a Reserve Component; the service member must become a Selected Reservist the day immediately following release from regular active duty service to qualify

TAMP eligibility is determined by the service (from which the member separated) and is documented in the Defense Enrollment Eligibility Reporting System (DEERS). For those who qualify, the 180-day TAMP period begins upon the sponsor's separation.

The **Continued Health Care Benefit Program (CHCBP)** is a premium-based health care program administered by Humana Military. Though not a TRICARE program, CHCBP offers continued health coverage (18–36 months) after TRICARE eligibility ends. (Unmarried former spouses may qualify for additional coverage.) Those who qualify can purchase CHCBP coverage within 60 days of the loss of TRICARE or TAMP coverage, whichever is later. (CHCBP enrollees are *not* legally entitled to space-available care at military hospitals or clinics.)

TRICARE Administration

The **Defense Health Agency (DHA)**, an agency under the direction of the Assistant Secretary of Defense (Health Affairs) manages the TRICARE program and is accountable for quality health care provided to beneficiaries. The DHA also serves as arbitrator for denied claims submitted for consideration by TRICARE sponsors and beneficiaries; its offices are located in Aurora, Colorado.

 NOTE:

Do not submit TRICARE claims to the DHA; claims are processed by TRICARE regional contractors (similar to Medicare administrative contractors) for different regions of the country and overseas.

TRICARE Service Centers

TRICARE regions are served by one or more **TRICARE Service Centers (TSCs)**, business offices staffed by one or more beneficiary services representatives and health care finders who assist TRICARE beneficiaries with health care needs and answer questions about the program.

Customer Service Representatives

A **customer service representative (CSR)** is employed at a TRICARE Service Center, provides information about using TRICARE, and assists with other matters affecting access to health care (e.g., appointment scheduling).

Health Care Finders

A **health care finder (HCF)** facilitates administrative activities, such as referrals to appropriate health care services in the military facility and civilian provider network. All beneficiary enrollment categories may use the health care finder, and the HCF also assists with preauthorization for procedures and services provided in a military treatment facility or civilian provider network. A *preauthorization* is formal approval obtained from a health care finder before certain specialty procedures and inpatient care services are rendered. A *referral* is a request for a member to receive treatment from another provider.

The TRICARE *civilian provider network* includes physicians and health care facilities that have signed a contract with a regional contractor to provide services to TRICARE beneficiaries. The civilian provider network accepts a negotiated rate as payment in full, files claims for beneficiaries, and does not require beneficiaries to sign documents to pay amounts above copayments or other cost shares (e.g., coinsurance percentage). This means that TRICARE beneficiaries will pay less out-of-pocket for health care services, and they will pay cost shares directly to the provider. The provider then submits a claim to collect the remaining amount due directly from TRICARE.

Military Health System Nurse Advice Line

The **Military Health System (MHS) Nurse Advice Line** allows TRICARE beneficiaries to receive advice from a registered nurse 24/7 when living or traveling in the United States or a country with an established military hospital or clinic. The registered nurse is available to answer health care questions, assess symptoms, provide recommendations for the most appropriate level of care, provide evidence-based instructions to treat minor ailments at home, help locate an urgent care or emergency care facility, and help schedule an appointment within 24 hours at a military hospital or clinic (when recommended by the nurse, and if enrolled at a military hospital or clinic).

 NOTE:

The MHS Nurse Advice Line is to be used *not* for emergencies that require immediate medical assistance. Beneficiaries who have an emergency should call 911 or go to the local hospital emergency department or an emergency service center.

Military Treatment Facilities

A **military treatment facility (MTF)** is a hospital or clinic located on military bases and posts around the world that provides inpatient and/or ambulatory (outpatient and emergency department) care to eligible TRICARE beneficiaries. The capabilities of MTFs vary from limited acute care clinics to teaching and tertiary care medical centers.

Beneficiary counseling and assistance coordinators (BCACs) are located at MTFs, and they are available to answer questions, help solve health care-related problems, and assist beneficiaries in obtaining medical care through TRICARE. BCACs were previously called *Health Benefits Advisors (HBAs)*. **Debt collection assistance officers (DCAOs)** are located at military treatment facilities to assist beneficiaries in resolving health care collection-related issues.

Case Management

TRICARE *case management* is organized under TRICARE utilization management and is a collaborative process that coordinates and monitors a beneficiary's health care options and services by assessing available resources to promote quality and cost-effective outcomes. The use of critical pathways, practice guidelines, and discharge planning can enhance the case management process. A **critical pathway** is the sequence of activities that can normally be expected to result in the most cost-effective clinical course of treatment. **Practice guidelines** are decision-making tools used by providers to determine appropriate health care for specific clinical circumstances. They offer the opportunity to improve health care delivery processes by reducing unwanted variation. The Institute of Medicine specifies that practice guidelines should be valid, reliable and reproducible, clinically applicable and flexible, a multidisciplinary process, reviewed on a scheduled basis, and well documented. *Discharge planning* assesses requirements so that arrangements can be made for the appropriate and timely discharge of patients from acute care or outpatient settings. (*Case management* also includes nurses or social workers as *case managers* who help patients and families navigate complex health care and support systems.)

Example: Inpatient records undergo quarterly review (using predetermined screening criteria) to identify individuals whose frequency of services or cost of services makes them candidates for case management.

Program Integrity Office

The DHA **Program Integrity (PI) Office** at the Defense Health Agency (DHA) is the central coordinating agency for allegations of fraud and abuse within the TRICARE program. The PI Office develops policies and procedures for the prevention, detection, investigation, and control of TRICARE fraud, waste, and program abuse. (According to health.mil, TRICARE fraud occurs when providers or other organizations deliberately deceives TRICARE to gain unauthorized benefits. TRICARE abuse occurs when providers or other organizations deliver procedures and services that do not meet medically necessity or professional standards.) It monitors contractor program integrity activities, coordinates with the Department of Defense and external investigative agencies, such as the the DHA's Office of Inspector General (OIG), and initiates administrative remedies as required.

The DHA's *Office of Inspector General (OIG)* provides advice, services, and support to the DHA, DHA activities, and subordinate organizations, and is assigned to other organizational entities within the DHA and members of the Office of the Assistant Secretary of Defense for Health Affairs. The DHA OIG administers the Department of Defense's inspector general programs, as such conducts, initiates, monitors, and supervises TRICARE audits, inspections, and investigations to deter abuse, fraud, and waste while promoting accountability, efficiency, and integrity.

TRICARE-authorized providers can be excluded from program participation if one of the following conditions applies:

- Any criminal conviction or civil judgment involving fraud
- Fraud or abuse under TRICARE
- Exclusion or suspension by another federal, state, or local government agency
- Participation in a conflict-of-interest situation
- When it is in the best interest of the TRICARE program or its beneficiaries

Example: A Colorado psychologist pled guilty to two felony counts of health care fraud, one felony count of conspiracy to defraud with respect to claims, and one felony count of criminal forfeiture. This judgment was the culmination of a six-year investigation of a counseling center where a billing-fraud scam involved submitting claims for services not provided as well as using an authorized provider's identification number to submit claims for services that were provided by an unauthorized provider. TRICARE will recover almost $500,000 in damages. The psychologist received a sentence of 21 months of imprisonment and three years of released supervision.

CHAMPVA

The **Civilian Health and Medical Program of the Department of Veterans Affairs (CHAMPVA)** is a comprehensive health care program for which the Department of Veterans Affairs (VA) shares costs of covered health care services and supplies with eligible beneficiaries. The Veterans Health Administration's Office of Community Care (VHA OCC), located in Denver, Colorado, administers the CHAMPVA program by:

- Processing applications
- Determining eligibility
- Authorizing benefits
- Processing claims

Eligibility for CHAMPVA

The *CHAMPVA sponsor* is a veteran who is permanently and totally disabled as the result of a service-connected condition or injury, died as a result of a service-connected condition or injury, was rated permanently and totally disabled as the result of a service-connected condition or injury at the time of death, or died on active duty and whose dependents are not otherwise entitled to TRICARE benefits. A *service-connected disability* is one that the Veterans Administration has concluded was caused or worsened by the Veteran's active-duty service. A permanent disability is one that is not expected to improve.

 NOTE:

A Veteran who is the qualifying CHAMPVA sponsor for their family may also qualify for the Veterans Administration (VA) health care program based on their own Veteran status. If both spouses are Veterans who qualify as CHAMPVA sponsors for their family, they both may also qualify for CHAMPVA benefits. Each time medical care is needed, they may choose to receive care through the VA health care program or by using their CHAMPVA coverage.

The *CHAMPVA beneficiary* is a CHAMPVA-eligible spouse, widow(er), or child. To be eligible for CHAMPVA, the beneficiary must be:

- The spouse or child of a veteran who has been rated permanently and totally disabled as the result of a service-connected disability by a VA regional office
- The surviving spouse or child of a veteran who died from a VA-rated service connected disability
- The surviving spouse or child of a veteran who at the time of death was rated as permanently and totally disabled as the result of a service-connected disability
- The surviving spouse or child of a military member who died in the line of duty (not due to misconduct) (However, these individuals may be eligible for TRICARE instead of CHAMPVA.)

NOTE:

For a CHAMPVA beneficiary who also has Medicare coverage, CHAMPVA is always the secondary payer to Medicare. Therefore, submit the beneficiary's claim to Medicare first. (CHAMPVA requires electronic submission of CMS-1500 claims.)

Veterans Choice Program

The Department of Veterans Affairs (VA) was established to fulfill President Lincoln's promise "To care for him who shall have borne the battle, and for his widow, and his orphan," by serving and honoring the men and women who are America's veterans. The *Veterans Access, Choice, and Accountability Act of 2014 (Choice Act)* was passed as a bipartisan response to health care access issues facing VA, and its expiration date was removed in 2017. The *Veterans Choice Program* provides enrolled veterans with health care access within their own community, allowing them to receive care from eligible non-VA health care entities or providers. Veterans eligible for the program: (1) had been waiting more than 30 days for VA medical care, (2) lived more than 40 miles away from a VA medical care facility, or (3) faced one of several excessive travel burdens.

The *Veterans Choice Program* is separate from the VA's existing program providing care to veterans outside of the VA system. Eligible non-VA entities or providers were required to enter into agreements with VA to furnish care, maintain the same or similar credentials and licenses as VA providers, and submit to VA a copy of any medical records related to care and services provided under the program for inclusion in the veteran's VA electronic medical record.

TRICARE Coverage

TRICARE coverage includes options, special programs, and supplemental programs, and TRICARE is the primary payer to Medicaid and TRICARE supplemental plans.

TRICARE Options

TRICARE offers two health care options:

1. *TRICARE Prime*: Military treatment facilities are the principal source of health care under this option.
2. *TRICARE Select* (formerly TRICARE Standard and CHAMPUS): This is a fee-for-service option.

TRICARE Prime

TRICARE Prime is a managed care option similar to a civilian health maintenance organization (HMO), which is available in certain geographic areas of the United States called *Prime Service Areas*. Enrollment in TRICARE Prime is required and guarantees priority access to care at military treatment facilities. Additional Prime options for active duty service members and their families include TRICARE Prime Remote, TRICARE Prime Overseas, and TRICARE Prime Remote Overseas.

A **primary care manager (PCM)** is assigned to provide most of the beneficiary's care, and the PCM is a military or network provider that is also responsible for referring beneficiaries to specialists, working with regional contractors to obtain for referrals/authorization, accepting copayments for covered health care services, and submitting claims.

- Active duty service members pay nothing out-of-pocket.
- Active duty family members pay nothing unless using the point-of-service option.
- All other beneficiaries pay annual enrollment fees and network copayments.

TRICARE Prime beneficiaries also receive care if they reside and work outside an MTF **catchment area**, the region defined by code boundaries within a 40-mile radius of an MTF. Note that certain TRICARE regions only allow a military doctor or medical clinic to serve as a PCM.

Catastrophic Cap Benefit

The **catastrophic cap benefit** protects some TRICARE beneficiaries from devastating financial loss due to serious illness or long-term treatment by establishing limits over which payment is not required. Under TRICARE Prime (and TRICARE Select), the *catastrophic cap* is the maximum a sponsor and family pay for covered TRICARE health care services each calendar year. This limits the amount of out-of-pocket expenses paid for TRICARE covered medical services. Out-of-pocket costs that apply to the catastrophic cap include:

- Enrollment fees
- Deductibles
- Copayments
- Cost-shares (or percentage) for covered services

TRICARE Select

TRICARE Select is a self-managed, preferred provider network plan available in the United States (It replaced TRICARE Standard and TRICARE Extra.) Beneficiaries schedule an appointment with any TRICARE-authorized provider, and referrals are not required for most primary and specialty appointments. However, preauthorization from a regional contractor may be required for some services. Beneficiary costs include:

- Enrollment fees
- Annual outpatient deductible
- Cost shares (or percentage) for covered services

TRICARE Select beneficiaries who receive care from a non-network provider will pay higher cost shares and may be required to submit their own health care claims. (An additional TRICARE Select option includes TRICARE Select Overseas.)

Additional TRICARE Health Plans

Additional TRICARE health plans include:

- *TRICARE for Life*
  - o Medicare-wraparound coverage for TRICARE-eligible beneficiaries who have Medicare Part A and B
  - o Providers submit claims to Medicare, which pays its portion
  - o Medicare then submits claims to TRICARE for Life claims processor
- *TRICARE Reserve Select(R)*
  - o Premium-based plan available worldwide for qualified Selected Reserve members and their families
  - o Requires payment of monthly premiums, annual deductibles, and costs shares (or percentages) for covered services

- o Beneficiaries schedule an appointment with any TRICARE-authorized provider
- o Seeking care from a non-network provider will result in higher costs shares, and beneficiaries may be required to file their own health care claims

- *TRICARE Retired Reserve(R)*
  - o Pemium-based plan available worldwide for qualified Select Reserve members and their families
  - o Requires payment of monthly premiums, annual deductibles, and costs shares (or percentages) for covered services
  - o Seeking care from a non-network provider will result in higher costs shares, and beneficiaries may be required to file their own health care claims

- *TRICARE Young Adult*
  - o Plan that qualified unmarried adult children can purchase after eligibility for "regular" TRICARE coverage ends at age 21 (or age 23 if enrolled in college)
  - o Provides comprehensive medical and pharmacy benefits
  - o TRICARE Young Adult-Prime Option works like TRICARE Prime
  - o TRICARE Young Adult-Select Option works like TRICARE Select

- *U.S. Family Health Plan*
  - o Additional TRICARE Prime option available through networks of community-based, not-for-profit health care systems in a limited number of regions of the United States (e.g., Johns Hopkins Medicine)
  - o All health care (including prescription drug coverage) is received a primary care provider selected from the network of private physicians affiliated with one of the not-for-profit health care systems
  - o Primary care provider assists in scheduling appointments with specialists in the area and coordinates health care
  - o *Ineligible* for health care at military hospital and clinics or from TRICARE network providers

- TRICARE Dental Program
  - o Voluntary dental plan for activity duty service members or National Guard/Reserve members and their families
  - o Single (one person) or family (two or more people) plans are available
  - o Beneficiaries pay monthly premiums and cost-shares, which depend on the sponsor's military status, pay grade, and location

- TRICARE Vision Care
  - o Benefits include eye exams
  - o Coverage for glasses or contacts depends on military status
  - o Referral and/or prior authorization may be required for vision care
  - o A combined *Federal Employees Dental and Vision Insurance Program (FEDVIP)* plan may be available to eligible uniformed service members, active duty family members, and survivors

TRICARE Special Programs

TRICARE offers demonstration projects or pilots and clinical trials that are tailored specifically to beneficiary health concerns or conditions. Some programs: (1) have specific eligibility requirements based on beneficiary category, plan, or status; (2) are for specific beneficiary populations while others offer services for specific health conditions; or (3) are limited to a certain number of participants or a certain geographic location. A **demonstration project or pilot** tests and establishes the feasibility of implementing a new program during a trial period. After the trial period, the program is evaluated, modified, and/or abandoned. A **clinical trial** is a research study that helps find ways to prevent, diagnose, or treat illnesses and improve health care; when enrolled, beneficiaries receive care that is considered the latest medicine or therapy but is not yet approved as a standard care. If, upon evaluation, it is determined that program implementation criteria are met (e.g., it is cost-effective and meets the intended needs of a population), the demonstration project is approved as a program, and enrollment is expanded to include all eligible individuals. (TRICARE was originally a demonstration project entitled the *CHAMPUS Reform Initiative [CRI]*.)

> **Example 1:** The *Chiropractic Health Care Program* emphasizes the recuperative power of the body to heal itself without the use of drugs or surgery. The program is available to active duty service members (including activated National Guard and Reserve members) at designated military hospitals and clinics.

> **Example 2:** The *TRICARE Comprehensive Autism Care Demonstration* program covers applied behavior analysis (ABA) services for all eligible TRICARE beneficiaries diagnosed with an autism spectrum disorder. The program includes a three-step process that includes diagnosis, referral and authorization, and scheduling an appointment.

> **Example 3:** The *TRICARE Cancer Clinical Trials* cover beneficiary participation in Phase I, Phase II, and Phase III studies, which are sponsored by the National Cancer Institute (NCI) or a regional contractor. Coverage includes all medical care and testing needed to determine eligibility and all medical care needed during the study (e.g., purchasing and administering approved chemotherapy agents, inpatient and outpatient care, diagnostic and laboratory services). TRICARE covers the costs for screening tests to determine eligibility for the clinical trial and the costs of participating in the cancer clinical trials. If enrolled in a clinical trial taking place at a military hospital or clinic, all outpatient care is provided free of charge. If referred to a civilian TRICARE-authorized provider, the patient is responsible for the same costs as for other TRICARE-covered services.

Exceptional Family Member Program and Military OneSource

The *Exceptional Family Member Program (EFMP)* is a program used to coordinate assignments to support families with special medical and educational needs. *Military OneSource Specialty Consultants* offer personalized consultations on such issues as education, special needs, and finances are available for military families with special needs. The service also offers customized research on community resources and appropriate military referrals. (Go to www.militaryonesource.mil for additional information.)

Supplemental Health Care Programs

Supplemental Health Care Programs (SHCPs) provide coverage by civilian health care providers to active duty service members and designated non-TRICARE eligible patients. Although authorizations and claims processing are administered by the TRICARE contractors, SHCP is funded separately by the Department of Defense and follows different rules than TRICARE.

TRICARE Billing Notes

The following is a summary of the nationwide billing information for TRICARE Select and TRICARE Extra out-of-network services. Providers of services are required to file these claims.

TRICARE Contractors

TRICARE contractors are grouped in large regional districts covering many states and overseas. Contact the nearest military facility to obtain the current address of the contractor assigned to your area, or access the TRICARE website at www.tricare.mil.

Claim Used

TRICARE accepts the CMS-1500 claim for professional services and the UB-04 claim for institutional services. If the patient has *other health insurance (OHI)*, as referenced on the DD Form 2642, attach the remittance advice to the TRICARE claim. This includes coverage such as automobile insurance and workers' compensation. If the other health insurance plan does not pay the claim, submit the exclusion section of its policy or a copy of the denial.

(A denial from an HMO or PPO stating that the patient did not use available services is not considered an exclusion.) If hospital care was provided for an accidental injury, submit a *DD Form 2527* (Personal Injury Questionnaire) that was completed by the patient.

- Providers receive a remittance advice from TRICARE third-party payers, which illustrates how claims were processed and the amount for which the enrollee is responsible. If a claim is denied, an explanation of the denial is also provided.

- Enrollees receive a TRICARE explanation of benefits (EOB), which is an itemized statement that includes the action taken by TRICARE submitted CMS-1500 claims. Patients who file claims directly with TRICARE submit a *DD Form 2642* (Patient's Request for Medical Payment) (Figure 16-3) and attach a copy of the provider's itemized bill to the claim. (Go to www.tricare.mil, click on Forms & Claims, click on Download a Form, click on Claims, click on Medical Claims, and click on the DD Form 2642.)

NOTE:

Inpatient and outpatient hospital (and other institution) claims are submitted on the UB-04 (CMS-1450). If inpatient or outpatient health care was provided at a civilian hospital, *a nonavailability statement (NAS)* must be submitted electronically. (Do not submit an NAS for emergency care provided at a civilian hospital.)

Claims Submission Deadline

Claims will be denied if they are filed more than one year after the date of service for outpatient care or more than one year from the date of discharge for inpatient care.

Allowable Fee Determination

TRICARE fee schedules are available from regional carriers. The TRICARE fee schedule must still be followed when TRICARE is a secondary payer.

Deductibles

All deductibles are applied to the government's **fiscal year**, which runs from October 1 of one year to September 30 of the next. This is different from other insurance programs, for which deductibles are usually calculated on a calendar-year basis.

Confirmation of Eligibility

Confirmation of TRICARE eligibility is obtained by entering the sponsor's *DoD Beneficiary Number* in the nationwide computerized Defense Enrollment Eligibility Reporting System (DEERS). The number is located on the reverse of the sponsor's uniformed services common access card (CAC) *or* DoD uniformed services identification (USID) card. (The CAC is a smart card that replaced the military identification card. Photocopying the CAC is permitted to facilitate eligibility verification and to provide health care services.)

Accepting Assignment

Accepting assignment for nonPARs is determined on a claim-by-claim basis. Be sure to indicate the provider's choice in Block 27 of the claim. All deductibles and cost-shares may be collected at the time service is rendered. When assignment is elected, the local beneficiary services representative can assist if there are problems collecting the deductible and cost-share (copayment) from the patient. The TRICARE contractor's provider representative can assist with claims review or intervene when a claim payment is overdue.

TRICARE has established a "good faith policy" for assigned claims when the copy of the front and back of the patient's uniformed services common access card (CAC) on file turns out to be invalid. If copies of the CAC are on file and TRICARE provides notification that the patient is ineligible for payment, the customer service representative (CSR) can help in investigation of the claim. If the investigation reveals that the

1. PATIENT'S NAME (Last, First, Middle Initial)

2. PATIENT'S TELEPHONE NUMBER (Include Area Code)
Primary ( )
Secondary ( )

3. PATIENT'S ADDRESS (Street, Apt. No., City, State, and ZIP Code)

4. PATIENT'S RELATIONSHIP TO SPONSOR (X one)
☐ SELF ☐ STEPCHILD
☐ SPOUSE ☐ FORMER SPOUSE
☐ NATURAL OR ADOPTED CHILD ☐ OTHER (Specify)

5. PATIENT'S DATE OF BIRTH (YYYYMMDD)

6. PATIENT'S SEX (X one)
☐ MALE ☐ FEMALE

7. IS PATIENT'S CONDITION (X both if applicable)
If yes, see #7 in section below
ACCIDENT RELATED? ☐ Yes ☐ No
WORK RELATED? ☐ Yes ☐ No

8a. DESCRIBE ILLNESS, INJURY OR SYMPTOMS THAT REQUIRED TREATMENT, SUPPLIES OR MEDICATION. IF AN INJURY, NOTE HOW IT HAPPENED. REFER TO INSTRUCTIONS BELOW.

8b. WAS PATIENT'S CARE (X one)
☐ INPATIENT? ☐ PHARMACY?
☐ OUTPATIENT?
☐ DAY SURGERY?

9. SPONSOR'S OR FORMER SPOUSE'S NAME (Last, First, Middle Initial)

10. SPONSOR'S OR FORMER SPOUSE'S SOCIAL SECURITY NUMBER OR DOD BENEFITS NUMBER (DBN)

11. OTHER HEALTH INSURANCE COVERAGE

a. Is patient covered by any other health insurance plan or program to include health coverage available through other family members? For patients overseas this includes National Health Insurance. If yes, check the "Yes" block and complete blocks 11 and 12 (see instructions below). If no, you must check the "No" block and complete block 12. Do not provide TRICARE supplemental insurance information, but do report Medicare supplements.
☐ Yes
☐ No

b. TYPE OF COVERAGE (Check all that apply)
☐ (1) EMPLOYMENT (Group) ☐ (3) MEDICARE ☐ (5) MEDICARE SUPPLEMENTAL INSURANCE ☐ (7) OTHER (Specify)
☐ (2) PRIVATE (Non-Group) ☐ (4) STUDENT PLAN ☐ (6) PRESCRIPTION PLAN

	c. NAME AND ADDRESS OF OTHER HEALTH INSURANCE (Street, City, State, and ZIP Code)	d. INSURANCE IDENTIFICATION NUMBER	e. INSURANCE EFFECTIVE DATE (YYYYMMDD)	f. DRUG COVERAGE?
INSURANCE 1				☐ Yes ☐ No
INSURANCE 2				☐ Yes ☐ No

REMINDER: Attach your other health insurances's Explanation of Benefits or pharmacy receipt that indicates the actual drug cost, amount the OHI paid, and the amount that you paid.

12. SIGNATURE OF PATIENT OR AUTHORIZED PERSON CERTIFIES CORRECTNESS OF CLAIM AND AUTHORIZES RELEASE OF MEDICAL OR OTHER INSURANCE INFORMATION.

a. SIGNATURE

b. DATE SIGNED (YYYYMMDD)

c. RELATIONSHIP TO PATIENT

13. OVERSEAS CLAIMS ONLY: PAYMENT IN US CURRENCY?
☐ No ☐ Yes

HOW TO FILL OUT THE TRICARE/CHAMPUS FORM
You must attach an itemized bill (see front of form) from your doctor/supplier for CHAMPUS to process this claim.

1. Enter patient's last name, first name and middle initial as it appears on the military ID Card. Do not use nicknames.
2. Enter the patient's primary telephone number and secondary telephone number to include the area code.
3. Enter the complete address of the patient's place of residence at the time of service (street number, street name, apartment number, city, state, ZIP Code). Do not use a Post Office Box Number except for Rural Routes and numbers. Do not use an APO/FPO address unless the patient was actually residing overseas when care was provided.
4. Check the box to indicate patient's relationship to sponsor. If "Other" is checked, indicate how related to the sponsor; e.g., parent.
5. Enter patient's date of birth (YYYYMMDD).
6. Check the box for either male or female (patient).
7. Check box to indicate if patient's condition is accident related, work related or both. If accident or work related, the patient is required to complete DD Form 2527, "Statement of Personal Injury- Possible Third Party Liability Defense Health Agency (DHA)." Download the form at https://tricare.mil/forms.
8a. Describe patient's condition for which treatment was provided, e.g., broken arm, appendicitis, eye infection. If patient's condition is the result of an injury, report how it happened, e.g., fell on stairs at work, car accident
8b. Check the box to indicate where the care was given.
9. Enter the Sponsor's or Former Spouse's last name, first name and middle initial as it appears on the military ID Card. If the sponsor and patient are the same, enter "same."
10. Enter the Sponsor's or Former Spouse's Social Security Number (SSN) or Patients DoD Benefits Number (DBN).

11. By law, you must report if the patient is covered by any other health insurance to include health coverage available through other family members. If the patient has supplemental TRICARE/CHAMPUS insurance, do not report You must, however, report Medicare supplemental coverage. Block 11 allows space to report two insurance coverages. If there are additional insurances, report the information as required by Block 11 on a separate sheet of paper and attach to the claim.
NOTE: All other health insurances except Medicaid and TRICARE/CHAMPUS supplemental plans must pay before TRICARE/CHAMPUS will pay. With the exception of Medicaid and CHAMPUS supplemental plans, you must first submit the claim to the other health insurer and after that insurance has determined their payment, attach the other insurance Explanation of Benefits (EOB) or work sheet to this claim. *The claims processor cannot process claims until you provide the other health insurance information.*
12. The patient or other authorized person must sign the claim. If the patient is under 18 years old, either parent may sign unless the services are confidential and then the patient should sign the claim. If the patient is 18 years or older, but cannot sign the claim, the person who signs must be either the legal guardian, or in the absence of a legal guardian, a spouse or parent of the patient. If other than the patient, the signer should print or type his/her name in Block 12a. and sign the claim. Attach a statement to the claim giving the signer's full name and address, relationship to the patient and the reason the patient is unable to sign. Include documentation of the signer's appointment as legal guardian, or provide your statement that no legal guardian has been appointed. If a power of attorney has been issued, provide a copy.
13. If this is a claim for care received overseas, indicate if you want payment in US currency.

DD FORM 2642, NOV 2018

Courtesy of Tricare, https://www.tricare.mil/

FIGURE 16-3 TRICARE Medical Claim–Patient's Request for Medical Payment (DD Form 2642).

CAC is invalid, refile the claim with a note stating: "We treated this patient in good faith. Please note the enclosed copy of the CAC that was presented at the time the treatment was rendered." *Do not send* your file copy of the CAC card. The provider should receive payment of the TRICARE-approved fee for these services.

TRICARE Limiting Charges

All TRICARE nonPAR providers are subject to a limiting charge of 15 percent above the allowed TRICARE fee schedule for PAR providers. Patients cannot be billed for the difference between the provider's normal fee and the TRICARE limiting charge (called *balance billing*). Exceptions to the 15 percent limiting charge include claims from independent laboratory and diagnostic laboratory companies, claims for durable medical equipment, and claims from medical supply companies.

Special Handling

1. Always make a copy of the front and back of the patient's uniformed services common access card (CAC) military identification card *or* DoD uniformed services identification (USID) card.

2. Check to determine whether the patient knows the next date of transfer. If it is within six months, it would be wise to accept assignment on the claim to avoid interstate collection problems.

3. A *Statement of Personal Injury–Possible Third-Party Liability Statement (DD Form 2527)* is required for all injuries that have been assigned ICD-10-CM codes in the S00-T88 category range. If there is no third-party liability, call the CSR for information on how to file the claim. (The *Federal Medical Recovery Act* allows TRICARE to be reimbursed for its costs of treatment if a member is injured in an accident that was caused by someone else.) (Go to www.tricare.mil, click on Forms & Claims, click on Download a Form, click on Claims, click on Medical Claims, and click on the DD Form 2527.)

4. Contact the regional contractor's representative if there has been no response within 45 days of submitting the claim.

Military Time

Time tracking using military time (Table 16-1) for providers is typically performed on a monthly basis, which allows for monitoring the time physicians spend with each patient. Provider office staff use the patient record to prepare the time tracking report, and it is used to manage office procedures (e.g., appointment scheduling, staff scheduling). As such, providers are responsible for documenting the start and stop time each time they provide patient care.

TABLE 16-1 Standard time and military time conversion table

Standard Time		Military Time	Standard Time		Military Time
12:00	A.M.	2400	12:00	P.M.	1200
12:30	A.M.	2430	12:30	P.M.	1230
1:00	A.M.	0100	1:00	P.M.	1300
1:30	A.M.	0130	1:30	P.M.	1330
2:00	A.M.	0200	2:00	P.M.	1400
2:30	A.M.	0230	2:30	P.M.	1430
3:00	A.M.	0300	3:00	P.M.	1500
3:30	A.M.	0330	3:30	P.M.	1530
4:00	A.M.	0400	4:00	P.M.	1600
4:30	A.M.	0430	4:30	P.M.	1630
5:00	A.M.	0500	5:00	P.M.	1700
5:30	A.M.	0530	5:30	P.M.	1730
6:00	A.M.	0600	6:00	P.M.	1800

(continues)

TABLE 16-1   (continued)

Standard Time		Military Time	Standard Time		Military Time
6:30	A.M.	0630	6:30	P.M.	1830
7:00	A.M.	0700	7:00	P.M.	1900
7:30	A.M.	0730	7:30	P.M.	1930
8:00	A.M.	0800	8:00	P.M.	2000
8:30	A.M.	0830	8:30	P.M.	2030
9:00	A.M.	0900	9:00	P.M.	2100
9:30	A.M.	0930	9:30	P.M.	2130
10:00	A.M.	1000	10:00	P.M.	2200
10:30	A.M.	1030	10:30	P.M.	2230
11:00	A.M.	1100	11:00	P.M.	2300
11:30	A.M.	1130	11:30	P.M.	2330

TRICARE Claims Instructions

Table 16-2 contains instructions for completing claims to be submitted to TRICARE Extra and TRICARE Select contractors. When reviewing the instructions, refer to the John Q. Public case study in Figure 16-4 and the completed CMS-1500 claim in Figure 16-5.

NOTE:

- Refer to Chapter 11 for clarification of claims completion (e.g., entering names, mailing addresses, ICD-10-CM codes, diagnosis pointer letters, NPI, and so on).
- Use these instructions when completing any claims associated with *Understanding Health Insurance*.

TABLE 16-2   CMS-1500 claims completion instructions for TRICARE fee-for-service claims

Block	Instructions
1	Enter an X in the *TRICARE* box.
1a	Enter the sponsor's DEPARTMENT OF DEFENSE (DOD) BENEFITS NUMBER as it appears on the reverse of the uniformed services common access card (CAC). *Do not enter hyphens or spaces in the number.*
	Note: The reverse side of the CAC, in the Medical block, states whether the sponsor is eligible for medical care from military or civilian sources.
2	Enter the patient's last name, first name, and middle initial (separated by commas) (e.g., DOE, JANE, M).
3	Enter the patient's birth date as MM DD YYYY (with spaces). Enter an X in the appropriate box to indicate the patient's sex. If the patient's sex is unknown, leave blank.
4	Enter the sponsor's last name, first name, and middle initial (separated by commas).

(continues)

TABLE 16-2 (continued)

Block	Instructions
5	Enter the patient's mailing address. Enter the street address on line 1, enter the city and state on line 2, and enter the five- or nine-digit zip code on line 3. *Do not enter the hyphen or a space for a 9-digit ZIP code. Do not enter the telephone number.* **Note:** Do not enter APO or FPO addresses as the mailing address. The patient's residence is the mailing address.
6	Enter an X in the appropriate box to indicate the patient's relationship to the policyholder. If the patient is an unmarried domestic partner, enter an X in the *Other* box.
7	If the address of the patient is the same as the sponsor, leave blank. Otherwise, enter the sponsor's mailing address. Enter the street address on line 1, enter the city and state on line 2, and enter the five- or nine-digit zip code on line 3. *Do not enter the hyphen or a space for a 9-digit ZIP code. Do not enter the telephone number.* **Note:** For an active duty sponsor, enter the sponsor's duty station address. For a retiree sponsor, enter the sponsor's home address.
8	Leave blank.
9, 9a, 9d	Leave blank. *Blocks 9, 9a, and 9d are completed if the patient has secondary insurance coverage (discussed later in this chapter).*
10a–c	Enter an X in the appropriate box to indicate whether the patient's condition is related to employment, an automobile accident, and/or another accident. If an X is entered in the YES box for auto accident, enter the two-character state abbreviation of the patient's residence.
10d	If DD Form 2527 is attached to the CMS-1500 claim, enter DD FORM 2527 ATTACHED. Otherwise, leave blank.
11, 11a–11c	Leave blank.
11d	Enter an X in the NO box. *Block 11d is completed by entering an X in the YES box if the patient has secondary insurance coverage (discussed later in this chapter).*
12	Enter SIGNATURE ON FILE. Leave the date field blank. (The abbreviation SOF is also acceptable.) **Note:** Entering SIGNATURE ON FILE means that the patient has previously signed an authorization to release medical information to the payer, and it is maintained "on file" by the provider. If the patient has not signed an authorization, the patient must sign and date the block.
13	Enter SIGNATURE ON FILE to authorize direct payment to the provider for benefits due the patient. (The abbreviation SOF is also acceptable.)
14	Enter the date as MM DD YY (with spaces) to indicate when the patient first experienced signs or symptoms of the present illness, actual date of injury, *or* the date of the last menstrual period (LMP) for obstetric visits. Enter the applicable qualifier to identify which date is being reported: 431 (onset of current symptoms/illness or injury) *or* 484 (last menstrual period). *If the date is not documented in the patient's record, but the history indicates an appropriate date (e.g., three weeks ago), simply count back to the approximate date and enter it on the claim.*
15	Enter the date as MM DD YY (with spaces) to indicate that a prior episode of the same or similar illness began, *if documented in the patient's record. Previous pregnancies are not a similar illness.* Otherwise, leave blank.
16	Leave blank.
17	If applicable, enter the first name, middle initial (if known), last name, and credentials of the professional who referred, ordered, or supervised health care service(s) or supply(ies) reported on the claim. *Do not enter any punctuation.* In front of the name, enter the applicable qualifier to identify which provider is being reported, as follows: DN (referring provider), DK (ordering provider), or DQ (supervising provider). Otherwise, leave blank. **Note:** If the patient was referred by a military treatment facility (MTF), enter the name of the MTF and attach DD Form 2161 (Referral for Civilian Medical Care) or SF 513 (Medical Record—Consultation Sheet).

(continues)

TABLE 16-2 (continued)

Block	Instructions
17a	Leave blank.
17b	Enter the 10-digit national provider identifier (NPI) of the professional in Block 17. Otherwise, leave blank.
18	Enter the admission date and discharge date as MM DD YY (with spaces) if the patient received inpatient services (e.g., hospital, skilled nursing facility). Otherwise, leave blank. *If the patient has not been discharged at the time the claim is completed, leave the discharge date blank.*
19	Leave blank.
20	Enter an X in the NO box if all laboratory procedures reported on the claim were performed in the provider's office. Enter an X in the YES box if laboratory procedures reported on the claim were performed by an outside laboratory and billed to the provider. Enter the total amount charged by the outside laboratory in $ CHARGES, and enter the outside laboratory's name, mailing address, and NPI in Block 32. (Charges are entered *without* punctuation. For example, $1,100.00 is entered as 110000 below $ CHARGES.)
21	Enter the ICD-10-CM code for up to 12 diagnoses or conditions treated or medically managed during the encounter. Lines A through L in Block 21 will relate to CPT or HCPCS Level II service or procedure codes reported in Block 24E. In the *ICD Ind* (ICD indicator) box, enter 0 for ICD-10-CM.
22	Leave blank. This is reserved for resubmitted claims.
23	If applicable, enter the prior authorization number. *Do not enter hyphens or spaces in the number.* Otherwise, leave blank.
24A	Enter the date the procedure or service was performed in the FROM column as MM DD YY (with spaces). Enter a date in the TO column *if the procedure or service was performed on consecutive days during a range of dates. Then, enter the number of consecutive days in Block 24G.* **Note:** The shaded area in each line is used to enter supplemental information to support reported services *if instructed by the payer to enter such information.* Data entry in Block 24 is limited to reporting six services. *Do not use the shaded lines to report additional services.* If additional services were provided, generate new CMS-1500 claim(s) to report the additional services.
24B	Enter the appropriate two-digit place-of-service (POS) code to identify the location where the reported procedure or service was performed.
24C	Leave blank.
24D	Enter the CPT or HCPCS Level II code and applicable required modifier(s) for procedures or services performed. *Separate the CPT/HCPCS code and first modifier with one space. Separate additional modifiers with one space each. Up to four modifiers can be entered.*
24E	Enter the diagnosis pointer letter(s) from Block 21 that relate to the procedure/service performed on the date of service to justify medical necessity of procedures and services reported on the claim.
24F	Enter the fee charged for each reported procedure or service. *Do not enter commas, periods, or dollar signs. Do not enter negative amounts. Enter 00 in the cents area if the amount is a whole number.*
24G	Enter the number of days or units for procedures or services reported in Block 24D. *If just one procedure or service was reported in Block 24D, enter a 1 in Block 24G.*
24H–24I	Leave blank.

(continues)

TABLE 16-2 (continued)

Block	Instructions
24J	Enter the 10-digit NPI for the: • Provider who performed the service *if the provider is a member of a group practice* (Leave blank if the provider is a solo practitioner.) • Supervising provider *if the service was provided incident-to the service of a physician or nonphysician practitioner* **and** *the physician or practitioner who ordered the service did not supervise the provider* (Leave blank if the incident-to service was performed under the supervision of the physician or nonphysician practitioner.) • DMEPOS supplier or outside laboratory *if the physician submits the claim for services provided by the DMEPOS supplier or outside laboratory* (Leave blank if the DMEPOS supplier or outside laboratory submits the claim.) Otherwise, leave blank.
25	Enter the provider's Social Security number (SSN) or employer identification number (EIN). *Do not enter hyphens or spaces in the number.* Enter an X in the appropriate box to indicate which number is reported.
26	Enter the patient's account number as assigned by the provider.
27	Enter an X in the YES box to indicate that the provider agrees to accept assignment. Otherwise, enter an X in the NO box.
28	Enter the total charges for services and/or procedures reported in Block 24. Note: If multiple claims are submitted for one patient because more than six procedures or services were reported, be sure the total charge reported on each claim accurately represents the total of the items on each submitted claim.
29	Leave blank. *Block 29 is completed if the patient has secondary insurance (discussed later in this chapter).*
30	Leave blank.
31	Enter the provider's name and credential (e.g., MARY SMITH MD) and the date the claim was completed as MMDDYY (without spaces). *Do not enter any punctuation.*
32	Enter the name and address where procedures or services were provided *if at a location other than the provider's office or the patient's home, such as a hospital, outside laboratory facility, skilled nursing facility, or DMEPOS supplier.* Otherwise, leave blank. Enter the name on line 1, the address on line 2, and the city, state, and nine-digit zip code on line 3. *Do not enter the hyphen or a space for a 9-digit ZIP code.* Note: If Block 18 contains dates of service for inpatient care and/or Block 20 contains an X in the YES box, enter the name and address of the facility that provided services (e.g., military treatment facility).
32a	Enter the 10-digit NPI of the facility entered in Block 32.
32b	Leave blank.
33	Enter the provider's *billing* name, address, and telephone number. Enter the phone number in the area next to the block title. *Do not enter parentheses for the area code.* Enter the name on line 1, enter the address on line 2, and enter the city, state, and nine-digit zip code on line 3. *Do not enter the hyphen or a space for a 9-digit ZIP code.*
33a	Enter the 10-digit NPI of the *billing* provider (e.g., solo practitioner) or group practice (e.g., clinic).
33b	Leave blank.

ERIN A. HELPER, M.D.
101 Medic Drive, Anywhere, NY 12345-9874
(101) 111-1234 (Office) • (101) 111-9292 (Fax)
EIN: 11-1234523
NPI: 1234567890

Case Study

PATIENT INFORMATION:

Name:	Public, John Q.
Address:	10A Senate Avenue
City:	Anywhere
State:	NY
Zip Code:	12345-1234
Telephone:	(101) 201-7891
Sex:	Male
Date of Birth:	03-09-1965
Occupation:	Retired
Employer:	

INSURANCE INFORMATION:

Patient Number:	16-1
Place of Service:	Inpatient Hospital
Primary Insurance Plan:	TRICARE Select
DoD Benefit Number	100 23 9678
Primary Policyholder:	Public, John Q.
Policyholder Date of Birth:	03-09-1965
Relationship to Patient:	Self
Secondary Insurance Plan:	
Secondary Insurance Plan ID #:	
Secondary Policyholder:	

Patient Status   [X] Married   [ ] Divorced   [ ] Single   [ ] Student

DIAGNOSIS INFORMATION

Diagnosis	Code	Diagnosis	Code
1. Mycoplasma pneumonia	J15.7	5.	
2. Type 1 diabetes mellitus	E10.9	6.	
3.		7.	
4.		8.	

PROCEDURE INFORMATION

	Description of Procedure or Service	Date	Code	Charge
1.	Initial hospital visit, level III	01-09-YY	99223	150.00
2.	Subsequent hospital visit, level II	01-10-YY	99232	75.00
3.	Subsequent hospital visit, level II	01-11-YY	99232	75.00
4.	Subsequent hospital visit, level I	01-12-YY	99231	50.00
5.	Discharge, 30 minutes	01-13-YY	99238	50.00

SPECIAL NOTES: Goodmedicine Hospital, Anywhere Street, Anywhere, NY 12345-1234. (NPI: 2345678901) Return visit one week.

FIGURE 16-4 John Q. Public case study.

HEALTH INSURANCE CLAIM FORM

APPROVED BY NATIONAL UNIFORM CLAIM COMMITTEE (NUCC) 02/12

☐☐ PICA

PICA ☐☐

| 1. MEDICARE (Medicare#) ☐ | MEDICAID (Medicaid#) ☐ | TRICARE (ID#/DoD#) ☒ | CHAMPVA (Member ID#) ☐ | GROUP HEALTH PLAN (ID#) ☐ | FECA BLKLUNG (ID#) ☐ | OTHER (ID#) ☐ | 1a. INSURED'S I.D. NUMBER (For Program in Item 1) 100239678 |

| 2. PATIENT'S NAME (Last Name, First Name, Middle Initial) PUBLIC, JOHN, Q | 3. PATIENT'S BIRTH DATE MM 03 DD 09 YY 1965 SEX M ☒ F ☐ | 4. INSURED'S NAME (Last Name, First Name, Middle Initial) PUBLIC, JOHN, Q |

5. PATIENT'S ADDRESS (No., Street) 10A SENATE AVENUE	6. PATIENT RELATIONSHIP TO INSURED Self ☒ Spouse ☐ Child ☐ Other ☐	7. INSURED'S ADDRESS (No., Street)
CITY ANYWHERE	STATE NY	8. RESERVED FOR NUCC USE	CITY	STATE
ZIP CODE 123451234	TELEPHONE (Include Area Code) ( )		ZIP CODE	TELEPHONE (Include Area Code) ( )

9. OTHER INSURED'S NAME (Last Name, First Name, Middle Initial)	10. IS PATIENT'S CONDITION RELATED TO:	11. INSURED'S POLICY GROUP OR FECA NUMBER
a. OTHER INSURED'S POLICY OR GROUP NUMBER	a. EMPLOYMENT? (Current or Previous) YES ☐ NO ☒	a. INSURED'S DATE OF BIRTH MM DD YY SEX M ☐ F ☐
b. RESERVED FOR NUCC USE	b. AUTO ACCIDENT? YES ☐ NO ☒ PLACE (State)	b. OTHER CLAIM ID (Designated by NUCC)
c. RESERVED FOR NUCC USE	c. OTHER ACCIDENT? YES ☐ NO ☒	c. INSURANCE PLAN NAME OR PROGRAM NAME
d. INSURANCE PLAN NAME OR PROGRAM NAME	10d. CLAIM CODES (Designated by NUCC)	d. IS THERE ANOTHER HEALTH BENEFIT PLAN? YES ☐ NO ☒ If yes, complete items 9, 9a, and 9d.

READ BACK OF FORM BEFORE COMPLETING & SIGNING THIS FORM.

12. PATIENT'S OR AUTHORIZED PERSON'S SIGNATURE I authorize the release of any medical or other information necessary to process this claim. I also request payment of government benefits either to myself or to the party who accepts assignment below.

SIGNED **SIGNATURE ON FILE**   DATE

13. INSURED'S OR AUTHORIZED PERSON'S SIGNATURE I authorize payment of medical benefits to the undersigned physician or supplier for services described below.

SIGNED **SIGNATURE ON FILE**

14. DATE OF CURRENT ILLNESS, INJURY, or PREGNANCY (LMP) MM 01 DD 09 YY YY QUAL. 431	15. OTHER DATE QUAL. MM DD YY	16. DATES PATIENT UNABLE TO WORK IN CURRENT OCCUPATION FROM MM DD YY TO MM DD YY
17. NAME OF REFERRING PROVIDER OR OTHER SOURCE	17a. / 17b. NPI	18. HOSPITALIZATION DATES RELATED TO CURRENT SERVICES FROM MM 01 DD 09 YY YY TO MM 01 DD 13 YY YY
19. ADDITIONAL CLAIM INFORMATION (Designated by NUCC)		20. OUTSIDE LAB? YES ☐ NO ☒ $ CHARGES

21. DIAGNOSIS OR NATURE OF ILLNESS OR INJURY Relate A-L to service line below (24E)   ICD Ind. **0**

A. J157	B. E109	C.	D.
E.	F.	G.	H.
I.	J.	K.	L.

| 22. RESUBMISSION CODE | ORIGINAL REF. NO. |
| 23. PRIOR AUTHORIZATION NUMBER | |

24. A. DATE(S) OF SERVICE From MM DD YY To MM DD YY	B. PLACE OF SERVICE	C. EMG	D. PROCEDURES, SERVICES, OR SUPPLIES (Explain Unusual Circumstances) CPT/HCPCS MODIFIER	E. DIAGNOSIS POINTER	F. $ CHARGES	G. DAYS OR UNITS	H. EPSDT Family Plan	I. ID. QUAL.	J. RENDERING PROVIDER ID. #
1	01 09 YY 01 11 YY	21		99223	AB	150 00	1		NPI	
2	01 10 YY	21		99232	AB	150 00	2		NPI	
3	01 12 YY	21		99231	AB	50 00	1		NPI	
4	01 13 YY	21		99238	AB	50 00	1		NPI	
5									NPI	
6									NPI	

| 25. FEDERAL TAX I.D. NUMBER 111234523 SSN ☐ EIN ☒ | 26. PATIENT'S ACCOUNT NO. 16-1 | 27. ACCEPT ASSIGNMENT? (For govt. claims, see back) YES ☒ NO ☐ | 28. TOTAL CHARGE $ 400 00 | 29. AMOUNT PAID $ | 30. Rsvd for NUCC Use |

| 31. SIGNATURE OF PHYSICIAN OR SUPPLIER INCLUDING DEGREES OR CREDENTIALS (I certify that the statements on the reverse apply to this bill and are made a part thereof.) ERIN A HELPER MD SIGNED MMDDYY DATE | 32. SERVICE FACILITY LOCATION INFORMATION GOODMEDICINE HOSPITAL ANYWHERE STREET ANYWHERE NY 123451234 a. 2345678901 b. | 33. BILLING PROVIDER INFO & PH # (101) 1111234 ERIN A HELPER MD 101 MEDIC DRIVE ANYWHERE NY 123459874 a. 1234567890 b. |

NUCC Instruction Manual available at: www.nucc.org   **PLEASE PRINT OR TYPE**

CARRIER

PATIENT AND INSURED INFORMATION

PHYSICIAN OR SUPPLIER INFORMATION

FIGURE 16-5 Completed TRICARE as primary CMS-1500 claim for John Q. Public case study.

Exercise 16.1 – Completing a TRICARE as Primary CMS-1500 Claim

1. Obtain a blank claim by making a copy of the CMS-1500 claim form in Appendix I.
2. Review the claims instructions in Table 16-2.
3. Review Figure 16-6, the Mary S. Patient case study.
4. Select the information needed from the case study, and enter the required information on the claim.
5. Review the claim to be sure all required blocks are properly completed.
6. Compare your claim with the completed claim in Figure 16-7.

ERIN A. HELPER, M.D.
101 Medic Drive, Anywhere, NY 12345-9874
(101) 111-1234 (Office) • (101) 111-9292 (Fax)
EIN: 11-1234523
NPI: 1234567890

Case Study

PATIENT INFORMATION:

Name:	Patient, Mary S.
Address:	91 Home Street
City:	Nowhere
State:	NY
Zip Code:	12367-1234
Telephone:	(101) 201-8989
Sex:	Female
Occupation:	Homemaker
Date of Birth:	10-10-1959
Employer:	

INSURANCE INFORMATION:

Patient Number:	16-2
Place of Service:	Office
Primary Insurance Plan:	TRICARE Select
Primary Insurance Plan ID #:	101 23 9945
Policy #:	
Primary Policyholder:	James L. Patient
Policyholder Date of Birth:	08-22-1944
Employer:	Turbodyne
Relationship to Patient:	Spouse
Secondary Insurance Plan:	US Navy
Secondary Insurance Plan ID #:	Dept 07 Naval Station Nowhere, NY 12367-1234
Secondary Policyholder:	

Patient Status	☒ Married	☐ Divorced	☐ Single	☐ Student

DIAGNOSIS INFORMATION

	Diagnosis	Code		Diagnosis	Code
1.	Fracture, distal radius, left (initial encounter)	S52.502A	5.		
2.	Fell at home	Y92.009	6.		
3.	Fell down stairs (initial encounter)	W10.8XXA	7.		
4.			8.		

PROCEDURE INFORMATION

	Description of Procedure or Service	Date	Code	Charge
1.	Closed manipulation, left distal radius	01-10-YY	25605-LT	300.00
2.	X-ray, left wrist, 3 views	01-10-YY	73110-LT	50.00
3.	X-ray, left forearm, 2 views	01-10-YY	73090-LT	25.00
4.				
5.				

SPECIAL NOTES: Fell down stairs at home today.

FIGURE 16-6 Mary S. Patient case study.

HEALTH INSURANCE CLAIM FORM

APPROVED BY NATIONAL UNIFORM CLAIM COMMITTEE (NUCC) 02/12

☐☐☐ PICA

1. MEDICARE (Medicare#) ☐ MEDICAID (Medicaid#) ☐ TRICARE (ID#/DoD#) ☒ CHAMPVA (Member ID#) ☐ GROUP HEALTH PLAN (ID#) ☐ FECA BLKLUNG (ID#) ☐ OTHER (ID#) ☐

1a. INSURED'S I.D. NUMBER (For Program in Item 1): **101239945**

2. PATIENT'S NAME (Last Name, First Name, Middle Initial): **PATIENT, MARY, S**

3. PATIENT'S BIRTH DATE: **10 10 1959** SEX M ☐ F ☒

4. INSURED'S NAME (Last Name, First Name, Middle Initial): **PATIENT, JAMES, L**

5. PATIENT'S ADDRESS (No., Street): **91 HOME STREET**

6. PATIENT RELATIONSHIP TO INSURED: Self ☐ Spouse ☒ Child ☐ Other ☐

7. INSURED'S ADDRESS (No., Street): **DEPT 07 NAVAL STATION**

CITY: **NOWHERE** STATE: **NY**

8. RESERVED FOR NUCC USE

CITY: **NOWHERE** STATE: **NY**

ZIP CODE: **123671234** TELEPHONE: ( )

ZIP CODE: **123671234** TELEPHONE: ( )

9. OTHER INSURED'S NAME

10. IS PATIENT'S CONDITION RELATED TO:

11. INSURED'S POLICY GROUP OR FECA NUMBER

a. OTHER INSURED'S POLICY OR GROUP NUMBER

a. EMPLOYMENT? (Current or Previous) YES ☐ NO ☒

a. INSURED'S DATE OF BIRTH MM DD YY SEX M ☐ F ☐

b. RESERVED FOR NUCC USE

b. AUTO ACCIDENT? YES ☐ NO ☒ PLACE (State)

b. OTHER CLAIM ID (Designated by NUCC)

c. RESERVED FOR NUCC USE

c. OTHER ACCIDENT? YES ☐ NO ☒

c. INSURANCE PLAN NAME OR PROGRAM NAME

d. INSURANCE PLAN NAME OR PROGRAM NAME

10d. CLAIM CODES (Designated by NUCC)

d. IS THERE ANOTHER HEALTH BENEFIT PLAN? YES ☐ NO ☒ If yes, complete items 9, 9a, and 9d.

READ BACK OF FORM BEFORE COMPLETING & SIGNING THIS FORM.

12. PATIENT'S OR AUTHORIZED PERSON'S SIGNATURE. SIGNED **SIGNATURE ON FILE** DATE

13. INSURED'S OR AUTHORIZED PERSON'S SIGNATURE. SIGNED **SIGNATURE ON FILE**

14. DATE OF CURRENT ILLNESS, INJURY, or PREGNANCY (LMP): **01 10 YY** QUAL. **431**

15. OTHER DATE QUAL.

16. DATES PATIENT UNABLE TO WORK IN CURRENT OCCUPATION FROM TO

17. NAME OF REFERRING PROVIDER OR OTHER SOURCE 17a. 17b. NPI

18. HOSPITALIZATION DATES RELATED TO CURRENT SERVICES FROM TO

19. ADDITIONAL CLAIM INFORMATION (Designated by NUCC)

20. OUTSIDE LAB? YES ☐ NO ☒ $ CHARGES

21. DIAGNOSIS OR NATURE OF ILLNESS OR INJURY ICD Ind. **0**
A. **S52502A** B. **Y92009** C. **W108XXA** D.
E. F. G. H.
I. J. K. L.

22. RESUBMISSION CODE ORIGINAL REF. NO.

23. PRIOR AUTHORIZATION NUMBER

24.

From MM DD YY	To MM DD YY	B. POS	C. EMG	D. CPT/HCPCS	MODIFIER	E. DIAG PTR	F. $ CHARGES	G. UNITS	H.	I. QUAL	J. RENDERING PROVIDER ID. #
1	01 10 YY		11		25605	LT	A	300 00	1		NPI	
2	01 10 YY		11		73110	LT	A	50 00	1		NPI	
3	01 10 YY		11		73090	LT	A	25 00	1		NPI	
4											NPI	
5											NPI	
6											NPI	

25. FEDERAL TAX I.D. NUMBER: **111234523** SSN ☐ EIN ☒

26. PATIENT'S ACCOUNT NO.: **16-2**

27. ACCEPT ASSIGNMENT? YES ☒ NO ☐

28. TOTAL CHARGE $ **375 00**

29. AMOUNT PAID

30. Rsvd for NUCC Use

31. SIGNATURE OF PHYSICIAN OR SUPPLIER: **ERIN A HELPER MD** DATE **MMDDYY**

32. SERVICE FACILITY LOCATION INFORMATION a. NPI b.

33. BILLING PROVIDER INFO & PH # (**101**) **1111234**
ERIN A HELPER MD
101 MEDIC DRIVE
ANYWHERE NY 123459874
a. **1234567890** b.

NUCC Instruction Manual available at: www.nucc.org   PLEASE PRINT OR TYPE

FIGURE 16-7 Completed TRICARE as primary CMS-1500 claim for Mary S. Patient case study.

TRICARE as Secondary Payer Claims Instructions

Table 16-3 contains modifications to the CMS-1500 claims instructions when a second CMS-1500 claim is generated with TRICARE as the secondary payer. In this situation, the patient's primary health insurance coverage is another payer, such as Medicare or an employer group health plan (e.g., BCBS).

 NOTE:

Use these instructions when completing any claims associated with *Understanding Health Insurance*.

TABLE 16-3 Modifications to CMS-1500 claims completion instructions when TRICARE is the secondary payer (Refer to Table 16-3 for primary CMS-1500 claims completion instructions.)

Block	Instructions
	Note: Blocks 11 and 11a–11c remain blank on a TRICARE as Secondary CMS-1500 claim.
1a	Enter the secondary policyholder's health insurance identification number (HICN) as it appears on the insurance card. *Do not enter hyphens or spaces in the number.*
4	Enter the *TRICARE as secondary* policyholder's last name, first name, and middle initial (separated by commas).
7	If the address of the patient is the same as the secondary policyholder, leave blank. Otherwise, enter the *TRICARE as secondary* policyholder's mailing address. *Do not enter the hyphen or a space for a 9-digit ZIP code. Do not enter the telephone number.*
9	Enter the primary policyholder's last name, first name, and middle initial (if known) separated by commas.
9a	Enter the primary policyholder's policy or group number.
9d	Enter the name of the primary policyholder's health insurance plan.
11, 11a–c	Leave blank.
11d	Enter an X in the YES box.
29	Enter the reimbursement amount received from the primary payer. Attach the remittance advice received from the primary payer to the CMS-1500 claim.

Courtesy of the Centers for Medicare & Medicaid Services, www.cms.gov.

Exercise 16.2 – Completing a TRICARE as Secondary CMS-1500 Claim

1. Obtain a blank claim by making a copy of the CMS-1500 claim form in Appendix I.
2. Refer to Figure 16-8, the John R. Neely case study.
3. Complete the TRICARE secondary claim for this case. Enter the patient account number as 16-3S.
4. Review the completed claim to be sure all required blocks are properly completed. Refer to Figure 16-9.

Case Study

ERIN A. HELPER, M.D.
101 Medic Drive, Anywhere, NY 12345-9874
(101) 111-1234 (Office) • (101) 111-9292 (Fax)
EIN: 11-1234523
NPI: 1234567890

PATIENT INFORMATION:

Name:	John R. Neely
Address:	1 Military Drive
City:	Nowhere
State:	NY
Zip Code:	12345-1234
Telephone:	(101) 111-9941
Sex:	M
Date of Birth:	10-25-1945
Occupation:	Retired Navy Captain
Employer:	
Spouse's Employer:	

INSURANCE INFORMATION:

Patient Number:	16-3
Place of Service:	Office
Primary Insurance Plan:	BlueCross BlueShield
Primary Insurance Plan ID #:	WXY7031
Policy #:	AS101
Primary Policyholder:	Janet B. Neely
Policyholder Date of Birth:	09-09-1945
Employer:	State College
Relationship to Patient:	Spouse
Secondary Insurance Plan:	TRICARE Select
Secondary Insurance Plan ID #:	001 06 7019
Secondary Policyholder:	John R. Neely

Patient Status   ☒ Married   ☐ Divorced   ☐ Single   ☐ Student

DIAGNOSIS INFORMATION

Diagnosis	Code	Diagnosis	Code
1. Abnormal ECG	R94.31	5.	
2. Coronary artery disease, native vessel	I25.10	6.	
3. Family history of heart disease	Z82.49	7.	
4.		8.	

PROCEDURE INFORMATION

Description of Procedure or Service	Date	Code	Charge
1. Established patient office visit, level III	03-10-YY	99213	75.00
2. ECG, 12-lead with interpretation and report	03-10-YY	93000	60.00
3.			
4.			

SPECIAL NOTES: Schedule stress test for tomorrow. BCBS paid $80 on claim.

FIGURE 16-8 John R. Neely case study.

REMITTANCE ADVICE ATTACHED

HEALTH INSURANCE CLAIM FORM

APPROVED BY NATIONAL UNIFORM CLAIM COMMITTEE (NUCC) 02/12

| | PICA | | | | | | | | | PICA | |

1. MEDICARE ☐ (Medicare#) MEDICAID ☐ (Medicaid#) TRICARE ☒ (ID#/DoD#) CHAMPVA ☐ (Member ID#) GROUP HEALTH PLAN ☐ (ID#) FECA BLKLUNG ☐ (ID#) OTHER ☐ (ID#)   **1a. INSURED'S I.D. NUMBER** (For Program in Item 1)
001067019

2. PATIENT'S NAME (Last Name, First Name, Middle Initial)
NEELY, JOHN, R

3. PATIENT'S BIRTH DATE MM 10 DD 25 YY 1945   **SEX** M ☒ F ☐

4. INSURED'S NAME (Last Name, First Name, Middle Initial)
NEELY, JOHN, R

5. PATIENT'S ADDRESS (No., Street)
1 MILITARY DRIVE

6. PATIENT RELATIONSHIP TO INSURED
Self ☐ Spouse ☒ Child ☐ Other ☐

7. INSURED'S ADDRESS (No., Street)

CITY NOWHERE   **STATE** NY

8. RESERVED FOR NUCC USE

CITY   **STATE**

ZIP CODE 123451234   **TELEPHONE (Include Area Code)** ( )

ZIP CODE   **TELEPHONE (Include Area Code)** ( )

9. OTHER INSURED'S NAME (Last Name, First Name, Middle Initial)
NEELY, JANET, B

10. IS PATIENT'S CONDITION RELATED TO:

11. INSURED'S POLICY GROUP OR FECA NUMBER

a. OTHER INSURED'S POLICY OR GROUP NUMBER
AS101

a. EMPLOYMENT? (Current or Previous) YES ☐ NO ☒

a. INSURED'S DATE OF BIRTH MM DD YY   **SEX** M ☐ F ☐

b. RESERVED FOR NUCC USE

b. AUTO ACCIDENT? YES ☐ NO ☒   **PLACE (State)**

b. OTHER CLAIM ID (Designated by NUCC)

c. RESERVED FOR NUCC USE

c. OTHER ACCIDENT? YES ☐ NO ☒

c. INSURANCE PLAN NAME OR PROGRAM NAME

d. INSURANCE PLAN NAME OR PROGRAM NAME
BLUECROSS BLUESHIELD

10d. CLAIM CODES (Designated by NUCC)

d. IS THERE ANOTHER HEALTH BENEFIT PLAN?
☒ YES ☐ NO   *If yes,* complete items 9, 9a, and 9d.

READ BACK OF FORM BEFORE COMPLETING & SIGNING THIS FORM.
12. PATIENT'S OR AUTHORIZED PERSON'S SIGNATURE I authorize the release of any medical or other information necessary to process this claim. I also request payment of government benefits either to myself or to the party who accepts assignment below.

SIGNED **SIGNATURE ON FILE**   DATE

13. INSURED'S OR AUTHORIZED PERSON'S SIGNATURE I authorize payment of medical benefits to the undersigned physician or supplier for services described below.

SIGNED **SIGNATURE ON FILE**

14. DATE OF CURRENT ILLNESS, INJURY, or PREGNANCY (LMP) MM 03 DD 10 YY YY   QUAL. 431

15. OTHER DATE QUAL.   MM DD YY

16. DATES PATIENT UNABLE TO WORK IN CURRENT OCCUPATION FROM MM DD YY   TO MM DD YY

17. NAME OF REFERRING PROVIDER OR OTHER SOURCE
17a.
17b. NPI

18. HOSPITALIZATION DATES RELATED TO CURRENT SERVICES FROM MM DD YY   TO MM DD YY

19. ADDITIONAL CLAIM INFORMATION (Designated by NUCC)

20. OUTSIDE LAB? ☐ YES ☒ NO $ CHARGES

21. DIAGNOSIS OR NATURE OF ILLNESS OR INJURY Relate A-L to service line below (24E)   ICD Ind. 0

A. R9431   B. I2510   C. Z8249   D.
E.   F.   G.   H.
I.   J.   K.   L.

22. RESUBMISSION CODE   ORIGINAL REF. NO.

23. PRIOR AUTHORIZATION NUMBER

24. A. DATE(S) OF SERVICE From MM DD YY	To MM DD YY	B. PLACE OF SERVICE	C. EMG	D. PROCEDURES, SERVICES, OR SUPPLIES (Explain Unusual Circumstances) CPT/HCPCS MODIFIER	E. DIAGNOSIS POINTER	F. $ CHARGES	G. DAYS OR UNITS	H. EPSDT Family Plan	I. ID. QUAL.	J. RENDERING PROVIDER ID. #
1	03 10 YY		11		99213	ABC	75 00	1		NPI	
2	03 10 YY		11		93000	A	60 00	1		NPI	
3										NPI	
4										NPI	
5										NPI	
6										NPI	

25. FEDERAL TAX I.D. NUMBER SSN ☐ EIN ☒
111234523

26. PATIENT'S ACCOUNT NO.
16-3S

27. ACCEPT ASSIGNMENT? (For govt. claims, see back) ☒ YES ☐ NO

28. TOTAL CHARGE $ 135 00

29. AMOUNT PAID $ 80 00

30. Rsvd for NUCC Use

31. SIGNATURE OF PHYSICIAN OR SUPPLIER INCLUDING DEGREES OR CREDENTIALS (I certify that the statements on the reverse apply to this bill and are made a part thereof.)

ERIN A HELPER MD   MMDDYY
SIGNED   DATE

32. SERVICE FACILITY LOCATION INFORMATION
a. NPI   b.

33. BILLING PROVIDER INFO & PH # (101) 1111234
ERIN A HELPER MD
101 MEDIC DRIVE
ANYWHERE NY 123459874
a. 1234567890   b.

NUCC Instruction Manual available at: www.nucc.org   **PLEASE PRINT OR TYPE**

FIGURE 16-9 Completed TRICARE as secondary CMS-1500 claim for John R. Neely case study.

TRICARE and Supplemental Coverage Claims Instructions

When the patient has supplemental health coverage (e.g., BCBS) *in addition to TRICARE*, participating providers submit just one claim. Claims completion modifications (Table 16-4) are made to the TRICARE primary claim (Figure 16-10).

 NOTE:

Use these instructions when completing any claims associated with *Understanding Health Insurance*.

TABLE 16-4 Modifications to TRICARE primary CMS-1500 claims completion instructions when patient has supplemental health coverage (Refer to Table 16-3 for primary CMS-1500 claims completion instructions.)

Block	Instructions
1	Enter an X in the *TRICARE* and *OTHER* boxes.
9	Enter the supplemental policyholder's last name, first name, and middle initial (if known) separated by commas.
9a	Enter the supplemental policyholder's policy or group number.
9d	Enter the name of the supplemental policyholder's health insurance plan.
11, 11a–c	Leave blank.
11d	Enter an X in the YES box.
29–30	Leave blank.

Courtesy of the Centers for Medicare & Medicaid Services, www.cms.gov.

Exercise 16.3 – Completing a TRICARE Primary with Supplemental Coverage CMS-1500 Claim

1. Obtain a blank claim by making a copy of the CMS-1500 claim form in Appendix I.
2. Refer to the Mary S. Patient case study (Figure 16-6), and select the information needed from the case study and the following list to complete the claim:
   - Supplemental policyholder: Mary S. Patient
   - Supplemental policyholder policy number: 123456
   - Supplemental policyholder health insurance plan: Aetna
   - Patient's Account No. 16-2SUPP
3. Review the completed claim to be sure all required blocks are properly completed.
4. Compare your claim with the completed Mary S. Patient claim in Figure 16-10.

HEALTH INSURANCE CLAIM FORM

APPROVED BY NATIONAL UNIFORM CLAIM COMMITTEE (NUCC) 02/12

PICA		PICA

1.	MEDICARE	MEDICAID	TRICARE	CHAMPVA	GROUP HEALTH PLAN	FECA BLKLUNG	OTHER	1a. INSURED'S I.D. NUMBER (For Program in Item 1)
	(Medicare#)	(Medicaid#) [X]	(ID#/DoD#)	(Member ID#)	(ID#)	(ID#)	[X] (ID#)	101239945

2. PATIENT'S NAME (Last Name, First Name, Middle Initial)	3. PATIENT'S BIRTH DATE	SEX	4. INSURED'S NAME (Last Name, First Name, Middle Initial)
PATIENT, MARY, S	10 10 1957	M [ ] F [X]	PATIENT, JAMES, L

5. PATIENT'S ADDRESS (No., Street)	6. PATIENT RELATIONSHIP TO INSURED	7. INSURED'S ADDRESS (No., Street)
91 HOME STREET	Self [ ] Spouse [X] Child [ ] Other [ ]	DEPT 07 NAVAL STATION

CITY	STATE	8. RESERVED FOR NUCC USE	CITY	STATE
NOWHERE	NY		NOWHERE	NY

ZIP CODE	TELEPHONE (Include Area Code)	ZIP CODE	TELEPHONE (Include Area Code)
123671234	( )	123671234	( )

9. OTHER INSURED'S NAME (Last Name, First Name, Middle Initial)	10. IS PATIENT'S CONDITION RELATED TO:	11. INSURED'S POLICY GROUP OR FECA NUMBER
PATIENT, MARY, S		

a. OTHER INSURED'S POLICY OR GROUP NUMBER	a. EMPLOYMENT? (Current or Previous)	a. INSURED'S DATE OF BIRTH SEX
123456	YES [ ] [X] NO	MM DD YY M [ ] F [ ]

b. RESERVED FOR NUCC USE	b. AUTO ACCIDENT? PLACE (State)	b. OTHER CLAIM ID (Designated by NUCC)
	YES [ ] [X] NO	

c. RESERVED FOR NUCC USE	c. OTHER ACCIDENT?	c. INSURANCE PLAN NAME OR PROGRAM NAME
	YES [ ] [X] NO	

d. INSURANCE PLAN NAME OR PROGRAM NAME	10d. CLAIM CODES (Designated by NUCC)	d. IS THERE ANOTHER HEALTH BENEFIT PLAN?
AETNA		[X] YES [ ] NO If yes, complete items 9, 9a, and 9d.

READ BACK OF FORM BEFORE COMPLETING & SIGNING THIS FORM.

12. PATIENT'S OR AUTHORIZED PERSON'S SIGNATURE I authorize the release of any medical or other information necessary to process this claim. I also request payment of government benefits either to myself or to the party who accepts assignment below.

SIGNED **SIGNATURE ON FILE**   DATE

13. INSURED'S OR AUTHORIZED PERSON'S SIGNATURE I authorize payment of medical benefits to the undersigned physician or supplier for services described below.

SIGNED **SIGNATURE ON FILE**

14. DATE OF CURRENT ILLNESS, INJURY, or PREGNANCY (LMP)	15. OTHER DATE	16. DATES PATIENT UNABLE TO WORK IN CURRENT OCCUPATION
01 10 YY QUAL. 431	QUAL.	FROM TO

17. NAME OF REFERRING PROVIDER OR OTHER SOURCE	17a.	18. HOSPITALIZATION DATES RELATED TO CURRENT SERVICES
	17b. NPI	FROM TO

19. ADDITIONAL CLAIM INFORMATION (Designated by NUCC)	20. OUTSIDE LAB? $ CHARGES
	YES [ ] [X] NO

21. DIAGNOSIS OR NATURE OF ILLNESS OR INJURY Relate A-L to service line below (24E)   ICD Ind. **0**

A. S52502A	B. Y92009	C. W108XXA	D.
E.	F.	G.	H.
I.	J.	K.	L.

22. RESUBMISSION CODE   ORIGINAL REF. NO.

23. PRIOR AUTHORIZATION NUMBER

24. A. DATE(S) OF SERVICE From / To	B. PLACE OF SERVICE	C. EMG	D. PROCEDURES, SERVICES, OR SUPPLIES (Explain Unusual Circumstances) CPT/HCPCS MODIFIER	E. DIAGNOSIS POINTER	F. $ CHARGES	G. DAYS OR UNITS	H. EPSDT Family Plan	I. ID. QUAL.	J. RENDERING PROVIDER ID. #
1	01 10 YY	11		25605 LT	A	300 00	1		NPI	
2	01 10 YY	11		73110 LT	A	50 00	1		NPI	
3	01 10 YY	11		73090 LT	A	25 00	1		NPI	
4									NPI	
5									NPI	
6									NPI	

25. FEDERAL TAX I.D. NUMBER SSN EIN	26. PATIENT'S ACCOUNT NO.	27. ACCEPT ASSIGNMENT?	28. TOTAL CHARGE	29. AMOUNT PAID	30. Rsvd for NUCC Use
111234523 [X]	16-2SUPP	[X] YES [ ] NO	$ 375 00	$	

31. SIGNATURE OF PHYSICIAN OR SUPPLIER INCLUDING DEGREES OR CREDENTIALS (I certify that the statements on the reverse apply to this bill and are made a part thereof.)	32. SERVICE FACILITY LOCATION INFORMATION	33. BILLING PROVIDER INFO & PH # (101) 1111234
ERIN A HELPER MD MMDDYY SIGNED DATE	a. NPI b.	ERIN A HELPER MD 101 MEDIC DRIVE ANYWHERE NY 123459874 a. 1234567890 b.

NUCC Instruction Manual available at: www.nucc.org   **PLEASE PRINT OR TYPE**

FIGURE 16-10 Completed primary TRICARE with supplemental coverage CMS-1500 claim for Mary S. Patient case study.

Summary

TRICARE is a regionally managed health care program for active duty and retired military members, their qualified family members, and eligible survivors of deceased uniformed services members. CHAMPUS (now called TRICARE) was created as a benefit for dependents of personnel serving in the uniformed services.

TRICARE regions are managed by lead agent staff, who are responsible for the military health system in their region. Lead agents serve as a federal health care team to support the mission of the Military Health System (MHS), which is the entire health care system of the United States uniformed services. The Defense Health Agency (DHA) coordinates and administers the TRICARE program.

TRICARE options include TRICARE Prime and TRICARE Select. TRICARE beneficiaries who have other health insurance (OHI) that is primary to TRICARE must submit documentation (e.g., remittance advice) when submitting TRICARE claims. TRICARE is the secondary payer to civilian insurance plans, workers' compensation, liability insurance plans, and employer-sponsored HMO plans. TRICARE is the primary payer to Medicaid and TRICARE supplemental plans.

CHAMPVA is a health care benefits program for dependents of veterans who are rated by Veterans Affairs (VA) as having a total and permanent disability, survivors of veterans who died from VA-rated service-connected conditions or injuries, and survivors of veterans who died in the line of duty and not from misconduct.

When completing TRICARE CMS-1500 claims for exercises in the textbook, assignments in the workbook, and case studies in SimClaim™, the following special instructions apply:

- Blocks 9, 9a, and 9d—Complete if the TRICARE beneficiary has a secondary or supplemental plan; otherwise, leave blank.
- Block 14—Leave blank.
- Block 15—Leave blank.
- Block 16—Leave blank.
- Block 20—Enter an X in the NO box.
- Block 23—Leave blank.
- Block 24H through Block 24I—Leave blank.
- Block 26—Enter the case study number (e.g., 16-5). If the patient has TRICARE as secondary coverage, enter an *S* (for secondary) next to the number (on the secondary claim).
- Block 27—Enter an X in the YES box.
- Block 32—Enter the name and address of the MTF.
- When completing secondary claims, enter REMITTANCE ADVICE ATTACHED in the top margin of the CMS-1500 (to simulate the attachment of a primary payer's remittance advice with a claim submitted to a secondary payer).

Internet Links

CHAMPVA: Go to *www.va.gov*, scroll down and click on the Health Care link, click on the Family and caregiver health benefits link, and click on the CHAMPVA benefits link.

TRICARE manuals: *manuals.health.mil*

TRICARE Plans: Go to *www.tricare.mil*, hover over Plans & Eligibility, and click on Health Plans. Select a plan to learn more.

Review

Multiple Choice

Instructions: Select the most appropriate response.

1. The health care program for active duty military members and their qualified dependents is called
   a. CHAMPUS.
   b. CHAMPVA.
   c. MHS.
   d. TRICARE.

2. Commanders of selected military treatment facilities for TRICARE regions are called
   a. health care finders.
   b. lead agents.
   c. service centers.
   d. sponsors.

3. Which manages the TRICARE program?
   a. Defense Enrollment Eligibility Reporting System
   b. Defense Health Agency
   c. Military Health System
   d. Military Treatment Facility

4. Which provides information from a TRICARE Service Center about using TRICARE and also assists with other matters affecting access to health care?
   a. Customer service representative
   b. Health care finder
   c. Military health system nurse advice line
   d. Primary care manager

5. A critical pathway is the
   a. approval process obtained from a health care finder before certain specialty procedures are provided.
   b. decision-making tool used by providers to determine appropriate health care for specific clinical circumstances.
   c. mechanism for surveillance of fraud and abuse activities worldwide involving purchased care.
   d. sequence of activities that can normally be expected to result in the most cost-effective clinical course of treatment.

6. The managed care option that is similar to a civilian HMO is called TRICARE
   a. Extra.
   b. Prime.
   c. Select.
   d. Standard.

7. The self-managed, preferred provider network plan available in the United States is TRICARE
   a. Extra.
   b. Prime.
   c. Select.
   d. Standard.

8. TRICARE nonparticipating providers are subject to a limiting charge of _____ percent above the allowed TRICARE fee schedule for participating providers.
   a. 5
   b. 10
   c. 15
   d. 20

9. Which is a comprehensive health care program for which the Department of Veterans Affairs shares costs of covered health care services and supplies with eligible beneficiaries?
   a. CHAMPUS
   b. CHAMPVA
   c. Medicare
   d. TRICARE

10. Which is reported on a TRICARE CMS-1500 claim in Block 1a?
   a. DoD Benefit Number
   b. DoD Identification Number
   c. National Provider Identifier
   d. Social Security number

Chapter Outline

Federal and State Workers' Compensation
    Programs

Eligibility for Workers' Compensation
    Coverage

Classification and Billing of Workers'
    Compensation Cases

Workers' Compensation and Managed Care

Forms and Reports

Appeals and Adjudication

Fraud and Abuse

Workers' Compensation Billing Notes

Workers' Compensation Claims Instructions

Chapter Objectives

Upon successful completion of this chapter, you should be able to:

1. Define key terms related to workers' compensation.
2. Describe federal and state workers' compensation programs.
3. Determine eligibility requirements for workers' compensation coverage.
4. Explain how workers' compensation cases are classified and billed.
5. Explain how managed care applies to workers' compensation coverage.
6. Describe documentation requirements for workers' compensation forms and reports.
7. Define appeal and adjudication as they relate to workers' compensation.
8. State examples of workers' compensation fraud and abuse.
9. Describe workers' compensation billing notes when completing CMS-1500 claims.
10. Complete workers' compensation claims.

Key Terms

adjudication

arbitration

Black Lung Program

Coal Mine Workers'
    Compensation
    Program

Employees'
    Compensation
    Appeals Board (ECAB)

Energy Employees
    Occupational Illness
    Compensation
    Program (EEOICP)

Federal Employees'
    Compensation
    Act (FECA)
    Program

first report of injury

Longshore and
    Harbor Workers'
    Compensation
    Program (LHWCA)

material safety data
    sheet (MSDS)

Mine Safety and Health
Administration (MSHA)

Occupational Safety and
Health Administration
(OSHA)

Office of Workers'
Compensation
Programs (OWCP)

on-the-job injury

permanent disability

state compensation fund

state insurance fund

survivor benefits

temporary disability

vocational rehabilitation

workers' compensation
board

workers' compensation
commission

Introduction

Federal and state laws require employers to maintain workers' compensation coverage to meet minimum standards, covering a majority of employees for work-related illnesses and injuries (as long as the employee was not negligent in performing the assigned duties). Employees receive health care and monetary awards (if applicable), and dependents of workers killed on the job receive benefits. Workers' compensation laws also protect employers and fellow workers by limiting the award an injured employee can recover from an employer and by eliminating the liability of coworkers in most accidents. Federal workers' compensation statutes (laws) apply to federal employees or workers employed in a significant aspect of interstate commerce. Individual state workers' compensation laws establish comprehensive programs and apply to most employers. CMS-1500 claims completion instructions are included in this chapter.

 NOTE:

Claims completing instructions in this chapter cover the CMS-1500 claim for procedures and services provided in a physician or other qualified health care practitioner's office or clinic. Institutional claims contain autopopulated data that has been abstracted and coded from patient records by the health information management department *or* by an electronic health record (EHR) in hospitals, skilled nursing facilities, inpatient hospices, and home health care organizations. (*Chapter 11 of this textbook contains general UB-04 claims completion instructions*, along with examples and a review assignment.)

Federal and State Workers' Compensation Programs

Workers' compensation insurance provides weekly cash payments and reimburses health care costs for covered employees who develop a work-related illness or sustain an injury while on the job. It also provides payments to qualified dependents of a worker who dies from a compensable illness or injury.

Federal workers' compensation programs are administered by the Office of Workers' Compensation Programs (OWCP) for civilian employees of the U.S. government. State workers' compensation programs are administered by workers' compensation boards or commissions, departments of labor, and other entities, and each state has its own workers' compensation laws.

Federal Workers' Compensation Programs

The U.S. Department of Labor's (DOL) **Office of Workers' Compensation Programs (OWCP)** is the agency that administers disability compensation programs. These programs provide wage-replacement benefits, medical treatment, vocational rehabilitation, and other benefits to federal workers (or eligible dependents) who are injured at work or acquire an occupational disease. The four programs are:

- Coal Mine Workers' Compensation Program
- Energy Employees Occupational Illness Compensation Program
- Federal Employees' Compensation Program
- Longshore and Harbor Workers' Compensation Program

Coal Mine Workers' Compensation Program

The **Coal Mine Workers' Compensation Program** (or **Black Lung Program**), enacted as part of the *Black Lung Benefits Act*, provides compensation to coal miners who are totally disabled by pneumoconiosis arising out of coal mine employment and to survivors of coal miners whose deaths are attributable to the disease. Eligible miners are also provided with medical coverage for the treatment of lung diseases related to *pneumoconiosis*. The *Division of Coal Mine Workers' Compensation* administers and processes claims filed by coal miners (and their surviving dependents).

Energy Employees Occupational Illness Compensation Program

The **Energy Employees Occupational Illness Compensation Program (EEOICP)** provides compensation and medical benefits to eligible employees and former employees of the Department of Energy, its contractors and subcontractors, or to certain survivors of qualified workers. The EEOICPA has two parts:

- *Part B* covers current and former workers diagnosed with cancer, chronic beryllium disease, beryllium sensitivity, or silicosis, and whose illnesses were caused by exposure to radiation, beryllium, or silica. Eligible individuals have worked at a covered Department of Energy facility or for a covered Atomic Weapons Employer or Beryllium Vendor during a specific time period. Certain individuals awarded benefits by the Department of Justice under the Radiation Exposure Compensation Act (RECA) are also eligible for EEOICPA Part B benefits.

- *Part E* covers Department of Energy contractor or subcontractor employees whose occupational exposure to a toxic substance was a significant factor in causing, contributing to, or aggravating their claimed illness. Eligible individuals worked at a covered Department of Energy facility during a covered time period. Certain individuals awarded benefits by the Department of Justice under the Radiation Exposure Compensation Act (RECA) are also eligible for Part E EEOICPA benefits.

The federal *Department of Labor's Office of Workers' Compensation Programs (OWCP)* is responsible for adjudicating and administering claims filed by employees, former employees, or certain qualified survivors.

Federal Employees' Compensation Program

The **Federal Employees' Compensation Act (FECA) Program** provides compensation benefits to civilian employees of the United States for disability due to personal injury or disease sustained while in the performance of duty. The FECA program also provides for payment of benefits to dependents if a work-related injury or disease causes an employee's death. Benefits provided under the FECA program constitute the sole remedy against the United States for work-related injury or death. A Federal employee or surviving dependent is not entitled to sue the United States or recover damages for such injury or death under any other law.

Federal Employees' Compensation Act (FECA) claims are submitted to the Division of Federal Employees' Compensation (DFEC), *FECA Claims Administration*. The FECA Claims Administration adjudicates new claims for benefits, manages ongoing cases, pays medical expenses and compensation benefits to injured workers and survivors, and helps injured employees return to work when they are medically able to do so.

 NOTE:

In 2020, the FECA program provided almost $3 billion in benefits to more than 197,000 workers and survivors for work-related injuries or illnesses. Of these benefits payments, over $2 billion was for wage-loss compensation, $790 million for medical and rehabilitation services, and $140 million for death benefits payments to surviving dependents.

 NOTE:

Federal agencies reimburse FECA for workers' compensation expenses through an annual *budget chargeback process*, which transfers funds from a responsible federal agency's budget (e.g., U.S. Postal Service) to the DFEC.

Longshore and Harbor Workers' Compensation Program

The **Longshore and Harbor Workers' Compensation Program (LHWCA)** provides compensation, medical care, and vocational rehabilitation services to employees disabled from on-the-job injuries occurring on navigable waters of the United States or in adjoining areas customarily used in the loading, unloading, repairing, or building of a vessel. (Injuries include occupational diseases, hearing loss, and illnesses arising out of employment.) The LHWCA also provides survivor benefits to dependents if the work injury causes, or contributes to, the employee's death.

LHWCA program benefits are typically paid by self-insured employers or private insurance companies on the employer's behalf. The *Longshore and Harbor Workers' Compensation Program Claims Administration* adjudicates new claims for benefits and manages ongoing cases.

Federal Department of Labor Programs

The Federal Department of Labor manages the following programs designed to prevent work-related injuries and illnesses:

- Employees' Compensation Appeals Board (ECAB)
- Mine Safety and Health Administration (MSHA)
- Occupational Safety and Health Administration (OSHA)

Employees' Compensation Appeals Board

The **Employees' Compensation Appeals Board (ECAB)** impartially and expeditiously hears and decides cases on appeal from decisions of the Office of Workers' Compensation Programs (OWCP). Board decisions are made in accordance with its statutory mandate, based on a thorough review of the case record as compiled by the OWCP. Injured federal workers have the opportunity for a full evidentiary hearing with the OWCP's *Branch of Hearings and Review* prior to review of the case record by the Board.

Mine Safety and Health Administration

The U.S. Labor Department's **Mine Safety and Health Administration (MSHA)** carries out provisions of the *Federal Mine Safety and Health Act of 1977 (Mine Act)* as amended by the *Mine Improvement and New Emergency Response (MINER) Act of 2006*. MSHA works cooperatively with industry, labor, and other federal and state agencies to improve safety and health conditions for all miners in the United States. The goals are to prevent death, illness, and injury from mining and to promote safe and healthful workplaces.

 NOTE:

U.S. federal mine safety laws were first enacted in 1911 and have since become increasingly stronger, culminating in the 1977 law.

Occupational Safety and Health Administration

The *Occupational Safety and Health Act of 1970* created the **Occupational Safety and Health Administration (OSHA)** to ensure safe and healthful working conditions for workers. Its goals are to establish and enforce standards and to provide training, outreach, education and assistance. OSHA has special significance for those employed in health care because employers are required to obtain and retain manufacturers' **material safety data sheets (MSDS)**, or *safety data sheets (SDS)*, which contain information about chemical and hazardous substances used on site. Training employees in the safe handling of these substances is also required.

Health care workers who might come into contact with human blood and infectious materials must be provided specific training in their handling (including use of Standard Precautions) to avoid contamination. Health care workers who might be exposed to infectious materials must also be offered hepatitis B vaccinations.

 NOTE:

Most OSHA records are to be retained for *five years* following the end of the calendar year that the records cover (unless a state's OSHA retention requirements are stricter). OSHA standards also state that employee exposure records, employee medical records, and material data safety sheets (MDSS) (or safety data sheet [SDS]) must be retained for at least 30 years. (The best practice is to retain records for the duration of employment plus 30 years.) *Exposure* means that an employee was subjected to a toxic substance or harmful physical agent in the course of employment through any route of entry. For example, a health care practitioner who experiences a "needle stick" has been exposed to a toxic substance (e.g., bloodborne disease).

State Workers' Compensation Programs

Each state establishes a **workers' compensation board** (or **workers' compensation commission**), a state agency responsible for administering workers' compensation laws and handling appeals for denied claims or cases in which a worker feels compensation was too low. There are two types of state workers' compensation insurance funds:

- *Competitive state insurance fund* allows employers the option to purchase workers' compensation insurance from the state or private insurance company.

- *Monopolistic state insurance fund* requires employers to purchase workers' compensation insurance through the state insurance fund only.

 NOTE:

In New York State (NYS), the maximum weekly benefit was $905 in 2019 (ranking fifth lowest in the country). (*www.wcb.ny.gov*)

State workers' compensation legislation resulted in the following types of coverage:

- **State insurance fund** (or **state compensation fund**): A quasi-public agency that provides workers' compensation insurance coverage to private and public employers and acts as an agent in state workers' compensation cases involving state employees.

- *Self-insurance plans*: Employers with sufficient capital to qualify can self-insure, which means they are required to set aside a state-mandated percentage of capital funds to cover medical expenses, wage compensation, and other benefits (e.g., death benefit to an employee's dependents) payable to employees who develop on-the-job illnesses and incur injuries.

- *Commercial workers' compensation insurance*: Employers are permitted to purchase policies from commercial insurance companies that meet state mandates for workers' compensation coverage.

- *Combination programs*: Employers in some states are allowed to choose a combination of any of the above to comply with workers' compensation coverage requirements (e.g., companies with a majority of employees who are at high risk for injury participate in the State Insurance Fund but may purchase commercial insurance coverage for office workers).

 NOTE:

The *State Insurance Fund* (or *State Compensation Board*) must offer workers' compensation insurance to any employer requesting it, thereby making the fund an insurer of last resort for employers otherwise unable to obtain coverage.

Eligibility for Workers' Compensation Coverage

To qualify for workers' compensation benefits, the employee must be injured while working within the scope of the job description, be injured while performing a service required by the employer, or develop a disorder that can be directly linked to employment, such as asbestosis or mercury poisoning. In some states, coverage has been awarded for stress-related disorders to workers in certain high-stress occupations, including emergency services personnel, air traffic controllers, and persons involved in hostage situations at work.

The worker does not have to be physically on company property to qualify for workers' compensation. An **on-the-job injury** would include, for example, a medical assistant who is injured while picking up reports for the office at the local hospital or a worker who is making a trip to the bank to deposit checks. These both qualify as job-related assignments. An employee sent to a workshop in another state who falls during the workshop would also be eligible for compensation, but not if injured while sightseeing.

 NOTE:

In a workers' compensation case, no one party is determined to be at fault, and the amount a claimant receives is not decreased by proof of carelessness (nor increased by proof of employer's fault). A worker will lose the right to workers' compensation coverage if the injury resulted solely from intoxication from drugs or alcohol or from the intent to injure themself or someone else.

Classification and Billing of Workers' Compensation Cases

The classification of workers' compensation cases impacts eligibility for medical treatment, vocational rehabilitation, wage replacement, and survivor benefits. The billing of workers' compensation cases for medical services requires an oversight process that verifies work-related injuries and illnesses and resultant treatment.

Classification of Workers' Compensation Cases

The injured employee's health care provider determines the extent of the disability, and cash benefits are directly related to established disability classifications. Federal law mandates the following classifications of workers' compensation cases:

- Medical treatment
- Temporary disability
- Permanent disability
- Vocational rehabilitation
- Survivor benefits

 NOTE:

The term *disability* associated with the following classifications does not refer to *disability insurance (or benefits)*, which are temporary cash benefits paid to an eligible wage earner who is diagnosed with disabilities as the result of an off-the-job injury or illness. This concept was discussed in Chapter 12.

Medical Treatment

Medical treatment claims are the easiest to process because they are filed for minor illnesses or injuries that are treated by a health care provider. In these cases, the employee continues to work or returns to work within a few days.

Temporary Disability

Temporary disability claims cover health care treatment for illness and injuries, as well as payment for lost wages. *Temporary disability* is subclassified as:

- *Temporary total disability*, in which the employee's wage-earning capacity is totally lost, but only on a temporary basis
- *Temporary partial disability*, in which the employee's wage-earning capacity is partially lost, but only on a temporary basis

Permanent Disability

Permanent disability refers to an ill or injured employee's diminished capacity to return to work. In this case, a provider has determined that although the employee's illness or injury has stabilized, the employee has been permanently impaired. The employee is therefore unable to return to the position held prior to the illness or injury. Subclassifications include:

- *Permanent total disability*, in which the employee's wage-earning capacity is totally lost, and the disability is total. (There is no limit on the number of weeks payable, and an employee may continue to engage in business or employment if wages, combined with the weekly benefit, do not exceed the maximums established by law.)
- *Permanent partial disability*, in which part of the employee's wage-earning capacity is permanently lost, and the disability is partial. Benefits are payable as long as the partial disability exists, except in the following circumstances:

- *Schedule loss of use*, in which the employee has a loss of eyesight, hearing, or a part of the body or its use. Compensation is limited to a certain number of weeks, according to a schedule set by law.
- *Disfigurement*, in which serious and permanent disfigurement to the face, head, or neck may entitle the employee to compensation (up to a maximum benefit, depending on the date of the accident).

Vocational Rehabilitation

Vocational rehabilitation claims cover expenses for vocational retraining for both temporary and permanent disability cases. Vocational rehabilitation retrains an ill or injured employee for return to the workforce, although the employee may be incapable of resuming the position held prior to the illness or injury.

Survivor Benefits

Survivor benefits claims provide death benefits to eligible dependents. These benefit amounts are calculated according to the employee's earning capacity at the time of the illness or injury.

 NOTE:

Providers who treat established patients for work-related disorders should create a compensation file (separate from the established medical record). Caution must be used to ensure that treatment data, progress notes, diagnostic test reports, and other pertinent chart entries pertaining to non-work-related disorders or injuries are not combined with notes and reports covering work-related disorders.

Billing Workers' Compensation Cases

Providers are required to accept the workers' compensation-allowable fee as payment in full for covered services rendered on cases involving on-the-job illnesses and injuries. An adjustment to the patient's account must be made if the amount charged for the treatment is greater than the approved reimbursement for the treatment.

State compensation boards (or state compensation commissions) and insurance payers are entitled by law to review only history and treatment data pertaining to a patient's on-the-job injury.

> **Example:** Patient A has been treated for diabetes by their doctor for the past two years. The patient was then treated by the same doctor for a broken ankle after falling at their place of employment. The patient was told to return in five days for a check-up. Three days after the original treatment for the broken ankle, the patient was seen in the office for strep throat. The doctor also checks on the ankle. The treatment for the throat condition should be reported in the patient's medical record; the progress report on the broken ankle will be recorded in the workers' compensation record.

Out-of-State Treatment

Billing regulations vary from state to state. Contact the workers' compensation board (or workers' compensation commission) in the state where the injury occurred for billing instructions if an injured worker presents for treatment of a work-related injury that occurred in another state.

Workers' Compensation and Managed Care

Both employees and employers have benefited from incorporating managed care into workers' compensation programs, thereby improving the quality of medical benefits and services provided. For employers, managed care protects human resources and reduces workers' compensation costs. For employees, the benefits include:

- More comprehensive coverage, because states continue to eliminate exemptions under current law (e.g., small businesses and temporary workers)
- Expanded health care coverage if the injury or illness is work-related and the treatment or service is reasonable and necessary

- Provision of appropriate medical treatment to facilitate healing and promote prompt return to work (lack of treatment can result in increased permanent disability, greater wage replacement benefits, and higher total claim costs)

- Internal grievance and dispute resolution procedures involving the care and treatment provided by the workers' compensation program, along with an appeals process to the state workers' compensation agency

- Coordination of medical treatment and services with other services designed to get workers back to work (research by the Florida Division of Workers' Compensation suggests that managed care may reduce the time it takes an injured worker to return to work)

- No out-of-pocket costs for coverage or provision of medical services and treatment; cost/time limits do not apply when an injury or illness occurs

Forms and Reports

Providers who treat workers' compensation patients have unique paperwork requirements, which can be time-consuming to complete. To reduce the administrative burden and increase provider participation, many states require submission of the CMS-1500 claim (instead of time-consuming paperwork) because it is easy to use and provides the information needed to process a workers' compensation claim.

When workers' compensation requires the submission of special forms and reports, they are submitted as attachments to the CMS-1500 claim and typically include the following:

- First report of injury
- Progress reports

In addition, an intake form is often completed for each new workers' compensation patient who seeks care for a work-related injury or illness. The intake form facilitates the provision of appropriate health care services.

First Report of Injury Form

First report of injury forms are initial reports completed by the provider (e.g., physician) when the patient first seeks treatment for a work-related illness or injury (Figure 17-1). (New York State adopted the CMS-1500 in 2018, replacing it for many previously required forms such as the previously required medical reports, and copies of patient records would be requested by its workers' compensation board to review the work-related medical necessity for procedures and services provided.) This report must be completed in quadruplicate with one copy distributed to each of the following parties:

- State workers' compensation board (or state workers' compensation commission)
- Employer-designated compensation payer
- Ill or injured party's employer
- Patient's work-related injury chart

 NOTE:

> There is no patient signature line on the first report of injury form. The law says that when a patient requests treatment for a work-related injury or disorder, the patient has given consent for the submission of compensation claims and reports. The required state forms may be obtained from the state board/commission. Necessary forms may be obtained from the personnel office where the employee works or from the workers' compensation Federal District Office listed under the United States Government listings in the phone book.

The time limit for submitting this form varies from 24 hours to 14 calendar days, depending on state requirements. It is best to make a habit of completing the form immediately, thus ensuring that the form is filed on time and not overlooked.

EVERY QUESTION MUST BE ANSWERED AND FORM SIGNED

INSTRUCTIONS
1. Enter answers to ALL questions and submit original to the Workers' Compensation Board within 72 hours after first treatment.
2. BE SURE to forward to the Workers' Compensation Board PROGRESS REPORTS and FINAL REPORT upon discharge of patient.

WORKERS' COMPENSATION BOARD
100 Main St, Anywhere, NY 12345-1234
PHYSICIAN'S REPORT

This is   First Report ☐   Progress Report ☐   Final Report ☐

DO NOT WRITE IN THIS SPACE

WCC CLAIM #

EMPLOYER'S REPORT   Yes ☐   No ☐

| 1. Name of Injured Person: | Soc. Sec. No. | D.O.B. | Sex   M ☐ F ☐ |

2. Address: (No. and Street)   (City or Town)   (State)   (Zip Code)

3. Name and Address of Employer:

4. Date of Accident or Onset of Disease: Hour: A.M. ☐ P.M. ☐   5. Date Disability Began:

6. Patient's Description of Accident or Cause of Disease:

7. Medical Description of Injury or Disease:

8. Will Injury result in:
(a) Permanent defect? Yes ☐ No ☐ If so, what?   (b) Disfigurement? Yes ☐ No ☐

9. Causes, other than injury, contributing to patient's condition:

10. Is patient suffering from any disease of the heart, lungs, brain, kidneys, blood, vascular system or any other disabling condition not due to this accident? Explain.

11. Is there any history or evidence present of previous accident or disease? Explain.

12. Has normal recovery been delayed for any reason? Explain.

13. Date of first treatment: Who scheduled your services?

14. Describe treatment provided by you:

15. Were X-rays taken?   By whom? — (Name and Address of Facility)   Date:
Yes ☐ No ☐

16. X-ray diagnosis:

17. Was patient treated by anyone else?   By whom? — (Name and Address of Provider)   Date:
Yes ☐ No ☐

18. Was patient hospitalized?   Name and Address of Hospital   Date of Admission:
Yes ☐ No ☐   Date of Discharge:

19. Is further treatment needed?   For how long?   20. Patient was ☐ will be ☐ able to resume regular work on:
Yes ☐ No ☐   Patient was ☐ will be ☐ able to resume light work on:

21. If death ensued give date: 22. Remarks:

23. I am a qualified specialist in: I am a duly licensed Physician in the State of: I graduated from Medical School: (Name)   Year:

Date of this report: (Signed)

(This report must be signed by Physician.)

Address: Phone:

FIGURE 17-1 Sample First Report of Injury form to be completed by provider.

The first report of injury form requires some information that is not automatically furnished by a patient. When the patient tells you this was a work-related injury, it will be necessary to obtain the following information:

- Name and address of the present employer
- Name of the immediate supervisor
- Date and time of the accident or onset of the disease
- Site where the injury occurred
- Patient's description of the onset of the disorder; if the patient is claiming injury due to exposure to hazardous chemicals or compounds, these should be included in the patient's description of the problem

In addition, the patient's employer must be contacted to obtain the name and mailing address of the compensation payer. Ask for a faxed confirmation from the employer of the worker with the on-the-job injury. If the employer disputes the legitimacy of the claim, you should still file the first report of injury form. The employer must also file an injury report with the worker's compensation board (or workers' compensation commission).

Completing the First Report of Injury Form

The *physician* is responsible for completing the first report of injury form.

Item 1

Enter the employee's full name as shown on personnel files (last, first, middle). Enter the employee's Social Security number and date of birth (MMDDYYYY). Indicate the employee's sex by entering an X in the appropriate box.

Item 2

Enter the employee's complete home address. This is very important, as workers' compensation disability payments, when due, will be mailed to this address. An incorrect address will delay receipt.

Item 3

Enter the complete name and address of the employer.

Item 4

Enter the date (MMDDYYYY) on which the accident or onset of disease occurred. Enter the time of the day at which the accident or onset of disease occurred, and check the appropriate box to indicate A.M. or P.M.

 NOTE:

> The date of the claimed accident must be specific. For example, if an employee was lifting heavy boxes on Tuesday (11/6) and called in sick on Thursday (11/8) because of a sore back, the date that is entered in Item 4 is 11/6.

Item 5

Enter the last date the employee worked after having the accident. If no time was lost from work, enter STILL WORKING.

Item 6

Enter the employee's word-for-word description of the accident. A complete description of the accident is required. Attach an additional page if space provided on the first report of injury form is insufficient.

Item 7

Enter the description of the injury or disease. Explain the physical injuries or disease (e.g., laceration, fracture, or contusion). Enter the anatomic part(s) of the body that required medical attention. Be specific, and indicate the location of the injured part when necessary (e.g., left middle finger, right thumb, left shoulder). Enter the location and address where the accident occurred.

Items 8 through 12

Enter as appropriate.

Item 13

Enter the date (MMDDYYYY) the patient initially received services and/or treatment.

Items 14 through 19

Enter as appropriate.

Item 20

Enter an X in the appropriate box.

Item 21

If the employee died as a result of the injury sustained, enter the date of death (MMDDYYYY). Notify the appropriate state agency immediately upon the work-related death of an employee.

Item 22

Enter additional information of value that was not previously documented on the form.

Item 23

Enter the physician's specialty (e.g., internal medicine), the state in which the physician is licensed, and the name of the medical school from which the physician graduated, along with the year of graduation (YYYY).

Be sure the physician or other health care provider dates (MMDDYYYY) and personally signs the report. Enter the physician's office address and telephone number.

Progress Reports

A detailed narrative progress/supplemental report (Figure 17-2) document any significant change in the worker's medical or disability status. This report should document:

- Patient's name and compensation file/case number
- Treatment and progress report
- Work status at the present time
- Statement of further treatment needed
- Estimate of the future status with regard to work or permanent loss or disability
- Copies of substantiating x-ray, laboratory, or consultation reports

The physician should *personally sign* the original and all photocopies of these reports. No patient signature is required for the release of any report to the compensation payer or commission/board. These reports should be generated in duplicate because:

- One copy is sent to the compensation payer.
- One copy is retained in the patient's file.

The physician is required to answer all requests for further information sent from the compensation payer or the commission/board. Acknowledgment of receipt of a claim will be made by the payer or the commission/board. This acknowledgment will contain the file or case number assigned to the claim. This file/claim number should be written on all further correspondence forwarded to the employer, the payer, the commission/board, and, of course, on all billings sent to the payer.

Appeals and Adjudication

When a workers' compensation claim is denied, the employee (or eligible dependents) can appeal the denial to the state Workers' Compensation Board (or Workers' Compensation Commission) and undergo a process called **adjudication**, a judicial dispute resolution process in which an appeals board makes a final determination.

Employee Name (First, Middle, Last)	Workers' Compensation #: _____
	Social Security Number: _____
Name of Employer:	Date of Injury: _____
	Disability Date: _____

Type of Report   ☐ Initial   ☐ Supplement   ☐ Final   ☐ Reopened

Treatment Now Being Administered:

Diagnosis:

Patient is under my care.	☐ Yes ☐ No	If no, care was transferred to: _____
Patient is totally disabled.	☐ Yes ☐ No	Patient is partially disabled. ☐ Yes ☐ No
Patient is working.	☐ Yes ☐ No	Date patient returned to work: _____
Patient may be able to return to work.	☐ Yes ☐ No	Date patient may be able to return to work: _____

Work Limitations:

☐ None: _____

☐ Cannot Work: _____

☐ Light Work: _____

☐ Weightlifting Limit: _____

Present Condition:

☐ Improved: _____

☐ Unchanged: _____

☐ Worsening: _____

Anticipated Date of Maximum Medical Improvement or Discharge:

☐ Weeks: _____

☐ Months: _____

☐ Specific Date: _____

☐ Undetermined: _____

Signature of Provider: _____   **EIN:** _____

FIGURE 17-2 Sample workers' compensation narrative progress (supplemental) report.

All applications for appeal should include supporting medical documentation of the claim when there is a dispute about medical issues. During the appeal process, involved parties will undergo a *deposition*, a legal proceeding during which a party answers questions under oath (but not in open court). If the appeal is successful, the board (commission) will notify the health care provider to submit a claim to the employer's compensation payer and refund payments made by the patient to cover medical expenses for the on-the-job illness or injury.

NOTE:

Adjudication is different from **arbitration**, a dispute resolution process in which a final determination is made by an impartial person who may not have judicial powers.

Fraud and Abuse

Workers' compensation fraud occurs when individuals knowingly obtain benefits for which they are not eligible (e.g., provider submits a false claim for workers' compensation coverage of patient treatment). *Workers' compensation abuse* occurs when the workers' compensation system is used in a way contrary to its intended purpose or to the law; fraud is a form of abuse. Penalties include fines and imprisonment, and most states offer a toll-free hotline to report fraud and abuse. Categories of fraud include:

- *Employer fraud:* Committed by an employer who misrepresents payroll amounts or employee classification or who attempts to avoid higher insurance risk by transferring employees to a new business entity that is rated in a lower-risk category

- *Employee fraud:* Committed when an employee lies or provides a false statement, intentionally fails to report income from work, or willfully misrepresents a physical condition to obtain benefits from the state compensation fund

- *Provider fraud:* Committed by health care providers and attorneys who inflate their bills for services or bill for treatment of non-work-related illnesses and/or injuries

Workers' Compensation Billing Notes

The following is a summary of the general nationwide billing information for workers' compensation claims. Local requirements will vary by state. Be sure to follow all the regulations established by your state commission.

Eligibility

For-profit company or corporation or state employees with work-related injuries are eligible for workers' compensation benefits. Coal miners, longshoremen, harbor workers, and all federal employees except those in the uniformed services with a work-related injury are eligible for federal compensation plans.

Identification Card

Some workers' compensation insurance plans issue identification cards (Figure 17-3), which are provided to employees who are eligible to receive workers' compensation coverage (because they are being treated for a work-related condition or injury).

Fiscal Agent

State Plans

Any one of the following can be designated the fiscal agent by state law and the corporation involved.

1. State insurance or compensation fund (not to be confused with the state's Workers' Compensation Board or Workers' Compensation Commission)
2. A third-party payer (e.g., commercial insurance company)
3. The employer's special company capital funds set aside for compensation cases

Federal Plans

Information may be obtained from the human resources officer at the agency where the patient is employed.

Underwriter

The federal or state government is the plan's underwriter, depending on the case.

**Brown Sweeney
Health Care Plan**

The Workers' Compensation Experts

EMPLOYER NAME: Green Consulting, Inc.
EMPLOYER POLICY #   12-3456789

To report a workers' compensation
injury, call (800) 555-1234

Payment processed in accordance with state's workers'
compensation treatment parameters and reimbursement rules
for submitted workers' compensation claims. Call Brown-
Sweeney Health Care Plan to obtain prior authorization for all
surgeries, medical imaging, durable medical equipment, and/or
any treatment that departs from treatment parameter rules.

**Submit all treatment authorization requests and completed
CMS-1500 claims to:** Brown-Sweeney Health Care Plan
P.O. Box 45392, Clay, NY 12041
(800) 555-1234

FIGURE 17-3 Sample workers' compensation identification card.

Forms and Claim Used

The forms used typically include:

- First report of injury form
- Narrative progress/supplemental reports
- CMS-1500 claim for professional services, depending on the state. (Some states also accept the UB-04 for institutional services.)

Claims Submission Deadline

The deadline for the first injury report is determined by state law. The deadline for submitting the claim for services performed will vary from payer to payer.

Deductible

There is no deductible for workers' compensation claims.

Copayment

There is no copayment for workers' compensation cases.

Premium

The employer pays all premiums.

Approved Fee Basis

The state compensation board or commission establishes a schedule of approved fees. Many states use a relative value study (RVS) unit-value scale; others have implemented managed care. Contact the state commission/board for information.

 NOTE:

For example, if CPT code 99204 is assigned a fee of $126.00 and RVS of 2.4, the reimbursement is $302.40. ($126 × 2.4 = $302.40)

Accept Assignment

All providers must accept the compensation payment as payment in full.

Special Handling

Contact the employer immediately when an injured worker presents for the first visit without a written or personal referral from the employer. Contact the workers' compensation board (workers' compensation commission) of the state where the work-related injury occurred if treatment is sought in another state.

No patient signature is needed on the first report of injury form, progress report, or billing forms. If an established patient seeks treatment of a work-related injury, a separate compensation chart and ledger/account must be established for the patient.

The first report of injury form requires a statement from the patient describing the circumstances and events surrounding the injury. Progress reports should be filed when there is any significant change in the patient's condition and when the patient is discharged. Prior authorization may be necessary for non-emergency treatment.

Private Payer Mistakenly Billed

When a patient fails to inform a provider that an illness or injury is work-related, the patient's primary payer (e.g., group health plan) may be mistakenly billed for services or procedures rendered. When the patient subsequently requests that the workers' compensation payer be billed instead, the workers' compensation claim may be denied. The patient must then initiate the appeal process with the workers' compensation payer (and the provider will be responsible for submitting appropriate documentation to support the workers' compensation claim). Any reimbursement paid by the primary payer must be returned.

Workers' Compensation Claims Instructions

Refer to Figures 17-4 and 17-5 as you study the claims instructions in Table 17-1.

NOTE:

- Refer to Chapter 11 for clarification of claims completion (e.g., entering names, mailing addresses, ICD-10-CM codes, diagnosis pointer letters, NPI, and so on).
- Use these instructions when completing any claims associated with *Understanding Health Insurance*.

TABLE 17-1 CMS-1500 claims completion instructions for workers' compensation claims

Block	Instructions
1	Enter an X in the *FECA* box *if the claim is submitted to the Division of Federal Employees' Compensation (DFEC), FECA Claims Administration.* Otherwise, enter an X in the OTHER box.
	Note: FECA is the abbreviation for the Federal Employee Compensation Act.
1a	Enter the patient's Social Security number. *Do not enter hyphens or spaces in the number.*
2	Enter the patient's last name, first name, and middle initial (separated by commas) (e.g., DOE, JANE, M).
3	Enter the patient's birth date as MM DD YYYY (with spaces). Enter an X in the appropriate box to indicate the patient's sex. If the patient's sex is unknown, leave blank.
4	Enter the name of the patient's employer.
5	Enter the patient's mailing address. Enter the street address on line 1, enter the city and state on line 2, and enter the five- or nine-digit zip code on line 3. *Do not enter the hyphen or a space for a 9-digit ZIP code. Do not enter the telephone number.*
	Note: If a state workers' compensation board or payer requires the patient's telephone number, enter it without a hyphen or space.

(continues)

TABLE 17-1 (continued)

Block	Instructions
6	Enter an X in the *Other* box.
7	Enter the employer's mailing address. Enter the street address on line 1, enter the city and state on line 2, and enter the five- or nine-digit zip code on line 3. *Do not enter the hyphen or a space for a 9-digit ZIP code. Do not enter the telephone number.* Note: If a state workers' compensation board or payer requires the employer's telephone number, enter it without a hyphen or space.
8	Leave blank.
9, 9a–9d	Leave blank.
10a	Enter an X in the YES box.
10b–c	Enter an X in the NO box.
10d	Leave blank. Note: For workers' compensation claims, duplicate claims or claims submitted as part of an appeal require entry of the appropriate condition code. The codes are: W2 (duplicate claim), W3 (level 1 appeal), W4 (level 2 appeal), and W5 (level 3 appeal).
11	Enter the nine-digit FECA number or the workers' compensation insurance policy number if a patient claims work-related condition(s) under the Federal Employees Compensation Act (FECA), the nine-digit FECA identifier assigned to the claim is entered. Otherwise, leave blank.
11a	Leave blank.
11b	Enter Y4 (as the reference code) in front of the vertical dotted line and the claim number assigned by the workers' compensation state fund or other payer in the space provided after the vertical dotted line. (Qualifier Y4 is entered to the left of the vertical, dotted line, and the agency claim identification number is entered to the right.)
11c	Enter the name of the workers' compensation state fund or other payer.
11d	Leave blank.
12–13	Leave blank.
14	Enter the date as MM DD YY (with spaces) to indicate when the patient first experienced signs or symptoms of the illness or injury. Enter the qualifier 431 (onset of current symptoms/illness or injury) to identify which date is being reported. *If the date is not documented in the patient's record, but the history indicates an appropriate date (e.g., three weeks ago), simply count back to the approximate date and enter it on the claim.* **Example:** For encounter date 06/08/YY, when the record documents that the patient was injured on the job three months ago, enter 03 08 YY in Block 14.
15	Enter the date as MM DD YY (with spaces) to indicate that a prior episode of the same or similar illness began, *if documented in the patient's record.* Otherwise, leave blank.
16	Enter dates as MM DD YY (with spaces) to indicate the period of time the patient was unable to work in his current occupation, *if documented in the patient's record.* Otherwise, leave blank.
17	If applicable, enter the first name, middle initial (if known), last name, and credentials of the professional who referred, ordered, or supervised health care service(s) or supply(ies) reported on the claim. *Do not enter any punctuation.* In front of the name, enter the applicable qualifier to identify which provider is being reported, as follows: DN (referring provider), DK (ordering provider), or DQ (supervising provider). Otherwise, leave blank.
17a	Leave blank.
17b	Enter the 10-digit national provider identifier (NPI) of the professional in Block 17. Otherwise, leave blank.
17a	Leave blank.
17b	Enter the 10-digit national provider identifier (NPI) of the professional in Block 17. Otherwise, leave blank.
18	Enter the admission date and discharge date as MM DD YY (with spaces) if the patient received inpatient services (e.g., hospital, skilled nursing facility). *If the patient has not been discharged at the time the claim is completed, leave the discharge date blank.* Otherwise, leave blank.

(continues)

TABLE 17-1 (continued)

Block	Instructions
19	Leave blank. Note: Some state workers' compensation boards or payers require Block 19 to be populated to provide additional information about the claim, using a string of characters that beings with *REF*. 19. ADDITIONAL CLAIM INFORMATION (Designated by NUCC) **REFX5985555–8B^^^0PGP^^^PWK09EAC00985621^^^NTEADD20220302** The text in Block 19 is interpreted as: • *Additional identifier indicator* REF • *State industrial accident provider number qualifier* X5 • *Workers' compensation board (WCB) authorization number* 985555-8B • *Three spaces* entered as ^^^ • *Osteopathic general practitioner WCB rating code* OPGP • *Three spaces* entered as ^^^ • *Supplemental claim information qualifier* PWK • *Progress report type code* 09 • *Service provided as part of an Expanded Access approval code* EA • *Electronic data interchange (EDI) transmission code* C00985621 • *Three spaces* entered as ^^^ • *Claim information qualifier* NTE • *Additional information qualifier* ADD • *Progress report date 20220302, which is March 2, 2022*
20	Enter an X in the NO box if all laboratory procedures reported on the claim were performed in the provider's office. Enter an X in the YES box if laboratory procedures reported on the claim were performed by an outside laboratory and billed to the provider. Enter the total amount charged by the outside laboratory in $ CHARGES, and enter the outside laboratory's name, mailing address, and NPI in Block 32. (Charges are entered *without punctuation*. For example, $1,100.00 is entered as 110000 below $ CHARGES.)
21	Enter the ICD-10-CM code for up to 12 diagnoses or conditions treated or medically managed during the encounter. Lines A through L in Block 21 will relate to CPT or HCPCS Level II service or procedure codes reported in Block 24E. In the *ICD Ind* (ICD indicator) box, enter 0 for ICD-10-CM.
22	Leave blank. This is reserved for resubmitted claims.
23	Enter any preauthorization number assigned by the workers' compensation payer. *Do not enter hyphens or spaces in the number*. Otherwise, leave blank.
24A	Enter the date the procedure or service was performed in the FROM column as MM DD YY (with spaces). Enter a date in the TO column *if the procedure or service was performed on consecutive days during a range of dates. Then, enter the number of consecutive days in Block 24G.* Note: The shaded area in each line is used to enter supplemental information to support reported services *if instructed by the payer to enter such information*. Data entry in Block 24 is limited to reporting six services. *Do not use the shaded lines to report additional services*. If additional services were provided, generate new CMS-1500 claim(s) to report the additional services.
24B	Enter the appropriate two-digit place-of-service (POS) code to identify the location where the reported procedure or service was performed.
24C	Leave blank.
24D	Enter the CPT or HCPCS Level II code and applicable required modifier(s) for procedures or services performed. *Separate the CPT/HCPCS code and first modifier with one space. Separate additional modifiers with one space each. Up to four modifiers can be entered.*

(continues)

TABLE 17-1 (continued)

Block	Instructions
24E	Enter the diagnosis pointer letter(s) from Block 21 that relate to the procedure or service performed on the date of service to justify medical necessity of procedures and services reported on the claim.
24F	Enter the fee charged for each reported procedure or service. *Do not enter commas, periods, or dollar signs. Do not enter negative amounts. Enter 00 in the cents area if the amount is a whole number.*
24G	Enter the number of days or units for procedures or services reported in Block 24D. *If just one procedure or service was reported in Block 24D, enter a 1 in Block 24G.*
24H–I	Leave blank.
24J	Enter the 10-digit NPI for the: • Provider who performed the service *if the provider is a member of a group practice* (Leave blank if the provider is a solo practitioner.) • Supervising provider *if the service was provided incident-to the service of a physician or nonphysician practitioner* **and** *the physician or practitioner who ordered the service did not supervise the provider* (Leave blank if the incident-to service was performed under the supervision of the physician or nonphysician practitioner.) • DMEPOS supplier or outside laboratory *if the physician submits the claim for services provided by the DMEPOS supplier or outside laboratory* (Leave blank if the DMEPOS supplier or outside laboratory submits the claim.) Otherwise, leave blank.
25	Enter the provider's Social Security number (SSN) or employer identification number (EIN). *Do not enter hyphens or spaces in the number.* Enter an X in the appropriate box to indicate which number is reported.
26	Enter the patient's account number as assigned by the provider.
27	Enter an X in the YES box to indicate that the provider agrees to accept assignment. Otherwise, enter an X in the NO box. (Some state workers' compensation boards require providers to accept assignment.)
28	Enter the total charges for services and/or procedures reported in Block 24. **Note:** If multiple claims are submitted for one patient because more than six procedures or services were reported, be sure the total charge reported on each claim accurately represents the total of the items on each submitted claim.
29–30	Leave blank.
31	Enter the provider's name and credential (e.g., MARY SMITH MD) and the date the claim was completed as MMDDYY (without spaces). *Do not enter any punctuation.*
32	Enter the name and address where procedures or services were provided *if at a location other than the provider's office or the patient's home, such as a hospital, outside laboratory facility, skilled nursing facility, or DMEPOS supplier.* Otherwise, leave blank. Enter the name on line 1, the address on line 2, and the city, state, and nine-digit zip code on line 3. *Do not enter the hyphen or a space for a 9-digit ZIP code.* **Note:** If Block 18 contains dates of service for inpatient care and/or Block 20 contains an X in the YES box, enter the name and address of the facility that provided services.
32a	Enter the 10-digit NPI of the facility entered in Block 32.
32b	Leave blank.
33	Enter the provider's *billing* name, address, and telephone number. Enter the phone number in the area next to the block title. *Do not enter parentheses for the area code.* Enter the name on line 1, enter the address on line 2, and enter the city, state, and nine-digit zip code on line 3. *Do not enter the hyphen or a space for a 9-digit ZIP code.*
33a	Enter the 10-digit NPI of the *billing* provider (e.g., solo practitioner) or group practice (e.g., clinic).
33b	Leave blank.

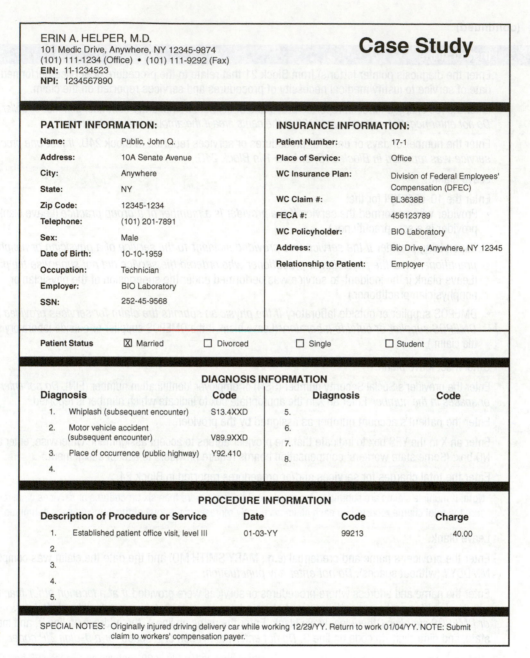

ERIN A. HELPER, M.D.
101 Medic Drive, Anywhere, NY 12345-9874
(101) 111-1234 (Office) • (101) 111-9292 (Fax)
EIN: 11-1234523
NPI: 1234567890

Case Study

PATIENT INFORMATION:

Name:	Public, John Q.
Address:	10A Senate Avenue
City:	Anywhere
State:	NY
Zip Code:	12345-1234
Telephone:	(101) 201-7891
Sex:	Male
Date of Birth:	10-10-1959
Occupation:	Technician
Employer:	BIO Laboratory
SSN:	252-45-9568

INSURANCE INFORMATION:

Patient Number:	17-1
Place of Service:	Office
WC Insurance Plan:	Division of Federal Employees' Compensation (DFEC)
WC Claim #:	BL3638B
FECA #:	456123789
WC Policyholder:	BIO Laboratory
Address:	Bio Drive, Anywhere, NY 12345
Relationship to Patient:	Employer

Patient Status	☒ Married	☐ Divorced	☐ Single	☐ Student

DIAGNOSIS INFORMATION

	Diagnosis	Code		Diagnosis	Code
1.	Whiplash (subsequent encounter)	S13.4XXD	5.		
2.	Motor vehicle accident (subsequent encounter)	V89.9XXD	6.		
3.	Place of occurrence (public highway)	Y92.410	7.		
4.			8.		

PROCEDURE INFORMATION

	Description of Procedure or Service	Date	Code	Charge
1.	Established patient office visit, level III	01-03-YY	99213	40.00
2.				
3.				
4.				
5.				

SPECIAL NOTES: Originally injured driving delivery car while working 12/29/YY. Return to work 01/04/YY. NOTE: Submit claim to workers' compensation payer.

FIGURE 17-4 John Q. Public case study.

NOTE:

ICD-10-CM categories S13 and V89 in the tabular list contain notes, which state that each code requires assignment of a seventh character. The "X" placeholder characters are included in the code so that the seventh character can be entered.

HEALTH INSURANCE CLAIM FORM

APPROVED BY NATIONAL UNIFORM CLAIM COMMITTEE (NUCC) 02/12

| | PICA | | | | | | | | | PICA | |

1. MEDICARE (Medicare#) ☐ MEDICAID (Medicaid#) ☐ TRICARE (ID#/DoD#) ☐ CHAMPVA (Member ID#) ☐ GROUP HEALTH PLAN (ID#) ☒ FECA BLKLUNG (ID#) ☐ OTHER (ID#) ☐

1a. INSURED'S I.D. NUMBER (For Program in Item 1)
252459568

2. PATIENT'S NAME (Last Name, First Name, Middle Initial)
PUBLIC, JOHN, Q

3. PATIENT'S BIRTH DATE MM 10 DD 10 YY 1959 SEX M ☒ F ☐

4. INSURED'S NAME (Last Name, First Name, Middle Initial)
BIO LABORATORY

5. PATIENT'S ADDRESS (No., Street)
10A SENATE AVENUE

6. PATIENT RELATIONSHIP TO INSURED
Self ☐ Spouse ☐ Child ☐ Other ☒

7. INSURED'S ADDRESS (No., Street)
BIO DRIVE

CITY **ANYWHERE** STATE **NY**

8. RESERVED FOR NUCC USE

CITY **ANYWHERE** STATE **NY**

ZIP CODE **123451234** TELEPHONE (Include Area Code) ( )

ZIP CODE **12345** TELEPHONE (Include Area Code) ( )

9. OTHER INSURED'S NAME (Last Name, First Name, Middle Initial)

10. IS PATIENT'S CONDITION RELATED TO:

11. INSURED'S POLICY GROUP OR FECA NUMBER
456123789

a. OTHER INSURED'S POLICY OR GROUP NUMBER

a. EMPLOYMENT? (Current or Previous) ☒ YES ☐ NO

a. INSURED'S DATE OF BIRTH MM DD YY SEX M ☐ F ☐

b. RESERVED FOR NUCC USE

b. AUTO ACCIDENT? ☒ YES ☐ NO PLACE (State) **NY**

b. OTHER CLAIM ID (Designated by NUCC)
Y4 BL3638B

c. RESERVED FOR NUCC USE

c. OTHER ACCIDENT? ☐ YES ☒ NO

c. INSURANCE PLAN NAME OR PROGRAM NAME
DFEC

d. INSURANCE PLAN NAME OR PROGRAM NAME

10d. CLAIM CODES (Designated by NUCC)

d. IS THERE ANOTHER HEALTH BENEFIT PLAN?
☐ YES ☒ NO If yes, complete items 9, 9a, and 9d.

READ BACK OF FORM BEFORE COMPLETING & SIGNING THIS FORM.

12. PATIENT'S OR AUTHORIZED PERSON'S SIGNATURE I authorize the release of any medical or other information necessary to process this claim. I also request payment of government benefits either to myself or to the party who accepts assignment below.

SIGNED _____ DATE _____

13. INSURED'S OR AUTHORIZED PERSON'S SIGNATURE I authorize payment of medical benefits to the undersigned physician or supplier for services described below.

SIGNED _____

14. DATE OF CURRENT ILLNESS, INJURY, or PREGNANCY (LMP) MM 12 DD 29 YY QUAL. **431**

15. OTHER DATE QUAL. MM DD YY

16. DATES PATIENT UNABLE TO WORK IN CURRENT OCCUPATION FROM MM 12 DD 29 YY TO MM 01 DD 03 YY

17. NAME OF REFERRING PROVIDER OR OTHER SOURCE
17a.
17b. NPI

18. HOSPITALIZATION DATES RELATED TO CURRENT SERVICES FROM MM DD YY TO MM DD YY

19. ADDITIONAL CLAIM INFORMATION (Designated by NUCC)

20. OUTSIDE LAB? ☐ YES ☒ NO $ CHARGES

21. DIAGNOSIS OR NATURE OF ILLNESS OR INJURY Relate A-L to service line below (24E) ICD Ind. **0**

A. **S134XXD** B. **V899XXD** C. **Y92410** D.
E. F. G. H.
I. J. K. L.

22. RESUBMISSION CODE ORIGINAL REF. NO.

23. PRIOR AUTHORIZATION NUMBER

24. A. DATE(S) OF SERVICE From MM DD YY	To MM DD YY	B. PLACE OF SERVICE	C. EMG	D. PROCEDURES, SERVICES, OR SUPPLIES (Explain Unusual Circumstances) CPT/HCPCS	MODIFIER	E. DIAGNOSIS POINTER	F. $ CHARGES	G. DAYS OR UNITS	H. EPSDT Family Plan	I. ID. QUAL.	J. RENDERING PROVIDER ID. #
1	01 03 YY		11		99213		A	40 00	1		NPI	
2											NPI	
3											NPI	
4											NPI	
5											NPI	
6											NPI	

25. FEDERAL TAX I.D. NUMBER SSN ☐ EIN ☒
111234523

26. PATIENT'S ACCOUNT NO.
17-1

27. ACCEPT ASSIGNMENT? (For govt. claims, see back) ☒ YES ☐ NO

28. TOTAL CHARGE $ **40 00**

29. AMOUNT PAID $

30. Rsvd for NUCC Use

31. SIGNATURE OF PHYSICIAN OR SUPPLIER INCLUDING DEGREES OR CREDENTIALS (I certify that the statements on the reverse apply to this bill and are made a part thereof.)

ERIN A HELPER MD
SIGNED DATE **MMDDYY**

32. SERVICE FACILITY LOCATION INFORMATION
a. NPI b.

33. BILLING PROVIDER INFO & PH # (**101**) **1111234**
ERIN A HELPER MD
101 MEDIC DRIVE
ANYWHERE NY 123459874
a. **1234567890** b.

NUCC Instruction Manual available at: www.nucc.org **PLEASE PRINT OR TYPE**

FIGURE 17-5 Completed workers' compensation as primary CMS-1500 claim for John Q. Public case study.

Exercise 17.1 – Completing a Workers' Compensation as Primary CMS-1500 Claim

1. Obtain a blank claim by making a copy of the CMS-1500 claim form in Appendix I.
2. Review the Mary S. Patient case study (Figure 17-6).
3. Select the information needed from the case study, and enter the required information on the claim.
4. Review the claim to be sure all required blocks are properly completed. Compare it to the completed claim in Figure 17-7.

ERIN A. HELPER, M.D.
101 Medic Drive, Anywhere, NY 12345-9874
(101) 111-1234 (Office) • (101) 111-9292 (Fax)
EIN: 11-1234523
NPI: 1234567890

Case Study

PATIENT INFORMATION:

Name:	Patient, Mary S.
Address:	91 Home Street
City:	Nowhere
State:	NY
Zip Code:	12367-1234
Telephone:	(101) 201-8989
Sex:	Female
Date of Birth:	10-10-1959
Occupation:	Clerk
Employer:	A1 Grocery
Address:	1 Main St, Nowhere, NY 12367
Telephone:	(101) 555-4561

INSURANCE INFORMATION:

Patient Number:	17-2
Place of Service:	Office
Primary Insurance Plan:	
Primary Insurance Plan ID #:	
Policy #:	
Primary Policyholder:	
Policyholder Date of Birth:	
Relationship to Patient:	
Workers' Compensation Plan:	State Insurance Fund
Workers' Compensation Claim #:	MSP9761
Patient's SSN:	467980123

Patient Status   ☒ Married   ☐ Divorced   ☐ Single   ☐ Student

DIAGNOSIS INFORMATION

Diagnosis	Code	Diagnosis	Code
1. Muscle spasms, trapezius	M62.830	5.	
2. Cervical osteoarthritis	M47.812	6.	
3. Accident at work (supermarket)	Y92.512	7.	
4. Work-related injury	Y99.0	8.	

PROCEDURE INFORMATION

Description of Procedure or Service	Date	Code	Charge
1. Office visit, established patient, level II	01-27-YY	99212-25	45.00
2. Trigger point injections (upper and medial trapezius muscles)	01-27-YY	20552	75.00
3.			
4.			
5.			

SPECIAL NOTES: Injured at work 01-20-YY. Return to work 01-22-YY.

FIGURE 17-6 Mary S. Patient case study.

HEALTH INSURANCE CLAIM FORM

APPROVED BY NATIONAL UNIFORM CLAIM COMMITTEE (NUCC) 02/12

[ ] [ ] PICA

1. MEDICARE	MEDICAID	TRICARE	CHAMPVA	GROUP HEALTH PLAN	FECA BLKLUNG	OTHER	1a. INSURED'S I.D. NUMBER (For Program in Item 1)
[ ] (Medicare#)	[ ] (Medicaid#)	[ ] (ID#/DoD#)	[ ] (Member ID#)	[ ] (ID#)	[ ] (ID#)	[X] (ID#)	467980123

2. PATIENT'S NAME (Last Name, First Name, Middle Initial)	3. PATIENT'S BIRTH DATE MM DD YY SEX	4. INSURED'S NAME (Last Name, First Name, Middle Initial)
PATIENT, MARY, S	10 10 1959 M [ ] F [X]	A1 GROCERY

5. PATIENT'S ADDRESS (No., Street)	6. PATIENT RELATIONSHIP TO INSURED	7. INSURED'S ADDRESS (No., Street)
91 HOME STREET	Self [ ] Spouse [ ] Child [ ] Other [X]	1 MAIN ST

CITY	STATE	8. RESERVED FOR NUCC USE	CITY	STATE
NOWHERE	NY		NOWHERE	NY

ZIP CODE	TELEPHONE (Include Area Code)	ZIP CODE	TELEPHONE (Include Area Code)
123671234	( )	12367	( )

9. OTHER INSURED'S NAME (Last Name, First Name, Middle Initial)	10. IS PATIENT'S CONDITION RELATED TO:	11. INSURED'S POLICY GROUP OR FECA NUMBER

| a. OTHER INSURED'S POLICY OR GROUP NUMBER | a. EMPLOYMENT? (Current or Previous) [X] YES [ ] NO | a. INSURED'S DATE OF BIRTH MM DD YY   SEX   M [ ] F [ ] |

| b. RESERVED FOR NUCC USE | b. AUTO ACCIDENT? [ ] YES [X] NO   PLACE (State) | b. OTHER CLAIM ID (Designated by NUCC)   Y4 MSP9761 |

| c. RESERVED FOR NUCC USE | c. OTHER ACCIDENT? [ ] YES [X] NO | c. INSURANCE PLAN NAME OR PROGRAM NAME   STATE INSURANCE FUND |

| d. INSURANCE PLAN NAME OR PROGRAM NAME | 10d. CLAIM CODES (Designated by NUCC) | d. IS THERE ANOTHER HEALTH BENEFIT PLAN? [ ] YES [ ] NO   If yes, complete items 9, 9a, and 9d. |

READ BACK OF FORM BEFORE COMPLETING & SIGNING THIS FORM.

12. PATIENT'S OR AUTHORIZED PERSON'S SIGNATURE I authorize the release of any medical or other information necessary to process this claim. I also request payment of government benefits either to myself or to the party who accepts assignment below.

SIGNED _____ DATE _____

13. INSURED'S OR AUTHORIZED PERSON'S SIGNATURE I authorize payment of medical benefits to the undersigned physician or supplier for services described below.

SIGNED _____

14. DATE OF CURRENT ILLNESS, INJURY, or PREGNANCY (LMP) MM DD YY QUAL. 431	15. OTHER DATE QUAL. MM DD YY	16. DATES PATIENT UNABLE TO WORK IN CURRENT OCCUPATION FROM 01 20 YY TO 01 21 YY
01 20 YY		

17. NAME OF REFERRING PROVIDER OR OTHER SOURCE	17a.	18. HOSPITALIZATION DATES RELATED TO CURRENT SERVICES FROM MM DD YY TO MM DD YY
	17b. NPI	

| 19. ADDITIONAL CLAIM INFORMATION (Designated by NUCC) | 20. OUTSIDE LAB? [ ] YES [X] NO $ CHARGES |

21. DIAGNOSIS OR NATURE OF ILLNESS OR INJURY Relate A-L to service line below (24E)   ICD Ind. 0

A. M62830   B. M47812   C. Y92512   D. Y990
E. _____   F. _____   G. _____   H. _____
I. _____   J. _____   K. _____   L. _____

22. RESUBMISSION CODE	ORIGINAL REF. NO.

23. PRIOR AUTHORIZATION NUMBER

24. A. DATE(S) OF SERVICE From / To MM DD YY MM DD YY	B. PLACE OF SERVICE	C. EMG	D. PROCEDURES, SERVICES, OR SUPPLIES (Explain Unusual Circumstances) CPT/HCPCS MODIFIER	E. DIAGNOSIS POINTER	F. $ CHARGES	G. DAYS OR UNITS	H. EPSDT Family Plan	I. ID. QUAL.	J. RENDERING PROVIDER ID. #
1 01 27 YY	11		99212 25	A	45 00	1		NPI	
2 01 27 YY	11		20552	A	75 00	1		NPI	
3								NPI	
4								NPI	
5								NPI	
6								NPI	

25. FEDERAL TAX I.D. NUMBER SSN EIN	26. PATIENT'S ACCOUNT NO.	27. ACCEPT ASSIGNMENT? (For govt. claims, see back)	28. TOTAL CHARGE	29. AMOUNT PAID	30. Rsvd for NUCC Use
111234523 [ ] [X]	17-2	[X] YES [ ] NO	$ 120 00	$	

31. SIGNATURE OF PHYSICIAN OR SUPPLIER INCLUDING DEGREES OR CREDENTIALS (I certify that the statements on the reverse apply to this bill and are made a part thereof.)	32. SERVICE FACILITY LOCATION INFORMATION	33. BILLING PROVIDER INFO & PH # (101) 1111234
ERIN A HELPER MD MMDDYY SIGNED DATE	a. NPI b.	ERIN A HELPER MD 101 MEDIC DRIVE ANYWHERE NY 123459874 a. 1234567890 b.

NUCC Instruction Manual available at: www.nucc.org

PLEASE PRINT OR TYPE

FIGURE 17-7 Completed Mary S. Patient workers' compensation as primary CMS-1500 claim.

Summary

The U.S. DOL Office of Workers' Compensation Programs administers programs that provide wage-replacement benefits, medical treatment, vocational rehabilitation, and other benefits to federal workers (or eligible dependents) who are injured at work or who acquire an occupational disease. Federal programs include the Energy Employees Occupational Illness Compensation Program (EEOICP), Coal Mine Workers' Compensation Program, Federal Employees' Compensation Act (FECA) Program, Longshore and Harbor Workers' Compensation Program (LHWCA), Employees' Compensation Appeals Board (ECAB), Mine Safety and Health Administration (MSHA), and Occupational Safety and Health Administration (OSHA). State programs include the following types of coverage: State Insurance (or Compensation) Fund; employer self-insured programs; private, commercial workers' compensation programs; and combination programs.

To qualify for workers' compensation, employees must be injured while working within the scope of their job description, be injured while performing a service required by the employer, or contract an illness that can be directly linked to employment. Workers' compensation cases are classified as (1) medical claims with no disability, (2) temporary disability, (3) permanent disability, (4) vocational rehabilitation, and (5) death of the worker.

Providers are required to accept workers' compensation reimbursement as payment in full. Balance billing of patients is prohibited. Many workers' compensation programs incorporate managed care to improve the quality of medical benefits and services provided, as well as to control costs.

The first report of injury form is completed when the patient first seeks treatment for a work-related illness or injury. The report is filed in quadruplicate with a copy distributed to the State Workers' Compensation Board (or Workers' Compensation Commission), employer-designated compensation payer, ill or injured party's employer, and patient's work-related injury chart. When employers initially deny workers' compensation claims, the employee has the right to appeal the denial. Detailed narrative progress/supplemental reports document significant changes in the employee's medical or disability status.

When completing workers' compensation CMS-1500 claims for exercises in the textbook, assignments in the workbook, and case studies in SimClaim™, the following special instructions apply:

- Block 14—Review the case study to locate the date of the on-the-job illness or injury.
- Block 15—Review the case study to locate the date of any prior episode of the same or similar illness or injury.
- Block 16—Review the case study to locate the dates the patient was unable to work.
- Block 20—Enter an X in the NO box.
- Block 23—Leave blank.
- Block 26—Enter the case study number (e.g., 17-4).
- Blocks 29–30—Leave blank.
- Block 32—If Block 18 contains dates, enter the name and address of the responsible provider (e.g., hospital).

Internet Links

California Workers' Compensation Institute: *www.cwci.org*

Federal workers' compensation resources: Go to *www.dol.gov*, scroll to Topics, and click on the Workers' Compensation link.

Mine Safety and Health Administration: *www.msha.gov*

National Workers' Compensation: Go to *www.workerscompensation.com*, click on State Info, click on any state, and click on the State Rules & Statutes tab to locate its workers' compensation laws and regulations.

Occupational Safety and Health Administration: *www.osha.gov*

State Compensation Insurance Fund of California: *www.statefundca.com*

WCC | Workers Compensation Consultations: Go to *workcompconsultant.com*, hover over the DIY menu, and click on State Work Comp Laws. Click on any state to view whether purchase of private insurance is permitted (competitive state insurance fund) or through a state fund is required (monopolistic state insurance fund).

Review

Multiple Choice

Instructions: Select the most appropriate response.

1. The Office of Workers' Compensation Programs (OWCP) administers programs that provide
    a. medical treatment.
    b. vocational rehabilitation.
    c. wage replacement benefits.
    d. all of the above.

2. Which federal Department of Labor agency is responsible for adjudicating and administering claims filed by Department of Energy employees, former employees, and certain qualified survivors?
    a. Employees' Compensation Appeals Board
    b. Mine Safety and Health Administration
    c. Occupational Safety and Health Administration
    d. Office of Workers' Compensation Programs

3. Which is the federal Department of Labor agency that is mandated to work cooperatively with industry, labor, and other federal and state agencies to improve safety and health conditions for all miners in the United States?
    a. Coal Mine Workers' Compensation Program
    b. Federal Employment Liability Act
    c. Mine Safety and Health Administration
    d. Occupational Safety and Health Administration

4. Which adjudicates new claims for Federal Employees' Compensation Act program benefits?
    a. Administrative Review Board
    b. FECA Claims Administration
    c. Office of Federal Agency Programs
    d. Office of Workers' Compensation Programs

5. The Employees' Compensation Appeals Board (ECAB) hears and decides cases on appeal from decisions of the Office of Workers' Compensation Programs (OWCP) in an impartial and expeditious manner. Prior to review of the case record by the ECAB, injured federal workers have the opportunity for a full evidentiary hearing with the OWCB
    a. adjudication mediation.
    b. arbitration intercession.
    c. branch of hearings and review.
    d. claims administration.

6. Material safety data sheets
    a. list activities and programs associated with employment-related hazards.
    b. contain information about chemical and hazardous substances used on site.
    c. govern communication and evaluation of chemical hazards in the workplace.
    d. may not be produced about non-hazardous materials in the workplace.

7. A state workers' compensation board (or workers' compensation commission)
    a. administers workers' compensation laws and handles appeals for denied claims or cases in which a worker feels compensation was too low.
    b. establishes a state-mandated percentage of capital funds to cover employees who develop on-the-job illnesses and incur injuries.
    c. provides workers' compensation insurance coverage to private and public employers and acts as an agent in cases involving state employees.
    d. requires employers to purchase workers' compensation insurance through the state insurance fund only, which applies to all states.

8. Which situation qualifies an employee for workers' compensation coverage?
   a. Cindy Frasier administered an injection to a patient and experienced a needle puncture; this required immediate treatment at the hospital and follow-up treatment by Cindy's primary care provider.
   b. Jenny Baker traveled to the local hospital from work to have lunch with friends who work there; after eating lunch, Jenny suffered food poisoning and underwent emergency care.
   c. Peter Mills attended an out-of-state conference for which reimbursement of expenses was preapproved; while attending a concert one evening during the trip, Peter fell and suffered a fractured radius in his left leg.
   d. Sally Jones left the doctor's office and stopped at the bank to deposit the day's accounts receivable; thereafter, while on the way home, Sally was injured in a car accident.

9. The judicial dispute resolution process in which an appeals board makes a final determination is called
   a. adjudication.   b. intercession.   c. mediation.   d. negotiation.

10. Which is typically completed when the patient initially seeks treatment for a work-related illness or injury?
   a. Billing information notes
   b. First report of injury
   c. Material safety data sheet
   d. Progress report

11. Which covers health care treatment for illness and injuries, as well as payment for lost wages, when the employee's wage-earning capacity is totally lost, but only on a temporary basis?
   a. Permanent partial disability
   b. Permanent total disability
   c. Temporary partial disability
   d. Temporary total disability

12. Vocational rehabilitation claims cover expenses for vocational retraining for
   a. permanent disability cases only.
   b. temporary disability cases only.
   c. temporary and permanent disability cases.
   d. Veterans Health Administration cases.

13. For employers, incorporating managed care into workers' compensation programs
   a. expands employee health care coverage.
   b. improves quality of medical benefits.
   c. increases the number of services provided.
   d. protects human resources and reduces costs.

14. Workers' compensation fraud occurs when
   a. individuals knowingly obtain benefits for which they are not eligible.
   b. payroll amounts or employee classifications are reported to a payer.
   c. providers submit claims for services received by employees.
   d. state compensation funds pay out workers' compensation benefits.

15. When a claim for workers' compensation benefits is denied, the patient must
   a. initiate the appeal process.
   b. refund the workers' compensation payer.
   c. reimburse the provider out of pocket.
   d. submit the claim to the employers' group health plan.

APPENDIX

I

Forms

You are welcome to copy the following forms for use when completing exercises in the textbook and workbook:

- CMS-1500 claim (black and white form suitable for photocopying)
- UB-04 claim (black and white form suitable for photocopying)

 NOTE:

The CMS-1500 claim and the UB-04 claim can also be printed by accessing the Student Resources online. Sign up or sign in at www.cengage.com to search for and access this product and its online resources.

HEALTH INSURANCE CLAIM FORM

APPROVED BY NATIONAL UNIFORM CLAIM COMMITTEE (NUCC) 02/12

			PICA						PICA	

1. MEDICARE □ (Medicare#)   MEDICAID □ (Medicaid#)   TRICARE □ (ID#/DoD#)   CHAMPVA □ (Member ID#)   GROUP HEALTH PLAN □ (ID#)   FECA BLKLUNG □ (ID#)   OTHER □ (ID#)   **1a. INSURED'S I.D. NUMBER**   (For Program in Item 1)

2. PATIENT'S NAME (Last Name, First Name, Middle Initial)

3. PATIENT'S BIRTH DATE   MM   DD   YY   **SEX**   M □   F □

4. INSURED'S NAME (Last Name, First Name, Middle Initial)

5. PATIENT'S ADDRESS (No., Street)

6. PATIENT RELATIONSHIP TO INSURED   Self □   Spouse □   Child □   Other □

7. INSURED'S ADDRESS (No., Street)

CITY   STATE

8. RESERVED FOR NUCC USE

CITY   STATE

ZIP CODE   TELEPHONE (Include Area Code)   (   )

ZIP CODE   TELEPHONE (Include Area Code)   (   )

9. OTHER INSURED'S NAME (Last Name, First Name, Middle Initial)

10. IS PATIENT'S CONDITION RELATED TO:

11. INSURED'S POLICY GROUP OR FECA NUMBER

a. OTHER INSURED'S POLICY OR GROUP NUMBER

a. EMPLOYMENT? (Current or Previous)   YES □   NO □

a. INSURED'S DATE OF BIRTH   MM   DD   YY   **SEX**   M □   F □

b. RESERVED FOR NUCC USE

b. AUTO ACCIDENT?   YES □   NO □   PLACE (State)

b. OTHER CLAIM ID (Designated by NUCC)

c. RESERVED FOR NUCC USE

c. OTHER ACCIDENT?   YES □   NO □

c. INSURANCE PLAN NAME OR PROGRAM NAME

d. INSURANCE PLAN NAME OR PROGRAM NAME

10d. CLAIM CODES (Designated by NUCC)

d. IS THERE ANOTHER HEALTH BENEFIT PLAN?   YES □   NO □   *If yes,* complete items 9, 9a, and 9d.

READ BACK OF FORM BEFORE COMPLETING & SIGNING THIS FORM.
12. PATIENT'S OR AUTHORIZED PERSON'S SIGNATURE I authorize the release of any medical or other information necessary to process this claim. I also request payment of government benefits either to myself or to the party who accepts assignment below.

SIGNED _____   DATE _____

13. INSURED'S OR AUTHORIZED PERSON'S SIGNATURE I authorize payment of medical benefits to the undersigned physician or supplier for services described below.

SIGNED _____

14. DATE OF CURRENT ILLNESS, INJURY, or PREGNANCY (LMP)   MM   DD   YY   QUAL.

15. OTHER DATE   QUAL.   MM   DD   YY

16. DATES PATIENT UNABLE TO WORK IN CURRENT OCCUPATION   FROM   MM   DD   YY   TO   MM   DD   YY

17. NAME OF REFERRING PROVIDER OR OTHER SOURCE   17a.   17b. NPI

18. HOSPITALIZATION DATES RELATED TO CURRENT SERVICES   FROM   MM   DD   YY   TO   MM   DD   YY

19. ADDITIONAL CLAIM INFORMATION (Designated by NUCC)

20. OUTSIDE LAB?   YES □   NO □ $ CHARGES

21. DIAGNOSIS OR NATURE OF ILLNESS OR INJURY Relate A-L to service line below (24E)   ICD Ind. |

A. |_____   B. |_____   C. |_____   D. |_____
E. |_____   F. |_____   G. |_____   H. |_____
I. |_____   J. |_____   K. |_____   L. |_____

22. RESUBMISSION CODE   ORIGINAL REF. NO.

23. PRIOR AUTHORIZATION NUMBER

24. A. DATE(S) OF SERVICE						B. PLACE OF SERVICE	C. EMG	D. PROCEDURES, SERVICES, OR SUPPLIES (Explain Unusual Circumstances)		E. DIAGNOSIS POINTER	F. $ CHARGES	G. DAYS OR UNITS	H. EPSDT Family Plan	I. ID. QUAL.	J. RENDERING PROVIDER ID. #
	From			To					CPT/HCPCS	MODIFIER							
	MM	DD	YY	MM	DD	YY											
1															NPI	
2															NPI	
3															NPI	
4															NPI	
5															NPI	
6															NPI	

25. FEDERAL TAX I.D. NUMBER   SSN □   EIN □

26. PATIENT'S ACCOUNT NO.

27. ACCEPT ASSIGNMENT? (For govt. claims, see back)   YES □   NO □

28. TOTAL CHARGE $

29. AMOUNT PAID $

30. Rsvd for NUCC Use

31. SIGNATURE OF PHYSICIAN OR SUPPLIER INCLUDING DEGREES OR CREDENTIALS (I certify that the statements on the reverse apply to this bill and are made a part thereof.)

SIGNED _____   DATE _____

32. SERVICE FACILITY LOCATION INFORMATION

a. NPI   b.

33. BILLING PROVIDER INFO & PH # (   )

a. NPI   b.

PLEASE PRINT OR TYPE

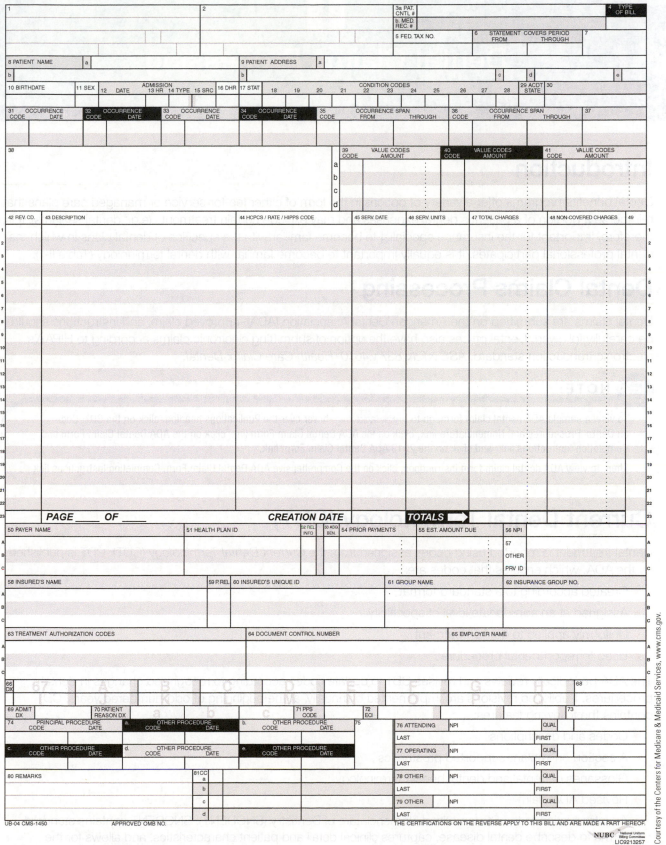

Introduction

Dental benefits programs offer a variety of options in the form of either fee-for-service or managed care plans that reimburse a portion of a patient's dental expenses and may exclude certain treatments (e.g., dental sealants). It is, therefore, important for the insurance specialist to become familiar with the specifics of dental plans in which the dental professional participates. It is equally important to become familiar with dental terminology (Table II-1).

Dental Claims Processing

Dental claims are submitted on the American Dental Association (ADA)–approved claim, and instructions should be carefully followed. Dental offices also have the option of submitting electronic claims according to HIPAA's electronic transaction standard, *ASC X12N 837 v.4010–Health Care Claim: Dental.*

 NOTE:

> To view a sample ADA dental claim form, go to www.ada.org, hover over the Publications heading, click on the CDT: Code on Dental Procedures and Nomenclature link, click on the ADA Dental Claim Form link, click on the ADA Dental Claim Form and Completion Instructions link, and click on the 2019 ADA Dental Claim Form link.
>
> Then, to view ADA dental claim form instructions, click on the Comprehensive ADA Dental Claim Form Completion Instructions link.

Current Dental Terminology (CDT)

Dental treatment is reported using codes assigned from the *Current Dental Terminology* (CDT). CDT is published by the ADA, which ensures that codes are:

- Created according to a standard format
- Assigned at an appropriate level of specificity
- Uniformly applied to dental treatment
- Used to report dental procedures

The ADA periodically reviews and revises CDT to update codes according to recognized changes in dental procedures. Published revisions are implemented biannually, at the beginning of odd-numbered years. CDT contains the following features:

- Codes and descriptions
- A section on implant-supported prosthetics
- Glossaries of dental and dental benefit terminology
- Revised ADA claim
- An introduction to the Systematized Nomenclature of Dentistry (SNODENT). SNODENT contains standard terms to describe dental disease, captures clinical detail and patient characteristics, and allows for the analysis of patient care services and outcomes

The *Current Dental Terminology (CDT)* is published by the ADA as a biannual revision. It classifies dental procedures and services.

Dental providers and ambulatory care settings use the CDT to report procedures and services. CDT also includes the Code on Dental Procedures and Nomenclature (Code), which contains instructions for use of the Code, questions and answers, ADA dental claim form completion instructions, and tooth numbering systems.

Example: Patient undergoes incision and drainage of intraoral soft tissue abscess. Report CDT code D7510.

 NOTE:

To view more about the CDT coding manual, go to www.ada.org, hover over the Publications heading, and click on the CDT: Code on Dental Procedures and Nomenclature link.

TABLE II-1 Glossary of common dental terms

Dental Term	Definition
abscess	acute or chronic, localized inflammation associated with tissue destruction
Academy of General Dentistry (AGD)	serves needs and represents interests of general dentists
Alliance for the Best Clinical Practices in Dentistry (ABCPD)	organization that encourages development of evidence-based prevention and treatment protocols through the process of organizing focused seminars
amalgam	alloy used in direct dental restorations; also called a *silver filling*
American Academy of Pediatric Dentistry (AAPD)	dedicated to improving and maintaining the oral health of infants, children, adolescents, and persons with special health care needs
American Academy of Periodontology (AAP)	dedicated to advancing the art and science of periodontics and improving the periodontal health of the public
American Dental Association (ADA)	promotes public health through commitment of member dentists to provide high-quality oral health care and promotes accessible oral health care
attrition	normal wearing away of the surface of a tooth from chewing
baby bottle tooth decay	severe decay in baby teeth due to sleeping with a bottle of milk or juice; natural sugars from drinks combine with bacteria in the mouth to produce acid that decays teeth
bitewing radiograph	x-rays of top and bottom molars and premolars
bruxism	involuntary clenching or grinding of teeth
calculus	hard deposit of mineralized material that adheres to teeth; also called *tartar* or *calcified plaque*
caries	tooth decay
crown	artificial covering of a tooth with metal, porcelain, or porcelain fused to metal
deciduous teeth	baby teeth or primary teeth
endentulous	having no teeth
endodontics	dental specialty concerned with treatment of the root and nerve of a tooth
fluoride	chemical compound that prevents cavities and makes tooth surface stronger
gingivitis	inflammation of gums surrounding teeth, caused by buildup of plaque or food
gum disease	*see* periodontitis
halitosis	bad breath
malocclusion	improper alignment of biting or chewing surfaces of upper and lower teeth
orthodontics	dental specialty concerned with straightening or moving misaligned teeth and/or jaws with braces and/or surgery
panoramic radiograph	single, large x-ray of jaws taken by a machine that rotates around the head
pedodontics	dental specialty concerned with treatment of children; also called *pediatric dentistry*

(continues)

TABLE II-1 (continued)

Dental Term	Definition
periodontics	dental specialty concerned with treatment of gums, tissue, and bone that supports the teeth
periodontitis	inflammation and loss of connective tissue of the supporting or surrounding structure of the teeth; also called *gum disease*
plaque	bacteria-containing substance that collects on the surface of teeth, which can cause decay and gum irritation when not removed by daily brushing and flossing
Prevent Abuse and Neglect through Dental Awareness (PANDA)	educational program that educates oral health professionals about child abuse and helps them learn how to diagnose and report potential abuse situations to appropriate authorities
prophylaxis	professional cleaning to remove plaque, calculus, and stains
prosthodontics	dental specialty concerned with restoration and/or replacement of missing teeth with artificial materials
radiograph	x-ray
scaling	removal of plaque, calculus, and stains from teeth
sealant	thin plastic material used to cover biting surface of a child's tooth
supernumerary tooth	extra tooth
tartar	*see* calculus

A

AAMA	American Association of Medical Assistants
A/B MAC	Part A/B Medicare administrative contractor
ABN	advance beneficiary notice of noncoverage
ACO	accountable care organization
ADR	additional documentation request
AHA	American Hospital Association
AHFS	American Hospital Formulary Service
AHIMA	American Health Information Management Association
AKS	Anti-Kickback Statute
ALJ	Administrative Law Judge
AMA	American Medical Association
AMBA	American Medical Billing Association
ANSI	American National Standards Institute
AOC	add-on code (edits)
APC	ambulatory payment classification
AP-DRG	All-Patient diagnosis-related group
APM	alternate payment model
APR-DRG	All-Patient Refined diagnosis-related group
ARRA	American Recovery and Reinvestment Act
ASC	Accredited Standards Committee
ASC	ambulatory surgical center
ASCA	Administrative Simplification Compliance Act
ASCQR	ambulatory surgical center quality reporting (program)

B

BBA	Balanced Budget Act of 1997
BCAC	beneficiary counseling and assistance coordinator
BCBS	BlueCross BlueShield
BCBSA	BlueCross and BlueShield Association
BIPA	Benefits Improvement and Protection Act of 2000
BPH	Basic Health Program

C

Ca	cancer or carcinoma
CAC	common access card
CAC	computer-aided coding
CAC	computer-assisted coding
CARC	claims adjustment reason code
CAT	computerized axial tomography
CCS	Certified Coding Specialist
CDAC	Clinical Data Abstracting Center
CDHP	consumer-directed health plan or consumer-driven health plan
CDHS	California Department of Health Services
CDI	clinical documentation improvement
CDI	clinical documentation integrity
CDM	charge description master
CDT	*Current Dental Terminology*
CERT	Comprehensive Error Rate Testing
CF	conversion factor
CfC	Conditions for Coverage
CHAMPUS	Civilian Health and Medical Program of the Uniformed Services
CHAMPVA	Civilian Health and Medical Program of Veterans Affairs
CHCBP	Continued Health Care Benefit Program
CHIP	Children's Health Insurance Program
CLIA	Clinical Laboratory Improvement Act
CMN	certificate of medical necessity
CMP	competitive medical plan
CMS	Centers for Medicare and Medicaid Services
CMS-1450	UB-04 claim used by institutional and other selected providers to bill payers
CMS-1500	Insurance claim used by noninstitutional providers and suppliers to bill payers
COB	coordination of benefits
COBRA	Consolidated Omnibus Budget Reconciliation Act
CoP	Conditions of Participation
copay	copayment
CPC	Certified professional coder
CPC+	Comprehensive Primary Care Plus
CPT	*Current Procedural Terminology*
CRI	CHAMPUS Reform Initiative
CSCP	customized sub-capitation plan
CSR	customer service representative
CSRA	community spouse resource allowance
CT	computed tomography

D

DC	direct contracting (payment model)
DCAO	debt collection assistance officer
DCG/HCC	diagnostic cost group hierarchical condition category (risk adjustment model)
DEERS	Defense Enrollment Eligibility Reporting System
DFEC	Division of Federal Employees' Compensation
DHP	Defense Health Program
DHHS	Department of Health and Human Services
DME	durable medical equipment
DME MAC	Durable Medical Equipment Medicare Administrative Contractor
DMEPOS	durable medical equipment, prosthetic and orthotic supplies
DNFB	discharged not final billed
DNFC	discharged not final coded
DoD	Department of Defense
DRG	diagnosis-related group
DSH	disproportionate share hospital
DSM	*Diagnostic and Statistical Manual*

E

E/M	evaluation and management
ECAB	Employees' Compensation Appeals Board
eCQM	electronic clinical quality measure
EDI	electronic data interchange
EEOICP	Energy Employees Occupational Illness Compensation Program
EFT	electronic funds transfer
EGHP	employer-sponsored group health plan
EHI	electronic health information
EHNAC	Electronic Healthcare Network Accreditation Commission
EHR	electronic health record
EIN	employer identification number
E/M	evaluation and management
EMC	electronic media claim
EMR	electronic medical record
EMTALA	Emergency Medical Treatment and Labor Act
EOB	explanation of benefits
EPO	exclusive provider organization
EPSDT	early and periodic screening, diagnostic, and treatment (services)
EQRO	external quality review organization
ERA	electronic remittance advice
ERISA	Employee Retirement Income Security Act of 1974
esMD	electronic submission of medical documentation system
ESRD	end-stage renal disease
ESRD PPS	end-stage renal disease prospective payment system
ESRD QIP	end-stage renal disease quality improvement program

F

FATHOM	First-look Analysis for Hospital Outlier Monitoring
FCA	False Claims Act
FCCA	Federal Claims Collection Act
FDCPA	Fair Debt Collection Practices Act
FECA	Federal Employment Compensation Act
FEHBP	Federal Employee Health Benefits Program
FELA	Federal Employment Liability Act
FEP	Federal Employee Program
FMAP	federal medical assistance percentage
FPL	federal poverty level
FQHC	Federally Qualified Health Center
FQHC PPS	Federally Qualified Health Centers Prospective Payment System
FR	*Federal Register*
FSA	flexible spending account
FSMA	Federal Services Modernization Act

G

GCPI	geographic cost practice index
GEM	general equivalence mapping
GEP	general enrollment period
GPWW	group practice without walls

H

HAC	hospital-acquired condition
HACRP	Hospital-Acquired Condition Reduction Program
HAVEN	Home Assessment Validation and Entry
HCERA	Health Care and Education Reconciliation Act
HCF	health care finder
HCPCS	Healthcare Common Procedure Coding System
HCQIA	Health Care Quality Improvement Act
HCRA	health care reimbursement account
HEAT	Health Care Fraud Prevention and Enforcement Action Team
HEDIS	Health Plan Employer Data and Information Set
HH PPS	home health prospective payment system
HHRG	home health resource group
HHVBP	home health value-based purchasing (model)
HICN	health insurance claim number
HIE	health information exchange
HINN	Hospital-Issued Notices of Noncoverage
HIPAA	Health Insurance Portability and Accountability Act
HIPDB	Health Integrity and Protection Data Base
HIPPS	health insurance prospective payment system (code set)
HIT	health information technology (standards)

HITECH	Health Information Technology for Economic and Clinical Health (Act)
HMO	health maintenance organization
HPMP	Hospital Payment Monitoring Program
HPSA	health personnel shortage area
HQRP	hospice quality reporting program
HRA	health reimbursement arrangement
HRRP	hospital readmissions reduction program
HSA	health savings account
HSSA	health savings security account

I

i2 Initiative	Investing in Innovations Initiative
ICD	*International Classification of Diseases*
ICD-9-CM	*International Classification of Diseases, 9th Revision, Clinical Modification*
ICD-10-CM	*International Classification of Diseases, 10th Revision, Clinical Modification*
ICD-10-PCS	*International Classification of Diseases, 10th Revision, Procedural Coding System*
ICD-11	*International Classification of Diseases, 11th Revision*
ICD-O-3	*International Classification of Diseases for Oncology, 3rd Revision*
ICHRA	Individual coverage health reimbursement arrangement
IDS	integrated delivery system
IEP	initial enrollment period
IHCIA	Indian Health Care Improvement Act
IHS	Indian Health Service
IME	indirect medical education (adjustment)
IMPACT	Improving Medicare Post-Acute Care Transformation Act of 2014
IPA	independent practice association (*or* individual practice association)
IPERIA	Improper Payments Elimination and Recovery Improvement Act
IPIA	Improper Payments Information Act of 2002
IPF PPS	inpatient psychiatric facility prospective payment system
IPFQR	inpatient psychiatric facility quality reporting (program)
IPIA	Improper Payments Information Act of 2002
IPO	integrated provider organization
IPPS	inpatient prospective payment system
IQR	inpatient quality reporting (hospital program)
IRC	integrated revenue cycle
IRE	independent review entity
IRF PPS	inpatient rehabilitation facility prospective payment system
IRVEN	Inpatient Rehabilitation Validation and Entry
IS	intensity of services
IS/SI	intensity of services/severity of illness

L

LA	lead agent
LC	limiting charge
LCD	local coverage determination
LGHP	large group health plan
LHWCA	Longshore and Harbor Workers' Compensation Act
LMRP	local medical review policy
LTCH PPS	long-term (acute) care hospital prospective payment system
LTCH QRP	long-term care hospital quality reporting program

M

MAC	Medicare administrative contractor
MAC	monitored anesthesia care
MACRA	Medicare Access and CHIP Reauthorization Act of 2015
MBI	Medicare beneficiary identifier
MCD	Medicare coverage database
MCE	Medicare code editor
MCR	Medicare contracting reform
MCHP	Maternal and Child Health Program
MCO	managed care organization
MCR	Medicare Contracting Reform (initiative)
MDC	major diagnostic category
MDS	Minimum Data Set
MedCAC	Medicare Evidence Development & Coverage Advisory Committee
MEDIC	Medicare Drug Integrity Contractors (program)
Medi-Medi	Medicare-Medicaid (crossover)
MEVS	Medicaid eligibility verification system
MFCU	Medicaid Fraud Control Unit
MHS	Military Health System
MIC	Medicaid integrity contractor
MIP	Medicaid Integrity Program
MIPPA	Medicare Improvement for Patients and Providers Act
MIPS	merit-based incentive payment system
MLN	Medicare Learning Network
MLTSS	managed long term services and supports
MMA	Medicare Prescription Drug, Improvement, and Modernization Act
MN	medically needy
MOON	Medicare Outpatient Observation Notice
MPFS	Medicare physician fee schedule
MR	medical review
MRI	magnetic resonance imaging
MSA	medical savings account
MS-DRGs	Medicare severity diagnosis-related groups
MSDS	Material Safety Data Sheet
MSHA	Mine Safety and Health Administration
MSI	Medicare Supplementary Insurance

MSN	Medicare Summary Notice
MSO	management service organization
MSP	Medicare Secondary Payer
MSSP	Medicare Shared Savings Program
MTF	military treatment facility
MUE	medically unlikely edit

N

NCA	national coverage analyses
NCCI	National Correct Coding Initiative (program)
NCD	national coverage determination
NCHS	National Center for Health Statistics
NCPCP	National Council for Prescription Drug Program (telecommunication standard)
NCQA	National Committee for Quality Assurance
NDC	*National Drug Code*
NEC	not elsewhere classifiable
NONC	Notices of Noncoverage
nonPAR	nonparticipating provider
NOS	not otherwise specified
NP	nurse practitioner
NPDB	National Practitioner Data Base
NPI	national provider identifier
NPP	Notice of Privacy Practices
NPPES	National Plan and Provider Enumeration System
NQF	National Quality Forum
NSF	national standard format
NUCC	National Uniform Claims Committee

O

OASIS	Outcomes and Assessment Information Set
OBRA	Omnibus Budget Reconciliation Act of 1981
OCE	outpatient code editor
OHI	other health insurance
OIG	Office of Inspector General
OMHA	Office of Medicare Hearings and Appeals
OPAP	outpatient pretreatment authorization plan
OPPS	outpatient prospective payment system
OQR	outpatient quality reporting (hospital program)
OSHA	Occupational Safety and Health Administration
OWCP	Office of Workers' Compensation Programs

P

P4P	pay-for-performance
PA	physician assistant
PAC	preadmission certification
PAC QRP	Post-acute care quality reporting programs
PACE	Program of All-Inclusive Care for the Elderly
PAHP	prepaid ambulatory health plan
PAI	patient assessment instrument
PAR	participating provider
PAT	preadmission testing

PATH	Physicians at Teaching Hospitals
PCA	progressive corrective action
PCCM	primary care case management
PCF	primary care first (payment model)
PCM	primary care manager
PCP	primary care provider
PDAC	Pricing, Data Analysis and Coding (Medicare contractor)
PDGM	patient-driven groupings model (home health)
PDMP	prescription drug monitoring program
PDPM	patient-driven payment method
PEPP	Payment Error Prevention Program
PEPPER	Program for Evaluating Payment Patterns Electronic Report
PERM	Payment Error Rate Measurement
PFFS	private fee-for-service plan
PHI	protected health information
PHO	physician-hospital organization
PHR	personal health record
PI	program integrity (office)
PI	promoting interoperability (programs)
PIHP	prepaid inpatient health plan
PIN	provider identification number
PIP DCG	principal inpatient diagnostic cost group
PlanID	national health plan identification number
POA	present on admission (indicator)
POR	problem-oriented record
POS	place of service
POS	point-of-service (plan)
PPA	preferred provider arrangement
PPACA	Patient Protection and Affordable Care Act
PPN	preferred provider network
PPO	preferred provider organization
PPS	prospective payment system
PQRI	physician quality review initiative
PRN	Provider Remittance Notice
PSC	program safeguard contract
PSO	provider-sponsored organization
PSO	patient safety organization
PSQIA	Patient Safety and Quality Improvement Act
PTP	procedure-to-procedure (code pair edits)

Q

QAPI	quality assessment and performance improvement (program)
QCDC	qualified clinical data registry
QDWI	qualified disabled and working individual
QI	qualifying individual (or quality improvement)
QIC	qualified independent contractor
QIO	quality improvement organization
QIP	quality improvement program (hospital)
QISMC	Quality Improvement System for Managed Care
QM	quality management

QMB	qualified Medicare beneficiary
QMBP	qualified Medicare beneficiary program
QPP	quality payment program
QPU	Quarterly Provider Update (published by CMS)
QWDI	qualified working disabled individual

R

RA	recovery auditor
RAC	recovery audit contractor (program)
RADV	risk adjustment data validation
RARC	remittance advice remark code
jRAVEN	Resident Assessment Validation and Entry (software)
RBRVS	resource-based relative value scale
RECA	Radiation Exposure Compensation Act
remit	remittance advice
REVS	recipient eligibility verification system
RHIO	rural health information organization
ROI	release of information
ROM	risk of mortality
RUG	resource utilization group
RVU	relative value unit

S

SEP	special enrollment period (Medicare)
SGR	sustainable growth rate
SHCP	Supplemental Health Care Program
SI	status indicator (or severity of illness)
SIA	service intensity add-on (payment)
SLMB	specified low-income Medicare beneficiary
SMRC	Supplemental Medical Review Contractor (program)
SNF	skilled nursing facility
SNF PPS	skilled nursing facility prospective payment system
SNF RM	Skilled Nursing Facility 30-Day All-Cause Readmission Measure
SNF VBP	skilled nursing facility value-based purchasing (program)
SNP	special needs plan
SOAP	subjective, objective, assessment, plan
SOI	severity of illness

SPR	standard paper remit
SSA	Social Security Administration
SSDI	Social Security Disability Insurance
SSI	Supplemental Security Income
SSN	Social Security number
SSO	second surgical opinion
SURS	surveillance and utilization review subsystem

T

TAMP	Transitional Assistance Management Program
TANF	Temporary Assistance for Needy Families (program)
TEFRA	Tax Equity and Fiscal Responsibility Act of 1982
TOS	type of service
TPA	third-party administrator
TPMS	total practice management software
TRHCA	Tax Relief and Health Care Act of 2006
TSC	TRICARE Service Center

U

UB-04	uniform bill implemented in 2004
UCR	usual, customary, and reasonable
UHDDS	Uniform Hospital Discharge Data Set
UM	utilization management
UOS	units of service
UPIC	Unified Program Integrity Contractor
URO	utilization review organization
USCDI	United States Core Data for Interoperability

V

VA	Veterans Affairs
VAN	value-added network
VBP	value-based purchasing (hospital program)
VM	value modifier

W

| WHO | World Health Organization |

Z

| ZPIC | Zone Program Integrity Contractor |

Bibliography

Books and Manuals

Accounts receivable management for the medical practice. (2009). Los Angeles, CA: Practice Management Information Corporation.

American Hospital Association. 2022. *Official UB-04 Data Specifications Manual 2022: Adopted by National Uniform Billing Committee (NUBC)*. Chicago, IL: American Hospital Association.

American Medical Association. (2021). *CPT 2022*. Chicago, IL.

Cunningham R. III and R.M. Cunningham, Jr. (1997). *The Blues: history of the Blue Cross and Blue Shield system*. Chicago, IL: Northern Illinois University Press.

French, L. L. (2018). *Administrative medical assisting*. Clifton Park, NY: Cengage Learning.

Green, M. (2023). *3-2-1 Code It!, 2022*. Clifton Park, NY: Cengage Learning.

National Uniform Claim Committee (NUCC). 2021. *1500 Health Insurance Claim Form reference instruction manual for form version 02/12*. Chicago, IL.

Optum (2022). *Coders' Desk Reference for ICD-10-CM*. Salt Lake City, UT: Author.

___ (2022) Coders' *Desk Reference for Procedures*. Salt Lake City, UT: Author.

___ (2022). *ICD-10-CM*. Salt Lake City, UT: Author.

___ (2022). *ICD-10-PCS*. Salt Lake City, UT: Author.

___ (2022). *HCPCS level II professional*. Salt Lake City, UT: Author.

___ (2022). *Uniform billing editor*. Salt Lake City, UT: Author.

Stuart, J.E. (1952). *The Blue Cross story: an informal biography of the voluntary nonprofit prepayment plan for hospital care*. Chicago, IL: Blue Cross Association.

Brochures and Bulletins

Choosing a Medigap policy: a guide to health insurance for people with Medicare. Washington, DC: Centers for Medicare and Medicaid Services.

CMS-1500 claim filing instructions. Indianapolis, IN: Anthem Blue Cross Blue Shield.

FEP service benefit plan brochure. Chicago, IL: Blue Cross and Blue Shield Federal Employees Program.

Health insurance, the history. Seattle, WA: Health Insurance Association of America.

HIPAA: Health care transformation to electronic communications (white paper). Bellevue, WA: Captaris, Inc.

Identifying and appealing health insurance claim payment issues. Chicago, IL: American Medical Association.

Medicare & you 2022. Washington, DC: Centers for Medicare and Medicaid Services.

Medicare and other health benefits: Your guide to who pays first. Washington, DC: Centers for Medicare and Medicaid Services.

Protecting yourself and Medicare from fraud. Washington, DC: Centers for Medicare and Medicaid Services.

The Blue Shield story: All of us helping each of us. Chicago, IL: Blue Cross and Blue Shield Association.

Understanding the choice you have in how you get your Medicare health care coverage. Washington, DC: Centers for Medicare and Medicaid Services.

Your guide to Medicare prescription drug coverage. Washington, DC: Centers for Medicare and Medicaid Services.

Your guide to Medicare's preventive services. Washington, DC: Centers for Medicare and Medicaid Services.

Your Medicare benefits. Washington, DC: Centers for Medicare and Medicaid Services.

Insurance Manuals

Basic manual for workers' compensation and employers liability insurance. Boca Raton, FL: National Council on Compensation Insurance.

CHAMPVA handbook. Denver, CO: VA Health Administration Center.

Medicare benefit policy manual. Washington, DC: Centers for Medicare and Medicaid Services.

Medicare claims processing manual. Washington, DC: Centers for Medicare and Medicaid Services.

Medicare contractor beneficiary and provider communications manual. Washington, DC: Centers for Medicare and Medicaid Services.

Medicare financial management manual. Washington, DC: Centers for Medicare and Medicaid Services.

Medicare general information, eligibility and entitlement manual. Washington, DC: Centers for Medicare and Medicaid Services.

Medicare integrity program manual. Washington, DC: Centers for Medicare and Medicaid Services.

Medicare managed care manual. Washington, DC: Centers for Medicare and Medicaid Services.

Medicare prescription drug benefit manual. Washington, DC: Centers for Medicare and Medicaid Services.

Medicare program integrity manual. Washington, DC: Centers for Medicare and Medicaid Services.

Medicare quality improvement organization manual. Washington, DC: Centers for Medicare and Medicaid Services.

Medicare secondary payer manual. Washington, DC: Centers for Medicare and Medicaid Services.

Office manual for health care professionals. Hartford, CT: Aetna.

Provider manual. Albany, NY: Empire BlueCross BlueShield.

State Medicaid manual. Washington, DC: Centers for Medicare and Medicaid Services.

TRICARE reimbursement manual. Aurora, CO: TRICARE Management Activity.

Journals, Newsmagazines, and Newsletters

AHA Coding Clinic for HCPCS Level II. Chicago, IL: American Hospital Association.

AHA Coding Clinic for ICD-10-CM and ICD-10-PCS. Chicago, IL: American Hospital Association.

CPT Assistant. Chicago, IL: American Medical Association.

Family Practice Management. Leawood, KS: American Academy of Family Physicians.

For the Record. Spring City, PA: Great Valley Publishing.

Healthcare Business Monthly. Salt Lake City, UT: American Association of Professional Coders.

Journal of Medical Practice Management®. Phoenix, MD: Greenbranch Publishing.

Journal of the American Health Information Management Association. Chicago, IL: American Health Information Management Association.

JustCoding News Inpatient and *JustCoding News Outpatient* (free e-newsletter). Marblehead, MA: HCPro, Inc.

Internet-Based References

learner.mlnlms.com—self-paced Medicare web-based training.

encoderpro.com—subscription service for CPT, HCPCS Level II, ICD-10-CM, and ICD-10-PCS.

hfma.org—Healthcare Financial Management Association (HFMA).

medicare.gov—official U.S. government site for Medicare.

med.noridianmedicare.com—Medicare fees and news (e.g., fee schedules, bulletins).

usa.gov—resource for locating federal government information on the Internet.

definitelyrealquotes.com—archive of historic quotes.

Software

EncoderPro.com. Salt Lake City, UT: Optum360.

SimClaim™. Clifton Park, NY: Cengage Learning.

Glossary

Note: Numbers in parentheses following a glossary term indicate the text chapter(s) in which that term appears as a key term.

21st Century Cures Act (5) 2016 legislation that requires submission of reports about Medicare Advantage and ESRD program risk adjustment model; prohibits *information blocking* of electronic health information (EHI) by actors, which include health care providers, health information exchanges (HIEs), health information networks, and health information technology (Health IT) vendors.

A

AAPC (1) professional association, previously known as the American Academy of Professional Coders, established to provide a national certification and credentialing process, to support the national and local membership by providing educational products and opportunities to networks, and to increase and promote national recognition and awareness of professional coding.

abuse (5) actions inconsistent with accepted, sound medical, business, or fiscal practices.

accept assignment (3) provider accepts as payment in full whatever is paid on the claim by the payer (except for any copayment and/or coinsurance amounts).

accountable care organization (ACO) (14) groups of physicians, hospitals, and other health care providers, such as DME suppliers, all of whom come together voluntarily to provide coordinated high-quality care to Medicare traditional fee-for-service patients and to control health care costs.

accounting of disclosures (5) HIPAA regulation that requires health care organizations to track medical information provided to third parties (e.g., attorneys, third-party payers, and Social Security disability offices) so that patients can be notified if there has been an inappropriate release of their medical information.

accounts payable (3) amount a business owes creditors and suppliers.

accounts receivable (3) amount owed to a business for services or goods provided.

accounts receivable aging report (4) shows the status (by date) of outstanding claims from each payer, as well as payments due from patients.

accounts receivable management (3) assists providers in the collection of appropriate reimbursement for services rendered; includes functions such as insurance verification/eligibility and preauthorization of services.

accreditation (2) voluntary process that a health care facility or organization (e.g., hospital or managed care plan) undergoes to demonstrate that it has met standards beyond those required by law.

accrual accounting (3) method that focuses on anticipated revenue and associated expenses; revenue earned and expenses billed are recorded even though third-party payer reimbursement has not been received and expenses have not been paid.

adjudication (17) judicial dispute resolution process in which an appeals board makes a final determination.

adjusted claim (15) payment correction resulting in additional payment(s) to the provider.

Administrative Simplification Compliance Act (ASCA) (11) implemented in October 2003 to prohibit payment of initial health care CMS-1500 claims that were not sent electronically, except in unusual situations (e.g., dental claims).

advance beneficiary notice of noncoverage (ABN) (14) document that acknowledges patient responsibility for payment if Medicare denies the claim.

advanced alternative payment models (Advanced APMs) (2) include new ways for CMS to reimburse health care providers for care provided to Medicare beneficiaries; providers who participate in an Advanced APM through Medicare Part B may earn an incentive payment for participating in the innovative payment model.

adverse effect (6) taking less of a medication than is prescribed by a provider or a manufacturer's instruction.

adverse selection (2) covering members who are sicker than the general population.

allowed charge (4) the maximum amount the payer will reimburse for each procedure or service, according to the patient's policy.

All-Patient diagnosis-related group (AP-DRG) (9) DRG system adapted for use by third-party payers to reimburse hospitals for inpatient care provided to *non*-Medicare beneficiaries (e.g., BlueCross BlueShield, commercial health plans, TRICARE); DRG assignment is based on intensity of resources.

All-Patient Refined diagnosis-related group (APR-DRG) (9) system that classifies patients according to reason for admission, severity of illness (SOI), and risk of mortality (ROM).

alternative payment models (APMs) (2) payment approach that includes incentive payments to provide high-quality and cost-efficient care; APMs can apply to a specific clinical condition, a care episode, or a population.

ambulance fee schedule (9) payment system for ambulance services provided to Medicare beneficiaries.

ambulatory payment classifications (APCs) (9) prospective payment system used to calculate reimbursement for outpatient care according to similar clinical characteristics and in terms of resources required.

ambulatory surgical center (ASC) (9) state-licensed, Medicare-certified supplier (not provider) of surgical health care services that must *accept assignment* on Medicare claims.

ambulatory surgical center payment system (9) uses the outpatient prospective payment system's relative payment weights as a guide for reimbursing ambulatory surgery centers.

Ambulatory Surgical Center Quality Reporting (ASCQR) Program (9) pay-for-reporting program that requires ambulatory surgical centers (ASCs) to meet administrative, data collection, reporting, and other program requirements, or receive a reduction of 2.0 percentage points in their annual payment update for failure to meet these program requirements.

Amendment to the HMO Act of 1973 (2) legislation that allowed federally qualified HMOs to permit members to occasionally use non-HMO physicians and be partially reimbursed.

American Association of Medical Assistants (AAMA) (1) enables medical assisting professionals to enhance and demonstrate the knowledge, skills, and professionalism required by employers and patients; as well as protect medical assistants' right to practice.

American Health Information Management Association (AHIMA) (1) founded in 1928 to improve the quality of medical records, and currently advances the health information management (HIM) profession toward an electronic and global environment, including implementation of ICD-10-CM and ICD-10-PCS in 2013.

American Medical Billing Association (AMBA) (1) provides industry and regulatory education and networking opportunities for members and offers the Certified Medical Reimbursement Specialist (CMRS) credential.

American Recovery and Reinvestment Act of 2009 (ARRA) (2) authorized an expenditure of $1.5 billion for grants for construction, renovation, and equipment, and for the acquisition of health information technology systems.

ANSI ASC X12N (4) an electronic format standard that uses a variable-length file format to process transactions for institutional, professional, dental, and drug claims.

ANSI ASC X12N 837 (5) electronic format supported for health care claim transactions.

ANSI ASC X12N 837I (11) standard format for submission of electronic claims for institutional health care services.

ANSI ASC X12N 837P (11) standard format for submission of electronic claims for professional health care services.

appeal (4) documented as a letter and signed by the provider, to explain why a claim should be reconsidered for payment.

arbitration (17) dispute-resolution process in which a final determination is made by an impartial person who may not have judicial powers.

assignment of benefits (3) the provider receives reimbursement directly from the payer.

audit (5) objective evaluation to determine the accuracy of submitted financial statements.

auditing process (10) review of patient records and CMS-1500 (or UB-04) claims to assess coding accuracy and whether documentation is complete.

authorization (5) document that provides official instruction, such as the customized document that gives covered entities permission to use specified protected health information (PHI) for specified purposes or to disclose PHI to a third party specified by the individual.

automobile insurance policy (12) contract between an individual and an insurance company whereby the individual pays a premium and, in exchange, the insurance company agrees to pay for specific car-related financial losses during the term of the policy; typically includes medical-payments coverage and personal injury protection (PIP) to reimburse health care expenses sustained as the result of injury from an automobile accident.

bad debt (4) accounts receivable that cannot be collected by the provider or a collection agency.

balance billing (9) billing beneficiaries for amounts not reimbursed by payers (not including copayments and coinsurance amounts); this practice is prohibited by Medicare regulations.

base period (12) period of time that usually covers 12 months and is divided into four consecutive quarters.

Basic Health Program (BPH) (16) health benefits coverage program for residents with low incomes who would otherwise be eligible to purchase coverage through the Health Insurance Marketplace; implemented by Affordable Care Act to give states the ability to provide more affordable coverage to residents with low incomes and improve continuity of care for people whose income fluctuates above and below Medicaid and CHIP income eligibility levels; states contract with one or more private insurance companies to provide coverage to eligible residents at affordable premiums.

BCBS preferred provider network (13) health care facilities, physicians, and other health care professionals that contract with BCBS to provide members with accessible, appropriate, cost-effective, and quality health care services.

benchmarking (2) practice that allows an entity to measure and compare its own data against that of other agencies and organizations for the purpose of continuous improvement (e.g., coding error rates).

beneficiary (4) the person eligible to receive health care benefits.

beneficiary counseling and assistance coordinator (BCAC) (16) individual available at a military treatment facility (MTF) to answer questions, help solve health care-related problems, and assist beneficiaries in obtaining medical care through TRICARE; was previously called *health benefits advisor (HBA)*.

benefit period (14) begins with the first day of inpatient hospitalization and ends when the Medicare patient has been out of the hospital for 60 consecutive days.

benign (6) not cancerous.

billing entity (11) the legal business name of the provider's practice.

birthday rule (3) determines coverage by primary and secondary policies when each parent subscribes to a different health insurance plan.

black box edits (5) nonpublished code edits, which were discontinued in 2000.

Black Lung Program (17) *see* Coal Mine Workers' Compensation Program.

BlueCard® (13) program that allows BCBS subscribers to receive local Blue Plan health care benefits while traveling or living outside of their plan's area, nationally, or in another country.

BlueCross BlueShield (BCBS) (13) independent and local BCBS companies that provide health plan coverage to Americans in all 50 states, the District of Columbia, and Puerto Rico; coverage is also provided to those who live, travel, and work internationally.

BlueCross BlueShield Association (BCBSA) (13) independent, community-based, locally operated BlueCross BlueShield plans that collectively provide health care coverage to more than 100 million Americans.

BlueCross BlueShield Global® (13) health care plans for employers, individuals, and students who live, work, and travel internationally; it represents a collaboration with *Bupa Global*, which offers international health insurance plans to individuals at home or who live, study, travel, or work abroad, including expatriates.

bonding insurance (1) an insurance agreement that guarantees repayment for financial losses resulting from the act or failure to act of an employee. It protects the financial operations of the employer.

breach notification (5) HIPAA rule that requires covered entities and their business associates to provide patient notification following a breach of unsecured protected health information.

breach of confidentiality (5) unauthorized release of patient information to a third party.

bundled payment (9) predetermined payment amount for all services provided during an episode-of-care.

business liability insurance (1) protects business assets and covers the cost of lawsuits resulting from bodily injury, personal injury, and false advertising.

C

cafeteria plan (2) also called *triple option plan;* provides different health benefit plans and extra coverage options through an insurer or third-party administrator.

capitation (2) prospective payment per patient for a prescribed period of time; provider accepts preestablished payments for providing health care services to enrollees over a specified period of time (usually one year or monthly).

carcinoma (Ca) *in situ* (6) a malignant tumor that is localized, circumscribed, encapsulated, and noninvasive (has not spread to deeper or adjacent tissues or organs).

care plan oversight services (7) cover the provider's time supervising a complex and multidisciplinary care treatment program for a specific patient who is under the care of a home health agency, hospice, or nursing facility.

carve-out plan (2) arrangement provided by a health insurance company to offer a specific health benefit that is managed separately from the health insurance plan.

case law (5) also called *common law;* based on a court decision that establishes a precedent.

case management (3) development of patient care plans to coordinate and provide care for complicated cases in a cost-effective manner.

case management services (7) process by which an attending physician coordinates and supervises care provided to a patient by other providers.

case manager (2) submits written confirmation, authorizing treatment, to the provider; include nurses and social workers who help patients and families navigate complex health care and support systems; also coordinate health care services to improve patient outcomes while considering financial implications as part of severity of illness and intensity of services [SI/IS] to address the balance of medical necessity, procedures/services provided, and level of care needed.

case mix (9) the types and categories of patients treated by a health care facility or provider.

case-mix index (9) relative weight assigned for a facility's patient population; it is used in a formula to calculate health care reimbursement.

case-mix management (9) allows health care facilities and providers to determine anticipated health care needs by reviewing data analytics about types and/or categories of patients treated.

case rate (9) predetermined payment for an encounter, regardless of the number of services provided or length of encounter.

catastrophic cap benefit (16) protects some TRICARE beneficiaries from devastating financial loss due to serious illness or long-term treatment by establishing limits over which payment is not required; the *catastrophic cap* is the maximum a sponsor and family pay for covered TRICARE health care services each calendar year, and it limits the amount of out-of-pocket expenses paid for TRICARE covered medical services; out-of-pocket costs that apply to the catastrophic cap include enrollment fees, deductibles, copayments, and other cost-shares.

catchment area (16) the region defined by code boundaries within a 40-mile radius of a military treatment facility.

Category I codes (7) procedures/services identified by a five-digit CPT code and descriptor nomenclature; these codes are traditionally associated with CPT and organized within six sections.

Category II codes (7) optional evidence-based performance measurement tracking codes that are assigned an alphanumeric identifier with a letter in the last field (e.g., 1234A); these codes will be located after the Medicine section; *their use is optional.*

Category III codes (7) temporary codes for data collection purposes that are assigned an alphanumeric identifier with a letter in the last field (e.g., 0075T).

Centers for Medicare and Medicaid Services (CMS) (1) formerly known as the Health Care Financing Administration (HCFA); an administrative agency within the federal Department of Health and Human Services (DHHS).

certificate of medical necessity (CMN) (8) prescription document for durable medical equipment, services, and supplies that is signed by the treating physician and submitted with the CMS-1500 claim to the DME MAC for reimbursement.

Civilian Health and Medical Program–Uniformed Services (CHAMPUS) (16) implemented in 1967 as the result of an initiative to provide military medical care for families of active duty members; designed as a benefit for dependents of personnel serving in the armed forces and the uniformed branches of the Public Health Service (PHS) and the National Oceanic and Atmospheric Administration (NOAA).

CHAMPUS Reform Initiative (CRI) (16) conducted in 1988; resulted in a new health program called TRICARE, which includes two options: TRICARE Prime and TRICARE Select.

charge description master (CDM) (3) *see* chargemaster.

chargemaster (3) computer-generated encounter form that contains a list of procedures, services, supplies, and revenue codes; chargemaster data are entered in the outpatient hospital facility's patient accounting system, and charges are automatically posted to the patient's bill (UB-04).

chargemaster maintenance (3) process of updating and revising key elements of the chargemaster (or charge description master [CDM]) to ensure accurate reimbursement.

chargemaster team (3) team of representatives from a variety of departments who jointly share responsibility for updating and revising the chargemaster to ensure accuracy.

Children's Health Insurance Program (CHIP) (15) provides health insurance coverage to uninsured children whose family income is up to 200 percent of the federal poverty level (monthly income limits for a family of four also apply).

civil law (5) area of law not classified as criminal.

Civilian Health and Medical Program of the Department of Veterans Affairs (CHAMPVA) (16) program that provides health benefits for dependents of veterans rated as 100 percent permanently and totally disabled as a result of service-connected conditions or injuries, veterans who died as a result of service-connected conditions or injuries, and veterans who died on duty with less than 30 days of active service.

Civilian Health and Medical Program–Uniformed Services (CHAMPUS) (16) originally designed as a benefit for dependents of personnel serving in the armed forces and uniformed branches of the Public Health Service and the National Oceanic and Atmospheric Administration; now called TRICARE.

claims adjudication (4) comparing a claim to payer edits and the patient's health plan benefits to verify that required information is available to process the claim, the claim is not a duplicate, payer rules and procedures have been followed, and procedures performed and services provided are covered benefits.

claims adjustment reason code (CARC) (4) reason for denied claim as reported on the remittance advice or explanation of benefits.

claims attachment (4) medical report substantiating a medical condition.

claims denial (3) unpaid claim returned by third-party payers because of beneficiary identification errors, coding errors, diagnosis that does not support medical necessity of procedure/service, duplicate claims, global days of surgery E/M coverage issue, NCCI program edits, and other patient coverage issues (e.g., procedure or service required preauthorization, procedure is not included in patient's health plan contract, such as cosmetic surgery).

claims examiner (1) employed by third-party payers to review health-related claims to determine whether the charges are reasonable and medically necessary based on the patient's diagnosis.

claims management (4) completion, submission, and follow-up of claims for procedures and services provided.

claims processing (4) sorting claims upon submission to collect and verify information about the patient and provider.

claims rejection (3) unpaid claim returned by third-party payers because it fails to meet certain data requirements, such as missing data (e.g., patient name, policy number); rejected claims can be corrected and resubmitted for processing.

claims submission (4) the transmission of claims data (electronically or manually) to payers or clearinghouses for processing.

clean claim (4) a correctly completed standardized claim (e.g., CMS-1500 claim).

clearinghouse (4) agency or organization that collects, processes, and distributes health care claims after editing and validating them to ensure that they are error-free, reformatting them to the payer's specifications, and submitting them electronically to the appropriate payer for further processing to generate reimbursement to the provider.

Clinical Data Abstracting Center (CDAC) (5) requests and screens medical records for the Payment Error Prevention Program (PEPP) to survey samples for medical review, DRG validation, and medical necessity.

clinical documentation improvement (CDI) (10) ensures accurate and thorough documentation in patient records through the identification of discrepancies between provider documentation and codes to be assigned.

clinical documentation integrity (CDI) (10) see clinical documentation improvement (CDI).

clinical laboratory fee schedule (9) data set based on local fee schedules (for outpatient clinical diagnostic laboratory services).

Clinical Laboratory Improvement Act (CLIA) (5) established quality standards for all laboratory testing to ensure the accuracy, reliability, and timeliness of patient test results regardless of where the test was performed.

clinical practice guidelines (2) define modalities for the diagnosis, management, and treatment of patients, and they include recommendations based on a methodical and meticulous evaluation and synthesis of published medical literature; the guidelines are *not* protocols that must be followed, and instead are to be considered.

clinical trial (16) research study that helps find ways to prevent, diagnose, or treat illnesses and improve health care; when enrolled, beneficiaries receive care that is considered the latest medicine or therapy, but is not yet approved as a standard care.

closed claim (4) claims for which all processing, including appeals, has been completed.

closed-panel HMO (2) health care is provided in an HMO-owned center or satellite clinic or by providers who belong to a specially formed medical group that serves the HMO.

CMS-1500 claim (2) claim submitted for reimbursement of physician office procedures and services; electronic version is called ANSI ASC X12N 837P.

CMS HCPCS Workgroup (8) develop and maintain HCPCS Level II; composed of representatives from CMS, Medicaid State agencies, the Veterans Administration, and the Medicare Pricing, Data Analysis and Coding (PDAC) contractors.

CMS Internet-only manual (IOM) (5) includes program issuances, day-to-day operating instructions, policies, and procedures that are based on statutes, regulations, guidelines, models, and directives; used by CMS program components, providers, contractors, Medicare Advantage organizations, and state survey agencies to administer CMS programs; also called *CMS Online Manual System*.

CMS Online Manual System (5) see CMS Internet-only manual.

CMS Quarterly Provider Update (QPU) (9) an online CMS publication that contains information about regulations and major policies currently under development, regulations and major policies completed or canceled, and new or revised manual instructions.

CMS transmittal (5) document published by Medicare containing new and changed policies and/or procedures that are to be incorporated into a specific CMS program manual (e.g., *Medicare Claims Processing Manual*); cover page (or transmittal page) summarizes new and changed material, and subsequent pages provide details; transmittals are sent to each Medicare administrative contractor.

Coal Mine Workers' Compensation Program (17) provides compensation and medical coverage to coal miners who are totally disabled by pneumoconiosis (black lung disease) arising out of coal mine employment, and to survivors of coal miners whose deaths are attributable to the disease.

coding (1) process of reporting diagnoses, procedures, services, and supplies as numeric and alphanumeric characters (called codes) on the insurance claim.

coding compliance (10) conformity to established coding guidelines and regulations.

coding compliance program (10) developed by health information management departments and similar areas, such as the coding and billing section of a physician's practice, to ensure coding accuracy and conformance with guidelines and regulations; includes written policies and procedures, routine coding audits and monitoring (internal and external), and compliance-based education and training.

coding conventions (CPT) (7)

> **boldface type** highlights main terms in the CPT index and categories, subcategories, headings, and code numbers in the CPT manual.
>
> **cross-reference terms** direct coders to a different CPT index entry because no codes are found under the original entry.
>
> > **See** cross-reference that provides direction to a different index main term or main term and subterm.
> >
> > **See also** cross-reference that provides direction to an additional main term.
>
> **descriptive qualifiers** terms that clarify assignment of a CPT code.
>
> **guidelines** define terms and explain the assignment of codes for procedures and services located in a particular section.
>
> **inferred words** used to save space in the CPT index when referencing subterms.
>
> **instructional notes** appear throughout CPT sections to clarify the assignment of codes.
>
> **italicized type** used for the cross-reference term, *See,* in the CPT index.

coding for medical necessity (10) involves assigning ICD-10-CM codes to diagnoses and CPT/HCPCS Level II codes to procedures/services, and then matching an appropriate ICD-10-CM code with each CPT or HCPCS Level II code.

coinsurance (2) also called *coinsurance payment;* the percentage the patient pays for covered services after the deductible has been met and the copayment has been paid.

commercial health insurance (12) for-profit companies, although some operate as nonprofit organizations, to which policyholders pay monthly premiums for coverage of medical expenses; individuals and groups are covered, depending on the negotiated contract; premiums and benefits vary according to the type of plan offered.

common access card (CAC) (16) identification card issued by the Department of Defense (DoD), which TRICARE enrollees show to receive health care services.

common data file (4) summary abstract report of all recent claims filed on each patient.

common law (5) also called *case law;* is based on a court decision that establishes a precedent.

comorbidity (6) concurrent condition that coexists with the first-listed diagnosis (outpatient care) (or principal diagnosis for inpatient care), has the potential to affect treatment of the first-listed diagnosis (outpatient care) (or principal diagnosis for inpatient care), and is an active condition for which the patient is treated and/or monitored.

competitive medical plan (CMP) (2) an HMO that meets federal eligibility requirements for a Medicare risk contract, but is not licensed as a federally qualified plan.

compliance program (5) internal policies and procedures that an organization follows to meet mandated requirements.

compliance program guidance (10) documents published by the DHHS OIG to encourage the development and use of internal controls by health care organizations (e.g., hospitals) for the purpose of monitoring adherence to applicable statutes, regulations, and program requirements.

complication (6) condition that develops after outpatient care has been provided or during an inpatient admission.

comprehensive assessment (7) must include an assessment of the patient's functional capacity, identification of potential problems, and a nursing plan to enhance, or at least maintain, the patient's physical and psychosocial functions.

Comprehensive Error Rate Testing (CERT) program (5) assesses and measures improper Medicare fee-for-service payments (based on reviewing selected claims and associated medical record documentation).

Computer Matching and Privacy Protection Act of 1988 (16) amended the Privacy Act of 1974 to regulate the use of computer-matching agreements by *federal* agencies when records contained within a system of records are matched with other federal, state, or local government records.

computer-aided coding (CAC) (6) *see* computer-assisted coding (CAC).

computer-assisted coding (CAC) (6) uses a natural language processing engine to "read" patient records and generate ICD-10-CM and HCPCS/CPT codes.

concurrent care (7) provision of similar services, such as hospital inpatient visits, to the same patient by more than one provider on the same day.

concurrent review (3) continued-stay review for continued appropriateness of care and medical necessity of tests and procedures ordered during an inpatient hospitalization.

conditional primary payer status (14) Medicare claim process that includes the following circumstances: a plan that is normally considered to be primary to Medicare issues a denial of payment that is under appeal; a patient who is physically or mentally impaired failed to file a claim to the primary payer; a workers' compensation claim has been denied and the case is slowly moving through the appeal process; or there is no response from a liability payer within 120 days of filing the claim.

Conditions for Coverage (CfC) (5) health and safety regulations that health care organizations, such as end-stage renal disease facilities, must meet in order to begin and continue participating in the Medicare and Medicaid programs.

Conditions of Participation (CoP) (5) health and safety regulations that health care organizations, such as hospitals, must meet in order to begin and continue participating in the Medicare and Medicaid programs.

confidentiality (5) restricting patient information access to those with proper authorization and maintaining the security of patient information.

Consolidated Omnibus Budget Reconciliation Act of 1985 (COBRA) (2) allows employees to continue health care coverage beyond the benefit termination date.

consultation (7) examination of a patient by a health care provider, usually a specialist, for the purpose of advising the referring or attending physician in the evaluation and/or management of a specific problem with a known diagnosis.

Consumer Credit Protection Act of 1968 (4) was considered landmark legislation because it launched truth-in-lending disclosures that required creditors to communicate the cost of borrowing money in a common language so that consumers could figure out the charges, compare costs, and shop for the best credit deal.

consumer-directed health plan (CDHP) (2) define employer contributions and ask employees to be more responsible for health care decisions and cost-sharing.

contiguous sites (6) also called *overlapping sites;* occurs when the origin of the tumor (primary site) involves two adjacent sites.

Continued Health Care Benefit Program (CHCBP) (16) premium-based health care program administered by Humana Military; though not a TRICARE program, CHCBP offers continued health coverage (18–36 months) after TRICARE eligibility ends.

continuity of care (2) documenting patient care services so that others who treat the patient have a source of information on which to base additional care and treatment.

contributory components (7) include counseling, coordination of care, nature of presenting problem, and time.

conversion factor (9) dollar multiplier that converts relative value units (RVUs) into payments as part of the Medicare physician fee schedule (MPFS) calculation formula.

Cooperating Parties for ICD-10-CM/PCS (6) AHA, AMA, CMS, and NCHS organizations and agencies that approve official guidelines for coding and reporting ICD-10-CM and ICD-10-PCS.

coordinated home health care (13) coordination between inpatient facility and home health agency to facilitate patient discharge home; patient is provided with home health agency care by a participating provider, and patient must require skilled nursing services on an intermittent basis under the direction of the primary care provider.

coordination of benefits (COB) (4) provision in group health insurance policies that prevents multiple insurers from paying benefits covered by other policies; also specifies that coverage will be provided in a specific sequence when more than one policy covers the claim.

coordination of care (7) provider makes arrangements with other providers or agencies for services to be provided to a patient.

copayment (copay) (2) provision in an insurance policy that requires the policyholder or patient to pay a specified dollar amount to a health care provider for each visit or medical service received.

counseling (7) discussion with a patient and/or family concerning one or more of the following areas: diagnostic results, impressions, and/or recommended diagnostic studies; prognosis; risks and benefits of management (treatment) options; instructions for management (treatment) and/or follow-up; importance of compliance with chosen management (treatment) options; risk factor reduction; and patient and family education.

covered entity (4) private-sector health plans (excluding certain small self-administered health plans), managed care organizations, ERISA-covered health benefit plans (Employee Retirement Income Security Act of 1974), and government health plans (including Medicare, Medicaid, Military Health System for active duty and civilian personnel; Veterans Health Administration, and Indian Health Service programs); all health care clearinghouses; and all health care providers that choose to submit or receive transactions electronically.

covered services (2) *see* schedule of benefits.

CPT Symbols (7)

- ● bullet located to the left of a code number identifies new CPT procedures and services.

- ▲ triangle located to the left of a code number identifies a revised code description.

- ►◄ horizontal triangles surround revised guidelines and notes. *This symbol is not used for revised code descriptions.*

- ; semicolon saves space in CPT so that some code descriptions are not printed in their entirety next to a code number; the entry is indented and the coder refers back to the common portion of the code description located before the semicolon.

- + plus symbol identifies add-on codes for procedures that are commonly, but not always, performed at the same time and by the same surgeon as the primary procedure.

- ⊘ forbidden symbol identifies codes that are not to be appended with modifier -51.

- ✗ flash symbol indicates that a code is pending FDA approval but that it has been assigned a CPT code.

- # number symbol precedes CPT codes that appear out of numerical order.

- ⟳ green reference symbol indicates that the coder should refer to the *CPT Assistant* monthly newsletter.

- ⟳ blue reference symbol indicates that the coder should refer to the *CPT Changes: An Insider's View* annual publication, which contains all coding changes for the current year.

- ⟳ red reference symbol indicates that the coder should refer to the *Clinical Examples in Radiology* quarterly newsletter.

- ★ star symbol precedes CPT codes that are reported for synchronous telemedicine services and require addition of modifier -95.

- ⋈ PLA symbol identifies duplicate proprietary laboratory analyses (PLA) tests.

- ↑↓ double arrow symbol identifies CPT Category I PLA codes.

criminal law (5) public law governed by statute or ordinance that deals with crimes and their prosecution.

critical care services (7) reported when a provider directly delivers medical care for a critically ill or critically injured patient.

critical pathway (16)   sequence of activities that can normally be expected to result in the most cost-effective clinical course of treatment.

Cures Act (5)   *see* 21st Century Cures Act.

***Current Dental Terminology* (CDT) (5)**   medical code set maintained and copyrighted by the American Dental Association.

***Current Procedural Terminology* (CPT) (1)**   published by the American Medical Association; includes five-digit numeric codes and descriptors for procedures and services performed by providers (e.g., 99203 identifies a detailed office visit for a new patient).

customer service representative (CSR) (16)   employed at a TRICARE Service Center; provides information about using TRICARE and assists with other matters affecting access to health care (e.g., appointment scheduling).

customized subcapitation plan (CSCP) (2)   managed care plan in which health care expenses are funded by insurance coverage; the individual selects one of each type of provider to create a customized network and pays the resulting customized insurance premium; each provider is paid a fixed amount per month to provide only the care that an individual needs from that provider (called a *sub-capitation payment*).

D

data analysis (3)   *see* data analytics.

data analytics (3)   tools and systems that are used to analyze (examine and study) clinical and financial data, conduct research, and evaluate the effectiveness of disease treatments.

data mining (3)   extracting and analyzing data to identify patterns, whether predictable or unpredictable.

data packet (11)   Format of electronic claims transmission, which are routed between provider and billing company, clearinghouse, or payer using the Internet or other packet-exchange network.

data warehouse (3)   database that uses *reporting interfaces* to consolidate multiple databases, allowing reports to be generated from a single request; data is accumulated from a wide range of sources within an organization and is used to guide management decisions.

day sheet (3)   also called *manual daily accounts receivable journal;* chronological summary used to manually track all transactions posted to individual patient ledgers/accounts on a specific day.

debt collection assistance officer (DCAO) (16)   individuals located at military treatment facilities to assist beneficiaries in resolving health care collection-related issues.

decrypt (5)   to decode an encoded computer file so that it can be viewed; convert data to a language that can be read.

deductible (2)   amount for which the patient is financially responsible before an insurance policy provides reimbursement (to the provider).

deeming (5)   CMS recognition of accreditation organization (e.g., The Joint Commission) standards that meet or exceed CoP and CfC requirements.

Defense Enrollment Eligibility Reporting System (DEERS) (16)   computer system that contains up-to-date Defense Department Workforce personnel information.

Defense Health Agency (DHA) (16)   an agency under the direction of the Assistant Secretary of Defense (Health Affairs) manages the TRICARE program.

Deficit Reduction Act of 2005 (5)   Created Medicaid Integrity Program (MIP), which increased resources available to CMS to combat abuse, fraud, and waste in the Medicaid program. Congress requires annual reporting by CMS about the use and effectiveness of funds appropriated for the MIP.

de-identification of protected health information (5)   process that removes identifiers from health information to mitigate privacy risks for individuals and thus supports the secondary use of data for comparative effectiveness studies, policy assessment, life sciences research, and other endeavors.

delinquent account (4)   *see* past due account.

delinquent claim (4)   claim usually more than 120 days past due; some practices establish time frames that are less than or more than 120 days past due.

delinquent claim cycle (4)   advances through various aging periods (30 days, 60 days, 90 days, and so on), with practices typically focusing internal recovery efforts on older delinquent accounts (e.g., 120 days or more).

demonstration project or pilot (16)   test and establish the feasibility of implementing a new TRICARE program during a trial period, after which the program is evaluated, modified, and/or abandoned.

demonstration/pilot program (14)   special project that tests improvements in Medicare coverage, payment, and quality of care.

denied claim (4)   claim returned to the provider by payers due to coding errors, missing information, and patient coverage issues.

deposition (5)   legal proceeding during which a party answers questions under oath (but not in open court).

designated record set (5)   group of records maintained by or for a covered entity and includes medical and billing records about individuals maintained by or for a covered health care provider; enrollment, payment, claims adjudication, and case or medical management record systems maintained by or for a health plan; or other records that are used by or for the covered entity to make decisions about individuals.

diagnosis pointer letters (11)   item letters A through L preprinted in Block 21 of the CMS-1500 claim; the letter next to an entered ICD-10-CM code in Block 21 is entered in Block 24E to indicate medical necessity of a procedure or service performed.

diagnosis-related groups (DRGs) (9)   prospective payment system that reimburses hospitals for inpatient stays.

***Diagnostic and Statistical Manual* (DSM) (9)**   classifies mental health disorders and is based on ICD; published by the American Psychiatric Association.

diagnostic cost group hierarchical condition category (DCG/HCC) risk adjustment model (14)   CMS model implemented for Medicare risk-adjustment purposes and results in more accurate predictions of medical costs for Medicare Advantage enrollees; its purpose is to promote fair payments to managed care organizations that reward efficiency and encourage excellent care for the chronically ill.

digital (5)   application of a mathematical function to an electronic document to create a computer code that can be encrypted (encoded).

direct contract model HMO (2)   contracted health care services delivered to subscribers by individual providers in the community.

direct patient contact (7)   refers to face-to-face patient contact (outpatient or inpatient).

disability income insurance (12)   *see* disability insurance.

disability insurance (12)   reimbursement for income lost as a result of a temporary or permanent illness or injury.

discharge planning (3)   involves arranging appropriate health care services for the discharged patient (e.g., home health care).

discharged not final billed (DNFB) (3)   patient claims that are not finalized because of billing delays.

discharged not final coded (DNFC) (3)   patient claims that are not finalized because of coding delays or incomplete documentation.

disproportionate share hospital (DSH) adjustment (9)   policy in which hospitals that treat a high percentage of patients with low incomes receive increased Medicare payments.

DME MAC (8)   process Medicare durable medical equipment (DME) claims for defined geographic areas.

downcoding (4)   assigning lower-level codes than documented in the record.

drug formulary (14)   list of brand name and generic prescription drugs covered by a health plan.

dual eligibles (15)   individuals entitled to Medicare and eligible for some type of Medicaid benefit.

durable medical equipment (DME) (8)   defined by Medicare as equipment that can withstand repeated use, is primarily used to serve a medical purpose, is used in the patient's home, and would not be used in the absence of illness or injury.

durable medical equipment, prosthetics, orthotics, and supplies (DMEPOS) (8)   include artificial limbs, braces, medications, surgical dressings, and wheelchairs.

durable medical equipment, prosthetics, orthotics, and supplies (DMEPOS) dealers (8)   supply patients with durable medical equipment (DME) (e.g., canes, crutches); submit claims to DME Medicare administrative contractors (MACs) who are awarded contracts by CMS.

durable medical equipment, prosthetics/orthotics, and supplies (DMEPOS) fee schedule (9)   Medicare reimburses DMEPOS dealers according to either 80 percent of the actual charge for the item *or* the fee schedule amount, whichever is lower.

E

Early and Periodic Screening, Diagnostic, and Treatment (EPSDT) services (15)   legislation that mandates states to provide routine pediatric checkups to all children enrolled in Medicaid.

eHealth Exchange (5)   health information exchange network for securely sharing clinical information over the Internet nationwide that spans all 50 states and is the largest health information exchange infrastructure in the United States; participants include large provider networks, hospitals, pharmacies, regional health information organizations, and many federal agencies.

electronic clinical quality measures (eCQMs) (2, 5)   processes, observations, treatments, and outcomes that quantify the quality of care provided by health care systems; measuring such data helps ensure that care is delivered safely, effectively, equitably, and timely.

electronic data interchange (EDI) (4)   computer-to-computer exchange of data between provider and payer.

electronic flat file format (4)   series of fixed-length records (e.g., 25 spaces for patient's name) submitted to payers to bill for health care services.

electronic funds transfer (EFT) (4)   system by which payers electronically deposit funds to the provider's (bank) account.

Electronic Funds Transfer Act (4)   established the rights, liabilities, and responsibilities of participants in electronic funds transfer systems.

electronic health record (EHR) (2)   global concept that includes the collection of patient information documented by a number of providers at different facilities regarding one patient.

Electronic Healthcare Network Accreditation Commission (EHNAC) (4)   organization that accredits clearinghouses.

electronic media claim (4)   *see* electronic flat file format.

electronic medical record (EMR) (2)   considered part of the electronic health record (EHR), the EMR is created using vendor software, which assists in provider decision-making.

electronic remittance advice (ERA) (4)   remittance advice that is submitted by the third-party payer to the provider electronically and contains the same information as a paper-based remittance advice; providers receive the ERA more quickly.

Electronic Submission of Medical Documentation system (esMD) (5)   implemented to reduce provider and reviewer costs and cycle time by minimizing and eventually eliminating paper processing and mailing of medical documentation, and to reduce costs and time for review contractors.

electronic transaction standards (5)   also called *transactions rule;* a uniform language for electronic data interchange.

embezzle (1)   the illegal transfer of money or property as a fraudulent action; to steal money from an employer.

emergency department services (7)   services provided in an organized, hospital-based facility, which is open on a 24-hour basis, for the purpose of "providing unscheduled episodic services to patients requiring immediate medical attention."

Employee Retirement Income Security Act of 1974 (ERISA) (2)   mandated reporting and disclosure requirements for group life and health plans (including managed care plans), permitted large employers to self-insure employee health care benefits, and exempted large employers from taxes on health insurance premiums.

Employees' Compensation Appeals Board (ECAB) (17)   hears and decides cases on appeal from decisions of the Office of Workers' Compensation Programs (OWCP) in an impartial and expeditious manner.

employer-sponsored group health plan (EGHP) (14)   provides coverage to employees and dependents without regard to the enrollee's employment status (e.g., full-time, part-time, or retired).

encoder (6)   automates the coding process using computerized or web-based software; instead of manually looking up conditions (or procedures) in the coding manual's index, the coder uses the software's search feature to locate and verify diagnosis and procedure codes.

encounter (6)   face-to-face contact between a patient and a health care provider (e.g., physician, nurse practitioner) who assesses and treats the patient's condition.

encounter form (3)   financial record source document used by providers and other personnel to select treated/managed diagnoses and procedures/services provided to the patient during the current encounter.

encrypt (5) to convert information to a secure language format for transmission.

end-stage renal disease (ESRD) (14) permanent kidney failure requiring dialysis or a transplant.

end-stage renal disease prospective payment system (ESRD PPS) (9) provides a single, per-treatment payment to ESRD facilities that covers all resources used in providing outpatient dialysis treatments.

Energy Employees Occupational Illness Compensation Program (EEOICP) (17) provides compensation and medical benefits to eligible employees and former employees of the Department of Energy, its contractors and subcontractors, or to certain survivors of qualified workers.

enrollee (2) *see* subscriber.

episode of care (home health) (9) period of time (two months) during which home health care is provided for a particular condition.

Equal Credit Opportunity Act (4) prohibits discrimination on the basis of race, color, religion, national origin, sex, marital status, age, receipt of public assistance, or good faith exercise of any rights under the Consumer Credit Protection Act.

errors and omissions insurance (1) *see* professional liability insurance.

essential modifier (6) *see* subterm.

established patient (7) one who has received professional services from the provider, or from another provider of the same specialty who belongs to the same group practice, within the past three years.

ethics (1) principle of right or good conduct; rules that govern the conduct of members of a profession.

Evaluation and Management Documentation Guidelines (7) federal (CMS) guidelines that explain how E/M codes are assigned according to elements associated with comprehensive multisystem and single-system examinations.

Evaluation and Management (E/M) section (7) located at the beginning of CPT because these codes describe services (e.g., office visits) that are most frequently provided by physicians and other health care practitioners (e.g., nurse practitioner, physician assistant).

evidence-based coding (6) coding auditor clicks on codes that CAC software generates to review electronic health record documentation (evidence) used to generate the code.

excess insurance (2) *see* stop-loss insurance.

exclusive provider organization (EPO) (2) managed care plan that provides benefits to subscribers if they receive services from network providers.

explanation of benefits (EOB) (4) document sent to the patient by the third-party payer to provides details about the results of claims processing, such as provider charge, payer fee scheduled, payment made by the payer, and patient financial responsibility. The Medicare EOB is called a Medicare Summary Notice or MSN.

express contract (2) provisions that are stated in a health insurance contract.

extent of examination (CPT) (7) includes comprehensive, detailed, expanded problem focused, and problem focused levels, based on physician documentation.

  comprehensive examination general multisystem examination or a complete examination of a single organ system.

  detailed examination extended examination of the affected body area(s) and other symptomatic or related organ system(s).

  expanded problem focused examination limited examination of the affected body area or organ system and other symptomatic or related organ system(s).

  problem focused examination limited examination of the affected body area or organ system.

extent of history (CPT) (7) includes comprehensive, detailed, expanded problem focused, and problem focused levels, based on physician documentation.

  comprehensive history chief complaint, extended history of present illness, review of systems directly related to the problem(s) identified in the history of the present illness, plus a review of all additional body systems and complete past/family/social history.

  detailed history chief complaint, extended history of present illness, problem-pertinent system review extended to include a limited number of additional systems, pertinent past/family/social history directly related to patient's problem.

  expanded problem focused history chief complaint, brief history of present illness, problem-pertinent system review.

  problem focused history chief complaint, brief history of present illness or problem.

external quality review organization (EQRO) (2) responsible for reviewing health care provided by managed care organizations.

F

face-to-face time (7) amount of time the office or outpatient care provider spends with the patient and/or family.

facility billing (3) *see* institutional billing.

Fair Credit and Charge Card Disclosure Act (4) amended the Truth in Lending Act, requiring credit and charge card issuers to provide certain disclosures in direct mail, telephone, and other applications and solicitations for open-end credit and charge accounts and under other circumstances; this law applies to providers that accept credit cards.

Fair Credit Billing Act (4) federal law passed in 1975 that helps consumers resolve billing issues with card issuers; protects important credit rights, including rights to dispute billing errors, unauthorized use of an account, and charges for unsatisfactory goods and services; cardholders cannot be held liable for more than $50 of fraudulent charges made to a credit card.

Fair Credit Reporting Act (4) protects information collected by consumer reporting agencies such as credit bureaus, medical information companies, and tenant screening services; organizations that provide information to consumer reporting agencies also have specific legal obligations, including the duty to investigate disputed information.

Fair Debt Collection Practices Act (FDCPA) (4) specifies what a collection source may and may not do when pursuing payment of past due accounts.

False Claims Act (FCA) (5) passed by the federal government during the Civil War to regulate fraud associated with military contractors selling supplies and equipment to the Union Army.

Federal Claims Collection Act (FCCA) (5) requires Medicare administrative contractors (previously called carriers and fiscal intermediaries), as agents of the federal government, to attempt the collection of overpayments.

Federal Employees' Compensation Act (FECA) Program (17) provides compensation benefits to civilian employees of the United States for disability due to personal injury or disease sustained while in the performance of duty; also provides for payment of benefits to dependents if a work-related injury or disease causes an employee's death; benefits provided under the FECA program constitute the sole remedy against the United States for work-related injury or death (because a federal employee or surviving dependent is *not* entitled to sue the United States or recover damages for such injury or death under any other law).

Federal Employee Health Benefits Program (FEHBP) (2) an employer-sponsored health benefits program established by an act of Congress in 1959 to allow federal employees, retirees, and their survivors to select appropriate health plans that meet their needs.

Federal Employee Program® (FEP) (13) began covering federal employees in 1960, provides benefits to more than 5 million federal enrollees and dependents, and underwritten and administered by participating BlueCross BlueShield plans.

Federal Employees' Compensation Act (FECA) (2) provides civilian employees of the federal government with medical care, survivors' benefits, and compensation for lost wages.

Federal Employers' Liability Act (FELA) (2) legislation passed in 1908 by President Theodore Roosevelt that protects and compensates railroad workers who are injured on the job.

Federal Medical Assistance Percentage (FMAP) (15) portion of the Medicaid program paid by the federal government.

federal poverty level (FPL) (15) income guidelines established annually by the federal government.

Federal Privacy Act (11) enacted in 1974 to prohibit a payer from notifying the provider about payment or rejection of unassigned claims or payments sent directly to the patient or policyholder.

Federal Register (5) legal newspaper published every business day by the National Archives and Records Administration (NARA).

Federally Qualified Health Center (FQHC) (9) safety net providers that primarily provide services typically furnished in an outpatient clinic.

Federally Qualified Health Center Prospective Payment System (FQHC PPS) (9) national encounter-based rate with geographic and other adjustments; established by the Affordable Care Act and implemented in 2014; FQHCs include a payment code on claims submitted for payment and are paid 80 percent of the lesser of charges, based on FQHC payment codes or the FQHC PPS rate.

federally qualified HMO (2) certified to provide health care services to Medicare and Medicaid enrollees.

fee schedule (2) list of predetermined payments for health care services provided to patients (e.g., a fee is assigned to each CPT code).

fee-for-service (2) reimbursement methodology that increases payment if the health care service fees increase, if multiple units of service are provided, or if more expensive services are provided instead of less expensive services (e.g., brand name vs. generic prescription medication).

fee-for-service plan (2) reimburses providers according to a fee schedule after covered procedures and services have been provided to patients.

Financial Services Modernization Act (FSMA) (4) prohibits sharing of medical information among health insurers and other financial institutions for use in making credit decisions; also allows banks to merge with investment and insurance houses, which allows them to make a profit no matter what the status of the economy, because people usually house their money in one of the options; also called *Gramm-Leach-Bliley Act*.

first report of injury (17) workers' compensation form completed when the patient first seeks treatment for a work-related illness or injury.

first-listed diagnosis (6) reported on outpatient claims (instead of inpatient *principal diagnosis*); it reflects the reason for the encounter, and it is often a sign or symptom.

First-look Analysis for Hospital Outlier Monitoring (FATHOM) (5) data analysis tool, which provides administrative hospital and state-specific data for specific CMS target areas.

fiscal year (16) for the federal government, October 1 of one year to September 30 of the next.

flexible benefit plan (2) *see* cafeteria plan and triple option plan.

flexible spending account (FSA) (2) consumer-directed health plan that allows tax-exempt accounts to be created by employees for the purpose of paying health care bills.

for-profit corporation (13) pays taxes on profits generated by the corporation's for-profit enterprises and pays dividends to shareholders on after-tax profits.

fragmentation (4) *see* unbundling.

fraud (5) intentional deception or misrepresentation that could result in an unauthorized payment.

G

gag clause (2) prevents providers from discussing all treatment options with patients, whether or not the plan would provide reimbursement for services.

gatekeeper (2) primary care provider for essential health care services at the lowest possible cost, avoiding nonessential care, and referring patients to specialists.

general enrollment period (GEP) (14) enrollment period for Medicare Part A and Part B held January 1 through March 31 of each year.

general equivalence mapping (GEM) (6) translation dictionaries or crosswalks of codes that can be used to roughly identify ICD-10-CM/PCS codes for their ICD-9-CM equivalent codes (and vice versa). *See also* legacy coding system.

GeoBlue® (13) international health care coverage for academic institution faculty/students/staff, employers, including non-profit organizations, individuals, and U.S. and non-U.S. academic institution faculty/students/staff who are short-term travelers and long-term expatriates.

global payment (9) one payment that covers all services rendered by multiple providers during an episode of care.

global period (7) includes all services related to a procedure during a period of time (e.g., 10 days, 30 days, 90 days, depending on payer guidelines).

global surgery (7) also called *package concept* or *surgical package;* includes the procedure, local infiltration, metacarpal/digital block or topical anesthesia when used, and normal, uncomplicated follow-up care.

Government-Wide Service Benefit Plan (13) phrase printed below the BCBS trademark on federal employee plan (FEP) insurance cards, which indicates that the enrollee has federal employer-sponsored health benefits.

Gramm-Leach-Bliley Act (4) *see* Financial Services Modernization Act.

group health insurance (2) private health insurance model that provides coverage, which is subsidized by employers and other organizations (e.g., labor unions, rural and consumer health cooperatives) whereby part or all of premium costs are paid for and/or discounted group rates are offered to eligible individuals.

group model HMO (2) contracted health care services delivered to subscribers by participating providers who are members of an independent multispecialty group practice.

group practice without walls (GPWW) (2) contract that allows providers to maintain their own offices and share services (e.g., appointment scheduling and billing).

grouper software (9) determines appropriate group (e.g., diagnosis-related group, home health resource group, and so on) to classify a patient after data about the patient is input.

guaranteed renewal (2) a provision, when included in a health insurance contract, that requires a health insurance company to renew the policy as long premiums continue to be paid.

guarantor (3) person responsible for paying health care fees.

H

HCPCS Level II codes (1) national codes published by CMS, which include five-digit alphanumeric codes for procedures, services, and supplies not classified in CPT.

HCPCS Level II code types (8)

    miscellaneous codes reported when a DMEPOS dealer submits a claim for a product or service for which there is no existing permanent national code.

    modifiers provide additional information about a procedure or service (e.g., left-sided procedure).

    permanent national codes maintained by the HCPCS National Panel, composed of representatives from the BlueCross BlueShield Association (BCBSA), the Health Insurance Association of America (HIAA), and CMS.

    temporary codes maintained by the CMS and other members of the HCPCS National Panel; independent of permanent national codes.

health care (2) expands the definition of medical care to include preventive services.

Health Care and Education Reconciliation Act (HCERA) (2) includes health care reform initiatives that amend the Patient Protection and Affordable Care Act to increase tax credits to buy health care insurance, eliminate special deals provided to senators, close the Medicare "donut hole," delay taxing of "Cadillac-health care plans" until 2018, and so on.

health care anywhere (13) concept that allows members of independently owned and operated BCBS health plans to have access to health care benefits throughout the United States and around the world.

health care finder (HCF) (16) facilitates TRICARE administrative activities, such as referrals to appropriate health care services in the military facility and civilian provider network, including preauthorization for procedures and services provided in a military treatment facility or civilian provider network.

Health Care Fraud Prevention and Enforcement Action Team (HEAT) (5) joint effort between the Department of Health and Human Services and the Department of Justice to fight health care fraud by increasing coordination, intelligence sharing, and training among investigators, agents, prosecutors, analysts, and policymakers; implemented as a result of the Patient Protection and Affordable Care Act (also called Obamacare).

health care provider (1) physician or other health care practitioner (e.g., physician's assistant).

health care reimbursement account (HCRA) (2) tax-exempt account used to pay for health care expenses; individual decides, in advance, how much money to deposit in an HCRA (and unused funds are lost).

health information technician (1) professionals who manage patient health information and medical records, administer computer information systems, and code diagnoses and procedures for health care services provided to patients.

Health Information Technology for Economic and Clinical Health Act (HITECH Act) (2) included in the American Recovery and Reinvestment Act of 2009 and amended the Public Health Service Act to establish an Office of National Coordinator for Health Information Technology within HHS to improve health care quality, safety, and efficiency.

health insurance (2) contract between a policyholder and a third-party payer or government program to reimburse the policyholder for all or a portion of the cost of medically necessary treatment or preventive care by health care professionals.

health insurance claim (1) documentation that is electronically or manually submitted to an insurance plan requesting reimbursement for health care procedures and services provided (e.g., CMS-1500 and UB-04 claims).

health insurance exchange (2) *see* health insurance marketplace.

health insurance marketplace (2) method Americans use to purchase health coverage that fits their budget and meet their needs, effective October 1, 2013, as a result of passage of the Affordable Care Act.

Health Insurance Portability and Accountability Act (HIPAA) (5) mandates regulations that govern privacy, security, and electronic transactions standards for health care information.

health insurance prospective payment system (HIPPS) code set (9) five-digit alphanumeric codes that represent case-mix groups about which payment determinations are made for the HH PPS.

health insurance specialist (1) person who reviews health-related claims to match medical necessity to procedures or services performed before payment (reimbursement) is made to the provider; *see also* reimbursement specialist.

health maintenance organization (HMO) (2) responsible for providing health care services to subscribers in a given geographical area for a fixed fee.

Health Maintenance Organization (HMO) Assistance Act of 1973 (2) authorized grants and loans to develop HMOs under private sponsorship; defined a federally qualified HMO as one that has applied for, and met, federal standards established in the HMO Act of 1973; required most employers with more than 25 employees to offer HMO coverage if local plans were available.

health reimbursement arrangement (HRA) (2) tax-exempt accounts funded by employers, which individuals use to pay health care bills.

health savings account (HSA) (2) Participants enroll in a relatively inexpensive high-deductible health plan (HDHP), and a tax-deductible savings account is opened to cover current and future medical expenses.

Healthcare Common Procedure Coding System (HCPCS) (1) coding system that consists of CPT, national codes (level II), and local codes (level III); local codes were discontinued in 2003; previously known as HCFA Common Procedure Coding System.

Healthcare Effectiveness Data and Information Set (HEDIS) (2) created standards to assess managed-care systems using data elements that are collected, evaluated, and published to compare the performance of managed health care plans.

Hill-Burton Act (2) provided federal grants for modernizing hospitals that had become obsolete because of a lack of capital investment during the Great Depression and WWII (1929–1945). In return for federal funds, facilities were required to provide services free, or at reduced rates, to patients unable to pay for care.

HIPAA Privacy Rule (5) HIPAA provision that creates national standards to protect individuals' medical records and other personal health information.

HIPAA Security Rule (5) HIPAA standards and safeguards that protect health information collected, maintained, used, or transmitted electronically; covered entities affected by this rule include health plans, health care clearinghouses, and certain health care providers.

history (7) interview of the patient that includes the following components: history of the present illness (HPI) (including the patient's chief complaint), a review of systems (ROS), and a past/family/social history (PFSH).

hold harmless clause (1) policy that the patient is not responsible for paying what the insurance plan denies.

Home Assessment Validation and Entry (HAVEN) (9) data entry software used to collect OASIS assessment data for transmission to state databases.

home health patient-driven groupings model (PDGM) (9) implemented in 2020 to replace *home health resource groups (HHRGs)*; relies more heavily on clinical characteristics and other patient information to place home health periods of care into meaningful payment categories; eliminated use of therapy service thresholds; resulted in unit of home health payment being reduced from 60- to 30-day period.

Home Health Prospective Payment System (HH PPS) (9) reimbursement methodology for home health agencies that uses a classification system called home health patient-driven groupings model (PDGM), which establishes a predetermined rate for health care services provided to patients for each 60-day episode of home health care.

Home Health Value-Based Purchasing (HHVBP) Model (9) designed to provide Medicare-certified HHAs with incentives to provide higher quality and more efficient care; HHA payments are adjusted for services based on quality of care.

home services (7) health care services provided in a private residence.

hospice (14) autonomous, centrally administered program of coordinated inpatient and outpatient palliative (relief of symptoms) services for terminally ill patients and their families.

hospital-acquired condition (HAC) (9) medical conditions or complications that patients develop during inpatient hospital stays and that were not present at admission.

Hospital-Acquired Condition (HAC) Reduction Program (9) encourages hospitals to reduce HACs by adjusting payments to hospitals that rank in the worst-performing 25 percent with respect to HAC quality measures.

hospital discharge service (7) includes the final examination of the patient; discussion of the hospital stay with the patient and/or caregiver; instructions for continuing care provided to the patient and/or caregiver; and preparation of discharge records, prescriptions, and referral forms.

Hospital Inpatient Quality Reporting (Hospital IQR) program (5) developed to equip consumers with quality of care information so they can make more informed decisions about health care options; requires hospitals to submit specific quality measures data about health conditions common among Medicare beneficiaries and that typically result in hospitalization; eligible hospitals that do not participate in the Hospital IQR program will receive an annual market basket update with a 2.0 percentage point reduction; part of the Medicare Prescription Drug, Improvement, and Modernization Act (MMA) of 2003. (The Hospital IQR program was previously called the *Reporting Hospital Quality Data for Annual Payment Update program*.)

Hospital Outpatient Quality Reporting Program (Hospital OQR) (5) a "pay for quality data reporting program" that was implemented by CMS for outpatient hospital services (as part of the Tax Relief and Health Care Act of 2006).

Hospital Payment Monitoring Program (HPMP) (5) measures, monitors, and reduces the incidence of Medicare fee-for-service payment errors for short-term, acute care, inpatient PPS hospitals.

hospital readmissions reduction program (HRRP) (9) requires CMS to reduce payments to IPPS hospitals with excess readmissions.

hospital value-based purchasing (VBP) program (5) health care reform measure that links Medicare's inpatient prospective payment system (IPPS) to a value-based system for the purpose of promoting better clinical outcomes and patient experiences of care; effective October 2012, hospitals receive reimbursement for inpatient acute care services based on care quality (instead of the quantity of the services provided).

hospitalist (11) dedicated inpatient physician who works exclusively in a hospital.

I

iatrogenic illness (6) illness that results from medical intervention (e.g., adverse reaction to contrast material injected prior to a scan).

ICD-10-CM coding conventions (6) general coding rules that apply to the assignment of codes, independent of official coding guidelines.

and when two disorders are separated by the word "and," it is interpreted as "and/or" and indicates that either of the two disorders is associated with the code number.

brackets used in the index to identify manifestation codes and in the index and tabular list to enclose abbreviations, synonyms, alternative wording, or explanatory phrases.

code also ICD-10-CM tabular list instruction that indicates two codes may be required to fully describe a condition with sequencing depending on circumstances of the encounter.

code first underlying disease appears when the code referenced is to be sequenced as a secondary code; the code, title, and instructions are italicized.

code first underlying disease, such as: *see* code first underlying disease.

code, if applicable, any causal condition first requires causal condition to be sequenced first if present; a causal condition is a disease that manifests (or results in) another condition.

colon used after an incomplete term and is followed by one or more modifiers (additional terms).

default code listed next to a main term in the ICD-10-CM alphabetic index and represents the condition that is most commonly associated with the main term or is the unspecified code for the condition.

due to located in the index in alphabetical order to indicate the presence of a cause-and-effect (or causal) relationship between two conditions.

eponym diseases and procedures named for people, such as Barlow's disease.

etiology and manifestation rules include the following notes in the ICD-10-CM Tabular List of Diseases and Injuries: *Code first underlying disease; Code first underlying disease, such as; Code, if applicable, any causal condition first; Use additional code;* and *In diseases classified elsewhere.*

Excludes1 note a "pure" excludes, which means "not coded here" and indicates mutually exclusive codes; in other words, two conditions that cannot be reported together.

Excludes2 note means "not included here" and indicates that although the excluded condition is not classified as part of the condition it is excluded from, a patient may be diagnosed with all conditions at the same time; therefore, it may be acceptable to assign both the code and the excluded code(s) together if supported by medical documentation.

in located in alphabetical order below the main term; to assign a code from the list of qualifiers below the word "in," the provider must document both conditions in the patient's record; ICD-10-CM classifies certain conditions as if there were a cause-and-effect relationship present because they occur together much of the time, such as *pneumonia in Q fever.*

in diseases classified elsewhere indicates that the manifestation codes are a component of the etiology/manifestation coding convention.

includes note appear below certain tabular list categories to further define, clarify, or provide examples.

laterality ICD-10-CM specifically classifies conditions that occur on the left, right, or bilaterally.

manifestation condition that occurs as the result of another condition; manifestation codes are always reported as secondary codes.

NEC (not elsewhere classifiable) means "other" or "other specified" and identifies codes that are assigned when information needed to assign a more specific code cannot be located.

NOS (not otherwise specified) indicates that the code is unspecified; coders should ask the provider for a more specific diagnosis before assigning the code.

other code when this word appears in an ICD-10-CM tabular list code description, the code is assigned when patient record documentation provides detail for which a specific code does not exist.

other specified code when this phrase appears in an ICD-10-CM code description, the code is assigned when patient record documentation provides detail for which a specific code does not exist.

parentheses enclose supplementary words that may be present or absent in the diagnostic statement, without affecting assignment of the code number.

placeholder use of character "X" as a placeholder to allow for future expansion of certain codes; used when a code contains fewer than six characters and a seventh character applies.

see directs the coder to refer to another term in the index to locate the code.

see also located after a main term or subterm in the index and directs the coder to another main term (or subterm) that may provide additional useful index entries.

see category instruction directs the coder to the ICD-10-CM tabular list, where a code can be selected from the options provided there.

see condition directs the coder to the main term for a condition, found in the index.

Table of Drugs and Chemicals alphabetical index of medicinal, chemical, and biological substances that result in poisonings, adverse effects, and underdosings.

Table of Neoplasms alphabetical index of anatomic sites for which there are six possible codes according to whether the neoplasm in question is malignant, benign, *in situ,* of uncertain behavior, or of unspecified nature.

unspecified codes when patient record documentation is insufficient to assign a more specific code, this (unspecified) code is assigned.

use additional code indicates that a second code is to be reported to provide more information about the diagnosis.

with when codes combine one disorder with another (e.g., code that combines primary condition with a complication), the provider's diagnostic statement must clearly indicate that both conditions are present and that a relationship exists between the conditions.

ICD-10-CM Diagnostic Coding and Reporting Guidelines for Outpatient Services—Hospital-Based Outpatient Services and Provider-Based Office Visits (6) developed by the federal government, outpatient diagnoses that have been approved for use by hospitals/providers in coding and reporting hospital-based outpatient services and provider-based office visits.

ICD-10-CM Index to Diseases and Injuries (6) an alphabetical listing of terms and their corresponding codes, which include specific illnesses, injuries, eponyms, abbreviations, and other descriptive diagnostic terms.

ICD-10-CM Index of External Causes of Injuries (6) arranged in alphabetical order by main term indicating the event; are secondary codes for use in any health care setting; capture how the injury or health condition happened (cause), the intent (unintentional or accidental; or intentional, such as suicide or assault), the place where the event occurred, the activity of the patient at the time of the event, and the person's status.

ICD-10-CM Official Guidelines for Coding and Reporting (6) prepared by CMS and NCHS and approved by the cooperating parties for ICD-10-CM/PCS; contain rules that were developed to accompany and complement coding conventions and instructions provided in ICD-10-CM; adherence when assigning diagnosis codes is required under HIPAA.

ICD-10-CM Tabular List of Diseases and Injuries (6) chronological list of codes contained within 22 chapters, which are based on body system or condition.

ICD-10-CM/PCS Coordination and Maintenance Committee (6) responsible for overseeing all changes and modifications to ICD-10-CM (diagnosis) and ICD-10-PCS (procedure) codes; discusses issues such as the creation and update of general equivalence mappings (GEMs).

ICD-10-PCS Official Guidelines for Coding and Reporting (6) prepared by CMS and NCHS and approved by the cooperating parties for ICD-10-CM/PCS; contain rules that were developed to accompany and complement official conventions and instructions provided in ICD-10-PCS; adherence when assigning procedure codes is required under HIPAA.

implied contract (2) results from actions taken by the health care facility or provider, such as registering a patient to provide treatment.

Improper Payments Information Act of 2002 (IPIA) (5) established the *Payment Error Rate Measurement (PERM) program* to measure improper payments in the Medicaid program and the Children's Health Insurance Program (CHIP); *Comprehensive Error Rate Testing (CERT) program* to calculate the paid claims error rate for submitted Medicare claims by randomly selecting a statistical sample of claims to determine whether claims were paid properly (based on reviewing selected claims and associated medical record documentation); and the *Hospital Payment Monitoring Program (HPMP)* to measure, monitor, and reduce the incidence of Medicare fee-for-service payment errors for short-term, acute care at inpatient PPS hospitals.

incident to (9) Medicare regulation which permitted billing Medicare under the physician's billing number for ancillary personnel services when those services were "incident to" a service performed by a physician.

indemnity plan (2) allows patients to seek health care from any provider, and the provider receives reimbursement according to a *fee schedule*; *indemnity plans* are sometimes called *fee-for-service plans*.

indemnity insurance (12) compensates policyholders for actual economic losses, up to limiting amounts on insurance policy, and it usually requires the insured to prove losses before payment is made (e.g., automobile insurance).

indented code (7) CPT code that is indented below a stand-alone code, requiring the coder to refer back to the common portion of the code description that is located before the semicolon.

independent contractor (1) defined by the *'Lectric Law Library's Lexicon* as "a person who performs services for another under an express or implied agreement and who is not subject to the other's control, or right to control, of the manner and means of performing the services. The organization that hires an independent contractor is not liable for the acts or omissions of the independent contractor."

independent practice association (IPA) HMO (2) *see* individual practice association (IPA) HMO.

indirect medical education (IME) adjustment (9) approved teaching hospitals receive increased Medicare payments, which are adjusted depending on the ratio of residents-to-beds (to calculate operating costs) and residents-to-average daily census (to calculate capital costs).

individual health insurance (2) private health insurance policy purchased by individuals or families who do not have access to group health insurance coverage; applicants can be denied coverage, and they can also be required to pay higher premiums due to age, gender, and/or pre-existing medical conditions.

individual practice association (IPA) HMO (2) also called *independent practice association (IPA)*; type of HMO where contracted health services are delivered to subscribers by providers who remain in their independent office settings.

initial enrollment period (IEP) (14) seven-month period prior to turning age 65 that provides an opportunity for the individual to enroll in Medicare Part A and Part B.

initial hospital care (7) covers the first inpatient encounter the *admitting/attending physician* has with the patient upon patient admission.

inpatient prospective payment system (IPPS) (9) system in which Medicare reimburses hospitals for inpatient hospital services according to a predetermined rate upon patient discharge.

Inpatient Psychiatric Facility Prospective Payment System (IPF PPS) (9) system in which Medicare reimburses inpatient psychiatric facilities according to a patient classification system that reflects differences in patient resource use and costs; it replaces the cost-based payment system with a *per diem* IPF PPS.

Inpatient Psychiatric Facility Quality Reporting (IPFQR) Program (9) pay-for-reporting program intended to (1) equip consumers with quality of care information to make more informed decisions about health care options and (2) encourage hospitals and clinicians to improve the quality of inpatient care provided to beneficiaries.

Inpatient Rehabilitation Facility Prospective Payment system (IRF PPS) (9) implemented as a result of the BBA of 1997; utilizes information from a patient assessment instrument to classify patients into distinct groups based on clinical characteristics and expected resource needs.

Inpatient Rehabilitation Validation and Entry (IRVEN) (9) software used as the computerized data entry system by inpatient rehabilitation facilities to create a file in a standard format that can be electronically transmitted to a national database; data collected is used to assess the clinical characteristics of patients in rehabilitation hospitals and rehabilitation units in acute care hospitals, and provide agencies and facilities with a means to objectively measure and compare facility performance and quality; data also provides researchers with information to support the development of improved standards.

institutional billing (3) involves generating UB-04 claims for charges generated for inpatient and outpatient services provided by health care facilities, which according to CMS include hospitals, long-term care facilities, skilled nursing facilities, home health agencies, hospice organizations, end-stage renal disease providers, outpatient physical therapy/occupational therapy/speech pathology services, comprehensive outpatient rehabilitation facilities, community mental health centers, critical access hospitals, federally qualified health centers, histocompatibility laboratories, Indian Health Service facilities, organ procurement organizations, religious non-medical health care institutions, and rural health clinics.

integrated delivery system (IDS) (2)   organization of affiliated provider sites (e.g., hospitals, ambulatory surgical centers, or physician groups) that offer joint health care services to subscribers.

integrated provider organization (IPO) (2)   manages the delivery of health care services offered by hospitals, physicians employed by the IPO, and other health care organizations (e.g., an ambulatory surgery clinic and a nursing facility).

integrated revenue cycle (IRC) (3)   combining revenue management with clinical, coding, and information management decisions because of the impact on financial management.

intensity of resources (9)   relative volume and types of diagnostic, therapeutic, and inpatient bed services used to manage an inpatient disease.

intensity of services (IS) (9)   determining whether provided services are appropriate for patient's current or proposed level of care (e.g., IV medications, heart monitoring, surgery).

International Classification of Diseases, 10th Revision, Clinical Modification (ICD-10-CM) (1)   coding system to be implemented on October 1, 2015, and used to report diseases, injuries, and other reasons for inpatient and outpatient encounters.

International Classification of Diseases, 10th Revision, Procedural Coding System (ICD-10-PCS) (1)   coding system to be implemented on October 1, 2015, and used to report procedures and services on inpatient claims.

International Classification of Diseases, 11th Revision (ICD-11) (6)   developed by the World Health Organization (WHO) and released in 2018 to begin the implementation process (e.g., translation into languages other than English).

internship (1)   nonpaid professional practice experience that benefits students and facilities that accept students for placement; students receive on-the-job experience prior to graduation, and the internship assists them in obtaining permanent employment.

interrogatory (5)   document containing a list of questions that must be answered in writing.

Investing in Innovations (i2) Initiative (5)   designed to spur innovations in health information technology (health IT) by promoting research and development to enhance competitiveness in the United States.

IPPS 3-day payment window (9)   requires that outpatient preadmission services provided by a hospital for a period of up to three days prior to a patient's inpatient admission be covered by the IPPS DRG payment for diagnostic services (e.g., lab testing) and therapeutic (or nondiagnostic) services when the inpatient principal diagnosis code (ICD-10-CM) exactly matches that for preadmission services.

IPPS 72-hour rule (9)   *see* IPPS 3-day payment window.

IPPS transfer rule (9)   any patient with a diagnosis from one of ten CMS-determined DRGs, who is discharged to a post acute provider, is treated as a transfer case; this means hospitals are paid a graduated *per diem* rate for each day of the patient's stay, not to exceed the prospective payment DRG rate.

K

key components (7)   extent of history, extent of examination, and level of medical decision making (except for Office or Other Outpatient Services).

L

lead agent (LA) (16)   serves as a federal health care team created to work with regional military treatment facility commanders, uniformed service headquarters' staffs, and Health Affairs (HA) to support the mission of the Military Health System (MHS).

legacy classification system (6)   *see* legacy coding system.

legacy coding system (6)   system that is no longer supported or updated, such as ICD-9-CM once ICD-10-CM/PCS replaced it effective October 1, 2015. (*See also* general equivalence mapping.)

legislation (2)   federal, state, county and municipal (city) laws, which are rules of conduct enforced by threat of punishment if violated.

lesion (6)   any discontinuity of tissue (e.g., skin or organ) that may or may not be malignant.

level of E/M service (7)   use of last number of each CPT evaluation and management services code to represent level of service provided.

liability insurance (12)   policy that covers losses to a third party caused by the insured, by an object owned by the insured, or on the premises owned by the insured.

lien (12)   pledges or secures a debtor's property as a guarantee of payment for a debt; may be used in a potential liability case, but use varies on a federal and state basis.

lifetime maximum amount (2)   maximum benefit payable to a health plan participant, such as annually or during a lifetime.

lifetime reserve days (14)   may be used only once during a patient's lifetime and are usually reserved for use during the patient's final, terminal hospital stay.

limiting charge (9)   maximum fee a nonparticipating provider (nonPAR) who does not accept assignment may bill Medicare patients for procedures and services provided.

listserv (5)   subscriber-based question-and-answer forum that is available through email.

litigation (4)   legal action to recover a debt; usually a last resort for a medical practice.

local coverage determination (LCD) (10)   formerly called *local medical review policy (LMRP);* Medicare administrative contractors create edits for national coverage determination rules that are called LCDs.

Longshore and Harbor Workers' Compensation Program (LHWCA) (17)   provides compensation, medical care, and vocational rehabilitation services to employees disabled from on-the-job injuries occurring on navigable waters of the United States, or in adjoining areas customarily used in the loading, unloading, repairing, or building of a vessel.

long-term (acute) care hospital prospective payment system (LTCH PPS) (9)   classifies patients according to long-term (acute) care DRGs, which are based on patients' clinical characteristics and expected resource needs; replaced the reasonable cost-based payment system.

M

main term (6) bold-faced term located in the ICD-10-CM index; listed in alphabetical order with subterms and qualifiers indented below each main term.

major diagnostic category (MDC) (9) organizes diagnosis-related groups (DRGs) into mutually exclusive categories, which are loosely based on body systems (e.g., nervous system).

major medical insurance (2) coverage for catastrophic or prolonged illnesses and injuries, which can include hospital, medical, and surgical benefits that supplement basic coverage benefits.

malignant (6) cancerous.

managed care (2) health care delivery system organized to manage health care costs, utilization, and quality.

managed care organization (MCO) (2) responsible for the health of a group of enrollees; can be a health plan, hospital, physician group, or health system.

managed health care (2) see managed care.

management service organization (MSO) (2) usually owned by physicians or a hospital and provides practice management (administrative and support) services to individual physician practices.

mandate (2) official directive, instruction, or order to take or perform a certain action, such as regulations written by federal government administrative agencies; they are also authoritative commands, such as by courts, governors, and legislatures.

manual daily accounts receivable journal (3) also called the *day sheet;* a chronological summary of all transactions posted to individual patient ledgers/accounts on a specific day.

mass immunizer (14) traditional Medicare-enrolled provider/supplier or a non-traditional provider that offers influenza virus and/or pneumococcal vaccinations to a large number of individuals.

material safety data sheet (MSDS) (17) contains information about chemical and hazardous substances used on-site.

meaningful EHR user (2) providers who demonstrate that certified EHR technology is used for electronic prescribing, electronic exchange of health information in accordance with law and HIT standards, and submission of information on clinical quality measures; and hospitals that demonstrate that certified EHR technology is connected in a manner that provides for the electronic exchange of health information to improve quality of care and that the technology is used to submit information on clinical quality measures.

meaningful use (2) objectives and measures that achieved goals of improved patient care outcomes and delivery through data capture and sharing, advance clinical processes, and improved patient outcomes; replaced by *quality payment program (QPM).*

Medicaid (15) cost-sharing program between the federal and state governments to provide health care services to Americans with low incomes.

Medicaid eligibility verification system (MEVS) (15) sometimes called *recipient eligibility verification system or REVS;* allows providers to electronically access the state's eligibility file through point-of-sale device, computer software, and automated voice response.

Medicaid Fraud Control Unit (MFCU) (5) investigates and prosecutes Medicaid provider fraud as well as patient abuse or neglect in health care facilities and board and care facilities

in all 50 States, the District of Columbia, Puerto Rico, and the U.S. Virgin Islands.

Medicaid integrity contractor (MIC) (5) CMS-contracted entities that review provider claims, audit providers and others, identify overpayments, and educate providers, managed care entities, beneficiaries and others with respect to payment integrity and quality of care.

Medicaid Integrity Program (MIP) (5) combats fraud, waste, and abuse in the Medicaid program; Congress requires annual reporting by CMS about the use and effectiveness of funds appropriated for the MIP.

Medicaid remittance advice (15) sent to the provider; serves as an explanation of benefits from Medicaid and contains the current status of all claims (including adjusted and voided claims).

medical assistance program (15) provides health care coverage to individuals with low incomes.

medical assistant (1) employed by a provider to perform administrative and clinical tasks that keep the office or clinic running smoothly.

medical care (2) includes the identification of disease and the provision of care and treatment as provided by members of the health care team to persons who are sick, injured, or concerned about their health status.

medical decision making (7) refers to the complexity of establishing a diagnosis and/or selecting a management option as measured by the number of diagnoses or management options, amount and/or complexity of data to be reviewed, and risk of complications and/or morbidity or mortality.

medical foundation (2) nonprofit organization that contracts with and acquires the clinical and business assets of physician practices; the foundation is assigned a provider number and manages the practice's business.

medical identify theft (5) occurs when someone uses another person's name and/or insurance information to obtain medical and/or surgical treatment, prescription drugs, and medical durable equipment; it can also occur when dishonest people who work in a medical setting use another person's information to submit false bills to health care plans.

medical malpractice insurance (1) a type of liability insurance that covers physicians and other health care professionals for liability claims arising from patient treatment.

medical necessity (1) involves linking every procedure or service code reported on an insurance claim to a condition code (e.g., disease, injury, sign, symptom, other reason for encounter) that justifies the need to perform that procedure or service.

medical necessity denial (14) denial of otherwise covered services that were found to be not "reasonable and necessary."

medical record (2) see patient record.

medical review (MR) (5) defined by CMS as a review of claims to determine whether services provided are medically reasonable and necessary, as well as to follow up on the effectiveness of previous corrective actions.

medically managed (10) a particular diagnosis (e.g., hypertension) may not receive direct treatment during an office visit, but the provider had to consider that diagnosis when considering treatment for other conditions.

medically unlikely edit (MUE) (10) used to compare units of service (UOS) with CPT and HCPCS Level II codes reported on claims; indicates the maximum number of UOS allowable by the same provider for the same beneficiary on the same date of service under most circumstances; the MUE project was implemented to improve the accuracy of Medicare payments by detecting and denying unlikely Medicare claims on a prepayment basis. On the CMS-1500, Block 24G (units of service) is compared with Block 24D (code number) on the same line. On the UB-04, Form Locator 46 (service units) is compared with Form Locator 44.

Medicare (14) federal health insurance program, authorized by Congress and administered by CMS, for people who are 65 or older, certain younger people with disabilities, and people with end-stage renal disease (ESRD).

Medicare administrative contractor (MAC) (5) an organization (e.g., third-party payer) that contracts with CMS to process claims and perform program integrity tasks for Medicare Part A and Medicare Part B, and DMEPOS; each contractor makes program coverage decisions and publishes a newsletter, which is sent to providers who receive Medicare reimbursement. Medicare transitioned fiscal intermediaries and carriers to create Medicare administrative contractors (MACs).

Medicare Advantage (14) see Medicare Part C.

Medicare-approved amount (14) amount a physician or supplier that accepts assignment will be paid, which may be less than the actual amount charged; Medicare pays part of the Medicare-approved amount, and the beneficiary pays the remainder; applies to Original Medicare.

Medicare beneficiary identifier (MBI) (14) replaces SSN as health insurance claim number on new Medicare cards for transactions such as billing, eligibility status, and claim status.

Medicare code editor (MCE) (10) software program used to detect and report errors in ICD-10-CM/PCS coded data during processing of inpatient hospital Medicare claims.

Medicare contracting reform (MCR) initiative (2) established to integrate the administration of Medicare Parts A and B fee-for-service benefits with new entities called Medicare administrative contractors (MACs); MACs replaced Medicare carriers, DMERCs, and fiscal intermediaries.

Medicare Cost Plan (14) type of Medicare health plan available in certain areas of the country, which works similarly to a Medicare Advantage plan; if the beneficiary receives health care services from a non-network provider, Original Medicare provides coverage, and the beneficiary pays Medicare Part A and Part B coinsurance and deductibles.

Medicare coverage database (MCD) (10) used by Medicare administrative contractors, providers, and other health care industry professionals to determine whether a procedure or service is reasonable and necessary for the diagnosis or treatment of an illness or injury; contains national coverage determinations (NCDs), including draft policies and proposed decisions; local coverage determinations (LCDs), including policy articles; and national coverage analyses (NCAs), coding analyses for labs (CALs), Medicare Evidence Development & Coverage Advisory Committee (MedCAC) proceedings, and Medicare coverage guidance documents.

Medicare Drug Integrity Contractors (MEDIC) Program (5) implemented in 2011 assists with CMS audit, oversight, anti-fraud, and anti-abuse efforts by identifying cases of Medicare Part D fraud and abuse, thoroughly investigating the cases, and taking appropriate action.

Medicare Hospital Insurance (14) see Medicare Part A.

Medicare Improvement for Patients and Providers Act (MIPPA) (2) Benefit programs that support states' and tribes' eligible Medicare beneficiaries to help lower costs of Medicare premiums and deductibles.

Medicare Integrity Program (MIP) (5) authorizes CMS to enter into contracts with entities to perform cost report auditing, medical review, anti-fraud activities, and the Medicare Secondary Payer (MSP) program.

Medicare-Medicaid (Medi-Medi) crossover (14) combination of Medicare and Medicaid programs available to Medicare-eligible persons with incomes below the federal poverty level.

Medicare Medical Insurance (14) see Medicare Part B.

Medicare medical savings account (MSA) (14) used by a Medicare beneficiary who is enrolled in Medicare Part C (Medicare Advantage) pay for health care services; Medicare pays the cost of a special health care policy that has a high deductible, and Medicare annually deposits into an account the difference between policy costs and what Medicare pays for an average enrollee in the patient's region; money deposited by Medicare is managed by a Medicare-approved insurance company or other qualified company, and it is not taxed if the beneficiary uses it to pay for qualified health care expenses.

Medicare Outpatient Observation Notice (MOON) (14) standardized notice provided to Medicare beneficiaries that they are outpatients receiving observation services and are not inpatients of a hospital or a critical access hospital (CAH).

Medicare Part A (14) helps cover inpatient hospital care, skilled nursing facility care, hospice care, and home health care; the UB-04 (CMS-1450) claim is submitted for services.

Medicare Part B (14) helps cover physician and other qualified health care practitioner services, outpatient care, durable medical equipment, and preventive services; the CMS-1500 claim is submitted for services.

Medicare Part C (14) an alternative to the Original Medicare Plan that bundles Medicare Part A, Part B, and Part D coverage, and may offer extra benefits such as dental, hearing, vision; formerly called Medicare+Choice; currently also called Medicare Advantage.

Medicare Part D (14) helps cover the cost of band name and generic prescription drugs according to a drug formulary.

Medicare Part D coverage gap (14) the difference between the initial coverage limit and the catastrophic coverage threshold as described in the Medicare Part D plan purchased by a Medicare beneficiary; a Medicare beneficiary who surpasses the prescription drug coverage limit is financially responsible for the entire cost of prescription drugs until expenses reach the catastrophic coverage threshold; also called Medicare Part D "donut hole."

Medicare Part D "donut hole" (14) see Medicare Part D coverage gap.

Medicare Part D sponsor (14) organization (e.g., health insurance company) that has one or more contract(s) with CMS to provide Part D benefits to Medicare beneficiaries.

Medicare physician fee schedule (MPFS) (9) payment system that reimburses providers for services and procedures by classifying services according to relative value units (RVUs); previously known as Resource-Based Relative Value Scale (RBRVS) system.

Medicare Prescription Drug, Improvement, and Modernization Act (MMA) (2) adds new prescription drug and preventive benefits and provides extra assistance to people with low incomes.

Medicare Prescription Drug Coverage (14) *see* Medicare Part D.

Medicare Pricing, Data Analysis, and Coding (PDAC) contractor (8) responsible for providing suppliers and manufacturers with assistance in determining HCPCS codes to be used; PDACs replaced SADMERCs (statistical analysis durable medical equipment regional carriers).

Medicare private contract (14) agreement between Medicare beneficiary and physician or other practitioner who has "opted out" of Medicare for two years for *all* covered items and services furnished to Medicare beneficiaries; physician/practitioner will not bill for any service or supplies provided to any Medicare beneficiary for at least two years.

Medicare Remittance Advice (4) an electronic remittance advice (ERA) or standard paper remit (SPR) sent to providers by Medicare administrative contractors, which contain details about claims adjudication and contains information about payments, deductibles and copayments, adjustments, denials, missing or incorrect data, refunds, and claims withheld due to Medicare Secondary Payer (MSP) or penalty situations.

Medicare risk program (2) federally qualified HMOs and competitive medical plans (CMPs) that meet specified Medicare requirements provide Medicare-covered services under a risk contract.

Medicare Savings Program (14) implemented as part of the Medicare Catastrophic Coverage Act of 1988 and later expanded by other legislation to provide relief for individuals who have limited income and resources so that the federal and state (and even some county) governments help pay for Medicare costs (when certain conditions are met).

Medicare Secondary Payer (MSP) (14) situations in which the Medicare program does not have primary responsibility for paying a beneficiary's medical expenses.

Medicare SELECT (14) type of Medigap policy available in some states where beneficiaries choose from a standardized Medigap plan.

Medicare severity diagnosis-related groups (MS-DRGs) (9) adopted by Medicare in 2008 to improve recognition of severity of illness and resource consumption and reduce cost variation among DRGs; bases DRG relative weights on hospital costs and greatly expanded the number of DRGs; reevaluated complications/comorbidities (CC) list to assign all ICD-10-CM codes as non-CC status (conditions that should not be treated as CCs for specific clinical conditions), CC status, or major CC status; handles diagnoses closely associated with patient mortality differently depending on whether the patient lived or expired.

Medicare Shared Savings Program (MSSP) (14) mandated by the Patient Protection and Portable Care Act (PPACA) to facilitate coordination and cooperation among providers to improve quality of care for Medicare fee-for-service beneficiaries and to reduce unnecessary costs through the creation of accountable care organizations (ACOs).

Medicare special needs plans (SNP) (14) covers Medicare Part A and/or Part B health care for individuals who can benefit the most from special care for chronic illnesses, care management of multiple diseases, and focused acute care management; such plans may limit membership to individuals who are eligible for both Medicare and Medicaid, have certain chronic or disabling conditions, and reside in certain institutions (e.g., nursing facility).

Medicare Summary Notice (MSN) (9) notifies Medicare beneficiaries of actions taken on claims.

Medicare supplemental plan (11) covers the Medicare deductible and copay or coinsurance amounts that patients pay for receiving health care through Medicare.

Medicare Supplementary Insurance (MSI) (14) *see* Medigap.

Medication Therapy Management Programs (14) available to Medicare beneficiaries who participate in a drug plan so they can learn how to manage medications through a free *Medication Therapy Management (MTM)* program; the MTM provides a list of a beneficiary's medications, reasons why beneficiaries take them, an action plan to help beneficiaries make the best use of medications, and a summary of medication review with the beneficiary's physician or pharmacist.

Medigap (14) supplemental plans designed by the federal government but sold by private commercial insurance companies to cover the costs of Medicare deductibles, copayments, and coinsurance, which are considered "gaps" in Medicare coverage.

member (13) BCBS enrollee or subscriber.

member hospital (13) hospital that has signed a contract to provide services for special rates.

Merit-Based Incentive Payment System (MIPS) (2) eliminated PQRS, value-based payment modifier, and the Medicare EHR incentive program, creating a single program based on quality, resource use, clinical practice improvement, and meaningful use of certified EHR technology.

message digest (5) representation of text as a single string of digits, which was created using a formula; for the purpose of electronic signatures, the message digest is encrypted (encoded) and appended (attached) to an electronic document.

metastasis (6) spread of cancer from primary to secondary site(s).

metrics (3) standards of measurement, such as those used to evaluate an organization's revenue cycle to ensure financial viability.

Military Health System (MHS) (16) entire health care system of the U.S. uniformed services and includes military treatment facilities (MTFs) as well as various programs in the civilian health care market, such as TRICARE; the MHS is managed by the Defense Health Agency (DHA).

Military Health System (MHS) Nurse Advice Line (16) allows TRICARE beneficiaries to receive advice from a registered nurse 24/7 when living or traveling in the United States or a country with an established military hospital or clinic.

military treatment facility (MTF) (16) hospital or clinic located on military bases and posts around the world that provides inpatient and/or ambulatory (outpatient and emergency department) care to eligible TRICARE beneficiaries.

Mine Safety and Health Administration (MSHA) (17) carries out provisions of the *Federal Mine Safety and Health Act of 1977 (Mine Act)* as amended by the *Mine Improvement and New Emergency Response (MINER) Act of 2006*; works cooperatively with industry, labor, and other federal and state agencies to improve safety and health conditions for all miners in the United States.

Minimum Data Set (MDS) (9) data elements collected by long-term care facilities.

minimum necessary standard (5) key protection of the HIPAA Privacy Rule based on sound current practice that protected health information should not be used or disclosed when it is not necessary to satisfy a particular purpose or carry out a function.

moderate (conscious) sedation (7) administration of moderate sedation or analgesia, which results in a drug-induced depression of consciousness.

modifier (7, 8) two-digit or two-character code attached to the main CPT or HCPCS Level II code; indicates that a procedure/service has been altered in some manner (e.g., modifier -50 indicates a bilateral procedure).

monitored anesthesia care (MAC) (7) provision of local or regional anesthetic services with certain conscious-altering drugs when provided by a physician, anesthesiologist, or medically directed CRNA; monitored anesthesia care involves sufficiently monitoring the patient to anticipate the potential need for administration of general anesthesia, and it requires continuous evaluation of vital physiologic functions as well as recognition and treatment of adverse changes.

morbidity (6) pertaining to illness or disease.

morphology (6) indicates the tissue type of a neoplasm; morphology codes are reported to state cancer registries.

mortality (6) death.

multiple surgical procedures (7) two or more surgeries performed during the same operative session.

N

narrative clinic note (10) using paragraph format to document health care.

national codes (1) commonly referred to as HCPCS Level II codes; include five-digit alphanumeric codes for procedures, services, and supplies that are not classified in CPT (e.g., J-codes are used to assign drugs administered).

National Committee for Quality Assurance (NCQA) (2) a private, not-for-profit organization that assesses the quality of managed care plans in the United States and releases the data to the public for its consideration when selecting a managed care plan.

National Correct Coding Initiative (NCCI) program (10) developed by CMS to promote national correct coding methodologies and to eliminate improper coding practices.

National Council for Prescription Drug Programs (NCPCP) Telecommunication Standard (11) standard format for retail pharmacy.

national coverage determination (NCD) (10) rules developed by CMS that specify under what clinical circumstances a service or procedure is covered (including clinical circumstances considered reasonable and necessary) and correctly coded; Medicare administrative contractors create edits for NCD rules called local coverage determinations (LCDs).

National Drug Code (NDC) (5) maintained by the Food and Drug Administration (FDA); identifies prescription drugs and some over-the-counter products.

National Individual Identifier (5) unique identifier to be assigned to patients has been put on hold. Several bills in Congress would eliminate the requirement to establish a National Individual Identifier.

National Plan and Provider Enumeration System (NPPES) (5) developed by CMS to assign unique identifiers to health care providers (NPI).

National Practitioner Data Bank (NPDB) (5) implemented by Health Care Quality Improvement Act (HCQIA) of 1986 to improve quality of health care by encouraging state licensing boards, hospitals, and other health care entities and professional societies to identify and discipline those who engage in unprofessional behavior; restricts ability of incompetent physicians, dentists, and other health care practitioners to move from state to state without disclosure or discovery of previous medical malpractice payment and adverse action history; impacts licensure, clinical privileges, and professional society memberships as a result of adverse actions; includes Health Integrity and Protection Data Bank (HIPDB), originally established by HIPAA, to further combat fraud and abuse in health insurance and health care delivery by serving as a national data collection program for reporting and disclosing certain final adverse actions taken against health care practitioners, providers, and suppliers.

National Provider Identifier (NPI) (5) unique identifier assigned to health care providers as a 10-digit numeric identifier, including a check digit in the last position.

National Standard Employer Identification Number (EIN) (5) unique identifier assigned to employers who, as sponsors of health insurance for their employees, need to be identified in health care transactions; it is the federal employer identification number (EIN) assigned by the Internal Revenue Service (IRS) and has nine digits with a hyphen (00-0000000); EIN assignment by the IRS began in January 1998.

National Standard Format (NSF) (5) flat-file format used to bill provider and noninstitutional services, such as services reported by a general practitioner on a CMS-1500 claim.

nature of the presenting problem (7) defined by CPT as a disease, condition, illness, injury, symptom, sign, finding, complaint, or other reason for the encounter, with or without a diagnosis being established at the time of the encounter.

neoplasm (6) new growth, or tumor, in which cell reproduction is out of control.

network model HMO (2) contracted health care services provided to subscribers by two or more physician multispecialty group practices.

network provider (2) physician, other health care practitioner, or health care facility under contract to the managed care plan.

Never Events (9) medical errors that should never occur (e.g., wrong-site surgery) and adverse events that are unambiguous (clearly identifiable and measurable), serious (resulting in death or significant disability), and usually preventable.

new patient (7) one who has *not* received any professional services from the provider, or from another provider of the same specialty who belongs to the same group practice, within the past three years.

newborn care (7) covers examinations of normal or high-risk neonates in the hospital or other locations, subsequent newborn care in a hospital, and resuscitation of high-risk babies.

noncovered benefit (4) any procedure or service reported on a claim that is not included on the payer's master benefit list, resulting in denial of the claim; also called *noncovered procedure* or *uncovered benefit*.

nonessential modifier (6) supplementary words located in parentheses after an ICD-10-CM main term that do not have to be included in the diagnostic statement for the code number to be assigned.

nonparticipating provider (nonPAR) (3) does not contract with the insurance plan; patients who elect to receive care from nonPARs will incur higher out-of-pocket expenses.

nonprofit corporation (13) charitable, educational, civic, or humanitarian organization whose profits are returned to the program of the corporation rather than distributed to shareholders and officers of the corporation.

Notice of Privacy Practices (NPP) (5) document that includes an individual's health privacy rights related to protected health information (PHI) and communicates how health information may be used and shared.

nursing facility services (7) performed at the following sites: skilled nursing facilities (SNFs), intermediate care facilities (ICFs), and long-term care facilities (LTCFs).

O

Obamacare (2) nickname for the *Patient Protection and Affordable Care Act (PPACA)*, which was signed into federal law by President Obama on March 23, 2010, and created the Health Care Marketplace.

observation or inpatient care services (7) CPT codes used to report observation or inpatient hospital care services provided to patients admitted and discharged on the same date of service.

observation services (7) furnished in a hospital out-patient setting to determine whether further treatment or inpatient admission is needed; when a patient is placed under observation, the patient is categorized as an outpatient; if the duration of observation care is expected to be 24 hours or more, the physician must order an inpatient admission (and the date the physician orders the inpatient stay is the date of inpatient admission).

Occupational Safety and Health Administration (OSHA) (17) ensures safe and healthful working conditions for workers; its goals are to establish and enforce standards and to provide training, outreach, education, and assistance.

Office of Managed Care (2) CMS agency that facilitates innovation and competition among Medicare HMOs.

Office of Workers' Compensation Programs (OWCP) (17) administers programs that provide wage replacement benefits, medical treatment, vocational rehabilitation, and other benefits to federal workers (or eligible dependents) who are injured at work or acquire an occupational disease.

Omnibus Budget Reconciliation Act of 1981 (OBRA) (2) federal law that requires providers to keep copies of any government insurance claims and copies of all attachments filed by the provider for a period of five years; also expanded Medicare and Medicaid programs.

on-the-job-injury (17) occurrence when the employee is either injured while working within the scope of the job description, injured while performing a service required by the employer, or succumbs to a disorder that can be directly linked to employment, such as asbestosis or mercury poisoning.

open claim (4) submitted to the payer, but processing is not complete.

open-panel HMO (2) health care provided by individuals who are not employees of the HMO or who do not belong to a specially formed medical group that serves the HMO.

operative report (10) varies from a short narrative description of a minor procedure that is performed in the physician's office to a more formal report dictated by the surgeon in a format required by the hospitals and ambulatory surgical centers (ASCs).

opt-out provider (14) provider who does not accept Medicare and has signed an agreement to be excluded from the Medicare program.

organ- or disease-oriented panel (7) series of blood chemistry studies routinely ordered by providers at the same time to investigate a specific organ (e.g., liver panel) or disease (e.g., thyroid panel).

Original Medicare (14) includes Medicare Part A and Medicare Part B.

orthotics (8) branch of medicine that deals with the design and fitting of orthopedic (relating to bone disorders) devices (e.g., braces).

Outcomes and Assessment Information Set (OASIS) (9) group of data elements that represent core items of a comprehensive assessment for an adult home care patient and form the basis for measuring patient outcomes for purposes of outcome-based quality improvement.

outlier (9) hospitals that treat unusually costly cases receive increased Medicare payments; the additional payment is designed to protect hospitals from large financial losses due to unusually expensive cases.

out-of-pocket payment (3) established by health insurance companies for a health insurance plan; usually has limits of $1,000 or $2,000; when the patient has reached the limit of an out-of-pocket payment (e.g., annual deductible) for the year, appropriate patient reimbursement to the provider is determined; not all health insurance plans include an out-of-pocket payment provision.

outpatient (6) person treated in one of three settings: health care provider's office; hospital clinic, emergency department, hospital same-day surgery unit, or ambulatory surgical center (ASC) where the patient is released within 23 hours; or hospital admission solely for observation where the patient is released after a short stay.

outpatient code editor (OCE) (10) software that edits outpatient claims submitted by hospitals, community mental health centers, comprehensive outpatient rehabilitation facilities, and home health agencies; the software reviews submissions for coding validity (e.g., missing fifth digits) and coverage (e.g., medical necessity); OCE edits result in one of the following dispositions: rejection, denial, return to provider (RTP), or suspension.

outpatient encounter (9) includes all outpatient procedures and services (e.g., same-day surgery, x-rays, laboratory tests, and so on) provided during one day to the same patient.

outpatient pretreatment authorization program (OPAP) (13) also called *prospective authorization* or *precertification;* requires preauthorization of outpatient physical, occupational, and speech therapy services; acupuncture; spinal manipulation/chiropractic; and habilitative services.

Outpatient Prospective Payment System (OPPS) (9) uses ambulatory payment classifications (APCs) to calculate reimbursement; was implemented for billing of hospital-based Medicare outpatient claims.

outpatient visit (9) *see* outpatient encounter.

outsource (4) contract out.

overlapping sites (6) *see* contiguous sites.

overpayment (5)   funds that a provider or beneficiary has received in excess of amounts due and payable under Medicare and Medicaid statutes and regulations.

P

palliative care (14)   provision of comfort care, such as pain management and symptom relief, instead of treatment to cure an illness.

parent/newborn claim (15)   submitted for services provided to a newborn under the parent's Medicaid identification number.

Part A/B Medicare administrative contractor (A/B MAC) (5)   see Medicare administrative contractor.

partial hospitalization (7)   short-term, intensive treatment program where individuals who are experiencing an acute episode of an illness (e.g., geriatric, psychiatric, or rehabilitative) can receive medically supervised treatment during a significant number of daytime or nighttime hours; this type of program is an alternative to 24-hour inpatient hospitalization and allows the patients to maintain their everyday lives without the disruption associated with an inpatient hospital stay.

participating provider (PAR) (3)   contracts with a health insurance plan and accepts whatever the plan pays for procedures or services performed.

past-due account (4)   one that has not been paid within a certain time frame (e.g., 120 days); also called delinquent account.

patient account record (3)   also called patient ledger; a computerized or manual permanent record of all financial transactions between the patient and the practice.

patient assessment instrument (PAI) (9)   classifies patients into groups based on clinical characteristics and expected resource needs.

patient-driven payment model (PDPM) (9)   case-mix reimbursement system that connects payment to patients' conditions and care needs instead of the volume of services provided; impacts intermediate care facilities, long term acute care facilities, and skilled nursing facilities.

patient ledger (3)   see patient account record.

Patient Protection and Affordable Care Act (PPACA) (2)   focuses on private health insurance reform to provide better coverage for individuals with pre-existing conditions, improve prescription drug coverage under Medicare, extend the life of the Medicare Trust fund by at least 12 years, and create the health insurance marketplace.

patient record (2)   documents health care services provided to a patient.

Patient Safety and Quality Improvement Act (5)   amends Title IX of the Public Health Service Act to provide for improved patient safety by encouraging voluntary and confidential reporting of events that adversely affect patients; creates patient safety organizations (PSOs) to collect, aggregate, and analyze confidential information reported by health care providers; and designates information reported to PSOs as privileged and not subject to disclosure (except when a court determines that the information contains evidence of a criminal act or each provider identified in the information authorizes disclosure).

payer mix (2)   different types of health insurance payments made to providers for patient services.

pay-for-performance (P4P) (9)   initiatives that link reimbursement to performance criteria so that the right care is provided for every patient every time; right care is effective, efficient, equitable, patient-centered, safe, and timely; as such, despite the patient's ethnicity, gender, geographic location, and socioeconomic status, patients receive "right care."

Payment Error Prevention Program (PEPP) (5)   required facilities to identify and reduce improper Medicare payments and, specifically, the Medicare payment error rate. The hospital payment monitoring program (HPMP) replaced PEPP in 2002.

payment error rate (5)   number of dollars paid in error out of total dollars paid for inpatient prospective payment system services.

Payment Error Rate Measurement (PERM) program (5)   measures improper payments in the Medicaid program and the Children's Health Insurance Program (CHIP).

payment system (9)   reimbursement method the federal government uses to compensate providers for patient care.

peer review (4)   appeal process that involves review of aby a medical reviewer (e.g., nurse) or a medical director (e.g., physician), and if an appeal is escalated, an independent external reviewer (e.g., physician with same specialty as provider) may assess the appeal.

per diem (9)   Latin term meaning "for each day," which is how retrospective cost-based rates were determined; payments were issued based on daily rates.

performance measurements (2)   strengthen organization accountability and support performance improvement initiatives by assessing the degree to which evidence-based treatment guidelines are followed and include an evaluation of results of care.

permanent disability (17)   refers to an ill or injured employee's diminished capacity to return to work.

personal health record (PHR) (2)   web-based application that allows individuals to maintain and manage their health information (and that of others for whom they are authorized, such as family members) in a private, secure, and confidential environment.

physical examination (7)   assessment of the patient's body areas (e.g., extremities) and organ systems (e.g., cardiovascular).

physical status modifier (7)   indicates the patient's condition at the time anesthesia was administered.

physician incentive plan (2)   requires managed care plans that contract with Medicare or Medicaid to disclose information about physician incentive plans to CMS or state Medicaid agencies before a new or renewed contract receives final approval.

physician incentives (2)   include payments made directly or indirectly to health care providers to serve as encouragement to reduce or limit services (e.g., discharge an inpatient from the hospital more quickly) to save money for the managed care plan.

physician query process (6)   when coders have questions about documented diagnoses or procedures/services, they contact the responsible physician to request clarification about documentation and the code(s) to be assigned.

physician referral (2)   written order by a primary care provider that facilitates patient evaluation and treatment by a physician specialist.

physician self-referral law (5)   *see* Stark I.

physician-hospital organization (PHO) (2)   owned by hospital(s) and physician groups that obtain managed care plan contracts; physicians maintain their own practices and provide health care services to plan members.

Physicians at Teaching Hospitals (PATH) (5)   HHS implemented audits in 1995 to examine the billing practices of physicians at teaching hospitals; the focus was on two issues: (1) compliance with the Medicare rule affecting payment for physician services provided by residents (e.g., whether a teaching physician was present for Part B services billed to Medicare between 1990 and 1996), and (2) whether the level of the physician service was coded and billed properly.

place of service (POS) (7)   the physical location where health care is provided to patients (e.g., office or other outpatient settings, hospitals, nursing facilities, home health care, or emergency departments); the two-digit location code is required by Medicare.

point-of-service plan (POS) (2)   delivers health care services using both managed care network and traditional indemnity coverage so patients can seek care outside the managed care network.

poisoning: accidental (unintentional) (6)   poisoning that results from an inadvertent overdose, wrong substance administered/taken, or intoxication that includes combining prescription drugs with nonprescription drugs or alcohol.

poisoning: assault (6)   poisoning inflicted by another person who intended to kill or injure the patient.

poisoning: intentional self-harm (6)   poisoning that results from a deliberate overdose, such as a suicide attempt, of substance(s) administered/taken or intoxication that includes purposely combining prescription drugs with nonprescription drugs or alcohol.

poisoning: undetermined (6)   subcategory used if the patient record does not document whether the poisoning was intentional or accidental.

policyholder (2)   a person who signs a contract with a health insurance company and who, thus, owns the health insurance policy.

practice guidelines (16)   decision-making tools used by providers to determine appropriate health care for specific clinical circumstances.

preadmission certification (PAC) (3)   review for medical necessity of inpatient care prior to the patient's admission.

preadmission review (3)   *see* preadmission certification.

preadmission testing (PAT) (6)   completed prior to an inpatient admission or outpatient surgery to facilitate the patient's treatment and reduce the length of stay.

preauthorization (3)   health plan review that grants prior approval of patient health care services.

precedent (5)   based on a court decision that is legally binding and follows the doctrine of *stare decisis* for deciding subsequent cases involving identical or similar facts; *stare decisis* is Latin for "the thing speaks for itself," which means it require courts to apply precedent law in the same manner to cases with the same facts.

precertification (3)   *see* preauthorization.

pre-existing condition (4)   any medical condition that was diagnosed and/or treated within a specified period of time immediately preceding the enrollee's effective date of coverage.

Preferred Provider Health Care Act of 1985 (2)   eased restrictions on preferred provider organizations (PPOs) and allowed subscribers to seek health care from providers outside of the PPO.

preferred provider organization (PPO) (2)   network of physicians, other health care practitioners, and hospitals that have joined together to contract with insurance companies, employers, or other organizations to provide health care to subscribers for a discounted fee.

premium (2)   amount paid for a health insurance policy.

preoperative clearance (7)   occurs when a surgeon requests that a specialist or other physician (e.g., general practice) examine a patient and give an opinion as to whether that patient can withstand the expected risks of a specific surgery.

prepaid health plan (2)   capitation contract between a health plan and providers who manage all of the health care for a patient population and are reimbursed a predetermined amount of money either monthly or annually.

prescription management (2)   controls medication costs using a variety of strategies, which include pharmacy benefit managers, cost-sharing copayments or coinsurance, disease management programs, electronic prescribing, drug formularies, drug utilization review, generic substitution, manufacturer drug rebates, negotiated prices, and prescription mail services.

present on admission (POA) (9)   condition that exists at the time an order for inpatient hospital admission occurs; when a condition develops during an outpatient encounter, including emergency department services, observation care, or outpatient surgery, and the patient is admitted as a hospital inpatient, such conditions are considered *present on admission*.

preventive medicine services (7)   routine examinations or risk management counseling for children and adults exhibiting no overt signs or symptoms of a disorder while presenting to the medical office for a preventive medical physical; also called "wellness visits."

preventive services (2)   designed to help individuals avoid problems with health and injuries.

primary care manager (PCM) (16)   assigned to provide most of a TRICARE beneficiary's care and is a military or network provider that is responsible for referring beneficiaries to specialists, working with regional contractors to obtain for referrals/authorization, accepting copayments for covered health care services, and submitting claims.

primary care provider (PCP) (2)   responsible for supervising and coordinating health care services for enrollees and preauthorizing referrals to specialists and inpatient hospital admissions (except in emergencies).

primary health insurance (3)   associated with how a health insurance plan is billed—the insurance plan responsible for paying health care insurance claims first is considered primary.

primary malignancy (6)   original cancer site.

principal diagnosis (6)   condition determined, after study, that resulted in the patient's admission to the hospital.

prior approval (3)   *see* preauthorization.

prior authorization (3)   *see* preauthorization.

privacy (5)   right of individuals to keep their information from being disclosed to others.

Privacy Act of 1974 (5)   forbids the Medicare regional payer from disclosing the status of any unassigned claim beyond the following: date the claim was received by the payer; date the claim was paid, denied, or suspended; or general reason the claim was suspended.

private health insurance (12)   *see* commercial health insurance.

private fee-for-service (PFFS) (14)   health care plan offered by private insurance companies; not available in all areas of the country.

privileged communication (5)   private information shared between a patient and health care provider; disclosure must be in accordance with HIPAA and/or individual state provisions regarding the privacy and security of protected health information (PHI).

problem-oriented record (POR) (2)   a systematic method of documentation that consists of four components: database, problem list, initial plan, and progress notes.

procedure-to-procedure (PTP) code pair edits (10)   automated prepayment NCCI program edits that prevent improper payment when certain codes are submitted together for Medicare Part B covered services.

professional billing   (3)   involves generating CMS-1500 claims for charges generated for professional services and supplies provided by physicians and non-physician practitioners (NPPs), which according to CMS include nurse practitioners, physician assistants, clinical nurse midwives, certified registered nurse anesthetists, and clinical nurse specialists.

professional component (7)   supervision of procedure, interpretation, and writing of the report.

professional liability insurance (1)   provides protection from liability as a result of errors and omissions when performing their professional services; also called *errors and omissions insurance*.

professionalism (1)   conduct or qualities that characterize a professional person.

Program for Evaluating Payment Patterns Electronic Report (PEPPER) (5)   contains hospital-specific administrative claims data for a number of CMS-identified problem areas (e.g., specific DRGs, types of discharges); a hospital uses PEPPER data to compare its performance with that of other hospitals.

Program Integrity (PI) Office (16)   responsible for the worldwide surveillance of fraud and abuse activities involving purchased care for beneficiaries in the Military Health System.

Programs of All-Inclusive Care for the Elderly (PACE) (14)   provides a comprehensive package of community-based medical and social services as an alternative to institutional care for persons aged 55 or older who require a nursing home-level of care (e.g., adult day health center, home health care, and/or inpatient facilities).

prolonged services (7)   assigned in addition to other E/M services when treatment exceeds by 30 minutes or more the time included in the CPT description of the service.

Promoting Interoperability (PI) Programs (2)   focus on improving patient access to health information and reducing the time and cost required of providers to comply with the programs' requirements; previously called EHR incentive programs.

property insurance (1)   protects business contents (e.g., buildings and equipment) against fire, theft, and other risks.

prospective cost-based rates (9)   rates established in advance, but based on reported health care costs (charges) from which a prospective *per diem* rate is determined.

prospective payment system (PPS) (9)   issues predetermined payment for services, such as bundled payments, capitation, case rates, and global payments.

prospective price-based rates (9)   rates associated with a particular category of patient (e.g., hospital inpatients) and established by the payer (e.g., Medicare) prior to the provision of health care procedures and services.

prospective review (3)   reviewing appropriateness and necessity of care provided to patients prior to administration of care.

prosthetics (8)   branch of medicine that deals with the design, production, and use of artificial body parts (e.g., artificial limbs).

protected health information (PHI) (5)   information that is identifiable to an individual (or individual identifiers) such as name, address, telephone numbers, date of birth, Medicaid ID number, medical record number, Social Security number (SSN), and name of employer.

public health insurance (2)   federal and state government health programs (e.g., Medicare, Medicaid, CHIP, TRICARE) available to eligible individuals.

Q

qualified diagnosis (6)   working diagnosis that is not yet proven or established; reported for inpatient cases only.

qualified disabled working individual (QDWI) (14)   helps individuals who qualify for the QMBP, SLMB, or QI programs by automatically qualifying them for extra assistance paying for Medicare drug coverage.

qualified Medicare beneficiary program (QMBP) (14)   program in which the federal government requires state Medicaid programs to pay Medicare premiums, deductibles, coinsurance amounts, and copayments for individuals who have Medicare Part A, a low monthly income, and limited resources, and who are not otherwise eligible for Medicaid.

qualifiers (6)   supplementary terms in the ICD-10-CM Index to Diseases and Injuries that further modify subterms and other qualifiers.

qualifying circumstances (7)   CPT Medicine Section codes reported in addition to Anesthesia Section codes when situations or circumstances make anesthesia administration more difficult (e.g., patient of extreme age, such as under one year or over 70).

qualifying individual (QI) (14)   state program that helps pay Part B premiums for people who have Part A and limited income and resources.

quality assessment and performance improvement (QAPI) (2)   program implemented so that quality assurance activities are performed to improve the functioning of Medicare Advantage organizations.

quality assurance program (2)   activities that assess the quality of care provided in a health care setting.

quality improvement (QI) (2)   involves continuous and systematic actions that result in measurable improvement in the provision of health care services and the health status of targeted patient groups.

quality improvement organization (QIO) (2) performs utilization and quality control review of health care furnished, or to be furnished, to Medicare beneficiaries.

Quality Improvement System for Managed Care (QISMC) (2) established by Medicare to ensure the accountability of managed care plans in terms of objective, measurable standards.

quality management program (2) *see* quality assurance program.

quality payment program (QPP) (2) helps providers focus on quality of patient care and making patients healthier; includes advanced alternative payment models (Advanced APMs) and merit-based incentive payment system (MIPS); replaced the EHR Incentive Program (or Meaningful Use), Physician Quality Reporting System, and Value-Based Payment Modifier program.

Quarterly Provider Update (QPU) (3) published by CMS to simplify the process of understanding proposed or implemented instructional, policy, and changes to its programs, such as Medicare.

qui tam **(5)** abbreviation for the Latin phrase *qui tam pro domino rege quam pro sic ipso in hoc parte sequitur,* which means "who as well for the king as for himself sues I this matter." It is a provision of the False Claims Act that allows a private citizen to file a lawsuit in the name of the U.S. government, charging fraud by government contractors and other entities.

R

radiologic views (7) studies taken from different angles.

recipient eligibility verification system (REVS) (15) also called *Medicaid eligibility verification system (MEVS);* allows providers to electronically access the state's eligibility file through point-of-sale device, computer software, and automated voice response.

record linkage (2) allows patient information to be created at different locations according to a unique patient identifier or identification number.

record retention (5) storage of documentation for an established period of time, usually mandated by federal and/or state law; its purpose is to ensure the availability of records for use by government agencies and other third parties.

Recovery Audit Contractor (RAC) program (5) mandated by the Medicare Prescription Drug, Improvement, and Modernization Act of 2003 (MMA) to find and correct improper Medicare payments paid to health care providers participating in fee-for-service Medicare.

re-excision (6) occurs when the pathology report recommends that the surgeon perform a second excision to widen the margins of the original tumor site.

referral (7) a patient who reports that another provider referred them.

regulation (5) mandated guideline written by administrative agencies (e.g., CMS); regulations interpret laws and mandates.

regulatory law (5) *see* regulation.

reimbursement specialist (1) *see* health insurance specialist.

relative value units (RVUs) (9) standardized measures used to determine MPFS pricing amounts that are adjusted to reflect the variation of practice costs from area to area; the standardized measures include physician work, practice expense, and malpractice expense.

release of information (ROI) (5) ROI by a covered entity (e.g., provider's office) about protected health information (PHI) requires the patient (or representative) to sign an authorization to release information, which is reviewed for authenticity (e.g., comparing signature on authorization form to documents signed in the patient record) and processed within a HIPAA-mandated 60-day time limit; requests for ROI include those from patients, physicians, and other health care providers; third-party payers; Social Security Disability attorneys; and so on.

release of information log (5) used to document patient information released to authorized requestors; data is entered manually (e.g., three-ring binder) or using ROI tracking software.

remit (4) *see* remittance advice

remittance advice (4) electronic remittance advice (ERA) or standard paper remit (SPR) sent to providers by third-party payers that contains details about claims adjudication, including information about payments, deductibles and copayments, adjustments, denials, missing or incorrect data, refunds, and claims withheld due to secondary payer, third-party liability, or penalty situations. Medicare administrative contractors send providers a *Medicare Remittance Advice.*

remittance advice remark code (RARC) (4) additional explanation of reasons for denied claims.

report card (2) contains data regarding a managed care plan's quality, utilization, customer satisfaction, administrative effectiveness, financial stability, and cost control.

requisition form (3) document electronically or manually submitted to a health care organization that serves as provider orders for outpatient services.

resequenced code (7) CPT codes that appear out of numerical order and are preceded by the # symbol (so as to provide direction to the out-of-sequence code).

Resident Assessment Validation and Entry (jRAVEN) (9) java-based data entry system used to enter MDS data about SNF patients and transmit those assessments in CMS-standard format to individual state or national databases.

resource allocation (3) distribution of financial resources among competing groups (e.g., hospital departments, state health care organizations).

resource allocation monitoring (3) uses data analytics to measure whether a health care provider or organization achieves operational goals and objectives within the confines of the distribution of financial resources, such as appropriately expending budgeted amounts as well as conserving resources and protecting assets while providing quality patient care.

respite care (14) the temporary hospitalization of a hospice patient for the purpose of providing relief from duty for the nonpaid person who has the major day-to-day responsibility for the care of the terminally ill, dependent patient.

respondeat superior **(1)** Latin for "let the master answer"; legal doctrine holding that the employer is liable for the actions and omissions of employees performed and committed within the scope of their employment.

retrospective reasonable cost system (9) reimbursement system in which providers reported actual charges for care after each encounter, and payers provided reimbursement according to a fee schedule, a percentage of billed charges, or a *per diem* basis.

retrospective reimbursement methodology (9)   *see* retrospective reasonable cost system.

retrospective review (3)   reviewing appropriateness and necessity of care provided to patients after the administration of care.

revenue auditing (3)   assessment process that is conducted as a follow-up to revenue monitoring so that areas of poor performance can be identified and corrected.

revenue code (3)   a four-digit code that indicates location or type of service provided to an institutional patient; reported in FL 42 of UB-04.

Revenue cycle management (3)   process that typically begins upon appointment scheduling or physician order for inpatient hospital admission and concludes when reimbursement is obtained or collections have been posted.

revenue management (3)   process that facilities and providers use to ensure financial viability.

revenue monitoring (3)   involves assessing the revenue process to ensure financial viability and stability using metrics (standards of measurement).

rider (2)   special contract clause stipulating additional coverage above the standard contract.

risk adjustment (14)   method of adjusting capitation payments to health plans, accounting for differences in expected health costs of enrollees.

risk adjustment data validation (RADV) (14)   process of verifying that diagnosis codes submitted for payment by a Medicare Advantage organization are supported by patient record documentation for an enrollee.

risk adjustment model (2)   provides payments to health plans that disproportionately attract higher-risk enrollees and uses an actuarial tool to predict health care costs based on the relative actuarial risk of enrollees in risk adjustment covered health plans.

risk adjustment program (2)   lessens or eliminates the influence of risk selection on premiums charged by health plans and includes the *risk adjustment model* and *risk transfer formula*.

risk contract (2)   an arrangement among providers to provide capitated (fixed, prepaid basis) health care services to Medicare beneficiaries.

risk of mortality (ROM) (9)   likelihood of dying.

risk pool (2)   combines a group of enrollees' medical costs to calculate managed care premiums (for enrollees); allows higher costs of less healthy patients to be offset by relatively lower costs of healthy patients.

risk transfer formula (2)   transfers funds from health plans with relatively lower-risk enrollees to health plans that enroll relatively higher-risk individuals, protecting such health plans against adverse selection.

roster billing (14)   streamlines the process for submitting health care claims for a large group of beneficiaries for influenza virus or pneumococcal vaccinations.

rural health information organizations (RHIO) (5)   type of health information exchange network that brings together health care stakeholders within a defined geographic area and governs health information exchange among them for the purpose of improving health and care in that community.

S

schedule of benefits (2)   outlines services covered by a health insurance plan.

scope of practice (1)   health care services, determined by the state, that an NP and PA can perform.

second surgical opinion (SSO) (2)   second physician is asked to evaluate the necessity of surgery and recommend the most economical, appropriate facility in which to perform the surgery.

secondary diagnosis (6)   coexists with the primary condition, has the potential to affect treatment of the primary condition, and is an active condition for which the patient is treated or monitored.

secondary health insurance (3)   billed after primary health insurance has paid contracted amount, and often contains the same coverage as a primary health plan.

secondary malignancy (6)   tumor has metastasized to a secondary site, either adjacent to the primary site or to a remote region of the body.

security (5)   involves the safekeeping of patient information by controlling access to hard copy and computerized records; protecting patient information from alteration, destruction, tampering, or loss; providing employee training in confidentiality of patient information; and requiring employees to sign a confidentiality statement that details the consequences of not maintaining patient confidentiality.

self-insured (or self-funded) employer-sponsored group health plan (2)   allows a large employer to assume the financial risk for providing health care benefits to employees; employer does not pay a fixed premium to a health insurance payer, but establishes a trust fund (of employer and employee contributions) out of which claims are paid.

self-referral (2)   enrollee who sees a non-HMO panel specialist without a referral from the primary care physician.

separate procedure (7)   follows a CPT code description to identify procedures that are an integral part of another procedure or service.

sequela (6)   residual late effects of injury or illness.

service location (13)   location where the patient was seen.

severity of illness (SOI) (9)   extent of physiological decompensation or organ system loss of function.

single-path coding (3)   combines professional and institutional coding to improve productivity and ensure the submission of clean claims, leading to improved reimbursement.

single-payer health system (2)   national health service model adopted by some Western nations (e.g., Canada, Great Britain) and funded by taxes. The government pays for each resident's health care, which is considered a basic social service.

site of service differential (9)   reduction of MPFS payment when office-based services are performed in a facility, such as a hospital or outpatient setting, because the physician or other qualified health care professional did not provide supplies, utilities, or the costs of running the facility.

Skilled Nursing Facility Prospective Payment System (SNF PPS) (9)   implemented to cover all costs (routine, ancillary, and capital) related to services furnished to Medicare Part A beneficiaries and generating *per diem* case-mix adjusted payments for each admission as part of a *patient-driven payment model (PDPM)* using a minimum data set and and relative weights developed from staff time data.

Skilled Nursing Facility Value-Based Purchasing (SNF VBP) Program (9)   implemented with the intent of rewarding quality and improving health care; SNFs have an opportunity to receive incentive payments based on performance.

skip tracing (4)   practice of locating patients to obtain payment of a bad debt; uses credit reports, databases, criminal background checks, and other methods.

skip tracking (4)   see skip tracing.

SOAP note (10)   outline format for documenting health care; "SOAP" is an acronym derived from the first letter of the headings used in the note: Subjective, Objective, Assessment, and Plan.

    assessment   contains the diagnostic statement and may include the provider's rationale for the diagnosis.

    objective   documentation of measurable or objective observations made during physical examination and diagnostic testing.

    plan   statement of the physician's future plans for the work-up and medical management of the case.

    subjective   part of the note that contains the chief complaint and the patient's description of the presenting problem.

socialized medicine (2)   type of single-payer system in which the government owns and operates health care facilities and providers (e.g., physicians) receive salaries; the VA health care program is a form of socialized medicine.

source document (4)   the routing slip, charge slip, encounter form, or superbill from which the insurance claim was generated.

special enrollment period (SEP) (14)   enrollment in Medicare Part A and Part B available outside of the general enrollment period due to special circumstances, such as individuals covered by a group health plan *based on current employment* as long as the individual or spouse (or family member if the individual is disabled) is working, and the individual is covered by a group health plan through the employer or union *based on that work*; individuals covered by a group health plan *based on current employment* whose employment ends or group health plan insurance *based on current employment* ends, whichever occurs first; or individuals who serve as international volunteers for at least 12 months and who volunteer for a tax-exempt non-profit organization and have health insurance during that time when volunteer work stops or health insurance outside of the United States ends, which occurs first; usually there is no *late enrollment penalty* if individuals enroll during a special enrollment period.

special report (7)   must accompany the claim when a CPT unlisted procedure or service code is reported to describe the nature, extent, and need for the procedure or service.

specified low-income Medicare beneficiary (SLMB) (14)   federally mandated program that requires states help pay Part B premiums for people who have Part A and limited income and resources.

spell of illness (14)   formerly called *spell of sickness;* is sometimes used in place of *benefit period*.

staff model HMO (2)   health care services are provided to subscribers by physicians and other health care practitioners employed by the HMO.

stand-alone code (7)   CPT code that includes a complete description of the procedure or service.

standards (2)   requirements established by accreditation organizations.

standby services (7)   cover providers who spend prolonged periods of time without direct patient contact, until provider's services are required.

Stark I (5)   responded to concerns about physicians' conflicts of interest when referring Medicare patients for a variety of services; prohibits physicians from referring Medicare patients to clinical laboratory services in which the physician or a member of the physician's family has a financial ownership/investment interest and/or compensation arrangement; also called *physician self-referral law*.

state compensation fund (17)   see state insurance fund.

state insurance fund (17)   a quasi-public agency that provides workers' compensation insurance coverage to private and public employers and acts as an agent in workers' compensation cases involving state employees.

statutes (5)   also called *statutory law;* laws passed by legislative bodies (e.g., federal Congress and state legislatures).

statutory law (5)   see statutes.

stop-loss insurance (2)   provides protection against catastrophic or unpredictable losses and includes aggregate stop-loss plans and specific stop-loss plans.

sub-capitation payment (2)   each provider is paid a fixed amount per month to provide only the care that an individual needs from that provider.

subpoena (5)   an order of the court that requires a witness to appear at a particular time and place to testify.

subpoena *duces tecum* (5)   requires documents (e.g., patient record) to be produced.

subrogation (12)   process of the third-party payer recovering health care expenses from the liable party.

subscriber (enrollee) (2)   individual who joins a managed care plan; subscribers also purchase traditional health insurance plans.

subsequent hospital care (7)   includes review of patient's chart for changes in the patient's condition, the results of diagnostic studies, and/or reassessment of the patient's condition since the last assessment performed by the physician.

subterm (6)   qualifies the main term by listing alternative sites, etiology, or clinical status; it is indented two spaces under the main term.

superbill (3)   an encounter form that contains a list of common diagnoses and ICD-10-CM codes and procedures/services and CPT/HCPCS Level II codes, which is used in the physician's office to capture encounter data for billing purposes.

supervising physician (11)   a licensed physician in good standing who, according to state regulations, engages in the direct supervision of nurse practitioners and/or physician assistants whose duties are encompassed by the supervising physician's scope of practice.

Supplemental Health Care Program (SHCP) (16)   provides coverage by civilian health care providers to active duty service members and designated non-TRICARE eligible patients; authorizations and claims processing are administered by TRICARE contractors.

supplemental health plan (12)   covers the deductible and copay or coinsurance of a primary health insurance policy.

surgical package (7)   see global surgery.

surveillance and utilization review subsystem (SURS) (15) safeguards against unnecessary or inappropriate use of Medicaid services or excess payments and assesses the quality of those services.

survivor benefits (17) claim that provides death benefits to eligible dependents, which are calculated according to the employee's earning capacity at the time of illness or injury.

suspense (4) pending.

T

Tax Relief and Health Care Act of 2006 (TRHCA) (5) created the Hospital Outpatient Quality Reporting Program (Hospital OQR) that is a "pay for quality data reporting program" implemented by CMS for outpatient hospital services.

technical component (7) use of equipment and supplies for services performed.

telemedicine (7) provision of remote medical care an interactive audio and video telecommunications system that permits real-time communication between you, at the distant site, and the beneficiary, at the originating site; an alternative to in person face-to-face encounters.

temporary disability (17) claim that covers health care treatment for illness and injuries, as well as payment for lost wages.

third-party administrator (TPA) (2) company that provides health benefits claims administration and other outsourcing services (e.g., employee benefits management) for self-insured companies; provides administrative services to health care plans; specializes in mental health case management; and processes claims, serving as a system of "checks and balances" for labor-management.

third-party payer (2) a health insurance company that provides coverage, such as BlueCross BlueShield.

total practice management software (TPMS) (2) used to generate the EMR, automating medical practice functions of registering patients, scheduling appointments, generating insurance claims and patient statements, processing payments from patient and third-party payers, and producing administrative and clinical reports.

transfer of care (7) occurs when a physician who is managing some or all of a patient's problems releases the patient to the care of another physician who is not providing consultative services.

Transitional Assistance Management Program (TAMP) (16) provides 180 days of premium-free transitional health care benefits after regular TRICARE benefits end, but it is temporary (similar to COBRA benefits when an employee resigns from a non-military job).

transitional pass-through payments (8) temporary additional payments (above the OPPS reimbursement rate) made for certain innovative medical devices, drugs, and biologicals provided to Medicare beneficiaries.

treatment, payment, and health care operations (TPO) (5) activities defined by the HIPAA Privacy Rule, including *treatment* (provision, coordination, or management of health care and related services among health care providers or by a health care provider with a third party, consultation between health care providers regarding a patient, or the referral of a patient from one health care provider to another); *payment* (various activities health care providers take to obtain payment or be reimbursed for their services and of a health plan to obtain premiums, to fulfill their coverage responsibilities and provide benefits under the plan, and to obtain or provide reimbursement for the provision of health care); and *health care operations* (certain administrative, financial, legal, and quality improvement activities necessary to run its business and to support the core functions of treatment and payment).

TRICARE (16) health care program for uniformed service members, retirees, and their families around the world; provides comprehensive care coverage to all beneficiaries, including health plans, special programs, prescriptions, and dental plans.

TRICARE beneficiary (16) includes uniformed services sponsors and dependents of sponsors.

TRICARE Prime (16) managed care option similar to a civilian health maintenance organization (HMO), which is available in certain geographic areas of the United States called *Prime Service Areas*; priority access to care at military treatment facilities is also guaranteed.

TRICARE Select (16) self-managed, preferred provider network plan available in the United States.

TRICARE Service Centers (TSCs) (16) business offices staffed by one or more customer service representatives and health care finders who assist TRICARE sponsors with health care needs and answer questions about the program.

TRICARE sponsors (16) uniformed service personnel who are active duty, deceased, retired, or members of the National Guard/Reserve.

triple option plan (2) usually offered by either a single insurance plan or as a joint venture among two or more third-party payers, and provides subscribers or employees with a choice of HMO, PPO, or traditional health insurance plans; also called *cafeteria plan* or *flexible benefit plan*.

trust the index (6) concept that inclusion terms listed below codes in the tabular list are not meant to be exhaustive, and additional terms found only in the index may also be associated to a code.

Truth in Lending Act (4) *see* Consumer Credit Protection Act of 1968.

two-party check (4) check made out to both patient and provider.

type of service (TOS) (7) refers to the kind of health care services provided to patients; a code required by Medicare to denote anesthesia services.

U

UB-04 (11) insurance claim or flat file used to bill institutional services, such as services performed in hospitals.

UB-04 flat file (5) series of fixed-length records used to bill institutional services, such as services performed in hospitals.

unassigned claim (4) generated for providers who do not accept assignment; organized by year.

unauthorized service (4) services that are provided to a patient without proper preauthorization or that are not covered by a current preauthorization.

unbundling (4) submitting multiple CPT codes when one code should be submitted.

uncertain behavior (6) it is not possible to predict subsequent morphology or behavior from the submitted specimen.

underdosing (6) taking less of a medication than is prescribed by a provider or a manufacturer's instruction.

uniformed services (16)   U.S. military branches that include the Army, Navy, Air Force, Marines, Coast Guard, Public Health Service, and the North Atlantic Treaty Organization (NATO).

unique bit string (5)   computer code that creates an electronic signature message digest that is encrypted (encoded) and appended (attached) to an electronic document (e.g., CMS-1500 claim).

unit/floor time (7)   amount of time the provider spends at the patient's bedside and managing the patient's care on the unit or floor (e.g., writing orders for diagnostic tests or reviewing test results).

United States Core Data for Interoperability (USCDI) (5)   standardized set of health data classes and constituent data elements for nationwide, interoperable health information exchange (HIE); *data classes* are the aggregation of various data elements by a common theme or use, such as patient demographics, and *data elements* are the most granular level at which a piece of data is represented in the USCDI for exchange, such as patient date of birth.

universal health insurance (2)   goal of providing every individual with access to health coverage, regardless of the system implemented to achieve that goal.

unlisted procedure (7)   also called *unlisted service;* assigned when the provider performs a procedure or service for which there is no CPT code.

unlisted service (7)   *see* unlisted procedure.

unspecified nature (6)   neoplasm is identified, but no further indication of the histology or nature of the tumor is reflected in the documented diagnosis.

upcoding (5)   assignment of an ICD-10-CM diagnosis code that does not match patient record documentation for the purpose of illegally increasing reimbursement (e.g., assigning the ICD-10-CM code for heart attack when angina was actually documented in the record).

usual, customary, and reasonable (UCR) (13)   description of amount commonly charged for a particular medical service by providers within a particular geographic region; used for establishing allowable rates.

utilization management (3)   method of controlling health care costs and quality of care by reviewing the appropriateness, efficiency, and medical necessity of care provided to patients prior to and after the administration of care.

utilization review (3)   *see* utilization management.

utilization review organization (URO) (2)   entity that establishes a utilization management program and performs external utilization review services.

V

value-added network (VAN) (4)   clearinghouse that involves value-added vendors, such as banks, in the processing of claims; using a VAN is more efficient and less expensive for providers than managing their own systems to send and receive transactions directly from numerous entities.

value-based purchasing (VBP) (9)   CMS effort to link Medicare's inpatient prospective payment to a value-based system for the purpose of promoting better clinical outcomes for patients by improving health care quality.

value-based reimbursement methodology (2)   compensates providers for the quality of care provided to patients as measured by patient outcomes.

vocational rehabilitation (17)   claim that covers expenses for vocational retraining for both temporary and permanent disability cases.

voided claim (15)   claim Medicaid should not have originally paid, resulting in a deduction from the lump-sum payment made to the provider.

W

wage index (9)   adjusts payments to account for geographic variations in hospitals' labor costs.

whistleblower (5)   individual who makes specified disclosures relating to the use of public funds, such as Medicare payments. ARRA legislation prohibits retaliation (e.g., termination) against such employees who disclose information that they believe is evidence of gross mismanagement of an agency contract or grant relating to covered funds, and so on.

withhold arrangement (2)   allows a health plan to retain a percentage of payments *or* pre-established dollar amounts that are deducted from a provider's service/procedure fee, capitation payment, or salary payment; those amounts may or may not be returned to the provider, depending on specific predetermined factors (e.g., contract language).

without direct patient contact (7)   includes non-face-to-face time spent by the provider on an outpatient or inpatient basis and occurring before and/or after direct patient care.

workers' compensation board (17)   state agency responsible for administering workers' compensation laws and handling appeals for denied claims or cases in which a worker feels compensation was too low.

workers' compensation commission (17)   *see* workers' compensation board.

workers' compensation insurance (1)   insurance program, mandated by federal and state governments, that requires employers to cover medical expenses and loss of wages for workers who are injured on the job or who have developed job-related disorders.

Z

Zone Program Integrity Contractor (ZPIC) (5)   program implemented in 2009 by CMS to review billing trends and patterns, focusing on providers whose billings for Medicare services are higher than the majority of providers in the community. ZPICs are assigned to the Medicare administrative contractor (MAC) jurisdictions, replacing Program Safeguard Contracts (PSCs).

Index

Page numbers followed by *f* and *t* indicate figures and tables, respectively.

A

A/B MAC (Part A/B Medicare administrative contractor), 125
AAMA (American Association of Medical Assistants), 18*t*
AAPC, 18*t*
Abbreviations, in ICD-10-CM coding, 183–184
ABN (Advance beneficiary notice of noncoverage), 309, 378, 511–513, 512*f*
Abnormal findings, 216
Abuse
  Anti-Kickback Statute (AKS), 130*t*
  Civil Monetary Penalties Law, 131*t*
  Deficit Reduction Act of 2005, 134*t*
  defined, 148
  False Claims Act, 130*t*
  Health Care Quality Improvement Act (HCQIA), 131*t*
  Medicare Drug Integrity Contractors (MEDIC) Program, 134*t*
  preventing, 148–150
  Program Integrity (PI) Office, for TRICARE, 579–580
  Program Safeguard Contractors, 133*t*
  surveillance and utilization review subsystem, 553
  workers' compensation insurance, 616
Accept assignment, 77, 413, 554
  versus assigment of benefits, 413
  Medicare, 497, 508–510
Account record, 82
Accountable care organizations (ACOs), 143, 505
Accounting of disclosures, 162
Accounts payable, 62
Accounts receivable, 62
Accounts receivable aging report, 114, 114*f*
Accounts receivable management, 62, 79–80
Accreditation, 40, 44
Accrual accounting, 62–65
ACOs (Accountable care organizations), 143, 505
Active duty family members, 582
Active duty service members, 582
Acupuncture, 291*t*
Adaptive behavior services, 290*t*
Additional documentation request (ADR), 364
Add-on code (AOC) edits, 365, 366*t*
Adjudication, 99–101, 100*f*, 614–615
Adjusted claim, Medicaid, 553*f*
Adjustment claim, 436
Adjuvant chemotherapy, 290*t*
Administrative Law Judge (ALJ), 110
Administrative Simplification (Title II, HIPAA), 150–164

electronic health care transactions, 151
HITECH Act, 159–161
privacy and security standards, 152–153
privacy rule, 157–158
protecting patients from identity theft, 161–162
release of information, 162–164
release of protected health information, 153–157
security rule, 158–159
unique identifiers, 150–151
Administrative Simplification Compliance Act (ASCA), 401
Admission review, 470
ADR (Additional documentation request), 364
Advance beneficiary notice of noncoverage (ABN), 309, 378, 511–513, 512*f*
Advance care planning, 272*t*
Advanced alternative payment models (Advanced APMs), 49, 50
Adverse effects, 198, 199
Adverse selection, 36
Affordable Care Act, 32, 549
Aggregate cap, 339
AHA (American Hospital Association), 468
AHIMA (American Health Information Management Association), 18*t*
Aid to Families with Dependent Children, 544
AIDS patients, release of PHI for, 156
Alcohol intoxication, 198
ALJ (Administrative Law Judge), 110
Allergy, 290*t*
Allowable fee, 474, 585
Allowed charges, 101
All-patient diagnosis-related groups (AP-DRGs), 340
All-patient refined diagnosis-related groups (APR-DRGs), 242
Alphabetic index, 181–182
Alternative payment models (APMs), 50, 507
Ambulance fee schedule, 323–324
Ambulatory payment classification (APC), 348–350, 498
Ambulatory surgery, 216
Ambulatory surgical center (ASC), 332–333
Ambulatory surgical center payment system, 332–334
Ambulatory Surgical Center Quality Reporting (ASCQR) Program, 333–334
Amendment to the HMO Act of 1973, 30
American Association of Medical Assistants (AAMA), 18*t*
American Health Information Management Association (AHIMA), 18*t*
American Hospital Association (AHA), 468

American Recovery and Reinvestment Act of 2009 (ARRA), 31, 49, 134*t*
Americans with Disabilities Act, 5
Anatomic pathology, 287*t*
Anatomic site is not documented, 196
"And" coding, 187
Anesthesia by surgeon, CPT coding modifiers, 253*t*
Anesthesia section, CPT, 18*t*, 274–277
  assigning codes, 274
  modifiers, 275
  qualifying circumstances, 275
  time reporting, 276–277
Anesthesia time, CMS-1500 claims, 418
ANSI ASC X12N, 95
ANSI ASC X12N 837, 151
ANSI ASC X12N 837I, 404
ANSI ASC X12N 837P, 404
Anti-Kickback Statute (AKS), 130*t*
AOC (Add-on code) edits, 365
APC (Ambulatory payment classification), 348–350, 498
AP-DRGs (All-patient diagnosis-related groups), 340
APMs (Alternative payment models), 50, 507
Appeals, 107
  for denied claims, 85
  workers' compensation insurance, 614–615
Appeals process, 65
Appendices, CPT, 234–235
Appointment scheduling, 62
APR-DRGs (All-patient refined diagnosis-related groups), 242
Arbitration, 616
ARRA (American Recovery and Reinvestment Act of 2009), 31, 49, 134*t*
Arrow symbol, 237
ASC (Ambulatory surgical center), 332–333
ASCA (Administrative Simplification Compliance Act), 401
ASCQR (Ambulatory Surgical Center Quality Reporting) Program, 333–334
Assignment of benefits, 77, 413, 474, 618
Assistant surgeons, CPT coding modifiers, 252*t*
Association health insurance, 445
Attestation, 51
Attitude, professional, 11–12
Audit, 137
Auditing process, 379
Authorization, 152
Automated voice response, 551
Automatic enrollment in Medicare, 492–493
Automobile insurance, 446

B

Bad debt, 114
Balance billing, 550
Balanced Budget Act of 1997 (BBA), 30, 31, 324, 510
Base period, 447
Basic Health Program (BPH), 543
Batch submission, 334
Batch uploading, 94
Batched remittance advice, 105, 106
Batches, 96
Benchmarking, 52, 94, 363
Beneficiaries, 101
   CHAMPVA, 591
   counting, 339
   Medicare, 401
   TRICARE, 576–577
Beneficiary counseling and assistance coordinators (BCACs), 579
Benefit period, 494
BenefitsCheckUp, 571
Benign, 193
Bilateral procedure, CPT coding modifiers, 250t
Billing and claims processing, 64
Billing entity, 420
Billing notes
   BlueCross BlueShield, 473–474
   Medicaid, 554–555
   Medicare, 518–520
   TRICARE, 584–587
   workers' compensation insurance, 616–618
Biofeedback, 289t
Biopsy, 53t
Birth date, CMS-1500 claim, 408, 429t
Birthday rule, 71
Black box edits, 147
Black Lung Benefits Act, 606
Block 21, CMS-1500 claims, 413–415
Block 24, CMS-1500 claims, 415–417
Blocked unindented notes, 239
Blood, 494
Blue reference symbol, 237
BlueCard®, 471, 473
BlueCross BlueShield (BCBS), 467–489
   billing notes, 473–474
   business structure, 469
   claims instructions, 474, 475–477t, 478–481f
   claims submission deadline, 473–474
   Federal Employee Program® (FEP), 472
   fee-for-service plans, 470–471
   Health Care Anywhere, 473
   indemnity plans, 471
   managed care plans, 471–472
   Medicare supplemental plans, 472
   network participation, 469–470
   origin of, 468
   preferred provider networks, 469
   secondary coverage, 482, 482–486f, 482t
   utilization management, 469–470
BlueCross BlueShield Association (BCBSA), 468–469

BlueCross BlueShield Global®, 473
Bonding insurance, 11t
Boxed notes, 182
Brackets, in ICD-10-CM coding, 184
Breach of confidentiality, 153, 164
Breast cancer screening, 53t
Bundled payment, 318
Business liability insurance, 11t

C

C codes, 302
CAC (Computer-aided coding), 177, 178f
CAC (Computer-assisted coding), 63, 177, 178f, 372, 373f
Cafeteria plan, 36
Call-back method, 163
Cancer
   breast cancer screening, 53t
   chemotherapy, 290t
   primary malignancy, 194–195
   secondary malignancy, 195
   Table of Neoplasms, ICD-10-CM, 182, 192–197, 194f
Cancer of unknown primary (CUP), 195
Capitation, 34, 499, 550
Carcinoma (Ca) in situ, 193
Cardiovascular services, 290t
Care management fee (CMF), 50
Care management services, 272t
Care plan oversight services, 270t, 271t
Career opportunities, 4–5
Carve-out plan, 26
Case law, 124
Case management, 84, 470
Case management services, 271t
Case mix, 321
Case rate, 318
Case-mix groups (CMGs), 352
Case-mix index, 321
Case-mix management, 321
Cash flow, 84
Catastrophic cap benefit, 582
Catchment area, 582
Category I codes, CPT, 233
Category II codes, CPT, 233, 292
Category III codes, CPT, 233, 293
CDACs (Clinical Data Abstracting Centers), 132t
CDI (Clinical documentation integrity), 370–372
CDM (Charge description master), 72, 75–76
CDT (Current Dental Terminology), 151
Cell phone pictures of patients, 152
Centers for Medicare and Medicaid Services (CMS), 2, 27, 320, 543
   manual system, 332
Central nervous system assessments/tests, 290t
Certificate of medical necessity (CMN), 309, 310f
Certified Electronic Health Record Technology (CEHRT), 51
CHAMPUS Reform Initiative (CRI), 575, 584
Change management, 13

Charge capture, 63
Charge description master (CDM), 72, 75–76
Chargemaster, 72, 75–76, 379
Chargemaster maintenance, 75
Chargemaster team, 75
Check digit, 150
Chemistry, 287t
Chemotherapy, 150, 290t
Child living with both parents, 71
Child of divorced parents, 71
Children's Health Insurance Program (CHIP), 543, 545, 568, 568t, 569–570f
Chiropractic Health Care Program, 584
Chiropractic manipulative treatment, 291t
Chronic diseases, 214
Civil law, 124
Civil Monetary Penalties Law (CMPL), 131t
Civilian Health and Medical Program of the Department of Veterans Affairs (CHAMPVA), 30, 580–581
Civilian Health and Medical Program–Uniformed Services (CHAMPUS), 30, 575–576
Civilian provider network, 578
Claims adjudication, 99–101, 100f
Claims adjustment reason codes (CARC), 107
Claims attachment, 97
Claims denials, 64
Claims examiner, 4
Claims instructions
   BlueCross BlueShield (BCBS), 474, 475–477t, 478–481f
   Commercial insurance, 449–453t, 453–456f
   Medicaid, 555–557t, 559f, 561f, 568, 568t, 569–570f
   Medicare, 520–521, 521–523t, 524–527f, 528, 529f
   Medigap, 528, 529f
   TRICARE, 588, 588–591t, 593–595f, 596, 599, 599t, 600f
   workers' compensation insurance, 618, 618–621t, 622–625f
Claims management, 92–93
Claims processing, 77–81, 98
   BlueCross BlueShield, 473–474
   insurance claim cycle, 98f
Claims rejections, 64
Claims review, 470
Claims scrubbing, 85
Claims submission, 93–98
   claims attachment, 97
   electronic submission of Medicare claims by providers, 96
   resubmitting claims, avoiding, 97–98
Claims submission deadline
   BlueCross BlueShield, 473–474
   Medicare, 519
   TRICARE, 585
   workers' compensation insurance, 617
Clean claim, 96
Cleanliness, 14
Clearinghouse, 93
Clinic notes, 385
Clinical Data Abstracting Centers (CDACs), 132t

Clinical documentation improvement, 370–372
Clinical documentation integrity (CDI), 370–372
Clinical immunology services, 290t
Clinical laboratory fee schedule, 324
Clinical Laboratory Improvement Act (CLIA), 131t
Clinical Laboratory Improvements Amendments (CLIA) of 1988, 158
Clinical practice guidelines, 40
Clinical trials, 583
Clinical validation denials, 107
Clinically denied claims, 64
Closed claims, 105
Closed-panel HMO, 35
Cluster coding, 180
CMF (Care management fee), 50
CMG payment rates, 352
CMG relative weights, 352
CMGs (Case-mix groups), 352
CMN (Certificate of medical necessity), 309, 310f
CMS (Centers for Medicare and Medicaid Services), 2, 27, 320, 543
    manual system, 332
CMS HCPCS Workgroup, 300
CMS Internet-only manual (IOM), 125
CMS Online Manual System, 125
CMS Primary Care Initiative, 322
CMS Quarterly Provider Update (QPU), 332
CMS reimbursement methodologies, 316–360, 318t
    case-mix management, 321
    changes to, 323
    data analytics, 320–321
    fee schedules, 323–332
    overview, 317–318
    payment systems, 322–323, 332–355
CMS Standard EDI Enrollment Form, 151
CMS transmittals, 125, 127f, 332
CMS Web Interface, 51
CMS-145, 27
CMS-1500 claims, 77, 78f, 81, 401–423
    and 837, 404
    assignment of benefits versus accept assignment, 413
    attachments, 407
    billing entity, reporting, 420
    blank claim, 405f
    Block 21, 413–415
    Block 24, 415–417
    data entry, 407–410
    dates of service, 415–416
    diagnosis coding, 413–415
    early & periodic screening, diagnosis, and treatment (EPSDT)/family planning, 416
    EMG treatment, 416
    final steps in processing, 422
    insurance file set-up, 423
    mailing addresses, 409–410
    maintaining files for practice, 422–423
    modifiers, 417–418
    national provider identifier, 410–412
    national standard employer identifier, 419

patient and policyholder names, 409
place of service, 416
procedures and services, 416
processing assigned paid claims, 423
provider names, 409
recovery of funds from responsible payers, 410
reverse of, 402f
secondary claims, 420–421
submission of, 403t
Coagulation, 287t
Coal Mine Workers' Compensation Program, 606
"Code also" coding, 189
Code number format, CPT, 234
Codes for Special Purposes, ICD-10-CM, 208
Coding, 3
Coding analyses for labs (CALs), 379
Coding audits, 371
Coding compliance, 362
Coding compliance programs, 362–370
    comprehensive error rate testing program, 363–364
    Internet links, 396–397
    medical review, 364–365
    National Correct Coding Initiative, 365–368, 366t
    recovery audit contractor program, 370
Coding conventions, ICD-10-CM, 181–190
    "and," 187
    "code also," 189
    "due to," 188
    "in," 188–189
    "see also," 189
    "see category," 189
    "see condition," 189
    "see," 189
    "with," 188
    abbreviations, 183–184
    alphabetic index, 181–182
    code assignment and clinical criteria, 190
    codes for reporting purposes, 183
    cross references, 189
    default code, 190
    etiology and manifestation rules, 187
    excludes notes, 185–186
    format and structure, 182–183
    includes notes, 185
    inclusion terms, 185–186
    other, other specified, and unspecified codes, 185
    placeholder character, 183
    punctuation, 184–185
    seventh characters, 183
    tabular list, 181–182
Coding errors, 113t
Coding for medical necessity, 372–381
    advance beneficiary notice of noncoverage (ABN), 378
    auditing process, 379
    case scenarios, 381–384
    coding and billing considerations, 378
    guidelines, 373–374
    Internet links, 396–397

Medicare code editor, 380
Medicare coverage database (MCD), 379–380
operative reports, coding from, 389–393, 390f
outpatient code editor, 380
patient records, 378, 384–389
Coding Guidelines, ICD-10-CM, 209–217
    accurate reporting, 211
    ambulatory surgery, 216
    assigning codes, 212–213
    chronic diseases, 214
    codes from A00–T88.9, Z00–Z99 U00–U85, 211
    diagnosis, condition, problem, or other reason for encounter/visit, 212
    diagnostic coding and reporting guidelines outpatient services—hospital-based outpatient services and provider-based office visits, 210–217
    documented conditions that coexist, 214
    encounters for circumstances other than a disease or an injury, 212
    encounters for general medical examinations with abnormal findings, 216
    encounters for routine health screenings, 216–217
    level of detail in coding, 212
    patients receiving diagnostic services only, 215
    patients receiving preoperative evaluations only, 215
    patients receiving therapeutic services only, 215
    routine outpatient prenatal visits, 216
    selection of first-listed condition, 210–211
    signs and symptoms, 211–212
    uncertain diagnoses, 213–214
    Z codes, 212
Coding manuals, 176
Coding validation denials, 107
Cognitive assessment and care plan services, 272t
Coinsurance, 27, 101, 474, 498
Collections, 65, 112–114
Collections reimbursement posting, 65
Colon, in ICD-10-CM coding, 184
Colonoscopy, 53t
Combination code, 213
Combination programs, 608
Commercial insurance, 444–466
    automobile insurance, 446
    claims instructions, 449–453t, 453–456f
    commercial health insurance, 445
    disability insurance, 446–447
    group health insurance, 445, 461, 461–462f
    individual health insurance, 445
    Internet links, 463
    liability insurance, 447–448
    secondary coverage, 457, 457t, 459–460f
Commercial workers' compensation insurance, 608
common access card (CAC), 577
Common data file, 101
Common law, 124

Communication, 12
  professional, 12
Community spouse resource allowance
    (CSRA), 546
Comorbidity, 214
Compact disc media, 96
Competitive medical plan (CMP), 31
Competitive state insurance fund, 608
Compliance monitoring, 85
Compliance officer, 362
Compliance program guidance, 362
Compliance programs, 137–138
Complication, 214
Comprehensive assessment, 270t
Comprehensive Error Rate Testing (CERT)
    program, 133t, 136t, 363–364
Comprehensive examination, 263
Comprehensive history, 263
Comprehensive Primary Care Plus (CPC+), 50
Comprehensive/component edits, NCCI, 369
Computer Matching and Privacy Protection
    Act of 1988, 576
Computer software, 551
Computer-aided coding (CAC), 177, 178f
Computer-assisted coding (CAC), 63, 177,
    178f, 372, 373f
Concurrent care, 261
Concurrent review, 470
Conditional primary payer status, 514
Conditions for Coverage (CfC), 128
Conditions of Participation (CoP), 128
Confidentiality, 152
  breach of, 163
  Internet and, 163
Conflict management, 12
Consolidated Omnibus Budget Reconciliation
    Act of 1985 (COBRA), 31
Consultation, 268t
Consultation referral form, 68f
Consultations, 268–269t, 287t
Consultations (clinical pathology), 287t
Consumer Assessment of Healthcare
    Providers and Systems (CAHPS), 51
Consumer Credit Protection Act of 1968, 111
Consumer-directed health plans (CDHPs),
    43–44
Contiguous or overlapping sites, 196
Continued Health Care Benefit Program
    (CHCBP), 578
Continuity of care, 44, 384
Contributory components, 262, 265
Conversion factor, 326
Coordination of benefits (COB), 70
  sustainability, 97–98
Copayment (copay), 27, 474, 498, 554
Correct Coding Initiative (CCI), 368–369
Cosmetics, 15
Cost measures, 53f
Counseling, 261
Covered entities, 95, 95f
Covered services, 26
CPT (Current Procedural Terminology), 3
CPT (Current Procedural Terminology), 73,
    231–297

anesthesia section, 274–277
appendices, 234–235
category I codes, 233
category II codes, 233, 292
category III codes, 233, 293
code number format, 234
code ranges, 242
coding procedures and services, 243–245
conventions, 242
descriptive qualifiers, 239–240
Evaluation and Management (E/M) section,
    255–273
guidelines, 238, 239f
index, 241–245
main terms, 241
medicine section, 289–292
modifiers, 245, 246–255t, 276
modifying terms, 242
notes, 239
overview, 231–232
radiology section, 282–286
relative value units, 233
surgery section, 278–282
symbols, 235–237, 238f
unbundling CPT codes, 369–370
unlisted procedures/services, 238
Credentials, 18, 18t
Credit, 111
CRI (CHAMPUS Reform Initiative), 575, 584
Criminal law, 124
Critical care services, 270t
Critical pathway, 579
Current Dental Terminology (CDT), 151
Current Procedural Terminology (CPT), 3
Custodial care services, 270t
Customer service, 12
Customer service representative (CSR),
    TRICARE, 578
Customized sub-capitation plan (CSCP), 35
Cytogenetic studies, 287t
Cytopathology, 287t

D

Data analysis, 85
Data analytics, 85, 320–321
Data capture, 63
Data mining, 85
Data packets, 403
Data warehouses, 85
Dates of service, 415–416
Day sheet, 82
Days in accounts receivable, 84
DCAOs (Debt collection assistance officers),
    579
DD Form 2642 (Patient's Request for Medical
    Payment), 585, 586f
Deadlines for claims submission
  accept assignment, 617
  approved fee basis, 617
  BlueCross BlueShield, 473–474
  Medicare, 519
  premium, 617
  TRICARE, 585

workers' compensation insurance, 617
Debt collection assistance officers (DCAOs),
    579
Decryption, 151
Deductibles, 27
  BlueCross BlueShield, 474
  Medicaid, 554
  TRICARE, 585
Deeming, 128
Defense Enrollment Eligibility Reporting
    System (DEERS), 577, 585
Defense Health Program (DHP), 575
Deficit Reduction Act of 1984, 324
Deficit Reduction Act of 2005, 134t, 139, 152,
    344
Delayed claims, 97–98
Delinquent account, 112
Delinquent claims, 112
Delinquent payment, 113t
Delivery/birthing room attendance and
    resuscitation services, 272t
Demonstration project, 583
Demonstration/pilot program, 504
Denial rate, 85
Denials and rejections management, 85
Denied claims, 64, 106–110, 113t
  appealing, 107–111
  types of, 107
Dental claims, 401
Department of Health and Human Services
    (DHHS), 3, 33
Department of Labor programs, 607
Department of Veterans Affairs (VA), 581
Dependent, 70
Dependent continuation, 27
Deposition, 124, 615
Dermatological procedures, 290t
Descriptive qualifiers, 239–240
Designated health service, 132t
Designated record set, 158
Detailed examination, 263
Detailed history, 263
Diagnosis coding, 63
Diagnosis pointer letter, 413
Diagnosis-related groups (DRGs), 340
  coding for, 343
  coding validation, 371–372
  decision tree, 341f
Diagnostic and Statistical Manual (DSM), 350
Diagnostic cost group hierarchical condition
    category (DCG/HCC) model, 502
Diagnostic services, 343
Diagnostic test results, 386–387
Dial-up, 96
Dialysis, 289t
Digital format, 151
Digital subscriber line (DSL), 96
Direct contract model HMO, 36
Direct contracting (DC) payment model, 322
Direct patient contact, 271t
Disability income insurance, 446–447
Disability insurance, 446–447
Disc, 96
Discharge planning, 470

Discharge services, 268t

Discharged not final billed (DNFB), 64

Discharged not final coded (DNFC), 64

Discontinued services, CPT coding modifiers, 247t

Disfigurement, 610

Disproportionate share hospital (DSH) adjustment, 340

Disproportionate Share Hospital (DSH) payments, 549

Disruption in electricity or communication, 401

Diversity awareness, 12

Division of Federal Employees' Compensation (DFEC), 606

DME (Durable medical equipment), 299, 519

DME MACs, 308

Documentation
electronic health record, 46
HCPCS Level II code requirements, 307–309
health care, 44–46
patient records, 44–45, 308–309
problem-oriented record, 46

Domiciliary services, 270t

"Donut hole," Medicare Part D, 503, 503i

Downcoding, 113

DRGs (diagnosis-related groups). See Diagnosis-related groups (DRGs)

Drug Abuse and Treatment Act, 130t, 157

Drug abuse patients, release of PHI for, 156

Drug assay, 286t

Drug utilization review, 470

Dual eligibles, 550

"Due to" coding, 188

Durable medical equipment (DME), 299, 519

Durable medical equipment, prosthetics, orthotics, and supplies (DMEPOS) dealers, 299
fee schedule, 325, 325f
HCPCS Level II code requirements, 309, 310f

E

Early and Periodic Screening, Diagnostic, and Treatment (EPSDT) services, 416, 547

Economic reality test, 10

eCQMs (Electronic clinical quality measures), 49–53, 135t

Education and training, of health insurance specialists, 5–7, 6t

EFT (electronic funds transfer), 103

eHealth Exchange, 135t

Electronic clinical quality measures (eCQMs), 49–53, 135t

Electronic data interchange (EDI), 94–96, 151

Electronic flat file format, 93

Electronic funds transfer (EFT), 103

Electronic Funds Transfer Act, 111

Electronic health care transactions, 151

Electronic health information (EHI), 135t

Electronic health record (EHR), 43–53, 159
certified EHR technology, 49
meaningful use measures, 49
meaningful users, 47–49
patient record documentation in, 384–385

vendor, 51

Electronic Healthcare Network Accreditation Commission (EHNAC), 93

Electronic media claims (EMC), 93, 151, 407

Electronic medical record (EMR), 47

Electronic remittance advice (ERA), 93, 102

Electronic submission, 96

Electronic Submission of Medical Documentation System (esMD), 80, 135t

Electronic transaction standards, 151

Eligibility
Medicaid, 543–544, 546–547, 555
Medicare, 492
TRICARE, 576–577, 585
workers' compensation insurance, 608, 616

Emails, 161

Embezzle, 11

Emergency (EMG) treatment, 416

Emergency department services, 269t

Emergency Medical Treatment and Labor Act (EMTALA), 131t

Empire BlueCross HMO, 471

Empire HealthChoice HMO, Inc., 471

Employee fraud, 616

Employee Retirement Income Security Act of 1974 (ERISA), 30–31

Employees' Compensation Appeals Board (ECAB), 607

Employer and union health plans, 505

Employer fraud, 616

Employer liability for independent contractors, 9–10

Employer tax identification number (EIN), 419

Employer-sponsored group health plan (EGHP), 515

EncoderPro.com Expert software, 368

Encoders, 176

Encounter, 178–179

Encounter form, 73, 379

Encryption, 151

Endocrinology, 290t

End-stage renal disease (ESRD), 491

End-stage renal disease prospective payment system (ESRD PPS), 334–335

End-stage renal disease quality improvement program (ESRD QIP), 335

Energy Employees Occupational Illness Compensation Program (EEOICP), 606

Enrollees, 26

Enrollment in Medicare, 492–494

Episode of care (home health), 336

Eponyms, 181, 191

EPSDT (Early and Periodic Screening, Diagnostic, and Treatment) services, 416, 547

Equal Credit Opportunity Act, 111

Errors and omissions insurance, 9

Essential modifiers, 191

Established patient, 259

Ethics, professional, 13

Etiology and manifestation rules, 187

Etiquette, 11–12

Evaluation and Management (E/M) section, CPT, 255–273

classification of evaluation and management services, 258
clinical examples, 267
commonly used terms, 259–261
documentation guidelines, 257
examination, 263
history, 263
level of E/M service, 259, 262, 263–264
level of medical decision making, 261–262
medical decision making, 263–264
nature of the presenting problem, 265–266
office or other outpatient services, 261–262
overview, 257–258
place of service, 257
services guidelines, 258, 262–263
special report, 266–267
subsections, 267–273t
type of service, 257–258
unlisted service, 266–267

Evidence-based coding, 177

Evocative/suppression testing, 287t

Examination, 263

Exceptional Family Member Program (EFMP), 584

Excess insurance, 26

Excludes1 note, ICD-10-CM coding, 186

Excludes2 note, ICD-10-CM coding, 186

Exclusive provider organization (EPO), 35, 471

Expanded problem focused examination, 263

Expanded problem focused history, 263

Explanation of benefits (EOB), 9, 70, 93, 103f, 104

Express contract, 25

Extension codes, 180

Extent of history, 263

External quality review organization (EQRO), 39

Extranet, 96

F

Face-to-face time, CPT, 260

Facility billing, 64

Facility coding, 73

Facsimile transmission of PHI, 163

Fair and Accurate Credit Transaction Act of 2003 (FACT Act), 133t

Fair Credit and Charge Card Disclosure Act, 111

Fair Credit Billing Act, 111

Fair Credit Reporting Act, 111

Fair Debt Collection Practices Act (FDCPA), 111

Fair Labor Standards Act, 10

False Claims Act (FCA), 130t

Family planning, 416

Federal Claims Collection Act (FCCA), 130t

Federal Employee Health Benefit Plan (FEHBP), 30

Federal Employee Program® (FEP), 472

Federal Employees Dental and Vision Insurance Program (FEDVIP), 583

Federal Employees' Compensation Act (FECA), 29, 606

Federal Employers' Liability Act (FELA), 29

Federal Financial Participation (FFP), 549

Federal Medical Assistance Percentage (FMAP), 549

Federal Mine Safety and Health Act of 1977 (Mine Act), 607

Federal poverty level (FPL), 550

Federal Privacy Act, 423

Federal Register, 83, 124, 126*f*

Federal surety bond, 140

Federal workers' compensation programs, 605–607

Federally Qualified Health Centers Prospective Payment System (FQHC PPS), 335–336

Federally qualified HMO, 30

Fee schedule, 26

Fee schedules, CMS, 323–332. *See also* CMS reimbursement methodologies
　ambulance, 323–324
　clinical laboratory fee schedule, 324
　durable medical equipment, prosthetics, orthotics, and supplies, 325, 325*f*
　Medicare physician, 326–332, 327*f*

Fee-for-service plans, 26, 37, 445, 470–471

Financial Services Modernization Act (FSMA), 111

First Report of Injury forms, 611–614, 612*f*

First-listed diagnosis, 210

First-look Analysis for Hospital Outlier Monitoring (FATHOM), 133*t*

Fiscal agent, 554, 616

Fiscal year, 585

Flexible benefit plan, 36

Flexible spending account (FSA), 43

Forced number, 179

Foreign body/implant definition, 240

Formulary, 445

For-profit corporations, 469

Fragmentation, 113

Fragrances, 15

Fraud, 378
　defined, 148
　employee fraud, 616
　employer fraud, 616
　examples and outcomes of, 149*f*
　preventing, 148–150
　provider fraud, 616
　workers' compensation insurance, 616

Front-end edits, 96

G

G codes, 302

Gag clauses, 38

Gastroenterology, 289*t*

Gatekeepers, 38, 471

Gender rule, 71

General behavioral health integration care management, 272*t*

General enrollment period (GEP), 493

General equivalence mappings (GEMs), 172–173

Genetic counseling services, 290*t*

Genomic sequencing procedures, 287*t*

GeoBlue®, 473

Global payment, 318

Global period, 279

Global surgery, 278

Gramm-Leach-Bliley Act, 111

Green reference symbol, 237

Group, 51

Group health insurance, 28*t*, 445, 461, 461–462*f*

Group health plan requirements (Title IV, HIPAA), 166

Group model HMO, 35

Group practices without walls (GPWW), 36

Grouper software, 336

Guaranteed renewal, 27

Guarantors, 66

Guidelines, CPT, 238, 239*f*

H

H codes, 303

Habilitative services, CPT coding modifiers, 255*t*

Hair, 14

Hand care, 14

HAVEN software, 336

HCFA Internet Security Policy, 164

HCPCS (Healthcare Common Procedure Coding System), 3, 208–315
　anesthesia modifiers, 275
　assigning codes and modifiers, 311
　code sections, 306
　documentation and submission requirements, 307–309
　Internet links, 312
　level I codes, 299
　level II codes, 3, 298–315
　miscellaneous codes, 302
　modifiers, 302–303, 303–304*f*
　organization of, 301–307
　permanent national codes, 301–302
　responsibility for, 300–301
　temporary codes, 302–303

Health and behavior assessment and intervention, 290*t*

Health care, 25

Health Care Access, Portability, and Renewability (Title I, HIPAA), 146, 147–148

Health Care and Education Reconciliation Act (HCERA), 32

Health Care Anywhere, 473

Health care audit and compliance programs, 136–147

Health care documentation, 44–46

Health care finders (HCF), TRICARE, 578

Health Care Fraud and Abuse Control Program (HCFAC), 148

Health Care Fraud Prevention and Enforcement Action Team (HEAT), 141–142

Health care provider, 2

Health Care Quality Improvement Act (HCQIA), 131*t*

Health care reimbursement, 26, 29*f*

Health care reimbursement account (HCRA), 43

Health information exchanges (HIE), 135*t*

Health information technicians, 5, 6

Health information technology (HIT) standards, 47

Health Information Technology for Economic and Clinical Health Act (HITECH Act) of 2009, 31, 49, 134*t*, 159–161

Health insurance, 23–33
　characteristics of, 37–42
　claims, 2
　commercial, 445
　coverage statistics, 28
　defined, 26
　glossary of terms, 28*t*
　group, 445, 461, 461–462*f*
　individual, 445
　major developments, 29–33
　private, 445
　regulations, 31
　secondary, 457, 457*t*

Health insurance exchange, 32

Health Insurance Marketplace, 32–33, 55

Health Insurance Portability and Accountability Act (HIPAA), 132*t*, 147–166, 403
　administrative simplification, 150–164
　breach notification, 160
　electronic health care transactions, 151
　fraud and abuse prevention, 148–150
　HITECH Act, 159–161
　identity theft protection, 161–162
　Internet links, 167
　overview, 147
　privacy and security standards, 152–153
　privacy rule, 157–158
　provisions, 148*f*
　release of information, 162–164
　release of protected health information, 153–157
　security rule, 158–159
　Title I, 147–148
　Title II, 148–165
　Title III, 165–166
　Title IV, 166
　Title V, 166
　unique identifiers, 150–151

Health insurance prospective payment system (HIPPS) code set, 336

Health insurance specialists, 1–22
　associations and credentials, 18, 18*t*
　career opportunities, 4–5
　defined, 4
　education and training, 5–7, 6*t*
　independent contractor, 9–10
　job responsibilities, 8–9
　professional appearance, 14–15
　professionalism, 11–15
　scope of practice, 8*t*
　telephone skills, 15–17

Health Integrity and Protection Data Base (HIPDB), 131*t*

Health Maintenance Organization (HMO) Assistance Act of 1973, 30

Health maintenance organizations (HMOs), 34, 35, 471

Health plan identifier (HPID), 150, 411

Health reimbursement arrangement (HRA), 43–44

Health savings account (HSA), 43, 44

Healthcare Common Procedure Coding System (HCPCS). *See* HCPCS (Healthcare Common Procedure Coding System)

Healthcare Effectiveness Data and Information Set (HEDIS), 40

Healthcare Integrity and Protection Data Bank (HIPDB), 132

Hematology, 287*t*

Hernandez v. Lutheran Medical Center, 124

High-risk pools, 445

Hill-Burton Act, 30

HIPAA. *See* Health Insurance Portability and Accountability Act (HIPAA)

History, defined, 263

HITECH Act (Health Information Technology for Economic and Clinical Health Act), 31, 49, 134*t*, 159–161

HIV patients, release of PHI for, 156

HMOs (health maintenance organizations), 34, 35, 471

Hold harmless clause, 2

Hold harmless payments, 350

Home Assessment Validation and Entry (HAVEN), 336

Home Assessment Validation and Entry (HAVEN) software, 336

Home health patient-driven groupings model (PDGM), 336

Home health procedures/services, 291*t*

Home health prospective payment system (HH PPS), 336–338

Home health resource groups (HHRGs), 336

Home health services, 496

Home Health Value-Based Purchasing (HHVBP) Model, 338

Home services, 270*t*

Horizontal triangles symbol, 236

Hospice care, 496

Hospice payment rate, 338, 338*t*

Hospice payment system, 338–339, 338*t*

Hospice Quality Reporting Program (HQRP), 339

Hospital discharge services, 268*t*

Hospital Inpatient Quality Reporting (Hospital IQR) program, 133*t*, 134*t*

Hospital Outpatient Quality Reporting Program (Hospital OQR), 134*t*, 350

Hospital Payment Monitoring Program (HPMP), 133*t*

Hospital quality improvement program (QIP), 346

Hospital readmissions reduction program (HRRP), 346, 347

Hospital reimbursement repayment program, 134*t*

Hospital value-based purchasing (VBP) Program, 346

Hospital-Acquired Condition (HAC) Reduction Program, 347–348

Hospital-Acquired Condition Reduction Program (HACRP), 346

Hospital-acquired conditions (HACs), 344–346

Hospital-Issued Notices of Noncoverage (HINN), 511

Hospitalists, 403, 412

Hospitalization, 494

I

Iatrogenic illness, 199

ICD-10-CM (*International Classification of Diseases 10th Revision, Clinical Modification*)

  "and," 187

  "code also," 189

  "due to," 188

  "in," 188–189

  "see also," 189

  "see category," 189

  "see condition," 189

  "see," 189

  "with," 188

  abbreviations, 183–184

  alphabetic index, 181–182

  CMS-1500 claims, 413–414

  code assignment and clinical criteria, 190

  codes for reporting purposes, 183

  codes for special purposes, 208

  coding conventions, 181–190

  coding manuals, 176

  cross references, 189

  default code, 190

  etiology and manifestation rules, 187

  excludes notes, 185–186

  format and structure, 182–183

  includes notes, 185

  inclusion terms, 185–186

  Index of External Causes of Injury, 200–201

  Index of External Causes of Injury, ICD-10-CM, 200–201

  Internet links, 217

  mandatory reporting of, 177

  medical necessity, 177–178

  other, other specified, and unspecified codes, 185

  overview, 173–175

  placeholder character, 183

  punctuation, 184–185

  seventh characters, 183

  Table of Drugs and Chemicals, 198–200

  Table of Neoplasms, 192–197

  tabular list, 181–182

  Tabular List of Diseases and Injuries, 204–208

  updating, 176–177

ICD-10-CM (*International Classification of Diseases 10th Revision, Clinical Modification*), 171–229

  general equivalence mappings, 172–173

ICD-10-CM Index of External Causes of Injury, 200, 201*f*

ICD-10-CM Official Guidelines for Coding and Reporting, 209–217, 371, 373

ICD-10-CM Tabular List of Diseases and Injuries, 205*f*

  coding guidelines, 209–217

  external cause codes, 206

  health status and contact with health services codes, 206, 207*f*

  morphology of neoplasm codes, 207–208

  structure of, 205–206

ICD-10-PCS (*International Classification of Diseases, 10th Revision, Procedure Classification System*)

  coding manuals, 176

  defined, 175

  mandatory reporting of, 177

  overview, 173–175

  updating, 176–177

ICD-11 (*International Classification of Diseases, 11th Revision*), 179–180

ID-9-CM (*International Classification of Diseases, 9th Revision, Clinical Modification*), 172–173

Identification cards, 616

Identity theft, protecting patients from, 161–162

Identity Theft Prevention Program, 133*t*

Immune globulins, 289*t*

Immunization administration for vaccines/toxoids, 289*t*

Immunology, 287*t*

Implied contract, 25

Improper payments, 140, 363

Improper Payments Elimination and Recovery Act of 2010, 503

Improper Payments Elimination and Recovery Improvement Act (IPERIA) of 2012, 363

Improper Payments Information Act (IPIA) of 2002, 116

Improper Payments Information Act of 2002 (IPIA), 133*t*

Improvement activities, 53, 53*t*

Improving Medicare Post-Acute Care Transformation Act of 2014 (IMPACT Act), 353

"In" coding, 188–189

Inclusion terms, ICD-10-CM coding, 185–186

Inclusive dates of similar services, 418

Income-first approach, 546

Indemnity insurance, 445, 446

Indemnity plans, 26, 471

Indented codes, 234

Indented parenthetical note, 239

Independent contractor, 9–10

Independent practice association (IPA) HMO, 36

Independent review entity (IRE), 110

Index

  CPT, 241–245

  HCPCS Level II, 304–305, 306

Index of External Causes of Injury, ICD-10-CM, 200–201

Index to Diseases and Injuries, ICD-10-CM coding, 190–203

  Index of External Causes of Injury, ICD-10-CM, 200–201

  main terms, subterms, and qualifiers, 191, 191*f*, 192*f*

  steps for using, 202–203

  Table of Drugs and Chemicals, 198–200

  Table of Neoplasms, 192–197

Indian Health Care Improvement Act (IHCIA) of 1976, 549
Indian Health Service (IHS), 549–550
Indirect medical education (IME) adjustment, 340
Individual, 51
Individual coverage HRA (ICHRA), 43
Individual health insurance, 28t, 445
Individual practice association (IPA) HMO, 36
Inferred words, 242
Information blocking, 135t
Infusions, 289t
Initial enrollment period (IEP), 493
Initial hospital care, 268t
Injuries. *See also* Workers' compensation insurance
   automobile insurance, 446
   disability insurance, 446–447
   First Report of Injury forms, 611–614, 612f
   ICD-10-CM Index of External Causes of Injury, 200, 201f
   liability insurance, 447–448
   special accidental injury rider, 27
Inpatient benefits, 554
Inpatient cap, 339
Inpatient coverage, 473
Inpatient neonatal intensive care services, 272t
Inpatient prospective payment system (IPPS), 339–348
Inpatient Psychiatric Facility Prospective Payment System (IPF PPS), 350–352, 351f
Inpatient Psychiatric Facility Quality Reporting (IPFQR) Program, 351–352
Inpatient Rehabilitation Facility Prospective Payment system (IRF PPS), 352
Inpatient Rehabilitation Validation and Entry (IRVEN) software, 352, 353f
Inpatient services, 268t
Institutional billing, 27, 64, 231
Institutional coding, 73
Instructional notes, CPT, 239
Insulin pump malfunction, 200
Insurance claim cycle, 92–105, 92f
   adjudication of claims, 99–101, 100f
   claims management, 92–93
   electronic data interchange, 94–96
   Internet links, 116
   payment, 102–104
   processing of claims, 98, 98f
   remittance advice reconciliation, 102–104
   submission of claims, 93–98
Insurance claim files
   batched remittance advice, 105, 106
   closed claims, 105
   denied claims, 106
   maintaining, 105–106
   open claims, 105
   rejected claims, 106
   remittance advice documents, 105, 106
   source documents, 105
   unassigned claims, 106
Integrated delivery system (IDS), 36
Integrated provider organization (IPO), 36

Integrated Querying and Reporting Service (IQRS), 131t
Integrated revenue cycle (IRC), 65
Integrated revenue management, 65
Intensity of services (IS), 242
International Classification of Diseases for Oncology, 3rd Revision (ICD-O-3), 208
International Classification of Diseases, 10th Revision, Clinical Modification. See ICD-10-CM (*International Classification of Diseases 10th Revision, Clinical Modification*)
International Classification of Diseases, 10th Revision, Clinical Modification (ICD-10-CM), 3
International Classification of Diseases, 10th Revision, Procedural Coding System (ICD-10-PCS):, 3
International Classification of Diseases, 10th Revision, Procedure Classification System. See ICD-10-PCS (*International Classification of Diseases, 10th Revision, Procedure Classification System*)
International Classification of Diseases, 11th Revision (ICD-11), 179–180
International Classification of Diseases, 9th Revision, Clinical Modification, 172–173
Internet, 96
Internet links
   coding compliance programs, 396–397
   coding for medical necessity, 396–397
   commercial insurance, 463
   Health Insurance Portability and Accountability Act (HIPAA), 167
   ICD-10-CM (*International Classification of Diseases 10th Revision, Clinical Modification*), 217
   insurance claim cycle, 116
   level II codes, HCPCS, 312
   Medicaid, 571
   Medicare, 539–540
   revenue management, 87
   TRICARE, 601
   workers' compensation insurance, 626
Internship, 6–7
interprofessional telephone/Internet consultation, 272t
Interrogatory, 124
Intoxication, 198
Investing in Innovations (i2) Initiative, 135t
IPPS 3-day payment window, 242, 342
IPPS 72-hour rule, 242
IPPS transfer rule, 344
IRVEN (Inpatient Rehabilitation Validation and Entry) software, 352, 353f

J

Jewelry, 15
Job description, health insurance specialist, 8–9
jRAVEN (Resident Assessment Validation and Entry) software, 354, 355f

K

K codes, 303
Key components, 262–263

L

Laboratory reports, 386–387
Laboratory section, CPT, 286–288t
Laboratory services, CPT coding modifiers, 254t
Late charges, 85
Lead agents (LA), 576
Leadership, 12–13
Ledger, 82
Legacy classification system, 172
Legacy coding system, 172
Legislation, 29
Lesions, 192
Level I codes, HCPCS, 299
Level II codes, HCPCS, 208–315
   assigning codes and modifiers, 311
   code sections, 306
   documentation and submission requirements, 307–309
   Internet links, 312
   miscellaneous codes, 302
   modifiers, 302–303, 303–304f
   organization of, 301–307
   permanent national codes, 301–302
   purpose of, 299–301
   responsibility for, 300–301
   temporary codes, 302–303
Level of care audits, 371
Level of E/M service, 259
Liability insurance, 447–448
Lien, 448
Lifetime maximum amount, 27
Lifetime reserve days, 494
Limitation of liability (LOL), 511
Limiting charges
   Medicare, 329, 508
   TRICARE, 587
Line of duty care, 581
Listserv, 128
Litigation, 115
Local coverage determinations (LCDs), 364, 365, 379–380, 513
Local medical review policies (LMRPs), 380
Location of service adjustment, 331
Longshore and Harbor Workers' Compensation Program (LHWCA), 606–607
Long-term care hospital quality reporting program (LTCH QRP), 352–353
Lost charges, 85
Lost claims, 113t

M

M+C, 104
MACs (Medicare administrative contractors), 125, 136t, 138, 146, 307–308, 364–365, 491, 518, 519f
Magnetic tape, 96
Main terms, 191
Major diagnostic categories (MDCs), 340
Major medical insurance, 30
Malignant, 192
Malpractice expenses, 326

Managed care alert, 67

Managed care organizations (MCOs), 34–35, 551

  case management, 41

  physician's practice and, 37

  prescription management, 41–42

  primary care provider, 38

  quality assurance and performance measurement, 38–39

  second surgical opinions, 41

  utilization management, 41

Managed care plans, 471–472

Managed health care (managed care), 26, 33–42, 445, 550–551

  characteristics of, 37–42

  consumer-directed health plans, 43–44

  defined, 33–34

  history of, 34

  managed care organizations and plans, 34–35

  models, 35–36

  physician's practice and, 37

Managed long term services and supports (MLTSS), 551

Management service organization (MSO), 36

Mandated services, CPT coding modifiers, 253t

Mandates, 30–31, 38

Mandatory claims submission, 510–511

Mandatory reporting, 177

Manifestation, ICD-10-CM, 184

Manual daily accounts receivable journal, 82

Mass vaccination programs, 535

Material safety data sheets (MSDS), 607

MCE (Medicare code editor), 340, 380

MCOs (Managed care organizations), 34, 551

MDCs (Major diagnostic categories), 340

Meaningful EHR users, 47–49

Meaningful use, 49

Meaningful use payment adjustments, 49

Medicaid, 30, 542–573

  billing notes, 554–555

  cards, 555

  Children's Health Insurance Program, 545, 568, 568t, 569–570f

  claims instructions, 555–557t, 559f, 561f, 568, 568t, 569–570f

  coverage, 547–549

  dual eligibles, 550

  eligibility, 543–544, 546–547, 555

  Internet links, 571

  managed care, 550–551

  mandatory benefits, 547

  medical necessity, 553–554

  Medicare-Medicaid (Medi-Medi) crossover, 530, 530t, 531f

  mother/baby claims, 565, 565t, 567f

  optional benefits, 548

  overview, 542

  participating providers, 550

  preventive health care services, 548–549

  Programs of All-Inclusive Care for the Elderly, 545

  remittance advice, 555

  as secondary payer, 550, 562, 564f

  special groups, 544–545

  spousal impoverishment provisions, 546

  surveillance and utilization review subsystem (SURS), 553

Medicaid eligibility verification system (MEVS), 551, 552f

Medicaid Fraud Control Units (MFCUs), 140

Medicaid integrity contractors (MICs), 134t

Medicaid Integrity Program (MIP), 134t, 139–140

Medicaid remittance advice, 552, 553f

Medi-Cal, 543, 571

Medical assistance programs, 543

Medical assistant, 4–5

Medical care, defined, 25

Medical decision making, 261–262, 263–264, 264f

Medical foundation, 36

Medical genetics, 290t

Medical identity theft, 133t

Medical liability reform (Title II, HIPAA), 165

Medical malpractice insurance, 11t

Medical necessity, 4, 177–178, 371, 373, 553–554

Medical necessity denial, 511

Medical nutrition therapy, 290t

Medical records (patient records), 44–45

  coding for medical necessity, 378

  documentation, 44–45

Medical review (MR), 138, 364–365

Medical treatment, workers' compensation, 609

Medical/accidental injury coverage, 554

Medically managed, 373–374

Medically necessary services, 497

Medically needy, Medicaid, 544

Medically unlikely edits (MUEs), 365, 367f, 419

Medicare, 30, 490–541

  advance beneficiary notice of noncoverage (ABN), 511–513, 512f

  applying for, 493

  billing notes, 518–520

  claim used, 520

  claims instructions, 520–521, 521–523t, 524–527f, 528, 529f

  claims submission deadline, 519

  conditional primary payer status, 514

  durable medical equipment (DME) claims, 519

  eligibility, 492

  employer and union health plans, 505

  enrollment, 492–494

  experimental and investigational procedures, 506

  Internet links, 539–540

  mandatory claims submission, 510–511

  nonparticipating providers (nonPARs), 507–509, 508t

  opt-out providers, 510

  overview, 491–492

  Part A (Hospital Insurance), 491, 494–497

  Part B (Medical Insurance), 492, 497–499, 501

  Part C (Medicare Advantage Plans), 104, 492, 499

  Part D (Prescription Drug Plans), 492, 502–503, 503t

  participating providers (PARs), 507, 508t

  as primary payer, 513–514

  private contract, 510

  reimbursement, 549–550

  roster billing for mass vaccination programs, 535, 536t, 537–538f

  as secondary payer, 515–516, 517f, 532, 532t, 534f

  split/shared visit payment policy, 519

  telehealth, 520

Medicare Access and CHIP Reauthorization Act of 2015 (MACRA), 49, 135t, 326, 507

Medicare administrative contractors (MACs), 125, 136t, 138, 146, 307–308, 364–365, 491, 518, 519f

Medicare Advantage organizations, 104

Medicare Appeal Council, 110

Medicare beneficiaries, 401

Medicare beneficiary identifier (MBI), 493

Medicare Benefit Policy Manual, 311

Medicare card, 67f

Medicare Catastrophic Coverage Act of 1988, 505

Medicare Choice, 104

Medicare code editor (MCE), 340, 380

Medicare contracting reform (MCR) initiative, 31

Medicare Cost Plan, 504

Medicare coverage database (MCD), 379–380

Medicare demonstration projects, 401

Medicare Drug Integrity Contractors (MEDIC) Program, 134t

Medicare Electronic Health Record (EHR), 50

Medicare Evidence Development & Coverage Advisory Committee (MedCAC), 379

Medicare fee-for-service, 31, 116, 140, 142, 519

Medicare Improvement for Patients and Providers Act (MIPPA), 31

Medicare Integrity Program (MIP), 132t, 138–139

Medicare Learning Network (MLN), 364

Medicare medical savings account (MSA), 500

Medicare National Coverage Determinations Manual, 311

Medicare outpatient observation notice (MOON), 495

Medicare Part D coverage gap, 503

Medicare Part D sponsor, 502

Medicare physician fee schedule (MPFS), 50, 326–332

  CMS manual system, 332

  formula for, 327f

  location of service adjustment, 331–332

  nonparticipating providers, 329

  nonphysician practitioners, 331

  participating providers, 328

Medicare Prescription Drug, Improvement, and Modernization Act of 2003, 31, 133t, 177, 232, 491

Medicare Pricing, Data Analysis and Coding (PDAC) Contractor, 299

Medicare Reconsideration Notice, 110

Medicare Redetermination Notice, 110

Medicare Remittance Advice, 93
Medicare risk programs, 31
Medicare Savings Program, 505
Medicare Secondary Payer (MSP), 401, 515
Medicare SELECT, 505
Medicare severity diagnosis-related groups (MS-DRGs), 242, 340, 344
Medicare Shared Savings Program (MSSP), 142–143, 505
Medicare Summary Notice (MSN), 81, 93, 329, 330f, 517, 518f
Medicare supplemental plans, 472
Medicare Supplementary Insurance (MSI), 505–506, **506**
Medicare, Medicaid, and SCHIP Balanced Budget Refinement Act of 1999, 350
Medicare-approved amount, 496, 497
Medicare-Medicaid (Medi-Medi) crossover, 530, 530t, 531f
Medication
    Medicare Part D (Prescription Drug Plans), 492, 502–503, 503t
    medication therapy management services, 291t, 504
    Medicine section, CPT, 233
    National Drug Code (NDC), 152
    prescription drug monitoring program, 43
Medication therapy management programs, 291t, 504
Medicine section, CPT, 233
Medigap, 472, 505–506, **506**
    claims instructions, 528, 529f
Member hospitals, 468
Merit-based incentive payment system (MIPS), 49–50, 50, 52, 52, 134t, 135t, 507
Message digest, 151
Metastasis, 214
Metrics, 84
Microbiology, 287t
Military Health System (MHS), 575
Military Health System (MHS) nurse advice line, 579
Military OneSource Specialty Consultants, 584
Military time, 587, 587–588t
Military treatment facilities (MTFs), 575–576, 579
Mine Improvement and New Emergency Response (MINER) Act of 2006, 607
Mine Safety and Health Administration (MSHA), 607
Minimum assistant surgeon, CPT coding modifiers, 252t
Minimum Data Set (MDS), 354
Minimum Data Set for Post Acute Care (MDS-PAC), 352
Minimum monthly maintenance needs allowance (MMMNA), 546
Minimum necessary standard, 157
MIP (Medicare Integrity Program), 132t, 138–139
MIPS (Merit-based incentive payment system), 50, 52, 52, 134t, 135t, 507
Miscellaneous codes, HCPCS Level II, 302
MLN (Medicare Learning Network), 364
Moderate (conscious) sedation, 291t

Modified adjusted gross income (MAGI), 544
Modifiers
    anesthesia, 275–276
    CMS-1500 claims, 417–418
    CPT, 245, 246–255t, 275
    HCPCS Level II, 275, 302–303, 303–304f, 311
    physical status, 275
Molecular multianalyte assays, 287t
Molecular pathology, 287t
Monopolistic state insurance fund, 608
Morbidity, 173
Morphology of neoplasm codes, 207–208
Mortality, 173
Mother/baby claims, Medicaid, 565, 565t, 567f
MSA (Medicare medical savings account), 500
MSI (Medicare Supplementary Insurance), 505–506, **506**
MSN (Medicare Summary Notice), 81, 93, 329, 330f, 517, 518f
MTFs (Military treatment facilities), 575–576, 579
Multianalyte assays with algorithmic analyses, 287t
Multiple codes, 213
Multiple modifiers, 254t
Multiple parenting, 179
Multiple procedures, 418
Multiple procedures, CPT coding modifiers, 251t
Multiple surgical procedures, 281–282
Mutually exclusive codes, NCCI, 366t
Mutually exclusive edits, NCCI, 369

N

Narrative clinic note, 385
National Cancer Institute (NCI), 584
National codes, 3
National Committee for Quality Assurance (NCQA), 40
National Correct Coding Initiative (NCCI), 132t, 140, 146–147, 365–370, 369
    add-on code (AOC) edits, 365
    column 1/ column 2 edits, 366t
    edits on Internet, 368–369
    medically unlikely edits, 365
    procedure-toprocedure (PTP) code pair edits, 365, 366t
    unbundling CPT codes, 369–370
National Council for Prescription Drug Programs (NCPCP) Telecommunication Standard, 404
National coverage analyses (NCAs), 379
National Coverage Determinations (NCDs), 83, 379, 380, 513
National Drug Code (NDC), 152
National individual identifier, 150
National Plan and Provider Enumeration System (NPPES), 151, 411
National Practitioner Data Bank (NPDB), 131t
National Provider Identifier (NPI), 150
National Quality Forum (NQF), 344–346
National Standard Employer Identification Number (EIN), 150

National standard employer identifier, 419
National Standard Format (NSF), 151
National Uniform Billing Committee (NUBC), 425
National Uniform Claims Committee (NUCC), 410
Nature of the presenting problem, 265–266
NCDs (National Coverage Determinations), 83, 379, 380, 513
NDC (National Drug Code), 152
NDC (National Drug Codes), 152
NEC (not elsewhere classifiable), 183
Neoplasms, 192
Net collection rate, 85
Network model HMO, 36
Network provider, 35
Neurology, 290t
Neuromuscular procedures, 290t
Never events, 134t, 319, 344
New patient, 259
Newborn care, 272t
No balance billing clause, 2
Noncovered benefit, 99, 110
Non-covered services, 26
Nonessential modifiers, 191
Non-face-to-face nonphysician services, 291t
Non-face-to-face services, 272t
Nonparticipating providers (nonPARs), 66, 329, 497, 502, 507–509, 508t
    accepting assignment on claims, 508–509
    limiting charge, 507–509
    waiver of Medicare billing contracts, 509
Nonphysician practitioners, 331
Nonprofit corporations, 469
NOS (not otherwise specified), 184
Not medically necessary, 108
Notes, CPT, 239
Notice of Exclusions from Medicare Benefits (NEMB), 369, 511
Notice of Privacy Practices (NPP), 157
Notices of Noncoverage (NONC), 511
NPPES (National Plan and Provider Enumeration System), 151, 411
Number symbol, 237
Nursing facility services, 270t

O

OASIS (Outcomes and Assessment Information Set), 336, 337f
Obamacare, 32
Objective part of SOAP notes, 386
Observation or inpatient care services, 268t
Observation services, 268t
Observation stay, 211
Occupational Safety and Health Act of 1970, 130t, 386, 607
Occupational Safety and Health Administration (OSHA), 607
Office of Inspector General (OIG), 580
Office of Managed Care, 30
Office of Medicare Hearings and Appeals (OMHA), 110
Office of the National Coordinator for Health IT, 135t

Office of Workers' Compensation Programs (OWCP), 605

Office or other outpatient services, 267t, 268t

Official Coding Guidelines for Physician and Outpatient Hospital Services, 373

Official Guidelines for Coding and Reporting, ICD-10-CM, 209–217, 371, 373

Official Guidelines for Coding and Reporting, ICD-10-PCS, 209, 373

Omnibus Budget Reconciliation Act of 1981 (OBRA), 31, 132t

One-day payment window, 323

online electronic medical evaluation, 272t

On-the-job injury, 608. *See also* Workers' compensation insurance

Open claims, 105

Open-panel HMO, 35

Operation Restore Trust, 150

Operative reports, 389–393

Ophthalmology, 289t

OPPS (Outpatient Prospective Payment System), 146, 302, 348–350

OPPS (Outpatient prospective payment system), 348–350, 349f, 498

Opt-out providers, 510

Optum360, 368

Ordering provider, 412

Organ or disease-oriented panels, 286t

Original Medicare, 491

Orthotics, 299

Osteopathic manipulative treatment, 291t

Other entity identifier (OEID), 150

Other evaluation and management services, 272t

Other health insurance (OHI), 584

Otorhinolaryngologic services, 290t

Outcomes and Assessment Information Set (OASIS), 336, 337f

Outlier, 340

Outlier payments, 350

Out-of-network provider, 66, 110

Out-of-pocket payment, 77

Out-of-state treatment, 610

Outpatient, 210

Outpatient code editor (OCE), 367, 368t, 380

Outpatient coverage, 473

Outpatient encounter, 349

Outpatient prenatal visits, 216

Outpatient pretreatment authorization program (OPAP), 471

Outpatient Prospective Payment System (OPPS), 146, 302, 348–350

Outpatient prospective payment system (OPPS), 348–350, 349f, 498

Outpatient surgery, 211, 216

Outpatient visit, 349

Outsource collections, 114

Overlapping sites, 196

Overpayment, 113t

Overpayment recovery letter, 144f

Overpayments, 140, 140–141t
  absence of provider liability for, 146
  examples of, 143
  provider liability for, 144–146
  reducing, 143–146

sample overpayment recovery letter, 144f

waiver of overpayment recovery, 143

P

PACE (Programs of All-Inclusive Care for the Elderly), 504, 545, 571

Paid claims error rate, 116, 138

Palliative care, 338, 496

Paper claims, 105, 401

Parens symbol, 236, 237, 239, 367

Parentheses, in ICD-10-CM coding, 184

Part A/B Medicare administrative contractor, 125

Partial hospitalization, 268t

Participating provider organization (PPO), 36

Participating providers (PARs), 66, 328, 497, 507, 508t, 550

Pass-through payments, 349

Past-due account, 112

Pathology section, CPT, 286–288t

Patient account record, 82, 82f

Patient assessment instrument, 352

Patient classification system, 353

Patient discharge processing, 64

Patient dumping, 131t

Patient Protection and Affordable Care Act (PPACA), 32, 134t, 140, 143, 345

Patient Safety and Quality Improvement Act (PSQIA), 134t, 165

Patient safety organizations (PSOs), 134t, 165

Patient(s)
  account record, 82
  billing, 65
  cell phone pictures of, 152
  identity theft, protecting from, 161–162
  ledger, 82
  managing, 65
  new, managing, 66–72
  records, 44–45
  registration, 62–63
  registration form, 69f

Patient-by-patient proportional method, 339

Patient-driven payment model (PDPM), 352, 354

Payer mix, 27

Payer of last resort, 448, 550, 571

PAYERID, 150

Pay-for-performance (P4P), 347

Payment, of claims, 102–104

Payment Error Prevention Program (PEPP), 132t

Payment error rate, 132t

Payment Error Rate Measurement (PERM) program, 133t

Payment errors, 113t

Payment systems, 322–323. *See also* CMS reimbursement methodologies

Payment systems, CMS, 332–355. *See also* CMS reimbursement methodologies
  ambulatory surgical center, 332–334
  end-stage renal disease prospective payment system, 334–335
  federally qualified health centers prospective payment system, 335–336

home health prospective payment system, 336–338

hospice payment system, 338–339, 338t

inpatient prospective payment system, 339–348

Inpatient Psychiatric Facility Prospective Payment System, 350–352, 351f

Inpatient Rehabilitation Facility Prospective Payment system, 352

long-term (acute) care hospital prospective payment system, 352–353

outpatient prospective payment system, 348–350

Skilled Nursing Facility Prospective Payment System, 354–355

Payment weights, 333, 340

PCM (Primary care manager), 582

PCP (Primary care provider), 38

Pediatric and neonatal critical care services, 272t

Peer review, 110

Peer Review Improvement Act, 131t

Peer-to-peer review, 110

Pending claims, 113t

PEPPER (Program for Evaluating Payment Patterns Electronic Report), 133t

Per diem, 317, 318, 319, 339, 344, 350, 354

Percentage of accounts receivable older than 30, 60, 90, and 120 days, 84

Performance measurements, 38, 233, 293

Performance-based incentive payment, 50

Permanent disability, 609–610

Permanent national codes, HCPCS Level II, 301–302

Permanent partial disability, 609

Permanent total disability, 609

Personal health record (PHR), 47

PFFS (Private fee-for-service), 501

Photodynamic therapy, 290t

Physical medicine and rehabilitation, 290t

Physical status modifiers, 275

Physician fee schedule, 498–499

Physician incentive plan, 38

Physician incentives, 38

Physician Quality Reporting System (PQRS), 50, 134t

Physician query, 371

Physician query process, 175

Physician referral, 38

Physician self-referral law, 132t

Physician Value-based Payment Modifier, 50

Physician work, 326

Physician-hospital organization (PHO), 36

Physicians, 45
  incentives, 38
  managed care and physician's practice, 37
  referrral, 38
  rendering, 412
  supervising, 411

Physicians at Teaching Hospitals (PATH), 132t

PI (Promote interoperability), 49, 53, 54t

Pilot tests, 583

Place of service (POS), 258, 416

Placeholder character, in ICD-10-CM coding, 183

PlanID, 150
Plus symbol, 236, 366*t*
Point-of-service (POS), 36, 471
Point-of-service device, 551
Poisoning, Table of Drugs and Chemicals, 198, 199
Policyholder name, CMS-1500 claim, 409
Policyholders, 26, 70
Post-acute care (PAC), 320
Post-acute care quality reporting programs (PAC QRP), 320
Postcoordination coding, 180
Posting late charges and lost charges, 85
Post-payment review, 139
Posture, 15
Potentially preventable emergency department encounters, 235
PPACA (Patient Protection and Affordable Care Act), 32, 134*t*, 140, 143, 345
Practice expense, 326
Practice guidelines, TRICARE, 579
Preadmission certification (PAC), 84
Preadmission review, 84, 470
Preadmission testing (PAT), 216
Preauthorization, 80, 84, 110, 578
Precedent, 124
Precertification, 84, 470
Precoordination coding, 179
Pre-edits, 96
Pre-existing conditions, 109
Pre-existing conditions clause, 77
Preferred Provider Health Care Act of 1985, 31
Preferred provider networks (PPNs), 469
Preferred provider organization (PPO), 36, 471–472
Premium, 26
    Medicare, 488, 493, 501, 505
    workers' compensation insurance, 617
Preoperative clearance, 268–269*t*, 268*t*
Preoperative clearance, CPT coding modifiers, 248*t*
Preoperative evaluations, coding, 215
Prepaid ambulatory health plan (PAHP), 551
Prepaid health plans, 26, 468
Prepaid inpatient health plan (PIHP), 551
Prepayment review, 139
Prescription drug. *See* Medication
Prescription drug monitoring program (PDMP), 43
Prescription Drug Plans (Part D), Medicare, 500*f*, 502–504
Present on admission (POA) indicator, 343, 345, 371
Preventing Health Care Fraud and Abuse (Title II, HIPAA), 148–150
Preventive health care services, 548–549
Preventive medicine services, 271*t*
Preventive services, 25, 497
Preventive services, CPT coding modifiers, 252*t*, 253*t*
Primary care case management (PCCM), 551
Primary care first (PCF) payment model, 322
Primary care manager (PCM), 582
Primary care provider (PCP), 38

Primary health insurance, 70
Primary malignancy, 193
Primary malignant site is no longer present, 196
Primary payer, Medicare, 513–514
Prime Service Areas, 581
Principal diagnosis, 210
Principal inpatient diagnostic cost group (PIP-DCG), 502
Prior approval, 84
Prior authorization, 84
Privacy, 152
Privacy Act of 1974, 81, 131*t*, 509, 575
Privacy rule, 157–158
Private contract, Medicare, 510
Private fee-for-service (PFFS), 501
Private health insurance, 445
Privileged communication, 152
Problem focused examination, CPT, 263
Problem focused history, CPT, 263
Problem-oriented record (POR), 46
Procedure statement, CPT, 244
Procedure/service coding, 63
Procedure-to-procedure (PTP) code pair edits, 365, 367*f*
Procedure-to-procedure (PTP) code pair edits, NCCI, 366*t*, 367
Productivity, 13
Professional appearance, 14–15
Professional associations, 18, 18*t*
Professional billing, 27, 64, 231
Professional coding, 73
Professional component, CPT coding modifiers, 253*t*
Professional ethics, 13
Professional liability insurance, 9, 11*t*
Professionalism, 11–15
    associations and credentials, 18, 18*t*
    attitude, 11–12
    change management, 13
    communication, 12
    conflict management, 12
    customer service, 12
    defined, 11
    diversity awareness, 12
    etiquette, 11–12
    leadership, 12–13
    productivity, 13
    professional appearance, 14–15
    self-esteem, 11–12
    team-building, 13
Program for Evaluating Payment Patterns Electronic Report (PEPPER), 133*t*
Program Integrity (PI) Office, 579–580
Program integrity contractors (RAC auditors), 141
Program Safeguard Contractors (PSCs), 133*t*
Programs of All-Inclusive Care for the Elderly (PACE), 504, 545, 571
Progress reports, workers' compensation, 614
Progressive corrective action (PCA), 364–365
Prolonged services, 271*t*
Promoting interoperability (PI), 49, 53, 54*t*
Prompt Payment Act of 1982, 104

Proper attire, 14–15
Property insurance, 11*t*
Proprietary laboratory analysis, 288*t*
Prospective cost-based rates, 318
Prospective payment system (PPS), 318
Prospective price-based rates, 318
Prospective reimbursement methodology, 318
Prospective review, 84, 470
Prosthetics, 299
Protected health information (PHI), 152
Provider fraud, 616
Provider notification/feedback, 138
Provider remittance notice (PRN), 81
Providers
    exclusive provider organization (EPO), 35, 471
    fraud, 616
    National Provider Identifier (NPI), 150
    network, 35
    nonparticipating providers (nonPARs), 66, 329, 497, 502, 507–509, 508–509, 508*t*, 509
    opt-out, 510
    ordering, 412
    out-of-network, 66, 110
    participating providers (PARs), 66, 328, 497, 507, 508*t*, 550
    primary care provider (PCP), 38
Psychiatric collaborative care management services, 272*t*
Psychiatry, 289*t*
PTP (Procedure-to-procedure) code pair edits, 365, 367*f*
Public health insurance, 28*t*
Pulmonary services, 290*t*
Punctuation, ICD-10-CM coding, 184–185

 Q

Q codes, 303
Qualified clinical data registry (QCDC), 51
Qualified diagnoses, 213–214
Qualified disabled working individual (QDWI), 505
Qualified independent contractor (QIC), 110
Qualified independent organization (QIO), 110
Qualified Medicare beneficiaries (QMB), 544
Qualified Medicare beneficiary program (QMBP), 505
Qualified registry, 51
Qualified working disabled individuals (QWDI), 544
Qualifiers, ICD-10-CM Index to Diseases and Injuries, 191
Qualifying individual (QI), 505, 545
Quality assessment and performance improvement (QAPI) program, 31
Quality assurance program, 38
Quality improvement (QI), 40
Quality Improvement Organization (QIO) Program, 31, 110
Quality Improvement System for Managed Care (QISMC), 40
Quality management program, 38
Quality measures, 52, 53*t*

Quality payment program (QPP), 49–53, 507
Quarterly Provider Updates (QPUs), 83
Qui tam, 124

R

RAC (Recovery Audit Contractor) program, 133*t*, 140–141
Radiation Exposure Compensation Act (RECA), 606
Radiologic views, 282
Radiology, 282–286
    complete procedure, 284–286
    CPT codes, 283–284*t*
    pathology and laboratory section, 286–289
    professional *versus* technical component, 285
Radiology services, 418
RARC (Remittance advice remark codes), 107
Readmission audits, 371
Recipient eligibility verification system (REVS), 551
Recombinant products, 289*t*
Record linkage, 43
Record retention, 136
Recovery Audit Contractor (RAC) program, 133*t*, 140–141
Recovery audit contractor program, 370
Recovery Auditor (RA) contractor, 139
Recovery of funds from responsible payers, 410
Red Flags Rule, 133*t*
Red reference symbol, 237
Reduced services, CPT coding modifiers, 247*t*
Re-excision of tumors, 196
Reference (outside) laboratory, CPT coding modifiers, 254*t*
Reference symbols, 237
Referral, 38, 268*t*, 578
Regulations, 124
Regulatory law, 124
Rehabilitative services, CPT coding modifiers, 255*t*
Reimbursement, 549–550
Reimbursement specialists, 4
Rejected claims, 106, 113*t*
Relative value units (RVUs), 233, 326
Release of information (ROI), 162–164
    breach of confidentiality, 164
    confidentiality and the Internet, 164
    facsimile transmission, 163
    log, 162
    telephone inquiries, 163
Religious nonmedical health care institution, 495
Remittance advice (remit), 9, 93, 102–104
Remittance advice documents, 105, 106
Remittance advice remark codes (RARC), 107
Rendering physician, 412
Reopened claim, 436
Repeat clinical diagnostic laboratory test, CPT coding modifiers, 254*t*
Repeat procedures, CPT coding modifiers, 251*t*
Report card, 40

Reproductive medicine procedures, 288*t*
Requisition form, 63
Resequenced codes, 237
Resident Assessment Validation and Entry (jRAVEN) software, 354, 355*f*
Resource allocation, 85
Resource allocation monitoring, 85
Resource utilization groups (RUGs), 354
Resource-based relative value scale (RBRVS), 498
Resources-first approach, 546
Respite care, 496
Respondeat superior, 9–10
Rest homes, 270*t*
Resubmitting claims, 64
Retrospective reasonable cost system, 317
Retrospective reimbursement methodology, 317
Retrospective review, 84, 470
Revene offsets, 166
Revenue auditing, 85
Revenue cycle management, 61–121, 63*f*
    accounts receivable management, 79–80
    auditing for, 83–86
    chargemaster, 75–76
    credit and collections, 111–115
    defined, 62
    denied claims, 106–110
    encounter form, 73, 74*f*
    established patients, managing, 72
    insurance claim cycle, 92–105
    insurance claim files, maintaining, 105–106
    insurance claim, processing, 77–81
    integrated, 65
    Internet links, 87
    monitoring for, 83–86
    new patients, managing, 66–72
    patient accounts, posting charges, 81–82
Revenue monitoring, 84–85
Revenue offsets (Title V, HIPAA), 166
Riders, 27
Right to control test, 10
Risk adjustment data validation (RADV), 503
Risk adjustment model, 32
Risk adjustment program, 32, 134*t*
Risk contract, 31
Risk of mortality (ROM), 242
Risk pools, 34
Risk purchasing group, 11*t*
Risk retention group, 11*t*
Risk transfer formula, 32
Roster billing, 401
    for mass vaccination programs, 535, 536*t*, 537–538*f*
Routine administrative Medicare claims process, 51
Rural health information organization (RHIO), 135*t*
RVUs (Relative value units), 233, 326

S

S codes, 303
Safety data sheets (SDS), 607
Same-day surgery, 211

Schedule loss of use, 610
Schedule of benefits, 26
Scope of practice, 8–9
Screenings, coding, 216–217
Second surgical opinion (SSO), 471
Secondary diagnoses, 214–215
Secondary health insurance, 70, 457, 457*t*
Secondary malignancy, 193, 195
Secondary payer
    Medicaid as, 550, 562, 564*f*
    Medicare as, 515–516, 517*f*, 532, 532*t*, 534*f*
    TRICARE as, 596, 596–598*f*
Security, 152
Security rule, 158–159
Sedation, 291*t*
"See also" coding, 189
"See category" coding, 189
"See condition" coding, 189
"See" coding, 189
Self-Disclosure Protocol (SDP), 137
Self-esteem, 11–12
Self-fund, 11*t*
Self-insurance plans, 608
Self-insured (or self-funded) employer-sponsored group health plans, 30
Self-pay reimbursement posting, 65
Self-referral, 36
Semicolon, 236, 280
SEP (Special enrollment period), 493
Separate procedure, 281
Sequela, 213
Serious reportable events, 345
Serious Reportable Events in Healthcare: A Consensus Report, 344
Serum, 289*t*
Service intensity add-on (SIA) payment, 339
Service station, 472
Service-connected disability, 580
Seventh characters, in ICD-10-CM coding, 183
Severity of illness (SOI), 242
SGR (Sustainable growth rate), 49, 507
SI (Status indicator), 348
Single-path coding, 73, 403
Single-payer health system, 28*t*
Site of service differential, 331–332
Skilled nursing facility (SNF), 495
Skilled Nursing Facility 30-Day All-Cause Readmission Measure (SNFRM), 354–355
Skilled Nursing Facility Prospective Payment System (SNF PPS), 354–355
Skilled Nursing Facility Value-Based Purchasing (SNF VBP) Program, 354–355
Skip tracing, 114
Skip tracking, 114
Small provider claims, 401
SNP (Special needs plans), 501
SOAP note, 386
Social Security Administration (SSA), 447, 492
Social Security Amendments, 131*t*
Social Security Disability Insurance (SSDI), 447
Social Security number (SSN), 419
Socialized medicine, 28*t*

Soft denials, 113*t*

Software
computer-assisted coding (CAC), 63, 177, 178*f*, 372, 373*f*
encoders, 176
Grouper, 336
HAVEN, 336
IRVEN, 352, 353*f*
jRAVEN, 354, 355*f*
Medicare code editor, 340
TPMS, 47

Source documents, 105
Special accidental injury rider, 27
Special enrollment period (SEP), 493
Special evaluation and management services, 272*t*
Special groups, Medicaid, 544–545

Special handling
BlueCross BlueShield, 474
Medicare, 520
TRICARE, 587
workers' compensation insurance, 618

Special needs plans (SNP), Medicare, 501
Special report, 238
Specified low-income Medicare beneficiary (SLMB), 505, 545
Spell of illness, 494
Split/shared visit payment policy, 519

Sponsors
CHAMPVA, 580
Medicare Part D, 502
TRICARE, 576–577

Spousal impoverishment provisions, Medicaid, 546
Staff model HMO, 35
Stafford v. Neurological Medicine Inc., 214
Stand-alone codes, 234
Standard paper remit (SPR), 93
Standards, 40
Standby services, 271*t*
Star symbol, 237
Stark I, Physician Self-Referral Law, 132*t*
Stark II, Physician Self-Referral Law, 132*t*
State insurance fund, 608
State insurance regulators, 115–116
State workers' compensation programs, 608
Status indicator (SI), 348
Statutes, 124
Statutory law, 124
Stem codes, 179
Stop-loss insurance, 26
Streamlined method, 339
Strike Force teams, 141
Student internship, 6–7
Sub-capitation payment, 35
Subjective part of SOAP notes, 386
Submission, HCPCS Level II code requirements, 307–309
Subpoena, 124
Subpoena *duces tecum*, 124
Subrogation, 448, 554
Subscribers (policyholders), 26
Subsequent hospital care, 268*t*

Subterms, 191, 192*f*, 242, 391
Superbill, 73, 74*f*, 379
Supervising physician, 411
Supplemental Health Care Programs (SHCPs), 584
Supplemental Medical Review Contractor (SMRC) program, 136*t*

Supplemental plans
Medicare, 421, 472
TRICARE, 581

Supplemental Security Income (SSI), 447
Supplier, 404
Suppression testing, 287*t*

Surgery
CPT coding, 278–282
multiple procedures, 281–282
separate procedure, 281
subcategories, 278
surgical package, 278–280, 279*f*

Surgical package, 278–280, 279*f*
Surgical pathology, 288*t*
Surgical team, CPT coding modifiers, 252*t*
Surplus lines market, 11*t*
Surveillance and utilization review subsystem (SURS), 553
Survivor benefits, 610
Suspended claims, 113*t*
Sustainable growth rate (SGR), 49, 507
Symbols, CPT, 235–237, 238*f*
Synchronous telemedicine services, CPT coding modifiers, 254*t*

T

T codes, 303
Table of Drugs and Chemicals, ICD-10-CM, 182, 198–200, 198*f*
Table of Drugs, HCPS, 304–305, 305*f*
Table of Neoplasms, ICD-10-CM, 182, 192–197, 194*f*
Tables, 182
Tabular list, 181–182
Tabular List of Diseases and Injuries, ICD-10-CM, 204–208, 204*t*, 205*f*
external cause codes, 206
health status and contact with health services codes, 206, 207*f*
structure of, 205–206
Taft-Hartley Act, 30
Targeted Probe and Educate (TPE) Process for Medical Review, 139
Tax Cuts and Job Acts of 2017, 33
Tax Equity and Fiscal Responsibility Act (TEFRA) of 1982, 31, 338
Tax Relief and Health Care Act of 2006 (TRHCA), 134*t*
Tax-related health provisions (Title III, HIPAA), 165–166
Teaching hospital, 44
Teaching physician, 45
Team-building, 13
Technically denied claims, 64
Telehealth, 520
Telemedicine, 235

Telemedicine services, CPT coding modifiers, 254*t*
Telephone inquiries, 163
Telephone skills, 17*f*
Telephone-availability policies, 16
Temporary Assistance for Needy Families program (TANF), 544
Temporary codes, HCPCS Level II, 302–303
Temporary disability, 609
Temporary partial disability, 609
Temporary total disability, 609
Termination of coverage, 110
Therapeutic drug assays, 287*t*
Therapeutic services, coding, 215
Third-party administrators (TPAs), 30
Third-party payer, 26–27, 37
Third-party payer reimbursement posting, 65
3-2-1 Code It! (Green), 172, 175, 176, 231, 372, 381, 425
Three-day payment window statutory provision, 323
Ticket to Work and Work Incentives Improvement Act (TWWIA), 571
Time reporting, anesthesia, 276
Total practice management software (TPMS), 47, 48*f*
Toxic effects, 199
Toxoids, 289*t*
Tracking resubmitted claims, 85
Tracking unpaid claims, 106
Transfer audits, 371
Transfer of care, 261
Transfusion medicine, 287*t*
Transitional Assistance Management Program (TAMP), 577–578
Transitional care management services, 272*t*
Transitional pass-through payments, 302
Transitional payments, 350
Transmittals, 125, 127*f*, 332
Treatment, payment, and health care operations (TPO), 157
Triangle symbol, 236
TRICARE, 574–602, 579
accepting assignment, 585
administration, 578–580
allowable fee determination, 585
beneficiaries, 576–577
billing notes, 584–587
case management, 579
CHAMPVA, 580–581
civilian provider network, 578
claim used, 584–585
claims instructions, 588, 588–591*t*, 593–595*f*, 596, 599, 599*t*, 600*f*
claims submission deadline, 585
contractors, 584
coverage options, 581–584
customer service representative, 578
dependents, 576–577
eligibility, 576–577, 585
family members, 576–577
health care finders, 578
history, 575–576
Internet links, 601

TRICARE (*Continued*)
  limiting charges, 587
  military time, 587, 587–588*t*
  military treatment facility, 579
  overview, 575–576
  as secondary payer, 596, 596–598*f*
  service centers, 578–579
  special handling, 587
  special programs, 583–584
  sponsors, 576–577
  supplemental coverage, 599, 599*t*, 600*f*
  supplemental health care programs, 584
TRICARE Cancer Clinical Trials, 584
TRICARE Comprehensive Autism Care
    Demonstration, 584
TRICARE Dental Program, 583
TRICARE for Life, 582
TRICARE Prime, 581–582
TRICARE Reserve Select(R), 582–583
TRICARE Retired Reserve(R), 583
TRICARE Select, 582
TRICARE Service Centers (TSCs), 578–579
TRICARE Vision Care, 583
TRICARE Young Adult, 583
Triple option plan, 36
Truth in Lending Act, 111
Tumors
  morphology coding, 207
  re-excision, 18
  Table of Neoplasms, ICD-10-CM, 182,
    192–197, 194*f*
21st Century Cures Act (Cures Act), 135*t*, 502
Two surgeons, CPT coding modifiers, 251*t*
Two-party check, 113
Type of service (TOS), 257–258

U

U.S. Equal Employment Opportunity
    Commission, 5
UB-04 claims, 27, 77, 423–443
  answer key, 438*f*
  blank claim, 406*f*
  claim development, 425
  correcting and supplementing, 436
  CPT codes, 424
  data specifications for, 425
  form locator descriptions and claims
    instructions, 426–436*t*
  HCPCS Level II codes, 424
  ICD-10-CM codes, 424
  ICD-10-PCS codes, 424

National Uniform Billing Committee, 425
  outpatient case, 437*f*
  overview, 424–425
  submission of, 403*t*, 425
UB-04 flat file, 151
UHDDS, 343
Unassigned claims, 106
Unauthorized services, 99
Unbundling, 113
Unbundling CPT codes, 369–370
Uncertain behavior, 193
Uncertain diagnoses, 213–214
Underdosing, 198, 199
Underpayments, 141
underwriters, 616
Unified Program Integrity Contractors (UPICs),
    136*t*, 139
Uniform Hospital Discharge Data Set
    (UHDDS), 343
Uniformed services, 575
Unique bit string, 151
Unique identifiers, 150–151
Unit/floor time, 260
United States Core Data for Interoperability
    (USCDI), 135*t*
Units of service (UOS), 365
Universal health insurance, 28*t*
Unlisted procedures/services, 238
Unpaid claims, 64, 106
Unspecified nature, 193
Unusual anesthesia, CPT coding modifiers,
    253*t*
Unusual cases, 401
Urinalysis, 287*t*
US Family Health Plan, 583
Usual, customary, and reasonable (UCR)
    basis, 474
Utilization management, 40, 84, 469–470
Utilization review, 41, 84, 469–470
Utilization review organization (URO), 41

V

Vaccines, 289*t*
Value Modifier (VM), 50
Value-added network (VAN), 93
Value-based purchasing (VBP) program, 334,
    346–347
Value-based reimbursement methodology, 37
Veterans Access, Choice, and Accountability
    Act of 2014 (Choice Act), 581

Veterans Choice Program, 581
Vocational rehabilitation, 610
Voided claim, 553*f*

W

Wage index, 349
Waiver of Medicare billing contracts, 509
Waiver of overpayment recovery, 143
Wellness visits, 271*t*
Whistleblowers, 134*t*
"With" coding, 188
Withhold arrangement, 34
Without direct patient contact, 271*t*
Word substitution, CPT, 244
Workers' compensation board, 608
Workers' compensation commission, 608
Workers' compensation insurance, 11*t*,
    604–627, 606
  accept assignment, 617
  adjudication, 614–615
  appeals, 614–615
  approved fee basis, 617
  billing, 610
  billing notes, 616–618
  claim used, 617
  claims instructions, 618, 618–621*t*,
    622–625*f*
  claims submission deadline, 617
  classification of cases, 609–610
  eligibility, 608, 616
  federal programs, 605–607
  First Report of Injury forms, 611–614, 612*f*
  fiscal agent, 616
  forms, 617
  fraud and abuse, 616
  identification card, 616, 617*f*
  Internet links, 626
  managed care, 610–611
  overview, 605
  premium, 617
  private payer mistakenly billed, 618
  special handling, 618
  state programs, 608
  underwriters, 616

Z

Z codes, 212
Zone Program Integrity Contractor (ZPIC)
    program, 133*t*, 139